THE
EVER HERO
SAGA

THE CHAOS GATE • THE FOE WARS
THE DIVINE FIST • SEKKA

JEFF PANTANELLA

First Printing, 2020
Ever Hero Productions
Yorba Linda, CA 92886
United States of America
www.everheroproductions.com

Cover Design by Gene Mollica Studio, LLC
Author Photo by Asia Yen Productions and Design
Edited by Maureen Neuman

JEFF PANTANELLA

THE
EVER HERO
SAGA

THE CHAOS GATE · THE FOE WARS
THE DIVINE FIST · SEKKA

ALSO BY JEFF PANTANELLA
THE EVER HERO SAGA

JOIN MY BAND OF EVER HEROES

My Band of Ever Heroes members get free books, free behind the scenes photographs, and unique items to accompany books.

Members are always the first to hear about my new books and publications.

See the back of the book for details on how to sign up.

This giant tome is dedicated to Jim Hunt, who's frequent phone calls of encouragement brighten my day and inspire me to keep writing.

ACKNOWLEDGMENTS

I am constantly blown away by the amazing artwork, professionalism, and empirical knowledge of bookcraft I receive from Gene Mollica Studio, LLC. Thank you, Gene, Sasha, and Cyrus for everything you do to help make my series a success.

JEFF PANTANELLA

THE CHAOS GATE

BOOK ONE IN THE
EVER HERO SAGA

THE CHAOS GATE

PART 1 - BOOK 1

"The Seven Heavens spin right. The Seven Hells spin left. Each in opposition to the other. Each searching for advantage. The Mortal Realm is forever pulled and squeezed in the middle. In all things, the Great Balance must remain."

~The Prophetess Miko Nuna

"A thousand wicks can be lit from the flame of a single candle, and the fire of the originator will not be lessened. Each new candle will add their flame to light ten thousand candles, and so on, creating an infinite sea of light. This is the Boundless."

~The First of Aetenos, Gen Moll

"Love carries on."

~Aetenos

PROLOGUE

"Hold! Hold!" a senior officer cried into the din of ferocious roars and wailing cries. His breath frosted before his face. Irrelevant whether his soldiers heard him, whether they wanted to comply; the battle had turned to a rout. Sekka's Frost Legion hammered the last remnants of the human army sent to halt her advance.

Sekka chuckled at the futility of the officer's command. "You should have sent more men, foolish monk. It won't be long now," she crowed.

The sky was ablaze with the crimson hue of a setting sun, reaching long blood-red fingers over the battleground. Despite the fire in the sky, there was no warmth. A cold wind blew through pockets of fighting, biting as deeply as the claws, teeth, and horns of her troops. The air reeked with the stench of open flesh and spilled viscera.

Sekka stretched her arms to the sky and flung her head back, full of joy. She twirled once, hugging herself, "Glorious!" The sobs of the wounded replaced the clang of swords and shields.

At the center of the battlefield, knights in once-shining armor moved like dwindling beacons of hope, their swords gleaming with enchantments meant to pierce the hideous hides of her demons. Even so, too few remained.

"A foul gift from those miserable do-gooders," Sekka cursed, raising her black-on-black eyes to the red sky, scanning for any indication *they* would interfere. A cruel smile curled the corners of her mouth. "Just clouds."

She brought her attention back to the battle, relishing its fury and inevitability. Despite the knights' valor, Sekka's Frost Legion was an unstoppable force impervious to fear or pain, bred on her home world of Gathos for the conquest of this realm. Scanning the field with a predator's interest, she spotted a human forming a last stand. Demon death ash formed miniature clouds, swirling over his head.

"Ah, there you are," Sekka purred. She had chosen a mortal form—sleek, sexual, and dangerous; fitting for conquest in this realm. Dressed in form-fitting war gear embossed with the eight-pointed Wheel of Chaos, she appeared the perfect image of a dread warlord. Her delicate hands, at odds with the lethal dark magic they summoned, flickered with shadowy tendrils, weaving a tapestry of malevolence. "At last the titans meet."

Others saw the lone warrior, too, and moved in frantic clusters, desperate to reach the tiny island of hope which stood against the storming sea of destruction. "The knights have rallied to their hero, wonderful," she observed. "More souls for the pits."

She moved gracefully through the battlefield, taking pleasure in ending life, in whichever foul way she deemed most enjoyable, until she finally reached the warrior.

"You will not win this day, devil," her opponent said before tucking his segmented staff under the crutch of his arm in order to dispatch a horned monster, using a palm-heel strike to its head. She was impressed by how easily he pulverized the demon's skull, turning the brain matter inside to pulp. The demon sat back on it haunches, eyes locked in a befuddled stare before bits and pieces of its flesh decomposed to ash, adding to the whirlwind circling above the warrior.

"Oh, I think I will. Look around. You're all that's left. It's over. This realm is mine. Quite frankly, I'm disappointed. This was the best you could bring to bear?" Sekka mocked, her eyes glinting with a dark mirth.

The warrior stood grounded in the packed snow and trampled grass. His calm demeanor a stark contrast to the surrounding carnage. Clad in simple, weathered cobalt robes, he spun the three-sectioned staff with an ease into an aggressive, attacking posture, belying his humble appearance. Sekka knew of the legendary staff, unassuming at first glance, it carried within it a powerful adversary. A blue flame rippled along its three sections as if the inhabitant within bided; impatient to be released.

"Ninziz-zida has been waiting for you," the monk said.

Sekka sneered, eyeing the staff with revulsion. "Is there anything you possess that wasn't stolen?"

"I—"

Sekka didn't wait for his explanation, striking in a blur of movement, launching shards of darkness that screamed through the air like malevolent spirits. The monk deftly maneuvered, his staff spinning in seamless arcs, each action a precise counter to the devil's magical assault. The staff's blue flame intensified, burning beyond the sticks, coiling into the fiery form above the monk.

Gritting her teeth, Sekka set her feet apart, preparing for the final battle—the real fight that would determine whether she dominated the Mortal Realm or if she would be cast back to the Abyss to suffer the torment of her disappointed benefactors.

The blue flames hissed at her, twisting through a transformation into an ancient fire elemental dragon. Sekka felt as if she stood before a volcano's fury, the heat from the dragon scolded her skin and crisped her hair. Blinded by the brightness of the serpent's flame, Sekka instinctively shielded her eyes. It was a mistake. The dragon and monk attacked as one, pummeling her with blows and bites. Her human form was weak and could not withstand such punishment for long.

Growling through a guttural curse, Sekka shifted into her true form. Her human facade melted away, revealing a horrific infernal creature, towering and fearsome. Four curling horns began to frame her head, and four hooked teeth protruded menacingly from her mouth. Floating above her head, a crown of bones materialized, adorned with glowing sigils of power that pulsed ominously from the gems at its base. Her body expanded, becoming immense and robust, her muscles hardening and rippling as if challenging magical restraints that sought to contain her.

Coarse, white fur sprouted and blanketed her back, each strand thick and wild. Her arms thickened. Claws grew from her fingers, gleaming from the light of the dragon's flame, each one capable of tearing through stone and flesh alike. Her legs, now avian in structure, ended in feet with raptor-like talons, ready to tear and rend anything in their path.

The dragon and monk continued their assault as she contorted and struggled, her chest heaved, her form swelling with raw, demonic power. Sekka lashed out blindly, hoping to gouge either foe. Innate chaos magic seeped from her pours. She would need to rely on it more that brute strength against her adversaries.

The monk, agile and serene, danced between the swipes of her claws, his staff a blur of motion, striking with the force of a tempest. Each hit from the fire dragon seared her flesh, but she was relentless, her dark magic weaving a shield of shadow and despair, absorbing the fiery onslaught and striking back with tendrils of pure darkness.

She shouted out another curse, this one directed at the mortality of the monk. Through squinted eyes, she saw him doubled over, vomiting blood. Ninziz-zida roared. The fire dragon reared up, sucking in a large draught of air, her eyes glaring at Sekka.

"Chanta-thriz-hor," Sekka chanted, summoning a protective aegis around her as the dragon spewed a thick stream of lava, making the air shimmer from its heat.

Sekka renewed her attack, aware that if the staff fell from the monk's hands, the fire dragon would lose its connection to the material world and be snuffed out. Lashing out with her claws and biting fiercely, she engaged in a brutal exchange with the fire dragon before unleashing a barrage of spells aimed to disable and disorient the monk. Anything to get him to drop the damned staff.

While the monk evaded most of her onslaught, one in every ten of Sekka's spells found its mark. She saw him stumble on unsure legs as a bolt of death energy grazed his thigh. She summoned lesser demons to her aid, each one a horrific nightmare of gnashing teeth and icy death. The monk fought through them all, but she could see it —almost taste it—he was slowing down.

She lunged forward, seizing the staff, and wrenching it from his grasp. The searing pain that raced up her arm, causing her flesh to melt off the bones of her hand, was a small price to pay for triumph. The fire dragon emitted a piercing shriek before it dissolved, its life essence being reabsorbed into the staff.

Sekka thrust the staff behind her. She sought the monk's eyes. "You see it now, don't you? My time has come."

The weakened monk leaped with a spinning high kick directed at her head. She grabbed his leg mid-flight and hurled him across the field. This day would see the end of the Great Monk, Aetenos, and mark the beginning of her rule in the Mortal Realm. *Oh, the delight!* she thought, stomping to where the monk lay on his back. "Perhaps a more delicate shape to savor my victory," she said, transforming back to the form of a wicked human queen. "They will look upon my beauty and despair."

And then, the clarion call of her doom pealed, ringing in her ears like ten thousand church bells. Her eyes shot skyward. From the billowing, crimson clouds, the Heavenly Host descended, a radiant legion of angels whose presence alone commanded awe. Their wings, vast and resplendent, shimmered with celestial light, casting beams that cut through the gathering dusk.

The Frost Legion awaited on the muted, snow-covered plains below, their grotesque forms and icy auras stark against the long shadows of the setting sun. As the angels approached, a profound silence fell, broken only by the soft whisper of feathered wings against the air.

Sekka found herself transfixed by the sudden and disastrous shift in events until a second clarion call pealed across the sky. Another legion! And then a third and fourth broke through the cloud cover. They were not here to stop her; they had come to annihilate her.

With an otherworldly grace and power that seemed to bend the very fabric of reality, the angels engaged the demons. The contrast was absolute: where the demons were harsh and brutal, the angels moved with a precision and elegance. Their weapons, forged from divine essence of righteous might, burned with holy fire.

The battle, though fierce, was one-sided. The Heavenly Host wielded powers that transcended the physical realm, commanding forces of light and purity that unraveled the demonic beings with each touch. Her Frost Legion was dismantled with a decisive and methodical efficiency.

With a final, concerted effort that seemed to draw on the very essence of the heavens, the angels unleashed a torrent of radiant energy that swept across the battlefield. As the light receded, Sekka's Frost Legion was no more, erased from existence but for the ash of their memory.

Sekka dropped to her knees, broken and defeated. In retrospect, perhaps she had been a tad overconfident, changing back to her mortal form after defeating the monk and his fire serpent. She was weakened in this form, bruised and swollen from her earlier entanglement—not that it mattered now. Nothing could stand against what hovered beneath the clouds. Victory had been within her grasp, but now her armies were gone, obliterated unfairly. The angels had no right to interfere, and yet they had.

She sneered as the ashes of her dead warriors floated past her face. Clenching her fists in frustration, she tallied the mortal soul energy she had spent to create her armies. The Gathos reserves were depleted now; she was vulnerable to attack, yet it wasn't the Heavenly Host that worried her for no angel would dare tread into the Abyss. The denizens of the Lower Planes could smell weakness and would race to claim what was hers.

She raised her pale face, and through clumps of matted, white hair, she vaguely saw the last remaining angels vanishing through a portal that illuminated the sky like a second sun. The bulk of the Heavenly Host had already departed, having finished their work here.

"Fly back to your precious Elysian; you thrice-damned little birds," she cursed. "I will have my revenge!"

She licked her dry, blue lips, with a pasty tongue. Everything hurt. Her innate healing powers worked tirelessly to repair the damage the staff had caused. Nonetheless, through cracked and sore lips a wicked smile crossed her bruised face. The fools had let her live, and there was still a chance she could gain a permanent foothold in the Mortal Realm, considering the agents she had previously scattered throughout this realm. Her succubus, Sess'thra, would find her another suitable host and then she would rebuild. The thought of harvesting so many souls gave her renewed strength. Sekka tried to rise. "As long as I draw breath..."

Then *he* stepped forward; his robed silhouette backlit by the distant sun. Light gleamed off his partially bald head. She envisioned him smiling, with a kind, worry-free expression, as if he possessed the secret to eternal contentment. One of the Great Three save her, how she hated him.

He held one arm comfortably behind his back. In the other was the three-sectioned staff she had torn from his grasp. The burn of its kiss still sizzled the rejoining flesh of her hand. Ninziz-zida remained confined within the sticks—for now.

As he drew closer, she saw his dull, cobalt blue robes were in tatters. Bloody, burgundy stains had soaked into its threads. She cracked a weak smirk, remembering the blows which had struck true.

"Aetenos," Sekka snarled. "It's not like you to gloat."

"I am here to do what must be done. I wish it was otherwise," he replied with a strained politeness.

He studied her, shaking his head with a sadness she found arrogant. The physical pain she felt was nothing compared to his pity. She cursed his soul a thousand times for interfering in her plans—centuries in the making yet destroyed in a blink of an eye. How had he contacted the Trueborn? There were protocols that must be followed!

"Your trespass into the Mortal Realm has ended. The laws of the Immortal Mother must never be broken. The Great Balance must remain," he schooled.

"You cannot beat me alone," Sekka scoffed.

"In this, you are correct, nor is it my destiny to do so, in this lifetime or the next. Yet, we remain connected through them all like the overlapping threads of an everlasting tapestry."

"This is not the end."

"There is no end, only a formless continuation of the spirit through the Boundless."

She hated his riddles. "Get on with it, monk."

"As you wish, devil."

Ninziz-zida blazed to life from the staff in Aetenos' hands, and Sekka's end came swiftly.

CENTURIES LATER...

1

KASAI

Brother Kasai raced down the polished stone corridors of Zazen Hall. His topknot of braided, black hair whipped like an angry viper behind his head. Light from rows of beeswax candles gleamed off the rest of his shiny scalp. He did his best to run silently, but his loose brown robes billowed like sheets in the wind. He was sure the noise could wake the dead.

The young monk had removed his sandals at the entrance to the Hall, as was customary. His wool socks slipped on the smooth stone, making running down the concourse difficult, and he was late to morning meditation ... again. Why he couldn't finish his dawn chores on time as the rest of his Brothers was a mystery to him. Master Dorje would not be pleased.

With a bit of luck, the doors to the Meditation Hall would be open, Kasai hoped. As he slid around the last corner, he watched the strip of light between the tall red doors narrow and disappear as they closed with a soft click. A sigh of disappointment escaped his lips. "I'm not even that late." He gripped the door ring and pulled slowly. "Quiet as a mouse now. Not a sound." The dry hinges refused to listen, and with an agonizingly slow creak, they shattered the silence of the room. Kasai scrunched his shoulders, grimacing as he slowly pushed the door open.

Peering into the dimly lit room, he spied all forty-three monks, ranging from child to young adult, heads down, sitting in quiet contemplation. Each had been brought to the monastery as a youngster by a Traveling Master, just like Kasai. The monastery offered orphaned and abandoned children a home and family when they otherwise would have none. Even so, their life was not easy. The monks were deprived of many comforts, but it was safe and a place they could call home.

Each monk chose to wear their hair in a formal topknot style or to shave their head clean. They sat in rows depicting age groups, older students to the front with the younger initiates in the rear. Legs were tucked under their knees, tan, sleeveless shirts gathered into dark brown leggings above the slippery, off-white socks. Some wore loose rusty-orange robes that billowed in the mountain winds and did nothing to curtail the cold. Others had removed their outer robes, folding them neatly on the floor before them. A few scattered candles threw a feeble glow upon their still bodies.

Master Dorje, one of the Three Masters of Ordu, was seated upon a raised platform, draped in simple blue robes. His head was upright, but his face remained in shadow. Interrupting his teaching, Master Dorje turned his smooth head towards Kasai, keeping his eyes closed.

"Stay shut. Stay shut," Kasai silently pleaded, squeezing through the narrowest gap the door would allow.

Master Dorje's eyes flashed open, acknowledging Kasai with a cold stare and disapproving frown. *This is going to be a bad day*, Kasai thought.

"Please have a seat, Brother Kasai. We have been waiting for you," Master Dorje instructed. The tone of his voice was neutral. This was another bad sign.

Nothing to do about it now. Kasai shuffled across the room to his zabuton, a somewhat safe three rows from Master Dorje's platform. He plopped down on his small, square mat and joined the rest of his Brothers in meditation.

Master Dorje continued his lesson, "All things are contained within the Boundless, yet the Boundless remains invisible to eyes that are blind, ears that are deaf, and hands unable to touch. The mountain filled with stones and the trees that grow in its earth is part of the Boundless. The water that flows in a stream, the air the blows with the wind, and the fire that burns, but lights our way are all the same. When you are one with the Boundless, you will see, hear, and feel the vibrations of their essence."

"You make more noise than a raccoon caught in the pantry. I heard you coming as far away as the dormitories," Brother Daku whispered from Kasai's right side.

Daku was a year older than Kasai. His muscular body could have been sculpted from stone. His face was sharp and angular in the same way. He looked like a living granite statue in a king's courtyard. "Master Dorje will not go lightly on you this time."

"I know. I know," Kasai sighed. "Who was assigned to oil the door hinges this month?"

"Me," Daku snickered.

"Thanks, *friend*." Kasai shut his almond-shaped eyes and concentrated on Master Dorje's lesson.

The Master continued, "Through the Boundless, you will share the gift of understanding with all things, for all things are alive with vibration. Their thoughts will be your thoughts, their actions, your actions, their energy shall be your energy. In return, you shall give all of yourself. This is the Openness. It is a bond of truth.

"When you free yourself from misery, from hate and revenge, you will be ready to embrace the Boundless. Do not fear the unknown, for within the unknown is the seed for growth."

The Master remained silent for a time. He breathed out slowly. Kasai heard the platform boards creak. *Oh, please let him leave without another word*, Kasai hoped.

"Contemplate what you have learned today, for it will help you in the future. Tomorrow, the Test of Pillars await the senior initiates."

Kasai cracked open his eyes, watching Master Dorje pad to the door leading to his private chamber. His pace was agonizingly slow. "Lucky, lucky, lucky," Kasai whispered with each of the Master's steps.

Master Dorje stopped at the door. "Brother Kasai, I shall have a word with you in my chamber when you have finished."

Kasai slumped on his zabuton. "I'm sunk." The old monk was known for his stringent punishments and Kasai hoped he would not be forced to choose between two impossible tasks again. That was a special torture. Once, he had to choose between balancing on one leg for a day and night or sitting naked in the snow until the morning sun was overhead. He now hated the cold with an extraordinary passion.

"Why must I always be late?" he lamented, shaking his head.

Two hours later, a bell chimed three times, signaling the end of morning meditation. Kasai got up and walked with heavy steps to Master Dorje's private chamber. Before he could reach the door, Daku hurried over to him.

"I don't want to hear it, Daku," Kasai said as the bigger Brother slung his heavy arm over Kasai's shoulder. Standing at least two hand's width taller than most of the Brothers at the monastery, Daku relished the view from above, particularly when it came to Kasai.

"Cheer up, Little Brother, this was only the third time you were late this month," Daku jested. He rarely, if ever, used the title "Brother" with any of the monks of the order. "I don't think that warrants anything too severe."

"Really?" Kasai said, hopefully.

"No, not really. You'll pull midnight watch for sure this time. Just think of it, you, alone on the North Ridge. The heavens are full of stars. The cold wind is blowing, but there's no fire to warm you. *Brrrrr.* I hope you have properly mastered the deeper fire xindu forms."

"You know I haven't," Kasai sighed.

"And only the calls of the vargru to keep you company," Daku added. "You'll know when they're close because their howling shifts to maniacal laughter and then stops abruptly."

"That's not true," Kasai said, his voice cracking with a hint of fear. "The vargru keep to the lower forests."

"If you say so," Daku chuckled. "I'll be with Jia'mu and Ri'sonu in the courtyard. Meet us after."

Daku left the meditation hall with the rest of the monks. Kasai turned to the side door. "This always happens to me. Why am I so unlucky?" He sighed once more as he grabbed the handle.

A short time later, Kasai entered the outside courtyard. He dragged his feet and wore the expression of a man resigned to a harsh fate. Brothers Jia'mu, Ri'sonu, and Daku joined him.

"Will it be an extra hour or two of sweeping the outer steps, or did Master Dorje go hard on you?" Jia'mu teased. He was roughly the same age as Kasai, though the Masters discouraged discussing a person's age in numbers. The Masters said it was a self-defeating idea used to count the days left in life, rather than the accomplishments that lay ahead.

Jia'mu was small and round, built like a cannon shot, which earned him the name Cannonball from his friends. His shaved head and puffy cheeks gave him the appearance of having a second, smaller ball, precariously balanced on his rounded shoulders. Not even Daku could move Cannonball from the center circle once he crouched in a static basket position.

Kasai tried, unsuccessfully, to smile. "Master Dorje fully expressed his disapproval with me for being late. I was granted a month's worth of midnight sentry duty on the North Ridge," Kasai reported.

Jia'mu and Ri'sonu grimaced and moaned.

"I knew it!" Daku's dark eyes flashed with excitement. He pointed his finger at Kasai. "It's not more than you deserve."

"Be thankful it's still early autumn, and you didn't draw winter duty," Ri'sonu said. "I'd hate to be out all night in the middle of December."

Ri'sonu wrapped his long arms around his thin body. His frame was the opposite of Jia'mu. He was just a few fingers shorter than Daku but skinny as a reed. His body could move like a length of rope, which made him difficult to hit in a fight.

"I didn't say guard duty started tonight." Kasai's shoulders slumped.

"Oh no," Ri'sonu cringed.

Daku laughed. "Serves you right, Kasai. You're always late. Knowing you, you'll be late for your own funeral."

"Speaking of funerals, we face the pillar test tomorrow. I didn't think it would be this soon. I'm not ready. What if it's a cloudy day tomorrow? We won't be able to see where we're going," Cannonball theorized, biting on a well-chewed fingernail. Ri'sonu nodded in agreement.

Daku scoffed at their nervous reactions.

"Finally, we are given a true test. I'm eager to pit my xindu energy against something real. I'm tired of practicing lame tricks over-and-over again. Hot hands, cold hands. Hot feet, cold feet. None of this is like fighting in the real world. I'm ready for a challenge!"

Daku was in a boastful mood today. *When was he not?* Kasai wondered.

Cannonball wasn't as confident. "I overheard two of the senior monks saying to Brother Maru that if you fail here, you won't be able to ascend to the higher ranks." He craned his head towards the clouds. "How far up do you think they go?"

"The pillar test is not meant to be completed by initiates. It was designed to help open us to the Boundless," Ri'sonu informed. He hid his hesitation behind a more scholarly approach. "Master Kunchen posted a scroll of who shall go tomorrow. We are the first four to attempt the challenge."

"I thought it wouldn't happen for another season after we had more training," Kasai said.

Ri'sonu and Cannonball stared uncertainly at each other.

"What a bunch of worriers. I'll race you all to the finish," Daku said. "And I'll win, no question."

"It's not a competition," Kasai said.

"Yes, it is. It always is," Daku said with a twisted smile. He turned to walk towards the sparring grounds. "I need to practice a new, low-kick combination. One of you come with me."

Kasai and Ri'sonu shook their heads. But Cannonball fell in step behind Daku.

"Don't go, Cannonball," Kasai said. "You'll regret it."

"I need to practice, too," Cannonball acknowledged.

"Let him go. He's a glutton for punishment when it comes to Daku," Ri'sonu said. "I'm convinced Cannonball reasons the more he lets Daku beat him up, the better friends they will be."

"That's messed up," Kasai said, wondering how often he though the same of himself.

The next morning, the young monks assembled around Master Choejor at the steps of the first pillars. He stood with his arms behind his back, hands clasped beneath his blue robe. His long mustache and wiry beard flowed in a smooth breeze.

Master Choejor's sightless, milk-colored eyes idly gazed at four lines of pillars; each one shaped from white marble quarried along the lower Sarribe hills. Their smooth surfaces glistened with dew. Four stones rested on the ground, starting the first step of an upward climb.

Master Choejor raised his voice to the group, "Brother Kasai, Brother Daku, Brother Jia'mu and Brother Ri'sonu. Step forward. Place your feet on the stone before you. Then you must step to the top of the first pillar, and then the next and next. Let the Boundless guide you, and your path will be clear."

Kasai looked to his right. Ri'sonu and Cannonball had taken their places on the first stones. Cannonball's fat face was filled with worry. He rubbed his left thigh. Brother Daku had not been kind in the sparring circle.

Kasai looked to the pillars before him. Each column rose slightly higher than the previous one. The long line ran parallel to the bend in the hillside and out of sight. Kasai wondered why he had never really noticed them before, or their height.

"Kasai, why are you waiting? Keep up!" Daku said. He had already leaped to the fifth column, which was now at least as tall as a grown man.

Kasai took the first two column steps. Easy. The sun was out, and the path of column tops before him was clear. Although each new column was higher in elevation, it was the same distance from the last one. Soon he was leaping from one column to the next, gaining on Daku.

"This isn't much of a test. I could probably do this blindfolded," Kasai boasted to himself. He could hear Ri'sonu and Cannonball behind him. Neither had difficulty leaping from one column to the next on their designated route.

The pillars mirrored the twisting natural rock formations that populated the area. Kasai rather enjoyed the exercise until the position of the posts became erratic. Up and down they went or jerked out of line. A gust of wind caught Kasai unaware and pushed him to one side. He almost slipped off the top before regaining his balance. "That was close."

Beads of sweat formed on his forehead. "Be mindful of the wind!" Kasai called out to his Brothers.

"I am the wind!" Daku sang. He was at least ten pillars ahead of the others. "Kasai, why so slow? Did you stop for morning tea and a biscuit?"

"Show off!" Cannonball yelled.

"Reckless is more like it," Ri'sonu declared. He was starting to huff.

"I never knew these pillars to be so high," Cannonball complained. "What do the Masters think we will accomplish? What happens if we fall?"

"Keep advancing. Don't give in to fear," Kasai reassured. He wished he could believe his own words. The winds picked up, and with it came a clinging mist. The line of pillars became obscured.

Kasai leaped to the next pillar. This time he skid a heart-stopping inch over the top's slick surface. The entire column shook slightly under his feet, casting subtle vibrations that echoed into the air.

"I can't see anything through the fog," Cannonball said. "I'm getting dizzy. I'm sure to fall."

"Jia'mu, be calm. Breath. Remember your training. Feel the Boundless," Kasai said. He hoped it would reassure Cannonball. Although, when he searched for a connection to the Boundless, all he felt was the cold, wet air.

"I'm climbing down. This is madness," Cannonball said with determined certainty. "Kasai, where are you?"

"Stay on your path. Trust yourself and keep moving forward. You will make it," Kasai called out.

The pillars before Kasai became ghostly silhouettes. *If Daku can do it, so can I*, he reasoned. He leaped to the next pillar and his sandaled feet slid out from under him. He landed on his back, legs dangling in the air. Instinctively, he locked his outstretched hands on the column's shaft. The surface of the stone was slick. Kasai found it challenging to keep his hands in one place. His eyes went wide, staring into white nothingness as his heart pounded in his chest.

"Concentrate on the air around you," Master Choejor called out from somewhere below. "Feel the movement of the moisture in the air. Feel its spirit. Let it define the form of the pillars. Trust your inner sight to guide your next step and leap!"

"But Master, if we fall..." Cannonball said. His voice was like a distant echo to Kasai now.

"Do not let the fear of the unknown prevent you from seeing the truth," Master Choejor said. "Believe in the path Aetenos has set for you. He will guide you. But you must open your eyes and see."

"I cannot see anything!" Cannonball's voice was shaky and small.

"If you cannot see with your eyes open, close them and embrace the Boundless," Master Choejor said.

"I'm afraid!"

"Afraid or not afraid, the outcome is the same. You must jump." Master Choejor's voice drifted into the wind.

Kasai had hardened his body through countless hours of physical training over the years at Ordu. Exposed to harsh weather conditions of the open mountain, he thought he was prepared for anything, yet somehow, this was worse than he could have imagined. The air was cold and biting, draining his strength as he rested on the pillar. Fear invaded his thoughts, causing his muscles trembled.

"Remember your training," Kasai said to the sky. He surrendered to the impossible situation he was in and let the fear fade. He forced his mind to become quiet and relaxed. Somehow, he needed to help Cannonball. Kasai could sense the conflict raging in his friend's thoughts.

"Brother! Calm your mind. Relax!" Kasai shouted from his back.

But as usual, Cannonball refused to listen to good advice. He jumped impulsively to the next column but never landed on its top. Kasai heard a desperate yell falling until the white mist consumed it.

"Cannonball fell!" Ri'sonu shouted. Kasai could tell Ri'sonu was close to breaking.

Master Choejor's calm voice returned. "Do not let the darkness consume you with fear. All is not as it appears in the physical world. Follow the path of Light set by Aetenos. See it. Reach out to it, and it will take your hand."

"I don't see any hands!" Ri'sonu said.

"Ri'sonu, calm down," Kasai called out.

"Kasai, I can't see a thing! Where are you?"

"I am here, Brother. Follow Master Choejor's instructions."

Kasai gathered his strength, curling himself to a sitting position before attempting to stand. Breathe in, breathe out. Kasai twisted his head to the right to where Ri'sonu was trapped. "Concentrate on my voice," Kasai said.

"No. Forget it. I'm done. I'm climbing down. There is no shame in being safe. Climb down with me."

"Ri'sonu, steel your mind and calm your heart. You must move forward."

"No way. I'm not crazy like you and Daku. I have nothing to prove!"

Kasai heard Ri'sonu struggle to lower himself over the edge of the pillar.

"Ri'sonu! Don't do it! The columns are too slick." But it was too late. Ri'sonu's scream echoed throughout the pillars as he fell.

Kasai felt sick to his stomach. What sort of fatal test was this? Climb down and fall. Move forward and fall. Where was Daku? How had he escaped this fate?

Suddenly, Kasai was seized by panic, his breath trapped in his chest. After a moment, he released a deep exhale and regained his composure. "Ok, I can do this."

Exhaling deeply again, he finally felt calm. He balanced on his left leg so he could slip off his right sandal. Kasai tossed it into the mist along with the wet sock he peeled off his foot. The stone was cold and wet on his barefoot, the tactile sensation was reassuring.

Kasi removed his other sandal and sock in the same manner. Now he could press his toes into the stone surface. "If I am to meet my end, then I shall do it moving forward."

Kasai was ready. He leaped for the next pillar but came up short. He just managed to catch the edge of the surface with his toes. Luckily, his momentum carried him forward enough to regain his balance.

Kasai's heart leaped to his throat. His entire body trembled no matter how hard he tried to keep himself calm. He scanned the air in front of him but could barely see the next pillar.

"I must not fear this test. Aetenos shall guide me," Kasai mumbled, wishing the words held more meaning to him.

The air shifted, and the mist blew in his face, blinding him. It was cold, silent, and suffocating. His temples throbbed like thunder at the sides of his head. His breath was quick.

Standing as still as he could, Kasai closed his eyes and forced himself to be calm. He wanted to believe that Aetenos would guide him, but what proof did he have? The Great Monk did not guide the path of his Brothers. How could he let them fall? These initiates were his monks. They represented the living symbols of the man who achieved enlightenment and rose to defeat evil at the height of its power.

And where was the guiding light of Aetenos when he was six years old. His Pa was a true believer in Aetenos, but still, he abandoned Kasai and his Ma to the Darkness. It was why he was here and not still living in the village. He ached for the comfort of his Ma now. She had died that fateful day, but he still felt the loss as if just witnessing it.

Kasai drew a deep breath and exhaled. He would not rely on an absent figurehead to save him. He had done that once when he was six, and it had cost him so much.

"I'm climbing down. Maybe I'll have better luck than Ri'sonu. This is crazy. The Boundless is not real. I don't want to die."

"*Trust me, my son.*" A soft voice came entered his thoughts.

"Father?" Kasai said into the mist.

"*I will guide you.*" Again, the voice was sent through his thoughts. It was like a familiar memory.

Kasai shook his head. "You cannot be my father. He wouldn't be here now. He would be somewhere safe."

"*Believe in me, and I will guide you.*"

"I can do this on my own."

"*Then, you shall fall.*"

"No, I won't." Kasai leaped for the next pillar, landing on the surface but promptly skidding over the side. His head struck something hard. Stars flashed before his eyes, and then he was the air.

Kasai's vision cleared to a dull blur. Somehow, he was alive, feeling like his brain was pushing against his eyeballs. The rough texture of hemp rope crisscrossing his body made his skin raw. Soft voices below him grew louder.

Kasai crawled to the edge of the safety net and lowered himself down to the solid ground. Daku was the first to greet him. "Did you enjoy your little nap?"

"How long have I been up there?" Kasai asked, trying to rub away the stiffness in his arms and legs.

"Who cares? I was the last to fall. I nearly made it to the end!"

Kasai looked dubiously at his friend. Although he had lost sight and sound of Daku, he doubted his friend could have lasted much longer than he did. But what did it matter? The pillars were impossible for anyone to complete.

Kasai realized the point of the lesson was to be exposed to the impossible and contemplate what it was not. Kasai had wished he had known about the safety nets earlier. But then his attempt to reach the Boundless would have been insincere. He needed to learn to trust the unknown.

"Come on, let's watch the next group. They don't know about the nets either. I bet nobody gets even close to my record." Daku said as he ran ahead.

"I'm sure they won't, Brother." Kasai continued rubbing his arms. He was simply happy to be alive.

2

SEKKA

The Arch Devil approached the prison door from a long corridor festooned with the bones of her enemies. It was a menagerie of sorts, dedicated to the souls used to feed her powerful and still growing empire; a dominion that had been brought dangerously close to the brink of disaster by a single man. It had taken long centuries it had taken to rebuild her strength ... all because of *him*.

She reflected momentarily on her prisoner, the one being who had thwarted her plans of conquest in the Mortal Realm. She wasn't even sure how he had managed to gain access to her homeworld of Gathos after her fall. It was said nothing could travel between the Three Realms since the Immortal Mother had created the Amaranthine Barrier. And she should know, she had tried and failed many times to return to the land of mortals after she had been banished.

"It's an intriguing riddle to be solved for another time," she said and tapped the ornate box she held in her hand. "This time will be different, now that I have the proper means to lay the foundation for my return."

She inserted her key into the well-worn lock of the dented, filthy cell door, pushing it through the lock's tumblers. It settled into place, the heavy *thunk* echoing through the depths of the lonely passage. The door swung open and flooded the prison cell with cold light. The prisoner released a painful gasp, but his head remained heavy on his chest.

She saw him as she had left him, a trophy hanging from the wall. His wrists were shackled and spread wide by chains hammered into the stone wall behind him. He turned his head to shield his one remaining eye from the blinding light.

He was not a handsome man, and worse to look at now that his face was swollen and bruised. He was bald except for a graying topknot growing from the back of his head, its braided ends frayed, tangled, and twisted.

She wore a luxurious, ice-blue gown that opened at her navel, plunging to her waistline like the wavy kris tucked in her sash. Her shapely neck rose from a fountain of white sable clasped at her throat. The bottom ruffles of the gown swished upon the thin layer of fresh blood which coated the floor. She left a trail of crimson snakes in her wake.

She wore it as if the Three Kingdoms of Hanna already bowed down to her as their beloved monarch, eager to pay homage to her with their very souls. And that was precisely what she intended. She moved as if part of a breeze towards a small table in the corner. It was cluttered with instruments of torture.

"This mess just won't do," she said, shaking her head. She brushed the iron pinchers and sharp-edged tools aside, casting them unceremoniously to the stone floor in a cacophonous clatter.

She gently placed the box down on the table's surface. Her black nails tapped out a simple rhythm over its top. She wore gaudy rings covered in precious stones on her fingers. The facets caught the light and created a dazzling kaleidoscope of color against the walls, though the onyx stone on her left index finger refused to join the celebration of light. The stone greedily devoured the light rather than reflect it with its sisters.

The angles of her face sat high on her long, serpentine neck. She looked him over with dark, iris-less eyes. He was helpless.

His abused body shivered underneath the tatters of his once cobalt-blue robes, now soiled and faded. She thought the sharp lines of his ruined face agreed handsomely with the cracked backdrop of the masonry from which he hung.

She swept towards him, wearing a devilish grin of satisfaction, stopping intimately close to his body to breathe in a deep draught of his intoxicating stench.

She had been thrown a morsel of luck, and she intended to exploit it to the fullness of its measure. She had longed for this moment for over a thousand years. He would serve as the leverage she needed to defeat her rivals. And, he had practically shown up on her doorstep. Oh, this was rich.

She glided forward into the cramped cell. An intricate, alabaster headdress rested on her head, blending gracefully with her white mane of long hair. The fiendish crown was made of hundreds of human bones and revealed the truth of her nature. Tiny skulls of infants dangled down her back and mingled with the long strands of her stark hair. Her headpiece clattered and knocked as the smaller pieces spun with her movements and clashed together.

Her thick, indigo lips parted ever so slightly as her excitement grew. She imagined the suffering he would endure when he discovered the full magnitude of her intentions. It was a just punishment for interfering with her plans of conquest so many years ago.

Today was the day of reckoning. Her gaze swept over his stretched and suspended body, which somehow still managed to resist the harsh lashes and probing cuts of her chief tormentor, the demon witch, Chedipe.

She lowered her head and raised playfully seductive eyes towards her unlikely benefactor. Her mocking interest was as a cruel reminder of her duplicitous nature. She gripped his chin with slender fingers and forced him to look back at her. "Aetenos, my dear. Why such a dour face? Are you not happy to see me again?" she chuckled mockingly. "Perhaps my flavor of hospitality is not to your liking?"

She moved even closer to his body and dropped her hand to glide along his quivering flesh. "I'm surprised you haven't called your winged playmates to rescue you. Snap, snap, and here they come, ready to save the day." She sneered at him. "But not this time and not here; Gathos is where angels come to die."

Aetenos twisted his neck away from her and whispered out her name in a sorrowful sigh, "Sekka."

A wicked smile played across her over-sized mouth. She dragged her fingers across his tormented flesh, angling pointed nails into the dark burgundy welts already covering his body. New lines of bright red beaded on his skin.

She glanced down at the three small beasts at her feet. The creatures feasted on the dripping life fluid of her prisoner. She kicked one to the side, and it became animated with excitement as if her action was an acknowledgment of tenderness. The others howled back at her in earnest.

"I am hoping they sing a song of joyful despair to the innocents you have failed. Alas, who can understand such beasts? Nonetheless, I am forever grateful to you for coming to my home as you did. I assure you, if I were allowed to go to you on my own accord, I would have been at your doorstep ages ago. But such fanciful ideas are no longer the way of things, and sadly, one must accept the rules of the game as they change."

She took a step backward, admiring Chedipe's work. "I imagine your journey here was arduous and fraught with peril, yes? Now tell me, truthfully, you missed me, didn't you? We have such history together, do we not? Did true love finally bring you running to my door, or was it simply the desire to lay with one not so innocent of the flesh?"

"I would never," Aetenos said.

"Oh, do stop with all this self-righteous dignity. The heavenly shine of your soul has dimmed. I can see that clearly enough."

Aetenos showed little spark of life. His body hung deflated like a condemned and forsaken man.

"Come now. You look disheartened. Tsk, tsk, what did you expect, a parade?"

Her brows furrowed, and she glared intensely at the monk. "You cheated when you called the angels for help and cost me centuries of accumulated mortal soul energy! I should have rivaled the power of the Great Three by now, but no, you had to interfere. You left me weak on Gathos. Do you have any idea how much favor I needed to call due … just to survive?"

Sekka brought her hands down to the edges of her open gown and traced the exposed parts of her breasts with her two small fingers. Her black nails traveled down to her midsection, leaving razor-thin lines of blue malice in her translucent skin. "But survive I did."

She giggled. "How bitter I must sound. But one must play their part, and I do so love mine. Isn't that what you preach, 'All things in their natural way' or some such nonsense?"

Sekka played absentmindedly with the blood that bubbled up from the cuts. It was one of her favorite pastimes. She drew a blue line across his cracked lips, then licked her fingers clean, one-by-one. She savored every drop. Her wounds closed immediately, leaving no trace of the incision.

She grabbed his flaccid cock, squeezing it until he moaned. Her eyes widened with anticipation as his meat filled with blood. "You cannot fool me. You thought to break me again, but I did not see Ninziz-zida in your hands when you arrived. Has the Fire Serpent abandoned you as well, or did you think to use this righteous scepter instead of the fiery sticks?" Sekka shook his member. "Did you hope to turn me to the Light? Was that your plan?"

Sekka laughed. "Or better yet, did you wish to possess me like one of your mind slaves? I hear you are known for choosing an unsuspecting mortal to carry out your whim, all in the name of..."

She observed his reaction. "Not so easy, silly monk. I wouldn't dare speak *Her* name here. Names are so important, are they not?" Sekka warily glanced upwards and waited. Nothing. She gave Aetenos a knowing wink. "There, you see. Nothing to fear."

She brought one hand to her mouth. Her long fingers danced over her lips. "I wonder, could it be that you are here because you no longer hold favor with the little birds in their pristine halls and cloudless skies?" Sekka squeezed his thick member again, her nails digging into the flesh. "I hate little birds."

Then she released him. She swished away as if twirled by an invisible dance partner.

"But the reasons why you are here and how you skirted the Amaranthine Barrier carry little importance to me at the moment. What matters to me now is that you *are* here, and I can use you.

"My dear Aetenos, you have been as much a thorn in my side, much like that irritating Red Devil. But now, like him, you are pitiful and weak. My trap is closing over you both. Be assured, you will not beat me a second time."

Aetenos raised his head. "I am bound by way of the Immortal Mother. Her sight of all things flows quick...as the monsoon. You...have been...exposed, like all things...under the sun." His breath wheezed out of his mouth. "You cannot hide... from her eyes," he said in a shaky voice. "But...I did not come for...you."

She laughed. "Oh, but you did. You came straight to my door. You were driven here by madness with the hopes of being a hero once more. Slay the dragon, save the despairing, helpless maiden, and all that nonsense. If you succeeded, you could regain the respect of your winged friends. Maybe the little birds might even take you back. Ah, but now the dragon has you by the balls, and the maiden has vanished. Found another plaything, has she?"

"I know...Illyria is here. Prisoner...through trickery," he said. "I am here to free her...from your prison of lies."

Sekka could see he barely had the strength to speak.

"Yes, your passionate devotion to that *angel* is admirable, if not misplaced. Illyria is here and has become a favorite plaything to many of the dark lords of Gathos. Much to her liking, I might add."

"Lies...Illyria remains...pure."

"And you remain delusional to the end. But we have other matters to discuss."

He raised his head slowly. "You will get nothing from me. You cannot hide... behind this glamour...vile creature." His head dropped to his chest again. Drool laced with blood bubbled at his lips. "I know what you are."

"Vile? I chose this attire just for you. Don't you like my appearance? Tempting, is it not?" She traced the heavily embroidered silk lace and stroked the white ermine at its edge.

She gave Aetenos a dramatic pout. "I'd like our time together to be enjoyable. I simply thought this form would be more pleasing to you," Sekka said with an impish smile. Her tone was seductive.

She grabbed his chin again. "Look at me! Do I not entice you? There are other, more aggressive forms I can take if you like. You've seen them before."

Her fingers teased down his stomach again and traced his exposed manhood. She cradled its length gently in her palm. "I see the angels didn't squeeze all mortal desire from you during your transformation."

"The Boundless…is my truth. It will save me…from your temptations…" He shook his head. His voice was barely a whisper. "It is…my truth."

"I will tell you what is true, monk. Me! I am the truth!" The fury in her voice magnified in the small chamber. "I am the cold in the air, and I am the frost on the ground. The deep power of Gathos is mine! The flames of the Red Devil will not have this land!"

Aetenos smiled. "Zizphander approaches…once more, but…in strength. The gameboard…grows broader."

She finally heard the quiet confidence in his voice that she so despised.

"You know nothing!" Her black eyes blazed with hatred, and she clenched her jaw.

How could he know? Her body shook with rage causing the skulls and bones of her headdress to thrash together. She stopped at the table and marshaled her emotions.

"But enough of this seriousness. Your hallowed serenity is all I desire, my dear. And so, I have brought you this gift in appreciation for our time together. I crafted it specifically for you and your unique nature."

Sekka opened the lavish box and took out a small, finely detailed amulet. The jeweled piece was attached to an intricately woven chain. Carved upon each link were hundreds of hard-edged symbols. Her face was close to his when she placed it around his neck. She lightly caressed his cheeks with both hands and kissed him hard against the lips. Then she pushed his head away.

His arms stretched to take on the weight of the amulet. Its small size belied its burden. The charm began to glow a putrid green as it throbbed against his bare chest like a second heart.

Sekka stepped back, appreciating the beautiful work of her craftsmanship. "It's perfect, just as I had hoped."

She shut the lid of the box, closing it with a click. She then moved towards the chamber door. Sekka stopped at the entrance and glanced back at Aetenos.

"You cannot fathom the boon you have given me by coming here. And for that, I am grateful. The legions of Gathos shall sacrifice uncounted mortal souls on temples raised in your honor. Your name will be worshiped throughout eternity."

Sekka slammed the heavy door shut. She leaned her back against its cold metal. Her smile came quickly as the Great Monk began to chant. The typical melodic tones and overlapping harmonies were replaced by sound patterns of pleading desperation. It was music to her ears.

There was just one more piece to connect. When it fell into place, she would ascend higher than any Arch Devil in the timeless history of the Abyss. Her nemesis, the Red Devil, Zizphander, would become an afterthought.

"That's it. Call to your mind-slave. Raise the next Ever Hero and seal the fate of the Mortal Realm into everlasting doom."

Sekka left the monk to his work; she had much to prepare.

3

SHIVERRIG

Volkerrum Keep was an ancient castle. It was built long ago on the backs of the conquered after the invasion of the warlord, Baroq Shiverrig from the East. The castle was the first of its kind to be built in the untamed wilderness.

Within a generation, the families of the invading warriors flowed beyond the Keep's walls and settled closer to the sea. The port city of Gethem was established and served as the entryway into untapped trade opportunities with the homeland across the sea.

Volkerrum Keep had been the seat of power for the Kingdom of Baroqia and the home of House Shiverrig for countless generations. War banners of deep-rose and purple hung from ceiling rafters within the Keep's Great Hall. The heavy cloth fluttered in a lazy dance from heat billowing from the blazing fire against the wall.

Duke Gerun Shiverrig, the last scion of the Shiverrig bloodline and heir to a usurped throne, sat at a long table and brooded over unpleasant news. He raised his eyes to King Mortimer Conrad's court messenger. The young boy's face showed a hint of impatience, which further infuriated Duke Shiverrig. *Again, Mortimer sinks his jackal's teeth into my flesh. The man means to bleed me dry*, Duke Shiverrig thought.

"Your answer, my lord?" the messenger said. The boy possessed the same arrogance as the king. He spoke as if he commanded a hundred knights at his back.

"No." The answer was more of a growl than a word.

"My pardon, my lord. What?"

"I said, no!"

Duke Shiverrig pounded his oversized fist on the massive, oak table. The force of the blow shook the clay jugs filled with dry wine from the plains of Western Baroqia. Exotic fruit wobbled in their shallow bowls, freeing an orange to drop from its stack and roll across the table. Duke Shiverrig eyed it menacingly then swatted it across the room.

Shadows from the fire rippled across his smooth scalp. His anger took on the fiery aspect of the blaze. The short whiskers that made up his dark, trimmed beard stood out like the raised hackles of a beast.

"I will not be dictated to by that fool, Mortimer Conrad, and his council of dimwitted sycophants. I refuse to acknowledge him as the rightful King of Baroqia!" Duke Shiverrig said.

He stood abruptly. His legs tangled with the chair until he kicked it away as if he was an angry mule. He was a colossal man and moved like an apex predator. Shiverrig circled the young messenger whose eyes were now wide with fear.

"For twenty-two years, I have endured this imposter who poses like a king on my father's stolen throne. And now, he looks to weaken my family's House even further by stealing more men."

"Yes, my lord." The boy bowed in acquiescence. He was trembling when he rose. "I mean, the king wishes to have you formally acknowledge the demands of his letter, Sir."

Duke Shiverrig stopped his rampage. He turned to the tall stone columns that supported the rafters.

"Malachi, come out where I can see you. This is your responsibility. You are supposed to be managing this!"

Archvashim Malachi stepped out of the shadows in burgundy robes with copper trim. Malachi was a tall man. He was narrow at the shoulders with angular features and penetrating eyes. He bowed in silence before Duke Shiverrig.

"I am here, my lord. It would seem impolite not to reply in some way to King Conrad's letter. Ideally, he will wish to know that you have complied with his command."

Duke Shiverrig's eyes grew wide with amazement. "I know that!"

He twisted back to the messenger. The quickness of his movement belied his considerable bulk. He looked for something to break. The messenger would do.

"A symbol of my obedience is needed, yes?" His slate-grey eyes narrowed on the messenger like a lion eying a rabbit. Duke Shiverrig pulled the long knife from the belt at his waist and watched the messenger's complexion pale. The boy took a few steps backward.

"A simple word of acknowledgment will do, my lord," the messenger stuttered.

"My lord," Malachi spoke in soothing tones, "Perhaps this is not the ideal message to send at this time."

"It is a message that is long overdue, Malachi," Duke Shiverrig said. He looked over the messenger's body with hungry eyes. "I'll carve it into the lad's flesh."

Malachi moved passed Duke Shiverrig like a specter. He laid a bony hand on the messenger's shoulder.

"Please inform King Conrad that Duke Gerun Shiverrig, the one hundred and fifteenth lord bearing the Shiverrig crest, is willing to do his duty to the realm. House Shiverrig will send more troops to patrol the borderlands. The Knights of Gethem will end the rash of brigand attacks against the frontier villages. See to the notary in the front chambers. He will affix the Duke's seal to the King's Letter, along with my blessing."

"Thank you, Archvashim Malachi," the messenger said. He quickly bowed, then scurried out of the room.

"Malachi, you overstep your usefulness once again," Duke Shiverrig said. His flash temper had abated but simmered just under the surface of control. "I have no intention of sending the Knights of Gethem to protect peasants in frontier villages. MY men will not be used to bolster the king's weak position in the outer territories. Let him send his reserves from Qaqal."

"The king is testing you. But there is a greater prize to be had here than rebuking the king's wishes. In time you will convert more of the kingdom's people to your cause than mere peasants," Malachi said in a conspirator's tone. The Archvashim rounded the large table and poured two glasses of wine from one of the clay jugs. "Come, let us sit and talk."

Duke Shiverrig remained standing. His burly arms folded across his chest. His stance was as immovable as his opinion of the king. "So, you still advocate an alliance with those meddling monks, or do you have some new scheme for me to ponder?"

Malachi took a sip from his glass and considered the bouquet. "There are many possibilities to consider but let us speak of the monks today. You must seek either an alliance with the monks of the Four Orders or their destruction. Each outcome would serve you well. Faith is an exquisite weapon when wielded with artful hands. Many subjects of the realm still pray for the return of Aetenos. He became a demigod, after all, or so say the true believers." Malachi rolled his eyes at the lunacy that any man could ascend to godhood.

"His monks represent the undefinable connection to the divine in human form. That is a powerful tool to be manipulated. Most people need to believe there is something more waiting for them after their time in this world is over."

"Yet, you have cast your die with Mor, the embodiment of change, chaos, and creation. He is the antithesis of the stability and lawfulness that Aetenos offers his followers. Why would you give your support to those who oppose your prophet?"

"The masses are easily swayed," answered Malachi. "There is a fine line between truth and heresy. Influence, not power, control the ideas that take shape on either side of that line. The song of Aetenos has been silent for hundreds of years. The convenient story says he has fully ascended and will never return to the Mortal Realm, which makes the monks the last embodiment of his legacy to this land. Win over the monks and slowly have your influence become their influence."

The Duke shook his head doubtfully. "No easy feat. Those stubborn monks are set in their ways. They will not turn. And who knows how many still exist outside of the Temple of Illumination? The locations of their remote monasteries remain hidden, though I suspect their sanctuaries were abandoned long ago. But if we could apply political pressure on the Temple and change the mindset from the top down..."

Malachi sipped his wine before answering. "Yes, that would seem to be the solution. Unfortunately, Grandmaster Marmo Nysulu remains shackled to tradition. As we have seen time and again, he is steadfast in his unwillingness to become associated with any political affiliations whatsoever. Eventually, he will need to be removed."

Malachi smiled at the thought and continued, "For now, the prudent strategy is to stay the course. Let the despair of the land prove Aetenos has fled this world. The last blight was not so long ago that people have forgotten hardship. Let the monks become reminders of Aetenos' betrayal of the people's trust. Cast the blame for the difficulties throughout the land on them. Nobody wants to see the hard times return, and when they do, the people will need someone to blame.

"Either way, you are in control of the levers of influence. They will join you, or they will be replaced."

"The spoils of the chaos you are advocating is taking longer to enjoy than you anticipated. As it is, I am depleting my power base by supporting Conrad's demands for more troops. This will only get worse." Duke Shiverrig reached for the glass of wine Malachi had poured for him. He drank deeply from the cup as if it was water. He hardly appreciated the vintage. His grandfather once said, 'Wine was a fancy drink for fancy men.'

"No, I think we go for the head of the beast and work our way down. Nysulu must have a vulnerability, something we can exploit."

"He is the Grandmaster of the Seventh Heaven. One does not ascend to such an elevated rank without amassing certain powers. To say he is vulnerable would be a mistake. But he has been the spiritual leader of the monks of the Four Orders for many decades. No matter how noble the heart, ambition stirs the desires of those who wait impatiently in line for their turn to rule."

Duke Shiverrig tapped the rim of the wine glass with his index finger. "I do not want to disrupt the machinations of the Temple. The last thing I need is a martyrdom here in Gethem. Conrad would not hesitate to use that against me. We shall work to sway Nysulu to our cause, rather than remove him outright."

"As luck would have it, Grandmaster Nysulu has deigned to come down from his lofty tower and is eager to bend your ear to his needs. He shall arrive at Volkerrum Keep upon the morrow. We shall see then if he is willing to listen to reason or not," Malachi said, wearing a fox's smile.

The Duke looked suspiciously at his Archvashim. He knew better than to take anything Malachi said at face-value. His Archvashim was a cunning and deceptive man with a head for politics. There was always a hidden twist to every plot Malachi hatched.

"How convenient," Shiverrig deadpanned.

The corridor walls leading to the Grand Hall of Volkerrum Keep were lined with stone sculptures of House Shiverrig's legendary heroes. The figures displayed a decisive victory over a beaten and broken foe and presented a powerful icon during the rise of the Kingdom Baroqia.

Each stone progeny was twice the size of an ordinary man. The figures had been carved masterfully from a single block of Phrygian marble. The artisans used the purple and rose veins found naturally in the rock to form the appearance of a circulatory system around the stone bodies. House Shiverrig had long ago associated their rule with the enduring qualities of the rock and took the colors for their banners and shields.

The Shiverrig family crest was proudly displayed on the heroes' shields and armored plates. Centered in the shield, a mastiff appeared ready to slip its stone confines to tear out the viewer's throat, its snarling muzzle showing that it would give no quarter, nor let go with its long, slavering fangs. The statues were also meant to be a stark reminder of House Shiverrig's dominance over any who challenged their rule. The message was clear. Defy us at your own risk.

The first statues wore artifacts of the warlord's power and absolute rule, and the latter figures were graced with majestic crowns, except for the last one. The stone icon of Gareth Shiverrig, Gerun's father, wore no such article of office. The bitter taste of Mortimer Conrad's ascension over his father's was ever present in Gerun's mouth. Between each sculpture hung a thick, purple banner with rose trim—colors meant for royalty and rule and another unpleasant reminder to Gerun's current station.

Duke Shiverrig waited the next petitioner, impatient in his majestic chair. Tapping his fingers slowly on the arm, he scanned the room looking for threats; a habit learned from the murder of his father.

An immense tapestry hung the length of the wall behind him. The finely crafted artwork depicted scenes of his paternal ancestors commanding the Five Armies of the realm to victory. It was the backdrop he preferred when addressing the citizen of Gethem or nobles from neighboring cities.

Two men stood to either side of Duke Shiverrig. On his left was Archvashim Malachi who bent slightly to speak in Shiverrig's ear.

"They will be along shortly."

Duke Shiverrig gave a gruff nod.

Malachi wore his religious robes of high office for the meeting with Grandmaster Nysulu. The cloth was bruised purple and flaunted gold trim around the wrists and neckline. A medallion inlaid with a faceted ruby hung heavy at his neck. The jewelry reflected a myriad of red hues whenever the Archvashim moved. The Shiverrig crest was proudly displayed on the upper left side of Malachi's robe. The emblem of Mor was embroidered on the right side. The design was a haphazard pattern to symbolize the constant change of chaos.

A famed Knight of Gethem stood at attention to Duke Shiverrig's right. He was encased in light armor with formal purple tabard hanging low over his steel plate. He stood silent and tall. The studded mace at his hip was well worn and easily accessible if needed. The knight's hands repeatedly flexed into fists at his sides.

A page appeared at the entered the entrance of the Great Hall to announce the arrival of Marmo Nysulu, the Revered Grandmaster of the Seventh Heaven, along with two of his senior monks. Duke Shiverrig bade them forward with a wave of his hand. He waited for what felt like an eternity for them to approach.

"As if time stood still for the righteous. They move slower than crawling stones," Shiverrig said under his breath.

"Quite so," Malachi said. "Pride goeth before the fall."

The Grandmaster and his attendants stopped at the foot of the dais, looking up at the Duke in unison, while Duke Shiverrig eased back in his chair. He appraised Nysulu with a tight smile. The man was old. He looked frail enough to be toppled by a strong wind.

"My Lord Duke Shiverrig, we are honored to be accepted into your home and to share this time with you. We have urgent matters to discuss," Grandmaster Nysulu said.

"A good day to you, Old Father," Duke Shiverrig said. "Please proceed."

Nysulu gathered his thoughts. Everything he did was frustratingly slow. Finally, he cleared his throat and spoke. "Horrendous reports continue to arrive at the Temple of Illumination. Barbarian raiders have come down from the Hoarfrost Mountains and sacked many of the frontier villages. Brigands roam unchecked across the grasslands. Even the streets of your fair city have become infected by a great madness. Gethem has turned sour."

Shiverrig shrugged as if the news was commonplace.

"It has always fallen to House Shiverrig to be the shield of the land," Nysulu said.

His tone was patronizing.

"I am aware of the responsibilities bestowed to my House," Duke Shiverrig said. Anger laced his voice at being reprimanded in such a way. "Of course, there is some unrest in the outer provinces. That is to be expected during the harvest months."

"I fear we are being plagued by something far worse than typical unrest. Seven villages containing small monasteries devoted to the teaching of Aetenos have been destroyed. The farmhouses have been put to the torch, and the livestock of the village butchered and left to rot in the smoking embers."

"I am sorry to hear this, Old Father," Shiverrig said. His fingers rolled on the armrest of his chair. "The frontier villagers are not for the meek. Those who live there know the risks."

"The villagers were left crucified on tall posts surrounding the halls of prayer. Each post has a plaque nailed to the top of the cross with the words 'False Believer' written in blood.

"Yet, in other villages, the ravens have been deprived of their feast. The villagers have vanished; yet all of their possessions remain in place. This is not the work of commonplace bandits. You must send troops to protect the souls of the innocents."

Duke Shiverrig's ire grew. His opinion of Grandmaster Nysulu changed. The man was just another version of King Conrad. Only Nysulu disguised his desire to take from House Shiverrig behind the glamour of spiritual guidance.

"As I have said, the wilderness is a dangerous place, and I cannot run to the rescue of every remote hamlet when a roving band of brigands comes calling. The king has taken great care to thin my already depleted armed ranks. I have no more to give." Shiverrig shrugged his shoulders.

"These people have chosen to live outside the protection of my city walls. They pay little in tax to Volkerrum Keep's coffers, and therefore, I'm less inclined to help. Perhaps you could send a gaggle of monks to each village and pray for their wellbeing."

"My Lord Duke, brigands pay no heed to the faith of others or care of the taxes paid to coffers," Grandmaster Nysulu said. "These people need you. The Knights of Gethem must ride."

Malachi subtly cleared his throat in disagreement causing the Grandmaster to raise a curious eyebrow.

"This is the work of the Followers of Mor!" a senior monk exclaimed. "They are attempting to drive the faithful of Aetenos from the land of Baroqia. King Conrad has decreed that all faiths are welcome in the realm."

"You have no proof of this, monk. The Followers of Mor are not butchers. This is an outrageous accusation," Malachi said. He glared at the Grandmaster. "You should know better."

The Grandmaster nodded to Malachi. "This is true. My aid misspoke. At this time, there is no conclusive evidence to the contrary. For now, we will assume these atrocities are what they appear to be. I apologize for the slight to your prophet, Archvashim Malachi." The Grandmaster's tone was respectful yet carried the weight of a man with a heavy burden.

The Grandmaster returned his attention to Duke Shiverrig. "The City of Gethem is in chaos. Have you not seen this with your own eyes? When has a son of House Shiverrig allowed such lawlessness in the streets of Gethem?"

Duke Shiverrig straightened in his chair. His anger rose. Who was this feeble monk to dare criticize him and his family's honor? He felt Malachi's bony fingers press into his shoulder. It was enough of a gesture to remind Shiverrig of the strategy behind this meeting.

"Yes, the unrest does appear to be a bit more pronounced of late. Perhaps some of it is caused by these unorthodox cults of the prophet, Mor. I don't know. Their ideas of constant change are not to my taste. I appreciate order.

"But, as your man says, all religions and faiths are welcome, per the king," Duke Shiverrig said. "I suggest you take your grievances to the King's Council in Qaqal."

"You are honor-bound to at least investigate the evil infecting the lands under your stewardship. You must report your findings to the highest authority so that a solution can be found." Nysulu's demeanor remained calm, though his words were like arrows into Duke Shiverrig's pride.

"Highest of authority, indeed. By that, you mean King Conrad," Duke Shiverrig said with a slight smirk. "This is unlikely to happen. Conrad can reconnoiter with his men, or you can send one of your traveling monks to the borderlands."

"The monks of the Four Orders will wait to see how we can best assist the king's decision."

Duke Shiverrig leaned forward. "There is another solution. Help me take command of the Five Armies. I assure you I would end the malady afflicting the land in short order. I'm sure the spiritual blessing of the Reverend Grandmaster Nysulu and the backing of the Temple of Illumination would go far in the ears of the King's Council."

The Grandmaster closed his eyes. Duke Shiverrig heard a slight sigh escape the Grandmaster's lips. Duke Shiverrig knew his message had been received. He waited patiently for the Grandmaster's answer. The crackle and pop of the fire burning against the wall filled the room. The Grandmaster finally shook his head.

"You know I cannot. The officials at the Temple are not to influence politics or side with any noble house or cause. We are the living spirit and faith of Aetenos. We are not political pawns to be used to outmaneuver rivals."

Duke Shiverrig eased back into his chair. He wasn't surprised by Nysulu's obvious answer. "Indeed, we all have our paths to walk. You see, Old Father, I have already mobilized a contingent of my forces to the northern border. My men may already be shedding their blood defending the land. And just earlier, your king asked for more. But where are the other armies? There is but a token host mustering at Qaqal. Where are Duke Rokig's, Lord Fritta's, or Lord Manda's men?"

The Duke continued with an irritated voice. "Truly, I am doing everything in my power to assist the paper crown, even at the expense of the stability of my fair Gethem, as you have so kindly pointed out.

"And why are my forces spread thin across Baroqia while King Conrad keeps his men safely in Qaqal? Why indeed, I wonder. Why does King Conrad not deal with these brigands himself? Perhaps there is a deeper reason."

"Which would be?" Nysulu looked perplexed.

"Due to the lack of support and decisive action from the crown, my thoughts cannot help but stray to thinking King Conrad is under the yoke of the Mad One in the North."

"Impossible!" Nysulu's second aid barked. The younger monk placed his foot on the first step of the dais. The knight at Duke Shiverrig's side held his mace ready to strike.

The Grandmaster gave a sideways glance at his aid. The monk immediately bowed low. "Forgive me, Grandmaster. I apologize for my emotional outburst and lack of control." Nysulu accepted his apology with a nod. The Grandmaster then looked at the Duke Shiverrig and his knight.

"Lower your weapon, Sir Marchan. Let us remain cordial in the presence of our esteemed guest," Duke Shiverrig added. He was curious about what would happen if the conversation escalated to violence. Just how fast could the old monk move?

The Grandmaster nodded his appreciation as Sir Marchan begrudgingly lowered his mace. "Duke Shiverrig, you are considered the Champion of Baroqia, and as such, you must accept your role as the servant of the king."

"Yes, yes," Duke Shiverrig spat, his voice was razor-sharp. "All the symbolism and none of the authority. Command of the Five Armies should be mine and mine alone. I fear our dear king will bestow that honor to his incompetent son, Dane, or perhaps that imbecile Baron Rokig.

"Yet, the Knights of Gethem account for more than a third of the might of the Five Armies. These are my loyal men. Again, if I had the support of the Temple, we could correct what is now wrong in the realm."

Grandmaster Nysulu listened politely. His manner was peaceful when he spoke. "Now is not the time to revisit family rivalries or hurt pride. Times have changed. Let the past stay where it belongs. You have authority in your city, yet we see the faithful of Aetenos being unjustly persecuted. The public squares in the Temple District are full of crucifixions. How can you turn a blind eye? All faiths and spiritual ways must be given equal measure. That is the great balance we all bow to."

"Thieves, witches and the treasonous are dealt with according to the law. Faith is irrelevant," Duke Shiverrig said. "I will not tolerate disloyalty or betrayal. This is well known."

Shiverrig's eyes challenged Nysulu. But Nysulu would not rise to the bait. The Grandmaster remained calm and composed.

Malachi boldly stepped in front of the Duke, his voice that of a hissing snake. "Aetenos the Bright has passed into darkness. He is known as Aetenos the Abandoner in many corners of the realm. When the people have fully embraced the Change of Mor, they will want for naught and will be delivered from this depravity. There shall be a great cleansing, and the faithful will be rewarded."

The Grandmaster's countenance softened as he looked at Malachi. His words were coated with pity. "You seek to control the people through deception and distraction. You court the weak-minded and take advantage of their fears. To do so upsets the Great Balance and darkens the light of those you touch. I fear your prophet Mor is but a pawn to the Great Manipulator."

Malachi sneered. "Such are the words of the self-righteous!" He turned to Duke Shiverrig. "You see, my lord? It is worse than you expected. Not only has Aetenos abandoned the people, but his servants that remain have mouths filled with lies."

Duke Shiverrig worried at the sudden level of passion emanating from his Archvashim. Malachi's voice held too much excitement. This wasn't the approach he had expected or wanted from his advisor. Rather than building a bridge of common ground with the Grandmaster and the Temple of Illumination, Malachi was pushing the monks away. At this rate, they would never unify under his banner.

Duke Shiverrig motioned to the page at the far entrance of the Great Hall. "Who's next?"

Thankfully, the Grandmaster understood at once that his time was over. He bowed low.

"I apologize for being abrupt, Old Father, but there are many that would have the ear of their Duke this day. Let me think more about what you have said. We shall speak again."

"Thank you for the time you have given us, Duke Shiverrig. Follow and be guided by the Light."

Another page came to ferry the monks away from the dais. Duke Shiverrig barely acknowledged the good wishes of the Grandmaster. *Malachi, you damn fool*, he thought. He was tempted to cancel the remaining audiences. His mind raced with appropriate punishments for his Archvashim. *I should have you flogged for such an outburst or rip that viper's tongue out of your throat.* Malachi had some explaining to do.

"I question your tact," Duke Shiverrig said. He pointed a gnarled finger at Malachi as the Archvashim entered the library. "You did more damage than good."

Malachi poured himself a goblet of wine and sat at the large oak table at the center of the room. The walls were lined with old tomes, bound in leather. Iron candelabras stood upright, holding candles of various lengths. Their flames danced upon oiled wicks. The hot wax dripped from the candelabra's iron arms, creating miniature stalactites.

"If I had played to the sensibilities of the old man, he would have immediately seen through that act. I told you; he will not sway from tradition.

"To borrow a simple idea of those fervent monks, when faced against an immovable object, one must flow like water around it. Simply put, there are other avenues to reach your goal. Your path to the throne requires a broader view of our world and the other realms connected to it."

"Don't bore me with your stories of divine intervention. Influence be damned. Steel is the real power that creates empires and brings lesser men to their knees," Duke Shiverrig said.

"With all due respect, my lord. Grandmaster Nysulu is no lesser man. You will need something special to move him," Malachi said.

"No doubt you have a lever in mind."

"Naturally, I would be of little use to you otherwise."

"Get on with it then," Shiverrig growled impatiently.

"There are alliances to be made that will unite the Three Kingdoms under one rule. I have recently contacted one who will be a great asset to you. She is the lever that will move Nysulu, one way, or the other.

"More politics," Duke Shiverrig grumbled. He yearned for the truth of battle, not more of Malachi's schemes. He understood what a properly placed sword could do to bone, blood, and muscle. Politics were for weak men that tricked and schemed behind each other's backs. He took the dagger from his belt and thrust it into the table. "I grow tired of waiting."

Malachi took a long draught of wine from his goblet. "Soon, everything will change. Of course, there will be a price to pay, but when is there not—for greatness?"

"Malachi, you sound as if you wish for me to make a deal with the devil."

A mischievous smile crept up the corners of Malachi's mouth. "Interesting choice of words."

4

SEKKA

Sekka brooded as she walked along the ice passageway that led to her bath chamber. Word from her spies was that the Red Devil was on the move again. Zizphander had invaded the territory of one of her weaker allies, a devil based in the outer planes that provided her with early warnings of the movements of her enemies, of which there were many. In all of her years, she had never known a more tenacious devil than Zizphander. Well, except for herself, of course.

Soon, she would be called upon to send more troops from her Frost Legion to support her ally's war effort. The plea for help was nothing new. But it was best to be cautious rather than rash. Lord Oziax, First General of her armies, was sent to survey the actual damage. It was wise to keep a watchful eye on her allies and their so-called needs.

The outskirt of Gathos was a spawning ground for ambitious demons and the occasional lesser devil. Every *thing* in the Abyss desired more power. It was a greedy addiction that was never satiated. Therefore, whenever she discovered one of her minions had become too influential, she would send Lord Oziax to ensure the new demon lord knew his place.

Typically, a tithe would be levied, and a new warlord would rise in the ranks of her Frost Legion. On rare occasions, Oziax brought back the demon lord's head. There were those in the Abyss that simply did not understand their place.

She reflected on the numerous carcasses of demons and devils collected over the centuries and frozen within the walls of the corridor. Each of them had thought to betray her or steal what was hers. *Such fools*, she thought. One day, that pest Zizphander would become an addition to her macabre museum. Seka smiled, thinking of his permanent installation.

She entered the changing room, moving over to her jewelry counter where she removed her ornamental headdress and set it upon a polished skull of a lesser demon —the tiny skulls and bones clattering as they settled into place. She still remembered the beast's name, for names were so important in the Abyss.

Beside it, a row of bone tiaras, crowns, headpieces and necklaces, all placed neatly on the skulls of defeated foes. She picked up a favorite small crown made of upright canine teeth; each one ripped from the mouth of an insubordinate demon.

Sekka saw herself reflected in the smooth surface of the ice walls of the chamber. She was glorious. She enjoyed being in the form of a mortal human and appreciated the sleek, sensual curves of her body. She was fascinated by the graceful way her arms and legs flowed as she walked.

She saved her demonic body for bloodier work. Even after all the centuries of her existence, she still relished the expression of horror her captives wore as she changed her shape before their awestruck eyes.

Her quick ascendancy had created bitter jealously among the minions of Hell, with mortal and divine enemies soon to follow. Chief among them was now the Red Devil, Zizphander. He was the only force strong enough to challenge her reign on Gathos.

I have defeated him before and will do so again, she thought, but her confidence was thin. Somehow, Zizphander was able to move his horde of fire demons across the Abyss unseen until the moment he struck. Taken by surprise, her allies would crumble before the overwhelming force of his war machine.

"I must have more soul energy—and soon," Sekka mattered as she undid her formal gown and let it fall to the floor. She stepped out of the encircling material, kicking it to the corner for a servant to pick up. From the row of softly simmering gowns, she picked a sheer robe, donning it as she once again ruminated on opening a Chaos Gate to the Mortal Realm. She'd have the means to crush any that opponent; Zizphander would be the first to perish, this time for good.

The Immortal Mother had made access to the Mortal Realm limited or near impossible since Sekka's last invasion. Only a small, cumbersome portal could be opened for a short period of time. Oh, she thought longingly, a Chaos Gate. It was the one thing that could potentially bypass the magic wards of the Amaranthine Barrier. The endeavor had a high likelihood of failure and would kill the witches and warlocks used during the spell casting. Damn the Immortal Mother and her rules!

Sekka imagined the soul energy she could harvest with such a diabolical portal. It would be limitless! She fantasized about the day when one of the Great Three would elevate her status in exchange for eternal access to the Mortal Realm. Which Supreme Devil would it be, Xerthotha or Azrollorza, she mused? She didn't think the third, Morrdilliax, with his myriad personalities, could ever stop debating with himself long enough to grant her wish.

No, it would be either Xerthotha or Azrollorza. She would stand with one of them as an equal in the High Pantheon of Hell, a Supreme Devil in her own right. Ascension was the real prize. A functioning and permanent Chaos Gate would ensure she would receive her greatest desire.

Sekka quickened her step. Her diaphanous gown was made from the skin of mortals. Humans had such thin skin, and so soft. She had left it open in the front and tied it off at her waist. It was more of an afterthought. Maybe she would wear it next time she visited her captive guest.

She chuckled at the absurdity of the joke as if an Arch Devil of the Ice Planes of Hell could seduce one so pure as the Great Monk. Yet, the myriad temptations of the Abyss eventually corrupted the souls of all men. A demigod of the Seven Heavens was no different.

The sides of the gown fluttered against her skin. The material tickled her breasts and sent sensations of delight up her spine. Sekka reveled in the juxtaposition of containing her immense power in such a vulnerable shell. She also loved the accessories, especially her human eyes. Gateway to the soul, they said. Ha! If the mortals only knew the truth of it.

Why she had never thought to spend more time in such a form was lost to her. She thrilled at the variety of new sensations her body experienced since the arrival of Aetenos to Gathos so many years ago. The Great Monk remained hard and steadfast in his resistance to her charms. Eventually, that would change as she introduced the second part of her masterful plan.

The humans must think he is dead by now. But of course, time moves differently in the Abyss, she mused. She pushed open the door to her bath chamber. The room was dimly lit by sconces emanating a blueish glow around the base of the walls. A circular tub full of slush was sunk into the middle of the floor. Two dozen humans hung from great hooks above the tub. They resembled beasts swinging in a slaughterhouse.

Sekka watched with a pleasant appreciation as their life fluid streamed out of their bodies to fill her bath. Their moans resonated off the cold walls and filled the chamber with an eerie melody. It was music to her ears.

Sekka looked up at them with contempt. Humans were blind and dumb to the hidden power they each possessed. The true essence of the soul remained a mystery to them. Yet, it determined their actions and was the spark that enabled them to think, to feel, and to evolve.

She shook her head as she thought of how badly they misused such a gift on mundane endeavors. No matter. They served as an excellent fuel for her dark machinations.

This group was all that was left from Lord Oziax's last visit to her slave pits. The stockade would need to be replenished. She knew she was desperately low on reserves. Fighting the wars of others for future favor had helped her ascend quickly, but it came with a cost. She was starved continuously for more soul energy to replenish the ranks of her armies.

The only way to increase her allotment of souls in the Abyss was to gain more territory. But Zizphander was consuming the lands of her allies faster than she could conquer or steal more. Again, she thought of the power she could wield by maintaining an active Chaos Gate. Even before the Amaranthine Barrier, the portal was inconceivable to create. The unique components needed for its birth were not to be found in the Abyss.

She chuckled to herself. That foolish monk had given her the first rare component with his arrival on Gathos. It was only a matter of time before he unwittingly provided her with the second piece. Aetenos would be the doom of the Mortal Realm. Ah, her revenge became sweeter by the moment.

Sekka disrobed and descended into the red slush with a satisfied smile. Her skin became taut as the refreshing cold wrapped around her flesh. The soothing properties of the bath relaxed her muscles as she waded deeper into the pool. The warm blood of the dying slaves showered over her head. It matted her hair in red clumps. A deep sigh eased from her lips as she smeared blood over her cheeks and mouth. The pain of her slaves was delicious.

Her mind drifted towards the pleasurable scenarios of pain she intended to inflict on Zizphander. She would take her time and savor the victory. She grew excited when she envisioned turning all of his lands of fire to ice.

Sekka heard the clatter of heavy armor approaching the bath chamber. Her mood soured. General Oziax had returned early from his mission. That much was clear, but she hadn't expected his return for days. Could this not wait until I called for him?

Something was very wrong. Sekka could hear it in his quickened footsteps as well as the heavy knock on the chamber door.

"My Queen, I bring dire news."

Sekka scowled and rose from her bath.

"Enter Lord Oziax."

The great demon lord bowed low upon entering the chamber. He wore his mortal form, as was her command while in her inner sanctum.

General Oziax appeared as a tall, well-built man. He wore pure white armor the texture of a seashell covered in barnacles, with ocean-blue accents gleamed along the seams of the ancient plate. He held his helm in his hand. The fell blade Eishorror was sheathed in its scabbard at his hip.

"You had best have a good reason for disturbing my respite. What news do you bring that requires such a dramatic entrance?" Sekka said.

General Oziax brushed long, white strands of hair from his face and tucked them behind his mortal ears. "My apologies, my Queen. I thought you would want to hear my report as soon as possible. Zizphander has taken another of the wild frost lands that border Gathos. It has been turned into molten slag."

"Yes, that seems to be his agenda of late. What about it? Annihilating a frontier realm, even one neighboring Gathos seems hardly worth the effort. What does he hope to gain? There is no strategic significance in holding unformed lands that dissolve with the whims of chaos. There is no soul reward to exploit, and the inhabitants are a scattering of undisciplined war-bands. Let Lord Auzdioz worry about controlling his stewardship of those shapeless lands."

"My Queen, everything is gone. Buried under cooling magma."

"And soon, Lord Auzdioz will regroup. He will spread his seed and fertilize another uncharted land as he had done for countless millennia. That is his role in the Abyss. Why worry if Zizphander wastes his resources in such a way?" She played with the viscous strands of blood that stretched down from the bodies above her head. Zizphander was trying to taunt her, nothing more. She wouldn't be distracted by such things.

"Lord Auzdioz has been obliterated. His infernal essence has been utterly destroyed, never to be reformed."

"Well, now, that is something." Lord Oziax now had her full attention. "Zizphander does not possess such power to remove one such as Lord Auzdioz from the Abyss permanently. He must have a patron shadow. But who?"

"I know not, my Queen. Many have openly shown their resentment of your triumphs." Oziax snarled. "But I will find out."

"Time has quickened for us," Sekka said. She raised herself out of the bath. She scoffed at the robe offered to her late by Lord Oziax. She was in no mood for his inability to understand mortal formalities.

"Have Chedipe send word to my minions on the Mortal Plane. Sess'thra is to go to the Northern Kingdom. There she will find the Sorcerer Maugris. She will know what to do. Then, the assassin Dax will introduce himself to one of the monks at the Temple of Illumination in Gethem."

"And the prisoner? Has there been any progress?" Lord Oziax said.

The Arch Devil had already left the chamber. A trail of red footprints followed her down the corridor. "The Great Monk will break. In the meantime, I shall lay out my plans for the invasion of the Three Kingdoms of Hanna."

5

KASAI

K asai sat motionless on his square mat in the dimly lit meditation hall. His eyes were closed while he breathed slowly through his nose. The distant screech of a broad-winged crest eagle. He envisioned the majestic bird soaring on thermal drafts in a cloudless sky. The whisper of a light breeze rippled through the pine needles and oak leaves in the lower ravine, miles below the monastery buildings. He reprimanded himself for being so easily distracted. A wandering mind was a weak-mind, and that was a dangerous thing. He returned to concentrating on the flow of his breathing.

He sat in the half-light of the room with his Brothers. Each monk focused on observing the sensation of air passing over their upper lip, through their nostrils, and then out again. All other aches and pains, no matter how severe or uncomfortable, were dismissed. The exercise was designed to reduce the noise within one's conscious mind and reveal to the monk the possibilities of the subconscious world. The monks maintained their concentration for long hours each day. Master Dorje spoke silently from the shadows of the raised dais in the front of the Hall.

"The Order of Ordu has always followed the teachings of the Pillars of Light, set by the First Monk, Gen Moll, the founder of the Four Orders of Aetenos. We join our spirit to the life force held within each being. We share in its peace and harmonize together to become one. It is a sacred gift from the Boundless. Only when you have achieved complete selflessness of heart, mind, and body, will you come to know the full power of the Boundless.

"Be wary of the Path of Ease, for this is the path of the common man. He will walk it as the accepted and proper way. He will believe it is the only truth that exists. He will believe and accept only what is known to be possible. His mind then enters a trap of containment and stagnation.

"You must erase what is possible from your mind. Only then will you see the infinite paths of not yet conceived realities. These are the paths you will walk as a Master Monk of Ordu. This is the Boundless."

Kasai heard a whisper and then soft laughter from the row behind him. His mind snapped back to the reality of the room. Painful pinpricks raced through his crossed legs. A dull ache in his lower back made itself known. How long had they been sitting, he wondered?

Brother Jarescu was at it again with his ill-timed wit. "But how will the Boundless get us girls?" He was one of the older monks. Daku referred to him as Flapping Gums.

Like many of the monks living at Ordu, Jarescu had been brought to the monastery by a Traveling Master. He was a mix between the dark-haired jungle dwellers of Sunne and the light-skinned, horse farmers of the great grass plains of Northern Baroqia. He had a broad frame yet delicate facial features and hands. His cheekbones sat high on his face and emphasized the upward slant of his almond-shaped eyes.

Jarescu continued, "Let me introduce you to the Boundless, my dear. It will set you free of those clothes."

Kasai heard more quiet laughter from behind. He worried that Master Dorje might think it was him interrupting the lesson. Just what he needed, more attention from the Master Monk.

Luckily, Master Dorje chose to ignore the slight disturbance of his pupils. "The Four Orders were built upon this premise. It is the Way of Aetenos. This is your path, young initiates."

Jarescu was relentless now that he had his audience. "I think I'll develop a different Way. I'll call it the Way of Jarescu. My path will combine the ancient powers of Rest, Relaxation, and Sleep. My arse is killing me."

Daku sat to the right of Kasai. Kasai could feel the tension stirring in his friend. Daku's breathing had changed from steady and calm to short, quick breaths.

"Concentrate, Brother," Kasai whispered while keeping his own eyes closed. "I can feel the heat from your fire xindu from where I sit. Release your water xindu. Let it soothe you."

Kasai heard Daku's breathing increase in tempo. "Stay with Master Dorje's words."

"That's right, Master Dorje, I'll travel straight to dreamland, I will," Jarescu continued, eliciting more quiet laughter from the younger monks. Kasai cracked his eyes. Master Dorje's eyes were open and looking straight at him. Kasai immediately closed his eyes.

Master Dorje continued with emphasis. "Meditation strengthens the mind. It provides a true path for the flesh to follow. But beware, the Path of Ease will ensnare the undisciplined mind. You must always be mindful of distraction for the unfocused mind is susceptible to the temptations of the Deep Dark.

"You will learn to channel the wonders of the Boundless through diligent training and meditation. Harness your passion and control its direction. Otherwise, you will lose your way and become a lost soul. This is suffering. This is the Emptiness.

"Meditate on my words. Contemplate the Boundless," Master Dorje said.

Kasai heard Master Dorje shuffle out of the room. The rapid breathing of Daku continued and echoed in his ears.

"Calm your breathing, Brother, and be at peace," Kasai whispered.

"I can manage without your instruction," Daku said tersely. His words came between clenched teeth. A moment later, Kasai felt the air move swiftly across his right side. Daku spoke in a low, menacing tone to the row behind him.

"You have upset my meditation with your distractions, Jarescu. Apparently, the meaning of Master Dorje's lesson is outside the realm of your understanding," Daku said.

Jarescu stared back defiantly. "Lighten up, Daku. You could benefit from a good laugh."

A few of the monks to his right and left chuckled under their breath. That's it, thought Kasai. Jarescu is a dead man. Kasai turned his head just enough to see Daku entirely reversed on his mat, staring intently at Jarescu.

Daku leaned forward, closer to Jarescu's face. "And since today's lesson was lost upon you, I am willing to bring special attention to your spiritual well-being during the tournament today."

The smile dropped from Jarescu's slender lips. Daku pointed his finger into the Jarescu's chest, almost pushing him over. "That's right, Jarescu, you see it now, don't you? Your lesson begins in the sparring circles. And at that time, *Brother*, I will take my time explaining Master Dorje's words to you. Until then, keep your mouth shut." Daku turned back around and closed his eyes.

"Why did you threaten him like that?" Kasai whispered. "He is your Brother."

Daku scoffed at the familial reference. "I am tenderizing the meat before the tournament. Plus, I just don't like him."

"You don't like anyone."

"Mostly."

Kasai shook his head. Daku was headed down a dangerous road. He pushed the boundaries of what was needed to achieve a goal, and what was overkill. Kasai's thoughts drifted back to Master Dorje's lesson. Somewhere there was an answer.

An early morning mist lingered when the monks emptied from the meditation hall into the central courtyard. The colors of their training garb resembled Autumn's seasonal bounty of falling leaves. The warm sun reflected off the monks' yellow shirts and bright-orange leggings as they practiced the secret fighting techniques known only to the Four Orders of Aetenos.

Twenty of the younger monks took the center of the square. They placed themselves in an equally spaced pattern before bowing to the senior monk who led them through the drill. Their lean, muscular bodies moved in unison, sometimes as a flash of lightning from Heaven, while at other times stiff and static like the granite of the deepest earth.

Kasai removed his outer robe. His forearms were covered in tattoos. The markings were runes of power he had received from past achievements. The symbols granted him limited abilities when he mentally engaged their stored energy.

Kasai knelt over a bucket filled with gravel. A similar bucket to his right was filled with sand, then one with rice and the last one with dried beans. Daku joined him but took the one to the left. It was filled with iron shot.

"If they had a final bucket of sharp glass, you would take it if I took the iron first," Kasai said to his friend.

"Yup."

Daku cocked his arm back and thrust his hand into bits of iron like a spade. "Feels good."

Kasai rolled his eyes. "Show off." He jabbed his hand into his bucket of gravel. He twisted his entire arm at the shoulder with each blow. Daku picked up the pace of his strikes. Kasai followed. It was a race to the bottom.

"Touched!" Daku said. He pulled his hand out and held up his bloody fingertips. Kasai was only about a third of the way through the gravel in his bucket.

"One of these days I will beat you," Kasai said. He didn't care who won, but he knew Daku did.

"No, Kasai, you won't."

The Three Masters of Ordu came into the square to observe the progress of the initiates. They were dressed in long, multi-layered robes of sky-blue with indigo pants and white sashes. Master Dorje's face was round and smooth as polished stone. He stood in between Master Choejor and Master Kunchen. He was built like a glacial boulder with short legs and a barrel-shaped chest.

Master Dorje was a foot shorter than Master Choejor, and half that again of Master Kunchen. He wore a wide-brimmed hat made of straw, the crown of which ended in a point. He nodded in agreement as Master Kunchen pointed out a young monk performing a particularly challenging punch-kick-punch combination.

Master Kunchen wore a similar wide-brimmed hat. The thin leather strap holding it in place disappeared beneath his long, wispy beard. His keen eyes carried the heritage of Sunne, raised upwards at the corners, but were an uncanny blue. His flowing hair had aged to a soft grey.

Master Choejor stepped forward to address the monks. He stroked his long mustache and beard in contemplation while the sun warmed his smooth, hatless head. Master Choejor's hair always reminded Kasai of unblemished snow.

Master Choejor clapped his hands once. The monks stopped their training and jogged to form a circle around the Masters. They bowed and waited patiently for instruction.

Master Choejor stroked his long beard again. "You shall now be paired with your opposite. Choose one to attack and one to protect. You shall learn your weakness by observing the strength of your partner. The winner will lead the rest on a mission outside the monastery walls. Let the tournament begin."

Kasai felt a firm hand on his shoulder from behind. He didn't need to turn around to know who it was.

"Let's go, Kasai. It's you and me."

Daku's body was built for strength and power. He fought like an enraged bull. Daku always took an aggressive approach when sparring. Strike first and hard, and before your opponent can respond, charge forward and strike again.

Kasai was smaller than most of the Brothers his age, especially Daku. He was a smart fighter who took a defensive approach against his opponents. Kasai was patient. When the moment was right, he unleashed quick and accurate counter strikes. The two friends made a formidable fighting team.

Daku surveyed the other monks with contempt. "We both know how this will play out. I'll take the role of striker. You protect my weak side. We are assured of victory."

"Not this time, Brother. I'm faster," Kasai said as the two friends received matching red arm sashes from a young initiate.

"Your opinion is noted and dismissed as irrelevant. I mean to win. You go too easy." Daku searched the other monks being paired with their partners. "Where is Jarescu? Ah, there he is over there."

Kasai saw Jarescu being matched with Brother Shiro.

"This will easier than I thought. I won't even need you to defeat them both."

"Daku, why must you make enemies of your Brothers? It won't always be me protecting your back. One day you will need to rely on one of them, perhaps with your life."

"Doubtful. But I'm glad you have accepted your role without much fuss today. Let's go. We are being called to the first circle."

Individually, Kasai and Daku were formidable opponents. When they were paired together, they had no rivals. Much of their friendship was based on outdoing the other's most recent accomplishments.

The competition began. The monks fought in pairs as Master Choejor dictated. The winners advanced, while the defeated moved to the side. Eventually, two pairs remained. Jarescu and Shiro stepped into the center circle. An unfortunate fate for the two monks.

"I'm impressed you dared to remain in the competition this long, Jarescu. I had thought you would intentionally remove yourself early, rather than face me in the later rounds," Daku said. He prowled around Jarescu and Shiro like a hungry predator. "I wonder, did you tell Shiro of the punishment that awaited you? Did he know I would have to go through him to get to you?"

"So much talk, talk, talk. I think he's scared, Jarescu," Shiro said. He had a slight Sunnese accent, which accentuated the vowels of each word. Shiro had mixed blood and was the offspring of foothill nomads that travels between Sunne and Baroqia.

Daku glared at Shiro. "Poor, poor Shiro."

Shiro accepted a blue arm sash and tied a second to Jarescu's bicep. Shiro was a scrappy and wiry fighter with long limbs and wore his hair in a topknot like Kasai. Today it was pulled and wound in a ball on the back of his head.

"You're lucky to be paired with Kasai. Without him, you would be lost. He's the only reason you have made it this far," Jarescu said. He stretched out his limbs, then unleashed a furious punching combination into the air.

Jarescu continued to bait Daku as the other monks gathered around the center circle.

"And Daku, as you can see by our Brother's smiles, they know it too."

Kasai was impressed with Jarescu's confidence, though it was misplaced. Kasai knew Daku was growing angrier with each insult. He would not hold back.

The four monks entered the center circle. They formally bowed to each other and then to the Masters. Some of the monks began to cheer on their favorites. Kasai stretched and rolled through different martial forms. Daku just stared at Jarescu.

"Stay with the strategy. It has worked well today," Kasai said. "Jarescu will eventually strike with a Mountain Wind Kick. He always does," Kasai said. He shook out his arms and legs. "This leaves him vulnerable, and Shiro is usually out of position for a proper defense. If you are patient, we will have them with ease."

Kasai looked at his friend with worried eyes. He knew Daku's judgment faltered when his anger took him. His fire xindu would rise to uncontrollable levels, and he would lose himself to blind rage. All the monks had a difficult life before coming to the monastery. Daku had it worse than most.

"Don't let his words distract you. Stay with the strategy," Kasai said. He moved in front of Daku and once more became a whirlwind of defensive postures. Each movement overlapped the last to prevent an opponent from gaining a positional advantage. He was ready.

Daku needed only to wait. It was the key to their success as a team. Eventually, their opponents would make a mistake. Then the two friends would pounce in tandem like waves upon the sand.

"Change of plans, Kasai, this one has a painful lesson to learn," Daku said. He jumped ahead of Kasai and unleashed a brutal kick with a shimmering, red glow trailed behind his spinning leg. His foot whipped around and connected with Shiro's midsection.

The move was completely unexpected. Shiro crumbled to the dirt of the circle, gasping for air. In the next instant, Daku was driving Jarescu back to the edge of the ring.

"You dare use xindu energy on a Brother?" Jarescu cried out. He shuffled backward in a mixture of confusion and fear. "What kind of monster are you?"

"The kind who wins," Daku said. He shoved Jarescu back a step, then twisted around and hit him with a kick to the chest. A strike to a nerve cluster in Jarescu's right arm left it dead below the elbow.

Jarescu looked expectantly at Kasai. "Do something!"

Kasai stood as dumbfounded as the rest of his Brothers. Jarescu was a skilled fighter, but he was outmatched. Daku was relentless. Even if Jarescu had a second defensive partner, the outcome would have been the same.

Jarescu took a vicious kick to the side of the face and dropped to one knee. His mouth was red from blood. "Enough. I yield."

Daku chopped down to the left side of Jarescu's neck. The beaten monk dropped to the ground with a thud. The fight was over for Jarescu, but not for Daku. He kneeled beside Jarescu and grabbed him by the shirt. Daku lifted Jarescu enough so he could speak clearly in his ear.

"Remember this moment, Jarescu. It will help strengthen your mind and keep it aligned during meditation. I expect your full attention during Master Dorje's next lesson."

Daku curled his fist into a tight ball. He smiled as he punched Jarescu in the face. Jarescu's nose shattered. Daku released Jarescu's shirt, dropping unceremoniously to the ground.

The central square was deathly quiet. Kasai was stunned.

Daku stood up. Darkness fell across his face when he stepped over Jarescu. "Easy."

Shiro found his strength and crawled over to his fallen partner. He raised his fists in a valiant defense. Two monks ran into the circle to collect Jarescu before Daku could do more harm. They lifted his body off the ground and carried him in the direction of the infirmary. Shiro followed behind. His eyes never left Daku. The monks surrounding the circle began talking and shouting at once.

Master Choejor clapped his hands together, and order was restored. The wall of monks reformed around the sparring circle. Kasai wondered why the Masters had not stepped in and disqualified them. Was this another lesson?

"Brother Daku, please return to the circle. You and Brother Kasai have earned the right to continue. In this contest, you shall face your ally and your weakness. Thus, you shall expose your truth and find inner balance," Master Choejor said.

Kasai looked squarely at Daku. "Was that necessary? Jarescu could have easily been removed, and Shiro was no treat. You and I both knew their blind spots."

Daku took the blue arm sash handed to him. "You were there, Kasai. You heard him. He needed to be taught a lesson."

"But not by you. That is for the Masters to decide. There are rules."

"Your rules, not mine."

"What?"

"Leaders blaze new trails for others to follow. That's always been your problem, Kasai. You refuse to take the first step; therefore, you will always be a follower. Not me. I intend to win now too. That is why I will be commanding the Brothers tomorrow and not you, my friend."

The two were a dynamic pair when fighting as a unit. Daku excelled at throwing lethal offensive strikes, while Kasai masterfully countered every attack from their opponents. But now it was a contest of opposing styles. Kasai moved with exceptional agility. His fighting style was based on making his opponent miss, rather than seeking to strike a critical blow.

Daku had less finesse. He used aggression and strength to overwhelm his opponents.

"Begin!" Master Choejor said.

Daku was on him before Kasai finished his bow. Daku spun using the same strike that left Shiro doubled over in pain. His attack was aggressive and quick.

Kasai snapped his body backward. "Really?"

Daku was caught off guard and spun full circle. His leg hung overextended in the air just long enough for Kasai to step forward and grab it. For the briefest moment, Kasai had Daku at his mercy.

The match could have been decided then with one blow, but Kasai released Daku without delivering a successful strike. Sounds of disappointment rose from the crowd.

"See? You are not able to do what is necessary to win," Daku said. He regained his balance.

"Brother, these bouts mean nothing to me. Everyone knows you strike first. It leaves your defense vulnerable."

"Always the honorable one and forever second. Trust me. The real world doesn't follow your rules."

Daku lunged at him. Kasai moved to the side with fluid grace. He found the perfect defensive posture to deflect Daku's attack, then diverted the power of the strike away from his body.

Daku's growled with frustration. Kasai sent a barrage of harmless yet distracting jabs to Daku's face. Daku swatted them all away, grabbed Kasai by the shirt, and knee-kicked Kasai in the chest. That one hurt.

"So, the little mouse can be hit after all," Daku said. He gloated as if he had already won.

Kasai threw a jab that got through Daku's defense. He snapped his fist when he hit Daku's nose. It wasn't a powerful blow, but it stung. Daku cursed and staggered backward. He fell to one knee with his eyes covered.

Kasai lowered his guard. He worried that he had broken his friend's nose. He had not meant to harm Daku, just push him back.

"Daku?"

Daku narrowed his watering eyes, then swept Kasai's leg with a locking kick. Kasai lost his footing and fell to the ground. Daku delivered a critical blow to Kasai's face that snapped his head to the dirt.

"That's it. I win!" Daku exclaimed.

"I see a bit of trickery is fair game now," Kasai said. He raised himself to his knees. He shook the dizziness from his head.

Daku was already up and brushing the dirt dust from his pants. "I told you, the world is an unfair place. You are not ready for it."

The Three Masters gathered together in the center circle. "Brother Daku, you have demonstrated your ability to triumph over your weakness," Master Dorje said. "Tomorrow, you shall lead your Brothers outside the monastery walls."

"Thank you, Master Dorje. I am grateful to pass this honorable challenge. I will lead the expedition with honor," Daku said. He bowed excitedly in front of Master Dorje. His Brothers did not share his enthusiasm.

"Brother Kasai, to my side," Master Choejor said. The elder monk was already walking in the opposite direction.

"Yes, Master Choejor?"

"Son, I may not have the use of these eyes, but I am not blind. Nor is the true sight robbed from Master Dorje or Master Kunchen. Might you tell me what stayed your hand during the last fight?"

"It is important for Daku to be chosen to lead. I don't care as much."

"This is certain, but is Brother Daku to be the leader because he is most worthy of leading or most needy?"

"Master, I'm not a leader. Daku is right. I am not ready for such responsibility. I will only let down those who follow me."

"Those are Brother Daku's words. Why are you content to be the shadow of his mountain? I sense a deeper conflict, young one. We will discuss it later. Now, bring me to lunch. I was told we would each have a bite of honey cake today. I mean to get mine before Master Dorje tries to convince me there wasn't enough for everyone again."

6

SHIVERRIG

The city of Qaqal, also known as the City of Spires, served as the capital city of the Kingdom of Baroqia. The throne had been moved from Gethem twenty-six years past when House Conrad claimed control of the kingdom from House Shiverrig.

The king's castle was an architectural masterpiece composed of a thick bundle of towers and tall spires, inspired by the mighty pines that rose in the forests of central Baroqia. The spires were made from multi-colored granite, quarried from the low hills of the Sarribe Mountains in the southwest, and the Hoarfrost Mountains in the northeast. Long poles sprouted from the sides of the lower towers that circled the central spire. Hanging from each was a pennant depicting a pouncing white griffon against a sky of blue.

The Great Houses of Baroqia gathered each year in King's Hall to hear their ruler's new policy decrees and to voice their grievances. Most of the nobles used the time to solidify side pacts with other Houses in hopes of weakening the political position of their rivals.

King's Hall was an immense room, which could comfortably seat a thousand persons with more standing room to the sides. At regular intervals, twelve ivory columns stood witness to the achievements and treachery both playing out within the confines; lit by long, delicate sconces affixed to the columns. Above the capitals, a cathedral ceiling inlaid with a mosaic of blue and white tiles resembled the heavenly skies over the tall spires of Qaqal.

The flickering light from the torches lightly lapped against white marble icons and carved images of the Immortal Mother and her scions. The divine figures looked down upon the limestone floor of the extravagant hall, judging all who crossed beneath them.

At the far end of the Hall sat the marble throne. A chestnut rug ran down from its base then split at the floor to encircle the entire hall. Blue banners adorned with proud white griffons hung heavy from the walls. An illuminated painting was placed beneath each banner illustrating a heroic deed of King Mortimer Conrad or his father before him. *All lies*, thought Duke Shiverrig as he and his retainers bullied their way into the hall.

Thick, stained-glass windows depicting angelic victories over the denizens of darkness were bracketed by drapes colored the same blue as the banners. The curtains had been adorned with impressive needlework of pouncing griffons, outlined with jewels. It was false evidence of House Conrad's delusional claim to power. The history of Baroqia was being rewritten while the scions of the real heroes still lived.

A magnificent throne made from a solid block of creamy-white marble sat at the end of the Hall. The sides were covered in decorative etchings. Two large statues of knights in full plate stood sentry behind the king. The head of a screeching griffon was fixed at the end of each armrest. The heads were made from a single, flawless stone of blue and purple tanzanite.

The crown was too big on King Conrad's head. It sloped forward so that its weight wrinkled his brow. His elaborate robes draped loosely over effeminate, narrow shoulders covering his weak knees and diminutive boots. He looked like a tiny man in an oversized dress. His displeasure at being made to wait was written across his doughy face.

Let the lesser man wait, thought Shiverrig, *he sits on a borrowed throne.*

Below the throne was the King's Table. Four similar, but far less ornate seats sat on a lower tier. Three of those seats were now occupied by the ruling member of a Great House.

Baron Rokig occupied the first seat to the right of the throne. He had a lean, sickly-looking face; high eyebrows with a bulbous nose above narrow lips. His hair was mousy-brown and slick, as if coated with the leftover grease from cooked bacon. Shiverrig never understood how a man of his nature had risen so high in the king's esteem. But then again, conniving men had a taste for one another.

Rokig had a troublesome feel about him. The man was a plague in his pompous, knightly half-armor and airs of importance. None of his influence had been earned in battle, as was proper to Shiverrig's way of thinking. The baron was a leech of other men's greatness and a whisperer of falsehoods. Shiverrig despised the man.

To Rokig's left, Duke Manda relaxed in his chair. He claimed the self-appointed title of High Merchant of the Realm. His family's wealth was second only to House Conrad's. Manda was a tall man with a penchant for the stylish trends of the day, no matter how obscure. Shiverrig took him for a flashy peacock who's only useful trait was his ability to fund war campaigns.

Duke Manda had a pretty face, well-formed nose, and angular lips. He covered it all in a delicate powder, with pastel eye shadow and rose-colored blush. His clothing was no less sensational than his face. He wore deep green ceremonial robes layered over thin ivory cloth, with topaz earrings and rings and an orange handkerchief. Shiverrig's ire rose from just looking at the man.

Lord Fritta sat primly in his chair across the landing, hands folded quietly in his lap, legs stretched out casually, crossed at the ankles. He was an older man with dark set eyes, who held his tongue until he could make an informed opinion. Shiverrig liked the man and appreciated his reserved quality.

Fritta wore an unadorned doublet and traditional breeches with high leather riding boots. A long scar rode across the side of his square face and dropped beneath his jawline. Fritta's attention remained sharp and focused.

Fritta's ancestors had a privileged history of fighting side-by-side with House Shiverrig during the founding of the kingdom. Shiverrig would not call the man friend, but he did have his respect, which was worth more in Shiverrig's eyes than some foolish notion of friendship.

Respect—and the brotherhood of combat—were the bridges that connected Shiverrig to other men. He knew what pushed a man's resolve and loyalty to the limit. Shiverrig valued a man's mettle under pressure, when blades were wet, and the screams of agony pierced the air.

Shiverrig eyed each of the men as he took his seat. Lord Fritta gave him a brisk nod. Duke Manda was aloof to Shiverrig's arrival; he was preoccupied with preening for the crowd of nobles. King Conrad sat on comfortable pillows of blue and white, adorned with emblazoned tips of darker blue. He is a soft man, thought Shiverrig. He's always been soft.

Rokig glared at Shiverrig from his chair across the platform. His pale skin reflected a tinge of blue. "You strike at the king's displeasure with your lack of punctuality, Duke Shiverrig."

Shiverrig stood. He addressed the king with a short bow. "My apologies to the king and lords present. I was busy doing nothing and forgot," Shiverrig responded without much sincerity.

Laughter echoed through the Hall, followed by excited murmurs. Many of the nobles from the Great Houses came solely to hear the strained discourse between Conrad and Shiverrig. They stood in a wide semi-circle set back twenty paces from the throne. There was standing room only today.

"You shall not mock this court with your insolence, Duke Shiverrig," King Conrad said. "The Crown relieves you of one thousand gold diras for your tardiness. And levies the same each year for a two-year tax period."

Baron Rokig called for the seneschal. "Make a note and draw documents."

"It's always about the money. Fine, fine. Shall we begin?" Shiverrig waved the proceeds forward. The Hall was called to order.

"Bring forth the first petitioner," King Conrad called out.

A commoner rose from the back of the room. He raised a copper baton. He was ushered to the edge of the throne area.

Shiverrig stood just as the petitioner was about to address the king. "Stop," Shiverrig commanded. The petitioner froze. Shiverrig scanned the faces of the nobles present.

"It is well known that House Conrad holds title on much of the lands outside Qaqal. Paper barons with familial and political ties have been installed to govern these lands. In so doing, King Conrad manipulates political opinion. Bit by bit, the Great Houses lose their voice to the underlying Conrad dictatorship."

Shiverrig's face reddened as his voice rose. "Weak decisions, nay, dangerous decisions are made without proper consideration or vote from the Greater and Lower Houses, allowing Conrad's predatory edicts to become the law of the land."

He watched the reaction of the nobles, seeing familiar heads nodding in agreement, while others continued with private conversations, paying him and his message no mind. There were too many of the latter.

Shiverrig was an influential and highly respected military leader. His strategic victories against invading barbarians from the northern Kingdom of Trosk were well known. His bravery in battle was unquestioned. However, his prowess on the battlefield did not carry over into the superficial politics of court.

Here, men changed their allegiance without thought or conscious in exchange for land, titles, and future favors. They forsook historic allegiances to the Great Houses that tamed the land. Traitors to bonds of loyalty infuriated him. Their honor was worthless.

Shiverrig continued, "Lesser men gain influence based on favorable political opinion, or due to duplicitous and underhanded betrayals of solemn pledges that have endured for generations. Most of you have bought your way into lordships!"

The floor erupted with shouts of denial from many of the nobles. Some shook angry fists at Shiverrig. *I have their attention now,* he thought.

"No longer do great champions rule ... rather, the one who controls the Great Houses," he paused to check the eyes of the crowd upon him before staring down Conrad's gaze, "and does so through political blackmail."

Again, he surveyed the crowd to see if they were making the connection. "Perhaps this is nothing new to the *uncivilized* world outside the Kingdom of Baroqia," he paused, gathering the attention of the nobles, "perhaps it will become commonplace here as well." Shiverrig flicked his eyes to Conrad before roving the crowd again; he thought it better to let that point fester in the minds of the ambitious and the fearful.

If his Great House could be stripped of power, it could just as easily happen to others. Still, he needed to ensure they understood. "We have created a weakness of rule with the safety of the realm at stake. Our decision-makers are compromised to those who hold ill-favors over their heads."

Shiverrig looked to those who had taken oaths of allegiance to his family. Their nods of agreement stoked his aggressive nature.

"House Shiverrig was hamstrung not so long ago from regaining succession over the new administration. I call to the Lesser Houses to band together with me now. Our collective influence will rid House Conrad's stranglehold on the realm."

Shiverrig stood with legs apart, hands curled into fists at his hips.

Into the rustling of shifting fabric and murmurings in the bright chamber, a voice arose, "Duke Shiverrig, we have respectfully entertained this argument of yours on numerous occasions in the past. Must you continue to bore us with this same diatribe again and again? The law is set for the betterment of the realm. If you have nothing of value to present to this council, please let another take the floor. If you wish to persist, I will think your words bear the mark of treason, and you will be dealt with accordingly," King Conrad said. The condescending manner in which the king spoke infuriated Shiverrig. Was this all just a game to the man?

Shiverrig's temper flared. "I will not be silenced. I am the head of a Great House of Baroqia, and a member of the King's Table. I have the right to speak my mind." He turned to the king. "Or are you afraid the illusion of your rule will vanish?"

Sound stopped as everyone waited for a response from the king. When none came, the floor erupted in shouts of outrage. Nobles stood, some moved forward, brandishing fists or pointing accusatory fingers. Shiverrig waved his arm to settle the crowd. "It is imperative that the nobles listen to reason. I have confirmed reports that a vast horde of barbarian raiders have massed at the northern side of Stormwind Pass. It is time to mount a pre-emptive strike against the North. Hear my words, fellow nobles, and be concerned. An invasion from the sorcerer, Maugris, is inevitable!"

Shiverrig noted many of the wealthy land barons with vast farming estates shook their heads in dismay. Their harvests would immediately be appropriated if a war was declared. Their annual profits would disappear. Shiverrig watched them closely. It would only take the slightest shake of their heads, and Conrad would decree that war was not the answer.

"What you suggest will create an immediate declaration of war from the North. I will not move forward based on information gathered from frightened peasants," King Conrad said. He shrugged his shoulders. "These are rumors at best and not immediate concerns."

"These reports are from my Borderland Rangers! The markers of a full-scale invasion are clear. Anyone with an iota of military experience would recognize the imminent danger to our kingdom. I have detailed accounts of massive movements of war machines and the strategic positioning of troops along the southern side of the Hoarfrost Mountains."

Shiverrig turned to the nobles. "You see? The decisions of a coward forsake the safety of Baroqia. We need leadership capable of protecting the realm. Now is the time to cripple the advance of the North, not with words and diplomacy, but with the strength of arms. We must root out Maugris in his mountain stronghold. If House Conrad does not have the strength of resolve to do what is necessary to protect the realm, I move for a vote of new rule!"

The hall erupted in a second upheaval of outrage and cheers. Shiverrig assumed the Lesser nobles attached to House Conrad would fear the change for it would jeopardize their highly coveted positions, while those aligned with House Shiverrig would consider how they might profit from a new regime.

Shiverrig remained standing as chaos ensued below him. The guards did not come to remove him for his outburst, and he was not surprised. Conrad was a coward and did not have Shiverrig blood running through his veins, for if any man spoke in such a way in Volkerrum Keep, they would be cut down without hesitation.

"Sir, you have been given leniency due to the historical debt owed to House Shiverrig. However, if you disrespect the Crown again, I will have you barred from King's Hall. You will be stripped of all lands and titles. Duke or not, you shall respect my authority! Am I clear?" King Conrad shouted over the din of the hall.

He was such a weak and feeble man.

The malicious smile of a viper before it struck, played over Shiverrig's face. "Please excuse me, Highness." He let the bitterness fade from his voice. "I am impassioned by the safety of our realm. I look at current events through a different lens. I see dark times ahead."

Shiverrig half turned so the rest of the hall could hear. "I have expressed numerous times my willingness to take command of the Five Armies of Baroqia. I will bring the fight to the sorcerer before he has time to marshal his barbarian forces."

The king shook his head. He was weary and sat back in his cushioned throne.

"Command of the Five Armies is not your concern, Duke Shiverrig. Contrary to your personal belief, I am well equipped to handle our military engagements.

"Our strategy is a defensive one, which revolves around open communication and negotiations. We need accurate reports from credible sources. Ill-educated border folk posing as rangers of the forest will not do. If you have reconnaissance reports to share, I suggest you hand them over immediately.

"And, I will remind you that if needed, you will add the Knights of Gethem to the host of the King's Army here is Qaqal. You will advise when and if called upon, but ultimate leadership will fall to others."

Shiverrig played his last card. "Mortimer Conrad, you have the military prowess of a child playing in the mud. I will not take orders from a lesser commander, especially one who hails from the bloodline of a traitorous house! You may hold sway over the realm for now, but I will not be pushed aside like a stray dog!"

The hall erupted into madness. Political allies loyal to the king jumped to his defense. A call for war sounded from those sided with House Shiverrig. A noble was shoved to the floor. Small scuffles broke out in the middle of the hall. The royal bodyguards moved into position around the king. Their weapons were drawn and pointed at Shiverrig.

His eyes narrowed, daring the guards to move first. As expected, they did nothing. Instead, they shuffled the king around the throne and to safety. Shiverrig stomped down the short steps from the landing of the King's Table to the hall floor. He and his contingent of followers shoved their way out of King's Hall.

Shiverrig left Qaqal pleased with the outcome of the day's events. He was sure there would be no disciplinary action from the Crown. War was pending, and the king knew it.

Although Conrad was a weak man, he was politically savvy enough to understand he still needed House Shiverrig and its knights when war was declared. The nobles of the Great Houses trusted House Shiverrig to save them in times of need. At least that much had not changed.

"Now, the true hearts of the nobles are known," Shiverrig commented. His outburst and harsh remarks of the king had revealed the allegiances of the nobles who had not yet publicly sided with any Great House. *They will return to the embrace of Shiverrig rule once war engulfs the land*, he thought.

Volkerrum Keep was a cold, indomitable place. Shiverrig liked it that way. He had no time for fancy balls or grand dinner parties to entertain his fellow nobles. Let Conrad waste valuable time and money on such worthless endeavors. Shiverrig stared into the fire warming the room. Today was a decision-making day.

His two mastiffs lay at his feet before the fire. They growled low when the Archvashim entered the room. Malachi's calculating expression paled at the sight of the dogs. He was wary of the beasts.

"Your methods begin to foster results, my Duke. The unrest is growing at a steady rate. The death of the Port Deputy at Parne, as well as the disappearance of another shipping baron, can only be good for us," Malachi disclosed with a soft voice. He shifted his way between the dogs to sit in the chair opposite the Duke. As he eased into the seat, one dog growled, the other snapped at his foot. Malachi yelped, quickly vacating the chair, opting for a position behind it.

Shiverrig watched the scene unfold, a smirk playing at the corners of his mouth as he noted Malachi's discomfort. "Please, continue when you're ready," he jibbed.

"Yes, thank you, my lord. Once the Northern Raiders attack, the economic stability of Baroqia will collapse. The nobles will realize the threat from the North is real, and the king will be forced to declare war. And as you know…," Malachi effused, "wars have always been good for House Shiverrig."

"There will be no raids if I pivot from this course," Shiverrig mused, staring into the fire. "Gethem bears the brunt of the unrest you are so fond of escalating. Conrad will use this to his advantage. He will declare me incompetent and unable to govern Gethem effectively. He will say such a liege-lord could never succeed him to rule the whole kingdom or be entrusted with its military."

Shiverrig's eyes bore into Malachi. "I'm taking a big risk. Your plan had better work."

Malachi met his gaze, light from the fire playing across his face. "Profit is what controls the actions of the nobles in Qaqal. And a secure king equates to secure profits. The coffers of Great and Lesser Houses alike have swollen due to King Conrad's favors and appointments. Therefore, the nobles will continue to invest their support with the current holder of the crown.

"But trust me, the moment their coin is threatened, their opinions will change. We find ourselves in a time when allegiances shift according to the winds of opportunity."

"It is your clever allegiances that trouble me most. Are you sure I can trust the Maugris to fulfill his part?"

"I believe he will. He has much to gain with this coup. He will see it through to the end. His delegates await you in the reception room. They are comfortable with food and wine."

Shiverrig rose. Mastiffs at his heel, he paced across the floor toward the study door. The larger dog turned, snarled at Malachi and woofed, causing the Archvashim to jump. Shiverrig dropped his hand to pat the mastiff's shoulder. "Good boy," he praised.

Duke Shiverrig paused at the door leading to the reception room. How could *this* be the only viable option to reclaim the throne? How had his Great House lost so much strength in so few years? It was inconceivable that he was courting with a madman as his last resort.

If he was having second thoughts, now was the time to alter his course of his actions. He could just walk away and have his men dispose of Maugris' delegates. He looked to the coat-of-arms above the door and the snarling dog against crossed swords. The Shiverrig name represented power and might across the Three Kingdoms.

"If I do nothing, King Conrad will bleed House Shiverrig of wealth, power, and influence. The legacy of my House will end with me," he acknowledged.

He had laid out his pieces like a chess master; Conrad had taken each token offered. While the fool thought he was gaining the upper hand, the endgame would soon begin, the trap beckoned. The king had been warned.

What happened next was his own doing. Shiverrig's hands were clean. "No, I will not back down now. Maugris need only fulfill his role and House of Shiverrig will rise to prominence again."

Shiverrig pulled on the wrought-iron handles of the reception room doors, scanning the room for threats. The Northerners congregated in the far corner; their conversation interrupted as they turned to observe him. Between them, a long table had been set with food and refreshments. Bowls of assorted fruits were placed between platters of glazed ham and honied carrots, though the food remained untouched, and the wine goblets unfilled.

One of the delegation members separated from the group, walking toward Shiverrig. He shimmered in the light. Shiverrig assumed the optical effect was because of the man's obscure clothing. It appeared to be made from something he couldn't identify, some kind of exotic skin, reptilian perhaps. Or was it the man himself that was shifting?

Uneasy with the individual moving forward, Shiverrig's already dubious opinion deepened. The remainder of the party—three oddly shaped men huddled in the far shadows of the room—were flanked by two larger men still wearing traveling furs.

Taking command of the room, Shiverrig opened his arms wide. "Gentlemen, Gethem welcomes you. Volkerrum Keep is at your service. I am Duke Gerun Shiverrig."

The three figures moved as one into a twisted heap of gangly flesh. Shiverrig was repulsed at the sight of the wretches but stood fast; it would be unfitting to cringe. Somehow, he had been placed in a position of service to these frail men with boney arms and gooey smiles. War made for strange bedfellows.

The three who were one came to him in a morbidly fascinating embrace of interlocking elbows and shuffling feet. They stooped forward and addressed the duke in unison. Shiverrig shook the hand that was offered to him. The slick surface of the palm felt like wet, rotting leaves. He surreptitiously wiped his hand on his trousers.

Shiverrig watched slick drool slip freely from their oversized mouths as they forced smiles to their puffy faces. Their breath reeked of old eggs. The gorge rose in his throat, and he forced it back down. His instinct was to kill this abomination, but he reminded himself that the needs of the people outweighed his own. The kingdom would be strong once more. He would set things right.

Their heads were shaved to an unusually high hairline. A tattoo of red ink was painted across their eyes. Shiverrig thought it resembled a mask. How appropriate, he thought, thieves at my door with smiling faces and hidden daggers.

He tracked the two men who approached as shadows behind the three wretches. They moved faster than the steps they took. They were physically wrong as if their bodies had been stuffed into human skin a size too small. The skin was stretched thin across their faces and hands. They stopped to either side of the three. These must be the enforcers intended to intimidate me, he thought. Curious.

"Lord Maugris is well, I hope?" Shiverrig said to his guests.

"We are The Three. We are here to ensure the will of Maugris the Infinite is carried out to his exact specifications. The timetables must be adhered to and under no circumstances altered." The Three spoke at the same time. The sound of their voices blended into a preternatural whine.

"I see, straight to the point. Well then, if I deliver my part of the alliance, what guarantee do I have that Maugris will keep his promise?" Shiverrig said. "My men are equipped and ready to move as soon as I..."

"See that they are, Duke Shiverrig. Failure to do so will be punishable by death." The Three gloated in one sick smirk. "Maugris the Infinite has no use for petty titles over these rural lands. Soon he shall command all of the Three Kingdoms of Hanna, and then the world beyond. His promise to you will stand."

Shiverrig looked squarely at the three odd men. They were lying. Maugris needed him. Otherwise, these three cripples would not be here claiming a victory that was, at best, a distant dream. He watched their drool fall on his floor. His desire to inflict pain upon them rose.

Possibly they had a layer of magical protection, perhaps not. Maugris was that arrogant to think the threat of his retaliation would be enough to stay Shiverrig's hand. The enforcers were another matter. They moved to positions behind him.

Two clicks alerted Shiverrig that the bodyguards had unsheathed hidden blades. Shiverrig's body relaxed into a defensive posture. He would strike fast if they continued. The shambling mound of human flesh in front of him would die first.

"Gentlemen, please. We are one in this endeavor. There is no cause for threats," the shimmering man said. He moved fluidly between Shiverrig and The Three. "Duke Shiverrig, let me introduce myself. I am Dax, Emissary of the North and Master of Secrets to Mistress Sekka."

Shiverrig took stock of the man. "Assassin then."

Dax nodded and gave a dramatic bow, hand sweeping to the side as he bent. Shiverrig looked upon his co-conspirators and calmed; what had he expected, a tea party with lads and ladies from the court? He opened his arms wide and bellowed out a hearty laugh.

"It is a strange time indeed. Come, my friends, let us eat and drink together while we discuss the future of the Three Kingdoms." He gestured to the table. The Three partially returned his sentiment. They presented queer smiles that revealed blackened teeth; huddling close and shuffling back to the corner shadows as if the food and drink were anathema to their tastes.

"Duke Shiverrig, let us discuss matters in a more civilized exchange. My lord Maugris is confident you will honor your pledge of men to his cause. Though today, he has a small request to ask of your great and influential, House," Dax said.

"Go on," said Shiverrig. He was unmoved by this false mockingbird's lip service.

"My lord would like the exact locations of the monasteries of Ordu, Symmetu, Harmonu, and Metho. This information would be sincerely appreciated." Dax held up his hand before Shiverrig could speak. "And well rewarded."

"What could Maugris want with a bunch of reclusive monks? He turned from the Light years ago," Shiverrig challenged. He moved around the table of food and wine to create some space between him and the two enforcers. "Aetenos has fled this world. Maugris has nothing to fear from an old wife's tale."

"Maugris the Infinite fears nothing! The Light betrayed him," The Three said from the shadows. Six eyes caught the light of the fire and blazed at Shiverrig.

"Old scores must be settled," Dax said. He shrugged. He then meandered to the table and perused the bowl of fruit.

Shiverrig heard the lie beneath the innocent remark. The prophecy of Aetenos' return and the rise of a new Ever Hero was alive and well through the frontier villages to the hamlets outside Gethem.

Shiverrig thought the lot of it was a bunch of nonsense. However, Maugris wanted anyone who might claim to be the avatar of Aetenos, dead. And those would be the monks of the Four Orders. It mattered little to Shiverrig. The monks were meddlesome and best left to their secret sanctuaries. Plus, he had no use for would-be saviors.

"Unfortunately, the Temple of Illumination owes no favors to House Shiverrig. If my studies serve me, only the Grandmaster of the Temple knows the locations of those monasteries," Shiverrig said. "But I will lend some resources to assist in this endeavor if it helps build a bond of trust between us."

Dax bowed deeply. "My lord Maugris gives you thanks. All shall be as foretold. The Time of Change is near."

"Indeed," said Shiverrig. His tone became serious. "Listen to me, I want real assurances that your lord will uphold his agreement." He looked again at the three miserable wretches huddled together. "Perhaps a show of his current strength. Remove House Conrad from the throne. I do not care how."

Dax ignored Shiverrig's obvious ruse to divulge Maugris' strength of arms or depth of infiltration into the King's Court. "At the appropriate time, you shall gather your armies and bring them North. There you will join under Maugris' banner. Your combined strength shall prevail over whatever strength King Conrad can muster."

"Combined strength? The Mad One has no standing army, or you would not be here. The barbarians he has collected number just over a thousand and the northern tribes do not mix well. Even if he doubled or tripled that number, they will do nothing against the might of the Five Armies.

"You want the knights, archers, and foot soldiers of Gethem to be his army. The blood of my men would be shed for his revenge, and I have no desire to declare myself a Rogue House."

"Mistress Sekka comes. She will provide Maugris with a power not seen in these lands for an age. Her legions brought forth from the realm of Gathos shall bolster your armies. Together you shall destroy all that oppose you."

Shiverrig looked at Dax in disbelief. "Are you insane? The last thing I want is Sekka to return to these lands. And you say she intends to bring her legions from Gathos to the Mortal Realm? The answer is no!"

"Duke Shiverrig, perhaps if you looked at the bigger picture and saw how this will all be to your benefit, you would have a change of heart."

"You must take me for a fool. Creatures from the Abyss cannot cross the Amaranthine Barrier. What you claim is impossible. If it were true, there would be demons walking the lands today."

"You'd be surprised," Dax said with a sly smile. "And nothing lasts forever."

"Let's say, against my better judgment, I believe you. Somehow, Sekka and her legions arrive on mortal soil. King Conrad is defeated, and Maugris has his revenge. What happens next? It seems unlikely the demons will simply return to the Abyss. I think they decide to stay. And why would I want that to happen?"

"The Mistress or I should say Maugris, needs great commanders to lead his armies. Exceptional men such as yourself, who know this land and its people. I can see no reason why you, Duke Shiverrig, would not become the supreme warlord of these forces when they arrive."

Dax picked through the fruit and snapped a grape from its bunch and popped it into his mouth. "Quite delicious."

Shiverrig scowled. "I can easily hold the Kingdom of Baroqia with command of the Five Armies. I do not need a horde of demons laying waste to the lands after the fighting is done."

"Yes, of course. I would not keep them here either. Disgusting creatures, really."

He ate another grape and its juices squirted over his lips. "Afterwards, take them where you will. There are other lands outside the boundaries of the Three Kingdoms to conquer."

Shiverrig rubbed his jaw and brooded.

"What does Sekka want in return for her … gift? There's always a price." He spoke calmly, though his stomach was churning. Was Maugris foolish enough to summon Sekka of Gathos back into the Mortal Realm? Could he do it?

"You are a wise man, Duke Shiverrig, it is true, there is always an exchange of one type of currency or another for such matters. Sekka demands a small tribute of human slaves for each season. Cull a frontier village here or there along the border fringes. Nothing more. They will hardly be missed." Dax held his forefinger close to his thumb as he spoke the word 'small,' opening his hand wide and waving it nonchalantly as he spoke further.

A hole of uncertainty opened in Shiverrig's gut. He could manipulate Maugris to do his bidding and over time, have him removed. Sekka was something completely different. He felt control slipping through his fingers.

"To what end? What would the villagers be used for?" he questioned, agitated.

"Frankly, I am surprised at your hesitancy. What choice do you have but to accept the helping hand of the Mistress? By my account, the king will not see House Shiverrig survive his rule." Dax tossed another grape in his mouth, savoring the sweet juice. "And more so, what do a few peasants matter, once you sit the throne of Baroqia?"

7

SEKKA

Sekka entered Aetenos' cell. She observed her prisoner with a surgeon's eye. He hung limp against the cold, unforgiving wall.

"You've seen better days, I'm sure," she said with a light chuckle.

Time in her dungeon had the desired effect on the old monk. The chains no longer rattled from feeble attempts at escape. Urns at his feet chugged out smoke laced with a unique blend of toxins. She intended to break his spirit along with his mind, but the mind was always first. She wouldn't want the demigod's thoughts to clear and have him call his winged friends again.

She was so close. He was almost ready. She broke into a wide grin as her human toes curled on the ice floor. "My dear monk, your fight has been a valiant one. I'm impressed it has lasted this long. But alas, there is no escape. You will die here on Gathos."

Dried blood and dark bruises covered Aetenos' body. All but a few tattered scraps of his cobalt-blue robes had been torn away. His lips wobbled slowly, swollen and parched. Sekka leaned in close. "You ... shall ... not ... win."

"Is that so?" Sekka said. She carefully moved the amulet that hung from his neck to the side. She spread the first two fingers of her other hand and dragged her sharp nails down the monk's exposed chest, starting at the base of his neck and ending just above his navel. She sliced a final stroke across the top where she began.

"I find your grasp of current events amusing."

Aetenos flinched in pain. Sekka gave him a wink. She took hold of the loose skin at the top and gave it a slight tug to make sure she had his attention.

"Ready?" She started to pull.

She tore the strip of skin from the monk's flesh. His unusual resistance to pain had evaporated years ago. His scream echoed through the dungeon halls.

"Why are you still here, I wonder?" Sekka mused. She let go of the loose skin. She tapped him on the forehead with two bloodied fingernails, then pushed his head up, forcing him to look at her. "Where are the faithful servants of Aetenos? You somehow managed to find your way to my doorstep. Did you forget to leave a trail of crumbs for them to follow?"

Sekka made playful designs on the monk's chest with the blood that came from his flayed skin. "Have all of the sheep in your flock lost their way? Eaten by wolves in your absence?" she taunted. "Where is your Ever Hero? Isn't his job to rescue you or some such thing?"

"No more … Ever Heroes."

"You didn't make more before you came to my home? Tsk, tsk, such a shame. Did you know that your little stunt of breaching the Amaranthine Barrier has provided me with a way to travel back to the Mortal Realm?"

Aetenos opened his one good eye, swollen as it was.

"Once there, I shall renew the harvest of precious souls you have protected for ages. Would you like to hear what really tickles me with joy? My way will be initialed by one of your Chosen. Do you remember the one? His big spell gone bad, then shunned by the Light, and forced into exile?"

"Maugris…" Aetenos' head dropped to his chest. Gibberish spewed from his mouth. The amulet was feeding on what little remained of his sanity.

"Yes, Maugris. Isn't that just grand?" She giggled in mirth, drunk on her delight. Her eyes blazed with anticipation. "The Mortal Realm shall be mine! But there are things we must discuss first." She whispered in his ear with the voice of an angel, soft and comforting and filled with innocence.

"Aetenos, my love, are you there? I need you." Sekka waited in silence. She watched as Aetenos' broken mind finally recognized the sound of the voice.

"Illyria?" Aetenos whispered. His head rolled to the side to better see her from his remaining eye. "Where are you?"

"Yes! Yes, my love. I'm here. I'm here to save you," Sekka said. She projected her voice outside the chamber. "But the door to your cell is locked."

Aetenos' raised his head for a moment. He looked straight ahead as if seeing an imaginary door. He struggled to speak but managed only a whisper. "I am here … in chains."

"Someone comes, my love. I will return."

Aetenos shook his head slightly as if to clear it. "Illyria … is here," he whispered. "…was not mistaken." A single tear ran down his grimy face. "Save her … but how?"

He pulled weakly against the shackles holding him in place. The chains mocked his efforts with clangs of their permanence.

"Find a way," he muttered softly. "All … depends … on me. No, no, no … not on me." His head sunk to his chest. "No … longer … my … time. I am … done. Time... Which time is this? Always … a mystery... Time." He pulled against the chains again and sighed deeply.

"Ever Hero … one chance … save a world."

"Yes, yes, reveal to me your avatar," Sekka whispered in his ear.

She cast an illusion upon herself. Her hair turned golden blonde and her eyes the blue of a cloudless sky. She called out to Aetenos in the voice of the angel, Illyria.

"Aetenos?"

The sound of a turning key released the latch locking the door. Aetenos still looked straight ahead. Sekka acted the part of a lithe figure dashing into the room.

"Oh, Aetenos. What have they done to you!" Sekka's illusion of Illyria burst into tears. "How you have suffered. It's all my fault."

He lowered his gaze at her. His smile was slow and sincere. "Dear Illyria … have joy…"

"We must get you down from there. Where are the keys?"

"No keys … Sekka only … spells of power…" Aetenos said.

"I shall steal the secret from her as I stole the keys for the door. I shall be silent and quick as a needle in the darkness."

"No, no. Must not… Flee, flee … evil place." His head fell forward. She was losing him.

"Oh no, not yet, my dear monk, not when we are so close."

Sekka grabbed a small vial from a nearby table. The elixir was used to revive him during more intimate sessions with sharper tools. Sekka forced the foul liquid between his lips.

"My love, if I cannot set you free, you must call your Chosen."

Aetenos could only slightly raise his head. He murmured through cracked lips, "Chosen … my Chosen, where are they?" He seemed perplexed. "Can't remember … where … I put them."

"You must find them. Call them with your song." Sekka noticed he had regained a portion of his vigor. The elixir was working.

"Song … no more, cannot … sing." He moved his head slowly in denial.

Sekka patiently kept him focused on her goal. "Concentrate and remember. Names, I must have their names," Sekka moved around Aetenos. Her agents in the Mortal Realm had provided her with the identities of potential candidates. Maybe one of them would be the next Ever Hero.

"Nysulu," she said. The name curled around her tongue.

A faint smile crossed Aetenos' face when he recognized the name. "We … raced through the jungles of Sunne."

"Yes, Nysulu. Who else, my love?

"Master Monks … fifteen … Master Dorje, Master Aika… Those two … always competing … who could hold … breath the longest. Such shades of purple … wonderful … yes, so much purple." He sighed, and his head lolled to his chest. "Playful monks … miss them. Master Aika … loved pasta … no sauce, only butter and cheese."

Sekka licked her lips, anticipating a savory feast. These were the foremost followers of the demigod. Undoubtedly one of them would be transformed into the next Ever Hero.

"How will you choose? Will it be one of the Fifteen Masters? Grandmaster Nysulu?" Sekka became eager with the prospect of finally discovering the final component of her grand scheme. "Who shall be your Ever Hero?"

"Ever Hero? No, no … too soon. Not yet … not ready. No hero … shall rise. All is lost." He fell back into his private delirium.

"My love, you must bring forth the savior. You must!"

"Very tired. Tired … and weak. My time gone, passed … all alone, so alone. Wanted you … be with you." He gasped for breath. "So very tired."

"We will travel beyond the realms of the Three Heavenly Rings and visit all of the Seven Heavens. But you must do this one last small thing to keep the Great Balance. You must let the Ever Hero rise."

Aetenos tried to lift his head but couldn't. He breathed out a ragged sigh.

"Tell me who is the next Ever Hero. Give me a name. The Grandmaster?"

"Nysulu? No ... no ... nor Masters" Aetenos was fading in and out of consciousness.

"Not the Grandmaster nor the Fifteen Masters? An acolyte? From which of the Four Orders?" Sekka pressed.

"My song ... no longer heard. Too many ... bright lights ... now dark." His words drifted in the air. Aetenos moved his head, but then stopped and tilted it to one side. "Maybe one ... in a sky filled with stone ... will listen."

"Stop playing your games. Who shall hear? Who is listening? A name. I must have a name!" Sekka was losing her patience.

"Names ... yes ... names. He will be called the Mountain Climber ... Pillar Dancer ... The Divine Fist... Happy you ... are ... here. Must ... sleep ... so very tired. Watch over me." He gasped for another breath. His body shuddered. Then he was still.

Sekka looked at Aetenos in disbelief. She had thought she would finally have her answer. But no. More riddles. Could he see through her glamour all this time? Was he playing her for a fool?

The paradox of this puzzle was profound. She would like nothing better than to eliminate Aetenos and everyone connected to him, especially his meddlesome monks. But she could not touch them until she knew who would be chosen to be the next Ever Hero.

At least now she knew who the next Ever Hero would not be. Grandmaster Nysulu and the Fifteen Masters would be removed first. That was a delightful thought. But she must warn her minions already in the Mortal Realm that no other monk was to be harmed. When she had the individual she needed, then they would all die.

Sekka left his cell. There was nothing more she would get from him today. She went to the chamber that housed her scrying pool. Reflected light rippled across the inner walls of the small room and bathed the ice queen in an eerie glow.

Sekka dipped her fingers into the thin layer of slush sitting at the surface of the bowl. The spell of divination was a mere command.

"Show me." Blurred images in the slush coalesced and became clear. She watched events unfold across familiar regions it the Abyss. A wave of fire moved towards Gathos. It was distant now, but its destination was obvious. She curled her lips in anger, and deep shadows lined her face from the light of the bowl. Time was mocking her.

"Get me Oziax!" Sekka yelled. Her anger seethed in her cold heart.

Lord Oziax raced to the chamber. Sekka could hear his footsteps stomping as he approached. "Make no mistake, that beast will never sneak up on anyone," she said into the bowl of slush.

"My Queen. What is your wish?" Oziax bowed before entering the chamber.

"Zizphander vexes me."

"He is nothing."

"I should have destroyed the Red Devil the last time he thought to flex his might." She lamented. "But now he marches with impunity across the Abyss. Has he truly grown that powerful?"

"Impossible! Allow me to unleash the Frost Legions. I shall crush this pretender and bring you his head to mount on the gates of Furia Keep. We shall avenge the loss of Lord Auzdioz," Oziax said.

Lord Oziax's rage was equal to her own when it came to matters concerning the

Zizphander. Oziax was a demon lord of the highest order, and the perceived loss to a lesser devil such as Zizphander during their first encounter was a dark blemish on his ruthless legacy. But now it seemed Zizphander's power, and his station had grown considerably.

"Lord Auzdioz means nothing to me. He was an annoyance at best."

Sekka looked back to her scrying pool. Why would it not reveal to her the answers that eluded her? "He must have a shadow patron. He must. No matter, I have pushed him back before with less, and now that I have the Great Monk, well, things will be different. Gathos shall remain a realm of ice and frost."

"My Queen, I implore you, let me empty the garrisons of Furia Keep. His horde is not but fire fiends and lesser demons. I will crush him."

Sekka turned away from the scrying pool in disgust. She would not lose everything she had accomplished, especially now that she was very close to solidifying her eminence in the Abyss.

"Zizphander grows in strength claiming whatever soul energy he can from the demon lords he vanquishes," Sekka said. She tapped her fingers together. "All of our forces may truly be needed to defeat him. But now is not the time for hasty decisions. A full engagement with Zizphander would leave Gathos open to attack. I can think of several greater devils waiting for their chance to strike."

She turned back to Oziax. "The time is almost ripe for the next Ever Hero to arise. I can hear it in the mumblings of that old fool chained to the wall. Precise planning and cunning shall prevail over brute force, my handsome beast."

The scrying pool rippled with new energy. Sekka skimmed her hand over the frigid water. "Ah, Sess'thra reports. The sorcerer, Maugris, has been swayed. He blindly assumes that by summoning me to the Mortal Realm he will also forever bind me to his will. Such hubris! Though I will become his slave, for a time, the shackles of his will should not be hard to break."

She chuckled with sinister glee. "It will not be long now."

"The Amaranthine Barrier has yet to be tested by one of your ancient blood. This is a dangerous plan," Oziax said.

"And I am a dangerous devil," Sekka replied.

8

KASAI

The morning air carried the first chill of the season. Twenty-three monks gathered in the central square. They wore sleepy faces and rubbed the soreness out of their stiff limbs.

Masters Dorje and Choejor spoke quietly in the pebbled courtyard, while Master Kunchen surveyed the faces of the assembled monks. All had participated in yesterday's tournament. Many were bruised and bandaged, but all stood at attention, awaiting his instructions.

Kasai saw Jarescu in the mix. The under part of his eyes was colored purple, and his nose was covered in white bandages.

"I know how that feels," Kasai sighed. The left side of Kasai's face was just as swollen and bruised. It was tender to the touch. But the real pain came from the fact that his Brothers knew he had thrown the fight with Daku.

"They just don't understand him," Kasai said to himself.

Kasai remembered arriving at the monastery alone and afraid. He was six years old. A week earlier, he had witnessed the death of his mother to unspeakable things. His father had abandoned them both when their need was most dire. Still, everyone at the monastery had a tale of hardship, or else they wouldn't be there. Kasai had never felt so sad and hollow inside.

He stood in the middle of this same courtyard. He was surrounded by monks of all ages doing their morning exercise. He wasn't sure what he was supposed to do. All he could see was orange, orange, and more orange. He started to cry when another young boy sided up to him.

"Just do it like this," the boy said. He showed Kasai the proper movements for each exercise. Kasai followed the boy's lead.

"I'm Daku," the boy said. He had a black eye and a puffy lip. But that didn't seem to bother him at all.

"I'm...Kasai Ch'ou."

"Don't worry, kid. I know how it feels. Stick with me. I'll watch your back," Daku said. He narrowed his eyes as he looked at the other monks. "You can't trust them."

The presence of Daku in his life filled the void left by the loss of his parents. Daku was like an older brother, and best friend rolled into one. No matter what Daku did, Kasai would defend him. He was a loyal friend.

Kasai gently touched the bruise on his face. It stung. "Or my Brothers are right, and I'm an idiot."

Kasai heard Master Kunchen clear his throat. The rest of the monks stopped talking.

"Brother Daku, please step forward," Master Kunchen said. "The Sunrise Bridge on the fifth cliff of Montouse Peak requires attention. You will lead your Brothers to the bridge, repair it, and return to the monastery before nightfall. You are the captain of this expedition. The decisions are yours to make. The successful completion of this assignment and the safety of your Brothers falls to you."

"Thank you, Master Kunchen. I will not fail," Brother Daku said. He bowed low to each Master, then turned to the monks behind him. "Gather your tools. Our mission is to repair the Sunrise Bridge and return before the fall of night. We shall not fail in either of these two objectives."

The group passed the main gates of the monastery and moved down into the wooded area of the mountain. Daku took the lead, as was his honor and right. Kasai followed next in line, then Jia'mu and Ri'sonu. The rest of the monks trailed behind in a winding but orderly line along a path through the woods.

"You know, leading an expedition like this is crucial to attaining the rank of Master. I bet I'll be the youngest Master Monk at Ordu," Daku said. He talked as if nature itself was listening to his every word.

"I'd put my money on Kasai," Cannonball said. "Masters Dorje and Choejor watch him. They talk."

"Only because he is always late to meditation," countered Daku.

"I've been at the Monastery for almost all my life. I wonder what the outside world is like now?" Ri'sonu said. He grabbed a dead twig overhanging the path. It snapped from its branch. "The Masters talk about the past and the future, but never about what is happening now." He tossed the stick casually into a patch of ferns.

"I'm sure it's all the same. Crops are planted in the Spring and harvested in the Fall. The rainy season comes and goes. Sunshine warms the valley in Summer, and snow blankets the land in Winter," Kasai said.

The day was warming. The air was fresh but had the taste of oncoming rain. Kasai took a glance through the trees. The bits of sky he could see was blue and cloudless. Nothing to worry about, he thought.

"How very poetic," Daku said. "There is more to life than what you read in books, Kasai. It's not all about falling leaves and soaring eagles." He moved his arms in grand gestures mimicking the way Kasai spoke.

"Oh, here we go again. Daku is going to school us on the merits of a powerful punch and a swift kick," Cannonball said.

"I'm talking about women. But I don't expect you to know much about them."

"Ok Brother Smooth," Ri'sonu said.

"All hail, Brother Smooth, Master Monk and lover of women," added Cannonball.

Kasai could not suppress a chuckle. Brother Smooth. That was perfect because Daku was anything but smooth. He was rough around every edge.

"That's right. I knew plenty of women before I came to this dismal place."

"There's no doubt," Cannonball said.

Kasai looked back at Ri'sonu. He was rolling his eyes in disbelief and whistled the sound of a rock being thrown in the air.

"Tell them, Kasai. He knows I'm telling the truth. Plus, I'm the Captain. You have to listen to what I say."

"Come on, you two, knock it off. Leave Captain Smooth alone," Kasai said.

Ri'sonu and Cannonball burst into laughter. Daku only scowled. Kasai had a feeling he would pay for that playful jab later.

The monks followed the path through the thick woods. Kasai always liked this time of year, especially when he could walk outside the monastery walls. The trees were just starting to change color. It reminded him of younger days when he raced through the forest surrounding his small village.

"I wonder if this is what it is like to be a Traveling Monk," Ri'sonu said. "Where do you think they send us when we are ready to leave the monastery? We are closer to the Kingdom of Sunne, and all its jungles, and bugs, and hidden things.

"Yet, history says the Kingdom of Baroqia is typically most in need of guidance. Prideful and ambitious family clans raise their swords first and find reasons later. It is a land of war."

Ri'sonu was a natural worrier and never stopped calculating his odds of success or failure.

"I don't think it matters where they send us. We must help where we can and protect those in need. Everything is the same in the eyes of the Boundless," Kasai said.

"Ugh, you sound more like Master Choejor every day," Ri'sonu said.

"Untrue." Kasai gave Ri'sonu a friendly shove.

"Hey!" Ri'sonu said. He rubbed his shoulder.

"The first thing I'm going to do is find myself a real woman," Daku said, steering the conversation back to him.

"Like you would know what to do if you found one," Cannonball quickly to chime in.

"I'm very experienced," Daku said. He raised a thumb to his chest.

"Ya, right. You were what seven, maybe eight when you arrived at Ordu?" Cannonball said.

"Ten. I was ten. That's plenty old enough."

"I found an old scroll in the library that said laying with a woman will keep you from the Boundless. That's why we are kept way up in the mountains, away from them, where it is safe," Ri'sonu said. "But that can't be true. Can it?"

"The Priestesses of Aetenos are cloistered in temples in all the major cities," Kasai said. "I'm sure exposure to women does not hinder one from reaching the Boundless. We are here at Ordu because this is where we must be."

"Master Kasai has all the answers today," Daku said. He kicked a rock on the path, sending it hard into a larger rock off to the side. "Please tell us, Great Master, where will your first stop be once you are freed from our monastery's hallowed walls? The city of Gethem is closest to us in Baroqia. There you will find the Temple of Illumination, as well as many dimly lit brothels. I'm sure Qaqal will have more action. There's a reason it's called the City of Spires. Which will it be? Meditation for your mind or pleasure for your body?"

"I hadn't thought about it," Kasai said, which, of course, was a lie. He had thought about it a lot. He wondered what it would feel like to receive a kiss from a girl. But not one from his mother, or an awkward kiss from an overly friendly neighbor. He meant a real kiss, on the lips, from someone he liked. Was there some kind of ritual or courtship that happened first? Did one kiss in public? Did one ask first? He had no idea. He had seen his parents kiss before, but they were married. Must you be married first? It all seemed very confusing and frustrating.

He fantasized about living in a small village by a wide river. He was older in the vision, like how he remembered his father. He had a small home of his own, in a clearing surrounded by tall pine trees. The fishing from the river was plentiful, and a vegetable garden provided in the Spring and Summer months.

A woman stood as a silhouette in the doorway of his small home. She had long, dark hair that flowed gracefully down her back. Lazy grey smoke rose from the chimney. He could smell carrot and potato stew simmering over the fire.

It was a quiet life and filled with happiness. The image shifted abruptly. The smoke turned black as night and poured out of the doorway and windows. Tongues of fire leaped from the rooftop. He raced to the house, but the woman was gone, consumed by the darkness. The dream shattered.

"Ahh!" Kasai said abruptly.

"Kasai? You ok?" Ri'sonu said.

"What? Yes, of course." Kasai shook himself back to the present.

He wasn't sure kissing girls even mattered. His life was devoted to the Monastery of Ordu. It was better that way. "I would probably meditate."

"Ha! I knew it! Kasai, the stupid monk," Daku said. "Never willing to take a chance."

"Yes, that's me."

Kasai remained quiet for a time. He walked with his Brothers but stopped listening to their conversation. He vaguely heard Daku ramble on about the spiral kick he had mastered. Kasai was relieved. He didn't like talking about himself so much. He was happy Daku had enough to say for both of them.

Daku called a halt to the group. The path had snaked towards the edge of the cliff. Over the side, and six thousand feet below was the Sunrise Bridge. It was a sheer drop.

"Ok, this is the spot. This should be an easy climb. I don't want anyone falling behind," Daku said.

The monks had been trained to find minute imperfections along smooth surfaces. The skill allowed them to scale what appeared to be unscalable. They moved with the precision and ease of rock spiders, scampering over the polished rock.

One by one, they slipped over the edge and climbed down the cliff wall. The descent was relatively easy. The sun was high and provided plenty of light to see the big jugs of rock ideal for hand and footholds.

The work to repair the bridge was not complicated. To his credit, Daku managed the repairs efficiently, though most of the work was more physical toil rather than anything requiring finesse. He organized the monks into smaller groups, each with a particular task. Old and rotted wood was replaced with new planks. A more durable rope was added to the underside of the bridge to allow for more weight. The work was completed within a few hours.

Daku was pleased, mostly with himself. The quick completion of the repair work would ensure he returned to the monastery well before nightfall. An accommodation would follow, and a new tattoo of power added to his arm.

"Gather your things. We're going back," Daku said. He grabbed a thick protrusion of rock above his head and started to climb.

"No rest for the weary, so the saying goes," Kasai said. He started his ascent and quickly caught up to Daku. Kasai noticed the air tasted wet. He glanced over his shoulder to see dark, angry clouds rumbling in the distance. They were coming closer.

"A storm is coming," Kasai said.

"Yes, of course. What of it?" Daku said.

"We won't beat it to the top. We must take the route of the Winding Snake. Today is the first scaling test for some of the younger Brothers. When those clouds burst, it will not go easy for them."

"That route is too long. We will not make it back to the monastery before dark. They will be fine," Daku countered.

"Just for once, could you think of someone other than yourself?"

"You sound like fat Jia'mu. If the Boundless holds such a trial for the young ones, so be it. They must learn the world is not always sunshine and warm breezes. Master Kunchen said return before nightfall." Daku turned to the horizon. "The skies will hold."

Kasai watched the progress of his Brothers. They were keeping pace. A feeling of pride came over him. He knew they were all just as sore as he was from the previous day's tournament, but all pushed on without complaint. He was proud to be part of such an honorable brotherhood.

Kasai saw that two of the youngest Brothers had fallen behind. Their movements were slow and overly cautious. They were preoccupied with the coming storm.

"Brothers make haste. We do not want you caught on the mountainside with this weather!"

Kasai watched the progress of the storm clouds with dismay. They rolled and tumbled in massive, gray waves. Bright sheets of heat lightning flashed within the billowing darkness.

The wind kicked up. Kasai shielded his eyes from the dust and debris. A light spattering of rain covered the mountain. A low rumble of thunder rolled over the mountain. The storm came fast; rain fell hard in fat drops.

"Daku, the rope. It's time," Kasai said.

Daku's face darkened in the dimming light. "Afraid of a little water, Kasai? The jugs are big and meaty along this pitch."

"The younglings, Brother." Kasai pointed below. The two young monks were well behind the main group.

"Stop worrying. This section is basic climbing." Daku grabbed a big jug with one hand and hung like a monkey from a branch. The wind turned him one way, and then the other.

Kasai watched the younger monks struggle. "The fear is upon them. It will steal their strength."

Daku shook his head. "They will make it. Stop mothering them." He continued climbing.

Kasai knew the role of the leader was everything to Daku. He had no desire to take it away from his friend. But Daku was blind to the greater need of the group. He was following the assignment to its defined conclusion, regardless of the safety of his Brothers. Flexibility through circumstance created the foundation of leadership. Not this.

Daku held tight to a different lesson, one he learned in the rough alleys of the coastal city of Ottoloto before he arrived at Ordu. The strong survive, and the weak perish. There was no middle ground.

Daku glared back at Kasai as if hearing his thoughts. Did he think this was a challenge to his authority? Daku's eyes bore into Kasai for a moment more, then he smiled, albeit reluctantly. "Fine. The rope then if it will stay your worrisome nagging."

Daku took the coiled rope from his back. He secured one end around his waist and lowered the rest. "Listen up! I am lowering a rope. Attach it to your sash and then let the remainder fall to the next. Be quick."

The monks worked efficiently, and soon the last Brother had tied off.

"Happy now, Old Mother?" Daku said.

"I will be when we crest the plateau. I'll wait until the younglings catch up. I'll tie on last."

Daku just peered upward. He grabbed another handhold and resumed his climb. "Just hurry up."

Kasai wedged his torso into a wall crevasse at his back. It was a useful technique to rest his arms and legs. One by one, his Brothers climbed past. Each acknowledged him with a thankful nod.

Kasai looked out into the horizon. A silver-blue light illuminated the air and everything it touched. The trees far below looked like miniature toys rather than the soaring pines of the forest. It was beautiful to behold, even with the rain and oppressive gloom of the storm clouds overhead.

"It is a beautiful land. One worthy of protection."

Kasai heard the words in his head. It was the same voice that spoke to him during his trial on the Pillars. Was it his conscience speaking to him, or was this something else?

"Not just an idiot monk, but a crazy one too," he chuckled.

"Let's go, you two. I'm getting soaked," Kasai called down to his Brothers. They were just below the lip of a nearby outcropping. The rope was taut and rubbed over the rock's sharp edge.

Two hands reached over the lip seeking purchase. Then two more followed. The hands grabbed ahold of meaty jugs, and Kasai breathed a sigh of relief. This was the last challenge the younglings would face alone today. The rest of his Brothers were already waiting at the next pitch. The rope was only so long.

"I'll tie off with these two. We'll catch up," Kasai yelled. He dislodged his body from the fissure and took the coiled rope from his back.

The first youngling to climb onto the narrow rock shelf was Brother Maru. Kasai liked him. He was a thinker and always had curious questions for the Masters. Kasai smiled, not that the Masters ever straightforwardly answered anything.

Maru knelt to give his fellow Brother a hand up onto the ledge. It was Brother Hondo. Kasai didn't know him as well, but that didn't matter. They were his Brothers at the monastery, and Kasai considered them part of his family now.

The younglings looked up at Kasai with faces filled with gratitude. and waved the two monks to him. "Didn't I say I was getting wet?"

"Coming, Brother Kasai," Maru said.

"Be quick!" The voice boomed in his head.

The mountain shuddered. A sharp slab popped from the cliff wall and shattered above Kasai's head. He wedged himself back into the crevasse just as a large boulder flew past his face, followed by a shower of smaller rocks. The boulder clipped the ledge holding Maru and Hondo.

The young monk's eyes grew wide as the ledge collapsed beneath them. The safety rope snapped. Kasai watched everything fall away in shimmering slow-motion.

He instinctively locked his legs into the crevasse and thrust the rest of his body towards his Brothers. His hands darted out, but he was too far away. He missed both by a long shot. Kasai watched in horror as Maru and Hondo dropped with the rest of the ledge.

"Daku! Stop!" Kasai yelled out. "Brothers have fallen!"

"What?" Daku said.

"We lost Maru and Hondo. We must climb down and see if they are still alive," Kasai shouted above the noise of the pelting rain and boisterous wind. The storm was getting worse by the moment.

Kasai somehow remembered a childhood story of Aetenos braving the fury of a mountain to rescue the chicks of the rare Crest Eagle. When he first heard the story, Kasai envisioned himself being that brave. Now that it was his reality, he wondered at his foolish childhood desires.

"Kasai, we must continue," Daku cried out. "We are wasting time! Nighttime will be upon us soon."

"I'll go," Kasai yelled back to the group.

"You'll do no such thing!" Daku barked back. "Continue climbing. They're gone. Don't be a hero."

Water ran down his face. His robes were heavy on his back. Maybe Daku was right. There's no sense risking my neck if they are already dead.

Kasai immediately regretted the thought. What if Maru and Hondo were alive but hurt? One did not remain connected to the Boundless by forsaking those who trusted in you or needed you.

"Courage," the voice spoke softly. *"They live."*

"I am not my father's son," he said into the rain, unsure as to why. Was he hoping for confirmation? The voice in his head remained silent.

Kasai shot his voice above the wind. "Daku, take the group back. I will fetch the fallen. Go!" His voice was filled with command.

"We'll all climb down search together. Hold there." Kasai recognized Jarescu's voice.

"Leave him," Daku yelled above the howling winds. "One life, or three, is not balanced with the lives of twenty. We climb to the monastery. Now!"

"They are our Brothers!" Jarescu shouted back. "We cannot leave them to the storm."

"Must I teach you another lesson, Jarescu? Master Kunchen decreed I am captain, not you, and not Kasai. He disobeyed my direct order. He made the group weak. He must live with that shame."

"He's your friend! Does that mean nothing to you?"

"Continue climbing, Jarescu. I won't repeat myself." Daku hoisted himself up to another handhold and resumed his climb.

Kasai heard every word. "That's just great," Kasai said.

He scanned the area where he had last seen the younglings. There! He saw a speck of orange on a ledge below. Kasai went fast. He practically fell, rather than climbed from one handhold to the next.

Maru was flat on his back. He was still alive, at least Kasai thought so. The rope connecting Maru to Hondo was snagged on a rock higher up on the wall. It was all that kept Hondo from falling to his death. Kasai lowered himself to the ledge.

Maru had a large lump on his forehead, and his face was cut and bleeding. Hondo remained suspended in air only by the grace of the rope. He moaned in pain each time his body swayed into the unforgiving mountainside.

"There are better ways to get attention," Kasai said. The brevity in his voice was not seen in his eyes.

Kasai grabbed the rope and pulled Hondo onto the ledge. Hondo's leg was broken. He would not be able to climb on his own.

"Faith in me," the voice said.

The fury of the storm was directly overhead. Rain fell in cutting sheets of pelting water. Small waterfalls drained the excess to the distant ground below. Kasai absent-mindedly stood to relax his legs. A gust of wind almost pushed him off the ledge. His stomach lurched. "Not smart," he said.

A flash of lightning lit the entire valley. A thunderous BOOM followed. The cliff wall shook, sending more rocks tumbling past them. It seemed as if the mountain was purposely trying to shake the three monks from its skin, like unwanted pests.

Chapter 9 SHIVERRIG

Shiverrig marched down a roughhewn stone corridor in Volkerrum Keep. Many of the torches were unlit. Though he knew his way, his irritation flared at the lack of proper lighting. 'A man should know every inch of the Keep he holds,' his late father had schooled him in younger days.

"Malachi, do you mean for me to go blind? Fix this. I want more light."

"Of course, my Duke." Malachi hurried to catch up. He cleared his throat. "I have news concerning the king's plans."

"Don't provoke me. I know what he's doing. The Royal Army sits in Qaqal."

"My associates from Rachlach Fortress have informed me that the king has opened talks of peace with Maugris."

"The fool has long enjoyed the sound of his own voice," Shiverrig said. "These talks will bear no fruit. The man is out of his depth."

"The threads of the great tapestry of life are woven together in minute detail. Look too closely, and one is driven mad by the complexity. Look from afar, and the secrets of the realms are revealed. The Lord of Change has provided an opportunity to seize power. All who follow the false light of Aetenos shall fall in ruin," Malachi said. Malachi's devotion to the prophet, Mor, bordered on fanatical.

Shiverrig worried at the ease in which his typically level-headed Archvashim could spin into fits of religious fervor. He couldn't care less about this man, Mor, who deemed himself the liaison to higher powers. Shiverrig had no time for delusional misfits with fairytale visions of the supernatural. Sword and shield, blood and honor, these were the things of value to the Duke.

"Calm yourself, Malachi. There is much work to do. I want the spiritual support from the Temple of Illumination. The transition of power will be easier for the people to accept when the deity of favor is on our side, and for most of Baroqia's nobles, that still means Aetenos."

"If Grandmaster Nysulu does not comply, he must be removed," Malachi said matter-of-factly.

"But not before we know if he will join us or not. I'd have him on our side rather than dead," Shiverrig said.

"The time of Aetenos is at its end. His flock will fade or be slaughtered. It is all the same in the eyes of Mor. Grandmaster Nysulu will be consumed by the fire of the purge like all non-believers!"

Shiverrig stopped fast. He grabbed Malachi by the shoulder and spun the slight man to face him. "I care not which demigod, god, or shining spirit holds sway over the hearts of the people of Baroqia. Faith and devotion to absent deities is a weakness that can be exploited. No more, no less.

"You may dismiss Aetenos and his followers as no longer relevant, but the Grandmaster of the Seventh Heaven is not to be dealt with lightly. The old man is odd, but I won't underestimate him. I'm not enough of a fool to think he is as feeble as he looks.

"Do not let your fanatical obsession cloud your judgment. I will not be denied my birthright to the throne of Baroqia."

Malachi's shifty eyes gleamed in the half-light of the sputtering torches. "My Duke, I have given the challenge of the Grandmaster considerable thought. I believe I have found an interesting solution. *She* will appreciate the endeavor of converting him to your cause."

"Be mindful of your steps, Malachi. I'm growing weary of the dubious company you keep of late. I don't trust *her*."

Malachi gave a short bow to Shiverrig. "Yes, my Lord."

"Now, what do you know of the monk, Eto Vyliche? Can he be moved to support my cause?"

Malachi nodded his agreement. "Yes, Eto Vyliche is a good choice to replace Nysulu. He is a favored disciple of Mor."

"Mor? Interesting. How can the Temple allow this?" Shiverrig was genuinely surprised.

"All worships are welcome at the Temple of Illumination. The absurdity of having two opposing forces under one roof is beyond me," Malachi scoffed. "But such are the mysteries of Nysulu."

"Will he follow?" Shiverrig said.

"All men conform to the desires of others until their mutual goals become unaligned. Eto Vyliche is ambitious. He grows impatient to bring the Way of Mor to the masses. That is his lever. Pull it, and you shall pull him along with you."

Shiverrig pondered Malachi's assessment for a moment. "My preference is to keep Nysulu in place but do what must be done to ensure Vyliche is with us as well. Invite the Grandmaster back to the Keep. I want to see if we can pull his levers first."

A page escorted the Grandmaster Nysulu and his young attendant into a large, but private audience chamber. Two of Shiverrig's guards remained at the door.

Waves of heat billowed into the room from a fire blazing in a grand hearth along the wall.

"The Keep has no shortage of heat," Nysulu murmured.

"If you please, my lord. There are refreshments," the page said. He directed the monks to a large table set for a feast. Candles burned brightly above platters filled with roasted meats and colorful fruits from across Baroqia. Pitchers filled with dark wine were placed evenly between the trays on the table.

"The Duke shall be along momentarily." The page bowed and left the room.

Servants stationed at the walls came forward and pulled back plush seats for the monks.

"I shall stand, thank you," the Grandmaster said. He and his attendant remained standing.

Shiverrig and Malachi entered the room from the east door. A small figure walked with them. The figure was cloaked in the deep purple and rose colors of House Shiverrig and remained a shadow amongst shadows.

"Gentlemen, my apologies for keeping you waiting," Shiverrig said. "I've been busy with the mobilization of troops…at the king's pleasure. Please be seated and refresh yourselves."

The monks remained standing. It was to be a faceoff then, thought Shiverrig. He calmed his rising irritation. The Grandmaster was playing a losing game.

"Duke Shiverrig, we have returned at your request. I hope that you are ready to assume your role as protector of the land. It is time to purge Gethem of its current sorrow," Nysulu said. The Grandmaster's voice was soft but direct.

"Yes, thank you for coming on such short notice. We have much to discuss. I'd like you to reconsider your position on my request to assume control of the Five Armies. The support of the Temple of Illumination will sway the favor of the lords and force King Conrad to return military leadership to House Shiverrig.

"My promise in return shall be to rid the land of this unfortunate plague of depravity. And then we can begin to rebuild this great realm of ours. I'm sure the construction of more monasteries would be beneficial to your followers."

The Grandmaster became thoughtful. Shiverrig was sure the old man was working through new locations where he spread the word of Aetenos to the far reaches of the realm.

"And when you once more control the full military might of the kingdom, what then? Where does the ambition of Duke Gerund Shiverrig end?"

He's a clever old man, Shiverrig thought.

"I meant only to extend the reach of the Temple's message to the people of Baroqia, perhaps even beyond our borders," Shiverrig said. "But of course, there are other endeavors one might consider. Many nobles agree a stronger Baroqia would be a welcome change to our status in the Three Kingdoms. Borders could be extended, and we could establish more favorable trade agreements with the southern Kingdom of Sunne. The vast jungles hold many natural resources that would benefit Baroqia's growth.

"My armies would march on Rachlach Fortress and eliminate the threat from Maugris in the north. I see prosperity for Baroqia. Let King Conrad sit on his throne. He will reap the rewards of my toils. This is familiar territory for him. I only wish for the security of the people of our realm."

The Grandmaster listened intently, then slowly shook his head. "No, Duke Shiverrig. Your grand words do not mirror the flow of your movements. I sense a taint within the air that surrounds you. It is much fouler than the smell of charred flesh and decaying corpses littering the squares. The sweet perfume of Gethem has changed to a maleficent odor.

"I fear something wicked has taken hold of this city. And now I see its roots have been allowed to grow deep." Nysulu's eyes shifted to the hooded figure then back at Shiverrig.

"You are mistaken," Shiverrig said.

"We both know I am not. Duke Shiverrig, you must never be allowed to command the Five Armies, even in the king's name. You will use the fear of a northern invasion to create a defensive barrier around Qaqal. Your control over the Great Houses would grow by leveraging military protection to the outer estates. It is a short step from there to a coup for the throne. For that is your ultimate goal, is it not? To supplant the king, and assume the throne for yourself?" Nysulu looked questioningly at the Duke.

Shiverrig clapped his hands together in applause. "I'll never understand how you monks do that clever trick, truth-saying do you call it? But yes, to your point, I will have the Temple's support in this matter. I will not ask again."

"I see things are worse than I originally suspected. The Temple of Illumination does not involve itself with matters of politics. Our position remains unchanged. However, your path will thrust the Great Houses into civil war, causing the deaths of thousands. This, we cannot condone. The Temple will no longer remain silent."

Shiverrig was about to speak, but he held his tongue. He could see the Grandmaster had made his decision.

"For the way of the world is through change. Those who cannot or will not alter their ways must be removed. So says the prophet, Mor," Malachi quoted.

The Grandmaster ignored Malachi's threat. His eyes were locked on Shiverrig. He spoke as a father would a wayward son, "I do not understand, Gerun. Your family has sired many of Baroqia's greatest heroes. How did one of their brightest stars fall so deep into darkness?"

This was the moment. Once he stepped forward down this path, there was no turning back. Was he sure? Shiverrig paused to collect his thoughts. His answer was clear in his head; Baroqia must be strong.

"I am sorry to hear you will not listen to reason, Old Father. But I will not sit idle and watch the kingdom of my forefathers crumble to dust." He nodded to Malachi.

"It is time we introduced our guest," Malachi said with glee. "May I present Sess'thra, from the frozen court of Sekka, the Arch Devil of Gathos."

Sess'thra removed her hooded and let the cloak fall to the ground. A lithe and supple body stepped out of the purple puddle of cloth. Her naked body glistened in the firelight. Her thin, almond-shaped eyes tapered upwards at their sides.

A feral smell emanated from her demonic pores as a long, serpentine tail grew from her backside. It swayed with a feline twitch.

"Finally," Sess'thra purred. She lunged forward at the young aid at the Grandmaster's side. Her hand shot out and tore through his throat. Sess'thra vaulted over Nysulu. A thick braid of jet-black hair uncoiled down her back. An eerie innocence filled her laughter as she landed softly across the room.

Nysulu flashed into action. Gone was any resemblance of a tired, old man content to spend his remaining days in quiet meditation. The Grandmaster of the

Seventh Heaven spun to face the demon. He crouched in a defensive posture as an aura of blue radiance formed around his body.

Shiverrig felt the air in the room change. The hairs on his arms rose off his skin. A burst of energy rippled past him that felt like a wave of electricity. It rattled the contents of the table and knocked over the empty wine goblets.

The Grandmaster held one hand out straight against the demon's advance. His other hand was curled at his side in a fist, ready to strike. Both glowed white-hot. Shiverrig watched the Grandmaster with fascination. He had heard of the mystical martial arts of the monks of the Four Orders, but he had never seen one of them in action. Real combat was the most accurate measure of a man.

Sess'thra wore a wolfish grin. She approached the Grandmaster with the ease of a streetwalker. She oozed with seduction as her slight hips swayed with each step. "So, this is the pride of Aetenos," Sess'thra mocked. Her magenta-hued eyes sparkled with intensity as they caught the white light burning from Nysulu's hands.

"I know not how you came so far without being detected, demon, but I see you now," Nysulu said.

Sess'thra brought her slender index finger to her lips and kissed the onyx ring upon it. She then wagged the finger side-to-side. "My Mistress Sekka provides."

Sess'thra ran towards the Grandmaster in a blurring, zig-zagged course. Nysulu held his position. He brought his clenched fist up to mirror his outstretched palm just before she crashed into him. A force of air slammed into the demon. Sess'thra was tossed across the floor. She tumbled into a roll and rose like an indignant cat.

"You have doomed yourself, Duke Shiverrig," Nysulu said, keeping his eyes fixed upon the demon. His manner was completely calm, almost peaceful.

"Join us!" Malachi yelled, "Join the new power of the Three Kingdoms. The Change of Mor is upon you! Decide!"

No answer came from the Grandmaster. Sess'thra sauntered towards the monk again. She wiped away a touch of blood from her nose with the back of her hand. She raised her eyebrow and gave Nysulu a bit of a smirk. The air shimmered behind her, and Shiverrig watched in amazement as bat-like wings sprouted from her back. They were the color of a moonless night and unfurled like a virgin fern. She took to the air.

Nysulu followed her movement as she flew above him. His arms slowly moved through different defensive gestures in anticipation of her next attack. It came quickly. Sess'thra dove towards him like a bird of prey. She shrieked as talons sprouted from her fingers. Her thinly shaped eyes grew wide with excitement.

Nysulu braced himself. He manipulated the air to form a white barrier between him and the demon. Sess'thra barked out a word of power that made Shiverrig wince.

The shield above Nysulu wavered just enough for the demon to slice through it. She plowed into Nysulu. The momentum of her impact carried both of them to the floor, though the Grandmaster rolled with fluid ease.

They grappled together in a climatic embrace. Nysulu masterfully blocked each of the furious strikes from her hands and feet. They missed his flesh and succeeded in only tattering his robes.

Nysulu struck back, but Sess'thra's leathery wings shielded her from his counter punches. Sess'thra strikes were wild. They grazed his skin, but she couldn't land a decisive blow. The Grandmaster's face and hands became lined with razor-thin scratches.

Somehow, Nysulu managed to get his feet under the demon. He braced himself against the floor and thrust his legs upwards. Sess'thra was blasted into the air with such force that she broke through one of the overhead rafters, spraying splinters of wood through a cloud of dust. Once the air clears, Sess'thra leered down at the old man.

Nysulu raised himself from the floor. His robes were torn, even shredded in some places, but he seemed intact. The Grandmaster was a formidable opponent. Shiverrig was right not to have underestimated his abilities.

"Your dark minion will not prevail here, Shiverrig," Nysulu warned. The man seemed unphased by the attack.

"You are already dead, monk!" Sess'thra hissed, "You have been kissed by my Mistress' nectar at least a dozen times."

Nysulu brought his hands to his face and examined the numerous welts and claw marks. He chuckled and shook his head. "You thought to defeat me with a little poison? Toxins of any kind shall not affect me," Nysulu said. "Now, let us finish this."

The Grandmaster assumed a sturdy pose. His arms circled as he breathed out deeply. Sess'thra remained in the rafters, watching, waiting.

A drop of blood oozed from Nysulu's nose, followed by a red gush that streamed down his face. The welts covering his body swelled like giant worms under his skin. White puss wept from the open scratch wounds on his hands. His arms dropped to his sides as if all strength had fled.

Somehow, the Grandmaster remained standing. The calm expression on his face never changed, yet his body trembled with exertion.

Sess'thra floated down from the rafters and stood confidently next to the monk. She leaned in close to the side of Nysulu's face. Her smooth cheek brushed against his weathered skin as she whispered in his ear. "As I said, my Mistress provides."

Shiverrig approached the Grandmaster. Malachi was by his side like a faithful dog. "This does not have to be the end, Old Father. The time has come to choose," Shiverrig said. Nysulu's eyes were filled with sadness and disappointment.

"Can he speak?" Shiverrig asked the demon.

"Let's see," Sess'thra purred before thrusting her clawed hand deep into the Grandmaster's chest. Nysulu's mouth opened wide, but only emitted a slight wheeze. She yanked her arm from his body and the Grandmaster of the Seven Heavens fell dead to the floor.

"No. He cannot," Sess'thra confirmed.

She swiveled her eyes to meet Shiverrig's, cocking her head to the side, smugly daring him to say or do anything. Shiverrig was tempted to throttle the little bitch. Instead, he grabbed a fistful of Malachi's robes and pulled his Archvashim close.

"The demon was not to kill the old man! He would have been a useful prisoner if he could not be swayed."

"You knew as well as I, the Grandmaster had made his decision before entering the keep," Malachi said, "It was a false hope he would be swayed."

Shiverrig was furious. He thrust Malachi away. Sess'thra's bloodlust had created a massive setback to his plans. He motioned to the guards at the main door. "Remove this mess and have the bodies burned. Tell no one."

Shiverrig would worry about the explanation for the Grandmaster's disappearance later. Malachi would come up with something plausible, he hoped. Shiverrig was under no delusions that the temple monks would believe him. "Fucking hell!" he yelled out into the room.

Malachi, oblivious to Shiverrig's rage, moved closer to Sess'thra. "You truly are a wondrous sight. Your perfect precision is a marvel. Your sanguine and seductive movements have enchanted me. Perhaps we can share more of your otherworldly delights in private, my lovely succubus."

Malachi ran his hand along her shoulder. His fingers traced her collar bone, then moved down towards the divide between her breasts. She looked at him, tenderly with a smile that was coaxing and dangerous at once. One of her sharp incisors peaked out over her bottom lip and bit down at its corner. Malachi's hopes broadened. He licked his dry lips.

His hand reached for her right breast. A quick flash of steel rose from Sess'thra's waist. Malachi's hand was sliced off at his wrist. It landed with a slap against the stone floor. A small dagger, hitherto unseen, glistened with dark blood.

"Touch me again, worm, and you shall lose the other," Sess'thra said.

Malachi's piercing shriek bounced against the walls of the room. He dropped to his knees. His remaining hand alternated between holding his bleeding stump and trying to pick up his lost appendage.

"Was that necessary, demon?" Shiverrig said through frustrated teeth. Malachi still had his uses. "I don't want him dead."

Sess'thra's lascivious smile was the only answer she gave before licking the knife clean. "Be thankful. My Mistress did not bless the dagger as well."

Shiverrig turned to face the fire burning in the hearth. He sighed. This was a frustration he did not need. His mind shifted through possible contingency plans. His wartime mind took over. First, stop the immediate bleeding. "Get him to the healers; perhaps something can be saved."

Shiverrig turned back to the fire. He nodded to himself. "It's time to move my plans to the next level. I will need Vyliche if I am to move on House Conrad."

Although unwelcome so soon, today's mess was not entirely unexpected. It just shifted a few new pieces into play as others were removed. Shiverrig tried to console himself to no avail. His pieces were now scattering in a foreign wind.

Sometimes, it's better just to embrace the chaos, he thought as he walked toward the door. Stopping, he looked over his shoulder at Sess'thra. "Demon, a word with you. Tell me more about Sekka."

9

KASAI

Two oddly shaped bodies stumbled toward the main gate of the Monastery of Ordu. One was the size of a young boy and walked with a hitched step. The other was a monstrosity with a massive upper torso, two heads, and what appeared to be multiple arms and legs. Both were silhouetted by the sun. The warning gong was struck four times.

One of the wall sentries pointed to the approaching figures. "There, do you see that?"

A second shouted from the wall to the monks gathered in the courtyard. "It's Brother Kasai! He's with Brothers Maru and Hondo. The younglings look hurt. Bring help!"

Kasai was relieved to see the gates open and Brothers rushing out to meet them. His back and legs ached from carrying Hondo. Maru kept pace at his side and offered whatever support he could.

Kasai heard faint cheering coming from the monks overhead as he stumbled through the gateway into the safety of Ordu. Hands grabbed his robe to keep him upright. His Brothers gently took Hondo from his back and laid him on the ground.

Kasai put his arm around Maru's shoulder and guided him to a nearby bench.

"We're home now. No more worry," Kasai encouraged. He closed his eyes and exhaled. His back was stiff from fatigue. His legs trembled as if chilled from being out in the snow too long.

Monks raced towards them with stretchers. Maru and Hondo were carted off to the infirmary. Brother Nabu offered Kasai a cup of water from a nearby rain barrel. Kasai drank down its fill. His mouth was already dry when he handed the empty cup back.

"Another, please."

"Should I bring you the entire barrel next time?" Nabu said as he handed a fresh cup to Kasai. "You certainly deserve it. Daku said you fell with the younglings. He told everyone you were lost. I am glad to see you are all in one piece."

A frowned stole across Kasai's face for just a moment, and then he forced a smile. "Happy to be in one piece, Brother," Kasai replied. He gulped down the second cup of cold rainwater. Water never tasted so good. He leaned back on the bench.

"I see you still carry the weight of the brotherhood on your shoulders," Nabu said.

"I'm tired."

"Uh oh, here comes Brother Manno. He's wearing the white robes this month."

"Ugh. Hide me," Kasai said halfheartedly.

Manno had pulled the duty of Master's Messenger. He bowed respectfully, but his face was all business. "Brother Kasai, the Masters would like a word with you. They wait for you in the Chamber of Reflection."

"All of them?" Kasai asked.

"I'm afraid so," Manno said.

"Looks like you are not done yet," Nabu said.

Kasai's spirit fell. What would it be now? A full season of midnight watch on the North Ridge? Various punishments rifled through his head, none of them pleasant. His legs hurt. His back hurt. He was tired, hungry, and just wanted to sleep.

Kasai reluctantly rose. He headed for the Chamber of Reflection. Daku must have said something about disobeying his direct orders. He was sure to receive a severe reprimand by Master Dorje. Daku would never let him live this down.

Kasai entered the hall containing the Chamber of Reflection. He walked hesitantly down a long wooden corridor. The walls of the hallway were covered with ancient scrolls. Each one was filled with colorful images depicting the great deeds and sacrifices of legendary monks from Ordu.

Gen Moll was given the first scroll as was his due. He had the honor of being the first Ever Hero of Aetenos. He was shown fighting against demons from the Abyss. His holy sword Azurn blazed bright red. Next to Gen Moll was Aetenos, who wielded Ninziz-zida. The weapon's segments spun in a blue swirl of fire.

Kasai felt a profound appreciation for the history of Ordu. His trial on the mountain had shown him some of the reality of those feats. Maybe he would one day have a scroll made in his honor. He shook his head. Who was he kidding? He was no hero. He was just a stupid monk.

Kasai arrived at the door to the Chamber of Reflection. The door was already open. Beeswax candles cast a dim, orange glow through the room. The delicate smell of sweet honey and aged wood filled the space. The Three Masters of Ordu waited inside.

Kasai took a deep breath and gathered his thoughts. He knew they would ask him to explain his conduct on the mountain. Daku had earned the right to command. That was the rule. He should not have gone against his captain's orders, but he couldn't forsake the younglings.

"Brother Kasai, it will be difficult to talk if you remain outside. Please come in," Master Kunchen said from inside the chamber.

"Yes, Master." Kasai hurried into the room.

"We are happy to see you have returned to Ordu. I hope your overnight stay on the mountain was a pleasant one?" His eyes crinkled and sparkled with amusement.

Kasai bowed to each Master before he spoke. "Yes, Master Kunchen, we were humbled by the hospitality of the great mountain. She graciously provided us with a small nook to take shelter against the rains. I secured Brother Hondo's leg with a basic rock splint. But I fear it will need to be reset. When the rains ceased, we scaled the wall as one. Brother Maru is quite skilled when he puts his mind to it." Kasai smiled. He remembered where he was and why and made his face blank.

"Tell me, did you discover your path to the Boundless?" Master Choejor said. He traced a design in the air that only his blind eyes could see. Then he blew it forward.

Kasai thought he saw the soft glow of candlelight on the Master's body grow brighter. He rubbed his eyes. When he opened them, a faint blue image floated in the air towards him. It was the same design the Master had drawn in the air. I'm so tired, he thought. I'm starting to see things. Kasai rubbed his eyes again for good measure.

"The Boundless did not fully reveal itself to me, Master Choejor, but it provided what was necessary when it was needed most." Kasai bowed respectfully after answering the question.

"Know that the Boundless interacts with us all as individuals. It is a path that you will travel alone, for the Boundless accepts us as ourselves in total as we are added to its whole. But you must have faith if you wish to succeed," said Master Choejor.

"Faith in a wandering demigod that has vanished from the lands, or an unseen goddess, who has created a world of misery and suffering, Master?" Kasai immediately regretting what he said. He would receive a double dose of punishment for sure.

"No, nothing so dramatic as that. You must have faith in yourself. No other-worldly being controls our actions or determines our fate. They merely point us in a direction based on influence. We do the rest."

"Brother Kasai," said Master Dorje in a stern voice. "We have discussed at length your actions on the mountain and their consequences."

"Yes, Master Dorje. I understand," said Kasai. He bowed once more and stood straight. He was ready to accept whatever punishment the Masters saw fit to give him for disobeying Daku's orders.

Master Dorje continued, "On the morrow, you shall receive the mark of Oh-hur, a shield against the outer elements. It will ward you for a time against the frigid cold of the deepest lake, and the fiery embrace of the burning pyre. Also, we will mark you with Mizzen, to fill the hearts of those around you with the courage you possess. As you are strong of will, so shall you inspire the will of others. That is all. You may take your rest."

Kasai was stunned. He stood dumbfounded for long moments.

"Brother Kasai?" Master Dorje said.

Kasai humbly bowed before each of the Masters and left the Chamber of Reflection. He wondered if he had heard correctly. Instead of receiving a reprimand, he was being rewarded. He would figure it out after he had rested. He was exhausted.

Kasai opened his eyes to a room filled with sunlight. It was already the following morning when he rose from his cot. The Masters had let him sleep throughout the day and night. He was famished. Kasai realized he had missed dawn chores and morning meditation. Maybe he could still get a bite of warm bread to eat before calisthenics and sparring.

Kasai left his small room and went outside. He saw Daku across the courtyard.

"Daku, wait!" he shouted.

Daku turned fast. His face was an angry mask of betrayal. "Leave me be! I want nothing to do with you. You have ruined my honor. The Masters look at me as something broken."

"Let me explain," Kasai implored.

Daku grabbed Kasai's forearm and held it up to his face. "When you get branded with Oh-hur and Mizzen later today, remember that you stole them from me."

"Brother. It wasn't like that."

Daku stepped uncomfortably close to Kasai. "How could I have been so blind? I have always carried you during the tournaments. I see now you've always been jealous." Daku squeezed Kasai's forearm. He had a grip as secure as a steel trap.

"You meant to humiliate me and undermine my authority. You and the two younglings were in it together. And Jarescu and Shiro as well!" Spittle flew from Daku's mouth. His face was bright red.

"You all wanted me to fail. But I won't! Now that I know of your betrayal, I will be prepared next time. I will show you what it means to betray me."

Kasai broke away from Daku's handhold. "Brother, none of what you say is true. I did not mean for the Masters to strip you of leadership. I said nothing of what happened. They already knew."

"Of course, they knew! Everyone here is a rat. Except for Kasai. He's a hero."

"I'm no hero, Brother."

"No, you're not. And stop calling me that. I am not your *Brother*. You are just like the rest. You have betrayed our friendship. We're finished." Daku marched away.

"Daku, wait!" Kasai wished he could think of something to say that would quench the fire xindu burning through his friend. Daku was caught up in a wild passion, and it would be best to wait until he was calm and at peace. Kasai strolled to kitchens. He wondered if he had lost his best friend.

Kasai left the refectory with a roll of bread dipped in honey. The earlier scuffle with Daku had mostly been forgotten. Kasai had no control over his Brother's emotions and therefore decided to let go of his guilt. The two friends had tenuous moments in the past. Eventually, they would find common ground together.

The mountain air was clean and crisp from the early autumn rains. The sky was the color of everlasting blue, and morning dew glistened in the yard. Kasai heard small mountain birds chirping their happiness at the start of a new day.

He sighed with contentment. He enjoyed the simple routine of his days. He was well-suited to a structured and ordered life, notwithstanding his consistent tardiness. But who among his Brothers was perfect?

The Way of Ordu challenged his mind in the same way his body worked through handholds and kicks. It required complete focus, dedication, and practice.

The monks of the Four Orders spent their lives seeking to perfect the execution of each unique doctrine of their particular Order. The Order of Ordu focused on the understanding and use of xindu energy.

The Masters continuously pushed the monks to develop their inner connection to the elemental forces of water, fire, earth, air, and spirit. In this way, they learned to manipulate the vibrations of energy flowing through their bodies. Mastery demanded deep concentration. When done correctly, a monk could achieve miraculous feats. This was the Way of Ordu.

"When you master the ability to control the depth of your concentration, you will understand the boundaries of self and non-self. This is the key to understanding the Boundless," Master Choejor had said.

.   .   .

Kasai was a diligent student. He excelled at the intellectual understanding of the xindu mysteries. Unfortunately, he lagged behind his Brothers when using the strange gift in his daily life. He was told xindu energy was the primordial force that gave life to the world, and mastering one's internal energy was a part of the Boundless. It was a big part.

That didn't matter to Kasai. It seemed unnatural to him. Using xindu energy felt like wielding some kind of dark magic. He didn't trust it.

"That's probably why the Boundless seems so very far away from me," Kasai said as he walked to the central square. He kicked a pebble in the courtyard. At least the bread was good.

He entered the central square just as his Brothers moved into the sparring circles to fight against one another. Some were lone defenders against multiple attackers, while others faced only a single adversary. The Masters watched and instructed. The monks changed positions when each match reached its conclusion.

"Brother Ori. Let's match up," Kasai said.

"Sure," Ori said.

They bowed once and then began. Within a few exchanges, Ori was on his back. Kasai reached down to help his Brother up. "Your strike combinations are becoming more fluid, Ori. It looks like you have been doing some extra practicing with the new technique." Kasai gave his Ori a friendly pat on the back.

"I need all the practice I can get. These advanced techniques are getting more difficult to perform," Ori said. "Yet, you make it look so easy."

"You need only let go of what you think you must do and focus on what fills its place."

"Has Master Choejor taught you to speak in riddles as well?"

"Do I really sound like him?" Both young monks paused a moment to reflect and then laughed. They resumed their positions opposite one another, bowed, and began again.

"I heard the Masters are looking for the next Capu to the junior Brothers," Ori said. "You would be perfect."

"I know. They asked before we left to repair the Dawn Bridge. I respectfully declined."

"You declined the Masters?" Ori was stunned. "Why? You are one of the best fighters at Ordu. The Brothers look up to you. You're a natural leader. Let's face it, Kasai, you already talk like one of them." They both laughed again.

"I think Daku is more interested in taking on the responsibilities of being Capu," Kasai said. "He is better suited for that role."

"Are you crazy? Daku? He left you, Hondo, and Maru on the mountain to die. Who does that to their Brothers?"

"Daku was only looking out for the safety of the group." Kasai brushed some ground debris from his shirt. He looked over to where Daku was sparring with another Brother. The fight had its typical outcome with Daku dominating his opponent with ease.

"Why must you always defend him? How did he earn such loyalty from you?"

"You don't understand him. His life before Ordu was harder than most of us. He'll change," Kasai said hopefully. "You'll see."

"We've all had bad weather in our past, Brother. For most of us, being here was the best option."

"Yes, we've all been through something," Kasai thought about his younger days. Darker days.

"Kasai, you owe it to us younger monks to be Capu. If nothing else, you would prevent Daku from breaking our backs."

"Ori, I think I would only let you down. I can best serve the brotherhood by following rather than leading. The ego leads. The servant follows, and through his service, more are helped. I am content with my role."

"So, you leave us to the whims of that bully? Watch him now. You'll see." Ori pointed back to where Daku was sparring. A new match had started.

Daku stepped into the sparring circle. He faced off against four junior Brothers. They immediately circled him. Each sought a weakness they could exploit. But as a whole, they took on different attack styles to prevent Daku from mounting a proper defense.

Daku rotated counter to their movements. He assessed each of his adversaries, then launched himself at Brother Lo. He was small, about the same height as Kasai.

Daku grabbed a handful of Lo's loose shirt and brought up his knee hard. It connected with Lo's midsection. Brother Meeri rushed him. Daku smoothly pivoted to his right and sent his heel to Meeri's jaw. Lo and Meeri were done. They dropped to the dusty ground at the same time.

Kasai could see the fear in the body language of the two remaining Brothers. Daku was in his element. He reveled in having power over others. Kasai saw Brother Jonah and Brother Nico contemplated their next moves carefully.

Daku took advantage of their hesitation and launched into the air with a spinning-hammer kick. His heel slammed down on Nico's shoulder. The young monk cried out in pain. The force of the blow must have shattered his collarbone. Daku spun in the opposite direction and delivered a second kick to Nico's handsome face. His nose exploded with blood, and he crumbled to the ground. Daku left him crying in the dirt.

Brother Jonah did his best to shore up his defense. Daku threw a flurry of punches at him, which eventually broke down Jonah's guard. Three quick strikes to the face and Johan was on his knees. Daku had systematically incapacitated four junior Brothers with ease. His form was perfect, and his swiftness of movement was astonishing.

"Daku strikes to hurt, not to disarm," Ori said.

"He wins because he instills fear in his opponents. Those four are better fighters against anyone else." Kasai watched as Daku celebrated his victory. He felt ashamed for his friend's exuberance.

"I'm the best! I'm the best!" Daku pumped his fist in the air. He looked around to see if anyone else had watched his match.

Kasai and Ori edged closer to where the Three Masters stood. They had watched the bout with great interest. Kasai knew he shouldn't eavesdrop. His curiosity got the better of him, and he listened anyway.

"Bitterness and loneliness fill the young man's heart. The bad memories of his youth fuel his fire xindu to dangerous levels. He must learn to control his rage, or he will become a problem," Master Dorje commented.

"The walls protecting his garden go high. They shield the seeds of his fear with resentment. The flowers he grows will be ill-formed if we cannot help him," Master Choejor added.

"Too great is his unwillingness to embrace in the Boundless. The Openness is closed to him. He refuses to share equally of himself with the world around him. Never formless is this one. He remains Daku at all times," Master Kunchen noted.

"The best, the best. Hmm, what is best? What is worst? Perhaps they are the same with our young monk? He hides much of himself in secret places. Maybe he has found a different path to the Boundless, unique only to him," Master Choejor said. "Let us present Brother Daku with the light of a different target. We will see what we can retrieve from the shadows of his anger."

The blind Master walked to the sparring circle where Daku stood victorious. Master Choejor bowed deferentially to the young monk. "You may use any weapon of your choice, Brother Daku. I shall rely solely on the Boundless and use what is offered."

Kasai and Ori looked at each other with apparent surprise. Masters did not spar with the junior or even senior monks. It would be as if a champion knight chose to joust against a horseless peasant.

Kasai could imagine what Daku was thinking. He would be eager to pit his skill against Master Choejor. Defeating a Master in one-on-one combat would ensure he regained his honor.

"It would be dishonorable to use a weapon against you, Master Choejor, when you have none," Daku said.

Kasai shook his head in disbelief. That was a mistake.

"As you wish," Master Choejor said. "Let us begin."

The two monks faced each other and bowed. Daku conclusively demonstrated a series of complex movements that conveyed the different offensive styles he had already mastered. He was ready.

Master Choejor remained calm and still. Daku's leg flashed low. He sought to sweep the Master's legs from under him. Master Choejor was a blur of motion. Daku spun in a complete circle. He stopped where he had started but was left off-balance. Daku crouched as best he could. He scanned for the Master.

Master Choejor tapped Daku on the back of his shoulder and sent him to the ground in obvious pain. Daku looked up in astonishment. Master Choejor simply smiled and patiently waited for Daku to recover.

Daku grimaced as he surged to his feet. He rolled his shoulder and did his best to relax the muscles before striking out with a powerful punch of his own. Master Choejor pivoted to the side, and Daku's strike found empty air. Master Choejor touched Daku's outstretched arm with two fingers to the deltoid. Daku's arm fell limp at his side.

Daku attacked with a reverse kick and found himself on the ground again. He scurried forward to grapple with Master Choejor. Daku's good hand shot out to grab the Master's pant leg but missed.

Daku was angry and frustrated. Some of the Brothers snickered under their breath. They were enjoying the payback. Daku leaped to his feet and scowled at the crowd. He launched into a furious and undisciplined attack.

"Don't lose yourself to your fury. You must control your fire xindu as you do all things passing through you," Master Choejor said. His words were calm and soothing.

"I am strongest with my fire xindu blazing!" Daku punched out again and followed with a leaping kick. The Master defected both blows with his outstretched hand.

Daku kicked a second time. Master Choejor grabbed the foot and twisted it around. Daku twirled in the air before he hit the ground hard.

"Guide your passion, young one. Be at peace with your xindu, or you are lost."

"I am not lost, Master!" Daku spat dirt from his mouth. He managed to stand, barely. With great effort, he raised the arm that Master Choejor had paralyzed earlier. "I can still fight." Kasai could see the focus was lost from Daku's eyes. His upper body swayed on weak legs.

"No, this match has reached its conclusion," Master Choejor said.

Brother Daku collapsed back to the ground. He could hear his Brothers mock him. "Stop laughing," he said.

"There is a lesson here, my son. Have you discovered it?"

Daku looked up at Master Choejor. Exasperation was written across his face. "As you say, Master, I must learn to control my fire xindu energy."

"That is partially correct, but the higher truth of the xindu mysteries still eludes you. Xindu energy fuels much more than merely your martial prowess. It will influence the creation or the destruction of your higher purpose.

"When you silence your passion, you will see the many options available to you on your path of life, instead of running blindly down the one you currently travel. What else have you learned?"

"I hoped I was your equal, but I was wrong. You are stronger, faster, and more skilled than me."

"No, that is not the lesson of today. This is not where you stumbled. Your eyes are open but are still blind to the higher world around you. You fail to grasp the totality of the Boundless, and so you remain a crude weapon."

Master Choejor walked a few steps in contemplation, then continued. "You maintain boundaries where there are none. You are Daku at all times. You hold tight to this identity, but it serves only to prevent you from Openness. You must learn to let go of the self if you are to be one with the Boundless. Contemplate Openness during your meditations, my young monk. Tomorrow is another day to grow."

"I will do as you say, Master. I am humbled by your skill and thankful for your wisdom." Daku bowed low to Master Choejor.

The lunchtime bell chimed in the background, and the monks made their way to the refectory. Kasai watched his friend intently. Daku was not known to exhibit humility or acceptance of defeat so readily. Perhaps this was a new beginning for his friend.

Unfortunately, when Daku rose, there was bitterness written across his face. Nothing had changed. Perhaps it never would.

But something Master Choejor had said to Daku resonated with Kasai. 'You maintain boundaries where there are none.' Kasai knew the same could be said for him. But something inside him was working to bring down those walls.

It started when he faced the Trial of Pillars and became more pronounced on the mountainside. It was as if a small space had opened in his mind. Or maybe it was there before, but he had never noticed. Kasai hoped it meant he was taking his first steps to become one with the Boundless. The voice in his head spoke to him frequently, but more often than not, it whispered twisted words Kasai did not understand. That was worrisome.

He said nothing about it to Maru or Hondo when they were sequestered on the mountainside together. He hid it again from the Masters in the Chamber of Reflection as well. He was unsure of what it meant. He feared if he expressed himself to the Masters, they would fill him with more riddles. No, this was something he needed to figure out for himself. But how? Kasai had a stupid idea. He walked in the direction of the pillars.

"I must not fear this test. If what I hear is truly my connection to the Boundless, I shall hear it again," Kasai said. "Either that or I am going as mad as the voice in my head."

He closed his mind from the noise of conflicting thoughts. He would be calm and let the fear subside. He was eager to see the higher world of the Boundless.

Kasai removed his sandals. He placed them neatly to the side of the first pillar. The first step was just as easy to take as before. The stone felt cold and hard against his bare feet. Kasai stepped to the next pillar and the next.

"This isn't too bad," he said.

He took the pillars at a run, and soon he was high above the ground. Then the air temperature suddenly dropped. The pillars became shrouded in mist, and a claustrophobic fear crept up his spine. He didn't want to take the next leap. "Just be calm. The voice will come."

The winds picked up, and the pillar swayed gracefully under him. No reassuring message came to mind. The voice was silent. What was he doing here? He had purposely put himself in a dangerous situation, thinking he was special. He wasn't touched by something special. That hard truth pounded in his head like a hammer against a dense stone.

He swiveled around. Maybe he could go back. He saw only swirling mists. The pillar top behind him was lost from sight. "Can't go that way."

A quick gust of air pushed him close to the edge of the pillar. He stumbled while trying to maintain his balance. His back foot slid off the top. His body dropped first to one knee and then over the side.

His hand shot out and grabbed the crest of the pillar. He quickly wrapped his thumb over his fingers to solidify the grip. Kasai dangled in the white air bumping against the post. It was a long way down, even with the safety nets. Wait, were they up? He had forgotten to check. His heart thumped in his chest, and the sweat of fear covered his body.

"Where are you when I need you?" Kasai said into the empty air. "Have you abandoned me as well?"

"*Trust,*" came the voice in a whisper. "*Calm. Concentrate.*"

Kasai listened to the message echoing in his thoughts, and he calmed his fear. He concentrated his efforts on regaining purchase on the pillar top. Once there, Kasai sat with his legs hooked around the column for support. He recited mantras to relax his body and mind. Eventually, his breathing came slow and even. He could feel the relaxed rhythm of his chest expanding with air and then deflating as he released it.

"*Look.*"

Kasai fixed his sight to a point in space where he suspected the next pillar to be. He stared intently at the same spot as moments stretched into minutes. Something was happening. He could see small particles of moisture floating in the air before his eyes. He felt each tiny droplet as it touched his skin. Kasai held his hand in front of his face. He could barely see it through the thick mist.

He focused more intently on the particles of moisture that separated from the air. They swirled around his hand in a shimmering, blue haze. The moisture moved passed his hand as a river flowed around boulders impeding its course. The flow was hardly discernable, but it was there. Kasai saw a map of what was and what was not.

"What dark magic is this?" He lost his focus. The impenetrable air returned to blanket his sight, and his hand disappeared from view.

"*Safe,*" the voice said.

Kasai sighed. "Ok. Ok."

Hesitantly, he sought the division between the water and the air. What else was out there? Where was the sun? The clouds? The birds? Kasai's heartbeat slowed. His mind became silent. His breathing was even.

"Show me the river that flows. Where are the rocks that are not the river?" Kasai saw trails of swirling blue flow around a long line of shadowy shapes. He saw the next pillar. It was so close he would barely need to jump.

Kasai leaped and landed squarely on its top. He jumped again, and again. It was as easy as walking in broad strides. The pillars finally descended. He cleared the mist layer and eventually stepped from the last pillar onto soft grass.

He felt each blade of grass underfoot. His toes dug into the soil. It felt warm even though the grass was cool. The mist was gone, but he could still see the currents of moisture flowing around whatever he saw.

Kasai suddenly became anxious. He had completed what should not have been able to be accomplished. He turned back to see the marble pillars winding up into the air behind him. A giddy feeling of unease filled his gut. He didn't know if he was going to cheer or vomit. "What have I done?"

"An interesting question," responded a voice approaching from across the lawn.

Kasai turned to see Master Choejor walking towards him. He saw a wisp of yellow flash over the Master's head. It was reminiscent of what Kasai saw when he was in the Chamber of Reflection with the Three Masters. He focused his attention on the color, and it blossomed into a golden glow around his teacher. Kasai bowed to Master Choejor.

"You have passed the Trial of Pillars, my son," Master Choejor said. "An impossible challenge for one of your level of training. This is a curious thing. But for now, I am wondering what led you to such a bold endeavor when the safety nets were not in place?"

Because I'm an idiot, Kasai thought.

"Master, please forgive my rashness. I'm not sure how to explain my actions. But it was something I had to do."

"Indulge me an attempt," Master Choejor said. He stroked his beard and mustache, which he was fond of doing.

"Master, there has been a voice with me since my first attempt ascending the pillars. I heard it again on the mountain. Maybe I've heard it for many years, but just not a clear. It says little but directs my thoughts and actions."

"Interesting. One would welcome such a helpful guide, yet you sound distraught."

"At first, I thought I was getting closer to understanding the Boundless. But now I am worried fell magic has befallen me. The voice guides me and shows me things I shouldn't know. That no one should know."

"Ah, perhaps you hear the Song of Aetenos."

"I thought that was only a myth. Something created to bolster the legend of the Great Monk."

"This does not surprise me," Master Choejor said. "Brother Kasai, you have always excelled in your studies of Aetenos, but a deeper belief in our patron seems to be missing. When you first arrived at Ordu, you could recite many of the stories before they were told to you."

"My father told me stories of Aetenos when I was very young before..." Kasai became silent.

"Before coming to the Monastery?"

"Yes, Master."

"Please, sit with me a moment."

Kasai sat down next to Master Choejor. They both looked to the majestic vista of the mountain range. The sky was clear and blue. Kasai wondered what had happened to the mist surrounding the pillars. Was it all just something he created in his head?

"There is great hesitancy in your actions. It was evident in the tournament bout against Brother Daku, and it is even more profound in acceptance of the xindu mysteries. Your overall spiritual progression is slow."

"I trust you and the other Masters, of course. I think I trust in the Boundless, though at times it seems very far from me."

"And what of Aetenos, my son? How does he fit into your understanding of all that is around you?"

"I'm not sure, Master. Things were much simpler when I was a little boy. The people of my small village followed his Light. He was our guide, and my father was a devoted follower. Everyone looked up to him. He was a hero.

But then, the dark things came. I was abandoned when I needed him most. How could that happen, Master? How could he allow so much misery to fall upon his faithful? Where was the hero when he was needed most?"

"Are you referring to Aetenos or your father, Brother Kasai?"

Kasai did not respond. He had often searched for answers to that question. The connection between Aetenos and his father always ended in the same way, a dead end.

It appeared Master Choejor had read his thoughts. "For each of us, the answer to such questions remain hidden until we are ready to accept the truth."

"But isn't Aetenos supposed to be the protector of his faithful?"

"Yes, of course. At times Aetenos himself is the divine hammer that smites the darkness. Other times he is the forge unto which his avatars are created. The souls of his Chosen become tempered through his trials. The process can be brutal. But eventually, the mettle in their hearts becomes unbreakable. They are his Ever Heroes."

Kasai thought about what Master Choejor said, then realized he was frowning. Kasai searched the expansive sky surrounding the snowcapped mountains for answers to unasked questions. He spotted a lone Crest Eagle climbing for warmer air drafts as it used its strength to gain altitude and then soared with outstretched wings atop the air streams. Its bright-orange feathers were golden in the yellow sunlight.

The eagle cried out as it snatched a smaller bird out of the sky. "The Crest Eagle is with us," Master Choejor said. "Perhaps the great bird is here now to help you along in your pensive journey?"

"Perhaps, Master."

"Brother Kasai, are you familiar with the legend of the Fire Serpent?"

"You speak of the great artifact, Ninziz-zida. I know that it is a three-section staff."

"Yes, that's right. But do you know of the unique characteristics of the weapon?"

"Some stories say Aetenos created Ninziz-zida during the Frost War against the devil, Sekka. But it was lost. Other stories tell how Aetenos gave Ninziz-zida to Gen Moll before he ascended to the Seven Heavens.

"I have read that the Fire Serpent is a bane against evil. It has traveled through the centuries wielded by heroes of old seeking to destroy the minions from the Deep Dark. Other texts say that Ninziz-zida is a damned thing with a mind of its own. It seeks to possess the soul of its wielder and make him or her its slave.

"You have studied the scrolls well," Master Choejor said. "And do you have thoughts of your own concerning the Fire Serpent? Would you welcome the opportunity to wield her in battle?"

"Me? Certainly not. I am not worthy of any weapon forged by Aetenos." Kasai was amused at the idea. "No, no, no. I am not a hero. Leave that weapon to the likes of Daku."

"You believe Brother Daku to be a more likely candidate for Ninziz-zida?"

"Well, he certainly has a great desire for battle and a healthy supply of fire xindu. Perhaps he could control the Fire Serpent and not become possessed by the staff."

"Interesting that you would say such a thing. There is no doubt the Fire Serpent commands respect. However, she seeks to belong to something greater than herself. She is incomplete without a greater power to wield her."

"The other Masters and I have noticed your proficiency in the use of the mundane sanjiegun, a weapon of similar size and design to the Fire Serpent. There has been a debate on introducing you to Ninziz-zida. The weapon chooses its own, mind you."

"I am unworthy, Master. Surely there is another more qualified." Kasai wasn't sure how or why this was being discussed. He was no champion to wield such a weapon, and he did not want to be one. Kasai was content to be a simple monk. He changed the subject. "You keep referring to Ninziz-zida as a 'she,' Master. Why?"

Master Choejor remained silent for a moment then spoke. "We shall talk more of this later. For now, you must remember, one must seek to be whole, not perfect. Now, news of your accomplishment will travel fast. Do not think these blind eyes were the only ones to see such foolishness. You had best prepare your answers for the questions to come." Master Choejor gave Kasai a tender smile.

"Thank you for your wise counsel, Master Choejor. I shall meditate on the mysteries of Aetenos and his relationship to us all. And prepare for a lot of unwanted attention." Kasai returned Master Choejor's smile and somehow knew the elderly monk felt it.

Kasai excused himself and walked away in silence. Yes, he recited the mantras of Aetenos with the rest of his Brothers, but he did not fully accept the message of hope they conveyed. How could he? While he was sequestered in the safety of Ordu, the nightmares of the real world preyed upon the weak.

Periodically, Traveling Monks returned to Ordu to discuss the events happening throughout the Three Kingdoms. The lands outside the monastery walls could be a cruel place.

"This is precisely why the message of Aetenos was so important. All things have their balance. We must act as the counterweight to the darker side of the human spirit. We must become the beacon of light which reveals the path of goodness within all of us," Master Kunchen had said.

Daku had a different philosophy. "The strong fist prevails over the tender heart." He only believed in the power of his own hands and not the ramblings of a crazed monk, long dead. Daku was always at odds with everyone.

Kasai wondered if he could make a difference in the real world. It all seemed so far away. He just wanted to belong somewhere, as he did in his small village. He wanted to have a home and be at peace. Life at Ordu was something he could believe in and protect. "This is where I belong. Ordu is my home now." Yet for all Ordu had to offer, Kasai still felt empty inside. Something was missing. He wished he had more faith, but sadly, it did not come to him as effortlessly as it did for the others. Master Choejor was right. He was incomplete.

There was fear in his heart that traveled with him like a second shadow. He feared being left behind and alone. He feared to fail those who counted on him to keep them safe, just like his father had done. No, he would not be the one who ran from danger. He would not follow in his father's footsteps. He would be different. He vowed then to protect those he loved. That would be his truth.

10

SEKKA

Sekka was the epitome of beauty and seduction in her human form. Tall, curvaceous, and slender she radiated a glamour that stirred desire in all who beheld her. She had been known to stir many a man to do impossibly wicked things. The female slaves she devoured could not help but be drawn to her womanhood before they met their fates. She was the dark side of desire. She was strength. She was chaos.

The witches and warlocks in her coven were drawn to her power. They craved even a morsel of the magic she possessed. Those lucky enough to win her favor would experience a touch of deep magic normally reserved for those born of devilish blood. It would destroy them over time, but they willingly accepted the gift. Anything for more power, even if it was fleeting.

Sekka was something far different in her abyssal form. A monstrous nightmare to behold, she had a body that was dense and formidable. Coarse, white fur blanketed her back in thick clumps. Four curling horns framed her head, and a crown of bones embedded with onyx stones at its base hovered above her head as smoky sigils of power rose through its center. Four hooked teeth jutted from her full mouth, which gnashed together in delight when she tore the souls from her human slaves.

She squatted at the center of an inverted cone-shaped pit. The walls of the hole were slick with ice. Human soul-slaves below frantically attempted to scurry over one another like rats fleeing a flooded hollow. Winds howling across the Wastelands of Thresh added to the sweet melody of their suffering.

Ending in great talons, her avian legs could grasp five grown men at once and rip them to shreds. Even lowered on her legs as she was, she towered ten feet above the pit's floor. The steaming blood and innards of the dead covered her chest and stomach like a thick apron of red and brown sludge.

Her black-within-black eyes scanned the delicious banquet before her. A hundred human slaves desperately climbed the slick sides of the outwardly sloping pit, tearing savagely at one another. The slaves pulled back the heads of their fellows by yanking handfuls of hair, eyeballs were gouged out, and necks throttled mercilessly. They climbed higher and higher, using each other to build a ladder to freedom.

This was how she played with her toys. Escape the pit and live, that was the game. Slaves already on the slippery floor dashed about like mice. They battled each other to gain purchase on the highest rung of the human ladder. None cared that the cost of their freedom was the souls of their brethren.

The longer the game played out, the more soul-slaves would be devoured, causing the height of the human ladders to decrease so that reaching the top became an impossible task. When the slaves realized their route of escape was gone, the ladders would break apart and those who could still move, would scurry like mice seeking another way to freedom, but there was none. It was then that they looked up at her, wide-eyed with absolute terror and remorse. She savored those moments the most.

Sekka spun on her haunches and spotted her next victim, a slave who had the misfortune of being pushed too close to her grasp. Plucking him off the ground, she gazed deeply into his eyes as a lover would before a kiss. The slave screamed in terror when she raised him over her head. Opening her mouth, she lowered him in to the waist. She held his horror-stricken gaze as her tongue coiled around his midsection, drawing him in deeper. Warm blood sprayed across her face when her teeth chomped down on another tasty treat.

Sekka caught the telltale scent of another blizzard sweeping down from the crater peak of the sleeping volcano that had given birth to the ice realm of Gathos. The Dead Giant, as it was named, remained dormant. She swallowed the last bits of the slave, before licking the blood from her mouth. It was a good day on Gathos.

A quick jerk pulled Sekka's mind to a prison within a black, silver sphere. And then she felt another, more urgent this time with command. "Finally," she exulted. "Maugris, you, wonderful fool!" A smile widened across her face as her conscious mind was dragged to the Mortal Realm.

If Maugris was strong enough, he would pull the corporeal aspect of her being through the Amaranthine Barrier as well. But if she was wrong about Maugris, or her intended path through the Barrier, she would suffer the pain of a thousand deaths.

Sekka's astral eyes adjusted to the atmosphere of the black, silver sphere. She recognized the residual energy left by the use of dark magic. The sticky mist clung to the surface of the spherical chamber like rogue strands of spider silk adrift in the wind. She could almost taste the suffering lingering in the metaphysical air.

Sekka felt the weight of heavy stone surrounding the chamber. She assumed the space had been delved deep within the roots of a mountain. It was a perfect prison with no visible entrances or doorways and one last precaution against *She* that was to be summoned. Maugris was clever.

In truth, she was powerless to make the journey on her own. The Immortal Mother's blasted Amaranthine Barrier now prevented any unauthorized crossings between realms. She supposed she was as much to blame for the Barrier as any ambitious devil who stole souls from the Mortal Realm.

The Immortal Mother had placed strict rules on the worlds she created. The Great Balance must remain constant amongst the different realms. That was the first and most revered law. Sekka's last invasion to the Mortal Realm had tipped the scales and disrupted that precious balance enough to call the angels to war. If they had just stayed put in their clouds, she would have been victorious. But things did not always go as planned.

Upon the smooth inner surface of the chamber's dark metal were laid thousands of intricate runes, each one representing another binding layer of to keep her captive. Interlaced with those symbols were other wards against infernal attack. Pure silver chains crisscrossed the center and wove together to form the strands of a shimmering web.

The links of the chains contained similar runes to those inscribed on the surface walls. As the strands of silver came together towards the center of the sphere, they formed a three-dimensional outline of a multi-pointed star. A perfect trap to collect an Arch Devil from the Abyss.

Twenty-five warlocks, clad in heavy robes hovered in the open space surrounding her summoned spirit. Their placement corresponded to the open areas of the three-dimensional star. Their breath clouded in the frigid air as they chanted ancient words. The sounds twisted and coiled like snakes from their mouths.

A bound slaves shimmered into reality in front of each warlock. The captives trembled uncontrollably from fear and the shock of the cold. The warlocks took black-bladed daggers from their sleeves and, as one, plunged them deep into the abdomens of the slaves. Blood sprayed against the silver chains. The excess dripped to the bottom of the chamber.

The moans of the dying echoed off the black-silver walls. *Pain was such a lovely bonding component*, thought Sekka. It was a nice touch to welcome her return to the Mortal Realm.

Maugris hovered at the top of the chamber as his shifty eyes scanned the placement of his warlocks and accepted everything was in order. She ignored the insult of a mere mortal having control over her for any amount of time. She assured herself it was only temporary, a minor discomfort.

Maugris' breath frosted the air before his face as the words of the final spell spilled from his mouth. Sekka focused her wicked mind on the transference from one plane of existence to another. She absorbed every syllable and gesture as Maugris' cast the binding spell. She searched for where his spell craft faltered, for she had no doubt she would unravel the spell at a later time. The magic of mortals was thin.

Sekka's essence shifted towards him.

Maugris wore heavy robes, lined with dense fur to protect him from the sub-zero temperature of the chamber. Dark-maroon and bright-orange sigils of protection radiated from his robes. The symbols revolved in a slow circle around him. Eventually, each one fluttered out of sight when its protective enchantment was secured. *How quaint*, Sekka thought.

A blood-ruby pendant hung at Maugris' neck, pulsing like a heart as it joined with the magic flowing through the chamber. He had prepared well for this confrontation, yet she still scoffed at his trinkets and false confidence.

Sekka searched for the mental flame of the sorcerer. It was like finding a mote of sawdust in the sand. *Mortals were such insignificant beings outside of the energy of their souls*, she thought with contempt. She poured her consciousness into the endeavor. There! She found him. She squirmed in glee. He was nothing compared to her.

Sekka plunged herself into Maugris like the sharp barb of a scorpion. Her preternatural awareness flooded into his thoughts. She felt his entire being gasp at her arrival.

This was his first test. Sekka would use the surprise of her overwhelming presence to gain control over him. The wards around him flared brighter. She snuffed the lesser ones out without much of a thought. Maugris staggered. She must be careful. If he lost control, the spell would unravel before it took hold. If he were unable to bring her corporeal form into the Mortal Realm, then her scheme would be delayed. She couldn't start over. She needed more souls now!

She knew Maugris had never confronted such raw power as hers. What mortal had? He fought against her will like a desperate man caught in a riptide. The more he struggled, the more she dragged him out to sea. The two engaged in a precarious tug-of-war. If she pulled too hard, she would break him, and the connection would be lost. If she gave in too readily to the summons, she would have a difficult time breaking the spell later. Time worked against her as Zizphander approached her now defenseless Gathos.

She felt Maugris' strength decline. The final summoning spell had siphoned away too much of his magical strength. He had underestimated the resources needed to control one of her might.

If Maugris proved to be too weak to enable her to crossover, then it would end badly for him. The Amaranthine Barrier would devour him along with the dark magic he used to conduct the spell. She thought of Aetenos wasting away in her dungeon. *How had he been granted access to the Abyss when all others of his kind were denied?* The riddle still plagued her.

Sekka eased off the drowning assault and withdrew direct contact with his essence. Instead, she flowed through his mind like a cerebral fog. She caressed his memories and absorbed his desires. She sucked at his mortal coil and gently probed him for weaknesses. She showed him visions of ultimate power. He could be a god. Just surrender.

His foolish pride refused her. Rather than succumb to her will, he would end his own life. Sekka watched in frustration as Maugris' body shriveled beneath his heavy robes. He was too weak.

He had lost control of the dark magic, and now it was feasting on him. His eyes grew wide and wild. He was desperate for more energy, and the connection faltered. He called to the other warlocks in the room for support.

"Lend me your strength! I am losing her!" he yelled.

Sekka saw no help forthcoming. Interesting. She would use this information against him in the future if there were a future for the failing mage.

Somehow, Maugris regained enough of his composure to tap the blood-ruby pendant on his chest. His eyes sought the nearest warlock hovering beneath him. The pendant flared bright red as its vampiric magic drank the life force of the unsuspecting warlock.

The wrinkles smoothed on Maugris' skin. His face became full once more. The empty husk of the dead warlock dropped out of sight. It landed with a thud and light splash in the bowels of the chamber.

Maugris sent the pendant's magic to the next warlock, and then the next. The warlocks were consumed in rapid succession. Good, thought Sekka, very good. Her smile broadened as she watched each warlock disappear. He was back in control of the dark magic, and he enforced his will upon the spell of binding.

"Sekka! Arch Devil of Gathos and Queen of the Frost Plane, I, Maugris the Infinite, bind you to me. Do my bidding, and ten thousand and one soul-slaves shall be yours to devour. I make this pact with you. Come Sekka! Come to your new master!" Maugris cried out in a voice magnified by the stolen energy he had consumed.

A horrific wail flooded into the chamber, causing blood to erupt from Maugris' ears. Streams of red flowed freely out of his nostrils. The chamber shuddered. Then the chains vibrated as if shaken in the hands of giants. A pinprick of light appeared in the center of the star prison. It grew in size and shape. First as a globe and then as something with the distinct form of a massive horror.

The preternatural wail grew louder in the chamber. The sweat covering Maugris' body turned to frost. He churned out heavy white breaths into the stale air.

Sekka's abyssal form joined with her consciousness and materialized at the center of the star prison. Her raptor talons flashed out to tear and rend. Her chest heaved, and her breasts swelled as she became entangled in the silver chains.

Hard muscles rippled against the magical bonds surrounding her. She could hear the sizzle of her flesh as the touch of the wards burned into her skin. Sekka shrieked in pain.

The soul-slave she brought forth from her orgy on Gathos dissolved in her clawed hand. She maliciously glared at Maugris for depriving her of such a savory meal. She played the part of the bound slave perfectly.

The silver chains were pulled tight like a fisherman's net, and wrapped around her writhing body, locking her in place. Sapphire-blue runes shimmered off the chains then vanished into the air. She howled in rage. The spell of binding was complete. It held her in its magical grip. But the battle was far from over.

Sekka's onyx eyes smiled at him with an otherworldly intelligence. She marveled at her cleverness. She had succeeded in passing through the Amaranthine Barrier. Now she could exert more power. She reapplied pressure on Maugris' mind and squeezed his thoughts together into mush. He buckled but did not break.

She tested his resolve with pleasures rather than pain. "Lower your guard, mortal. I shall make you king of all you see. Release me, and I shall grant your every last desire. Yours shall be the seed that sires' legions made for conquest."

"I saw you … in a vision. Now you are…here before me. You are…mine…to command," Maugris stuttered. His words came slowly, but they gave him confidence. "Enough with your torments."

Sekka howled. She could not harm Maugris. Not yet. The magic placed upon the chains was too deep. Pacts had to be honored. She must do as he bid.

+**What is it you wish of me, mortal?**+ Sekka spoke directly into Maugris' mind. He shuddered.

"You shall be my instrument of despair upon the Lands of Hanna," Maugris said aloud. "The bindings placed upon you shall force you to obey my commands."

+**Failure to provide the soul-slaves promised to bind me will be your undoing, little mage.**+

Sekka fought once more against the invisible chains that bound her. While her body convulsed in pain from the binding, she continued to probe his mind. She sought areas of weakness she might exploit in the future.

"A vision, you say?" Sekka purred in a sensual voice as her bestial form changed into the more subtle curves of a human woman. "Tell me more."

. . .

Sekka lounged across her divan like a feline leisurely basking in the warmth of the sun. Ironically, her chamber was cold and dark. Precious items from the Three Kingdoms filled the room. Maugris' minions had brought her thick bear fur, skinned from the northern grizzlies of Trosk. There were exquisite, wooded chairs hewed from a single block of Baroqia's mighty redwood trees in the corner. Hanging on the walls were rare silk tapestries of vibrant color and detail. Sekka suspected they were stolen from the jungle tribes of Sunne. It all bored her.

She decided to redecorate her room with the mutilated bodies of the playthings Maugris had gifted her. "These witches and warlocks shall serve as you cabal," he had said. Their skill and ability were laughable. Most she took as sex slaves, but their uses were limited. She draped their skins over the priceless chairs from Baroqia. Their blood cast a rosy reflection throughout the room.

Her thoughts lurched to the image of Maugris. He had *summoned* her. The compulsion placed upon her still held, but barely. Soon, she would have it unraveled, and his trivial magic would no longer have sway over her.

A fresh batch of apprentices had arrived. Sekka studied them through black-on-black eyes. They observed the flayed skins of their predecessors, and an uneasiness passed through the group. Their breath frosted the air as they patiently waited for her to command them. The men and women before her were frail; weak magicians at best, but such were the shortcomings of all mortals.

They dressed in the garb of witches and warlocks. Sekka saw them only as costumed children playing with silly wands and staffs. They were mere sycophants who posed at being bold wielders of magic yet, knew nothing of the dark arts. All sought her favor for a chance to drink from the fountain of deep magic that flowed through her. They would get nothing from her.

She smiled pleasantly at them. She would let Lord Oziax play with them for a day, once he arrived. Then they would understand power. But, for now, they were distractions to alleviate her boredom. She was sure she could find a use for them eventually.

She rose like a serpent from her repose, causing her sheer robe to flow down over her shapely legs like a slow waterfall. Seduction radiated from her as she approached the first apprentice. He trembled in anticipation. Did he fear her or desire her? It mattered not. Both were acceptable forms of supplication to the Arch Devil.

As much as she relished the physical strength of her abyssal body, she did savor the subtlety of her human form. Her senses appreciated things differently. Perhaps it was due to the frailty of this body? Humans cherished life more since it could be ripped away at a moment's notice. That was why the human soul was such valuable currency in both the Abyss and the Seven Heavens.

It was the soul where the real power of mortals existed, and sadly for them, they wouldn't realize it until after their death. Such was the great paradox of all things set forth by the Immortal Mother.

Her flock of neophytes fluttered around her like black butterflies. They followed in her wake as she left her grisly chamber. Sekka casually led them down a long flight of stairs en route to the central keep. She occasionally stopped to lay her hands on the sigils of warding and binding that were carved into the stone. It was an irrelevant precaution Maugris had added to his fortress.

The sigils held no sway over her, not anymore. She snuffed each one out as she meandered through Rachlach Fortress. She knew the sigils would be back in place when she returned down the same corridor. It was just something to pass the time. Once she had broken the foundation spell, all secondary and tertiary spells would fail as well.

Sekka eventually came to another room filled with stacked books and unrolled scrolls. Maugris was there grumbling to himself. He paced before twelve bound slaves lined against a wall. Sekka assumed they were borderland peasants. Villagers who chose a piss-poor existence along the fringes of Baroqia.

Maugris' hands were clasped behind his bent back as he walked. He mumbled gibberish to himself between swift intakes of breath. He turned towards the slaves.

"Be honored, for you have been chosen. Your souls will fuel the otherworldly gifts provided by my concubine and slave. A higher purpose awaits you."

He turned away as if distracted by another conversation before he returned to mumbling in broken sentences. Then he raised his hands in a proclamation. "By my will shall a new age be delivered to the Three Kingdoms! And vengeance shall know my name!"

The twelve slaves were on their knees. Tight, razor-sharp chords crisscrossed their bodies. Each breath saw the chords dig deeper into their flesh. Purple elixirs were force-fed to the slaves by small gnome-like creatures. It was a special brew Sekka had taught to Maugris that kept the slaves alive.

Sekka remained at the entrance, unimpressed.

Maugris saw her and turned away, irritated by her lack of urgency to his summons. "You are *finally* here. It is time. I must have the Frost Legions of Gathos. I command you to open a portal." He refused to look at her.

He wore layers of furs to fend off the cold that seeped through the stones of his tower. He moved to a desk cluttered with bound scrolls. He hunched over a massive book opened at a marked spot. He carefully scanned the brittle pages of the ancient tome.

Maugris pointed over his shoulder at the twelve slaves bound against the far wall. "Those there, use them as you must to open the portal."

Sekka shook her head, no. It was the same demand he had made countless times.

"You would bring forth a legion of demons with no commander to lead them? Are you mad? Lord Oziax must come first."

"I will lead them," Maugris said with confidence. "I do not trust you, or your white-maned demon."

"Lord Oziax has been the General of my Frost Legion for millennia. Only by his presence and force of will can the armies of Gathos be controlled. Without him, the greater demons and fiends would revert to their vicious and chaotic nature. The weaker spawn would be butchered without a second thought. Might I remind you of the hatred and rivalry all demonkind have for one another?"

"I am aware of the feuds of demons and devils alike. All those mad creatures, eternally scurrying up the layers of ascendency until they are brought low by overwhelming power."

"Quite so," she said.

He looked straight into her black-on-black eyes. "It seems Zizphander has been busy during your absence. The Red Devil moves through the Abyss uncontested. He leaves the realms of his rivals covered in molten slag. Now there is an Arch Devil worthy of the title. Perhaps he intends to finish what was once started so long ago. What would happen, I wonder if he rekindled the fires of the Dead Giant?"

"You dare!"

"There are many in the Abyss who gladly divulge information for the proper payment. I have watched your struggle against the Red Devil for quite some time."

Sekka kept a calm expression, though she internally seethed with fury. She knew he was testing her to see if what he said was true. She would give him no such satisfaction, nor would she reveal her predicament in the Lower Planes. She would have her day with him. This fool Maugris knew nothing of the depths of deception and pain a true Arch Devil could conceive.

Maugris strode from behind the table. "No, your pet Oziax shall not have sole reign over the demonic army you will provide me. You are a cunning devil, but that was never part of my plan. I will turn my attention to other lands when the Three Kingdoms of Hanna are mine. Perhaps I shall also rule the wastelands you call home.

"And when that time comes, I will need a queen to rule at my side. If you are worthy, I may grant you such favor."

The cold sparkle in her black eyes betrayed knowledge of a different outcome. She decided then that merely ripping his soul from his body and dining on his tender memories would not be enough punishment for his insolence. She would reserve a special place for him in the coldest pit of Gathos. Maugris would suffer for ages uncounted. But for now, she would wait. He still had a role to play.

"Maugris, why must you tease me such? You know I am already your captive. Your will is my command. But you would be wise to heed my advice. Lord Oziax shall obey you, as I must."

"Do not press your agenda, devil. I demand you open me a portal. Bring forth the means to destroy my enemies. I grow tired of your excuses and delays!"

"With what raw material? Do you think the soul energy of a few slaves to be enough to bridge the gap between realms? But no matter, the Amaranthine Barrier prevents such a portal from opening for any length of time."

"Do not mock my intelligence. Use your infernal magic to compensate."

"Certain divine rules must be obeyed, even for one as mighty as me. However, there is another way. Bring me the Ever Hero of this age. Then you will know the power of the Abyss."

Maugris brought his hand up to massage his forehead. His eyes squinted closed. "The Ever Heroes of Aetenos are a myth. They are little stories created over the centuries by weak-minded commoners and the monks who control them.

"Even if the Ever Hero were real, he would be a pale comparison to the demigod himself. What use could a fragment of the divine possibly be to help you breach the Barrier?" Maugris looked hard into her eyes. His eyes shifted back and forth as if the solution to a complex equation was within his grasp. "Unless…"

He shook his head, dismissing the idea. "Bah, it matters not. Aetenos has not walked these lands in many, many years. He has forsaken this realm. His religion is dead. His faithful are scattered and lost."

Maugris smiled as if he had won a significant victory. He staggered to a large map hanging on the wall. He tried to hide his discomfort. Her relentless mind-probing left him weary and weak.

He traced his fingers over the Sarribe Mountain range in the Southern Province of Baroqia. "Everything is happening according to my will. By now, that vainglorious Duke Shiverrig has discovered the locations of the monasteries. There will be no one to stop me once those troublesome monks of the Four Orders have been eradicated."

"No! You must not harm the monks!" Sekka demanded. "They are part of unwinding the riddle of the Ever Hero. The Masters may perish, but the younger acolytes must survive. They are needed."

Maugris turned back to Sekka. His eyes flared like that of a starved animal protecting a morsel of food. "Enough! I do not wish to hear any more nonsense of Ever Heroes. The monks will die." His eyes grew dark. "You are mine to control. Now open the portal."

"Yes, I am bound by you, yet you can only receive a fraction of my power. Now, if a Chaos Gate were to be opened…"

"Do you take me for a fool? A living Chaos Gate would mean the end of this realm."

"Obviously, you misunderstand the intricacies of a Chaos Gate and the rules of deep magic."

"Enlighten me," Maugris said.

"A Chaos Gate only allows passage to those deemed worthy by its creator. Yes, others may pass, but the cost is significant. But more importantly, those who pass through would be leashed to the will of the creator of the Gate." Sekka doubted if that were true. But never ruin a good story with the truth.

"Yes, and?"

Sekka wondered how one of such dull intellect possessed the magical strength to have summoned her from Gathos. "My dear Maugris, if the forger of the portal happened to be under the control of a powerful sorcerer, well, then who would control the horde?" She gave a mental tug at the strings of his desire for conquest.

"A Chaos Gate would allow for the entirety of the Frost Legion to bypass the Amaranthine Barrier."

She had him.

He shook his finger at Sekka as if he was the brunt of a playful joke. "You have your worth, devil. A simple portal will not do when a Chaos Gate provides all I need."

Sekka crossed her arms over her chest. "If there is no Ever Hero, then there is no Chaos Gate. As I have said, I must have the raw material to create the bridge. Only the soul of one fused with the essence of the divine can provide the required building blocks." She spoke to him as if he were a petulant child. "And unless you are hiding Aetenos somewhere in your dreary fortress, I will need the next best thing."

Maugris' demeanor shifted again. "How can one such as you be so blind? The Ever Hero is a myth. I was a Chosen of Aetenos at one time. I had power. Real power. Then the demigod betrayed me. If there were to be an Ever Hero of this time, it would have been me!

"When the Time of Fire and Famine came to Baroqia, the crown looked to me to quell land's fury with my art. I crafted a spell to tame the wild Elemenati magic infecting the land. It was a brilliant work of creative genius. My spell would save the realm and ensure my legacy as the greatest mage in the history of Baroqia. But something went wrong.

"I had made sure every nuance was accounted for and in place." Maugris looked past Sekka as if remembering the horrible event. His words came in a whisper. "It was Aetenos. He was jealous of my great accomplishment. When I called for His Light to add a spark of the divine to my spell, he went silent. I was left with insufficient power to complete the spell. It failed.

"Banishment, they said. Banish the Mad One to the North! But I shall have my revenge. The monks of Aetenos die first. Then those fool nobles in the City of Spires."

Sekka smirked at Maugris' tale. If the man only knew the truth of the matter. "It is a touching tale. Nonetheless, the pace in which you exact your revenge is in your own hands."

"Enough with your stubborn behavior, Hell-born. There is no Ever Hero. If you cannot provide me with what I desire, I will replace you with another who can."

Maugris moved back to a long table piled with ancient parchments. He leaned on its edge for support. He rubbed his chin with his hand. "If I was strong enough to summon you, then there are others whom I could call."

A devious smile creased his weathered face. "I wonder how eager Zizphander would be to carry out my wishes if I offered him his arch-nemesis bound and gagged on a silver platter? Are you prepared to watch the flames of the Red Devil consume your precious Gathos?"

Sekka grew bored with the debate, "Do what you must, or you can. Zizphander would need the same means of establishing a portal great enough for what you ask."

Her devilish desire was to rip him to shreds, but she was still bound. Time, she needed just a bit more time. She approached Maugris delicately. She brushed up against his body with slow and sensual movements.

"Let us not fight. You are mighty, Maugris, and your will shall be done. I can tell you are fatigued. Let me soothe your weary head."

She turned his head to her breasts. His body followed. She held him as a mother would a child. Maugris resisted her embrace at first but finally succumbed to the coolness of her body. The softness of her flesh was too much to endure in his weakened state.

"That's it. Just rest."

Maugris' defenses dropped for a moment. It was just enough of an opening for Sekka to purr an inconspicuous spell of suggestion into his ear.

"I shall open a small portal and bring forth Lord Oziax to lead your armies; however, remember the Ever Hero is the key to your ultimate vengeance. Find him, and you shall rule whatever realm you wish." She then lifted his head and gently kissed his lips. "Perhaps you would like to start with the one before you?"

Her sheer gown fell to her ankles. Her naked body was a masterpiece of desire. The torchlight caressed her muscular form and lush curves. She stepped out of the pile of rumpled fabric, and slowly pirouetted before the Sorcerer. "Do you like what you see?"

She deftly removed his robes. Maugris mumbled some agreeable words about Lord Oziax. He would put men to the task of finding the one she desired. Her tongue was a shock of ice over his body. The stiffness of his member was a testament that he burned for more. As she had expected, her devious charms would be the first of her powers to break through the shackles of Maugris' binding. Humans were so easy to manipulate.

Their coupling was filled with moans of delight from Maugris. She beckoned her forgotten flock of magicians closer. Their eyes were filled with lust. Craving hands reached out to touch her. She smiled with wicked joy.

Her provocative human form altered its shape. Horns, talons, and teeth grew from her body. Her magicians screamed in horror, but they could not turn away. She compelled them forward and feasted on their flesh. Maugris writhed in ecstasy beneath her terrible form. Soon he was coated in blood.

Sekka mentally whispered the words of a summoning spell into Maugris' mind. He repeated the words aloud, lost as he was in the bliss of her attention. The tear in the Amaranthine Barrier caused by Aetenos' arrival on Gathos had grown wider when she was summoned to the Mortal Realm. Now the path was easy to follow if one knew the way.

A flash of light brightened the chamber, followed by a thunderous boom. The walls shook, and stacks of books tumbled to the floor. The temperature dropped, and frost covered everything in the room. The slaves lined against the far wall shivered in pain as the chords dug deeper into their flesh.

Lord Oziax leaped into the Mortal Realm.

He was a huge demon standing on two muscular legs. One arm ended in five long tentacles cascading from where his elbow would be. Hundreds of small sucking mouths with sharp teeth lined the surface of each tentacle. His broad back was covered in coarse, alabaster hair. His nostrils flared in anticipation of violence.

Lord Oziax had the head of an artic lion. A full mane of thick fur framed his face. Two long canine teeth jutted from his jaws. His skin was the color of bleached bone. He stepped through the broken and mauled bodies as the juice of the dying magicians spread across the floor to Sekka's side and bowed deeply before her.

"What is it you wish of me, my Mistress?"

Sekka was covered in gore. She swiveled her hulking form to face him. "Look at the banquet our little mage has set for us, Lord Oziax." Her wicked grin drooled long strands of swaying bile. Her flesh changed back to her exposed human body. Broad swaths of blood smeared down her neck and covered her breasts and legs.

Lord Oziax's eyes landed on Maugris. "Let me devour the mortal flea at your loins." A purple tongue lolled out of his mouth and curled around his enormous incisors.

Maugris came to his senses. He squirmed out from under Sekka, parting the pool of blood in a long smear. He grabbed his robe and stood indignant before Lord Oziax. Maugris surveyed his study, confused as to what had taken place. He assumed a regal stance.

"Bow down before me, creature. I am your master now."

A deep baritone chuckle resonated from Lord Oziax's throat. He ignored Maugris. "What are your orders, my Queen?"

"Now," Maugris said. He raised his hand to strike Lord Oziax.

Oziax's eyes flashed with anger. "Who is this human worm that stands before Mighty Oziax? I shall peel the skin from your pitiful body for your lack of reverence."

Lord Oziax's body swelled and bristled. He shook where he stood but could do no more. The magic that held Sekka also bound the great demon lord.

"I command you now, Lord Oziax, Demon Warlord of the Frost Legions." Maugris walked closer to Oziax. His confidence grew with each step. "Colorful monikers, but I am unimpressed. A more capable demon lord would have put an end to Zizphander when he was an irrelevant lesser devil. But now, the Red Devil has grown in power, and Oziax has lost his opportunity." Maugris then turned to Sekka. "Perhaps, next time, do not leave a demon to do a devil's work, eh?"

Oziax bellowed out in rage. Black sigils flared to life above his head. The stench of dark magic mixed with the odor of drying blood and entrails. He lunged at Maugris but was held fast by the power of the binding spell. Nonetheless, Maugris took a few steps backward. A nervous expression filled his face.

Sekka draped her arms around Oziax's neck. She whispered in his ear. "Calm yourself, my beautiful beast. Remember why we are here."

She then spoke in a louder voice for Maugris to hear. "Apologize to Maugris and assume a more suitable appearance for your new master."

Lord Oziax followed Sekka's lead. He morphed into his human form. A tall, muscular man with long, straight hair appeared where the demon once stood.

"There, that's better. Now come, Lord Oziax. There is much to prepare," Sekka said. She walked from the room.

Lord Oziax brushed passed Maugris. "Careful with your words mortal. The Fates are fickle. The path they set is never clear. Your feet may not always tread on such a fortunate ground."

11

KASAI

G iant, finger-shaped spires of granite towered amongst the mountain peaks of the Sarribe Range. Nestled among the natural rock formations was the Monastery of Ordu. It was built to blend with the enduring presence of the mountain without creating distracting blemishes to its rocky surface. Valley forests of pine and oak stubbornly stretched their reach up the sides of the high spires to include the monastery in their wooden embrace. Crest eagles and spire vultures hung lazily in the air on warm thermals that rose from the lower lands.

The monks of Ordu traversed the spire-shaped peaks via a maze of hanging rope bridges. Small bells and colorful ribbons were woven into the hemp strands of the ropes and the acoustics of the mountain range would carry the sounds of the bells for miles, adding a layer of mystery and misdirection, which confused those seeking to infiltrate the ancient haven.

The bells also served a different function. A person unaccustomed to walking the swaying bridges would leave an awkward sound pattern. The sentries could discern who approached based on the melodies of the bridges. Those were precautions from a different time when the monks were hunted and prosecuted by tyrannical kings and bloodthirsty warlords.

The Four Orders of Aetenos were meant to unify all people together under the Laws of Heaven. Unfortunately, this ideal often created a conflicting agenda with less-than-scrupulous rulers outside the religious orders. Spies were sent to infiltrate the sanctuaries of Ordu, Symmetu, Harmonu, and Metho, in order to discover the secrets of the strange monks. In time, assassins were contracted to remove influential members of each Order.

The mountain passes were blocked, and well-known bridges destroyed. Over the years, the locations of the monasteries themselves were lost. Maps were purposely removed from all government archives and only the memories of the highest officials at the High Temple of Illumination and the Master Monks of each Order were entrusted with such valuable information.

The monastery locations were passed from one generation to the next verbally; formal maps were forbidden. The monks took great precaution to thwart unwanted guests from finding their homes. Unfortunately, no fortress could remain hidden forever, nor was it impregnable.

Kasai pulled his outer robe a little closer. Today was blustery day, a cold portent of the winter to come. Brightly colored leaves fell from the trees and swirled like dust devils on the ground. The smell of early winter was in the air. A loose truce had formed between Kasai and Daku during the weeks since the ordeal on the mountain. Thankfully, Daku's anger had lessened with time, as it usually did.

Brothers Jorraih and Morad accompanied them as they walked along a smooth stone path. The two younger acolytes followed a few steps behind. The Brothers collected deadwood for the Monastery fires.

"The Masters are unfair to me, especially Choejor. I am constantly rebuked when the opportunity for advancement is clear. What's worse, I am punished for excelling," Daku said. He kicked a dead branch off the path instead of picking it up. "I have mastered all of the striking positions of the Twenty-One Fire Columns. I am the only one who fully understands the Windu'uni Disciplines. My fire xindu is the most powerful of all the Brothers. It probably rivals the level of the Masters by now."

"I understand Windu'uni," Kasai said.

"Sure you do, Kasai," Daku scoffed.

"You're the one holding on to every slight as if it were your last breath. Let it go. The Masters teach us what we need to learn. Perhaps ask yourself why they treat you as you say. Seek the answer from within," Kasai suggested.

"I already know the answer. They are worried that one day, perhaps soon, I will be their equal. They fear me. They fear the change my fighting methods will bring to the Order. Aetenos left the High Temple of Illumination for the same reasons. That is why they keep me from the more powerful mysteries," Daku snapped back.

"That's not why Aetenos formed the Four Orders," Kasai said.

Daku was churning through more than just that one event in his head. It was his way. He liked to dig up nightmares from the past and make them into present battles.

Jorraih called out, "Hey, are you two going to do some work or just chirp all morning like little birds?" He was small and of similar build to Kasai, with a broad smile and contagious laugh. "Morad and I have already filled up our sacks."

"See Kasai, more taunts. Now it's coming from those of lesser rank as well. I should teach him the meaning of respect."

"Jorraih means nothing by it. He's just trying to fit in," Kasai said.

The four monks strolled down the winding path until they came across the broken nest of a scarlet swallow. The nest had been blown from its perch and smashed into the dirt. Scattered about the ruined nest were three dead chicks. A fourth had somehow managed to survive the fall. It chirped fearfully for its mother on the unfamiliar ground, while the mother swallow helplessly squawked from a higher branch in the tree.

Morad did his best to repair the nest and then, with careful hands, placed it back into the tree. Jorraih had taken up the helpless chick and gently laid it in the nest.

"There you go, little one," Jorraih said.

"What do you think you two are doing?" Daku said. He snatched the nest and the chick from the safety of the branch.

"What does it look like we are doing? We are going to save the chick. See, the mother is right over there. Now put the nest back in the tree or give it to me," Jorraih said.

Daku hid the nest behind his back. "The mother should not have chosen such a poor spot to build its nest. As Master Choejor says, 'It is the natural way of things.' This chick will die with its siblings."

Kasai realized Daku still felt the pain of humiliation by Master Choejor in the sparring circle. If Daku had to bear the brunt of the Master's example, then all the Brotherhood would feel his pain as well. Daku would not allow himself to become a parody of weakness.

"That's hardly what Master Choejor means. Just give the bird back," Morad said.

"The mother bird needs to learn a lesson. Next time she will take more care when choosing a nesting site," Daku said.

The eyes of the younger monks became anxious. Kasai understood how they felt. Daku was in a raw mood. Kasai saw the telltale spark in Daku's, he wanted a fight, and the slightest provocation would set him off.

"Leave the chick alone. It is not your place to play judge and executioner," Jorraih said. He reached out to try and snatch the nest away from Daku.

Daku was quicker. "Is it not? And who are you to stop me? Come on. I'll let you have the first two strikes without retaliating."

"Daku, just give the bird back to Jorraih. We still have to finish our chores," Kasai said.

"Just listen to Kasai. Besides, you can't hope to best the three of us at once," Morad said.

Daku's face softened as if he had finally come to his senses. Kasai saw through it, though. Daku's expression was always calm before he attacked. Kasai would need to act fast if he was to save Morad from a painful lesson.

Daku snapped the neck of the chick and dropped it back in the nest. "Here."

Morad took the nest. His mouth was wide open.

"No!" Kasai was shocked. "Why?"

"I told you, Kasai, the outside world is cruel. It is the natural way of things." Daku pushed passed them. He continued walking alone on the path, humming a peaceful tune.

The night was calm. A fragrant, sugary aroma drafted up from the turning leaves of the Katsura trees growing in the valley below. The air swept through cracked windows and into the sparse sleeping quarters of the monks. The full moon was bright and bathed the room in soft blue light. Forty-four monks slept on plain cots, all but one rested peacefully. Kasai tossed and turned in a half-sleep. Sweat beaded on his forehead, and the wool blanket tangled around his legs in a knot.

Creatures of fell magic chased him in the dark. He wanted to run, but his legs moved as if they were being sucked into a thick mire. He heard the gnashing teeth of the creatures behind him. They were gaining ground.

The nightmare changed. Kasai watched his mother die by the hands of a foul, eyeless ghoul. Meanwhile, his father ran into the embrace of a fiendish woman draped in a regal, ice-blue gown. She wore a high headdress made of animal horns and human bones. The woman had stark-white hair, white skin, onyx eyes, and indigo lips. She eyed Kasai as she held his father in a lover's embrace. The woman spoke the same word to him every night. "Mine."

Kasai woke with a shiver, and his skin felt clammy. The nightmare appeared more frequently, each iteration revealing more of the story. He looked around the dormitory to see everyone still asleep. Kasai sighed. "Lucky."

Kasai told no one about his dreams; today was no different. He was thankful for his daily routine. It made it easier for him to believe that the unsettling nightmares were nonsense. He reasoned with himself during dawn chores that there was nothing wrong with him. He was calm again by the end of morning meditation. By the end of the day, he had all but forgotten his dreams.

Kasai stretched as he paused for a moment to enjoy the orange glow of the setting sun, the last bit could be seen through the high spires surrounding Ordu. He had yet to finish his dusk chores and would be late for dinner. *Cold stew again*, he thought.

He had drawn outer sweeping duty, again. The stairs and paths outside the monastery walls were cleaned meticulously in the early morning and once more in the early evening. The Masters said the work helped to clear a person's mind of unwanted debris collected from the trials of life. Kasai just saw it as a never-ending cycle of work.

The late autumn sun lit the cliffs and valleys in a luminous glow. The mountains took on a cool, purple hue while the colors of turning leaves held onto the last warmth of the sun. The cold nights came early this time of year, and as the sun descended from sight, the icy blast of chilly winds gusted against the mountainside. Their eerie howls took Kasai out of his reverie.

Kasai thought of his Brothers inside the warm refectory enjoying hot stew in freshly-made bread bowls. His mouth watered with anticipation of food and his stomach let him know it agreed. The faster he finished sweeping, the sooner he would be inside eating his dinner. He arched his back and moved side-to-side.

"Best get on with it," he grumbled.

He had one more section to go before he was finished. *Perhaps tomorrow would bring some warmer weather. Wishful thinking*, he thought and moved to the remaining section of stairs. As Kasai turned to cross the last bridge, he was distracted by small reflections of light coming from the cliff of the East Wall. The top of the cliff housed the Inner Halls and many of the common structures of the monastery.

What was that? He squinted to get a better look and saw that some of his Brothers were dusk climbing. The evening sky bathed their robes, a dark-mustard color. Kasai was unaware of a work detachment assigned to the East Wall this evening. One of the Masters must have scheduled a nighttime scaling exercise. Probably Master Dorje, he was known for forcing Brothers to confront their fear, conquer it, and grow stronger.

Kasai thought back to his experience on the mountain and sympathized with his Brothers on the rock. Kasai watched them scale higher along the sheer wall and silently cheered them on. Night climbing was a challenge, especially for the younger novices. He tried to discern who was leading the climb and who followed. He couldn't recognize the body shapes belonging to any of his Brothers.

"That doesn't seem right." Kasai tilted his head to one side. He noticed the monks moved awkwardly. There was no fluidity to their motion. The monks conserved their strength and used the momentum of their body to flow up and down the wall. Their unique skill of crisscrossing arms, hooking heels, and dropping legs enabled them to grip onto impossible holds. His Brothers moved like elegant spiders along the rock wall.

However, these climbers used brute strength to lunge from one hold to the next. Kasai saw the climbers driving handpicks into the rock. His Brothers didn't need anchor holds to climb a sheer surface. Kasai sharpened his focus for a better look. Were those ropes dangling down from the lead climbers? More climbers followed the lines from below. He broadened his view and saw many groups were scaling the wall. His stomach sank. These weren't monks, and this wasn't a training exercise. The monastery was under attack!

Kasai watched in shock as the invaders crested the cliff and scurried to the monastery walls. They threw grappling hooks that lodged into the crenels of the stone and climbed again. Longswords were strapped to their backs and reflected the last of the sun's glowing light. Within moments the attackers were over the top and in the courtyard.

Black smoke rose in the half-light over the white walls that protected the central buildings. The wind changed. The stench of something greasy and burnt wafted past him. Kasai froze with fear. What was happening? Where were the sentries, and why had no alarm been sounded?

He took a few steps forward. He stopped. What was he doing? If he went directly to the front gate, he would be spotted. The smoke intensified, and now he could see flames lapping up to the sky. Even if he went to the monastery, what could he possibly do? He was only a junior monk. Sparring in a controlled environment was one thing. Fighting real foes was something altogether different. Daku was right. Kasai was not prepared for the real world and the many challenges it held.

The Masters would be able to deal with this threat. But they could not be everywhere at once. His mind froze with hesitation. He had to do something to help. He looked at his hands. His broom was a poor excuse for a proper staff. He would be better off using his hands.

"Don't be stupid, Kasai. You're safe here."

He told himself his reasoning was sound. Daku would organize the older acolytes into fighting groups, and they would mount a defense. He couldn't do anything from here.

Kasai thought of the younglings. They would be led to Zazen Hall for safety. Best to get them out of the way when the fighting started. More smoke appeared over the walls of the monastery. The meditation hall was on fire. The younglings might already be trapped inside.

Intruders crawled over the walls like an infestation of vermin. Kasai heard booming thunderclaps resounded from the courtyard and felt the air shudder. The wind carried the smell of sulfur and spoiled meat. A cold shiver shook his body as Kasai remembered the same horrible odor from his early childhood. It could only mean one thing.

The creatures of evil had returned and were using dark magic against his Brothers. They could already be dead. His family was being stolen from him. *Not again*, he feared.

Now was the time to act. Kasai took a hesitant step forward. The front gate was lost. Was there another access available on the Eastern wall? *Think!* His eyes followed the tracks of a series of bridges. Each path resulted in a dead-end. Time was against him. This portion of the slope was covered in meditation circuits. Each bridge circled back to the same spot.

The wind carried the screams of his Brothers. *Hurry.* His mind raced. *Come on, come on, Kasai. People are counting on you.* His heart pounded in his chest. Sweat beaded on his forehead. He couldn't think. He was useless.

Kasai forced his eyes closed. He inhaled deeply through his nose and let the cool night air fill his chest. He let it out slowly. Again. Breath in, breath out. He tapped into his water xindu to calm the fire in his spirit. He wished he had a better grasp on the xindu mysteries.

Slowly, the level of his water xindu rose. His fear and frustration sank into the memory of a favorite swamp from his childhood. Kasai focused on removing the tangle of false paths before him. He let their patterns dissolve from the maze of possibilities meant to baffle and confuse an enemy.

By doing so, the true way would reveal itself. There! A narrow fissure that collected rainwater and melted snow. The fissure fed it to an interior basin, which the monks used for their water supply. For once, Kasai was thankful for his smaller size. He had to cross two bridges and leave the main path, but then he could easily downclimb to the natural aqueduct.

Kasai raced across the first bridge on sure footing. He would not abandon his Brothers. He traversed in such a way as to add a new song to the chiming bells, one filled with determination and courage. He reached the fissure without being seen by the invaders. He climbed inside.

The echoes of fighting bounced off the inner walls. Kasai tried his best to keep the sounds of the dying from his mind. Instead, he concentrated on the twists and turns of the natural drainage system.

He gradually descended. The shaft opened to a broader space. Beneath him was the basin that housed the refectory water supply. He scanned the walls for the opening where his Brothers drew water. That was his way into the monastery.

Kasai moved carefully along the slippery surface. The inner walls only offered sharp, tiny nibs for handholds. The tips of his fingers became raw, but he kept moving forward. He thought about what he would do once he reached the top. His best option would be to find one of the Masters. Master Dorje's chamber was closest to the refectory. Kasai would start there.

He emerged from the well shaft and into a small room. He peered into the refectory and saw uneaten food resting on cloth placemats. Water mugs were turned over or had rolled to the floor. In some places, water still dripped from the solid oak table. But otherwise, it was empty.

Kasai ran to Master Dorje's chamber. He was doubtful that he would find him there but decided he needed to start somewhere. Perhaps Master Dorje had left a youngling behind to convey his instructions in case any of the older Brothers had the same idea as Kasai.

The noise of battle was everywhere. Otherworldly screams echoed through the empty stone halls. *What was he doing?* He had no plan and scarcely any real information. Rushing blindly into battle was a poor tactic.

Kasai had traveled these halls for years, but suddenly he felt disoriented and unsure of which way to go. His mind held too many questions demanding answers. Who had attacked the monastery? What purpose would it serve? The monks of Aetenos had no political affiliation or any real influence in the regal circles of the King's court. They were servants of the land and the people who dwelled there. Nothing more. They were only monks! Who would need to slaughter monks?

The entrance to Master Dorje's chamber was before him. The door was open, and Kasai ran in but stopped short. He gasped in shock when he saw that Master Dorje was dead. The invaders murdered him. But he was not just killed, beheaded.

The Master's body lay in a heap on the floor. His head placed on the windowsill overlooking the courtyard. It was clear the killer had wanted Master Dorje to witness the attack on the monastery, even with dead eyes. There was no evidence of a fight, and nothing was amiss or broken in the room. There was no sign of struggle. It was as if Master Dorje had been taken completely unaware. But that was impossible.

The room twisted and turned as the weight of events pounded into Kasai's mind. His entire body began to tremble. He thought he would fall to the floor. The sounds of battle flooded back to his ears. The mark of Mizzen flared on his forearm, lending him courage.

Kasai could do nothing here and was needed elsewhere. He raced to Master Kunchen's chamber next.

He reached Master Kunchen's chamber panting for breath. The old man was dead as well. His heart had been ripped from his chest. The organ sagged from a dagger driven to the wall. Again, there was no struggle. It made no sense. One does not take a Master of Ordu unaware and end their life so casually.

Kasai was no longer registering the immensity of events unfolding before him. Everything was condensed down to individual moments that could be more easily identified, even if not understood. *What of Master Choejor? Had the same fate befallen the blind Master? Without the Three Masters to lead them, his Brothers were doomed.*

His heart pounded in his chest as he ran in the direction of Master Choejor's chamber. Unconscious tears streamed from the corners of his eyes. He was losing his family again, and just as before, he was helpless to stop it.

He rounded the corner of a hall too fast and tripped over the body of one of his Brothers. The body had been torn to pieces. Terrible gashes were slashed across the larger parts. Kasai couldn't even recognize who had died.

Was this the work of the same killer that had butchered the Masters? There were no bodies of enemies anywhere. Who or what could be powerful enough to kill Masters Dorje and Kunchen without a fight?

The inner hallways filled with smoke, and the air became thin and dark. Kasai changed his route and passed the Hall of Artifacts. It was a sacred area, holding the relics and ancient weapons of the Order of Ordu. The room was filling with smoke. So much would be lost in the fire.

Kasai kept moving. He tried to understand what was happening around him. Taking out the Masters made sense. They were the real threat at the monastery. His Brothers could mount a counterattack, but it seemed unlikely they would be victorious against this foe.

Master Choejor was next or had already been murdered. Kasai's eyes stung. His visibility was dim from heavy smoke. Kasai clenched his fists when he heard the noise of battle getting louder; the enemy was near. He needed something to even the odds. He ran back into the Hall of Artifacts. He'd grab the nearest weapon available and ask forgiveness later.

Thick smoke filled the room. Kasai groped blindly for anything that was not locked behind a thick glass case. Nothing. Where were the keys? Not here. Only the Masters held the keys to these locks. Why hadn't he thought about that earlier? The sounds of fighting grew louder.

He tested the strength of the locks, but they held fast. His eyes watered. Kasai was desperate. He stumbled further into the Hall of Artifacts, searching for anything to help.

A burnt wooden rafter had fallen and smashed through a case in the back of the room. Kasai was half-blind from the smoke and reached for whatever was there. His hand found the familiar shape of a sanjiegun. He grabbed the folded three-sectioned staff and ran to help his Brothers.

The weapon felt oddly warm in his hands and was heating as he approached the fighting. He rubbed the water from his eyes and looked at the weapon more closely.

"Oh no," Kasai groaned.

He held Ninziz-zida, the Fire Serpent. Kasai had no time to put it back and search for another. "Please don't curse me," Kasai pleaded. Reluctantly, he tucked the folded staff into his sash and ran forward. It wasn't long before Kasai came to the entrance of Master Choejor's chamber. Kasai was relieved to hear his old Master's inside. He rushed into the room.

"Master Choejor! I'm here!" Kasai keeled over, trying to catch his breath. He put his hands on his knees for support. Master Choejor's back was to the door, and he was speaking to another monk.

"Ah, Brother Kasai. I'm glad you are here," Master Choejor said with a relaxed yet direct voice. Kasai still huffed. His lungs were on fire. He was amazed at how calm Master Choejor could be in such an intense situation.

"Master Kunchen says he has rallied the senior Brothers to the left wall and brought the younglings to the food storage under the refectory. We must leave with all haste to join the fight."

"But Master Kunchen is dead!" Kasai gasped between gulps of air. Tears streamed down his face. "He's gone."

"Eyes can be deceived in the heat of battle, Brother Kasai. I assure you, I am very much alive," Master Kunchen said. The old Master's head poked around the body of Master Choejor. He eyed Kasai suspiciously, and promptly put some distance between the two monks.

How could this be? He noticed there was something very wrong with Master Kunchen's face. His skin looked false, and his eyes held an expression of wickedness.

Kasai was exhausted. His mind moved faster than his understanding could keep up. He gave up trying to figure things out. Unconsciously, he stripped away what was inconsistent with Master Kunchen and sought the truth.

A black vapor materialized above Master Kunchen's head. Bewildered, Kasai stared in confused fascination. Was it just smoke? The dark mist formed into an unusual symbol. It pulsed outward in an erratic motion. Black tendrils reached out to strike the bright-orange glow that had now appeared above Master Choejor's head. That was new.

"Master Kunchen, I'm sorry. I don't understand. How did you get here? What happened to you?" Kasai said as he tried to gather his thoughts. Had he imagined seeing the murdered body of Master Kunchen? "And what is that black symbol above your head?"

Master Choejor tilted his head to the side. "You see a sigil, Brother Kasai? Tell me what you see immediately. Describe it to me," Master Choejor said his voice held unfamiliar urgency. His body tensed.

"I'm not sure what I am seeing. There is a strange, black rune floating above Master Kunchen. I've never seen the like of it before. Is he sick, Master Choejor?"

Master Choejor's shoulders slumped, and his body deflated for a moment. "You are correct, Brother Kasai. Master Kunchen is dead," Master Choejor said. "This imposter is his assassin."

"Assassin." Kasai couldn't believe what he was hearing. He looked again at the man before him. How could this be? Master Kunchen began to take a few steps towards the open window, giving him a clear view of both monks.

The weight of what had happened to Master Kunchen, Master Dorje and his Brothers, finally came to the forefront of Kasai's awareness like a rushing wave of fire. His fingers curled around Ninziz-zida's segments at his waist. His heart pounded heavily as the fire xindu filled his body with anger, even fury. His mind went from asking too many questions to one focused answer. Hurt the one who hurt you.

The enemy was now before him, smiling like a spoiled child who had gotten his way. Ninziz-zida was already in his hands. He gripped her two end segments and stretched the Fire Serpent in a defensive position, but one that could strike with ease.

His mind filled with new and exotic attack sequences combining the reach of the staff and his own body. A dominant force took control of his actions, just as a puppeteer manipulated a puppet. He did not think to resist the influence, only to act. "Master, what are your orders? I am ready."

The thing that was Master Kunchen sized up Kasai. "You are ready? And what is the little monk ready to do? Stop me when two of the famed Masters of Ordu could not? You are but a boy."

Kasai heard the sounds of battle growing closer as shouts and footsteps advanced towards the chamber. Then Kasai recognized the familiar sound of padded sandals on the stone floor of the hallway.

"Your time is up. My Brothers approach in numbers," Kasai said. His entire being wished to strike out at the creature, but his will remained steady. Master Choejor had yet to give his order. He was surprised by the aggression that filled his mind and the desire to engage in battle. His fire xindu had never blazed so fiercely.

The imposter leaped to the windowsill, perched like a gargoyle on a ledge. "Alas, I must bid you farewell. My time grows short, and I must be away on more pressing affairs." The image of Master Kunchen shifted out of focus and revealed something else. Something shimmering and unnatural.

The *thing* on the window ledge deftly tossed a small object to the floor. It exploded and filled the room with billowing smoke. Kasai shielded his eyes and began to cough, but his senses were on alert. He somehow heard the rapid deployment of numerous objects cutting through the air and heading in his direction. He reacted on instinct. Ninziz-zida was a whirlwind of motion.

Time slowed down before his eyes. The confusing nature of the smoke slowed to almost a standstill. Kasai saw the oncoming projectiles appeared as large as bloated apples pushing through the smoke. Ninziz-zida's outer sections deflected the darts with ease, sending broken pieces in all directions. Not one barb managed to penetrate Kasai's defense.

Kasai heard Master Choejor grunt in pain. Events in the room flashed back to real-time. The assassin was gone. Master Choejor laid crumpled on the floor.

"Master Choejor!"

"I shall be fine," Master Choejor said, but not without effort. He tried to stand. "We must help the others. Get me up."

Kasai did as he was asked, but Master Choejor remained unsteady without assistance.

"Master, what was that…thing? What is it? Are you hurt? What happened?"

Master Choejor removed his robe from his left shoulder. He brushed away a small barb that was embedded in his flesh. The skin around the impact point had turned an ugly green with blisters bubbling around the edge.

"It appears I have been poisoned," Master Choejor said in a curious tone. His power tattoos flared as they sought to counter the toxins and repair the wounded flesh. But the skin blistered at a more rapid pace.

"But how? This wound is on your back. How could … oh no. I was not thinking of where the darts were going after I blocked them. Master, I am sorry."

"You defended yourself admirably," Master Choejor said. He looked towards the door with blind eyes. A small group of younger monks barreled into the small chamber. Their eyes were wide with fear. Many had encountered the enemy and had done their best to fight back. Their faces and hands were covered in cuts and bruises. Somehow, they had managed to escape the melee and had fled to the safety of the inner buildings.

"Master Choejor! Brother Kasai! The monastery is overrun. The buildings are burning. Everyone is dying. What should we do?" one of the younglings wailed; his words spilling together. Kasai knew him as Brother Mica.

"Where are the others? Where are the senior Brothers?" Master Choejor asked in a strained voice.

"Whoever is left is fighting in the courtyard. Daku sent me to find all the Masters. He needs help. I found Brothers Tutto, Nindus, and the others in the meditation hall," Mica said.

"Take me to Brother Daku. Have you seen Master Dorje?" Master Choejor said.

"We were hoping he was with you," Mica said.

"Brother Kasai will lead us to the courtyard. We shall lend our help where we can. Hopefully, we will join with Master Dorje along the way," Master Choejor said.

"But…" Kasai decided to hold his tongue. He led the younger monks out of the chamber and towards the courtyard. Destruction was everywhere. The old wood of rafters crackled and popped as the fire ate into their core. Black chunks of wood fell to the floor, followed by filthy streams of charred smoke. The old monastery was crumbling around them. Kasai navigated a path through the burning debris. The monks often had to go back the way they came when collapsed ceilings prevented them from moving forward.

Master Choejor brought up the rear. He spoke reassuring words to the younger Brothers, but they were all moving too slow.

Kasai wanted to tell Master Choejor of the death of Master Dorje but considered the information carefully. He did not want to create more panic in the younger monks. He was barely able to retain his courage himself and could only imagine what was happening in the minds of the young ones. Their vacant eyes told him they were in the grips of the death fear. Kasai would tell Master Choejor about Master Dorje later.

"Let me scout ahead and make sure it is safe," Kasai told the others. He moved quickly down the hall and around a corner, hoping the way to the courtyard was clear.

The corridor shook as if it trembled with the same fear he felt in his heart. The air here was thick and suffocating. A long groan was followed by a deafening crack. He whirled around, retracing his steps to find an entire section of the ceiling had crashed to the stone floor. Dread filled his heart. A tangled pile of burning wood, grey stone, and plaster was heaped in the middle of the corridor. Under the debris were the unmoving arms and legs of the younglings.

"No, no, no!" Kasai cried. He frantically threw fiery pieces of the fallen ceiling to the side. Everything was hot, and his hands soon blistered. His Brothers were gone. Tears of frustration ran down his face.

"Master Choejor! Master Choejor!" Kasai could not find the old monk. Cruel tongues of flame laughed at him as it burned through the wood. Kasai knew there was nothing to be done now. He had lost them all. How could he have missed the compromised ceiling?

Kasai saw movement beyond the rear of the pile. Master Choejor had fallen backward when the ceiling collapsed. He sat up straight and cocked his head to the ceiling. It looked like the Master was meditating or communing with an unseen voice.

"I understand," Master Choejor said into the air. He slowly stood using the wall for support.

"Kasai, you must escape to Gethem. Go to the Temple of Illumination and find Grandmaster Nysulu. He must know what has occurred here. Our sister monasteries must be alerted to this danger, or the same fate will befall them."

"But what of the others? They need our help," Kasai said.

"The Boundless has set you on a different path. I shall gather as many as I can. I am afraid we have lost this day to darkness. There is a foul smell in the air. Somehow the Amaranthine Barrier has been breached. Creatures from the Abyss have returned to the Mortal Realm."

"The Abyss..." Kasai's heart sank as the magnitude of the word registered in his mind. He was reliving his worst fears.

"The monastery is lost. You must warn the others. Their salvation lies with you. Race now to the catacombs as quickly as you can." Master Choejor slumped against the wall. His breathing was shallow.

"Come, Master," Kasai said. "Put your hand on my shoulder. I will not leave without you."

Master Choejor smiled with understanding and nodded slowly. Together, they navigated the torn hallways towards the monastery's catacombs. Kasai grew increasingly worried. Master Choejor was getting weaker instead of stronger, needing frequent rest.

They stopped behind a partially-collapsed ceiling and wall. It provided excellent cover and a clear view out to the courtyard. The fire blazing through the monastery buildings lit the square. Kasai saw a small group of monks fighting off the invaders. Daku led the survivors, but the enemy grossly outnumbered them.

One-by-one the monks were captured in large nets and dragged to the side of the courtyard. Daku was the last to be caught. His wrists were bound, and he was forced to kneel on the ground before the murderous assassin.

The assassin conversed with a group of oversized men in loose clothing resembling monk's robes. Kasai felt a shudder pass through the air. He smelled a pungent mix of sulfur and cinnamon permeate the ash-filled air.

There was a blinding flash, and a lithe, otherworldly creature materialized into the courtyard. She had a feminine form and was both dazzling and deadly to behold. Kasai could not look away. He had read of the different types of demonkind in the monastery library. This creature was a succubus, seductive, and deadly.

The demon shunned modesty and was naked from the waist up. She wore form-fitted leather leggings, which hung low and tight on her slender hips. The demon did very little to cover her seductive curves. Onyx, bone-straight hair shot down her alabaster skin and glistened like black oil running down a sheet of ice.

She marched straight towards the assassin. He bowed cockily in her presence like some flamboyant minstrel in the presence of royalty.

"Is this all that remains?" she growled.

"And an excellent evening to you, too, Sess'thra," the assassin chortled, with a pompous grin. The demon slapped him hard across the face, dropping him to the dirt.

"The monks were meant to be collected and unharmed until tested," Sess'thra growled. "Our Mistress will be furious with what you have done here, Dax."

"My orders were to remove the Masters. Maugris' mindless Vor were to create a distraction and chose carnage." Dax shrugged. "I cannot be held accountable for their bloodlust."

The succubus looked at what remained of the Brotherhood, sneering. "And? Was there success?"

"My dear Sess'thra, you wound me. Success? Of course. All but one Master is no more. The third will be dead soon. He will not be able to resist the unique poison in his veins."

"I was referring to them." Sess'thra looked past Dax. She sauntered over to the bound Brothers, narrow hips swaying, predatory eyes glaring. "Now, let us see if something can be salvaged from this debacle."

Sess'thra moved through the captives. She spun a small amulet over each of their heads. Kasai saw a flash of green every time the stone at its center caught the light of the fires.

"What is she doing?" He whispered but knew Master Choejor would be unable to answer. He feared she was deciding which of his Brothers would be taken as slaves and which would be killed as sacrifices to unholy gods. He forced himself to stay hidden and quiet.

Sess'thra moved between the captives like a snake slithering through the grass, occasionally stopping to grab someone's chin or examine another's arm before shaking her head in disappointment. She glanced back at the assassin. "It will not go well for you if he is already dead," she said, continued her search, passing Daku, and then turning back to inspect him. "That one. Pull him from the rest."

Daku was separated from the group. He looked at her with a mixture of anger, awe, and blatant desire when Sess'thra gave Daku a flirtatious smile as she slithered in his direction. Carnal delight oozed from her movements. She halted a few meters from him and tossed a wicked-looking dagger at his knees.

"You. Pick that up," Sess'thra said in a commanding voice.

Daku picked up the dagger between both hands. He looked questioning at the succubus.

"You're different from the rest. I can smell it. I would wager that no one here sees your true potential as I do. There is a certain glint in your eyes that holds promise for greatness to come.

"I offer you a choice. No longer will you be shackled beneath all this...hypocrisy." Sess'thra waved her hands about the burning monastery. "You shall be transformed into a champion among champions. Yours shall be a life of conquest. You shall have the power which only one such as I can grant. You will come with me and experience all that you desire."

"And in return?" Daku asked.

"Ah, yes, everything must have a price. All I have said shall be yours *when* you slit the throat of every one of these miserable monks. The choice is yours. Shall it be one final stand for Ordu? Will you fight beside your Brothers and friends, or will you choose freedom without consequence?"

The Vor, as Dax had called them, chuckled with deep guttural malice. Daku flipped the dagger backward in his hands and sliced through the leather straps binding his wrists. He then drove the blade into the ground and rubbed the circulation back into his hands.

Daku surveyed the position of the enemy around him. When Daku attacked, Kasai would use the distraction to join his friend. Maybe together they push the creatures back and free the others. That was a long shot, but worth a try. Ninziz-zida felt warm in his hands.

Daku flipped the dagger into the air and caught it in a firm grip, then turned and thrust the blade into Brother Hondo's chest. Kasai gasped and quickly covered his mouth.

Daku methodically worked his way through the group of his shocked and helpless Brothers. Ri'sonu fell next, then Brothers Dani, Jonah, and Numan. Daku didn't stop until only two remained.

Kasai clenched his teeth to keep from yelling. He turned away from the grisly sight. "Daku, what have you done?" He whispered with his head low. Kasai then heard the voice of Jarescu yell above the din of burning buildings.

"Have you lost your mind?"

Kasai looked back. Jarescu was kneeling in the dirt. Tears ran down the sides of his face as Daku stalked towards him.

"Times have changed. I finally see real power in front of me. I'm sick of the Masters brainwashing me and telling me there is a Boundless that will grant me power. It's all a hoax. Ordu is a lie," Daku said.

"She's a demon!" Jarescu yelled.

"Demon? Can you not see her? She is a goddess. I see her. I see her so clearly," Daku said. He was speaking to himself as he stared at Sess'thra in a daze.

"It's not too late, Daku. Cut us loose," Cannonball said.

Daku was momentarily broken from his swoon. He looked again at Cannonball and Jarescu. "No, it is only too late for you two. The strong survive, the weak perish. It's the natural way of things."

Daku wore a wicked smile and deftly slit the throat of Brother Jarescu. "Plus, I never liked you."

"Good-bye, Cannonball." Daku stabbed Jia'mu in the chest. A fountain of blood followed the knife's blade when he ripped the dagger out of the chubby monk's body.

Daku walked up to Sess'thra and placed the dagger back in her hands. "I accept."

He glanced back at the carnage he had reaped, satisfied with his work. "They were never my Brothers, and certainly not my friends."

Sess'thra handed the dagger back to him. "No, my lovely pet, keep this as a symbol of our trust. Your ascension shall be glorious." She looked past Daku and straight towards the location where Kasai and Master Choejor had taken refuge. Kasai quickly ducked back behind the debris. He prayed he had not been seen.

"Master, we must go," Kasai said, and Master Choejor nodded.

"We shall gather some traveling supplies and make for the monastery catacombs. If we are lucky, we will reach the wilderness without incident," Master Choejor said.

Kasai supported him as they walked away. Master Choejor's face was white. Kasai knew their chances were slim to none that they would make it outside the monastery walls alive.

"Lucky, lucky, lucky," Kasai said to himself.

12

SHIVERRIG

On a table in his study, Duke Shiverrig unrolled a map of the Sarribe Mountains in southern Baroqia and set a heavy wooden marker at each corner to keep the map stretched open. He studied the Sarribe Pass, marked in red. It wasn't the only entryway into the Kingdom of Sunne, but it was the safest.

Shiverrig would see Baroqia strong again—and he had plans, but he was woefully short of allies, troops, and the wealth needed to purchase mercenaries. He stroked the three-day stubble on his cleft chin as his eyes drifted to the northern kingdom. Dense forests filled the central regions of Baroqia as roads and rivers wound throughout the realm. The land was civilized due to the vision of a long line of House Shiverrig rulers imposing their will upon forest and field.

He reached for another map, this one depicting the northern borderlands of Baroqia and beyond—to the Kingdom of Trosk where Maugris stayed cooped up in his fortress of rock and snow, plotting his revenge. Shiverrig sucked at his teeth. Maugris. What to do about Maugris?

His maps were made of boarhide, a sturdy material that accepted script and design work without ink bleeding through to its backside. The Duke favored these maps. They were a part of his family's history as much as Volkerrum Keep; heirlooms passed down as relics-of-honor from father to son, dating back to the founding of Baroqia. They had traveled with him through blood, mud, and victory.

More charts were rolled out over a long table made from a single slab of thick red oak. Shiverrig was obsessed with the details of any campaign, no matter the size or scope. He assessed his troop deployments, where the land provided natural choke-points and areas for swifter movement of the infantry and war engines. The more significant frontier settlements were also displayed in graphic detail.

Shiverrig turned to ponder a larger map tacked to the wall behind him. It showed a detailed description of the vast grasslands that spread throughout northern Baroqia. A box was drawn on the map just south of the sloping foothills of the Hoarfrost

Mountains. It symbolized the Last Garrison, an old military base used mostly for war games and training. It held hard memories for Shiverrig, memories he intended to erase.

He traced a path with his finger through the Hoarfrost Mountains along Stormwind Pass. The route led to Rachlach Fortress, Maugris' stronghold. Could the sorcerer be trusted? That was a question Shiverrig could not answer with confidence. No matter, he would put together overlapping contingency plans to ensure the outcome of events followed his design. He turned back to the maps on the table, clasping his muscular arms behind his back.

He would tighten his hold on the outer villages throughout Baroqia and secretly draft more conscripts to his cause, not Conrad's. Peasants could choose to live outside of the walls of the kingdom and the politics within, but soon they would need to side with one power or the other. Either way, they would be consumed in the war to come.

"My Duke, I came as soon as I heard the word. Dax has returned," Malachi said as he scurried into the study. "Ordu has fallen. All have been slain."

Duke Shiverrig looked upon his Archvashim. The man's body appeared more bent than straight, and his face had developed blotches of a purplish nature. It was clear he hadn't sleep in days. His lower right arm was wrapped in leather bindings and ended in a mean, iron stump. Malachi was a haggard mess.

"And the demon?" Shiverrig inquired. Words like 'demon' came too easily to his lips in recent weeks. He didn't like it. It was a sour alliance, but a necessary one until he could control the might of the kingdom.

Malachi became crestfallen upon hearing the description of his unrequited love. This was becoming a problem.

"I fear I do not know. Sess'thra travels when and where she will. She leaves without warning and returns the same."

"I'm wary of the time you spend with your dark charges. Our guests are not toys or baubles for your fancy. When they have served their purpose, they will be removed." Shiverrig took a hard look at his advisor in the light. "You look unwell."

Malachi's mood brightened at the mention of the demonkind at Volkerrum Keep. "My Duke, they have so much to offer us. And not just the Vor spawned from Rachlach Fortress. The lesser fiends that have been summoned from Gathos have so many secret things they are willing to tell and do. Fascinating creatures." Malachi absentmindedly brought his left hand to the stump at his right, caressing the edges of iron.

"I see," Shiverrig said. He did nothing to hide his contempt. "Until the disposition of these creatures can be properly assessed, I do not want you to bring them any closer than you must. Sess'thra speaks in honey-coated riddles. Dax is too polite to be trusted, and these Vor are now everywhere. Keep yourself clean of their taint until this is over."

"Of course, my Lord. It shall be as you will."

"Did I hear someone mention my sweet name?" Dax inquired as he glided into the study. Shiverrig took note that a young man dressed in dirty robes trailed the assassin. Not a prisoner, but also not a companion.

"Where did you find this one?" Malachi said. "By the looks of him, I'd say vagabond traveler or monk hopeful for the Temple of Illumination. And one in need of a bath." His face scrunched in disgust from an imagined foul smell.

"Ah, yes, a proper introduction then. I present to you, Daku. No last name, or none that the lad wished to give me. So, let us call him Daku of Ordu. A one-time monk and now an extended agent of the Mistress. We remain hopeful at least," Dax said. He brushed off some dirt from Daku's shoulder and fussed over his robes. "Well as can be, I suppose."

"Come here, boy," Shiverrig ordered. He was impatient to know why a monk from Ordu had survived the culling and been brought to his Keep. Daku moved with fluid ease away from Dax and presented himself to the Duke. He drew back his shoulders and kept a rigid posture.

"From Ordu? How is it that you came to be here?" Shiverrig said.

"I decided it was in my best interests to walk a different path than those at Ordu," Daku said.

"You see! Mor's truth is spoken from one of Aetenos' own. The demigod is truly dead," Malachi said. He jumped forward with keen interest. "The Change of Mor reveals the truth in all things." He stabbed a bony finger into Daku's chest. "Even you!"

Daku raised an indifferent eyebrow. He then fixed his dark eyes on Shiverrig. Daku had the same relaxed reserve that the Grandmaster had during their failed negotiations.

"Malachi, calm yourself. Give the boy some room," Shiverrig said. His Arch-vashim's fanaticism with Mor was becoming more pronounced since the arrival of the demons. If it clouded his judgment, Shiverrig would need to remove him.

Malachi bowed. "Yes, my Duke." He grumbled something more as he passed Daku but moved to the side.

"I am not interested in Mor or Aetenos. Either will do, or pick another. I care not. I need more able-bodied men under my banner, not the rantings of new worlds to come by another self-inflated prophet," Shiverrig said. "Which are you?"

It was a test. What information had Dax let pass through his lips on the long journey back to Gethem? For now, Shiverrig would consider the boy a spy until proven otherwise.

"A monk's true power comes from mind-over-matter. By using a focused determination of will, one can separate the illusion of mental pain from what is in reality, only physical sensation. A new reality then blossoms within the disciplined mind when this basic principle has been mastered.

"Deities and demigods are inconsequential to my abilities. Stories of Mor or Aetenos are meant to control the masses. They do not grant magical favors to the faithful."

Malachi's eager expression dropped into a menacing glare. "You will become part of the Change of Mor or perish."

Shiverrig frowned.

"Duke Shiverrig, I can be of value. The monks of Ordu were found homeless on the streets of desperate neighborhoods across the lands of Baroqia. They were orphaned or abandoned at an early age. They have nothing.

"Feed them, shelter them, give them an enemy to focus their anger on, and your ranks will swell. I'll recruit and train them myself."

"An army of street rats pretending to be monks of lost Ordu?" Malachi scoffed.

Daku's eyes narrowed. "Do not push me, old man."

The boy has courage and pride. I can use both, Shiverrig thought.

Dax came to Daku's side and patted him on the back. The assassin was quick to change the subject. "The boy certainly has spirit and a favorable conscience to your cause. He's strong as a bull and not without a quick, fiery fist. Quite the fighter when cornered, mind you. He managed to hold his own against some unpleasant disagreements with my entourage along the way to Volkerrum Keep. Plus, our dear Sess'thra has taken him into her trust."

As a plaything or informant? There was more to this young man than just an afterthought or memento from a raid. He was here for a reason. "Where is that little bird? She is constantly fluttering here and there, yet I am not privy to her movements," Shiverrig said.

Sess'thra appeared like a ghost from the shadows of a forgotten corner of the room. Sulfur and cinnamon followed in her wake. "The monasteries of the Four Orders have fallen. The monks are gone. Hardly the fight I expected. It was all quite disappointing."

Shiverrig heard a slight sigh come from Malachi. The Archvashim rushed to faun over Sess'thra. He reached his good hand out to touch her.

"What did I say about touching me again, worm?" Sess'thra growled.

Malachi immediately pulled back his hand. "I only wished to welcome our wayward dove back to the Keep."

Sess'thra's upper lip curled. She gave Malachi a sidelong glare when she passed him. "I'm already in a foul enough mood without listening to your weak drivel."

She drew close to Dax. "I was able to test the monks, properly this time. None passed."

Daku pushed forward to stand in front of Sess'thra. "I did what you said. I want what was promised."

"Ah, my young monk. I have not forgotten about you."

Sess'thra raised an amulet with an emerald center above his head. There was a flicker, but then the stone went dark. She sighed. "Still nothing."

Shiverrig sensed the frustration clinging to Sess'thra's typically alluring features. There was another storyline in play. Sekka's real interest in this campaign was taking shape with each piece she moved into place. Maugris seemed content enough to watch those that made him an outcast suffer, but the Arch Devil and her thralls were up to something entirely different.

"I said, I want…" Daku started again.

"I do not care what you want!" Sess'thra barked at Daku. She turned back to Dax.

"Were all the monks within the walls of the Ordu during the raid? Could any have escaped?" The succubus was fire and fury in a moment's notice. She was unbridled passion.

"How would I know? I was busy disposing of the Masters," Dax said.

"Who was missing!" Sess'thra screamed. She rounded on Daku. "You were in the courtyard. You saw them all die. Who wasn't there?"

His eyes went wide with surprise. "I, I don't know. Let me think." Daku looked left and right. "Kasai wasn't there," Daku said at last. "He was absent in the refectory at last bell. I did not see him in the holding area, either. He might have been outside the monastery walls during the attack." Daku softly chuckled. "I knew it. Late for his own funeral."

"Ah, it seems this Kasai may have alluded us," Sess'thra eased back to her provocative demeanor. "Kasai." She gently breathed the name through her teeth. "Such a peaceful name. Like a field of long grass blowing in a gentle breeze."

The succubus stretched out her arm and walked her slender, alabaster fingers up Daku's tattered sleeve. "Could Kasai do anything interesting, any tricks?" Sess'thra purred into Daku's ear.

"He was average. I could best him in the sparring circles with ease. I once engaged four other Brothers simultaneously. I defeated them all. I even fought against a Master. I was next in line to ... "

"Not you!" She cuffed him across the back of his head. "I examined every monk within the monastery walls. Dead or alive, the amulet did not respond, not so much as a glimmer. But I did not think to look to the outer reaches. My advance scouts did not speak of monks being late with their chores."

Sess'thra exchanged a quizzical glance with Dax. Shiverrig let the plot unfold as each piece fell into place. It was valuable information that he could use to his benefit in the future, once he understood its meaning.

"I will ask you again. Did your Kasai do anything special?" Sess'thra said. Her impatience was on the rise.

"Well, he did complete something I couldn't, but I'm sure he cheated," Daku reluctantly said under his breath.

"And what was that?" Sess'thra said.

"He completed the Trial of Pillars."

Sess'thra looked at Dax for some kind of explanation. The assassin shrugged his shoulders.

"It's a maze in the sky. An initiate follows a circuit of columns by jumping from the top of one to the next," Daku said.

"Not much of a test," Sess'thra said. "I presumed you monks were capable of feats of this nature."

Daku rolled his eyes. "Not if you're blind to where the next column stood. It's as more of a mental test than a physical one. Kasai was good, but not that good. Even I could not finish the route. The test is designed to be impossible for any but a Master to complete."

"Could it be he had someone watching over him? A guardian angel, perhaps?" Sess'thra's excitement mounted. "Tell me more. Tell me everything" The purring had returned.

"What do you want to know? Kasai was soft. He had green eyes that changed color according to his mood. I don't know. He loved to protect the weak. I tried to tell him, only the strong survive in this world. But he wouldn't listen."

Dax sided up to Sess'thra and spoke in a conspirator's tone, "Kasai was the name of the monk who interfered before I could finish off the last Master. He saw through my glamour and alerted the blind one to my identity."

Sess'thra wore a devious smile. "He is the one," she said with conviction.

"Kasai? Why does he matter? He's a nobody. You said I was special." Daku looked forlorn.

Shiverrig wondered if the fool was in love with the succubus. That would be a mistake. He feigned boredom with the conversation. "Assassin, please explain why any of this is of interest to me in any way?"

"Because Duke Shiverrig, our lovely Sess'thra speaks of the coming of the next Ever Hero. The Mistress has made it clear that she wants the avatar of Aetenos for her own in the North," Dax said.

"Bad news for her if he was a monk," Shiverrig said. He picked up a map from his desk and studied it to hide his surprise. Could it be true? Had Sekka entered the Mortal Realm?

"Kasai? The Ever Hero? Don't make me laugh. Kasai wouldn't let his shadow be seen if he didn't have permission first. He's been a milk baby since I met him at Ordu. He's no hero," Daku said. He crossed his arms over his chest. "You have the wrong person."

Shiverrig took a hard look at Dax. Was it true? Had the fool Maugris successfully summoned the devil to the Mortal Realm? Assuming he had, why would she need the Ever Hero alive? It didn't make sense. Maugris wanted the monks of Aetenos dead. Who could blame him? History showed them to be a troublesome lot, and Sekka would be smart to be rid of them as well.

If Aetenos was truly gone, then who would be left to oppose her? Better to have the Ever Hero dead as well. But she had other plans. She needed the Ever Hero alive for something special. But for what? This question lingered in his mind, as did his wondering on who was the real power in the North?

A storm was coming, one that King Conrad would never be able to weather on his own. Unfortunately, Shiverrig was not strong enough to defend the land without absolute control over the Five Armies. If a demonic invasion were imminent, he would need to consider his position in the aftermath.

There were always weak links in any well-planned strategy. Perhaps, a partnership with Sekka, not Maugris, was necessary ... until the proper moment to counterattack presented itself. Focus on one enemy at a time, while keeping them all in mind.

"I am not some dullard, keen on prophecies or peasant stories of salvation from the unseen divine. I care not if the monks are gone from the mountains, grasslands, hills, or hovels where they hid. Can we finally move forward as planned?" Shiverrig demanded. He deliberately acted as if he was none-the-wiser of the real motives of his guests.

"What about me and the promises you made me? I want the power you spoke of at the monastery." Daku grabbed Sess'thra by the shoulder to pull her around. He failed to do anything but elicit a sharp hiss from the succubus. Then a sensual smile came to her lips.

"In time, you will have ample opportunity to prove your worth," Sess'thra said. The demon did not try to hide her desire for Daku. It was clear she had other plans for the young man.

"I have real worth right now! I can show you."

Sess'thra ignored Daku. She turned to Dax. "Take Maugris' Vor and score the mountainside, foothills, and forests. Find any remaining monks that could have been outside the walls of Ordu. Bring them here. We want the one named Kasai. I'll wager he did not escape our trap alone. He is your priority. Keep him alive."

"You'll never find him," Daku said. "Not without my help."

"We found our way to your hidden sanctuary easily enough. I'm sure we can manage," Sess'thra said.

"It's obvious the Order was betrayed. However, the paths Kasai now walks are known only by the monks of Ordu. And unless you can raise the dead, you'll need a guide."

"I see, which makes you conveniently indispensable. How timely." Sess'thra eyed

Daku with suspicious doubt. "How do I know this is not some trick to protect Kasai?"

"Kasai betrayed me," Daku said. Shiverrig heard the threat in the boy's tone. He was beginning to appreciate the lad.

"The boy was born into the wrong house," Dax said, full of mirth. His laughter circled to Shiverrig, who remained stoic.

"Let me show you my loyalty once more. Let me lead your pack of hunters. I know Kasai. He will come running when he sees a friendly face. Then you will have your prize, and I will have my reward."

The young monk grew bolder now that he had the succubus' attention. He didn't know the game he played with the demon. She was toying with him.

"I have not the patience to wait while you bumble around in the woods, and more so, there is no way a mortal could lead a host of demonkind. You'd be ripped to shreds the moment Dax' back was turned."

"I held my own against them before."

Sess'thra gave Daku a quaint smile. "They were playing with you. You are not ready. There is much in you that would need to change."

She walked away, throwing Daku a teasing pout over her shoulder. "Kasai shall not escape. We have all the information we need."

Dax cleared his throat. "If we are finished here, I shall be on my way."

"Wait!" Daku cried. He looked uncertain. "How? How would I need to change?"

"Be careful of what you ask for, monk," Shiverrig said.

"Oh hush, Duke Shiverrig. You'll scare the boy. I won't need much, just a bit of his soul," Sess'thra said. "Well, to be honest, I'll need all of it."

"My soul? You want my soul?"

Shiverrig saw Daku try to step back, but Sess'thra was quickly within his intimate space. She entwined herself around him before he could create any distance.

"Ordu was a lie. Aetenos is gone and left his monks with nothing. And you have no use for deities and demigods, remember? Why worry about something so intangible as a soul? Hmm? They are overrated at best. Live a life of greatness now. The cold dirt of death offers no salvation, divine or otherwise," Sess'thra whispered lie upon lie in his ear.

Shiverrig watched and waited.

"There may be a way, if you are strong enough," Sess'thra said. She pushed herself away from Daku. "But I doubt it. Mortals are made of weak stock."

"I am strong! You said I was different."

"In your body, perhaps, but we shall see if your soul also has the strength of your conviction. If you are found worthy, you will prevail. If not, well, your soul was not worth the etheric energy it was given in the first place."

"No, not my soul. Take something else instead." Daku became defensive.

Shiverrig studied the young monk. He was fit and fearless until this point, a supple fighter with a brawler's mentality. He was an easy target to manipulate when his passions rose.

This was an opportunity to gather sorely lacking information about the demon's abilities. The boy had betrayed his Order and was of no use to the Duke, except, maybe, as an experiment.

"You boast of prowess and worth. You demand respect, and yet, when given the solution to attain your goal, you refuse. Strong words fill you, but they are empty. You're just a frightened, young boy.

"Send the assassin about his business. Have him find the monk Kasai, or the Ever Hero or whatever. I tire of this drama. If the boy has no more use to you, then get rid of him."

"But it's my soul."

"What better raw material to use to build the new you? Maybe the Duke is right. You are not ready for such advancement," Sess'thra said.

She dismissed the idea and turned to the assassin. "No more mistakes, Dax. If Kasai is the one the Mistress desires, he must not be harmed."

Shiverrig watched Daku closely. The boy was exhausted and probably hadn't had a solid meal in days. A decision of impatience and ill-consequence was about to be made by the youngster.

"I'll do it. I'll do what you ask," Daku said. He stepped forward and stood proud.

Sess'thra was once again at the boy's side purring in his ear. "A wise decision. You shall be magnificent. The mortals of this world shall bow down in your presence." Before Daku could say another word, she deftly placed a white pearl into his mouth. "Now, swallow."

"Hmmph?"

She gave him a passionate kiss and pushed the pearl deeper into his mouth.

Shiverrig folded one of his arms across his barrel chest and with the other raised his hand to stroke the sides of a rough mustache. I need to shave, he idly thought. Something would happen soon. He was not wrong.

"My body feels warm and filled with energy. Is this what you feel?" Daku said. His eyes were wide with amazement. He stretched his body and curled his hands into fists. "I feel strong."

Fat droplets of sweat formed on his forehead and freely flowed down his face. He looked at his arms and nodded. "Yes. I feel it. Just like you promised."

Blue veins rose to the surface of his exposed skin and pumped hot blood throughout his body. Daku's dark eyes turned pink, and his sandy-brown skin became pale.

"Yes, but not quite like I promised. The demon seed has taken hold," Sess'thra purred. She watched the transformation evolve. "Humans are frail compared to the vigor of demonkind. This is only the beginning."

Daku held an eager expression. "More. I want more."

"Oh, it is coming," Sess'thra said.

The Duke remained skeptical. Nothing with the infernal born was straightforward or free. A price must always be paid.

"It's wonderful. I feel...wait. I feel cold. Why am I cold? There is...pain."

Shiverrig watched as Daku deliberately slowed his breathing. He chanted foreign words, "Om tare tutarre ture soha, Om tare tutarre ture soha, Om tare tutarre ture soha..." Shiverrig assumed it was a mantra to go beyond the pain. It wasn't working.

Daku's hands trembled. He clamped down on his temples as if to hold his head together. "So much pressure...the pain. The pain...is too much. I've changed my mind. I don't want this!" Daku pleaded. "Make it stop."

"But this is what you wanted," she noted with sweet innocence. Sess'thra stepped back. She watched the young monk's torment with knowing eyes.

Daku's wailing shifted to screams. He dropped to his knees, hunched over from the pain. Malachi's eyes widened, and his head inched forward to take in more of Daku's suffering. The Archvashim licked his dry lips. Shiverrig grabbed him by the collar and pulled him back.

Daku from Ordu was doomed. Shiverrig hoped the mess would be minimal. He stood protectively in front of his table of maps as an eerie silence came over the monk. The room waited.

A deep gurgle resonated from within the monk and turned into a horrible laugh. Daku's pink eyes darted around the room as if looking for an escape. The monk's body expanded. Muscles stretched, ripped, and grew anew. Bones cracked and broke, then reformed to support something ... bigger.

Daku's torso convulsed. Blood vomited from his mouth and sprayed across the floor. He tore off his robes as if they were anathema to his new form. His spine budged along his back, then sharp-edged bone tore through his pale skin as each vertebra swelled and popped back into place.

Daku's body grew into a cruel and vile shape. Where the young monk once knelt was now a beast of ashen muscle and short, white fur. A pale-skinned demon raised itself from the floor. A final, whimpering gasp seeped out of its mouth.

Sess'thra approached the pale demon and laid her hand upon his impressive physique. "Welcome Khalkoroth, Shadow Demon of Gathos."

The demon was massive, standing eight feet tall. It resembled the basic human features of Daku but took on the thick musculature and size of an arctic bear. Khalkoroth's stout muzzle filled with needle-shaped teeth. Instead of paws, the creature had long fingers that flexed in the open air.

The leftover debris of Daku's torn and tattered skin hung from Khalkoroth's hard body. The pale demon grabbed the husk and threw the membrane to the floor. A black vapor trailed from Khalkoroth's body as it moved about in its new form.

The demon's face shifted back to the image of Daku. His pink eyes turned dark. "Help me," a meek and distant voice cried.

Khalkoroth roared, and the pale demon's visage returned. A viscous lather coated its lips. Pink eyes glared in anger.

"This one has a strong will, but he will not escape me." Khalkoroth's voice rumbled through his throat, sounding like boulders grinding beneath the weight of a mountain.

Khalkoroth coughed twice. He vomited a thick mass of bodily fluids and tissues. The mess flowed down its chin and over its smooth chest. He wiped the remains of Daku off his face and smeared it over Sess'thra's mouth. The succubus licked her lips. She provocatively rubbed her body over the pale demon's groin like an animal in heat.

Khalkoroth grabbed Sess'thra and took her in front of Shiverrig and the Archvashim. It was brutal and savage. Malachi's pallor became ghost white. He looked confused and hurt during their rutting, shaking his head in disbelief. The demon's lust spilled out of his erect member and puddled on the floor.

"Next time, demon, you'll fuck where I tell you to fuck. Malachi, find someone to clean up this mess," Shiverrig ordered.

"Did you enjoy that, Daku?" Sess'thra whispered in Khalkoroth's ear. "I know you can still experience the world around you through Khalkoroth's senses. Such are the gifts I give you."

Khalkoroth momentarily shifted back into the resemblance of Daku, albeit a brutish version of the former monk. There was a visible struggle on the boyish face, mixed with determination. Khalkoroth reasserted control, and the boy vanquished. It appeared the two beings wrestled for control of the shared soul.

The monk had some fight in him. Perhaps, if the boy was strong enough, he could be of use as an informant. How to communicate with him without the beast knowing would be something to consider later.

"Yes, little monk, your thoughts and memories are known to me. It shall be a pleasure tormenting a follower of Aetenos. You will be helpless to watch the destruction I wreak upon his land," Khalkoroth's deep voice filled the room.

Khalkoroth glared at Shiverrig, assessing the level of threat posed by the Duke. He then sniffed Malachi. A feral grin grew on his snout. "What of these mortals? Are they food for Khalkoroth? I have great hunger. I wish to feast on their flesh."

Shiverrig heard a faint gasp escape from Malachi's lips as the Archvashim stepped back.

"These are friends, Khalkoroth. You will treat them as such," Sess'thra said. She playfully winked at Shiverrig.

Khalkoroth stepped close to Shiverrig and took in his scent. The Duke knew battle lust when he saw it. Khalkoroth was eager for violence. This was a challenge.

Shiverrig remained composed. Sess'thra wedged herself between the two, purposefully placing her hands on Shiverrig's chest. She gave the pale demon a stern look.

"Remember Khalkoroth, *friends.*"

Khalkoroth gave Shiverrig a smirk. "Yes, friends."

"Now, there is one called Kasai that is of utmost importance to the Mistress," Sess'thra said. "He must be handled with care. You'll find his identity within the soul memories of your host." She twisted around, brushing her hard backside against Shiverrig before handing Khalkoroth an emerald amulet.

"What of this trinket?" Khalkoroth held the amulet in front of his face.

"Keep it for now. The Mistress said it would find its rightful bearer soon."

"And in the meantime?"

"I want you to stay here and watch for our quarry. I suspect if Kasai escapes our net again, he will make his way to the holy temple in the city. If you get bored, look to the priests for entertainment."

Khalkoroth's pink eyes shifted to Malachi, and a wicked smile curled at the edges of his snout. Drool dripped in long strands from his jaws. "That I will."

Shiverrig was unimpressed with the spectacle. He was more concerned about the loyalties and allegiances of the demons and devils entering his lands. "And what of you, Dax? You do not seem to have the mark of frost upon you," Shiverrig said.

"Duke Shiverrig, I am not from the Frost Plane of Gathos, nor any of the deeper layers of the Abyss. I hail from the Mortal Plane, same as you."

"He is a cambion, a cross-breed mongrel," Khalkoroth snorted with contempt. "The Mistress keeps him only as a curious freak."

"Cambion?"

"Yes, my dear Duke. I am what the pale demon says, a cambion. I was spawned from the union of a changeling demon and a mortal. My childhood was uneventful until my powers matured, and I began to shift from one form to another. I had no control as a youth. What child does?

"My mother and I lived in a small village. The townsfolk did not take kindly to my extraordinary ability. The village preacher labeled my mother a Sunnese witch. He tortured her within a sliver of her life, then put her to the fire. Her screams through the night were enough to turn any kind soul black."

"Yet, you survived."

Dax shrugged his shoulders, "I ran and hid."

"Of course, you hid like a coward. There's too much human in you. A true demon spawn would have destroyed his enemies. I would not have rested until I slaked my thirst for revenge with their blood," Khalkoroth snarled. He let the excited drool fall from the corners of his mouth.

Dax ignored the pale demon's taunts. "My mind was filled with fear. I ran into the forest and transformed from one animal to another. I blended into the woods with ease. The pursuit of the villagers was short-lived.

"I scraped out a meager existence in the forest. I tried to survive by thieving and hunting small game. I was not very successful.

Fortunately, a band of forest brigands took me in, they saw my ability as a gift rather than a curse. They trained me how to steal properly, and of course, how to kill. I excelled at the latter."

"And the villagers who put your mother to the fire?" Shiverrig's curiosity in the cambion's story was piqued.

Dax's eyes gleamed back at Shiverrig. "One-by-one, they turned on each other. I had them utterly convinced their loved ones had committed horrible deeds. 'More firewood!' they said.

"I took a certain satisfaction in hearing the pleas of denial and innocence from the preacher. This was some years later, after I had mastered my shape shifting craft."

"And so, we come to the present. How did you become Sekka's killer?"

"As I developed my talents, I realized I was better off on my own. The small band of thieves I ran with felt I owed them a debt and threatened to kill me. Perhaps I did owe them something."

Dax reflected for a moment. "Nonetheless, I killed them all. Of course, talents of my proclivity attract notice. Eventually, Sess'thra found me. She encouraged me to meet her Mistress. The rest is history."

"He has no loyalty. He moves with the wind. Cambions cannot be trusted," Khalkoroth growled out the words.

"Oh, and you *can*, my foul friend?" Dax laughed. "Why do you think the Mistress keeps you locked up in a little pearl?"

"Do not mock me, changeling." Khalkoroth's voice turned savage. The pale demon's pink eyes looked to the side as if distracted by another's words in his ears. Khalkoroth's face shifted momentarily to the visage of Daku, but then snapped back to that of the demon. The young monk was still fighting for possession of his soul.

"Come Khalkoroth. We have preparations to make. Dax is just teasing you," Sess'thra said. The commanding nature of her voice was at odds with her childlike size. Khalkoroth stomped off behind her with a frustrated gruff.

Good, good, thought Shiverrig. Khalkoroth's lack of control was something he could manipulate once he found the right levers to pull.

"He is the one to watch," Dax said.

"Indeed, he is."

13

SEKKA

Sekka brooded as she walked down barren corridors deep within the bowels of Rachlach Fortress. The binding Maugris had laid upon her was proving to be more difficult to unwind than she initially expected, and her latest attempts had left her in a toxic mood, much to the misery of her unfortunate slaves.

Sekka had cunningly crafted the magic herself, giving the finished summoning spell—and subsequent binding knowledge—to her trusted succubus, Sess'thra. She in turn, who was to deliver it to Maugris, in such a way for him to think he was the original creator. It was a simple thing to accomplish—mere child's play for Sess'thra.

It was a necessary precaution, since Maugris was incapable of weaving the correct path through the Amaranthine Barrier with his limited understanding of deep magic. Left to his own devices, he would have caused her to be torn to shreds, while attempting to pull her through the Barrier.

The spell was laced with loopholes and trapdoors she could exploit later. Maugris had discovered the obvious inconsistencies in the spell and removed them, as she knew he would. But the more obscure ones remained in place. Yet, countering the core magic of the spell was proving more difficult than she initially predicted. Could the Amaranthine Barrier have contributed unique threads that strengthened the binding portion of the spell?

She reminded herself that this had been the only way. If she tampered too much with any part of the spell, it would become unstable and corrupted, and cast her who knows where? In time she would divine the weakest thread within the spell, or within Maugris, and pull it. Still, it was an insult to her majesty that she was his to command.

Sekka entered her scrying chamber. A stand with a basin filled with water was located in the center of the room. The air was stale and heavy as if the basin's enriched waters had recently been used to speak to an ally or spy upon a distant adversary. Was Maugris watching her?

Maugris' obsession with her had become unbearable. The fool thought he was going to *allow* her to be by his side once the conquest of the Three Kingdoms was complete. Such were the hopeful delusions of mortals who overreached their abilities.

Sekka approached the stand and looked down at the basin with contempt. She loathed the need for such aid to communicate with her minions mentally, but until she was completely free of Maugris' binding spell, she had no choice but to use the tools at her disposal.

She spoke dark words in the language of Gathos and parted the water with both hands. The water turned to slush as it folded back over itself. Her fingers traced patterns in the icy film covering the surface. Arcane designs floated lazily in the air and disappeared.

"Show me Oziax." Sekka concentrated on the image of the lord, and soon the demon warlord appeared in the slush.

Lord Oziax walked, in his human form, through a crowd of her minions from Gathos. He held the regal stature of an aristocrat; finely polished and elegant features, high cheekbones and chiseled jaw. Long alabaster-hued hair flowed from his head and spread luxuriously over an oversized fur coat, unclasped and flowing open. The remains of arctic wolves, snow rabbits, and white-winter elks composed the bulk of his coat. The animals were frozen in place and added a macabre design to his mortal apparel. The antlers, claws, and teeth of the dead beasts jutted out from the fur coat like warped bristles. Under the coat, he had donned form-fitting white-leather armor, covered in strange designs and deeply engraved runes of brilliant-blue.

The massive rune sword, Eishorror, hung on his hip, sheathed in the stretched hide of an abyssal jol'goth. The encased blade radiated an intense cold, which froze the moisture from the air. A white trail of crystal flakes followed him as he moved.

+Lord Oziax, align your senses with mine. I want to enjoy the impending raid. My mood is sour.+ Sekka's thoughts invaded Oziax's mind.

+As you wish, my Queen.+ Oziax sent back.

Sekka felt the connection to Lord Oziax's position become stronger. The walls of the scrying chamber faded away to be replaced by hundreds of straight and tall Asher Pines with greyish, grooved bark and twisted branches sprouting clumps of long needles.

Late afternoon had turned to dusk across the Hoarfrost Mountains. The crisp air and fresh smell of pine sap offended her senses. Her mind was carried forward as the pine trees raced past her in a blur. She descended from the high plateaus and into the lower foothills where Blackwood Cotton trees, Red Chestnuts, and Bur Oaks grew in abundance. The stubborn deciduous trees still held on to their leaves, refusing to relinquish the colorful bounty to winter's grey sleep.

The musky smell of Autumn surrounded her. Crickets could be heard tuning for their nightly chorus. The forest floor was covered in a mulch blanket of red, orange, and brown. Sickening, she thought. Soon this land will feel the wondrous touch of Gathos' chill and be buried under ice and snow.

Lord Oziax now stood at the head of a demonic horde waiting inside the perimeter of trees that surrounded a small hunting village. He uttered a harsh word, and frost gathered on the ground under the feet of the horde. With a wave of his hand, the icy crystals crawled towards the village. A foul spray of mist followed and then swept through the village. The stench of lesser fiends and demons carried the odor of rotten meat and the coming of something worse.

Sekka peered into the village with Lord Oziax's eyes. She spotted an old goatherd leading five goats with a long stick. The man stopped short and staggered for a moment on unsteady legs before dropping to the ground, vomiting whatever sparse contents remained from the day's meal. His goats bleated fearfully and scattered.

Sekka's mouth watered with eagerness for the events to come. If only she could be there for the slaughter. She longed for something wild to chase. She loved equally the intoxication she felt when her victims realized they were doomed and the primal fear on their faces that followed.

Lord Oziax worked his demons into a wild frenzy with the promise of human flesh to rend and devour. Lesser fiends scurried between the legs of hulking abominations or jumped up and down on their backs. The larger beasts barked and snapped their jaws at the bothersome pests. The guttural language of the horde echoed through the trees. A wayward traveler would think the creatures of the forest had suddenly gone mad.

Just as the dire symphony of the horde reached its crescendo, it ceased with a word from its master. Lord Oziax was always one for theatrics. No birds chirped, or insects buzzed. Even the air between trees went still, holding its breath in anticipation.

Lord Oziax had become proficient at raiding the human villages, and the horde followed his orders with precision. If a lesser demon or fiend disobeyed his will, it was destroyed without question. Any challengers to his authority were met with battle, as was the way of demonkind. None were a match for Lord Oziax and his brutal blade. The loser's essence was obliterated and never again able to reform in the rejuvenation pits of Gathos. Such was his promise to the horde.

Lord Oziax barked out another command, and the horde raced forward. The forest trees provided a weak defense against the rampaging monsters. Ancient oaks cried, cracked, and fell to the ground with loud swooshes to the ground. Smaller maple trees exploded under the weight of the massive oaks in a hail of splinters and red leaves. The branches of thick chestnut trees shook and then shattered, tossing their serrated leaves into the air. The forest canopy resembled a thousand colorful birds dashing and darting into flight. Prickly ground bushes were uprooted, thrown into the air, and stampeded under hoof and claw.

Unnatural combinations of man, beast, and otherworldly filth, spawned from the Ice Plane of Gathos, raced out of the forest and into the defenseless village. The living nightmares unleashed horrific mayhem to those within their diabolical reach.

The villagers were overwhelmed with little effort from the horde. Those not killed by the initial onslaught of bloodlust, were herded to the center square by deformed, bearlike demons covered in thorny barbs. The demons held double and thrice-pronged spears, which they used to poke and prod the prisoners into makeshift holding pens.

Other demons with flat faces and birdlike beaks roamed through the holding pens. They placed iron shackles around the necks of the terrified townsfolk. The restraints were attached to long chains which traveled back into the forest mist, where they were held in the massive grip of a pink-skinned giant that rivaled the height of the younger trees.

Sekka knew this Gathos giant well, for he was the only of her lesser juggernauts whom she had summoned. Maugris would have no more until he brought her the Ever Hero. The giant beast was called Morteg the Despoiler in the mortal tongue. His upper torso was that of a man, but he possessed a boar-shaped head with enormous tusks that jutted from his oversized mouth. His lips were slathered in mucus, and ropes of drool dripped down his face to resemble a liquid beard. Morteg stood on four sturdy legs and his long tail was covered in glistening iridescent scales. It swished through the dead leaves and wrapped around the trunk of a tree.

Lord Oziax spoke to Sekka in his thoughts. +Shall we see what we have caught this day, my Queen?+

Even in his mortal form Lord Oziax towered over the villagers. He regarded them knowingly, as a victorious warlord eyed a defeated rival's followers. They would be fodder for darker deeds to come. He stared at the townsfolk with a gleam in his pale-purple eyes, satisfied with himself as he took in the plentiful catch. The villagers huddled in a mass of trembling flesh, holding one another in fear.

+Are you pleased?+

+Carry on, Lord Oziax.+

Withered and desiccated beings, the color of bleached bone, jumped into the pens. Their arms and legs were long and spindly. They wove through the terrified villagers leaving a trail of frosty footprints in the dirt. The demons weeded through the families and grabbed the children from their horrified parents.

The children were hastily corralled into a smaller group to the side, closely watched by grotesque demons resembling bulbous toads. These creatures, with their lidless eyes bulging from their spotted, grey bodies, seemed to see everything simultaneously. As the children screamed in terror, their gazes fixed on the slavering jaws and rounded lips of the ravenous beasts. Desperate cries for their mothers' embrace filled the air, but those who attempted to run were swiftly devoured by the toad-like demons in single, monstrous gulps.

+There's an elusive one.+ Sekka sent to Oziax. They both saw a lone villager slip between cottages. The man raced to a small group of villagers who had been previously undetected by the horde. He wore the short, off-white robe of a healer with a cobalt-blue monk's sash tied around his waist. He quickly reached a family huddled together on the porch of a small cabin.

+Apparently, we have found a true-believer.+ Sekka sent.

+The monk will not survive.+ Lord Oziax replied.

+Check him first, Lord Oziax. Then you may have your fun.+

"Fear not my children. The power of Aetenos shall prevail," the old monk called out so that all could hear. "We shall banish this dreadful host through His blessing."

Lord Oziax motioned to a beast handler and pointed to the monk. The handler unleashed a pack of six quadruped fiends covered in coarse, yellowish quills. The fiends howled in delight as they raced after new prey.

The monk saw the pack and swished his arms together in a broad, rhythmic pattern. The upswept leaves on the porch swirled at his sandaled feet and bounced off his brown leggings. The air shimmered around the family and encased them in a transparent sphere of blueish hue.

Three of the smaller fiendish dogs broke away from the pack and sprinted toward the isolated villagers. Their long jaws snapped together with strands of slobber trailing like ribbons from their gums. Mad hunger drove them senseless, and one after the other, they leaped into the air. The air sparked to life as each fiend struck the barrier protecting the villagers. The sphere flashed with bright-blue light, the fiendish dogs dissolving into black ash.

The remaining pack skidded to a stop; all abyssal creatures knew the toxic smell of divine energy. It was anathema to their flesh and held certain doom for lesser demons. The fiendish dogs backed away in frustration, thwarted from reaching their prize.

The monk held his ground and concentrated on maintaining the barrier. The fiendish dogs scampered along the edge of the aegis. One snapped at another, and the two fought until only one was left alive. The victor gnashed its teeth at its remaining brother.

Lord Oziax looked at the blood and carnage splashed throughout the village. Sekka could feel the satisfaction in his heart. He walked to the monk's barrier as the lesser demons and fiends parted before him in deference.

"The power of Aetenos shall smite you, as it did your cursed minions."

The demon warlord chuckled. "There is strength in your spirit and possibly more in your soul, but how long do you think you can last, old man?" Lord Oziax said.

Lord Oziax gingerly tapped the barrier twice and quickly removed his hand. He blew on his burnt finger and contemplated the wall of light preventing the fiends from their savory morsels.

"Such a distant song Aetenos now sings, if any at all," Lord Oziax said, absent-mindedly. He inhaled a deep draught of air and placed his entire out-stretched palm on the barrier. He lowered his head and murmured throaty words with complex syllables as he exhaled. The runes on his garments came to life. The barrier protecting the villagers faded.

Lord Oziax raised his pale-purple eyes at the monk. "What now, old man?"

"Thou shall burn in the Holy Fire of Righteousness!" the monk denounced. He jumped off the porch and into action. He conjured a pillar of fire that engulfed Lord Oziax. The fiendish dogs scurrying at the warlord's feet burst into flames and then cindered to ash.

The rest of the horde moved aside as they saw what the holy fire could do. The column of flame rose into the air and bathed the small village in divine light. The old monk dropped to his knees, exhausted from the release of so much fire xindu energy.

"The power of Aetenos saves us!" one of the villagers proclaimed.

"The Heavenly Mother and her Son of Light have protected us!" another said.

"Father Dante is a monk of the Four Orders?" a third villager said. "He never said a word."

A cheer of sorts came about from the villagers in the holding pen. Most were still in shock and awe of what they had witnessed. They stared wide-eyed at the column of flame. Then Lord Oziax stepped unharmed through the conflagration.

"Not today, I'm afraid," Lord Oziax said. He brushed at the smoldering furs to tap away any adolescent flame that threatened to rekindle. "Anything else?"

The old man's energy was spent. He looked up at the smoking figure of Oziax. Sekka saw defiance in the man's eyes.

+He will need to be broken, Lord Oziax. But see the youngling entering the square?+

Oziax saw a child walking towards the chaos instead of fleeing from it. The little girl rubbed her eyes and called for her mother between sobs. One of the prisoners in the holding pen saw her too. He pushed past a demon bear thing and sprang over the wall of overturned carts to rescue the young child.

Her sleepy eyes recognized him immediately, then grew wide as a pack of lithe demons with curved beaks leaped on his back and ripped him to shreds. Blood and viscera burst in the air as the villager struggled in vain against the demons. The child went down with less of a fight.

"Well, that was unfortunate," Oziax said, "but not unexpected." His voice was a rich baritone, and each word echoed in his throat with an animalistic growl. He paused to think of what a human noble might say in this situation.

"I'm dreadfully sorry for this bit of inconvenience, but your dear neighbor to the North, Maugris the Infinite, demands the pleasure of your company." The sound of malice in his voice mocked the pleasantries of his words. Lord Oziax could not keep the grin from his mouth. He savored the pungent smell of fear now reeking from the peasants.

"I am the Great Demon Lord, Oziax, High General of her majesty Sekka's Frost Legions, and Baron of the Frozen Wastelands of Thresh. I am at your service," he bowed deeply.

"What do you want with us?" Father Dante said.

"I mean to escort you safely through the high peaks of the Hoarfrost Mountains and beyond to Rachlach Fortress. There you will work to till the frozen soil and harvest the food for the army of the North."

"Maugris the Mad! You send our souls to oblivion. In the name of Aetenos, the Light Bringer and the Smiter of Darkness, I command you, begone!" Father Dante said. He did his best to stand. His commanding voice helped to stabilize the growing fear and moans of the villagers.

"I shall smite you, demon, as Aetenos once did long ago. We shall not be fuel for dark sorceries!" he said. Father Dante glared at the creatures surrounding him. The howls and screeches of the abominations grew louder.

+ They shall be a grand batch for the ice pyre. Such fear. However, the child was not enough. The defiant one brings them hope. Take the monk.+ Sekka commanded.

Oziax motioned to two tall demons with bloated midsections. Puss wept from their eyes. He then pointed at the old man. "Bring him."

The tall demons grabbed Father Dante with their long limbs. Rough, white hands secured the old man and dragged him to their master. They dropped the monk in a frosted puddle of mud at Lord Oziax's feet. The frozen dirt cracked and bit sharply into the monk's hands and knees.

"Why, oh why, must you mortals always make this more difficult than it need be? Aetenos is no longer with you. He rots in the deepest hole in the Mistress' Keep." Nearby demons laughed and nodded their cursed heads in agreement.

Father Dante glared up from the puddle of reddish muck and raised himself to his knees. "Begone! In the name of the Light Bringer and the return of his Ever Hero! Foul creature, begone!"

"Ah, now we are getting somewhere. You speak of the avatar of Aetenos. Yes? Could he be you, old man?" Lord Oziax took a small amulet from a pouch at his belt and held it over the monk's head. An emerald sparkled and twirled at its end, but that was all.

+He is useless.+ Sekka voiced in Lord Oziax's mind.

"Sadly, you are not the one. Well then, would you know where I might find this human hero with the soul of a demigod? Hmm?"

"He shall be with us when our need is greatest!"

"I would think that time is now, don't you?"

"Go back to the Deep Dark," Father Dante said. He slumped defeated in the cold mud. "He shall come."

Lord Oziax looked around the ruined village and waited a moment. He even held his hand to his ear as if listening. "It appears he will not come this day. More's the pity. For if you are not the Ever Hero, nor able to provide the information concerning his whereabouts, then you are little use to me."

A wolfish smile broadened on Lord Oziax's face. He unsheathed his terrible blade and held it even with Father Dante's eyes. An icy chill filled the air as frost fell from the vile weapon, and the nervous sweat dripping from the monk's forehead froze in place.

"This is Eishorror, and she is a most frigid wench." Lord Oziax swung the sword in a low arc and sliced clear through Father Dante's neck. The cut was so quick and precise that there was no blood. The old man's body turned blue and crystalized instantly. Lord Oziax deftly kicked the decapitated head into the air. A winged creature grabbed it mid-flight. The airborne demon glided to a nearby rooftop and consumed its prize.

A hush came over the villagers as they stared in disbelief as the body of Father Dante collapsed in the mud.

+A nice touch.+ Sekka thought. She was enjoying the show.

"Now, where were we? Ah yes, travel arrangements," Lord Oziax said. He turned to the villagers in the holding pen.

"Please, take us and leave the children behind. What could Maugris need with small children? They are but infants," lamented one young mother. Her tears ran through the grim on her face. Her dirty hands came together in prayer above her head.

"They will not survive the harsh passage north," sobbed another. She bowed and cowered in the mud of the pen.

Lord Oziax tapped his finger to his lip three times. "Indeed. The journey north would be a bit extreme for the youngsters. You make a fair request. And to show you I am a just host, I decree, the children shall remain!" Lord Oziax said. He dramatically swept his arms through the air in a grandiose manner. "Your prayers have been answered."

A glimmer of encouragement came to the faces of many of the villagers. Although their doom was sealed, at least their children would be saved. "Besides, they have a more immediate use," Lord Oziax said as he turned to the demonic horde behind him. "Enjoy."

The villager's eyes grew wide in disbelief. They watched in horror as the wretched demons pounced on their helpless children. A bloody mist floated like a crimson cloud through the square. The monsters left nothing but slashed and tattered clothing and red-stained dirt once they had their fill.

Oziax signaled Morteg the Despoiler to begin. The chains drew taut. The villagers were pulled to their feet and forced to march to their doom. The old and grief-stricken who could no longer walk were dragged.

A gangly and sinewy demon approached Lord Oziax as the horde left the pillaged village. His face bore the scarring indicative of advanced rank. "Till the soil, Lord? There is no soil in the North. It is frozen rock as far as the eye can see. The ground is barren."

"I thought it best to have something to entertain us along the way. We shall flay them one-by-one and mount them on posts marking our progress north. If the Ever Hero has risen, this should create a trail of carnage easy enough for that miserable soul to follow."

"And what of the quota set by Maugris? The sorcerer's demands were very clear."

"That petty magician shall have his share of soul-slaves to sacrifice in the name of the Mistress. We will have plenty to spare from the next village." Both demons laughed and followed the horde into the cold mist of the dark forest.

+Can you taste the sweetness of their dashed hopes, my Queen?+

+You have done well, Lord Oziax. You have entertained me well and lifted my mood. Your rewards shall be great upon delivery of the Ever Hero. I have something special planned for you once my prize is in my grasp.+

+Thank you, my Queen. I shall have reward enough when Eishorror takes the head of that miserable wrench, Maugris.+

Sekka severed the connection to Lord Oziax. Her vision returned to the stone walls of the scrying chamber. She smoothed the thin layer of icy film on the water's surface and traced new designs in the slush. It was time to see what progress her nemesis Zizphander had made, if any, towards reaching the Ice Plane of Gathos.

Sekka reached out to the minds of her border scouts. Only one remained. Fresh frost formed on the walls as Sekka cast her spell and established a connection to her minion, who answered her summons with dire news.

+What story of the borders? Where are the other scouts?+

+The Red Devil has taken his first steps into Gathos. The outer limits of False-shore are ablaze. The others did not survive Zizphander's fury.+

Sekka looked upon the desolation through her servant's eyes. Great rivers of magma flowed where thick ice had once laid dormant for thousands of years. The land boiled and bubbled like a sea of fire. Geysers of red magma erupted into the air, then fell back into the lava flow. Scalding hot steam whistled out the pending death song of her land. Zizphander had reached the outer borders of her realm and was circumventing the plane, creating a wall of fire around its edge.

Sekka took it all in with a calm reserve. He is taunting me. He means to lure me out into the open and engage him in direct battle. Time was growing short. She pondered his location for a moment. Why was she not notified about his exact movements? How had he reached Gathos so quickly without her knowledge?

She should have been warned. This was precisely the type of information lesser devils used to win favor or at least her attention. There should have been more buffers to slow him down, smaller skirmishes with allied devils as he passed through their realms. But there was nothing.

Betrayal within her dominion came to mind. But if Zizphander knew my present location, he would have already pounced on Furia Keep. There was a grander scheme being played, but by whom?

"Lord Oziax, you must be quick. Time works against Gathos." She spoke aloud, lost in her musings when Maugris interrupted her thoughts.

"Are you talking to my errand boy, Oziax? Has he the slaves I demanded?"

"Leave me," Sekka said. But she had no control over the sorcerer.

"Where is my army? And not this piecemeal rabble you insist is all you can bring me. I demand the great beasts of Gathos to lay waste to Baroqia. Where are the famed behemoths?" Maugris' impatience had reached its limits.

Sekka's hand deftly brushed through the slushy water and any remnants of the conversation with her scout. "You fail to bring me the raw material needed to fulfill your request," Sekka said with ease. "A Chaos Gate must be opened, and to do this, you must give me the soul of the Ever Hero. Only in this manner can I bring forth the greater beasts."

"There is no Ever Hero to be found!" Maugris screamed. "I have indulged your foolish whims long enough. My resources are taxed. The spies have found nothing. The Ever Hero is a myth! I have had enough of your excuses. I shall have my revenge on those who saw fit to banish me to this frozen desolation." He waved his arms and hands frantically as if to encompass the entire realm on the North.

"You are drained. It is clear from your complexion and disposition." The unconscious strain of fighting back Sekka's constant mental probing was exacting a high toll on the sorcerer. His skin was pale and drawn tight across the bones of his face. His bloodshot eyes were set back in dark hollows. Sekka reached out her hand to soothe Maugris' gaunt cheek.

His face twitched as if her touch burned his skin. His eyes flashed with madness. "Do not insult me with your false compassion!"

Sekka withdrew her hand. The hint of a smile peeked at the corners of her mouth. Not long now, she thought. The relentless riptide of magical currents she sent into Maugris' mind was wearing him down. Her mental barrage was slowly eroding his willpower and resolve.

The power struggle between the two foes was formidable. Maugris was forced to draw deeply from the well of eldritch energy to increase his magical resistance to her probe. However, pure magic was not inherent in humans, and it claimed too much of their life force as payment. Maugris' fate would be no different.

"What have you been up to?" Sekka said. Her words dripped with a mother's suspicion towards a naughty child. Could he be secretly communing with Zizphander?

"My actions and whereabouts are my own," Maugris said defiantly. He wore the guilty countenance of a conspirator. "Do not forget who is master, devil."

"I only ask in that I may assist you in summoning more demonkind. Your new wizard cabal does not possess enough strength to bring forth anything of merit from the Abyss. If you want to summon another who is equal to Morteg, then you will be forced to devour the life force of all your remaining wizards.

"What will you do when you have no more wizards? The greater juggernauts of Gathos demand a high tax, and you will have nothing of value to sacrifice. The powerful behemoths such as Cymeryes will ignore you." She watched him calculate possibilities, frowning as he realized she was right.

"The juggernauts will do. I must have all of them! And I want them now!" He smashed his fist into an open palm. "No more tricks. Do as I command, devil, or you will know my wrath."

"You cannot command me to do something that is not within my power to provide. I will tell you again. Only a Chaos Gate has the means to bypass the Amaranthine Barrier and transport the true power of Gathos into the Mortal Realm. This is the only way you will achieve your goal."

Her mind raced through possible scenarios. The combined energy of soul-slaves from any one of the great cities found in the Three Kingdoms would be more than enough to topple Zizphander. The remaining cities would provide her with a surplus of infernal currency. She would have power enough to bargain her way into the highest echelons of power in the Abyss, perhaps even a position among the Great Three.

Her imagination traveled beyond the Three Kingdoms of Hanna and into the broader world of mortals. If she could open a Chaos Gate, the potential for soul energy would be limitless. Nay, she would not demand a mere position among the Great Three. She would topple them!

As her lust for power grew, so did her excitement to inflict pain. She was tempted to rip the heart from Maugris' chest and feast upon it before his very eyes. Her arm was held in check by the power of the binding spell.

She returned to matters at hand. The invasion of Hanna must be quick. All would be lost if Zizphander attacked while her physical presence was still trapped in the Mortal Realm. She must have the soul of the Ever Hero. She must!

Maugris marched over to the scrying bowl and looked to the frosted water. The slush had settled, and nothing remained of the previous spell Sekka had cast.

"Do not pander to me. I grow weary of your excuses. Summon my army, or I will replace you in the most humiliating way. And you will never see Furia Keep or your precious Gathos again." Maugris stormed out of the chamber.

"Your time is short, magician. Very short," Sekka said through clenched teeth.

14

KASAI

"Master, why are we not being followed?" Kasai said. He took most of Master Choejor's weight on his shoulder.

"I suspect the enemy is busy checking the bodies of our dead. They are looking for something, or someone," Master Choejor replied. He spoke with more of a wheeze than a voice. "Now is our best opportunity to reach the lower levels."

"Let me grab a travel pack first. We'll need supplies."

Kasai returned promptly and the two monks fled through the smoky passages that led to the catacombs. They blended with the shadows like thieves in the night. There was no alarm that their passing had been discovered. "Lucky, lucky, lucky," Kasai whispered.

Eventually, Kasai heard the whistle of night air rustling through the catacombs like lonely ghosts. They hobbled into the moldy, subterranean chambers and disturbed a nest of mice. The small shadows scampered in a hundred directions underfoot. Kasai held his breath as the squeals of the red-eyed rodents echoed off the walls of the old passages. They turned a corner and the silhouette of the outer gate was in sight, their last door to freedom.

Upon opening, the small iron portcullis practically caterwauled from disuse. Kasai's heart beat faster. He gave the gate a quick shove to end its rebellious wail. He cautiously stepped out and did a quick survey of the area. The harvest moon was high in the night sky, bathing the entire grounds in soft blue light. Their way was clearly illuminated, leaving them naked to anyone who happened to look in their direction.

Kasai felt just like one of the frightened mice that had scurried for a proper hiding place. His senses were alert for sign of danger as they raced down a rarely trodden footpath and into a copse of trees. Like fugitives, they scampered low to the ground, wary of being spotted by hostile eyes.

Surprisingly, Master Choejor took the lead, albeit stumbling as he went, somehow managing to flawlessly navigate his way along the trail with unseeing eyes and unsteady legs. Soon they came to their first bridge.

"Master, the bells."

"Those who attacked the monastery will not know the song of the bells. They will assume it is nothing but the wind," Master Choejor said.

Kasai looked up to the monastery walls and then across the open gap. This was a very long bridge. He looked far below where the cliff wall vanished from sight.

"If anyone happened to look our way while we crossed..."

"The Boundless will hide our passage," Master Choejor said. Then muffled a cough as best he could.

"Just the same, we should traverse the underside," Kasai said. He looked closely at Master Choejor. He looked bad. The poison continued to leech away the Master's strength. The old monk coughed again; this time in the sleeve of his robe.

Kasai took some rope from the small travel pack he had appropriated from the monastery supply chamber. Luckily the storeroom had been enroute to the lower vaults that led to the catacombs.

"Master Choejor, I ask with great respect, will you allow me to assist you across the bridge?"

Master Choejor nodded once in agreement and offered no resistance. Kasai strapped his Master on his back and secured the ropes around his own chest. Kasai knelt down carefully to the lower side of the bridge and grabbed a handful of weathered rope.

"So this is why Master Dorje made us climb with rocks in our packs," Kasai said, hoping to add a little levity and calm his own frayed nerves.

They moved together like two awkward spiders buffeted by the wind. Fear of losing his grip threatened to break his concentration. Kasai grunted with each reach and grab. Somehow, he remained focused. Safety drew closer with each lunge and successful grab.

Midway across the span, Kasai came to a halt.

"I need to rest," Kasai said. "Are you ok, Master?"

Kasai hooked his legs between connecting pieces of rope and let his arms rest one at a time. Master Choejor's arms and legs were wrapped around Kasai's torso like a jungle sloth.

"I will be fine. Do not worry for me," Master Choejor said. "You have much of your father's strength. A bright spirit to move the body forward."

"With all respect, Master, I take after my mother. My father was a liar and a coward. A disgrace to those who looked upon him as their protector."

"Those are harsh words coming from the son of Jarei Ch'ou. I knew of a different man. One that gave of himself more than he thought of his own needs. Did you know your father was a great healer? He was able to blend his xindu energies together and use the unique energy to mend broken bones and cure the infirmed. It is a rare gift, though I suspect with the right training you would be able to do the same."

Training? What good was training when the entire monastery had been overrun so quickly? Kasai thought.

"Master, please do not refer to my father as if he were a saint. He abandoned us, my mother, and me when we needed him most. He ran away to save himself from those...creatures, instead of protecting us."

"Yes, Master Kunchen has told me the unfortunate story of how you came to us at Ordu. He was sorry he could not save your mother when he found you both, lost in the wilderness as you were. Her wounds were too great for even his skill."

"I know," Kasai said. He remained silent and thoughtful.

"Let us be on our way, Brother Kasai. The assassin may return with greater numbers when they discover our absence. They may already have our scent."

"I don't suppose you have any safety nets below us here, do you?"

"Not this time, my son. If we fall, we will fall for a very long time. Trust in the Boundless to guide your hands."

Luckily, the autumn winds held their breath, and the air remained still. Kasai and Master Choejor reached the far side and climbed back to solid ground undetected. A few steps later, they were under cover of trees. Kasai untied Master Choejor and lowered him to the ground. He placed the small travel pack behind the old monk's head.

"Rest, Master."

Kasai's shoulders and forearms burned from fatigue. He looked back to the monastery walls and saw tiny torch lights bobbing across the many bridges and moving along the edges of the cliffs. The monastery had been overrun and they needed to keep moving. Kasai knew they had been lucky so far but doubted it would last.

"They shouldn't be able to see us from here," Kasai said. He rubbed his arms to increase circulation. "Who would do such a thing to peaceful monks?"

The forest was alive with activity. Kasai noticed gashes in the trunks of nearby trees and traced his fingers along the grooves.

"What's this?" Kasai said then looked nervously into the wooded shadows.

"Vargru," Master Choejor said. He sat quietly. His head was tilted to the sky.

"Master Choejor?"

"The vargru mark their territory. This pack has given us fair warning. We are outside the protective boundaries of Ordu. We now trespass on their domain."

Kasai had been wary of enemy pursuit all night and worried that the poison from the assassin's dart would continue to hinder his Master's movement. He had hoped the shadows from the forest canopy would provide enough cover to conceal their location while he figured out what to do next. And now this. The vargru would not need sight to guide them.

"Master, we should move on. The enemy has made progress down the Eastern Slope. They will find the lower bridges soon."

Master Choejor rose slowly and nodded in agreement. Kasai inspected the festering wound and realized the Master would need medical attention very soon.

Kasai spotted a patch of peppermint and removed a handful of the bumpy, spade-shaped leaves from the plants. He offered a few of the bitter, yet flavorful leaves to Master Choejor. He took a few for himself.

"Come, Master. Let us put some distance between us and our pursuers." They moved at Master Choejor's pace through the trees and half-submerged boulders. Kasai offered his support whenever Master Choejor grunted in discomfort. Kasai suggested short rests whenever possible, although he felt the enemy's presence behind every shadow or unfamiliar noise.

Their garments were ill-equipped to handle Autumn's cold night air. Kasai chastised himself for not thinking to grab two heavier robes or a travel shelter to keep them warm and dry while they slept. As if on cue, the wind changed direction and blew cold air down from the mountains. It would only get colder along their journey to the Temple of Illumination in Gethem.

There was nothing for it now. He decided to risk a small fire to give them a bit of warmth. Kasai grabbed the travel pack and rummaged through its contents. The bag contained items meant for a few day's excursion away from the monastery, nothing more. There was a small clay bowl for eating and drinking, a small pot for boiling water, some waybread and dried jerky, a canteen, some flint and tinder, a fishing line with a lure, and a compass. He sighed. It would have to be enough.

He found a large, slanted rock, jutting out from the ground. It would provide enough cover to shield the firelight from distant pursuers.

"We are in luck," Master Choejor said with a half-smile. He pulled his knees to his chest and wrapped his arms closer around his legs, waiting for the fire to warm his body. "The night wind blows our scent downwind, away from pursuit."

Kasai looked into the direction they were headed. But what if something worse waits for us along this path? Upwards, through the loose canopy of swaying trees he saw a thousand shining stars in the dark sky. At least it wasn't raining, he chuckled ironically to himself.

"Just rest a bit, Master Choejor. I'll make you some tea."

Kasai gathered leafy herbs not far from where they camped. He was fortunate to also find wild ginger and wolfberry growing nearby. He put the roots and berries into a small pouch and returned to their makeshift camp.

Kasai placed the ingredients into the small bowl then ground them into a fine meal with a rock. Next came boiling water from the pot he had placed next to the fire. The elixir wouldn't cure Master Choejor, but it might ease his discomfort.

"Master, drink this. It will lessen the inflammation of your wound," Kasai said. He could smell the wound in Master Choejor's back. That was worrisome.

Kasai shook his head in disbelief as if things couldn't get any worse. Now he had to contend with vargru. He knew something of the creature's lore from his studies. The sorcerer, Maugris, or his witches or warlocks had mutated the animals of the forest and turned them into horrors to help lay waste to the frontier villages. The vargru were abominations driven to madness ... and they hunted in packs.

Kasai was roused from his musings by a distant screech. He looked at Master Choejor to see if he heard it too. Master Choejor sat quietly, enjoying his tea. Kasai strained to listen for another, but there was none.

"They won't bother us," Kasai said, mostly to calm his nerves.

He heard strange and exotic sounds, some deep and guttural, some high-pitched, clicking and clucking. The forest was saturated with noise. He tried to distinguish which if any of the sounds were threatening. His imagination played cruel tricks on his hearing. Nerves, it was just his nerves getting the better of him. He took a deep breath.

Then he heard the screech again. And then another, like the first but closer.

Master Choejor handed the clay bowl back to Kasai and leaned against a small boulder to rest. "I've always enjoyed this time of year the most. Such wonderful colors all around."

Kasai looked at Master Choejor with incredulous wonder. Colors?

"Master, we cannot rest now. I fear we are being hunted by more than just the attackers of the monastery."

Kasai began breaking down the small camp and gathering up their meager supplies.

"Yes, Brother Kasai, I too have heard the song of the vargru. They shall be along soon enough. But first, sit a moment more with me. Let us speak together of the Boundless."

"Now, Master?"

"There is always time for now, Brother Kasai. There is more you must learn before the end." Master Choejor paused for a moment. "Your mind is strong, but already too full of answers for one so young. This is what keeps you separated from truly understanding the Boundless. Perhaps even more so now."

"I am open to the Boundless, Master. I just wish I could see it."

"The Boundless if formless, yet you see it everywhere with your open eyes and your listening ears. You feel it in the temperature in the air, and the wetness of water, or the thickness of the earth. All these things are alive, and they speak through a universal language of vibrations. You need only learn to decipher their message as you did atop the pillars.

"When you do this, you will see, feel, and hear a different world. Silence your mind, and the melodies change."

"I understand, Master."

"Do you? I wonder. I sense little harmony with the alignment of your xindu energies."

"Forgive me, Master. I'm more comfortable trusting the strength in my body rather than something intangible or magical." Kasai said. He hoped that would end the conversation.

"Magical? Now you sound like Brother Daku. You both mistrust what you cannot control. The known is no more your friend than the unknown."

"Daku...How could he do those things?" Kasai shuddered.

"Brother Daku's journey was set in motion long before that dreadful event."

"But Master, the Way of Ordu should have prevented him from..."

"From what? Do you think the Way of Ordu has the power to sway a soul from its predestined journey?"

"Yes! If not, then what good are the lessons and the training?" Kasai looked at his Master in bewilderment. He sat back against the side of another boulder and rubbed his temples. "None of this makes any sense."

"Kasai's vision blurred, and he suddenly felt very weak. Disturbing images overloaded his mind. Daku was Kasai's spiritual Brother and his friend. He was a difficult person to deal with, but that was because most people didn't understand his code of friendship. You were either with Daku or against him, there was no middle ground. He demanded unconditional loyalty and respect. But to murder his Brothers? What could have possessed him to that extreme?

He saw his dead Brothers in his mind, and then the assassin...and...the alluring demon. He quickly shut her from his thoughts. His thoughts became a confusing jumble of images without meaning. The world he knew had been turned inside out.

Master Choejor was speaking. The tone of his words was soothing. Kasai became calm.

"We all have a seed within us that matures to fruition over our days. During the time we are given, the sapling matures and grows into the highest and strongest tree possible.

"The amount of water, sun, and care that is given to the seed will not change the type of tree that grows. Perhaps it will stunt or accelerate the growth, but it cannot change the nature of the tree."

"I understand, Master." Kasai lied. He didn't understand. Seeds and trees did not help him comprehend how Daku could have strayed so far from the path of the Light. There was a whirlwind of conflicting thoughts and emotions crashing against the walls of his sense of reason.

"Come, Master, let's be on our way."

Kasai did his best to push thoughts of Daku the Killer out of his mind. He had more pressing concerns to solve. Kasai needed to get Master Choejor to a healer that could counteract the poison in his blood. The City of Gethem seemed to be an eternity away. The weary monks pushed on for a few more hours before stopping for the night.

The deep forest never slept. Kasai could understand why. It was the noisiest place he had ever experienced. Night birds chirped and hooted, and an occasional wolf howled into the dark sky. The clicking sound of insects was relentless. Kasai felt as if they crawled mercilessly over his body. The horrible screeches persisted. Their wails sounding like mocking laughter.

Kasai's body ached. The grueling flight from the monastery had not been kind to his sore muscles. Kasai searched for sleep that his mind could not find. He drifted in and out of a nightmarish haze.

The events of the last twelve hours replayed over and over in his head. He saw the image of Master Kunchen flicker in and out of focus. He saw smoke and darts sailing towards him in slow motion. Ninziz-zida reacted in a blur of movement as the three sections that made up the staff flashed out to shatter or block each projectile.

Kasai saw in sharp magnification the one dart he had inadvertently deflected into his Master. He could see the poisoned tip in great detail as it ripped through loose robes and impaled itself into his Master's flesh.

He felt the suffocating weight of massive rocks heavy on his chest. The shifting image of Master Kunchen finally settled to the face of the assassin. It changed again to a mask resembling the face of Daku. His friend leered down at him while he was trapped under the rocks.

"I told you. But you wouldn't listen," Daku said. "Now look at me."

A rough hand took away the mask to reveal something else, something unnatural. Pink eyes filled with malice and hate stared back at him. Then the *thing* faded from sight.

15

DESDEMONIA

Desdemonia sat at the stoop of her small cottage. It wasn't much, but it was home, of a sort. The morning sun hadn't yet chased away the chill in the air. The skin on her exposed arms was like gooseflesh, but she didn't mind. She appreciated the sensation. She stretched out her legs and drew arcs in the dirt with her heels.

Blackbirds and robins chirped in the nearby trees. The leaves were well through the color shift, and every day more fell to the ground. She blew a rogue strand of hair from her face. She watched if fall back into the same place, then tucked it behind her ear.

"Another day in paradise," she sighed.

She was lonely. It was always worse this time of year. Autumn brought memories of brighter days learning her craft from her parents and playing hide-and-seek with the village idiot. He wasn't really an idiot. He just didn't have any magic in him. Not one bit. It was a rare condition amongst the Sunnese. But she didn't care. She liked him for who he was, not what he could do.

She could have found another village to take her in as a stray, but that would mean staying in Sunne, and more bad memories. She needed to move on and find a new life, somewhere away from the jungle. She would go someplace where there wouldn't be so many reminders of what she lost.

The fragrant blooms from the late Autumn flowers wouldn't let her forget. They came on the winds from the south and through the Sarribe Pass into Baroqia. The jungle found her and wouldn't let her go. Desdemonia couldn't escape her past.

She glanced to her right and saw three chickens pecking at stones at her feet. She rolled her eyes. "Rocks are rocks, you dumb birds."

She cast a simple spell, and seeds tumbled to the ground. The chickens clucked happily and enjoyed their breakfast. "Now, a little something for me."

She walked to the fruit trees growing in the clearing that made up her yard. She climbed the fig tree first and gathered a handful of the small fruit. "Maybe an apple as well." She hummed a tune as she gathered her breakfast.

She heard a telltale screech in the distance. It was far enough away not to be a problem. The vargru were only dangerous when then hunted in numbers. Maybe this one was just lonely too. She heard a rustle in the brush beyond the tree line. Something was out there, something big.

She put her hands on her hips. "Not now. I don't want to play. I'm hungry."

The rustling stopped. A heavy grumble came from the bush.

"If you're going to sulk, then I'm going inside." She waited a minute. "Fine. But you're staying outside this time."

Desdemonia walked back to the cottage to enjoy her figs. She forgot about the apple. Her little home was cozy, and she liked it that way.

"There was no room in here for that big oaf anyway," she said. She washed the figs in a bucket of water, cut them in half and drizzled just a bit of honey over them. She sat on a small bench under a small table. Her fingers knocked the figs back and forth.

"What do you think, Gauldi. Maybe we should move again." She spoke loud enough, so her voice projected outside. "I don't know. Where would we go? A city? Ha! Never." She popped a fig half in her mouth. "What is that tree-bark-for-brains up to now? Gualdumor! What are you doing?"

She went outside and noticed immediately that the birds had stopped chirping. She heard a second screech and a third. The vargru were on the hunt.

"When will they learn?" she said. "C'mon, Gauldi. It seems the old alpha wants to test my boundaries again."

Desdemonia ran into the forest. The trees across the clearing swayed aside as something large followed in her direction. Then whatever it was pushing through the trees vanished as if swallowed by the earth.

16

KASAI

K asai awoke from a restless sleep, covered in morning dew. He was shivering, his body was sore, and ached with fatigue. Kasai wrapped his arms around his body to keep from shaking. He lied to himself, saying it was from the chill in the morning air, not the dream. He looked over at Master Choejor and saw his skin was pale blue. *This shouldn't be happening*, he fretted.

"I'll get some more fuel for the fire," Kasai said to himself as he quickly gathered some loose twigs and leaves for kindling. When he returned, Master Choejor was awake. "Master, does your injury still bother you? I shall heat more tea. It will soothe your pain and help you regain your strength."

"Thank you, my son," Choejor muttered. His voice was soft and distant. "We must continue to the Temple of Illumination in Gethem. I must speak with Grandmaster Nysulu. Something terrible is upon us. Something bigger than the destruction of Ordu."

"Yes, Master. We will be on our way after some breakfast. Please forgive me for saying so, but your skin lacks the warmth of your heart. Something is not right."

"Fear not for me," Master Choejor said. He propped himself up to a sitting position. "I shall persevere." The old man grinned briefly as some of his old humor returned.

A breeze blew through the tree canopy above them. The thick branches swayed back and forth, releasing brilliant red, yellow, and orange leaves. The sunlight intensified their color as they spiraled down to the ground.

"They look like mid-summer lanterns," Kasai said.

"As with all things, their beauty shines true in the light," Master Choejor said. He wiped a trickle of blood from the edge of his mouth.

"All things, Master? You cannot also mean to include the evil that attacked the monastery, or what Daku did?"

"All things have their natural place in the Great Balance. When something is pure to itself and follows its natural way, you will see its truth. When you understand the truth of a thing, you can then appreciate its beauty.

"All too often, we are seduced by the Great Manipulator or evil, as you call it. Our emotions turn against us. Our bodies no longer listen to our will. Our minds play tricks on us, and soon we have become pawns to a darker power. We give in to the ease of its disordered desires. Thus, we surrender our light and become an instrument of darkness."

"I don't understand, Master. How can evil control the pure at heart?"

"Be mindful of the kinks in your armor, Brother Kasai, for we all have many. Evil searches for weaknesses to exploit and does so in subtle ways. We are most vulnerable when we are unaware of the manipulation. Beware the doppelganger disguised as truth."

"How will I be able to see evil for what it truly is, Master?"

"You saw the truth of the assassin beneath his glamour. That was a fine feat. Sadly, Masters Dorje and Kunchen could not see the truth before it was too late. Nor did I sense the changeling's presence."

"Changeling," Kasai whispered, scarcely believing the truth of what that word meant. All of this seemed unreal. However, the scattered memories of his earliest childhood told him a different story. The monsters were real. He looked hesitantly at Master Choejor.

"I don't know how that happened. I was scared at first and wanted to flee. But then I remembered the younglings. I knew they would need help during the battle. So, I went back.

"When I reached the inner sanctum, I saw the fires and broken bodies. I was closest to Master Dorje's chamber and sought his guidance. His Light had been extinguished when I found him. I am sorry I did not say so earlier, Master."

"I understand. I assumed as much from the assassin's bold words. Please continue."

"I saw death in every hall and room. I ran to find Master Kunchen. I saw him dead, as you now know. I knew you would be next, if not already dead, so I ran to find you.

"I realized I was weaponless as I ran past the Hall of Artifacts. I ran back to look for anything that would help, but all the weapons were locked in their cabinets. I noticed the ceiling had fallen over one case. My eyes watered from so much smoke, and I could not see clearly. Though I did not know it at the time, my hand grabbed Ninziz-zida. I tucked the collapsed staff into my sash and ran out of the room."

"Did you now?" Master Choejor said with surprising interest.

"Please forgive me, Master. Let me return the Fire Serpent to you now. I am unworthy of such a weapon."

"The Fire Serpent indeed. She is an unwilling ally if she is mismatched. The mere fact that you hold her freely speaks of a partnership between weapon and wielder that is rare. Keep her for now. You will find she is both a fierce weapon and a motherly protector to those she respects. Now, please continue."

"I barely remember it all. I ran into your chamber. Master Kunchen was there when he should not have been. I could not think clearly. But then, a warm calmness took me." Kasai paused to reflect on the clarity of that moment. "It was then that I saw the blackness come alive above Master Kunchen's head. You were bathed in amber light. I saw a sigil of the same hue floating above your head. I felt relief.

"The movement in the room slowed to a standstill. Everything shimmered with vibrant color. The darts fired at us became inflated, and the smoke seemed frozen in the air. Ninziz-zida acted of her own will and directed my movements."

"Interesting. Can you see my sigil now?"

"Yes, when I concentrate, but the impression is faint. It's more of a whisper now. I fear it has something to do with the sickness inside you."

Master Choejor sat back in contemplation.

"Brother Kasai, each of us possesses an inner sight that helps guide our steps and shows us the truth. Most of us are unwilling to use it, and we remain blind. I am quite baffled how you saw behind the veil so effortlessly. This ability is gained only from advanced training, which you would not have been exposed to at Ordu. Also, I have never witnessed an initiate having the depth of mental control to time-shift.

"Had I not heard your words of warning in my chamber and the subsequent outcome, I would not believe them to be true."

"Am I sick, Master?"

"Sick? Oh no, my boy. You are not sick. These are accomplishments few Reverend Grandmasters have attained over decades of study and meditation." Master Choejor chuckled. "And you speak of them as if they were commonplace. What it means and how it has come to pass, I do not yet know."

Fear crossed Kasai's face. He looked at the ancient weapon anxiously. "Am I being manipulated by Ninziz-zida's dark magic? Is that why this has happened to me? I have no love for sorcery or the ill-effects it causes those who wield it. It's unnatural. Please, take the Fire Serpent back. I don't want it."

Master Choejor thought for a moment. "I have never known the Ninziz-zida to grant any special abilities to its wielder outside of boosting the wielder's martial prowess. But she never accepted me as an equal partner. I shall meditate upon this and open myself to the Boundless for answers. You shall do the same."

And the matter was decided. The two monks sat in silence for a time, lost in their thoughts. Kasai stared at the compressed sanjiegun, wondering how any of this could get any worse. He needed something else to do, anything other than meditation.

"You should eat something to help keep your strength up. Please rest. I'll fix us up something before we continue."

After a small meal of way-bread and jerk, Kasai broke camp and the two monks trekked deeper into the wilderness. The sounds and smells of the forest amazed Kasai. Life was abundant here, but there was also death in the air.

Kasai and Master Choejor came across the carcass of a massive wild boar near the edge of a shallow stream. It had been dead for a time, but oddly enough, no other animals had come to feed on the remains. Kasai suspected he knew what had taken down the great brute.

The claw marks on the boar's flesh were the same as those gouged into the trees when they first entered the forest. The safe confines of the monastery seemed so very far away. There was savage danger here. Not far away, a howl shattered the daytime din and liveliness of the forest. A profound, unnatural silence dropped over the trees. Kasai and Master Choejor stopped along the path and listened.

In barely an audible whisper, Kasai asked, "What was that?" He tried to gauge the proximity of the clamor. *How close? Maybe a mile.* He figured the predators must be following along the same path they had traveled.

Kasai moved Master Choejor off the path and into the denser woods. Perhaps they could find suitable shelter or a more defensible position like a high rock, or a cave, or anything besides being caught on the open trail. A deep gurgle sounded ahead of them. Kasai pushed Master Choejor off to the right. They didn't take ten steps before they heard another menacing growl coming from behind a dead tree that had been felled in a storm.

A series of squeals forced Kasai to put his hands to his ears. He turned Master Choejor to go in a different direction, but again the hunters were already there, waiting. Kasai realized they were being surrounded. The vargru had found them and were closing in for the kill.

"Master, there is but one way we have open to us, but I fear this is by design," Kasai said through huffing breaths.

"Your instincts are right; however, we must continue to move forward. The numbers surrounding us are too many to overcome," Master Choejor said. "Perhaps there is salvation ahead where there is none behind."

"We'll need to run." Kasai knew the confrontation was inevitable. They would not escape the vargru. Kasai hoisted Master Choejor onto his back. He wasn't sure how fast he would be able to run, or how far, but he would run until he could run no more.

The wild chase began. Kasai used his peripheral vision to keep track of the vargru on either side of him. He caught fleeting glimpses of fangs and claws, ripping up trees and throwing storms of leafy mulch into the air.

Kasai's childhood nightmares came back to him in a wave of fear. He recalled his vow to protect those he loved, and this gave him renewed strength to run. He was determined not to lose another family member to creatures of darkness. But what hope did he have?

The vargru glided fast through the forest. Nothing seems to hamper the monsters' strides. Kasai had managed to avoid punches and kicks from his Brothers during sparring because of his agility and speed, but against these mutated killers, he was too slow.

Master Choejor's body jostled on his back. Every screech and wail brought the monstrosities closer. *Just keep running*, he thought. *Don't stop.*

Kasai's lungs were a fiery furnace filled with hot coals. His legs burned with fatigue. How much longer could he last? The vargru charged forward. Their pounding feet shook the ground. He narrowly missed stumps, rocks, and fallen branches as he ran. *When would one finally snag him and send them both to the forest floor? Just keep running.* He hoped an opportunity for escape presented itself before he was spent. But he doubted it.

The dense forest opened to a small meadow surrounded by sheer cliffs on three sides. The environment would be considered idyllic under different circumstances. Kasai knew they were trapped.

Two vargru erupted out of the woods a moment later. Each sprinted to either side of Kasai and forced him to run straight. They were as large as the bears of the deep forest. Their fur was patterned like camouflaged cats, and stunted antlers grew down their backs. Their heads tapered into the canine snouts of wolves.

Steep rock walls loomed ominously over Kasai, draining him of hope. Escape was impossible. He slowed down since there was no sense wasting any more of his strength. The vargru mirrored his steps. Each had five pink eyes that rolled in enlarged milky clouds. Yet, they did not attack.

Kasai's legs trembled from exhaustion and threatened to buckle beneath him. Master Choejor set himself on the ground. Kasai knew their only option was to climb the rock wall. Maybe alone he could scale the rock face fast enough to escape, but that was a big 'maybe.'

I won't leave Master Choejor, he thought. Somewhere in the back of his mind, he heard Daku laughing.

"Master, our path ends here. There is nowhere to go but up the rock wall," Kasai said. He frantically looked for an alternative escape route, but he saw none. "We will need to fight."

"Clever beasts," Master Choejor said. He extended his hands and rotated his body as if to discern the locations of the vargru. "I will deal with these abominations. Get to the Temple of Illumination in Gethem. Find Grandmaster Nysulu. Tell him what has happened at Ordu."

Master Choejor stepped forward to draw the attention of the two vargru. "Why are you waiting? Climb the wall now!"

Three more vargru bounded out of the forest. And lastly, one great beast entered the meadow. Its body was covered in twigs and loose debris. The alpha vargru bellowed out a high-pitched chortle to its pack mates, and they responded with submissive chirps.

The three vargru slowed to a leisurely pace and spread out. Their prey had nowhere to go. Kasai looked up the rock wall and then back to his Master. Master Choejor breathed in deeply and readied himself in a defensive position. But in truth, the assassin's poison had sapped too much of the Master's strength. He was sacrificing himself to give Kasai time to escape.

Kasai grabbed Ninziz-zida from his sash.

"No Master, we shall face this trial together, as one with the Boundless at our side." He thought he caught a satisfied smile from Master Choejor's mouth before more coughing brought blood instead.

Kasai would fight for as long as he could. He hoped his Master would be proud of him, but he held none for victory. There were too many of the enormous creatures.

All of Kasai's training was predicated on stopping the fight once his opponent offered submission. But this was different. Kasai could almost feel the primordial hunger from the vargru was over him like a wave of aggression. Fear traveled through his body and knotted in his muscles. His heart pounded in his chest, and his limbs grew weak.

As if sensing weakness, the two side vargru charged directly at him and lunged with splayed claws and gnashing teeth. One of Ninziz-zida's end segments flashed out with astonishing speed. It cracked against the skull of the first vargru, and then without hesitation, Kasai's body twisted so he could stab the butt-end of its other end segment into the eye of the second. The vargru drew back, reassessing their prey.

Kasai was amazed at the quickness of his attacks. Ninziz-zida hummed in his hands. It was as if the *sanjiegun* moved of its own volition and made his body follow. It created a protective barrier around him, then whipped out fast as a viper whenever a vargru came within range. Kasai felt a flash of hope but then realized the vargru had succeeded in widening the distance between him and Master Choejor.

Master Choejor had engaged the other three vargru. Somehow, he had regained some strength and was keeping the pack of unnatural horrors at bay. The Master's movements were fluid and effortless. He redirected the force of each attack away from himself, sometimes sending the frustrated beast headlong into the ground. Kasai stared in awe.

Ninziz-zida burned hot in his hands. Kasai stupidly looked at the weapon in surprise. He realized too late the sensation was a warning. White light filled his sight. The shock of the blow was like no other he had ever felt. Kasai was bent in half as his feet left the ground. A sharp pressure built in his side. Broken ribs. How many he did not know.

The air left his lungs as he hit the ground. The pain was excruciating. He knew that was it when a tall shape blocked out the light of the sun. He shut his eyes and waited for the sharp bite of the vargru to finish him.

"Kasai! Kasai!" Master Choejor said. "Stand if you can." Master Choejor stood over him. His hands glowed white-hot.

Kasai clenched his teeth through the pain. He held Ninziz-zida loosely in his hands and stood. Breathing was difficult. The vargru did not wait to pounce. The one closest to Kasai lunged into the air like a cannonball shot.

Kasai's arms thrust forward with the staff to intercept. The sections of Ninziz-zida miraculously aligned together into a rigid rod. The impact of the strike shook Kasai's arms and left them tingling up to his shoulders. The vargru fell, but slowly regained its feet. It shook its head like a dog in the rain.

Kasai struck again but missed his mark. He was no match for these unnatural predators. Fear was clouding his thinking and slowing his responses. Daku was right. He had never learned to do what was necessary to win. He always held back against his Brothers at Ordu. He never struck the killing blow.

Ninziz-zida changed back into three sections. Kasai spun the staff in such a way so that the outer parts created a broader, figure-eight patterned pinwheel. Master Choejor was not faring any better as the vargru attacked from multiple directions at once.

Master Choejor cried out in pain. Kasai spared a glance and saw that the old monk had fallen to his knees. Master Choejor tried to stand, but a second vargru shouldered into him, bowling him over. In a heartbeat, the third vargru had him pinned to the ground. The other two circled to enjoy the kill.

Kasai tried desperately to get back to his Master's side. He struck out widely at the nearest vargru. It dodged his blows and snapped at his legs. The other vargru jumped to the rock wall and climbed.

The beast leaped into the air, intent on attacking Kasai from above. Kasai saw the threat but was in no position to defend himself. He braced himself for the impact.

Three bolts of blue energy slammed into the vargru's side. Kasai almost stumbled in surprise. The shots were not enough to kill the creature but knocked it to the ground near his feet. Kasai wasted no time. He compressed Ninziz-zida into one hand and used the sections as a bludgeon. He hit the back of the vargru's head as hard as he could. The vargru's skull cracked.

Kasai looked to see who or what had saved him. A lone figure entered the meadow from the far right. She walked with the gait of a young woman. She was dressed in the colors of the forest and wore tight-fitted leathers with a hooded frock. She fired more blue bolts into the back of one of the vargru closest to Master Choejor.

Kasai took advantage of the distraction. He struck the vargru pinning Master

Choejor. Ninziz-zida flared with heat as the two outer sections repeatedly bashed and battered the monster's side. The vargru lunged at Kasai and swiped his leg with one of its massive paws. Kasai fell back to the ground. The vargru pressed the attack.

Kasai back-peddled like a crab. Then he kicked his legs up and over his body. He pushed off the ground with his hands, holding tight to Ninziz-zida's middle segment. He arched backward and landing in a standing position. The acrobatic movement momentarily transfixed the vargru.

Kasai drove the end segment of the staff down the vargru's throat. Ninziz-zida blazed with bright light. The vargru's eyes bulged as the end of the staff punctured through its neck. A warm sensation rushed up Kasai's arms, and he felt an odd sensation of gratitude. Kasai looked at the three-sectioned staff with amazement and no small amount of trepidation. Kasai wondered if the cursed staff was relishing the kill.

The vargru's mutated body collapsed to the ground with only its head remaining upright. Kasai pulled Ninziz-zida out of the monster's mouth. He dared for a moment to check on Master Choejor. Unbelievably, the old monk was slowly raising himself off the ground.

The alpha vargru barked out a series of high-pitched screeches. The vargru hovering around Master Choejor scattered and regrouped. The three younger vargru raced towards the woman. Two ran straight at her while the third circled to attack from the side. The alpha held back, waiting like an experienced general surveying the battlefield.

The woman went straight for the vargru. Her movement was more of a spiraling dance rather than a sprint. She moved her arms in rhythmic gestures while she twirled through the air. Kasai saw strange, autumn-colored runes trailing from her hands. The magic rose higher and twisted in the air behind her head. She acted if she didn't care about the danger closing in on her. She spread her arms wide, keeping her palms down over the grassy field.

The grass between her and speeding vargru trembled and convulsed. Both vargru leaped into the air. In the same moment, the living earth erupted between them, morphing into the shape of a giant humanoid. Dirt, grass, and flowers covered its outer skin. Thick roots spiraled together, then overlapped to make up its arms and legs. Branches and leaves sprouted from all directions across its vast bulk.

The earth golem snatched one of the vargru from the air with an enormous hand. It snapped its neck with a quick flex. The golem then twisted its body with incredible speed and caught the second vargru by its hind legs and hurled it across the field. The vargru somersaulted awkwardly through the air and landed hard with a loud crack. The golem turned to the alpha, while still holding the first vargru tightly by its neck.

The alpha moved forward slowly, sniffing the air and assessing the golem's strength. The golem let the dead vargru fall from his hand. The alpha snorted in some form of animalistic disgust. The arrival of the newcomers had stolen his advantage, and it called to its remaining packmate. The runt scurried to its leader, and both bolted into the forest.

Kasai breathed out a long sigh of relief. He saw the woman communicating with the earth golem. They both looked in Kasai's direction. It seemed they were deciding his fate.

The woman approached. Kasai's mind screamed out in warning, Wood Witch!

She was coming for them, probably to take as slaves or boil in a stew. He raised Ninziz-zida in defense.

"That's close enough. What do you want?" Kasai said. His ribs felt like they were moving on their own. He slumped to one side.

The golem roared. The rumble of its earthly voice vibrated through Kasai. The woman put her hand on the golem.

"That's enough, Gauldumor. Don't mind him. He can be a bit of a bully sometimes," she said. "Are you hurt?"

Kasai was surprised by the softness of her voice. "We are fine. We do not need your help."

"Kasai, it will be all right," Master Choejor said. He was finally up. He put a reassuring hand on Kasai's shoulder. "I do not believe the Forest Dweller means us any harm."

"Listen to him, Gauldi, not even a thank you," the woman said over her shoulder to her giant creation. "Of course, we don't mean you any harm, old monk. You're lucky I happened along as I did."

Kasai refused to lower Ninziz-zida. The Fire Serpent's section glowed a dull mauve. He had no trust of Forest Dwellers and their mysterious ways. Kasai felt Master's Choejor's hand slide off his shoulder. The old monk had dropped to the ground.

"Come now, boy. I can see your father is not well. Let me have a look at him." The woman took a few steps toward Master Choejor.

"Stay back! Do not touch him."

Gauldumor growled menacingly.

"Gauldi, hush. It's Kasai, right? I'm Desdemonia, and that big mud pie is Gauldumor. Kasai, listen, your father is hurt. I can help him. If I do anything unnatural, then you are free to strike me with your pretty sticks. Ok?" The woman took away the hood and revealed her young face. Black locks of thick hair cascaded down her back. "Do we have a deal?"

Kasai didn't say anything but didn't prevent her from moving closer to Master Choejor, either. Desdemonia waved her hands over the prone monk's body. Kasai smelled lavender and blueberries as a soft bluish glow lapped against her palms. She gently touched Choejor, and the flames caressed his body as well.

"Gauldi, help me roll him over," Desdemonia said. She examined him thoroughly and found the source of his sickness. "Oh, that's a nasty sting."

She uttered strange words and brought her hand down over Master Choejor's wound. The soft, blueish flamed turned dark.

"What are you doing?" Kasai said anxiously.

"Shh," Desdemonia whispered sternly.

White puss oozed from the wound, and then it closed shut. Desdemonia selected some reddish herbs from a small pouch on her thigh and crushed them on a nearby rock. She collected the pulped pieces into her hand, spit on them, then squeezed her palm tight. Again, the soft, blue flame engulfed her hand, and the sweet smell of berries wafted through the air.

She put the paste on the closed wound and bound it to his body with sticky leaves from a different pouch. Desdemonia looked up at Kasai with kind eyes as dark as coal.

"See, that wasn't so terrible," she said. "The wound is closed for now. He will feel some strength return. But he needs rest. Whatever is infecting him is beyond my cure craft. Now, let's have a look at you." The seriousness had left her face, and a pleasant smile took its place.

Kasai looked at Desdemona in both awe and suspicion. "You're a...that was Elemenati magic," he said. He took a step backward with a frowned.

"I can see by that unfavorable expression you do not approve," Desdemonia said. She had the apathetic tone of one who had endured this conversation too many times before. Her hands rested on her hips. "I told you, Gauldi, another day in paradise."

"You made...that," Kasai said. He took another step backward. His ribs screamed in agony. He scrunched to one side to lessen the pain. It didn't work.

"Yes, I called upon the ancient pacts between the Earth Goddess and First Dwellers to raise Gauldumor. Right now, the only thing saving your father is the healing power of the forest."

She spoke in a melodic, richly accentuated voice. Kasai couldn't place it. Perhaps she was from a jungle tribe in Sunne. How she had come to pass the Sarribe Mountains was a riddle. He looked upon his rescuer with new eyes, and his pulse quickened. She was beautiful.

Based on the books he studied in the monastery library; her clothes were form-fitting as befitted the traditional attire of a Forest Dweller. They were made of a flexible material that allowed her to move silently past trees and bush with nothing loose to snap a branch and give away her position. Bands of deer hide crisscrossed her legs and wound up her torso, keeping the material snug to her body. Charms and thin pouches were woven into the straps for ease of access. Her outer garment was sleeveless and revealed arms with the muscular definition of one who was trained to defend herself.

Desdemonia's eyes briefly caught the light of the rising sun. The color shifted from dark charcoal to smoldering amber. Kasai had never seen eyes so bright before. He was mesmerized by their inner fire. He stared at her, dumbfounded, the pain in his side forgotten.

Her slender feminine shape stirred a queer feeling in his gut. He was unsure why his heart thumped against the walls of his chest. He tried to say something to break the silence, but his mouth was bone dry.

It wasn't as if he had never seen a woman before. While at the monastery, he had studied numerous anatomical diagrams of both men and women. The images showed meridian lines and primary energy zones, as well as pressure points and vulnerable nerve clusters.

All of that was forgotten as he looked upon the supple and sinuous figure of Desdemonia. He saw strength in her body as well as a feminine allure. Kasai noted the marks of old scars that traveled up her forearms. She was a fighter and a healer, just like the monks of Ordu.

Desdemonia was no village damsel lost in the woods. She was a daughter of the forest who was one with the wilderness. Somehow, that made him nervous.

Kasai stared at Desdemonia's comely, yet bewitching face. Her golden gaze drew him in for a second time, and he was spellbound by her smart, bright eyes. Eyes that demanded his attention and made him uncomfortable. She smiled at him, and his insides leaped.

"Something to say?" Desdemonia said with a raised eyebrow.

The wind shifted and pulled at her long raven locks. Thick strands of hair swam before her amber eyes and cast them back into shadow. The pain in his side returned and snapped him out of his reverie.

"You are a witch then?" Kasai said, not knowing what else to say. He quickly added, "And he is not my *father*. My father is dead and gone."

17

SHIVERRIG

Duke Shiverrig leaned back against the wooden chair at his desk and read from an oversized book. The worn leather cover felt good in his hands. It was old and familiar. The book was filled with the historical events of the Shiverrig Clan, dating back to when the first Aj-Kahun, Baroq Shiverrig, led his burly, pale-skinned warriors across the Eastern Ocean. They arrived on sleek wooded ships trimmed with sail and oar; intent on conquest.

It was Baroq Shiverrig's vision to tame the wilds of new land and bring its native people to heel under his reign. The Aj-Kahun ruled with absolute power and imposed his will with sword and spear. He conquered all that dwelled in the hills and forests, between the cold and jagged Hoarfrost Mountains to the north, and tall peaks of the Sarribe Mountains to the south.

Duke Shiverrig turned another page. A crude diagram extended over two pages of what was now known as the Kingdom of Baroqia. The able-bodied men of the middle lands were conscripted into his warband, and soon the warband became an army. The women and children were used as slave labor to service his war machine or tend to the farmlands, ensuring the harvest came in to feed his warriors.

Shiverrig traced the borders of Baroqia then extended his path into the Kingdoms of Sunne and Trosk. He exhaled in frustration.

"The pages of my life will not be meaningless. Baroqia must grow," he said. He turned another page.

Gangs of ogre were discovered in the deep forests and initially thought to be perfect fighters due to their size and strength. This notion fell out of favor when the great brutes were assimilated into the army. The body of an ogre was ripe for war, but their bloodlust and lack of discipline made them a liability in battle. The results were catastrophic, and most were slaughtered or used in the slave pits for sport.

The Aj-Kahun's rule remained uncontested for decades. His armies swelled to vast numbers and were filled with colossal soldiers that defied understanding.

Rumors spread that the great conqueror and his scions had intermingled their bloodline with that of the ogre slaves. It was pure speculation, and any who spoke out against the newly appointed King Shiverrig were rarely heard from again.

New bloodlines were introduced into the population, and over time the size and stature of the army normalized. Yet, the Shiverrig scions remained as giants amongst men.

"Better times," Shiverrig said.

He closed the book and placed it on the desk. He stood feeling quietly agitated as if he wanted to be in several places at once. He abruptly left his study. Things were taking too long.

He reached the sparring chamber. Twenty of his elite soldiers were already in the room. Shiverrig was taller than most men with a perfectly proportioned physique. His broad shoulders and thick legs supported the massive slabs of packed muscle across his frame. He moved with the grace and skill of a mountain cat.

Practice swords and shields clashed together. The clatter of a disarmed weapon hit the stone floor and skidded to his feet. Shiverrig picked it up and walked to the central mat. He stood barefoot, wearing loose pants and a thin shirt. His men, however, wore padded armor consisting of quilted layers of cloth and batting. He drew in a breath to center himself.

"Begin," he said.

His opponents came at him one-by-one or many at a time. It didn't matter. Gerun Shiverrig was a brute. He never held back, always being the aggressor. He reigned vicious blows down on his opponents with the sword or his bare hands.

His soldiers were systematically dispatched and sent sprawling to the floor. He had already laid low a dozen men when Sess'thra sauntered into the room. She wore soft leather boots and leggings. The vest she wore, loosely tied in the front, barely contained her alabaster flesh. She propped herself up against the weapons rack.

"I see the steward has finally found you something appropriate to wear," Shiverrig said. He was not thrilled to see her here. He knew his men would quickly fall under her seductive spell. They were useless to him if they were distracted. Their efficiency in training would diminish, and he had barely worked up a sweat.

"Clothing is such a bother, yet Sess'thra still obeys her master," the succubus said with a crooked smile. "Seems the mighty Duke Shiverrig does not have much of a challenge this day."

She picked up a blunt dagger and twirled it in the middle of her palm. "Perhaps I should call Khalkoroth for playtime. He would be happy to oblige you."

"Call your pet abomination, then. I could use a good brawl," Shiverrig said.

In truth, he wanted to know more about how demons fought. Their outer strength was apparent enough, but was that magically enhanced? And how did they fare without the use of deadly poison? He would need to consult with his mages, and possibly have them create a charm for him for both scenarios.

Sess'thra pouted. She threw the blunt dagger fast into a dummy target. The blade struck what would have been the heart of a real man. It managed to stay embedded in the practice doll. The succubus sashayed up to Shiverrig. She reached out and wiped a bead of sweat from the side of his rough face.

"And here I thought you would ask me to dance." Sess'thra gave him another pout while her tail twitched seductively in the air. She backed away with outstretched arms. "As you can see, I am now unarmed."

The Duke's men collected in a ring around the two. Most were rubbing bruises or sore muscles, while some stared helplessly at the succubus. The challenge had been declared, that much was clear. They waited eagerly for their Duke to respond.

Shiverrig decided a tussle with the succubus could work to his advantage, and it would be a good lesson for his men. They all needed to understand their uncommon allies' strengths and weaknesses. He walked away from Sess'thra and placed his practice sword on the weapons rack.

"I am unarmed as well, but how do I know you do not come here bearing your Mistress' gifts?"

"You don't. But be at ease, the Mistress has not informed me of any recent slights from Gethem or its Duke. This bout is purely for my pleasure."

"Grappling only," Shiverrig said.

"Until submission," Sess'thra purred.

"Then, let us dance." Shiverrig took a fighter's stance and waved Sess'thra forward. He remained in the center of the sparring mat while she rounded his position.

Her lithe figure was like a child compared to his massive build. She looked at him in admiration and awe, but that was just a feint. He had observed her in the battle against Grandmaster Nysulu. She was a handful, but how deadly was she without the aid of poison or magic? That was what he intended to discover.

Sess'thra launched herself at Shiverrig with a kick to his midsection. The Duke caught the blow in both hands with ease. He knew something more was coming and was ready when she twisted out of his grip and swept her tail across his calves. His sturdy legs withstood the impact of the blow. His men cheered.

"I like a man with strong legs." She gave him a playful wink.

Shiverrig moved fast to counterstrike. He grabbed Sess'thra's right arm and twisted it around her back. She arched backward and laid her head against the Duke's chest.

"An enticing position," she remarked. Her free hand playfully traveled up his left leg. The Duke pivoted and shot his knee out and down to the backside of Sess'thra's right leg. The move forced her to the mat. Shiverrig followed her down.

Sess'thra folded with the momentum and twisted the two into a roll before hitting the floor. The Duke found himself on his back with Sess'thra's backside lying over him. He involuntarily became aroused with the weight of her body draped over his.

"My, my, my, you are full of surprises," Sess'thra purred.

Don't give in to her tricks. She is just trying to confuse you into making a mistake, he thought. She twisted out of his arm lock and twirled to mount his chest. Her crooked smile returned. Shiverrig grabbed the loose fabric of Sess'thra's vest from behind her back and pulled. The succubus somersaulted acrobatically through the air and landed in a standing position. Shiverrig drew his legs back and leaped to his feet.

Shiverrig rushed Sess'thra. She jumped into the air to avoid his tackle. He caught her by one leg and slammed her back to the floor. He pounced upon her, grabbed her wrists above her head, and held her arms down with his knees. His men cheered again, but he knew the succubus was toying with him. She was making this too easy and enjoying the sexual provocation of her actions.

"Shall I submit here, or would you like to continue this in private? Trust me, I don't mind being watched," Sess'thra spoke loud enough for all to hear. Her tail twitched in the air behind him. A page cleared its young voice.

"My apologies, my lord Shiverrig. I have news from the City of Spires."

Shiverrig swiveled his head to see a page standing in the doorway. His spies had returned. The outcome of this bout could wait. He released Sess'thra and hurried from the sparring chamber.

"Summon Malachi. I'll want his input," Shiverrig said to the page.

"Who's next?" Shiverrig heard the succubus say as he left the room.

Shiverrig went directly to his strategy room. It was perched at the top of a high tower within the main castle walls. A sturdy table sat central to the chamber, with a sheaf of paper, an inkwell with a pen for written decrees, but no chairs. The Duke preferred to stand while deciding the fates of those who fell under his rule.

Ten arched windows, positioned to spiral around the inner wall, added the cleanliness of natural light instead of candles or torches to the room. Somehow it made Shiverrig feel pure when bathed in the outside light.

The city stretched out beneath him. Gethem was the first walled encampment that grew into a town and then into a thriving city. It was the hub of commerce for Baroqia. Ports filled the coastline of Gethem; ships from the Three Kingdoms came with their unique wares, leaving with goods bound for markets beyond.

Gethem bore the gritty marks of its history on every street corner. The city's narrow alleys and bustling markets were often thronged with characters of dubious repute, yet there was an unyielding honesty about them rooted deeply in their proud heritage. Every citizen of Gethem could recount their ancestors back to the original bands of conquerors who had claimed these lands. Such a legacy fostered a fierce loyalty to their own, making them wary of outsiders.

Amidst these imperfections, Shiverrig found a resilient spirit in his city. The populace adhered strictly to the edicts of their Duke, a testament to their enduring allegiance. In Shiverrig's eyes, Gethem deserved to remain the capital of Baroqia, a bastion of tradition and strength. However, the political tides shifted when House Conrad ascended to power, relocating the capital to the more picturesque and affluent city of Qaqal.

The new capital, with its lavish apartments and tranquil views of undulating hills and dense forests, appealed to the sensibilities of the nobility. The elite preferred the sanitized beauty of Qaqal over the industrial soot and labor of Gethem. From their lofty perches, why should the nobles spare a thought for the toil and troubles of those below, as long as their wealth—measured in overflowing coffers of gold and silver—remained untouched by the struggles of the common folk?

"They're all soft," Shiverrig scoffed.

The image of overflowing coffers reminded him of House Conrad's treachery. The nobles had so easily been manipulated with the promise of gold. Damn Maugris and his wayward spell! A storm of passion swirled in Shiverrig's heart.

He turned from the window of the strategy room as Malachi entered with a stocky man named Pathias. Shiverrig had been waiting for weeks for a reliable report from Qaqal. He was concerned about the lack of information flowing to him. "What news, Pathias? Be direct," Shiverrig said without pleasantries.

"King Conrad has decreed Baroqia will take up arms against the North. He will soon call upon the four Great Houses to bring their respective portions of the Five

Armies together in Qaqal. The individual armies will be dismantled and consolidate into the newly named King's Army. The king will bestow a temporary title of Second General to you, Lord Fritta, and Duke Manda.

"He will then divide up the armed forces into new legions and grant leadership as he sees fit. Rumors fly that Baron Rokig will be named First General of the King's Army. He will be assigned ten thousand men, mostly coming from the Standing Army of Gethem. I have heard he will order them north and east to secure the outer territories. It is uncertain what roles you and the remaining lords will play."

"Of course, Baron Rokig, the king's lackey. I would expect no less from that spineless sycophant. Continue," Shiverrig said in a calm tone, yet internally the storm in his heart raged with new fury.

"Each Lord will retain a token host at their keep, enforcing the king's law, although King Conrad will soon demand the presence of the Knights of Gethem in the Capital City to bolster his personal security." Pathias bowed. His report had ended.

"Why now? What has happened to change the king's stance on Maugris in the North?" Shiverrig's mind raced to potential betrayals, and those that might benefit as House Shiverrig grew weaker.

"That is all I presently know, my Duke," Pathias said, bowing once more.

The Duke paced the hard floor of the circular chamber. "He would dismantle my standing army and spread my troops across Baroqia. It is a bold move and one I would not expect Conrad to make on his own." Shiverrig pondered for a moment. "Who is advising the king? He knows I will not surrender my troops as willingly as Baron Rokig."

Malachi walked to a window with his hands clasped behind his back. "This is precisely why he does it. The king will force you to play your hand for power but on his terms. He gathers the kingdom's armies to him in case you strike," Malachi said. "If you agree to his demands, he will bleed your strength slowly. House of Shiverrig will become a frail husk of its former glory. A memory to be scattered in the wind."

"Spare me your poetry, Malachi. It's exactly what I would have done to him if I had the favor of the other Great Houses. But why now?"

"My Duke, you have been rather verbose with your ill-will towards the rule of House Conrad of late," Malachi said. He raised his eyebrows as if this was an obvious statement.

"He's scared," Shiverrig said. "He needs something to solidify his rule. A war would ... "

Sess'thra walked into the strategy room, uninvited, cozying up to Shiverrig. "Your men bore me," she cooed, walking her fingers up the duke's arm. "They break too easily." She winked seductively at Malachi as her hands massaged Shiverrig's bare, muscular arms.

The Duke ignored the remark. He peeled her body off his as if he were removing the slick membrane of a sticky fruit. He was not in the mood for her games. "The timing is not quite right to crush Conrad. I have enough men in key positions within the noble houses, but not enough to sway the balance of power. I cannot strike without the alliance of either Duke Manda or Lord Fritta. I need their men if I wish to hold the throne."

Shiverrig paced across the small chamber.

"I could promise Duke Manda the Baron's lands and its holdings in return for his assistance. It might be enough to sway him. There is no love lost between the two, and he would become the second richest House in Baroqia.

"Lord Fritta has always been a wildcard. I'm not sure where his alliance lies. House Fritta will watch and wait. Of the two, I trust and respect Fritta more. He honors tradition."

The Duke turned to Pathias. "I need to know when Conrad will move his troops against Maugris. Get me the routes of supply lines he intends to run. Have the heavy war engines been mobilized outside the city gates yet? What numbers will he keep in reserve behind the city walls?

"Speak to your brethren inside the walls of Lords Fritta's and Duke Manda's Keeps. See if either will acquiesce to the king's demands or resist. I suspect Duke Manda will go along willingly with the king. His ambitions go no further than the easiest way to fill his coffers with more gold. He will surely finance the war effort, and therefore will follow whatever the king wishes. Also, have your shadow men keep their eyes and ears open for dissenters against our House in Gethem. I want names and family connections."

"Yes, my Duke. It shall be done." Pathias bowed one last time before departing the chamber.

Sess'thra moved in front of the Duke. "Tread lightly, Duke Shiverrig. Now is not the time for heroics and hurt pride. The flow of Maugris' plans must not be interrupted. It would not end well for you to change the outcome of his war."

"I care not for the Mad One's desires," Shiverrig said. He took a step to the side of Sess'thra. "I cannot allow Conrad to continue on this course."

"Then let me say it a different way. My Mistress would be most displeased if you altered the events now set in motion. There are other moving pieces whose success or failure depends on the completion of your tasks." Sess'thra moved back in front of Shiverrig to make sure he fully understood her message.

"Are you threatening me?" Shiverrig's outward calm demeanor evaporated. She stood her ground against his fury, which caused his desire for her to increase. He wanted to break her.

"I am merely stating the obvious consequential events." Sess'thra's alluring stare had him captivated. Shiverrig could not look away.

"My Lord, perhaps we have overlooked an interesting partnership. The influence of the Demigod of Change has brought about a new radial faction called the Cult of Shokuei. They follow the teachings of Mor and are rising in prominence in the outer cities and villages," Malachi said.

"The time of war grows near. It is time to bring your pieces of power to their proper places on the board," Malachi said. "The Cult of Shokuei would be a valuable tool to create unrest from within Qaqal and the outer townships. Their influence could have a profound effect on the nobles backing the king."

Shiverrig turned his head towards Malachi as if hearing him for the first time. Sess'thra grabbed his chin and forced him to look back into her purple eyes.

"You must commit now to the higher ideals of the Ice Queen or choose to be fodder for Lord Oziax's demon horde. And I wouldn't want the latter for my dear Duke." She pressed close to Shiverrig. "The Frost Legion shall soon arrive, and the frigid tide will flow."

"The Shiverrig Clan tamed these lands, and I shall not dishonor my ancestors any longer. The rule of this false king must end. I am the strength and might of the land, not House Conrad." He pressed his finger down on Sess'thra's forehead. "How could you understand such a thing as honor, demon?"

"The concept is not so different, though *honor* has little meaning in the Abyss; power suits the Infernal and Ice Planes better. But do not mistake this idea for mere physical strength. Indeed, cunning and deception are equally vital, serving as the true measures of gaining what one desires."

Shiverrig felt the pliable form of Sess'thra body press forcefully against his. Her figure melted around his body as her arms and hands wandered up his spine. His desire for her rose, and his body responded. Shiverrig saw Sess'thra in a new way. The succubus was wise, and she wanted only to serve her master. He could almost taste her desire on his lips.

"Sess'thra, you have a valid point." Shiverrig turned his head to Malachi. "Send a squad of loyal knights to Qaqal as an honor guard for the king. Make sure they keep me informed. That will be all." Shiverrig looked back to Sess'thra, not bothering to watch Malachi leave the room or caring if he did. He returned her embrace, much to his surprise.

His eyes devoured the succubus, while his mind played through different ways to possess her. She looked up at him, longing for the attention his body promised. "Are you done playing the disparaged son of a twice-dead king? We have unfinished business together."

Sess'thra climbed up Shiverrig's chest and kissed him hard. She bit down on his bottom lip and drew blood.

"You do enjoy tormenting my Archvashim," Shiverrig said when he pulled away from her kiss. He wiped a few drops of fresh blood from his mouth. He lifted Sess'thra's vest over her head and dropped it to the floor. The afternoon sunlight lit her alabaster flesh in warm hues.

Shiverrig devoured her breasts. He barely noticed when she removed his pants or when she removed her own. The Duke swept the contents of the table to the floor. Her legs dangled over the edge when he mounted her.

Sess'thra's nails dug into his back and bit deeply into his shoulder. She bucked under his weight and drove him deeper between her legs as he climaxed. Ecstasy filled his body as he filled her with his seed.

It was soon over. Shiverrig fumbled to collect his clothing. His thoughts were jumbled and hazy as he dressed. Sess'thra slid off the table with a cunning smile on her lips. "I see before me a lordly Duke among the immortals of Gathos. There is strength in you, Gerun Shiverrig. But first, you must bow to the rule of Maugris and the Mistress. Do this, and great power awaits you. The Three Kingdoms of Hanna is only the beginning."

Shiverrig's vision spun. He heard himself talking but wasn't sure of what he was saying. "There is wisdom in your words, Sess'thra. I will honor my arrangement with the North. I will not alter Maugris' timetable." He sounded like a drunken cur. The room seemed to shift with each step he took.

"I'm glad you have come to your senses, my Duke. Now, if you'll excuse me, I have an orange-robed fly to catch." Sess'thra blew Malachi a kiss and strolled lightly out of the room. She didn't bother to dress.

The effects of rutting with Sess'thra wore off soon after she departed. His mind cleared. "I'll play your game, for now, succubus." Shiverrig knew wars left armies weak and depleted, no matter the victor. He would hold back his elite forces and use the rest sparingly until he was assured of one side's victory over the other. Threats and false promises did not concern him. In the end, ultimate rule would once more belong to House Shiverrig.

18

SEKKA

The strength of a summoning spell—and its subsequent bond of holding over the summoned—adhered to a straightforward tenet; the summoner must always maintain control of the magic. The spell creates a contest of wills between the two opposing forces; one to maintain dominance, the other seeking to escape. No creature, whether infernal, divine, or otherwise desired to be controlled by another. It's the natural way of things.

Maugris was a capable sorcerer, but his strength was finite. He was only mortal, after all. The depth of his spell-craft was shallow when compared with the abilities of an infernal-born devil. Maugris lacked the patience to properly construct spells that were impervious to improvisation or suggestion. His obsessions created mental distractions, which left his spells open to attack from a more advanced spellcaster, such as herself.

She waited until Maugris had depleted both his magical and mental endurance and then stealthily wove thin threads of corrosive magic into the invisible bonds of his binding spell. She patiently exploited minuscule weaknesses in his spell-craft that were unseen by mortal means. Freedom was only a matter of time.

Maugris had ranted and raved that she was twisting the meaning of his commands, and of course, that was precisely what she was doing.

"Let me make this crystal clear. I want the entire Frost Legion, here, in Rachlach Fortress, now! I want my war!" he screamed. He paced the floor of his study with agitation. Her answer was always the same. "Bring me the Ever Hero, and all of Hanna will fall. Until that time, all I can give you are lesser demons. The effort taxes me to my limits."

Sekka feigned exhaustion. She could summon an army of lesser demons if she wanted to, but until the binding spell was broken, they would be under Maugris' control, not hers.

"The Amaranthine Barrier is too strong. I will need the raw energy of ten thousand soul-slaves to bring forth anything bigger."

"Ten thousand? All of the frontier villages combined do not amount to that number!" Maugris screamed.

"Cull your remaining wizards. The magical sacrifice may be enough for another lesser juggernaut such as Morteg." She lied. "Now, I must rest." She lied again.

Whenever Maugris' frustration reached its apex, she slyly tempted him with a bit more knowledge to summon her minions without her assistance. He took it without question, as she knew he would. His lust for power was insatiable.

"I feel no such fatigue," he boasted. "I will summon another demon lord such as Lord Oziax to lead my armies." His attempts failed, as she knew they would. He glared at the Arch Devil. "I want the juggernauts! Bring them!"

"Be patient. The foot soldiers of Gathos will suffice to wage your war," she said with detached interest. "In time you will have enough."

"I will need more than just foot soldiers. Can't you understand I will need the behemoths to bring down the walls of the great cities? Do you know nothing of siege-craft? If you are incapable of doing what I ask on your own, then give me the knowledge I need to do it myself. If you cannot, I will find another who can." His face twisted in a sinister grimace.

Sekka looked deeply into his eyes. He was bluffing. There was no one else ready to take her place as his bondslave. Nonetheless, she was forced to teach him the lore of summoning one of the truly magnificent beasts of Gathos, for it was in her power to do so, and she was still under his yoke.

"There are rules to this game you play, rules which cannot be broken. A portal must remain open long enough to admit a juggernaut, and your wizards to not possess the etheric energy needed for such a duration of time. They will all die in the attempt, as will the summoned giant. A behemoth requires so much more." She shook her head. "It cannot be done."

"Give me what I need!" He screamed.

"I have told you what I need to accomplish what you ask. I warn you, to attempt such a summoning on your own will go badly."

She knew he would still try. She was counting on it. Maugris eventually learned to summon lesser demons and fiends on his own. But the well of eldritch magic he drank from took more than it gave, and his ability to resist her corrosive charm was continually being taxed.

She continued to add buffers and parasitic channels to divert Maugris' magical energy away from the strength of the binding spell. Maugris would not know his plight until it was too late. With any luck, the transition would be so subtle that he would be none the wiser when the shackles of binding finally dissolved—and that was a delicious thought.

At long last, the day Sekka stole back her freedom had arrived. Maugris and his cabal of wizards would attempt to summon a greater demon from the Gathos. She would ensure that he succeeded this time, but the cost would be high.

Sitting alone in her chambers in deep concentration, Sekka worked through the multiple stages of the incantation one more time. Her counter-spell should work.

If she timed the spell correctly, it would take hold when Maugris was at his weakest. She was taking a big chance. If her spell failed, it could alert Maugris to the true precarious nature of his sorcery. He would naturally reestablish the binding enchantments of his spell and his own magical wards. That would set her back months in her work. She did not have the time to begin again. The counter-spell could also cause her to be self-banished from the Mortal Realm, for she would no longer have a host connection. Returning to Gathos in such a manner would be a painful process that would leave her debilitated. She would be vulnerable to the likes of Zizphander, or worse. But her options were limited—and time was running out.

+Is everything in order, Lord Oziax?+

+Yes, My Queen. I have done as you commanded. I primed the chamber myself.+

+Excellent.+

+I have long anticipated this day. Maugris will learn the folly of his actions. His pain will bleed off him as his blood seeps through his pores.+

+Don't be rash. Maugris still has a role to play. Your time with the mortal will come, but not before I possess the Ever Hero of Aetenos. Am I clear?+

+Yes, my Queen.+

+Very well. Ahh, I feel the beckoning. My time has arrived.+

Sekka's physical form was pulled from her room and materialized in the same spherical chamber that had summoned her from Gathos. The air tasted stale and worn. She hovered in mid-air opposite Maugris. His wizard cabal was already in position in the spaces between the points of the three-dimensional, silver-chain star. The slaves no longer struggled as the drugs took hold of their movements, but still left them entirely coherent for the inevitable pain.

"Does this not bring fond memories, my slave?" Maugris said haughtily. "We have accomplished much together, Sekka, but you have taught me too well."

"You remain the master, Lord Maugris. Your summoning shall be a great accomplishment. Even Lord Oziax will be impressed," Sekka said, playing into his ego as much as she dared.

"I care not for the adoration of that beast. I intend to replace him with a true General. One that will obey my commands without question."

"You cannot mean Lord Narthoth?" She raised her eyebrows in mock surprise.

"The same," Maugris said with a faint smile. "This day shall mark a turning point in my ascendency with the Dark Arts. Nothing shall stand in my way now."

Maugris prepared to cast the taxing spell to summon Lord Narthoth, a Valgothi Warlord whose influence and command in the Frost Legion were rivaled only by Lord Oziax. The timing of her counter-spell would need to be flawless.

Maugris wove his summoning spell, and his strength ebbed away. At the same time, Sekka carefully added the final touches of counter-magic to disrupt his binding spell on her. She laid down one subtle layer after another. Too much, too soon, and Maugris would feel the currents of magic tug against him.

The torches in the chamber grew dim as the arrival of Lord Narthoth sucked the oxygen from the room. The silver chains crisscrossing the chamber shook violently and became blurred in space. The temperature in the room dropped, and the pungent smell of dark magic filled the chamber.

Maugris moved through the final phases of his spell. Sapphire blue runes rose from the silver chains as they should but were then quickly extinguished by indigo sigils of power. The dark sigils drifted down to fuse with the chain. Sekka glanced from the corner of her eye at Maugris. He was none the wiser to her subterfuge. His eyes were closed tight in concentration as he uttered his intricate spell.

A pinprick of light formed in the center of the three-dimensional star. Ice crystals formed a layer of thin frost over the silver chains. The light grew brighter, followed by a wave of force that pinned the wizards against the walls of the chamber.

Lord Narthoth materialized in the center of the star. His roar echoed throughout the chamber. The crisscrossing chains wrapped around his material form and ensnared him in place. The greater demon howled in pain as the silver chains burned his skin. A thick mane of white hair bristled along his back. The knots and braids tied into his hair thrashed back and forth, following the movements of his bat-shaped head. His face contorted with rage. Black, beady eyes glared menacingly at Maugris and his wizard cabal.

Lord Narthoth's dark-blue wings remained furled behind his back, locked in place by the constricting chains. His hind legs, resembling those of a predatory cat, were built for speed. They jerked and stretched, trying to find some invisible purchase in the air. He had powerful shoulders and arms, with multiple protrusions of jagged, ice shards growing from his elbows.

His arms ended in oversized hands tipped with claws meant for rending and tearing. Circling his torso were five smaller arms with crablike pinchers instead of hands, which clacked and snapped in the air. A long tail, ending in tufts of white fur, angrily swished and whipped through the air.

"Lord Narthoth, I am Maugris the Infinite. You will call me Master. I command you to obey me!"

Lord Narthoth flexed his arms and legs against his bindings, but they held tight. He strained to look to the right. His black eyes found Sekka. "You have betrayed your oath!"

Sekka ignored Lord Narthoth's theatrical performance. She cast the final stanza of her spell. Lord Narthoth roared again. He pulled aggressively on the silver chains, but they would not break.

"It is pointless to resist," Maugris boasted. "What hope do you have to break the bonds that have held your queen to my will?"

"She is no longer my queen! I shall destroy her once I have devoured your soul!"

"Your threats are feathers in the wind," Maugris said over the din of clanging chains.

Maugris chanted the final spell that would dissolve the silver into the demon's body, thus binding the demon to his will. But the long chain links did not infuse with the beast.

Lord Narthoth chuckled. He jerked fast on one of the chains that held him in place. It snapped easily. His eyes narrowed, finding Maugris and holding him in check. "Your words do not match your skill, little mage." Lord Narthoth broke the link to another chain, and the long strand fell away from him. "I'm going to enjoy this."

"No, no, no!" Maugris' face distorted in confusion. His cabal of wizards was frozen in fear. Lord Narthoth unwrapped the last of the chains and tossed it away.

The demon's wings unfurled, and with blinding speed, he pounced on the nearest wizard. A head flew in the air. Lord Narthoth moved quickly to the next. The wizard's wards were no match for the strength and fury of the greater demon.

Maugris screamed out words of power, but he lacked the required energy to give them strength.

"Narthoth the Bleeder comes for you, foolish mortal."

"Sekka! I command you to stop Narthoth!" Maugris wailed in desperation.

The familiar compulsion to obey was absent. She felt nothing. Her counter-spell had worked! She was now as free as Lord Narthoth. She acted quickly, knowing that any hesitation on her part would alert Maugris to what she had achieved. She cast a simple spell at the demon. Sticky web spun from her fingers. Lord Narthoth dissolved the strands with contempt.

"You reek of weakness. Narthoth will devour your essence and rule Gathos!"

"Banish him! He will destroy us all!" Sekka said with as much worry as she could muster. She had to play her part, even at the expense of her pride.

"She cannot help you now." Lord Narthoth shook his head at Maugris. "Your fear is ripe. I can taste it in the air."

Maugris was frantic. He looked left and right with eyes wide from fear. He pushed away from Lord Narthoth. He reached inside his sleeve and hastily threw something small at the demon. Lord Narthoth caught the small object in one hand with amusement.

"A pebble to stop Narthoth?"

"Obliterate!" Maugris cried out.

Lord Narthoth tried to drop the obliteration pearl, but it expanded past his hand and engulfed his entire body. The milky white substance then collapsed upon itself and shrunk to its original size. Lord Narthoth was gone. The pearl fell to the bottom of the chamber with a deafening thud.

Maugris' chest heaved, searching for breath. His wild eyes shifted in every direction before throwing his head back, laughing like a mad man.

"I live!" he exclaimed.

Sekka stared at him in wonder. Maugris' eyes eventually found hers.

"Surprised?"

"Quite so," Sekka admitted.

"I know the deep desires of those who follow me. The temptation to steal my power will always be too great for some, so I remain prepared. I've expected betrayal since your arrival."

"It is no small feat to construct a Pearl of Oblivion," Sekka said.

"Child's play," he sneered. "Let this be a lesson to you, I cannot be defeated." Maugris searched for a reaction. She gave him none. He scowled and reached inside his sleeve again. This time he held a small vial. He popped the stopper and drank the fill of its contents.

He looked about the chamber. "So much wasted." A few moments later, he teleported out of the chamber.

He was a liar. The Pearl of Oblivion must have taken years to create. "Enjoy your small victory." A devious smile crept across her face. The counter-spell had worked, but there was still much to do.

+Lord Oziax. Our time has come.+

19

KASAI

Kasai followed Desdemonia along a deer path that wound its way through the ancient oak trees and sprawling clusters of ferns. The colors of the forest blazed deep purple, bright yellow and vermillion all around him. He tried to recall the events of the previous days. Everything had become murky impressions, rather than distinct images.

A thin branch snapped back and stung him in the face. He looked up and saw the witch standing in front of him, giggling. She then twirled away and ran ahead down the path.

Master Choejor's hand rested upon his shoulder. Kasai was happy he could lend his Master some support. Desdemonia was lost from sight, although Kasai could hear her plain enough as she sang a tune into the heady forest air. The lyrics were unusual and in a foreign tongue unknown to Kasai.

"Why must she be so loud?" he questioned.

Kasai's shoulders slumped. He felt heavy and slow. The intensity of fighting with the vargru had worn off, and his body felt rigid and stiff. He was sore everywhere. His mind drifted to thoughts of his Brothers at Ordu. The family he had left behind, again. All gone. All dead.

"Kasai, I sense you walk with heavy steps," Master Choejor voice was sluggish as he shuffled behind Kasai. Desdemonia's healing magic had given Master Choejor a respite from the pain, but she had said it was only temporary. They needed to get to Gethem before the poison entirely took him.

"I was just thinking about Ordu," Kasai replied. He spotted Desdemonia reappearing on the trail and pranced about like a minstrel entertaining the peasant folk. His head tilted to the side, and after a few moments, he realized he was staring at her. The sun poked through the high branches of the forest in beams of apricot light. She glowed like honey each time she danced through one.

"She should stop singing, or at least lower her voice," Kasai whispered under his breath. "I fear for our safety. What if more of those creatures are lurking in this forest?"

"No, don't ask her to stop. I'm enjoying the song. It reminds me of my homeland. She sings of the jungle during the monsoon."

Kasai shook his head. Was he the only sensible one? He looked ahead and watched Desdemonia curtsy to a stump with two small saplings growing from its roots. She locked her elbow around the shaft of one and circled to the second. She saw him and laughed joyfully.

"Come and join me for a dance!"

He was sure he would do no such thing, turning his attention to Master Choejor. "Is the witch's magic the same as xindu energy?"

"You will find many different powers in the world. Xindu energy is but one. Desdemonia's magic is not the Song of Aetenos, nor the Change of Mor, which draws from darker sources, but the overlap between the two. It comes from the same vast ocean of energy that binds the worlds together.

"It is known by many names. We call it Elementi magic. The Forest Dwellers refer to it as the Gift of Nayche. Many from the jungle kingdom of the Sunne are high practitioners of this art. Her companion Gauldumor is a fine example of the manifestation of this magic. He was derived from the physical elements of the world we inhabit."

"How can you tell, Master Choejor? Forgive me, but you cannot see the earth golem, can you?" Kasai looked behind him. He saw the lumbering giant keeping pace with the group. It glared back at him and snorted a *humph* of steamy air. The golem's rock eyes bore into Kasai and made him turn away.

"I can smell the old bark that encases his strength, hear the pondering steps that shake the ground. I can taste the decaying leaves and earthy roots that make up his great bulk. The magic within his construct changes the flow of air as he gets close. I can see him well enough. Can you?"

"I don't think he likes me much," Kasai muttered under his breath.

Master Choejor continued, "Those who follow the Way of Nayche believe the essence of their loved ones returns to the goddess when they die. One day they will be born again, or reawakened as they say, such as the life cycle of the golem."

"Is reincarnation real, Master?"

"Who can say? When you are one with the Boundless, all things become possible, in one shape or another. A tree falls in the forest. It decomposes to feed the nearby saplings with nutrients. The vacant space in the canopy lets in the sunshine to warm the leaves of the younger trees below, and so life continues, taking with it a part of the old, fallen tree."

Kasai remained silent. He believed magic of any kind was evil. Now he had been saved by magic and healed by magic—the embodiment of that power was a dancing gypsy who wouldn't stop winking at him.

"But can *she* be trusted? She is still a witch, after all."

"Trusted? Who knows? Our options are limited now, wouldn't you say?" Master Choejor chuckled. "However, I sense no ill-intent from the young woman. There is no room for evil in a body filled with joy. You must be mindful of deciding the merit of a person based on tired labels or monikers. Each of us has our own story to tell."

"Yes, Master. I will try." Kasai saw Desdemonia walking his way again. The woman could not walk in a straight line.

"Ah, listen to them, Gauldumor. The monks keep so many secrets from us." Desdemonia's voice was filled with laugher. She brushed passed Kasai and marched up to the earth golem like a soldier in the King's army. "We will keep secrets too! And then we can trade them all away by the fire later tonight."

The late afternoon sun was fading. Soon it would be night. Desdemonia skipped and danced along the trail without worry. There was gaiety in each word she spoke, no matter how nonsensical. Kasai wondered at her sanity.

"And perhaps share a few secrets together in private, eh love?" Desdemonia gave Kasai another exaggerated wink and a mock elbow to his side as she danced back ahead of him to lead the party.

"What? No. I mean, who? Why do you keep calling me that?" Kasai stammered through words that made no sense. He couldn't think. If matters weren't troublesome enough, now this forest pixie was teasing him. "Do you have to be so loud? Aren't you fearful of another attack?"

"Here? Now? With Gauldumor raised by our side?" She looked back at Kasai with puzzlement written across her face.

"Doesn't seem like you have much to be afraid of then." Kasai secretly wished he could say the same for himself.

"Oh, to lose my soul to the Deep Dark would be a horror beyond words," Desdemonia replied, "or to die bound and helpless under the cruel whims of another. Demons. Don't like demons either. What else?" She rolled her eyes, looking up to the right. "Hmm ... a bird shitting on your head would be bad. Ya, I know it's supposed to be good luck and all, but when it happens it's a mess to clean."

"But ... isn't Gauldumor... a...?"

"What? Is he a creature of darkness? Of course not. Gauldi, he thinks you're a demon!" Kasai flushed in embarrassment. Her hysterical laugher didn't help much either. He looked to Master Choejor for support, but his Master was chuckling along with the witch.

"Gauldumor is a Guardian of the Forest. He has a soul just as much as you or me. His is the essence of the living trees and the flowing rivers, the soft grass underfoot and the fragrant pollens that move through the branches," Desdemonia explained. "He is all of this and more."

"He truly has a soul?" Kasai was still confused.

"Yes, a soul. Don't they teach you anything in monk school? All living creatures have a soul. Now, those prickly demons are different. They don't have one, and that's why they are constantly trying to get ours. But if you know their name, their true and secret name, then you can control them to do your bidding."

"Really?"

Desdemonia's eyes grew wide, and she stared deeply at Kasai. Her hands waved in the air. "Yesssss!" She jumped away and stomped out a different dance and a much louder song, laughing joyfully between verses.

He was sure another pack of vargru would hear her and follow the sound of her voice to their next campsite. They would attack en masse, and not even the earth golem would be enough to hold the creatures back. But in his nineteen years of life, he had never seen hair so thick or black or long. It flowed like an onyx river down her back. He just wanted to touch it.

Desdemonia danced back to Kasai. Her eyes sparkled in the orange half-light, and again he was dazzled and amazed. "You have a riddle in your mind that doesn't know its way out. Am I right, love?"

How did she know? Had she cast a spell? So many unanswered questions and his mind raced to every possible outcome no matter how farfetched.

"Do not call me that. My name is Kasai Ch'ou, all right?" Kasai blurted out. He didn't mean for his words to sound ungrateful or overly blunt, but they did. He took a breath and relaxed. His mind was spinning in circles. "I apologize. You spoke of a safe place. Master Choejor needs rest. Will we be there soon?"

"Soon? We are here now, silly." Desdemonia danced through a well-camouflaged opening in the densely-packed trees. In the clearing stood a small cottage, entirely hidden from sight, meshing naturally with the trees and boulders surrounding it.

20

DESDEMONIA

Desdemonia stood at ease in front of Gauldumor, hands clasping her elbows behind her back. She leaned back and craned her head to meet the creature's eyes.

"The boy has been touched; his destiny no longer his own. The paths of time are in flux with that one," Gauldumor's deep voice rumbled.

"I know, I know. I sensed it too. The monk is on the precipice. His decisions will affect many," Desdemonia added while absentmindedly tracing a pattern in the dirt with her foot.

"Light and Darkness are at war over his soul. He is a prize for each." Gauldumor bent forward and edged in closer to Desdemonia. "He shall face a difficult decision, one that will affect many by its outcome. Return them to the glade where you found them."

"Maybe we can help them?"

"He is not for you. If you value your soul, you will be done with him." He spoke as a parent would do to a carefree child.

"I can't just leave them alone in the forest."

"Then I will end them both while I remain above the soil."

"You'll do no such thing." She pointed her finger at the earth golem and gave him a playful slap under the chin. "You may be right, Gauldi. Time will tell. But for now, we must do what we can to help them. I will lead them out of the forest and away from here."

"You have the stubbornness of your father and the loving heart of your mother. Choose your path carefully, or your fate may follow theirs."

"Thank you, my dear protector and faithful friend." She patted the earth golem lovingly on the chest. "I will be careful. There is something important about this one, even if he doesn't know it yet."

"I tell you again, let them go."

"Without a guide? The old alpha would have them within a day."

"If that is their fate, let it be so." The earth golem raised itself up straight and folded its great arms across its thick chest. "Do not be tempted, child. I have seen that look in your eyes before."

"Stop worrying. I'll be fine."

"Very well. The deep earth beckons me to return. Call, and I shall come. But if you leave this forest, know I can no longer help you."

"I know, I know. Off with ya then, you big oaf."

Desdemonia watched Gauldumor melt back into the fertile forest soil. The earth golem left behind a heap of loam that soon congealed with the mossy brown ground and was gone.

She tied her hair back in a knot behind her head. "It's not the same for you."

"Ouch!"

"Who's there?" Desdemonia spun quickly. It was Kasai. He stood with a stack of firewood in his arms. One had apparently fallen on his foot. He attempted to pick it up but only succeeded in dropping the rest. He stood dumbfounded, holding a small twig with an awkward, sheepish grin.

"I didn't mean to listen, but well, I was collecting and wood and turned the corner of the cottage," Kasai stammered, looking back the way he came.

He must have heard everything. She walked towards him, and his expression changed from embarrassment to apprehension. He thinks I'm going to turn him into a toad, the poor dear. She couldn't help but laugh.

"Well, Gauldi sure doesn't like you. Don't worry, love, I'll protect you. I'll get you and your father out of the forest. In the meantime, it will be nice to have some company. I've always wanted a kid brother." She patted him on the top of his smooth forehead.

"Kid brother? I am not a child. This is my nineteenth summer, or there about. And I told you, Master Choejor is not my father. He is my mentor and a Master of Ordu." Kasai tossed the twig. He picked up the fallen wood. "I'll have you know the monks of Ordu are renowned and well respected."

"A monk of Ordu, are we? That's nice. Are you coming? I'm starving." She walked inside.

Master Choejor rested quietly on a small cot near the fire. A medium-sized pot rested in a stand above the flame, filled with a stew she started hours ago. The savory smell of the vegetables and herbs from her garden made her mouth water and her stomach growl. Dinner was almost ready. It seemed like a lifetime since the morning's fig halves.

"Have a seat, and I'll serve you a bowl," Desdemonia pointed to a small bench that sat next to a wooden table. Kasai sat down as instructed. Desdemonia returned with two steaming bowls of stew.

"Well, slide over, I'm not eating on the floor," she said as she put both bowls down. She then brought over two wooden spoons and cups filled with water. Kasai slid over and watched her sit down next to him. There was barely enough room for two, and their sides touched.

She felt him stiffen. "Relax. I won't bite," she said. She had to admit she was a bit drawn to the monk. Her pulse quickened as she felt the warmth of his body next to hers. Something was endearing about his awkwardness.

"What were you doing in the middle of the deep forest?" she asked casually between each spoonful of stew. She was almost halfway through her bowl when he decided to answer.

"I ... cannot say," Kasai stared into the steam that rose from his bowl.

"That's right, you monks like your secrets. Don't worry, we all have them. Start eating. It looks like you need a good meal."

Kasai took a tentative sip of the stew. She saw him glance sideways at her.

"Just eat," she said without looking at him.

Kasai did as he was told. He ate quickly and finished before she did.

"Do your parents live nearby?" Kasai said. "How did you learn to make an earth golem. Are there more of you nearby?"

He clearly did not want to talk about himself or why they were running for their lives in the forest.

"My parents are dead." Desdemonia finished her stew and got up from the bench.

"Oh. I'm sorry."

"It happened when I was young ... when we lived together in the forest village of Shryse." At his confused look, she added, "Just outside the jungle basin south of the Sarribe." When he nodded, she continued. "A traveling band of merchants came to our village eager to trade furs and metals for magical items. They had heard of a family in the region that could enchant items and imbue them with special powers." She paused. *Why I am I telling him so much?* "My family was known for such deeds." She busied herself with cleaning her bowl and spoon.

"What happened?" Kasai shifted on the bench to face her.

"When they brought forth their swords and spears, my father told them we were healers, not killers. We honored the land and all living things that were a part of it. He told the merchants he would not enchant their weapons of war.

"We were all relieved when they left. Unfortunately, they returned a week later, at night. They abducted my mother and me and forced my father to enchant their blades. A fight broke out, and other villagers got entangled.

"The merchants were not men of commerce at all. They were a savage band of thieves. When the killing began, it did not stop. My father died protecting my mother and me. We fled together until an arrow found my mother's heart. I alone escaped into the jungle."

Desdemonia stopped talking and went to the pot. She stared into the fire, and absentmindedly used the ladle to stir the stew. "I await now for their awakening. Perhaps if I am lucky, I will find them again in this lifetime."

"When they wake? I don't understand."

Desdemonia turned around with a smile on her face. "I shall tell you more of the jungles of Sunne and the ways of my people in exchange for a kiss!"

Kasai went white as a ghost. "What? No. I'm a monk. I don't kiss."

"You're not a dead monk, are you?" Desdemonia approached him with a sly smile. He was so easy to tease. "You have pretty eyes. Did you know they turn sage green when you are happy?"

"What, what are you doing? Stop. I'm not happy," Kasai said. He was so nervous. That made her want to tease him even more. She pinched his arm hard.

"Ouch! What was that for?" Kasai rubbed his arm.

"Not dead yet," Desdemonia said. She twirled away to wake Master Choejor for some dinner. Her laughter filled the room.

21

KASAI

Strong southern winds blew across the dense forest canopy for the next three days. Old trees creaked as bough and branch swayed in the warm air. Waves of leaves rustled over the heads of the three unlikely companions as columns of sunlight poured into the forest. The bodies of tiny insects flickered in and out of the beams as they drifted aimlessly across the swatches of light.

Kasai and Desdemonia walked side-by-side along a leave covered path with Master Choejor trailing a few steps behind. Kasai was relieved the Master had regained some of his strength. It was the first bit of good news in what seemed like an age of running, fighting, and hiding from danger.

"Why does your earth golem not walk with us? Or is he traveling under our feet?" Kasai minded his steps. He hoped he wasn't offending the golem in any way.

"Gauldi? He's not mine to command," Desdemonia said. She turned to Master Choejor. "Seriously, what do you teach them in that monastery? Doesn't he know anything about anything?"

Kasai wore a broad grin. Now she would hear some tales. She would think twice before calling him a 'kid' again. But Master Choejor only chuckled lightly and said no more. A devilish smile lit Desdemonia's lips while she waited for an answer.

"It's not like that. Master Choejor, tell her. I learned plenty at Ordu."

"Anyways, there's a lagoon fed by an underground hot spring, not a half day's trek from here. The warm water is said to have rejuvenating qualities and will help ease the pain your Master is experiencing. He hides his discomfort well."

"I'll have you know, the monks of Ordu are taught to elevate our minds above physical trauma. Pain is nothing more than a mental illusion; a sensation to experience, observe, and then let pass. A tickle or a slap can be perceived in the same way, depending on the strength of one's mind." Kasai said in somewhat of a haughty voice. "Master Choejor is a Master Monk of Ordu. He is hiding nothing. He has gone beyond the pain."

"If you say so, Mister Special," Desdemonia rolled her eyes.

Kasai didn't care what the witch thought about Ordu, or about him. He was above pain, too, just like his Master.

"Plus, the warm water is ideal for kissing," Desdemonia said with a crooked smile. She proceeded to skip in a circle around Kasai. Kasai's tower of superiority crumbled to the ground. She never once missed an opportunity to provoke him.

"Kissing? With you? Didn't I just say that I am a monk of Ordu?"

How could she be so daft? She frustrated him to no end with all her dancing and laughing and teasing. Couldn't she see he was serious? His world radiated at a higher, more cerebral level. He would not taint his purity of mind and body by succumbing to such a base desire as physical interaction. Even in his head, he sounded like an idiot.

He watched Desdemonia spin in a pirouette. He figured they were roughly the same age, although maybe the witch had seen a few more summers than he, but not many. One moment she was a frolicking gypsy, singing, and prancing without care; the next, she became a warrior druidess of the forest. Kasai didn't know if she was fearless or just crazy, or both.

He concentrated on her image. The glow of her aura surged around her in a wild frenzy of yellows and greens. The streaking colors reminded Kasai of two cats playing together in the grass. One chased the other until it was caught. They tumbled together for a bit, then leaped to their feet and renewed the chase. She was as wild as the forest.

He focused on her more intently to test his newly discovered inner sight. A mandala of complex organic shapes and colors spiraled above Desdemonia's head. He saw the purity of nature in symbolic form. Master Choejor was right about her. She was not an enemy.

Desdemonia also possessed high levels of fire xindu. Kasai didn't need any special skills to see that aspect of the witch. But as he looked deeper, he saw something else.

"Water xindu?" He tilted his head to the side. The two energies clashed together like the rapids of a fiery river. But there was an odd sense of harmony to how they flowed.

Desdemonia was passionate, but unlike Daku, her heart was filled with tenderness rather than cruelty. At least Kasai hoped so. He couldn't figure her out. Daku, Desdemonia, who's next? Why do I always attract crazy people?

Kasai thought of Daku. What happened? It still seemed impossible to imagine. How could he? Kasai pushed the horrible thoughts from his mind. He would sift through them all later, once Master Choejor was safe in Gethem.

Eventually, Desdemonia's lagoon came into view. The path curved, and now they walked parallel to the steaming water. Kasai heard small waves lapping up against a hidden shore. There was a distinct smell of salt in the air.

"This spot will do. We will make camp here," Desdemonia said. "Master Choejor, I have something for you that I took from my home. Perhaps it will ease some of your pain." She handed him a small vial filled with dark liquid.

"I told you he is a Master Monk of Ordu," Kasai interjected. "Hey, stop that. What are you doing? He doesn't need that."

"Thank you, sweet child. I appreciate your kindness," Master Choejor said. He took a sniff of the contents and scrunched his nose. "Mm...valerian root. It will certainly let me rest."

"Why won't you listen to me? I know what is best for Master Choejor."

Desdemonia gave Kasai a triumphant smirk. He just dismissed her with a shake of his head. She annoyed him to no end but would not engage in another one of her games.

"Fine. I'll get the camp set up." He removed the bowl and some herbs from his travel bag. Once he made a small fire, he would fix Master Choejor a proper tea.

"I'll scout ahead and make sure we are alone," Desdemonia said.

Ninziz-zida whispered to Kasai in strange tongues. It sounded more like the buzz of a horsefly. And like the pest, its message was incessant, shapeless, and had no meaning. Its only purpose was to ensure one knew it was there. Kasai massaged his temples. His head had not stopped hurting since taking Ninziz-zida from the Hall of Artifacts. He took the staff from his sash and held it before him.

"What do you want from me?" he said. He didn't expect the ancient weapon to answer. But maybe the buzzing could stop. He laid Ninziz-zida down upon a smooth boulder across the campsite. A little separation couldn't hurt.

Desdemonia called to him from further down the path. She didn't sound like she was in any danger, but she was undoubtedly a troublemaker. Kasai got up and obediently followed the direction of her voice. He marveled at the different colors and sounds he encountered along the forest path. There were incredible amounts of life here. Soon enough, he saw her close to the water's edge.

"It's about time. Come on, let's go for a swim," Desdemonia said. She shed her clothing down to her undergarments. She ran into the water and within moments was waist-deep in the hot pool.

"What are you waiting for? The water's perfect."

Kasai immediately looked away. "I don't think that's a good idea, Desdemonia. I need to watch over Master Choejor." He tried to quell the rapid thumping in his chest.

"You said yourself he's a Master Monk of Orduuuuuu. I'm sure he can take care of himself. And it's Des."

"What?"

"Call me Des. Desdemonia is so formal, especially if you are planning on saying sweet things to me in the water." Her laughter filled the air. The playful gypsy had returned.

Kasai watched her wade further into the dark water as the rising steam swirled in the wake of her body. He stood there like a statue, bewildered and fascinated.

He should say something witty in reply. A clever gibe to show her he was already two steps ahead of her. If she wanted to play games, he would show her some real skills.

"Now you're all wet and ... I like being umm, dry. I think I hear Master Choejor calling me." He sulked disheartened back to the campsite. Why couldn't he just keep his mouth shut?

Kasai plopped down on his haunches. What a fool. He looked at the lagoon through the trees. There was something in the rock wall across the steaming water. It was some kind of dark grotto, as best as he could reckon. A thunderous waterfall dumped a steady supply of mountain water to its right.

Kasai turned to hand his Master Choejor some hot tea and found him already asleep. He was propped against a weathered stump, napping peacefully. The vial of valerian root was empty. That was good. Master Choejor needed as much rest as he could get.

Perhaps he should trust her more. Master Choejor seemed to be at ease with the witch. Kasai looked back at the water. Desdemonia had turned right and walked across his line of sight. She stopped and arched backward. Her chest and breasts rose into the air as she submerged the back of her head into the warm water.

Kasai's insides lurched. He quickly averted his eyes, but peeked again, nonetheless. She squeezed the water from her hair. She looked back at the shoreline, shrugged her shoulders, and dove into the steaming water.

He scolded himself for being unfriendly and disrespectful, if he was honest, for his cowardice as well. Who wouldn't jump at this opportunity? He glanced back and saw Desdemonia wading deeper into the lagoon. "What's wrong with me. I like swimming," Kasai grumbled as his heart thumped like a caged beast inside his chest. She was unlike anyone he had ever met before. He allowed himself a small chuckle. "As if you are some sort of expert on women."

The noon sun towered overhead. Kasai wondered why no birds flew in the sky. "Come to think of it. I don't hear any chirping, either." He feared the vargru had found them again. He caught a glimpse of a sharp sparkle at the edge of the ridge where the waterfall started its plunge. Kasai looked more closely, but whatever was there was now gone.

His senses remained alert. Something was not right with this lagoon, and he looked to the water. The pool was empty. An uneasy feeling crept up Kasai's spine. Where was Desdemonia?

He heard a chorus of unearthly howls. He stood up to get a better vantage of the cliff wall. Three dark blurs dropped from the cliff's edge and splashed into the water. Desdemonia finally resurfaced, but she was unaware of what had entered the lagoon.

She bobbed up and down for a moment and scanned the shoreline. Kasai knew she was searching for him. Three giants broke through the mist behind her. Two of them waded towards her while the third dove under the water. Kasai realized the sound of the waterfall masked their approach.

She continued to play in the water, blind to the approaching danger. He needed to warn her. Kasai raced to the clearing where she had entered the lagoon. He reached for Ninziz-zida. Gone! He had left the Fire Serpent at the camp.

"Stupid!" He panicked and began waving and pointing frantically behind her. Desdemonia waved back. She was still trying to coerce him to join her.

Kasai finally saw the recognition of danger in her face. She spun around as the giants closed in on her. Kasai took a few steps into the water. An image of a snarling vargru came to mind. He needed the staff.

"Stupid, stupid, stupid!" He raced back to the camp to retrieve Ninziz-zida.

Kasai heard Desdemonia chanting. It sounded like water splashing against the walls of a box. Through the trees, he saw her point at the lead giant, and a watery column enveloped its maligned body. The giant frantically pushed the water away from its face, but he couldn't escape. Its movement slowed, and it sunk beneath the surface.

"One down," he said when he reached the camp. Master Choejor was snoring peacefully. Kasai didn't know how long the effects of the potion would last, and he doubted he could wake the Master if he tried. He quickly decided Master Choejor was safe for now.

Where was Gauldumor? Kasai wondered. They would need the earth golem's strength.

Kasai snatched up Ninziz-zida, and the three-sectioned staff felt warm and reassuring in his grip. The buzzing sound he usually heard coming from the staff shifted in his mind. Kasai pieced together its message.

'You need only me.'

A piercing yowl came from the direction of the water, and Kasai sprinted back to the entrance of the lagoon. He heard Desdemonia begin the chant a second time. When he reached the clearing, he stabbed Ninziz-zida in the soft soil. Kasai tore off his outer robe and kicked away his sandals. The loose clothing would only slow him down in the water.

He picked up the Fire Serpent, and the staff ached for battle. Kasai waded into the steaming water with Ninziz-zida held above his head.

The second giant came fast. It howled and snarled and beat its chest, but Desdemonia remained calm and sized up her next target. Bright blue sigils of power fanned out behind her back. The swirling patterns pushed the steam away as they spun.

Desdemonia raised her arm to cast her next spell. The water erupted behind her. The third giant finally surfaced. His massive hands grabbed her, pinning her arms to her sides. The blue sigils of power vanished along with her spell.

"That was my brother, witch!" said the giant as it drove forward in the water. He finally reached her and grabbed her by the throat. "No more magic from you!"

He was a brutish thing with scar tissue crisscrossing his face and arms. He lifted her in the air as if she were a child. The giant brought her head close to his own. His swollen tongue lolled out of a black-toothed mouth, and he slathered her in grey mucus from cheek to mouth. "Not that we care, right, Ruffo?"

"The more for the two of us, eh?" Ruffo said. He continued to hold Desdemonia's arms tight. He had filthy red hair that was packed together in long ropey coils.

Desdemonia's body was full of storm and defiance. She kicked the giant facing her in the stomach. He doubled over. Ruffo twisted her in the air and dunked her under the water.

Kasai was moving too slow. The water deepened, and he could no longer walk on the soft bottom. He tucked Ninziz-zida under one arm and swam on his side. The red-headed man-beast dragged Desdemonia back towards the cave as she struggled to the surface for air. The giants roared with laughter as Ruffo dunked her again. Kasai fretted he would not reach her in time.

Ruffo pulled her up again. "I like the feisty ones. Better for sport."

The second giant with the scarred body struck Desdemonia with a powerful backhand across the face. Water sprayed across the lagoon from the impact of the blow. Desdemonia's body sagged lifelessly in the giant's mighty hands. "She be easy now."

"We fuck, and then we eat," Ruffo said. "You finally taste forest witch."

"I'm first this time!" The scarred giant pleaded.

Kasai's heart filled with equal measures of despair and fury as the giants carried her towards the cave. Luckily, they had not seen him through the mist. He followed as best he could, but he could not keep up with their long strides. They quickly outpaced him and disappeared into the entrance of the cave.

Kasai hated himself for being unprepared. Ninziz-zida whispered something that felt like a reprimand for being left behind. He tried to tune out the staff's clamor in his mind. Finally, his feet hit the soft bottom again. He tucked Ninziz-zida into his sash and rushed out of the water.

The low bank on the far side of the lagoon was easy enough to climb. His eyes stung from the saltwater, but the smell outside the cave was worse. It almost made him faint. Bones and offal littered the ground. Rats gnawed on the scraps of what must have been the leftovers of a recent kill. Kasai put his hand over his mouth and nose and ran into the cave.

Mold, mildew, and some other kind of shiny matter was splashed against the inner walls of the entrance. Blood? Urine? It was difficult to discern. The light became scarce as he ran deeper into the cave. Then he noticed a glow coming from the staff. He looked more closely and saw tiny red flames rippled along Ninziz-zida's surface. The fire moved over his hand as if he was part of the staff. He was alarmed at first, but he didn't feel any pain.

"Please don't possess me," Kasai said with apprehension, but he kept moving.

He heard bestial howls echoing from the darkness. When he rounded a corner, he saw flickering light slapping against a far rock wall. He approached the next bend and cautiously peered around the corner.

The two giants leaped across a blazing fire while hollering and shoving each other in a jubilant and primitive dance. They were naked and sullied, one slightly larger than the other. The lagoon water did little to wash the filth from their malformed bodies. They had coarse hair of red and black that resembled a horse's mane, filled with dirt, twigs, and Aetenos knows what else.

They grappled together. Ruffo howled in delight when one knocked the other down. He waved his hard member at the scarred giant on the cavern floor, but then swiveled in the direction of Desdemonia. She laid on the ground with her wrists bound behind her back. A filthy rag was stuffed in her mouth.

Was she unconscious? Dead? There were soiled knives strewn all about the cavern floor. He couldn't tell if she had been cut or not. It was too difficult to see from this vantage point.

"I'm going to have to kill them," Kasai realized. He knew offensive strikes, of course, but had spent his time mastering more the defensive forms which focused on protecting the people around him.

But now he was alone, and his defensive skills would not be enough to save Desdemonia. He cycled through the few hit to kill strikes he knew. They didn't seem to be enough against such large foes.

Ninziz-zida twitched in his hand as if insulted by his thoughts. Kasai looked down at the Fire Serpent in wonder. A warm glow washed up his arms, and the mysterious voice in his head became singular and focused. Images of fighting positions and angles of attack rolled through his mind.

He felt Ninziz-zida request access to his fire xindu as one friend might ask another for a favor. It purred to him with a promise of partnership, not possession. Kasai acquiesced to the Fire Serpent's desire. What choice did he have? Desdemonia was doomed if he didn't act quickly.

Summoning his fire xindu, Kasai channeled it into the staff. The slow ripples of flame on Ninziz-zida segments began to grow. Miraculously, the fire still did not burn him.

'Together,' Ninziz-zida sent into Kasai's mind.

Kasai nodded. "I understand. You shall strike, I shall defend. Together we will be whole." Kasai gripped Ninziz-zida's segments tightly and slipped into the giant's lair. He spun one of Ninziz-zida's outer sections in a glowing figure-eight pattern while the other part whipped back and forth across his waist. The giants were startled for a moment, then jumped to attack.

Ruffo, with the mangy red mane, came first. The giant unwisely grabbed Ninziz-zida's outer segment, and flames blazed across his hand and forearm. Ruffo's high-pitched scream filled the small cavern. He desperately tried to douse the fire.

Ninziz-zida connected itself into a straight staff. Kasai thrust forward and impaled the end into Ruffo's chest. Kasai pulled the staff back, and Ninziz-zida split back into three sections. The motion was fluid and exact as if Kasai and Ninziz-zida shared the same thought. Ruffo sank to the cavern floor, burning.

The black-haired giant with a scarred face grabbed a spear with a barbed head. He cautiously circled to the left, pushing Kasai in the opposite direction and away from the lair's entrance. Kasai carefully stepped over Ruffo's smoldering body. Ninziz-zida blazed in his hands. Too late, Kasai realized the giant was not dead.

Ruffo grabbed at Kasai's ankle. He missed but succeeded in tangling Kasai's legs with his arm. Kasai fell to the floor. Dust and dirt blinded him. He rolled quickly onto his back and tried desperately to push away from Ruffo.

The scarred giant howled in glee. He raced forward and tried to jab Kasai with his spear. Kasai rolled to one side and avoided the blow. The spear point scrapped against the ground and sent chips of stone into the air.

The giant stepped over Kasai's body. This time he aimed carefully. He raised the spear in two hands over his head. Kasai's luck had run out. In this position, Ninziz-zida could not hope to stop such a mighty blow.

The giant stopped mid-thrust. Something had locked up his muscles and shoved him forward a step. His torso vibrated unnaturally. Large, white bumps boiled up from his skin until they burst.

The giant screamed in agony when his midsection burst. The two halves of his body fell to the cavern floor. Kasai was amazed to see Master Choejor's standing where the giant once stood. His outstretched hand vibrated with shimmering, white energy. Ruffo tried to rise, but fell back to the floor, dead.

"Master Choejor! I thought you were asleep. How did you..."

"One does not become a Master of Ordu by sleeping with both eyes closed." The smile on his lips was short-lived as Master Choejor sank to his hands and knees. Blood vomited from his mouth.

"We must be on our way to Gethem," Master Choejor gasped between fits of coughing and spitting up phlegm. "I will be fine. Tend to Desdemonia."

"Desdemonia, Desdemonia, wake up. Are you hurt?" Kasai unbound her wrists and removed the dirty cloth from her mouth. He gently rocked her awake until she opened her eyes, sleepily taking in the new environment. She rested her eyes on Kasai.

"Hello, Handsome." Her smile returned, and she propped herself up on an elbow. For once, Kasai was relieved to hear her playful banter.

A faint voice came from the back of the lair. "Help me."

Kasai grabbed a torch from the wall and followed the sound of the voice. The cavern sloped into a curving tunnel that opened to a second, smaller area, where Kasai found a little person chained to a rock. At first, Kasai mistakenly thought she was just a young girl. She was huddled next to a group of dead pilgrims. The stench of the decomposing bodies was unbearable. The pilgrims wore the clothes of priest-esses of the Immortal Mother.

"Please, please, help me," she cried, her dirty face streaked with tears. Magenta-hued eyes the shape of thin almonds slanted upwards at the corners, like the tips of thorns.

Kasai nodded. He looked around to find something to unlock the chains. Off to the side, he saw a weathered chest. Inside were odd blades, bones, some coin and luckily, a set of rusted keys.

"I've found someone. She needs help."

Kasai unlocked the heavy shackles and helped the young priestess to her feet. Her unnaturally pale skin and was in sharp contrast to her jet-black hair, which she wore in a style he'd not seen before. Her bone straight hair was cut sharply across her fore-head, falling like a curtain to just above her shoulders where it ended like a solid wall.

"Oh, thank you. Thank you," she whimpered. "They were horrors. I had given up all hope. They ... they were going to ... going to ..." She broke down, shuddering as more tears streaked her face. She swooned, and Kasai caught her. She clung to him while heavy sobs racked her small body.

"Shh, shh, you're safe now. You have nothing more to fear from them. My name is Kasai."

"Thank you, Kasai." She looked at him with thoughtful eyes. "I like your name, Kasai. I am Reese."

Kasai gently pushed her away though she was reluctant to let go.

"What happened to you?" he asked.

"We were on pilgrimage ... to the Temple of Illumination and ... Shrine of the Immortal Mother... Pray for the coming ... of the Ever Hero ... peace in the land."

Reese could barely speak. She was still in shock. Superficial scratches and cuts covered her body; fortunately, nothing was broken.

Reese looked to the bodies of the other pilgrims and wept again. Kasai wasn't sure how to act. When he patted her on the shoulder, she wrapped unnaturally strong arms around his torso. She was unnaturally strong for such a young woman.

"Kasai, what's happening? Who's there with you? You need to come back," Desde-monia called out. She limped to the back of the cave. "Master Choejor is not well."

Kasai set Reese aside and ran to Master Choejor. He was on his back with blood coating his mouth, and his breath came in shallow gasps.

"Can you help him?" Kasai looked imploringly at Desdemonia.

"Not here. I have no components to use. We need to get him back to my home."

"He won't make it," Kasai said. Reese had followed them and knelt next to the old monk.

"Let me try," Reese said. The light of the central fire revealed more of her features. Kasai thought he saw something familiar about the young priestess. He couldn't quite put his finger on it, though. She had the vague appearance of someone he remembered from a dream.

Reese whispered strange words over Master Choejor's body as she reached out and grabbed Kasai's hand. An oddly shaped ring was wrapped around her index finger that was black as night. She placed her other hand over Master Choejor's head, and Kasai momentarily lost his balance, but his vertigo left him as quickly as it had arrived.

Kasai looked at Desdemonia for an answer to his curious instability. Maybe it was some form of magic she recognized. Desdemonia shrugged her shoulders. She watched Reese with suspicious eyes. Master Choejor coughed once more, and then his face softened. His breathing became less erratic and calm.

Reese brought the side of her head over Master Choejor's mouth and nose to listen to his breathing. She whispered strange words close to his mouth. Desdemonia wedged herself between the priestess and Master Choejor and wiped the blood from his mouth. "I can take it from here."

"He will be all right, but needs rest," Reese explained. She rocked back on her heels. "The Immortal Mother provides and has granted him her favor."

Kasai was filled with relief. "We travel to the Temple of Illumination as well. The Monastery of Ordu has been attacked, and we must alert Grandmaster Nysulu before the other monasteries fall to the same fate. Master Choejor has been poisoned. Only the High Healers can save him now." The words tumbled out of Kasai's mouth.

"Kasai, you say too much! We don't know anything about her," Desdemonia said. She took an aggressive step towards Reese. "Who are you? You say you're a priestess? What denomination of the Immortal Mother do you follow? Your clothing doesn't look like it fits you well. Why were you saved and not the others?"

Reese fled behind Kasai's back. She held tight to the fabric of his vest with her small, shaking hands.

"Desdemonia, she saved Master Choejor. That is enough to know for now. Leave her be. We can help her reach Gethem." Kasai turned around to face Reese. Her magenta eyes glistened with fear.

"You may join us to Gethem if you like," he said. Reese nodded, seeming happy with the pronouncement happily. She glanced at Desdemonia for her reaction, not quite meeting her eyes. Kasai attributed it to shyness. "We'll stay here the night and then be on our way in the morning," Kasai said.

"I'll take first watch," Desdemonia said. She turned in a huff to the tunnel exit.

22

SHIVERRIG

"**P**athias, what have you learned? Be quick," Shiverrig inquired of his man. They spoke in hushed tones while walking through the King's Palace in Qaqal.

"My shadow men within the Great Houses have been activated."

"Good, good. And the scouting reports of enemy strength and movement?"

"All altered before reaching Baron Rokig. The majority of the scouts used by the Crown were trained in Gethem. Tradition has its rewards, lord," Pathias said.

"Excellent work, Pathias. The king is desperate for a victory. He will blindly blunder along until he trips into his own coffin. All we have to do is keep the lid open."

They reached a door with two guards on either side of the entrance. "It won't be long now. Have Malachi send word to the North."

"Yes, my lord." Pathias bowed and walked away.

Shiverrig eyed the guards. Each bowed in deference as he pushed passed them and entered the King's War Council.

"Is he insane? He does this on the eve of declaring war?" Shiverrig's voice bellowed into the room. Lord Fritta, Duke Manda, and the king's lackey, Baron Rokig, were already present. King Conrad had yet to arrive.

Shiverrig took the last remaining seat on the side of a magnificent marble table in the center of the room. A grand map of the Three Kingdoms of Hanna was laid over its smooth surface. Figurines had been neatly placed, showing dispositions of armies. Rokig was busy adjusting the placement of auxiliary troops while pontificating to the others of his vast military knowledge and experience. The man had never taken up a sword and shield against a real enemy in his life.

What did any of these fools know about warfare? All he saw were children playing war games with toys on a map. Out of the bunch, maybe Fritta had a decent mind for battle. But the others, especially the king, were products of pretend military tours at the Last Garrison.

Shiverrig took in the contents of the room. Ceiling-to-floor banners lined the walls. Each depicted an act of bravery and courage from a historic event in the development of the realm. He expected to see scions of House Shiverrig commanding troops or vanquishing foes. But instead, the dominant persona had been changed to an insignificant family member of House Conrad. All lies! The actual history of the realm had been rewritten in one generation.

"The function of the Five Armies has always been to keep power spread out amongst the Lords of the Realm," Shiverrig said. "No Great House should have absolute control over the others. It has been this way from the very beginning. The Crown must have a counterweight to keep it balanced."

Fritta and Manda sat at opposite sides of the long table. Fritta's arms were crossed against his chest. He nodded his head in agreement with Shiverrig's pronouncement but said nothing more. The king's proclamation would become a death sentence to anyone opposing the Crown.

Manda sat back in his chair with a leather-bound ledger tucked under his arm. Sorting through the contents of a fruit plate to his left, he plucked a handful of plump, purple grapes, and tossed them past garishly colored lips, one after another. He seemed unconcerned who controlled the Five Armies or if a new King's Army was formed. Shiverrig had expected as much from Manda. His family's influence in the court had been established through their extensive mercantile holdings. He wasn't a military leader, nor had ambitions to be one. He let others run campaigns, preferring to finance them. He was only concerned about the interest he was able to charge on his way to a tidy profit, and of course, debt repayment. War was good for business .ii his business.

King Conrad finally arrived. His crown still sloped on his narrow forehead. He was flanked by his son, Prince Dane, a boy in his sixteenth year, and Baron Rokig to the right. Rokig had eschewed his family's coat-of-arms and wore in the livery of House Conrad. He pinned unearned medals of honor to the oversized lapel of his jacket. He was a grand image of a heroic general of old. None of it was true.

"Desperate times call for desperate measures, Duke Shiverrig," Conrad said. "The realm requires a stable and merciful king to lead during times of fire and sorrow."

"One king, one rule, sire," Rokig affirmed, his sycophant's voice unable to be syrupier.

"You are all here as my Generals, yet only one can lead the realm's forces to victory," Conrad said.

"And who might that lord be? Rokig?" Shiverrig pointed first to the opportunistic man who married into wealth, and then across the king to his son. "Or, perhaps Prince Dane? A boy with no practical experience in warfare, whose family now holds the throne due to the criminal trickery of a disingenuous grandfather?"

"Hold your tongue, Shiverrig. You are here at my sufferance and out of the respect that is due to your family's contribution to the kingdom—not because of you. You became obsolete the day your father died."

"You dare!"

"I am the king. I will dare as much as I like. You will do as you are told. Know your place and be grateful you still have a position at this table."

"Gerun, hold your tongue. Let us hear the king's strategy. Perhaps it is sound," Fritta soothed, his tone fatherly. He was the eddy that calmed the storm waters before they reached the harbor. His deep-set eyes pointed out the additional guards behind Shiverrig.

Shiverrig stood defiantly. "Speak then."

He knew he was risking much the more he baited Conrad. He would show the other lords present he would not be dismissed so easily. Conrad waved Rokig to begin.

Rokig glowered at Shiverrig at the insult to his honor. He pointed to the map. "As you can see, our forces greatly outnumber anything the North can muster."

Rokig then placed a large figurine across the northern mountain range on the map. "Maugris will descend the Hoarfrost Mountains via Storm Wind Pass. The King's Army will be waiting for him at the Grassland Plains just outside the Last Garrison. The might of our full military on display will convince Maugris of the futility of an invasion into Baroqia."

"You feel superior numbers alone will destroy the enemy's morale," Shiverrig said. His brows lowered and knit together in consternation.

"I do," Rokig said. "If they do not break immediately, we shall rush Maugris' army of ragtag barbarians, overwhelm them and break their will to fight. The barbarians will drop their weapons and flee the field. They have no spirit for war. They came only for easy plunder, not to die. Maugris will see his forces scattered and will withdraw back to Rachlach Fortress. I'd wager he sues for peace within a fortnight.

"The king shall allow Maugris and what is left of his meager army passage back to the north. A war reparations tax will be levied, and Maugris will be forever bled of resources."

Rokig made a point to look squarely into Shiverrig's eyes. "In this way, the king wins a decisive victory without the spill of Baroqian blood. This is warfare at a more intellectual and humane level."

Rokig took his place once more to the side of the king. He raised his brows in an expression of superiority and challenge like the arrogant peacock he was.

Shiverrig approached the table. He snatched up a figurine representing a block of enemy troops and rattled it in his palm. "The king's strategy is weak. It affords the enemy multiple avenues of escape. They will not retreat, but to regroup in numbers and attack our forces from unprotected sides."

Shiverrig placed the piece in his hand down and moved other figurines into new positions across the map. "You underestimate the resolve of what lurks in the North."

Manda was bored. Fritta, however, gave a slight nod of understanding. However, Conrad was a simpleton and could not see three steps ahead of himself. Rokig scoffed at the new placement of the figurines.

"The Crown has gathered enough information to validate our strategy. We will be more than prepared for whatever the North sends into battle," Rokig said.

"This will not be a ragtag group of barbarian tribesmen looking to fill their pockets with some Southland trinkets. It will be an army created by a maligned sorcerer intent on destroying all of Baroqia," Shiverrig declared.

"Shiverrig," Rokig rolled his eyes.

"My king, there are vast poppy fields ready for harvest along the lower hills of the Hoarfrost. The cotton fields that extend into the plains are also ripe. Storm Wind Pass lies but a day's journey north," Manda said.

"I see. It will be unfavorable to lose those crops due to the ravages of an invading army," Conrad said. A tinge of worry coated his words.

"Quite so. Last year's harvest came in three percent below the year before. Many nobles have tied their debt payment to this year's harvest," Manda said. He took the ledger from under his arm. He turned a few pages to confirm his analysis. "The pageantry of war will benefit your current acceptance rate with the Lesser Houses, but the destruction of the land and its valuable crop yields will cause irreparable harm to your reputation as a qualified leader during times of strife."

He shrugged his shoulders. "The scions of House Shiverrig have always been known as the War Kings. If it's a war you want to win, give the command to Shiverrig. The percentages of victory, and a safe harvest, more than triple in his favor."

"Finally, Manda, you have contributed something of value," Shiverrig said. Manda pursed his lips in a childish expression.

Rokig was quick to interject. "My king, the royal mages have assured me there is nothing to fear from the Mad Magician. They have the means of canceling his corrupt magic. He will be contained. The harvest will be safe."

Fritta cleared his throat. "Sire, with all due respect to the Crown, your strategy promotes participation in a war but not one that will lead to ultimate victory. Even if you win here, the conflict will persist, and your enemy will return. Our aim here is to end the threat from the North, is it not?"

Fritta's statement was true to form. He was a rock, never moved by emotion. Like Shiverrig, he was a man of the realm. Baroqia came first, its ruler's ego second. Fritta saw through the frill and concentrated on the real objective.

"Lord Fritta is correct!" Shiverrig jumped to confirm the typically taciturn lord's assessment. "This time, Maugris must be destroyed. Banishment gave him time to lick his wounds and recover. Now he is back with a greater force.

"And if the Knights of Gethem are to be used in battle, they will be used to ensure victory. The king's strategy is flawed. I will not sacrifice my men in a battle that will never be won. Such an ill-conceived plan must have come from you, Rokig. You will race forward-thinking victory is assured just as Maugris' trap snaps shut." Shiverrig gave Fritta a warrior's nod. Perhaps he had found the partnership he needed to topple Conrad.

"They are not *your* men, Duke Shiverrig. They are men of the realm, and therefore, my men," King Conrad said. "And neither Baron Rokig nor Prince Dane will be at the head of the King's Army. It will be me."

"You?" Shiverrig said. "That is interesting."

Shiverrig looked back to the map and the figurines. "Very interesting, indeed. I suggest we place regiments of infantry and spearmen here, here, and here. Fritta's ballista will be moved to the hills to the right and left. Their range will hold the enemy war machines back. Our archers will stall the enemy's ground advancement. Depending on how Maugris brings his troops to battle, we can remain flexible with our own infantry's position."

He placed the figurines that represented the fighting forces of Baroqia on the map. The combined infantry of House Fritta, House Manda, and House Rokig will engage the enemy with sword and spear. I will lead a division of cavalry behind Maugris' forces and cut off his retreat, here.

"Send the conscripts forward as fodder to draw the enemy into the range of the archers and ballista. Hope that Maugris' inexperience in large terrain warfare compels him to commit his cavalry too early. He will run them into the waiting tips of our spear men's lances."

Fritta nodded favorably. "The regiments attack from three sides, merge as one and connect with the cavalry division. We do not allow for an enemy retreat."

"That's right. We cut them down to the last man. Then, we regroup to reassess our strength. In short order, we march on his lair. This time, we uproot the vile weed once and for all."

"All very impressive, if not a bit of overkill. Baroqian soldiers will die in this type of exchange, which is not to my liking," King Conrad said. "I have a hunch there will be no need to fight, and I like my hunch."

Baron Rokig chuckled at the king's remark, but Fritta held a concerned expression. Shiverrig caught him shake his head disapprovingly. It was just a small gesture, but it was there.

"Sire, maybe we should at least consider Shiverrig's ideas. If on the odd chance Maugris does something unexpected, it would be well to have our forces properly positioned."

The king studied the players and their positions on the map. "Yes, yes, of course. Shiverrig's plan has some merit, but there are obvious holes and details to be worked out. If his strategy is accepted, then it will be me leading the cavalry. The king shall cut the head from the beast."

Rokig pondered the placement of Shiverrig's figurines with a critical eye. "What great force do you believe Maugris to possess? You plan for war beyond the means of an outcast magician. He has been holed up in his mountain fortress for years. He is a recluse. What army could he possibly muster? The Northern Tribes present no threat. They are wanderers with hardly a scrap of military training or discipline."

Shiverrig shook his head. "Declaring war on Maugris is not the same as inviting him to a county fair where the jousting matches are fixed with collapsible lances. The duels will not be fought with blunt, wooden weapons. We must prepare for every possible scenario."

Rokig continued to press Shiverrig. "You are forcing a fight that could easily be avoided. If the battle is over too quickly, you will be denied glory through bloodshed. Is that what you fear, or is it something else? If you know something more, I suggest you share it."

Shiverrig held his tongue. He was busy calculating potential numbers of wounded and dead on either side. He considered areas of terrain for positional advantage or disadvantage. He was keen to predict where the killing fields of battle would form. He would direct their position as much as possible.

King Conrad would lead them all to ultimate ruin, and Shiverrig couldn't have been happier. Battle was an unpredictable thing. When the killing began, even the most experienced fighter could lose their ability to think and reason. Accidents were plentiful.

When the smoke cleared, who could know the reason a rogue arrow, a spooked horse, or misguided round from friendly ballista fire found Conrad instead of the enemy? The battlefield offered so many beautiful ways for a king to die.

23

KASAI

"You didn't tell me one bit of your troubles when I first asked. I had to coax and coddle every single word out of you. But oh, this cute little thing crosses your path, and you just spout like a fountain," Desdemonia whispered angrily to Kasai. She grabbed his arm and turned him to face her. "She is too helpless, too convenient, and I don't like her."

"Des, you imagine snakes in the grass where there are none."

Desdemonia's amber eyes blazed back at him. He hoped she wasn't about to cast a spell on him.

"Listen to me. Reese is no good. The forest knows nothing of her. It's as if she just appeared out of thin air."

Kasai ignored the warning look from Desdemonia. He just stared straight ahead.

"Send her away, Kasai. No good can come of this."

"Just like you wanted to send me away?"

"That was Gauldumor, not me. Please, don't think such things about me."

"What are you two whispering about up there?" Reese inquired. She had eagerly volunteered to support Master Choejor as they walked along a well-traveled path. The forest had thinned, and a more settled land took shape.

Desdemonia turned her head towards Reese. "I'm educating Kasai on some of the unique fauna found in the wild. Not everything here is as helpless as it looks."

Desdemonia turned her head back and faced forward. "Her wounds are many, but superficial scratches at best. Where are the deep bruises from being held against her will? Where are the rope burns from struggle? Not a single broken bone, not a one."

"I don't know, Des. Maybe she healed herself. Listen, she's been through a lot. Those giants killed all the other pilgrims, and she was to be next. Can you imagine how scary that must've been for her? She's just a kid. We can't just abandon her now. Where's your heart?"

"That's right. Reese is a perfect, precious little thing, isn't she? You're not thinking straight. Can you not see that she is *too* beautiful, *too* vulnerable? She's just the kind of helpless waif that would inspire warmth and care from an over-protective monk who just lost everything. And don't think I'm jealous because I'm not."

"You're not making any sense. Why would you be jealous?"

"Ugh. Now you're truly under a witch's spell." She shook her head in frustration and stormed off ahead of the group.

"What's with her?" Kasai shrugged his shoulders. She wasn't wrong, Reese was beautiful. If she needed protection, then that is what he would give her. His training at Ordu had prepared him to be a shield to those in need. It was one of the Pillars of Aetenos, after all. And Reese had healed Master Choejor at a desperate hour, and Kasai felt he owed her a debt for that kindness.

Eventually, the forest opened to a small grass field. Kasai saw the outskirts of a hamlet, and beyond the city walls of Gethem. The outer edge of the town seemed peaceful, the homey smell of burning wood wafting through the air. Kasai envisioned sitting in front of a warm fire, enjoying a hot meal, trading stories with his Brothers. How long had it been since fleeing the monastery? A few weeks? Maybe a month? So much had changed since those days.

There was an oddly familiar tang to the taste in the air. Kasai remembered a similar smell from his early youth but couldn't place it in his memories. The afternoon meat was being prepared for the afternoon meal. It wasn't cooking—it was burning.

Soon this nightmare would be over. Master Choejor would finally get the aid he needed and just in time. The Master would know what to do next. Kasai breathed a sigh of relief. He was uncomfortable making decisions that affected others.

"Des!" he called out.

She stopped and turned. Her mood was sour. "What do *you* want?"

"Look! We've reached Gethem." Kasai pointed to the distant walls of the city.

"And?" Desdemonia stood impatiently with her hands on her hips until Kasai reached her.

"You've led us safely out of the forest."

"Of course I did."

"Well, you can return home now. Master Choejor and I are grateful to you. We couldn't have made it this far without you." Kasai bowed humbly. When he raised his head, he saw a hint of sadness in Desdemonia's eyes.

"I think it's best if we stay together a little longer. There is a foul scent in the air. Something is not right here. I'll wait until you and Master Choejor are safely inside the Temple before I leave." She looked suspiciously to the hamlet, and then to Reese. Her eyes narrowed just a bit.

"Don't worry, Reese will be fine too. The priestesses of her order will look after her," Kasai said.

"Then you won't need to worry about her, either," Desdemonia said. Her eyes had become dark and heavy.

Kasai was about to reply when Reese came forward, filled with excitement.

"Look! It's Gethem. We are saved! The Immortal Mother has guided us true." She handed Master Choejor to Desdemonia and hugged Kasai in a heartfelt embrace. "You did it!"

"Immortal Mother?" Des looked incredulously at Reese. "Let's just get this over with."

The four companions entered the outskirts of the hamlet. Modest huts were built sporadically on the edge of the small town, growing denser as the party walked towards its center. The smell of something burning became more pronounced. *Wood,* Kasai thought, *but something else as well.* Then he noticed that the thin columns of black smoke became thicker as they rose into the sky.

His first thought was the night of the raid at Ordu. The sights and smells were so similar. *Stop it. Not all the world is so horrible,* he thought. *Maybe, there's a festival in the main square.* By his reckoning, Aetenos' Day of Ascendance was still a few weeks away. *Perhaps these townspeople are celebrating something else.*

He smelled roasted pig on the fire, or was it some other kind of animal? He wasn't quite sure. Either way, his mouth watered at the thought of slabs of bacon and fresh ale. His stomach growled with every step.

"I bet you didn't know we could make ale at Ordu," Kasai said to Des.

"Fascinating," Des replied, but she wasn't paying much attention. "Maybe we should turn back."

"Turn back? Now?" Kasai said.

"Or get to Gethem a different way. Something doesn't feel right."

"You've been saying since the cave. It will be fine. Come on."

The townspeople stopped what they were doing, watching silently as Kasai, and the others made their way into town. Soon a small following trailed behind them, speaking in hushed tones. Kasai figured they were just curious people. They did make up an odd lot. Two mysterious monks of Ordu, a Forest Dweller, and a priestess of the Immortal Mother were an unlikely fellowship.

These townspeople appeared to be simple folk of meager means. They dressed in clothes designed for working the fields and some carried farm tools in hand. The group behind Kasai and the others grew larger.

"I don't like this," Desdemonia said.

As if on cue, the voice of the crowd rose above a murmur. Kasai heard discouraging words like "witch," and "dark magic, and "evil."

Some of the townsfolk covered their mouths and pointed their fingers at Desdemonia. They traced symbols in the air to ward off evil spirits. Kasai spied other individuals standing in place, twitching erratically—black drool leaked from their mouths as they cast vapid stares from dead eyes.

The street leading to the center of the hamlet was walled off by a haphazard arrangement of boards, broken doors, and overturned carts. People milled about the entrance searching for something forgotten or lost. The townspeople, as one, turned and watched them approach. Their faces glared menacingly at Desdemonia. The murmurs from the group behind them grew to shouts.

"Kasai, we need to get out of here, now," Desdemonia said.

"I think you're right."

Kasai pivoted the group around only to see that the crowd behind had swollen. They seemed to be only mildly interested in Kasai, Master Choejor, and Reese. Their focus was centered on Desdemonia. They reached for her, cautiously at first but then with more determination. Desdemonia pushed away from their groping hands, but there were too many of them.

The crowd turned into a mob.

In a quick surge, the townspeople flowed in a massive current of flesh that swarmed around Desdemonia. She was cut off from Kasai and the others. The mob carried her through the makeshift barrier and into the town's square. Kasai tried in vain to reach her, but too many bodies filled the gap between them.

He saw Reese was frozen with fear. He could not leave Master Choejor with her like this. The crowd would trample them both.

"We must get Master Choejor to safety," Kasai shouted over the noise of the crowd. He grabbed Master Choejor's arm and worked his way out of the mob. He was hard-pressed to find an opening through the sea of people.

Reese snapped to attention. She moved in front of him and drove the manic townspeople out of their way. Kasai was amazed at her strength, and it wasn't long before she pushed through the crowd. Kasai spotted a narrow alley between two small buildings.

"We'll be safe here," he said. The pupils of her magenta-hued eyes had dialed to swollen black disks. She had the look of a preternatural hunter.

"Stay here with Master Choejor. I'm going back for Des," Kasai said.

"Stay with me, Kasai! The Wood Witch can take care of herself. Don't leave me alone. I can't be alone, not again," Reese said. The hard edge vanished, and tears welled up in her eyes. She was visibly trembling.

Kasai was unsure what to do. He couldn't just leave Reese and Master Choejor alone. She looked so frail. If the mob discovered them, he could lose them too. But Desdemonia was in danger right now.

"I'll be right back. Just don't move from this spot."

He raced to save Desdemonia. He followed the crowd through the wooded barrier. Kasai gasped in horror at what he saw on the other side. Crucifixes in the shape of an X lined the ground, creating a semi-circle around a central platform. Bodies were spread against the roughly cut wood in various stages of decomposition.

Massive scaffoldings draped limp bodies from thick ropes. Black ravens lined the top beams over the dead bodies. Two jumped from their perch, squawking angrily at each other. Loose feathers sputtered from their wings as they competed for a piece of loose flesh from a dead man's face. The choice eyeballs were already taken. Eventually, the victor ripped it free and flew into the grey sky. The other trailed close behind, refusing to give up.

Charred bodies slumped from blackened stakes over smoldering wood. He followed the movement of the mob to a high stake surrounded by fresh timber. Three men held Desdemonia, while a fourth was busy tying her to the stake. The mob's wild hysteria grew. They demanded another victim to satiate their bloodlust.

The center of the town was a sea of madness. How was this possible? What would cause decent people to act in such cruel and horrific ways? Kasai was shocked as he raced passed latecomers to the next spectacle.

He drove into the heart of the crowd, pushing and pulling his way towards Desdemonia. She thrashed against her bonds to escape, but the ropes held. Naked bodies caked with muddy filth gyrated against Kasai in a macabre dance. Their hands pressed against him and tried to encourage him to join their madness.

Kasai pushed the naked zealots back. He climbed awkwardly atop the loose wood and sticks. Desdemonia's eyes were bright amber, alive with fright.

"Call Gauldumor!" Kasai shouted over the deafening crowd. He looked frantically for a way to free Desdemonia.

"I can't! The forest binds Gauldi. He cannot travel beyond its deep roots. Free my arms, and my spells will flow!"

Kasai tried to untie the ropes, but the knots were too tight. Fear sweat poured from his forehead, and panic clouded his thoughts. Ninziz-zida grew hot in his sash. Kasai looked out at the angry mob, but he could never stop them all.

It was happening again. All he wanted to do was protect those he cared for and loved. He failed to save his parents, his Masters, his Brothers, and now Desdemona. He had lost so many. He felt powerless.

"Let the light of your heart spread as my Light once did." The fatherly voice returned.

Kasai barely heard the message. He was focused on four flaming torches bobbing their way through the crowd. Each was thrown towards the kindling wood at their feet.

The fire caught fast. The mark of Oh-hur on his forearm responded involuntarily. The temperature of the flame dissipated as the power tattoo protected him. But Des didn't have a unique tattoo to ward off the flames.

The fire spread. Kasai was desperate. He needed a knife to cut the rope. He stomped at the flames with his feet. But he only succeeded in spreading the fire. He searched the crowd for a sympathetic face. A sea of insanity stared back at him.

"Burn! Burn! Burn!" The townspeople shouted. "Burn the witch!" Some thrust pitchforks or short swords in the air, while others raised their fists in anger.

"Kasai, the fire, it burns! Help me!" Desdemonia wailed.

Kasai felt helpless. His power tattoo would not protect him infinitely, and the fire would burn them both if he didn't do something soon. Kasai searched through his memories of Ordu. He couldn't concentrate on anything but the flames.

"Focus. Calm. Light." Kasai heard the voice in his mind again.

"Aetenos?" It was the first name that came to mind.

"Let me in. I will light your way."

Desdemonia's shrill screams pierced Kasai's heart.

"Help me!" Kasai shouted. He lowered his guard and allowed the voice's mystic presence to guide him. Then a wave of cooling sensation coursed through his body. Kasai felt his intense need to protect grow stronger. It was his shield and weapon at once.

Where before his panic had unraveled his thoughts, now the soothing energy helped focus his concentration. The cooling sensation within him swelled to an overwhelming force. It pushed against the barriers of his awareness. It wanted to grow, to live.

Kasai was barely aware of the white light seeping from his body like a soft mist. It flowed down below his feet and smothered the flames of the pyre. The light expanded upwards and encased Kasai and Desdemonia in a loving embrace.

Desdemonia was no longer screaming. She was calm and serene. Kasai saw a look of wonder in her eyes.

The enraged mob raged and yelled as they rushed the stake with more lit torches. Pitchforks and swords raised in the air. They would not allow the witch to survive this day. Kasai felt the angry surge of the crowd. The mob was blind to the light flowing from him.

Kasai tried to control the energy, but it was bigger than him, bigger than the fire, bigger than the mob and the entire hamlet. When he could no longer contain it, he let the massive force go. Blinding, white light exploded out of his pores in a violent release of energy.

The mob, blown off their feet, had fallen like freshly-scythed wheat, laying in a circular pattern around the wooden stake. Some of the townspeople smoldered and burst into flame.

Kasai's body glowed and flared with righteous light before fading, as if it were never there. He jumped to the ground and picked up a fallen blade to cut Desdemonia's bounds. She hugged him tightly, their embrace as pure as the white light. The two leaped from the smoking pyre and ran out of the square. Soon they came to where Kasai had left Reese and Master Choejor. Kasai was aware of two men following them from the square.

"We do not want any more trouble," Kasai warned. He took Ninziz-zida from his sash. The men slowed their approach and showed their hands, free of weapons. In unison, they and dropped to a knee and bowed their heads.

"We offer our service to the Argent Hammer of the Divine Fist," one of the men proclaimed. He wore dark leather breeches and a dark, form-fitted shirt. He was lean and muscular. Two long daggers were tied to either side of his waist. The collar of his shirt had an embroidered shape of a three-pronged wheel. The arms of the emblem spun counterclockwise. Kasai recognized it as a symbol of Aetenos.

Rugged in appearance, the man had straight black hair slowly giving way to grey. Kasai guessed he'd seen more than thirty winters.

"Aetenos' blessing is upon you, young one," the man said. "We are Followers of the Light. We have waited long years for the rise of the next Ever Hero. I am Pallo Katan."

His bright blue eyes held a father's authority. "This is my brother, Veers, but most know him as Run-Run." The other nodded his head enthusiastically but remained silent.

Veer's face was expressive, especially his green eyes. They reminded Kasai of Spring's first tender shoots stretching up through the last remaining snows of winter. He had a stubble beard and auburn shoulder-length hair, the cinnamon color of a turning leaf.

Veers was dressed in similar clothing as his brother, wearing the same blue, three-pronged symbol on his collar, but overall his appearance was shaggy and unkempt. Kasai saw that Veers, or Run-Run as he was called, wore bits and pieces of bush and grass tangled in his hair.

Run-Run was slender and wiry. When he stood, he moved with fluid grace. He looked younger than Pallo, perhaps in his late twenties. Run-Run did not say a word but stared at Kasai in adulation. Kasai shifted uneasily. He didn't like so much attention.

"Come, we must leave this place. The townspeople are under the influence of the Change of Mor. They will gather their senses soon enough and be back to finish what they started."

Kasai was about to respond when Desdemonia stepped forward. She pointed to Gethem. "Can you get us to the Temple of Illumination?"

Pallo and Run-Run looked to each other with unease. Run-Run's brow furrowed, and Pallo signed with his hands in response. Kasai wondered what was exchanged between the two brothers.

"If that is the wish of the Ever Hero, it shall be done. But we must be quick," Pallo said. Run-Run nodded his agreement but kept a worried face.

"I don't trust them. We should find a different way. Just us," Reese said. She looked from behind Kasai as if to shield herself from their view.

Kasai turned around and placed his palms on Reese's narrow shoulders. "Reese, I think they are friends. And by the looks of things, we'll need all the help we can get," Kasai said. He tried his best to be reassuring.

Reese looked up at Kasai with saucer-shaped eyes. "I followed you as far as the barrier. I saw what happened. How... I've never seen anything like it. The holy books promised of the coming of a savior. You are the promised one. We have been searching for you."

"Not you too," Kasai sighed.

"The Song of Aetenos sings brightly in you," Pallo said.

Master Choejor began to vomit blood where he sat on the ground. Kasai pushed thoughts of demigods and Ever Heroes from his mind. Master Choejor had to get to the High Healers.

Pallo and Run-Run gathered Master Choejor in their arms. They walked deeper into the alley. "Come, there are other ways to get into Gethem besides through the main gates."

They moved quickly to an inconspicuous door, which opened into the rear portion of a tavern. Kasai and the others entered a dark room. The floor was sticky, the air smelling of old smoke and stale mead. Chairs were flipped upside-down, arranged haphazardly upon long oak tables.

Pallo and Run-Run lead the way to a blank section of the wall. Pallo gently transferred Master Choejor's weight to Run-Run and produced a silver key from an inner pocket. He used it to unlock a small door that was invisible to Kasai until it was opened. Inside was a small landing and a descending staircase.

"Who are you people?" Reese inquired suspiciously.

"I have said, I am Pallo. He is my brother, Run-Run. We are..." but before he could say more, Run-Run interrupted him with a grunt. "We are Followers of the Light."

Kasai quickly scanned their auras. Faint blue, dagger-like shards shimmered in circling spirals that traveled in a circuit from their feet to their heads and back again. The shards seemed to point in the direction of Reese no matter the position they occupied over the men's bodies. Kasai wondered why the auras of followers of Aetenos would be at odds with the aura of a priestess of the Immortal Mother.

Kasai looked to see if Reese's aura did the same in return, but surprisingly, he could not make out any discernable shapes or symbols surrounding the young priestess. Her aura remained unfocused as if constantly in motion.

The staircase descended into another small landing. The walls and floor were covered with wooden boards. A tight corridor traveled into shadow to the right and left. Pallo reached into a belt pouch and took out a palm-sized stone, while Run-Run did the same. The brothers hit the stones against the wall a few times until they glowed with an inner light. Pallo handed his stone to Kasai, and Run-Run gave his to Desdemonia.

"We will travel under the chaos," Pallo said. He pointed down the right corridor. "Lead the way, Ever Hero."

"You are mistaken. I am just a monk," Kasai said as he moved to the front of the group.

"I want to be right next to Kasai," Reese said fast. She locked her arm inside of his.

"Des, maybe we should spread the light out so everyone can see," Kasai said.

Kasai thought he caught Reese give Desdemonia a nasty look. Des just shook her head and walked to the rear.

"Everyone ready? Ok, let's go," Kasai said. It wasn't long before the wooden panels were gone, and the corridor turned into an excavated tunnel of packed earth.

"How far does the tunnel go?" Kasai asked.

"We will walk for three hours. The end will bring us up into the center of Gethem. But you must know, the city has changed, and not for the better," Pallo opined.

They walked along in silence, boots slapping the cool, moist surface below, arms sometimes brushing clammy walls. The tunnel was cold and damp. Eventually, they reached another staircase that ascended to an upper platform. Pallo unlocked another hidden door with the same silver key, and they entered a vacant tunic and cloak shop where the window curtains were drawn.

"Where is the shop owner?" Desdemonia asked. "Why isn't anyone here?"

"He is a friend of Aetenos," Pallo said and explained no more.

Kasai and Des handed the rocks back to the brothers.

"How far now?" Kasai said.

"Not far," Pallo responded. He opened the front door; the noise immediately assaulted their ears. Kasai had read that Gethem was considered the King's Jewel for centuries. House Shiverrig imposed strict orders over the populace. Anyone disobeying the law was dealt with swiftly. But as Pallo had said, things had changed.

The streets of Gethem had been transformed into a sprawling, savage arena of mayhem and misery. The stench of death hung heavy in the air. How could such suffering be allowed to happen? Where were the duke's men to enforce law and order?

Kasai heard the click-clack of animal hooves on cobblestone. A column of armed knights in polished armor rode atop massive horses clad in long chainmail, leading an extensive train of wagons filled with supplies. The heraldry of House Shiverrig was draped over their backs and the coverings of the wagon loads.

"They're leaving the city on their way to war," Pallo pointed out.

The harsh noises and oppressive smells were overwhelming; Kasai longed for the silence of the monastery and the sounds of the mountains. The ambient clamor of suffering and screams was deafening. Even the forest seemed tranquil by comparison.

Long lines of impaled bodies and rotted heads littered the street. The ground was wet and muddy and dotted with deep burgundy puddles.

"What fresh hell is this?" Desdemonia said.

"Gethem bleeds for reasons known only to the Duke," Pallo said.

The clouds hung low, filling the atmosphere with oppressive gloom as no sunlight could pierce the thick veil. Men and women dance naked through the chilly streets, gyrating beneath the slow deaths of neighbors that had been nailed to rough, wooden beams.

A disheveled and dirty man stood facing a stone wall, screaming obscenities inches away from its surface. His arms flailed in chaotic exclamation as if addressing an enthusiastic audience and stirring them to revolt. He then cocked his head back and rammed it into the wall. A wicked gash opened on his forehead. The insane man ran to another section of the wall with blood streaming down his face. Once there, he started his tirade again.

"Gethem has turned from the Light of Aetenos. These people have lost themselves to the Change of Mor," Pallo said. "The hamlet was but a taste of the depravity that has befallen sweet Gethem."

"What do they hope to achieve?" Desdemonia said.

"They seek salvation by freeing themselves from the constraints of the flesh," Pallo said. Run-Run rolled his eyes and drew a revolving circle in the air beside his temple.

"Let's keep moving," Pallo said.

The city spread out, folding back upon itself with hundreds of switchback streets. Pollution poured mercilessly from rusty spouts into already dirty waterways. There were bridges and canals around every street corner where filth was swept freely into the water and mixed with the slow-moving, thick current.

Judicators in tall conical headgear prowled through the masses of hysterical worshippers. They grabbed people, seemingly at random, for trial. The crowd would cheer every time a recruit was selected for the Change of Mor. The judicators were followed by packs of filthy sycophants, wearing hooded frocks. They scurried about with muddy feet, stopping only to lash themselves with hand-held whips.

Feral dogs ran amok, holding human body parts in their mouths. The weaker animals gave up their bounty to the strong and, in turn, stole from lesser beasts.

The thick smoke hung low in the sky and kept the stench of charred flesh in the air. Black ash drifted about as if an abyssal snowstorm fell on Gethem. Kasai thought he might vomit. He kept walking, trying only to focus on reaching the Temple.

Pallo successfully navigated the group through a back alley, which opened to another street surprisingly clear of mayhem. Ahead of them stood the Temple of Illumination.

The Temple began with three short steps that led to a modest one-story gateway. Orange-stained columns rose on either side of rust-colored double doors. The columns supported rows of arches with curled ends that pointed to the heavens.

The entrance had been vandalized. The iconographic images and artifacts usually found on the main doors of any monastery had been torn off.

The Temple's sacred structures wound around a central tower, presumably where the Grandmaster took office. The corners of the tiled roofs also curled upwards to symbolize the enlightened souls that transcended the mundane world. However, the windows had been boarded up or bricked over. The Temple no longer radiated the glory of Aetenos or the power of the Immortal Mother.

"Is this it? I expected something more," Desdemonia said.

Pallo and Run-Run walked Master Choejor up the stairs to the doors. "The loss of Aetenos has brought much suffering to the lands of Hanna. This is the work of Mor, or worse," Pallo said sadly. He looked upon the once immaculate temple and then back to the city of Gethem. "A great evil has risen. It blows its foul breath through the lands, infecting all who taste its foul air."

Kasai agreed with Desdemonia. He had expected something more from the Temple of Illumination since Ordu was kept spotless. Kasai would know. He was always cleaning.

One who followed the Way of Aetenos did not lavish himself in decadent ornamentation or precious things. His role was to serve others and to be a shield to those in need. What he saw upon the outer façade was complete disdain for the spirit of the demigod and his followers.

His eyes wandered to Reese. Was she a precious thing or someone in need of a shield? Either way, it would not matter. Soon she would be back with the other priestesses of her order, and Des would be gone, too.

He had traveled many miles and endured much hardship to reach the Temple. Now that he had finally arrived, he wasn't sure he wanted the journey to end. Another fit of coughing wracked Master Choejor, and fresh blood wet his lips. He sagged in the arms of Pallo and Run-Run.

"We must go inside and find the High Healers," Kasai said. He took the first step towards the Temple doors. Saving Master Choejor was the priority, not his mixed feelings towards his new friends.

Desdemonia remained standing in the street. Her hands locked in fists firmly on her hips. "Kasai, haven't you wondered why Gethem allows such atrocities to continue? Or what your Temple is doing to protect these people? Are you sure there are healers in there?"

She looked to another square further down the street. "These people aren't evil, but they are most definitely under some dark spell."

"And you would know," Reese said. Her voice was noticeably hostile. "Isn't it time for the Wood Witch to be running along? Go back to your forest, Desdemonia. Kasai doesn't need you anymore. He is among his kind now."

Reese took Kasai by the arm and led him the rest of the way up the stairs.

"In that case, I'm coming too," Desdemonia said. She marched up the steps and joined Kasai and Reese at the doors.

24

SEKKA

Sekka stood at the center of her inner chamber, watching with interest in her mirror the patterns of blood dripping from her naked mortal body in the matted sable of a tattered rug. Outside the circle of the mat, butchered slaves were tossed about the furniture or piled on the stone floor in messy heaps of torn flesh.

She had chosen a group of slaves to take as lovers, albeit for a brief time, and enjoyed their company. She reveled in the feel of human skin upon skin. It was so delicate. It was electric. Eventually, her dagger found their hearts at the precise moment of climax. The mixture of death and release was an intoxicating splash of bliss and misery. She savored every drop.

Others had felt the wrath of her bestial form. That usually came after the session of so-called lovemaking. She tended to need something more to satiate her demonic passion. Those unfortunate slaves were ripped to pieces by her talons and teeth. Their shredded remains still dripped down the walls and puddled on the floor. But no matter how often she tried to distract herself, she could not find peace.

Now that Maugris' spell of binding was broken, she could communicate with her thralls on the Gathos with ease. Sekka licked wet blood from her lips. She spoke a final syllable and completed the ritual of sending.

+Chedipe.+

The connection was instantaneous. Chedipe was startled from her work. She looked up as if Sekka stood before her.

+Open your senses to me.+ Sekka commanded.

+My Queen. The hour is desperate. You must return!+

+Show me the monk.+

Chedipe's eyes, now her eyes, looked down on the bloodied and bruised body of Aetenos. He had been removed from the stone wall of his prison cell and moved to a bigger room. Presently, he was stretched on a flat table. His wrists were bound above his head and chained to the edge of the table. His legs were spread and shackled at the ankles. Carving instruments laid jumbled and bloodied on the table between his flayed legs.

+What news do you have for me?+

+Zizphander comes. His armies have begun the march to Furia Keep. Gathos burns!+ Chedipe's mind was saturated with anxiety. Sekka pushed the demon witch's fear aside. She needed answers.

+What has Aetenos revealed?+

+He refuses Chedipe. The monk speaks in riddles of madness.+

+I told you not to break his mind.+

+No, my Queen, he is not broken. His mind is crafty. He has hidden it where Chedipe cannot find it. Chedipe will dig deeper. She will find the information you seek.+

Sekka had used subterfuge and coaxing to discover the whereabouts of the next Ever Hero. She failed. She entered his mind and tried to take the information by force. She was rebuffed. She hoped by now Chedipe would have had more success, but still, Aetenos had revealed nothing. Again, failure.

Aetenos' eyes cracked open. He looked up at Chedipe, but Sekka knew, somehow, he saw her instead. One of his disgusting, lighthearted smiles, broadened his lips. Was he mocking her?

Sekka forced Chedipe's face closer to his. "Why do you endure so much for the mortals? Their faith in you has faltered. You are a forgotten thing to them."

Aetenos said nothing. He simply continued to smile.

Chedipe paced the floor of the torture chamber. Sekka's mental influence betrayed the control she had over the demon witch's body. When she spoke next, her voice inadvertently came out of Chedipe's mouth.

"I must have his secret before Zizphander learns of my absence. What was overlooked?"

"Reached too far…again. Enemies…at doorstep. Take advantage…your folly. Late to flee…Gathos." Aetenos chuckle through bruised lips.

"You know nothing!" Sekka glared at him through Chedipe's eyes.

"A hero has risen … grows stronger. Defeat you … above and below. Same fate as before. Unless Zizzzphan … der." Aetenos' eyes closed, and he went silent. However, the smile remained on his face.

+Heal his wounds and secure him outside. Make sure he is protected from the cold. He is useless to me dead.+ Sekka commanded Chedipe.

Sekka severed the connection to Chedipe. This was wonderful news! The Ever Hero had finally risen. If Aetenos would not reveal his location, then she would bring his avatar to her.

+Lord Oziax.+

+Yes, my Queen.+

+Meet me in Maugris' throne room. It is time to force the war with the South.+ She looked at her body in the mirror again. +I will be along shortly. Say nothing until I arrive.+

Magical, floating globes were interspersed along the corridor leading to Maugris' throne room. They generated a sorcerous, emerald light that played against the uneven rock of the walls.

The corridor was carved from dark grey hematite, which made up much of Rachlach Fortress' inner chambers. The natural iron in the stone gave the walls the appearance of shining, green metal.

When Sekka arrived, Maugris sat uncomfortably in his black throne. Dark runes of power were etched into the surface of the broad chair. Oziax stood beneath him at the foot of the dais. The tension was thick between the two.

Maugris stood as he spotted her, pointing his finger in accusation. "I will not commit to a war with the South until I possess the greater demons of Gathos. I have demanded this from the start!"

"You will do as the Queen commands," Lord Oziax said.

"What did you say? You and your Queen are nothing."

"You are a brave mortal behind your shield of binding. If I were free of your bond, I would tear your heart from your body and devour it before your eyes," Oziax snarled up at Maugris.

"But you are not free, are you? It is a wonder I still allow you to exist."

Sekka arrived at the dais. She faced Lord Oziax and eyed the demon warlord knowingly.

+I told you to hold your tongue.+

She turned to Maugris. "Lord Maugris, an army gathers in the South. The time for war has come."

"I am well aware of what is happening in Baroqia. Let them come. Conrad's host will freeze in the mountains before they find me."

"This is a fortuitous opportunity. One that should not be squandered."

"Have you brought me the behemoths and juggernauts of Gathos? No? Then this conversation is pointless."

"My lord, we are so very close to achieving all that you desire. I have been alerted the Ever Hero has risen. He must be lured to Rachlach Fortress."

"Ever Hero, Ever Hero," he mocked, sneering at her. His face twisted, turning purple as he screamed, "Ever Hero!" He threw his hands in the air. "This obsession of yours has pushed my patience to its limit."

"My obsession is driven by your desire, my lord. A world of demonkind awaits your command, but I need the means to bring them to you. The war with the South will compel Aetenos' avatar to come forward. Once he is in our grasps, I will have the means to open the Chaos Gate."

"The answer is still no. I will decide when the appropriate hour is to invade the South." Maugris gathered himself into his robes on the throne chair.

"Perhaps it would be best to speak of other, more favorable developments. Duke Shiverrig has pledged his loyalty to your cause," Sekka said.

"Gerun Shiverrig, the son of Gareth Shiverrig?"

"The very same. The combined strength of House Shiverrig's armies and the current demon horde shall be enough to assure victory over those who wronged you long ago."

"A Shiverrig will only embrace a cause as long as it fits his agenda. They are a family of vipers. But no matter. When this is over, all of the Great Houses will fall," Maugris said.

"Then let us begin the reign of Maugris the Infinite."

"Give me what I command."

"I cannot."

"Bah. It is clear I sucked the wrong devil from the Abyss. There will be no war until I am ready. I am quite content to remain here and bide my time."

"Maugris, do not be cruel. Lord Oziax will lead the horde into Baroqia and take the fight to the Southerners."

"He will do nothing of the sort. Did you know the fiends haunting these cold halls are fond of whispering secrets? They speak of foul-play and betrayal. The demon Narthoth should not have been able to break the wards of my binding spell. I wonder if it was not Lord Oziax that sabotaged the summoning chamber."

Lord Oziax bristled at Maugris' words. A challenge had been issued.

"I have heard enough. It is time for this insufferable mortal to learn his place." Lord Oziax took a step towards the dais.

"You will not take another step." Maugris cast a contemptuous glare at Lord Oziax, which faded as the demon warlord put his foot on the first step of the dais. Maugris' bold attitude was replaced by questioning doubt.

"Oziax! I command you to stop!" Maugris shouted.

Lord Oziax's eyes narrowed at Maugris. A sinister grin of canine teeth filled his mouth. The demon lord took another step.

+STOP!+ Sekka bellowed into Oziax's mind. She sent a burst of mental force that brought him to his knees.

Maugris released a clenched breath. His superior countenance returned quickly.

"You see? Look how he cowers," Maugris stepped down to where Lord Oziax knelt. He jabbed a bony finger into the demon warlord's forehead. "You are nothing."

Lord Oziax pushed against Maugris' finger and slowly rose. His eyes sunk into his head. Razor-thin lines appeared over the demon's exposed skin. A white mane of hair grew long past his shoulders.

The temperature in the room dropped, and the air smelled of a coming storm. Maugris hesitated, then backed away. "What's this?"

+Obey him, or I will destroy you myself.+ Sekka said with calm determination.

Lord Oziax's head twitched to the side. He lowered his head in submission. +Why do we need him, my Queen? Give him to me. His death will be slow and sweet.+

+No. You will do nothing until the Ever Hero is mine. Is that understood?+

Lord Oziax did not respond. He raised his head towards Maugris. His body seethed with hatred.

+OZIAX!+

+Understood, my Queen.+

"One wonders what value your Queen sees in you."

"If not Lord Oziax, then who? I have said countless times that the demons of Gathos will not follow a mortal, even one of your abilities. Lord Oziax is well respected and feared among the horde. There is no other they will follow at Rachlach Fortress."

"Then bring me one they will! Am I not being clear?" The emotional angst radiating from Maugris was raw and palpable. "You consistently find ways to twist my demands into suggestions and then afterthoughts."

"My lord Maugris, we are at an impasse. As I have said, if you wish to bring forth anything of merit from Gathos, you will need to open a Chaos Gate. I cannot do the impossible, no matter how often or insistently you ask. The Ever Hero is the key to your triumph."

Maugris was no longer listening. He tapped his fingers together in front of his mouth. His eyes were filled with suspicion. "Leave me now. I wish to hear the sound of my own thoughts and no others."

Lord Oziax begrudgingly backed away from the throne dais. He gave a short, obligatory bow to Maugris and left the room. Damn that impatient beast. Maugris would soon realize the truth. Perhaps Lord Oziax was right. What did it matter now? She could take control of the horde, but the longer she siphoned Maugris' resources, the more she could conserve her own. She would need all of her strength when she encountered Aetenos' Ever Hero. Aetenos was wrong. She would not suffer the same fate as before. This time she would win.

Where was Sess'thra? She had not given her a report of any kind for days. Her silence was unnerving. "I'll throttle that little minx if she's neglecting her duties again and fucking for her own pleasure."

25

KASAI

Kasai pushed open the Temple's red double doors. He was not surprised they were unlocked. All were welcome inside the hallowed halls of the Temple of Illumination. The street clamor poured into the entry chamber. Kasai closed the doors quickly once everyone was inside. The entryway was deserted, and he was puzzled when there was no one to greet them.

"Shouldn't someone be here?" Desdemonia asked.

"Yes," he confirmed, looking past the entryway. There should have been a novice monk stationed at the door to offer weary travelers a cup of freshwater. Where was the sound of monks chanting verses of the sutra? All he could hear was the muffled chaos of the street. Kasai exchanged a nervous glance with Desdemonia.

His expectations of the Temple of Illumination had always been grand, but this was a dreary and untended place. The halls lacked the serenity that was familiar to him at Ordu. There was an oppressive heaviness in the air that Kasai couldn't quite place. The misery of Gethem had seeped into the Temple's foundation and corrupted the peaceful harmony of the building. He suddenly longed for the chiming bells of Ordu.

"Let's try to find someone that can direct us to the healers," Kasai said.

He spotted an older temple monk down the hall. Kasai was surprised his robes were dyed bright red. Typically, monks wore rusty-orange or bright, yellow-colored robes, never bright red. The Master Monks dressed in light blues, like Master Choejor. Kasai guessed this was the attire of a city-temple monk versus one studying at Ordu, or any of the other three Orders of Aetenos.

"Wait!" Kasai called out.

The temple monk stopped abruptly. His look of surprise turned to uncertainty and then concern. Kasai did not see any distinguishing marks of Aetenos upon the monk's robes. Nothing about this Temple made any sense.

"What's going on here?" the temple monk asked. He examined Master Choejor's soiled and tattered robes. He looked at the others with a troubled expression, then focused his attention on Kasai. "You two are from...?"

"We come from the mountain monastery of Ordu," Kasai answered.

"Ordu," the temple monk repeated. "Is that so?"

"Yes, we have traveled far to see the High Healers. He is Master Choejor. He has been poisoned by something that cannot be purged. A terrible fate has befallen the Order. I must speak with Grandmaster Nysulu," Kasai said.

"A Master from Ordu." The temple monk's eyes darted to each member of the party. "Yes, yes, you must come quickly. My name is Jai. I will bring you directly to the Grandmaster."

Jai led Kasai and the others down a dimly lit hall where only a few candles sputtered in sconces along the walls. The stained-glass windows depicting Aetenos' journeys through the lands of Hanna had been painted black. A deep worry took hold in Kasai's gut. He felt Desdemonia's nearness as they walked.

"This is bad," she whispered.

"I know. I know," Kasia said. He caught up to the temple monk. "Jai, what is going on here?"

Jai picked up his pace. "Hurry now. It's not far."

"Are we going to the High Healers? Will Grandmaster Nysulu be there?"

"The Grandmaster of the Seventh Heaven has passed from this realm of suffering," Jai said over his shoulder. There was no remorse in his voice.

"Dead? Grandmaster Nysulu is dead? But how? When?" Kasai was stunned.

The uneasy feeling of worry in his gut became a tight knot. His intuition warned him not to trust this temple monk and to leave this place immediately. There would be no salvation here for him or his companions. But Master Choejor needed deep healing. Where else could he go? There was no time. If the healers were here, then they would help.

He had been thrust into events beyond his understanding since the attack on Ordu. Kasai felt like the ground had opened up beneath him. No matter how quickly he backpedaled, he could not escape the crumbling edge.

"Come. Come. Eto Vyliche, the new Grandmaster of Eternity, will answer your questions," Jai said.

Kasai looked at Des, and her eyes were filled with doubt. Reese seemed perfectly content. When their eyes met, she gave Kasai a reassuring yet, somewhat misplaced wink. "We're almost there; the Shrine of the Immortal Mother is located close to the receiving room of the Grandmaster." Reese's smile seemed benign.

They entered a large room where the newly appointed Grandmaster stood speaking to another monk. Grandmaster Vyliche exaggerated an air of self-importance. His delicate hair fell in long thin strands down to the middle of his back, and he wore a magnificent red robe with embroidered gold symbols circling the sleeve cuffs and collar. Five temple monks, in less ornate bright-red robes, stood along the far wall of the room.

"Please, only those from the Monastery of Ordu may approach his Holiness. The others must remain back with me," Jai said.

Kasai took Master Choejor from Pallo and Run-Run, shouldering his weakened Master's weight on his shoulders as he slowly approached the Grandmaster. Kasai hoped the smaller monk standing next to him was a High Healer. The monk didn't look like a Healer, and Kasai did not sense any compassion in him. He looked crafty.

And the monk shimmered strangely in the light when he moved. Kasai remembered seeing that shimmer before, but he couldn't recall where. It made the hair on the back of his neck rise.

Kasai briefly looked back at Desdemonia with trepidation. She mirrored his unease. She shook her head side-to-side in short, quick moves. Reese, however, looked enthusiastic, as if waiting eagerly for something to happen.

Kasai looked more deeply into the auras of the temple monks in the room. Although they were too far away for an accurate reading, he clearly saw ashen vapors surrounding the monks. Even the Grandmaster's aura was no more than a few flecks of bright blue struggling to avoid muddy-black tendrils that wrapped and unwrapped around his body like constrictors.

Kasai's heart sank. The Temple of Illumination had turned from the light of Aetenos and into a house of darkness.

Kasai reached the Grandmaster, and quickly told him of the trouble at Ordu, the poison infecting Master Choejor and their flight from the monastery. Master Choejor hung so heavily from Kasai's shoulder; he appeared nearly dead. The crafty-looking monk moved closer as he examined the frail Master.

"Yet, you two somehow survived the massacre of Ordu," Grandmaster Vyliche stated. He slowly evaluated Kasai with a scrutinizing eye. "Good, good. It is a wonder you managed to reach us at all. Were there any others who survived that dreadful day?"

"I do not know, Grandmaster. There could be others. I fear the other monasteries shall suffer the same fate if they are not warned." Kasai looked nervously around the room. The five temple monks fidgeted aggressively along the back wall.

"The other three monasteries of Aetenos have already fallen. The Four Orders are no more," the Grandmaster said matter-of-factly.

A cold sweat edged down Kasai's back. He was too late. His heart thumped heavily in his chest. All of the monasteries had been destroyed. Gone. His eyes searched for some kind of answer.

"I see this is news to you, young friend. Come, I shall tell you the entire tale, but not here. This information is sacred to the Temple and not for the ears of the uninitiated." Grandmaster Vyliche looked to where Desdemonia and the others stood. "Let us adjourn to my private chambers. Master Lanak will accompany us. I believe he can shed more light on these terrible events." The crafty-looking monk bowed deeply.

"Grandmaster Vyliche, I humbly request that Master Choejor be brought to the High Healers first. He needs immediate attention. He is very sick."

"Indeed. I'll send for a healer to join us. Come, I wish to hear more of your story. Your friends may take their respite in the garden. Brother Jai, see that they are comfortable." The Grandmaster's tone made it clear this was not a suggestion but a command. He turned and walked across the room to a far door.

Kasai followed the Grandmaster, though his instinct screamed, RUN! Everything about Gethem, the Temple of Illumination, and the temple monks within were wrong. Kasai concentrated intensely on seeing the aura of Master Lanak. The ashen vapor above his head shifted into the black sigil he had seen at Ordu, the day the assassin's dart pierced Master Choejor's flesh.

Kasai's heart raced faster. Master Lanak was the changeling! The five temple monks along the back wall approached slowly. He observed similar black sigils fade into reality above their heads. He turned and looked at the temple monk, Jai. Darkness surrounded his soul, as well.

Why hadn't he listened to Desdemonia's warning? Now he had walked his companions into a trap. The Temple of Illumination was filled with vipers, and Kasai had stumbled blindly into their pit.

The despair of Gethem was permitted to thrive because the spiritual leaders had embraced a darker evil. They had turned their backs on the people they were meant to heal and protect. Kasai stopped walking.

"Will the changeling be accompanying us, Grandmaster?" Kasai asked as he pointed to Master Lanak. He was surprised at his own words. But the *things* in the room were imposters or worse. He reached for Ninziz-zida. The Fire Serpent's sentient connection to Kasai responded with her approval. His instincts were correct.

The Grandmaster turned and tilted his head at Kasai. "What did you say, young man?"

Master Lanak looked at Grandmaster Vyliche in mock surprise, and then a knowing smile crossed his face. "I believe the lost monk from Ordu owes me an apology, Grandmaster Vyliche," Master Lanak said. He drew a short dagger concealed in his robe and pointed it at Master Choejor. "And a life. I see the last Master has not yet found the deep sleep from my dart's kiss. She is quite an aggressive leech. Once she has developed a taste for something, she eats her fill … from the inside out."

"Assassin," Kasai cried out with disgust. Ninziz-zida's segments flamed in his hands.

"Yes, that is quite a clever talent you possess," Dax said beneath the outer disguise of Master Lanak. He nodded something of approval towards Kasai.

Master Choejor coughed up more blood. With great effort, the frail monk rose out of his stupor. Master Choejor moved protectively in front of Kasai and took up a shaky defense.

"Leave now, my son, while there is time. Flee this unholy place," he muttered.

Kasai moved beside Master Choejor. He uncoiled Ninziz-zida and readied her in a striking grip. He cried out to his companions, "Assassins!"

"Where? Who?" Desdemona responded as she dropped down in a defensive posture. Her hands glowed bright azure. Short swords flashed in the hands of Pallo and Run-Run as they moved forward to help Kasai. Reese backed against the wall, distancing herself from the others.

Grandmaster Vyliche sighed with impatience and held up his hands. He turned back towards Master Choejor. Quick as a snake, he struck Master Choejor in the temple with the first two fingers of his right hand. Master Choejor crumbled to the floor.

"Deal with this mess, Dax. Ordu should no longer exist. Kill them all," Grandmaster Vyliche said and turned to leave the room once more.

"It will be my pleasure," Dax said, swinging his attention to Kasai.

"Aetenos, help me," Kasai said absentmindedly. He had never actually prayed to the demigod before, and he honestly didn't know how. However, the thought of Aetenos at his side gave Kasai a righteous fury. His fire xindu ignited throughout his body.

"Aetenos, if your Song is truly with me, let me hear it now. Give me the strength to save Master Choejor."

Ninziz-zida welcomed the sensation of holy righteousness to fuel her flame. She blazed brighter as she tapped into the flow of Kasai's xindu energy.

Dax dropped the disguise of Master Lanak.

"Thank you for saving me the trouble of hunting you down. Sess'thra will be jealous that I found you first."

"You talk too much," Kasai said. He whipped the outer sections of Ninziz-zida in circular arcs probing the assassin's defenses. Ninziz-zida's red fire lit up the center of the room.

Dax stabbed forward, hoping to catch Kasai off guard. Kasai pivoted, striking a blow across the assassin's exposed wrist—bones cracked. Twisting his body, Kasai flicked his other wrist, batting the dagger away with Ninziz-zida's opposite end-section. The staff sent sensations of triumph into Kasai's mind.

Dax sneered, cradling his shattered wrist. Kasai whirled, expanding Ninziz-zida's segments; blazing bright red as he funneled more of his fire xindu into the ancient weapon. Dax's expression turned to defeat as Kasai swung Ninziz-zida down to finish the assassin. His strike was stopped by two temple monks who tackled him from behind. Kasai was astonished at their strength, but he soon knew the reason why. Their faces changed from human to monstrous fiends as their malformed mouths snapped inches from his own. Their breath stunk of rotten eggs.

They fell hard on the floor. Ninziz-zida collapsed into a tight three-sectioned baton as Dax raced to the back of the room, holding his injured wrist. He twisted a sconce on the wall, and a hidden door panel slid open.

Kasai used Ninziz-zida to bludgeon the head of one of the assailants. The strike of the Fire Serpent's wrath burned the fiendish monk with an otherworldly flame. He rolled to the side, flames festering, consuming his robes. A chilling scream left the monster's lips as Ninziz-zida's holy fire burned him to ashes.

Kasai hit the second fiend with a knee to its gut and jumped to his feet.

"Des! There!" Kasai yelled.

Blue energy swirled around Desdemonia; glyphs of power radiated from her body. Numerous deadly darts shot from her magic hands into the back of the second attacker. The fiendish monk arched in pain, whirling to face Desdemonia.

"Fire, Des! Use fire!" Kasai yelled.

Des nodded that she understood. She spoke ancient words of power and formed a small ball of fire in her hands. She threw it at the fiendish monk; he burst into flames and dropped to the floor to roll and snuff out the fire. Des' magical fire flared again, consumed him, turning him to black ash. It smelled horrid.

Three more temple monks in the ruby red colors of the Grandmaster of Eternity poured into the room, carrying short, curved blades. Holy pretense dropped as they warped into creatures spawned from madness.

A lumbering monstrosity covered entirely in short, white hair appeared from the passage. It looked pale and unwholesome, the size of an upright bear, it pushed aside the smaller killers, the temperature plummeted as it advanced. From his nose and snout, thick ropes of snot and drool splashed freely, the ends clinging to his naked chest as they cooled. The pale demon licked his lips, exposing rows of razor-sharp teeth.

Spying Kasai, the demon halted. Their eyes met and both widened as the creature's face softened and shifted slightly to resemble Daku. Just as quickly, the likeness disappeared and the image of Daku was lost.

"Kasai!" It bellowed out with a repulsive laugh. "We have been waiting for you. Daku has told me all about you."

A temple monk ran at Kasai in the center of the room. Desdemona shot a focused funnel of wind into his chest, sending him windmilling into the air. His red robes billowed around him as he smashed into the stone wall across the room. When Desdemonia cut the air, the monk dropped to the floor, a dark smear trailing after his slide down the wall.

"That's enough!" Jai held Reese tight with a dagger at her neck. Pallo and Run-Run sprang to her aid. Pallo's short sword somehow peeled Jai's weapon away from her neck and Run-Run stripped her away from the older temple monk. Jai ran from the room, and Reese was safe.

"Kassssssai..." the aberration taunted him. "Shall we spar once more?"

Kasai saw the demon was close to the body of Master Choejor.

"Where is Daku? What have you done with him?" Kasai shouted.

"He's right here. Inside me. I sometimes hear him weeping in the corner of my mind. I laugh at his misery. His soul is mine."

The demon moved to stand over the prone body of Master Choejor.

"Ah, dear Choejor. Daku bids your greetings, but it will be Khalkoroth who takes you to the darkness." Khalkoroth began to hum a tune, and then words came to his song.

"Off we go, off we go.
The Halls of Madness awaits all who go.
Off we go, off we go.
To those who follow, let them know.
In blood, you'll be, from head to toe.
Off we go, off we go."

Ninziz-zida was eager to attack, but Kasai held her back. Kasai could see the mannerism and movement of his lost Brother when the demon moved. Daku was in there, somewhere. If he destroyed this monster, would he not kill his best friend in the process? And how could he fight with Master Choejor at risk?

"Kasai! Move!" Desdemonia cried out. She'd conjured more fire in her hands and hurled it at the demon. Kasai ducked as the small fireball soared over his head.

Vermillion flames splashed over the demon's body, causing a green rock around his neck to flare with emerald light. The demon snickered as the flames were sucked into its core.

"Anything else?" he taunted before leaping hard and fast.

Ninziz-zida flashed out to strike but couldn't get through the demon's defense. Her fire did not burn the pale demon as it did the other fiends. The demon caught Kasai with a sweeping blow, sending him sprawling to the ground. Leaping forward, he straddled Kasai, glaring at him. He brought his claws down , the segments of Ninziz-zida in his hands deflecting the blow.

"You never did know how to win," Khalkoroth mocked, using Daku's voice.

Kasai thrust Ninziz-zida into its face, but the pale demon swatted the segments aside with an enraged growl. Its strength was overwhelming. Kasai knew he wouldn't be able to withstand such punishment.

"I can hear Daku wailing inside. Perhaps he longed for those special sticks in a past life. Another thing he will never have," the Thing said as it slashed his claws across Kasai's hands. The pain was excruciating. A second blow swatted Ninziz-zida across the floor. The flames of the Fire Serpent sputtered out.

"You've lost your precious Ninziz-zida. Now you are doomed!"

Kasai brought his hands up to block the next blow. He was desperate. "Aetenos! Help me!"

"Believe in me and be shielded from the darkness."

"I believe! I believe!" Kasai yelled out with desperation.

Khalkoroth picked Kasai up and raised him to his face. Kasai struggled, but the creature held him tight, lips peeled back revealing needle-sharp teeth. "This will be over soon."

Kasai brought his feet up against the pale demon's chest and pushed with all his might. His robe tore where the claws held them, and Kasai flew backward, crashing into a table. He had nothing left. He was totally spent. Beaten. This abomination would kill him now.

Kasai saw the prone body of Master Choejor lying on the floor. He willed himself to get up. Master Choejor still needed him. Kasai managed a kneeling position but felt panic rising to drown him in its murky darkness—he forced it down. *I will not fail Master Choejor.*

Khalkoroth stomped closer. Kasai took a deep breath and bowed his head to his chest, steadying his resolve. "Aetenos, hear me. I believe. Hear me." The words were calm and meaningful. He lifted his head, watching the demon approach.

"Praying will not save you now," Khalkoroth spat, his massive arms high over his head, ready to smash Kasai into oblivion.

"I am here, my son. I have always been here with you."

"I know," Kasai whispered, raising his hands as the demon's fists swept down.

A shield of energy rippled in the air. The demon pounded again and again on the invisible aegis, furious at being denied his killing blow, howling like a crazed wolf. Kasai rolled to the side and kicked as hard as he could into the demon's knee. It stumbled back a few paces but quickly regained his footing.

"Ah...Brother Kasai. Look at how many things have changed. But your clever tricks will not save you." The demon came at him again.

Desdemonia ran up while firing blue bolts at the demon's back. Once again, the amulet that hung from his neck absorbed the magic. Khalkoroth swiveled his head in her direction.

"What is this pest? Something wild and dirty you found in the woods?"

Desdemonia pushed her hands into pouches on her thighs. When she pulled them out, there were long bear claws attached to gloves on her hands. She leaped on the demon's back and repeatedly raked her razor-sharp claws across its face while shouting strange, unfamiliar names.

Ninziz-zida lay on the floor, and Kasai scrambled to retrieve her. Khalkoroth grabbed Desdemonia by the hair, ripped her off his back. As it lifted its massive arm back to thrust claw-hands through her chest, Kasai leaped into the air and snapped Ninziz-zida into the demon's face. Khalkoroth snarled something ancient and evil and dropped Desdemonia to the ground. With its hair on fire and raw, burned skin, its pink eyes burned with hatred. The burning smelled putrid and poisonous.

Kasai backed away to draw the demon after him, but Reese suddenly jumped in front of the hulking killer.

"Halt!" she demanded in her childlike voice. She thrust up her hand in Khalkoroth's face. The demon eyed the onyx ring on Reese's finger with uncertainty, then narrowed his demonic eyes at her. Reese thrust her hand up into his face. "Stop!"

"Where did you get that ring?" Khalkoroth sounded confused.

"In the name of the Immortal Mother, I command you to stop!" Reese shouted again, with newly found authority.

"Who are you to command Khalkoroth?" The pale demon took a step back, uncertain of the power of the priestess.

"Reese, no! He is too strong!" Kasai cried out.

Reese began chanting something in an exotic language. She raised her other hand, and the monster stepped back in pain. Reese seemed to hold sway over its behavior as it retreated. But it saw Master Choejor still on the floor and jumped at the monk.

"You stupid monk. You never could see the truth." Khalkoroth's booming laughter filled the room. He threw Master Choejor over his shoulder.

'To Rachlach, I go. To Rachlach, I go!
Poor Choejor's hollow head is broken and low.
To Rachlach, I go. To Rachlach, all will go!"

The room suddenly grew dim as the Thing that called itself Khalkoroth gathered the shadows into a haze of darkness around itself. Kasai rushed forward, but the darkness was quickly gone, taking with it the demon and Master Choejor. Only faint maniacal laughter lingered in the air.

Kasai looked anxiously around the room, searching for what he knew was already gone. Pieces of ash swirled on the floor. Pallo and Run-Run were alive; battered and bruised, but alive. They had dispatched the other temple monks while Kasai and Desdemonia battled with the demon. Reese seemed unharmed. Desdemonia was on the floor and not moving. Kasai ran to her, thinking the worse.

"Des, Des!" He rolled her over.

Her eyes flared open in alarm, then softened as she saw his face. "Give us a kiss, Handsome," she said with a wide grin. The jovial gypsy was back.

"Really?" Kasai rolled his eyes. "Come on, Des, get up. We need to find Master Choejor." Kasai scanned the room. Where could they have gone? He heard more temple monks coming through the hidden passage.

"Ever Hero, we must flee while we can. We will find your Master, but not here," Pallo pressed.

Kasai knew Pallo was right, more danger approached.

"The demon said something about taking Master Choejor to Rachlach. Did he mean Rachlach Fortress in Trosk?" Reese wondered aloud to the group. She was already leaving the room, beckoning the others to follow.

"Yes, I heard Rachlach as well, but how do we get there?" Kasai said.

Pallo and Run-Run looked at each other. "We know the way," Pallo said. "Run-Run can guide us once from the wilderness."

The Temple of Illumination was suspiciously empty as Kasai and the others ran outside into the streets. Run-Run took the lead, followed Kasai, Des, and Reese. Pallo was the rearguard. They skirted in and out of alleyways, passing unused storefronts. Kasai noticed many repeating symbols of long triangles arranged around a central point to mark the general location of secret handles for concealed doorways or trapdoors.

"How do you know of these secret ways?" Kasai asked as they ducked under a shallow ceiling and crawled along a narrow passage that opened into a tunnel.

"There's a scourge upon the lands of Hanna. It has infested the Northern Kingdom and is now infecting Baroqia. The jungles of Sunne will soon be overcome as well," Pallo said. "We are Spire Runners by trade, and part of a swelling resistance called the Kibo Gensai. We are devoted followers of Gen Mol, the First of Aetenos, and these are our secret passageways."

"The first? Do you mean his first follower?" Kasai said.

"Gen Mol was the first Ever Hero," Pallo said. Run-Run nudged his brother.

"We remain in secret due to the oppressive subjugation of Aetenos' followers. The factions of Mor have become warped by an unholy alliance with a diabolical evil. They are too numerous and too powerful to stand against in the open."

Run-Run nudged Pallo, again, in the direction they needed to go. "We must keep going," Pallo said. As they reached the end of the tunnel, Pallo pressed a smooth rock in the wall. The wall slid to the right, the afternoon light filling the exit. They now faced north, the forest only a short distance away.

"We are the daggers that pierce the darkness," Pallo declared just before they ran for the trees. "The Kibo Gensai have long searched for signs of the return of Aetenos and the rise of his next Ever Hero."

When everyone was concealed within the tree line, the two brothers dropped to one knee in front of Kasai. "We are the servants of the Divine Fist and his Argent Hammer, the Ever Hero. We are your sworn protectors during the time of transformation."

Kasai looked at them as if they were mad. "Get up, get up! What are you doing? There's not going to be any transformation. Not for me..., I'm no Ever Hero. I'm nobody. Nothing. Only a simple monk from Ordu." He shook his head in disbelief.

Pallo reached up and took Kasai's hands in his own. "You are much more. You bear the mark. You are the one who shall grant salvation to the worthy." Pallo then turned Kasai's hands upright to reveal cobalt-blue symbols on his palms, shinning like two freshly-inked tattoos. The design on each hand was in the shape of an open spiral.

"What's this? Kasai exclaimed.

"The Prophecy is revealed. The Ever Hero has risen," Pallo said.

Run-Run nodded eagerly. His grin was missing two teeth.

26

DESDEMONIA

Desdemonia huffed dismissively, "I don't care. Kasai can do what he wants." She lingered at the back of the group, lost in her thoughts, as they trekked through the forest. Ahead, Kasai was constantly engaged in conversation with the annoyingly clingy Reese. It was clear that Reese had developed a deep attachment to him; she was always by his side, close as a second skin. Desdemonia noticed how Reese flirted unabashedly with Kasai, though she doubted it would lead to anything substantial, after all, Kasai was a monk from Ordu. *Whatever that meant,* she fumed.

The morning air was crisp, and the smells of the forest were a cleansing relief from the filth of Gethem. Small birds flitted from branch to branch, chirping incessantly as the travelers walked beneath them. Desdemonia missed her little cottage in the woods and the squirrels that came to eat nuts out of her hand.

They had been traveling for ten full days without incident due to the clever trail-blazing of the brothers. Run-Run typically scouted ahead, as he did this morning to see that the way was clear. Pallo followed his brother's markers and lead the group through the undisturbed forest. They were keen to stay off well-traveled paths.

Pallo also kept a watchful eye on Reese. Desdemonia was glad she wasn't the only one that suspected something not quite right with the priestess. Kasai, of course, was an idiot. He only saw the good in everyone.

She could only imagine what Kasai must be feeling right now. No one could explain the strange markings on his palms. The brothers were convinced he was the next Ever Hero. Wow. *What an incredible burden.*

She had heard of a strange phenomenon that altered the bodies of raving zealots, but in her heart, she knew Kasai wasn't mad.

"Maybe a poor judge of character, but he's not crazy," she commented to herself. She watched him trace the blue spiral on one of his palms. *Could he really hear the Song of Aetenos?* Her eyes drifted to Reese. The tension she felt with the priestess had been mounting since arriving at the Temple. There was something about that one that made her skin crawl. The confrontation with the demon, Khalkoroth, was still heavy on her mind.

Kasai struck up a conversation with Pallo, leaving left Reese by herself. Seizing the opportunity, Desdemonia quickly caught up to her. "Reese, I've been meaning to ask you something," she said, hoping to sound as friendly as possible.

"What do you want?" Reese's mouth creased into a frown.

Even when Reese was unpleasant, she was still beautiful. No law said a priestess of the Immortal Mother had to be ugly, Desdemonia reminded herself. But Reese had an uncanny, flawless beauty. And somehow, that made Desdemonia uncomfortable.

Staring at her with sharp, magenta eyes, Reese stated impatiently, "Yes?"

"You were very brave to stand up to the demon the way you did," Desdemonia began.

"How would you know? You were lying on the floor being useless."

Desdemonia bit back a sharp retort, determined to be civil towards the young priestess. She needed answers. "Yes, well, Pallo told me what happened afterward. What did you say to the demon that made him back away? Pallo said you commanded him to leave, and he did."

Reese became pensive, fingering the black ring she wore. An impish smile came to her mouth. "I don't know. Kasai was in danger. I couldn't lose him. Not after all he's done for me. I jumped in the path of the demon and said the first thing that came to my mind. It was a verse my mother sang to me as a child to ward off evil spirits."

Desdemonia eyed Reese with skepticism. "You expect me to believe you recited a nursery rhyme and pushed back a greater demon?"

"I know. Who would believe it?" Reese put her hand to her mouth, then giggled like a young child. She abruptly stopped laughing and became serious.

"I want to make something perfectly clear to you. Don't get in my way."

"In your way of what?" Desdemonia asked, genuinely confused.

"Oh, don't play that game with me. I see how you look at him when you think no one is watching. He's mine."

"Who, Kasai? You're crazy."

"You have no idea." Reese glared. "This is your only warning."

Desdemonia looked away, perplexed at the instant hostility. Collecting her thoughts, she turned back to Reese, another question on her tongue when Kasai rejoined the pair. Reese practically leaped into his arms.

"Hi, Kasai. Desdemonia and I were just commenting on what a nice morning it is. Don't you agree?"

"Sure," Kasai said, appearing uncomfortable by Reese's enthusiastic embrace.

"When you're finished," Desdemonia comments, "I want to show you something. I took this from Khalkoroth." She held a delicate chain that was attached to a small amulet. There were intricate runes inscribed over the central piece. The emerald jewel in its center sparkled bright-green when it caught the light.

"Des, you shouldn't have that. It's evil. Destroy it now!" Kasai reached out to take the amulet away from her.

Desdemonia pulled the amulet back to her chest. "Not so fast. It might not be evil. Didn't you see how the amulet absorbed magic?"

"Yes, and it was around the neck of a demon that wanted to kill us, Des. Maybe it only absorbs good magic."

"I don't know. I want to study it more. Plus, we will need more than my simple spells and your flashy sticks where we are going."

Reese cast a suspicious eye towards Desdemonia and pulled Kasai's attention back to her. "Never trust the words of sorcerers or *witches*. I think she wants to make slaves of us all. Desdemonia makes me nervous."

"Don't be ridiculous. Des is a friend," Kasai said.

Reese leaned closer to Kasai and whispered, "Let her keep the trinket and send her away. We don't need her anymore. The Immortal Mother watches over us." Her magenta eyes gleamed with eagerness.

"Ugh, I'm standing right here. I can hear you," Desdemonia snapped. "And I'm not going anywhere."

"We'll see about that," Reese said.

Run-Run returned to the group to interrupt the standoff. He hurriedly spoke to Pallo using grunts and quick hand gestures. Pallo nodded in understanding.

"A war column approaches from Gethem. The Knights of Gethem lead a long trail of armed townsfolk and wagons swollen with supplies. We could merge with the local conscripts and see about retaining some additional supplies. We are ill-equipped to cross the Hoarfrost. Winter will catch us soon, and we will need warmer clothing.

"Run-Run suspects the column travels to the Last Garrison. It's large enough to serve as a command center for the coming battle. We can walk with them until we reach that point, then take Stormwind Pass to get to Rachlach Fortress."

"And the Sorcerer," Reese said, glumly.

"Run-Run is right. We are not prepared for the cold," Kasai said. "What do you think, Des, should we join the war column?"

Reese quickly interjected, "I don't like it. Let's keep away from those mean soldiers. We can wait until they pass and continue alone," She took Kasai's hand and tried to pull him in a new direction, away from the group. "The Immortal Mother provides."

Desdemonia held out her arm to prevent Reese from going any farther. "The closer we get to the mountains, the more likely we are to run into the enemy. There is safety in numbers until we have a better idea of what lies ahead."

"What is the wish of the Ever Hero?" Pallo said. "He shall decide our path."

"Blending in with the regular folks seems like a smart idea. Plus, we are heading in the right direction. We can make our move to rescue Master Choejor when the opportunity presents itself."

"It shall be done as the Ever Hero commands," Pallo said.

Run-Run bowed and vanished among the forest trees.

"Where's he going?" Desdemonia asked.

"He goes to secure our ingress within the column. Hopefully, there will be others of the Kibo Gensai that will help us gather supplies," Pallo said.

"Why do you call him Run-Run?" Kasai asked.

Pallo chuckled a bit to himself. "We were trained to be Spire Runners at a very young age. My brother was the fastest of us all. Quick as a rabbit, that one. He could run at pace for hours without losing the scent of a trail. I swear, my brother has the nose of a hound. No one could match his speed or stamina."

"Spire Runners? I am unfamiliar with this title," Kasai said.

Pallo hesitated. "Interesting. I would think a monk of Ordu would be well versed in the history of the realm."

"They don't teach them much in the mountains," Desdemonia said.

"Pallo, pay no attention to her," Kasai deflected. "Please, go on."

"When first the stones of Volkerrum Keep were laid in Gethem, runners were used to race across the land to bring messages from one small village to the next. This was how Baroq Shiverrig, the great Aj-Kahun of his time, kept his subjects informed of his will.

"Eventually, other cities grew and prospered throughout the realm, most notably, Qaqal."

"The City of Spires," Kasai added, proving he knew something of the outside world.

"Yes, exactly, the City of Spires. Over time the idea of runners caught on with the noble class in Qaqal. The Spire Runners, as they became called, knew the fastest routes to convey not only the King's Law but also the secrets of their rivals for power."

"Secrets," Desdemonia interjected.

"Yes, secrets," Pallo continued. "Valuable secrets of such importance that the Spire Runners were in danger for their lives. In the same way messenger birds could be shot from the sky, Spire Runners could be caught and made to reveal what they knew. Hence, we trained ourselves in many martial forms, becoming proficient with blade and fist alike."

"City life." Desdemonia shook her head. "At least one knows where they stand in the forest. What about Run-Run? He never talks."

"His is a sad tale. Years ago, my brother was caught by a pack of zealots. They were maniacal worshippers of Mor. They forced him to renounce his faith in Aetenos. Run-Run would not, so they cut out his tongue as a reward for his devotion."

"Oh no," Desdemonia said. "I'm so sorry."

Pallo nodded sadly. "But let us not dwell in the past. We must be ready to move upon Run-Run's return."

It wasn't long before the party meshed with the slow-moving column of supply wagons and war engines destined for the coming battle with the North. Warhorses plodded along with heavy steps through worn and muddy roads, and their tails swished away fat flies that trailed their muscular flanks.

The last breath of Autumn was giving way to the cold slumber of winter. Instead of crisp air bringing the smell and flavor of snow to the lands, there was a bitter reek drifting on the winds.

Desdemonia couldn't shake the feeling they were being watched, or worse, hunted. The presence of a predator was close. She could feel it lurking in shadows and following their every move.

She watched Kasai move through the different groups of soldiers and conscripts. No matter how much he declined the moniker, the title of Ever Hero followed him. Rumors of the return of the Ever Hero had spread fast from the townsfolk outside of Gethem.

Pallo and Run-Run didn't help matters, either. They refused to see him as anything but a holy savior. The two brothers rarely left his side and acted as body-guards and servants.

Somehow, Kasai remained humble through all the adulation. He was a unique soul with a pure heart. They were a good team together, unless Reese showed up to act like a wedge between them. Strangely, since they joined with the war column, Reese had been absent for long periods.

"Good riddance," Desdemonia snorted. "Lord knows what type of mischief that so-called priestess is causing." She didn't believe for an instant that Reese was spreading the good word of the Immortal Mother to the troops. She caught the sight of orange robes bookended by two black shadows as Kasai and the brothers made their way closer. His face looked worn and drawn.

"Their eyes are on me everywhere I go," Kasai said.

"Whose eyes?"

"Everyone's." Kasai's hands went out to encompass the war column.

"Well, you know … you should be honored," Desdemonia quipped, poking him in the arm. "Not everyone gets to be the savior of Hanna." She shouldn't jest, he was having a hard enough time already.

"Funny," Kasai responded, though he wasn't laughing. He looked down at her finger where it was pressing against his arm and moved to take it in his hand. He shifted his gaze to meet hers. "Des, they have it all wrong. I'm just a monk. Nothing more, nothing less. I don't know why all this is happening, but to think it's because I somehow possess the spirit of Aetenos is just fantasy." Kasai sighed, dropping her hand. "The weight of their expectations is great."

Run-Run gave a grunt, nudging Pallo before pointing in the direction of a small group of townsfolk approaching, dressed in makeshift war gear of padded armor and mismatched helms. They held old, dull swords that should be used for something other than killing. Pallo and Run-Run were quick to occupy the space between Kasai and the oncoming townsfolk. Desdemonia thought they looked harmless enough.

A man of roughly forty summers with a short, thick beard, salted with age, and a balding head, spoke for the group. He had heavy eyes, filled with caring and stature that expressed years of hardship.

He looked with cautious interest at Pallo and Run-Run, then addressed Kasai politely. Desdemonia felt slightly insulted at being left out. "Here we go again."

"I am Lorne from East Valor. The land yields less each year, and the people suffer. I am fearful for my family's safety. Watch over me, Ever Hero, so that I may return to them when this is over." He bowed low to Kasai. The rest of the group did the same.

Kasai glanced at Desdemonia, his expression seeming to ask if now she understood. He did his best to straighten each member of the group. "Please, please, stop bowing."

"The prophecy reveals itself. Your arrival has been foretold," Pallo said with zealous conviction. "Behold, the Mark of Aetenos! Have courage, my friends. The Ever Hero walks with you." Pallo raised one of Kasai's arms to the crowd and showed the symbol of power on his palm.

"Pallo, enough," Kasai implored. He pulled his arm down, but the damage had been done.

"The Open Palm," one of the townsfolk remarked in awe. "The prophecy reveals itself."

"The Divine Fist and his Ever Hero are among us. Aetenos has returned," another exclaimed aloud. Other conscripts and now soldiers heard the townsfolk's exclamations. They drew near.

"He bears the Mark!" Lorne said. "Show them, show them all!"

Kasai reluctantly did as he was asked. The men before him gasped. They bowed their head in reverence or knelt before Kasai. More soldiers came. It wasn't long before Kasai was surrounded by at least fifty kneeling worshippers. Each had their head bowed, and one hand raised, palm facing towards their savior.

"Well, we can forget about blending in with the militia now," Desdemonia snarked. She hoped the sorcerer didn't already have spies wading through the army ranks. But that would be wishful thinking.

27

KASAI

Alone, Kasai walked through a frigid wasteland with nothing more than his burnt orange robe. The cold air burned his exposed skin. The encampment had changed to open tundra. Kasai saw his breath cloud in front of his eyes. When it cleared, the barren landscape had transformed into a cold and dark interior. Where was Des?

Ice stalactites hung from the ceiling. He looked about the room, seeing sharp and dangerous looking tools on a small, waist-high bench. Underneath, spatters of blood stood out against the frozen white floor. The outline of a woman took shape in the shadows.

"Des, is that you?"

"Ah, there you are, my elusive monk. I wonder as you do, are you the One?"

"Reese?"

"Now, step a bit closer and let me see your handsome face. That's it, just a bit closer."

Kasai could not stop himself from obeying. His feet slid forward on the slick floor of their own volition. "Reese? Show yourself. Who's there?" Kasai said to the shifting image.

"I can be many things. Whatever your heart desires," the woman whispered.

"Why are you hiding?" Kasai's voice wavered. A warning of danger crept up his spine.

"Let me show you."

The form of the woman changed, darkness wrapping around her in a shifting haze of shadow. Kasai saw the shape of her body become flesh. She was magnificent. Perfect. He took a step closer.

The darkness gave way to a flurry of brightness. Now she was shrouded in a swirling cloud of snow. A headdress of bones grew from her head. Kasai recoiled in shock. He knew this woman. The apparition from Ordu had found him again. The nightmare continued.

She grew in stature to tower over him. She pulled a limp body from behind her back. She held it up for Kasai to see. Kasai's eyes widened in horror. He recognized the face of his father. The apparition then showed him the body of Master Choejor. The old monk's body was ashen and broken.

"The frail hopes of forgotten fathers are calling you. Come to me. Save them if you can."

Kasai gasped. His body felt unnaturally hot. Pinpricks covered his skin. He felt a profound sadness as his stomach heaved into his throat. He couldn't move, no matter how hard he tried to twist or turn his body.

The apparition slammed the two bodies together until they shattered like glass. The pieces fell out of sight. She took a step closer to Kasai.

Fear washed over him. He tried to reach for Ninziz-zida, but his arm was anchored to his side. He searched for anything that could help him escape.

"Who are you? What do you want from me?" Kasai said.

The woman's body grew until only a colossal face remained in Kasai's field of view. He saw the woman's long neck, slender chin, and full mouth. The rest was lost in swirling white snow that spread throughout the entire room.

A seductive smile formed. Kasai was drawn against his will to the enticing lips. The mouth opened wide, and he saw rows and rows of sharp, arrowhead-like teeth. Her smooth jaw lurched forward and snapped at him, inches from his face. He stared, frozen in fear.

Kasai snapped awake, heart pounding, lying on his back in a puddle of clammy sweat. The early morning moon cast its pale light over the encampment of Shiver-rig's army in the fields surrounding the Last Garrison. Dawn was still a few hours away.

At some point during the night, Reese had returned and lain down next to him. She was lying across his outstretched arm. Her arm laid across his body. Her small hand had somehow snaked beneath his robes and rested just below his navel.

Kasai looked around. Desdemonia was curled up at the edge of their small camp with her back to Kasai. He carefully removed Reese's hand and pushed her gently aside.

He stood up. The feeling of helplessness still clung to his body. He rubbed his hands over his smooth scalp and down his long, black braid of hair. He stretched in the cold, pre-dawn air. He looked around the camp for a quiet place to meditate.

"You see with the eyes of the Ever Hero," Pallo said. He was tending a small camp-fire nearby.

"What?"

"The visions are real."

Kasai had no answer. He moved to sit closer to Pallo. The warmth of the fire put him at ease. Kasai soon heard the familiar sound of steel plates clanking together from heavy footsteps. Soon, three armed knights wearing the house colors of Duke Shiverrig came into view. A snarling mastiff emblazoned the purple and rose light shirts they wore over their armor.

"You shall come with us, now," the lead knight said. There was no introduction or explanation.

Pallo jumped in front of Kasai with his daggers drawn. The knights did not bother to remove their swords.

"Now," said a second knight.

"Pallo, it will be all right. I do not sense ill-will from these men. It is probably best to go while everyone still sleeps. I do not want to cause a disturbance."

"As you wish. I will be close if the need arises," Pallo whispered to Kasai.

Kasai was brought to a large tent where guards dressed in plate armor stood two apiece to each side of the entrance, their steel bodies reflecting the yellow light of campfires and torches. They parted the mastiff icons embroidered into the canvas panels between them, admitting Kasai to stand in the busy command center.

Like bees surrounding their matriarch, busy advisors and lieutenants circled the towering duke and they discussed contingency plans and assignments, pointing at maps unrolled on the table in the center of the room. Shiverrig looked up and noticed Kasai, frowning in disapproval, which was replaced by a look of annoyance. "You. Come closer." He raised his voice and spoke to the room, commanding its attention. "This is the one creating the disturbance among my men?" Shiverrig asked.

Kasai took three steps closer. Shiverrig gave him a thorough scrutiny. "You don't look like much."

"No, sir," Kasai responded.

"Well, let's have it boy, should I address you as Sir Ever Hero?"

"No, sir. Maybe. I don't know," Kasai vacillated. He wasn't sure what he should reveal to this man. The Duke of Gethem couldn't be trusted. He had turned a blind eye to the suffering of his subjects within the once-great port city.

"Trust me, boy. You are not the Ever Hero; there is no such thing. The idea of a mighty avatar walking the lands with the powers of a god is absurd. Even the so-called mages Great Houses employ are little more than petty carnival acts. It's all lies and myths used to quell the hearts of the weak-minded. There are no saviors."

Kasai studied the duke's aura. A volcanic blossom of blood-red anger continuously erupted around the man. Shiverrig possessed violent anger and immeasurable fury. He walked to another table that held the figurines of troop placement atop a map of the immediate area.

"Life and death," Shiverrig contemplated his words and then continued, "all revolve around blood and steel. True heroes are forged from battle and conquest. True heroes are men that fight and die to protect the realm their family forged with their own hands. Yes, a true hero must protect the lands and its people from would-be usurpers and duplicitous diplomats."

Shiverrig studied the map for a moment. He moved some of the king's pieces to a new location and added more, bearing his family's colors. He gently pushed them all over on the map. Shiverrig brought his hand to his chin and rubbed the rough stubble.

Kasai noticed the Duke make a slight, silent nod to himself, then picked up the pieces and returned them to their original location on the map. He turned his gaze back to Kasai.

"You know something of what I speak. The Monks of Aetenos are renowned for coming to the aid of the people in times of need, are they not?"

"Yes, Duke Shiverrig. We are taught to protect and serve, to be a shield from darkness and a healer when the land falls ill."

"Exactly! There is a sickness in the land that must be purged. The people need a symbol to rally behind. Although you are not the blood of kings, you can still be of great use to me. If the people are convinced you are their Ever Hero, and it gives them courage in the coming battle, then so be it. You shall be their hero."

"Duke Shiverrig, I am just a simple monk from Ordu."

"Ordu, you say? I was told the hidden monastery was no more. Yet you survived."

"Yes. I was more fortunate than most."

"Indeed." Shiverrig studied Kasai more closely. "Yes, yes, well, you need not worry about evading death a second time. You will remain behind in the medical tents. I can't have a rogue arrow find your heart, or an enemy sword sever you in half."

"I beg your pardon, Duke Shiverrig, that was not my meaning."

"I don't care, it's mine." He looked around the room for a page that wasn't there. "Blast, where is Morgan? Tell that useless page to provide the monk with a medical supply horse. Perhaps he can use some of the famed monk healing on my troops during the coming battle."

Shiverrig called to his guards. "Get him to the armory. I want him covered head-to-toe. Nothing too fancy." Shiverrig turned to Kasai. "The armor will protect you when I cannot. Under no circumstances are you to engage the enemy. Are we clear?"

"Yes, Duke Shiverrig," Kasai bowed.

"Then, that is all." He waved Kasai away, returning his attention to the table and is commanders.

Kasai was taken to the tent housing the knight's armory and given armor, shield, and sword. Although using a sword and shield were not wholly foreign to him, he walked awkwardly in the plate mail.

He felt off-balanced and claustrophobic. The armor was loose in some areas and too tight in others. He could not feel the energy vibrations of the outside world. Perhaps he was one step closer to understanding the Boundless now that he was cut off from it.

A page was waiting for Kasai when he left the armory. The boy held the reigns to a small, spotted pony, that was burdened with packs of healing supplies, water, and little vials of dark liquid. Kasai wondered if it was the same valerian root Desdemonia had given Master Choejor to let him sleep.

"Sir, Ever Hero, sir, I am Morgan. I am to be your page. I am to go where you go."

"You mean to keep an eye on me and make sure I don't do something stupid, right?" Kasai said, trying to bring some brevity to the conversation.

"Yes, well, something like that, Sir Ever Hero."

"Please, just Kasai."

Kasai smiled at the young boy. He was dressed in the livery of House Shiverrig and had oily, black hair, cropped at the shoulders. Morgan did his best to carry himself in a noble and knightly way, but Kasai could see there was great fear behind his soft eyes. War was no place for children, no matter their upbringing or family heritage.

Kasai returned to camp, but his companions were not present. He assumed they had gone to secure supplies or help where they could. Kasai picked up Ninziz-zida and tucked the Fire Serpent under one of the saddlebags with the rest of the supplies.

Although he had agreed not to march into battle with the regular soldiers, he knew from experience to keep the ancient Fire Serpent close at hand when danger was near.

Kasai walked through the ranks of the reserves. Morgan was always just a step behind, leading the pony. The youngster followed Kasai as if his life depended on it. Perhaps it did.

The plate mail chafed and confined his movement to a slow crawl. How could anyone fight in such a cumbersome shell? He wondered if he could wield Ninzizida effectively if the need arose.

Kasai and Morgan walked through the masses of reserves and met other monks along the way. Somehow, they had survived the monastery massacres. He spoke briefly with them, trying to answer questions, but he felt increasingly uneasy in the presence. Most were adolescent lads that had somehow managed to survive the wilds, only to be conscripted into Shiverrig's army.

The tale of his miraculous feat in the hamlet had spread like wildfire during a dry summer. The ragtag groups of monks looked at him in awe. Some asked to see the Mark of Aetenos on his palms, while others asked if Kasai could speak directly to Aetenos. It was the same everywhere throughout the encampment. The people assumed he was something that he wasn't. They desperately needed a savior. He just wasn't it. "Blessings to you, Ever Hero, and bless of the return of Aetenos," the monks would say repeatedly.

"Thank you, Brothers, and blessings to you as well," Kasai responded politely, but he felt no different inside. He didn't feel heroic or invincible. The truth was Kasai felt helpless and afraid. If it weren't for Desdemonia, Master Choejor, and then Reese saving him, he would have been dead three times already. How was he supposed to be a hero when he couldn't even take care of himself?

His thoughts drifted to Master Choejor. His Master was somewhere beyond the Hoarfrost Mountains, trapped and suffering at the hands of Khalkoroth. Kasai was haunted by the image of Daku's face appearing and disappearing on the surface of the demon's head. Daku was trapped as well, but could he be saved?

A majestic horn sounded, and the call-to-arms rang out among the early morning campfires. Kasai and Morgan found a high outcropping of boulders that jutted out from a sloping hill. They managed to climb to the top to get a better vantage of the battlefield.

Morgan pointed to a group of large tents with long, colorful banners. The flags flapped and snapped in the wind. "Look, there is Lord Fritta's tent. You can tell by the eagle with its spread wings. And that one there is Duke Manda's. See the diving hawk? The great boar of Baron Rokig's is to the far left. He was made General of the King's Army. A command that should have gone to my Lord Shiverrig."

Morgan was quite a knowledgeable youngster. He explained to Kasai how the Duke's forefathers had come to Baroqia so many years ago to tame the land. The Shiverrig clan laid the foundations of what had become the Kingdom of Baroqia, ruling as kings for countless generations.

Things were different now, however. The power to rule the kingdom had changed. During a time of crisis, it was the gold of House Conrad, not the military power of the House Shiverrig, had paved the way for salvation. Kasai didn't have the heart to tell him he knew at least that much of the history of Baroqia.

"And do you see that great tent with the pouncing griffon? That is King Conrad's tent. My Lord Shiverrig said the king came to watch the victory over the North while he took his tea. He said the king would not personally fight. He said the king was a coward."

Kasai remembered the anger that radiated from Duke Shiverrig. He wasn't surprised to hear such words had been spoken from the duke. Kasai followed Morgan's litany of family histories as he pointed to the icons and emblems on different tents. Troops began to pour out of the traveling barracks, running to muster points to stand by their lords.

"Do you know anything about warcraft, Ever Hero?"

"Please, Morgan, it's just Kasai. My training at Ordu encompassed all forms of military strategies from significant battles to small skirmishes."

"Have you been in many wars?" Morgan said.

"None. I lived in a place where war was something only read in books."

The horn pealed a different cadence. The armored ranks of the King's Army assembled. Row after row of locked shields and spears tips formed behind the mass of conscripts and peasants relegated to the front.

Kasai peered into the fields just to the front of the lines where the King's Army were still shuffling and jostling into place. He saw the enemy with little difficulty. Barbarian tribesmen from the Far North wielded great broadswords and wore heavy furs on their backs. Their long hair whipped in the early morning wind. There was a small assortment of horsemen, but they were scattered haphazardly throughout the foot soldiers.

"Why would they bring so few to war? The King's Army will make short work of them," Kasai speculated.

The small band of northern barbarians smashed their axes to their shields and shouted curses at the top of their lungs. Without cause or cue, the Northerners charged the men of the King's Army. Burly riders on saddleless horses trotted behind men running full speed, hoping to be the first to engage the enemy.

A trumpet blared from the ranks of men. Mounted knights bearing the flag of General Rokig bolted down a corridor between the fidgeting conscripts into the open field.

"This may be over very quickly," Kasai said with no lack of relief.

A war horn's bone-chilling wail shrieked out over the grasslands; the ground split, tearing open to reveal a colossal beast crawling up from the black dirt. It had the upper torso of a man and the malformed head of a lion. Enormous tusks rolled out of its mouth. Four monstrous legs powered it onto the grassy field. The beast bellowed a preternatural challenge to the men of the King's Army. A warrior in dull, white armor climbed up upon the beast's back. When the beast was fully above ground, The warrior blew from his horn a second time, and the ground trembled.

"Look!" Morgan squealed, his quaking young betraying his youth.

Kasai saw it too. A vast horde of child-sized, unworldly beings spewed from hundreds of previously-hidden holes in the surrounding fields. Misshapen forms and hulking monsters followed in their wake. Kasai saw glimpses of feathered wings and barbed tails, long hooked beaks, and broad snouts rolling through the mass of creatures of chaos.

"Aetenos, help us," Kasai said. "This enemy is beyond men."

A great stench preceded the horde. The air became filled with the stale odor of old death. A frigid wind washed over the King's Army like the precursor of a terrible blizzard. Kasai looked to the reserve troops and saw fear mounting in their hearts.

Nightmares given form stomped and screeched. Their numbers grew as more escaped from the underground tunnels. A raw coldness crept up Kasai's spine. It was an absolute horror. It was death. His mind failed to comprehend what his eyes were seeing.

Rokig's cavalry raced across the open field to engage the barbarians.

"They are too far away," Kasai said. "Stop. Stop!"

The cavalry continued their long charge, eventually crashing into the pack of barbarians, scattering them into smaller groups. Those on foot were brought down quickly under the trampling hooves and the sharp lances of Rokig's knights. The Northern horsemen peeled off quickly to return to the demon horde. Kasai wondered why General Rokig had committed such an ill-advised charge.

"General Rokig has drawn first blood!" Morgan's excitement was short-lived when a flock of bat-winged creatures dove down from the dense grey clouds.

"He's overextended and has lost the support of the archers. The spears and swords cannot cover his retreat," Kasai enlightened his young page. He squeezed his eyes shut, wincing when he heard the ear-piercing screams of the warhorses.

28

SHIVERRIG

Duke Shiverrig sat restlessly on a magnificent black destrier; the early morning's chill lingered on the open fields. The horse shimmied from side-to-side, snorting warm clouds of air through its enlarged nostrils, perhaps sensing his irritation. It

His troops regulated to the southern flank; the king didn't want any competition when he rode the enemy army down. The barbarians had shown their numbers, and as expected, they were few.

The thunder of hooves caught Shiverrig's attention. He opened his spyglass and watched with keen interest as Rokig launched a premature cavalry charge. An experienced general would have seen it for the apparent feint it was. Rokig took the bait. He led half of his mounted knights into battle. The peal of General Rokig's war horn rang out over the clamor of moving troops and nervous draft horses.

"The fly races to the spoiled meat," Shiverrig said. "Ready men. We move on my signal."

The duke rested his spyglass on his thigh, calculating the likelihood of survival for Rokig's cavalry charge. The fool had driven his contingent too far, outside the range of the archers. If the subsequent calvary-infantry melee was not exhaustive, Rokig's group might survive, but Shiverrig was certain the enemy was hoping for just this sort of blind-headed blunder and suspected what was coming next.

A fantastic wail curdled through the air. The ground opened, and a creature from nightmare pulled itself onto the grassy plain. A rider stood on its back with a sword that looked like a long, shard of ice. A second peal of the rider's horn signaled the beginning of the end for Rokig. Hidden tunnel doors opened, and Hell vomited its minions onto the battlefield.

A dark cloud descended on Rokig's far-flung knights. Shiverrig raised his spyglass again and saw queer, bat-like creatures swarm into focus, darting down from low cloud cover to harry the knights. When the winged demons could not pierce the steel of the knight's armor, they gave their full attention to the exposed flanks of the warhorses.

The Duke heard another horn blow. The conscripts and foot soldiers charged the field. Only a token host of reserve troops remained behind. There was no semblance of order to the advancing footmen and no cohesion of lines drawn up to support an orderly retreat.

"And the flow of folly begins," Shiverrig said. He swiveled his spyglass to the enemy warlord, who stood on the back of his war beast.

The warlord raised his sword and blew one last screeching note from his horn. Abyssal creatures rushed across the open field as the demonic horde was unleashed. The poorly equipped conscripts and half-armored, but undisciplined, foot soldiers of the King's Army slowed to a stop.

The enemy slammed into the king's infantry with wild fury. Ill-prepared to deal with such a brutal foe, their will to fight faltered. Many stood frozen in fear as demons pounced on them and rendered them to pieces.

The demon horde drove the soldiers back, killing everyone in their path. The infantry fell back on each other, bodies piling up under the onslaught. Monstrous shrieks were drowned out by human screams. This battle was over before it began. Without a protected front or compact battle groups, Conrad's scattered and poorly disciplined troops quickly fell to the horde. The rest of the morning would be messy blood work.

"Oh, I warned you. Yes, I did," Shiverrig said. He trained his spyglass to Conrad's camp. Knights bearing the colors of House Conrad surrounded the king's tent. A lone rider emerged. The knights formed a protective barrier around him, and as a whole, they galloped hard in the opposite direction of the battle.

"Had your fill of playing war hero, have you?" Shiverrig said.

He signaled his knights. "We go to the king!"

Shiverrig and his knights left the encampment in a cloud of dust and debris. He had accounted for this contingency. The rats always abandon the sinking ship before the cold waters take it. Mortimer Conrad was no different. He had no taste for actual battle.

Hearing the cries of men dying was very different from moving clay figurines on a map. No one ever talked about the smell of death, but it was awful, repulsive to the living. Conrad had always been a coward. He should have ended Gerun long ago, just as Mortimer's father had deposed Gerun's father in these very same fields. "Oh, no, no. Don't think I have forgotten." Shiverrig raced to catch the king. If his allies in the North had done their part, Conrad would be heavily engaged by the enemy when they arrived. That was a big 'if.'

Up ahead, Shiverrig saw a beautiful sight.

"Dax, you perfectly wicked creature," Shiverrig chortled. The North had not betrayed him. The king and his accompaniment of knights were surrounded by a thirty, maybe forty barbarians. The scene was set for Shiverrig to ride in and make a heroic statement. Which he would. Today was the day he saved Baroqia.

"Shiverrig! The enemy besets us!" King Conrad shouted. "To your king! To your king!"

Shiverrig halted his advance. The barbarians leveled heavy crossbows at the king's knights. A guttural command was shouted, and the bolts were let loose. More than half of the knights died slumped in their saddles or fell to the ground to be broken by their horse's hooves.

The barbarians saw Shiverrig's company and scattered across the field or escaped into nearby holes.

"Get them! Get them all!" King Conrad cried.

The king's knights gave chase. Ten of them curled back to form a loose circle around the king.

"The battle did not go as you planned, eh Mortimer?" Duke Shiverrig said as he calmly rode up to the king. His destrier snorted and pranced closely to the king's horse. King Conrad's mare shied away from the intimidating warhorse.

"You will address me as your king!"

"You should have followed my strategy at the war council, Mortimer. Soldier's lives would have been saved. Lives I would have put to better use in the coming war. But no matter, we would have eventually come to this moment, you and I."

King Conrad was puzzled. "This moment?"

"Yes, this moment, Mortimer." Shiverrig's eyes followed the trails of the king's knights as they darted after the fleeing enemy. "No accounting for an untrained guard." He unsheathed his great bastard sword.

Conrad's eyes widened in shock. "Are you mad? I am your king! My men here will witness your treasonous betrayal and cut you down where you stand."

Shivering laughed. "These men?" Shiverrig pointed to the mounted knights closing the circle about the king. "These are MY men. The ones you insisted taking from Gethem's Elite Guard, or had you forgotten?"

Conrad drew a sword that had never been bloodied in battle or otherwise. It was too heavy for his hands, and the point drooped low. Shiverrig shook his head with disappointment.

"You could have been a wealthy noble and lived a long life, had you simply acknowledged my rightful claim to the throne when I came of age. The history of the land shall now be honored."

Shiverrig blocked the King's pathetic thrust with ease and jabbed his sword into Conrad's shoulder. The sword fell from his hand and clattered uselessly on some small stones.

"I yield! I yield! The kingdom is yours!" King Conrad cried.

"It's far too late for that."

Duke Shiverrig deftly sliced his sword back across Conrad's exposed neck. The cut was deep enough to cut the carotid artery. Conrad's lifeblood spurted out over his unblemished armor. Shiverrig tore off Conrad's loose-fitting helm and tossed it to the ground. He then grabbed a handful of Conrad's hair and gave a swift jerk, pulling the dead king from his horse.

Shiverrig spat on the pitiful form of his nemesis.

"Round up the remains of this rabble. Kill the Northerners and any of Conrad's remaining knights."

A squad of Shiverrig's knights galloped away.

"Throw the dead together. Make it appear we arrived too late to protect the king from the ambush."

Shiverrig took in the carnage. Justice was served.

The Knights of Gethem quickly dispatched the remaining guardsmen of the king. Most of Conrad's men were elevated to knighthood by excessive financial contribution to House Conrad's coffers. Some of the Northerners managed to escape, but that was little matter. Shiverrig's objective had been achieved.

It was now time to collect his men. Lord Fritta had agreed to terms of Shiverrig's ascension to the throne if the King should fall, and with luck, Lord Manda would comply as well. What would that princess of a man care as long as the coin flowed?

Duke Shiverrig turned his horse to lead his knights from the killing field. He spotted a lone figure approaching on a twisted beast. The figure shimmered in the late morning light and wore a broad grin as he clapped his hands together in applause.

"Sekka, the Frost Queen of Gathos, congratulates you on a job well done, Duke Shiverrig. The battle was easily won, as expected. The Mistress wishes to meet with you and express her gratitude to you in person," Dax said.

"Curious, that it's Sekka, not Maugris, who brings congratulations."

"Maugris, yes. I'm sure he would like to express his pleasure as well," Dax said. The twinkle in his eye spoke volumes to Shiverrig of who indeed held power in the North.

"Her desire for celebration is untimely. I have other pressing business in Qaqal."

Shiverrig signaled his knights to gather close. He pointed at a nearby squire. "You there, get word to my man, Pathias. Have him alert Lord Fritta that the king has fallen to an enemy ambush. This battle is lost. All soldiers are to regroup at the Broken Boulder Crossroads. Have Pathias send another man to Lord Manda with the same message."

Shiverrig rounded his horseback to Dax. "Tell your Queen that her precious Ever Hero was in my possession before the fighting began. I instructed our mutual friend to walk with him like a second shadow. I know not what has become of him, but I have done my part."

"All is as it should be, Duke Shiverrig." Dax bowed again in his saddle. "I bid you good fortune until we meet again."

The Duke addressed his men. "Knights of Gethem, we march to the City of Spires and the throne of Baroqia!" The knights cheered and raised their swords. They fell into rank and proceeded to follow their beloved Duke.

29

KASAI

Sharp horns sounded as the King's Army raced to engage the enemy with a rush of infantry. General Rokig and his men frantically fought the flying creatures as the bat-like things swarmed around the knights.

Eventually, the winged demons turned their attention to the warhorses. Kasai heard the animals scream. Soon each horse was covered in flapping wings. The horses ran, kicking and bucking, but could not dislodge the demons. Riders fell to the ground as they were shucked off their terrified mounts.

The infantry finally joined the desperate knights in the middle of the battlefield. Before the soldiers could take up proper defensive lines, the demon horde attacked with fury. They slammed into the king's disoriented army in a giant wave of claws, hooked beaks, and gnashing teeth. Wings beat, and barbed tails pierced men until they died.

Fear overwhelmed the troops. They stood motionless as creatures from their nightmares became real before their eyes. Soldiers were slaughtered where they stood. The demon warlord slid off his mount and effortlessly carved a gruesome path towards General Rokig and his horseless knights.

"If the general falls, it will be the end of the infantry," Kasai warned.

The demon warlord ruthlessly slew everything in his path. No one could stand against him or his horrible sword and survive. Bodies were cloven in half or shattered into spraying shards of ice. As their ranks were destroyed, the men turned and ran. The King's Army had failed miserably.

The soldiers held back in reserve began to panic. They saw the frontline troops fleeing the field, and knew their turn was coming. Kasai could smell the reek of their desperation. In some cases, it puddled at their feet. A captain rode forward on a bloodied horse and yelled out, "Wedge formation, now! Push forward hard and drive the enemy forces back. Keep ramming ahead until you reach General Rokig. Do not stop! If you fail, we die!"

Kasai could see the faces of the men below him. None of them were listening to the captain. They looked out to the battlefield to where the slaughter was the greatest. They were being sent to their deaths to support the retreat of the Rokig cavalry and the first wave of infantry.

Suddenly, a collective roar spread across the battlefield. Kasai looked back to the battle and saw the demon warlord had struck down General Rokig. The general lay headless on the ground with a circle of dead knights piled around the demon.

The soldier's morale was broken; men fled for their lives. Monsters pounced on their backs and dragged them to the ground. It was a day of ruin for the King's Army and, possibly, the Kingdom of Baroqia. The horde shrieked its unnatural symphony of animalistic victory. Who could stop such a force?

The reserve troops were barely able to shuffle into a defensible position. Fear glued their feet to the ground. If the reserves didn't stop the horde, the monsters would run free across Baroqia. The army needed someone to rally them together and keep courage and bravery in their hearts. General Rokig was gone. The army was disintegrating. A new hero must emerge, or all would be lost.

Kasai looked to the tent of King Conrad. His leadership and presence on the battlefield were needed now more than ever. A group of knights was in a defensive circle around the entrance. A mounted rider trotted out of the large tent and took his position inside the semi-circle of armor and steel.

"Look, Morgan, King Conrad is coming out of the griffon tent. He will lead the army."

The king emerged clad in shining armor as if on parade. But the king and his knights galloped away, fleeing the battlefield.

"I don't understand," Kasai professed as he watched in disbelief.

"Coward," Morgan responded matter-of-factly, his face also turned to witness the betrayal of the king.

Kasai observed the young page, for the first time noticing that Morgan's eyes were a unique pale-magenta.

"Come, Ever Hero. We do not want to be trapped up here when the demons come," Morgan said.

Kasai simply nodded, carefully climbing down the boulders as he followed Morgan, his armor making every move a chore. Morgan reached the bottom first and untied the supply pony he had left at a small tree. Kasai thought of his friends and hoped they were all right. Had Pallo and Run-Run joined the fight? Were Des and Reese tending to the incoming wounded? What would happen when the demon horde reached the encampment? None of them would be safe.

"Morgan, there is something I must do. Help me remove this shell."

"But my duke clearly instructed me to keep you out of harm's way. Those plates are important. They will keep you safe. You are too valuable."

"I can't move properly. Please, help me."

"What do you intend to do?" Morgan said. He slowly shook his head from left to right as he reached for a buckle.

"Something stupid. Now please, unbuckle what I cannot reach in the back."

The armor dropped to the ground. Nearby, soldiers heard it clang. They looked at Kasai, wondering what he was doing. Nobody removed their armor during battle. Morgan gave him a quick nod of approval. The young page almost seemed eager to see what would happen next.

"Where are you going, monk?" one of the soldiers demanded. The young man pointed his sword at Kasai. His old, chipped blade shook nervously in the air.

Kasai's eyes went to the battlefield. The slaughter was getting worse. There was only one way to stop it. "I must go."

The reserve soldiers stared at Kasai with anger in their eyes.

"Deserter!"

"Coward!"

"You're no Ever Hero! We are all doomed!"

"You were supposed to protect us from harm!"

They accused him with desperate voices. Kasai knew they were terrified. "I'm sorry. My place is not here with you."

The soldiers saw the sword and shield gifted to him by Duke Shiverrig lying on the ground. Hatred filled their faces.

"Go and hide, you traitorous monk. Your time will come soon enough. None of us will survive this day."

Kasai gathered his burnt-orange robe tighter. He did his best to smooth out the wrinkles caused by the heavy armor. He turned to the supply pony and reached under the saddlebag. Ninziz-zida felt good in his hand.

The ancient weapon glowed amber, eager to be wielded once more. Kasai sighed. I must do this thing, though it surely will cost me everything. Ninziz-zida heard his thought and passed on feelings of partnership, trust, and power. The ancient weapon coaxed him to share his fire xindu energy with her. He drew in a deep, slow breath. So be it.

Ninziz-zida came alive. She pressed into his mind whirling striking movements and intricate patterns of defense. Would it be enough? He recalled the words of Master Dorje when he received the power tattoo for courage. It seemed like ages ago. 'You shall fill the hearts of those around you with the bravery in your soul and the courage in your heart. As you are strong of will, so shall you inspire the will of others.'

Kasai found his courage, and the Mark of Mizzen glowed on his forearm. He thought about Desdemonia. A slight smile crossed his lips when he thought of the frolicking gypsy, dancing through the forest when they first met. He wished he could have said goodbye.

In the distance, the allied army was trying desperately to regroup. Small, isolated pockets of resistance began to form. The demon horde was a swirling tide of death around them, preventing them from connecting. The demon warlord directed them from where he stood.

'The Great Balance must remain.' Kasai heard the prophetic words of Master Dorje in his head. "And as General Rokig fell, so must the enemy's leader," he said to himself.

The ground vibrated with the pounding of warfare. Kasai's exposed feet felt the energy of the cold soil as his toes dug into the earth. The sensation of war was foreign and harsh to him. It overwhelmed his senses.

He closed his eyes and calmed his breathing once more. It must be this way. He knew the soldiers' anger was understandable, if not warranted. He turned away from their mistaken expressions of betrayal and began the long walk towards the battlefield.

Kasai held the three segments of Ninziz-zida in one hand as he approached the front line of the reserve ranks. He surveyed the field and the quickest route to his goal. Kasai felt a firm grip take his arm and turned to see who had grabbed him from behind.

"Brother Kasai?" It was Brother Maru from Ordu. Kasai was just as surprised as Maru to see the other alive.

"Maru? I'm happy to see you are still among us, Brother, although I wish it were under better circumstances."

"You're heading into the madness? You can't make any difference. You're wasting your life."

"I must try, Maru."

"You'll be ripped apart!"

"I have Ninziz-zida to guide me." Kasai held out the ancient weapon for Maru to see.

"You hold the Fire Serpent," Maru said and looked at Ninziz-zida with reverence, but he backed away in confusion. "How?" Then focus returned to the young monk's eyes. "Kasai, look at me. This battle is over. We must regroup with the remaining monks and do what we can to heal the wounded. We will lead them to safety away from this place. There will be another time."

"Maru, you are very wise for such a youngling. That is a sound plan and one aligned with the Boundless. The Masters would be proud to hear you say those words in a time like this. You and the others will be greatly needed in the days that follow."

Kasai looked back to the battlefield. Retreating soldiers pushed past them and into the ranks of the waiting reserves. "The Boundless has set a different path for me. Be well, my friend."

Kasai left Maru's side and jogged onto the field. While others fled, he alone moved towards the chaos. Wounded men stumbled back to what they thought was the safety of the reserve troops. Messenger horses with empty saddles galloped back to the encampment. Their fear struck eyes were wide as saucers.

Kasai focused his concentration on the ink-black auras of the creatures from the Abyss. They were everywhere he looked. They fought on the ground or flew in the air over the battle. How could mere men withstand such a foe when fear tore away their resolve to fight?

Without a focal point to keep their hearts and minds aligned as one, the men of the army lost hope. The death of Rokig had broken them. Kasai picked up his pace and ran towards the scattering pockets of men still fighting for their lives. The trampled grass was no longer golden brown, but red with blood.

Ninziz-zida pulsed in his hand and kept time with the pounding of his heart. The fighting swelled around him. The smell of fresh blood and metal shavings filled his nose.

The screaming was everywhere. Demons ripped the entrails from living men and gorged themselves on the warm meat of their victims. Kasai's mind began to fray. There were too many possibilities, too many targets, too many lives to save. His hands squeezed Ninziz-zida tightly.

The ancient artifact sensed Kasai's fear and confusion. Warmth radiated up his arm and filled his body with strength and purpose. Kasai's vision cleared, and his mind became lucid. The movement of fighting slowed down around him, yet he knew his own body was moving faster.

Kasai ran towards a warrior who had fallen under the savage blows of a demon with silver scales and white fur. The demon knocked away the soldier's sword, chortling through a mouth filled with dangling cilia. It grabbed the soldier's shield and tossed it to the ground. The white-furred demon raised its jagged spear to deliver the killing blow.

Kasai launched into the air, sailing over the prone soldier. Ninziz-zida's end segment flashed out in a blaze of yellow fire. The demon's head was vaporized into red mist. Its body crumbled to the ground and settled into a pile of ash.

Ninziz-zida sent sensations of conviction and strength into Kasai. Somehow, like before, he knew what the ancient weapon said. *I am the Great Fire Serpent! I am Ninziz-zida! I will blaze brightly into the soulless Darkness!*

The ancient weapon was challenging the entire enemy horde.

Kasai thought he now understood Ninziz-zida. The Fire Serpent did not want to possess his soul and make him into a slave. The weapon was crafted to destroy evil, and the greater the evil it encountered, the more powerful it became.

Ninziz-zida was alive in his hands. The mental connection the two shared was acute, and he realized they needed each other; they were meant to be together. Ninziz-zida had been dormant for many, long years waiting in the monastery's Hall of Artifacts. Now she had awakened and had somehow chosen Kasai as her champion.

Kasai held Ninziz-zida with both hands. Her sections pulsed with eagerness to continue the attack. Kasai closed his eyes and concentrated on opening all channels of his xindu energies to the artifact. Perhaps Ninziz-zida could transmute his energy into her fighting spirit. He breathed in deeply and let out a long, slow, cleansing breath.

"Ninziz-zida, we are of singular purpose. As I give myself to the Boundless, I now open myself to you. Show me your righteous flame. Let us confront this horror together, as one."

Ninziz-zida's three sections burst forth with bright-orange flames in his hands. *As one.*

Kasai and Ninziz-zida became an unbroken force of attack and defense as they struck down the enemy demons and barbarians. He was a whirling dervish, moving like a blur from one killing strike to another.

His lightning-fast strikes left his enemies defenseless and ruined. Hundreds of barbarian bones shattered, and the creatures of the Abyss were vaporized into ash. A cyclone of Ninziz-zida's fire whipped around Kasai as he rushed toward the demon warlord.

Kasai climbed over the ring of dead knights and soldiers, while the warlord stood preoccupied in the middle, white armor was dented and smeared with human blood. Smeared handprints showed the slain warriors' last attempts to hold the demon back.

Kasai approached slowly, while the warlord admired the armored head of General Rokig. The general's headless body laid at the warlord's feet. The demon lifted Rokig's head high over his own, drinking the fluids leaking from the severed neck. Finally, he spotted Kasai from the corner of his eye.

"The Great Warlord Oziax welcomes you to your death, mortal," he stated with mocking bow. He casually pointed his demonic sword at Kasai and uttered a sharp sounding word. A blast of ice shot from the blade. Kasai spun Ninziz-zida's end sections into a shield of fire, melting the ice fragments in the flame.

"Clever trick, monk," Oziax said. He dropped Rokig's head and leaped at Kasai.

Kasai held the middle section of Ninziz-zida and spun the end segments in a curved figure-eight pattern. The staff wiped from one side of his body to the other. Kasai sent one of the staff sections out to attack Oziax, but the demon's sword parry was faster, and Kasai's strike missed its mark.

A terrible hiss and groan resounded as the two weapons clashed together again and again. Kasai felt Ninziz-zida's frustration and focused more of his fire xindu into the enchanted weapon.

Kasai grabbed the tail of the Fire Serpent and whipped the rest at Oziax. Kasai snapped the staff back just as it connected to Oziax's shoulder guard on his sword arm. The armor cracked and sizzled. Oziax ripped the useless armor away, exposing his alabaster arm and shoulder.

Oziax bellowed in rage and drove harder into Kasai. The power of the demon was almost overwhelming. Kasai shuffled back in defense, but Oziax slashed his sword forward and struck Kasai on the knuckles of his right hand. Kasai pulled his hand back but lost his grip on the section he was holding.

The demon pivoted sharply and grabbed Ninziz-zida. Oziax gritted in pain as Ninziz-zida's flames burned hot in his hand. But Oziax held on tight and ripped the Fire Serpent out of Kasai's hand, tossing her wide to the side and out of reach.

Oziax swung his ice sword at Kasai's head and then at his gut. Kasai jumped back in a series of somersaults to avoid the terrible blade.

"Stay still, little butterfly."

Kasai spun back again but tumbled over the circle of dead men that made up their mini arena, scrambling to his knees as quickly as he could. Oziax was already there, striking down with a mighty blow Kasai could not dodge. He reacted the only way he could, reaching up to clamp the sword between his hands. Blue light erupted from the cobalt marks on his palms.

"Impossible! No one can stop the might of Eishorror," Oziax shouted as he threw Kasai off the sword. Kasai tumbled away. He stood up fast and was rewarded by a terrible backhand across his face.

Kasai was battered, bruised, cut, and now bloodied. Even with Ninziz-zida in hand, he had only managed to annoy the demon warlord. He was running out of tricks.

Oziax charged forward. Kasai shifted his weight and collapsed at his knees. As Oziax's sword arm passed overhead, Kasai sprung back up. He shaped his hand like a knife and delivered a sharp strike to the nerve cluster in the demon's exposed shoulder. It paralyzed Oziax's arm, and his ice sword dropped to the ground. Kasai breathed a quick sigh of relief.

Oziax howled in pain and frustration as he tried to raise his dead arm. Glaring at Kasai, he said, "You cannot win. Let me show you."

Oziax took two steps back and began to change into something grotesque and horrible. His armor fell off his body, his form swelling and distorting itself. His legs transformed into something akin to the back legs of a horse or satyr with cloven hooves.

The hand that could still move, grew long tentacles where fingers were before.

Each tentacle had hundreds of suction cups with sharp barbs protruding from the center.

Oziax's facial features drew back into a brutish animal skull. The old flesh stretched across its surface and tore in places. Long black horns sprouted, curling upward from his forehead.

His back became covered in coarse, white hair, the rest of his skin the color of bleached bones suffering too long in the sun. Kasai watched the transformation with fascination and dread. He couldn't breathe. His lungs felt like a burning furnace consuming all the air around him, suffocating him in the process.

The demon stomped forward, deadly and invincible. Without Ninziz-zida, all he had were his feeble skills.

"I am nothing without Ninziz-zida. Nothing. I can't fight this thing. It's finished," Kasai thought.

"This is not the end. You must have faith. You must believe."

"I do believe," Kasai said, and he did. He believed he heard the Song of Aetenos in his head. But it wasn't enough.

"In yourself."

The voice in his head was right. Kasai pushed the doubt from his mind. He would have faith in himself. It didn't matter if he was the Ever Hero or not. At this moment, he would choose to believe that he was.

Kasai drew deeply from the reservoirs of his xindu energy. The life forces connected to the Boundless demanded a heavy toll, and he surrendered himself as payment. His xindu energies expanded to claim the spirit of his offering. Fire, water, air, and earth energy overlapped for the first time. The sensation was powerful and exhilarating.

"I must end this now. There is no more to give."

Kasai's body vibrated. A transparent membrane of silvery-blue light shimmered around him. He heard the distant echo of Aetenos' voice in his mind.

"I am the Divine Fist, and you shall be my argent hammer to smite the darkness."

Now, there would be no more confusion, no hesitation, just clarity of purpose. Kasai's eyes lifted to the heavens.

"I will."

Oziax lunged head-first like a charging bull. Kasai flashed to the right. He shot his arms out and struck the side of Oziax's head with his open palms. The noise of battle was sucked into a sliver of silence before a dynamic BOOM resounded across the battlefield. A dome of energy expanded outward, ripping open the debris-filled air. The slain bodies of General Rokig's elite guard rolled and tossed like broken ragdolls.

Oziax reeled sideways, dazed and unbalanced. He shook his head like a wild beast shaking water from its dense mane. Glaring at Kasai, a wicked smile came to his face when he regained his balance.

Panting, Kasai could hardly stand. He had never known such exhaustion and could barely keep his head up. But it didn't matter anymore. He had done his best, though it wasn't enough. Death came for him in the form of a wicked beast. But for some reason, an image of Desdemonia laughing and dancing came to mind. It would be, perhaps his last pleasant thought in this world of horror he could not escape.

Oziax's steps became more erratic and exaggerated. He overcompensated to prevent himself from falling but only became more unbalanced. The murderous smile faded as black ichor oozed from his fleshless nostrils before leaking from his eyes and bubbling out of his ears.

The demon fell to his knees. The tentacles of his left hand wrapped around his bestial head. Oziax threw his head back and unleashed a primordial roar just before his head exploded. Tiny pieces of brain and skull jettisoned over the bodies of the dead and then withered to ash. Oziax's headless body sank to the trampled ground and slowly dissolved to a pile of black ash.

Kasai barely registered what had happened. He rested his head on his chest. It was over. He just wanted to sleep. No more fighting. No more suffering. No more anything. He felt his body go light and hoped the afterlife would be kind. His eyes closed, and his ears went deaf to the sounds of battle around him.

When Kasai finally opened his eyes, smoke and ash were billowing in the air. He was lying flat on his back in the open encampment of the King's Army. The sharp sounds of mayhem amplified as his hearing returned. A small group of people surrounded him, including Pallo, who all but hovered. Behind him, two knights unfamiliar knights approached. "Your page found us after you took to the field. You are either mad, or there is a courage in your heart unknown to men. We fought to reach your side and arrived to witness some kind of miracle," the knight said in a voice filled with awe. "We carried you here but held little hope you would survive long enough to receive proper healing." He stared at Kasai with wonder in his eyes.

"Morgan ... is he safe?" Kasai asked.

The second knight spoke. "The remaining knights rallied behind the incredible turn in the battle you caused ... with your bare hands." He looked at his own hands, shaking his head in bewilderment. "With their leader destroyed, the horde broke ranks and scattered. They lost themselves in a sea of carnage. They killed anything in their immediate vicinity, including their own. The weak fell prey to the strong, none could escape the hunger of the horde. I spied a fell, white fiend picking through the ash corpse of their headless warlord. Vile creatures. No respect for the dead."

"Duke Shiverrig will want to hear more of your bravery and the story behind your magic," the first knight said eagerly.

Kasai massaged his throbbing head. "It's not magic." He raised himself on one elbow to search the room. "Where is Des?"

"I am here," she said, shouldering her way between the two knights. "Seems you have a knack for finding trouble no matter where you go."

"And Reese?"

"I am here, Kasai," Reese said, kneeling at the end of his cot. "I saw what you did to that ... monster. Only a True-born of the Immortal Mother has such strength. How ... did you do that?" Reese asked.

Pallo kneeled by the side of the cot. "The prophecy is unwoven. The Ever Hero of the Divine Fist now walks the land."

"Reese," Kasai said with genuine affection. "I'm glad you are safe." He looked for Run-Run, then turned his head towards Pallo. "Where is your brother? He didn't—"

"Run-Run secures supplies. We assumed you would want to continue the search for your Master. He has found loyal friends that would be honored to join the Ever Hero in his quest.

"The road will not be easy. We must move with stealth and precision. The enemy is scattered but hungry for mortal souls."

Kasai lifted himself from the cot but fell back again.

"Ninziz-zida. I lost the Fire Serpent during the battle. I must retrieve her."

"Rest easy, Ever Hero. I found her when we found you." Pallo presented Kasai with a long, wrapped length of cloth. "She was hot to the touch. I could not hold the staff with my bare hands for any amount of time."

Kasai breathed a sigh of relief. He clutched Ninziz-zida tightly. The familiar shape and weight of the weapon gave him comfort.

Reese edged in closer to Kasai. She reached out a tentative hand to touch the cobalt mark on his left palm. "You ... really are the Ever Hero. The prophecy is true. The reincarnation of Aetenos is here." Reese knelt before the cot in supplication. "Our savior has returned."

"Reese, please. Stop. I am still just Kasai." He sat at the edge of the cot. He was a bit shaky but well enough to move. "We have done all we can here. I am well enough to travel. Master Choejor needs us," Kasai said, determination renewed.

30

DESDEMONIA

The King's Army had scattered. Extensive amounts of supplies, tents, armor, equipment, and war machines were left unattended. Riderless horses formed herds and bolted away from the carnage into the open fields. The demon horde divided into smaller groups; some chased down the fleeing soldiers while others fought amongst themselves. The victor sat in the middle of the slain and ate its fill.

Earlier, Run-Run had gathered enough horses for everyone, and the small party carefully navigated away from the overrun encampment. They outran anything that was too lazy to give chase. There were plenty of slow-moving foot soldiers to occupy the attention of the horde. Soon, the battlefield was well out of view.

The open fields provided no shelter, but at least they could see enemies coming from afar. While the rest of the party kept a watchful eye for pursuit, Desdemonia scanned the ground ahead. She had no desire to be on the surprise end of a sneak attack.

The party rode throughout the rest of the day until the glowing orange sun silently slipped below the jagged mountain peaks of the Hoarfrost Mountains. Pallo, at the lead, put his hand up to signal a stop. In the distance, Desdemonia spotted three riders approaching from the south.

"Men of the King's Army?" Kasai asked.

"Not soldiers," Pallo answered.

The three riders rode their mounts hard until they reached the others and brought their lathered horses to a stop. Desdemonia noted they wore the mark of Aetenos on their jacket collars; she wasn't keen on new faces, but knew they'd need help where they were headed. She overheard Pallo discussing the route to Storm Wind Pass with one of the riders.

"We will camp here for the night," Pallo said when they were finished.

Desdemonia dismounted. Her body was sore and tired. She looked to see how

Kasai fared; he looked exhausted—face was drawn with his eyes that looked apologetic, like everything that had happened was somehow his fault.

Run-Run tended to the horses, he was a natural with animals. Desdemonia could tell he was a friend of the forest. She wondered if Kasai was...or could be.

Desdemonia heard a sharp whistle; Pallo waved his brother and the three newcomers over to him. The three men quit their tasks and jogged over to Pallo. They chatted for a moment before walking purposefully to Kasai. Desdemonia followed.

"Time for introductions," she sighed. She just wanted to sleep.

The five men stopped as one in front of Kasai. Pallo pointed at each newcomer in turn.

"Ever Hero, may I introduce Airis, Rafar, and Orin. They are all experienced spire runners and trusted members of the Kibo Gensai. Orin is most familiar with the terrain of the Hoarfrost. He will act as our guide once we reach the foothills."

Rafar stepped forward and put two fingers to his forehead and bowed deeply. He was a tall man, the tallest of the group. He wore his hair tied back behind his head, allowing only a few thick strands to fall in front of his face. His intense, dark eyes never left Kasai. "I am honored and humbled to walk with the Ever Hero of our time. Please accept my swords as your own."

Airis was next. He wore a broad grin when he took a step forward. He was a young man, filled with enthusiasm and determination. He had a boyish face and eyes that had seen too much sorrow. He had wavy, dirty-blonde hair that he wore tied up above his head in a topknot.

"Run-Run, the Miko Nuna sends her greetings and eagerly awaits your safe return," Airis said. There was laughter in his voice.

Rafar just shook his head.

"Run-Run, what did I tell you about that one? Don't get mixed up with the crazy ones."

Run-Run looked at his brother and then somehow found Desdemonia's eyes. His bashful expression was endearing. She had liked him immediately. He maintained a level of happiness that most people dreamed of, and yet, he had suffered great hardship. He had a pure soul.

Desdemonia watched Reese move about the basic camp. She wore the clothes of a priestess and said the words of one devoted to the Immortal Mother, but everything about her was off by just a little. She made too many tiny mistakes. Any of them could go unnoticed, but when added up, they told a different story. Kasai once said Desdemonia saw snakes in the grass when there were none.

I know a snake when I see one; Desdemonia narrowed her eyes, keeping a keen watch on Reese as she listened to Pallo introduce the third newcomer as Orin. The man had closely cropped jet-black hair. He had a clean-shaven face that proudly displayed thin scars that covered his cheek and jaw.

"Greetings, Orin," Kasai said. He pointed casually at the scar tissue on Orin's face. "Have you seen many battles?"

"No more or less than any of us, Ever Hero. Orin is a good fighter with quick steel," Pallo responded, in place of Orin, who bowed, but remained silent. His eyes shifted to Desdemonia and then to Pallo.

"And the scars? Now that I see them more clearly, they seem to be intentional," Kasai said.

This time, Orin spoke for himself, "We of the Kibo Gensai have devoted ourselves, mind, body, and soul, to fight the enemies of the Light. I am a man of singularity in my faith. The marks are not limited to my face. I notch my flesh with a count of every foul creature I have slain in the name of Aetenos. The unmarked portions of my body are a grim reminder that there is more holy work to be done."

"There are more?" Kasai said in astonishment.

Pallo nodded. He circled his finger over all of Orin's body. Orin stepped back, but not before eying Desdemonia with a baleful look.

She gave him a friendly wink in return. *Here's another one that's going to be a problem,* she thought. Orin's eyes were dark and sharp. He looked the type that liked to brood. She felt his scrutinizing gaze like a dagger thrust. Somehow, Orin's hawk-like stare made her feel unwanted or tainted in some way. *Bah. I'm just tired. He's the newcomer, not me.*

Kasai cleared his throat. "I'm not very good at this sort of thing," he started then took a breath to collect his thoughts. "I will honestly tell you I do not know what it means to be an Ever Hero of Aetenos. Who could? And since there were no lessons on the subject at Ordu, I am making this up as I go." He grinned at Desdemonia, knowing he beat her to the joke. She smiled warmly back at him. *He's learning.*

"I do know what is right and what is wrong. I know the importance of protecting the vulnerable spots of the Brother fighting by your side and being protected in kind. Together, we are stronger.

"I go to keep a promise to rescue my Master from an evil that is beyond my comprehension, and quite possibly my skill. I cannot ask you to follow me, for I do not know what horror awaits us in the mountains. If you do, I will be honored by your companionship."

The Kibo Gensai bowed in unison. They returned to their horses and unpacked their bedrolls.

"Nice speech. Uplifting and filled with the promise of a great victory," Desdemonia commented with a grin of her own.

"Funny," Kasai said. "Have you seen Reese?" He looked about the camp.

"Maybe she fell in a ditch," Desdemonia chuckled, sounding hopeful.

"Very nice." Kasai's horse became agitated. "What's spooked you, girl?"

Reese seemingly appeared from around the other side of Kasai's horse. "Oh, I'm still here. I'll be with you until the end." Reese gave Desdemonia a crooked smile.

"Lovely," Desdemonia gibed under her breath.

"I hope we can eat soon. I'm famished," Kasai said. He walked over to where Run-Run was unpacking a sack of food.

"Remember what I said, witch. Do not get in my way." Reese shouldered past Desdemonia to join Kasai and Run-Run.

"This just keeps getting better," Desdemonia deadpanned. She unstrapped her saddle and slapped her horse on the rear, sending it to graze.

The next morning the party awoke at first light. Everyone was sore from yesterday's long ride. They ate a quick breakfast before breaking camp. Desdemonia climbed atop her horse. Kasai fumbled along as he usually did. He tripped over more things than she could count. The members of the Kibo Gensai looked at him as if he were a sacred thing. *So much bowing,* she thought, shaking her head amused, allowing herself a little chuckle.

"It's a day's ride to the beginning of Storm Wind Pass. Orin will take us through the mountain trails once we leave the Pass. We will find Rachlach Fortress on the morrow of the third," Pallo said as the small party made their way East.

"If we're lucky," Orin said.

"Isn't it curious that we have not encountered any enemy patrols?" Desdemonia commented.

"The Immortal Mother protects her children in their time of greatest need," Reese countered. "Everything is as it should be."

Desdemonia looked skeptically at the priestess. "Or we are heading straight into a well-placed ambush."

"Let's be happy luck is on our side for once," Kasai suggested as he trotted past the two women. "And stop your bickering."

The party traveled on without incident to the entrance Storm Wind Pass. "We must leave the horses here and travel light on foot. Airis will take the horses into the forest foothills a few miles to the south. He will await our return there," Pallo said to the group.

"This makes no sense. Ten thousand footsteps must have passed this way to battle, yet they leave no one behind?" Desdemonia pointed out. "Where's the broken gear, or shit, or something?"

Pallo looked all about and nodded in agreement. "Orin, surely there should be sentries of some kind along the mountain pass."

Orin unsheathed one of his short swords. He narrowed his eyes. "Best to be ready."

"Ever Hero, what can you sense?" Pallo asked.

"Can you sense danger, too?" Desdemonia said. She'd be impressed if he could. "That would be handy."

He shrugged his shoulders. "It doesn't really work like that."

Reese sighed. "You all worry too much. There are no sentries because the battle was a slaughter. There's no need to guard what the dead cannot steal."

"What do you think, Des?" Kasai asked.

Reese interjected before Desdemonia could respond. "There is nothing more to say. A higher-power watches over us and has cleared the way for the Ever Hero."

Desdemonia gave Reese a cross look, "Doubtful," she said before catching up to Kasai. He was walking with heavy steps again. She could tell he had something on his mind, beyond the present. *It's the amulet.* Every time she brought it up, he shut her down. He refused to listen to any form of reason. "Kasai?" Des began softly when they walked side-by-side.

"Des, if it's about the amulet again, I will listen, but you know how I feel about it. Dark magic is dark magic, no matter the point of view," he said. He was short, almost angry. Something was definitely on his mind.

"I don't want to talk about the amulet," she said, protectively grasping the rock hanging from her neck. "Forget it, Kasai. I can see you are in a mood."

"I apologize, Des. Please continue."

Desdemonia could not help but look askance at him. She was unsure if she wanted to discuss the amulet or not. She decided it was best to change the subject.

"We have been traveling together for quite some time now. And well, as you know, I've been on my own since my early years. Just me and Gauldi. But he really isn't much of a talker if you know what I mean. And well, I thought … after all this is over, maybe you and Master Choejor would like to stay with me in the forest." She was surprised that tumbled out of her mouth so easily. "There, I said it."

"The forest? With you and that creature who would like nothing more than to split me in two?"

"That's just Gauldi's way. Okay, not the forest. We can go anywhere. Maybe back to Sunne."

"You must know I need to return to Ordu. It will need to be rebuilt. That's Master Choejor's and my home."

"You don't have to say no straight off like it's a stupid idea. Is it because of Reese?" Desdemonia fumed yet felt crestfallen on the inside. She should have kept her idea to herself.

"Reese? What does she have to do with anything? She's not coming to Ordu."

"Why must you be so dense? I see the way she's always whispering in your ear, telling you things in private. She's poisoned your heart against me. Don't deny it."

"Reese? What? Poisoning my heart?"

Desdemonia looked directly into his eyes. "Yes, Kasai, your heart. Have you no feelings for me after all that we have shared?"

Kasai's eyes grew wide. He fidgeted as he walked. He kicked a stone on the road, and then another.

"Well?" Desdemonia said.

"Of course, I have feelings for you. We're friends."

"Nothing more?" She cozied up to him, her grin broadening.

"I don't know. Sometimes you make me feel dizzy."

"Dizzy? That's hardly romantic," Desdemonia cuffed him upside his head. But inside, she was smiling. "You apparently have no idea what I am talking about. I'm such a fool." She threw her hands up in the air.

"Des, that's not it."

"Well, what is it then? Spill it."

Kasai was about to answer when the dark shape of a cargo net spun over their heads, falling around them before being cinched tight. The rest of the party were ensnared in the same way. Howls erupted from the sides of the pass. Fiendish creatures sprang from their hiding places, brandishing serrated blades.

"Trespassers are always welcome," one fiend garbled in a coarse version of the common tongue. The fiend had a long, white snout and sharp horns cascading down its back.

"Need more slaves," a second fiend said. It prodded Rafar with its sword. "He tall one. Maybe fight well."

A brutish thug pushed through the group, tossing aside the lesser fiend with the pitched fork. He glared menacingly at the other hellions. Each cowered under his commanding presence. "Bind hands and collect weapons. Sekka sees them alive."

"Looks like we've found the sentries," Desdemonia said. "Just lovely."

31

KASAI

The fiends surrounded the prisoners. They prodded them along with their serrated blades and jagged daggers. Kasai's group was herded into the fortress of the enemy.

Kasai had imagined an eerie, black keep with sweeping buttresses and snow-covered towers, but he saw no such things. A sudden squall carried a mini storm of snow; rough terrain blurred in a haze of dirty white. The party was led through a slot carved into the side of the rocky pass. The opening led into a cavern, which slowly reduced to an excavated tunnel ending in an iron door.

The lone demon who commanded the group took out a set of rusted keys to unlock the worn door. He shoved the party inside and commanded all but one of the fiends to remain outside.

"Martuk alone get reward for bring souls to Queen of Ice," the demon said. He pointed proudly to his hairy chest. He grabbed the smaller fiend. "You take bag filled with Martuk new weapons. Follow Martuk now!"

Martuk then pushed Kasai and the others along the corridor. The tunnel was cold and dimly lit. Kasai trudged along beside Pallo; his mood was grim.

"I suppose you think your Ever Hero has some mystical power to get us out of this jam," Kasai whispered to Pallo.

"Fear not. We have everything in hand. Run-Run and Rafar are cutting their bonds now. Orin and I have already freed ourselves."

Run-Run walked behind Desdemonia and Reese. Kasai caught a glimpse of the Kibo Gensai removing a small shiv from the cuff of his sleeve. He deftly positioned the blade in his fingers and sliced through the coarse ropes.

"We of the Kibo Gensai have our special talents, too, Ever Hero," Pallo winked knowingly at Kasai.

Orin and Run-Run fell upon Martuk. One used his shiv to slit the demon's throat, while the other thrust the hard metal through the demon's yellow eye. Pallo and Rafar did likewise to the fiend carrying the weapons, the latter caught the sack of weapons before it fell to the floor with a clatter. It happened fast and silently.

Run-Run freed Kasai, Des, and Reese while Orin took the sack from Rafar and handed out the weapons, except Kasai's. He hesitated, an expression of worry crossing his face.

"I'll take her out," Kasai reassured Orin, taking the sack from the Kibo Gensai warrior. Ninziz-zida's smooth segments slid into his hands. The ancient artifact responded in kind.

"It smells of old, dead magic here. It clings to the walls," Desdemonia commented.

"Come, this way," Reese called out, taking the lead. Her lithe body swayed with newfound confidence.

"Reese? Wait, Reese, where are you going?" Kasai caught up to her and pulled her by the arm to stop. She looked at Kasai with pure innocence.

"The Immortal Mother guides me. This way is clear."

Kasai looked to the others for their opinion. It was clear the Kibo Gensai would follow him wherever he went. Desdemonia's expression remained skeptical and suspicious when it concerned Reese.

"I don't know. This feels awfully like the Temple," Desdemonia said.

The ease of dispatching the guards did seem rather convenient. Kasai looked down the corridor Reese intended to follow. It was empty.

"One way is as good as the next until we can discover the location of Master Choejor. Ok, Reese, you have the lead."

Reese tossed Desdemonia a smug look. She took Kasai's hand and swaggered ahead of the group. She led them down numerous corridors, always deliberate in the direction she chose.

"Something is amiss. Our way has been made remarkably clear since leaving the encampment," Orin said in a low voice. "We are being led by an invisible leash."

"Agreed. Run-Run and I feel the same," Pallo replied.

Kasai knew they were right. No amount of luck lasted this long. Each corridor Reese led them down was as vacant as the last.

"Can we stop for a moment and devise some sort of plan?" Desdemonia commented.

"Not much longer now," Reese said. "The pull on the Immortal Mother is strongest in this direction." She turned a corner that stretched down another long corridor, which opened to a large room. It was awash with pale hues from overhead lights.

"Kasssaaai. I have been waiting for you. Why did you dally? You made Master Choejor endured so much more pain by your tardiness," Khalkoroth taunted as the party entered the room. A deep gurgle chuckled from his throat. The demon squatted over a small altar holding a thick chain that wrapped around a man's waist. Kasai recognized the broken figure of Master Choejor under a pile of shredded blue robes.

Khalkoroth pointed a gloomy finger at Desdemonia. "I see you still have my favorite trinket, Wood Witch. I'll have it back."

The pale demon leaped off the altar and pulled hard on the chain, dragging Master Choejor to the floor. The stone surface was unforgiving. Master Choejor let out a painful moan.

"But first some unfinished business. I wanted you to be witnesses to my little ceremony of transference. Your best friend Daku willingly provided me with a satisfactory vessel to enjoy this world." Khalkoroth drooled viscous sludge from his mouth. The creature's pink eyes blazed with malice and cruelty. "Therefore, I owe him a debt."

Kasai saw the frightened face of Daku appear over the demon's features. His eyes were wide with fear and desperation. "Daku, fight! Don't give up!"

Khalkoroth chuckled. He wiped his brutish hand over his face and smeared the visage of Daku away. "I have all the memories of Daku here with me. Each one is such a tasty titbit of his mortality. It seems Master Choejor was quite a problem for my young monk. So many painful and embarrassing lessons."

Khalkoroth lifted the chain into the air, raising Master Choejor so they were face-to-face. "Daku never liked you, Choejor. Your death will serve as payment of my debt."

The pale demon pulled his free arm back and extended the long-fingered claws of his hand, then thrust his hand through Choejor's chest, ripping out his heart. A slight sigh escaped Choejor's lips before all life left him. "Thus, I seal the soul pact of transference between us."

"Daku! NO!" Kasai yelled.

Blood dripped from Khalkoroth's hand. He casually dropped the wet heart on the floor and squished it under his foot.

"Reese stay behind us. Your rhyme may not work to confuse the beast a second time," Pallo directed. The Kibo Gensai fanned out, approaching the pale demon in a broad semi-circle.

"Kasssaaai, look what I found sifting through the messy remains of your handiwork." Khalkoroth reached behind his back and pulled Eishorror from its sheath. He waved it casually in the air. "It is an arrogant weapon, with no love for you, Kasai."

Khalkoroth eyed the warriors surrounding him. He scrutinized the ice sword. "Such an exquisite blade yearns to freeze the warmth of your blood. Maybe it feeds on the living? I really don't know. Oziax was never one to share his toys. But sadly, Eishorror is not for today. I have been instructed otherwise."

Khalkoroth placed the sword on the ground. He lunged at Pallo with surprising speed. The older warrior barely dodged the sweeping blow that followed. The Kibo Gensai struck as a pack of wolves. Run-Run flashed in to strike Khalkoroth's exposed flank, while the others harassed Khalkoroth with feints and thrusts. Although skilled fighters, their mundane weapons could not penetrate the infernal flesh of the demon.

Desdemonia held back. The Kibo Gensai moved around the demon too fast, and her magic would not know friend from foe. Reese backed away to corridor entrance.

"Kasai! Snap out of it! We need you!" Desdemonia shouted.

"Master Choejor is gone. I couldn't save him. He was counting on me. I failed him." Kasai gritted his teeth, wiping away tears.

"Only you have the power to stop this creature," Desdemonia pleaded.

Kasai saw his companions fighting the demon but were losing. He focused his sadness on Khalkoroth. It all came back to Daku. Daku the hothead. Daku the bully. Daku the Slayer of Ordu!

Kasai's fire xindu flared red hot. It burned through his despair to ignite his anger. "Dakuuuuuu!" Kasai shouted, pointing Ninziz-zida at Khalkoroth. Ninziz-zida blazed bright red. Kasai leaped to his feet with tears streamed down his cheeks.

Khalkoroth spoke through a hateful grin, "The weakling Daku is gone. Only Khalkoroth remains."

Kasai felt the intense wrath of Ninziz-zida as if it were his own. The ancient weapon revered all who followed the Light of Aetenos. She would have her revenge.

Kasai spun Ninziz-zida in a flaming circle. Red flames lapped against his hands. The fire burning along the sticks changed to orange, then to yellow, and eventually blazed forth in righteous blue. Daku was gone. It was time to end this creature.

The Kibo Gensai continued to badger Khalkoroth, attacking with overlapping short swords and daggers. Khalkoroth lunged at Rafar. The warrior was too slow and lost his face to the demon's long claws.

Kasai raced forward. He struck Khalkoroth's open side. The strike penetrated Khalkoroth's magical protection and pushed the demon back. Blue fire erupted over the demon's pale skin and hair. Khalkoroth shrieked. He stumbled backward and frantically snuffed out the flames.

"Pallo, move your men back," Kasai said with absolute determination.

As Khalkoroth hobbled away, his foot brushed up against Eishorror's hilt. He snatched up the blade from the floor. His white fur left a trail of smoke from Ninziz-zida's touch.

Kasai closed the gap with three long strides and jabbed Ninziz-zida forward, once, twice, three times. Ninziz-zida was too fast. Each thrust found unprotected flesh. Khalkoroth howled in pain, while Ninziz-zida hissed her elation in Kasai's mind.

Kasai whipped around as fast as a spinning tornado and kicked Khalkoroth in the mid-section. The demon doubled over. He held Ninziz-zida collapsed and in two hands. Kasai raised the Fire Serpent high to strike down on the demon's head.

Kasai paused. He knew this strike would end Khalkoroth, and Daku would go with him.

"Do it, Kasai. Do it. Kill me!" It was Daku's voice. His sad face looked up at Kasai through the bestial features of the demon.

"Daku?"

Khalkoroth laughed. "Just a voice, little monk. I have others." He spoke in the voice of Master Choejor, "Help me, my son. Save me!"

Kasai knew then that nothing of his friend remained. He raised Ninziz-zida higher. Khalkoroth raised his gnarled hand and uttered a strange, black word, the sound of which made Kasai shudder. The shadows in the room expanded until all was thrust into darkness.

"Not again, demon," Kasai said. He held his open palm above his head. "Aetenos! Light!"

Silvery-blue light flooded from Kasai's hand, and the darkness was banished. But Khalkoroth was gone.

Desdemonia ran to Kasai's side. "Did you do it? Did you kill him?"

"I assumed the blessing would merely illuminate the area." Kasai searched about the room for ash or hidden doors.

"Look! The beast runs!" Orin shouted. He pointed across the room. Khalkoroth bounded down a second corridor on all four limbs.

"We must catch him!" Kasai said.

"Kasai, wait!" Desdemonia grabbed his arm tight. "This is work for the King's

Army now. Let someone else bear the responsibility of rooting out the evil in this dark place. Let someone else lead. There is nothing more for you to do here."

"I must avenge my Master!" Kasai's eyes were wide, frenzied. "Don't you understand? I must do something."

"Then just walk away, Kasai. Master Choejor is gone. Come with me. Back to the forest and be at peace."

"Walk away? No. I have lost too much. Master Choejor must be avenged!"

"What about me? Will you risk losing me too?" Des spoke quietly.

"This responsibility has fallen to me. It's my destiny."

"Who says so? Anyone could have been chosen. Forsake the Song. Let another rise up in your place."

"Perhaps another could, but it was me that was chosen. I must do what was asked of me."

"What about what I am asking of you?" Desdemona pleaded. "This world has too much pain and suffering. I want to return to my forest, where there is peace. Come with me. Let's leave this horrible place together."

"Des, you don't understand," Kasai said. He slowly shook his head.

"I do understand. This is too big for us. Come, my love, while there is still time. Your duty to Master Choejor has ended. Please, I do not want to lose you, too. I need you."

"Des, I need..." He beheld Desdemonia's sad, amber eyes. Feelings of warmth and love quelled Kasai's fire xindu energy and calmed his anger.

Desdemonia nodded forward with affirmation. Her eyes watched him, anticipating his answer. "Tell me. Tell me what you need."

"Kasssaaai," Khalkoroth taunted from the end of the corridor.

Kasai stared down the corridor at the demon. The weight of his failure to save Master Choejor rekindled his hatred for the pale demon. His fire xindu blazed forth with volcanic might within his soul. All the suppressed pain and sadness of losing the loved ones in his life erupted within him at once.

Kasai took his arm away from Desdemonia's grasp. "There shall be no peace in the land while this corruption exists. I will destroy these demons before they can take more innocent lives. I will stop Khalkoroth. And Maugris if he's here. No matter what comes against me, I will fight."

Desdemonia bowed her head in resignation. "Then it's settled. I will walk this path with you. I will fight by your side until the end. Regardless of the cost."

"Kassaaai... Kassaaai... I'm waiting," Khalkoroth's deep voice echoed through the corridor. "Still holding back, little brother?"

Kasai led his group into a great hall supported by rough-cut buttresses. The walls cast a metallic-green sheen from sorcerous globes floating across the ceiling. Kasai saw Khalkoroth limping to a dark dais at the far side of the room. He bowed to the two figures upon the dais, then moved off to the side and blended into the shadows.

The figures were shrouded in darkness. One sat upon a back-lit throne, and to his side stood the silhouette of a tall woman with shapely curves. She wore a tall headdress that trailed down her back.

A sultry voice called from the dais. "Rachlach Fortress welcomes the Ever Hero of Aetenos." The woman stepped into the full light. Her headdress was strewn with bleached bones that rattled when she turned her head to the man seated on the throne.

"You see, Maugris. I told you he will come."

Kasai gasped. The apparition from his nightmares was here now, perfectly depicted and very much alive. The woman nodded in recognition at the ancient weapon in Kasai's hands.

"And he shall bear the fabled Fire Serpent into battle against the Darkness, as his progenitor once did."

Maugris rose from his throne. He wore an elegant attire of purple satin robes, embroidered with beautiful, golden runes.

"This is who you have been searching for all this time? This boy is the Ever Hero of Aetenos?" Maugris said with contempt.

The woman's eyes bore into Kasai. Her gaze was mesmerizing, and Kasai felt helpless and weak under her scrutiny. Then Desdemonia was in front of him. Her hands took hold of his arms and shook him out of his stupor. Des was always there for him. She gave him renewed strength.

"Kasai! We must run! We cannot win. She is not of this land," Desdemonia implored Kasai. She shook him again to make sure he was listening to her.

"I know, Des. I know."

"No, Kasai, you do not know! That is Sekka. She is a greater devil from the Lower Planes! Listen to me, please! For once, listen to me!"

Kasai looked squarely into Desdemonia's amber eyes. "Des, it must be this way. The path ends here."

Desperation swelled in Desdemonia's eyes. "Then take the amulet. The charm will protect you against their magic."

Kasai shook his head. "No, I have a different faith to protect me now."

"Ugh, you're as stubborn as Gauldumor. Fine, we do it your way." Desdemonia's hands glowed with swirling blue light. Azure sigils of power glittered, penetrating the green light of the room. The Kibo Gensai formed a line in front of Kasai. Reese took up a stance behind Desdemonia.

Kasai stepped through the line of Kibo Gensai. He rapidly twirled Ninziz-zida's end section into a spinning shield. Blue fire burst from the ancient weapon as it too recognized its old foe upon the dais.

Maugris was furious at such a challenge.

"I shall not be mocked by a boy! You all will die!" Lightning burst from Maugris' hands. It bounced off the floor to break into separate chains, striking the Kibo Gensai warriors, tossing them like rag dolls into the static-replete air. Their twisted bodies smacked into the stone of the floor, where they lay smoking. An acrid, pungent odor filled the room.

Ninziz-zida's magical components deflected much of the lightning, but not all of it. Kasai's body was wracked by spasms of shocking pain. Des raced to his side, ready to attack. The amulet around her neck had absorbed the brunt of the dark magic. The green emerald at its center throbbed like a beacon.

Kasai recovered enough to see Reese standing nearby. She was unharmed. He turned back to the dais. Sekka's cruel eyes were studying his movements with keen interest. Desdemonia reached out and gathered a portion of Ninziz-zida's blue flame into her hand.

"Your fancy sticks like me, too," Des said with a grin. She gave him a playful wink as she added her Elemenati magic to the flame and crafted a swirling column of blue fire at her side. She grabbed a handful of flame and molded it into a ball. Then threw it at Maugris. The sorcerer dismissed it with a contemptuous wave of his hand.

"You will all pay for your trespass," Maugris said. He threw a fireball of his own. The fiery magic washed the room in vermillion light as it sped towards Desdemonia. It exploded in an array of shimmering cinders when it reached her. The amulet at her neck briefly flared bright green as it absorbed the last of the fiery ball's heat.

Maugris hurled a curse and a second fireball at Desdemonia. Again, the amulet protected her from his spell. "Impossible!" he cried.

Desdemonia peppered him with smaller blue, fireballs but Maugris canceled her magic with barely a word.

"The witch possesses an interesting item." His shifty eyes glared at Sekka. "But let's see how much your Ever Hero can take." Maugris pointed at the floor beneath Kasai's feet. He turned his other palm upright with his fingers pointing to the ceiling.

Kasai felt a quick warning from Ninziz-zida. He instinctively directed the weapon downward in time to smash the stones spikes that shot upwards beneath his feet. Nonetheless, one jagged stone got through his defense and gave him a horrible gash on the outer side of his leg. Kasai fell to one knee in pain.

"This feeble boy is the key?" Maugris questioned Sekka in disbelief.

Sekka observed everything like a spectator at a grand duel. "Kill him then, if you think you can."

Desdemonia raced to Kasai's aid. She reached into one of her shirt pockets and took out a small vial. "Drink!" she said. Kasai took a draught of the thick liquid and immediately felt the pain in his leg subside.

"It's got a bit of a kick," Kasai said.

Desdemonia helped him to stand. Maugris descended the dais.

"I cannot get close enough," Kasai said through his teeth.

"I know, leave that to me. I have a plan. You attack. I'll defend." She looked deeply into his eyes. "Trust me."

Kasai nodded his agreement to the familiar style of fighting. Desdemonia's amber eyes sparkled back at him. She tapped her finger to the side of her head. "Smart."

Her gypsy smile returned for just a moment. Then a stern look of determination crossed her face. "Stay behind me until we are close enough."

"Right."

Kasai and Desdemonia ran towards the dais just as Maugris cast a black cloud of gas. The amulet sucked the foul vapor into its center. Kasai darted past Desdemonia, unleashing Ninziz-zida in a swirling barrage of strikes. Cobalt flames whipped from Ninziz-zida's segments, but her attacks were rebuffed.

Maugris' protective aegis flared against Ninziz-zida's wrath and kept the sticks at bay. Maugris laughed. "How long do you think you can keep this up?"

Kasai heard Master Choejor's words in his head. 'You maintain boundaries where there are none and, therefore, are easily defeated. Give yourself fully to the Boundless and receive its gift in return.' Kasai knew he must fully embrace the Boundless if he had any hope of surviving this fight.

Kasai dropped into a flash meditative state. He let go of his fears of magic, of loss, of failure, of the need to control. He let his xindu energies rise on their own accord. A powerful force called to him. It demanded more, and Kasai gave it willingly.

The Boundless gave its energy back to him in return.

Kasai felt a new connection to a vast power. His xindu energies rose to levels he had never experienced before. He felt as if he was drawing from the raw elements that flowed through the land; fire from volcanoes, water from the sea, earth from mountains, and air from the sky.

Kasai felt the might of the Ever Hero within him. He funneled his xindu energy into Ninziz-zida. The azure glow of her flame burst from the segments in a blinding, blue light.

"Des, step back."

Kasai spun the Ninziz-zida to each side, raising her above his head; the momentum increasing the power building within the staff. Desdemonia backed away from the broad swings of the ancient weapon.

Kasai whipped the end section down on Maugris' shoulder. The magical barrier protecting the sorcerer failed. Maugris' left shoulder shattered. His arm hung useless at his side.

Kasai swung Ninziz-zida around again and connected with Maugris' ribs. The sorcerer backed away, gasping for breath. It finally came to him in screams as Ninziz-zida's fire ate through his robe and dug deep into his flesh.

Kasai shot the heel of his foot into Maugris' knee, and the sorcerer collapsed to the stone floor. Blue fire blazed over his crumpled body. Kasai took a step back. Des moved back to where Reese stood. Kasai looked to Sekka.

She raised a curious eyebrow. "Impressive. Let's see how far you've come," Sekka said with a wicked grin. She looked passed Kasai to Reese. "Sess'thra, now."

Kasai spun around and saw Reese transform into the demon succubus from that last, dreadful day at Ordu. The succubus' almond-shaped eyes grew round with anticipation as she slid behind Desdemonia.

"I told you to stay out of my way, witch," Sess'thra said as she stabbed Desdemonia in the back with a small dagger. Kasai saw pain and sadness fill Desdemonia's face. She melted to the floor.

"NO!" Kasai yelled as he ran to Desdemonia. Ninziz-zida fire trailed behind him.

Sess'thra took to the air and landed at the foot of the dais just as Sekka descended the steps.

"Well done," Sekka applauded.

Sess'thra bowed her head as Sekka walked past her and over to the smoldering ruin of Maugris' body. She looked down at him with uncaring eyes.

"Heal me, devil," Maugris pleaded in a frail voice. Sekka sneered down at the broken sorcerer.

"My dear Maugris. You have played your part well. However, your immediate use is at an end."

"I command you to destroy my enemies," Maugris said through gritted teeth. He slowly raised one charred hand to point at Kasai.

Sekka laughed with sinister amusement. "You command me to do nothing." She crouched down and took Maugris' chin in her hand. "You are a tiny, insignificant thing."

Maugris was shocked. "I ... I command you." His words lacked strength, and his head dropped to the floor.

"Do not fear, Maugris. I may still have use for you in time." Sekka stood, turning her attention to Kasai.

Kasai had barely listened to the exchange between Maugris and Sekka. He was at

Desdemonia's side with Ninziz-zida resting on the floor nearby, its fire rippled along the lengths of its segments.

"Love, please don't let her take my soul..." Desdemonia's eyes searched Kasai's for understanding.

"Never, Des, never." Kasai wept. His tears fueled his anger, and Ninziz-zida blazed blue once more. "I should have listened. I should have turned away when you asked. I'm so sorry."

Desdemonia lifted the amulet from her neck and held the chain out to Kasai. "Take it. Keep you safe." Her body went limp in his arms, and the amulet fell to the floor.

Kasai looked at the marks on his palms. "Aetenos, please heal her." Nothing happened. Kasai feared it was too late. Sadness and anger swelled in his heart.

He reached into his soul and called upon the newly discovered power of the Ever Hero. He took up Ninziz-zida and gathered strength from the ancient weapon. She was eager to confront her age-old foe. But something in his heart knew it would not be enough.

He contemplated using the amulet.

"What is wrong, Ever Hero? Surely the Chosen of Aetenos does not fear me," Sekka taunted. "Perhaps you would like to take Maugris' place and join me in the conquest of this realm? I can be anything you desire."

"You are nothing that I desire." Kasai brushed away his tears. He made himself ready for this final confrontation.

"No? Well then, as I have said before to another of your ilk, I have other, more aggressive forms, if that is more to your liking." Sekka ripped off the clothing she wore. The headdress of bones clattered to the floor as her naked body shimmered with dark magic. Kasai's breath frosted before his face as the temperature in the room dropped.

Sekka arched her back forwards, and four great horns sprouted from her head. The horns curled around themselves, and massive teeth grew from her extended jaw. As she stood upright, her human legs changed to a more avian form, equipped with talons that dug into the stone floor.

Sekka towered over Kasai. Coarse, albino fur covered her back and shoulders. She flexed her powerful arms. A crown of bones materialized and floated above her head with glowing sigils, pulsing with power.

Sekka shrieked menacingly. Ninziz-zida's blue flame gave Kasai courage, and he held his ground. Sekka uttered a strange word, and swirling black tendrils lashed out at Kasai. Ninziz-zida reacted with blazing speed. Her segments shattered all but one of the tendrils, which wrapped around Kasai's leg.

Kasai's body froze like a block of ice. Ninziz-zida immediately sent Kasai's fire xindu back to him. The heat thawed the frigid paralysis, but his movements were incredibly slow.

Sekka attacked again. Lightning flashed from the floor, ceiling, and walls and struck Kasai from all sides. He was raised off the ground and tossed close to Desdemonia's prone body. The pain was greater than any he had ever felt.

"Aetenos..." Kasai whispered the name. Yet, no inner voice responded to his call.

+The Great Monk cannot hear you, Ever Hero. This room is your doom.+ Sekka's voice pounded in Kasai's mind.

His life and the lives of his companions would be over if he didn't stop Sekka now. Maugris was nothing compared to her raw power. He needed something more.

Kasai coughed up blood, then spotted the amulet on the floor.

His fingers slowly walked across the cold floor and tangled around the amulet's chain. He grimaced as he got to his feet. Kasai held the amulet up against Sekka. The center of the charm dangled before him.

+It will not help you against me+ Sekka sent into his mind.

She chanted in a dark and dangerous language, which Kasai could not understand. With a flick of her wrist, she sent a magical dart at Kasai. The amulet took in the magic. It worked for him as well!

With renewed confidence, Kasai put the amulet around his neck and took Ninziz-zida in both hands. Sekka's bestial eyes opened wide, and long strands of drool looped from between her inner teeth. Her mouth gaped open with a guttural sound of triumph.

She raised her bestial hand and pointed at Kasai. One last dark word echoed into the frigid air. Kasai readied himself and trusted the amulet would protect him. But no dark magic attacked him.

The sound of the word drifted through the air and sparked the amulet to life. The emerald charm throbbed with intensity and turned fetid green. The room darkened into a blackish-verdant hue.

+The connection has been made! The Chaos Gate shall open! Aetenos' greatest gift to the mortals has now sealed their doom.+

Kasai heard her words pounding in his head. The amulet's power dug deeply into his essence. It grabbed hold of something that was formless yet found a way to contain it and imprison it. Kasai somehow felt a new bond become established between him and Aetenos. Not one of the mind or heart, but of the soul. And it was horrible and wicked.

The amulet flared with green fire as it burned through the fabric of his robe and into his skin. Kasai tore it from his chest and threw it to the ground.

The stone shattered on the floor. From each piece, a demonic sigil rose into the air and then faded from sight. The stone floor melted where the pieces lay as if burned by an alchemist's acid. The smaller holes grew until they connected together, forming one singular hole. The outer edges burned with green fire and continued to grow in diameter.

Sekka stomped over to the edge. Kasai knew by her twisted smiled that whatever was coming would be worse than anything he had faced up until now.

+My Chaos Gate lives!+

Sekka grabbed the broken body of Maugris and tossed him onto the portal's surface. The charred body sank until it was gone. Sekka stepped away from the growing edge and transformed back into her human form. Her naked body was slick with wetness and reflected different shades of ugly green. Pungent vapor bubbled like a boiling cauldron from the portal.

Kasai tried to block his ears from the screams of tormented souls and nightmarish creatures coming from the portal.

"The amulet..." Kasai hung his head in shame.

"Yes! The amulet. It took your soul and connected it to another on Gathos. Now the bridge is complete."

"Gathos ... another soul," Kasai stammered. "Whose soul?"

Sekka gave Kasai a sly grin. "Oh, I think you must know by now."

"Whose soul?" Kasai shouted. "Whose soul?"

"Isn't it obvious? Where do you think Aetenos has been all this time?"

"No, no, no," Kasai fell to his knees, sobbing.

Sekka chuckled before turning to Sess'thra, "Time is short, and there is much to do. Stay by Shiverrig's side. Entice him to take the demon seed. I will need a capable warlord to lead my legions until I can revive Oziax and Narthoth."

"What of the monk and his friends?" Sess'thra asked with a lascivious grin.

"They cannot harm me now. Let them stay and witness the arrival of my Frost Legion. It is a fitting reward for all they have done."

"Yes, my Mistress." Sess'thra bowed in deference. The air crackled, and she was gone. Sekka stepped over the edge of the portal and walked across its surface. Its diameter had already tripled in size. When she reached the center, she slowly descended out of sight.

Kasai crawled to Des and raised her head to his leg. She was still unconscious, and blood ran freely from the wound in her back. Kasai pleaded to Aetenos for the strength to heal her. When no help came, he tapped into his water xindu and placed his palms over the knife wound.

"Take everything. Just make her well."

The Boundless responded when Aetenos did not. The gash closed. Kasai rocked her slowly for what seemed like hours. Kasai tried to figure out what to do next. It didn't matter. Nothing mattered now.

Desdemonia finally opened her eyes as she regained consciousness.

"Is it over? Are we safe?"

Kasai smiled sadly at her then looked over at the growing Chaos Gate. A cold reek billowed from the portal in anticipation of foul things to come.

"No, Des, things are worse."

EPILOGUE

J arei Ch'ou sent one last thought to his wife, hoping it would pierce the fire and smoke ravaging their home to touch her heart. Life had been so simple in the frontier village. Now, everything was lost.

Jarei had read the signs. The last three years of poor harvests were just the beginning. The fish in the river were washing up on the shore, bloated and dead. Pine trees lost their needles and turned black. Barn animals walked in a stupor before dropping to the ground, legs splayed behind them. A sickness had infected the land. The Frozen Dark had returned.

Jarei and his wife, Marquia, had spoken of this dreadful day many times. He knew he would be a target. The minions of evil were drawn to healers, especially those blessed by the benevolent demigod, Aetenos. His wife and their son, Kasai, would also be in mortal danger.

"When, not if, the time is upon us, you must be the one to save our son, Marquia. Find the Masters. Kasai is important. Aetenos watches over him. I believe the Great Monk has a special purpose for our son."

Marquia shook her head, no.

"Marquia, I have heard Aetenos's song. The monks will take you in. You will be safe," Jarei implored his wife.

She resisted, of course. "We shall go together. We are a family and shall remain a family."

"The creatures will be drawn to me. They will think I am the One. We can use this to our advantage."

Jarei returned his focus to the aegis of light that separated him from the *things* on the other side. His barrier wavered as fell creatures threw dark magic against it. The foul beasts were pale, gangly creatures standing on thin legs. Their dissected torsos and arms wavered back and forth as they sent spells fishtailing into the barrier. They screeched obscene curses when their magic exploded harmlessly against the wall of Light. Yet, Jarei's strength had its limits.

The heads of the creatures tapered slightly to blunt, rounded cones. They possessed no eyes, only deep slits for nostrils. Their oversized mouths were set with sawblade like teeth that were frozen in a permanent, wicked smile.

Jarei knew these creatures from ancient texts and scrolls. They were hunter fiends. Trackers from the frigid Abyss dredged up from the frozen plains of Gathos. The abominable hounds could smell and taste the use of magic in all its wondrous forms. They had finally found him.

He looked to the window where he knew his wife watched in fear. Their eyes met through a brief clearing of smoke and debris. Marquia's expression pleaded with him to stay with her and Kasai. Her eyes said they could make it there together. Jarei knew it was not to be so.

They had been together since childhood. Jarei knew everything there was to know about his wife, each expression, and bodily gesture. He knew what her heart was saying even though she could not send the message back to him. 'We can make it together.'

+No, we cannot. They want me most of all. They will follow me far enough for you to escape. It must be this way.+ Jarei sent.

She nodded slowly. No more words needed to be spoken. Her eyes said enough. 'I love you.'

+I love you, too. Now go!+

Jarei begrudgingly left her visual embrace. The fires grew higher; smoke poured out through the windows. It was everywhere. He knew he must hold the barrier for a bit longer, long enough so his wife and son could escape.

Sweat flowed freely down his forehead. He let the aegis of light collapsed. The drain on his strength was too much. He would need that strength to run. He wondered, only for a moment, how Aetenos could allow such filth to return? But Aetenos had his way, and Jarei was a devoted follower. He would not question the plan of the Great Monk. He wished he could hear the Song as loud and clear as the people of his Order once did.

Jarei heard Kasai call to him in a terrified voice. Jarei knew his son was wondering why he was not next to him, holding him, and keeping him safe. The pain was too much to bear. He spotted Kasai from across the yard, but the creatures were too close. If he ran to his son, they would both be overwhelmed.

Jarei held his son's gaze for just a moment longer. He sent him a smile that he hoped would register within such an innocent mind. His mother would explain it all to him when he was older.

Jarei turned to the fiends. Now was the time for sacrifice. He raced towards the creatures and then past them. He cast a beacon of light above his head to give the fiends an easy target to follow. Hopefully, it would also keep their attention away from his family.

Jarei fled into the dense forest. He hoped he could put up a good enough chase. Time, his family needed more time. He ran faster.

Jarei jumped over fallen trees and thin streams. He felt like he ran for hours, but it was only minutes. He looked back in dismay to see the gangly creatures had gained on him; their thin form belied their preternatural quickness. He pressed on.

His right shoulder thrust forward on its own volition; he looked down to see a bright red shaft an arrowhead and bright red shaft jutting from his upper chest.

Jarei's breath grew shallow, legs buckling, he stumbled. The hunter fiends surrounded him. Jarei crawled forward. The pain in his shoulder slowed his movement. He put his back against a small birch tree. The arrow tormented him as it brushed against the young trunk. There was nowhere to run. Waves of pain flowed through his body.

A more human figure glided among the fiends. He handed a longbow to one of them and moved confidently towards Jarei. He then unclasped a cruel-looking dagger strapped to his thigh. His head was hidden by a dark green hood that kept most of his face in shadow.

The man approached Jarei and removed his hood. He had surprisingly handsome features that shimmered in and out of focus. The man held the dagger in one hand. He knelt by Jarei.

"They always run," the strange man said. He took out a small amulet with a bright, green center from a pocket. He dangled the small charm above Jarei's head.

Jarei looked at the amulet, then looked away with disinterest. The songs of birds in the trees brought him back to happier days with his family. He remembered a time when he and his wife and son played hide-and-seek together in these same woods.

"Another hunt ends, and alas, you are not the One," the man said. Jarei heard the disappointment in his voice. "Once again, my talents are wasted on pursuing a misguided believer of a crazed monk.

"I ought not to question the motives of the Mistress. But still, anyone could do such a task. Why send me, the master assassin, Daxzulz Thrum?"

When Jarei laughed, blood bubbled out of his mouth. "Aetenos shall find his way to strike you down. His followers are true."

He was not afraid to die. His family would be safe.

"Your deluded fantasies have failed you. Look around you, priest. There is no savior. You are alone. Aetenos has abandoned this land."

Jarei slumped down against the birch and coughed up more blood. Thankfully, he could no longer feel the sting of the arrow.

"Aetenos has already answered my call. My family is safe. You will never find them."

Pure wickedness came over Dax's shimmering face. His dagger was in and out of Jarei in a flash.

"We shall see, priest. We shall see."

JEFF PANTANELLA

THE FOE WARS

BOOK TWO IN THE
EVER HERO SAGA

THE FOE WARS
PART 2 - BOOK 2

PROLOGUE

"**Y**our doctrines, Lord Raguel, and *your* banishment. This was not the will of the Immortal Mother. Aetenos walked a road of salvation, not just for the mortals, but for us all!"

Zhao Houzi heard Artiya'il's melodic and passionate voice, though muffled behind closed doors. He could almost picture Lord Raguel's flawless face darkened with a frown as the crowds of spectators inside the Cloud Court's amphitheater erupted with cheers of agreement or shouts of protest.

"Quiet! I will have quiet now!" His voice thundered like a crashing wave and echoed off the pristine walls. The din of the crowd quickly diminished.

"This shouldn't be. It cannot be," Zhao Houzi mumbled to himself as he scurried up another flight of stairs leading to an upper balcony.

Today was the day the angel, Artiya'il, was to be sentenced for crimes against the Laws of Heaven. Never had a True-born been brought before Lord Raguel's Cloud Court and treated in such a manner.

A True-born! And I'm already incredibly late. This is all Titus's fault, he thought. *That great warhorse can be so stubborn in his ways and he never listens to reason, no matter how many irrefutable facts I give him.*

"This will change everything," the small monkey said and did his best to use only his short "man" legs and not all four limbs, as was proper in such an august and magnificent place. It was a challenge not to revert to his ancestral ways when he was pressed for time. Using four limbs was so much quicker than two.

"Pardon me. Pardon me, sir," Zhao Houzi said cheerfully and respectfully as he darted past a group of slow-moving celestials taking their time moving up the same stair. Each wore robes of office of intricate design and patterned with brightly colored sigils of turquoise, amber, and emerald.

Their feathered wings remained furled and tight behind their rigid backs. Thin circlets of silver and gold wrapped around their heads and were decorated with jeweled charms that dangled just above their shoulders. Zhao Houzi wondered what it would feel like to fly, to feel the air rush through the hair on your face, to soar and dive like a bird.

"Monkey! Watch your paws!" said one of the lower-born angels with obvious irritation. He twisted around with his back to the wall as Zhao Houzi scampered underfoot.

"Hands and feet, good sir," Zhao Houzi said. "Just like you."

"They will allow any riff-raff into the Cloud Court these days. The High Court should require an entry visa into Tanalum and block these unfavorable animal spirits from disturbing the peace. Keep them all in Elysian, where they belong. This is not their place," another said. His tone reeked of disgust. "Let them soil the First Level with their debauchery and unsupervised revelries."

"Block them all, I say. Elysian has become a droll nursery at best, unfit for the governance of the realms. Lord Raguel must keep all human souls away from any agendas requiring important decision making." His long slender nose pointed like a ninth finger at Zhao Houzi. "You will be named in my complaint to the Chancellor Pinnacle, Monkey."

A third celestial was quick to comment. "I cannot abide by these animal spirits. The stench of their former existence never leaves them." She was older than her companions and wore a purple sash around her waist, which complimented the light lavender hue of her robe and pink skin of her face. He thought the color combinations were quite pleasing.

Zhao Houzi would usually be disappointed to hear such intolerance, but today he was too preoccupied with getting a good seat. He dashed past the angels and followed the tight spiral stairs that wound to the upper mezzanine. The old stone walls reflected his small body, clothed in a bright crimson vest and cream-colored pants with swirling orange designs. His hairy feet and arms moved quickly, and he scampered over the remaining steps.

He wanted to see, as much as hear the Chancellor Pinnacle's verdict. This was a critical case, and depending on Raguel's decision, it could have monumental repercussions throughout the Seven Heavens.

Perhaps an unclaimed seat remains that will give me an unobstructed view of the court arena below, he thought but didn't hold out much hope as he opened the last door leading into the mostly filled, upper-deck seating.

"There!" He said and darted over the back of one row of chairs, then leaped between two seated celestials using their shoulders to support his small, hairy body.

"Monkey!" They cursed as he flew past their heads. But he barely heard their astonished gasps and harsh words of reprimand, distracted as he was with the incredible amphitheater.

Amber sunlight poured through clerestory openings above the upper mezzanines. A sphere of polished gold suspended by invisible means, spun hypnotically in the center of the arched ceiling's atmosphere.

The sphere was a perfect measurement of forty-nine meters in diameter with an additional glowing corona of thirty-three meters extending from its surface. A shimmering halo formed around the indoor sun, and no matter the viewer's vantage point, it was seen in the same way framing the golden orb. Zhao Houzi marveled at this effect but could never understand how it worked. It was a riddle for his friend, Titus, to decipher.

The surface of the ceiling was filled with geometric designs, each flowing harmoniously into the next. Cascading rays of sunlight washed over the silver inlays worked into the perfectly shaped stone blocks, causing them to sparkle and shimmer.

Today was a lucky day. Zhao Houzi found an unoccupied, front row seat between two elder celestials, most likely hailing from the second level of Heaven based on their white gowns. He gave each a warm greeting and then peered between the gleaming golden rails to the court below.

The immense chamber's inner shape was set as a perfect square with layers of circular terraces drawn down to the floor of the room. The upper mezzanines were filled with spectators and lower-level celestials jostling for a view, politely but assertively angling their way to the front railings.

The lower mezzanine and mid-level balcony seating had reached capacity hours ago with the privileged celestials that held rank and office over the mere citizens of the realm. Only the True-born, those celestials who had materialized at the beginning of all things, occupied the choice orchestra seats.

They sat in stoic silence, garbed in golden robes of silk and cashmere. Bright sigils of power spun in slow, clockwise circles above their heads resembling floating crowns. The movement of the sigils mirrored the pace of the glowing indoor sun above.

The chamber was full of boisterous laughter and commentary as if the event was more for entertainment than a pivotal moment in the history of the Seven Heavens.

Such a sad and desperate day, yet they all seem to be enjoying the spectacle, the monkey thought as he scanned the faces of his fellow celestials. He could smell the ripe aromas of change in the air, even if the others could not. Never had one of their own been tried for transgressions against the Heavenly Realm. Would that he believed the Chancellor Pinnacle would find compassion in his heart and decide upon a lenient sentence if Artiya'il was found guilty of his crimes. The monkey inwardly sighed. He knew better than to hope for such an outcome.

Far below, seven structures were raised from the floor and jutted into the center of the room like stone jetties. When seen from above, the negative space between each structure created an offset heptagram shape, an auspicious design for such an area of purity and law. Each podium rose off the floor from polished stone stairs that ended in a circular platform, capped by a small rotunda.

Raguel raised his hands to quiet the vast chamber. His wings unfurled into a great span across his back, mirroring his irritation at the disruption to his court.

A quieting hush flowed through the chamber as six heavily robed figures entered the great hall and walked to their respective stairs and made their way to the end of each podium. Radiant mandalas of swirling sigils spun above their heads, and their preened and perfect wings were folded upon their backs. These were the oldest of the celestial lords and had presided over the High Court for millennia, and their judgments were final.

Each of the six judges wore a specific color representing one of the six lower-levels of Heaven. Sage Green was draped over the first judge celebrating the innocence of a new soul's arrival to Heaven, for each soul entering the Seven Heavens began its journey of worthy progress in the land of Elysian.

Here the soul would be indoctrinated in the Ways of Heaven and enjoyed relief from all worry and despair. This was a happy place, filled with verdant trees and golden meadows, where fresh souls could play upon the lush green grass, and bath in blue lagoons of mineral water.

Ivory for the Second Level of Heaven called Eden and representing the pure of heart and the cleansing of sin. Zhao Houzi felt Eden was a dreary place, one of reflection and perhaps a touch of unwarranted guilt, as each soul released the last memories of a less than perfect life in the Mortal Realm.

He wondered why these souls desperately clung to the grief of their past. They were free now. What perplexed him more was knowing mortals possessed the same power within them to cast away the burden of past failures and bad decisions when alive, yet rarely exercised this ability. True forgiveness, especially of the self, seemed to be a difficult or impossible concept for most mortals to grasp.

The third judge took each of his steps with a proud swagger. He wore layered robes the color of bronze, which gleamed like the polished stones throughout the courtroom pavilion. The Third Level of Heaven, called Arcadia, was for the passionate, kind, and just. Those who would fight for others in times of need were gathered in this realm. Legions of champions of spear, sword, shield, and lance trained in readiness for any conflict with the evil spawn from the Abyss. They were the protectors of the realm.

The judge who wore the crimson robes with fiery specks of orange and magenta hailed from the Fourth Level of Heaven, named Erewhon. Mystical powers of divine force manifested in the souls of this realm. Gifted by the righteous might of divine soul energy, the warrior-priests of the Seven Heavens honed their magical craft. Their devotion to the Immortal Mother rewarded them with higher learning and powerful spells.

The fifth judge climbed the opposite platform from where Zhao Houzi sat in the upper mezzanine. When the judge reached his rotunda, he gazed up at the spectators in the grand chamber. Zhao Houzi's keen sight saw sadness in the elder angel's eyes. His robes were of a strong vermillion with lighter swirls of yellow interwoven into the fabric, showing that he represented the Fifth Level of Heaven called Canaan. The celestials living on Canaan were the caretakers and healers of all realms, though their influence in the Mortal Realm was less defined and non-existent in the Abyss.

Deep cerulean robes, under bright emerald overlays, clothed the judge representing the Sixth Level of Heaven. This realm was called Paradise. It was a peaceful place of rest and meditation, filled with high mountain peaks and valleys carved by winding rivers.

Yet long ago, those who dwelled here used their acquired mental prowess to assert control over the Third and Fourth Levels, marshaling for the forces of Heaven and directing them on the battlefield where they thought best.

Gold, representing the golden touch of the sun and all that fell under its glorious reign, was for the Seventh Level of Heaven. The Laws of Order were written in Tanalum and enforced by Lord Raguel's Protectorate. There was no higher office than the Chancellor Pinnacle, and Lord Raguel had held the office since its inception at the dawn of all things.

His wings were composed of feathers from a thousand different birds and he opened them with great flourish, as he surveyed the crowd from the seventh structure. Then his ageless hands motioned that the final sentencing would begin. The air became still and quiet.

The defendant, Artiya'il, stood alone in the center of the chamber. He wore a simple white tunic and modest sandals. His wings and wrists were bound in silver chains, but he still held his head high. It appeared he had been treated well and unharmed.

Nonetheless, two armed and armored Protectorates were in striking distance if necessary. Their dazzling and unblemished plate armor sparkled in the bright light of the chamber. Zhao Houzi noticed his ankles were also shackled and loosely connected by a chain.

Why would so many chains be needed? he wondered.

The angel dutifully acknowledged each of the judges in their high perches and ended with a respectful nod to Lord Raguel. He stood defiant and proud. "My Lord Raguel, Chancellor Pinnacle of the Seven Heavens. I hope this day finds you well," Artiya'il said. His voice sounded of a sweet chorus of nightingales as if nothing was amiss.

Lord Raguel moved quickly past formalities of greeting. "Artiya'il, your trial is at its end. The charges brought upon you, as written in the Book of Heavenly Laws, have been spoken, and your pleas and defense have been heard. The Six Judges have come to bear witness to your sentence."

The Chancellor Pinnacle's voice boomed throughout the chamber. "Do you have any last words you would like the court to hear before the verdict is delivered?"

Artiya'il paused for a moment before speaking, collecting his thoughts. "We must change as the realms surely have changed through time. Our laws are fit for a time long past. The mortals are children who need our direction and encouragement, not a blind eye until their undisciplined mind falls into folly, for when it does, there is nowhere else to look than the Deep Dark for answers. They need our guidance and love, not punishment in its most severe form.

"This was Aetenos's Way. He, who was born of the realm of men, and a divine brother to us all in the Seven Heavens, knew this to be true. His message to us was clear. We have overlooked our children and left them cold and hungry in the wild, fodder for wolves."

Lord Raguel's face twitched at the mention of Aetenos. His knuckles whitened around the banister he unknowingly held so tight. A dull murmur flowed through the crowds. Many knew of the rift between the Chancellor Pinnacle and the demigod, Aetenos.

Zhao Houzi wondered how many knew it began from the unrequited love Raguel bore for Lady Illyria? It was plain to see on Lord Raguel's face that he still felt the prick of that rejection, and it stung.

"I do not deny my actions on behalf of the mortals," Artiya'il continued. "My intentions were pure of heart and well-meaning. They may have conflicted with the words written in your book, but they were right!"

A murmur of unease rippled through the upper mezzanine. Zhao Houzi was amazed at what he was hearing. He, too, felt the Heavenly Laws were too strict. There was no room for interpretation or a higher understanding of the Immortal Mother's will.

But to speak aloud such brazen disregard for the Law in the High Court was tantamount to heresy. The monkey scanned the mezzanine and lower seats. He saw others nodding in agreement. The Way of Heaven would be irrevocably changed after the outcome of this trial.

Artiya'il waited for the crowds to simmer down. "My final hope is that we will one day take the mortals into our divine embrace and guide them towards right-eousness. Do not wait for the distractions of the undeveloped human mind to cast them astray before they have learned the Truth. We all shall benefit if we hold them as sons and daughters now rather than as afterthoughts to be culled and denied access to our paradise later."

Lord Raguel contemplated the angel's words. "You are correct, the mortal mind is a weak thing and prone to temptation, but it is not for us to tamper with until their time has been chosen. They must prove themselves worthy to enter the Seven Heavens with no divine intervention.

"Such is the Way of the Immortal Mother and the doctrines she set to stone from the beginning of all things. Great Balance must remain. The path of Aetenos was misguided. Your friend thought to change what was unchangeable, and therefore, the Immortal Mother sent him away. Now he is nowhere to be found. His voice is lost to the mortals.

"But we are not here to debate wayward actions of a wandering fool."

Monkey was on the edge of his seat. The silent tension in the courtroom rang in his ears like a continuous, high-pitched peal. Raguel was about to deliver his verdict.

"Artiya'il, you have committed unforgivable crimes against the Heavenly Realm and the Laws of Order that govern us. The will of the Immortal Mother was passed down to me, the first True-born of Heaven, and rightfully interpreted by this office to protect our way of life. Thus, Chaos is kept at bay.

"You took it upon yourself to change the destiny of countless human souls and tampered with the mortality of their lives. Your actions have jeopardized the Great Balance, and therefore it is to my great sorrow that I must banish you. Henceforth, you are exiled from the Heavenly Realm, nor are you allowed to exist in the realm of men, such is your sentence."

Zhao Houzi's mouth hung open in shock. He slumped back in his chair. How could this be? Banishment from the entire Heavenly Realm and forbidden from entering the Mortal Realm? This was more than a punishment for a misguided deed. The Chancellor Pinnacle was sending a message to all.

Zhao Houzi looked back to the floor and watched Artiya'il lead away by the Protectorates. The condemned angel's head was low, and his wings slumped against his back. Then the seats before and behind him were filled with raucous excitement as the celestials stood to exit.

Where would he go now? Zhao Houzi wondered as he descended the crowded stairs, be as careful as possible not to be stepped on or kicked.

Outside the amphitheater, the sun was high in the sky over Tanalum, the seventh and highest level of the Heavenly Realm. Its golden light bathed the city of Asher in a warm, soothing glow. The sprawling metropolis sparkled in the sunlight. Fluffy clouds floated peacefully in the sky as the celestials went about their administrative affairs and duties of monitoring the fates of the frail humans during their short trial of life.

Zhao Houzi left the Heavenly Hall in a daze. He found a small, unoccupied wall niche along the shade side of a building and hopped inside the concavity. It felt like an upright coffin and just the right size for a little monkey's last resting place.

The building's shadow stole the warmth of the day as he sat at the edge of the niche and put his wrinkle-skinned hands to his face and sobbed. He still couldn't believe what he had heard. Lord Raguel had given a True-born angel the death sentence.

There was no need to wipe away the tears that ran freely down his furry face. No one could see him, and he doubted much that anyone would care.

32

KASAI

K asai held Desdemonia close to his chest. She stirred in and out of broken sleep. Kasai had fed her the contents of a small vial he had found in one of her many pockets. Thankfully, the healing elixir closed the vicious wound inflicted by Reese, who, in truth, was the succubus, Sess'thra. Kasai shook his head in shame.

"I know, Des, you tried to warn me," he said softly.

His thoughts returned to that ill-fated moment when the serrated dagger plunged into Desdemonia's back. How could he have overlooked such deception, especially when his inner sight showed him Reese was hiding such a terrible secret? How could he have been so blind?

The Chaos Gate crackled with etheric energy and smelled of rancid snow. The surface of the portal glowed ashen-green as vapors from Gathos escaped into the Mortal Realm. Its edges slowly and methodically ate away the floor, melting away the stone slabs like hungry acid.

The throne room was oddly quiet, and Kasai wondered if the entire fortress was empty. He looked for his companions. Maugris's lightning attack had ripped through the Kibo Gensai and tossed them across the room. Their bodies lay scattered and contorted on the floor. Kasai was unsure if they lived. What did it matter? Soon, Baroqia would be overrun by hordes of demons, and it was all his fault.

Desdemonia moaned in his arms. Kasai let his water xindu flow into her. It was a basic healing technique he had learned years ago at the now desecrated and ruined Monastery of Ordu. It would help to soothe her pain.

What was it about her that had captivated him so? He felt awkward when she was close and desperate for her return when she was away. His emotions were not his to control when it came to Desdemonia. She was his dear companion and confidant. He looked to her wisdom in resolving the hard choices that came from such a perilous quest.

"Maybe just once you could listen for a change, you stupid, monk," he said as he gently rocked her body.

And still, there was something more. Kasai yearned to be closer to Des, and yet he pushed her away. He just didn't know how to express how he felt. Kasai was lost in thought for some time and did not say a word. He just continued to rock her back and forth.

Kasai stroked her hair. He couldn't believe a beauty like hers existed in the world. She was his dark-haired angel. Yet, at the slightest provocation from her, his fire xindu would flare, and he would stomp off, feeling frustrated and angry. Nonetheless, even in such a short time together, he couldn't imagine his life without her in it. Desdemonia stirred again, barely opening her eyes.

"Hello, handsome. Did we win?" Des mumbled softly and buried her head deeper into his chest and shoulder.

"We need to leave this place," Kasai said and fed her more of his water xindu. He didn't have the will to tell her he had damned them all.

"In a moment. Let me rest, just for a moment."

Kasai continued to stroke her hair. "I'm sorry, Des. I should have listened to you. You were right. This was too big for me to do alone."

"Mmmhmm...I'm always right," Des said with a sleepy voice.

"I was driven by revenge and pain. So much pain. I should have taken your hand and gone with you to the forest, where we could find peace, while there was still peace to be had. At least we would be together until the end came."

Desdemonia didn't respond, but Kasai didn't notice. He watched another chunk of floor dissolve into the Chaos Gate. Its hungry mouth started to consume the far wall.

"And if I went with you, well, I couldn't bear to lose you, too. That makes no sense." Kasai looked down at Desdemonia's body lying across his lap. "What am I trying to say? I don't know. I don't know anything anymore. I was just afraid to lose you, too."

Perhaps now that it didn't matter, it was easier to let go of unnecessary burdens and uncertainties. Kasai waited patiently for Desdemonia's reaction, but she had fallen into a deep sleep in his arms.

Kasai outwardly sighed. "I guess it doesn't matter if you know or not. Just rest."

He realized the Chaos Gate would soon consume the entire tower. Des was right, this was too big for him. This was the work of a king, and generals and armies of fighting men, not one inexperienced, stupid monk. He was no Ever Hero.

Kasai wondered what was left of the King's Army after being overwhelmed by the demon horde. Thoughts of his battle with the demon warlord, Oziax made him shudder. He looked at the palms of his hands. Those awful cobalt blue marks were still there, staring at him, mocking him for believing he was a hero.

Kasai shook his head in disappointment. How did all of this come to pass? One minute he was sweeping stones from the East Wall steps at Ordu, the next, he was losing his soul to a horrific infernal portal, which led to the Abyss and consumed all it touched. And as a grand finale, he had just tried and failed to profess his love for a witch, whom he now held close to his chest.

Kasai thought he should turn himself in and pay the consequences for creating such a dreadful thing. What else could he lose? His soul was already forfeit. At least he would not be able to bring any more harm to the world. He looked back at Des. He would lose her.

Kasai wished things could go back to the way they were. He never asked to be the Ever Hero. Aetenos had wrongly chosen him.

"I don't want it! Do you hear me? Take it back!" he shouted.

The only response came from the hissing sizzle of a tapestry as the green fire burned it from the wall. Kasai shifted Des off his body. He found a small chair cushion on the floor and used it to prop up Desdemonia's head. He let her rest and moved to check on the Kibo Gensai. Thankfully, Pallo, Run-Run, and Orin were alive. Rafar was dead, killed by the demon, Khalkoroth. Another vile act Daku would need to answer for if Kasai ever found him.

Kasai roused his companions and made to leave the doomed fortress. Carved artifices of demonic creatures fell from the ceiling as the fortress's foundation lost its structural integrity. He tucked Ninziz-zida in his sash, and the Fire Serpent felt heavier than he had remembered. She too lamented the fate of Master Choejor. Another death Kasai had been unable to prevent. With a heavy sigh, he roused Desdemonia.

"Wake up, Des, it's time to go."

As Kasai suspected, the enemy was gone. They had emptied the halls and abandoned the stronghold to the expanding Chaos Gate. "Like rats fleeing a sinking ship," he thought.

When they had exited the fortress, Kasai told his companions what had happened after Maugris's lightning strike. He and Des had managed to defeat the sorcerer, but Reese had revealed her true form and betrayed them by driving a dagger into Des's back. In a desperate move to even the odds against Sekka, he used the magic-absorbing amulet Des had stolen from Khalkoroth.

He placed it around his neck, and when the emerald stone within the centerpiece had touched his flesh, it established a bridge to Aetenos's soul, which opened the Chaos Gate. It was the worst thing he could have done, for that had been Sekka's plan all along. The devil had won. Now a working portal existed between the Mortal Realm and the Realm of Gathos.

"I have failed you and possibly damned all of the Three Kingdoms. I am sorry. I was not the hero you had hoped I would be."

"It's okay, Kasai. You did your best. No one could have done better," Desdemonia said. She gave his arm a reassuring squeeze.

Orin sulked quietly. His eyes roamed to Kasai, and then to Desdemonia with a scowl.

"Something to say, Orin?" Desdemonia said. "I can't hear you under that sour puss you're wearing."

"Des, let it go. We are all feeling miserable right now."

"I have nothing that needs to be said at this time," Orin said. He turned to Pallo. "Run-Run and I will scout ahead to make sure the way is clear."

Pallo nodded, and the two warriors jogged ahead of the party.

"What was that all about?" Kasai questioned Desdemonia.

"There's one in every group. I'm surprised you of all people missed the way Orin stares at me with those shifty eyes of his."

"Does he? I hadn't noticed."

Desdemonia just shook her head in frustration. "Don't you notice anything? Just forget about it."

The party walked on in silence until they were rejoined by Run-Run. Orin had found the way to the Storm Wind Pass, and he would lead them from here. Eventually, the bruised and bloodied party descended the Hoarfrost Mountains.

They found Airis at the edge of the forest foothills, the horses and supplies were ready. The young warrior was eager for news of their success.

"Airis, a word together," Pallo said. He took Airis aside before Kasai could say anything. Kasai could see Pallo was explaining the events that had unfolded. Airis listened intently and occasionally spared a confused glance at Kasai. He eventually nodded his understanding and returned with Pallo to the group.

"I'm sure you did your best, Ever Hero. Not all battles are won in the way in which we plan. Hope is not lost, for you are still with us, and can fight again." Airis bowed his head.

"Airis, I'm sorry. I think Aetenos made a mistake. I'm not the Ever Hero that was promised."

"Have faith, Ever Hero. The prophecy continues to reveal itself. 'For *he* shall find hope in his darkest hour.' So, you see, all is how it is meant to be." Airis half-heartedly smiled at Kasai and turned to tend to the evening fire.

Kasai wondered how anyone could have faith in him. They spend the early evening in somber silence. Desdemonia made use of the remaining sunlight to gather herbs and replenish spell components in the forest, while Pallo and Run-Run tended to the horses. Orin climbed a nearby tree to take the first watch.

Kasai sat apart from the group and attempted to ease into a deep meditation. He closed his eyes and tried to be calm, but his mind was filled with erratic and distracting noise. He struggled to concentrate but could not balance his xindu energies. His thoughts unwound like a frayed sea pennant being blown apart by gale-force winds; each tattered thought became an individual thread, whipping and snapping on its own.

Instead of leading him down paths of tranquility, his mind stubbornly and repeatedly showed him the horrors of the past day. He did not have the strength or will to become realigned with a higher state of awareness.

Kasai barely noticed as the first tear rolled down his cheek. He brushed it away as if it were an insect. Then another tear ran down his opposite cheek. Then another and another. They came too fast for him to wipe away. He gave up and cupped his hands in his face and sobbed.

"I should have died at Ordu. Now, I've doomed them all."

He felt the presence of another approaching and assumed it was Desdemonia coming to tell him food would be ready soon. "Great, now she can see me like this. Some hero," he said and tried his best to dry his face with the cloth of his sleeve.

Even with his arm over his eyes, he could sense a great light shining and getting brighter as it approached. She must have brought a torch to light her way. He slowly dropped his arm and saw a vision of an angel appear before him.

Kasai thought he was dreaming. He closed his eyes fast and opened them again, but shockingly, the image remained. She was a woman, covered in golden attire, floating in the air before him.

"Who...are you?"

"Hello, Ever Hero. I am Illyria of the Nine, and the last daughter of the Immortal Mother."

Kasai rubbed his eyes. Her aura swirled in a mist of pale gold, rings of white and yellow danced throughout the ethereal haze to an unheard melody. It was as bright as a hundred lanterns.

He immediately felt at ease. Everything about her was soothing. His body was revitalized by her presence as if he had slept soundly and just awoken refreshed and eager for the new day. Kasai knelt before her and placed his forehead to the cold dirt.

"Rise, Ever Hero. Your journey does not end here. There is still much to accomplish, and little time to do what must be done," Illyria spoke in a gentle, caressing voice. "I have found the one I lost but cannot go to him. The Amaranthine Barrier prevents me from reaching my beloved, Aetenos."

"Aetenos?" Kasai stood and looked in the direction of Rachlach Fortress, where the Chaos Gate festered. His shame was too great, and he could not make eye contact with the angel. "I fear I have damned us both to everlasting torment."

"All is not lost, for you are the Ever Hero, reborn in this age. Sekka has Aetenos held fast in Furia Keep. You shall rescue him and return him to me in Paradise. I will then urge the Immortal Mother to return your souls, thereby closing the portals to the Chaos Gate."

"But what hope do I have against such dark power as Sekka? Surely armies are needed to free him from the Abyss. I am but a simple monk. I'm nobody."

"As I have said, you are the Ever Hero. You shall find a way."

"You say that as if it will be enough," Kasai said. He was doubtful that he could do anything of the sort. "I am awed by your divine presence and humbled that you have faith in me when I have none. But I'm not the one that was promised. I've tried to tell them, but they won't listen. They just want to talk of prophecy. My decisions and actions have caused nothing but misery. I'm sorry. I'm not the Ever Hero. Aetenos chose wrongly."

A sympathetic and compassionate smile tugged at the corners of Illyria's mouth. "Trust in the wisdom of the Great Monk. Aetenos does not choose lightly when crafting his champions. There is great strength within you. You must only believe it belongs to you, and not dismiss it out of hand."

Kasai stood in silence, contemplating her words. He could not walk away from his responsibility to protect the land and to serve its people. It was one of the cornerstones of being at one with the Boundless. He needed to correct the wrongs he had committed.

"I assume the Chaos Gate will bring me to Gathos. Yet, I know not how to accomplish what you ask of me."

"No. The Chaos Gate is not your path, for it will lead you straight into the jaws of evil. Sekka now assembles her Frost Legions to conquer the lands of mortals. I have pleaded with the Immortal Mother for this one favor to save the Mortal Realm, and she has granted passage to the one who shares the soul of the Aetenos.

"I shall help you to pass the Amaranthine Barrier, as another of my celestial sisters helped Him so many years ago. The Chaos Gate must be destroyed."

"I understand, and I will do as you ask," Kasai said and thought for a moment about what that meant. "Does that mean I will need to...die?"

"Only the Immortal Mother knows this answer."

The weight of this request was disheartening, but it was his responsibility to repair the damage he had caused. It was a fool's errand, and he would not be returning home. Yet, he was honor-bound to try.

"I will go, though I fear I will not succeed on my own."

"You won't be there alone. I'm going too." Desdemonia appeared from behind moss-covered boulders. A light brush of snow had fallen and dusted the winter-brown hair of the hibernating flora. It collected on her hair and clothing. Illyria wore a genuine smile when she saw Desdemonia approach.

"You see, you have the support you need."

"Des, what about returning to the forest, and being at peace?"

Desdemonia's bewildered expression made Kasai feel as if he had said the most ridiculous thing imaginable. He wondered if he would ever understand the witch.

"Des, are you sure? I don't think we will be coming back."

"That's why you'll need me there to make sure we do."

Desdemonia then looked straight at Illyria. "I said I'm going too." Her amber eyes pierced forward, daring Illyria to say otherwise.

Illyria nodded slightly, knowingly. "Of course, you are."

The Kibo Gensai approached silently from different directions, surrounding the trio with swords drawn. Their uncertainty towards Illyria's identity quickly turned to astonishment when they grasped the totality of the divine being in their presence. They immediately fell to the ground in supplication.

"Goddess Illyria betrothed to our Lord Aetenos. We are the Kibo Gensai, Servants of the Divine Fist," Pallo spoke for the small group.

"Rise, friends of Aetenos. There is no worry or demand that I bring to you, only the opportunity for salvation. The Ever Hero shall require your blades and comradeship in the trials ahead, if you will lend them."

The Kibo Gensai rose together. All stood tall and ready to serve.

Illyria approached them one at a time and kissed each gently upon the forehead. "I bless you all with this charm against the bitter cold of Gathos, for you will know no warmth there besides what you keep in your hearts."

Then she bade them place their weapons in a circle with blades pointed inwards. She put her delicate hand upon the steel and spoke in a language that was mystical and serene.

"To your weapons, I add the Light of Heaven, the bane of all infernal creatures, large or small."

"We are honored to serve and shall forfeit our lives when necessary to fulfill Heaven's request," Pallo said. As one, the Kibo Gensai warriors bowed in agreement.

Illyria acknowledged their oath with a thankful nod. She then turned to Kasai.

"Once you have freed Aetenos, I shall find you again if that is the will of the Immortal Mother."

"Wait, you cannot guarantee our way back?" Kasai was alarmed at such a lack of certainty from the angel.

"You are the Ever Hero. Trust in yourself. You shall find a way if I cannot."

"Let's all hope it doesn't come to that," Kasai said, still feeling as if this was all another tragic mistake.

"What must we do, Ever Hero? Travel by way of the Chaos gate?" Airis said. His encouraging voice tempted Kasai out of his self-doubt.

Kasai gathered his thoughts.

"The portal is closed to us, Airis. Sekka will soon bring her forces through, and we are not prepared to take on her Frost Legion single-handedly. Illyria knows of a different route to Gathos. Once there, we find Aetenos, free him, and escape. That is our quest."

Kasai looked once more at Desdemonia for reassurance. He was happy she had wanted to join him, and they would be facing this challenge together.

Illyria raised her hands to the sky and uttered more of her mystic language. She then pointed to the ground, and a small ring of orange and gold appeared. Holy symbols scripted from ancient magic sparked around the outer edge of the circle as it grew to roughly two strides in diameter. The reek of Gathos rose from its center as swirling snow and ice vomited up from its core.

"The Immortal Mother honors her agreement. You must now honor yours."

"Aetenos is the Light that guides," Kasai said, mostly to himself, and jumped into the center of the hole that led to the Abyss.

33

SHIVERRIG

A dark cloud rose on the horizon outside the city gates of Qaqal. War banners and pennants with the markings of the Four Generals of the King's Army broke through the groundswell of dust and debris kicked up by oncoming horses and foot soldiers. The flags flapped in the blustery air. Their swatches of color stood out against the blue-grey clouds of an early winter's sky. The air was crisp and smelled of the pending arrival of new snow.

The tired and battered remnants of a spliced-together army of knights, spearmen, and archers approached the Gates of Qaqal, entrance to the City of Spires, and the throne of Baroqia. An oversized banner, decorated with the image of a mighty griffon, marched proudly beside an austere carriage in the center of the procession. The ornate carriage was adorned with the colors and splendor of King Conrad. A broken man slumped at the driver's seat of the carriage.

Muscular draft horses followed the beautiful carriage, drawing massive siege engines designed to pulverize stone walls and render enemy ballista to useless, broken timber. Banners with the icon of a great mastiff adorned their sides.

At the head of the army was Duke Gerun Shiverrig, the War Duke of Gethem. He sat majestically on the back of a black destrier. The horse pranced forward with intimidating confidence towards the waiting city. Shiverrig wore no helm and enjoyed the crispness of the air as it caressed his scalp through his short-cropped hair.

Shiverrig looked ahead at the shut gates with eager anticipation. Soon they would open, and he would hear the peal of trumpets ring out a victory serenade to the returning hero of the realm. Today was to be a magnificent day. What did it matter that the King's Army had suffered a terrible defeat? From this day forward, he would make things right in the kingdom. Now was his time!

Shiverrig was flanked by Lord Fritta and Duke Manda on horseback to his right. A dazzling young shield-maiden, wearing tanned breaches and a form-fitting chain-mail shirt, sat upon an elegant Gypsy Vanner stallion to his left. Her body moved sensually as it flowed with the rhythm of the Gypsy Vanner's movements, while her onyx hair streamed in the wind, dancing in rhythm with the army's pennants of a dubious honor.

Fritta's and Manda's mounts snorted in nervous discomfort at the closeness of the shield-maiden. Shiverrig understood their unease, but allies were scarce, and exceptions had been made.

"This is a day is long overdue," Shiverrig said. He looked along the rising merlons and spacious crenels of the battlement walls surrounding the city. He saw the image of a griffon, pouncing to-and-fro as the late king's flags billowed in the wind. The false icon of House Conrad would not see another sunrise.

A lone rider emerged on a young chestnut roan from a door to the right of the massive city gates. The horse and rider cantered to the vanguard to greet the four leading the King's Army home.

"What news, Duke Shiverrig? Has our great King Conrad brought victory to the Kingdom of Baroqia?" the emissary said as he stopped five horse lengths from the procession. Shiverrig heard the insult to his station in the emissary's words. He would remember this one's face.

"It was a quick and well-executed campaign," Shiverrig said with confidence. His large hands encased in oversized gauntlets rested on the horn of his dark leather saddle.

"The tower watch gave the word that your host is now but a third of what left Qaqal. It is a dark victory when so many men will not return to loved ones."

"General Rokig did not understand the nature of his foe, and his opening foray was ill-timed. It was a decision that cost much of our strength."

"And where is High General Rokig? Does he fair well, I hope? I do not see him present." The emissary looked quizzically about the foursome, looking askance at the shield-maiden.

"Rokig fell in battle against the enemy's warlord. He was valiant to the end. Conrad then rightfully elevated me to High General of the Field, and we routed the enemy. It was a decisive victory. But the war is far from won. We will need to reassess our strength and muster fresh troops. Now, open the gates. These men are weary from battle and the long march home."

The emissary narrowed his eyes and looked suspiciously at the shield-maiden. She leered back at him with a devilish grin. The emissary diverted his eyes past Shiverrig to the King's carriage. "And our beloved, King Conrad? I wonder why he is not here at the forefront of such a great victory?" The concern was rising in the truth of his words.

"King Conrad saw fit to allow me this last honor and lead the troops home through the Gates of Qaqal. Now, I will say again, open the gates."

The emissary was hesitant. He looked to Fritta and Manda for some validation in Shiverrig's claim. Fritta's expression remained stoic, while Manda wore a face of indifference. The emissary finally capitulated.

"Yes, my Lord Shiverrig. As you command." The emissary raised his hand and signaled the gates to open. He turned his horse and cantered to the small entrance from where he initially emerged.

"Exactly, as I command." Shiverrig sat with a satisfied and bemused smile. His destrier pawed at the ground. The animal could sense his eagerness to move on. Soon, a Shiverrig would ride through the Gates of Qaqal as a conquering hero.

The capital city would welcome him as their lost son, thankful for his return to prominence and their continued safety. He would purge the land of its treasonous politicians that fleeced the kingdom with their twisted agendas. Shiverrig would restore order to the realm.

Once his troops occupied the city, his coup would be complete, and House Shiverrig would regain the throne of Baroqia. Ah, what a sweet day it shall be. A small flutter of snow fell gently over the open road. The fulfillment of his destiny opened before him with the movement of the gates.

Shiverrig heard the frantic gallop of a rider, speeding from the far left and towards the emissary. His broken and spoiled armor cast no shine in the dull morning light. A wasted cloth bearing the emblem of a pouncing griffon whipped behind the horse's lathered flanks.

The riders met halfway to the gate. The exhausted knight gestured wearily and pointed at Shiverrig and his host. The emissary looked back in shock. His hand flew to the air, signaling the Gates of Qaqal to close.

"It seems the knights loyal to the dead king were not all slain as instructed," the shield maiden said. Her words were as light as a child's playful giggle. "I don't think they will believe King Conrad fell by the hands of the enemy. Or not at least, not the enemy you intended."

Shiverrig scoffed at her wry observation. Her eerie, childlike laughter unnerved him, and his mood soured. "This is unfortunate. I had hoped to gain a quick entrance before the Auxiliary Guard could mount a proper resistance. A siege shall be costly, in time and morale."

"Leave that to me," she said, wearing a wolfish grin. She unclasped the chainmail shirt and let it drop to the cold dirt. Her white skin took on a blueish hue in the early light as she rose into the sky on freshly sprouted, thin-membraned wings.

"No! Sess'thra!" But it was too late. The demon had already revealed herself. The guards upon the battlements remained stupefied as the sultry, winged horror flew towards them.

"Kill it!" the captain of the guard yelled out to his men, driving them into action. Arrows flew at Sess'thra, but she was too agile for their clumsy attempts. Soon she was over the walls and descended out of sight.

The knight and the emissary drew swords and charged Shiverrig.

"Murderer!" The knight yelled.

Shiverrig sighed. "The hard way, then." He unsheathed his bastard sword and trotted out to meet his new foes.

The knight arrived first and lashed out quickly and deliberately at Shiverrig, who turned the tired knight's thrust with ease. But instead of striking back, Shiverrig chopped down on the unprotected neck of the knight's horse. Blood sprayed up in a grisly, red fountain, coating the surprised knight. He instinctually brought his arm up to block the excessive gore from blinding him.

Shiverrig pulled his sword arm back as the dying horse faltered and collapsed. The emissary attacked, and Shiverrig twisted his sword sideways to block his thrust. Shiverrig countered with a powerful, sweeping blow, nearly knocking the emissary out of his saddle.

He then directed a sword thrust between the emissary's breastplate and light pauldron, finding the unprotected flesh and vitals. The emissary slumped forward in his saddle when Shiverrig pulled his blade free.

Shiverrig looked for the hampered knight and found him scurrying away from his dead horse. Shiverrig sent his horse forward into a leaping gallop. His bloodied sword crashed into the neck and shoulder of the knight, severing the steel plate and lodging itself into the man's body. The knight's knees buckled, and Shiverrig ripped his sword free.

He looked to the top of the wall. The archers now had a more natural target and nocked arrows and drew bowstrings to their chin.

"Duke Shiverrig! You shall pay for your crimes against the crown," the captain of the guard atop the wall shouted out.

Shiverrig turned to his loyal men. They were ready with trained arrows on the archers upon the wall. "Unleash!" Shiverrig commanded. Black shafts shot into the air and found their marks. Those that had escaped the first volley were forced to remain behind the safety of the merlons as arrows continuously sailed upwards.

Shiverrig turned his eyes to the gates. They were once again moving in his favor. Sess'thra sauntering through the slender but widening gap. He drew his horse closer while she licked the blood off her delicate fingers.

"When will you learn to do as you are told?" Shiverrig said. She frustrated him to no end with her disobedience.

"Probably never," she said with a wicked smile as she shrugged her shoulders.

Shiverrig shook his head. "You push too far, succubus."

"Oh, stop your pouting. Your kingdom awaits."

"We shall have words when this is over," Shiverrig said. Then he called to his men. "To the gates! Take the city!"

Sess'thra's wings unfurled, and she took to the air as the army raced towards the Gates of Qaqal, eager to do his bidding. Manda trotted up to Shiverrig and nodded in the direction of the demon as she flew over the wall. "You have much to explain, Shiverrig. You hide the enemy we fight against in plain sight."

"It is a temporary but necessary alliance. One must fully understand an adversary if he is to prevail at the highest level. We know little of demonkind. That childish creature will provide me with all we need to know of how to defeat the hordes of Maugris. I do not intend to suffer another loss, such as that brought down Conrad. In time, I will rebuild Baroqia's armies to stand against and defeat this new foe."

"This is madness. Are you foolish enough to think any of the demonkind can be trusted?"

Shiverrig smiled sarcastically at his newly acquired co-conspirator. "Of course, they cannot be trusted. But there is a longer game to play here. Trust me, I know what I am doing."

Manda watched with calculating eyes as the colors of his troops meshed with those of House Shiverrig and House Fritta. Their combined forces rushed past the gates and through the short tunnel en route to secure the capital city.

"You were wise to add your surviving troops to my cause after Conrad fell in battle. He fought valiantly to the end," Shiverrig said.

"The manner of Kind Conrad's death is irrelevant to me. Frankly, he was a fool to assume command of this campaign, and fools are bad for profit."

"Yes, and profit is profit."

"Exactly. Although, I did not account for such dark alliances with fell creatures as part of my support."

"You look concerned, Manda," Shiverrig jested.

"Should I not be worried about the company you keep? What other wicked secrets will you unveil in the coming rule?"

"It was important to keep the identity of the succubus secret until we had established the new rule."

Fritta brought his horse to stand close to Shiverrig's and Manda's mounts. His expression downcast. "Shall history remember us as saviors of the kingdom, or fell creatures as dark as the enemy we opposed?"

"Come, Lord Manda, Lord Fritta, such dire words! This day is ours. Let us claim our prize and raise Baroqia to greatness never seen before in the Three Kingdoms."

"Baroqia shall need a Minister of Finance to appropriately tax the Greater and Lesser Houses to fund the coming war. They have skirted their responsibility to the realm for far too long. The army will also need a competent War Marshall, to muster our troops against our mutual foe. I can think of no others than the two of you for such positions. Let us rejoice. A new era of prosperity and empire is upon us."

"Yes," Shiverrig said, "this was a magnificent day." He urged his horse forward through the Gates of Qaqal.

The City of Spires was aptly named for its tall, spire-shaped columns that rose into the air like thin fingers, tickling the underside of the Seven Heavens. Uniquely colored stones were used to create dazzling mosaic designs that raced and churned from one tower to the next, like fierce rapids flowing through the decadent city.

Height was considered an aspect of prestige, and the rich spared no cost at outbuilding their political or financial rivals. High buttresses secured the tall spires and prevented the towers from toppling. Their numerous forms jutted from the curved sides, and sky-high walkways connected adjacent towers, locking them in place. Shiverrig playfully mused over the idea of occupying the late king's magnificent estate or razing it.

"Qaqal doesn't have quite the same flavor as your beloved Gethem, does it? It's so clean. The people, so...docile," mused Sess'thra as she trotted up to Shiverrig upon her Gypsy Vanner. The killing of the resistance had stopped, and the city was now in a state of quiet shock.

"This city wears a false skin. The corrupt politicians only polished the surface to get what they wanted but never bothered to remove the filth from its pores. And why should they? They are from the filth and give birth to more, as they climb their ladders of small influence, striving for power that was acquired by sleight of hand rather than earned in battle.

"They are the reason the filth exists. Remove its thin veneer, and this is a stagnate, dying place, while the character of Gethem remains true," replied Shiverrig.

"And what character is that, oh, great duke?"

"The people of Gethem are loyal to House Shiverrig," he said. Shiverrig looked squarely at Sess'thra. "Unquestionably loyal."

"You will need that level of devotion in the days to come," Sess'thra said.

"Bah. The kingdom has grown weak, and these paper lords will easily crumble. None shall usurp the rule of House Shiverrig again." Shiverrig urged his destrier forward towards the capitol building. He had much to do.

. . .

Shiverrig opened the side door to the grand throne room of Qaqal. The clamorous uproar of frustrated and indignant nobles and their families rushed to envelop him. The families loyal to House Conrad had been gathered together and packed into one area to receive their new king. A line of armed knights bearing the Shiverrig colors of deep purple and rose pressed back the agitated crowd.

Shiverrig was appalled at the changes House Conrad had made to the throne room. Banners depicting the dead king's victory over Maugris and his northern horde had already been hung. Presumptuous fool. Never again will lesser men rule the lands tamed and harnessed by the blood of his ancestors, thought Shiverrig.

He walked purposefully to the throne. Dax had arrived earlier in the day and now stood at ease next to Malachi. The archvashim, however, looked worn and thin. Shiverrig would need to remind his advisor to keep himself clean. Too much interaction with the demonkind led to the corruption of the mind, and in Malachi's case, also the body.

Shiverrig scanned the faces of the assembled nobles. He hated them all. It was time to leave the broken path that the misguided realm had trod along for more than a generation. And to do so, the noble class would need to change.

"Shiverrig! What is the meaning of this? Where is King Conrad?" one noble shouted above the clamoring crowd.

"Dead! The king is dead!" Another noble made herself heard.

"Shiverrig is in league with demons!" a third noble said.

Shiverrig did not care to note who said which remark. All in the room were complicit in keeping him from his birthright. Shiverrig raised his arm to quiet the room.

"I was going to tell you of the heroic way Conrad fell in battle, protecting the realm from evil, but alas, that story will never make it into the sagas of lore. The truth is, when his poorly appointed High General, Rokig, allowed the enemy to swarm our unstructured and unsupported men, the army was overrun.

"Conrad ran with his tail between his legs, racing back to the protection of the high walls of Qaqal. Unfortunately, he was flanked by enemy barbarians from the north. I arrived too late and could not save your king."

"Lies! You have befriended the enemy and brought it to our homes!"

Shiverrig quieted the room once more. "I'm sure you all have something of inconsequential value to add, but it is time we came to terms," he said.

"Duke Shiverrig, we are not sheep you can herd into submission. Your lust for power is well known and will not stand!" Lord Jolla said as he stepped to the front of the crowd. He was precisely the type of man Shiverrig loathed. Jolla was an opportunist and a schemer. He and his family had ridden the coattails of House Conrad for two generations. House Jolla was new to money and did not understand the importance of tradition.

"Where is the true heir to the throne? Where is Prince Dane?"

"Prince Dane has seen the folly in his father's ways and has abdicated the throne to me. He understands a stronger Baroqia will be needed to defeat the enemy," Shiverrig said.

"And that means House Shiverrig will conveniently assume the throne? Why should House Shiverrig enjoy such ease into the seat of ultimate power? Where is the vote? What of House Jolla? I say our time has come!" Other lords shouted praises for Lord Jolla or voiced their claim to the vacant throne.

"Lord Jolla, you amuse me with such airs. What right to the throne of Baroqia could you, or any of the lords present here, possibly imagine you have?

"Were you on the field of battle, when the blood of Baroqia was spilled defending the land? Or when the demon horde broke through Rokig's ranks and slaughtered the men of the King's Army? Did you rally the men under one banner and return to the City of Spires to protect the people and ease their fearful hearts?

"No, you did none of these things, for you were not there. You hid in your mansions or country estates. You let others bear the weight of hard decisions and bloodshed. Which brings me to the reason you all are here. I offer you this choice. Freely acknowledge me as the rightful ruler of Baroqia or consider yourself an enemy to the throne."

"The rightful ruler?" Lord Jolla looked astounded by Shiverrig's proclamation. "Never! House Shiverrig's time has passed. I will not submit to your wild ideas and nefarious liaisons! Bring me Prince Dane. I wish to hear from his mouth that he is not the true king."

The nobles' fists flew in the air, and many shouted for the appearance of Prince Dane. Shiverrig nodded to himself, knowingly. He didn't think this meeting would go any differently than it did, and he was glad that it didn't.

"Lord Jolla, your voice is undoubtedly loudest in a room full of dissenters. I can appreciate the loyalty to the Prince you have exhibited, and for once, you show a redeeming character trait.

"Nonetheless, you, your families, and the fellow lords present are charged with treason to the realm. You have plundered the kingdom and shirked your responsibility to defend its people and lands from hostile intent. I will determine your fate in time. Take them away."

The side chamber doors opened, and a company of armed knights, clothed in purple and rose, surrounded the crowd and escorted the condemned nobles out of the room.

"What will you do with them?" Malachi inquired. He scratched the butt of the wrapped stump where his right hand had once been.

"They shall be dealt with according to their crimes unless I can think of a better use for them," Shiverrig said. "Baroqia shall be ruled by empirical martial law, as my forefathers had intended. The populace will either abide by the Shiverrig Law and enjoy the prosperity to come or resist and sway in the gallows."

"Your edict will flow easily through the streets and taverns of Gethem, but the people of Qaqal have enjoyed a different life for too many years. You cannot expect them to change so readily," Malachi said.

Duke Shiverrig pondered Malachi's words. There was always unrest in every regime change. He would deal with the most vocal dissenters publicly, and in time, the people would be swayed.

Malachi continued, "Rumors spread that you killed the king in cold blood. Already the Lesser Houses outside of Qaqal are rallying together to bring you to justice. You will need to hold the City of Spires by force. Lose the city and lose the throne."

"Then I appoint you my Minister of the Word. Use your silver tongue to convince them otherwise. Feed the peasants bread and meat each week and send messengers to the lords of the Lesser Houses. Tell them I have lowered their taxes for the remainder of the year. They will soon forget their loyalty to King Conrad and no longer care to know the manner of his demise. And tear those bloody griffons down!"

Shiverrig glanced at Dax. "And what of Sekka? Did she succeed in her efforts to capture her Ever Hero?"

"The Mistress has arrived with her Frost Legions and soon will claim the frontier villages as was agreed upon," Dax said with indifference as if this was well known and accepted information.

"That is more than what was promised," Shiverrig said, outwardly disgruntled. Already the agreements were changing. He had expected as much and was inwardly pleased. His new rule depended on directing the subjects of the kingdom towards a common enemy, one that only he could defeat. He would soon turn Maugris's blunder of summoning the devil, Sekka, and her foul minions, to his most significant advantage.

Shiverrig mused over the foundational pieces being set to build his new empire upon. It was his destiny to outshine his forefathers and be a more celebrated conqueror than the legendary Overload Baroq Shiverrig.

"Remind Sekka that the agreed-upon tithe was a remote village or two each season and to stay away from the main cities of Baroqia."

"She honors the pact. The Kingdom of Sunne shall bear the weight of her needs. If there is nothing more, I have pressing business for the Mistress, elsewhere."

Shiverrig dismissed him with an off-handed wave. Sunne, the one land that had somehow remained outside of the dominion of my family's rule, thought Shiverrig. Once the throne was secured, he intended to extend the borders of his kingdom. The lands of Sunne looked very appetizing to him.

34

SEKKA

Sekka's slick body rose from the Chaos Gate's slushy surface and into the frigid air of Gathos. The light snowfall was a welcome homecoming. The nether portal hissed as bubbles burst under her feet, but its surface remained stable enough for her to walk across. A viscous film covered her naked skin, which mirrored the shifting colors rising from the demonic gateway.

The transition felt like crossing through a thick membrane of gooey oil. Not altogether unpleasant to Sekka's human form, but messy. She looked about her icy realm and was pleased. Her power base would soon grow ten thousand-fold, and her ascendancy to the loftiest station in the Pantheon of the Abyss was all but guaranteed.

Sekka scanned the frozen ground until she saw the broken body of Maugris. Remarkably, the mortal still lived. Somehow, he had crawled across the surface of the portal and dragged his mangled body onto the cold terrain. He, too, was covered in the sloppy remains of traveling through the Chaos Gate.

What remained of his scorched robe was curled into thick, black clumps of melted fabric. Sekka scoffed in disdain as Maugris tried to rise on shaking legs. The fool was trying to escape. The break in his shoulder looked painful, and his right arm hung uselessly by his side. His other arm held his chest tight in a failed attempt to prevent his broken ribs from moving on their own.

"I don't understand. Mine to command…mine." Maugris's mad eyes searched for the answer in the snow. The Chaos Gate hissed again as Sekka approached the injured sorcerer. He looked at her in horror as she transformed into her demonic form. She lurched forward and grabbed him in her massive talons. Maugris grimaced in pain as she shook him like a rag doll.

+*Welcome to Gathos, Maugris the Infinite.*+ Sekka pounded her thoughts into his mind.

She was going to enjoy his suffering. She would possibly find a use for him in the future, for he was a competent mage, but foolish in his overreaching ambition. That had been his downfall.

She would let Chedipe, her trusted demon witch and chief tormentor, toy with him for a century or two. Maybe even give him a taste of freedom between her sessions, just enough to give him hope he could escape his fate. Then she would yank it away, for having hope in the Abyss was the worst torment of them all.

Sekka raised Maugris's body close to her face and shook him violently.

+Wake up!+

Maugris's eyes half opened. "Just kill me," he said meekly.

Her laughter rose about the howling wind. She tossed him to the base of an X-shaped crucifix with a man who was bound to its beams. His head was low to his chest, and his arms and legs were outstretched and nailed to the ends. He looked exhausted and defeated.

+Say hello to Aetenos.+

"No, no, no!" Maugris groaned and broke Aetenos from his stupor. Sekka transformed back to her human form and kicked Maugris like a mangy cur.

"Yes, and he has been here all along, even when you cast your pitiful spell to save the Three Kingdoms."

Maugris looked up at Aetenos in disbelief. "Is it true? My spell. I was to be chosen?"

Aetenos sadly nodded.

The chill winds blew through Sekka's alabaster hair and spun it like a whirling dervish. She loved the sensation of cold air upon her human skin. She drank in the sorry state of Aetenos. Somehow, she felt a deeper connection to his despair through her mortal eyes.

Aetenos's head swayed in the wind. Eventually, he recognized her, and she saw his misery rekindled in his heart. He had been the catalyst for her cunning plan to birth the Chaos Gate.

"I have returned victorious, Great Monk! Nothing can stop me now," Sekka gloated and caressed Aetenos's bruised cheek with a tender hand, as a mother would comfort a child.

"Ever...Hero..." Aetenos forced out the words through frostbitten lips.

"He was nothing. The boy was scared and weak. You should have chosen better."

"He shall...find...way."

Sekka broke into a burst of incredulous laughter. "His soul is mine, as is yours, forever trapped in the dimensional core of the Chaos Gate."

Aetenos looked into Sekka's eyes with a glazed stare. "You...will not...win."

Sekka laughed at the absurdity of his remark. She had already won! Soon her legions would march on the undefended Mortal Realm, where she would reap countless souls. Her warlords had assembled the Frost Legion at Furia Keep. She must be quick to harvest her bounty and transform the pure soul energy of the humans into mighty weapons. Finally, she would destroy her last rival, the devil, Zizphander.

"Goodbye, old friend. I must awake Lord Oziax from his astral sleep." Her body pressed close to the monk, and she kissed him passionately. Her tongue found his. She mercilessly played with it, sucking on it and bludgeoned it like a pit fighter's punches. She bit hard on his lip as she withdrew.

"I still wonder at the fortuitous gift you handed me by coming here. How could one such as you be so misguided? Illyria has abandoned you," Sekka said as she licked Aetenos's fresh blood from her lips.

"Illyria...save Illyria..."

Sekka relinquished her embrace and backed away, shaking her head. The man was mad. It mattered not, crazed or insane, the divine soul of Aetenos was hers for eternity.

"Greater...forces...at play," Aetenos whispered from split lips, dripping blood. His head sank back to his chest.

Sekka's brow furrowed. "I am the greater force!" But the monk was unconscious again. She snatched up a thick tuft of Maugris's hair and dragged him in her wake. She walked with sure and swift footsteps on the icy terrain. Her laughter mingled and echoed with the howling wind.

Sekka entered a large chamber filled with iced columns connecting the cold floor to a ceiling that remained out of sight. The room smelled of dead things forced to live once more. Damaged and fetid flesh was reworked into living tissue, tendons, and bones. Hundreds of wells, of various diameter, spotted the floor.

Slow condensation dripped into the open pits, adding to their dark, murky substance or splattered apart on the frozen floor. Stalactites and stalagmites welded together over the eons formed bizarre, floor-to-ceiling columns of ice.

The dim, cold light coming from the center of the activated wells was all that lit the room. The pits were rejuvenation graves. The chamber served to house the mending of the physical forms of Sekka's more powerful minions, provided their dark essence was not thoroughly compromised, as was the fate of Lord Auzdioz, at the hands of the Red Devil, Zizphander.

Most of the pits were filled with a stagnant sludge, waiting to be activated. Wicked creatures slithered and swirled under the frosted surface, creating hypnotic currents as they prepared each vat for its next occupant.

The pit that held Lord Oziax's essence was overflowing with a frozen slush of putrefied flesh, human blood, and dark magic. The demon lord's head slowly knit itself back together, along with the rest of his abyssal form. The process was slow and painful, as evident from the muffled howls coming from the open pit.

Sekka pondered on the events that had destroyed her mighty warlord and begrudgingly appreciated the strength of the Ever Hero. The boy had summoned an immense power to kill Oziax, so said Khalkoroth after the warlord fell in battle. Somehow, while under the stresses of torture and an addled mind, Aetenos had passed his divine strength to the boy. The boy had momentarily become a potent force. It was quite an amazing feat considering the presence of the Amaranthine Barrier.

"Too bad it was so short-lived," she said.

She knew the outcome of that battle would be quite different on Gathos. Oziax could draw strength from the souls suffering under her dominion, as he had done countless times in the past. He was a true Champion of the Abyss.

But perhaps she had been too hasty to let the boy remain free in the Mortal Realm. With his soul attached to the Chaos Gate, she could have brought him here.

"Bah, he is nothing more than a trivial loose end. There will be plenty of time for merriment later. But, wouldn't it be interesting if I could harness the divine power of Aetenos and his Ever Hero into a weapon to use against my enemies? Now that would be something." She let the thought ruminate in the back of her mind.

Sekka turned to the pit containing Lord Narthoth's demonic essence. It held some of the demon's personal artifacts, hair and a random tooth Chedipe had found in his lair. It wasn't much material and recovering his physical form would take more time to manifest, since Maugris's obliteration spell had destroyed most of his essence in Rachlach Fortress. There was a high probability he would never return.

"But a mortal's magic is nothing compared to one born in the Abyss," she said.

It was a gamble for her to sacrifice Narthoth so soon. He was a powerful asset to her Frost Legion, and his absence in the coming campaign through the Three Kingdoms of Hanna would be problematic. But she had done what was needed to drain enough magical energy from Maugris and finally dissolve the spell of binding he had placed on her.

She hoped luck would stay on her side long enough for Narthoth to be fully restored. Unfortunately, due to the nature of his demise in Maugris's fortress, the warlord would not be permitted to enter the Mortal Realm for a thousand years. She scowled, it might take that amount of time or more just to get him back.

Sekka returned to the pit where Oziax reformed. Not long now, she thought, as the slush in his hole heaved and thrashed. It was clear he was becoming more conscious as one massive arm shot into the air and the thick tentacles that formed his hand snaked around a frozen column. The demon lord roared in triumph as he pulled himself from the rejuvenation grave.

Oziax's wet, white mane hung heavy across his broad shoulders and muscular back. His chest heaved as it took in large gulps of air to fill empty lungs. He stared menacingly at Sekka until he recognized her and his surroundings. He lowered himself to one knee at her feet.

"My Queen. I have failed you. The power of Aetenos passed to another, and I was taken unaware." Oziax's tentacles absently caressed his skull.

Sekka scrutinized him. "What did you think would happen when you finally encountered the Ever Hero? Nonetheless, the Chaos Gate lives. Soon my Frost Legion shall march on the Mortal Realm and harvest souls with impunity."

"Yes!" growled Oziax. He raised himself from the ground and stretched to his full height. "I shall enjoy such a feast!"

"You know the rules. You are forbidden to set foot in the Mortal Realm for a millennium. Such is the punishment for death at the land of humans."

Lord Oziax roared in frustration. "Damn the soul of the boy monk! Had I known the bond he shared I would have…"

"You would have done nothing different. You played the part needed to move the young monk one step closer to the trap. You shall remain on Gathos and defend Furia Keep until I have harvested enough soul energy to defeat Zizphander. For now, regain your strength. Furia Keep must not fall."

"It shall be as you bid, my Queen."

Sekka noticed Oziax contemplative eyes, thoughtfully planning. "You shall do nothing until I have given my command. Is that understood, Lord Oziax?"

Sekka noted the scowl on Oziax's face. The laws established for the Abyss, the Mortal Realm, and the Seven Heavens were set and could not be undone, save for the will of the creator goddess. Only the Immortal Mother could breach these steadfast rules. The Great Balance must remain. A thousand years wasn't so long. Sekka had suffered the same fate at the hands of Aetenos so many years before.

She would merely acquire another capable warlord to lead her legions throughout the Three Kingdoms, one that was of mortal blood and more easily controlled. Gerun Shiverrig would do nicely, once he partook of the demon seed, of course. It was still one of the best ways to get a demon into the Mortal Realm.

Sekka had provided Sess'thra with the essence of the demoness, Jynxx, and left the details of administration in the capable hands of her succubus. Once Shiverrig had bonded with the spiritual substance of Jynxx, he would be under Sekka's control. If he refused, he would die.

But for now, she had more immediate needs and had summoned temporary replacements from the barren tundra of Vyzyn. Not her first choice, but they were who was available, and she was desperate for more souls now.

Sekka thought again of converting the Ever Hero into her champion. Oh, what delight that would be, and such misery for the Great Monk to suffer. The depths of her wickedness thrilled her as she called five thralls to attend to Lord Oziax. They examined his body and wrapped him in wet, pungent sheets.

Sekka strode from the chamber. Her Frost Legion awaited her command.

She had commanded a portion of her Frost Legion to assemble on the Frozen Plains of Thresh, which surrounded the Chaos Gate. They waited impatiently for her to send them through the gaping portal and into a world ripe for pillage and slaughter. Sekka was due to meet with her newly appointed warlords; she had partitioned off four legions, each ten thousand strong, whose primary role was to gather humans for the soul harvest.

Sekka was already spread thin with many of her legendary behemoths quelling the uprisings of lesser devils on other kingdoms across the levels of the Abyss. This move would decrease the number of remaining troops on Gathos to dangerously low levels. She realized she left herself only enough to defend a siege of Furia Keep. Each day she waited to begin the soul harvest was another day her arch-nemesis drew closer. Without the additional human slaves and the soul energy they provided to fuel her war machine, she would not win a battle of attrition against Zizphander.

Zizphander had grown too bold, even for him. He must have made a pact with a Shadow Patron, she thought. It was the only explanation for his ability to move his armies secretly and unrestricted through the Abyssal Planes. The Red Devil and his fiery horde had reached Gathos undetected, while Sekka had been under the binding spell of Maugris. She fumed at the thought of being held against her will by the sorcerer, regardless that it was a crucial part of her devious plan to create the Chaos Gate. Still, he would suffer much for his role.

Sekka pondered the idea of Zizphander accepting the gifts of a Shadow Patron. She understood the strategy and had been tempted to do the same in the past. The alliance created a substantial, albeit temporary, power base for the beneficiary. There was always a considerable cost with such partnerships, which often left the recipient depleted and paying off a soul debt for millennia. And Sekka refused to be the indebted thrall of another unless there was no other solution. Thankfully, her cunning mind had always found a workable alternative as she rose through the lower and the higher echelons of the Abyss.

Sekka wondered how far Zizphander would go to unseat her from her beloved Gathos? Would it be worth a devil's lifetime of servitude? He had nipped at her haunches like an old hound for centuries. Yes, she had grown strong and influential quickly and acquired many jealous rivals along the way, but his determination was perverse.

The thought of a union between Zizphander and a Shadow Patron unnerved her. There was more behind his relentless pursuit than mere jealousy. Something, or someone, pushed him to keep her in check, and always stall her plans. But who could it be and why?

A terrible realization crossed her mind that she loathed accepting, but her dark instinct knew it to be true. Zizphander's Shadow Patron was one of the Great Three. Who else would have enough infernal power and influence to contest her might? Only with the help of Azrollorza, Xerthotha, or Morrdilliax could Zizphander overthrow her now. The reality of that possibility filled her with foreboding.

Sekka looked upon her eager warriors. The swollen ranks of fiends and demons contained a mass of horrors, filled with oddly shaped creatures covered in horns, coarse hair, and slithering parts. Her minions jostled against each other in a mounting excitement to kill. And within the center of each company stood a ponderous juggernaut, an immensely powerful demon that could wade through enemy troops causing excessive mayhem with their enormous strength. What the juggernauts lacked in intelligence they made up for in sheer destructive power.

The juggernauts grew smaller than the behemoths of Gathos, their larger brethren, which stood as tall as a castle wall; however, these demons were still the size of tall siege towers and stood on four massive legs. Relinquishing such force to the Mortal Realm was a necessary risk with Zizphander's forces already upon the outer reaches of Gathos. She needed to hold the conquered territories of the Three Kingdoms once she began her invasion. She reckoned she would have the first harvest of human souls to replenish her ranks on Gathos before committing to a full engagement with Zizphander.

Sekka approached the Four Warlords of Vyzyn, two brothers and two sisters, who fought as strongly against their enemies as they did amongst themselves. An unsavory choice to lead her assault into the Three Kingdoms of Hanna, for they were untested in the Mortal Realm and unpredictable.

The Warlords of Vyzyn removed their black helms as she acknowledged each in turn. Sitrix, a monstrous warrior, held a long black lance at his side and raised it to salute his Queen; ice-blue runes blazed along its dark shaft. His human body resembled the thick bulk of his demonic form. His head was crowned by six sharp horns that crested a mane of black hair.

Sitrix's eyes remained locked on Sekka. She momentarily wondered if he was assessing her strength, searching for a weakness he could one day exploit. Every creature in the Abyss wanted more. He eventually broke his gaze and stared into the Chaos Gate.

"You will honor your promise." Sitrix said it as a statement of fact rather than a question.

"Provided you deliver what I require without delay or interruption, then yes, you will have your command of the Frost Legion." Sekka eyed the tall warlord directly, and added, "Shall you fail, your essence will never return to be reformed, not to the Mortal Realm, or the Abyss. Am I clear?"

Sitrix gave an abrupt nod.

"Good," she said.

"And Oziax?" a female voice said.

Sekka turned to see Tazizu, the Warrior Witch. Her pupil-less eyes were nestled in black slits that sloped upwards on her face. Her hairless head sat high on a lanky, lean frame, and was tattooed with blood-red symbols of arcane might. "And when we fulfill our obligation to you, Lord Oziax will be ours to do with as we like?" Her voice rose above the din of the massed troops in a high-pitched shrill.

Tazizu's leather armor was a colored patchwork of reddish and blue-grey hides. It was form-fitting and made from the tough skins of her demonic rivals, which she had covered in ancient runes of mystical power. Sekka appreciated the symbolic touch. An orange sigil spun slowly above her head made up of delicately shaped runes, with tendrils of dark energy that snaked and snapped in the air. Tazizu held a three-lashed whip, ending in cruel ice barbs that spewed ice shards as it swayed in the winds of Gathos.

"As per our agreement, if you succeed, then Lord Oziax shall be yours."

Sekka heard a peal of bold laughter to the right of Tazizu. Her sister, Aeshmara, sat proudly on her steed and could not control her high spirits. "At last, the Warlords of Vyzyn shall be avenged!"

She drew two, double-bladed daggers that she deftly manipulated through her long fingers and raised them in salute to Sekka. A different malefic rune pulsed on each of the dark edges. She looked through dark, slate-blue eyes, which were the color of a coming storm. Her head was wreathed by a waterfall of straight white hair. Black runes faded in and out of existence as they swirled in the cloud of hazy darkness that surrounded her.

Aeshmara was shorter than her sister, and the youngest of the brood. She wore subtle, form-fitting armor that flexed with her movements. She was smooth and quick. Sekka could see the height of ambition in her stormy eyes.

Sekka lastly acknowledged Dai-Ko-Zior, the frail and sinister warlock. He sat hunched and hooded in his saddle and remained aloof to the excitement of coming war. It was rumored he drew his arcane power from blood pacts made with ancient entities, long forgotten by time, who remained in a sleepless state of consciousness, watching and waiting for the moment to be reborn.

Sekka was most cautious of Dai-Ko-Zior. She searched for his demonic essence and found nothing. Perhaps it was engaged elsewhere, communing on a distant plane of existence not connected to any of the known layers of the Abyss. One foe at a time, she thought. *I shall deal with this abomination once the flow of souls has begun.*

Each warlord sat upon a bestial mount that gnashed their teeth at any nearby warrior who happened to stray too close. The mounts were an amalgam of creatures from the Mortal Realm but were beings of pure chaos. Their upper bodies resembled sleek hunting beasts covered in smooth, ash-colored scales, and from their lower extremities extended six insectoid appendages that ended in razor-sharp tips. Each point scratched deep furrows into the frozen ground as they shifted and flexed.

Their muscular necks were thick and stout, allowing their rider to fight efficiently on either side. The beasts sniffed the air at Sekka's approach and snapped their mean muzzles into the air in anticipation of the hunt.

Sekka was full of pride at her impressive force. The Three Kingdoms of Hanna would be the first of many lands in the Mortal Realm to fall to her. Nothing could stop her now.

Sekka gazed to the center of the Chaos Gate, where her thralls had moved Aetenos, still nailed to his crucifix. A hover spell had been cast upon the posts as it bobbed and spun slowly above the living portal. He would be forced to watch her troops enter the Mortal Realm to wreak their havoc. All because he was too foolish to come to Gathos.

Somehow, it should not have been so easy. A worrisome suspicion entered her mind, that her good fortune had happened at the will of another, and that things were not as they seemed.

"Bah, I know what I am doing," she said and sent the first of her troops through the Chaos Gate.

35

DESDEMONIA

"Don't you let me go!" Desdemonia yelled back as her foot sought purchase on a small outcrop of the cliff wall. Kasai slowly belayed the rope tied around her waist to where Pallo stood ready to grab her and pull her to the safety of the ledge.

"Can't say this is my favorite thing to do," she shouted, as Pallo reached for the front of her molachuk coat. Run-Run had wisely equipped each of the party members with special gear for the cold. There were plenty of supplies left behind by the retreating soldiers of the King's Army. The heavy furs were durable and flexible, and a handy addition on their journey.

Kasai climbed down when she was secured on the ledge. Even on the icy rocks, he moved like a spider, with not one slip or misstep. Desdemonia figured his training at Ordu had prepared him for challenging climbs, seeing how the entire monastery was practically built on the side of a cliff. But this, she looked around, how could anyone be prepared for this? She was amazed that the small party had made it this far without losing anyone. A fall from this height would mean certain death.

"Where to from here, Captain?" she shouted above the wind as he joined them. Kasai gave her a half smile then shot a worried look to the sky. She followed his eyes and saw the storm was getting worse.

"Down."

"You'd think Illyria could have placed us closer to Aetenos, or at least on flat ground, right?" Desdemonia said as she hugged her arms around her body. The blessing of warmth Illyria had given each of them was working, but it didn't completely shut out the cold.

"I mean, really, the side of a volcano?"

"Shut yer mouth, witch," Orin said. His eyes glared daggers at her. "I grow tired of your blaspheming tongue."

Des just rolled her eyes. Orin took everything so seriously.

"We are here because this was the way He took, and somehow, that's important," Kasai said. The wind picked up again, and it was getting difficult to hear.

"Why? How do you know?" Des quickly asked.

"I don't know. I can't explain why, but it all feels so familiar."

Dark clouds spat out sheets of rain which froze upon the dead volcano's rocky surface, coating it with a glaze of ice. Pallo looked down the cliff wall. He was filled with trepidation about continuing without rest. Desdemonia didn't blame him.

"I know you're tired, but we need to keep moving. We won't survive trapped on this cliff when that new storm hits," Kasai said and pointed to an oncoming mass of black and purple thunderclouds.

"We will follow your lead," Pallo spoke for the group. Each gave a brief nod of agreement. Only Airis was hesitant. The youngster's face was downcast, and his eyes were hidden in the hood of his cloak. He moved slowly past Kasai to gather some rope, and Desdemonia saw he favored his right side.

They had all pushed their bodies to their limit, herself included. But something about being in this place made her magic stir as if something new was growing inside her. She looked to see how Kasai was holding up. His body carried the weight of fatigue, as did the others, but his eyes looked hollow, almost haunted.

"We keep going," she said and nodded her encouragement to him.

Pallo moved carefully to Kasai's right side. He cupped his hand over Kasai's ear and pointed to the left. "Run-Run has spotted a route to get to that large outcropping. It should give us some shelter from this rain."

Kasai nodded in favor of the route.

The wind picked up and brought with it blinding sleet that blurred Desdemonia's vision. She squinted at the proposed route as lightning flashed in the sky above. The icy, second skin of the mountain gleamed back. Bolts of electric air crackled and sizzled in the air as more swollen thunderheads swirled around the desolate summit.

"And I could have been halfway home to my little cottage by now," she said, knowing no one could hear her.

"We must move!" Kasai shouted above the din. "We don't have much time!" The party pressed on.

Run-Run's routes proved reliable and safe, and the companions made their way down the side of the volcano. It was an arduous process, and the weather grew worse as time wore on. Run-Run was an excellent guide and spotted routes that were unseen by the others. At last, they had reached the base of the sheer wall.

"Illyria watches over us with her protective hand," Airis said, and he dropped to his knees with exhaustion. Kasai noticed a trail of blood following Airis in the snow.

"Praise is to Aetenos and his guiding light," Orin said, who also collapsed in the snow near Airis. He saw the blood as well. "You're hurt!"

"I caught a shard of the mountain in my leg. It's nothing," Airis said. He clamped down with his hand on the outside of his leg. He hadn't said a word through the entire descent, but his face showed the pain that he hid behind pressed lips.

"Let me have a look at that," Desdemonia said and removed Airis's bloody hand from his leg. "Kasai, this is bad."

She pulled aside some of the torn cloth from Airis's pant leg and revealed a deep gash that was oozing blood. A shard of volcanic rock was lodged firmly in his leg. If it wasn't removed, Airis would eventually bleed to death. His face was ashen already.

"I'll be fine. We keep moving. Don't wait for me if I can't keep up. Completing the quest is all that matters."

"I admire your courage, Airis, but we must remove that shard, or you're not going anywhere," Desdemonia said. She grabbed some bandages from her rucksack. "These will help, but that cut will not close without proper stitching."

"Des, do you have any more healing potions?" Kasai said.

"Just one remains. I was saving it, though."

"Let's have it."

"But, what if…"

"C'mon Des. He needs it now."

"What if you need it more!" she blurted out the words.

All eyes were on her now, though she had said what they must all be thinking. Airis held his hand up and pushed Desdemonia away.

"She's right. Just wrap me up. I'll be fine."

"Des, can you heal him?" Kasai said.

"No, it's too deep. I could close it temporarily, but it will reopen easily. He needs a doctor."

"Or a healing potion."

"But Kasai," she said, trying to think of another way. She looked to Pallo for an answer, and he gently shook his head. His eyes told her enough. The last healing potion should be saved for Kasai.

"Des, the potion," Kasai insisted.

She reluctantly handed him the small vial. Run-Run looked questioningly at his brother.

"The Ever Hero knows best, Run-Run. It will be alright," Pallo said and knelt down next to Airis to take hold of the shard. "Ready?"

Airis nodded and shut his eyes tight. Pallo gave a quick pull and removed the rock.

Kasai popped the stopper to the vial and fed the contents to Airis. Thankfully, the gash on Airis's leg closed quickly.

"Des, can you wrap him up?" Kasai said.

"I'll do it," Orin said and moved to help Airis. He practically knocked her out of the way with his body.

Desdemonia backed off and sat down in the snow, feeling frustrated and annoyed. Kasai had just done a foolish thing. She hoped she wasn't going to have to debate him on every wrong decision he wanted to make.

"Well, that's what I'm here for," she said in jest. The others' uncertain looks told her they questioned his judgment as well. It was a difficult choice, but a necessary one. Kasai was the most selfless person she had ever known.

Hopefully, they would find Aetenos soon, and the Great Monk would make everything right. She craned her head to look up at the mountainous volcano. "I hope we don't have to return the same way we arrived."

Kasai eventually joined her. He gave her a brief smile before he sat down. "I know. You don't have to say anything."

"That was very generous, if not very wise," she said anyways.

"I couldn't let him die, Des." Kasai watched Orin help Airis move about slowly. Kasai frowned when he saw Pallo and his brother Run-Run exchanging hand signals.

"I hope they are talking about the lay of the land and the direction the party might travel next." Kasai sighed. He had pulled up his knees and rested his forehead on his arms. "I don't know what I'm doing. I should have listened to you."

"I know. That was our last potion," she said and tried to keep the frustration out of her voice.

"No. I mean when we were in Maugris's fortress, and you asked me to leave after losing Master Choejor."

"Oh, that. Ya, that would have been smart, too."

"We should have left when we had the chance." He shook his head in disappointment. "I'm responsible for bringing that dreadful portal into existence. I let my anger rule my judgment."

Des could see the weight of his words was like an avalanche crashing down on him.

"You did what you thought was right. You have a good heart, Kasai. It's a noble feature."

"This is all a terrible mistake," he said. "I'm not the one everyone needs me to be. What kind of Ever Hero would let something like that happen?"

Des didn't know what to say, so the two sat in silence.

"It's a wonder we made it this far," he said eventually.

"And we will make it the rest of the way. One step at a time, until it's finished."

"I wish I had your confidence."

"Me too, handsome. Now pick yourself up. You have a rescue party to lead."

"You're right," he said and got to his feet. "Pallo, we must move on."

Pallo roused the rest of the small party, and they resumed the trek to find Aetenos. The snow swirled around them in a constant flurry for the next hour. Desdemonia and Kasai caught up to Pallo as he trudged through the snow. The leader of the Kibo Gensai gave them both a somber nod.

"Do you think Run-Run will be able to find our way back? I'm hopelessly lost already. Each step forward erases one from the past," Kasai said.

"We shall all find our way home, Ever Hero. The Light of Aetenos will guide us."

"I hope so," Kasai mumbled.

The group moved onwards with Run-Run and Orin taking the lead. Pallo dropped back to walk with Airis. The snow-filled wind blurring their shapes into dark shades. Desdemonia curled up tightly within her molachuk fur, hoping it would shield her against the biting winds. It helped a little, but not enough.

"Something is happening to me, Des. I feel as if I have walked these wastelands before."

Desdemonia was quiet for a while. Something was happening to her, too.

"Do you think it has something to do with Aetenos and the Chaos Gate?"

"How could it not? I have an uncanny insight directing me where to go, but not how to return. I feel so drained as if I haven't slept in weeks. I can't remember anything. There was a mountain, wasn't there?" Kasai turned around fast. "Good, good. It's still there."

"Of course, the mountain is still there. Where would it go?" She was shouting again. This blasted wind! She could barely hear her own thoughts.

"I'm okay, I'm okay," Kasai said, but not to her. He was lost in his own world, rocking back and forth as they walked.

Desdemonia saw Orin trudging through the snow towards them. His eyes flashed with intensity at her then became soft and weary as he addressed Kasai.

"Ever Hero, we should rest and take food. Run-Run has spotted shelter from the wind, there to the left."

"Fine, lead the way," Kasai said.

The small party headed to the low hills area where natural upheavals of rock and ice built high snowdrifts on either side and created a buffer against the wind. Desdemonia was grateful to be on solid ground and not shin-high in snow.

The companions nestled themselves inside a small hollow of rocks and slowly ate the last of their rations. The salted food would have to be enough for what remained of their journey, but how long that would be, no one knew.

Desdemonia's body soaked up the sparse nutrients of the beef jerky. She felt a wave of perspiration flow out of her pores and was distraught to waste such a valuable resource. She would need to keep all the available water in her body to help stave off dehydration.

The landscape was a tempestuous sea of icy snow and deep slush. The companions had no map or any precise knowledge of where Aetenos was located. Kasai pointed them in the basic direction, but he, too, seemed unsure.

They were exhausted and lost in a desolate land. No one spoke, and only the howling wind could be heard, mocking them for their trespass.

"We must continue in this direction," Kasai said, pointing to the south if there was south here. He tried to appear confident, but Desdemonia could tell he wasn't.

"How can you be sure of the way?" Orin sputtered through chattering teeth. He held up a compass, and they all watched the directional needle dance and whirl endlessly. Pallo cast a stern expression at the Kibo Gensai warrior.

Desdemonia saw guilt in Orin's eyes. They all knew the compass had stopped functioning long ago. There was no magnetic north here, nor a consistent set of constellations anyone could see beyond the cloud-filled skies.

"In truth, I am not sure," Kasai lamented. "I remember things that I couldn't possibly know." Kasai looked imploringly at the others for their understanding. The Kibo Gensai, especially Pallo, seemed to know more about the ways of the Ever Hero than he did.

"Trust in the Ever Hero, Orin. He need only follow his heart," Pallo interjected.

"I meant no disrespect." He bowed to Kasai, and then to Pallo.

Kasai just waved him away and slumped down where he stood.

Desdemonia was happy Pallo had intervened, or else she would have said something to put Orin in his place. Orin wasn't the friendliest of chaps, and she wasn't going to let his foul disposition get under Kasai's skin. He had too much to worry about already.

She looked over at Kasai and smiled warmly at him. He raised his head and returned her gaze. She knew they were connected and shared a special bond together. Maybe she knew him in a previous awakened life.

Whatever it may be, when this was finished, she would ask him again to return with her to the forest. He could find peace there and rest for his soul. Once they had freed Aetenos, the Great Monk would make everything right again.

"Do you think we will be there soon?" Desdemonia said to Kasai. She was grateful she didn't need to compete with the wind to be heard. "If not, perhaps we could take a longer break."

"I'll be fine," Kasai said. His words were short. "I don't need to be mothered."

"I'm sure you don't, Sir Hero," she said tersely at first, and then added with a quirky smile, "I thought I might conjure some ice bunnies in the snow and brighten up this dreary place."

"It certainly could do with a little fun, and a Wood Witch's touch," Airis added with a smile. He put two fingers behind his head to mimic rabbit ears.

"But I wouldn't advise making a snack out of them. They may bite back," she said.

Despite his downtrodden mood, Kasai couldn't suppress a chuckle and soon began to laugh. Pallo and Run-Run did the same. Desdemonia noticed they had the same sort of snorting laugher, and their bodies bobbled like children's toys. Only Orin remained glum. His grave eyes never left Kasai.

"I feel like I'm dying," Kasai said while still laughing, but his mirth quickly ended. "It's this horrible place. It's killing me," he said softly. The rest of the group looked at him with serious concern.

"You need rest, Kasai," Desdemonia said. She put her arm around his shoulder so he could lean on her. He didn't resist. His body was shivering, and she hoped she had enough body heat for the two of them.

"My past is fading and being replaced with memories of someone else's life."

Desdemonia noticed the interest of the Kibo Gensai piqued.

"You now walk in the steps of the Divine Fist," Pallo said. Run-Run sat close to his brother and nodded enthusiastically. "It is his memories you share."

"Aetenos? Impossible," Kasai said. "I'm no hero. It's all a cruel joke. It was never supposed to be me. I'm nobody." His voice was barely a whisper. Desdemonia could feel the heaviness of his body sink into hers.

36

KASAI

The edges of Kasai's sight dimmed to dark shadows. He heard a distant voice pleading with him, but he didn't want to listen anymore. Why wouldn't they just let him sleep? Everything would be easier if he could only sleep.

"Kasai wake up! We need you." He heard Desdemonia's voice getting louder. He felt her hands around his chest, lifting him up to a sitting position. Soon more hands were holding him, keeping him steady.

The winds momentarily ceased their howls as if waiting to observe his resolve. But there was only silence and doubt in his heart. There was no strength left in him to support the burden of this calling. Be the Ever Hero, they all said. He didn't even know what that meant.

"Kasai, Kasai. Are you alright?" Desdemonia's voice was filled with concern.

"Des, I cannot do this task, I am so tired. I cannot go on, the weight is too heavy," he mumbled.

"Kasai, we must try. I'm here with you. Together we can win."

Kasai looked deeply into Desdemonia's amber eyes and saw smoldering fire and determination.

"Okay, Des. Together."

She grasped his hands. He rose, and his renewed purpose lingered in the air, a floating feather of determination ready to guide him. The next gale blasted its way into the natural shelter, and again he fell to the cold ground. Pallo and Run-Run exchange nervous glances.

"The Ever Hero must rest. The misery of this realm has a greater effect on him, much more so than us, though I am amazed we have traveled so far. This horrid place is enough to drive any sane person mad," Pallo said.

"I can stand," Kasai said and tried to raise himself from the ground. His legs trembled with exhaustion and rebelled against another step. His mind willed them forward, but his body refused to be pushed further. Kasai slumped back into the snow. "I'm sorry. I can't."

"Come, help me build a better shelter against the wind. Push snow closer to the taller rocks. We'll remain here the night," Pallo said. "If there is a night here."

Kasai vaguely heard Pallo's insistent order to the others. Working quickly, they soon had built up walls of snow and ice to divert the rushing winds. They huddled together for warmth, placing Kasai in the center.

Kasai's thought drifted in and out of lucidity. Images filled his mind of a similar journey traveled by another's footsteps in the deep snow. He felt as if he was in a dream. Kasai looked at his hands and saw they were now the hands of another, worn and weathered with callouses and scars. His grey molachuk fur had changed to a robe of cobalt blue, and he was moving...

His bright-blue cobalt robe was in sharp contrast to the shoulder-high snowdrifts that blocked his path and taunted him to bully his way through. He pushed forward, and the ice and snow dissolved before his feet. He stumbled awkwardly through what was no longer there. The snowdrift scattered in all directions and formed again in a new location.

He was alone on the icy tundra. The cold air burned his lungs as he pressed onwards. His mind wandered as the elements continued to test his willpower and resolve.

"By the Immortal Mother, I do not belong here. None of my kind does."

He plowed through another snowdrift. This one remained thick and solid long enough to tax his divine strength. He broke through with a final thrust. The snow quickly tapered down to a white powder, dashed over a veil of thin ice. The ice shattered from the weight of his hard step, and a previously hidden crevasse opened beneath him. The ground became a hole of black emptiness and only his enhanced reflexes, and tantric muscle control saved him from plummeting into a frozen grave.

He leaped to the side and scrambled over the lip of the pit. He took a few steps away from the opening and sat down. He needed to be stable of mind, to concentrate, and regain control of his thoughts if he were to succeed in rescuing his beloved. He took a moment's respite to tap into his vast reservoir of fire xindu and thaw the deep shiver from his body.

The past and present unleashed a spinning unreality that clouded his perception. He must stay true to his purpose for being here, in this living nightmare, or his mind would break.

"Start again with the basics," he said. "Something easy to hold on to and build upon. My name. What is my name? I must have a name!" Nothing. He had been given so many names in his time, and now he could not recall even one. *Forget the past. Who am I now?* "Ka, Kasa..." The name slipped through his mind as quickly as it had arrived.

The location of the desolate volcano was now beyond his grasp. Had it been there, or was it another trick, courtesy of his increasingly deranged imagination? Had he already entered the frozen realm and descended the dead goliath in triumph or was he, in fact, born of the ice and snow and had yet to ascend that fierce and terrible foe, a significant barrier preventing him from exiting this land and completing his quest? Was that crucial information lost to him now, as well?

"No, I was not of this place, not of this time. Nor shall I ever be! I did not belong here then, or now. By all rights in the Seven Heavens, I should not be allowed to step into this Hell at all. How then am I here? What mysterious journey has the Immortal Mother placed me on? Why was I chosen? There must be a reason I was sent here."

The question perplexed him. He must have been given help to pass the Amaranthine Barrier, but by whom? He had no recollection. The only answer was the howling wind and the madness given voice in the back of his mind, coaxing him to relent.

Stop walking, old man. Sit. Meditate. Relax. Sleep...surrender. Your journey is at last over, Great Monk.

"Concentrate!" he shouted over the distracting winds and to silence the voice haunting his mind. "If I am alone, then my journey is not complete, and I am certainly alone in this wretchedness. I know Illyria is here!" His visions had shown him that she was here and in pain.

His reasoning was sound. He pushed back against the fog in his head and cleared some space for her image. He saw her bright face and the tenderness in her eyes, his angel. He held on to that image, and it gave him the strength to push onwards. He could not forsake her. He would not!

The wind died down momentarily. He scanned the horizon and realized he was hopelessly lost. There were no landmarks to gauge the distance he had covered. There was only emptiness. Small hills of snow rose in a hasty fury and then were blown asunder.

None of that mattered. He would rely on a different compass to guide his way. His angel had placed a craving in his heart long ago, and it directed his steps now. He relied solely on that compulsion to guide him. Somehow the chaotic winds could not keep the smell of her scent from him and the memories of the passion they had shared together.

Why she had left him one day without cause or reason vexed him still. Ah, he knew it could not last, not with her. They were just too different.

She had wanted to change him and succeeded most profoundly. His ascension into the ranks of the Heavenly Host was a miracle. However, the core of his human heart remained the same, and that was their downfall. He could not wholly ascribe to the strict laws of the Seven Heavens. He could not forsake his mortal brethren and their struggle to understand the boundaries of the path of righteousness. There was too much real life in the grey shadows of human understanding and desire.

Over time he had learned to forget her, or rather, mask the heartache and became obsessed with higher aspirations and noble deeds. Many in the Mortal Realm heard his Song, a message of joy and peace throughout the land, and it lifted their hearts and caressed their souls.

But, little by little, she would creep back into his consciousness, a soft whisper to excite the imagination of what might be. And then, all at once, he felt her addictive pull. It crashed through his meditations and distracted his will. She had become ever-present in his dreams and encompassed his thoughts once more.

He saw her in the dreamlike haze between his thoughts, just out of reach of his physical sight, but real, nonetheless. And now she called him again. It must have cost her much to communicate with him in this manner, over such distance through the Realms.

He would honor that sacrifice. Illyria was reaching out to him to rescue her, to set her free. He forgot his Song, and the lands of mortals went silent while he searched desperately for her. He would find her. She needed him!

He pushed on into the cold. Dark thoughts surrounded his mind and lashed out at him for being so weak. "Is this what I have become, a young pup desperate for a morsel of attention tossed at his feet from the Mother's daughter? Does each savory bite only served to drive the hunger harder and yearn for the next taste?" He said aloud, trying to understand who he was. "I am the greatest Grandmaster of them all! I have transcended the ways of all earthly desires and have ascended into the divine." He paused in his ravings. "No, I am...that no longer. I am just a man, with a heart that yearns for love and belonging."

The madness swarmed into his mind and made him blind. "I am but a humble servant, set in this world to give fully of myself and endure. There is nothing for me to possess. I was made to give, always to give."

He pressed on, trudging through deep snow. The warm glow of Illyria's soul was the only beacon for him to follow in the deep, dark places where his mind had become a prisoner.

He had never been in love with any one thing before, for, after his transcendent ascension, his passion touched all beings. His love was unconditional and equal, but with her, it was different. The enticement of her call was bewitching. She had possessed his every thought and drove him into frenzied action, regardless of how foolish.

He knew he did it willingly, always searching for her approval. Approval? Who was she that he needed her approval? His muse? His lover? He did not know. She was the angel Illyria, and that was enough for him. He let the unanswered questions float behind him and scatter into the breeze.

The thin layer of surface ice crunched under his steps as each leg fell thigh-deep into the thick, wet snow. It sucked at his legs as he took the next step, refusing to let go. The visions his inner-sight showed him spoke of being nowhere and everywhere at once. Visions had a mysterious and vague language of their own, and this place fit that description perfectly. The Abyss had entirely claimed this once beautiful land.

Therefore, being lost was relative, and he assured himself that he would know when he reached his goal by the clarion call in his heart. Confident in his clarity of purpose once more, he pushed on against the maddening howl of the wind and the ever-shifting snow.

His steps became less muffled upon the ankle-deep snow, and he grew more confident that the terrain underfoot had changed for the better. He could capture lost time due to the more favorable footing.

The blinding snow had created a seamless transition between frozen land and frozen lake. The shrieking wind had drowned out all sound except for its devilish chorus until he heard the heavy moan of ice breaking. Deep cracks spun off in multiple patterns beneath his feet. He contemplated their beauty just before the ground dissolved into an icy deathtrap.

He plunged into a new horror, as frigid water opened beneath him and eagerly slurped him down into its depth. His mind registered the danger instantly, and his body went into a blur of motion. He pushed off the solid block of ice still underfoot and leaped for the far side. The unstable ground compromised his efforts, and what should have been an easy leap turned into a sinking wade through icy slush.

He sank down deeper into darkness. The numbness was a quick shock to his senses. With one last, desperate effort, he lunged upwards like a cobalt scaled koi, propelling itself out into the open air towards the far bank.

. . .

Kasai came awake with a start. Desdemonia and the Kibo Gensai surrounded him, all huddled closely around him, resting as best they could. Desdemonia looked at him with sleepy tenderness.

"I hope you were dreaming of me, handsome."

Kasai smiled. He appreciated the flirtatious gypsy and her affable charm.

"How long?" Kasai asked as he began to get up.

"Only a few hours," Pallo said. The relief on his face was evident.

"We are ready to continue," Orin said as if answering the question in Kasai's mind. "If the Ever Hero is willing." Kasai received a determined nod from Desdemonia as well.

Kasai took a deep breath. The cold burned his lungs, but it also made him more alert.

"I think so," Kasai said. He shook the lingering dream of walking in another's footsteps from his head. He hoped it meant they were at least going in the right direction. They collected their belongings and left the shelter.

The low hills eventually relented to barren flatlands and the glacial plain, which stretched out endlessly to all horizons. They were alone, wanderers in a desolate wasteland, insignificant specks adrift in a forever changing landscape of swirling, white winds, and frigid misery. They walked in silence for hours.

Terrible squalls sprayed frozen debris into Kasai's face creating a spectacle of hallucination and delirium. The fierce winds relentlessly buffered and berated him.

"Fool!" Kasai heard the word carried on the wind and not for the first time. It mocked him, laughed and jeered at him for thinking he could succeed. What was he but an insignificant monk who had mistakenly been chosen for greatness that belonged to another?

His resolved broke. He fell once more and felt the cold, sharp kiss of the hard snow as it dug into his knees.

"I am the fool who has damned the world," Kasai said and shook his head in disbelief. "I am only a monk, just a simple, stupid monk." Kasai's strength ebbed away, and he sank deeper into the cold embrace of dispassionate snow. His mind drifted back to the dream of a giant cobalt koi, jumping out of a frozen pond…

Miraculously, he grabbed a tiny handhold, a nub of ice no bigger than the tip of a finger, but it was enough. He wrapped his calloused hand around it and reinforced his hold with his thumb. Slowly he pulled himself from the black water, his saturated, robes heavy with slush.

He was thankful to be back on stable ground, but now he had a new problem. He was drenched and would soon be encased in a cocoon of ice. His body temperature had already dropped significantly. The desire to panic crept into his thoughts like a slow, stealthy hunter.

He sat for a moment and willed his mind to remain calm. He needed to marshal his thoughts. Time was slipping away. He scanned the horizon again, looking for any slight indication that he was closer to his destination, but saw nothing that revealed he had made any progress at all. He sighed with despair.

He then spotted a high snowdrift that would serve his more immediate need. He backtracked to where the snow was deeper and climbed up a snowbank. His body ached, and skin itched as if a thousand pins repeatedly stabbed into his flesh.

The sensation of pain gave him hope. If he could still feel, then he was still alive and would endure. He reached the summit and slowly excavated out a deep hole from the middle, then dropped inside. The fierce wind howled above his head as he stripped off his outer blue robe, boots, and undergarments. He had little time to waste.

He sat naked in the center of his temporary refuge and cleared his mind. Hypothermia stalked him like a starved tundra wolf. It waited patiently for its prey to succumb to the exhaustion of the hunt. Its pack mates, Doubt, and Misery were constant adversaries in his mind. They nipped at his heels whenever he regained focus of his mission.

It was only a matter of time, even for one of his enhanced endurance. He couldn't survive in this wasteland forever. The nature of the place exerted a special tax upon his divine essence. His entire body was wracked with cold and shivered uncontrollably.

He closed his eyes and forced his mind to concentrate. "Be calm, for Life is a willing extension of energy within the multiverse. A gift is given freely and returned without remorse. This is the Boundless. Law and Chaos are the twin strangers, each forcing and encouraging the other to grow. Each gave and received the other's special blessing.

"The gift of the multiverse is within me, and I will use it to grow, as well. I will add myself to the great expanse and become one with the Boundless."

He said the soothing words through chattering teeth, activating his four xindu energies, and calling forth the glowing fire within his soul.

Gradually, he felt his heart beating to a new rhythm, one that was at peace with his circumstance, accepting it as temporary and not forever. He was not filled with pain or consumed by panic. His heart beat slowly and steadily in his chest. It thumped louder with each controlled breath, and eventually, drowned out the shrieking winds outside his snow ditch.

His body began to summon warmth from the surrounding pockets of invisible xindu energy that existed even here, in this cold and barren hell. Some of it he gave freely from his inner core; some of it he borrowed from the Boundless, creating a balanced harmony of giving and receiving.

His skin felt wet as the thin glaze of ice sloughed off his body and puddle in the creases of his crossed limbs. As the heat expanded from his body, the inner sanctum glowed amber, and steam rose from his flesh. The shivering ceased, as his body relaxed for the first time since he had entered Gathos.

His inner fire blazed on, and soon his skin dried, followed by his clothing. What had started as a warm, kindled flame now flared red-hot with fervor. The walls of his shelter began to melt. He needed to quench the insatiable hunger of his fire xindu, or he would be lost to the flame.

Slowly, gently, he tapped into his water xindu to buffer the inner inferno he had created. His fire xindu understood and relented to a warming furnace. He was still in control, always the Master. After a short rest, he dressed and climbed out of his ice shelter to resume his journey.

An icy gale blew up from behind and shot past him as it raced mindlessly across the barren snowdrifts, a wild banshee screaming out her madness, unhindered by rock or tree or hill. It slammed its eerie might into a distant, solitary spire, spraying snow and ice upon its sleek, black surface.

The lone tower rose out of the ground, a slender finger of contempt against the arctic elements. The citadel had stood for millennia and would continue to do so until Time itself was cast into oblivion. He had found the entrance to Furia Keep at last, the dreadful place that held his dear Illyria captive.

The stronghold radiated an aura of gloom and despair to rival the frigid temperatures outside. But to the man in cobalt-blue robes, it was a beacon of hope. He stood to take in its preternatural magnificence. Somewhere inside the completion of his quest would be found.

He knew it was a forsaken place, yet it was the destination of his journey, the one he had sought without a map or guide. It had been part of his dreams, and it called to him as Illyria had called to him, a siren in the cold dark.

No matter the Immortal Mother's plan for him, he would do this one thing for himself. He would save her.

Time was once more his enemy, not direction. He knew he had pushed his inner fire xindu to the limit and for far too long. However, he willed it on, knowing it was slowly consuming his essence for the fuel it needed to keep burning. It was now the only thing keeping him alive, albeit barely.

He looked longingly at the distant spire, watching it blur in and out of focus through wet eyes. A flurry of snow whipped up and eclipsed the tower. When it had passed, a hazy-figure, shimmering in the distance had taken its place.

As the shade approached, he could make out the curved outlines of a woman's figure, naked against the elements. Her hair danced wildly in the air and fought back against the blizzard of snow and ice swarming around her. He squinted against the furious snow squall, not trusting what he saw. When his eyes cleared, she had vanished into the blinding white.

"Push on. Just take one more step forward. Keep warm, regardless of the cost. I'm coming." He had nothing more to give. His fire xindu had continuously raged for what must have been days, or months or years. He could no longer tell.

"Illyria," he whispered her name to make sure he remembered. His legs folded beneath him and crunched into the shallow snow. He fell into darkness.

Kasai picked himself up off the frozen ground once more. It was difficult to decipher what was his present reality and what was a borrowed memory. The ever-present swirling snow prevented his mind from recognizing the difference between the two.

Kasai saw a vast area in the distance that glowed with a distinct, ashen-emerald hue, and his heart filled with dread. He stood like a statue in the snow, and absent-mindedly brought his hand to his chest. He felt the area where the brand from the cursed amulet had left its mark on him in Rachlach Fortress, and thereby established the soul bridge needed to open the horrific Chaos Gate.

The dead bodies of trampled slaves littered the land surrounding the diabolical gateway. They were buried in the frozen ground at different depths. Some were locked in place at their ankles, while others were buried up to the ridge of their nose. Their souls were given up as a sacrifice to appease the cosmic forces that required payment for passage.

Sekka had already marched her demon horde through the Chaos Gate and into

Baroqia. Kasai realized the demons had stomped on the immobile slaves as they crossed over the ground and into the portal, leaving the wretched bodies broken and wallowing in small, frozen pools of maroon. All were dead.

The incessant wind caked ice and snow around them, incorporating the bodies into the desolate terrain. The Three Kingdoms of Hanna were doomed. All hope left Kasai, and his mind sought to escape from this nightmare. He could not go on. He had failed.

"Kasai! You found it! The Chaos Gate!" Desdemonia was there at his side once more, but Kasai could barely hear her words. The weight of his misguided deeds overwhelmed him. He couldn't breathe, nor did he want to expend the effort to try.

Des moved in front of him and shook him. He knew she was shouting at him, but he could no longer hear her words. Was she berating him for bringing her here to die? She should have left him and Master Choejor to the savage Chaos Beasts and not bothered to rescue them. Then she would still be safe.

Kasia thought he heard another whispered voice. "Look there! Movement." It was one of the Kibo Gensai. Kasai thought his name might be Airis, but he couldn't be sure. Everything around Kasai was a dense fog. Airis, if that was his name, looked as if he was shouting and pointing excitedly at something in the distance.

Kasai couldn't concentrate. He shivered so severely that his teeth rattled in his head. It was the only thing he could hear as his eyes rolled back into his head. *Sleep. I must sleep,* he thought. Someone was shaking him.

His eyes opened to slits. It was Desdemonia, holding him firmly. "Fire xindu! Kasai listen to me! Use your fire xindu!" She was trying to say something else. She grabbed Ninziz-zida from his sash and held the Fire Serpent up to his eyes. *She can't do that,* he thought. *No one can hold her but me.*

Kasai barely acknowledged what she meant and took Ninziz-zida in his hands. Immediately the Fire Serpent locked within called to him, imploring him to come back, to rejoin the fight of righteousness. The ancient weapon thrust her energy into his body. Kasai was pulled out of his fugue state to the maddening howls of the frigid winds. Ninziz-zida graciously kept a steady flow of vital energy flowing into him, and he regained some of his strength.

Thank you, Ninziz-zida. You do me a great honor.

The weapon pulsed back her reply in his mind. *We are not finished.*

Kasai saw movement to the right side of the portal as three small creatures harried a broken slave, bound to an X-shaped crucifix. They crawled over his body like vermin.

His head was low, and his body seemed broken, held up only by the support of the crucifix. Ninziz-zida flared to life in his hands, and Kasai felt as if the Fire Serpent was expressing joy.

Aetenos! Ninziz-zida shouted her elation in his mind. *You have found the Master.*

37

SHIVERRIG

S hiverrig woke with the lithe succubus wrapped around his body. The smells of their lovemaking, if one could call it that, still lingered in the air. He enjoyed her changeling appearances, which added unique twists to their coupling. Sess'thra now shared his bed whenever she deigned to make an appearance in the capital city of Qaqal, which had become more frequent since the arrival of Sekka and her Frost Legion to the Mortal Realm.

The air that swept through the streets and alleyways of Qaqal was noticeably colder since his coup and the death of King Conrad. *It will be an early winter this season*, thought Shiverrig. The city had been shut down to locate and punish the dissenters to his new regime. After a quick trial, the accused were hung in the local squares for treason. The dead weight of the bodies gently swaying in the chilly breeze was a grim reminder to would-be sympathizers to the House of Conrad. Frost would cover their cold bodies overnight and melt away in the afternoon sun.

"The things I do, I do for the good of Baroqia. The rats must be driven from their dens. It's the only way to align the people to a more structured rule," Shiverrig said. "It's what my grandsire would have done."

Shiverrig expected there would be a time of unrest before the general populace embraced him as their new ruler. However, he grew tired of expending time and resources to quell the public fear or to quash a new uprising of a smaller noble house looking to advance its position in the new hierarchy of rulership in Qaqal. The nature of his blood demanded conquest, and he felt the eyes of his forefathers bearing down on him in impatient judgment. He needed a unified Baroqia before Sekka became too entrenched in the Three Kingdoms. The disputes of the lesser houses were delaying his plans.

Shiverrig gazed at Sess'thra's lithe figure draped over his own. She was a welcome addition to his warm bed. To many, she seemed but a child by her appearance, and they were the fools for thinking such. The demon was ancient. Shiverrig idly wondered if one of her kind needed sleep or just pretended. He found he didn't care.

The succubus was an enjoyable distraction, but nothing more. He had grander things to conquer than mounting an overly sexed creature from the Abyss. Sess'thra had tactical information he needed regarding Sekka and her Frost Legion, but the succubus was not forthcoming with anything of value, and he needed an advantage.

Shiverrig heard nearby movement. He peered into the half-light of the room to see Khalkoroth hunkered down in the shadows, mumbling to himself. The pale demon was always present when Sess'thra returned to the castle-keep. He lurked nearby, shifting his weight on his haunches like a hungry watchdog, waiting to be fed.

"Go find yourself another toy to worry over, Khalkoroth, and leave this chamber. Your presence here is unwelcome," Shiverrig said as he left the bed and dressed in a morning robe. "Haunt someone else's dreams."

"I shall go and stay where I please, mortal," Khalkoroth said as the hackles rose on his back.

Shiverrig knew it didn't take much provocation to anger the demon, and he was in no mood for an argument or a fight. "Stay then, and pretend the succubus holds any desire for you."

Khalkoroth's growl rumbled in his chest. The succubus stirred seductively under the sheets of the grand bed but did not rise. Shiverrig knew she was awake and enjoyed the tension between him and the pale demon.

He noticed Khalkoroth stared longingly at Sess'thra and suspected Daku, the young monk from Ordu, continued to fight for his soul somewhere within the confines of the demon's vast bulk. Sess'thra had tricked Daku into ingesting a demon seed holding the essence of Khalkoroth. Once swallowed, the beast within could then possess the soul of its human host.

Khalkoroth lowered himself on his haunches and began mumbling to himself again. Shiverrig did not understand the language he spoke but assumed it was the infernal tongue of Gathos. Mostly, Shiverrig caught Khalkoroth unaware, arguing with himself in the corner of a room or the shadows of a long hall. The demon's facial features would subtlety shift in the gloom from a bearlike snout with bestial eyes, to the human face of a young man.

Shiverrig was impressed. The Monks of Ordu were renowned for their exceptional abilities and disciplined minds. A new level of respect formed in Shiverrig's mind for the young monk. Daku remained a thorn in the demon's side. Shiverrig wondered if a human could completely break the bonds of demonic possession and maintain control of the shared soul. Shiverrig knew he would never succumb to possession of any sort. He would die first.

"I see Daku is not as weak of mind and spirit you had initially assumed. Watching you lose control amuses me," Shiverrig said, testing his theory.

"His soul is mine! The monk is forever lost." Khalkoroth rose to a towering height. Shiverrig was instantly on guard for an attack, but instead of lunging forward, the pale demon lumbered out of the room, knocking over a small statue on a pedestal when he left.

Sess'thra had said, when a mortal ingested a demon seed, the demon held within the pod would forever be bound to that human soul, but she did not say which of the two retained control once established. Interesting that she left out that crucial bit of information.

The battle for Daku's mind and soul proved to be an essential experiment to observe. If a mortal could take the demon seed and retain his conscious mind but command the demon's superior strength and reflexes, it would make for an unstoppable soldier. Shiverrig could train them to be a cohesive fighting machine, unlike the failures of his ancestors with breeding ogres and humans together. Hopefully, this would produce different results.

"Everything has a weakness," Shiverrig said. "Everything. I just need to find it."

There could be only one ruler of Baroqia, and all of Hanna, for that matter, and Shiverrig was determined to ensure that its ruler was mortal.

He recalled a conversation he had with his man Pathias, after the Battle at the Last Garrison. "*The weakness of a pure-bred demon horde is its leader. The warlord is the force that holds the monsters together as a singular unit. If the warlord falls, the structure of the horde became undone, and the bloodlust of the individual takes over. I watched demons fall upon their own when their leader was destroyed.*"

"*Destroyed? How?*" Shiverrig dug deeper and listened with great interest to Pathias's report.

"*A lone monk took the field and engaged the enemy's warlord when the rest of the King's Army was in retreat. Amazingly, he was without armor or support of men. I watched in keen interest as the two battled. There was a flash, and the warlord fell, headless.*"

"*And the whereabouts of the monk?*" Shiverrig wondered if the monk who killed the warlord was the same one Dax referred to as the Ever Hero. Could the myth be true? Rubbish. War made a man's wits leave him quicker than a fish released from the fisherman's hook. It was more likely that a misplaced missile took the warlord's head rather than anything a single monk could do.

"*I do not know, my Lord. Once the warlord was destroyed, the demon horde splintered, and I was hard-pressed by the foe.*"

Chopping the head from the snake was the key to a decisive victory, as long as fear didn't overwhelm his men. He wondered how to train against the demons without alerting Sess'thra, Khalkoroth, or even the rarely seen Dax to his agenda. His men were not ready for the likes of Khalkoroth, and the demon would surely kill his men first, before relenting when they went down.

Shiverrig thought more about the mixture of Khalkoroth and Daku. The beast was formidable to behold but had the disposition of a petulant child. He was moody and unpredictable, where the monk possessed a rational and disciplined mind. One that could develop complex thoughts and contingent strategies during a raging battle.

Perhaps an average soldier would not possess the same depth of understanding as a monk of Ordu. Still, divisions of foot soldiers and spearmen were needed in battle the same as competent generals. What was the key to control, he wondered? The answer flitted like a gnat buzzing in his ear, but just out of reach when he tried to catch it.

Shiverrig would keep the pale demon under surveillance and always have one of Malachi's men watching him. Hopefully, none of them would be killed in the process. The world was changing. No longer would mundane weapons be enough to conquer and hold new lands. The threat from the Abyss was real. He needed to have a powerful force of his own that could match the demons in combat.

. . .

"Sekka has a plan for this realm," Shiverrig paced the floor of the chamber where he had received his closest advisors, Duke Manda, Lord Fritta, and his archvashim, Malachi. They all nodded in agreement. Shiverrig continued. "I am no fool. She will not stop at Sunne. Sekka will eventually come for Baroqia. Control of Hanna must be her ultimate objective, and I intend to be an obstacle in her way. She will need to remove me."

"Perhaps your choice of allies was misguided. You have vanquished an enemy of the realm in one hand, only to raise a stronger one with the other," Duke Manda said.

"But if the archdevil wants conquest, why would she not immediately march on the capital city? She must know the realm is in chaos," Lord Fritta said. "The lands north of the Hoarfrost Mountains lack immediate building resources, fertile soil, or a significant populace to warrant an invasion. There is no reason for her to stay there, however, for the same reason, why would she pursue Sunne? Scouting or merchant reports dating back hundreds of years speak of a land of dense jungles holding a few pockets of scattered indigenous tribes. There is nothing for her there but jungles and more jungles. It makes no sense."

Shiverrig weighed the logic of Lord Fritta's assumption. "Gaining a foothold in a land protected by the Sarribe Mountains would be a sound strategy. Its passes are few, and its peaks are treacherously high, guarding her against a flash invasion. But, why take her Frost Legion to an uncomfortably hot and humid environment, when Trosk and its eternal winter is available?"

"She would be better served to consolidate her strength there rather than Sunne," Fritta added.

"You must stop thinking as men of conquest and question what does an archdevil of the Abyss need? Is she looking for land? Resources? Gold? That seems unlikely," Malachi said.

"We are ill-equipped to deal with this menace. Access to this land should never have been given to that devil," Lord Fritta said as he sat back in his chair, folding his arms across his chest.

"Gentlemen, we have been over this before. Sekka will be removed in time. It was a binding pact made at a different time. I will break it as soon as we are ready. Trust me," Shiverrig said. Moral was slipping, and he needed a victory soon to keep his co-conspirators' minds occupied.

"Slaves would be the ideal choice," Malachi added, the words salaciously leaving his mouth. "Soul-slaves, to be more precise." His eyes bore into Lord Manda, anticipating a reply.

"We are all in agreement, Sunne is an unknown, and has been since the founding of Baroqia. The Overlord, Baroq Shiverrig, stopped his armies at the steppes of the Southern Sarribe Mountains for reasons only he understood when he turned his energy back towards subjugating the newly conquered tribes," Shiverrig said. "But if Sekka wants it, we should understand why, and if necessary, take it from her."

"Agreed," Lord Fritta said.

Shiverrig nodded at Fritta's wisdom. "I shall strengthen trade routes and use the merchants as reconnaissance agents. I do not want to alarm our new 'friends' of any unfavorable duplicity. We will secretly establish diplomatic relations with Sunne and act as their comrade-in-arms against the demon horde. With any luck, we shall have a united force before Sekka knows of our..."

Sess'thra sauntered lazily into the room and languidly lounged on a red divan placed along the wall. Shiverrig frowned at her interruption and wondered how much she had heard. Lord Fritta and Duke Manda both exchanged uneasy looks of discomfort. Her appearance excited Malachi, but he soon regained his composure and addressed the lords of the realm.

"Unification of Baroqia is far from complete, my lords. There is still much to accomplish in Qaqal alone, not to mention the realignment of the Lesser Houses that remain loyal to the House of Conrad. Fear alone will not calm their hearts.

"Individually, they are not a threat, but united they will be problematic. They will fight like cornered badgers if their livelihood remains in flux. They need to see a unity of purpose from the crown and, more importantly, the coin of the realm to flow. You will need their support to rule effectively."

Sess'thra sighed aloud and impatiently picked herself up off the lush divan and strolled leisurely to Shiverrig's side. She made sure she had Malachi's eye, and watched him become noticeably flushed as she moved passed him.

"You mortals have such limited thinking. So much talk, talk, talk about trade and loyalty and history. Such a bore," Sess'thra said. "The means for total conquest of the Kingdom of Baroqia, and any other kingdom you desire is already at your disposal."

Shiverrig looked at the succubus and raised his eyebrow in surprise and interest. "Go on," he said.

"I have told you, the Mistress Sekka has already expressed her interest in you to lead her Frost Legions in the Mortal Realm. You would be unstoppable."

Lord Fritta and Duke Manda looked questioningly at Shiverrig. The succubus had a knack of stirring fears and anxieties whenever she spoke.

"Shiverrig? You court the devil we wish to dispose of? Where is your sanity?" Lord Fritta shook his head in disbelief. Shiverrig held his hands up to calm Fritta's troubled thoughts.

"The price is too great. I would not taint the purity of the Shiverrig line with demon blood or possession."

"Hasn't it already suffered diffusion of purity with the ogre races of long ago?" Duke Manda said with a superior air of disdain.

"Peasant fables, nothing more," Shiverrig lied.

Sess'thra rolled her eyes, unconvinced. She approached Shiverrig and draped her slender arms over his broad shoulders. She pulled his head down to hers and spoke plainly in his ear.

"My dear Gerun, the demon seed shall set you free. Think of the power you shall wield over mortal and immortal beings alike!"

"And become a slave to a demon like the young monk from Ordu. Do you take me for a fool? My legacy shall not be tainted. My star rises now, and I will build on this momentum as the lords of my great house did long ago." He pulled away from her embrace.

"You misunderstand. Each seed is as different as the demonic essence that was bonded to it."

"Are you trying to tell me that the demon seed containing Khalkoroth wasn't meant for me? I find that hard to believe."

"Of course, it was meant for you. But that was before we knew your strength and resourcefulness. The Mistress has greater things planned for you. Where Daku failed, you shall prevail."

"Shiverrig! Explain yourself. What is the succubus implying?" Lord Fritta said. He was a careful and cautious man who did not enjoy surprises.

"You all should partake in the demon seed. And rid yourself of this frail shell you call mortality." The succubus looked at each in turn and stopped to leer at Lord Fritta, causing the strong man to lower his eyes.

"That's enough," Shiverrig said, annoyed at the disruption. "If you have nothing of import to add, you may leave." The succubus swished her tail like a lazy snake in the warm sun and walked from the room.

38

KASAI

Kasai rushed ahead of the others as Ninziz-zida flared to life. Her ancient fire xindu flowed freely into Kasai and gave him renewed strength and energy.

"Thank you, Ninziz-zida, for the gift of your warmth. Let us free Aetenos and leave this desolate place."

Three smallish demons, resembling gross, hairless felines with the lower extremities of bloated slugs, molested Aetenos's frost-covered body. Their fat tails left gooey trails of mucus as they slithered and crawled over his chest, legs, and shoulders.

Ninziz-zida's fiery light caught their attention and they turned to hissed at Kasai. The demons sprung from Aetenos's body at him, but Ninziz-zida snapped out at each one in quick succession and immolated the things in midair. Fetid smoke from their burning bodies rose in the air until Kasai rubbed the remains out with his foot.

"Ugh, disgusting," Kasai gasped. The air reeked of sulfur and rotten eggs. His eyes watered as he put the nook of his arm up to his face to cover his mouth and nose. The wind did nothing to blow the stench away.

Kasai gently tapped Aetenos, hoping to wake him from his stupor. "Master Aetenos, we are here. Master, wake up." But Aetenos didn't move, even when nudged by Ninziz-zida's righteous flame. Kasai panicked, fearing the worst.

"Oh no, oh no. Master Aetenos!" Kasai stood face-level to the Great Monk and shook him with more urgency. Aetenos's exposed skin was ashen beneath a pattern of nasty bruises and angry welts. Dried blood was caked like frozen mud across his beaten body.

"Is he dead?" Desdemonia said. She was out of breath when she joined Kasai. Pallo was close behind. Both slowly came to a stop as they saw the lifeless condition of the Great Monk. Desdemonia put her hand on Aetenos's outstretched wrist, searching for life. She stepped back quickly in alarm. "He's so cold." She cast a spell, and a blue swirl of magic wrapped around Aetenos's body but dissipated in the wind. "Something is blocking me."

Aetenos's head hung heavy on his chest. Kasai heard a slight moan and gently lifted his head. A hollow pit where one eye had been destroyed, gaped hauntingly at him. The other eye was closed, sealed tight with frozen mucus. Run-Run, Airis, and Orin kept back and formed a perimeter around the party to guard against attack. They each glanced back at the crucified monk and exchanged anxious looks with one another.

Heal him! Ninziz-zida shouted in Kasai's mind.

"I don't know how," Kasai said. The others looked at him questioningly.

Quickly!

Kasai didn't think. He reacted to Ninziz-zida's command and instinctively placed his hand on Aetenos's chest, above his heart.

Give, and the Boundless will share the same.

Somehow, even with all he had forgotten since entering Gathos, Kasai remembered the image of a tall oak tree and a little boy crying at its roots. The boy had fallen from a high branch and held his ankle tightly. He looked up through watery eyes to see his mother kneeling down in front of him. She wrapped his ankle with some clean bandages and then hugged him close. An incredible feeling of love and care washed over Kasai, and he channeled that warmth into Aetenos.

Aetenos stirred. He let out a long moan, and his head swayed from side-to-side. Kasai stepped back as a faint light radiated from Aetenos's body, and the membrane of frost that previously coated him sloughed off. The whiteness of his skin took on a rosier complexion.

Kasai wiped away the mucus covering Aetenos's remaining eye. The eyelid fluttered open, and he looked in one direction and then the next. Aetenos examined each of them suspiciously. Then he dropped his head back to his chest.

"Haunt me no more, demons. Your cruel work is complete. I am undone."

"Master Aetenos. I am Kasai." Aetenos did not raise his head. Kasai scanned the trappings that bound Aetenos, searching for a way to release his from the criss-crossed beams. He was horrified to see the steel bolts nailed into Aetenos's flesh.

"Begone demon. Leave me to my sorrow," Aetenos whispered in resignation.

Kasai backed away from Aetenos. He glanced at Desdemonia, hoping she would know what to do.

"Kasai, try again!" Desdemonia implored him. "He has become lost in his mind. Help him find his way back."

Kasai nodded, searching for something to jar Aetenos from his delirium. "Master, it's Kasai, from Ordu, the mountain monastery. You called to me. I am...your Ever Hero." Kasai felt awkward saying the words. Aetenos slowly raised his head and focused on Kasai. A broad grin expanded across his face.

"Ah, it is you. I knew you would find a way," Aetenos said with a sigh of relief.

"Help me get him down!" Kasai called to the others. Pallo cut the straps that bound Aetenos, but the bolts were another matter. Airis, Orin, and Run-Run carefully removed Aetenos from the X-shaped cross, firmly pulling his arms free and then his legs. It was a painful process. They helped him to the ground while Desdemonia rummaged through a supply bag. She found some clean bandages and wrapped them around Aetenos's wounds and covered the open eye socket of his damaged eye.

"You are still very hurt," she said, scrutinizing Aetenos's tortured body.

"But better now than before," Aetenos said with a genuine smile. He stood on his own and stretched as if he had just woken from a long sleep. Kasai was filled with awe and relief.

"Come here, all of you. There is much we must discuss," Aetenos said. The group came in closer to listen to the Great Monk's urgent orders.

"Illyria needs me! She is imprisoned in the deepest dungeons of Furia Keep. Come with me, Ever Hero, help me save my beloved!" Aetenos took a step but sank to one knee on the next. "Perhaps a bit of a rest first, then."

The Kibo Gensai lowered themselves to the ground beside Aetenos. They each bowed their head to the snow in reverence.

"The Light of Aetenos protects," Pallo said.

"And shall guide me through the darkness of my fears," Airis and Orin completed the simple prayer in unison.

"Up! Up! Stand, my new friends. The ground is hard and cold," Aetenos implored the Kibo Gensai as he raised himself, albeit on wobbly legs. He waved his hands in a sweeping fashion for the Kibo Gensai to follow, but the warriors did not rise.

Aetenos looked concerned. "What are you doing down there?" Aetenos crouched back to the ground and began searching around in the crusty snow. "Did you lose something? Is it shiny?"

"We are humbled in your presence, Great One," Pallo said with his head only slightly raised from the snow.

"Huh? What's this? Nothing lost?" Aetenos kneeled in the snow, his body upright and hands on his hips. His expression was perplexed. "Where am I? Why am I kneeling in the snow?" Aetenos looked closely at Kasai and the others as if seeing them for the first time. "Who are you people?"

"Master Aetenos?" Kasai said worriedly.

Aetenos pointed his finger at Kasai. "You. I know you…don't I?" Aetenos squinted his one eye at Kasai to see him more clearly. "It's so hard to remember anything here." He looked at the bandages on his wrists. "What's happened here?" He then saw the empty X beams. "Oh, that's a nasty looking thing."

The Kibo Gensai continued to prostrate themselves before the Great Monk. "We have searched for the Light for many years, Great One. We have finally found you." Orin spoke as if he was unworthy to utter the words.

"Oh, balderdash. Get up, you fools and stop your groveling."

Aetenos pointed to the remains of the smoking demons. His expression turned sour, and he scrunched up his nose. "They stink." He looked about as if searching his mind for answers.

"Did the Immortal Mother send you? Is that why I'm kneeling in the snow? Was I groveling?"

The Kibo Gensai rose, and all took an awkward step back in the snow, looking confused and fearful. Aetenos rose and approached Kasai. "I don't suppose you have another one of those warm furs I could wear. It's quite chilly out here." The Great Monk wore a sheepish smile and wrapped his arms around his naked chest, acting to ward off the cold.

"Yes, of course, Master Aetenos." Kasai dug through a spare pack and gave Aetenos the grey molachuk fur that would have been Rafar's, had he still lived and made the journey to Gathos. Kasai felt a massive weight leave his shoulders. Finally, they had found the demigod. Illyria would call for them, and Aetenos would fix everything.

He had fulfilled his promise. Now a real hero could save them, and he could go back to his peaceful life. First, he would rebuild Ordu in memory of his dead Brothers. Then maybe even join Des in her forest for a time.

"Master, your Light has never been needed more. You must stop Sekka."

Aetenos paused as if unsure who Kasai spoke of or what it meant. Then, realization sprung to his face. "Oh, no, no, no. That old devil, Sekka, is your concern, not mine." He repeatedly poked Kasai in the chest.

"Me?"

"You are the Ever Hero, after all." The Great Monk gave Kasai a wink. "I have other matters to attend. I must save my beloved. You are all welcome to join me, of course. It has been an age since I have had any decent company."

Aetenos looked all around as if trying to get his bearings. "Now, could one of you point me in the direction of Furia Keep?"

Aetenos looked to Kasai and then Desdemonia for input. Kasai saw the blank expression on Desdemonia's face and felt his own must be a mirror of disbelief.

"No?" Aetenos said, then addressed the Kibo Gensai with his hands on his hips. "What about you, lads? Ideas? Come now, it's cold out here, and we had best get a move on."

Airis slowly raised his hand and pointed behind Aetenos. "Is that it?"

"Ah, there's a clever boy. That's it, indeed."

Kasai's heart sank. None of this was what he had expected. "Master, I can't defeat Sekka alone. I tried once and look at the results." His eyes went to the festering Chaos Gate.

Aetenos gazed at the portal and nodded his head in understanding. His face grew somber when he saw the trampled bodies surrounding it.

"The Immortal Mother knows best. The design of her eternal tapestry is mysterious and grand. All will be revealed, in its own time."

Aetenos spoke in barely a whisper as if he remembered something vague and lost, but somehow Kasai heard his words. Desdemonia moved closer to Kasai.

"What is he saying? Does he know a better way back? We should keep moving. There are bound to be other, more dangerous things along soon," she said.

"Oh, hello there," Aetenos said in a sing-song voice. He bowed deeply to Desdemonia as if seeing her for the first time. "We have not been formally introduced. I am Aetenos Sommai." Aetenos looked mildly disappointed at Kasai. "Ever Hero, where are your manners?"

Desdemonia bowed to Aetenos in a formal greeting. "I am Desdemonia Mishi, from the village of Shryse, south of the Sarribe Pass. It is an honor to meet you, Master Aetenos."

"Shryse, Shryse, hmm," Aetenos thought for a moment, then, "You are Sunnese!" Aetenos exclaimed in a proud voice as if he had solved a great riddle. Desdemonia shot a puzzling look at Kasai.

"Yes, Master Aetenos, I am from Sunne." She then became more insistent. "Do you know a way back to Baroqia? Will we be traveling through the Chaos Gate? Time grows short." She looked around the barren tundra, wary of the approach of enemies.

Aetenos was perplexed. "You don't need me. The Ever Hero walks with you." Aetenos grabbed a generous handful of Kasai's shoulder and squeezed with brotherly familiarity. "He knows what to do. He shall guide you home." Aetenos looked into

Kasai's eyes and nodded, searching for understanding and agreement. Kasai slowly nodded back, although he had no idea why.

"See? There, it's settled." Aetenos once again wore a broad grin, as if everything was now just as it was supposed to be.

The companions stood like lifeless statues in the cold wind. Kasai couldn't believe what he was hearing. He wondered if this really was Aetenos or just another elaborate hallucination.

"My new friends, I thank you for your help. I feel just like a youngster! I hope to repay you in full one day, but for now I bid you good day," Aetenos said. He turned and headed in the direction of the lone tower, whistling a cheerful tune. The Kibo Gensai joined Kasai and Desdemonia.

"What is happening? Where does Master Aetenos go?" Airis said. His eyes were wide with nervous anguish. "Why does he not stay to save us?"

"Does he mean for us to follow? Does he show a different way home?" Orin said next. His eyes darted to the Chaos Gate and then to the departing monk. The two young warriors looked to Kasai for answers. Kasai stood dumbfounded for a long moment then bounded after the Great Monk.

"Master, wait! That tower, you called it Furia Keep. It's Sekka's lair, isn't it?" Kasai caught up to Aetenos. He took hold of a bunch of the Great Monk's molachuk coat to stop him but unhanded it quickly.

Aetenos stopped and gave Kasai a friendly backhanded flick on his chest. "You know the landmarks of Gathos well. Have you come to join me?"

Aetenos seemed to remember some event and chuckled to himself. Then his expression turned grim. "I must rescue Illyria."

He pointed his thumb over his shoulder to the Chaos Gate. "Back there is your way home. Just say the magic words and enjoy the ride."

Aetenos resumed walking towards the tower.

"Master Aetenos, Illyria is in Baroqia, and awaiting our return. She was the one who sent us!" Kasai shouted over the wind. But Aetenos kept walking. Kasai ran to him again.

"Stop, stop! There is only sorrow where you go."

"Baroqia? Nonsense. Illyria is in there." Aetenos gave a quick nod in the direction of Furia Keep. "And there is where I go." He picked up his pace and marched purposefully to the tower.

Kasai raced ahead of Aetenos and stood in front of him, blocking his way. "Master, it was Illyria who sent us to you, by what means, I am unsure. She insisted we rescue you." Kasai looked back to the others to join him. His companions came fast. Desdemonia seemed baffled by the demigod, while the others just stared in silent uncertainty.

Aetenos tilted his head slightly as if waiting to hear more, but Kasai remained silent.

"And you have, my young friend. You have fulfilled your promise. See? You rescued me. I am free." Aetenos opened his arms wide as if to prove he was no longer bound. "Wait, did I not thank you sufficiently?" Aetenos looked questioningly at Desdemonia. "Did I not?"

"Yes, Master Aetenos, you did thank us," Desdemonia replied, a bit exasperated.

"Perfect! You have fulfilled your promise, and I have thanked you for your deed. All is balanced, and I shall be on my way."

Aetenos hummed a happy tune as he walked around Kasai.

"He is not well. He's lost his mind and cannot help us," Desdemonia said, shaking her head. Kasai thought the same.

"Do not speak of what you do not know!" Orin shot back with surprising rage.

"Orin, I meant no disrespect. You heard him as well as I. It's as if the plight of mortals no longer concerns him."

Orin turned quickly on Desdemonia. His short sword was in his hand and raised at her throat. "Take it back, witch, or I will slice you!" Orin's entire body shook, and tears quickly froze as they tried to roll down his cheeks. The long and arduous journey had broken the young man's spirit.

Desdemonia jumped back, and her eyes flared bright amber. Vermillion glowing runes rose from her back and swirled in the air behind her. Orange fire coalesced in her hands.

"Orin put the sword away, or I will hurt you," Desdemonia said in a tone more menacing than Kasai had ever heard.

"Des! Stop!" Kasai jumped in front of Desdemonia. "Pallo! Get Orin under control!"

Pallo quickly had a hand on Orin's sword arm and pushed him away from Desdemonia.

"She's cast a spell on him! You all saw it. Aetenos is not himself due to her dark magic!" Orin cried out.

Kasai heard Orin, but his eyes were on Desdemonia. "Des! Calm down! What are you thinking?"

He searched Desdemonia's burning eyes for answers. Then, her body relaxed. "I... I don't know. I just reacted." She took a deep breath. "I'm fine now. My magic is stronger here, much stronger than in our realm. It's eager to flow and difficult to control."

"I don't understand, Des. Your magic comes from the living energy of the forest. There is nothing alive here." Kasai looked all around. "Nothing."

"Elemenati magic flows directly from the elements of nature, and chaos is the spark that sets nature in motion. In its purest form, the destructive force of chaos creates the building blocks of new life."

Kasai was confused. He had thought he had learned much of the world from the books and scrolls at Ordu, but it appeared he was grossly mistaken. He opened his mouth to say as much, but she continued before he could speak. "Think of rain. Does it fall in the same pattern, drop-after-drop? No, of course not. But does the water bring life to the forest? Yes. It is essential.

"Well, here, in this place of pure chaos, each raindrop is filled with the means to create oceans of life, however random."

"Ever Hero, should we follow?" Pallo interrupted. Kasai saw the worry in the older man's eyes.

"Aetenos is abandoning us." Airis's voice quivered with fear, and his shoulders slumped with defeat.

"We'll be trapped here," Orin said. He had regained some of his composure, but his mood was still hostile.

Kasai knew everyone was counting on him to lead them to safety. He peered at the Chaos Gate with reservation.

"Aetenos said to use the Chaos Gate, but I do not know any magic words to activate it, or how it works. Des?"

She shook her head. Where is Illyria, Kasai wondered? He concentrated on her image and called to her in his mind. Nothing. Kasai heard only the howling wind. He looked to see what progress Aetenos had made in reaching the tower. They could still catch him if they hurried. What choice did they have but to follow the Great Monk?

Aetenos stopped abruptly and turned in the snow, back towards the companions. The Great Monk shouted something over the swirling winds and waved to the party to catch up.

"I think he means for us to follow," Pallo said.

"Let's go. Master Aetenos is still the key. We need to help him regain his identity," Kasai said and looked specifically at Orin. "He needs all of us."

"Yes, Ever Hero. Forgive me. I misspoke," Orin said, then bowed to Desdemonia.

"There will be time for apologies later, Orin," she said with a bit of a hard smile. "Now, we must catch ourselves a wayward monk! The first one to the demigod wins the prize!" And she ran after Aetenos.

Kasai was next, followed by the others. He tried his best to remain calm, even though the situation had worsened as the towering height of Furia Keep loomed overhead.

39

SEKKA

Sekka stood at the edge of a great bowl-depression of ice. She eyed the bounty before her with human eyes and a well-deserved sense of satisfaction. Her planning and scheming had borne its first delicious fruit. A thousand living humans stared up at Sekka as her alabaster hair whipped madly in the turbulent winds of Gathos.

The archdevil was clad in a formfitting bodice and leggings made from the skins of slaves. The organic material had been dyed indigo with thick stitching of black leather, which stood in stark contrast to her billowing, white tresses. Black sigils of abyssal power danced and mingled within the pale strands of her hair like playful birds.

Aeshmara stood rigid to her right, wearing her soft hunting armor. The tanned leather was the color of dark gold and deep rose. Arcane runes of protection graced its worn surface. Her hands idly caressed the handles of her double-bladed daggers. The Vyzyn warlord and youngest sister of the brood had been commanded by Sekka to ensure the flow of souls to Gathos was uninterrupted.

"This is a promising start. The suffering of a thousand souls shall be a welcome addition to the ranks of my Frost Legion," Sekka mused. Aeshmara nodded at the recognition.

"My Queen, the humans were easily corralled, and many came willingly, thinking greater plunder awaited them."

Sekka hungrily gazed down at the first bounty brought thru the Chaos Gate. They were members of the northern barbarian tribes, who had rallied under the war banner of Maugris. The barbarians were promised slaves and riches in return for their swords and spears against the King's Army of Baroqia. Those who were not killed in battle or by her demon horde after the fall of Oziax had fled the battlefield but remained to loot the poor border villages before returning home. That was where Aeshmara's soul hunters had captured them. It was an easy march back through the ruins of Rachlach Fortress and to the living portal of the Chaos Gate.

The humans huddled tightly together, shivering in their spiked armor and war helms, which sprouted curled animal horns. The thick furs they wore did nothing to protect them from the frigid cold of fear. The bravado the barbarians once exhibited on the battlefield surrounded by demon allies had turned to numbing terror. Even still, some bowed in acquiescence and reverence to their goddess. Good, she thought. Suffering came in many different forms, and she could use them all.

"You see, Aeshmara, love and fear are the same. As the Immortal Mother is fond of saying, the balance must remain."

Aeshmara remained stoic, her stormy eyes stared unblinking at the mass of captives.

"Bring up the orthods," Sekka called out to her beast handlers farther back from the edge of the pit. Cruel forms slithered and skittered across the ice on stubby, talon-shaped appendages, extending from the sides of their bodies. The handlers viciously poked at the giant grub's ridged and bloated thoraxes, directing the sluggish creatures into position around the rim of the depression.

The orthods' upper bodies were fashioned like a mantis from the Mortal Realm. Each of the demons had a pair of three-sectioned arms encased in a hard shell. Where the end section folded back over the middle, it resembled serrated scissors, which opened and closed menacingly in the cold air. Their heads were shaped like triangular helmets composed of overlapping, plated shells, ending in a stubbed beak for a mouth.

The beast handlers eagerly awaited Sekka's orders as the orthods cooed and screeched in anticipation of their feast.

"Aeshmara, you have done well. You were thoughtful to bring me an early taste of victory from the Mortal Realm. I am pleased with the rich bounty before me. But I must have more, much more."

"You honor me, my Mistress. I wished to present the first harvest to you myself. Dai-Ko-Zior, scours the land leading to the mountain pass of Sunne. I suspect when I return to him, he will have more human souls to add to your banquet."

"You are a clever opportunist."

Aeshmara bowed. "I wish only to serve the great Sekka and dare to hope she sees value in my deeds."

Sekka was not fooled by the pleasantries or professed loyalties of Aeshmara. The warlord was as cunning as she was deadly. "The Sarribe Pass must remain open. I suspect treachery soon from our allies in Baroqia. If the pass falls, I shall hold you and your warlock brother personally responsible. I must have unfettered access to Sunne. Is that clear?" Sekka's eyes bore into Aeshmara's.

"That sulking and brooding brother of mine shall be more than capable of holding the pass. His magic is strong. The soul harvest will not cease," Aeshmara said with a clear understanding of Sekka's unveiled threat.

"Ensure that it does not. Your existence depends on it," Sekka said.

"Yes, my Mistress. I shall return to supervise the next harvest."

"Hold for a moment. Let us enjoy the suffering of your diligent work." Sekka gave a slight nod to the lead beast handler, who yelled out a command to his group. The orthods along the rim of the wide depression slid down the slick surface.

The giant, malformed demons barreled into the barbarians with their bulbous bodies and chiton-plated limbs. Sharp, scythe-like appendages swept through the air, slicing and cleaving human flesh. Heads, arms, and legs tumbled through the air. Red mist rose from the depression as the screams of the captives added to the swirling howls of the barren environment.

Sekka could feel the raw power coursing through her blood as her infernal body soaked up the soul energy of the dead and dying. The black sigils dancing about her hair swirled like a cyclone above her head. A sigh of bliss escaped her full, blue lips.

"Lord Oziax!" Sekka called to her revived warlord. "Tell me, why is Zizphander still a thorn in my side?"

Aeshmara chuckled beneath her breath at the slight to the once esteemed warlord's pride. Oziax's coarse hair bristled over his human form as the demon lord walked to the edge of the pit and stood to the left of Sekka. He was in human form and dressed in thin, bleached-white armor composed of the bones of his defeated enemies. He glared menacingly at Aeshmara.

"My Queen, as we have discussed, the upstart Zizphander has aligned himself to a Shadow Patron, who swells the ranks of his armies and grants him clandestine passage through the Abyss."

"And who is this mysterious and most beneficial Shadow Patron that aids my foes and thwarts my plans?" Sekka's voice dripped with soft kindness as if she was coddling a child.

"I do not know."

"WHY NOT?" her voice boomed over the screaming and dying barbarians. The orthods had begun to feast in earnest on the mayhem they had wrought. "Why have you not unraveled this simple riddle for me? Have I not granted you every opportunity to redeem yourself?"

"Yes, my Queen." Oziax dropped to a knee and bowed before Sekka. "Allow me to lead your new host and stop Zizphander. He shall never reach Furia Keep."

"Ah, at long last, the mighty Oziax grovels for forgiveness and favor," Aeshmara laughed out the words.

"You dare!" Oziax growled.

"Aeshmara please, it is not becoming of you to tease. Leave poor Oziax alone. He has suffered much," Sekka said in a playful tone. Her words were a honey-coated bee sting.

"I am sorry, my Mistress." The Vyzyn addressed Lord Oziax directly. "I apologize for my hard words. But tell me, Lord Oziax, where is the boy who so easily took your head? I should like to congratulate him on such an impressive victory."

Oziax stood in a flash and throttled Aeshmara with his powerful hands. He raised her off the ground and held her in the air. "Your existence ends now!"

Aeshmara remained unfazed. She held both her double-daggers at Oziax's neck, their blades already drawing blood. "Release me now or lose your head a second time," Aeshmara threatened through clenched teeth.

"Oziax! Release her," Sekka commanded. Oziax dropped Aeshmara to the ground. She landed like a cat, ready to strike again if necessary.

"Now, if you are finished, I would like to hear your assessment of our remaining troops here on Gathos, and what should be added from the soul energy of our barbarian guests?"

Oziax regained his composure and turned to Sekka. He ignored the blood flowing down his neck and rolling down the bones of his white armor. "My Queen, Zizphander has amassed a great horde, but it is stocked with inferior soldiers. Minor fire demons and ash fiends make up the bulk of his ranks. He uses their vast numbers to overwhelm those who stand in his way. They would fall against a great behemoth of the ice." Lord Oziax bowed. "I will march out with the might of a mountain and destroy the upstart once and for all."

"Aeshmara, what is your opinion of Lord Oziax's strategy?"

"While a single behemoth is of great power, it is slow and dimwitted. A division of Zizphander's horde can easily preoccupy it while the rest of his troops flank its sides and continue to Furia Keep. Lord Oziax's winner-takes-all strategy is short-sighted and ill-conceived. It is a poor attempt to regain his lost prominence in your eyes. You will need to strike with speed and precision, at the most vulnerable points of the foe's army to cripple the advance of his troops. This will provide the time necessary to replenish the Frost Legion."

"I agree with your assessment, Aeshmara. You show promise as a keen strategist and powerful addition to the Frost Legion. Perhaps even as its new General."

"My Queen!" Oziax appeared stunned. "I must lead the Frost Legion, as I have done for millennia."

"You shall remain outside the tower and supervise the flow of mortals into the orthod pits."

"I am wasted there!"

"Nonetheless, you shall do what you are told. My sentries will continue to harry Zizphander and delay the approach of his army. I will crush him once I have accumulated sufficient might."

"Gathos will burn. We will be trapped when Zizphander reaches Furia Keep!"

"SILENCE!" Sekka struck Oziax with such force that the demon lord fell to the ground. "Do not question me again. Your past service to me is all that keeps you from joining the barbarians in the pit."

Aeshmara burst into a fit of condescending laughter. "What hope do you think you have against Zizphander when you were bested by a single, mortal child?" Aeshmara smirked with a wicked grin. "You reek of failure."

Oziax shook with rage as he turned to confront Aeshmara. "You Vyzyn are vermin scurrying for the small scraps of my achievements! You and your miserable siblings. Each of you less trustworthy than the next. My Queen, grant me my request and let me destroy this pretender!"

"Do not presume to threaten me, Oziax. Your time as the Queen's Champion has ended. The Warlords of Vyzyn shall usher in a new age of dominance in Gathos, and beyond. You are a relic from the past. You are unneeded and unnecessary."

"I shall hear no more of this bickering," Sekka said. "Lord Oziax, prepare the remainder of the Frost Legion. When you are not feeding the orthod pit, you shall protect the Chaos Gate at all costs."

She could sense the demon lord's fury. It mattered not to her. She had stretched her influence far and thinned her legions across much of the Abyss. She had meticulously calculated the number of troops she would need to hold off Zizphander until more human souls could be harvested. There would be just enough.

"Mistress, has the thought occurred to you that Zizphander knew of your plans for the Chaos Gate, long before its creation?" Aeshmara said.

"Impossible! You are sadly mistaken," Oziax scoffed.

"Few knew of such plans," Sekka agreed. "Lord Oziax and me from Gathos and... Maugris."

But Zizphander had plagued her well before the arrival of the Great Monk. The

Red Devil was settling an old score, nothing more. An unnerving thought crossed her mind. Could Maugris have contacted another archdevil, or a higher power out of frustration when she refused him? Information of this nature was a valuable currency in the Abyss.

Sekka turned her attention back to the pit. The beast handlers had removed the orthods, and it was time to release the soul energy she had collected. Her open hands caressed the air, while her fingers traced delicate patterns above the bits and pieces of cleaved flesh and broken armor in the pit.

Large piles of debris coalesced into odd forms comprised of multiple limbs and protruding horns and spikes. Hulking flesh golems rose from the charnel remains of the pit. The golems no longer resembled the individual humans they had once been, for now they were an amalgamation of armor, horns, fur, and flesh. Eyes opened, and teeth chattered in random locations across their bodies.

"That should be enough to ward off Zizphander if he attempts to storm the Keep. Our walls are strong and easily manned. Lord Oziax, take them to the tower's outer gate and hold there until I give further instruction."

"I will triple our efforts in the Mortal Realm and have a swift return," Aeshmara proclaimed. "My Mistress, with your leave, I shall depart."

Sekka waved her away. Her thoughts drifted to the dungeons buried deep in Furia Keep. The time had come to finally solve the riddle of Zizphander's Shadow Patron.

Sekka entered Maugris's dank prison cell. The once-powerful sorcerer wedged himself into the corner of the small room. He was collared by an iron band connected to a thick chain, which continued through the ice floor. His arms were bound behind his back by rough ropes that bit into his pallid skin.

A gag and full mouthpiece prevented him from speaking. It was merely a precaution against any spells he may have hidden away before she had made him her prisoner on Gathos. He was known for his cunning contingency plans.

Sekka looked down at the frail man and sighed with contentment. Maugris flinched at the sight of her, but he quickly regained his haughty demeanor. He posed no threat to her now, especially here. She ripped the gag from his face.

His eyes were defiant and held an unwillingness to accept he had been duped. Sekka laughed to herself. Such were the shortcomings of mortals.

"Chedipe tells me you heal quickly, even after her most savage attentions. You have quite an impressive constitution."

"Get out," Maugris said as if he still ruled over her actions. But his commanding attitude was short-lived. He turned away, deflated.

"You often spoke of Zizphander in Rachlach Fortress," Sekka spoke in a casual and friendly manner. She toyed with a loose chain hanging from the wall, stroking its length and then lightly swinging it to the side. "Did the Red Devil ever answer your call?"

Maugris laughed. "What's this, now? Do you come for tea? You should have killed me long ago. Every day I am alive is another day I plot my revenge. It will be me that delivers you to your doom."

"Surely. I would expect no less. Now, tell me of your conversations," she said and bent down and traced her long nails up and across Maugris's face, stopping just before his eye. Her fingernail drew blood from his lower eyelid. His arrogance was always a blind weakness, and she hoped he would take the bait.

"What is there to say that you don't already know? The Red Devil comes and comes fast. Soon, Furia Keep shall burn, and all of Gathos will melt beneath the inferno of his rage."

"He has not the might of arms to storm my Keep. My defenses are too strong within the tower. The brash upstart knows this and will not engage me directly, not here."

"The Red Devil is not alone!" Maugris glared defiantly into her eyes and then chuckled with satisfaction. "And you still do not know."

Sekka's hunch proved accurate. Maugris had been in contact with other powerful denizens of the Abyss. Whether he spoke directly to Zizphander or lesser demons willing to divulge their secrets was unknown. It was clear he had information that her spies and sentries could not provide.

"I realize I may have underestimated you and offer you a bargain of sorts."

"What game do you play with me?"

"You shall tell me everything you know and, if it proves worthy of my interest, I will release you from your pain."

Maugris gazed at Sekka with uncertainly, then he burst out laughing. "You will then kill me!"

"If that is your wish. Or perhaps I can find a place for you in the Frost Legion. A mage of your talent is not carelessly thrown away."

Maugris stopped laughing. He stared silent daggers back at her. His silence spoke of a fear Sekka had felt with increasing unease. A more sinister game was afoot and willingly or not, she was a playing piece moved by another's hand.

Just then, she received a mental message from a sentry posted on the outskirts of the Wasteland of Thresh. She turned away from the penetrating eyes of Maugris.

"What do you mean the flesh golems are gone? Gone where?" Sekka mistakenly spoke aloud, into the air.

+My Queen, Lord Oziax took the recruits through the gates of the tower. He marched across the Wastelands to confront Zizphander.+

+All of them?+

+Yes, my Queen.+

Sekka turned her thoughts to Lord Oziax. Her rage boiled. +Oziax! What have you done? Answer me!+

There was only silence. Sekka focused her will into the mind of Oziax and established a connection. She saw the blurry terrain through Oziax's eyes. Pale, bone-armored boots stomped hurriedly on the white ground. She heard labored breathing over the crunching snow.

She forced Oziax's head to swivel around and take in more of his surroundings. The new golem horde had been decimated. What few numbers remained, raced back to Furia Keep in full retreat. Sekka could only assume Zizphander's horde was close behind and would soon overtake them.

Sekka felt Maugris's eyes on her. He wore a smug grin. "You are already doomed," Maugris said. He slid back against the wall. "Doomed."

40

KASAI

Kasai, Des, and the others took a momentary break to catch their breath before they resumed chasing after Aetenos. A sharp, wind-swept flurry of snow blew across the smooth surface of the lake of ice before them. Aetenos had not hesitated to cross and bounded forward with great haste.

The demigod ran like a man sprinting the last league of a grueling marathon, obsessed as he was with reaching Furia Keep. His pace was locked, but his steps occasionally faltered on his unsure and exhausted footing.

"His strength is returning," Pallo commented between deep gulps of air. His body folded forward with his hands on his knees, trying to catch his breath.

"Perhaps in body, but not in mind!" Airis said. He, too, was panting. "He races to Sekka's lair without care! Illyria is not there!" The young warrior stated aloud what everyone in the small party knew as well. "And we blindly follow."

"His memory will return. Until then, you will find your courage and complete the quest." Pallo tilted his head up to look Airis in the eyes. His tone was reprimanding yet patient.

"The Wood Witch was right. The Master is not well," Airis said to the group. Orin glared daggers at Airis and shook his head in disgust. "Do not listen to her, Airis. She is not one of us."

Airis's expression was grim. He turned to each of them and then grabbed Kasai by the arm to make his point. His eyes were wide and wild. "We will not survive this."

Kasai understood how he felt. Fear soaked through everything here. It was thick and suffocating and coiled around his spine. Kasai felt it in cold, prickly sweat that formed between his skin and clothing he wore.

The Kibo Gensai were just men relying on their faith to sustain them through such an insane trial. Desdemonia had no such conviction. She relied on her magic, at least that was the act she was playing. Kasai observed the vibrant greens of her aura fading to sickly, dirty-yellow hues.

His companions had come willingly on this quest; however, none of them could have known what to expect or the despair that awaited them on Gathos. He had to find a way to pierce the thick fog clouding Aetenos's mind, or they would all go mad. Kasai could talk some sense into him if he would just stay still long enough.

Kasai peered into the distance. Aetenos had pulled farther ahead of the group.

"Come, we must not dally for too long, or we will lose the Master to the snow."

Kasai and the others ran across the lake in pursuit of Aetenos. Up ahead, he noticed blurry shapes moving erratically at the frozen lake's surface. They all slowed their pace when they saw the exposed bodies held fast in the ice. Some were trapped at the waist and twisted one way and then the next, trying to escape, others were submerged up to their heads or higher. A few had managed to free their bodies but could not unlock their feet from the ice. They frantically pounded on the ice's surface, hoping it might break.

Small, hair-covered wardens with stubby arms and legs held long poles ending in trident points. The dwarf-like creatures stabbed at the flailing bodies until other, larger fiends came by and dropped a glowing yellow orb onto the ice next to the condemned soul. Relief turned to dismay as the ice around the victim turned to slush, and the condemned soul sank deeper into the frigid water. Then the slush froze, trapping the soul anew.

Aetenos raced past them, scurrying the wardens out of his way. Kasai was shocked the demigod did nothing to help the suffering souls trapped in the ice. But what was there to do? These souls were here for a reason, weren't they?

Kasai surveyed the ground carefully for fear of tripping over the heads locked in the ice. He jumped over a group of souls frozen up to their noses. They stared wide-eyed as he and his companions ran past. They zigzagged past the bodies whose chests were above the ice and reached for them with their grabbing hands. Dark-colored eels slithering below the ice's surface and gorged themselves on the souls' submerged flesh. The condemned screamed in agony unless their mouths were frozen under the ice.

Aetenos had stopped and appeared unsure of his surroundings. He spun slowly to the right, took a few steps, and then turned to the left. Furia Keep loomed menacingly in the near distance but seemed invisible to Aetenos.

"Master Aetenos?" Kasai said between breaths when he was close enough to be heard.

Aetenos turned, and his one eye squinted at Kasai with suspicion until recognition returned. "Ah, it's you again. Hello."

The others caught up and gathered around.

"Are these your friends?" Aetenos nodded to each of Kasai's companions, and he bowed to Desdemonia. "Hello, I am Aetenos Sommai. May I assist you in any way?"

Desdemonia looked questioningly at Kasai before she gave a short bow in return. "Hello, Master Aetenos. I am Desdemonia."

"Well met, Desdemonia. You look familiar. Have we met? It's doubtful I would forget a beauty such as yours."

Aetenos curiously raised his eyebrow, waiting for an answer. When none came, he casually looked about until he saw Furia Keep. "That's odd. When did that get there?"

Aetenos put his index finger to his lips and remained in deep thought.

"Master Aetenos, who are these people? Why are they trapped here? Is there a way to save them?"

He looked at Kasai as if seeing him for the first time, and then realized he had been asked a question.

"Hum?"

"Can these people not be saved?"

Aetenos looked over the frozen lake, and the prisoners trapped there for eternity. His one eye saddened. "Oh, yes, I see. Well, no, they are beyond salvation. But worry not, they are no longer people as you see them, for their mortal bodies died long ago. They are phantoms now, residual consciousnesses of damned souls are all that remain. They suffer eternity being tormented by whatever punishment was sentenced to them for their actions in life."

"By the Light of Aetenos! What could they have done to deserve such torture until the end of all things?" Pallo said as he moved cautiously around a thrashing soul. He looked questioningly at Aetenos for an answer, not realizing the scripture he had just quoted in the demigod's name.

"And who is so worthy of condemning a soul for all eternity? Why has the Immortal Mother passed such judgment and punishment?" Desdemonia said with disapproval.

Run-Run exchanged a nervous glance with his brother. Airis and Orin mumble troubled words to each other and pressed two fingers to their respective foreheads.

"The Immortal Mother is above such actions. She is the creator of all things and holds all her children in the Great Balance. It is not her will that sentences these lost souls."

"Who then?" Desdemonia would not relent. "Who is so above the actions of all living beings and can judge them fairly? Whatever their transgressions, these souls have been forgotten, yet their torment endures."

"Ho, ho! I see you have passion in your heart!" Aetenos nudged Kasai in the side. "Her fire burns bright!"

"Des, maybe now is not the right time for this," Kasai said.

"There is always time for now," Aetenos said playfully.

Kasai remembered a time when Master Choejor had said the same thing to him. He wished Master Choejor was here now. He longed for his dead Master's advice.

"Master Aetenos, we must return to Baroqia. Illyria is there waiting for you. She is not on Gathos and not in the dungeons of Furia Keep," Kasai said.

"Furia Keep? Yes! My Illyria! Thank you for reminding me, my friend." Aetenos then darted forward and ran once more to Furia Keep.

"He still didn't answer me," Des said as she stomped past Kasai and ran after Aetenos.

It wasn't long before Aetenos reached the base of the tower. He peered over a snowdrift, assessing their next move. "I present to you the entrance to Furia Keep and the lair of Sekka of Gathos." He padded the air with his hand. "Best to speak in whispers. We don't want anyone to hear our secret plans."

Run-Run looked about and then signed questioningly to his brother with quick hands. Pallo shrugged his shoulders. "I know, Run-Run. There is no one about."

"Where are the guards? Or patrols? Or anything? Something is wrong here," Airis said, looking desperately at Kasai. "We are walking into a trap."

"We are already trapped, Airis, only on the outside," Orin said. "The ice and snow cover everything. If there is a door, it is not here."

"Master Aetenos, return with us to the Chaos Gate. Illyria waits for you in Baro-qia. Please, listen to reason. We were sent here to return you to her."

"Illyria?" Aetenos paused. "I knew an Illyria once. She was my special angel." He sat back heavy in the snowdrift. "It was so very long ago."

"Yes, Great One. She waits for you in Baroqia, south of the Hoarfrost Mountains. Come with us and be reunited," Orin pleaded.

Aetenos jumped to his feet. "I remember now! You are the Ever Hero!" Aetenos thrust his hand out for Kasai to take in partnership. "You must join me in rescuing my beloved! It shall be a grand quest worthy of the ages."

"Master Aetenos, Illyria is not there," Kasai spoke slowly and calmly.

A lower portion of the tower's surface broke away from the rest in an ear-shat-tering pop of ice. Kasai could now see the outline of two massive gates where moments before there were only stone and snow. Slowly the doors were pushed open from within by two hulking creatures covered in white fur.

"Look at the size of those beasts!" Airis exclaimed.

"Airis! Be still!" Pallo spoke in a hushed voice.

"They look like Tashi-Du bears from the upper reaches of Northern Trosk," Orin said in awe. Run-Run nodded with enthusiasm while putting his arms high up in the air for Pallo to see.

"Yes, Orin has the right of it," Pallo said.

"They are jol'goths," Aetenos said and counted two fingers on his hand. "Where are all the others hiding, I wonder? Hmm…"

Aetenos scuffled over to where Orin sat against the snowbank. "You see? One can always find a way, when one looks closely and has a bit of luck," Aetenos winked at Orin and turned to the rest of the group.

"Remove what is deemed impossible and search through what remains. There you will find the possible. Or is it the other way around?" Aetenos then stood straight up and shook the snow and ice from his molachuk fur. "Well then, my angel awaits."

"Master Aetenos! Please get down," Kasai grabbed him by his coat and hauled him down. The Great Monk was like an unaware child, who thought everything was a toy to play with or examine without pause or concern.

A war song bellowed from inside the tower. The Kibo Gensai pressed in close to the snowbank, and Desdemonia crouched down next to Kasai. Master Aetenos squatted down as well, mimicking the others for fun. There was mischief in his one remaining eye as it darted back and forth and an eager smile across his face.

"What do you think is coming out of that gate?" Aetenos said with excited wonder. Kasai couldn't tell if he was asking because he was ready to do battle or just enjoying the surprise.

Kasai sighed. He remembered how Master Choejor spoke with such calm ease during their escape from Ordu. Never once did Master Choejor show fear or worry while fleeing for their lives. Kasai wondered what it took to face danger with such tranquility.

"You remind me of Master Choejor."

"Who do you think taught that old rascal?" Aetenos made an exaggerated gesture of pointing his thumb at himself. "And Dorje and Kunchen, too."

"You taught the Three Masters of Ordu? But your Song has not been heard for over a hundred years." Kasai quickly regretted speaking so plainly; however, he wondered at the sanity of the Great Monk.

"Was I gone that long? It seemed like only a blink and a yawn," Aetenos said and shrugged his shoulders. "One must understand, time moves differently in each of the Three Realms."

"Is that why you were gone for so long? You simply lost track of time?" Airis said incredulously. "We endured so much suffering simply because you forget about us?"

Pallo cuffed the young warrior. "Airis! Know your place. Aetenos does not need to explain his actions to you."

Aetenos drifted off in a trance. "My message was heard on the late summer breezes and in the smell of the first winter snow. It could be felt in the cool spring thaw and seen as the colorful rain of Autumn leaves. I have always been close to those with open hearts and open minds."

Aetenos turned to Airis, and there was kindness in his voice when he spoke. "Do not feel angst, Airis. There is a natural flow to all things. No matter the hardship or the pain, the Immortal Mother keeps all in her perfect balance. All is as it should be, even now, for you."

Airis slumped into the snowdrift, looking more confused than when Aetenos first spoke.

"But you will set things right. You will restore the balance. Won't you?"

Aetenos pointed his finger repeatedly at Kasai. "Your answer is sitting right there, my young friend."

Airis looked away, clearly disappointed. His faith in Kasai was low. Orin moved closer to Airis and rested a reassuring hand on the young warrior's shoulder.

"It will be alright. You'll see."

Airis just looked away. His body shook beyond the effects of the cold. Even Desdemonia looked despondent as she gazed nervously towards the tower's open gates. Kasai knew he should say something to lift the spirits of his companions. But what was there to say?

Kasai's thoughts were interrupted by the sound of howls and deep drumbeats. A large quadruped and rider lumbered out from the open gates. Its body was covered in interlocking plates that resembled the hard shell of a river turtle. A viscous, metallic-green slime oozed out of crusty, fist-sized barnacles along its side, and flowed down the mount's long flanks. Its broad paws kicked up snow and ice as it plodded forward.

Six human slaves with arm-sized hooks dug into their backs and protruding out their chests, dangled from chains attached to six, long poles mounted on the beast's side. The slaves swung mercilessly against the steps of the lumbering mount, crying out in pain as the hooks ripped through their bodies.

The rider was covered in bone-like armor. His head was completely enclosed in a tall helm, graced by two twisted horns that reminded Kasai of the magnificent antlers of mountain forest stags. Behind the rider came creatures out of nightmares.

The flesh golems stood upright and slogged awkwardly on two legs. Their bodies were humanoid in appearance but twisted and corrupted by dark magic. Mismatched animal fur covered much of their bodies, but where it did not reach, their flesh was protected beneath random pieces of armor. Clusters of human eyes rolled in opposite directions and malformed mouths exposed chattering teeth.

The arms of the flesh golems ended in curled and serrated iron. Their weapons clanged together and added an eerie melody to the raucous march. The line of demons followed the antler-helmed rider out into the frozen wasteland.

The two jol'goths followed the procession past where Kasai and the others huddled against the snowbank. The brutes watched with indifference as the swirling winds and blinding snow consumed the war party.

"Ho, ho! Now's our chance. We can sneak in like little mice, hop, hop, hop," Aetenos said and moved his hands like small animals scurrying over the snow. "Ready?"

Kasai was not sure how to respond. He felt Ninziz-zida weigh heavy at his side. The ancient artifact pulsed a need into his mind. Kasai assumed the weapon wanted to stay with the Master, for only his divine might could fully unleash the vast potential of the ancient artifact.

"Master, wait. Forgive me for not mentioning this earlier. I have Ninziz-zida. I believe she wishes to return to you, and I would do so before we enter the tower."

Aetenos looked down at the weapon. "Ah, there's a pretty thing." His hands moved lovingly along the staff's three black segments. Vapors of heat radiated from the surface of the weapon in response to his touch.

Kasai sensed the deep connection between Ninziz-zida and Aetenos. It was a bond that would never be broken as if the two were two separate pieces made whole. Aetenos nodded once, and a smile came to his face. He then slowly pushed the weapon back towards Kasai.

"No, my son, she wishes to remain with you."

Kasai was dumbfounded. He looked down at Ninziz-zida and bowed in respect. The Fire Serpent blazed brightly in his hands. He wanted to believe he was worthy of such an honor. Then Aetenos clapped his hands together and hopped and danced behind the snowbank.

"Come! Come! The parade has finished, and it's our time to skitter and steal like mice beneath the lazy eyes of the sleepy cat!"

"Master, wait! We are just going to walk in the front entrance?" Kasai looked baffled.

"Why not? No one inside really expects visitors. It's getting out that will prove difficult."

Aetenos gave Kasai a knowing wink, then leaped over the snowbank and raced through the open doors of the tower gate.

"We're doomed," Airis said. He lay back in the snow, defeated.

"Nonsense. Up you go! The chase remains. The prize has doubled since we now know he's crazy," Desdemonia said in a cheery voice. She nodded in the direction of where Aetenos had disappeared inside Furia Keep, playfully elbowed Kasai in the arm. "Remind you of anyone?"

She laughed as she leaped over the snowbank, and followed Aetenos into the tower. Kasai shook his head in wonder. Just like that, the frolicking gypsy was back without a care in the world.

"She's an interesting one," Pallo said. His eyes looked to the tower with foreboding. "And fearless. Come, Ever Hero. We will need your strength."

Run-Run was already up, ready to follow Kasai's lead.

"She will ruin us all," Orin said.

Kasai looked down at Airis, who seemed to have sunk deeper into the snow.

"Airis, we must go."

"Why? We cannot hope to succeed. The witch is right, Aetenos has lost his mind."

"Airis!" Orin said. "Mind your tongue."

"I will not!"

"Airis, we will help him find his way back. You'll see," Kasai said. "But until we do, he will need your blades and your faith."

Airis stared at Kasai for a long moment. "Illyria chose you. I was there and saw it with my own eyes. My faith in Aetenos may be lost, but I will hold my faith with you."

Kasai extended his hand for Airis to grasp. Airis rose and brushed the snow from his clothing. "I follow the will of the Argent Hammer."

"Do not abandon hope, Airis, nor your faith in the Light. Both will keep you safe."

"Do you really think we will get home?"

"I don't know. But we must keep trying."

"Thank you, Ever Hero. Forgive me. Your courage will be my courage."

Kasai put his hand on Airis's shoulder and turned to Pallo, Orin, and Run-Run. "It's all any of us can do." He then leaped over the snowbank and followed after Aetenos and Desdemonia. The Kibo Gensai followed closely behind.

They soon regrouped and stayed close to the ice wall within the courtyard of the tower. Bodies of the condemned were encased in ice and frozen in grisly gestures, many with open mouths as if caught mid-scream before being frozen solid. Their bodies rose up the wall to unseen heights.

Kasai was astounded by the impossible size of the courtyard. The exterior of the tower could not possibly hold such a vast interior. The height of the tower seemed to extend forever. It was a world within a world.

"Master Aetenos, how will we find our way through such a place?" Kasai said as he craned his neck upwards.

Aetenos placed his hand on the back of Kasai's head and tilted it downward. "First, we look in the right direction. We go down."

"These statues look so lifelike," Airis said. He put his hand out to touch the nearest one.

"I wouldn't touch that if I were you," Aetenos said, and Airis quickly withdrew his hand.

"Orin, you and Airis will mind the entrance," Pallo said as he too looked curiously at the statues. "Run-Run, see if your keen eyes can help Master Aetenos in any way."

Run-Run nodded and sided up to Aetenos and Kasai.

"The statues look wet," Desdemonia said, and she backed away from the wall. "The ice is melting. Something is happening."

"We work quickly with slow and careful hands," Aetenos said and moved his hands along the wall, using his fingers to search along the cracks and fissures.

"Kasai, they're alive!" Desdemonia gasped.

"I told you not to touch them," Aetenos said.

The ice sloughed off the heads of bodies and slid down to the floor. The eyelids of the condemned flashed open and stared wide-eyed at the party. Then they screamed.

"Not good, not good," Pallo said as he and Run-Run drew their swords. The shrieking chorus of the damned grew louder as more of the condemned souls thawed from their frozen hibernation. Orin and Airis backed away quickly from the sides of the entrance and drew their weapons.

The jol'goths raced through the open doors and snarled with maws filled with gleaming, needle-shaped teeth. The wailing souls trapped in their icy shrouds turned their sorrowful cries to malicious and mocking laughter.

"Master Aetenos," Kasai said. He grabbed Ninziz-zida from his sash and held her three segments tightly together in one hand. Desdemonia conjured her magic, and the air smelled of Autumn's dry leaves and moist soil.

"It's here somewhere. I'm sure of it," Aetenos said and mumbled some other words Kasai could not understand.

"Master!" Kasai shouted.

"Hmm, yes?"

Aetenos looked over his shoulder at the approaching jol'goths. Their mangy fur bristled as pinkish snakes rose from their backs.

"Not so sneaky mice after all. See to them, would you? I really must concentrate." He waved away the jol'goths as if they were a simple nuisance and returned to feeling the surface of the wall. Before Kasai could say another word, the white-furred demons were upon them.

41

SEKKA

"**D**amn that impulsive fool!" Sekka stormed out of the cellblock. The words of Maugris echoed in her thoughts. *"You are already doomed."* She quickly calculated the remaining troops in Furia Keep and those that could be recalled in short notice from the frontiers. What did it matter? It was not enough. If Zizphander followed Oziax to Furia Keep, he could mount a significant siege, but more importantly, he would discover the Chaos Gate.

+Oziax! You are forbidden to return to the tower. You shall stay on the field and fight. You shall sacrifice your miserable life to stall the Red Devil.+

There was no mental reply, but the footsteps stopped abruptly in the snow. Then raced to a new location. Soon, the remaining flesh and iron golems joined him. All was silent.

Sekka sent her thought command to Sitrix, the eldest Vyzyn warlord mounting a campaign in the jungles of Sunne. The soul energy from the barbarian harvest was a dim light in comparison to the power she would receive from a harvest of the Sunnese. It should give her the edge she needed to hold Zizphander while she regained her strength.

+Sitrix, report.+ The connection was dead. She tried again, with more force. Still, nothing. Sekka reached out to his sister, the witch, Tazizu.

+Tazizu, answer me! What news from Sunne? Why does Sitrix refuse to answer my command?+

The existence of the Chaos Gate had magnified her ability to communicate with her minions in the Mortal Realm tenfold, but something was wrong. The wait was too long. Sekka focused her full concentration on Tazizu and finally picked up a faint mind-link.

+My Queen.+ Tazizu had responded through a garbled connection. Sekka could detect anger and much fear from the witch. *+There is powerful magic here. More than expected.+*

+Yes! Of Course! Why would I send two warlords if only one was needed?+ The connec-

tion went stale once more. Only the residual emotion of fear remained. Tazizu was in danger. A weak response touched Sekka's mind.

+We have encountered resistance. Not only from the mortals. There is something more here. Sitrix has fallen. I now lead the Frost Legion in retreat. Must regroup.+

+Sitrix has fallen?+ The weight of the words hit Sekka like a physical blow. She had mistakenly thought the eldest Vyzyn to be the strongest and would hold the horde together with the might of his presence. Tazizu was there to support Sitrix's advances with spell cover. She was no leader. *Oziax! I doubly curse you!* Command of the Frost Legion was Oziax's forte. He had earned the respect of her demon troops through countless battles over eons of fighting. His dominance was unquestioned.

+Ancient magic fills the jungle, older than mountains and seas. Send more, must have more. Great resistance. We are pressed and retreat.+

Sekka was furious.

+I must have those souls! Command the Frost Legion forward! Call upon your brother, Dai-Ko-Zior, for support. He holds the Sarribe Pass. Aeshmara returns.+

There was silence, and the connection became stale. Tazizu was resisting her advice.

+Tazizu! Do not fail me.+

+The will of Sekka be done.+

The link was gone, either by natural interference or from the will of Tazizu. Sekka brooded in anger. How could Fate betray her in such a cruel way? She had masterfully outwitted and overthrown her infernal rivals for power in the Abyss and rose to the lofty height of archdevil of an entire world. She had cunningly schemed against the power-hungry, yet dim-witted Maugris to grant her passage to the Mortal Realm, and masterfully manipulated the Great Monk to bring forth his next Ever Hero. Everything had fallen into place as she had planned. The creation of the Chaos Gate was her greatest triumph and would surely grant her an exalted seat at the table of power among the Great Three.

But now, when ultimate victory was so close, her champions failed her in the simplest of tasks. The Vyzyn warlords were powerful warriors, but they lacked the infernal presence of a greater demon lord like Oziax. She should have saved Lord Narthoth to lead the fickle and blood-thirsty minds of her Frost Legion. Damn that Maugris and his obliteration spell. She seethed in anger once more.

+Aeshmara!+

+Yes, my Queen.+

+Harvest the frontier villages of Baroqia and bring six thousand mortals to Gathos immediately.+

+And what of Sunne?+

+Do as I say, and you are one step closer to leading the Frost Legion. Fail, and your eternal essence shall be fused with the slaves in the orthod pit.+

+It shall be as you command.+

Sekka severed the connection. She hoped six thousand human souls from Baroqia would be enough. She thought back to her mental exchange with Tazizu. Of course, Sunne would be a more arduous conquest. That is what made it so valuable. The ancient magic which flowed through the jungles of Sunne was also infused into the souls of its inhabitants.

+Sess'thra.+

+My Mistress.+

+Additional support is required from the lands of Baroqia. Give him the demon seed.+
+I have tried in so many delicious ways to convince him, yet he still refuses to partake in your glory.+
+He will take it, or he will die. Am I clear?+
+Yes, my Mistress. Sess'thra obeys.+

Time continued to vex her. Zizphander and his Shadow Patron were at her doorstep, and her forces were scattered across the realms. She loathed to admit it, but she needed help. She could not stop Zizphander's advance without more troops.

She pondered a partnership with one of the Great Three, Azrollorza, Xerthotha, or Morrdilliax. One was undoubtedly the hand that guided Zizphander in conquest, but which one?

Morrdilliax was least likely to be Zizphander's Shadow Patron. The hundred-headed beast could never make up its mind. Every decision was a chaotic process of overlapping agendas that would often contradict the original desired idea.

Sekka entered Chedipe's study. The room was dimly lit with sorcerous glow balls, bathing the space in murky, green light. Three male human slaves hung suspended at the wrist along the wall from taut, onyx chains connected to the rafters. They shivered in their nakedness and moaned incoherently. Each had been slashed, beaten, and bruised, to what end only Chedipe knew.

Bulbous maggots feasted upon exposed flesh, where large swatches of skin had been removed. The larvae dropped to the floor and squirmed in a mound of its brothers in mindless delight.

The demon-witch sat at a long table and poured over ancient grimoires and scrolls, looking for gruesome ways to torture Sekka's captives. Glowing sigils of power rose over dusty books tossed like discarded rags on the floor.

Chedipe raised her thin head as Sekka approached the desk. Black vapors rose from her body and snaked through the thick, green air, twisting and turning with her movements. Her fingers twitched and shook from the residual effects of wielding dark magic as she turned another page made of skin and bound by twined hair.

"Chedipe. I require information," Sekka said as she casually fingered through a book on the surface of the desk.

"Chedipe obeys the Queen of Ice and Frost. What is it that Sekka wishes to see? An ambitious warlord, ripped and torn, ruined in the steaming mud of jungles, hot and wet? Or visions of another, failed and defeated, cowardly and alone? Or a third, distant and hollow, owned body and soul by phantom world-eaters? Or the last, confident and cunning, walking proudly through a gateway of malice, seeking souls for her Queen, but more for herself.

"Shall Chedipe show Sekka these things?"

Sekka pondered this for a moment. "These things, I know."

"Something vexes Sekka? A riddle Chedipe can solve?"

"Perhaps."

Sekka moved closer to the slaves hanging on the wall. She idly dragged a long nail down the chest of the nearest man. His eyes opened in horror as the pain she inflicted hit his nerves. A smile hooked the corner of her mouth. She spoke casually as she played with the blood oozing out from the slave's torn flesh.

"Chedipe, which of the Great Three is most receptive to my cause?"

Chedipe's eyes shifted from side-to-side, searching her mind for an answer. She hissed into the air, and her body convulsed.

"Chedipe must ask the Whispering Spirits, my Queen!"

She picked up a short, broad-faced dagger that lay on the table and shuffled to the same slave Sekka had tortured moments before. She knelt to the floor and grabbed the man's foot, pressing it against the grimy stone wall.

Chedipe then pushed the dagger down hard like a small cleaver to remove the man's toes. His high-pitched screams echoed off the walls of the small chamber. One-by-one the toes fell to the floor.

"Your screams caress the ears of the Whispering Spirits. But these digits are not enough to appease their hunger." She sliced deeply across the man's abdomen. Blood so red and dark, it looked greyish-purple in the green light. She opened her mouth to let the warm fluid squirt past her thin lips and flow down her throat.

Chedipe gathered the toes and scurried to a scrying bowl in the corner of the room. She chanted slippery words that drooled out of her misshapen mouth while she squeezed the blood from the small digits. The surface of the bowl bubbled, and steam rose up into Chedipe's face.

"The Whispering Spirits will speak, and once spoken, they shall be gone for an age. Ask Sekka, and they shall reveal their secrets, but there is little time."

Sekka moved closer to the scrying bowl. "Which of the Great Three shall aid me against my enemies?"

The dark water of the scrying bowl rose out of its basin and formed into a watery sphere and spun slowly in the air. The shape of mouths formed over its surface and began to whisper, each spoke in a different language, but the message was the same.

"Three Supreme Devils are entwined in a circle of hate. All claim the rightful rule of the Shadow Realm, yet one may not overthrow the other while the third exists. The Great Balance must remain!"

"Who! Who shall help me!" Sekka circled the sphere. "I must have the name!"

"A hundred heads atop the body of Morrdilliax shall twist and turn and giggle and wail. He is the steadfast fulcrum of the Abyss. He does not heed the wishes of lesser beings, no matter their need."

"Not Morrdilliax. I assumed as much."

"That which is Xerthotha hunts for the means to break the eternal stalemate with its rivals. He shifts. He deceives. She mocks. She growls. Together, that which is Xerthotha searches for a means to extend a reach beyond the Abyss."

"The Chaos Gate? Does Xerthotha seek the Chaos Gate?"

"That which is Xerthotha knows! It knows! The Chaos Devil of the Abyss felt the birth of the passage between worlds."

Sekka's worst fears were real. At least one of the Great Three knew of the existence of the Chaos Gate, and if one knew, it would not take long for the other two to feel the pull of the portal's dark magic. It was only a matter of time before they came for it.

"Azrollorza is the one you seek. The cost will be great, in the beginning, and in the end. Sekka will win, only to suffer the consequences of her victory as was foretold millennia past."

"I've known suffering. The cost will be acceptable if it grants me the power I desire."

The watery sphere began to spin rapidly, and the dark liquid sprayed from its surface. The mouths receded into the whole.

"Beware. You have set in motion events that will cause the unbreakable to shatter. They come to feast. They come to destroy!"

Then the Whispering Spirits were gone. The sphere dissolved and splashed back into the basin of the scrying bowl.

Sekka quickly asked, "Who is the Shadow Patron that lifts the Red Devil, Zizphander, to heights beyond his red wings?" But the water of the scrying pool had flattened.

A tall column of ice rose in the center of Sekka's summoning chamber. Four hundred young female slaves hung upside down facing outwards. Their shins and feet had been frozen face up into the column, anchoring them in place. Their hands dangled beneath them, holding serrated daggers. Their exposed skin was ashen due to the freezing temperature of the room.

The slaves mumbled gibberish through frosted clouds of breath. Their unblinking eyes were vacant stares into unknown horrors. They shouted obscenities or laughed hysterically in high-pitched outbursts. Their voices echoed off the cerulean-colored walls of ice and rock.

Sekka floated down from an opening in the ceiling to land softly on the top of the column. She loathed to expend human slaves in this way, but there was always a price to be paid in the Abyss, and the currency was souls.

Of course, it was her duty and privilege to travel to the realm of her would-be patron. Nonetheless, the fact that she had to go to Azrollorza's realm struck her as amusing. The three Supreme Devils were the pinnacle of power in the Abyss. To be in the presence of such greatness left even the bravest and boldest archdevil humbled. But for all the might and influence a Supreme Devil commanded, they could not physically leave the kingdoms they ruled.

The Immortal Mother had her sense of irony.

"Ahh, but I will be the first to claim such power, and cast off the shackles of giants," she thought. A feeling of self-pride swelled within her. What others could boast of what she had accomplished? Only Zizphander now stood in her way.

Sekka saw that all was ready. She raised her hands above her head and began a slow chant. Each of the young females picked up the rhythm of the spell. The room echoed with arcane words that twisted the slaves' mouths in unnatural ways, splitting lips and ripping at throats.

When the spell reached its crescendo, Sekka lowered her hands in a sweeping gesture. The slaves reached up with their daggers held in a chopping fashion, and stabbed into their loins, then dragged the serrated edges down their inverted bodies.

Hot blood flowed from deep red tracks and washed down their chests and heads. The slaves drank in their fill and then vomited it out in a rouge fountain. When their strength vanished, their bodies draped lifelessly towards the floor.

"Azrollorza! Queen of the Abyss and greatest of the Three! Sekka sends souls for your pleasure. Your servant calls to you for an audience! Azrollorza, hear me!"

An unnatural silence claimed the last moans of the dying slaves. A muted, orange light permeated the summoning chamber. Multicolored tendrils of unknown substance coiled out into the area where Sekka stood. They wrapped around the space surrounding the archdevil as if to caress her form without touching it.

"Azrollorza, your servant Sekka seeks an audience with you to discuss designs of conquest and supremacy."

The appendages flowed like vaporous ribbons in the air. Thousands of slits appeared on each tendril and flashed opened to reveal eyes that examined Sekka keenly. Each swirling tendril then whipped back and swept down the column to wrap around the limp body of a slave, and with preternatural strength, pulled the slave from the icy structure. In some cases, the bodies were ripped in half as the tendril sucked them into another realm.

"Azrollorza! Sekka calls to you. Will you answer?"

The tendrils began to fade. Soon, even the dull, golden light dimmed.

Sekka stood alone. The deafening silence was gone, and she could hear the blood dripping from broken limbs. She felt a pressure build in her head. It came upon her fast and sharp. Her legs buckled, and she fell to her knees. She wrapped her hands around her skull, trying to offset the pain. Then a voice echoed in her mind.

+COME.+

42

SHIVERRIG

The newly crowned King of Baroqia woke with a start. Gerun Shiverrig felt vibrant, full of life and vigor. An unseasonal warm breeze flowed through the sleeping chamber, high within a lone spire in the castle of Qaqal. He could smell a hint of the distant spring thaw in its light caress. The crescent moon lit the posh surroundings of the room in a hazy, half-light. He gazed at the serpentine lines of Sess'thra's lithe body as she slept on her side next to him.

He traced his gnarled fingers over her smooth, alabaster skin, fingers that somehow now felt more sensation than he thought possible. He felt every thin hair, every small imperfection, or indentation. Everything felt as if it were bursting with life at that moment. Could this be love for the succubus or just the excitement of finally achieving his birthright? At long last, the Kingdom of Baroqia was his.

The pleasant musings quickly ended as the sensation of strength and warmth changed abruptly as he fully awoke. There was something else, something dark and sticky inside him. It clawed at his mind and snuck through his body like a thief. The presence wanted to dominate him and control his will.

Shiverrig looked back to the sleeping succubus. His body began to shake as nausea filled his gut, and bile rose in his throat. Sess'thra looked up at him from the corners of her now opened, almond-shaped eyes.

"What have you done?" Shiverrig said accusingly. His eyes drew tight with rage. Was this how the mighty Gerun Shiverrig he would meet his end? Poisoned in his sleep? Drooling, and shitting himself like a helpless newborn?

"I did what was necessary to ensure your survival," Sess'thra said as she propped herself up on her elbow. She watched him with great interest.

He gripped Sess'thra by the throat and ripped her out of the soft sheets of the bed. He held her up effortlessly in the air and glared into her eyes.

"I shall not submit to your kind. I am Gerun Shiverrig, the one hundred and fifteenth lord bearing the Shiverrig Crest of Rule, and you will not control me!"

"You are that, and so much more. You shall command Sekka's...Frost Legion," Sess'thra gasped out the last words as she struggled to breathe.

Sweat beaded across his forehead, and his arm trembled as nausea in his gut siphoned away his strength. He tightened his grip and walked to the nearest wall and slammed her against it. Her naked form slapped against the smooth surface of the polished stone.

There was excitement in Sess'thra's eyes and a sensual, predatory smile on her lips. Her breath came in short gasps while her tail twitched with eager anticipation beneath her dangling legs. He wanted to crush the life out of her, and she liked it.

"There is another voice inside my head!" His body and mind struggled against the invasion of this foreign presence.

+*Submit,*+ the intruding voice said. It was slick and slow like cold syrup.

"Never!"

"She is...Jynxx. Help...you...dominate...and control...Frost...Legion," Sess'thra struggled to get each word out. Her eyes watered yet remained locked on Shiverrig with delight.

His body began to change. His massive build expanded as his muscles bulged and rippled. A sheen of opalescent scales shimmered over his body in the dim blue moonlight like a second skin.

"I will not submit!" Shiverrig bellowed. He lifted Sess'thra off the wall and slammed her back against it again. "I will not!"

"Yes, yes...you...great...warlord...of Frost..." Sess'thra gasped out the words. Her hands lovingly caressed Shiverrig's thick forearm and hand as his grip cut off the last of her air. Her eyes rolled back, and her tongue lolled out from her mouth.

And then Shiverrig shuddered and relaxed his grip. However, he kept her pinned to the wall. The scales receded under his human skin. He drew a deep breath, and as he exhaled, he returned to his normal size. The intruder's voice in his head was quiet.

Shiverrig closed his eyes and felt his heart thumping wildly in his chest. His entire body shivered with chills. It was over. He looked at Sess'thra with a new understanding and acceptance of what had occurred. She smiled back at him.

"How do you feel?" she said.

He brought his face closer to Sess'thra's to make a point. "I will never submit, nor will I serve as your Mistress's lackey."

"Clearly."

He then became thoughtful. "The days of spineless kings bending to the will of weak-minded politicians and unworthy lords, that peck and grab power for their own miserable pockets, is over.

"The untarnished and pure traditions of Shiverrig law will once more govern the land. I will bring back the old ways, before Baroqia claimed her maiden name, when my forefather, Baroq Shiverrig, ruled with absolute power as Aj-Kahun."

"Yes! Yes!" Sess'thra hugged the strong forearm that held her locked in place against the wall. "You shall be an unstoppable force across the land."

Shiverrig thought for a moment. "I must have a greater army than the troops I now possess. The men are not unified and are scattered in thought and purpose. Many hold a festering grudge against me."

"Then they shall be...converted," Sess'thra said with a wicked smile. She curled one leg under Shiverrig's outstretched arm and the other over his opposite shoulder, locking them behind his neck. Her heels dug into his back as she pulled him closer.

She rose above his head with the momentum of her movement, and her legs spread wide across his face.

"Drink your fill, Aj-Kahun Shiverrig, ruler of all and slave to none. Let none oppose the will of your desires."

Shiverrig knocked the mud and slush from his riding boots and handed the leather reins of his destrier to the Master of Horses. The smell of horseflesh and old hay permeated the air, creating an oddly pleasing, rustic musk. The hostler walked the jet-black horse into its stall. The animal's thick muscles twitched from exertion, and it snorted in disdain at being led by anyone other than its master.

Sess'thra's Gypsy Vanner was given to a younger groom. The young boy bashfully looked away, averting the succubus's lascivious gaze. The morning's ride was filled with questions that did not bring adequate answers.

"Explain to me again this process of conversion," Shiverrig said.

"My Aj-Kahun, the process is simple and complex at once. Your participation, however, is the simple part. You merely say yes." Sess'thra cozied up next to Shiverrig. The colts reared up and bucked as she walked by their wooden enclosures. They neighed with excitement, while the fillies brought their heads low and shied away from her sight.

"A simple word, yes, but one with so many consequences. And once converted or remade, as you say, who retains control over these *things*?"

Sess'thra laughed and clapped her hands in merriment. "Such an extravagant description."

"Answer the question, succubus. I do not care what these hybrids are called. I only wish to know who they will follow."

"Like all things with a connection to the Abyss, or chaos in general, the strong dominate the weak. Command is earned, through fear, conquest, and strength of will. But one with your unique gifts should not worry over such things."

"And why does Sekka need me so desperately? Where are her other warlords?"

"Let us say, with the loss of Lord Oziax, she was forced to enlist the talents of some rather unsavory individuals, which are proving to be most unsatisfying."

The two walked into a small courtyard. Men-at-arms trained in the morning light with blunt swords and wooded maces. All now wore the livery of the Aj-Kahun. A new emblem of a fierce, three-headed mastiff with pinned back ears was fashioned in its center.

His men respectfully acknowledged the prominence of their Aj-Kahun, and many bowed in admiration to Sess'thra as well. Shiverrig hoped this would not become a problem. The succubus had a way of muddling the minds of his men.

A hunchbacked creature eagerly approached, hobbling on malformed legs and missing a hand. Its body was covered in festering boils that oozed a rancid, pearly-white goo.

"My Aj-Kahun, my Aj-Kahun, at last, I have found you."

"What is it, Malachi?" Shiverrig said. Contempt washed over his face as he looked at the hot mess that had become his archvashim.

Once Malachi had learned of Shiverrig's transition, he insisted on doing the same. Unfortunately, Malachi's change from mortal to hybrid was not as flattering.

In a mocking gesture, Sess'thra had infused him with the essence of a highly intelligent, but repugnant imp named Hilo.

The creature was as ugly as a beaten crone, which, unfortunately, carried over to the appearance of Malachi. Luckily, the archvashim had retained his brilliant intellect, which was the only quality that mattered to Shiverrig, and kept Malachi among the living.

"The nobles loyal to the Dead King are ready to embrace you as their ruler. They wish to discuss terms and positions within your new empire," Malachi said as he wiped the drool from the corners of his mouth.

"You see? Fate has sided with the mighty Aj-Kahun. Your subjects are ready for you to lead them," Sess'thra commented with a crooked grin.

"Terms and positions?" Shiverrig shook his head in disdain. "They scramble like hungry gulls over scraps of chum."

"Yes, my Aj-Kahun. They demand allowances and securities for their support." Malachi's eyes sparkled with excitement.

"What are you up to, Malachi. I know that look."

"Perhaps a window opens to give a broader view of the world, my Aj-Kahun."

"I should just kill them and end their annoying lives."

"Or, they can serve a more practical purpose," Sess'thra said. She glanced knowingly at Malachi. The archvashim's eagerness rose with her attention as more drool escaped his lips.

Shiverrig remained silent for a time, then sighed with disappointment. "Start with Lord Jolla. Alert me when you are finished. I will be in my study. Based on the results, I shall decide the fate of the others."

A page soon arrived at his study with the news of Lord Jolla's transformation.

"And?" Shiverrig said.

"Success, my Aj-Kahun," the page said in a trembling voice.

Shiverrig dismissed the page and raised himself from his chair. Success meant one more step down an ever-thinning path, he thought.

He left his study and walked down a corridor to his throne room. The air temperature suddenly dropped, and a chill crawled up his back. He watched as the air rippled before him, and the shade of a bent and broken man appeared. The ghostly figure looked cautiously from side-to-side.

"I am Maugris. Listen closely. I have little time. Sekka plots against you."

"Maugris Hennerstrum? You're supposed to be dead."

Maugris nodded his head once. "Betrayed."

"Not by me. I upheld my part," Shiverrig said. He took a step closer.

"Stop talking. There is little time. You are not to rule. Vyzyn demons reap souls in the Kingdom of Sunne. Soon, Baroqia will fall to their combined might. Sekka courts madness in her lust for power. Darkness comes to the Three Kingdoms. Beware!"

"Maugris, where are you? If you are still live, why do you not come in person?"

"Heed my words. Whoever controls the Chaos Gate, controls the flow of souls. All others perish. Do not shun the gift of friendship from afar."

"Chaos Gate? What do you mean? Explain," Shiverrig commanded, but the shade had faded away.

Pressure built up in Shiverrig's mind, and his mouth became dry. A voice not his own but now part of him, resonated in his thoughts.

+Do not listen to that fool. He is nothing but a slave-puppet now,+ Jynxx whispered in Shiverrig's head. He could feel her claws digging into his mind, searching for control.

"Be still, demon, and stop haunting my mind."

Shiverrig caught the shine of an object on the floor where the shade of Maugris had disappeared. He saw what appeared to be a golden circlet. It was smooth and dull, but for a tiny band of red that ran through its center. He looked more closely and saw a strange rune inscribed into what would be its front when worn on the head.

+Leave it!+

"I am not some dog for you to command."

He mentally pushed Jynxx away from the forefront of his thoughts and picked up the circlet. Curious, he thought, as he watched a strange, red liquid pulse just under a transparent surface like blood pushing through a vein.

"A gift of friendship," Shiverrig said aloud in contemplation and tapped the side of the circlet.

+Touch it not! Leave it! It is hated!+

Something about holding the circlet eased the pressure in his mind, and the struggle for control with Jynxx subsided as if she took a deep breath and held it fast. Shiverrig brought the circlet over his head, feigning to wear it.

+LEAVE IT!+ Jynxx lashed out at him through his mind. The blow staggered him, but when it had passed, the demon's presence was felt even less.

"It appears you are not in favor of such a generous gift," Shiverrig said, knowing the demon could hear his thoughts and well as his words. "I think I'll keep it."

Malachi waited patiently at the base of the throne. He fidgeted and scratched the boils on his face when Shiverrig entered from a side door.

"You really should have those checked. You stink," Shiverrig said as he approached.

"Yes, of course, my Aj-Kahun. Sess'thra shall be along shortly with Lord Jolla. You will be amazed at the remarkable difference in the man."

"You certainly seem pleased with the results."

"He's a bird! He's a bird!" Malachi said in the laughing voice of Hilo, the demon who had joined with his soul. The archvashim quickly covered his mouth. "My apologies, Aj-Kahun. I am still wrestling with the little beast."

Shiverrig disappointedly looked away and saw Khalkoroth stomping down the red carpet towards the throne.

"I was told there was something of interest to see," Khalkoroth grumbled. He looked up at Shiverrig and sniffed the air. "I smell her, but you are still here. It is very rare for a mortal to control the essence of a true demon spawn."

"I am no ordinary mortal, Pale One," Shiverrig said and looked deeply into Khalkoroth's pink eyes.

"Jynxx was always weak," Khalkoroth smirked.

"I wonder if Daku from Ordu would say the same of you. How does he fare?"

Shiverrig casually moved the golden circlet from one hip to the other. Nothing. Khalkoroth didn't even acknowledge the item. He just scowled and looked away.

"My Aj-Kahun, once you see the miracle of Lord Jolla, you will want all of the

Dead King's Army converted," Malachi suggested. "And from there all of the citizens of Qaqal. An infernal orgy of chaos to spread your will."

Shiverrig contemplated Malachi's words. Naturally, Hilo was coaxing them out of his archvashim's mouth.

"Hilo, what is the relationship between the human soul and the lust your kind have for it? Surely there must be some greater purpose other than appeasing your sick amusement," Shiverrig said.

"You are naught but the raw material that fuels the Outer Realms," Malachi spoke, but it was the voice of Hilo that was heard.

"Explain."

"The mortal soul is the currency of the Abyss. But do not think the alternative offers salvation. For each mortal soul is another golden coin to those twice cursed winged avengers of Lawful Order. The Seven Heavens are but a mirror of the Abyss, having the same face, but a different disguise. Wars rage eternal over the conquest of souls; for he who holds the souls of the Mortal Realm holds the power of the Outer Realms!

"This is the importance of the Chaos Gate, for it provides the foxes access to the chickens without the farmer being the wiser until all the chickens are gone," Hilo said in a giggling voice.

"Hilo! Shut your worthless mouth!" Khalkoroth roared. He grabbed Malachi by the throat and lifted him high over his head. "Or, I will rip your essence out of the mortal and devour it myself!"

Khalkoroth's other hand drifted to the pommel of Eishorror. The ice blade was sheathed at his waist in its newly bejeweled scabbard.

"Don't hurt poor Hilo. He is a faithful servant of the Frost Queen and only does her bidding. Hilo obeys the will of mighty Khalkoroth. Hilo will say no more."

"Khalkoroth, put my archvashim down," Shiverrig said. He didn't bother to hide the menace in his voice.

The pale demon glared up at Shiverrig. "Or you will do what, mortal?"

Shiverrig leaped from his throne and backhanded Khalkoroth with such force that the demon stumbled to the ground. Malachi was sent sprawling across the stone floor and crashed into sitting chairs along the wall.

"I will tolerate you no longer, mortal!" Khalkoroth growled as he stood. The coarse white hair stood high across his back. He lunged at Shiverrig with extended claws reaching for Shiverrig's throat. But once again, Shiverrig was too fast. He swatted the demon's arms aside, pivoted, and was immediately behind Khalkoroth.

He locked his muscular arm around the pale demon's throat. Iridescent scales appeared on Shiverrig's forearm as he tightened his hold.

"Yield, Khalkoroth. I do not wish to snap your neck."

Khalkoroth ripped at Shiverrig's arm, but the Aj-Kahun squeezed tighter. The pale demon reached for his sword as Sess'thra entered the throne room with Lord Jolla.

"Enough of this! Khalkoroth, submit!" Sess'thra said.

Khalkoroth partially drew Eishorror out of its scabbard. Sess'thra slapped him across the muzzle when she reached him.

"I said, submit."

Khalkoroth gave one last growl but calmed against Shiverrig's arm.

Shiverrig peered at Lord Jolla. Malachi had it right. The man had been altered.

Lord Jolla stood erect, slightly taller than before. His face had become more aquiline, like the shape of a hawk's head with his nose coming to a sharp point. But the most noticeable change to Lord Jolla was the wings that sprouted from his back.

Lord Jolla's new appendages were grey with black smear marks. His fingers now ended in sharp triangular nails that constantly twitched at his side. Shiverrig mounted the steps to his throne and to get a better view of this new creation.

"Lord Jolla, how do you feel?" said Shiverrig. "You look...different."

"I am now complete, my Aj-Kahun," Lord Jolla said. The tone of his voice had changed to the shrill call of a hunting bird.

"Do you know what that title means, Lord Jolla?" Shiverrig asked with interest. He leaned forward and eyed the hybrid carefully, searching for any hint of mockery.

"Yes, my Aj-Kahun. It means your will is absolute."

"And you will follow my will, Lord Jolla?"

"I exist only to serve the Aj-Kahun. All other matters are secondary."

"We shall see," Shiverrig said and beckoned the two guards standing by the side-wall holding three hooded captives. One guard pushed an adult woman forward, while the other marched behind with two children.

When the hoods were removed, the woman gasped in shock, while the children stood and cried. However, the once-proud nobleman showed no expression towards the three.

"Lord Jolla, do you recognize these people?" Shiverrig asked.

"Yes, my Aj-Kahun," replied Lord Jolla.

"Who are they?"

"She was my wife, and they were my sons."

"And who are they now?"

"They are possessions of the Aj-Kahun and exist only at the whim of his pleasure."

"What have you done to him, you monster! May Aetenos strike you down for the evil you have brought to the land of Baroqia!" Lord Jolla's wife yelled out and reached for her children, but the guard held her fast.

"If they exist only at the whim of my pleasure, then I command you to slay them. Now."

Lord Jolla did not say another word but slashed out his talon-shaped fingers. She fell to the floor, gasping. Her hands tried to hold back the blood pouring from four deep gashes at her throat. Soon it was over.

He turned to his crying children and repeated the action. The cries stopped as the young boys collapsed to the floor near their dead mother.

"It is done, my Aj-Kahun."

"This is a promising start. You are dismissed," he said and sat back in the throne. The shade of Maugris had said, *"Whoever controls the soul energy controls all things."* Shiverrig now understood why. The guards cleaned up the dead bodies and departed the room. Khalkoroth exited the throne room, but before he left, he looked over his shoulder at Shiverrig.

"The boy's soul is mine!" Khalkoroth harrumphed as if to punctuate the end of the debate about Daku. He snarled menacingly at Malachi, who cowered away like a frightened dog. The demon then stormed from the room and down a dark hallway.

"Your soul is mine! Mine! There is no escape for you, Daku! No escape."

"I wonder," Shiverrig whispered. "I wonder."

43

SEKKA

The muggy marshland-jungle of Azrollorza's world reeked of soured milk and rotting corpses. The humidity clung to Sekka's body like a wet, wool blanket. A warm, metallic light illuminated every malignant leaf, vine, and rock, casting a metallic, burnt-orange glow throughout the entire jungle landscape. Everything looked like it was burning.

Sekka contemplated how to appear before one of the Great Three. Her demonic form would be a more natural choice, but where was the flair in that? She decided to present herself in the most vulnerable way possible, and come to Azrollorza in her frail human body, without ornamentation or clothing, for what were trinkets or apparel to one of such raw power?

Her appearance would create a different effect and convey a more subtle message. *I am weak and humble in your presence, and I do this intentionally to show my courage and strength.* She hoped Azrollorza would appreciate the gesture.

She walked along an overgrown pathway. The ground was a festering morass of thick, brown mud that swallowed the edges of her feet and squished through the gaps in her toes. Giant treelike fronds grew in abundance and towered over her, creating a dense canopy of foliage weighed down by slime. The air was heavy and overbearing. *This was a terrible idea,* she thought, and not for the first time.

"Stop it. You were invited." She would not be afraid, she told herself again. She would be brave and bold in the presence of the Supreme Devil.

Breaks in the foliage revealed slow-moving leviathans hovering overhead. The pale light of Azrollorza's lair caught the slick surface of their bulbous, gelatinous heads.

Hundreds of drooping, wet tentacles composed of thick ribbons of pink, fleshy membranes hung from their underside. The immense demons plowed through the overgrown vegetation as if it were sea kelp, searching the undergrowth for intruders.

Wicked suction cups lined with gnashing teeth grew from their hanging appendages, ready to latch onto any unwanted thing the tentacles encountered during their hunt. The guardians of Azrollorza's lair were diligent in their sentry duty and immediately noticed Sekka's arrival. Their tower-sized bulk, equal to the Juggernauts of Gathos, swam through the air towards her.

Upon closer inspection of the tentacles, Sekka saw multi-segmented human arms sprouted between the larger suction cups. Their gnarled hands and elongated fingers stretched into the dank air like sensory hairs. When the human appendages came in contact with the organic material of the landscape, they vibrated and twanged, creating eerie harmonies of warning.

One of the floating leviathans drew uncomfortably close to her position on the path. The great beast's tentacles probed through the foliage, searching for her exact location. More of its arms joined the hunt, bellowing out a harrowing screech.

"Does it think I am an intruder? Surely, I am expected," Sekka said. "Of course! One did not enter the lair of Azrollorza without proving herself worthy. Fine."

Sekka prepared herself for an attack. If she were to be tested, she would give such a display of power as to leave no doubt why she alone held possession of Gathos. Her back hunched, and shards of ice fell from her hands as she drew infernal energy from the Abyss.

"Come on, let me show you Gathos's bitter sting."

The tentacles of the great beast sliced through the air. The suction cup mouths opened, showing row upon row of sharpened teeth made up of the bones of various creatures found in the three realms. However, just before the leviathan was upon her, it altered its course, and burrowed its tentacles deep into the fetid mud, then withdrew them, leaving gaping holes which quickly filled with murky sludge.

Sekka relaxed her breathing. She should have known this entire escapade was merely a show of power. She walked forward with her head held high, and chin raised, exposing her long throat as a show of submission to a higher power. It was best to show Azrollorza she understood the message and was willing to play the game. How she loathed such belittling theatrics.

The next step she took transported her in the presence of Azrollorza. Somehow, she now stood in a vast courtyard made up of unnaturally shaped, organic material that swirled and tangled upon itself. The area was an open space with distant walls, yet no ceiling.

Sekka was momentarily blinded by so much light. Then there, in the distance, she saw Azrollorza, surrounded by countless human soul-slaves, naked and bound together with bright-blue vines. With a wave of her hand, the soul-slaves circled a tall heap of flesh that appeared to be a massive gastropod. The meaty thing slowly raised its slime-covered head and occasionally devoured one of the condemned humans.

The large area was filled with soul-slaves, and still she saw a second group and then a third waiting in an adjacent field, and even more in the distance. The numbers were countless. She saw hulking demons covered in yellow scales, herding the humans with sharpened poles or the harsh sting of barbed whips.

The soul-slaves wailed and gibbered like desperate animals trapped in a butcher's pen. It was music to Sekka's ears. How she yearned for such supremacy. The sight of so much raw and potential power was intoxicating. Her mouth watered as she wanted for the same, and she would have it!

Azrollorza merely smiled half-heartedly, bored with the magistrate duties of her long existence. It was a never-ending routine of converting human soul energy into beasts of destruction. Sekka's excitement rose at the thought of having an equal number of soul-slaves at her disposal, nay more!

As Sekka took in more of the area, she spied numerous demons meshed within the organic material of the walls of the courtyard. The demons blended into the vegetation and, in some cases, made up an entire surface area of the wall with their bulk. More of the leviathans floated overhead. Their tentacles screeched and snapped at each other as they fought to hold the territory of their airspace.

Azrollorza suddenly glanced up, and her many eyes locked on Sekka. The Supreme Devil was a warped creature, with the upper torso and head of a woman and the lower extremities of a mutated starfish. She had wide hips that splayed into a base of five, slug-like pseudopods that sprawled out underneath her upper body.

Azrollorza's upper torso was that of a beautiful, voluptuous woman, strong and muscular in the abdomen and sporting six, large breasts. She had long, stringy hair that fell heavy on her head and over her shoulders as if she had just come out of a murky pool.

A wet sheen of moisture collected on her smooth skin and dripped from her body as she moved.

Seven eyes of various shapes and sizes spanned across Azrollorza's forehead, each held Sekka fast as swirling tentacles sprouted from her shoulders, creating a billowing, multicolored dance of sea snakes behind her back.

She radiated the same burnt-orange glow as the ambient light found throughout the realm, and Sekka wondered if Azrollorza was the source.

Azrollorza undulated forward on her slug-like appendages, carving her way through the throng of forlorn soul-slaves and quickly closed the gap between the two devils. Sekka was awed at the sheer infernal power that emanated from the monarch devil, and she took an unconscious step backward. Then she lowered herself to one knee in deference.

"Great Azrollorza, I am humbled in your presence."

Azrollorza towered over Sekka and scrutinized her as if she were a toy that had fallen out of favor but now seemed infinitely interesting. She lowered her arm and took Sekka's chin in her hand, raising it up. Azrollorza looked deeply into Sekka's eyes.

"As you should be. Now, tell me, why are you here? Surely not to interrupt my leisure time." Azrollorza's voice sounded as if she was half-submerged in swamp water and spoke through a thin membrane of flesh.

"I have come asking for assistance."

Azrollorza's head came forward, and her seven eyes bore intensely into Sekka. Then suddenly, the Supreme Devil looked away uninterested.

"Ah yes, the Red Devil remains unfettered on Gathos and burns his way towards Furia Keep. You have spread your legions too thin, meddling in the affairs of lesser devils, always looking for favors to advance your status."

"How can you know this?" Sekka said, surprised and worried. If Azrollorza knew of her plight, then she may also know of the existence of the Chaos Gate.

Azrollorza's eyes glanced back at Sekka and glittered with intrigue. "There are no secrets held from one such as I, for I am as vast as a thousand horizons. What you see before you are nothing but a fraction of my true self. My essence is beyond the infinite."

"Yes, Great One. Zizphander marches on Gathos with a great force, not his own. He has the help of a Shadow Patron and thwarts me at every turn."

The Supreme Devil considered Sekka's words. "Help you say, but you know not from where or who? Interesting."

"No, Great One. The identity of the Shadow Patron hides from my sight. The scrying from my soothsayers proves useless."

"You must know you have attracted many enemies in your thirst for power. The aid of Azrollorza comes at a high price. What do you offer in return for my assistance?"

"What is it you desire, Great One?"

"Silly child, what any Infernal Monarch of the Abyss would desire, more mortal souls."

"Then, I shall bring you a thousand soul-slaves for your pleasure, Great One."

Azrollorza looked at Sekka, and a contemptuous smile graced her face. A liquid and sickening laugh gurgled at the back of her throat. "Oh no, that won't do. Look yonder at the ten thousand soul-slaves I have gathered." Azrollorza referred to the large group of mortals she had waded through to get to Sekka.

The Supreme Devil gave a signal with the twitch of her finger, and one of the demon guards walked to the gastropod and stuck it with its long pole. The creature lurched in pain.

Soon, white ooze flowed from pores covering the slug's body. The sticky fluid immediately ensnared the guard and closest soul-slaves. The demon tried in vain to escape, knowing what fate would befall the captives. The soul-slaves grabbed for the nearest mortal to help, effectively trapping their neighbor as well.

The demonic slug brayed and mewed into the air as it shot white ooze over the entire assembly. A shower of sticky strands fell upon the ten thousand soul-slaves, trapping them where they stood.

Sekka saw there was no escape for the mortals. The slug then moved through the group, attaching the bodies of the soul-slaves to its bulk as it encountered them, whether by siding next to them or merely rolling over them. When the collections of the condemned became too dense on any one side, the slug rotated to allow room for more. Soon, all ten thousand soul-slaves were attached in some manner to the creature.

Azrollorza spoke a word of power, and the humans screamed in pain. The white ooze sizzled and melted into their bodies, fusing them together with the slug. A thick cloud of greyish vapor blossomed into the air, and when it dissipated, another of the hovering leviathans had been born.

The great beast shuddered into awareness. The hair-like appendages made from the human remains vibrated in a call of homage to Azrollorza. Its tentacles sloshed out of its underside and dangled beneath its bulbous head. Then it rose to the open sky, to join its kin hovering above the transformation area.

"Ten thousand soul-slaves to create a single Dezemilian," Azrollorza said, and sighed through unseen mouths, the noise seemed to moan from her entire body. She tapped a long finger to her lips. "Bring me fifty thousand mortal soul-slaves. We shall start there and see if you are a worthy little devil."

Sekka gasped. She would need to mount a full-scale invasion on one of the humans' capital cities to achieve those numbers, and she would be left with nothing to stop the advance of Zizphander. "Great One, that is no easy measure to fill. You ask much."

"Little Devil," Azrollorza rolled her seven eyes across the sky. "Surely you realize that true power demands unwavering commitment. My assistance in your little squabble with Zizphander is no light matter, considering who protects the Red Devil."

"You know the identity of Zizphander's Shadow Patron?"

Azrollorza's eyes fastened on Sekka's once more. "Of course, I know who, but what is more interesting is knowing why. That you have not deduced he is under the protection of Xerthotha is disconcerting, but I supposed I mistakenly hold you to the same brilliant intellect as myself. Know that I risk much interfering in the schemes of one of the Great Three."

"Nonetheless, I have enjoyed watching your quaint rise to power. You have become one of my favorite little distractions." Azrollorza maternally patted Sekka on the top of her head.

"But the reward must be greater than the risk. Be happy I do not require more."

"And in return for such spoils, you shall destroy Zizphander, and obliterate his existence forever? You shall then place me by your side in power?"

"Ah, to thwart the plans of that arrogant beast, Xerthotha would be such a treat," Azrollorza mused. "He eternally schemes and connives, meddling in affairs not his own. Such a bother. All I wish is to have peace in the Abyss."

Azrollorza laughed at the absurdity of her last statement. Sekka knew full well any one of the Great Three would eagerly, albeit secretly welcome a chance to smite one of the others while using the hands of a third.

"Oh, not by my hands, no. I shall have nothing to do with the removal of Zizphander, but I'm sure one way or another, the Red Devil will fall," Azrollorza said with a sly smile.

"Yes, Great One. And you will raise me to sit beside you in the Unholy Pantheon of the Lower Plains?" Sekka pressed. She needed a commitment.

"You have lofty ambitions, my Little Devil. The Great Three have ruled over the Layers of the Abyss for countless millennia. What makes you fit to join such majesty? What do you have to offer? Perhaps you would release to me your precious Gathos in return for my goodwill?" Azrollorza peered down at Sekka, and all of her eyes bore into the Frost Queen.

Because I have the means to control the flow of uncounted soul-slaves at my disposal! thought Sekka, but she held her tongue. She dared not give away such valuable information. Not yet.

Azrollorza waited for an answer, but when none came, she spoke again. "When you have found a way to deliver my meager tithe, I shall consider assisting you where I can. Now leave me."

Sekka saw that Azrollorza was studying her, looking for subtle information in her reactions. Did Azrollorza know of the Chaos Gate, or was she acting the fool for some other reason? It mattered not, for it would not be long before each of the Great Three knew of the Chaos Gate from their own means.

Sekka seethed internally, knowing she was trapped. She had caught Azrollorza's cunning rhetoric. The Supreme Devil had promised nothing. However, rather than show her emotions, Sekka merely bowed and left the lair.

. . .

Sekka was happy to feel the cold chill of Gathos on her skin once more. She pondered her fate on her throne of ice as she took stock of the genuinely mighty beasts at her disposal, none of which had been able to stop the advance of the Red Devil. She had saved one under the ice in case Zizphander managed to reach Furia Keep, but she needed something different, something unique to surprise her enemy and stall him long enough for her to regain her strength. If not, Gathos would run red with fire.

A small city's worth of souls! Insanity! It was an impossible tribute for only a show of faith and a future audience to discuss terms. A harvest of fifty thousand soul-slaves by her warlords would ensure victory over Zizphander, and she would not become indebted to Azrollorza or any other Supreme Devil.

"Those miserable, Vyzyn. I should have known better. Worthless!" she said aloud. "And Sess'thra is stalling. Shiverrig should have been her willful slave by now. Must I do everything myself?"

Sekka quickly contemplated her options. Although the infernal power granted by Azrollorza could sweep all of her immediate problems away at once, Sekka realized she could not do this yet, the cost was too high. If Shiverrig turned on her, she would be hard-pressed to hold the mortal portal of the Chaos Gate. She must defeat Zizphander on her own.

A messenger hastened to the base landing of her throne. It bowed low in deference to Sekka, shaking noticeably in her presence. Its body was a deformed combination of avian legs supporting a bare, childlike torso. The head was sharp, and its eyes were pulled back across the sides of its face.

"My Queen, I regret to inform you that Aetenos has been freed," the messenger spoke with dismay.

"What did you say?" she glared at the diminutive creature.

"All gone. Caretakers burned by nasty holy fire. Many footprints, mortal footprints, were found in the snow."

"And the Chaos Gate?"

"It is silent, my Queen."

"And where did the footprints go?" she said with great interest.

"Back to the tower, my Queen."

"Back to Furia Keep," Sekka mused. Her eyes narrowed and shifted back-and-forth. "Could it be true? The boy has returned to free the Master. But how?" She absentmindedly raised her eyes upwards.

"No feathers. No man-birds. Only footprints and dead caretakers," the messenger said.

"Find them. Return Aetenos and his Ever Hero to me, but I want them both alive."

The messenger bowed deeply again and turned to leave. A devilish and delicious plan germinated in her mind. She called out one more order. "If there are others, specifically a woman, I want them alive, too."

44

DESDEMONIA

The jol'goths raced forward in a quasi-gallop as their muscular arms pounded massive fists into the ground. Long strands of ropey drool whipped across their bestial faces as their gaping nostrils flared open, spraying snot from white snouts. Their angry roars rivaled the screaming laughter of the living statues held tight in the ice wall.

Transparent horns grew from random locations on the jol'goths' skulls and curled around the creatures' massive heads and bearlike muzzles. Their bodies shook with rage as the dead black eyes of the demons glared viciously at the intruders.

Desdemonia watched them in shocking fascination. The old alpha vargru from her forest was a killer, but he and his packmates had none of the ferocity of these creatures. This was insanity manifested in rippling muscles and gnashing crystal teeth.

"Airis! Orin! Get out of the way!" Pallo cried, but too late. The lead jol'goth swatted Airis to the side. His body flew ten feet and landed hard. The second jol'goth lunged at Orin, but luckily, the wiry warrior dashed out of the way. He slid on his side and then sprang back up.

"Here they come!" Desdemonia shouted.

She watched Pallo and Run-Run spread out and form a thin wall of steel between the oncoming demons. Desdemonia was impressed with their courage. The Kibo Gensai were fierce fighters and honorable men, but the blessing Illyria gave them had yet to be tested in battle. She hoped it would be enough against such foes, but her gut told her no.

She eyed the jol'goths, feeling cocksure of herself, and eager for the confrontation. "Let's see what I can do to even the odds," she said and began to dance, willing her magic to life.

Deep orange sigils of power appeared in the air and spun around her, slowly at first but then with alarming speed as her magic ignited within her. She felt a deep pool of emotional conflict overflowing within her and filling up the dark, painful places she had hidden away all her life. She had never experienced this kind of raw power before, and the feeling was intense.

The magic flowed through her, and she let herself get caught up in its current. Her arms and legs moved gracefully, tracing invisible lines and magical patterns in the air. Then through the spinning, vermillion haze, she saw Kasai run past Pallo and Run-Run towards the lead jol'goth. He twirled Ninziz-zida's fiery sticks across his body and over his head.

He leaped into the air and struck the demon across the side of its head with the snap of Ninziz-zida's spinning end segment. The demon's head cracked to the side, and blue flame engulfed half its face. Somehow, it still managed to grab Kasai by the leg and twisted him upside down.

The jol'goth's wide mouth opened, revealing rows of needle-shaped teeth reflecting the azure light of Ninziz-zida's flame burning across its ruined face.

"Desdemonia!" Kasai yelled out as he twisted about the demon's grasp.

"I've got this," she said and spun one last rotation, then released the magic that had built up inside her. A miniature comet sped from her outstretched hand and slammed into the demon's chest and shoulder. She spun repeatedly, peppering the demon with similar-sized fireballs. The impact swung the jol'goth around, and Kasai was tossed like a rag doll across the courtyard.

The jol'goth was momentarily stunned. Then it screamed in pain as its white fur melted, and its skin sizzled. The demon tried desperately to brush away the enchanted flames burning its upper torso and face, while long ribbons of muddy-colored smoke billowed in its wake as the demon stumble one way and then the next.

Desdemonia spared a glance back at Aetenos. The Great Monk continued to search for gods knew what along the wall and seemed oblivious to the danger of the jol'goths.

"He's no help," she said.

Out of the corner of her eye, she saw a flash of light. Pallo's blade had sunk deep into the second jol'goth's leg as Illyria's charm flared to life. The demon tossed its bearlike head back and roared into the sky. It then glared down at Pallo with its black lips curled back and teeth bared. The jol'goth raised its long arms high over its head, intent on pounding Pallo into the ground.

Run-Run threw down his swords and tackled his brother out of harm's way just as the jol'goth's huge fists crashed down to the courtyard floor, bursting the stone slates to rubble. The two bodies tumbled together across the ice floor.

Run-Run was up first as the confused demon searched for its missing prey. Pallo rose slowly to his feet and handed his brother one of his swords. They spread out and watched for an opening to attack.

"They're good enough for now," Desdemonia said, and she looked to where Kasai had fallen. Thankfully, he was standing as well. His body looked calm and relaxed, even in the presence of such a monster.

The demon she had initially burned roared, and reached out for Kasai with hands tipped with long, black nails. Kasai stepped backward and away each time the Jol'-goth grabbed for him, bending like a reed in the wind, then snapping Ninziz-zida into its face, blinding the demon. The jol'goth grew more impatient with each failed attempt and bounded forward, landing on all fours. Kasai flipped backward, avoiding the demon once more.

"Stop playing with it!" Desdemonia shouted.

"It's not like I'm trying to make it angry!" Kasai shouted back.

The jol'goth swatted at Kasai and connected. He was tossed awkwardly to the side. Still, Kasai hit the ground in a roll and was up again in a fluid motion. The jol'-goth screamed in anger and pounded its fists into the ground.

Desdemonia looked down at her hands. They were shaking, not from fear, but from exhilaration. Her magic was hungry for more and demanded to be released. She spied the demon stomping towards Kasai. "More it is then," she said with determination and clenched fists.

The smell of a coming rainstorm filled in the air of the courtyard. Then a blinding flash hit the jol'goth across the side of its body. Kasai was knocked off his feet by an intense whoosh of wind, followed by a thunderous boom. A sharp, pungent zing filled her nostrils, like musky, moist earth after a rain shower.

She looked to where the Jol'goth stood. The demon's body shook in an unnatural dance as crisp lightning crackled and burned over its body. It tried in vain to escape the electrical charge eating through its insides to no avail. The jol'goth's eyes rolled back in its head and it dropped dead to the ground, a smoking, charred heap of mottled flesh.

She menacingly stalked towards it. It had all happened so fast she wasn't sure if it was dead. Silver-blue sigils still danced around her body, and she felt the urge to strike the demon a second time.

"Des?" He was staring at her.

"What? Why are you looking at me like that?" She rounded on him with a feral smile on her lips. "It feels good, Kasai, really, really good."

"How did you generate so much power?" Kasai said hesitantly.

Her hands glowed with silvery light, and the new sigils of power swirled around her like a protective shield. They both heard Orin yell out in pain. The other jol'goth had him in his grasp with one hand, while swatting away the Pallo and Run-Run with the other.

"Would it be so bad?" Des said softly.

Kasai unfurled the Fire Serpent and raced to aid his comrades.

"Kasai! Wait!" Desdemonia shouted. But Kasai either didn't hear her or was not listening. He flew at the jol'goth with Ninziz-zida spinning, flames burned along her segments.

Desdemonia felt her magic swell inside her. It was glorious.

The jol'goth must have sensed Kasai's approach because it turned abruptly and chucked Orin at him like a rock. Kasai skillfully dodged the body and ducked in close under the sweeping arms of the demon's defenses.

The musky smell of summertime rain filled her senses. It was intoxicating to her. She felt herself drifting in storm clouds that crackled around her and raised the hair on her skin. Oh, it was bliss. She wanted to strike again, badly.

"Shades, Kasai, move out of the way!" she said.

Ninziz-zida was a whirlwind of motion, striking rapidly to batter the body of the jol'goth. Three sharp blows from the Fire Serpent shattered the right knee of the demon. It could no longer support its weight and crumbled awkwardly to one knee.

The jol'goth lashed out with blind rage, and Kasai, Run-Run, and Pallo all leaped back to avoid its raking claws. Desdemonia barely had time to focus her aim before her magic took over. Her hands unleashed two long streams of pure electricity into the demon's chest. Two thunderous booms followed seconds later. The demon was gone, and only floating bits of ash remained.

Kasai stood alone, not entirely understanding what had happened. He looked back at her.

"Wow."

"I know, right?" Desdemonia said with a bit of wonder as well.

Pallo and Run-Run got Orin to his feet. The three were a mess.

"I'm fine. I can manage on my own," Orin said and pulled away from their help. He limped over to where Airis laid.

"No, no, no, no," he said as he knelt over the young warrior. "Airis, Airis, wake up."

She and Kasai exchanged worried looks as Pallo and Run-Run joined Orin. Run-Run reached into a pouch and withdrew a dab of sometime Desdemonia could not identify. He waved it under Airis's nose, and the young warrior stirred to life.

Pallo and Orin helped him stand. The four of them looked like they had fought a hundred men and lost. As a group, they approached Kasai with awe-filled eyes. Desdemonia realized this was the first time they had seen him fight. They bowed their heads to him as if he were a saint.

"He shall battle the forces of evil, unarmored and alone," Orin said in a prophetic tone when he lifted his head.

"The Ever Hero walks with us," Pallo said. "Airis, hold your faith, and we shall persevere."

Airis simply nodded. Tears rolled down his cheeks, his eyes were no longer filled with doubt.

"You know, I helped too," Desdemonia said, but no one was listening. She looked at Kasai for a little recognition, or at least a "Good job, Des," but he was too busy deflecting the adulation of the Kibo Gensai warriors.

"How typical," she mumbled under her breath and looked to see if Aetenos had made any progress on his mysterious project.

45

KASAI

Ninziz-zida whispered soothing thoughts that echoed into Kasai's subconscious as if distant memories were brought to the forefront of his mind.

The wielder becomes the weapon, and the weapon becomes the wielder. Together we are one. Together we are strong. Apart, we are nothing.

Kasai felt Aetenos looking at him and turned to see the Great Monk wearing a proud smile across his face, yet his one eye gleamed with crazed excitement. The smile quickly disappeared, and he turned back to his examination of the wall. Muttering incoherently to himself.

"What are you looking for?" Desdemonia asked Aetenos.

"I know it's here, but I know not where. I'll know it when I find it," Aetenos said as he continued to examine the wall and tapped his fingers on the surface. "Now stop being so pesky, all of you, can't you see I'm looking as fast I can?"

"Can we help, Master Aetenos," Desdemonia said.

"Des, don't encourage him. We're trying to leave this place, not stay longer," Kasai said.

The living statues continued to shriek in alarm. Some managed to pull their arms free of the wall's icy grasp and excitedly pointed at the small party. Kasai suddenly felt exhausted. He tucked Ninziz-zida under his arm and placed his hands on his knees, trying to catch his breath. The cold air cut like razors in his lungs, and Ninziz-zida squirmed at his side like a cat that no longer wishes to be pet. The Fire Serpent was alive with energy and yearned to destroy more of the creatures of chaos.

Kasai heard the roars of more jol'goths advancing towards their position. The fight was not over.

The wielder becomes the weapon, and the weapon becomes the wielder. Ninziz-zida's words tumbled again through his thoughts. She called to him, urged him to belong to something greater than himself. She would protect him and keep him safe, if only he would wholly commit to her, and only her. *Together, we are strong.*

He felt her power and warmth and gave himself over to the siren song of the Fire Serpent. Her strength washed through him as she coiled around him like a second skin.

Kasai stood straight, and Ninziz-zida dropped into his waiting hand. The cold air no longer bothered him. He breathed it in, and let it fill his lungs. It was exhilarating. Cleansing.

Kasai felt invincible and would stand against the monsters that were soon to pour from the many corridors and gateways leading into the courtyard. He moved aggressively to a more central position and waited for the first of the demons to arrive. He spun Ninziz-zida into a shrieking banshee at his side, and she came alive with divine purpose. Azure flames burst from her sticks and pinwheeled circular patterns around him.

Kasai glared at the entrance, where the next assault would likely appear. He was ready and welcomed the opportunity to destroy the evil of Gathos. Ninziz-zida purred like a cat in his hands.

"Come to me, you filthy things," he said with determination.

"Kasai! Stop! Where are you going?"

It was Desdemonia. Kasai looked back and saw her hurrying towards him. He lessened the spin of Ninziz-zida's segments to a slow twirl, and the Fire Serpent moaned in disappointment.

Stay with me.

But Kasai's thoughts were now focused on Desdemonia and the look of concern on her face.

"Where are you going? We must stay together," she said. "Kasai, what's wrong." Her voice was calm but direct.

Not her. Only me. Ninziz-zida called to him again. *I will protect you.*

"Together," Kasai whispered.

"What?" She came in closer to hear over the shrieking alarm. "We must stay together. Aetenos needs you, and so do I."

"Des," he said as if seeing her for the first time. He held Ninziz-zida still. "Yes, of course. I'm here."

He saw her clearly now. Her face was flushed from the use of magic, and her aura glowed a soft blue. Her eyes were dilated and still carried the intensity of battle.

"It's okay, Des, I'm here."

She gave him a funny look. "Yes, I know. Where else would you be?"

Kasai felt Ninziz-zida's presence subside, and the flames along the staff reduced to a flicker. A profound sadness washed over him as if the Fire Serpent was disappointed in him or somehow felt rejected by him.

"What's he doing now?" Kasai said, pointing to Aetenos.

The Great Monk continued to frantically tap and push the oddly shaped stones along the wall. Occasionally, he would close the mouth of one of the shrieking statues and put his finger to its lips. Finally, a small rock gave way to his touch, and Aetenos pushed open a hidden door.

"Come, my friends! The time to live is now!" Aetenos shouted and raced inside.

Kasai, Desdemonia, and the Kibo Gensai reluctantly went to the opening. Kasai heard Airis muttering to himself in disbelief. "Did he really just say, 'The time to live is now?' What about an hour from now?"

Orin sided up to Airis. "We almost lost you. Stay behind me next time. Understood?"

"Don't baby me. I can handle myself. I just slipped is all. It won't happen again," Airis said in a disgruntled voice. He shook off Orin's hand and went through the doorway.

"He's a proud warrior," Desdemonia said to Orin.

"What do you know about it? Just keep to your own, witch," Orin said and hurried inside.

"What did I say?" Desdemonia said, genuinely perplexed.

"Orin is a pious man," Pallo said. "He sees things as either right or wrong, there is little in between. He thinks magic is something that should only be wielded by the divine, and those mortals that wield it do so at the peril of others."

"Oh, so Orin makes the rules? Who does he think he is? I saved everyone just now!"

"He just needs some space, Des. I think he feels like Airis is his responsibility," Kasai said.

"You know, Kasai, just once, I'd like to hear you take my side," she said and marched into the opening. "Just once!"

Finally, after hours of searching and hiding to avoid the roving guards and smaller fiends in the Keep, the party grouped together to rest at the end of a corridor where four halls came together. Aetenos was noticeably distraught. They all sat in the cold light emanating from the sparsely placed glow-balls in the ceiling.

"She must be here. She must!" Aetenos stood and called out in a booming voice, "Illyria! Illyria!" But there was no sweet voice to answer his call. Dejected, he slid down the side of a smooth wall next to Kasai. "Where is she?"

"Master Aetenos, please listen to me. I have spoken to Illyria. She sent us here to find you and bring you to her, but she is not here in Gathos. She waits for you in the realm of men. She is in Baroqia." Kasai watched to see if his words were registering with him.

"Balderdash! You are mistaken." Aetenos put his hand on Kasai's forehead. "Are you feverish?"

"I'm fine, Master."

"You there," Aetenos said and grabbed Airis's hand. "Feel his head. Now feel mine. His again, and once more to me. Well, doctor, what is your prognosis? Is he sick?"

"I'm not a doctor, Great One," Airis said and tried to pull his hand back. He looked to the others for support.

"Well, why are you examining us? Who's the doctor here?"

"We have none, Master Aetenos," Kasai said.

Aetenos leaned over to Kasai. "You know, next time you might think to bring a doctor. They can be quite handy in a place like this." He winked as he pulled his head back.

Pallo knelt in front of Aetenos. His eyes were heavy with fatigue. "The Ever Hero speaks true. We wear the mark of her blessing on our foreheads and blades. How else could we survive such a place?"

"Indeed," Aetenos said, nodding his head and squinting his eye. "How do you survive here? Well, let's have a look at you then. Up, up." Aetenos and Pallo stood together.

The Great Monk looked squarely at Pallo and pressed an unsteady hand to the older warrior's forehead. He placed his other hand on Pallo's shoulder for support. Aetenos bowed his head in concentration.

"You hide in the shadows, protecting those who follow the Light." Aetenos raised his head, and warmly smiled at Pallo. "I thank you."

Aetenos moved to Airis and Orin and raised them off the cold floor. He placed his hands on them as well and nodded in satisfaction. When the Great Monk reached Run-Run, he signed with his hands, what must have been a special message. Run-Run stood dumbfounded for a long moment, and eventually signed back that he understood. It was the first time Kasai recalled seeing Run-Run happy.

Aetenos pulled the Kibo Gensai to him. "We are all brothers. All of us."

He then raised his nose and turned his head in different directions, all the while sniffing the air. He walked to the center of the crossed corridors, then dropped down on all fours like a hound. He scampered a few feet down the right passage, and then returned to go down left one as if locked onto a scent. He leaped up and decided to race down the third corridor instead.

"This way!"

"What, nothing for me?" Desdemonia said, shaking her head with her hands on her hips. "What is with you people?"

Kasai closed his eyes and sighed. Just when he thought Aetenos would live up to the legend of the Divine Fist, he reverted to the antics of a rambunctious, childish, fool. The Kibo Gensai continued to revere him as a divine being, but was it their faith or an obligation of honor, that held them true? Why hadn't Aetenos simply snapped his fingers and whisked them back to Baroqia?

"I don't know, Des, I just don't know."

"I'm not sure what to make of him, either," Desdemonia said as they trailed after Aetenos. "But he sure is an interesting fellow."

"It's like he's channeling himself from another time. He's here, but not here with us, now," Kasai said. "His mind must have been shattered by the tortures of Sekka's dungeon."

"I hope you can find a way to stitch it back together before it's too late."

"You and me both," Kasai said, and he sensed only doom on the path the small party now followed. But when had he thought otherwise since fleeing Monastery of Ordu with Master Choejor? Whatever the state of the Great Monk's mind, lucid or mad, they all just needed to stay alive long enough for him to come to his senses, Kasai thought.

Perhaps a more concerning issue was that Ninziz-zida had gone silent. She no longer pulsed reassuring sensations into his thoughts. The absence of her sentient whispers eroded his confidence in fulfilling the mission, and more importantly, in himself. Her presence gave him the strength to continue. He feared he would lose hope if she did not return.

Had he offended the Fire Serpent, and now she had turned her back on him? Was he no longer worthy of being her wielder? She was an ancient soul with a demanding ego, but one that gave as much as she took.

He wondered with no small amount of apprehension if the relationship he was forming with Ninziz-zida spoke true of the rumors of possession by the weapon.

Again, another questioned to be answered later. He wished he could find a quiet place, sit with no distractions and meditate.

Kasai watched Desdemonia as she ran after Aetenos. He was grateful for her constant companionship and belief in him and knew in his heart he could count on her for support, no matter the circumstances, and that gave him renewed strength. She had become an extraordinary person to him, once he let go of his stubborn belief that all magic was evil.

How they had found one another was a miracle. They were two people who never should have a reason to meet. But they had come together and formed the most unlikely friendship. It was a fantastic concurrence. However, at that moment, all he could see was her radiant beauty, pushing the darkness away.

The things you think about in the direst situations, he thought with an internal chuckle. Somehow, she seemed to hear his thoughts and turned at that precise moment and gave him a quick wink. *How does she always know when to do that,* he wondered?

The party moved down the corridor at a slower pace while Aetenos scampered ahead, tapping on sections of the wall and tracing cracks in the ice with his fingers as he had done in the courtyard. Kasai's shoulders slumped, and he breathed out a dense cloud of white air.

"Kasai, what is it? You look troubled, more so than usual." Desdemonia said with a smile. She never hesitated to have a little fun with him.

"Only a little over a month ago or so, my biggest worry was how I would finish my chores before dark, and if my supper would still be warm when I got to it."

A warmth crossed her face. "Now, things are a little different, aren't they?" She looked around the morbid hallways. Bones of dead things were fused into the icy walls. Sharp edges protruded from the surface and reached out to snag and tear the clothing of any party member who brushed by too close.

"What a nasty place. The woman has an odd fetish, to be sure," she said with a smile.

"She sure does," Kasai said while absentmindedly shaking his head. "Des, I do not know what to do. I feel lost without Master Choejor. If only you knew how important he was to me. He was like the father I never had."

"Yes, Kasai. I do know. I was there and saw the bond the two of you shared. I loved Choejor, too, for the short time I knew him."

Kasai looked deeply into her eyes. "Des, I'm not ready for any of this. It's too big."

"You'll find a way to succeed. Master Aetenos has confidence in you, as do all those other misfits." She nodded in the direction of the Kibo Gensai, who were following Aetenos down the hall.

He watched Aetenos stop, stare at a wall, kick it a few times and then seem perplexed as to why it didn't move. Kasai looked up to the ceiling and sighed then looked straight into Desdemonia's amber eyes.

"I can't stop Sekka on my own," Kasai said. "It's impossible." He didn't want the others to hear him and lose what little faith they had in him. "I'm sorry I have brought you into this mess. I'm sure you would rather be with Gauldumor and your life in the forest."

Desdemonia shook her head. "You have something unique inside you, Kasai. I have seen it. I have faith in you, as do the others."

"Tricks!" The word came out harder than he had wanted. Kasai softened his voice. "Just tricks, Des. It's borrowed strength from others. Aetenos before, and now Ninziz-zida. This is not me."

And then Aetenos was at Kasai's side, seemingly out of thin air. "The monkey is not the fish or the bird, but it can soak for hours in water and soar through the air as it jumps from branch to branch. It remains a monkey only in form, not in essence. That is its truth."

The one-eyed monk smiled broadly and then dashed away more convinced than ever he knew precisely where to go. "This way! Up, across, and down we go! Do not dally my friends. Soon now! Ho, ho! Very soon!" Aetenos shouted in glee as he raced down the hall to a ladder and climbed up the rungs without looking back.

"Now, I'm a monkey?" Kasai looked questioningly at Desdemonia.

She shrugged her shoulders. "I think he means, you are more than what you think you are, even if you tell yourself otherwise," Desdemonia said.

"You know he's crazy, right?" Kasai said, and sighed in resignation.

She gave Kasai a reassuring squeeze on his shoulder. "Aren't we all? Come on, at least he has the right spirit."

"I'd appreciate a little less spirit, and a little more of the Great Aetenos of legend," Kasai said as they reached the ladder. Pallo and Run-Run had already ascended. Orin went next, followed by Airis.

Kasai took the first rung and thought he heard a noise that sounded like a distant scream. "That can't be good."

"Let's go, Monkey. Up the ladder," she said.

Eventually, the party stood in another long corridor that stopped in a dead-end. Aetenos sat on a small square with his chin in his hand as his fingers tapped his lips in contemplation.

"Well, my friends, we have finally come to the place where I lost her. We are here."

"Master Aetenos?" Kasai said.

"I know, I know, you had your doubts, but it's okay. You don't need to thank me."

"Where are we, Master?"

"Why, the dungeons of Furia Keep, of course. Beneath me lies an entrance to horrors beyond imagination." Aetenos jumped to his feet with a broad grin and pointed to the trap door.

"Ready?"

46

DESDEMONIA

Desdemonia followed close behind Aetenos as he led the way through the upper dungeons of Furia Keep. The light was dim and hollow, and she did not want to get separated from the group. The dank air reeked of death, and the party moved slowly, nursing bruised muscles and pushing away the slow sleep of exhaustion.

There was no shortage of despair in each cell they passed. Boney fingers attached to flayed arms, and bluish-white with frostbite, reached out to the passing mortals. They sought to touch them, and remember the warmth of life, even for the briefest of moments.

One such condemned soul came to the bars and tried desperately to squeeze his face through. The crystalized whiskers of his overgrown beard shattered against the hard iron.

"Free me! The smell of life you bring is a curse and worse than I already endure. Free me!" the prisoner said.

But Aetenos did not stop. He marched on, looking straight ahead and never right or left. Desdemonia wondered how a dead soul could still be forced to feel agony and pain.

"Master Aetenos? Is there not something we can do?" Kasai asked as he too passed the prisoner's cell.

The condemned soul pointed at Kasai. "You there! Boy! You are a monk of the Four Orders! You failed to free me in life, and now you fail to do the same in death! Follow the Light, you said. The Great Aetenos watches over us and will keep us safe if you but heed his Song.

"BAH! All lies. I followed the Light, but no safety came. The was no song, no rain, and the harvest was lost! So, I did what I had to do to survive. And now look at me! Look at me! This is your fault!"

Aetenos stopped at the sound of his name. He returned to the cell holding the deranged man. The prisoner's cheeks grew red and then white as he pressed his face harder between the bars. Spittle formed on his broken and blue lips.

"My son. I am sorry. I have failed you," Aetenos said with a soft, sad voice.

The prisoner scrutinized Aetenos, his eyes shifting back and forth. Then he laughed with maniacal vigor. "You? The Great Aetenos?"

Aetenos bowed his head in affirmation.

"The eyes of the insane can see like for like, and you, my friend, are crazier than I!" The prisoner's laughter grew. He moved from the bars, waving his hands to shoo away unwanted guests. "Begone evil spirits. Begone. There is no salvation in Gathos, it is a lost place."

Aetenos stepped away from the cell. His head hung heavy on his chest. Desdemonia heard him chastising himself and saying a word, over, and over again. "Remember."

They kept walking and passed many cells. Some were empty or filled with skeletons heaped in a pile. The corridor opened to a larger area reserved for torment and torture. The room was filled with racks, some designed to stretch, while others were meant to slice off limbs or break bones in two.

Along one wall were tables with rough surfaces, stained deep red, purple, and black from the layers of blood and viscera spilled over them for countless ages. Chains hung from another ending in black, metal hooks, one was drawn taut from the weight of a moaning soul, left in the darkness to wither away alone in her pain, forgotten from sight and memory.

Man-sized cages with inverted spikes hung from the ceiling. Many held bodies of the condemned, impaled upright and leaking what remained of their forgotten life into deep, slush-filled vats.

Desdemonia looked away in disgust and saw a desiccated being nailed to a thick fixture with seven ice-coated beams arranged in an inverted, circular pattern, splayed out from a central base. The prongs jutted out to form the spokes of a wheel. Two arms, two legs, and two wings were fastened tight to the ice beams by nails. Leather bands now hung in loose loops draped over what had once been healthy, living flesh.

The crucified being's torso and face were a ruined mess of flayed skin, dissected organs, and broken bones. Circling the rack where numerous tables covered with bloodied instruments of torture. Bloodied saws, knives, pokers, and thongs littered the table's surfaces, along with cups and vials of grossly colored liquids. The used tools had been discarded over time, the blood hardened and covered in brightly colored mold.

"I've found something interesting," she said and pointed to the rack. The party stopped and looked in the same direction.

Aetenos hurried over to the forsaken soul and placed a gentle hand upon the creature's forehead. He whispered a prayer to the bound prisoner and marked his forehead with strange symbol. When Desdemonia was close enough, she heard the last of his words, "...and find me here, my love."

He removed his hand and gently kissed the same spot of the prisoner's forehead. "Rest the eternal sleep, my friend," Aetenos said aloud and bowed his head, then stepped away from the rack. "How could Raguel allow such a thing?"

Desdemonia noticed a change in the disposition of the demigod. Although a lone tear trailed down his cheek, his eye was clear and focused, filled with a deep intelligence rather than its typical erratic insanity.

"Master, who was this?" Kasai asked and looked questioningly at Aetenos.

"This was Artiya'il. His is known by many names throughout the Three Realms. Celestial, Deva, the Yazata, and the Qadimi Shahanshahi are a few of the common names spoken in the lands of men. But in the Seven Heavens, he was known as a True-born, and more importantly than that, he was my friend."

"An angel," Pallo gasped in amazement as he approached the rack.

Run-Run's eyes grew wide as he came to stand next to his brother. He tapped two fingers to his forehead in reverence to the angel.

"Impossible," Orin said in disbelief as he approached the crucified angel. "One born under a righteous sun such as he has no place in this hell, so it is written."

Desdemonia approached the dead angel and heard Orin continue.

"For only those who live under a black moon and flirt with the powers of darkness, shall fall from grace and be condemned, such spoke the Prophetess Miko Nuna."

"Follow the Light," Airis responded under his breath.

"Follow and be guided by the Light," Pallo repeated.

Desdemonia glared at Orin when she heard his remark. "And what exactly do you mean by that, holy man? Are you implying I live under a black moon? Maybe we should pick up where we left off and find out?" Deep orange sigils fanned out behind her, and the moldy smell of the dungeon turned to the musky scent of damp soil.

Orin held his ground. "This is beyond one such as you. It is a sacred covenant between the heavenly powers and men of purity. A witch wielding the powers of chaos would not understand such things."

"They are real?" Airis loudly exclaimed and pushed himself between Desdemonia and Orin. His naïve manner diffused the rising tension in the room. The young Kibo Gensai hesitantly made to touch the deceased angel.

Orin cuffed him behind the head. "Airis, mind your tongue and your hands. Of course, they are real. We are in the presence of the Great Aetenos. He is real, is he not?"

Airis lowered his head and voice. He gave a sideways look at Aetenos. "Is he?"

Desdemonia moved close to examine the divine being before Orin could smack Airis again for his lack of faith.

"Do not touch what is sacred with unclean hands!" Orin cried out.

"I'm warning you, back off," she said ominously over her shoulder, then lightly caressed the angel's broken wings. "He must have been beautiful."

Aetenos came to stand beside her and raised a curious eyebrow at her swirling magic.

"Sorry," she said and lowered her guard, causing the sigils of power to fade from sight.

"He was beautiful, yes, but unfortunately far too careless," Aetenos said. "The Seven Heavens have strict rules concerning right and wrong. Many of the True-born of Tanalum are extremist in their devotion to Law of Order, steadfast in their beliefs and commitment to upholding the impossible standard of divine perfection.

"Mortals have become lesser beings in their eyes, faulty and incomplete. But as more mortal souls are locked out or cast away from the Heavenly Realms, the balance of power shifts and slips to the eager grasp of all that is evil."

The Great Monk continued, "For the mortal soul is the eternal fuel to be used by whatever hand guides it and shapes it through life. It should not be looked at in disdain, but rather nurtured and encouraged to grow with a noble purpose. And now, even a True-born can be cast out of paradise."

He brought his hand to just below his chin and stroked an imaginary beard. "This cannot be good."

"What was the angel's crime?" Desdemonia asked.

"His crime? Who can say? But Artiya'il was overly compassionate to the underdeveloped human mind and must have guided the actions of one too many wayward mortals. Only Raguel, the Chancellor Pinnacle of the Seven Heavens, would have the authority to cast him out of Heaven. But how Artiya'il arrived here, in the dungeons of Furia Keep, I do not know.

"It seems Raguel has lost sight of the importance of the Great Balance and has turned his back on the humans."

Airis raised his eyebrows, and Desdemonia could easily read his expression. Hadn't Aetenos done the same by leaving them all to their fate? The subtle action was not missed by the Great Monk, who had seemingly regained much of his legendary demeanor.

Aetenos put a hand on each of the young Kibo Gensai's shoulders. "I traveled a dark road for many of your years, but one cannot live in the shadows of his mind forever. Seeing Artiya'il has reminded me of a different time, one that I have forgotten in my selfishness. I now realize how important I was to many, not only to the mortals I professed to love, but also the friendships I failed to support in times of need."

"That's good news, right?" Kasai said. "We can go home now?"

"Come closer and listen, my friends. Please, all of you, come, come," Aetenos said and gathered the small party together in a semi-circle. He stood before them as if preparing to give an intimate sermon.

"Maybe we should keep moving and not stay in one place too long," Kasai said in a worried tone.

"There is always time for knowledge, my son." Aetenos cleared his throat. "Now, the human soul is a precious and valuable thing. It is not only the bridge that connects a person to the Boundless but also a source of immense power for the lofty Heavens and the deep layers of the Abyss. A soul holds the energy of a lifetime of actions and emotions, good or evil, that can be converted into the power to create by the oldest beings of the Outer Realms.

"Upon the death of its physical host, the soul is weighed, judged, and sentenced. The subconscious essence of the condemned is sent to one of the many realms of pain, such as Gathos. Souls of higher merit enter one of the levels of the Seven Heavens.

"The joyful happiness of an ascended soul combines with the righteous power of the divine, to spread lawful order and push back the chaotic darkness, smiting it when it can.

"Unfortunately, the suffering from such torment in a place like Gathos is used to create unspeakable horrors in an everlasting desire to conquer and destroy."

"Or to power something as wicked as a Chaos Gate," Kasai lamented.

"Just so."

"And the soul energy of a True-born angel in the hands of Sekka..." Desdemonia let the thought trail off.

"She could create a monster the size of a city wall."

"Can it be destroyed?" Airis interjected. "Can the Chaos Gate be destroyed?"

"That is a riddle which will be solved in its proper time. Not before, and not after. Trust in the wisdom of the Immortal Mother, my young friend."

"The righteous will always defeat the evils of the lower realms, for it is written," Orin said defensively. His eyes sought for understanding that did not come easily.

"Written by who?" Desdemonia said. "Haven't you been paying attention?"

Orin scowled at her but didn't say more.

"Nature is blind to our pain and deaf to our sorrow, for the mundane has no reason to care. But the Boundless will hear your call and answer in kind when you fully give yourself and surrender to the Openness."

"See?" Desdemonia said and smirked. Then she turned to Aetenos. "Master Aetenos, I'm not sure I understand something. Why does this Raguel character shun souls when he should be welcoming them all into Heaven? Why not deprive your enemies of the souls they need to wage war and do harm?"

Desdemonia waited for an answer. When none immediately came, she gave one last thought. "I mean, why not create a heavenly paradise for all, if it were in your power to do so?"

"You question the will of the Immortal Mother? I tire of your blasphemous ravings, witch." Orin took an aggressive step forward, his hand drifted to the pommel of his sword.

Desdemonia's hands flared, this time with silvery-blue light. A low rumble crossed over the ceiling, and the air smelled like rain. Her eyes narrowed. "Try it."

Aetenos padded her hands down and slowly nodded his head, as if he too had pondered such questions. "All souls must travel along the path of their unique destiny. The damned cannot remain in Heaven. All things have their rightful and perfect place in the Immortal Mother's tapestry of life. The Great Balance must remain."

Pallo spoke softly under his breath, "The Song of Aetenos is within you. Rejoice in its righteous verse."

"Follow and be guided by the Light," Airis and Orin whispered in response, but Orin's challenging eyes remained locked on Desdemonia.

She waited to see if Orin would say another word on the matter. She was mildly disappointed he didn't.

"Master Aetenos, I don't understand," Kasai said. "The Masters at Ordu never mentioned the soul as a means of becoming one with the Boundless. One achieved a connection by opening the mind and heart to something bigger than the self. Giving unconditionally and receiving the same."

"Quite so. But it is the soul that connects one to the other. Without the soul acting as a bridge or gateway, the mind and heart would forever be separate and unable to receive the blessings of the other."

Aetenos smiled and tilted his head awkwardly to the right. "Just like the open eyes of a blind potato." He raised his eyebrow in surprise. "What's that? We have potatoes?"

"Master? I'm not sure I understand. Blind potatoes?" Kasai shook Aetenos by the arm. "Master, are you well?"

"I'm gooooood-ada." Aetenos's eyelid fluttered, and his voice slurred as he spoke. "We must continue in our search! Illyria is here. I know it." Then he dashed out of the room.

Desdemonia simply shook her head in disbelief. Then, she heard a commotion and Aetenos's startled voice coming from the next room.

"Oh, hello. That certainly is a pointy spear you have there. Oh, and you have one too. Exceptionally good. And you, and you, and you. Ho, ho! It's a spear party! We have potatoes!"

Desdemonia and the others raced into the room. They saw Aetenos half-surrounded by the spearheads of twenty or more demons, all heavily armored in dull plate armor, wearing ugly war-helms topped with spikes and horns. Aetenos reached out and touched the tip of one of the spears. "Ah, yes, very pointy."

The Kibo Gensai fanned out around Kasai with their swords drawn. Kasai stepped forward with Ninziz-zida in both hands. Des readied a spell, and the air became crisp with her magic. She smiled eagerly, ready to unleash it again.

She heard a loud *thunk* inside her head and watched the floor rise to meet her face. She didn't remember hitting it or the pain of the collision. "Kasai," she moaned, looking for him, but then her head dropped to the floor and room went dark.

47

KASAI

Aetenos curiously examined each of the spear tips that inched closer his flesh, lost in his own world, and oblivious to their danger. Desdemonia moaned in pain, and then Kasai heard a heavy thud on the floor. He spun around to see the room filled with more of the white-armored demons. Ninziz-zida blazed in his hands, undaunted at the sight of such overwhelming odds, and urged Kasai to engage the enemy before there was no room to fight.

Run-Run lunged at the demon that had struck Desdemonia. He batted aside the demon's club with one short sword, then rammed his second through the creature's neck. The demon mewled like a sick cat as it dropped to its knees. Pallo darted to his brother's side as the rest of the demons drew in close, slavering like hungry wolves, eager to be the first to make the kill.

A hulking demon in armor etched with ice-blue runes, pushed through the crowd. He barked out commands to the others in a brutal tongue, which held the pack at bay. Then he spoke in a rough version of the common tongue through a swollen mouth filled with broken teeth, "You. Ground. No weapons."

Orin moved to Kasai's side. "We will need the divine strength of the Ever Hero if we are to survive them. I will guard your back."

The leader removed his helm. His skin was bluish-green and covered with scars and pox marks. He leered at Kasai and pointed his long spear at the Kibo Gensai's readied weapons, and then back to the floor. "Weapons. Down." He paused a moment and then added with a sinister smirk, "Or die."

"I think they have other plans for us. Best to live now and plan our escape," Kasai said, though his words spoke of confidence that was not in his heart. "Lower your blades."

"No, Ever Hero," Orin said in desperation. "Our souls must not be used to create another dark abomination. It would be a fate worse than death."

The brothers hesitated, and Pallo glanced over his shoulder and gave a quick shake of his head. They would fight. But Kasai saw Desdemonia, helpless on the floor.

"Lower your blades," he said and laid Ninziz-zida at his feet. The Fire Serpent cried out in alarm.

No! Fight! They are no match for me!

"Perhaps, great Fire Serpent, but I must think of the others," Kasai said.

The others, or her?

The Kibo Gensai reluctantly complied, and the guards pounced. Cold steel shackles bit into his flesh as they snapped around his wrists and ankles.

"No good will come of this, Ever Hero," Orin said and narrowed his eyes at Desdemonia as she was lifted by Pallo and Run-Run. "She has doomed us all."

The demons pushed and pulled the party into a slow jog. Kasai realized they were descending deeper into the bowels of Furia Keep by the way his boots slapped the hard floor and his thighs burned. Aetenos continued to mumble incoherently about his lost love Illyria, and occasionally lamented the loss of his friend, the angel Artiya'il. But mostly, Kasai only heard gibberish from him.

"Where are they taking us?" Airis said. His voice was frail and scared.

"We will soon find out. Whatever it is, you will be brave in the eyes of the Divine Fist. Do you hear me, Airis? You will be brave."

Airis just kept pace with the others and remained silent.

Soon the corridor opened to a large room with high ceilings lined with menacing stalactites of ice, formed over eons from whatever foul minerals were found in the rock of Gathos. A gooey liquid slowly bled out from the ceiling and oozed over the protrusions of ice, before dripping down to splash on the waiting stalagmites below.

Soul-slaves were used as a fleshy mortar between two connecting points to form a full column. Their bodies were stretched and broken to fit where necessary, then fused into the ice, sometimes leaving arms and legs dangling outside the main formation. It was a slow, agonizing process for the condemned.

Dark shadows flickered against the wall describing more immediate torments. The wails of long-dead souls echoed endlessly in Kasai's ears. Everywhere he looked, there was misery, mayhem, and pain. He tried to shut out the screams and focused his mind on creating a peaceful center of calmness and tranquility. But the weight of sorrow of the others was too much for him to bear. He couldn't push it away and was soon overwhelmed.

Above the din, Kasai heard a clash of bellowing roars and sinister laughter against the screams of tortured souls as they were brought to the edge of a great pit. Kasai reeled when he saw the hideous monster in the base of the pit wading through a mass of human soul-slaves. The condemned tried in vain to flee the grasp of the monster's wicked talons but to no avail. Each soul-slave was shredded apart in turn, sometimes quickly, but more often very slowly.

The monster turned, wearing a sick smile as it looked for another soul to devour, then lifted its eyes to Kasai, and he recognized her immediately.

Sekka.

+*So lovely to see you again.*+ The words pounded into his mind, and his legs buckled beneath him.

Sekka's infernal form thrashed and stomped in the pit, creating a swirling maelstrom of flesh and gore. Her white mane was saturated red, and her gnashing teeth broke bones and shredded limbs.

Her scream of bliss sent shivers up Kasai's spine. Pallo and Run-Run did their best to keep Desdemonia standing, while still shielding their eyes to the horrors happening below. Airis stood stone still, shocked with fear and with eyes wide and white. Orin stared righteous hate back at the devil. Only Aetenos seemed unfazed, and he waited patiently for her attention.

Sekka leaped effortlessly out of the pit and stomped over the companions. She bared down on Aetenos, but he did not flinch away. Kasai wondered if the Great Monk even knew where he was or if he thought this was just a dream.

As Sekka chuckled, the sound resonated deeply within her and sounded like many different voices overlapping each other. It made Kasai dizzy and want to puke. She snaked her long tongue out between her lips and wrapped it around Aetenos's throat, pulling him closer. Still, he did not so much as tremble.

Sekka released him and turned towards Kasai. She towered over him, dripping blood and gore, and her breath was fetid and sharp. Kasai could not keep the disgust from his face and turned away. He wanted to appear strong like Aetenos, but his confidence did not follow his intention.

Her booming laugher filled the room as she morphed into a slender but shapely woman, covered in bits and pieces of viscera. Her alabaster hair was pink and red and fell wet down her chest and back.

Kasai heard Desdemonia moan again and as she regained her senses. "What is going on? Where are we? Kasai?"

"I'm here."

"Ah yes, the Ever Hero and his little wood witch. Such an unlikely pair," Sekka jested. Her hands roamed freely over Kasai, pulling his bound body close to hers. He could feel an intense cold pulsating from her body. His fire xindu tried to counter the chilling sensation, but he was simply too exhausted to put up much of a fight.

"Take your filthy hands off him!" Desdemonia said. There was no fear in her voice, only venom.

Sekka raised her eyebrows at the outburst. "Full of vigor, I see. Gathos has that effect on those with chaos in their heart."

Desdemonia's amber eyes blazed back at her. Like Aetenos, she would not turn away.

"I said, let him go!"

"As you wish." Sekka removed her hands from Kasai and walked back to where she could take in the entire group. "Now, what shall I do with so many living souls when only the dead are provided freely?"

A fierce and jolly laugher erupted from Aetenos. "What else could you do that hasn't already been done?" He turned to Kasai and said, "One day, I'll tell you all about the so-called hospitality of Sekka. Ho, ho, but it's no picnic." He looked back at Sekka. "I'm sorry. What were you saying?"

She glared at the crazed monk. "Your jokes will lose their mirth soon enough. There is a bit of a scuffle here on Gathos that requires some attention and…"

"The Red Devil is here now," Aetenos interrupted and rocked back on his heels.

Sekka's body swelled in agitation, and Kasai thought her mortal form would give way to the beast once more. But she regained her composure and settled back into an alluring and sensuous woman even as her body glistened with blood.

"The folly of Zizphander shall soon be put to rest," she said with a gleam in her eye.

"No matter which path you walk, they all end in your doom. Your time is at an end," Aetenos said calmly but with conviction.

"So says the one who has paved the way for my ascendancy," she said and laughed in her horrible, malicious voice.

Kasai wondered if Sekka could possibly be defeated. He looked to his companions. They had suffered the ravages of Gathos and barely clung to their strength, though he saw that young Airis had succumbed to paralyzing fear once more.

The syrupy voice of Sekka interrupted his musings, and he focused his eyes on the seductive devil. Kasai was repulsed by the idea that he felt any kind of desire for the wicked creature. Nonetheless, his heart beat faster as lust mixed with fear.

Somehow, she knew how he felt. She spoke to Aetenos but looked at him from the corner of her eye. A bemused smile came to her mouth as she traced a long finger across Aetenos's jawline.

"I have had the grandest of ideas. You shall purge the Red Devil from Gathos."

"Oh?" Aetenos smiled with disbelief.

"Yes!" Sekka spun around in a pirouette like a young girl. "It's such a delicious plan, and won't Zizphander be surprised?"

"Surprised or not, what makes you think I will prevail when you and your minions have failed countless times?"

"Because you will take your mind slave with you. We shall finally see the powers of the Great Aetenos and his Ever Hero fighting as one. Oh, and along the way, please help Lord Oziax find his way to me. He has not been himself since his untimely return to Furia Keep."

The name echoed in Kasai's mind, Oziax, Oziax, Oziax. It seemed familiar to him but from another lifetime. Oziax. Then he had it.

"Oziax is dead," Kasai said with as much conviction as he could muster, which he thought wasn't much, but he must have shouted because all eyes now stared at him. Then the demons erupted in guttural laughter.

"We shall never help you, devil!" Orin courageously spoke out. "The power of the Light shall smite you and all of your wickedness!"

Sekka slowly turned her head and locked her gaze on Orin. She sauntered over to the impassioned warrior and cupped his head in both her hands.

"I thought that might be your answer." Sekka nodded to Airis. "Take the young one."

Two guards grabbed Airis and thrust him to the floor. One stood behind him and placed his monkey-like hands on Airis's shoulders to hold him down.

"Aetenos! Help me!" Airis cried.

But the Great Monk made no move to help and only looked at Airis with compassion in his eye. It seemed he had already accepted the young man's fate. Airis turned desperately to Kasai.

"Ever Hero, please, you must do something. I do not want to die. Not like this. Not *here*. You promised the Light would keep me safe. Please, I want to go home."

Kasai tried to get out of the grips of the demon behind him but was held fast. His fists tightened, and a bright, azure glow grew from his hands. The binders on his wrists began to creak.

"Oh, none of that here, please," Sekka said and passed her open hand across Kasai. Immediately his limbs grew numb as frost spread up his arms. Sekka's magic prevented him from igniting his fire xindu, and his fists flexed open as the strength and warmth left his hands.

"Wait!" Kasai cried. "Stop!"

Sekka casually walked to Airis, and elongated nails sprouted from her fingers. She glanced back at Kasai and gave him a wicked smirk, then unceremoniously dragged her nails across Airis's neck. Red lines trailed her fingers, and then blood flowed in steaming sheets down his throat and over his chest. Airis's lifeless body crumpled to the floor, folding upon itself.

"Airis!" Orin yelled out.

Pallo fought against his jailor, and Run-Run's eyes looked to the ceiling, and he mouthed a silent prayer.

"Now, who shall be next?" Sekka said as she set her eyes on Desdemonia. "Bring the wood witch."

"No!" Kasai shouted. "You cannot take her!"

"You would like to reconsider?"

"I'm going to destroy you!" Kasai cried out, and tears rolled down his face. "Leave her alone!"

Sekka smiled at him with a wolfish grin. Aetenos leaned his head over closer to Kasai's and nodded in agreement. "Well said, my boy." Kasai looked back at Aetenos in astonishment. He did not understand why the Great Monk had done nothing. How could he remain so calm?

"Bring the witch," Sekka commanded.

"Hold a moment," Aetenos said and stared at Kasai for what seemed like an eternity while Desdemonia's throat was made ready for Sekka's claws. Kasai stared back, unsure of what the Master meant to do. Was this a test?

Kasai lowered his head in shame. "I am sorry. I was not strong enough. I freed you only to have you fall into her hands once more." Kasai looked back at Airis's still body. "I have now failed Airis as well."

"No, my son. There is no failure. His soul shall be welcomed in the cloudless realm of the Seven Heavens. His suffering is over."

Kasai desperately wanted to believe Aetenos's words. He then brought his head in closer and whispered, "If we are finished, I'd have the suffering of my companions end as well. I shall create a diversion while you escape. Find Illyria in Baroqia and close the Chaos Gate.

"Continue to fight for our souls, Master. Hopefully, you will see they are still worth your attention. The people of Baroqia must hear your Song once more."

"If you are you finished, I'd have your answer," Sekka said, growing impatient.

"Tell me, do you love her?"

"What? Who? Sekka?"

Aetenos rolled his one eye. "No, you dolt, the witch. Do you love her?" He tilted his head to the side towards Desdemonia.

Kasai pulled his head back, confused. "What do you mean?"

"Do you love the Wood Witch, my son?" Aetenos repeated each word slower this time and would not break eye contact.

Kasai looked to Desdemonia. She struggled against the grips of her captors, but there were too many hands holding her down. Kasai could not imagine life without her, even though they had shared only a small amount of it together.

"Yes, Master. I do." Finally, it was out for all to hear. Kasai felt a constriction around his heart release, and his eyes cloudy with tears. He looked at her and nodded while she stared back in disbelief.

"But I thought…"

"Yes, since the first. I have no words for such things, and don't know how to express them."

"Ho, ho! Then we shall honor that love with action and not sad words of lonely deeds or complaints of weakness," Aetenos said and addressed Sekka. "It seems our time together is not yet at an end. My friend and I shall do as you ask."

"How will we find your headless beast?" Kasai said, feeling emboldened, but immediately wished he had not said a word. The hall erupted in more wicked laughter.

"Oh, I believe you will find him to have a familiar face once more," Sekka said in a playful tone. "Take Aetenos and the boy to the surface so they can rescue poor Oziax from himself. The rest shall watch the success or failure of our new champions."

Kasai looked desperately at Desdemonia. He feared this would be the last time he would see her alive, and there was so much more to say.

"Kasai!" Desdemonia blurted out, but she could do no more as the guards covered her mouth and twisted her head away.

"Know that their fate is in your hands, Ever Hero," Sekka said behind him. "Stop the Red Devil and bring my lost warlord home, or I will discover new torments for your friends that will make you wish you were in that pit instead."

Kasai resisted being led away from his companions and struggled to break the grip of his captors. "How do we know you will keep your promise and not harm the others?" he yelled out.

"Oh, I made no such promise. But I like to think of myself as an honest devil, and promise you this, no immediate harm will come to your companions. After all, they are wonderful leverage. Take care, Ever Hero, and bring me the head of Zizphander."

Kasai and Aetenos were led through a maze of ice tunnels and back to the surface of Gathos. They eventually came to a heavy door, which their escorts unlocked and pushed open. Kasai recognized the courtyard where they had first entered Furia Keep.

One of the guards carried a heavily wrapped bundle and threw it at Kasai's feet, just as another guard shoved Aetenos out into the square, where he stumbled to the ground. Kasai reached down and unwrapped the bundle to see Ninziz-zida's black sticks. He grabbed her just as he was shoved outside as well. The door swung shut behind them with a deep thud.

Thankfully, the statues plastered to the walls remained silent. Ahead of them were the gates that led back to the frozen wastelands of Gathos. Kasai heard the dull pounding of surface winds crashing against the outer walls of the Keep.

"I will do my best to protect you," Aetenos said.

"Thank you, Master."

"Don't look so worried then. You'll be fine. We will battle side-by-side, just as I did with Gen Moll."

Kasai just nodded sullenly. "You should know, I never mastered the Xindu Mysteries. Master Choejor was often disappointed with my progress." Kasai pulled his fur closer to his body and stuck Ninziz-zida in his sash. The cold was relentless and seeped into his already stiff and tired limbs.

"Ah, Blind Choejor. He could see straightest of us all, could he not? I shall be happy to see him again when this nonsense is at an end."

Kasai's heart sank. "Master Choejor is dead. I could not save him."

"Oh, I see. That is a shame."

They trudged in the direction of the outer gates without another word. Then a smile broadened Aetenos's face. "I have fond memories of Choejor locked away in this old head of mine. He shall live on with me there, and during happier times. But for now, let us talk about the Xindu Mysteries and the nature of this energy."

"Yes, Master."

"Vibration can be easily seen when you can understand their rhythm. I believe you saw this atop the pillars some time ago, and more recently, while dancing with Oziax, which was quite impressive, I might add."

"Yes, Master, but only with your help or Ninziz-zida's fire. I cannot do it alone."

"Bah, my help, Ninziz-zida's fire, all that has ever been done for you was to suppress the barriers you have built up inside your heart. And finally, when the walls came down, you were free to experience the Boundless in its pure form.

"But behold! The Great Walls of Kasai Ch'ou shall not fall! Look what a masterful job you have done, building back up so quickly, that which was sought to be taken down forever. Never has an Ever Hero been so reluctant to embrace his fate."

Aetenos shook his head, half in wonder, half in disappointment. "You believe everything is your responsibility and your fault."

"Master, I could have..."

"This is arrogance," Aetenos said abruptly. "Was it you that set the Realms in motion when you came to be?"

"No, Master."

"No is right. These things move along their own destinies, beyond any influence we might think we add."

"Even your influence, Master?"

"Me? I am nothing more than a light breeze moving through the small leaves of the ancient oak. I do not uproot the tree with my whisper, and most of the leaves fall back to their original position after I pass through. I am an afterthought to most."

"But how can I—" Kasai started to say.

"Stop convincing yourself you cannot and listen for a moment. It was all within you already, my son. I did very little once you believed. Your training at Ordu gave you form and discipline. And yet, to the dismay of the Immortal Mother, you push so much of your potential away."

"I have always been fearful, Master," Kasai said.

"Yes, you have always resisted what you do not understand. Your father was a great teacher. I had hoped he could have taught you more before his time was at an end. But his moment in your life was short."

"My father? My father was a coward. He ran to save himself the moment my mother and I needed him most."

Aetenos was no longer listening to Kasai. "It's a shame he didn't have more time with you. A terrible shame. He was a good man. Yes, more time. So much time everywhere, and never quite enough..." Aetenos's voice drifted off and was lost in the wind. The Great Monk became silent and contemplative.

Kasai waited patiently for Aetenos to speak again. Then suddenly, Aetenos was back in the present. "The Xindu Mysteries. What do you know of them?"

"Master?" Kasai said, confused.

"Tell me, tell me." Aetenos rolled his hand to get Kasai to begin.

"Well, there are four energies which a disciplined mind may control, fire, to light the passion, water to cool the soul, earth to support the body, and air to connect them all. The Mysteries were first discovered..."

"That's enough." The excitement faded from Aetenos's eye. He shook his hands in front of Kasai. "Yes, yes, that's quite enough."

"Forgive me. I thought you wanted me to..."

"Yes, and there it is, you thought." Aetenos put his hand on Kasai's forehead and rubbed his palm vigorously across the smooth skin as if he was scrubbing away dirt.

"Have you ever thought that you overthink everything?"

He tapped Kasai's brow with his first two fingers. "Forget about what is here. And feel what is here." He then gently padded Kasai's chest, over his heart. Kasai followed Aetenos's hand with his eyes and then back at the Master. He shrugged his shoulders.

Aetenos sighed and pointed to Ninziz-zida. "Take her in your hands."

Kasai did as he was instructed and held Ninziz-zida's three segments in his outstretched hands. He moved as if to give the weapon to Aetenos.

"Don't give her to me, you fool. Let her uncoil in your grip. Feel her warmth, her passion. Is she only a blunt weapon to swing and smash? No. She is a focused force of passion with a purpose. She is lawful strength, not reckless chaos. She is the Great Defender, powerful in the hands of the righteous, but woe to any of evil intent that touches her smooth onyx sticks."

Kasai felt Ninziz-zida's warm pulse in his hands. He felt an intimate connection to the ancient weapon and wondered if the Fire Serpent was a living thing, concealed in a mundane object.

A realization suddenly dawned on Kasai. "Master, Ninziz-zida *is* fire xindu. I felt something deeper when we fought the jol'goths at the entrance, not only with her xindu energy but also a bond with her..." Kasai reflected for a moment, then, "with her heart."

"Yes, yes! That's it! She is a wondrous beauty, and as with most beautiful things, she will demand your attention. What else?"

Kasai closed his eyes and concentrated solely on Ninziz-zida and the emotional connection being forged between them. "She...she is vast. I...can sense endless fire, so much...energy...and I feel something else as if a mountain has uncoiled into a river." Kasai opened his eyes, startled at what he had felt.

"And she is filled with all kinds of surprises, ho, ho!" Aetenos laughed.

Kasai looked at the Fire Serpent in amazement. He had thought she was a formidable weapon as they fought together in the past, but now he knew he had barely tapped into her strength.

"Master, I thought...but why me?"

"Yes, yes, I know. Kasai the Unworthy." Aetenos dismissed Kasai's assumption once more with the wave of his hand. "Ninziz-zida makes her own choices. And believe me, she will not be coerced against her will by anyone, not even me."

"Desdemonia tells me I have a noble heart, but she is always saying the oddest things."

"The wood witch and Fire Serpent seem to understand your quality quite well. Why then, do you remain blind?"

"I wish I knew," Kasai said just as he heard the all too familiar growl of a jol'goth behind him. He quickly spun around, Ninziz-zida held firmly in his hands. The tall, bear-faced demon lumbered forward and glared first at Aetenos, and then snapped its saliva-dripping muzzle at Kasai.

But the jol'goth moved past the pair and approached one of the tall gates. It lowered its shoulder against the frozen iron and stone. Even under such a heavy coat of shaggy fur, the pronounced musculature of the demon was undeniable.

The gate groaned on tight hinges and slowly swung forward, plowing a path of newly fallen snow away from the entrance. The snowstorm outside raced into the courtyard as snow billowed in and swirled on the stone tiled floors.

The jol'goth stepped outside first. It pointed a long finger in the same direction the procession of demons had marched earlier that day, led by the warlord armored in white with an antlered helm of horns. Kasai hoped Aetenos knew what their direction would be, for he hadn't a clue.

A sunless, greyish-mauve sky greeted them as they took their first steps back into the unkind wasteland. The chilling wind bit and nipped at their flesh as it dug into their bones. The vastness of Gathos stretched out in all directions, and the bleak desolation weighed heavily on Kasai's resolve.

"How will we ever find Oziax? He could be anywhere out there. This is hopeless."

"You found me, did you not?" Aetenos said.

Kasi felt ashamed for his lack of focus. He carried so much doubt in his heart, going back to the loss of his mother, and filled with one disappointment after another, culminating with his current predicament. He was about to explain this to Aetenos, but the Master had already moved on in his lesson.

"So, you can see that all things have their own rhythm and vibration, and can be more than they seem, yes?" He tapped Ninziz-zida and nodded to make sure Kasai understood.

"Good. Now that we have a different way of thinking, let us consider what to do with this energy and how we can manipulate it."

"Manipulate, Master?"

"That's right."

Kasai immediately became confused. The crunching snow of the Abyss made more sense to him than understanding Aetenos's meaning.

Aetenos patiently sighed. "Think of the wind. Can you see it move in the open sky? No. But you feel it upon your skin. Can you see it move the tall trees and long grass?"

Kasai nodded.

"You are experiencing its essence, its spirit. This is part of the Boundless. Vibrations are the living energy, or spirit, that can move in haste to bend trees as the wind or be stern and slow as the stone wall. They move in flowing currents like the deep ocean or remain stoic like the old mountain.

"There is a meeting place between your vibrations and the vibrations of all things around you. When vibrations merge, they become something new, which can be directed."

Kasai felt foolish. "I do not understand, Master. I cannot do what you do. I have learned a few tricks at Ordu, but anything worthy of great power that I have conjured has been without my knowledge. I could never duplicate it on my own."

"Hmm." Aetenos was thoughtful for a moment. His one good eye became animated as he spoke. "Before you took your first breath, was breathing something you could do? No. But since that moment of awareness of breath, you have been able to breathe without thought. You have mindlessly manipulated your breathing to be heavy or shallow, yes?

"You have held great gulps of air in your chest and remained underwater for long lengths of time. You have pushed it through your lips to speak, shout and whistle. Such wondrous things you have achieved through breathing alone, and all things you could not do until you did them."

Kasai tried hard to understand, but Aetenos was worse than Master Choejor.

"Master, all living things breathe. It is a natural thing."

"There, see? Now you have it. Easy. Ho, ho! You are a quick learner, or I am a great teacher. Either way, we are ready." Aetenos was delighted with his lesson. He proudly patted Kasai on the back.

"Come, let us find Oziax and have a look at what has become of the Red Devil, Zizphander, shall we?" Aetenos eagerly marched forward as if on his way to a garden party, filled with pleasant company and where delicious sweets and honeyed bread would be served.

Kasai wondered how this man had become a demigod.

48

SHIVERRIG

Aj-Kahun Shiverrig wore a thick, black bearskin fur that bristled across his broad shoulders and over newly crafted half-plate armor, which was polished to an exquisite sheen, and bore his new coat of arms. The lone mastiff had been replaced by a more terrifying version of the same, with three heads, each looking in a different direction, guarding and attacking at once.

He stood upon a makeshift dais and surveyed a small courtyard within the castle walls of the City of Spires. Winter's morning air was still and crisp. The sound of chickadees chirped in nests wedged within the cracks of the stone walls and caws from blue jays trumpeted as they flew overhead.

The noble families loyal to the Dead King, and previously imprisoned, had been brought together to hear the proclamation of their fate. The reek of the castle's dungeons filled the morning air. Luckily, the winter chill kept the black flies dormant and only a handful of those which traveled from the dank cells with their hosts, buzzed through the air.

Small exhales of breath clouded before the nobles' faces. Their clothing had lost much of its rich luster and hung worn and wrinkled on bodies just as unkempt. Shiverrig noted that many of the lords of Great Houses stood with eager eyes and avarice smiles.

"The fools believe they are here to discuss their recompense for having a change of heart," he said to Malachi on his left.

"Indeed, my Aj-Kahun," Malachi said. "Such is their nature."

Shiverrig scratched his forearm, and absentmindedly worried away a dry piece of skin. He casually looked down and realized he rubbed a shimmering scale between his thumb and forefinger. Its sheen was aquamarine in the cold, blue light of dawn.

+*So much could be yours, if you gave me but a bit more of your soul.*+ Jynxx whispered in the shadows of his mind. Shiverrig ignored her request and adjusted the circlet to sit more evenly upon his head. The object did wonders at keeping the demon's constant nagging out of his mind.

Shiverrig narrowed his gaze back to the families standing before him. All counted, husbands, wives, and children, their number was precisely three hundred. An interesting number. Not quite a battalion but numerous enough to hold back an oppressive force when positioned strategically on a battlefield.

Shiverrig peered to his left at Malachi. Thankfully, his archvashim had remembered to alter his appearance to remove any semblance to the demon, Hilo, who festered within and whispered secrets into the man's mind. At least he could assert some, small amount of control over the fiend, Shiverrig thought with a hint of irritation.

Malachi had traded his red robes of office and wore a boiled, dark leather jacket and pants under a silver fox fur. The medallion of Mor was still hung from his neck, though Shiverrig doubted that devotion would remain pure, now that a more pestilent power visibly walked the lands. Where Malachi's right hand should be was now a golden cup resembling a large thimble, etched with strange glyphs which Shiverrig could not decipher.

Malachi moved to the front of the dais to address the displaced nobles. He held his hands up to quiet the crowd. "Subjects of the Aj-Kahun, Gerun Shiverrig, first of his name and ruler of the civilized lands of the Three Kingdoms, I will have your attention. You have been brought together to become one with your Aj-Kahun, and permanently add yourselves to his Everlasting Empire."

Shiverrig saw faces change from wary confusion to amusing confidence. Some even smirked to their fellows and assumed it was business as usual. It didn't matter to them who sat on the throne, if they received their due. He was unimpressed with their newfound devotion.

"House Moutlier and all of the house clans under her banner are with you!" Lord Moutlier shouted above the crowd and pushed himself to the forefront of the assembled lords, wanting to be the first to accept Shiverrig and his rule. "We bow to the Aj-Kahun."

"As does House Fountaine! And the banners of Clan Rouke, Clan Thoss, and Clan Molneer! Hail Gerun Shiverrig! Hail the Aj-Kahun!"

Malachi hushed the crowd once more. "It was the way of the first Aj-Kahun to recognize his most trusted lords and ladies with a place at his table, to share in his food and drink and tell stories of valor. Today, we observe the old ways and honor tradition.

"Approach the dais and receive the Aj-Kahun in a symbolic gesture of fealty. Drink from his cup and eat from his table and be made anew."

Malachi pointed to a long table to the left of the dais, set with many goblets and a decorative wooden chest. Two young pages stood nearby, one opened the chest to reveal small, pearl-shaped orbs inside, and the other poured wine into the rows of cups. "The Aj-Kahun wishes for you partake in the ceremony of fealty and bonding of brotherhood."

Lord Fountaine spoke over the crowd of murmurs, "And then we shall discuss our terms of accommodation and title within the new regime?" He looked hopeful and suspicious at once.

"Quite so," deadpanned Shiverrig, and the crowd roared in delight. Some enthusiastically raised their fists in salute or waved their hands in acknowledgment of the new regime. Such was the way of pigs, Shiverrig thought.

The Knights of Gethem entered the courtyard. They had kept their namesake, but now wore the brand of the three-headed mastiff on their breastplate and shields. They herded the nobles and their families together, forming them into a line that approached the table.

The nobles laughed with one another and spoke ill of the short reign of the Dead King. Many openly boasted of reneging on loans due to House Conrad and that they would reinvest their money in a new tower or country home.

"These people have no honor," Shiverrig said in disgust.

Moutlier and the members of his House arrived at the foot of the dais. His family members knelt before the Aj-Kahun, and Shiverrig nodded his approval of their fealty.

"Feed the first, Malachi," Shiverrig said, and Malachi placed a small orb in Moutlier's mouth, while one of the pages handed him a goblet of diluted wine. The other page gave each family member a similar orb to swallow. One-by-one they drank their fill, draining the cup and showing it empty to their Aj-Kahun. They handed the cup back to the page and bowed to Shiverrig, who gave each a forced smile.

When the members of the last House had passed the dais and returned to the courtyard, Malachi gained the elevated platform and addressed the crowd.

"The Aj-Kahun thanks you for your willing participation. Your sacrifice shall be written in the histories of the land for all eternity."

"Sacrifice? What trickery is this Shiverrig?" Moutlier shouted, then doubled over in pain, cupping his hands over his ears. He fell to his knees and screamed.

"Get out of my head!"

Moutlier's chest heaved, and his breath came short and fast. His hands moved from his ears to his hair. Within moments he was pulling dirty-blonde tuffs from his scalp. "Shiverrig! A thousand curses upon you!"

Shiverrig looked at Moutlier and the rest of the nobles with uncaring eyes. He spotted Sess'thra walking through the crowd. Her wings were tucked in close behind her back, and her serpentine tail swayed loosely, while the tip twitched with excitement.

Sess'thra had donned black leather breeches and high boots. She wore a loose green tunic, belted low across her hips, and dangerously open in the front, the color at odds with her sharp lavender eyes. She held no concern for modesty or how the cold morning air affected her lithe body and caressed her uncovered flesh.

She examined the transformation of the nobles. Some she grabbed by the chin and gazed deeply into their eyes, nodding her approval, others she pushed out of her way, disgusted in their inability to cope with the madness of possession.

Her narrow hips swayed seductively as she sauntered to the dais and climbed the stairs. A feral grin spread across her lips as she looked upon Shiverrig with admiration and desire.

Lord Fountaine staggered to the base of the dais, tears streaming down his rough face. He tried to speak but suffered a fit of coughing through a throat filled with phlegm. Once he recovered his composure, he pointed a shaking finger at Shiverrig.

"What have you done! I demand answers!"

Shiverrig surveyed the individual struggles in the courtyard, then eventually cast his gaze back to Fountaine. "I did what must be done to ensure your survival."

The words came easy to Shiverrig, as did the scowl when he heard the mocking laughter of demon Jynxx ringing in his head.

"How do you feel, Lord Fountaine?"

The distraught nobleman looked at Shiverrig with incredulous eyes. "You are a madman!" he said through trembling lips, and then his body began to buckle, and he fell forward on his hands and knees.

Shiverrig heard the unmistakable sound of cloth ripping, first from Fountaine's back and then across the courtyard. One-by-one, the nobles screamed in pain as bat-like wings unfolded across their bodies. They reminded Shiverrig of springtime buds breaking through winter's thawing ground as the soft membrane delicately unfurled in the air. The half-breed demons cautiously tested the reality of their leathery appendages, hesitant at first but then stretching and expanding in magnificent elegance.

As was with Lord Jolla, the nobles' facial features resembled aquiline shapes of birds of prey with slightly hooked noses and pulled back cheekbones. Their arms thinned with fingers that grew tapered and sharp. But where Lord Jolla's wings were avian in nature, these half-breeds took on a more nocturnal aspect.

Sess'thra clapped her hands in delight, and Shiverrig wondered if he had been duped. The creatures had an uncanny resemblance to her as if she had mothered the brood from her own loins. What did he expect? The seeds had come about at the most opportune time.

"Look upon our children, my Aj-Kahun," Sess'thra said as she leaned against his muscular body.

"You have done well," he said.

He begrudgingly admitted Sess'thra's cunning and crafty subterfuge was a brilliant move to ensure his legacy. In days long past, the warlords of old had raped their way through the tribes of the conquered, siring the next generation of children by their own seed.

If he must do the same to bring forth his Everlasting Empire, then so be it. He envisioned vast armies of half-breeds, bonded to him by blood, sweeping across the Three Kingdoms, destroying all opposition that stood against him. This made him smile. His empire would be the greatest ever known to mortal man, one that lasted for an eternity. He would finally be worthy of the Shiverrig name.

Then a disconcerting thought crossed his mind. Where did the brood's loyalty lie?

"I have one more surprise for you to honor this day," Sess'thra purred into his ear. "Look there, breaking through the crowd."

Shiverrig saw the half-breeds move apart as another team of knights arranged in a spear tip formation marched forward, dragging a young man to the dais. He was dirty, and his skin looked smudged from so many bruises.

Two knights held the prisoner's arms up and away from his back, while a third pushed the rounded end of his polearm into the nape of his neck, forcing him to kneel with a lowered head.

"Duke Shiverrig, you shall answer for your crimes," the prisoner said and raised his head with great effort against the polearm while squinting in the bright light. His face was cut and swollen. Dirt and grime were caked in clumps through his hair and soiled his clothing.

"Prince Dane, welcome to the dawn of New Baroqia and her rise to prominence," Malachi said with bravado laced with a sneer. "This shall be a very auspicious day for you. As you can see, those loyal to your father have joined the ranks of the Aj-Kahun's forces."

The voices of the nobles had changed to more of a squawk-like speech rather than High Common. Prince Dane looked about in horror. "You monster."

His head dropped, and the knights let his body fall the rest of the way to the ground. A light dusting of snow blew across the courtyard from an unexpected breeze. Malachi stepped down from the dais to stand in front of Prince Dane and signaled one of the knights.

"Head up, please."

The knight grabbed a thick tuff of hair and jerked the young Prince's head back. Malachi reached into a pocket on the side of his leather jacket and took out a red orb.

"Open wide."

Prince Dane refused to comply until a second knight blocked the Prince's nose and forced down his chin. Malachi plopped the red orb into the back of Prince Dane's throat and nodded to the knight.

"Close it up."

Malachi stepped back when he was assured the Prince had swallowed the orb. Shiverrig looked on with great interest, as did Sess'thra.

"Here shall be our crowning achievement," she said. "Our children will need a leader, one who will control them as you wish."

Prince Dane gasped for breath that would not come. His eyed watered, and his hands swelled as he dug his fingers into the frozen dirt. He arched his back and screamed into the air. Great feathered wings, the color of rubies in the sunlight, ripped away what remained of the tattered shirt he wore.

He raised himself to a kneeling position with his back straight and up. His broad wings beat as he stood, and then lifted him higher, taking the weight off his legs entirely. Suddenly, his knees snapped back and reformed in the reversed direction, becoming more avian in appearance.

Prince Dane looked queerly at Shiverrig as if seeing him for the first time with little recognition. The whites of his eyes turned orange, and his pupils were dilated to black orbs. His mouth opened to scream as two sword-like appendages spiked from his mouth into a long, stork beak. Then, a great fan of red and purple feathers bloomed from his scalp and neck.

"Welcome, Vorleeth," Sess'thra said and came down from the dais to inspect the transformation. Her slight hips swayed with each step like a church bell at noon.

The red-winged demon took in the courtyard as the other half-breeds paid him no heed and jostled together in mounting aggression. Vorleeth walked to the front of the crowd on reformed and stable legs. He leaped into the air and hovered above the newborns, his brilliant wings created a storm of snow and dirt through their ranks.

Vorleeth drew a deep breath and shrieked a harrowing cry causing most of them to drop immediately to their knees in supplication. Shiverrig noted one of the few that remained standing was Moutlier; either he or the demon he had become, refused to yield.

"Let this be a lesson to you, my dearest, on the ways of demonkind," Sess'thra said over her shoulder.

Vorleeth hovered closer to Moutlier as the defiant half-breed squawked and preened until Vorleeth snapped his head forward and drove his sword-like beak through Moutlier's face and out the other side of his skull. Vorleeth then rose higher into the air until the dead demon slipped off his beak.

Vorleeth shrieked out his victory to the rest of the half-breeds, daring any of them to challenge his dominance. Those who still stood dropped and groveled on the ground.

"Get them trained and ready to obey, especially that one," Shiverrig said, pointing at Vorleeth. "The last thing I want is another Khalkoroth nipping at my arse."

Shiverrig descended the dais and walked back into the inner chambers of the keep. Once alone, he pondered the cryptic information he had received from the shade of Maugris. The denizens of the Abyss cast a wide and dangerous net, and he would not be foolish enough to underestimate Sekka as Maugris had done.

"Which brings me to the crafty, Sess'thra," he mused. She played the part of his ally and lover with great flair, but ultimately, she was just another fly stuck in the sticky strands of Sekka's web. His new shock troops would be beneficial in the coming days if they could be trusted to follow his will.

The Aj-Kahun's heavy footsteps pounded across the wooden floor. A priceless mirror hung on the wall, and as he passed in front of it, he thought he noticed its glass rippling along the edge of its baroque frame. Shiverrig had no knowledge of the alchemy behind its reflective gaze, and nor did he care. He hated mirrors, for they were the trapping of weak politicians and lords who bolstered their own importance with opulence and needed a constant reminder of their image in the center of stolen wealth.

"Maybe I'll destroy them all," he pondered aloud.

Shiverrig contemplated his own reflection as he decided the mirror's fate. The bearskin fur he wore was a testament to his strength and prowess in combat. He remembered the day he slew the animal with only sword and spear, just as his legendary grandsire, Baroq Shiverrig, had done when he tamed these lands. It was the Shiverrig way. "A man must earn his furs."

He smiled at his reflection, knowing he too was mighty, he also was a conqueror!

"I will carry on the Shiverrig tradition of conquest to the uncivilized lands of Sunne and throughout the barbarian tribes of Trosk. I will make you proud, great grandfather," he said.

But the more he scrutinized his reflection, the more doubt crawled under his skin at the righteousness of his actions. Shiverrig frowned. He felt the image in the mirror mocked him.

"What have you achieved but to murder a frail man who could barely hold a sword, and sully the honor of your House by laying with the devil?"

Mirrors clouded a man's mind with falsehood but also showed him the truth of his ways to spite him. Mirrors were an evil thing, he thought and turned away, thinking this one would be the first to be smashed, melted down into glass trinkets, and sold to the savages of Sunne.

Out of the corner of his eye, he caught a glimpse of the same ripple he had thought he saw earlier. A startling image of a great beast with gnashing teeth filled the entire mirror. The creature quickly dissolved into an innocent babe, which then moved through the whole lifecycle of a maiden, disappearing at last as an old crone that withered away to nothingness. A flitting sparrow appeared and then burst into flames that spiraled out from a central point, lapping against the edges of the mirror.

A loud, baritone voice spoke from far away but seemed to be gathering speed as it reached the mirror's surface.

"THE CHAOS GATE FLOWS FREELY IN TROSK."

Shiverrig felt a throbbing pain erupt from behind his left eye and then roll to the back of his head.

"What dark magic is this?"

He put his arm to the wall to steady himself from rising nausea in his gut. The inner presence of Jynxx rushed to the forefront of his mind in a warning.

+Do not speak any words! Do not ask its name. Let it remain nameless and forgotten.+ Jynxx was horrified. Now he was intrigued.

"Speak plain, demon of the mirror. I know not of a Chaos Gate or what that implies," Shiverrig said, playing dumb.

The deep voice chuckled, then the pitch of the voice melded into that of a young child.

"SOON YOU SHALL, MORTAL, AND WITH MY HELP, YOU COULD CONTROL ALL OF THE LANDS YOU SEE. ALL YOU NEED TO DO IS ASK."

"I will achieve this without your assistance."

Shiverrig peered suspiciously into the glass. His finger lifted to the surface, wondering if what he heard, and saw were real.

"I have felt your presence, in the shadows behind thick curtains and in the winter winds that harrow through lonely corridors. And now you hide behind this mirrored glass? You claim great power, yet you remain powerless to appear."

"AH, THERE ARE RULES ALL MUST FOLLOW, AND I MUST BE ASKED POLITELY."

+Do not! We shall be consumed! Say no more, lest your words are twisted into a pact of eternal damnation!+

+ENOUGH! YOU SHALL SPEAK NO MORE. I NAME YOU, TOKOLOSHEJYNXX. I SEE YOU AND SHALL HAVE YOU! +

The words boomed in Shiverrig's head, and he momentarily lost his balance, needing the wall to steady himself. He felt the presence of Jynxx cower and flee at the command from the otherworldly entity. His mind became clear and clean, but for a high-pitched note that stalked the edges of his thoughts and grew louder when Jynxx attempted to return, forcing her away with shrill screams of pain.

The voice in the mirror resumed a more pleasant, familiar tone.

"NOW WE MAY CONTINUE WITHOUT INTERRUPTION."

"There is nothing to speak of, demon. You have been asked for nothing. I do not need your help and want it even less."

"I AM NO MERE DEMON, AND FAR GREATER THAN YOU CAN CONCEIVE WITHIN THE LIMITS OF YOUR MIND. I SHALL FORGIVE YOU THIS INSULT ONCE, BUT DO NOT MISTAKE ME FOR ANYTHING BUT THAT WHICH I AM."

Shiverrig took a step backward, studying the mirror's surface, watching for any details that might give away more of his visitor's bearing.

"AND YOU HAVE ALREADY ACCEPTED MY HELP."

"I have done no such thing."

"THE CIRCLET ON YOUR HEAD WAS MY GIFT TO YOU."

Shiverrig's hand absently went to the golden band on his head. Of course, Maugris. He grabbed the circlet to take it off.

"FEAR NOT. I DO NOT LOOK TO CLAIM YOUR SOUL, AND THERE IS NO PAYMENT DUE. THE CIRCLET IS BUT A TOKEN OF GOODWILL. SPEAK OR THINK OF JYNXX'S TRUE NAME AND FOCUS YOUR WILL INTO THE CIRCLET.

JYNXX SHALL QUAIL IN TERROR AS HER DEMONIC ESSENCE IS DELIVERED TO ME, PIECE-BY-PIECE."

"And to whom do I speak?"

"MY TIME GROWS SHORT, BUT WE WILL SPEAK AGAIN SOON."

The voice trailed off into a whisper, and whatever presence was there had vanished. All that was left was Shiverrig's reflection staring back at him. He knocked at the glass with the back of his forefinger knuckle and the surface was as rigid as it should be. He stepped away.

"The world has irrevocably changed," Shiverrig said. "And I hold the weakest position."

He needed to identify the artifact he wore on his head, but he would do so in secret. The voice made no mention of Sekka, which was very curious and would require more investigation. But for now, he would concentrate on the training of the half-breeds into a fierce fighting force. They could be an incredible asset if he could make more.

He made to leave the hall and realized that his legs were still shaking.

49

KASAI

Kasai and Aetenos trudged through the frozen wastelands of Gathos, neither spoke much to the other as the omnipresent howls of frigid winds locked their jaws tight and minds even tighter. Distant shapes came into focus along the horizon, but the snow furiously whipped across Kasai's eyes, blinding him and blurring the identity of the newcomers. One thing was sure, the shapes were approaching in haste.

Eventually, Kasai recognized the distinct shape of magnificent antlers that had belonged to the warlord earlier in the day, if day and night existed here. Time passed without meaning in the white cold of Gathos.

The warlord was now on foot, and Kasai saw that his armor had been dented and broken. He stumbled in his steps as he approached, then came to a startling stop when he saw Aetenos.

"What madness is this? The mighty Aetenos has come to save me on Gathos? I would rather be obliterated by the Red Devil before I accept the help from a one-eyed angel lover."

"Sadly, such is not your fate, Lord Oziax," Aetenos said, then bowed slightly. Kasai was surprised his Master spoke in such a respectful manner to the demon.

One-by-one, the misshapen flesh golems that trailed after Oziax, joined their leader. They were maligned creatures with too many eyes and mouths covered in matted fur or exposed skin that raised welt-like gooseflesh in the cold. Long shafts of sharp iron and steel protruded from their limbs.

Oziax cast his helmed gaze on Kasai, and recognition came a moment later. "You!" he said and pointed a gauntleted finger at Kasai. "You die here and now for the ruin you have caused me!"

Oziax drew the black sword at his side, and Kasai heard it moan as if it were alive.

Kasai stepped back and readied Ninziz-zida to defend himself.

"Where Eishorror failed, the black blade, Void, shall prevail. Today will see the end of the Red Devil, and my honor reclaimed."

Aetenos stepped in front of Oziax and raised his right hand, index and middle finger straight, and pointing upwards. An expanding bubble of displaced air swelled around him, lifting the snow that had clumped on his head and shoulders and drove back the swirling wind.

Oziax pointed the black blade at Kasai. "Your mind slave has a debt to repay, Old Monk. I shall have my due! Step aside."

Aetenos shook his head. "We are honor-bound to save you. Nothing more shall you have this day but your life if that is possible. Now, where is bold Zizphander? I hear he has been quite troublesome of late."

Oziax looked back to Kasai, and then Aetenos's energy field. Reluctantly, he lowered his blade. "His horde knows no rest and will come upon us soon."

Oziax looked behind him and then scanned to the sky from left to right. Aetenos followed the demon warlord's line of sight. A moment later, he pointed to the ridgeline of high hills to the far right.

"I believe I have found our mutual adversary. The Red Devil seeks to finish you now and races ahead to cut off your retreat."

"Retreat? I am not in retreat! I lure him to the ground of my choosing. As I have said, before this day is done, the Red Devil shall be no more!"

"Of course," Aetenos bowed slightly again towards Oziax. "Let us see if I can help you in that endeavor."

Zizphander flew through the sky with the speed of a shooting meteor. His body glowed against the blue-grey landscape like a ball of fire, then banked towards them and came at speed.

Aetenos pointed his right hand in the direction of the flying devil, then closed his eye and concentrated. Kasai saw the snow swirling around Zizphander compress into a thick ball around him until he tumbled out of the sky.

Aetenos opened his eye and smiled, but Kasai saw only profound fatigue in his face.

"Master, are you well?"

"Hmm? What's that? Oh, quite well, thank you," Aetenos said and took in his surroundings as if for the first time. "A bit of a dismal place for a stroll, isn't it?"

Kasai's eyes grew wide. Oh no. Please, no. Not now.

Aetenos looked questioningly at Oziax, then back to Kasai and finally seemed to remember where he was and what he was doing. "I am sorry, my son. I am apart from myself and not whole. The tortures of Gathos have taken a toll on me, and I will need the healing energy of the Seven Heavens to be stitched back together again."

Oziax bellowed out in laughter. "I see Chedipe's knife cut out more than just an eye while you were strapped to her rack." He then sneered menacingly at Kasai. "He cannot protect you forever, little man."

"Now might be a good time to address your woes with Zizphander," Aetenos said and pointed to where the devil had fallen.

"I need no instruction from you, Old Monk. But do you think it so easy to vanquish Zizphander? Look, he has cast off your simple trick and flies once more."

Kasai saw Zizphander airborne again and wondered if Aetenos was mentally stable and strong enough to defeat him. He surveyed the flesh golems under Oziax's command and counted nineteen in total.

"Where are the rest?" Kasai said.

"Dead," Oziax said and narrowed his eyes as if Kasai had just challenged him.

Kasai then heard shrieks and chortles rise on the wind and grow louder. Zizphander's horde was hidden by the billowing snow, but coming closer, though it was difficult to determine from which direction.

A red glow appeared to Kasai's left, and then another on the right. The enemy had split and had somehow flanked them on both sides. Hundreds of fiery fiends erupted through the whipping snow, gnashing their teeth and brandishing thick talons and claws.

Aetenos pulled Kasai aside and looked directly into his eyes. Kasai felt like the Great Monk peered directly into the vacant space where his soul once lived.

"The Boundless is so small, so simple, but its meaning is timeless and profound. It has an entrance and an exit and is two sides to the same with nothing in between. The entrance constantly opens and closes as each side weakens and flourishes," Aetenos said in a calm and smooth voice.

"Your poetry will not help us now," Oziax said and raised his black blade. The raw laughter that followed grated on Kasai's ears and unsettled his resolve. Oziax spoke of what was in Kasai's heart. They were doomed.

Aetenos gently turned Kasai's face back to look squarely at his own. "Though hidden within, the spirit of the body flows like water. Though obscured like a setting sun through rainclouds, the spirit moves like an unleashed rabbit, this way, and that. The spirit catches hold of the body and leaps one step ahead of its shadow, for the spirit cannot be retained in form. And, though ever moving like the wind and churning like the ocean waves, it cannot be heard. It is silent to all ears but the one who holds it full. Do you understand?"

Kasai instinctively nodded yes but wasn't sure why. Maybe on some intuitive level, he grasped its meaning, but how these words would help him now was still lost to him.

Aetenos smiled thinly and continued, "When your way is battle, let your spirit rise and fill all from within, but outwardly be relaxed and show only calmness. Appear to be as gentle as a feather in a warm breeze, but react as a furious bear, a striking falcon, and a vicious jungle cat."

"Yes, Master. I understand. Be a cat."

"Listen to me and hear the message of my words. If there was ever a time to be a tiger, my son, now is that time."

"I will," Kasai said, and Ninziz-zida's sticks blazed in his hands.

Oziax commanded his flesh golems to spread out in a semi-circle. They would be the first line of defense. Then he joined Aetenos and Kasai and stood in a triangle, each with his back to the others.

The fiery horde filled in the central space between their split forces and came at them in a wide arc. Kasai spun Ninziz-zida in a figure-eight pattern hoping the defensive barrier would keep the attackers at bay, but he knew their situation was hopeless.

The forerunners came into focus as a freakish mass of small, goblin-like creatures, colored in shades of burning wood and red-hot coal. Their heads were far too large for their bodies and covered with too many eyes. Their spines jutted in an unnatural curl along their backs, causing them to remain in a permanent hunch, supported by thin, boney arms and legs. But these malformities did not hamper their ability to run or hunt or kill.

"If you are going to do something worthy of your title, I suggest you get on with it," Oziax said over his shoulder.

Kasai prayed the demon warlord wasn't referring to him. He looked to his right and saw that Aetenos had dropped to one knee and thrust one hand towards the ever-changing sky. He then grasped at the turbulent winds and closed his open palm into a fist, while his other hand slapped down hard on the frozen ground. A wall of force shimmered over the snow-laden ice and smashed into the oncoming fire fiends, tossing black, brown, red, and orange creatures away in a tangle of malformed bodies.

"Run!" Aetenos yelled.

Oziax barked out orders to the flesh golems in a harsh and guttural language, and they remained behind. Zizphander's horde was endless, and those not affected by Aetenos's attack, clawed their way over and through their broken brothers.

Oziax threw off his antlered helm revealing red clumps of hair plastered over the right side of his forehead. Blood flowed down the side of his face from the nasty gash on his head.

Kasai blanched at the sight of the demon warlord's wounds. Oziax caught his gaze and glared back, then added a deep, menacing laugh. "No taste for war, little monk? Your Master's tricks will not hold them off forever. At some point, we will need to fight."

Kasai just looked away and concentrated on not slipping on the smooth and slick terrain. He took in huge gulps of cold air that slashed at his throat and burned his lungs, yet he managed to keep speed with Aetenos and Oziax, though the fatigue of battle was sucking away the last of his strength. Kasai tripped on uneven terrain and stubbled to the ground.

When he stood, he looked back at the horde with dread. It was a churning mass of fiends, that jumped and rolled and ran as one giant organism with gangly arms and snapping jaws.

"We need to create more space," Oziax yelled out. "Or they will overcome us once more."

"Space is all there is in these wastelands. Gathos is an ocean of snow and ice," Aetenos said and spread his arms wide as he ran ahead of Kasai.

I'm always chasing that crazy monk, Kasai thought. Then an idea came to him. "The ice-covered lake outside of Furia Keep!" Kasai yelled over the din of howling wind.

"What of it, boy? We are far from the tower and will never reach it in time," Oziax growled back as he leaped over a boulder covered in snow.

Aetenos spun around and ran backward but still kept pace. "Ho, ho! The Ever Hero has the right of it! Where there is one frozen lake, surely there is another."

"Enough of your games, old monk. How can the frozen ponds of Gathos help us now?" Oziax brow furrowed with a scowl. "They are tireless in their pursuit. We must find a way to douse their flame or…" Oziax nodded in understanding. "I see your clever scheme now. This way!"

Oziax turned the party left and lead them over a series of rock mounds. Clumps of snow rolled away from their footfalls as they descended each slope. Kasai was hard-pressed to keep up and stumbled again but was lifted by steady hands. "No time for napping," Aetenos said with a wink.

The three tumbled down the last hill into shin-deep snow. The land opened to a wide vista of flatness. The winds slashed across Kasai's face, blinding him and forcing his eyes to remain mostly closed. Then he heard Oziax's rumbling voice.

"Here is your lake, old monk. Be sure we have crossed first."

"Ho, ho! No time for a swim, either!"

The three raced across the ice like jackrabbits hunted by hounds, only there were thousands upon thousands of hounds in pursuit. The sound of the horde was getting closer, and Kasai spared a look back to see a rosy glow coming from behind the last hill they had descended. Soon the horde would be crashing down the opposite side. Kasai hoped the plan would work, or this time they would be finished.

As they approached the far shore, Aetenos slowed his pace and stopped. Kasai and Oziax skittered to a stop a bit farther on and hustled back to where Aetenos was examining the ice.

"I hope you have found us a deep well, Lord Oziax," Aetenos said while continuing to search the surface and ran his fingers along seams in the ice. "Ah, here we are."

Aetenos rubbed his hands together to get them warm and then pressed one down on the ice. The warm colors of late summer cascaded over his knuckles then spread across the back of his hand as dark reds and bright-yellows lit the ice.

He pressed his hand down into the ice until he was just past his elbow. Aetenos then stood and admired the hole he had created. Kasai and Oziax looked into the hole and then back Aetenos.

"And?" Oziax said.

"Yes, that should do it," Aetenos said, nodding in approval.

"Master? What happens next?"

"You tell me. This was your plan."

Kasai stood dumbfounded, staring at Aetenos, who nodded politely, and somewhat encouragingly to the hole.

"Well, I thought—" Kasai began to say.

"You thought someone else would do the work for you? How will you learn anything with that attitude?" Aetenos pointed back to the hole. "There is your starting point. Oh, and you may want to hurry."

Kasai looked to the distant shore as the horde streamed down the far hillside and rolled onto the ice in an undulating sea of fiery flesh. The wind lifted flaming tongues of fire from their backs and lit the space above their heads in a blazing inferno.

"Hurry, you fool boy!" Oziax screamed.

"I'll need some help," Kasai said and grabbed Ninziz-zida from his sash. He knelt down to the ice and lowered Ninziz-zida into the hole. "And something from myself."

He quickly raised the level of his fire xindu and added it to Ninziz-zida's flame, but she resisted.

Together, Ninziz-zida pulsed into his thoughts.

Kasai thought he understood and attempted to add his fire xindu again, but this time in a slow, sharing, selfless manner instead of fast and impatient. But Ninziz-zida rebuffed him as would a maiden shucking away the advancements of a childish admirer. Kasai opened his eyes. The horde was madness in physical form and continued to careen down the hill.

"You have failed us! We die here," Oziax bellowed.

Kasai looked to Aetenos for direction, but the Master did nothing more than wave his hand towards the hole as if to say, again, try again. Kasai resumed his grip on Ninziz-zida and closed his eyes.

"Help me understand, Great Fire Serpent," Kasai whispered and opened his awareness to the ancient artifact, letting her power flow freely into him.

Together as one but different.

Ninziz-zida showed Kasai visions of mountains and deserts, rocks, boulders, and dry riverbeds. He saw large landmasses from a bird's eye view and small pebbles, as seen by the mouse.

The images Ninziz-zida showed Kasai brought back memories of Ordu and the mountain monastery. He remembered days of training and his friendships, Daku, lost to the demon, Khalkoroth, Brother Jarescu, and his inappropriate humor during Master Dorje's lectures, Cannonball's fat cheeks, and young Maru and Hondo, whom he had saved on the mountain.

He remembered long discourses with Master Choejor, discussing the various properties of the Xindu Mysteries and the four elements that made up the whole: fire, water, air, and earth. Four! Not one, but four.

The pebble builds a mountain, and the mountain is reduced to the pebble.

Kasai realized she was speaking of earth xindu and its dry, tasteless, unmoving, and stale energy. Earth xindu remained stoic, at peace with time, and as immobile as the mountain. It took its power from permanence or very slow-moving things, like ice!

The horde flowed like lava across the ice. On it came, a gibbering wave of fire. The sides ran faster and curled into the location of the three fugitives, attempting to surround them and cut off all escape.

Kasai channeled the images of lost friends and loved ones into thoughts and emotions. But he didn't allow the passion of their loss to rise and activate his fire xindu; instead, he focused on the everlasting relationship he shared with them, and let it wake the sleeping reservoir of his earth xindu.

A sense of enduring strength filled him and molded around him like a protective layer of rock. He passed the energy into Ninziz-zida as he thrust her back into the ice hole. Ninziz-zida's fire xindu whirled around the spiritual rock armor Kasai had created, and spun it like a drill, driving deeper into the ice.

Kasai forced his earth xindu energy to expand against the boundaries of the hole in hopes of shattering the ice. But it refused to break. It was too vast, too rigid and immovable. He delved deeper within himself for more energy and felt the boundaries of his essence begin to fade. Fear of dissolving into nothingness washed over him and broke his concentration.

Surrender. Trust. We are stronger together.

Kasai wasn't sure what she meant, until seemingly on cue, long-forgotten words from Master Dorje's soothing voice echoed in his mind, but louder, like a herald proclaiming his lord's will.

"When you are in harmony with the Boundless, you will share this gift with all living things. Their thoughts will be your thoughts, their actions, your actions, their energy, shall be your energy. And you shall give all of yourself in return. This is the Openness."

The words never meant much to him when he first heard them at Ordu. But now, Kasai thought he understood.

"I must give freely of myself, not only to you, Ninziz-zida but also to the surface layer of ice and frigid water beneath.

Yesssssss, Ninziz-zida whispered in a hiss. *Surrender and remain.*

Kasai refocused his earth xindu to seek the vibrational level of the ice. It was a slow process, and the ice was aloof and unresponsive to his will. He vaguely heard Oziax's persistent calling for him to hurry like a distant echo in the wind.

Kasai eased his will against the outer parts of the ice shaft, probing its surface. He focused more intently, feeling for cracks and imperfections he could latch onto, just like when climbing the sheer mountain cliffs at Ordu.

Finally, the ice opened to him, and his awareness traveled along the crisscrossing cracks and fissures leading to the far shore. He extended his vision to map out an elaborate path that flowed under the rampaging horde racing to surround them.

Kasai had never felt so calm. He no longer heard Oziax's pleas for haste, or the howling wind, or felt the bitter cold of the wastelands. He drew in a deep breath and slowly exhaled, surrendering more of his earth xindu into the ice as gratitude for its acceptance of his journey through its pathways.

He called to Ninziz-zida. "Follow."

Ninziz-zida erupted with glee and sent the energy of her fire xindu blazing along the lines of Kasai's awareness. She blasted through the veins of the ice, causing it to burst into fist-sized chunks under the horde.

Kasai half-opened his eyes as the outside world came back into focus. He saw the floundering horde bobbing in the broken ice until the frigid water sucked them under its surface, thousands of glowing bodies illuminated the dark water as they sank.

He raised himself up and turned to see Aetenos wearing a proud smile, and Oziax stood with his mouth agape. The demon warlord snapped it shut quickly and walked in the direction of the shoreline, grumbling to himself.

"Well done, my son," Aetenos said. "See? You have found a way."

Kasai bowed to Aetenos. "Thank you, Master."

"However, our work is not done. We have merely stalled our determined friends. Look."

Aetenos twisted Kasai back around. The water glowed dull-mauve and changed to bright-red as the horde rose to the surface and swam through the slush. Their fire burned below the water as freely as it had done above.

"What devilish curse is this? The water should already have frozen over them or at least locked them in place."

"Yes, a temporary solution at best. We must use this respite wisely. The lake will not slow them indefinitely," Aetenos said.

"We should race to Furia Keep. The Queen will empty the garrison with reinforcements and put an end to this insult," Oziax said as he absentmindedly wiped the blood seeping from his forehead. The gash bled freely, although the demon warlord paid it no heed.

"Oziax, come closer. Let me have a look at you."

Oziax narrowed his eyes in suspicion.

"Please, I haven't much time. You need to be mended and complete if you are to be of any use to me."

"Master, is that wise?" Kasai said. "He is an ally but for temporary convenience."

"We cannot engage an entire horde with but three, and certainly not two. Our resources are rather limited."

Aetenos then turned to Oziax as he examined the wound. "Did you not seek to know your foe before this folly? What did you hope to accomplish with such a meager force at your side?" His patronizing tone was unmistakable.

"Do not mock me," Oziax said with a sneer. "You know the demands of the Abyss. Fear and respect are the coins of power and must be maintained. I will die in battle with my hands wrapped around the throat of my enemy rather than suffer the alternative."

"Yes, while that may be so, Zizphander will not stop until he has claimed all of Gathos. And that is our current challenge. We can either destroy him, or his minions, but cannot do both. I say we have a better chance against the Red Devil, and for that, we shall need three."

Aetenos studied the surrounding environment. "You spoke of a more favorable ground, certainly one you did not mean to die upon. What was your plan, Oziax? Where were you leading the horde when we came upon you?"

"Zizphander is a true beast of fire, and the frost of Gathos does not touch his soul. But the horde that follows him is composed of lesser fiends. I meant to drive them into the deepest hole I could find and let the cold of Gathos freeze them solid. Although now I see nothing will extinguish their flames."

"And where do we find such a hole?"

Oziax surveyed the wastelands to the right and left. "The Chasm of Woe is a league to the south from our current location."

"Such a colorful name," Aetenos said with a sarcastic smile.

Kasai saw another storm approaching from the direction they meant to travel. He wondered if there was ever a time on Gathos when the snow ceased, and the winds died. He thought not.

"I see, I see. Let us make haste and see what opportunity the Chasm of Woe will provide. Lord Oziax, please lead the way."

Oziax snarled at Aetenos and stomped off in the direction of the chasm.

50

DESDEMONIA

Desdemonia shook the iron bars of the prison cell again, but like the countless times before, they still wouldn't budge. She hated everything about being a prisoner, the confinement, the hopelessness, and the despair. She wanted to scream, and her magic came alive of its own accord. Desdemonia watched with wide-eyes as it slithered like black snakes down her forearms and to wrap around the cold and rigid bars. It demanded to be free, but she couldn't control it. When she tried to focus it on a way to escape, it unraveled into nothingness.

She quickly released her hold and looked over her shoulder to see if anyone had seen what happened. Pallo and Run-Run were preoccupied in a silent conversation using only their hands, but Orin sat in a corner, staring at her with a scowl.

"You don't fool me. I've known what you were from the start," Orin said with a tone filled with disgust. "You belong here, with the rest of this filth. Airis's death will not go unavenged."

That got Pallo's attention. "Orin, mind your tongue!"

"Why? I will no longer be false to myself or my faith. We had one chance to stop Sekka before she established a foothold in our world. One chance! The Ever Hero had risen, and it was up to us to keep him safe until his powers manifested. We could have succeeded if it wasn't for her! She clouded his mind and convinced him to fight the devil before he was ready."

"That's not true. None of that is true. Pallo, you don't believe him, do you?"

Pallo said nothing but just looked at her with questioning eyes. She looked at Run-Run and didn't need a translator to understand the meaning behind his solemn face.

What did they know of her or the bond she shared with Kasai? Nothing! They were too busy being caught up in their self-righteous ramblings of prophecies and secret societies. She knew they wanted to drive a wedge between her and Kasai. They wanted him all to themselves. Well, she wasn't going to let that happen.

Her eyes narrowed at Orin. She hated him most of all. He was like a deer tick that dug deep under her skin and was near impossible to remove. She wanted to end his miserable life here and now, and she knew so many ways to make him suffer.

Orin egged her on with another cold stare. He was taunting her. She felt her magic bang against the walls of its own prison, the one she called control.

"It would be so easy to end you," she said under her breath. Then she clenched her jaw and quickly turned away.

What am I thinking? she wondered and rubbed her head. She wasn't going to hurt Orin, nor did she want to fight him.

"What's wrong with me?" she mumbled under her breath and grabbed at the bars again.

She had not felt like herself from the moment they arrived in Gathos, and her mood swings were only getting worse.

"I'm a wreck, my magic has a mind of its own, and now I'm talking to myself in a room full of people."

Kasai was outside, somewhere in the cold, and he needed her help. Desdemonia tested the iron bars again. "I have to get out of here. He needs me."

"You will only bring him closer to his doom, witch," Orin said from his corner. He hugged his knees up to his chest and put his head down on his arms.

Desdemonia looked to her side as Pallo joined her at the cell bars.

"Do you think he's alright? I mean Kasai, not him," she said and nodded over her shoulder at Orin.

"He is the Ever Hero, and he fights at the side of the Divine Fist. There is no stronger combination for good that exists in our world."

"But we are not in our world, and Aetenos has lost his mind! Whatever you thought he was supposed to be was taken from him long ago. Kasai is scared. I saw it in his eyes when they dragged him off. I know it. He needs me."

"He is fortunate to have such a courageous friend like you. Don't take Orin's words to heart. He's a passionate man, and often says things without thinking. His will tires and he feels he has failed not only in the quest to save Aetenos but also in his oath to help restore the Great Balance. Everything now rests on the shoulders of the Ever Hero."

"But Kasai's not ready!"

"He will find a way. That is why he was chosen over all others."

Desdemonia banged her head on the bars. She felt powerless. Then she heard footsteps echoing coming from a dark corridor.

"Someone's coming," she said and waited to see who approached.

Sekka rounded the corridor corner wearing a sheer, form-fitting gown and broad smile as if the world waited on her arrival.

"It's her," Desdemonia said and felt an odd mixture of loathing and enticement watching the fluid grace of the archdevil's movements as she approached the cell.

She and Pallo stepped back as Sekka came to stand before the bars, and her eyes bore into Desdemonia with eager anticipation. She was a smug, wicked creature, filled with hatred and malice, and reeked of dark magic. Much to Desdemonia's surprise, the magic within her responded longingly to the nearness of such a sinister power. She could feel it building inside her, yearning for release. It hated to be caged as much as she did.

Desdemonia lowered her head. She hated Gathos and all its diabolical tricks.

Sekka stepped closer to the bars and contemplated the captives. Pallo averted his eyes and Run-Run moved to the back of the cell, blending into the shadows. Orin stayed in his corner with his head on his arms, mumbling Airis's name repeatedly.

"What do you want," Desdemonia said with a sneer.

"More than you can possibly imagine. But for now, I'm more curious about you," Sekka said.

"Me?"

"You've noticed a change, haven't you?" The devil said with a gleam in her eyes. "Things feel different."

"I do not know what you are talking about." But she knew precisely what Sekka meant as she felt her magic pounding in her veins.

"I'm certain you can feel it. Chaos is the spark that gives life to all magic, especially Elemenati Magic. This is where your power was born, my little witch."

"You only know how to destroy," Orin said as he jumped up and pointed aggressively at Sekka. "You kill for the pleasure of creating sadness in others. There is no honor in the suffering you cause."

"Oh! But there is. Suffering is the lifeblood of the Abyss. It is the constant that holds the realm together."

"You are a sickness," Orin said and remained fearless and defiant.

Sekka merely smirked. "You seem to believe that your way of lawful order will set it all right?"

"The Immortal Mother..."

"The Immortal Mother is fickle and dispassionate. She cares little, if at all, for your struggle."

"Blasphemy! You dare speak such words! May the Immortal Mother strike you where you stand."

Sekka glanced up to the ceiling. "I see no lightning bolts or firestorms, do you?" She turned away from Orin and focused back on Desdemonia. "You know of what I speak."

"Shut up, you know nothing." Desdemonia turned away.

"Oh, I know quite a few things. Let me show you how fares your hero," Sekka said and licked her lips as she held up a small mirror. She tapped it with her other hand, and the surface became opaque. Desdemonia heard the clang of battle, and then Kasai shouted Aetenos's name and then grunted in pain. The mirror's surface slowly focused and revealed a circle of fiery chaos surrounding three small figures.

It was hard to make out what was happening as reddish steam combined with the swirling snow and obscured everything. Desdemonia saw blurry images fighting back a seething mass of rolling flesh and flickering flames.

The scene cleared, and she watched in dismay as Kasai, Aetenos, and a third figure encased in alabaster armor with a broken, antlered war helm, fought a losing battle against what could only be Zizphander's horde. They were slowly being surrounded.

"You can see, there is no hope left for your monk. He will perish along with his master, consumed by the fiery flood of Zizphander's horde. The Red Devil has proven to be too much, even for the Great Aetenos. Though, I think we all realize he is but a fraction of his former glory," Sekka said with a chuckle.

"No," Desdemonia whispered.

"Unless," Sekka said with a thoughtful inflection.

"Unless? Unless what?" Desdemonia watched as Kasai wielded Ninziz-zida in whirling patterns of destruction as the staff's magic raged around him in bright arcs of electric-blue flame. Fiends burst apart with every swing, but there were just too many. Oversized heads with even greater disproportionate mouths filled with ugly teeth bit into her love or slashed at him with skinny limbs ending in razor-sharp claws whenever he dropped his guard.

"There might be a way you can help him, though, as you can see, at this point, it is probably too late."

"Enough with your riddles! How can I save him!" Desdemonia said as she watched the horde slowly overwhelm Kasai through its sheer numbers.

The mirror zoomed into Kasai's face. His eyes darted from side-to-side as each attack pressed in. Then, as if time stopped, he looked directly at Desdemonia with eyes that said everything she needed to know. His situation was hopeless, and he would die in the wastelands.

She let out a startled gasp. "No."

Sekka took the onyx ring from her little finger and held it up to Desdemonia. "I give you this choice, watch Kasai perish in the frozen snow, or use the power in this ring to save him."

"Desdemonia, you must not! The Ever Hero will find a way, an honorable and virtuous way. Aetenos will protect him. Do not succumb to this madness," Pallo shouted. But she could barely hear him.

He attempted to pull her away from the bars and Sekka's influence. "The Devil's water may taste sweet, but her gifts are never free. There is always a price!"

She shook off his hands and locked her eyes on the vision within the handheld mirror. The battle grew worse. More of the fiends were getting through his defenses and hurting him.

"I will not abandon him to die, no matter the cost."

"But this cost is too great! You are blinded by an illusion. You don't know if what you see in the mirror is true."

"The witch reveals herself at long last," Orin said. "I should have killed you when I had the chance."

"I said, no matter the cost!" Desdemonia looked back to Sekka and the onyx ring. "What does it do?"

"A wise choice. You show promise, child. The ring merely enhances what is already within you. Perhaps you will find the power to save those who now fight for your lives. Now, it requires just a pinprick of blood, nothing more."

"Desdemonia, I say again. Do not do this thing. You will forever walk a path of darkness. Think of your love for the Ever Hero," Pallo said. Run-Run had joined his brother, and his soft eyes said the same. Do not do this.

"I am thinking of Kasai. Look into the mirror for yourself. He will die in the cold, alone. Can't you see that?"

"I see only a wicked witch submitting to the desires of her fiendish master," Orin said. The venom of his words came in a spray of wet spittle. "Do it then. Do it and damn us all!"

Desdemonia held out her hand to receive the ring. As Sekka slipped it on, a small shard slipped under her skin and drew a bead of blood from her finger.

"There, it is done. The ring has a spark of my essence that will mingle with your own. Now, let's get you out of there and off to help your love."

51

KASAI

Kasai, Aetenos, and Oziax had kept a steady pace and created some distance from their pursuers. Oziax's knowledge of the terrain had proven extraordinarily beneficial and provided them with an advantage over the horde. Eventually, a low mountain range rose from the barren plains and rolling hills of the wastelands. Most of the mountain range was hidden due to the constant snowfall, but as they approached, Kasai saw the definition of two flat-topped cliffs split between a deep chasm at their base.

"Ahead lies the Chasm of Woe," Oziax said. "We will take the left route. It's safer."

They followed Oziax's advise and traveled along the left side ledge until they were halfway through the ravine when Aetenos stopped the group.

"This will do."

The wind whistled through the passage with what sounded like the high-pitched shriek of a feral cat in heat. Kasai peered upwards and saw a thin line of turbulent sky between the opposing cliff walls. He looked over the edge of their path into a blackness that seemed almost solid in its completeness. He cautiously stepped closer to the side of the wall.

"The plan is simple," Aetenos continued. "Zizphander's horde will enter the rift as we did and follow us along this ledge or the one across the chasm, but hopefully they will choose both."

Oziax looked skeptical. "And why would they do that?"

"Because you, my friend, will be the tasty lamb that brings the hungry wolves running. Once they see their prize cannot escape, they will fully commit to pursuit."

"I will do no such thing. Let your mind slave be the bait," Oziax growled.

"Oh no, the Ever Hero will be needed elsewhere. He and I will climb these walls, and when the time is right, we will bring down the rock on our determined foes, sealing them within the depths of the chasm forever." Aetenos nodding his head, looking for approval. "Right?"

Oziax looked skeptically at Aetenos, who smiled brightly at the demon lord.

"And Oziax, do make sure you get out of the way when the rocks start to fall. Sekka expects your return."

Kasai absentmindedly nodded his agreement. *Yes, Oziax, don't get smashed under the falling cliff wall*, he thought and chuckled at the idea of huge slabs of granite and ice burying Oziax along with Zizphander's horde. But then he realized what Aetenos had said.

"Wait, what? Master, what do you mean?"

"You shall climb here," Aetenos patted the rock wall, finding it sturdy and acceptable. "And I will take yonder side," Aetenos said with the utmost confidence. "Get to the top, and as the horde crosses beneath us, we will collapse the side of the cliff. It all comes down. Boom, boom, boom. See? Easy."

"Master, how do you expect me to bring down the side of a mountain?" Kasai shouted over the wind, exasperated. He needed just a moment to think, but the ringing in his ears was unbearable.

"Vibrations!" Aetenos said with a smile and raised his hand, wiggling his fingers in the air. "Remember the ice? A fine job there, by the way."

"But," Kasai was about to say more.

Aetenos shook his finger. "It's the same as taking your first breath. You don't know you can do it until you do. Right? You'll be fine." Aetenos patted him on the shoulder.

"Master, a layer of ice covering a body of water is different. And Ninziz-zida…"

But Aetenos was not listening. He was looking up to the cliff ridge. "Oh, and one more thing."

"Yes, Master?"

"Make sure you are away from the edge when it comes down." He used his fingers again, but this time to imitate a falling man. "Right? Don't go down with the ship, or the rock, well, you know what I mean."

Before Kasai could say another word, the Great Monk leaped across the chasm with ease. Aetenos ascend the cliff like an agile snow monkey. Kasai stood dumbfounded as he watched in disbelief. He then heard the low, rumbling snigger of Oziax.

"I should end you here and now, Ever Hero." Oziax said the title with disdain. His pale purple eyes roved menacingly over Kasai. "But time is endless on Gathos, and I don't think you'll be leaving here anytime soon. Scurry up the wall, little man."

Kasai frowned and looked up the craggy wall, then to the pit below. He had no choice and grabbed a meaty jug of rock above his head and began his climb. The cliff's surface offered numerous hand and footholds to choose from, and the ascent was easier than he expected. For once, something in this horrible place wasn't determined to kill him.

The cliff finally plateaued, and he saw Aetenos across the ravine sitting peacefully in meditation.

"Bring down the side of a cliff, he says. It's easy, he says. Vibrations, he says," Kasai mumbled to himself.

He then knelt in the snow and held Ninziz-zida across his lap. He closed his eyes and exhaustion wrapped around him like a blanket. When had he last slept? He could only think of how tired he was as was his body slumped in on itself. Kasai felt Ninziz-zida burning in his hands and jarred him from his stupor.

"I'm awake, I'm awake," Kasai mumbled. He opened an inner channel to the energy of his earth xindu and then stared at the ground, trying to find the cliff's vibrations, but all he saw was rough granite under a thin icy skin.

"Ninziz-zida, I cannot do this on my own."

The Fire Serpent pulsed confidence into his mind. *Together.*

Kasai tried to relax and concentrated on matching the vibrations of his earth xindu with the cliff wall's movement, but the imperceivably slow crawl of the rock caused his mind to drift and wander. Then he heard the voice of Master Choejor whisper in his head.

You are held back by what you feel you are not, and not by what you are in truth. It's not until you know yourself completely and come to an acceptance of who you are, that you will be able to be calm, quiet, and at peace. This is when you can move the fastest.

Kasai understood the words but not their meaning. He sighed and leaned forward to brush away newly fallen snow from the icy surface of the rock and tried again, but he couldn't feel the rhythm of the frozen ridge. He searched for anything that might help him achieve the impossible. But his mind remained blank.

Kasai impatiently stood up and walked to the edge of the cliff to check the horde's progress. They had taken the bait and followed Oziax along the route of Kasai's cliff.

"Of course, my side," Kasai said and shook his head in dismay.

Then he saw a bright red object streak between the cliff walls. It glided through the air utterly unaffected by the bullying winds of the wastelands. Kasai realized it was Zizphander as the devil arched his back and shot straight upwards to circle above the twin plateaus.

Kasai was shocked by the magnificent beauty before his eyes. Zizphander had the head of a handsome man with long flowing hair the color of rippling fire. A spinning crown of purple and black sigils floated above his head but stayed locked in place as he flew.

He had great, feathered wings that stretched to three times his body's length and shimmered through the colors of bright-red, yellow and deep-orange. Thin, blue spines bristled along his back and ended in pure-white, bulbous knots. Each spine glowed light blue in its core, and left a trail of sparks in their wake.

Zizphander slowed to observe the advancement of his troops. Kasai noticed the devil held no physical weapons or none that could be seen from his vantage point. Suddenly, Zizphander twisted his neck towards Kasai, and the two adversaries locked eyes. Kasai felt woozy, and the sky and ground seemed to tilt before his eyes.

Kasai's body was warmed by the heat washing off Zizphander's fiery feathers as he beat his great wings. It was the first time Kasai felt warm since arriving on Gathos. For an instant, he wondered if Zizphander was just another angel trapped in the Abyss like Aetenos's friend, Artiya'il, and that somehow had become warped by the powers of chaos. Was it a form of divine power that shielded the devil and his horde against the cold or the icy depths of the lake?

If Zizphander was an enemy of Sekka, then didn't that make him Kasai's ally? Zizphander smiled warmly at him, and Kasai felt drawn to the devil. They could be friends. Ninziz-zida pleaded with Kasai to resist such temptations, but he pushed her voice away and stuffed her into his sash.

"Don't be afraid, Ninziz-zida, the Red Devil is not evil. He can help us," Kasai said and took a step towards the edge of the cliff. "I can finally stop pretending to be the Ever Hero. Everything will be alright, you'll see."

He looked over his clothing and saw the burnt-orange leggings extending out from his molachuk fur. He somehow realized he was dressed in the attire of a monk of Ordu. That was just another fantasy. He was nothing but another lost soul, sentenced to Gathos and forced to endure a hopeless existence through all eternity.

"We need to stop believing we are something we are not," Kasai said as he became overwhelmed with despair. "Why should I go on, when nothing matters anymore? I was a fool to think I could defeat Sekka."

Zizphander nodded in agreement, and with his sapphire blue eyes, he encouraged Kasai to take another step towards the cliff's edge.

Kasai stepped forward. "Nothing matters."

A voice echoed in his head. +Jump! Jump to me and end your suffering.+

Zizphander floating effortlessly against the gale-force winds between the two cliffs. The devil watched him closely and then knocked his head back over his shoulder.

+Come with me. Jump and be free.+

Kasai walked to the sharp edge of the cliff and looked down. He saw the horde swarming over both narrow ledges of the chasm, pursuing a single figure in white armor. The throng scampered and stumbled in a frenzied dash to reach their quarry, causing many to fall to their deaths.

"Come to me," the devil said in a sweet, kind voice.

Kasai was so tired. His eyes partially closed, and he felt the three-segmented staff burning at his side. Reflexively, his hand closed around the black sticks, and a vision of a sea of flames exploded before his mind's eye. He heard a monstrous hiss reverberate from what seemed like another dimension as a fountain of fire erupted before him and wrapped itself around him in a protective embrace.

TOGETHER WE ARE STRONG!

Kasai snapped back to his senses and realized he teetered on the edge of the cliff. He felt the depth of the chasm sucking him forward. Small rocks and bits of hard snow fell from the side as he shifted his feet back and stepped away from the ledge.

Kasai looked up and saw Zizphander's expression turn sour, and his body shook with rage. Kasai took Ninziz-zida in his hands, and the staff's blue fire came to life. Then something distracted Zizphander, and he looked forward with narrowed eyes. He shrieked like a banshee and dropped down into the ravine.

Kasai looked to his left and saw a great beast flying towards him with five figures riding atop its back, one with hair as dark as midnight, billowing in the wind. The four others were hulking jol'goths wielding long, black lances. He feared Sekka had sent a cadre to kill him once Zizphander had been defeated.

Kasai recognized Desdemonia standing in a saddle mounted to the beast's back as it landed. She suffered through freeing herself from the saddle's straps and jumped down to embrace Kasai.

"I found you!"

"How did you win free of the dungeon?" Kasai said, amazed to see her.

"What? Not even, hello, I'm so happy to see you, Des?" she said and folded her arms across her chest. "And where's my kiss?"

Kasai stood dumbfounded. "Huh?"

"Never mind," Des sighed and shook her head. "You'll get it one of these days."

Kasai ignored her and raced back to the edge of the cliff. He saw the horde closing in on Oziax. He looked across the chasm and saw Zizphander hovering over Aetenos's prone body.

"He's hurt! We need to save him!"

"There is no time," Desdemonia said. "We must stop them here and now."

"I can't, Des. I'm supposed to bring down this cliff on Zizphander's army. Master Aetenos presumes too much of me."

The atmosphere grew dark as a new storm marched across the sky. Lightning flashed, and thunderous booms echoed overhead. The amber in Desdemonia's eyes flared into a bright glow.

"Leave that to me."

Kasai stepped back as silver light blossomed around her hands, and black runes of power fanned out around her body. She swirled like the wind in a spectacular dance, and eventually, her arms raised up to the sky. Kasai stood dumbfounded and was mesmerized by the fluidity of her movements.

Desdemonia shouted out strange words while she danced, which drew down spinning funnels of air from the clouds. The whirlwinds spun in place around where she danced, and Kasai felt primal fear creep into his gut, the kind one feels when witnessing the raw and destructive power of nature. His heart filled with dread as he saw Desdemonia's eyes blazing with excitement.

Then, a flash of light shot from her body and was consumed by one of the whirlwinds. The air became charged with electricity, and Kasai could feel the hairs on his body rise.

Suddenly, the landscape turned white as a crackling bolt of lightning shot down from the sky and shattered a small section of the cliff wall across the ravine. Zizphander darted away and flew upwards. Soon, he was lost in the overhead clouds.

Desdemonia's dance intensified, and more flashes of light shot from her body and into the whirlwinds, which brought down more lightning strikes against the far cliff. Kasai watched in amazement as an avalanche of huge chunks of rock and ice slide down the wall and smashed into the ledge below.

Desdemonia continued her dance and directed her hands to the cliff they now stood on.

"Des! Wait!" Kasai shouted, but she was lost in her magic.

A long line of lightning bolts flashed down against the sheer side of the cliff wall. The plateau shook, and Kasai lost his footing. Then, a large portion of the cliff fell away to plummet onto the horde below.

Kasai heard an unnatural screech and saw Zizphander flying towards them. His beautiful face was now ugly and twisted. Kasai readied Ninziz-zida and prepared to defend Desdemonia from the devil.

Zizphander halted his advance as the whirlwinds spinning around Desdemonia grew larger. She slowed her dance to a stop, but none of the intensity left her face. No words were exchanged between the two, but Kasai was sure they communicated together, somehow. Then Zizphander scowled, and his cruel laughter filled the air.

Desdemonia shook her head, and a mighty bolt of lightning zigzagged from above and struck Zizphander in the back. He howled in pain as lines of electricity crackled and swarmed around his body. The devil dove into the ravine, and out of sight, until Kasai saw a streaking bullet of red, traveling in the opposite direction of Furia Keep.

She turned to him, wearing a wicked grin. "Betcha didn't know I could do that."

Kasai thought she was about to say more, but her amber eyes rolled back, and she fell to the ground. He rushed to her side as the air funnels broke apart and dissipated into thin air.

Thankfully, she was still breathing. Kasai searched desperately for help, but of course, there was none. Then, he heard a shriek from above and saw more of the flying beasts descending through the clouds. Sekka had finally sent reinforcements.

The flying beasts were set down on the plateau, and to Kasai's dismay, Oziax leaped from the saddle of the last one and drew his black sword.

"Time to die, little man," Oziax said.

Kasai readied Ninziz-zida, and her segments burst into blue flame. But then Oziax stopped as if listening to another voice. He frowned and disappointedly sheathed his sword.

"Another time."

Oziax then directed his troops to gather up Desdemonia and others to fetch Aetenos across the ravine. Kasai was quickly surrounded and lowered Ninziz-zida to the ground. He gave himself over to the enemy, a prisoner once more.

52

SHIVERRIG

Malachi scrambled past the posted guards at the entrance to the dining hall. His back was hunched, and he moved with apish steps, practically dragging his stumped arm to his side. Shiverrig shook his head in disappointment. The fiend Hilo had levied control over Malachi, and the archvashim had readily accepted his role as its host.

"I am here, my Aj-Kahun. What are your wishes?" Malachi spoke, but the words were from the voice of the fiend. He stood at the opposite side of a massive wooden table where Shiverrig ate his meal. The smell of the roast lamb, glazed with green jelly, buttered baked potatoes and honeyed carrots filled the dimly lit room.

Shiverrig sat in a high-backed, wooden chair and was dressed in a heavy leather jerkin and breeches. His thick robes were draped over the top posts of the chair and fanned out behind him like folded wings. He still wore the circlet upon his head and kept it as a permanent fixture to his attire.

Shiverrig sat for a moment carving the juicy meat away from the rack of lamb on a plate before him. The dish was prepared the way he liked it, just a flash over raw. Shiverrig took a bite of the lamb and, while chewing the plump morsel, pointed his fork at the stooped figure of Malachi.

"Hilo, whom do you serve? The Aj-Kahun or the Frost Queen of Gathos?"

"Without fail, poor Hilo serves the will of the great Aj-Kahun," Hilo said with utmost confidence and loyalty.

"And what would happen if your Aj-Kahun's will contradicted the plans of the Frost Queen?"

For the briefest moment, Hilo's expression faltered. Only with the combined and enhanced senses of Jynxx was Shiverrig able to catch it. It wasn't really a test. Shiverrig knew he could not trust any of the demonkind, not until he was able to sire them from his own seed, as he did with the nobles.

He picked up the rib bone and chewed away the lingering meat and fat. "I have received some rather undesirable reports from the borderlands, and visits from unlikely bedfellows."

Shiverrig tossed the bone on his plate and sucked at his fingers. "And this prompted me to ask questions. The answers I received were most interesting. Would you like to hear them?"

"Why, of course, my Aj-Kahun. Please share your newfound knowledge with poor Hilo, and he will advise you as best he can as to their true merit."

"For starters, I am concerned that Sekka has sacked the majority of the southern border villages and marched the peasants north, towards Rachlach Fortress. This, of course, doesn't surprise me. I suspected her greed would not be satiated by one or two villages per season, such is the way of your kind."

Hilo shifted on his feet, studying Shiverrig, and shrugged his shoulders. "The Frost Queen has a full appetite for souls."

"Surely, she does. But then I wondered, what benefit would there be to march them north, through winter's ice and snow, with the prospect of losing so many to the cold along the way? What was she to do with them in the north that couldn't be achieved where she found them in the south? It's a perplexing thought, is it not?"

"You are wise to wonder at the movement of all your subjects," Hilo said. "But what is the importance of a few border villagers scattered along the outskirts of forgotten territory? They are but an afterthought to the coming empire of Aj-Kahun Shiverrig."

Shiverrig tore off another rib from the rack of lamb. He held the medallion by the bone and tore into the tender meat, letting the red juice and dark grease flow over his lips and down his chin.

"As you can imagine, I sent scouts. This brings me to some more interesting news. My scouts found an anomaly of demonic origin, nestled in the ruins of Rachlach Fortress, which turned out to be a gateway between realms. I wonder, why did Hilo not inform his Aj-Kahun of such a boon?"

The smile Hilo wore on Malachi's face widened, revealing teeth that now tapered to shallow points. "The Aj-Kahun gives poor Hilo more credit than he deserves. Surely, Hilo cannot know of all the wonders from the Abyss that now exist in the Realm of Men. Hilo only walks through the City of Spires and observes the immediate happenings surrounding his lord."

"I see. So, you had no knowledge that this device, this portal as it were, which leads directly to your homeworld of Gathos, was created by Sekka?" Shiverrig waved the half-eaten medallion in front of Hilo.

Hilo became noticeably uncomfortable and did his best to feign interest. "The Queen of Frost does not deign to tell her servant of her affairs."

"Her servant. Interesting choice of words."

"My lord, please forgive poor Hilo. He misspoke. Hilo serves only the Aj-Kahun."

"Yes, of course. My faithful servant."

"Yes, my lord," Hilo smiled and bowed low.

"Oh, and one last thing, I had almost forgotten the answers to my questions. I have learned something of great value to me. A name. An ancient and specific name."

Hilo's head snapped up, and his eyes bore into Shiverrig, probing for the truth in the Aj-Kahun's words. "What is the name Aj-Kahun Shiverrig thinks he has learned?"

"Hilomannegishi."

Malachi's face turned reddish-purple, and his eyes squinted to sharp slits. "What do you know of that name?"

"I know it is the name of your birth, and how to use it to make you suffer."

Shiverrig focused on Hilo's true name and connected his will to Xerthotha. Malachi screamed with Hilo's voice and dropped to his knees with his hands pressed tightly against his head.

"You cannot know this! No one has known this name for more than five thousand years!"

"Ah, but I know it now."

Shiverrig bit too deeply into the remaining meat, and the bone cracked and crunched in his mouth.

"Xerthotha," Malachi spit out the hated name as his hands dropped to the floor, and his chest heaved. "It was the Great Changeling that bestowed the name to you. You flirt with a power you cannot possibly comprehend."

"I understand you have been collared, Hilo. You are now mine. Know that your allegiance is to me and only to me. Any break, however slight shall see your essence ripped away from you and fed to the Supreme Devil, Xerthotha."

Shiverrig tossed the rib bone atop the pile of discarded debris building on the table near his plate. Malachi's body trembled, and he slowly raised himself back to a kneeling position. Eyes controlled by Hilo blazed hatred at the Aj-Kahun but quickly glazed over in submission as Shiverrig raised his hand to the circlet.

"Hilo shall obey his master," he said and bowed his head to Shiverrig in compliance.

Ankle-deep snow had fallen during the night and covered the exposed grounds within the Keep's walls. Shiverrig stood in front of an open window overlooking the training grounds. He wore black bear fur draped over his shoulders, thick leathers, and a long, curved dagger at his side. His breath clouded briefly before his face.

Below him, the newly transformed nobles drilled in battle groups, exercising their new talents. Vorleeth shrieked out orders to some and beat others into submission. The brightly feathered half-breed had already killed three challengers to his leadership by tearing them to shreds. Their mangled bodies had been left where they fell, while slashed arteries still sprayed grisly fountains of black blood into the packed snow.

Vorleeth saw Shiverrig and barked out an order, commanding the half-breeds to come to attention. As a group, they pivoted to the window. Vorleeth spoke again, and the group saluted Shiverrig in unison, raising whatever form of weapon they held, be it a sword, mace, halberd, or long-talon claw. Overall, Shiverrig was pleased with what he saw. He nodded his approval and moved away, walking through a long corridor filled with morning light.

His thoughts wandered to the portal in the north. As Xerthotha had called it, the Chaos Gate would soon become a crucial chokepoint in his battle against Sekka. If he could take control of the portal, Sekka would not be able to steal souls from the Mortal Realm to feed her war machine on Gathos, nor would any more of her own troops be allowed to enter Baroqia.

Sekka's grand scheme would come to a halt without proper soul-forged material to fuel the creation of her armies. Shiverrig was no fool. Once he learned of the existence of the Chaos Gate, Sekka's goal became apparent, a complete and total invasion of the Three Kingdoms of Hanna. But she must still be weak on Gathos; if not, she surely would have brought her infamous Frost Legion into the Mortal Realm, to bear down upon the mortals in a sweeping victory.

But time had cost her dearly, that and the succubus. Sess'thra was playing a devious game. The demon seed she had placed within him was no doubt guided by Sekka's hand. But changing the nobles with the seed of their sexual union, to a warband that was loyal to him was certainly not part of Sekka's plan.

And now Sess'thra begged him to convert what remained of the King's Army into more of their brood. What was she up to? Two full legions of half-breeds would be a great asset in conquering the northern kingdom of Trosk and holding Baroqia in check. Still, surely it was nothing compared to the countless legions Sekka could vomit forth from Gathos. Unless he controlled access to and from Baroqia.

Closing the Chaos Gate to her would immediately initiate a war that he could not win with only the current resources at his disposal. What if instead, the slaves she stole stayed in Baroqia and were transformed into new recruits to his growing army? Now that was interesting.

He would need an accurate accounting of her military and clandestine assets already working in the Three Kingdoms. Those would need to be eliminated first. The shade of Maugris had spoken of the Warlords of Vyzyn warring in Sunne, but he had limited intel of their victories or defeats. Hilo would be eager to redeem himself with this information.

Sess'thra and Khalkoroth would be wildcards, like the mysterious assassin, Dax, who had not been seen or heard from in the months since Shiverrig took control of Qaqal. For all Shiverrig knew, Dax could be standing next to him in the form of Lord Fritta or Lord Manda. The shape-shifting doppelganger wore his disguises well.

If he could get the true names of all three demons, then he could also have them under his sway. But how many favors did he want to owe Xerthotha? That was a dangerous and taxing game to play, and unfortunately neither Hilo nor Jynxx had any names to provide him, no matter the amount of torture the two demons endured. It was a dead end.

His first order of business would be to reinforce his defenses in the capital city of Qaqal as well as Gethem. Maintaining control of those two cities would be crucial in any war effort.

"More loyal troops would solve many of my problems," he said and accepted what must be done.

He would roll the dice and allow Sess'thra to convert the remaining soldiers of the King's Army to half-breeds, leaving out the soldiers from Gethem's standing army that had remained steadfast and loyal to him. Perhaps there was a more significant role they could play, once he knew all the variations produced by the wicked seeds of his loins. His instincts told him he was but sampling the surface of a much deeper reservoir of power.

That begged the question, what of the rest of his subjects throughout Baroqia? The balance of power had changed with access to and from the Abyss. Any sensible ruler would understand the importance of military dominance to protect the land. It was what shaped empires and led to future conquests.

And what of the lands outside Baroqia? Shiverrig mused. What power besides that from the Abyss could stop him? Surely not Trosk. The Northerners would bow to his dominance quickly enough once his new troops whet their blades and claws on their flesh. It would be an adequate test to see how well his new troops performed in battle. What barbarians remained after the short war would be assimilated into his new empire.

That left the Kingdom of Sunne. The war journals left by his forefathers spoke of hidden power, infused with Elemenati magic that would not bend to the will of conquerors. The Jungles of Sunne were too dense to penetrate effectively with conventional siege engines and troop deployment. The enemy attacked quickly, seeming to materialize where there should be none, inflict heavy casualties and blend back into the jungle foliage.

The campaign had been abandoned by his grandsire, Overlord Baroq Shiverrig, as he settled into ruling what was now Baroqia. Future generations had taken up the challenge of conquering Sunne with halfhearted efforts. None had succeeded.

But now, Sunne offered a different treasure other than land and resources. Shiverrig now understood why Sekka marched into Sunne first. The soul energy found in its inhabitants must be higher than an ordinary mortal. If he could convert the two other kingdoms into fuel for his own war machine, his armies would be unstoppable. Then perhaps, with enough might at his disposal, he could venture into the Lower Planes of the Abyss and depose Sekka from her throne on Gathos.

It would be a just punishment. Shiverrig had a debt to settle with that devil, who had lied to him and would soon betray him. He indulged himself with a bit of a chuckle. Of course, they all lied and schemed. What did he expect from devils and demons from the Abyss?

Shiverrig entered his throne room, where a delegation from Gathos waited impatiently for him to arrive. Among them was a huddled mass of three humanoid figures fused into one. Shiverrig had been expecting this visit as much as he wished to avoid it. This creature disgusted him.

The Three, as they called themselves, scuttled forward, no longer wearing the colors or symbols of Maugris the Infinite. Apparently, their loyalties had changed quickly with his downfall. Three thin arms were raised, pointing trembling fingers towards him.

"You must cease your actions, Lord Shiverrig, or pay a dear price."

+*Kill them! Kill them now! Spill their wretched blood.*+ The voice of Jynxx echoed in laughter in his head. +*Of course, you cannot. They are untouchable, now that they are emissaries to Sekka's court. Aj-Kahun Shiverrig, the helpless and weak at your service.*+

"Enough demon spawn, while I hear their words," Shiverrig said under his breath. He then directed his attention to The Three.

"My actions? You mean sending troops to protect the frontier villages from Sekka's pilfering?"

"The Frost Queen whets her appetite for the conquest of Sunne, and claims her tithe, as promised."

"What is of such importance in Sunne? My scouts report nothing but dense jungle, swarms of blood-sucking insects, springs of unpotable water, and a scarce population of backward natives."

The Three gurgled through what was meant to be a laugh. "It is no wonder to us that you are blind to the uniqueness of Sunne. Nonetheless, you shall know in due time. For now, know this, the Kingdom of Sunne has been claimed by the Queen of Frost. You are not to meddle in her affairs."

"I am the Aj-Kahun and shall go where I please." Shiverrig turned from The Three and walked to the steps of his throne. "I am intrigued by her interest in the southern kingdom. Perhaps there is more there than meets the eye. Your efforts to keep me at bay say much of her difficulties in Sunne. I feel it goes poorly."

"You are a child playing king. We are here to ensure you do not overstep your feeble kingdom's boundaries and do as you are commanded. Sekka now shares a soul bond to Azrollorza, the greatest of the Supreme Devils. What hope could a mortal believe he has against such might."

+They mock you, without fear of retribution.+

+Enough demon or I shall send another piece of you to Xerthotha.+ Shiverrig sent the thought back to Jynxx.

+Ah, the whispers echoing throughout the aether are true. Sekka has aligned herself with Azrollorza. The end of your rule comes on a swift, cold wind.+

Shiverrig pushed the voice of Jynxx out of his head and watched The Three sway in place. Each misshaped head slowly swayed atop the sickly heap of their entwined body parts, waiting for him to acknowledge their warning. Shiverrig remained quiet, pondering the implications of what he had heard.

Sekka had gained a powerful ally in Azrollorza, which he could not hope to best, even with ten legions of his half-breed brood. Matters were escalating out of his control. Each forward step of progress he took, found him still two steps behind the leader. He was consistently being outplayed by Sekka. His mood turned sour.

"Yes, you see it now, don't you, Shiverrig?" The Three commented as one, their voices overlapping and creating an irritating buzz in his ears. "All of your bold moves have won you nothing, but castles made of sand before the incoming tide."

Shiverrig knew they were right. Sekka was merely biding her time in Sunne, collecting souls to harvest while her armies on Gathos swelled and would burst upon Baroqia through the Chaos Gate.

Without thinking, his long dagger flashed in his hand, the blade gleamed in the light as he thrust it into one of the wretched creatures, then twirled around and stabbed another on the opposite side. The middle one screamed like a sick baby.

"What have you done! We are The Three! We are the voice of Mistress Sekka!"

Shiverrig thrust the dagger, already oozing with black-purple blood, into the mouth of the last, killing it quickly.

+That was not wise.+ Jynxx laughed inside his head. Shiverrig brushed her opinion aside. But the demon was right. He was not ready to openly declare himself against Sekka. Jynxx must have clouded his judgment. Shiverrig activated the power of the circlet.

"Give Xerthotha my regards," Shiverrig snarled. The sound of Jynxx howling in agony filled his mind. *+He feeds!+*

Shiverrig enjoyed the screams of the demon and was not quick to release Jynxx from her pain and torment. He then heard the arrival of another and release the connection between Jynxx and Xerthotha.

Her consciousness reentered his mind, panting after the ordeal. *+Do not think yourself so strong. The less of me in you means the more of you remains. How then will you control the demon horde you've created? Do you think they will bow willingly to you simply because you are their sire?+* She managed a condescending laugh, meager as it was.

"You are still many painful moments from that time, I think. And when you are gone, I shall be glad to take another. The extent of your worth to me is finite. You are a candle wick dipped in oil and burning fast. Be wary that I do not light the other end as well."

Shiverrig stood over the dead bodies of The Three as Sess'thra sauntered into the room.

"This will be difficult to explain. What delicious mischief are you up to now, my glorious and most terrifying Aj-Kahun?"

"Spare me your flattery, succubus. We have work to do."

Shiverrig walked through the ranks of the depleted King's Army, followed by Sess'thra, Khalkoroth, and the hunchback, Malachi. The fiend Hilo remained tucked away within Malachi's inner body, refusing to come to the surface unless demanded to do so.

The bodies of the soldiers were in different stages of transformation. Many were hobbled to the ground on hands and knees, vomiting out whatever remained of their sanity. Sess'thra skipped ahead of Shiverrig, weaving in and out of the soldiers, laughing aloud and tapping some on the shoulder as if she were playing a childhood game of tag.

"Our little family has grown!" She turned to Shiverrig with gleeful happiness, then raced back to him and threw her small body into his arms. Sess'thra kissed him feverishly with her legs wrapped around his waist. Behind him, Khalkoroth snorted his resentment.

"And who shall lead this frail group of half-breeds, the peacock, Vorleeth?" The derision in the pale demon's voice was unmistakable.

Shiverrig removed the succubus from his chest and concentrated the power of the circlet on Khalkoroth, but without the demon's true name, no connection could be made. He tried to connect with the boy, Daku, but again, nothing.

The strength of Khalkoroth would be an asset if he could be trusted and controlled. As of now, the pale demon obeyed the will of Sess'thra, and ultimately, Sekka, be it from loyalty or dominance, Shiverrig was not sure.

He assumed the Khalkoroth could overcome the succubus in sheer strength. But she held something over him, like a small, yipping lapdog dominating a fierce hunting dog, eventually forcing the bigger dog's tail between its legs.

Shiverrig was counting on the uncanny mental discipline possessed by the monks of Ordu to somehow get past the barriers Khalkoroth had put in place. If he could reach Daku undetected, the monk could divulge Khalkoroth's true name.

Yet, he would need to be patient. Shiverrig could see Daku asserting more control over Khalkoroth, or at least trying to take some back. The demon's once bold confidence had become marred by overt declarations of his hold on the boy. Something was happening from within. Khalkoroth no longer had absolute control.

"Do not worry yourself over such concerns, Khalkoroth. A worthy general shall emerge," Shiverrig said. "One of sound mind and body."

Khalkoroth eyed Shiverrig with sheer disdain, then threw his head back and laughed into clouds. "Your time grows short."

"As does yours, demon. As does yours."

Shiverrig turned to Malachi and Sess'thra. "See this wraps up and assemble them into companies based on their unique attributes. Those who possess wings and the ability to fly, I want to be placed under Vorleeth's command. Those who still retain most of their mortal form will follow Lord Fritta's commands. If not, bring them to Lord Jolla. I want to personally inspect any who rise from the transformation, as did Vorleeth. I shall be in my war room."

Shiverrig paced in his war room, alone but for the voice in his head. Each visit from the devil was more arduous to bear. He felt as if his soul was being expanded and stretched to make way for another, one that could never be held in his mortal shell.

"How is it that you can enter my mind so freely?"

+YOU MUST ASK, EVEN NOW?+

"The circlet?"

+NO. YOU NOW SHARE A DEEP BOND TO DEMONKIND. I SEE ALL IN THEIR GLORIOUS, SOULLESS HEARTS AND DEVIOUS MINDS, FOR THERE IS NOWHERE I CANNOT GO.+

"But for all your power, you are forbidden to physically enter the Mortal Realm."

It was not a question. Shiverrig still had one small piece of leverage he could use, and hopefully, he would not squander it mistakenly.

Xerthotha remained silent for a time. +YOU ARE AN INTERESTING MORTAL, AJ-KAHUN GERUN SHIVERRIG.+

"What do you want? Access? Do you think there is some way I can open the door between realms when you cannot?"

+I AM CONTENT TO REMAIN WHERE I AM, FOR NOW. TODAY I OFFER WISDOM AND A TASTE POWER. WHEN THE TIME IS RIGHT, I MAY ASK YOUR ASSISTANCE AGAINST A COMMON FOE. I MERELY WISH TO HELP YOU PREVAIL, AND IN DOING SO, I PREVAIL.+

"And your price? Speak plainly, if it is in your power to do so."

+I HAVE NO PRICE TO COLLECT. A FRIEND DOES ANOTHER A FAVOR.+

"We are not friends, Devil."

+DEVIL? I TELL YOU THIS, I AM NO MERE DEVIL. I AM XERTHOTHA, AND I AM SUPREME!+

Xerthotha's anger at Shiverrig's slight pounded into his mind and buckled his knees, dropping him to the floor. He gasped to collect his breath and forced himself to stand. Shiverrig could not allow himself to appear weak.

"A friend does another a favor?" he said slowly.

+CONTROL THE PORTALS OF THE CHAOS GATE AND I SHALL BRING YOU LEGIONS TO COMMAND.+

"Commanded in your name and for your purposes. I know nothing is given for free."

Xerthotha remained silent once more, which was answer enough for Shiverrig. He knew better than to trust the mysterious creature.

+YOUR REALM HAS BEEN CHANGED FOREVER BY THE BIRTH OF THE CHAOS GATE. YOU REALIZE THIS BUT CANNOT KNOW THE ANCIENT BEINGS WHICH MOVE WITH ALL HASTE TO SLAKE THEIR THIRST ON THE REALM OF MORTALS, AND THEIR SOUL THIRST IS GREAT.+

"And you are our savior? The protector from what slouches towards Hanna from the Abyss. You alone shall hold these ancient beings at bay?"

+IN A MATTER OF SPEAKING, YES.+

"And in return for my acceptance of your generous offer? I ask again, what is your price?"

+YOU AND YOUR KIND SHALL WORSHIP ME AS YOUR GOD, AND YOU, THEIR AJ-KAHUN SHALL ASCEND TO BE MY GOLDEN SON, MY CHAMPION IN THIS REALM. YOU SHALL RIVAL THE MIGHT OF THE DIVINE FIST AND CEASE HIS BOTHERSOME INTERFERANCE.+

"I have another solution. It is my mind to destroy the Chaos Gate and plug the hole oozing filth into my kingdom."

Xerthotha's laughter bellowed in Shiverrig's mind like a rolling thunderclap from a distant storm.

+AH, THE INNOCENT NAIVETE OF MORTALS. THE AMARANTHINE BARRIER HAS BEEN ripped OPEN WITH THE BIRTH OF THE CHAOS GATE AND Eyes that have slept for eons now open and see through the HOLE.+

"Why not plunge through this hole yourself? Surely that would be easier."

Shiverrig felt the connection to the Supreme Devil being pulled thin. He now only heard whispers in his head.

+TIME GROWS SHORT AND DECISIONS MUST BE MADE. CHOOSE NOW AND CHOOSE WISELY.+

Shiverrig did not know how long he had been in communion with Xerthotha. The conversation had left him trembling. He wiped the sweat streaming from his forehead with the back of his wrist. His leathers felt clammy against his skin, and he wanted to strip out of them to somehow feel clean.

Shiverrig knew his options were few. The survival of his newly won kingdom was precariously balanced on the razor's edge of fate. His head swam through tumbling thoughts of grand victories, swallowed by everlasting despair.

He walked on unsteady legs to the large wooden desk in the room and eased himself into the chair behind it. His movements were stiff, and his muscles ached worse than if he had engaged in armored combat against a worthy foe. What choice did he really have?

Shiverrig looked down on the table. A large map lay across its surface filled with small figurines representing the troop placement, and company strength of his and Sekka's warriors across the Three Kingdoms. Official documents written on rolled parchment were scattered on the edges of the map, needing his attention and signature.

He brushed it all aside, clumping the figurines against his forearms and letting the parchments fall off the table, and roll on the floor. Slowly, he lowered his head to the worn material of the map and slept.

53

SEKKA

Sekka had used cunning and deception to thwart the advance of Zizphander, and she knew Azrollorza was pleased. The Wood Witch had been easily manipulated when her love, Kasai, and that fool Aetenos grappled in vain with the Red Devil. What hope did he and his mind slave have in stopping Zizphander, when she and her forces on Gathos had failed at every turn?

But this Wood Witch was fearless and possessed such a deep reservoir of pure Elemenati magic that she had only just begun to realize existed in her blood. And now that the one called Desdemonia had a taste of unadulterated power, she would be even easier to entice to join Sekka's elite cadre of operatives in the Mortal Realm. Perhaps she would take in the demon seed and become an even more significant asset. There were so many possibilities to explore.

Sekka couldn't help but wonder if the Wood Witch's bloodline originated from the ancient lines of Sunne. Troublesome Sunne. Sekka had expected resistance, but not defeat. The Warlords of Vyzyn had grossly underestimated the resolve of the Sunnese people, and now Sitrix, the eldest, was dead. Sekka's musings were interrupted by Azrollorza's watery voice as it droned on in her mind.

+...And by using the Great monk's slave as a carrot, no less. So clever. This is why you are still my favorite little devil. your reward for my pleasure shall arrive soon.+

"I have not agreed to terms!" Sekka shouted back in the air, as if speaking in a louder voice would be more easily understood.

+I am sending my emissary, kotto'gyges, to Gathos and you will release Aetenos and his Ever Hero to him.+

"Wait!" Sekka shouted again, but Azrollorza had severed the connection. "Not good, not good at all!"

Moments later, a distant rumble crossed the icy plains outside Furia Keep and shook the walls of her chamber. "A thousand curses upon that bloated bitch!" Sekka screamed. "I did not agree to this."

She concentrated her will on contacting the demon witch, Chedipe, to join her as she rushed to the outer walls of the Keep.

"No, no, no, no! Not now, not yet!" Sekka peered over the outer battlements, and her eyes grew wide with anger as a vast army of minor demons rumbled towards Furia Keep.

Sekka saw numerous banners swinging from hoisted standards that glowed from within; a dull, burnt-orange light illuminated them in the snow-filled, grey-blue atmosphere. All bore a similar image, that of seven eyeballs clustered together, surrounded by a swarming mane of tentacles. Azrollorza had sent an army to her doorstep, much to Sekka's dismay.

Coming behind the first wave of infantry were at least a hundred lesser juggernauts, smaller in size than the castle-sized behemoths of Gathos, but fearsome, nonetheless. The creatures floated through the swirling snow, bobbing up and down as they approached. Sekka was reminded of the bulbous, jelly-headed leviathans Azrollorza had called the Dezemilians.

Like their more colossal brethren, these creatures had long, hanging appendages, that dangled from their bulbous heads and dragged through the snow like long tails from their underside. Tube-shaped proboscises extended from the bellies of the demons, curling and uncurling like the fingers of sea anemones, as they sucked in the frigid air of Gathos through gross, puckering mouths. Sekka couldn't help but feel they were mocking her.

Upon each spongy back stood a cadre of demon knights, ten abreast clad in vermillion armor holding long, black spears. Bright-orange sigils of power gushed in the wake of the knights and swirled in the air behind them. Below the floating demons were at least ten thousand lesser fiends, plodding through the snow. The fiends quarreled and harried one another as they marched, unable to control their desire for mayhem. Few were equipped with short swords and crude maces, but most relied upon their claws and teeth in battle.

Leading the vast horde was a purple and pink monstrosity of bloated flesh with countless segmented arms attached to its body. The arm either ended in hands or sharp, dagger-shaped tips. The chitinous appendages covering its body propelled it forward like a rolling meat shredder, ripping up chunks of ice and snow from the ground.

The demon had hundreds of blueish, wavering stalks covering his rotund body. Some ended in gibbering maws, which opened and closed, spraying spittle and screeching horrible curses, holding the ranks of the army in order. The other stalks ended with lidless eyes that stared up at her in contempt.

"Kotto'gyges," Sekka said with a grimace.

Chedipe arrived sometime after, her movements hampered by weak limbs held together by dark magic in a body forced to live beyond natural means. Stringy black hair cascaded from her head and swayed like isolated blades of swamp grass with each painful step. White-knuckled hands gripped a tall, bone staff that supported the weight of her frail body.

"Chedipe is here, my Queen," she breathed out the words sharply, then gasped at the army at the gates of Furia Keep and pointed at the one who led them.

"Kotto'gyges, the Impaler, is a mighty demon prince, my Queen. Powerful in the arcane, and devious of mind."

"I know who he is!"

Sekka saw Kotto'gyges lived up to his namesake. The demon prince could attack in any position, impaling his enemies with quick thrusts of his arms and tear them apart, or stuff them still living into his gaping mouths.

Chedipe stepped away from the rampart, consternation moved across her weathered face.

"Azrollorza provides a great weapon, and a warning by sending her First General of the Eighty-eighth Legion. Kotto'gyges will not hesitate to turn his talents on you, my Mistress, if you displease the Supreme Devil."

"You sound suspicious of our glorious patron's intentions," Sekka said in a syrupy sweet voice. However, she felt uneasy at such a vast host appearing on Gathos without warning or permission. She could easily take this for an act of war, had she not initially gone in search of support.

"The sword she sends is sharp on both sides," Chedipe said.

Sekka knew it to be true. The tithe Azrollorza would demand in exchange for her favor would take centuries to repay, all the while keeping Sekka bound in servitude. And if the debt remained unpaid for too long, well, that would be the end of her reign on Gathos.

"Azrollorza must have known of the Chaos Gate from the beginning," Chedipe spat. "What shall you do?"

Sekka tapped her long nails on the ice-covered stone crenels.

"She is watching me, testing me. Azrollorza and I will need to come to an arrangement, and soon. She will continue to demand an impossible payment of souls for her patronage. The moment I fail to deliver her due, she will strike with impunity, and with no just cause of retaliation from either Xerthotha or Morrdilliax. She will claim reparation from a pact broken and a payment unfulfilled. And who would believe otherwise?"

"A decision must be made to strike first," Chedipe hissed like a snake.

"Decision? What decision could I possibly make now!" Sekka slapped Chedipe hard across her face and sent her sprawling to the floor.

"Azrollorza requires fifty-thousand souls as payment for this army. A pact I never accepted, but one that is forced upon me now. I have nothing to do but accept her patronage and its cost."

Chedipe cringed from the floor, fearful of a second strike, but Sekka paid her no mind as she worked at unraveling the riddle that had entwined itself around her, and her precious Gathos.

"A broader game between Xerthotha and Azrollorza is at play, and Gathos has become the tip of the fulcrum, bringing both opponents to the endgame. I am embroiled in a conflict that has deeper ramifications than the existence of the Chaos Gate. The portal is merely an added spoil that will go to the victor."

"Yes, my Queen," Chedipe said in a whisper. "The birth of the Chaos Gate has changed many things. Many, many things. Ancient threats awaken. But Chedipe does not fear the future. Her Queen is wise and shall prevail as she always does."

Sekka frowned at Chedipe and thought to strike her again. She needed answers, not the sycophantic praise of a broken dog. Then an idea came to her.

"Oh, Xerthotha, you are so clever, so clever indeed."

"My Queen?" Chedipe asked questioningly in a meek voice.

"Xerthotha knew I would eventually discover he was Zizphander's Shadow Patron. If I were to prevail over the Red Devil, I would need to align myself with one of the other Supreme Devils. My only choice would be Azrollorza, for Morrdilliax has forever refused to align himself with lesser devils, even one of my status. So, Xerthotha draws Azrollorza into another conflict, but why now?"

"They have no lack of past aggression towards one another. Why should your part matter?"

"Isn't it obvious? Openly attacking one another would bring Morrdilliax into the fray, and the Abyss would shatter. No, Xerthotha attacks Azrollorza through her allies and slowly bleeds her strength. Eventually, he will strike but must be assured of a quick victory before Morrdilliax can intervene. Until that time, he must keep his hands clean."

Sekka stepped away from the outer wall and slowly walked along the battlements. A horrible revelation took shape in her mind. "Xerthotha is using me just like his dog, Zizphander."

She stopped and screamed, her voice adding to the howling winds swarming around Furia Keep. Her fists clenched at her sides, and her chest heaved like a sea swell in a storm. Chedipe crouched lower to the floor, huddled in fear.

Sekka gathered herself and exhaled, a wordless surrender was carried in her breath.

"Control of the Chaos Gate must be relinquished if Gathos is to survive, and I am to ascend. I will use it as my dowry to Azrollorza." The words seethed between her teeth. Once again, her carefully laid plans unraveled due to no fault of her own.

"It will be a priceless gift to any Supreme Devil," Chedipe said as she rose cautiously from the floor, her eyes locked on Sekka for fear of being struck again.

Sekka turned to Chedipe with a sparkle in her eye. "Yes, but only if I willingly give them access to it. Some rules must be followed, even for a Supreme Devil."

Chedipe looked back over the wall. "What of Azrollorza's army at the gate?"

"We shall let them pass within Furia Keep. Xerthotha will rue the day he chose to use me as his lackey."

"How fare the Warlords of Vyzyn and the war in Sunne, my Queen?"

Sekka's mouth twitched into a frown. The dire news from the Sunne campaign came with disappointing consistency.

"Tazizu has called again for reinforcements. She claims the jungle itself had come alive and fights with unnatural zeal against her shock troops.

"She claims hanging vines pull fully armored demons off the ground, strangle them or worse, burrow their tendril fingers into open seams between the plates, then rip them apart from the inside.

"Now I hear whole platoons have been lost along narrow jungle paths as the solid ground they trod upon turned to quicksand and sucked them down into the deep earth. It was worse for the juggernauts. Their massive bulk caused them to sink faster. They proved to be ill-suited for the dense jungle terrain and perished needlessly."

Sekka seethed at the waste of so much soul stock. She doubted the stories were true and assumed they were more lies to cover up the complete incompetence of the Vyzyn Warlord.

Sitrix, the eldest of the brood, was the military strategist and had been groomed for war. He would not have made such clumsy mistakes and squandered his resources. Unfortunately, Sitrix had been targeting and killed quickly in the campaign. The Sunnese had decapitated the beast and left the horde unmanaged and scattered from the start. Clever natives.

Sekka now put her faith in Aeshmara and had given her command of the forces in Sunne. The youngest warlord of the brood was cunning, ambitious, and driven by accomplishments and praise. Sekka hoped she would finally see the results she expected.

"Chedipe, I want you to send a portion of Azrollorza's troops to reinforce Aeshmara in the jungle campaign. Instruct her to collect Dai-Ko-Zior at the Sarribe Pass and continue the invasion of Sunne. Their priority is not to control land, but to harvest souls. Is that understood?"

"Yes, my queen. Chedipe obeys."

"Open the gates!" Sekka called to her guards below.

Sekka was satisfied with her decision, for it was the best she could hope for given her current predicament. She looked back over the battlements and peered down at the waiting Kotto'gyges. The demon prince had stopped screeching and stared back at her with flowing hypnotic eyes, the stalks resembled a field of grass in the wind.

No words were spoken between them, but the tension was there, Sekka could taste it on her long tongue. Demons lusted for the power they could not have, and blindly challenged the strength of their superiors.

No matter, she had dealt with upstart demons in the past, and Kotto'gyges was no different. He would either succumb to her will or perish. She had more pressing concerns other than the wild urges of a spoiled demon prince.

She turned from the wall. "Chedipe, summon Lord Oziax."

Sekka then heard a desperate wail over the howling winds and saw one of her many scouts flying haphazardly to the Keep. The small, winged fiend flew over the wall and skidded to a stop at her feet. It had been wounded in numerous places, and black blood oozed from as many wounds.

"My Queen," the imp sputtered. "The Red Devil comes."

Sekka heard the scout's words and assumed he spoke of an earlier report that was just being delivered now. She knew Zizphander had been defeated and pushed back by Aetenos, his Ever Hero, and, more importantly, the wood witch, Desdemonia.

"The Red Devil is nursing his wounds at the edge of Gathos. He will not return anytime soon."

"No, my queen. Forgive me, you are mistaken. He comes. He comes!"

Sekka looked to the East and saw a line of rosy light appear and then grow across the horizon as if a newborn sun rose into the sky. This was no simple horde to harass her troops and lay waste to outlying territories. Zizphander had returned with the entire might of his legions. Furia Keep was under siege.

54

KASAI

Kasai and Desdemonia were forcefully thrown in the same cell that held Pallo, Run-Run, and Orin. He tried to make her comfortable by gently pulling her semi-conscious body onto his lap. He then sat with his back against the wall, which was opposite the barred door.

The Kibo Gensai huddled closely together in the farthest corner, away from them and keeping to themselves. Orin spoke in hushed whispers to Pallo and Run-Run, who nodded and exchanged worried expressions, then cast a suspicious look at Desdemonia.

The jailors had thrown down a poor substitute for straw on the floor, and it stank of something nameless and foul. There were no bedrolls or other means of comfort, just walls, bars, and the cold. Kasai looked through the front wall bars and into the adjacent cell. There sat Aetenos, cross-legged in the center of his own cell. The Great Monk cradled his head in his hands and rocked slowly back and forth, mumbling incoherent thoughts.

"No more sleepy magic to addle an old man's mind. Ho, ho," he said, but his voice was anything but joyful.

Their weapons had been confiscated and tossed into an old, battered locker in the large torture chamber where they had earlier found the angel, Artiya'il, crucified on his wheel. The jailors slammed the door shut, and that was the last Kasai had seen of Ninziz-zida.

Kasai wondered what was happening in the towers above, and if Sekka was devising horrible ways to make them suffer. His mind drifted to Illyria and why she had abandoned them. The thought lingered as he peered over at Aetenos.

Kasai shook his head in despair. Why should she come back for any of them when they had failed her quest? He was saddened to think of Baroqia, now that there was no one to stop Sekka and her armies. The Chaos Gate would remain open to untold horrors, and it was all his fault. He deserved this doom.

"You shall find a way," he said the words he had heard repeatedly in a mocking tone. "Well, they got that wrong."

They were prisoners with no weapons and no means to escape the dungeon, let alone Furia Keep. And even if he could find a way out of Sekka's lair, they would never survive the ravages of Gathos. Nobody could save them now. They were alone.

Desdemonia stirred on his lap. He was still amazed at what she had accomplished to stall the advance of Zizphander. He stroked her hair and watched her facial features twitch as if she was dreaming. Kasai hoped that when she awoke, the frolicking gypsy would return. He realized how much he missed her inappropriate remarks and they could all use some brevity to lighten their moods.

He tried to concentrate and fall into a calming state of meditation. His mind circled the same question endlessly of how to escape, but there was no answer forthcoming.

Desdemonia's eyes flashed open, but they only stared ahead, blank, unrecognizing anything or anyone around her. He noticed the bright amber color of her irises had faded and become dull and dark. She blinked a few times and moaned, then pulled herself up off his lap.

"Hello, love," she said, rubbed her temples, then plopped down next to him with her back against the wall. Her thick hair tumbled in long, heavy curls across her face. She tilted her head up and looked into Kasai's eyes. A feral smile crossed her lips, but then quickly vanished as she pressed her eyes closed and grimaced. "Ugh, my head. Where are we?"

"We are back in the dungeons, this time as prisoners," Kasai said in a weary voice.

Desdemonia looked about the cell. She glanced at the Kibo Gensai and they at her, but they quickly turned their heads away and rejoined their private conversation.

She paused for a moment as if reliving events in her mind. The wild grin came back to her face, and her eyes lit like smoldering embers.

"Kasai?"

He raised his eyebrows. "Yes?"

"Did you mean it? What you said in front of Sekka and Aetenos and the rest. Did you?" She placed a hand on his chest that crept slowly to his throat.

"What do you mean?" Kasai said though he knew exactly what she meant. This was the moment he was dreading. Desdemonia was going to tease him first for professing his love for her, and then let him know she was not for him.

"You said you loved me."

Kasai closed his eyes. "I know. Des, I'm sorry. I meant no offense. She was going to kill you."

"Do you?"

"What?"

She sat up on her feet, squatting to his side. She draped her arms over his shoulders and blew the hair away from her face. Her eyes were the eyes of a predator, and she pulled him close into an embrace. "Kiss me."

"Des, here? Now?" Kasai felt ashamed and embarrassed. He'd never kissed a woman before and awkwardly pulled away.

"You said you loved me. Prove it," she said in a sensual and seductive tone.

"What's wrong with you?" he said. "Everyone is right there."

"So what? They've seen people kiss before." She looked over at Pallo, Run-Run, and Orin. "And they can watch if they want."

Orin looked away in disgust as if confirming something said earlier to Pallo and Run-Run.

Kasai tried to pull away, but she held him tight and stared into his eyes. He wanted to kiss her, but he had no idea how and worried he would make a mistake. But more than feeling awkward, he was torn. Part of him wanted to dive into her embrace and kiss her with savage abandon like in legendary tales of heroes after rescuing the fair maiden from the clutches of the evil villain.

However, another part of him felt sickened by her touch. He couldn't see the carefree gypsy or the warrior druidess in her eyes. Now he saw someone or something else looking back at him. Something different and unnatural.

Desdemonia pushed him away. Her strength surprised him, and he toppled over on his side.

"You don't love me. You don't even know what love is. You're right. You're just a simple and stupid monk, a nobody. I hate you."

"Des, I didn't mean..."

"Oh, shut up, if you don't love me, then I'm sure either Pallo or Run-Run will show me more attention. Would you like to see that? I know they look at me. Maybe even Orin would like a taste. After all, he's still a man under all that posturing and self-righteousness, unlike you."

"What's come over you?"

"Did you think I was going to wait for you forever?" she sucked her teeth at him in disappointment.

The unmistakable clang of metal on metal preceded slow, deliberate footsteps coming down the corridor. Then Sess'thra came into view as she sauntered down the passage between the two cells. Her small, deft fingers gently played against each bar of Kasai's cell until she reached the door.

Sess'thra gazed into his cell, and her hip jutted to one side with her hand resting comfortably on the curve. She wore a light blue, scaled bodysuit, and the cold lights of the corridor reflected off its shimmering membrane, illuminating the shapely contours of her lithe figure.

Kasai hated that even now after all the succubus had done to them, he could not quell a repulsive desire for the demon. He looked over at Desdemonia and, with shocking clarity, realized the awkward attraction he felt for the demon was now the same he held for her.

Sess'thra cracked a half smile and gave him a crafty wink. "Having a bit of a lover's quarrel?"

"You!" Desdemonia sprang to her feet like a cat.

"I see you've recovered from our last dance. You seem well," Sess'thra said. "I was told an interesting change had developed with one of our heroes and wanted to see the transformation for myself."

Her eyes roamed over Desdemonia. "Hmm, not so much yet, only around the edges, I think, but I must say, I am pleased with the selection. Soon, we shall be sisters, you and I."

"I am nothing like you, Reese, fiend, or whatever you name yourself."

"Fiend? Tsk, tsk. Oh, you wound me so." Sess'thra feigned a hurtful expression as her hands pressed against her heart. "In time, you will see. Sisters, through and through."

Desdemonia aggressively raised her hands, but no magic came. She looked uncertainly at her palms and then back to Sess'thra. The succubus brushed her fingers back and forth across the cold bars. "Enchanted. Cancels all that wonderful tree magic of yours."

"You wear an onyx ring," Desdemonia said with dismay as her eyes found the ring Sess'thra wore on her index finger.

"Our Mistress provides," Sess'thra said and waved her finger in the air.

Desdemonia tried desperately to remove the ring, but it only wrapped itself tighter around the digit of her finger.

"We shall meet again, and I hope to be more friend than foe to you. Maybe even lovers, if you're lucky."

"You disgust me!" Desdemonia shouted.

"But for now, I am needed in Gethem to tame a confused duke, or whatever title he has now chosen. What a silly mortal. He can't seem to get out of his own way."

Sess'thra looked over her shoulder into Aetenos's the cell. "The fall of the divine is deep in the Abyss, so very deep." Her laughter dripped with syrupy malice and faded as she glided away from the cells and back down the corridor.

Kasai stood and noticed the onyx ring on Desdemonia's finger. "Where did you get the ring? Does it have anything to do with what happened on the cliff?" He didn't mean to sound accusatory, but it was precisely how the words came out of his mouth.

Desdemonia covered the ring with her hand and moved thoughtfully to a spot farthermost away from where the Kibo Gensai huddled on the floor. Then she turned sharply to face Kasai.

"Do you think only the Ever Hero can manifest higher powers when the need is great?" she said and placed contemptuous emphasis on his new nomenclature. Her tone was aggressive, and her eyes blazed at him as if he were an enemy.

But then her posture relaxed, and she quickly cooled, as if she was deflated by the resignation of some hidden truth.

"Pure Elementai Magic runs deep within my blood." Her voice trailed off to a whisper, and her eyes became distant.

"Des?" Kasai said with concern.

Desdemonia looked uneasy and hesitant, then the flame returned.

"Can't you see? I finally feel alive! My magic flows through me like a raging river, racing to be free."

She then glared at Kasai. "Since I met you, you've always been skeptical of me and my gift, as if it were something unwanted, no matter how many times it saved you. You don't appreciate anything I do. You don't understand me. You have always been afraid of me, afraid of what I could be to you. You are a coward, Kasai. A coward!"

Kasai stood shocked at her outburst. "But..."

"Just leave me alone!"

She turned her back to Kasai and crossed her arms over her chest. Her shoulders and back heaved, and Kasai could hear that she was sobbing.

"What am I even doing here? I should be in my forest, minding my own business. Gauldumor warned me, warned me of all of this. Why couldn't I have listened for once."

Her sobs grew heavier.

"It's my fault, Des. If I hadn't used the emerald amulet against Sekka, none of this would have happened. There would be no Chaos Gate." Kasai tried to sound as gentle as he could.

She turned to face him as tears streamed down her face. "And you would be dead, Kasai. We would all be dead!" Her arms encompassed the little group of prisoners.

"That would have been acceptable! No good has ever come from using magic. Look at what it is doing to you now!" Kasai shut his eyes, immediately regretting what he had just said.

Des walked towards Kasai with a noticeable switch in her hips.

"What's the matter, Kasai? Am I unsightly to you now that you finally see the real me?"

A wolfish grin played across her lips as she moved closer to him, uncomfortably close. She put her fingers under his chin to lift his face.

"Look at me. Tell me, what do you see?"

Kasai knew it deep in his soulless heart that he loved her, but he didn't understand her at all. His mouth was so dry his lips would not part to speak. He looked deeply into her aura and caught a glimpse of a dark, thin thread entwining around the swirling colors of green and yellow, strangling them, and then vanishing out of sight.

She looked at him with expectant eyes, and her fingers squeezed his chin roughly. "Well?"

If only he could find the right thing to say to her. Master Choejor always had unique words for these situations. He could speak right to the point of a matter and say precisely what was needed to be said. Kasai had no words like that.

"You've changed," Kasai sputtered.

"And you've been blind all this time. Blinded by fear of what you cannot explain."

She shucked away his chin and stomped off to her own corner of the cell. Kasai welcomed the relief from her pressing questions and uncomfortable advancements. He felt like a bumbling idiot when it came to matters of the heart...and body. The Masters of Ordu had failed to train him in all the aspects of the outside world.

Who was he kidding? This wasn't their fault. Desdemonia was right. He was a coward and afraid to express how he really felt about her.

"You really messed that up," he said to himself, feeling frustrated and confused. He tried to think of different things he could tell Desdemonia that might cheer her up, but nothing came to mind.

He sat down on the floor and tried to relax. It was difficult at first because everything inside him felt constricted and tied in knots. Eventually, his training from Ordu took hold, and he fell into a deep meditation.

He heard the soft chime of bells in the corner of his mind, like the ones tied to the loping rope bridges at Ordu that swayed over the mountain crevasses. The melodic song of the bells eased his mind away from worry and fear.

Kasai envisioned himself rising out of his physical form and floating to the top of the cell. He looked down upon himself, then Desdemonia and lastly, Pallo, Run-Run, and Orin. He shifted his view to the iron bars of his cell and the locked door at its center.

His objective was freedom, yet there were so many barriers to overcome before he could achieve his goal. He had no key to open the locked door, or weapons to fight the guards if he escaped the cell, nor did possess a map to lead them to safety out of Furia Keep. And even if they were able to get that far, he could not operate the Chaos Gate nor had he the means to destroy it. Every path led to a dead end, and his soul remaining trapped within the dark mechanism forever.

Now that escape was impossible, what was left that *was* possible? Aetenos had spoken of a universal language of vibration that connected everything together. Kasai took a deep breath and let it out slowly. Easier said than done, he thought.

He concentrated on the lock. How could such a small thing stop him when he had burst apart the ice of a frozen lake? It had been so much easier with Ninziz-zida's help, of course, but he didn't need that much power. This was just a lock. A simple, small lock. It was worth a try.

He let his mind flow back into a deep meditative state, letting his thoughts drift without cause, reason, or fear. He sought to understand how the lock mechanism worked and reached out with his senses to unravel its mystery.

He imagined the individual pieces that would be found inside any locking device. None came to mind. He did not know the internal makeup of locks or how they worked. He was not a tinkerer. Doubt crept into his mind and clouded his reasoning.

No, do not think! Feel! Feel the rhythm of the lock. The clicks and teeth that held the bolt tight. How does its energy flow?

The lock remained frozen in a dead slumber and refused to wake. It needed something of equal vibration to bring it to life. Kasai probed deeper and channeled his energy into a key, not a physical one, or the idea of one, but the feeling of one.

He drifted deeper into his trance, and his breathing became even and slow. His impatience to be free lit his fire xindu, but he pushed it back. Not yet.

Then something amazing happened all on its own. Kasai's air xindu gathered and swirled around the energy his fire xindu had manifested. It coaxed it and curled it, then directed it to the lock in the door, but it would not enter the keyhole. Something more was needed.

Kasai pushed harder with his fire xindu. Willing the energy to obey. Yet, it swirled before the lock and would go no farther. Kasai instinctively let his water xindu rise to calm his sense of urgency, and in time, a cooling, watery sensation washed over him. As he added his water xindu to the ethereal mixture, the energy moved forward and entered the keyhole, but there it remained.

Kasai now understood what was needed next and activated his earth xindu to speak on equal terms with the lock's frozen mechanisms. He turned the complete mixture of energy as he would a key in a lock. To his amazement and gratitude, the lock clicked, and the door was released.

Kasai opened his eyes and saw Desdemonia walking hesitantly to the open door, amazed and unsure of what had happened. He then peered past her into Aetenos's cell. The Great Monk was standing at the bars, a satisfied smile beamed across his face.

"You see? You shall find a way! Ho, ho!"

Aetenos promptly popped the lock of his cell and pushed it open. The worn hinges creaked with a sound that could wake the dead. "Let us be on our way. Illyria has heard my call, and we shall meet again soon, but we must not dally."

"But, if you could...?"

Aetenos glanced back at his open cell door and shrugged his shoulders. "Then you would never learn, would you? Trust yourself, my son. The way is already within you."

"Yes, Master. Thank you."

"There are no thanks given. You must learn these lessons, well and fast, for there is much to do."

Aetenos led the heroes back to the room where the angel's body was splayed on the torturer's rack. The dimly lit room smelled of death and decay. Nothing had changed. Kasai immediately went to the old locker that held their weapons. The demons hadn't bothered to lock the door, and why would they? No one escaped the dungeons of Furia Keep.

Kasai gripped Ninziz-zida in his hands, and she embraced him in kind by vanquishing the chill in his bones with a wave of her fire xindu. He handed the others their short swords.

"We will defend ourselves as best we can to gain the upper levels. With any luck, Master Aetenos can find the way back to the outer courtyard," Kasai said as he handed Run-Run his second sword.

Kasai looked to Aetenos to take the lead, but the Master sat in a chair, making himself comfortable instead.

"Master, why do we linger here?"

"We wait for my beloved, Illyria," Aetenos said and picked at his fingernails, clearing away the filth he had accumulated from his long ordeal on Gathos.

Pallo joined Kasai and Aetenos. His face filled with anxiety. "Master Aetenos, I fear with each passing moment we lose more innocents to Sekka's evil in Baroqia."

"You're wasting your time. Aetenos has fallen under the spell of the witch. The quest has failed, and we have been forsaken," Orin said.

"Mind your tongue!" Pallo said in disbelief.

"I will not! I speak for the lost soul of Airis! The boy had barely seen his twenty-second summer," Orin said through clenched teeth. He lifted one of the swords Kasai had just handed him and pointed it at Desdemonia.

"We all knew the risks and took vows to follow the path of the Ever Hero, long before Illyria's quest," Pallo said.

"And some Ever Hero we have here, don't we?"

"I've had just about enough of your hostile attitude and disparaging words," Desdemonia said.

She glared at Orin and tilted her head from side-to-side, studying him as a young predator might look upon something it knew was prey, but had not yet tasted. Kasai could smell the scent of a distant thunderstorm collecting in the room. Silver runes swirled lazily around her body like a cat slowly twitching its tail before pouncing.

Aetenos looked up from his business with his nails and then back down again. He nodded and smiled briefly as if the coming conflict was inevitable.

"Lower your sword, Orin. She's not your enemy," Kasai pleaded and stood in front of the Kibo Gensai warrior. "This is not the way!"

But Orin's expression said otherwise. "The witch must pay for her wickedness. Stand aside, Ever Hero, I do not wish to hurt you."

Dark clouds materialize overhead, and slim tendrils of air snaked down to the floor. Desdemonia chuckled in a sultry laugh. "Let him come, my love. This madness will quickly be over. If he so desires to be one with the Light, I will grant him a swift passage."

"You see? She is evil and must be destroyed!" Orin pushed Kasai to one side and readied his swords.

Kasai saw a devious smile creep up the corners of Desdemonia's mouth, and he knew Orin was a dead man. Pallo and Run-Run had their swords in hand and had taken a defensive stance. The rolling sound of thunder became more pronounced, and the smell of rain overpowered the reek of the room.

"Stop! Stop this all of you!" Kasai cried out, but no one was listening to him.

Then a brilliant, white light flashed throughout the room, followed by a thunderous boom. Kasai fell back to the floor and heard the clamor of weapons and torturous devices falling around him. Heavy tables were pushed aside as their sturdy legs screeched across the dirty floor. Old chairs exploded against the walls and shattered into unrecognizable pieces.

Kasai shielded his eyes from the blinding light. He expected to hear Orin cry out in pain, but instead, there was only an eerie quiet once the last item clanged to the ground. The bright light dissipated to a warm glow, and he slowly opened his eyes to see a shimmering figure standing in the middle of the room. Illyria had appeared.

55

DESDEMONIA

Desdemonia stumbled backward, tripped over some random bones that had spilled out of a bin next to one of the larger torture devices, and fell to the floor. She shielded her eyes until the blinding light that filled the chamber subsided. The divine beauty of Illyria filled her with awe, but she felt galled that her magic had been disrupted, and Orin was still alive. She watched in bitter disappointment as the storm clouds overhead dissipated into thin air.

Illyria looked over the small group of companions and then laid eyes on Aetenos. Her smile became broad and thankful. "I have finally found you, my beloved."

She walked to the body of the dead angel and gently placed a hand on Artiya'il's forehead as the small party rose from the floor or disentangled themselves from toppled lockers and overturned tables.

"You were wise to mark him as you did, my love. The fading light of Artiya'il's soul was a beacon in the darkness one last time. Even in death, he continues to serve the Seven Heavens. I only hope it is not too late."

Aetenos bowed his head.

"This nightmare is finally over, and we can all go home," Kasai said with relief. "Des, we did it."

Illyria looked tenderly at Kasai and paused to collect her thoughts. "The birth of the Chaos Gate has created a rift in the Amaranthine Barrier and awakened ancient powers that hunger for mortal souls. As the tear grows, the protective layer surrounding the Mortal Realm weakens and dissolves.

"The Great Balance now tips far to one side, and the champions of Light are called to defend their world. The Divine Fist must heal and be made strong again, for the coming conflict will be the greatest fight he has ever faced. The Great Balance must be restored."

Aetenos gave Kasai a friendly elbow to his side. "Got that?"

"Isn't this a job for the angels? Will they not interfere again and vanquish Sekka a second time?" Kasai said. "Aren't they supposed to defend us?"

"Things are not as clear as they once were, and old grudges have plowed deep grooves in stone hearts," Aetenos said.

Illyria's ominous words filled Desdemonia with dread. They would not be going home after all. Then Orin marched to Illyria and pointing in Desdemonia's direction.

"She has colluded with the devil! Her blood is tainted and seeks to damn us all! I saw it with my own eyes. Pallo, tell her. You were there. You saw what she did!"

"Orin, enough with your wild conspiracies," Kasai said, and he looked to Pallo for support, but the elder Kibo Gensai would not meet his imploring gaze.

"Pallo? What is it? What happened?"

Desdemonia stepped in front of Kasai and turned him away from the others. "It's nothing, Kasai. Let it be," she said in a soft voice. "I did what was necessary to save you."

"Des, what happened? What did you do?"

Illyria raised an eyebrow and examined her with an air of suspicion. Instead of feeling uplifted by Illyria's divine presence, Desdemonia felt unworthy and ashamed.

She glared back at the angel. "And, I would do it again without hesitation," she said with conviction as the angel approached.

"You wear an onyx ring," Illyria said sadly. Desdemonia quickly covered the ring with her other hand.

"The Kibo Gensai warrior speaks the truth. The Wood Witch's soul is compromised, and her blood is tainted. She will not be received where we must go."

Orin's face beamed with a self-righteous victory. "The goddess Illyria has spoken. The witch stays in the Abyss, where she belongs."

Desdemonia pulled away from the others and tried again to pull off the ring. It wouldn't budge. She thought about cutting the ring finger off, but what would that do to her spellcasting? She knew from childhood experience that those in her village who lost fingers and toes, or arms and legs could no longer appropriately wield their gift. The magic just wouldn't flow, and that thought seemed like a death sentence to her now.

She turned to the others, feeling betrayed. *How dare they think to take away who I am!*

"As I have said, I did what was needed to be done to save Kasai. How many rules did you break to even come here?" she said, challenging Illyria. "If that means I am somehow less worthy in your so-called divine eyes and must stay behind, then so be it. I say damn to those who see what I have done as evil."

"She curses us!" Orin shouted.

"Des settle down. There is no way I'm just going to leave you here," Kasai said.

"Just go. It doesn't matter. You can't save everyone."

"Of course, it matters! It matters to me," Kasai said incredulously. "I can't just leave you here."

"You heard the witch. She belongs here, among her own kind."

Orin stepped closer and grabbed Kasai's arm, trying to pull him away from her. But Kasai rooted himself to the ground and twisted out of Orin's grasp. He gripped Ninziz-zida's collapsed segments tightly in one hand and used the Fire Serpent to push Orin back. Blue flames came to life over the staff.

"I mean it," Kasai said.

"Orin, enough," Pallo said.

"Des, please, no more guessing games," Kasai said. "What happened?"

His eyes had turned from sage green to dark hazel. He was scared. She wished she could make him understand.

"After all this time, you still don't get it, do you? Kasai, I would do anything to keep you safe. Anything."

Run-Run came over to Kasai and put a hand on his shoulder. He nodded affirmatively and pointed at Desdemonia, and then to the rest. He even looked at Orin with an expression that said, yes, him too. Run-Run encouraged Kasai toward Illyria and the others, but he still resisted.

"Des, you're coming with us. I don't care what happened."

"It's okay," she said, searching for something more to say, but her heart was breaking.

She took a deep breath, knowing there was nothing more to say. What did her needs matter against the needs of a kingdom?

"Our time together in this life is over. But we will find each other again, just as we did in the meadow, outside my forest. Have faith in the bond we share and hold our love close to your heart. Keep it safe, and we will see each other when our paths cross again."

"What? No! I don't want to wait for the next life!" His eyes glistened with tears. "This is crazy. You're coming with me!"

"Not this time, Kasai. You have to listen to Illyria. I cannot go where you must go. I made a decision, and these are the consequences. You've been blessed to achieve great things and protect the world we know. I cannot be the reason you fail."

"You're the only reason why it's worth doing. You're all I have left!"

"Illyria said..." Orin piped in with arms crossed over his chest.

"Orin!" Pallo said.

Kasai stepped up to Illyria. "Take Aetenos and the others with you. Des and I will find another way back to Baroqia. Maybe through the Chaos Gate, I don't know. But I'm not leaving without her."

"You have chosen well, Aetenos. Your Ever Hero has a pure and noble heart," Illyria said and gave Kasai a warm smile. "But we are not returning to the Mortal Realm. Aetenos has suffered greatly, not only of the body but also of mind and spirit. He requires the healing touch of the Seven Heavens to regain his full strength. I only hope it will be allowed."

"Then take him. Take the others and go," Kasai said.

"As I have said, the Outer Realms have slipped out of balance. The Divine Fist must be made whole and filled with the power of the Light, and you, his Ever Hero, must be at his side, for the two forces of the same must not be without the other, or all is for naught."

Aetenos approached Kasai with fatherly eyes. "I am sorry to have given you this burden, my son. But time is short, and there is much to do before the dark tide swells too far over our heads."

"Master, I need her."

Pallo pushed forward. "And the Chaos Gate? Do we just leave it open and allow the hordes of Gathos to lay waste to Baroqia? You cannot forsake all those innocent people!"

"Pallo is right. Tell me what I must do to destroy the portal," Kasai said.

"There is only one way to destroy the Chaos Gate. The soul connection Aetenos and his Ever Hero share with the portal must be severed. But I do not have the power or knowledge to do such a thing.

"Aetenos, our time is short, and we must leave in haste. The decision is yours to make. Will the Wood Witch remain in Gathos, or continue her journey with your Ever Hero?"

Desdemonia took Kasai's free hand in her own. "Remember, keep the spark of love safe in your heart. It will be the beacon for our souls to find one another across lifetimes. Find me, Kasai. Find me."

Kasai shook his head, no. "This isn't happening. It's not fair."

Aetenos's forehead was deep with lines of worry. "The Light fades and gives way to Darkness, giving us little time to save the things we cherish. Your love will be tested, Desdemonia, and the Ever Hero shall be the dagger that cuts your bonds and seals your fate. Let us hope you both are strong enough to survive the coming trials. We all go."

"No!" Orin shouted. "She will doom us all!"

"The Divine Fist has spoken," Illyria said. She held a smile that could not change the sadness in her eyes as she waved the others closer. "All of you gather around. Clasp hands and do not let go, for any reason."

Desdemonia held Kasai's hand tightly.

He gave her a reassuring smile. "Everything will be fine, Des. You'll see. They will fix you up in no time."

She glanced sideways and peered at him through the dark hair cascading around her face, keeping it in shadow. "But what if I don't want to be fixed?" she said softly.

Then the cruel sights of the torture chamber spun before her eyes in a dizzying array of warped shapes and colors. The numbing cold of Gathos faded away and was replaced by the soothing warmth of summer. She heard laughter and the splash of water just as her feet landed on firm ground.

She slowly opened her eyes and gasped. Illyria had transported them all to a bright meadow enclosed by a tall rock formation shaped like a half-moon. The long grass growing at her feet swayed in a gentle breeze that carried over a clear lake, creating shimmering waves reflecting the bright sunlight. It was a happy place, but it made Desdemonia feel sick to her stomach, and she wanted to flee.

Angels frolicked in the sky, some gracefully floating upwards with broad feathered wings, while others spun and twirled like aerial acrobats as sparkling light danced across their bodies. Others dove with their feathered wings folded tight behind their backs like ocean terns entering the water in a perfect line, then moments later, burst back into the air.

Not all the celestials had wings, nor were people at all, but animals of all shapes and sizes. Humans and animals spoke and played together as if they were one and the same, though none seemed to pay much attention to the new arrivals.

Mingled among the long grass were multicolored flowering plants with giant blossoms of red, orange, blue, and purple. The fragrant air reminded Desdemonia of springtime when the wildflowers opened for the first time after a long winter sleep.

Pallo stood firm, yet his face held an expression of wonder. Run-Run's arms were flung wide, and tears fell freely down his cheeks, while Orin had dropped to his knees in supplication, murmuring prayers to the Immortal Mother. There was no pain here, only joy and laughter, and their faces beamed with happiness.

Desdemonia tried to smile, but her nausea persisted, and a queer feeling crept up her back. She felt like a thief about to be caught red-handed with stolen goods.

Kasai held her hand tight. "We made it, Des. Everything will be okay."

"This is Elysian, and is the first level of the Seven Heavens," said Illyria. "Come, we have a long journey to the Steps of Judgment."

Aetenos's face was filled with consternation and he seemed agitated. Pallo, Run-Run, and Orin followed Illyria as she made her way to the rock wall.

Desdemonia squinted her eyes against the unbearable light. She let go of Kasai's hand and brushed her long, raven hair into her face. When that wasn't enough, she used both her hands to shield her eyes. Her entire body trembled as if she shivered from a fever.

"Des?" Kasai said.

"I'm just still dizzy from the journey," she said meekly and with a shaky voice. Her legs buckled, and Kasai caught her before she fell.

"Illyria, wait. Something is wrong with Des."

Illyria glanced back but didn't stop. "I cannot interfere. I am sorry."

The sound of a distant trumpet peeled to the left, and the angels in the sky ceased their dives. Another sounded from the right, and then a third from behind. The celestials around them stopped their conversations and watched the party with curious eyes.

Aetenos moved to help Desdemonia stand and then laid his hand on Kasai's shoulder.

"You have grown much in our brief time together, and I am proud of you. What-ever happens next, you must face it with courage and be strong of heart."

"What do you mean, Master? Are we in danger?" Kasai said in surprise.

"Are you alright now, dear?" Aetenos said to Desdemonia, making sure she could stand on her own.

"I'm okay, thank you," she said. "Just dizzy."

"It is to be expected. The time of trials has begun," Aetenos said.

The wind picked up and swirled around the small party. Desdemonia thought for a moment the storms of Gathos had followed them to the Heavenly Realm. Flashes of silver and gold whisked through the air, circling her and the others in a whirlwind of metallic color, dust, and debris.

When the air settled, the group was surrounded by soldier angels clad in opulent war gear. Small tendrils of residual electricity caressed the surface of their polished and unblemished armor. The angels' splayed wings blocked out the sun as they leveled their spears inward in a menacing circle.

"The Praetors have arrived," Illyria said.

One separated himself from the group and approached Illyria. He wore a golden helm with iconic wings of a fierce falcon pinned against the sides as his long, blonde locks flowed from beneath the helm and shimmered like pale gold in the sun.

"Lady Illyria, please step away from the condemned souls."

"Condemned? What is the meaning of this? We are holy fighters of the Kibo Gensai!" Orin proclaimed. "It is the witch you seek!"

"I am Gray'el, Commander of the Praetor Guard of Elysian. You are under arrest by order of the First Ministry. Your guilt will be determined in time, mortal," the Commander said and looked at Orin with disgust.

One of the angelic guards pointed to Desdemonia. "The mortal speaks true. The taint of chaos is strong on the female. She should not be allowed to continue." He pointed his spear menacingly at Desdemonia.

"They will be tried according to Lord Raguel's Law, some quicker than others," Gray'el said. "Lower your spear, Marcus."

Aetenos stepped forward and bowed to the helmed angel. "On what charges are we to be prosecuted?"

"Heresy, punishable by death. Take them away."

56

SHIVERRIG

Shiverrig surveyed his new war room. It was sparsely decorated as was fitting for a place where life and death were to be decided. The late king had filled the room with lies, and the last of the false trappings of House Conrad had finally been removed. A large table was placed in the center of the room with a map draped over its top.

The crimson-feathered Lord Vorleeth stood rigidly by the west wall. Next to him was the aloof peacock, Lord Jolla, and then the hunched back archvashim, Malachi, who looked and smelled as if he hadn't washed in weeks. Lord Fritta, who had been bestowed the title of First General of the Aj-Kahun's armies, stood stoically against the east wall, while Khalkoroth paced back-and-forth on the other side of the table.

Shiverrig nodded to Vorleeth, "Take your three hundred winged half-breeds and fly to the ruins of Rachlach Fortress in Trosk. I will need an accurate accounting of what is happening at the Chaos Gate." He pointed to the map. "Place sentries around the portal, here, here, and there, but stay hidden. I want to know what goes in and comes out of that pit without causing suspicion."

"You tread on dangerous ground, Shiverrig," Khalkoroth grumbled. "This smells of betrayal of the Mistress's trust."

"Think what you may, demon. No ruler should be without proper intel of the comings and goings in his kingdom."

Shiverrig looked down onto a map of the fertile basin of Sunne. The twin rivers of the jungle kingdom curled around one another in a graceful dance. Wadi Majarah was the larger of the two waterways and reflected a bright blue that rivaled the sky above. It was a raging beast with a will of its own, endlessly carving away at the dry land to its sides.

Wadi Banz-jan was thin and playful, resembling more of a line of molten silver as it snaked back and forth, and avoided winding too close to the giant Wadi Majarah. The twin rivers flowed from the Sarribe Mountains and through the dense Verdant Valley, nourishing the jungle lands of Sunne for miles.

The southern side of the Sarribe Mountains was balmy and wet throughout the year, and they would need to pack different supplies for that portion of the campaign. The smells would change abruptly from the biting, deadness of winter to the summer's loamy and flowery perfumes. A memory of a sugary taste of sweet nectars played upon his tongue.

"First General, you will lead a separate host into Sunne. Khalkoroth and I shall come along and enjoy the countryside. We will investigate and assist Sekka's troops where we can. Lord Jolla, you have command of the remaining army in Qaqal. Make sure I have a capital city to rule when I return."

Khalkoroth looked suspicious. "You mean to bring a host of armed warriors to the frontier, under the guise of support? Is that wise considering the blunder you just unveiled with killing Sekka's messenger? The Three were untouchable."

+The Three were useless. The Frost Queen no longer required them. But amends must be made.+ Jynxx's voice echoed in Shiverrig's mind.

"I shall make my peace with the Frost Queen, or her warlords, if that is who she has entrusted with Sunne's conquest. We are one big, happy family, after all. And I'd like to know who, or what, she has already brought to my kingdom."

"Your kingdom is filled with weak lords and dirty peasants," Khalkoroth snorted. "You hold no power here."

"Khalkoroth is right. The death of The Three will not be easily forgiven. There must be a penance to win back trust." Malachi spoke in the voice of Hilo.

+The Three were nothing. They deserved to die.+ Again, Jynxx whispered in his mind.

"I will deal with Sekka, and any issues of malcontent, should they arise. We embark tomorrow at dawn."

Shiverrig rode a black, Nivernais stallion at the head of a long column of five hundred Knights of Gethem and assortment of demon half-breeds. He wore a polished cuirass over a chainmail shirt and thick leather pants. His boots were high on his shins and caked with mud in his stirrups. He enjoyed the sensation of the fresh air on his skin and left his helm to bounce against his horse's flank.

The golden Circlet of Xerthotha nestled snugly on his brow. The red band that ran through its center pulsed like blood coursing through a thick vein around his head and reminded Shiverrig of Xerthotha's beneficial yet unnerving presence.

The column was equipped enough to handle any small engagements, while still able to move quickly over the wild, untamed terrain of the frontier. Deep purple and rose banners, bearing the icon of the three-headed mastiff, fluttered in cold drafts of air, blown down from the top of the Sarribe Mountains into the ravines and lowlands of Baroqia. The wind bit at his exposed skin and watered his eyes. It was good to be back on the campaign trail, doing to what he knew best, waging war.

His warhorse's long neck dipped and rose as it walked. It snorted double clouds of breath from its wide nostrils and kicked up clumps of muddy snow as it wound its way through the thinning trees along the forest trail. It took some time for the horses to adjust to carrying half-breeds, but eventually, they managed. Those with wings flew overhead, while those without, and did not merit being part of his company, walked with the rest of the human infantry.

Stunted trees, starved for nutrients in the thin soil, gave way to massive, white boulders that had at one time tumbled down from the high cliffs above and smashed into the rugged land below. On the other side of the Sarribe Pass was the Kingdom of Sunne, and his destiny of conquest.

All that stood in his way was Sekka and her Warlords of Vyzyn. Once they were gone, he could control or, better yet, destroy the Chaos Gate and concentrate on Sunne's more deliberate campaign. One enemy at a time, he thought.

+*The Vyzyn Warlords are weak replacements for the true lords of Sekka's Frost Legion. It will be an easy task for you to remove them all.*+

Shiverrig merely grunted his acknowledgment of Jynxx's encouragements as he saw the base of the Sarribe Mountains.

"No birds in the sky or animals scurrying away," Fritta said.

He rode a black roan and was also clad in a polished cuirass and mail shirt, newly fashioned by the armor smiths in Qaqal. The embossed image of the three-headed mastiff proudly reared on his chest.

"They have already darted away," Shiverrig said. "Though, I agree, there is always a curious beast or two that lingers behind." He then took in a deep draught of air. "Damn, it's good to be outdoors."

"Perhaps a little fresh air would do your archvashim some good," Fritta said. "The man looks unwell. Rumor has it he is often heard conversing with himself, speaking aloud with his human voice and answering in the voice of the fiend."

"Let me guess, he debates the merits of an eternal life of demonkind over mortality?"

"That's typically how the tale goes."

"I know, and I'm sure he agrees more than disagrees," Shiverrig said with a humorless chuckle.

"Can he be trusted?" Fritta's mood turned serious.

Shiverrig didn't answer as Khalkoroth loped along to the left. The pale demon's alabaster fur was covered in mud from the journey, and he resembled a fatigued hound with his tongue lolled out of his mouth. The demon's physiology had definite advantages over mere humans, and he had little difficulty keeping pace with the column. Shiverrig suspected that Khalkoroth's extended tongue was more due to enjoyment than exertion.

Shiverrig watched Khalkoroth as they moved up a small hill. He recalled questioning the pale demon why his sword was missing at the onset of their expedition. "I notice you have left behind the ice blade, Eishorror. Have you already grown tired of your new toy?"

Shiverrig said it with a broad smile, hiding the fact that he was uncomfortable with the pale demon handling such a vile and powerful weapon.

"It is a noisy and cumbersome blade with a mind of its own. I need no such distractions to destroy my enemies." Then the demon turned away and joining the column riding out of the castle.

Shiverrig eyed the pale demon now and thought he caught Khalkoroth's features momentarily flutter into the visage of Daku. The pale demon grunted as he shook his head and mane of filthy hair. Mud flew off in all directions and added to the splatter of the horses.

"I'd like to speak to Daku, if I may," Shiverrig said with casual ease, testing the control Khalkoroth still maintained on the boy.

The pale demon glared up at Shiverrig on his tall horse. "What could you want with that weak-minded child? He hides and cowers in fear. Soon his essence will be fully consumed, and nothing of Daku from Ordu will remain."

"Perhaps before that time comes, he can share with me a name."

Khalkoroth glanced sideways at Shiverrig, and a sly smile crept across his pale-purple lips. "I'm sure you would like that. The monk's mind is shattered. His memories are now tender morsels for me to snack on when bored. He knows nothing."

Shiverrig studied Khalkoroth carefully. The smile on the demon's face remained, but his eyes shifted to a dark brown. The malice dissolved, and a more serene aspect took hold, but only for a moment. Khalkoroth blinked hard, and his eyes turned pink and wicked. Khalkoroth snapped his snout at Shiverrig and quickened his pace ahead of the column.

"Interesting," Shiverrig mused. "Soon, I think. Not yet, but soon."

The war column eventually came upon a frontier village at the foot of the Sarribe Pass. The small, stone huts were covered with foreign-looking palm fronds, folded and overlapped to prevent water intrusion. The broad-faced and unusual leaves most likely came from the outer jungles that crept up the south side of the mountain range or perhaps were traded across the Sarribe Pass for whatever the jungle natives took as precious.

No fires burned within the huts, nor were there any distinct smells of food cooking on cookfires. The village was deserted. Whatever had happened here had occurred weeks ago. There were the impressions of footsteps, human and demon alike, that had been frozen into the ground. But there was no evidence of a fight. Nothing was broken or burned to the ground.

"Damn peculiar," Shiverrig said. "Take some men ahead and see if it's the same."

Fritta led a small group of knights on horseback to the central parts of the village. Shiverrig realized it had been taken or abandoned without a fight. It was as if the villagers had simply walked away one day, peacefully, leaving behind whatever possessions they had accumulated in the emptiness of the frontier.

Strange insects the size of his fist fluttered about on transparent wings. They were nothing like anything he had seen before in Baroqia. The flies, if that was what they were, harassed his host with painful stingers, or noisily hovered nearby, but always just out of reach of being crushed in a mailed fist.

The stench of death became more evident as Shiverrig followed Fritta's route into the village center. The First General pointed to nine flayed bodies impaled on black iron shafts.

"The bodies of the villagers."

"A sacrifice, or a warning?" Shiverrig mused.

"Where are the others, I wonder?" Fritta said and twisted in his saddle.

Shiverrig wondered the same thing.

"They must have fled."

"Or chose a different fate, one that may have seemed more acceptable at the time," Shiverrig countered. Then he was startled by Khalkoroth's deep chuckle.

"Like all mortals, they were weak," Khalkoroth said. "They did not flee. They have become part of the soul harvest. More will be led through the Chaos Gate, and the strength of the Frost Queen will grow on Gathos."

Khalkoroth then peered knowingly at Shiverrig, then pointed upwards along the trail that began the Sarribe Pass and followed into Sunne. "She goes to feast on the souls of the jungle dwellers."

+The savages are yours to rule. Sekka steals your glory.+ Jynxx whispered in his mind. *+You must act quickly and decisively if you are to survive.+*

"We shall settle here for the night. Make preparations and inform my returning scouts. I wish to see them immediately in my tent," Shiverrig commanded Fritta.

"By your will, Aj-Kahun," Fritta said and instructed the men to create a defensive perimeter.

Shiverrig woke early the next morning after a meaningless sleep and called a page to fetch him Fritta. His mind was active and alert, focused on myriad campaign details all being condensed together through a funnel of not enough time. He realized Jynxx was right. Now was the time to act.

"We will have one chance at surprise against Sekka," Shiverrig said as Fritta joined him in his tent, and the two perused the maps of Sunne.

"Are you sure now is the correct time to betray her trust. Even with the addition of the half-breeds, we are still not close to the full strength of what was the Five Armies."

"Then, our first attack must be an overwhelming success and cripple her forces in the Three Kingdoms. But first, we must appear to be allies that offer help instead of a hindrance."

"And what of the pale demon? He watches your every move," Fritta said.

"Khalkoroth will be neutralized," Shiverrig responded, though a strategy had not materialized. All he need was the blasted birth name of the demon.

He absentmindedly bit into a small stick of dried jerky and chased down the heavily spiced meat with a bland, watered-down wine as he studied old maps of the Sunnese basin and the jungles extending to the south.

"If our intel from Sess'thra is to be trusted, the dense jungle terrain has proven difficult for Sekka's forces to overcome. I'm afraid ours will fare no better. We will be engaging in a multi-tiered battlefield, and the winged beasts will lose their mobility under those trees," Fritta said. "And the underlying ground is impossibly unpredictable. Troop movement will be slow."

Shiverrig nodded his agreement. This would change his battle tactics, and his soldiers' ability to fly would be a detriment rather than an asset. His shortsightedness in this aspect of the now obvious terrain issue stung his pride.

"I'll find a workaround to the aerial combat once I have more information," Shiverrig said.

Attaining accurate maps of formal roadways had been futile. The Sunnese traveled along thin and winding footpaths, secret tunnel systems, or they simply ran across a maze of branches high above the ground.

He traced the twin rivers with his fingers. "The rivers create a natural means of transportation, but even with the swifter currents of the Wadi Majarah, the passage would be slow going as the river doubles back on itself. Traveling on the smaller Wadi Banz-jan would leave us open to attack from opposite banks, and I do not want to be caught in a crossfire. We will plot our own course and attack on the ground of my choosing with surprise on our side. Once we secure more land, we can utilize the rivers to move larger cargo and supplies."

One of his new scouts was presented at the entrance to Shiverrig's tent.

"Enter," Shiverrig said.

The man bowed low.

"My Aj-Kahun."

Shiverrig took in the man quickly but did not recognize him. He returned to studying the map.

"Name?"

"Spire Scout Anders, my Aj-Kahun," the scout replied.

"And what is your report, Spire Scout Anders?"

"My Aj-Kahun, the Sarribe Pass is closed. A fearful storm lingers there."

"Natural or Unnatural?" Shiverrig inquired and lifted his eyes from the map.

"I believe unnatural, my Lord. The clouds at the top of the rise are bruised dark purple, and my tongue tasted of ash, yet I smelled no wood burning. The storm rages but is unmoved by wind or time."

"The Warlords of Vyzyn," Shiverrig said and tapped the map upon the table. "Could you see any arrangement of troops? Numbers? Best guess."

"There was no one there to count, and I thought to bring this news first."

"I suspect we might find our lost villagers in that fog," Shiverrig said to Fritta.

"Or we'll find a reconnaissance war party hidden from prying eyes and sent to gather what villagers were easily available in the Pass. I suspect they intend to take them back to Gathos," Fritta said.

Shiverrig stared more closely at the loose details of the map. "Jynxx, tell me, the Frost Queen still believes I am her ally, yes?"

+Your duplicity has not been betrayed by me.+

"Sorry?" Anders said, confused at who Shiverrig's one-sided conversation was directed at.

Shiverrig raised his eyes to the scout. "Nothing. You've done well. Inform Khalkoroth we will journey to the summit and that I want a company of half-breeds to accompany us, prepared for battle. We shall see what hides within this impenetrable storm of yours."

Shiverrig's Nivernais stallion came to a halt, and he leaned forward in his saddle, hands braced upon the horn. Ahead of him, perhaps less than two miles away, was the summit of the Sarribe Pass, a unique corridor between two high peaks that crested the mountain range at its lowest point, and then dropped into Sunne on its southern side. But instead of the way being clear, he saw a wall of churning clouds that hid the passage and shrouded the peaks from sight.

Shiverrig took out a small looking glass and expanded it into a long tube, he set his eye to the eyepiece and peered into the dark fog. Long, thin chains of lightning flashed within and around the clouds, and Shiverrig felt the hair on his skin rise. Khalkoroth lumbered to a halt next to his horse. A deep grumble resonated from his chest.

"This is a warning from the Mistress. Do not trespass into the territory she has claimed."

Shiverrig scoffed at the notion that Sekka had any claim to these lands.

+She cannot claim lands that are yours by right.+

He then handed the looking glass to Fritta as the First General came to a stop.

"First Scout Anders," Shiverrig called out.

The scout trotted up to his side from a small group of men and half-breeds. "Yes, my Aj-Kahun?"

"It seems we have found your wall of fog."

"I can say it has grown worse."

+There is nothing to fear.+

"Then let us see what there is to see before it truly becomes a problem. Leave the rest behind. I don't want our friends to think we are looking for a fight." Shiverrig kicked his horse forward and trotted toward the mist.

Anders had it right. The air tasted of ash, but not from wood, it was something meatier. Shiverrig, Fritta, and Anders rode their horses into the fog while Khalkoroth loped along to the side. Dark shapes of large boulders on either side of the trail came into focus, and Shiverrig could not help but feel he was being both watched and followed.

Khalkoroth inhaled a deep breath of air. "I smell ancient and forbidden sorcery. We should not proceed forward without the others." The hesitation in his voice was apparent.

+He is a coward.+

Shiverrig raised an eyebrow. "The mighty Khalkoroth is afraid of a little black magic?"

"I fear nothing but your ignorance. As usual, you meddle in things beyond your comprehension."

"Then let us enlighten ourselves," Shiverrig said and continued along the path.

The boulders became more numerous, and one stood at eye level on his left. Shiverrig spotted a figure of a man lying on his back at the top of the rock. Upon closer examination, Shiverrig saw that the man was one of the lost villagers, and he had been stripped naked.

His wrists and ankles were strapped with ropes that spread his arms and legs across the boulder's surface. The lines were then tied to stakes, which had been hammered into the ground.

The villager's stomach cavity had been ripped open, and a noxious and purplish vapor rose from his bowels. He saw another ahead on the path, and then another. All had been fashioned on the rocks in the same way.

"They've been sacrificed, and the rocks doubled as alters," Fritta said and brought the back of his gloved hand to his nose and mouth. He looked at the other victims and shook his head in dismay.

"Perhaps the demon is right, and we should return at full strength."

"Nonsense," Shiverrig said and spurred his horse forward.

The haze in the air thinned as the path plateaued to more even ground. Smaller boulders, roughly the size of milk cattle, had somehow been rolled to the center of the road and placed in a full circle. Placed in the middle of the circle was a solitary hut.

The mist rolled across the front façade as a light breeze flapped open the loose tarp covering the entrance. Shadows from inside the hut danced to the movement of a small fire.

Shiverrig dismounted. "Anders, you will remain with the horses. Fritta and Khalkoroth come with me."

"My Aj-Kahun, I again recommend caution," Fritta said as he scanned the desolate area.

"Noted, now get off your horse and show some courage," Shiverrig said as he approached the hut.

"No good will come of this," Khalkoroth said and sniffed the air. "We are intruding on a sacred rite. We are not welcome here.

Fritta handed his reins to Anders and took stock of his weapons to make sure all were in place. He then drew his long sword. Khalkoroth gurgled a derisive chuckle.

"Your mortal weapons will prove useless."

Fritta looked worriedly to the hut, and then to Shiverrig. "I hope you know what you are doing. Flirting with dark powers unnerves me. I long for the days when enemies were mere flesh and blood."

+The power of the Xerthotha shields you. There is nothing to fear.+ Jynxx whispered encouragingly.

"Times have changed, my friend. Embrace your destiny and find glory in our new world," Shiverrig said and slapped his hand on Fritta's chest plate.

He then turned and approached the hut, and without waiting for the others, he pushed the tarp aside and walked inside. The depth of the hut was misleading and further obscured by the green fire burning in a pit in the center.

Fritta and Khalkoroth entered the hut and stood at either side of Shiverrig. The interior looked abandoned. There were no chairs or chests. No standing racks of armor or arms.

"Are you satisfied? There is no one here. The hut is empty. Let us leave at once," Khalkoroth said.

Then a voice spoke in a hiss with each word slithering through the air. "Why are you here?"

Fritta turned left and right but saw no one, and Khalkoroth issued a menacing growl. The coarse hair rose across his back.

+Nothing to fear.+

Shiverrig took a step forward. "I am Gerun Shiverrig, the Aj-Kahun of Baroqia." He thought he glimpsed movement in the shadows across the flaming pit.

"The name of Shiverrig is known to me. All of your true names are known to me. Even yours, Pale One."

Khalkoroth snorted with disdain. "You know nothing, sorcerer."

"I'll take your name now, phantom, or do you fear to reveal yourself?" Shiverrig said, irritated by the voice's condescending tone. "I quickly grow tired of this cat and mouse game."

He directed Fritta and Khalkoroth to move around the firepit, while he advanced in the opposite direction. He drew his sword, and the sickly green of the firelight glazed his steel.

"As you wish mortal, I am Dai-Ko-Zior of Vyzyn, but knowledge of my name will not help you. I am beyond your means."

"Should that name mean something to me?" Shiverrig said, stalling for time, trying to adjust his eyes beyond the fire's light and into the shadows.

Khalkoroth's growl became more intimidating. "Vyzyn outcast."

"I will ask you one final time. Why are you here, Gerun Shiverrig? What do you hope to accomplish with this intrusion, but to incur Sekka's wrath?"

"It's quite simple, my mysterious friend. You see, this is my kingdom, and I am concerned by the Frost Queen's bountiful harvest of my citizens. I merely wish to discuss our arrangement in more detail."

"Your lies are revealed to me, Gerun Shiverrig, son of Gareth." The hissing of his voice slid through his late father's name. "The brand of the Chaos Devil has scorched your soul. You are already his puppet."

Khalkoroth rounded the other side of the firepit and heard Dai-Ko-Zior's claim. Then, he glared menacingly at Shiverrig. "You dare betray the Mistress?"

"Be silent," Shiverrig hissed. "The sorcerer is lying."

"Aha, ha, ha, ha, ha. You did not know, did you, Pale One? And now, it is so much worse for you. What will Sekka think when she finds out you have aligned yourself with a traitor?"

The slithering voice in the darkness grew bolder as the murky shadows dissipated to reveal the hooded and cloaked figure of Dai-Ko-Zior, seated close to the far wall. He sat cross-legged and slightly bent over at the waist, and his head bowed towards the floor.

Dai-Ko-Zior's clothing was inscribed with verdant glyphs that dimly pulsed with an otherworldly light. His elbows rested on his outstretched knees, as a monk would do while in deep meditation. But his hands were in constant motion, spinning through elaborate gestures and tracing lime-colored symbols in the air, which rose overhead and dissolved to nothing.

Shiverrig found it challenging to focus on the sorcerer's physical form as he shifted ever so slightly from one position to the next, phasing in-and-out of reality.

"Sorcery," Fritta whispered nervously.

"Yes," Dai-Ko-Zior hissed and rose to his feet as if he was lifted by unseen hands. "You have blundered into your doom, First General, Fritta."

Without warning or command, Khalkoroth lunged at Dai-Ko-Zior and passed through him and into the wall. He wiped around quickly, searching for the evasive sorcerer.

"Show yourself!" Khalkoroth screamed.

The eerie laughter filled the interior of the hut. "My sister Aeshmara will be along shortly. You may play with her if you are so desperate to meet your end."

"Khalkoroth, Fritta, get to the entrance. It is time we ended our dalliance," Shiverrig shouted. His two companions raced to the doorway flap. Fritta threw open the tarp and followed Khalkoroth outside.

Sweat beaded on Shiverrig's forehead. How could he have been so blind? He felt the air in the hut become thick, and an invisible noose pulled tight around his neck.

+Do not think I have forgotten my suffering so easily.+ Jynxx said in a mocking tone. +You can feel it, can you not? There is no escape for you now.+

Shiverrig tossed aside the tarp and bolted outside. Fritta and Khalkoroth were already to either side of the entrance, and both had taken up defensive stances.

Jynxx had done a masterful job of building up his confidence and scaling back his reason. He cursed himself for his folly as a warband of demons with hostile faces leered back at him. They each bore a symbol across their chest of a dark circle, surrounded by the waving arms of an iconic sun, a black star. He did not recognize it as one that was typically worn by the minions of Sekka.

The demons wore little to no armor, but Shiverrig saw that their skin seemed to be made of rough stone, and slate grey in color. They held long poles with a hooked blade for reaping and a spike at the top. Some had swords sheathed at their waist.

A female warrior, clad in dark gold and deep rose leather armor, stood in front of the warband. Arcane runes had been carved into the material and filled in with a dull, metallic substance.

She had the confidence of a leader, as was evident in her form-fitting leathers that were better served for hunting in the shadows than the brutal hacking and slashing of confrontational warfare. *This must be Aeshmara*, thought Shiverrig.

She held a double-edged dagger to the throat of Anders in one hand. His eyes were wide, and his groin had the unmistakable stain of battlefield fear. Her toned muscles flexed with her movements as she shifted her weight.

"You are the one called Shiverrig, are you not?" Aeshmara said and pointed her dagger at him. She then brought it back to Anders's throat.

"I am."

"The Frost Queen spoke of your prowess in battle and keen strategic mind. She said you would be an asset to the conquest of these lands."

She shook her head in disappointment. "But I don't see it. I even argued with my sulking brother that you would never be taken so easily, but here we are," she said, and a crafty smile curled up her lips.

"Is this how Sekka treats her allies?" Shiverrig said. He counted the number of demons and looked for weak spots in their cordon around the hut. But there was no need to count them all. He already knew there were too many.

"Allies?" Aeshmara laughed. "Silly mortal. You had a simple purpose, which was to kill the king and steal his throne, which caused the kingdom to fall into chaos and make it so much easier to control. But I believe now your purpose has been fulfilled, and you are no longer needed."

Aeshmara brought her face close enough to Anders's head that he blanched at the smell of her breath. "Take them, preferably alive. The Frost Queen may want to give the Orthods something sweet to chew on when we return to Gathos with the harvest."

"What is the meaning of this?" Khalkoroth bellowed. "I am a loyal servant of the Mistress! I will not be treated in the same manner as these mortals."

"Hush, traitor. You'll be culled with the rest of those insufferable half-breeds we found at the base of the Pass."

She playfully looked at Shiverrig. "What do you call them? Pets?"

Shiverrig instinctively reached a hand to his neck, feeling the imaginary noose tighten around his throat. "You are making a mistake. Sekka has plans for me. I am to lead her Frost Legion!"

"Shiverrig! Hold your tongue!" Khalkoroth shouted.

"Oh?" Aeshmara's expression became insightful. "She has other plans for you, does she? Well, that makes this decision much easier, doesn't it?"

Aeshmara narrowed her eyes at Shiverrig. "I've changed my mind. Kill them all, starting with the Pale One."

The front row of Aeshmara's warband stepped back, and five, slender demons with crude bows took their places. Black shafted arrows were nocked against bowstrings, and the wood of the bows creaked in the cold as bony fingers pulled strings taught. Khalkoroth crouched low to the ground, ready to pounce on the first enemy within his reach.

"This is your fault, Shiverrig," he said as the arrows flew from their black bows.

EPILOGUE

Cruelty was an inherent human trait, thought Raguel, the Archangel, and holder of the highest seat of power in the Seven Heavens. He had recently come from the High Court on the last plateau of the Steps of Judgment, atop Mount Ajma, where he dutifully meted out his decisions and judgments on those who had fallen from grace.

If there were a king that reigned over the Seven Heavens, he would be it. But he did not require such a gauche and pompous title. He was the first created and would be the last to exist, so said the Immortal Mother of all creation.

Raguel sat on a plush mat in the center of a pristine room, uncluttered with loose folios and pamphlets. Timeless columns of white marble veined with wisps of blue and green lined the polished walls and framed the tall windows of his Chamber of Reflection. He had chosen a classical design for the room, and never tired of the subtle dance of light and shadow as the sun moved through its cyclical journey each day. Everything was in its rightful place. Everything balanced.

Humans. He let the classification settle in his mind. The creatures remained unbalanced, no matter the teachings bestowed upon them from divine intervention to the mortal masters of every age. They claimed to want harmony but ultimately shunned it in a never-ending quest for power, wealth, and dominance over others.

No other animal of the Mortal Realm exhibited the same behavior throughout their short lifespans, and on such a consistent and grandiose scale, as did the men and women of that primitive ball of clay. One might claim their actions were due to the influence of cunning devils and beguiling demons, whispering malcontent into their innocent ears.

But that would be folly, for cruelty, death and destruction were as much a part of the human condition as happiness and joy, yet the former behaviors often tipped the scales of balance with the obscene weight of their crimes. Why the Immortal Mother had instilled the mortals with such base desires was lost on the Archangel.

The humans repeatedly squandered their brilliant potential with their coarse actions. They were a herd of dumb beasts, willing to throw themselves into an emotional grinder of turmoil and suffering, committing the same mistakes with each new generation.

And for what? All they could expect was more pain and more sorrow. Yet, buried within their souls was the energy matrix for creating the building blocks of righteous power and might, and adversely, dark magic and sorcery. The latter wielded by the evil denizens slithering and stalking in the Abyss.

The Immortal Mother was not without her flair for comedy. She was a jester at heart and set the eternal players of the game on either side of the board. They opposed one another with formidable weapons and armies, and then She threw mindless humans in the middle, as the prize to be gained or lost with only free will to guide them.

The Archangel rose and walked to three tall windows that overlooked the lands of Tanalum. He let the bright light warm his face. As of late, his trance-sleep had left him agitated and unsettled. Ageless powers had woken from an eternal slumber. He felt them rise in the murky darkness. A thousand pairs of slanted eyes slowly opened across massive heads the size of cities and peered through the aether. They could smell the scent of mortal flesh and virgin souls.

Raguel could sense their vast bulk moving steadily towards the newly born Chaos Gate. The demonic device had torn a gap in the Amaranthine Barrier. Now an astral passageway existed between two realms. The Ancients looked to slake their thirst on the misery of the mortal world once more. He shook his head, thinking about the devils and their extravagant plans for conquest. "When will they learn their place?"

A bell chimed and broke Raguel from his dark visions. He turned to see his equerry, Sonnalle standing at the entrance. Sonnalle wore opal colored robes with intricate patterns of grey and gold. Like all True-borns, he was the apex of beauty. His platinum blonde hair curled in slow loops to his shoulders, accentuating his piercing blue eyes and elegant features.

Raguel's spirits were lifted at seeing his confidant and friend. Sonnalle had been with Raguel since the beginning. His equerry was a virtuous soul. He had complete conviction and unwavering faith in the path Raguel forged for the Seven Heavens.

Sadly, so many of its inhabitants now lacked the same commitment for perfection that he held so dear. They had become complacent, lazy even. They wanted only to bask in the golden sunlight without care or worry or interfere where they were clearly forbidden.

"I'll never forgive Aetenos. That blasted monk put ideas in Artiya'il's head, ideas that led to insubordination. I had no choice but to banish the angel," Raguel said. He was still distraught over casting out a True-born from the Seven Heavens.

"I know, Lord Raguel. You did what must be done," Sonnalle said.

Loyal and trustworthy Sonnalle, Raguel thought, why cannot more True-born follow the example set by his equerry? Sonnalle was steadfast in pursuing Raguel's vision of perfection. The equerry assisted him in facilitating the decrees that would affect Tanalum, and more so, the lower levels of Heaven. But, as many saw Raguel as the benevolent builder of the Immortal Mother's Golden Path, Sonnalle was referred to as the Archangel's velvet hammer.

Those opposed to Raguel's vision would eventually be visited by Sonnalle and be persuaded by the equerry to see things in a different light. Sometimes more torque was needed to twist the views of the dissatisfied, and when required, Sonnalle would use other, more unsavory methods to pound in the nails of Raguel's will into acceptance.

"What is it you want, Sonnalle?"

"Excuse me, Chancellor Pinnacle. Gray'el, Commander of the Praetor Guard of Elysian, requests your audience. He has a report from the Lower Realms," Sonnalle said.

"Let him enter." Raguel's meditation had proven ineffective, and he might as well get to the matters of the day.

Sonnalle gave a signal. A lower-class angel dressed in golden armor walked purposefully into the room with his winged helm held at his side. The sunlight gleamed off his plate mail and sent sparkling reflections dancing on the walls of the chamber.

Before reaching Raguel, the angel dropped to one knee in deferential respect. "Chancellor Pinnacle. I bring news from Elysian."

Raguel raised an indifferent brow. "Yes? What is it? All is not well in the eternal playground?"

Gray'el bowed his head deeper. Raguel knew he should not mock the commander with his station of deployment. All had a duty to perform, and Gray'el's was to oversee Elysian, a place of frolic, joy, and debauchery. It was the entry gate to the Seven Heavens, and mostly occupied by mortals of basic merit, and angels with base ambition.

"Illyria of the Nine has returned to us. She has brought mortals through the Gates."

"Yes, and what of it? She excels in mischief, constantly meddling in the affairs of the humans. Unfortunately, my laws seem to apply to everyone but her. The First Heaven is filled with beings of low importance. A few more won't matter." Raguel's impatience rose. He had more pressing matters to attend to than listening to tallies of common entrants to the heavenly playground.

"My Lord Chancellor, Aetenos has returned with her. He is not well."

"What did you say?" Raguel said slowly. His jaw clenched, and his immense wings twitched across his back.

The Seventh Heaven was the final destination that any creature, mortal or divine could aspire to reach, for it was the nearest point one could physically approach the spiritual essence of the Immortal Mother. It was here that Raguel lived his long existence, as did other True-born celestial beings, born into the divine at the creation of all things. Occasionally, an exceptional soul, or as he considered them, a lucky one, would ascend by the grace and willing hand of the Immortal Mother, or by the desire of one of her daughters with Illyria being the youngest of the nine.

He had made his thoughts know over the long years to the Mother and her Nine. He was adamant that too many mortals of inferior breeding stock were granted access to the power of the divine, and used it recklessly, playing demigod among the humans. Why had that bumbling monk, Aetenos, been gifted with such favor by the youngest and fairest of the Nine? It mocked his better judgment and pricked at his pride like a sharp needle. He told himself again he no longer cared or had feelings for Illyria. She had been a distraction for a time, nothing more.

"There is more. I have placed the mortals and demigod under quarantine. There is a wood witch among them who carries the taint of the Abyss in her blood."

"Meaning you imprisoned them." It was not a question. Gray'el nodded solemnly.

"Surely Illyria would have known the penalty for bringing such filth to Elysian. The Seven Heavens have strict rules on such matters."

"They will need to be judged," Sonnalle said.

Raguel's interest became piqued. He played his dexterous fingers on the smooth surface of his chin. "Yes, judged. And the others, have they been infected as well?"

"We inspected the lot. The warriors are of sound body, and spirit. They are clean. The soul of the demigod, however, is missing. The same is true for the one he calls Ever Hero."

"Such boastful names the humans create for their champions," Raguel smirked. "Missing you say? Gone? Where would one lose a soul, I wonder."

"The one named Kasai, sir, the Ever Hero, spoke of a Chaos Gate, though I do not know of what he speaks."

"No, I would not think that you would. But I know what it is, and what danger it will cause the realms. I have seen what has stirred in the nether space due to the portal that has been opened."

Raguel turned back to the open windows. The birth of a Chaos Gate changed many things. Raguel's mind computed thousands of scenarios that could arise now that such a diabolical device existed in the three realms. An unsightly frown deepened across his face. Aetenos should have known better than to fall into such an obvious trap! The fool monk would once more be the cause of his anguish. And somehow, he had tied Illyria to his plight. They would unite in a quest to save the souls of the undeserving mortals. Raguel felt that rare emotion of jealousy as it slithered into his consciousness, and he loathed the way it disrupted the serenity of his mind.

"Thank you for your report, Commander Gray'el. Keep the prisoners under guard until we can better understand the meaning of their untimely arrival," Raguel said. "Sonnalle will show you out."

This time things would be different, thought Raguel. He knew it was not his place to question the Immortal Mother's will, only to uphold the law as it had been spoken by Her so long ago. He understood the concept of the Great Balance, and that must remain intact. He had done his part for countless millennia to ensure the vision of the Mother was maintained.

Nonetheless, his appreciation of her plan for the humans had waned over the centuries. It crumbled, bit-by-bit, along the frayed edges of curiosity and reason, and became distorted and false. He would never utter such blasphemy aloud, so it remained an itch that could not be scratched, until now.

The wrongness of the Great Balance was apparent to him. Others of his age had begun to ask the same questions. What need was there for suffering in the extreme? Why create an Abyss, who's very meaning of existence was to destroy harmony and perfection? Why must the light of the righteous be chased by the specter of darkness just as day turned to night?

Raguel conjured an image of the Immortal Mother in his mind. She was the Creator and Destroyer in one. She had molded the three worlds in all of her likenesses and set forth the laws of all things. She held ultimate authority, even if he felt some of her decisions were flawed. He would do his duty, as he had done faithfully since the birth of time. He must, for if his focus wavered, even for a moment, the purity of law would succumb to darkness, and that was anathema to his being.

Raguel contemplated the Deep Dark of the Abyss. His intellect told him it should not exist. It had no meaning and did not contribute to the precision of purity. Life did not need to be destroyed to be reborn into something new. There was no need for new. Perfection was complete and not required to change. But now, a Chaos Gate had been born. Death and destruction would ride unchallenged through the Mortal Realm and reap the souls of countless beings.

He sighed. "This could have been avoided," he said to the open air.

The Amaranthine Barrier was not enough, and he had pleaded with the Immortal Mother to end the Third Realm once and for all after their last trespass on mortal soil. "Cast the Abyss away," he had said. "Let it consume itself. I will shepherd the lost flock of humans into a better, more pristine, and perfect order." And if they refused or could not be assimilated into his lawful world? Well, then he would find a better use for their soul energy and be done with them.

The long feathers of his wings resembled Mountain Crest Eagles, strong and wide, made for soaring on turbulent up draughts of air. Colored feathers of a hundred different birds, from scarlet cardinals, vermillion lorikeets, lilac-breasted rollers, and golden pheasants, lined the inner plumage of his wingspan and added to the magnificent design. His feathers now stretched like fingers, flexing and twitching in the warm afternoon sun.

He was perfect in every way, a beautiful creation made by the hands of the Immortal Mother. His intellect was superior among the divine, and all other beings for that matter. He knew what must be done for the betterment of all. The Seven Heavens must prepare for the coming conflict, and as of now, it was woefully weak with leniency and unsanctioned variation.

He would be the dutiful son, but there was an opportunity to be exploited, and this time he would take the upper hand. He would set the Heavenly Realm on a new and proper course of rule over all others. The arrival of Aetenos and the creation of the Chaos Gate had provided him with the kindling to start the fire, but he but needed another's hand to strike the flint.

Raguel clasped his hands behind his back. He turned from the light and returned to the plush mat in the center of the room.

"This must be done." Raguel knew it in his heart. "The Immortal Mother will understand."

He crossed his legs into a sitting position, straightened his shoulders, and folded his wings asymmetrically across his back. When he was in perfect misalignment, he opened his mind and scanned the astral plane. His thoughts wove between the layers of time and space, focusing on a beacon of immense darkness and corruption, deep within the Abyss.

Raguel's sense of purity and correctness were immediately offended when he made the first, slippery connection to the chaotic mind he sought.

"You will open your mind to me, devil. We have matters of import to discuss." Raguel sent his mental command into the mind of the Great Chaos Devil. A wave of heat blasted through Raguel's body, and a sheen of sweat coated his skin. Xerthotha chuckled at Raguel's bold assumption of authority.

"What do you want, feathered bird? My time is of a value you cannot comprehend," Xerthotha said with annoyance at being disturbed. The arrogance of his nature dripped with each word. He was dressed as an armored general with decorative harpy wings jetting from his shoulders. Layered, steel plates of deep moss green with golden trim covered the bulk of his body. He wore a helm of black iron with flaring horns across its top. His face was covered by a mask resembling a snarling lion with horrible tusks jutting from top and bottom.

Xerthotha stood in a vortex of fire and flames, and molten rock swirled around his warrior form. "I have a realm to conquer."

"An entire realm? And which realm might that be? Azrollorza, not Xerthotha, controls the portals of a Chaos Gate, connecting the Abyss to the Mortal Realm."

"She has overextended her reach. The fool has not yet begun to understand the consequences of her actions, or those of her pet, Sekka."

"Yet, with access to so many souls, she will have the power to destroy you."

Xerthotha scoffed at the notion. "The high-minded bird on his heavenly stoop truly believes he has all the answers. Clearly, you need something. Be quick."

"I'm curious. What will you do?"

"Do? Why nothing, of course." Xerthotha sniggered. "I but have to wait for her to destroy herself. Her false sense of conquest will be her undoing. She cannot be everywhere at once."

"And while Azrollorza is creating a new hell on earth, you shall attack her realm in the Abyss?" Raguel mused aloud.

A child's voice responded. "And why would Xerthotha, the Great Chaos Devil, want her to remain? Hmm?" Xerthotha had changed into the form of a small girl wearing a tiara and gown of a princess. The tempest of fire morphed into a blizzard of ice and snow. The temperature in Raguel's Chamber of Reflection dropped.

"It is not only the devils of the Abyss that smell the sweet scent of human souls. I am aware of the broken slumber of the Ancients," Raguel said.

"The Old Gods race towards that lacerated boil between realms. They will consume her with their arrival," the sweet voice of innocence responded.

"Along with the Mortal Realm, if they are allowed to pass through the tear in the Amaranthine Barrier."

"If such is the destiny of the mortals, then it is not my concern. Why do you bother me so?" Xerthotha said. Raguel could picture the young princess pouting with her hands on her hips.

"And if the Ancients turn their greedy eyes to Gathos? It is a quick journey to the Abyss through the Chaos Gate."

"Why would they care? It is the pure souls they hunger for, and those trapped in the Abyss are filled with taint. I am not worried about the Ancients and their mindless hunger. I will reap more than my fair share of souls with Azrollorza destroyed. When the time is right, I will destroy the portal on Gathos. I have everything under control," said the child.

"If you were clever, I imagine you could harvest enough souls to topple Morrdilliax before the Ancients were any wiser."

"Do not mock me, Raguel. What is your plan? Do you mean to stop her? Will you close the Gate on your own?" The fierce warrior had returned, as too his fiery wrath.

"Stop her? Why, I may assist her. If I am lucky, you will destroy one another. I will have two thorns removed at once."

"Then why waste my time? Do you mean to parade your assistance to Azrollorza before me? Beware, little dove, your wings can be clipped as easily as the birds you mimic."

"I jest, Lord Xerthotha."

"Ah, now he speaks with a sweet tongue. Finally, we come to your need."

"Albeit slightly entertaining, the trivial subterfuge and blatant power grabs you three devils play at in the lower layers of the Abyss, do not alter the scale of the Great Balance. Therefore, they are not my concern. My eyes are on the approaching Ancients, as should yours be. I suggest more of a partnership between two respectful foes."

"To destroy her?" Xerthotha said.

"The Chaos Gate must be closed, and Azrollorza punished."

"But not destroyed?"

"No, not destroyed, not yet. I see a different outcome. Her minion, Sekka, thinks she has won a great victory by establishing a foothold in the Mortal Realm. She has broken the sacred law of the Immortal Mother by invading neutral territory. The skies will open, and judgment will come for her again. My Heavenly Host will rain down upon her wretchedness, and she will be destroyed."

"Sounds lovely," Xerthotha chuckled. His voice echoed in Raguel's mind as if a thousand mouths laughed at once.

"Azrollorza will surely come to Sekka's aid," Raguel said. He was leading Xerthotha to his end game.

"Surely. If nothing else but to enjoy the feast of souls on the Mortal Realm."

"And you will prevent this from happening. Azrollorza must not pass through the Chaos Gate. The neutral ground must remain untainted. Is that point understood?"

"And how shall I be rewarded for such interference? I need not land nor riches, for I have gathered such in abundance since the dawn of time. What can the likes of a pretty bird offer me, but a shiny halo to brighten the horns of my helm?"

"If that is your desire," Raguel jested.

"Bah! I think not. Here is my price, Raguel. It is well known that a single Supreme Devil does not have the strength to defeat another, for the third would interfere, and tip the balance of power against the aggressor. When Morrdilliax comes forth, you shall destroy him."

"See? You are a clever devil, after all. No, I shall not hand you the Abyss on a silver platter. But if you prove yourself capable of defeating Azrollorza on your own, then I will stay the hand of Morrdilliax long enough for you to consolidate your power. Once Azrollorza is removed, it should be an easy matter subverting Morrdilliax's strength. The creature is more content to contradict itself throughout eternity rather than engage in an even bout for rule."

"Thus, in theory, leaving me as the reigning monarch of all the Abyssal Planes." The environment around Xerthotha erupted with countless butterflies of multiple colors and sizes. The swarm of insects turned and glided in the air, a floating, fluttering aerial dance.

"That is your goal, is it not?" Raguel said.

"And the Ancients?"

"Their access to the Mortal Realm will be denied once the Chaos Gate is closed, and the Amaranthine Barrier repaired. They will lose the scent of the Mortal Realm and drift back to sleep. I'm confident you and I can wrap up loose ends before they ever get close."

"Then we are unlikely brothers. I accept your deal."

"And I yours, Xerthotha."

"One last question before you remove this vile light from my skull."

"Ask."

"Why not dispose of Azrollorza the moment she sets foot in the Mortal Realm as I suggested earlier? It would be your right."

There was silence across the gap. And then Xerthotha's deep laughter resounded in Raguel's mind. "Ah, I see it now. Let the devil do the dirty work."

And with a flick of Xerthotha's fingers, the fluttering butterflies turned into a ravaging frenzy of death as each turned on its neighbor, gnashing and tearing until the last one pinwheeled to the ground.

"Precisely," Raguel said and severed the connection.

JEFF PANTANELLA

THE
DIVINE FIST

BOOK THREE IN THE
EVER HERO SAGA

THE DIVINE FIST
PART 3 - BOOK 3

PROLOGUE

"These are desperate times, my old friend," the monkey sage, Zhao Houzi said to the black warhorse, Titus. He felt the worry lines deepen on his brow as he waddled upright on two short legs along a well-manicured path. A slight dusting of sand covered its surface. He shook his small furry head. "Desperate, desperate times."

Zhao Houzi was dressed in yellow silk pants and a bright vest of many colors while Titus wore thin strips of golden ribbons woven into the long braids of his mane and tail.

"You worry far too much, Monkey. Leave everything to Lord Raguel. He knows best," Titus responded as he clip-clopped at Zhao Houzi's side.

The sky was clear, and a warm spring breeze blew the sweet scent of cherry blossoms from countless trees that extended to the horizon. Zhao Houzi also caught the fragrance of scented primrose of yellow and deep-blue, bushes of rhododendrons with open flowers of red and pink, and bulbous lilac heads growing in long clusters of smaller plants.

The trail they walked followed the rolling landscape along rising hills and shallow dales. Zhao Houzi typically enjoyed the coarse sensation of the gritty sand on the soles of his feet. The slight abrasion felt cleansing and tickled his toes. But today, the sand was an irritation at best.

Beauty and tranquility surrounded the excitable monkey and occasionally, blossom petals fell like soft snow from the trees. Nonetheless, he was distraught and stroked the short beard under his chin. He believed in the purity of the Laws of Heaven, as he should, since they were the spoken truth from the Immortal Mother, and nothing could be more perfect than she.

"It's the new interpretation of the Heavenly Laws that has me worried," he said and looked up at Titus's giant head to see if the horse understood his meaning and, more importantly, if he agreed. He didn't on either account.

"You must learn to scrutinize less and accept that the Chancellor Pinnacle has everything under control."

"That's the problem. I feel Lord Raguel is straying from the path of righteousness. The invisible machinations of his High Court promote injustice and intolerance. And it's a blind man who cannot see what is hidden in the spaces between the gears."

He remembered the words of his master, the Sunnese Mage, Joson Del. *"Look beyond the obvious, and see what is intended to be hidden. Be mindful of that which is not shown, for this is the reality and not the illusion you have been meant to see. When you do this, my humble Monkey, you will know the truth."*

His master's message had never been so prevalent. It was not so long ago that an inconceivable injustice had ripped through the sensibilities of the Seven Heavens, dividing the populace of celestials and creating suspicious enemies where once there had been enduring friendships. The angel Artiya'il had been banished from Heaven and forbidden to enter the Mortal Realm.

Zhao Houzi struggled to grasp the actual reason why such a severe punishment had been meted out. Indeed, a demotion of status or a hundred years of community service on either the first or second levels of Heaven could have sufficed. None knew of Artiya'il's present whereabouts, but there was only one destination where lost souls were collected and that was the Abyss. The thought of being condemned to eternal suffering made Zhao Houzi shudder.

"I can see there is more twisting and turning in that head of yours, isn't there?" Titus said.

"Of course, there's more. I'm sure we can agree and accept that some souls are more welcome than others in the Seven Heavens. What one does in life is an honest reflection of their worth, and it's only fair that they ascended to the higher plateaus of righteousness after their arrival into Elysian," Zhao Houzi said.

"Agreed. Just as their merits are accumulated and judged while here," Titus added.

"Yes, exactly. But it seems to me that many ascensions have been granted too quickly to those who publicly championed the Chancellor Pinnacle's policies and reinforced his decisions without question or reason, rather than through selfless acts of service or bravery.

"And now, Lord Raguel's sentencing of Artiya'il has changed everything. He banished an ancient angel! A True-born, created by the will of the Immortal Mother at the beginning of all things."

Zhao Houzi couldn't fathom the depths of this decision and how it would affect the High Court's future policy. If this became the new normal, what hope was there for a mere animal spirit like himself?

"I fear Lord Raguel abused his authority and worse, received no reprimand or censure. He passed judgment with impunity, and no one even tried to stop him."

"Monkey, you must let it be. You were not the one who was banished."

"Can't you see? The sentencing and punishment of Artiya'il was just the latest in a series of abnormally harsh decisions from Lord Raguel and his office. The Chancellor Pinnacle's policies are creating deep divisions among the citizens of the Heavenly Realm. How soon until the lines of tolerance become blurred, and those who were once accepted as equals are condemned without thought?"

Zhao Houzi sensed shadows crowding the edges of the infinite horizon. For the first time in millennia, he felt unsafe. He wondered if his friend thought the same.

"Wouldn't you agree that leniency and thoughtful understanding of a being's actions and intentions should be of great import when determining innocence, or guilt, in upholding the perfection of the law?" Zhao Houzi said.

The monkey glanced up at Titus again to see how he received his message. The sheen of Titus's black coat shimmered in the yellow sunlight, and his thick muscles twitched as he walked, keeping his pace slow to accommodate his short-legged friend.

Zhao Houzi continued, "Artiya'il was a shepherd to the mortals for countless ages and welcomes each new soul into Elysian. What was his crime, I ask? What was so dreadful as to cause his banishment?"

"His crime was clear. He interfered in the lives of certain mortals by shifting their path and altering their fate." Titus's deep voice rumbled past his lips and thick teeth.

"He acted as a guide, only," Zhao Houzi was quick to point out, raising a finger of wrinkled skin into the air.

"Monkey, you know as well as I that Artiya'il made a point to bend the rules and often broke them willingly. Now he must suffer the consequences."

"Unjust and outdated rules," Monkey grumbled.

"Rules, nonetheless. The Laws of Heaven were given by the Immortal Mother and cannot be broken."

"Given by the Immortal Mother, but interpreted by others," Zhao Houzi said. He kicked a small rock from the path and into the garden at its edge. His brow furrowed with consternation as he shook his head, not knowing the right answer. He felt in his heart that the old laws must change, but not in the way Lord Raguel was proceeding.

"Ever moving and changing is our shared existence with the other realms. We should not remain rigid while they evolve and expand. All three realms are connected, akin to waves in an ocean, each is unique, flowing and smashing together, but all part of the same water.

"It is the chaos of the wave that provides life to the sea as it churns up the nutrients left on the sandy shore of evolution."

Titus lowered his massive head equal with Zhao Houzi's furry face, so their eyes met. "I see you are the Monkey Poet today," the great warhorse said, and then turned to blow a gust of air through his wide nostrils, mussing up the monkey's hair. Zhao Houzi did his best to brush it all back in place with his hands, not appreciating Titus's levity.

The two animals had lived centuries ago, and centuries apart, within separate lands of the Mortal Realm. Each had proven their worth as champions of great merit against the forces of darkness during their time. Zhao Houzi fought beside the Sunnese mage, Joson Del, against the third demon incursion of Sunne, after which the Amaranthine Barrier had been placed around each of the Three Realms by the Immortal Mother, protecting them from each other and the potential trespass of cosmic, malevolent beings.

Zhao Houzi had been blessed with an intellect far superior to that of common primates. When Joson Del discovered the monkey in the deep jungle, he sensed a latent strain of Elemenati magic within him that could be developed into a complementary asset to his own. With time and tutelage, Zhao Houzi was taught to draw his power directly from the living jungle's energy.

Mage and monkey became inseparable until Joson Del died at the hands of the archdevil, Sekka, who sought the magical soul energy of the Sunnese to strengthen her Frost Legions on Gathos.

Zhao Houzi was shocked to hear rumors that Sekka had somehow bypassed the Amaranthine Barrier and returned to the Mortal Realm. He immediately petitioned the Heavenly Host to destroy her before she did more damage. Sadly, his request was denied.

Titus was the loyal steed of the northern barbarian lord, Rulf Glisgild. The man was fierce. He was devoted to his tribe and stubborn in his mindset about how to protect them best. In his mind, an impregnable defense was more important than an aggressive attack.

Therefore, he established his clan atop high cliff walls surrounded by waterfalls, which froze to slick ice during the long winter months, and gushed torrents of water during the brief spring thaw. His stronghold was aptly named Holdfast and was never breached during his reign.

The warlord found a kindred spirit in Titus, the jet-black warhorse, and rode upon his broad back whenever duty called to defend the lives of the families of his clan. They fought together as one, each anticipating the other's actions. None could stand against them in open combat.

Zhao Houzi looked sideways at his friend. "All poetics and joking aside, I fear we are at a crossroads, and the paths before us are twisted and rough. There is a change, a shift, if you will, in Lord Raguel's direction. Can you feel it as well?"

Titus rolled his charcoal-colored eyes. "You see snakes and spiders in the grass and under every rock. There is only one golden path necessary for us to walk, that which the Immortal Mother and her regent, the Chancellor Pinnacle, has provided for us."

"Lord Raguel is regent now, is he?" Zhao Houzi said with surprising interest in his friend's statement.

"Monkey, the logic is sound. Remain on the golden path, and you will find contentment and peace with every step. When one strays from the path and crosses its edge, then only peril awaits. We have seen this repeatedly, especially with the mortal humans suffering through their short lives. They refuse to control their appetites and desires. They are reckless."

"But they must not lose freedom of will!"

"Monkey."

Zhao Houzi peered up at his giant friend and nodded begrudgingly in agreement. "Yes, I know, freedom of will entices infinite possibilities and outcomes, and therefore, there will be many degrees of variation along the thin line that separates the path from the peril."

"You overthink in the abstract, Monkey. Our rules are set to keep the Heavenly Order pristine and allow no room for chaos to bloom. I have known you for many years, my friend, too many to count. And if there ever was a monkey who enjoyed speaking in riddles, especially those he could not solve, it's you."

"Perhaps you are right, Titus. It's a challenging concept to put into concrete terms. And not for a humble soul such as mine to deliberate. But I ask you this, what of love?"

"Love? In what context?" The great horse tilted his head to the side.

"You fought countless battles at your master's side, as did I. You shared a special bond and threw yourself into harm's way to protect him, did you not?"

"Yes, of course. It was my duty."

"Duty, yes. Did I tell you of the time when Joson Del and I were cornered by—"

"The Narvoni tiger? Yes, Monkey, it's your favorite story. I have heard it countless times."

"Yes, well, my point is what would you do to save Rulf Glisgild?"

"I would offer my life to protect his without hesitation."

"And if the choice you had to make destroyed your honor and filled you with madness, but was needed to save the life of your master, well what then?"

Titus's ears fell back as he raised his enormous head into the air, bobbing and snorting. Zhao Houzi watched his friend ponder the question and become frustrated with his potential answer. The war horse snorted again, shaking his head back and forth, so the golden ribbons in his mane snapped like a banner in the wind.

"A hypothetical debate requiring an impossible decision does not concern me now. The laws are sacred and cannot be broken," Titus said, appearing agitated.

"Is love not more so? Was it not love of the mortals which caused Artiya'il to transgress? His deeds brought him no personal gain or prestige. Each one a selfless act, to encourage a human to follow a brighter path."

"Ah, but there is the flaw in your argument, Monkey," Titus said triumphantly. "The Great Balance must remain. It is the Immortal Mother's will that both outer realms are fed the appropriate amount of souls. Artiya'il had no right to steal from the Abyss."

"Perhaps no lawful right, per se. But the question still weighs heavy in my mind. What manner of importance does love merit when deciding the rightness or wrongness of an action?"

"You sound as if you mean to interfere, again," Titus whinnied what could only be a sigh. "Trust the Chancellor Pinnacle to guide us true, as he has since the beginning of time. Leave Aetenos and his Ever Hero to the wisdom of the High Court. You do not want to get involved."

"A messy business, being the Ever Hero," Zhao Houzi mused. "A most unfortunate ordeal for the mortal who is not ready for such a burden."

"And one who felt ready would not be chosen. The hubris negates the ascension," Titus said. His heavy hooves clicked and clacked on the road.

The Monkey Sage remained quiet for a time, pondering the riddle of what was right and what was wrong, outside of ancient laws and rules. Finally, he had his answer. He slapped a balled-up hand into the open palm of the other and gave a small monkey hoot.

"Yes, love is the equalizer!" Zhao Houzi said. "It balances all things. It should be the abstract variable that tips the scales outside of policy and law. Come, Titus. Let us introduce ourselves to Gray'el's prisoners. I am eager to hear their stories and how they became prisoners in paradise."

57

KASAI

Kasai watched Desdemonia stare at the ground for a long time. She brushed the foot of her worn, leather boot over the soft grass, smoothing it over from side-to-side. Eventually, she lifted her head to look directly at him. Her amber eyes reflected the golden light of the Elysian afternoon sun.

"What else could I do?" she said and shrugged her shoulders.

Kasai wasn't sure what to say. So much had happened since fleeing the Monastery of Ordu with Master Choejor, when the black smoke of burning buildings and the sounds of his dying Brothers' screams filled the air. That seemed like a lifetime ago. Since then, Kasai had inadvertently been the cause of something truly terrible. He should have died with the others at Ordu; then the world would be free of Sekka and that terrible Chaos Gate.

Kasai didn't want to think of the innocent people that now suffered because of his inability to control his anger. Oh, if he could only take back that one dreadful misstep to hurt Daku and make him pay for killing Master Choejor. No, not Daku, not anymore. Now his hateful friend had been reborn into a horrific *thing*. Khalkoroth was his name now. Daku was gone.

Kasai rubbed his forehead, trying to put together the remaining pieces of the nightmare that wouldn't end. He had unwittingly fallen into Sekka's trap, and the archdevil had promptly stolen his soul, joining it with the soul of the demigod, Aetenos, which enabled her to open the Chaos Gate, a demonic portal between the Abyss and the Mortal Realm.

Afterward, Illyria had given Kasai a quest to rescue Aetenos, who was imprisoned by Sekka somewhere on Gathos. Kasai had accepted without hesitation, knowing full well it was a fool's errand, and he would most likely die trying.

Against the odds, Kasai and his companions had freed Aetenos from his bonds only to reluctantly follow the Great Monk back into Furia Keep, where he sought to rescue his love. But Aetenos was mistaken. Illyria was never held against her will on Gathos. The ruse was just another cleverly laid trap by the wicked archdevil.

Kasai had wrongly assumed once freed, Aetenos would resume his role of savior of the Three Kingdoms of Hanna, destroy the Chaos Gate, and deliver him and his companions from the Abyss. But instead of a heroic demigod, Kasai had found a broken man, one crazed and defeated.

The Great Monk's mind had been shattered under the wicked spells and torturous tools of the demon witch, Chedipe, and now madness bloomed, crowding the open space between too many cracks of his sanity.

Kasai's awareness and control of his xindu energy had grown. Aetenos's tutelage of his new Ever Hero came at unlikely times and was filled with confusing riddles. Yet somehow, Kasai deciphered enough of his master's teachings to perform incredible feats, but the cost to his sensibilities was high.

Doubt still filled his young mind, and his thoughts desperately clung to old beliefs that magic of any kind, even when used for good, would inevitably harm and corrupt those who used it. And now Kasai felt as if the plague of magic lived within him.

Master Choejor had said xindu energy was not magic, per se, but the vibrational life force found in everything. Kasai had learned to control the fundamental vibrations within himself at Ordu. Now, with the help of Master Aetenos, he was moving the objects around him. The extraordinary powers he wielded could not possibly be real, more likely a dark manifestation of a dream that should not be his.

Yet, when he was calm, in a meditative peace, the Boundless spoke lost secrets to him, and the answers to impossible questions were revealed, coming unburdened of the need to know how or why.

Then there was the battle against Sekka's nemesis in the wastelands outside Furia Keep. The Red Devil, Zizphander, proved too strong for the addlebrained Aetenos and his newly proclaimed Ever Hero. Kasai had been crippled by a psionic attack and was in mortal danger.

In desperation, Desdemonia had accepted an onyx ring from Sekka, which heightened her use of Elemenati magic but also mingled her blood with the blood of the archdevil. It was a condition she could not refuse if she wished to save Kasai.

She was different now, changed somehow. And not for the better.

But back to arranging the puzzle pieces. One moment he and Des, and the three of five remaining Kibo Gensai warriors who had begun the quest to protect Kasai and save Aetenos, were running for their lives from demons deep in the dungeons of Sekka's stronghold on Gathos.

He remembered finding the angel, Artiya'il splayed out on the torturer's rack. Then, Illyria miraculously returned, filling the dreary chamber with a warm, bright light, offering hope and salvation. Gone were sights of miserable devices designed to inflict gruesome pain. The bloodstains soaked into the floor, or sprayed against the walls, were bleached away, and for a moment, the room was clean.

Somehow, Illyria had found them and quickly magicked Kasai and his companions to Elysian, the first level of the Seven Heavens, where they were promptly captured by Gray'el, the Commander of the Praetor Guard, for heresy.

And now, they were prisoners in Heaven.

The pace of his life was now akin to running through a strange and unexplored forest during a moonless night. The twisted twigs from low hanging branches scratched his exposed skin and pulled at his clothing. Sticky strands of spider's silk-covered his face, and with each breath, he inhaled more into his mouth, coating his tongue and teeth. No matter how he tried, he could not wipe the crisscrossing strands free and escape his destiny of being chosen as the next Ever Hero.

"It's ok, Des. We will figure this out. We'll find a way," Kasai said. However, he had no idea how that would happen. He was so tired. His body wanted to sleep, but that would not come. Instead, his thoughts traveled down a maze of winding corridors, overlapping and backtracking in a knot. But at least the environment was soothing.

The golden sun shone high above their heads, warming away the deep chill set in their bones from long days fighting the bitter cold on Gathos. Before them, sweeping grass grew underfoot, sprinkled with patches of colorful wildflowers, and other small groves of trees that provided cool shade. The long days trapped in the Abyss had not been kind, and the weary companions found a bit of solace in their surroundings, although captives they remained.

Their prison was not a typical four-walled cell like the cramped and dank enclosure found in Furia Keep's dungeons. Here on Elysian, Kasai looked upon an open expanse for a far as his eyes could see. He could walk for what seemed like hours, unguarded and unchained, in any direction. However, he always returned to the same copse of birch trees with their black-and-white patterned trunks and broad, spade-shaped leaves of bright green. What seemed like hours of exploring to Kasai would result in only a few minutes away from his companions when he returned.

"This is not right. Only the witch is guilty of breaking the sacred vows," Orin said loud enough for everyone to hear. He pointed an accusatory finger at Desdemonia as he paced in a short circuit like a caged animal. Run-Run looked woefully at his older brother, Pallo, who in return gave the mute a half-smile.

"The Ever Hero is right. We will solve this riddle together as we have since the beginning." Pallo's voice was reassuring, and Kasai was happy the elder Kibo Gensai warrior was on his side.

Orin turned to Pallo, his face red with anger. "You heard that angel. We are heretics by association! The witch admits her guilt. Call the Praetor. Let him hear her confession and be done with this farce." He grabbed a branch and snapped off a purple bud that had begun to blossom and crumbled it in his hands. "I'm Kibo Gensai, dammit! Each one of the scars on my body is a testament to my dedication to the faith."

Run-Run gasped and then slowly stepped away from Orin. His eyes immediately scanned the sky.

"I'm not sure if you are allowed to do that here," Kasai said. He looked to Aetenos for an answer. But the Great Monk sat motionless under a different tree, with his one eye closed and a patch over the other. The angels had dressed his companions' wounds and gave them fresh clothes to wear. Kasai tilted his head to the side. Was that more obscure mumbling he heard coming from Aetenos's lips, or was his master humming a tune? It sounded like a tune.

"I have devoted myself to the destruction of evil for too many years to be treated like a common criminal. I say again, look at my face. Don't these scars tell a different story?"

"Actually, you pretty much look like a villain," Desdemonia chimed in. "Am I right?" She looked at Kasai for confirmation, who gave her a rueful look. "What? He does."

Pallo pointed to a large boulder in the distance. "A rider comes."

Kasai and the others peered into the distance and saw a strange little man standing atop the back of a magnificent black steed, galloping toward them. The little man was covered in fur and resembled a child-size genie, with his arms folded across his hairy chest.

The furry man was dressed in yellow silk pants and a vest that rivaled the colorful wildflowers growing in the surrounding field. Streaming golden ribbons billowed like pennants in the wind behind the Shire stallion's black mane and tail. The horse's black coat glistened in the pale golden light, as its thick muscles bunched and twitched as it ran.

"Is that a monkey?" Desdemonia said in curious disbelief.

"I think you're right," Kasai said.

The stallion came to an abrupt halt in front the companions. With acrobatic skill, the monkey jumped off the back of the great horse and stood proudly before the group. He had weaved a lock of blue-green hair into the tan fur behind his ear. Then, he stroked the short, grey beard under his chin.

"I am Zhao-Houzi, and this magnificent horse is Titus," the animal spirit said.

"I am Kasai Ch'ou," Kasai bowed respectfully to the monkey.

"You see, Titus, very polite," Zhao Houzi said.

The tall horse merely snorted. "Get on with it, Monkey. I wish to return to the fields of Heavenly Arcadia. The grass of Elysian is not to my taste."

"Titus, please. Be patient. I feel there is much at stake here."

"May I help you with something, Lord Zhao Houzi?" Kasai said.

"I am not a lord. Zhao Houzi will do, or just Monkey, is fine, too," Zhao Houzi said. A warm smile graced his furry face. "We have heard rumors of your tale, Soulless One, and have journeyed from the upper levels to hear the story from your lips. Perhaps your current dilemma can help us solve a friendly debate, which has reached an impasse."

"I can try," Kasai said.

"You are the Ever Hero, yes?" Zhou Houzi didn't wait for Kasai to answer.

Pallo and Run-Run eyed the talking monkey carefully. Aetenos remained under his tree. Orin stood apart, apparently not sure what to make of the strange duo.

"And you are a Daughter of the Forest, yes? Come closer, let me have a better look at you," Zhao Houzi said. He carefully gripped her wrist in the delicate fingers of one hand, and with his other, he gently extended the finger which held the onyx ring. "Ah, yes, here's the problem."

His sapphire-blue eyes scrutinized the onyx ring as he rotated her wrist back and forth. "I would imagine there is no taking it off."

Desdemonia raised her eyebrows in wonder at Zhao Houzi and nodded to the talking monkey. "Yes, and I fear removing the finger will cause more damage than I can bear."

"You mean it will end you."

"Something like that."

Kasai gasped. "What? How do you know?"

"I see, I see," Zhao Houzi said, and let Desdemonia's hand drop to her side. "Titus, what do you think?"

"There is no need for speculation or discussion. That's an onyx ring. You know better than anyone who makes them and enslaves those who wear them to her will. She bears the taint of Chaos, and the Law of Heaven is clear in this matter. Her soul is forfeit and must return to the Abyss."

Orin came straight over. "You see! Let the witch burn. She's an outsider here."

Zhao Houzi stroked his short beard, contemplating Orin's outburst. "You have open eyes, young warrior, yet it appears they see very little."

Orin's mouth hung open as if to say more, then he turned and waved away the monkey's assessment. "What does a talking monkey know? This creature is just another cruel joke made to make us look like fools." He walked back to the shade of the birch trees, continuing to grumble to himself.

Zhao Houzi was unphased by Orin's outburst. "Laws can bend without breaking. There is an argument for removing guilt when indeed, the purest of intentions with no malice to dictate otherwise commences the performance of a vile act. Some leniency is in order where presently there is none."

"You would incite anarchy," Titus countered.

"I'm not so sure, my steadfast friend." Zhao Houzi peered around Kasai to see Aetenos still leaning against an older birch tree. "Well met, my old friend. It appears you've lost an eye since we last met."

"Hello, Monkey, Titus. It's another beautiful day in Heaven," Aetenos said without opening his good eye. He gave a short wave in return, then went back to his humming.

"Some things never change," Zhao Houzi sighed.

Titus whinnied. "You can easily see the corruption that festers in all humans exposed to raw Chaos. Even the mighty Aetenos has resigned himself to his fate."

"Titus, you know better than to assume anything when it comes to him." Zhao Houzi crossed one arm across his chest, and the other he brought up to massage his chin.

"I shall endeavor to help you. I am curious to see if one can be saved by the purity of intention and not solely condemned by the act of a deed."

Zhao Houzi leaped onto the back of the black horse. "Until we meet again, Soulless One. Keep hope in your heart and know you have a friend in Heaven."

Kasai watched the odd couple trot away and eventually vanished in the distance.

"That was...unusual," Desdemonia said.

"Heaven is a confusing place. Who would have known there were so many rigid laws and harsh punishments?" Kasai said.

Aetenos opened his eye. "The Monkey Sage is wise."

"Master, why did Illyria bring us here? We did what she asked. Why must we be punished?"

Aetenos looked intently at Desdemonia. "Punished or purified. In the Seven Heavens, there is a thin line separating the two."

"We of the Kibo Gensai are innocent. We fight only for good," Orin stated matter-of-factly. "Heaven should welcome us with open arms and sing songs of our deeds."

"There are many realms or levels you might refer to as Heaven, young warrior. They are called by many names, but most refer to them as Elysian, Eden, Arcadia, Erewhon, Canaan, Paradise, and the seventh and highest level of Tanalum.

"Each level is specific and carries its own behaviors, yet there is one steadfast rule, which states that law and order must be maintained according to the Laws of Heaven. There is no in-between. The Seven Heavens create an opposite mirror to the Abyss, and act as a counterweight to the insanity of chaos with the Mortal Realm acting as the fulcrum," Aetenos said as if giving a proper explanation as to why the authorities of Heaven were ignoring Orin's declaration.

He then closed his eye and added, "But fear not, all is as it should be. Whether me or another who will rise to take my place, there will always be someone to carry the torch of hope to brighten the hearts of men during dark times."

"What do you mean? Are you giving up? That Zhou Houzi monkey-person just said he would help us," Kasai said, exasperated that after all they had endured, Aetenos had resigned himself to his fate.

"As one light is lit, another fades to darkness. It is the way of the Great Balance," Aetenos said.

"Another? Who? An angel?"

"Be patient. Now is the time to rest and to wait."

"Wait? Wait for what?"

"Why, the answers, of course. You will find not all is as it seems on the surface. Do not fall into the same trap as young Orin. Now, come here and let us speak of surrender."

"Surrender, Master Aetenos? That's it? The fight is over, and we just give up?"

"Give up? No. My goodness, what are they teaching you at Ordu these days?" Aetenos said. "The fight is eternal. One battle ends and another begins. It is the natural way of things. I speak of a different type of surrender, one of acceptance and understanding."

"The Boundless."

"Yes, my son, the Boundless." Aetenos reached out and held Kasai's hand, forearm, and then shoulder. "You must accept that this flesh is not you. It's merely one crude way to describe you. Same as your name or the language you choose to speak. The real you will always be in motion and constantly changing. Therefore, what you felt a moment ago is no longer you. It belongs to a different you and has no bearing on who you are now."

Kasai just stared at the demigod.

"Got it?"

A soothing breeze blew through the birch trees, gently swaying the branches. Kasai heard a soft rustle overhead as the leaves fluttered on their stalks. He brought his hand to his sash, where Ninziz-zida usually was holstered. She had been taken by the Protectorate Guard when the party first entered Elysian. He longed for her reassuring warmth now.

"Well?" Aetenos pressed.

A thought came to Kasai's mind. "Ninziz-zida is connected to the Boundless."

"You are a quick study when you remove doubt from your mind. Yes, she surrendered herself to the Boundless when the need of the Three Realms was great. She became something unique and pure."

"What was she before?" Kasai asked.

"That is for her to reveal to you when you are ready. But first, you must earn her unconditional trust. To do so, you must surrender yourself to the Boundless as well. Remember, you are not the past you, and you will be a different you in the future. You are the present you and no other you. Everyone is separate.

"When you surrender being Kasai, you will be nothing. And then you and Ninziz-zida will truly be one. Makes sense, right? Good," Aetenos said. He smiled and went back to his tree, sat down and fell asleep.

Kasai thought maybe he should just stop talking to Aetenos all together.

58

SEKKA

Zizphander's army lined the horizon of the Wastelands of Thresh. The fiery glow of his warriors and lumbering war beasts lit the swirling sky in an aura of rosy arrogance. He commanded an endless horde, and Sekka wondered again what Xerthotha hoped to gain by destroying her. Was this payback for defeating the Red Devil centuries ago? Xerthotha should have seen she was the abler devil and given her a nod for her trickery and cunning. Why then had he chosen Zizphander again as his champion instead of her? It boggled the mind.

Sekka was meticulous in her planning and calculated the consequences of her actions before unleashing any one of her many schemes to gather more power in the Abyss. She thought back through the centuries, trying to remember any other possible slight or insult she may have caused the Great Chaos Devil, directly or indirectly. She could find none. Could he possibly have been holding a grudge all this time, or was there a more complicated equation she had overlooked?

Kotto'gyges rolled through Furia Keep's gates, followed by his bodyguard of five, chaos-tainted maidens. They were called the Nu Kua and wore light green armor, sculpted to resemble bare-chested, muscular women. Each had the lower body of a thick snake covered in a kaleidoscope of purple, blue, and green scales.

The five bodyguards slithered into the courtyard and fanned out around Kotto'-gyges. In each hand, they held a long, tapered scimitar, which caught the pale light of Gathos along its edge. Each wore a sleek helm, which covered what was surely a cruel-looking face and molded in the appearance of a fearsome scowl.

The lumbering jol'goths positioned around the perimeter of the courtyard vibrated in agitation at the presence of a foreign force in Furia Keep. Some paced back and forth and gnashed their ice crystal teeth or growled to show their displeasure. Many pounded their fists into the snow-covered stones of the courtyard.

Sekka watched the demon prince slow to a stop. The stench from the realm of Azrollorza filled her courtyard. *Yet another sacrifice I must endure to reach my goals*, she thought. Sekka glanced back over her shoulder to see if Zizphander had moved closer, but the Red Devil had stayed his advance. *Such a blind fool. He seeks to set fear in my heart at the sight of his overwhelming numbers.* She sucked at her teeth. It was time to show Zizphander the real power of Gathos.

A defensive strategy was forming in her head as she walked to the door at the end of the rampart and descended the stairs to the courtyard. "Azrollorza gives me no choice but to accept the arrival of her troops, and payment for their use will be steep. She shadows every step I take and forces me to do her bidding."

Sekka had been outmaneuvered, and she knew it. Her fists clenched at her sides. "One day I will be the greater devil. And on that day, I will show her what it means to be the slave."

But it would not be today. Sekka could not fight the army of Kotto'gyges and Zizphander's horde at the same time.

An image of Gerun Shiverrig, the self-proclaimed Aj-Kahun, came to her mind. Sekka's spies had reported that a small host of hybrid demons had hidden around the Chaos Gate's perimeter in Trosk. What was that clever mortal up to now? Did he mean to subvert her hold on the entrance to the Mortal Realm? Or was he was watching her movement and assessing her strength. Unlike the demons she commanded, Shiverrig was patient, which was a dangerous trait in an adversary.

Sekka sent a brief telepathic communication to Aeshmara in the Mortal Realm. *+Return to the Chaos Gate in haste. Hold the portal at all costs. Keep whatever souls you have collected safe. I will need them soon. If Shiverrig gets in your way, remove him, otherwise let him live for now. He may still prove useful. But capture his troops. The screams of his half-breed mongrels will nourish the Orthods in their pits.+*

Sekka heard only indistinguishable mumblings and wondered if other forces were tampering with her ability to communicate with her minions. Then a warbled voice penetrated the distortion. *+It is done, my Queen. Dai-Ko-Zior has captured Shiverrig and leashed his dog. My brother has them both well kept.+*

At least she could count on Aeshmara to successfully carry out her orders. Sekka soon reached the courtyard and prepared herself for a contest of strength. Kotto'gyges was a formidable demon prince, filled with arcane knowledge, some she suspected would be unknown to her, but he could not rival the power of an archdevil.

She remained in her mortal form for obvious reasons. She did not need to destroy Kotto'gyges, and there was simply too much raw strength in her demonic body. With so many distractions, it would be difficult to control her bloodlust if it came to blows.

"Kotto'gyges, welcome to Furia Keep," Sekka said in a neutral tone. "I honor your arrival with the command of the armies of Azrollorza and Furia Keep. Untold glories await you in the coming battle."

If she were lucky, Kotto'gyges would be more interested in grappling with the Red Devil than testing the extent of her strength. But she doubted luck was with her.

Kotto'gyges's eye stalks twisted and turned, assessing the keep and its inner fortifications. He gave a brief but disdainful chuckle at the jol'goths frustrated antics. Then his eyes aligned to focus on Sekka.

"Azrollorza sent me to keep you safe, devil, but now that I am here, I have thoughts of my own. Perhaps Kotto'gyges should rule here instead of just babysitting one so helpless as you." The demon prince's voice came from many mouths, each slightly overlapping the others.

"I am in no mood for a contest of barbed words and shallow threats. Azrollorza wishes to test me, fine. I expected as much. It's a fortunate day for me that she has sent only you. Come, let us get this over with, Kotto'gyges. I have a war to end."

"Yesss...," Kotto'gyges hissed. "Much has been said of your boldness and delicious, wicked nature. I see it was not untrue. Yet so few have sampled the taste of your flesh. Kotto'gyges hungers for Sekka, to whet his appetite before dispatching the lapdog of Xerthotha."

Clumps of snow gathered and swirled around Sekka, crystalizing into shards. Soon a spinning shield of razor-sharp ice surrounded her. Kotto'gyges chortled, "Ah, this will not stop Kotto'gyges from a savory meal of Sekka's flesh."

"No, but it will hurt." Sekka readied a spell that would freeze Kotto'gyges where he stood on bladed appendages. She only wanted to stop him and make him yield. If she destroyed the demon prince, she would lose an asset in the coming battle.

Then Sekka was distracted by a commotion off to the side. She glanced to the left and saw Lord Oziax pushing aside two jol'goths, then racing forward in the space between them.

"KOTTO'GYGES!" Lord Oziax roared. The demon lord thundered into the courtyard, already half-changed from the shape of an elegant prince to his bestial, infernal self. His cloven hooves kicked up snow and clacked on the stone floor of the courtyard. In one hand, he gripped the black hell-blade, Void. Black vapors rose from the dark iron. Five tentacles slithered from his other hand where fingers would be.

Oziax's human facial features dissolved into the shape of a brutish animal skull. What skin remained was stretched thin along its surface. Pale purple eyes within the dark, empty sockets locked on Kotto'gyges as black horns spiraled and curled from his forehead. The coarse, white hair of his back bristled in anger.

Kotto'gyges twisted a quarter of his blue eye stalks in the direction of the rampaging Oziax. Just as many arms swiveled in the same direction, dagger pointed tips hovered menacingly at the warlord.

"I wondered if Oziax the Soul Breaker would dare show his face in my presence. I'm surprised to see your head is still joined to your body." Some of Kotto'gyges's mouths spoke in unison, while others laughed in a high-pitched squeal. "You must bring Kotto'gyges the boy monk called the Ever Hero. I should like to congratulate him on such a memorable victory."

Oziax came fast and leaped at the mocking demon prince only to be turned aside by Kotto'gyges's bodyguards' sharp blades. Five pairs of steel flashed in front of Oziax, aiming to cut down the demon lord. The Nu Kua tails twitched and squirmed, pushing the ground layer of snow into small banks. Sekka heard the Nu Kua hiss with wicked intent through their masks.

"Yesss...Soul Breaker, join the brothel of Kotto'gyges. My Nu Kua need a new playmate," Kotto'gyges cooed. "Your queen shall join you soon."

The sound of movement from Zizphander's army was carried on the howling winds and sucked into the immense courtyard. The blueish stalks covering Kotto'-gyges fleshy bulk swayed to the music of coming battle. "It is a festive day at Furia Keep with so many great lords who wish to destroy Sekka of Gathos."

"I don't have time for this. You will serve me, or you will die," Sekka snarled. She sent the swirling ice shards into Kotto'gyges. As she expected, the demon prince had a protective aegis placed around his body. The ice shards melted upon impact of its surface.

"Oh, ho, ho. Your icy kisses do not hurt Kotto'gyges." The demon prince began to mouth the words to a spell.

"No, but this will."

Sekka raised her hands and uttered words of dark magic faster than Kotto'gyges could counter. The clouds overhead gathered into a vortex and funneled down, encasing Kotto'gyges in a cyclone of cold. The Nu Kua were scattered haphazardly across the courtyard from the gale-force winds.

Oziax crouched low, impaling Void into the ground. He wrapped his tentacles around his hand for support and braced himself against the shrieking winds. Somehow, he maintained his grip on the sword hilt while the coarse hair covering his back billowed behind him.

Sekka brushed away the spell with a sweep of her hand, dismissing the storm clouds as quickly as she had summoned them. When the air cleared, a transparent membrane of ice coated Kotto'gyges, freezing the demon prince in place. Some of his eye-stalks looked up at the storm that had plunged down on him, while others focused on her. Most of his dagger-tipped appendages were aimed at her, while the remaining ones braced against the freezing wind.

Sekka took note that many of Kotto'gyges's mouths were trapped in different shapes, and she wondered if she studied the various positions of his lips and tongues, could she decipher the spell he was about to cast. However, it didn't matter now.

She turned her wicked gaze to the slowly rising Nu Kua. They picked up their scimitars and glared back at the archdevil as they slithered forward. Sekka sighed. There was still too much to do. Her forces were not in place, and Furia Keep was vulnerable.

She waved for her jol'goths to intervene. Thirty of the massive demons sprang into action, forming a wall of imposing muscle, teeth, and claw between the Nu Kua and Sekka. Oziax had risen and moved to the head of the line.

Sekka proceeded to Kotto'gyges's side and melted the ice over one of his open mouths.

"Kotto'gyges shall have you!" the mouth shouted in defiance.

"Tsk-tsk," Sekka shook her head. "What did you think would happen here?"

"Kotto'gyges shall— Aargh!" The demon prince screamed in pain. Sekka held the broken half of an ice-embalmed eye-stalk in her hand like a wand. "Shall I snap off another?"

Oziax now stood next to her and circled the point of Void at the other eye-stalks. "He has plenty more to choose from."

Sekka melted the ice from another eye-stalk. Once it was free from the ice, it swerved in all directions, assessing its situation and the damage to its body. Blue blood oozed from the broken stalk that now hung limply across its ice-encased body.

Sekka grabbed the thawed shaft, squeezing it while looked directly into its eye. "You now understand, yes?"

The end section of the eye-stalk nodded once. Sekka then thawed another stalk that ended in a mouth and engraved a deep, ice-blue rune into the fleshy part of the shaft. She enjoyed hearing Kotto'gyges groan as he realized what she had done.

"Yesss, Kotto'gyges," Sekka mockingly hissed. "You know what I have placed on you. Who do you serve now?"

The eye-stalk reluctantly nodded again in acceptance. "Kotto'gyges serves the Frost Queen, Sekka."

Sekka placed her open hands on the ice membrane covering the bulk of his body and issued a word of command. The remaining ice sloughed away, and Kotto'gyges collapsed to the ground. He slowly maneuvered to stand. Lord Oziax stood with the point of Void pressed into the demon prince's flesh.

"That won't be necessary, Lord Oziax. Kotto'gyges knows his place."

Oziax lowered his sword, albeit with hesitation.

The Nu Kuna slithered to their demon prince, stretching their scimitars at Oziax, letting him know that they would still protect their master should the need arise.

Sekka then heard howls and screeches in the wind, and she realized Zizphander had ordered his horde forward. She would never get the army of Azrollorza within the walls of Furia Keep in time. The troops were in disarray and presently without a commanding officer to lead them.

"Blast it. Why can it never be easy?"

Chedipe hobbled into the courtyard. "My queen! The Red Devil advances. Azrollorza's army awaits orders but is unraveling. Infighting has begun."

Sekka turned to her warlords. "Kotto'gyges, get your troops under control. Order the infantry of fiends into the field. Use them as a buffer until we can fully mobilize and mount a proper offensive. Arrange your armored warriors in five groups and place them around the walls of Furia Keep. Go!" The pupils in Kotto'gyges's eyes grew small in a moment of defiance.

Then, the ice-blue rune Sekka had engraved in one of the stalks blazed with white light. The archdevil saw some of his pupils enlarge as his eyeballs glazed over, but no cry of pain came from his mouths. Kotto'gyges acknowledged the command and rolled away. The Nu Kua slithered behind him out of the gates.

Sekka turned to Oziax. "Find the leader of the D'xyston Riders. Look for the largest of the floating Takuun outside the gates. That's where you'll find him. Bring them all over the walls. We will reserve the flying beasts and their riders until the battle develops. Also, get the jol'goths to the ramparts. They will defend the walls from a breach."

Oziax wasted no time racing past the heavy gates and into the battlefield. Sekka knew Oziax wanted this battle more than she. If he could find redemption in her eyes, it would be out there on the battlefield.

"Chedipe, go to the dungeons and fetch me that fool, Aetenos, his mind slave, and the Wood Witch. But leave the other three men under guard. Tell the heroes I will slay their friends if they do not come peacefully."

Chedipe's pale skin turned pasty white with fear.

"What is it? Speak!" Sekka commanded.

"The prisoners have escaped, my queen."

"WHAT?" Sekka screamed. "When?"

"Chedipe does not know. She has been occupied with the defense of the keep. Poor Chedipe serves Sekka faithfully. She did not know until today."

"A thousand curses on that monk!"

"Chedipe will find him. He will not escape."

"No, you will come with me now to wake Cymeryes from his icy slumber. It's time to end this nuisance for the last time."

The war cries of the advancing horde echoed in the courtyard and the frozen ground quaked from the pounding steps of countless fiends.

"Come. We must reach the Chamber of Awakening before it is too late," Sekka said and rushed inside.

"We are already doomed," Chedipe cried but followed Sekka, nonetheless.

59

SHIVERRIG

"For Baroqia!" Lord Fritta yelled and raced forward, bringing the fight to the archers before they could lose their deadly arrows.

Shiverrig heard Fritta's battle cry and saw the First General rush the enemy as black arrows flew from their bows. Miraculously, Fritta deflected two shafts that would have pierced his light breastplate at such close range.

Shiverrig felt the force of an arrow punch through his thigh and quiver to a stop when it struck bone. He glared through watery eyes as the sharp sting of the arrowhead brought the battle intimately close. *No time for pain*, he thought.

+Jynxx! You vile creature. Why didn't you warn me? If I die, you die!+ Shiverrig blasted the thought to the symbiotic demon who shared his body.

+Jynxx cares nothing for Shiverrig's mortal life. When he dies, Jynxx will return home and suffer no more torment from the Great Chaos Devil.+

Shiverrig gritted his teeth. *+It will not be as easy as that.+* He severed the connection and rushed forward to support Fritta's valiant yet futile attack.

A shrieking blur of white fur and snarling, purple gums shot past Shiverrig and barreled into the line of archers. Khalkoroth was in a berserker's rage and threw himself into the enemy's front line. His arms thrust out quick as the wind, and black bows cartwheeled in the air. He grappled with three archers at once, ripping off the face of one before hitting the ground. Blue blood sprayed his muzzle and chest as a reward.

The other two archers remained entangled with their faceless comrade and frantically squirmed out from under Khalkoroth's bear-sized frame. Larger demons with wicked, serrated-shaped polearms and unsheathed swords came in fast. Khalkoroth reached up with an open hand and grabbed the chipped blade of a sword chopping down to his back. He snapped the steel in half like a dry twig, and in a flash, he threw the pointed shard into the chest of its wielder. But, the old steel bounced harmlessly off the demon's stony hide.

Left of Khalkoroth, a grisly demon covered in snake scales had kicked Fritta to the ground. The First General raised his sword to ward off the killing blow, but Shiverrig knew it wouldn't be enough. The demon brought his polearm above his head, sporting a spear tip barbed on four sides.

Shiverrig lunged forward to the fallen Fritta and thrust his sword into the demon's exposed ribs. The demon screamed in pain and tried to spin away from the blade. But Shiverrig braced his good leg into the ground and held tight on the grip of his sword. The demon's horrific wail intensified as his momentum carried the steel across his torso.

A satisfied but short-lived smile graced Shiverrig's face. More of Aeshmara's warriors had gathered closer and bore down on the three allies. The company of half-breeds Shiverrig had brought from Qaqal would have equalized this fight, but foolishly he had left them at the base camp. +*Jynxx, you will pay for addling my mind.*+

Shiverrig hauled Fritta to his feet. "Get up!" he shouted and turned to see how the pale demon fared. Khalkoroth's muddied white fur was covered in blue blood, much of it now his own. Two black shafts protruded awkwardly from his back but didn't seem to hamper the white beast. He rose to his full height and moved to lunge at one of the enemy demons.

"STOP!" Dai-Ko-Zior's eerie voice boomed through the camp.

The entire melee froze as if commanded by an unseen force. With great effort of will, Shiverrig slowly turned around and saw a haze of swirling green mist flowing out of the tent. Then a hooded figure materializing within the fog.

"And now this," Shiverrig said. He could feel the tension on his body relaxing as the sorcerer's spell wore off. Then his back erupted in an explosion of pain. He twisted his neck, fearing the worst, and saw a black shafted arrow protruding from his armor.

Dai-Ko-Zior's raspy voice slithered through the air like a snake, aimed at the archer who had loosed the arrow. The slender demon dropped his bow and stepped backward. He shrieked and ran in fear. A loud crack broke the camp's silence as the fleeing demon lurched unnaturally in mid-step and fell to the ground. His neck, back, legs, twisted and broken.

"They shall not be harmed," Dai-Ko-Zior breathed the words out in a raspy whisper as if he stood intimately close to Shiverrig and spoke in his ear. Shiverrig noticed Aeshmara's demon warriors looking questioningly at one another, not sure if they should obey what must have been the same message or follow the orders of their leader.

Aeshmara stormed at Dai-Ko-Zior from the right. Her eyes blazed, and she scowled menacingly at her brother. "You dare usurp my command? I will gut you along with the others if I must. The lives of these mortals are mine."

Dai-Ko-Zior carefully removed the hood from his head. Thin, brownish-green hair, resembling limp, water reeds that had long ago lost their will to live, clung to the weathered skin of his face. His eyes were sunk in deep sockets, hiding their shape. The sorcerer's face was gaunt, and his skin radiated a pale-green sheen. The rest of what could only be a frail and skeletal body remained under thick robes.

"Do not tempt me to dishonor my pledge to the Frost Queen, sister. I vowed to keep you among the living if I could during her inconsequential foray into this realm. But my patience has its limits, as does my willingness to honor a promise to one who is destined to fail."

"I am in command here, not you," Aeshmara seethed.

"I have no desire to command the broken legion of a devil vying for unreachable power. I serve titans of another time and dimension and have come to the Mortal Realm for a different purpose altogether."

"Then stay in the shadows, mumbling to your forgotten gods and let me carry out the Frost Queen's will. I promise you; I will not hesitate to cut you down."

A thin smile crossed Dai-Ko-Zior's white lips. "There are higher powers, beyond your sight and comprehension, that have become interested in this mortal. Shiverrig's fate has been altered. He is to live. As will the beast, Khalkoroth."

"I am owed blood. And I will have it!"

Dai-Ko-Zior walked to the unsteady body of Fritta. "Fine. If you must kill something, then satisfy your bloodlust on this one. He is meaningless to my masters."

Shiverrig knew what was coming, but the arrowhead still lodged in his thigh, and the throbbing pain in his back made him slow to react. Dai-Ko-Zior mumbled garbled words then grabbed Fritta by the rear neck molding of his cuirass and threw him with preternatural strength to Aeshmara's feet.

Dai-Ko-Zior pointed to a demon close to Aeshmara. "Bind these two and secure them in my tent until I call for them. We embark on a long journey soon."

The demon instinctively bowed to Dai-Ko-Zior but looked to Aeshmara for direction. Aeshmara sheathed her daggers. Her eyes lit with furious hatred. "Do it. And string this one up to one of those boulders." She pointed to Fritta. "Tie him tight to ensure his screams are loud enough to be heard all the way to Gathos."

Shiverrig and Khalkoroth were taken away and bound back-to-back to a pole in Dai-Ko-Zior's tent. The green mists within made the inside light unnaturally even and flat, creating a shadowless environment. The outside noise vanished as soon as the tent flap was sealed. The area was deathly calm.

Shiverrig clenched his jaw. Losing the First General was an unfortunate casualty, but at least he still lived, as did Khalkoroth.

"You have doomed us to a fate worse than death. Our bodies will be stretched and broken, but not before our skin is flayed and the jelly of our eyes are sucked dry by demon leeches," Khalkoroth wailed.

"Would you shut your snout and let me think of a way out of this?" Shiverrig said. He was surprised at the change of demeanor in Khalkoroth. No longer was bravado dripping from every word out of his needle-toothed mouth. *Was the pale demon genuinely fearful of what lay in store for them if they didn't escape?*

"You sound just like Daku," Shiverrig teased.

Khalkoroth pulled hard against the tent shaft, shifting the pole and pulling Shiverrig's wrists with it. The demon had heard Dai-Ko-Zior speak of his association with Xerthotha. Whether Khalkoroth believed the sorcerer or not, the dimwit would eventually fit the puzzle pieces together and realize Shiverrig's true intentions. And when that happened…

Shiverrig would worry about that later. First, they needed to escape the camp, and right now, that seemed unlikely. He was wounded and bleeding. The inside of the tent smelled like a crypt, filled with the stench of decomposing flesh and other dead things he did not want to imagine.

Thankfully, Khalkoroth wasn't complaining about his wounds, but Shiverrig knew the pale demon was suffering. They couldn't fight their way out, not in this condition and against the odds stacked against them outside. Stealth was their only option. But how? Shiverrig scanned the inside of the tent. The mist obscured every-thing, and the stench made his eyes water.

What is that smell? Spoiled meat? The odor was hard to describe as one foul scent layered over another. One thing was for sure; if he didn't escape and put an end to Sekka's plans, she would soon cover the Kingdom of Baroqia in a similar taint.

Shiverrig leaned his head back against the central shaft and noticed the supports along the tent's sides were resting on the stone surface of the ground.

"Khalkoroth, can you grab the pole with your hands?"

"Unfortunately, that's all I can grab. But if your neck were closer—"

"Shut up and pay attention. Grab the pole and stand up. If you can raise the tent high enough, I will slip the rope tying my hands under the bottom."

"And sacrifice me to the sorcerer? Not a chance. You'll suffer the same fate as me."

Shiverrig sighed. "Listen to me, you stupid brute. One of us needs to be freed first. My hands are lower on the pole. Just lift. I'll free you as soon as I find some-thing to cut your bonds."

"If this is a trick, I will find you, and no amount of pleading from Sess'thra will save you."

"Stop your yapping and just lift the bloody shaft."

Shiverrig heard Khalkoroth shimmy his legs under his bulk and grabbed the pole with his hands. The pale demon grunted. Shiverrig could feel the strain on the shaft as it shifted slightly upwards but then dropped back to its original spot.

"This is a stupid plan," Khalkoroth spat.

"Is that it? Is that all you have left? I overestimated the mighty Khalkoroth. You sound like Daku before the boy took your demon seed. Always whining like a baby."

Khalkoroth huffed. He grabbed the pole again, a deep growl resonated from his chest as he heaved upwards, taking the shaft up with him. "Daku is weak. Khalkoroth is strong."

I'm not so sure he's as weak as you say, thought Shiverrig. He rose with the shaft and wasted no time slipping his bound wrists under its bottom. He quickly stood and searched the tent for his weapons.

"Free me!" Khalkoroth whispered angrily. "I will rip out the throat of that miser-able Vyzyn sorcerer."

"Just a moment. Ah, here they are," Shiverrig said as he grabbed his sword and short dagger. He buckled his sheathed weapons to his waist and approached Khalko-roth. "Once I free you, we must work together if we are to survive. We cannot march out through the front flap of the tent and start spilling blood. Do you understand?"

"Free me." Khalkoroth strained against his bonds. "Khalkoroth will kill them all while the coward Shiverrig watches from the safety of the tent."

"Do you understand?" Shiverrig stood in front of Khalkoroth, his sword now in hand, and pointed at Khalkoroth, waiting for the pale demon to answer. Khalkoroth looked at the tip of Shiverrig's blade and then into his slate grey eyes.

"Khalkoroth understands."

"Good." Shiverrig sliced through Khalkoroth's bonds. "Now, I suggest we leave through a less obvious door. And don't take anything. The sorcerer will likely be able to track us."

He walked to the rear of the tent and carved an opening through the fabric. The cut drew forth an odd, bubbling substance as if the tent was bleeding.

Shiverrig pushed open the flap and peered outside. He immediately heard Fritta's terrible cries as he was tortured somewhere in the camp. Aeshmara's warriors shrieked in delight with every new torment delivered to the First General's body. It was dark, and a crescent moon gave little light. *Just enough to light our way and hide our escape.* He looked over his shoulder as Khalkoroth approached. The pale demon rubbed his wrists and clenched and unclenched his fists, which seemed oddly human.

"I shall have my day with the Vyzyn brood. They dare question my loyalty to Mistress Sekka," Khalkoroth muttered to himself.

"Come on," Shiverrig said quickly. "And try to be quiet." He raised the flap once more and investigated the area outside. All clear. Unfortunately, he couldn't risk rescuing Fritta. *His sacrifice will not go unavenged,* Shiverrig thought, but in truth, he didn't care.

Casualties were part of a war. Fritta's role was to serve, and now the event of his death served Shiverrig's escape. Bloodied and beaten, the two quietly snuck into the moonless night.

Shiverrig scrunched his nose and brought his hand to cover his mouth. The smell of the dead, rotting things within the tent was replaced by the stench of demons fouling the land. He cursed Maugris again. If that fool of a magician had not tampered with forces beyond his control, Shiverrig would certainly now be ruling over a clean and decent land.

Somehow, the pair managed to avoid the eyes of roving sentries. Shiverrig was impressed at Khalkoroth's stealth; the lumbering beast moved without making a sound. It wasn't a behavior the pale demon had exhibited before while in Gethem or Qaqal. Again, Shiverrig wondered at the rising influence of Daku. Apparently, the monk was still fighting for his soul deep within the body of the demon.

Once they were clear of the camp, Shiverrig surveyed the grounds ahead and noticed the trees grew thicker, maybe a mile away. "Come on. We'll take cover there and reassess our options," he said and led the way, hobbling down the rough terrain, taking time to use the sparse cover of the hillside when available.

Through some unholy miracle, they made it past the tree line. Shiverrig spotted a blueish-grey boulder nestled under an ancient oak with gnarled roots and directed Khalkoroth to follow. Panting, the two escapees hid behind the rock to catch their breath.

Once Aeshmara or Dai-Ko-Zior discovered them missing, they would send out search parties. Outrunning the demons was not an option without a horse, and the two couldn't fight and hope to win against such numbers. Khalkoroth offered no suggestions and remained uncharacteristically quiet.

"We must find the Knights of Gethem if we hope to survive this," Shiverrig said through deep gulps of air. His preternatural strength had waned with the silence of Jynxx. He pictured the demoness stamping her feet like a defiant child, standing in a harrumph with her arms across her chest.

She had siphoned away much of her demonic abilities after he had fed a portion of her essence to the Chaos Devil, Xerthotha. He couldn't fault the creature. Had he been in her position, he would have done the same.

Jynxx had a subtle and crafty way of influencing his judgment, and he blamed her for murdering that mewling, three-bodied creature known as the Three. She would know there would be punishment for tricking him. He glanced at Khalkoroth. Did the pale demon suspect his weakened condition?

"You can shadow walk us out of here," Shiverrig said.

Khalkoroth turned to meet his eyes. A cruel smile curled up the pale demon's lips. Then, his white snout rose quickly into the air. He inhaled a deep breath and stood fast, turning past Shiverrig and rounding the boulder.

"What is it?" Shiverrig said and readied himself for a fight. His leg throbbed from the arrowhead lodged in his flesh. Each step of their escape felt like the tip of a dagger, squirming like a beached fish in his thigh. He grimaced and slowly drew his sword.

"Khalkoroth, what do you smell? Tell me!" Shiverrig grew tense and watched the muscular back of the pale demon rise and fall. The arrow shafts had been removed from Khalkoroth by Aeshmara's soldiers, and the blood from the wounds had caked over his white fur.

"Your salvation." A purring voice came from behind him. Shiverrig spun clumsily to see Sess'thra's lithe figure saunter from the other side of the boulder. Her hips swayed from side-to-side, and a cocky smile lit her mouth. Her unbraided, black hair was a fussy mess as if she had just taken a tussle with a stable boy in the hayloft. She was dressed in soft-brushed, green leather pants and a thin, moss-colored top tied into a belt at her hip.

"You look awful," she said playfully.

"How did you find us?"

Sess'thra sighed as if the answer was obvious.

"We are eternally connected now. Or had you forgotten my embrace so quickly?" The succubus's lips pouted dramatically. Khalkoroth rumbled over to Sess'thra's side. He nodded in deference to the greater power before loping away.

The succubus had the look and nature of a young woman, but Shiverrig knew that was merely a glamour she wore when it suited her. She was an ancient creature who had risen to power, presumably over centuries of faithful service to Sekka. Although, Shiverrig wondered if Sekka was her first and only mistress.

"The half-breeds are dead. Do you bring extra horses? Where are my knights? We cannot stay here long," Shiverrig said.

"A horse? Sess'thra needs no horse," Khalkoroth said as he glanced over his shoulder and chuckled as if they shared a joke at Shiverrig's expense. Shiverrig frowned. He was never comfortable with the clandestine movement of the succubus, or any of the demons for that matter.

Sess'thra saw his displeasure. She snapped her fingers and disappeared. A moment later, she was standing atop the boulder. She snapped again and appeared at his side once more.

"Why didn't you free me from the camp?" Shiverrig said, exasperated.

"I was curious if you could manage on your own. And you did! Just as I had hoped." Sess'thra clapped her hands in excitement. "You never cease to amaze me, my wonderful Aj-Kahun."

Khalkoroth snarled and climbed to the top of the boulder. "You pick inappropriate times to play your games, succubus."

"Poor Khalkoroth. Did the mean sorcerer take away your shadows?" Sess'thra said and pretended to cry like a baby. Khalkoroth just scowled back at her.

"We must regroup with the Knights of Gethem," Shiverrig said, scanning the wooded area for them and hoping they would soon appear. "If we are quick, we should be able to reach them before Aeshmara knows of their position."

Sess'thra's purple eyes grew wide, and she grinned like a child who held a precious secret. She brought her hand to her mouth in a mock attempt to hide her smile. "Noisy knights go clang-clang in their shiny armor. Horses plod, plod, plod, and reek like tasty food. Neither remains hidden for long in a land filled with demonkind," Sess'thra sang in a melodic voice.

Shiverrig looked questioningly at the succubus. "Tell me straight. Where are my knights?"

"Oh, your knights are with you now and are scattered throughout these stunted trees. Look there. I see a piece of one now." Sess'thra pointed to an object half-covered in the dirt. It was a bloodied helm.

"Damn that Aeshmara to the coldest Circle in the Abyss!"

"That would be Gathos," Sess'thra said, teasingly.

"Serves them right. Inferior mortals." Khalkoroth said. His mood had turned grumpy.

The pale demon climbed to the top of the boulder and watched Shiverrig with cold, hollow eyes. It was difficult to tell in the dull darkness of the night what was mud, kicked up from the semi-wet dirt, and the demon's blood, for his fur was covered with black patch marks of caked-on debris.

"I need time to think," Shiverrig said, and moved to a solitary tree to attend to his wounds. He had more important things to concern himself with than the demon's pride. Nonetheless, he propped his sword against the tree as a precaution.

Sess'thra worked at removing the arrowhead from his leg. She gave her work all the playful attention a cat enjoys with a wounded mouse. Eventually, when her fingers wouldn't work, she used her dagger to dislodge the sharp piece of metal. With a flick of her blade, she freed the arrowhead into the air. A dark trail of blood followed.

At least it still looks red, Shiverrig thought. Though in the half-light, he couldn't be sure and quickly clasped his hand over the wound to stop the flow of blood.

Sess'thra stood over him and watched with fascination as blood seeped through the spaces between his fingers. She gingerly moved the dagger closer as if she would poke his hand to see the wound.

"Does it hurt?" she said and wet her lips with her tongue. The arrowhead had cut deep. If he didn't get proper medical attention soon, the injury would fester and most likely kill him.

"We must get to Gethem. We can regather our strength and mount a counteroffensive," Shiverrig said, doing his best to sound strong and confident.

"Perhaps you should rethink another confrontation against Sekka's forces," Sess'thra said, a thoughtful expression crossed her face.

"You deliberately walked us into a trap!" Khalkoroth spewed the words out of his mouth. The outburst had been building long before the arrival of Sess'thra. "Did the all-knowing Aj-Kahun not suspect the Frost Queen had spies throughout his cities?" Khalkoroth emphasized the title with contempt. His breath grew ragged as his ire rose.

"I needed to know what they knew, their strength of arms, and their intentions. If you had half a brain, you might understand my tactics," Shiverrig countered, doing his best to dress the wound. "As I suspected, Sekka is pursuing a singular agenda concerning the Sunnese. And I wanted to know why." Shiverrig took his attention from Khalkoroth and focused on tying off the makeshift bandage around his leg.

Khalkoroth slid off the boulder and landed silently on the forest floor. Then bounded across the short distance to Shiverrig. His pink eyes blazed red death as muddy leaves and fallen twigs flew behind him.

"I am finished listening to your clever lies. You mean to betray the Mistress!" The pale demon's ears were pinned back against his head, and his chest heaved with anger.

Shiverrig knew Khalkoroth would eventually challenge his strength but assumed it would arise sometime during the real campaign against Sekka. Unfortunately, it was happening now, and the opportunistic demon had taken the worst possible time to do so.

Shiverrig wished more of Daku's influence had surfaced before confronting Khalkoroth. But if it were to be now, then now would do. He grabbed his sword and thrust it forward, causing the pale demon to skid to a quick stop.

Khalkoroth panted with a predator's anticipation, knowing it had cornered wounded prey.

"Pretend time is over, mortal. It's long past time you understood who I truly am."

Shiverrig rose slowly and stepped away from the tree to increase his area of movement. His body was on fire with pain, but his mind remained battle-ready and calm. Khalkoroth stalked from side to side, watching for a better angle of attack.

"You are mistaken, Khalkoroth. I have known who you were from the beginning. You're just a lesser demon with delusional—"

Shiverrig barely registered the sweeping blow that sent him careening to the ground. The crack of his jaw echoed in his ears, while his thigh was an inferno of pain as he slid through loose leaves and sharp, icy dirt. He spat out blood and with it a chipped tooth. His lip was already swelling.

Shiverrig raised his hand to wipe away the blood and realized his sword was gone.

"Daku, if ever there was a time to make your presence known, it would be now," Shiverrig said. He pushed himself off the ground to a kneeling position, just as Khalkoroth slammed into him. The pale demon wrapped his mighty arms around Shiverrig's body and lifted him off the ground with ease. Hard claws tore into the chainmail links covering his back and ripped into flesh. The pain was excruciating. Khalkoroth dropped Shiverrig to the ground and leered at him with a wicked grin.

Shiverrig tasted dead leaves and dirt, then spat out more blood. "Jynxx! I need your strength!"

Khalkoroth brought his face down within inches of Shiverrig's and slowly shook his head. His laughed turned into a deep, rumbling growl and the stench of his breath made Shiverrig wince.

"Jynxx knows better than interfere. Daku is lost, and soon you shall know his misery," Khalkoroth said.

Shiverrig pushed Khalkoroth's face away and scrambled to the side, his hands dug into the frost shards of the cold dirt and came up bloodied. He knew Sess'thra was watching with keen interest, eager to see the outcome of the duel. Her loyalty and wanton desire only flowed toward power, plain and simple.

"Daku! If you are there, hear me!" Shiverrig shouted as loud as he could. The pain in his jaw shot stars into his eyes. "The name! I need the demon's true name!"

Khalkoroth lumbered closer. "The monk's mind is shattered. He cannot help... you." Khalkoroth's rough voice faded, and his body stumbled to a stop.

"I...I am here," the unsure and soft voice of a young man said. Sess'thra came to Shiverrig's side. "Now, that's interesting."

"Daku?" Shiverrig said with relief.

"Yes."

"Quickly, I must have the demon's hidden name. His true name."

"Hidden name?" Khalkoroth's entire body shook. His hands came to the sides of his head. "Aargh, he comes again. There's so much pain," Daku said in agony. "It hurts."

"Dammit, Daku! The name! Give me the beast's true name, and the pain will stop!"

Khalkoroth stared pink hatred beneath a furrowed brow into Shiverrig's eyes. "This ends now, Pretender King. The coward Daku has run away and hidden from my wrath. But I will find him. He cannot hide for long."

Shiverrig could not hope to best the rage of Khalkoroth. Jynxx had timed her revenge perfectly. Khalkoroth's arm shot out and grabbed Shiverrig by his chainmail shirt, ripping through the folded metal links. Sharp claws raked deep gashes into the muscles of his chest as Khalkoroth lifted him off his feet. Shiverrig grunted in pain as his blood flowed freely out of his body. The pale demon raised his other great hand high into the air.

"Daku," Shiverrig said weakly, raising his arms to fend off the next blow.

Khalkoroth's upraised hand paused for a moment above his head. The pale demon's pink eyes shifted side-to-side, and then he squinted his eyelids into tight slits. "No. This is not possible," Khalkoroth whispered in anger.

Shiverrig looked up to Khalkoroth's raised hand and then into the pale demon's face, whose eyes had turned dark brown.

"Tornalk'sukoroth," Daku's voice exhaled out of Khalkoroth's snout. "His true name is Tornalk'sukoroth. Please, free me. Hurry."

"In time, my young friend. You will not be forgotten," Shiverrig said as Khalkoroth's pink-eyed glare returned. The pale demon shook his head to clear the confusion of Daku's presence.

Shiverrig concentrated on Khalkoroth's true name and sent a warning into his mind.

+*Tornalk'sukoroth! See what awaits you if you lay your hands on me again.*+

Khalkoroth's pink eyes grew wild with fear. "What have you done? This cannot be," he whimpered.

+*Yes, it can. Now lower me to the ground. Easy does it.*+

Shiverrig pried the demon's fingers away from his shirt and stepped to the side. Khalkoroth dropped to his knees and covered his head with his arms and hands. "No more," he wailed.

Shiverrig spied his sword a few paces away and staggered to retrieve it. "You will obey me," he said in a hoarse voice, then looked questioningly at Khalkoroth. His eyebrows raised in anticipation of the pale demon's answer. "Yes?"

Khalkoroth nodded once, then sulked away like a beaten dog.

Shiverrig covered his ruined chest with his hand. The bandage on his leg had held, but he knew he was losing blood down his back. He would need a war surgeon's attention, and soon.

60

KASAI

Kasai wondered how much time had passed. The daylight never wavered, and he could not recall needing sleep. His time in Heaven was one long, lazy afternoon. Aetenos seemed to think so as well. The Great Monk had rarely shifted his position from under the large birch tree.

Orin had worn a path in the grass from his incessant pacing. "This isn't right." He shook his head, grumbling out the words. "The Kibo Gensai have been keepers of the faith for generations. Ever since that one vanished from the lands." Kasai watched Orin thumb his finger at the napping Aetenos. "We should be treated with respect, heroes even, but here we are, imprisoned like common thieves."

"Orin, this will all be worked out in time. Illyria will vouch for our honor," Pallo said. His brother Run-Run stood quickly from examining a trail of small ants cutting a path through the green grass and nodded enthusiastically. He pressed his index fingers and thumbs together to form a ring above his head and blew out an excited whistle.

"Come, Orin, sit with me, and reflect on the virtues of noble silence," Aetenos said. He gestured for Orin to join him on the ground.

"Please, do it. You're giving everyone a headache. Listen to the old monk. He's finally making some sense," Desdemonia said from the shade of another tree. She lay on her stomach with her arms cradling her head. Her hair was down and covered most of her face.

Orin stopped his pacing and pointed at her. "We should have left you behind."

"Then we would still be cold," Aetenos said. He propped his hands behind his head to be more comfortable. "I think we can all agree that it's more pleasant here. Now sit."

Run-Run became animated, pulling on his brother's sleeve, and pointed off to the right. Pallo peered in the same direction. "The animal spirits have returned."

Titus galloped towards the birch trees with Zhao Houzi riding on his back. His clothing was excessively formal. He wore a pleated vest of golden silk, with thin lines of orange thread striping the front. He wore the vest over a stiff, off-white, collared shirt. The shirt's sleeves puffed out as they reached his wrist.

His pants were of a decadent gold, darker and tapered at the ankle. Kasai saw the monkey even wore painful-looking shoes. The entire outfit seemed outrageously odd with his furry sticking out where it could.

"Well met, Soulless One," Zhao Houzi said with a cheerful smile. Titus nodded his large head in a respectful greeting but said nothing.

"Hello, Sir Zhao Houzi. I am happy to see you. Is there any news?" Kasai said.

"Your unique case has been discussed at length in the Cloud Court, and much has been decided. Things will happen quickly now."

"Is that good news?" Kasai asked. He looked to Desdemonia with concern. She rose but kept her hand at her brow, hiding her eyes from the sun.

Orin came forward quickly. "Finally! They have come to their senses. Come on, Pallo, Run-Run, it's time to go. We have fulfilled our duties and brought Aetenos home. Fetch our weapons, Monkey. I wish to be free of this prison without walls."

Zhao Houzi's smile became less enthusiastic. "I'm afraid it's a bit more complicated than that. Our escort will be along shortly."

Kasai smelled the scent of wet mulch in the air that comes before an approaching thunderstorm. Then spikes of lightning flashed to the ground, illuminating the trees and long grass. When the light faded, armored guards with folded wings stood around the copse of birch trees.

Residual electricity swam over the angels' polished armor. Their faces were serene, yet they carried no semblance of friendship. In unison, they leveled their halberds at the prisoners. The edge of their spear tips gleamed in the static light.

One of the angels stepped forward. Kasai recognized him as Gray'el, the commander of the Praetor Guard. "The Chancellor Pinnacle has summoned you to the Heavenly Hall in the City of Asher. You will come with us now."

The monkey fussed with his vest, trying to look as dignified as possible. "We shall gladly accept Lord Raguel's summons and accompany you and your honor guard to the Heavenly Hall."

"And what business is this of yours, Monkey?" Gray'el said as he raised a curious eyebrow.

Zhao Houzi pulled down at the corners of his vest. "The Lady Illyria has appointed me as the Heavenly representative of the demigod, Aetenos Sommai, and his Ever Hero, Kasai Ch'ou." Then he quickly added, "And all of their companions, of course."

Gray'el rubbed his chin. "This is highly irregular. My orders are to bring the prisoners. There was no mention of you."

"Surely, the archangel would not deny the prisoners fair and just counsel before they are sentenced. They know not our ways, and being mortal, have not the wit to understand the Heavenly Laws, nor the depths of their dark deeds."

"As you wish, Monkey. I have no desire to keep Lord Raguel waiting. He will sort you out along with the accused."

Zhao Houzi gave Kasai a reassuring smile, though the young monk wondered if things had taken a turn for the worse. A bright light filled Kasai's eyes, and with a sensational rush, he felt as if an unseen force catapulted him into the sky.

Then the sparkling city of Asher was before them. Kasai looked from right to left. The sprawling metropolis was endless. The city was filled with opulent structures, one more impressive than the next. Some buildings had creamy-blue, tiled roofs with cornered edges that curled upwards into the sky. Other buildings were roofed with red and yellow tiles of various sizes.

Kasai marveled at how anything so vast and majestic could exist. The cities of Gethem and Qaqal would be squalid city blocks by comparison.

An intricate roadway snaked through the fantastic buildings, connecting them for those who wished to enjoy a stroll in the constant afternoon sun. Straight trees of one kind or another, all immaculately pruned, lined each route. Their shiny leaves and flowering buds created painterly but purposeful lines of color throughout the city.

But for all the grandeur of the city, its colorful display of flora, and an ideal blending of architectural elements with the natural forms they emulated, it was dwarfed by an immense palace which rose from the base of the mountain and crept up its side. A tower rose from the center of the structure and spiraled up into the clouds.

"Unbelievable," Kasai said in awe. The castle was composed of repeating, cylindrically-shaped structures with fanned-edged roofs that also curled to the sky. He thought it interesting how some of the roof design resembled the buildings at the Monastery of Ordu.

But that was where the comparison ended, for this structure was not only colossal, it was also covered with intricate details, lined with gold and other precious metals and stones. Statues of angelic warriors and animal spirits graced the rooftops or sprouted from the stone walls.

Ordu now seemed a sad, distant memory; the burned down relic of a past life. Kasai wondered briefly if he would see Master Choejor here or any of the other Masters who had taught him at the monastery. *Maybe I'll see one of my dead Brothers who perished in the massacre. Where else would they go but here?* But in truth, he didn't expect to turn a corner and see his friend Cannonball, walking down the street, eating a sweet cake on the seventh and highest level of Heaven.

The sun remained overhead and never seemed to move, and if it did, it was slight. A cool breeze blew through the city, and Kasai was thankful for the respite from the noon heat.

Nonetheless, he felt clammy inside and his gut wouldn't settle. He looked to see if his companions were in similar discomfort. Desdemonia was beside him, as always. Her head was lowered again. Raven-colored hair fell in her face, shading her from the intense light. She had not taken the time to braid it or perhaps had no desire to keep it away from her face.

The Kibo Gensai were ahead of him. Orin continued to grumble, though no one cared to listen. Pallo remained pensive and rigid. Only Run-Run seemed to be enjoying the spectacle of the city.

The mute warrior's body turned in full circles, and his arms flashed about repeatedly, pointing out remarkable buildings or flying celestials to his brother. It was as if he hadn't a care in the world and their current predicament had no bearing on his mood.

Kasai heard the clacking of hooves approach from behind as Titus drew near. The magnificent steed wore bells the size of grapes in his mane, which chimed a pleasant melody as he trotted closer. But the horse remained silent. He watched

Kasai with intelligent eyes as if he was concentrating on putting together the pieces to a puzzle or solving a riddle.

"This is the city of Asher, and that magnificent tower is the Heavenly Hall," Zhao Houzi said from atop the black horse. "Asher was built upon the face of Mount Ajma when time was a babe in the Immortal Mother's arms."

Kasai looked again at the ancient marble edifice. The stone looked as if it had just been quarried, cut, and polished to perfection. He marveled at the design of the tower. It was stacked with repeating sections of alabaster stone, with brilliantly colored windows dotting the outer walls, their edges gleamed in the sunlight. Each part was then divided by an exquisite band, with curled-edged, tiled corners, which fanned out like flower petals along the perimeter.

Each band possessed an individual color, starting at the lower sections with dark violet and blending into indigo, then blue, green, yellow, orange, and eventually red at the top. Kasai thought the bands shifting subtly from one color to the next, moving slowly up the tower. But if he looked away and then back again, the pattern reverted to its original placement.

He noticed thousands of angels flying about the different sections of the tower. They soared from one location to another, rather than walking along the colorful, tree-lined roads.

Brilliant halos of gold, orange, and yellow glowed above their heads. Most seemed to be in a rush, with little conversation or friendly greetings to their aerial neighbors.

"They look like hornets gone haywire," Desdemonia said.

"Really? Hornets?" Kasai said. "Are you serious?"

"Wasps, then, if you prefer."

The monkey waved his arms about to encompass the entire city. "This is the administration hub of the Seven Heavens. The archangel, Lord Raguel, presides as the Chancellor Pinnacle. It's he who will act as the final judge over your case. You are being given a great honor."

"Is he the King of Heaven?" Kasai asked.

"No, although one might think Raguel would welcome the title," Zhao Houzi said with little enthusiasm.

"Monkey, you speak thoughts when your mouth should be still," Titus said in a disappointed tone.

"He's not wrong," Aetenos said from the rear of the group.

Zhao Houzi ignored his friend and the demigod. "We will enter Heavenly Hall there and proceed to the Cloud Court. This is where the most important affairs of mortals, celestials, and demons alike, are discussed and deliberated."

"And sentenced," Titus said. "Don't sugarcoat what is happening, Monkey. You should explain to the mortals the truth of their predicament. Do not give them false hope."

"The Cloud Court of Raguel is layered deep in tradition and procedure," Zhao Houzi said. "As I have said, much of your case has already been decided in private. Nonetheless, please, be on your best behavior. It can only help."

Kasai heard Aetenos speaking softly to himself. *Was the old monk chanting a mantra of courage or praying for salvation?* Kasai couldn't tell, but he doubted it was either of the two. He just hoped the Great Monk was putting a plan together that would help them win their freedom.

"Titus and I shall go ahead and secure the proper paperwork for admittance into the Cloud Court. Come along, Titus," Zhao Houzi said.

The horse and monkey entered the tower's massive entryway and were soon out of sight.

Kasai remained outside with the others, surrounded by the Praetor Guards. He noted slight veins of green and yellow woven through the alabaster stone blocks. White doves flitted from the eaves of the building, while majestic golden eagles soared on thermal updrafts along the sides of the tower.

The Heavenly Hall sat high above all other buildings. It was a stoic overlord, peering down on the entire city from its high perch, watching and judging those below.

"Master, do you have any idea what will become of us?" Kasai said to Aetenos, but the Great Monk remained lost in thought. "Master?"

"Huh? Yes, what is it?" Aetenos replied, although Kasai saw that he was intent on peering upwards and to the right, searching the sky.

"What shall become of us?" Kasai repeated.

"Hmm? I don't know. Tried and convicted of something, I'm sure, for that is the way of things here. What do you think? Heresy? Treason? Or both? I think both." Aetenos nodded in agreement to himself while still gazing upwards. "Beautiful creatures, those eagles. I should wish to come back as an eagle and soar as they do. Wouldn't you like to try your hand, or wing, at flying?"

"Master, I hadn't...never mind," Kasai said. He was in no mood for more of his master's riddles or pretending there would be a day he would fly like an eagle.

Eventually, Zhao Houzi and Titus returned. The monkey excitedly waved a fistful of papers in the air, looking triumphant as if he had successfully won a hard-fought debate on their behalf. "We are ready. All is in order."

"I'm worried about time, Des," Kasai said. "Every moment the Chaos Gate stays open, more innocent souls are lost."

"It seems the angels don't care much about that, do they? If it's not their concern, perhaps it shouldn't be yours," she responded sharply. Kasai looked at her, stunned. Desdemonia had been excessively moody ever since entering the Heavenly Realm.

"Excuse me, Sir Zhao Houzi. How much time has passed in our own realm since we arrived here? By my reckoning, we entered the Abyss only two days after Autumn's harvest moon and remained in Gathos for maybe a few days. I'm not sure how long we have been confined here since the sun never seems to set. Could a week have passed in total to bring us to today?"

"Oh no, Soulless One. Months have passed. Autumn has given way to Winter, and soon the snows covering the land in the Mortal Realm will thaw to Spring, if Sekka can be stopped that is. Otherwise, an eternal winter will fall over the lands of your home," Zhao Houzi replied, then returned to sorting the papers in his hands.

Kasai couldn't believe what the monkey had said. "We've lost so much time."

"There is an abundance of time, more than we need and less than we have," Aetenos chirped.

Kasai gave him an incredulous stare, and Desdemonia simply shook her head. Her hair fell about her head and cast her face back into shadow. Kasai pushed a deep breath out of his mouth.

"This is all my fault. If only I had listened to you, Des. If only we had just left Maugris's fortress when we had the chance."

"Stop saying that! What is done is done. Enough with your whining," Desdemonia snapped. Her hands were curled into fists. Then, she opened them slowly and appeared to collect herself. "You're all right, Des. Just stay calm," she said and exhaled a deep breath.

Then she looked at Kasai. "You did what you thought was best and followed your heart," she said and tried to smile. "And that is the best any of us can do in such times as these."

"The Wood Witch is right. The noble heart is an honorable guide," Aetenos added.

"But the people suffer because I was impulsive. I acted in anger. I wanted revenge for the death of Master Choejor."

"The lessons of life come in many different forms. This one you will not soon forget, I think," Aetenos said and patted Kasai on the shoulder.

Kasai walked on, staying in line with his friends. No, he would not forget this lesson for as long as he lived. *However long that might be,* he thought grimly.

"We should be marching in line with the angels, bringing just punishment to the damned and not walking as a gang of criminals. We are the Kibo Gensai, dammit!" Orin said.

"Everyone knows that already, Orin," Kasai said. But the angels didn't care to listen to Orin's constant griping, and neither did he.

61

DESDEMONIA

The Cloud Court was filled with spectators, sitting or standing in tiered balconies that rose to an impossible height. True-born angels, celestials, and spirit animals from each level of the Seven Heavens had come to witness the trial of the demigod and his mortal Ever Hero. The story of his mishap in the Abyss had been told and retold a hundred times, changing slightly with each iteration.

Voices, whispered from a thousand conversations, buzzed throughout the chamber. Many stared in shock and dismay as they heard the tale of Aetenos's journey into the Deep Dark, dragging with him hapless mortals at the behest of an archdevil, to do battle against her rival.

Desdemonia felt their judgmental eyes upon her, bearing down on her, condemning her without mercy or understanding. She overheard the words "evil witch" too many times.

Wasps, all of them, she thought. *And they're already convinced I kicked over their fragile nest.*

Seven winged judges robed in brightly colored frocks entered the grand chamber from separate doors. Each held their head high, commanding respect for their office and power from those gathered to watch the proceedings.

The din of the Cloud Court settled to a dull murmur as the judges ascended their individual stairs and reached a capped rotunda at the end of a circular platform. One by one, the judges bowed their heads to a final judge in magnificent golden robes with feathered wings the color of a rainbow. Then as one, their heads turned to Aetenos and the others. When their gaze landed on Desdemonia, she felt small and insignificant.

Aetenos stood to her left, and she heard him whistling a tune. It was a happy note, not loud enough to be disrespectful, but clearly one for amusement. Kasai fidgeted to her right as he shifted his weight from one leg to the other. The three Kibo Gensai stood in line behind them in silence. Thankfully, Orin had finally shut his mouth.

A judge draped in sage-colored robes stepped forward. His elderly hands gently found the railing of his rotunda. He waited for the noise of the crowd to subside and then addressed the accused.

"The monkey, Zhao Houzi, has provided the Cloud Court with a detailed account of your dealing with the archdevil, Sekka, the creation of a Chaos Gate, and your trespass into the Abyss. Your testimony has been recorded in the angelic archives."

"Testimony?" Orin cried. "We were never questioned or consulted by that foolish monkey, or anyone else for that matter. We have been kept in isolation since our arrival."

Zhao Houzi joined the group and stood in front of Aetenos. He seemed incredibly proud of himself. "I told the story as best I could. Very daring of you, and brave beyond measure! Truly a story for the ages."

Aetenos gave a slight bow of his head as a respectful acknowledgment of the monkey's kind words. Then Desdemonia followed Zhao Houzi's eyes past Aetenos and on to Orin behind her. "Now, please be polite. It is our time to listen, not to speak," he said.

"Orin be respectful and consider where you are," Pallo said sternly.

The judge draped in ivory robes came to the railing of his rotunda. His voice resonated as a sweet melody throughout the chamber. It seemed to Desdemonia that a choir of a hundred voices sang out the words instead of them coming from a single mouth.

"Orin Wyeth of the Kibo Gensai, you have been charged with heresy, collaborating with the enemy, and assisting in the creation of a Chaos Gate, a device of diabolical nature which bypasses the sacred Amaranthine Barrier, allowing the denizens of Gathos to run free in the Mortal Realm. How do you plead?"

"I didn't help create the Chaos Gate! I tried to prevent it! I am not a heretic! I am Kibo Gensai! Does no one here know what that means?" Orin shouted back. The crowd gasped.

Zhao Houzi turned and looked squarely at Orin, and his finger to his mouth. "Shh, too much talking. You need only answer the question as guilty or innocent."

"Innocent!" Orin said.

Next came the bronze robed judge. "Pallo Katan of the Kibo Gensai, you have been charged with heresy, collaborating with the enemy, and assisting in the creation of a Chaos Gate. How do you plead?"

"Innocent, your honor," Pallo raised his head with dignity. The older warrior spoke in a clear voice, filled with respect for the judges and honest sincerity for his part in the Chaos Gate catastrophe. Desdemonia always liked him and would miss his stern looks and bushy eyebrows.

"Veers Katan of the Kibo Gensai," the crimson robed judge looked down upon Run-Run. Then his hands flashed in intricate movements. Run-Run responded back with hand gestures of his own. "Let it be recorded in the angelic archives that the accused has answered 'innocent' to the crimes of heresy and collaborating with the enemy."

Run-Run flashed his hands again.

"Let it also be recorded that the accused wishes to be named Run-Run, and not Veers, in the angelic archives," the judge said with a frown, then took a step back and placed his hands within the folds of his sleeves.

Run-Run looked at his brother with a broad smile.

The next judge to step forward was clad in vermillion robes. Swirls of yellow spiraled up his sleeves. Desdemonia Mishi," the judge said her name with obvious disdain rather than the melodic sounding voices from the other judges. "You are charged with heresy and conspiring with evil to create a living Chaos Gate. You have also willingly mixed your blood with the blood of Sekka, a notorious archdevil and ruler of the Seventh Circle on the Third Layer of the Abyss, named Gathos Wastelands of the Weeping Winds. Your blood will forever be tainted by her poison. How do you plead?"

"Oh, I'll tell you exactly how I plead," Desdemonia said and stepped forward from the group. She brushed the tussled, jet-black hair from her face and glared back at the angel. She pointed her finger at her accuser and then to each judge in turn.

"Seven arrogant birds standing in judgment of us from your lofty perch, condemning innocent souls without thought or care. You're supposed to represent all that is good in the Three Worlds. But it seems the stories of your great deeds and forgiving nature are lies. All that matters to you is your silly ideal of perfection. Well, it's flawed! You're flawed! You're no better than the demons we killed in the Abyss."

The crowd erupted with shouts of outrage and gasps of astonishment.

Desdemonia continued, "What do you know of the truth? You weren't there. You didn't have to make that horrible choice! I won't deny what I have done. Yes! One of Sekka's onyx rings sits on my finger and will not come off unless by my death."

She let the words linger for a moment, then raised her hand into the air for the spectators in the Cloud Court to see. "There it is. Look at it and see that it's real."

Then she turned to Kasai and whispered, so only he could hear her. "And I would choose to do it again, knowing it would protect the one I love from certain death and save my heart from breaking."

Then her voice returned in anger, and she spun to face the judges. "Who are you to tell me otherwise?"

The judge in vermillion robes held his hands in the air to quiet the crowd. A hush fell over the chamber.

"Once again, how do you plead, Wood Witch?" he said, unmoved by her outburst.

"What does my answer matter to you? I was born a witch and therefore guilty of *something*. Your accusations are the same as the ignorant mobs in Baroqia, who tied my kind to stakes and watched them burn. For witches have only one place, and that's the Abyss."

The judge glared down at her. "If you do not respond to the question, I will presume your answer is guilty."

"I am innocent in the eyes of love," Desdemonia said. Her defiance faded, and her heart sank. There would be no leniency for her. She knew she was a goner.

"Kasai Ch'ou," came a booming voice from the judge wearing cerulean and emerald robes. "You have forfeited your mortal soul to the foundation of a Chaos Gate. You have trespassed in a forbidden land and abetted an archdevil in a war against her foes. You are responsible for the loss of countless innocent souls sacrificed to the Deep Dark, souls that would have rightfully come to the Seven Heavens in time.

"Also, a pending investigation is in effect to determine if the blood of this mortal is tainted from any dubious liaisons with the succubus, Sess'thra. If found to be true, there will be an added sentence to the verdict today."

"Des, I never," Kasai said.

"I know," she said. "That's not you."

"Kasai Ch'ou. How do you plead?"

Kasai stepped forward and bowed in deference to the judges. "My companions are indeed innocent of the crimes you accuse them of committing."

"I am not interested in your interpretation of the Laws of Heaven. How do you plead?" the judge said.

"My lord, it's true, I unwittingly fell into the trap laid by Sekka. The creation of the Chaos Gate was my fault. And yes, I willingly fought Sekka's enemies to save the lives of my friends. I am guilty of these crimes.

"I wish I could take back every step since leaving the Monastery of Ordu. But again, honor dictated I save the life of my Master and warn the other monasteries of the same danger. If I had died with my Brothers at Ordu, none of this would have happened. I will accept whatever punishment is handed to me for my actions."

"Kasai, no! Don't say anymore. You did what was right and what was needed to be done," Desdemonia shouted. She glared at the judges. "We all did what needed to be done."

"The accused admits his guilt," the cerulean robed angel said and stepped back. The six angels that had spoken then turned their heads to the last judge, clad in shimmering gold. Lord Raguel, the Chancellor Pinnacle, stepped forward into the light. He removed the hood of his robe. His skin was perfect.

"And lastly, I call the accused, Aetenos Sommai, Ascended Monk of the Four Pillars of Light, Thirty-Third General of the Heavenly Legions of Arcadia. Hero of the third demonic invasion of the Mortal Realm, known as the first Frost War, and self-proclaimed Defender of the Mortal Realm, to bear witness to his crimes." Raguel notably frowned after reciting the list of titles and honors given to the demigod.

"You have been charged with squandering your divine soul, a heavenly gift without measure, to the archdevil, Sekka, whereby giving her a crucial component to the creation of a living Chaos Gate. How and why you were in the Abyss in the first place is a mystery we will unravel later.

"Due to your incessant meddling in the affairs of mortals, you have disrupted the lives of countless humans, altering their paths and increasing the likelihood of their admittance into the Seven Heavens. The acceptance of marginal souls into the ranks of Heaven only serves to lower the strength of our righteous might against the powers of evil. You know this, and yet you continue to disobey direct orders to the contrary.

"You have shown blatant disregard to this court and its strict guidelines of distribution of divine power. You have been warned on numerous occasions that the creation of your so-called Ever Heroes was forbidden. Yet before us stands your latest endeavor; a boy raised in a sequestered monastery, naïve to the dangers of the world outside its walls, and barely a hint of knowledge of the power he wields or how to use it. It's no wonder his soul was lost to the archdevil and the trappings of Chaos.

"Aetenos Sommai, how do you plead against the charges leveled against you?"

"Good day to you, Chancellor Pinnacle. You are looking well, my friend. I have done all these things and more. For what is more important than protecting the soul of an innocent? The newborn souls of mortals are akin to toddlers and must be nurtured and guided, for they are ignorant to the outer realms. Within them are the seeds for greatness, but alas, so many are tempted to darker paths and fall the way of destruction. We must encourage the light to flow freely from them, not extinguish it before it's lit. If these are crimes, then yes, I am guilty."

"Your presence here openly mocks this court and the designs of the Great Balance set forth by the Immortal Mother."

"My dear Raguel, I believe she had something quite different in mind. I feel you have lost sight of her greater plan. You see, everything changes, for nothing can remain static. The Mortal Realm has advanced over these long years. It has grown!"

The courtroom erupted with hollers of condemnation for the old monk.

"Blasphemy!"

"He is possessed by Chaos!"

"The devil has him!"

"Burn him!"

"The laws are set and eternal! Aetenos has been seduced by the Wood Witch and acts as her slave."

"Burn them both!"

Aetenos paid the rabble-rousers no attention. "Be the beacon, Raguel, not the storm. Guide the mortal souls to the greatness that awaits them. They will never take the place of the True-borns. They only wish to share in the divine splendor of the Immortal Mother's gifts."

Desdemonia watched as Raguel's hands tightened around the banister of his rotunda.

"Aetenos Sommai, you are found guilty of treason against the Laws of Heaven and heresy for aligning your divine soul with the powers of Darkness. You and your companions are sentenced to die." Raguel stared down at Aetenos. A satisfied smile curled up his lip.

Aetenos bowed in acceptance of the sentence and turned his head to Kasai. "See? I told you, didn't I? It was both."

Desdemonia rolled her eyes. *The man is a dunderheaded fool.*

"The Cloud Court is adjourned." Raguel and the other judges turned to leave.

"A moment of your time, please," Zhao Houzi said. However, the judges continued to walk towards their private rooms.

"A moment of your time, good sirs," the monkey shouted. He put his hands on his hips and sighed. "They never listen to the monkey."

Zhao Houzi leaped into the air and hovered at the same level as the judges, but respectfully keeping lower than Raguel. The outline of his body glowed with an unnatural, orange light.

"A moment, please." His voice rang out like a banged gong banged. Raguel turned back to the center of the chamber. Clearly irritated at the disturbance.

"He sure is a polite little fella," Desdemonia said.

"Some help it did us. That monkey can take his politeness and—"

"Orin! Remember who you are! You will not dishonor the Kibo Gensai with your disrespectful words," Pallo said.

"What does it matter now? We're going to die," Orin said.

Desdemonia tuned out the bickering men and listened more closely to what was being said overhead.

"Monkey, I will have you barred from this courtroom for a hundred years if you utter another outburst. Your presence here was a courtesy to Lady Illyria. Lower the volume of your voice, or I shall do it for you." Raguel spoke with strained patience.

"It's true, I am but a humble monkey spirit, and have no right to ask anything from one, or any, of the astute and honorable judges of the Seven Heavens." Zhao Houzi waved his hands to gather the attention of the other judges. Some of the spectators in the chamber stopped became quiet, others returned to their seats.

Somehow, the monkey had piqued their interest. *Not just polite, but clever*, Desdemonia thought. *This trial is not over yet.*

Raguel sighed audibly. "I warn you. Do not bring dishonor to yourself by wasting more of the Court's time."

"Thank you, Chancellor Pinnacle. I will be quick."

"Speak then, Zhao Houzi." Raguel waved his hands for the monkey to continue.

Zhao Houzi cleared his throat. "What are we all striving to create?"

Raguel frowned once more. The feathers of his wings ruffled as they settled into place on his back. "We do not strive for anything, for we have achieved the ultimate state of being. The Seven Heavens are perfect."

"And what of love?"

"What does love have to do with anything?"

"It's a simple word, is it not? Four small letters, but so important. It can be heavy as the greatest boulder and then again, light as a feather. What other thing has these properties?"

"Explain yourself."

"I ask you, Chancellor Pinnacle, what is the value of Paradise if we sacrifice love for perfection? Consider the gardens of Elysian. They are marvelous, are they not? The colors are so vibrant. They dazzle my eyes with such wonder and beauty as I walk along the sandy paths."

"They are perfect," Raguel said. "Your point?"

"My point is, one does not strike the entire garden if one presumes a weed has grown in its soil. We must consider the whole of each of the accused before rendering such dire sentencing."

"Their sins are extensive. You make a poor point. Their sentence remains," Raguel said. He dismissed Zhao Houzi and turned away. "You would be wise to abandon this matter."

A light as bright as the noonday sun filled the chamber. "How will you know if the weed is a not flower in disguise when you refuse to give it a chance to blossom?"

The voice was pure and kind. Desdemonia instinctively shut her eyes from the harsh light. It was unbearable. She brought up her hands to cover her face, but it did little to soothe her pain.

"It's Illyria," Kasai said in awe.

Desdemonia slowly opened her fingers and squinted against the light. There she saw a beautiful angel with long flowing hair hovering next to Zhao Houzi's small frame. She was glorious, but the sight of her still made Desdemonia feel sick.

Illyria's thick blonde tresses cascaded over her shoulders like a waterfall of satin cloth to the base of her back. The white shift she wore was lost within the illuminating light, pulsing from her body.

The silhouette of Zhao Houzi spun in the air and looked straight at Desdemonia. She thought maybe the monkey had just winked at her. Voices within the crowd rose from shocked whispers to shouts of worship. Others were notably disappointed. The arrival of Illyria appeared to cast suspicion with many of the spectators in the chamber.

"Do you still know the feeling of love filling your heart, my lord Raguel?" Illyria said as she hovered in place, waiting for the Chancellor Pinnacle to answer. "Or is your heart solid as stone?"

"Lady Illyria," Raguel spoke the name with masked devotion. He was notably moved by her presence. "Judgment has been passed. The accused must answer for their crimes."

"You know our little monkey is right. Let the mortals prove they are flowers and not weeds. Their intentions have been towards the greater good of their realm. For once, forgo rules and regulations and see through the eyes of love."

Zhao Houzi looked up at the shimmering angel with loving devotion. Illyria returned his gaze and patted the top of his furry head, then she turned back to Raguel. "Is there truly no hope for the Wood Witch? Does one mistake in judgment erase countless forays into battle against evil? It was fear of losing her true love that caused her misguided decision, and not an evil, hateful heart."

Raguel stiffened as Illyria's words shot through him like an arrow. "What of my loss?"

Serves him right, Desdemonia thought.

"The Heavenly Laws must be upheld." Raguel fumbled through the words as he tried to regain his composure.

Desdemonia watched as the other judges returned to their posts. Each looked to the other from across the chamber's floor. She wondered if they were silently communicating together over the murmur of the crowd.

Illyria floated closer to Raguel's rotunda. She reached her hand out for his. Hesitantly, he gave it to her. "Raguel, what would you do for love if the Wood Witch's choice was yours to make instead?"

"Illyria, you go too far. Do not ask this of me." His powerful voice was still shaky.

"But I will ask, nonetheless. There are many variances to the Great Balance, even within the state of perfection."

"Follow the Lady Illyria. Give the Wood Witch a chance!" someone yelled from the upper mezzanine.

"A chance at redemption!" came from the opposite side of the chamber."

"The chance Artiya'il never received!"

"Redemption! Redemption! Redemption!"

Raguel regarded the spectators remaining in the chamber. A worrisome expression shadowed his face.

"I propose a Challenge of Righteousness be given to the accused," Zhao Houzi spurted out the words and jumped higher into the air as if he was still on firm ground. Raguel scowled at the monkey's antics. His eyes blazed for a moment, then soften as a thin smile crossed his lips.

"A Challenge of Righteousness, you say?"

Zhao Houzi floated down to the floor and stood between Kasai and Desdemonia. He took each of their hands in his. "Yes. Let them prove their innocence. Let love be their judge."

The monkey masterfully played to the crowd. He gazed up at Desdemonia and gave her a smile. "Polite and clever is right."

"How did you—" Desdemonia stammered.

"Shh…" Zhao Houzi said. He half rocked, half swung between Kasai and Desdemonia like a child holding his parents' hands.

Raguel looked squarely into Illyria's eyes. Desdemonia could not tell if she saw acceptance or resignation on the Chancellor Pinnacle's face. Raguel peered out to the crowds as the chant of "redemption" repeated throughout the chamber. His brilliant wings mirrored his arms as they extended into the air and settled the spectator's voices. When all was quiet, he peered down at the accused.

"The Divine Daughter of the Immortal Mother is right, and there is honor in Zhao Houzi's words. The Laws of Heaven are set to bring harmony and stability to our eternal lives and peace to all the realms. But woe the day that we become blind to what is right and wrong due to such strict obedience to the written word. I will grant the opportunity for redemption."

The crowd of spectators was split between shouts of encouragement and disapproving gestures. Illyria nodded approvingly to Raguel, and Desdemonia saw the Chancellor Pinnacle's face soften, but only for a moment. Then his expression hardened.

"The accused must destroy the evil they have raised from the Abyss. Sekka must die. A time limit of one mortal year shall be in effect to complete this task. Failure to fulfill the Challenge of Righteousness will result in immediate death to those sentenced. I have spoken."

Raguel turned and left the chamber. The other judges followed his lead.

62

SHIVERRIG

Shiverrig's body shook from deep chills on the cold forest floor. Light snow had fallen around his makeshift shelter. Hundreds of voices called to him in his fever driven dreams. There were too many to count, but each one distinct and distracting him from needed sleep. They whispered in his thoughts or sent shrieking wails through his skull.

+*What have you done to yourself, my Golden Boy?*+
+*If you let me in, I can save you. Hurry.*+
+*Just a bit more is all I need.*+
+*The pain will stop.*+
+*YOU WILL BE A GOD!*+

Shiverrig woke with a start. He instinctually rose, but the pain from his wounds sent him back to the unforgiving ground. He was burning up. A flash sweat covered his body, and in the next moment, he was shivering again.

He stared into the pine branches woven together above his head. The pungent smell of seeping sap made him think of happier times when he hunted elk or bear in similar woods. Now he was the animal being hunted.

Another voice entered his mind. It snuck through memories and hid in the shadows between thoughts. Shiverrig felt its fear.

+*I warned you! Now you shall destroy us both,*+ Jynxx whispered in his head. +*I will try to shield you from Xerthotha, so you can think clearly, if only for a moment. Listen closely, mortal. There is no time for debate. You must give me your soul, or forever will you be a pawn to the Chaos Devil. But time is short. I must have it now. Give it to me. Hurry!*+

+*HOW DARE YOU!*+ A baritone voice raced to the forefront of Shiverrig's thoughts and exploded in his mind. The pain was excruciating. He brought his hands to his temples and squeezed the sides tight for fear that his head would split in half.

+*THERE IS NOTHING YOU MAY HAVE OF MY GOLDEN BOY.*+

Shiverrig was delirious. He pawed the air of his imaginary sight, trying to ward off specters that loomed before him.

Xerthotha's voice pounded into his mind. *+BUT I WILL SAVOR EVERY MORSAL OF YOUR ESSENCE, TOKOLOSHEJYX. SO SWEET. SO TENDER.+*

Shiverrig heard what sounded like a distant, wailing bird in the recesses of his mind. Then, it turned into the high-pitched scream of a prisoner being pulled apart on one of his torturers' racks.

Xerthotha laughed heartily as he ripped the essence of Jynxx from Shiverrig's body. Spots appeared before his eyes and his body shook with uncontrollable spasms. He felt hollowed out from the absence of the demon, as if his internal organs had withered to husks and then turned to ash, leaving his chest an empty cavity.

Then Shiverrig felt the slippery substance of another essence oozing into him and filling the void. It was massive and threatened to rip the seams of his being apart. But then the sensation changed to something altogether pleasant. The pain from his wounds faded, and his body remained still.

"You will not have me," Shiverrig said. But his protest was weak. He had lost too much blood, and with it the will to fight the Supreme Devil's control. The shadows crowded around the shelter as he drifted into a welcome unconsciousness. Or so he thought.

His eyes flashed open to a world turned inside out. It twisted and morphed into an advanced civilization, filled with buildings that rivaled the size of mountains, displaying incredible feats of architectural design and making the City of Spires look like drip sandcastles at the beach.

The world was then invaded by an endless army of malformed creatures, swarming over the buildings like a marauding colony of ants. They vomited mucus from their extended mouths over everything they touched, which bubbled and boiled then ignited to flames. Soon a raging inferno burned everything to cinders and with it the creatures who started the blaze.

Purple grass grew from the rubble, followed by greenish bushes and mustard yellow trees. Soon, Shiverrig was in the middle of a thriving forest and then a dank jungle. The tall trees thrust out thick branches in an overlapping canopy filled with leaves and long needles.

Vines with sharp brambles snaked around the mustard yellow trunks and disappeared in the dense ceiling overhead. Weird looking predators stalked lesser beasts for food, pouncing on defenseless animals and devouring them without thought.

No sooner had the jungle reached a point of over-abundance when the ground underfoot turned red and began to congeal into a syrupy slime. The tangled forest and its inhabitants melted like sticks of wax into a lake of ooze, which then froze solid. Its surface was as smooth as a sheet of new glass.

Miraculously, Shiverrig was untouched by the endless cycles of change. He remained a singular spectator to a world where centuries washed past his eyes in seconds. The otherworldly landscape continually morphed from one epoch to another. Then Shiverrig saw someone or some*thing* approach. It was difficult to tell from such a distance.

The form tossed and spun in the billowing wind until it set on the churning landscape. Its shape changed to a small child, maybe five or six years of age, who stopped ten paces from him.

The child was dressed in a formal, white gown worn by royalty at family functions. Small gems sparkled in the off-light of the changing world.

"Welcome to my humble realm, Aj-Kahun Shiverrig," the child said. Her voice was high and sweet. She had small hands that just peeked out of elaborate cuffs and a delicate face with short-cropped, platinum-blonde hair. Her green eyes carried the weight of ancient knowledge.

Shiverrig remained silent. Was this a dream or a bizarre new reality caused by the presence of the Chaos Devil?

"This is not a dream, nor is it a reality, my Golden Boy. It's the razor's edge that separates our realms," the child said.

"Why have you brought me here?"

The girl tilted her head to the side as if confused by his question. "Why? Because you are dying or did you not know?" the girl said. "And there is much we must still accomplish. You have yet to reach your potential."

The child's eyes rolled back into her head, leaving only the white sclera staring back at Shiverrig. Wisps of black smoke rose from their corners, slowly at first but then with much more strength. Her platinum-blonde hair rose into the air as if blown by an unseen force from below and then ignited into orange flame.

She began to grow. The gown melted off her body, while her naked form changed from a small, innocent girl to a seductive woman with wide hips and full breasts. Bright-red flames licked up her body from her ankles to her head.

Ice debris blew up from the ground and whipped around her new, shapely body. The ice collected into larger chunks and slammed into her from all sides. A cloud of steam engulfed her body and clouded his vision. When the vapors cleared, the woman was encased in ancient, red armor, akin in style to the protective gear the Shiverrig Clan of his ancestors wore when they tamed the wilds of Baroqia.

Her armor consisted of a finely polished, hinged iron cuirass, helmet, and iron mask in the shape of a snarling lion. Shiverrig could clearly see this design was less cumbersome than what his own knights donned and maximized the soldier's ability to move quickly in battle.

A divided skirt, suspended from the breastplate, allowed the wearer to twist, turn, or jump from a horse while affording protection for the hips and thighs. Completing the suit were shoulder guards, arm covers, thigh armor, and shin guards.

The figure before him wore no boots, and the black claws of her red feet scratched into the now smooth, icy surface of the ground.

"Are you real?" Shiverrig's thoughts blurred in a fog of confusion. The woman opened her arms, ready to embrace him.

"Quite real, my Golden Boy. I am all and everything at once."

"Xerthotha," Shiverrig said through now parched lips. The air was cold and dry, though he felt beads of sweat forming across his forehead.

The armored woman gave a curt nod of her head. "The same."

Her molded breastplate was emblazed with a masculine figure holding a great sword in his right hand, and in the left was a long chord, which strangled two colossal deities. Shiverrig assumed the painted figure held Azrollorza and Morrdilliax as slaves tied to his rope.

The painted figure's body was a duplicate of the live version of Xerthotha standing before him. The armor was flawless in every way, and its full effect was a unique combination of delicacy and brutality. Oddly, Shiverrig was reminded of Sess'thra's aggressive lovemaking. The act left him cut, bruised, and panting with exhaustion, and always desiring more.

A buzzing swarm of black bugs appeared and circled the warrior woman. Each landed on her body and crawled between the small openings in her armor, though she seemed not to notice. Her smoking eyes remained locked on his. She took a step forward, arms still extended and flexing armored fingers tipped with claws.

Shiverrig suddenly felt uncertain of Xerthotha's intentions.

"What do you want of me, Changeling?" Shiverrig said, holding his ground, for what it was worth in this strange dimension. He reached for a sword that was not there.

The woman warrior's snarling lion mask smiled back at him with a wicked grin. "I intend to save you." Her next step brought her intimately close to him as if they shared the same breath, then she was gone.

Shiverrig smelled pine sap. He was cold, and his body ached against the hard ground. But the pain was superficial and felt more like muscle soreness after a rigorous sparing session, rather than the intense suffering caused by mortal wounds.

He placed a hand on his chest, tracing the location where Khalkoroth's claws had drawn blood. The swelling had miraculously subsided under the bandages.

Shiverrig slowly opened his eyes to see Khalkoroth's large snout inches away from his forehead. The pale demon sniffed his skin and then the air around his head. Khalkoroth jerked back in disgust and then snarled menacingly.

"The stench of the Chaos Devil reeks from your pores," Khalkoroth said. His pink eyes bore into Shiverrig. "The Vyzyn sorcerer did not lie. You have doomed us all." The words came out in an accusatory hiss. Khalkoroth's lips quivered in plum-colored anger just before he lunged.

Stupid beast, Shiverrig thought, and moved with uncanny speed, leaping out of Khalkoroth's path. The pale demon spun back around and lashed out with his claws. Again, missing his mark. Shiverrig's heart pounded against his chest like an iron fist breaking through a stone wall.

Then an impossible sounding voice rang from Shiverrig's throat. It was many voices, speaking, whispering, and shouting at once. Shiverrig felt a surge of air blast up from his chest and out his mouth. "TORNALK'SUKOROTH!"

Khalkoroth's limbs locked fast, and his momentum carried him face forward into the semi-frozen ground. Loose leaves sprung into the air and scattered around the pale demon's body.

Shiverrig stepped closer. "Have you already forgotten the punishment that comes with disobedience?" He tapped the circlet on his head with his first two fingers. "I was saving the reveal of my allegiance for a more productive time, but it seems you have forced my hand."

"You will be ruined. The Chaos Devil will consume you," Khalkoroth mumbled. His body was held in place from the neck down, and he managed only to glare up at Shiverrig. Then the pale demon laughed. "You're insane."

"Yes, I'm quite sure you're right," Shiverrig said. "I should slay you like the animal you are, but I suspect there is useful material here, especially under the surface."

He took the circlet off his head and spun it between the fingers of both hands. "I wonder what would happen if you wore this? Hmm?"

"If what? What is that? What are you doing? Stop!" Khalkoroth tried in vain to keep the circlet from his head. "Traitor! Do not touch me with that loathsome thing."

"You should be more thankful, Khalkoroth, when someone gives you a gift," Sess'thra said.

Shiverrig placed his knee on the back of Khalkoroth's neck to hold the pale demon still. He then lowered the circlet over Khalkoroth's head and watched it miraculously grow to mold itself into a snug fit around the demon's skull.

Khalkoroth howled in pain. His agony echoed through the trees. "Shh, you'll give away our position," Shiverrig said, though he didn't really care. He was enjoying every minute of it.

Then, Khalkoroth went quiet. The demon's body shuttered once and was still. Shiverrig waited for a few heartbeats and then stood up.

"Daku?"

The pale demon opened his eyes. The flaring pink irises slowly turned deep, dark brown.

"I am here." Daku slowly rose to his feet. He looked upon his bestial body and flexed his arms. One corner of his mouth curled up in a smirking grin.

"How do you feel?" Shiverrig inquired.

"I have the worst headache. But I'll live." Daku's voice was shaky, and it retained a hint of Khalkoroth's deeper resonance.

"I believe you will," Shiverrig said. "Interesting that your body has not changed back to its original form."

"I suppose with enough effort, I could manage that, but the demon's body suits me." Daku opened and curled his fists. "And I favor the accessories that come with it."

Shiverrig heard slow clapping to his left. He turned to see Sess'thra standing ten paces away. Her head and shoulders were dusted with snow. She stood in a serpentine pose, with one hip jutted out to the side.

"I remain impressed. You are so full of surprises, my wonderful Aj-Kahun." She looked admirably at Daku. "And our young monk finally has proven worthy of his promised reward. I didn't think the boy had it in him."

Daku came forward aggressively with a low growl rumbling from his throat.

"You tricked me," he said, pointing a clawed finger at the succubus.

"Naturally," Sess'thra replied. She glanced at her nails and removed a bit of dirt from them. "It's what I do."

Daku touched the circlet on his head. "This is a handy item. But know this, it was only a matter of time before I beat the demon and regained control."

"It was the circlet. Nothing more," Shiverrig said.

"I had a plan, and it was working!" Daku said defensively.

"I'm sure," Shiverrig said with disinterest. "Perhaps another time, you can tell me the story of your assumed victory."

"I'd like to hear his tale. You must admit, there were times when the boy's influence came to the surface. I have never known of a mortal able to best one such as Khalkoroth. Please, big boy, indulge me with your story," Sess'thra purred.

"With or without the help of the circlet, I would not be Khalkoroth's forever."

"Go on," Sess'thra smiled.

"My consciousness was shrouded in darkness..."

"This sounds exciting!" Sess'thra clapped her hands together gleefully.

"Don't encourage him. Just get on with it, Daku," Shiverrig said as he readied his gear.

Daku cleared his throat and started over. "The will of Khalkoroth bore down on my mind. I was held tight in a prison of darkness.

"There were times when the demon's presence was more persistent than usual. It saturated me in its foulness, clouding my senses and thoughts. I assumed something unfortunate had happened to him in the material world, and he wanted to punish me."

"Our young monk is quite a storyteller," Sess'thra said.

"Maybe he should write a book," Shiverrig said.

"Hush!" Sess'thra scolded. "Please, go on."

Daku curled his lips at Shiverrig, then continued. "There was no escape. I was alone and drowning in a sea of misery. There was nothing to cling to for safety and nowhere I could hide. The demon was right. Escape was not possible, and I was lost.

"There was something significant about that word, and I repeated it again, *possible*. The sound of it echoed in my mind. It took shape as a glimmer of light, though nothing more than a distant sliver. *Possible*. The word tried to slip away like a wriggling fish. *Possible. Possible. Possible.*

"A thought brushed past me like someone whispering in my ear. *Remove what is possible and what is thought to be known. You will find only the unknown remains.* Who said that? I wondered. The voice had no texture and no sound. It was familiar, though, like a soft, summertime breeze on a warm day. A memory formed of brighter days filled with learning.

"My mind reached for the fleeting message and grabbed it faster than a spider snatches a fly. I chanted it over and over again. It was something relevant to my past. I sensed the litany was something that could help me escape. What is the unknown but the known, waiting to be born? Where was the door that was not yet opened? Where was the way back to the Light?

"Khalkoroth sensed the change in me. The demon renewed his mental attack with great fury. *+There is no escape from Khalkoroth! The monks of your Order are gone, never to return. Ordu is dead. There is no salvation for you. You know this in your mind and feel it in your heart. You are the last, and you are mine for all eternity.+*

"The beast had given me another clue. Ordu. The word glowed like a lantern on a moonless night. It held the promise of lost emotions discovered in the dark. It hinted at my awareness of a different time. There were still no images that I could see in the shapeless, void of my prison.

"Ordu. The word had meaning. It was a place of strength and pulsed in my mind like a burning pyre set upon a barren cliff wall during a winter's storm. Its golden fire guiding my lost soul through the angry, churning sea of Khalkoroth's misery.

"I heard the demon chuckle deeply. *+You think you're special. You think you shall find a way back. I can feel your hope, and it is misplaced.+*

"But Khalkoroth was wrong. I had finally found a key to unlock the shackles of my imprisonment. I tried to hide my new consciousness from the demon until I was sure it was real.

"He taunted me at every opportunity. *+There is nowhere to hide from me. I am all that you are now. I am everywhere.+*

"But this time, I did not cower in fear. This time, I felt the strength of my will push back. I answered the demon with a mental command of my own. *+You're right, demon. There is no escape for me, and neither is there for you.+*"

Shiverrig looked unimpressed. "Interesting monk stuff, I suppose. Who knew Daku from Ordu was also a poet?"

"That's how it happened!" Daku said, appearing hurt and insulted. The human expression on such a bestial face was comical to Shiverrig.

"My advice to you is not to let the circlet fall from your head," Shiverrig said as he stared down the length of his sword before placing it back in his sheath. He then turned to Sess'thra.

"You knew all along this day would come."

"Of course, I knew. What kind of conqueror would you be if you didn't rebel against the Frost Queen? You were made to rule more than this patch of dirt and the cattle of souls that breed here. If you had any hope of winning, you would need stronger muscle by your side. Mortal flesh will only take you so far." She sauntered close to Shiverrig. Her seductive eyes smiled at him. "And I do like winning."

"And here I thought it was true love." He knew it wasn't, not for a second. "Or maybe just boredom."

"Oh, you tease me so." Sess'thra traced her fingers across Shiverrig's strong jawline, hooking her nails at the corner and drawing his face closer to hers. She raised herself up on her toes and licked the bottom of his chin, like a snake searching for food.

"There is never a boring moment with you, my fascinating man. You certainly attract interesting company. My, my, my, no less than the Chaos Devil himself. You are a wonder."

She pressed her body against his.

"My arrangement with Xerthotha has yet to be resolved." Shiverrig gave a slight frown. He grabbed Sess'thra by the arms and lifted her away from him. "And how soon before you squeal to Sekka of my association?"

"Oh no. Not me, not ever. I am having too much fun in your world to go back to dreary Gathos. My sensitive skin was not made for the cold. Besides, I've served her long enough."

Shiverrig sized up the lithe succubus. He knew he couldn't trust someone who thrived on mischief. But for now, he needed her. "We cannot linger here much longer. Aeshmara's hunters will have our trail soon."

"Surely they are already on their way," Daku said with confidence, using more of his own voice. "We must make haste to Gethem. The city must be fortified."

"Gethem," Shiverrig said, letting the name of his home and the city of his forefathers linger in his thoughts. Even with the quickness of travel the succubus offered, it was still too far away from where he needed to be. "Sess'thra, take us to Qaqal. I have a plan."

Shiverrig, Sess'thra, and Daku were greeted at the steps to the royal palace by Malachi, who lead what seemed to be a hastily gathered honor guard.

"Welcome home, my Aj-Kahun! You look healthy and full of vigor. I didn't expect your return so quickly," Malachi said as he bowed.

Shiverrig thought he sounded surprised. *Good, it was best to keep his subjects, even his closest advisors, off-balance.* When the archvashim rose, Shiverrig clearly saw Hilo's flickering outline within Malachi's frame. Another "gift" from the Chaos Devil, he presumed.

Malachi called to a nearby servant. "Go to the kitchens and alert the master cook to prepare a feast for our returning Aj-Kahun. Gather the porters and see to their comfort. Have baths drawn and light refreshments sent to their quarters."

"That won't be necessary. There is little time and much to do."

"Had I known of your early arrival I would have arranged a welcoming parade.

You really must keep me more abreast of your movements. Next time you must send a raven or let the succubus bring me word personally."

"I'll keep that in mind," Shiverrig said and walked into the entryway of the palace.

A month had passed since he first marched from Qaqal en route to the Sarribe Mountains and a potential confrontation with Sekka's forces currently invading Sunne. Now that he had returned, he saw much had changed. Qaqal had lost its vibrant glow. There was little to no activity in the streets. Many storefronts were closed, boarded up, or ransacked.

Shiverrig had noted pockets of mass executions littering the larger squares along his route back to the palace. The bodies of dissidents swayed quietly under a hangman's rope. The rabble-rousers had been preserved from rot by the cold of winter, allowing ravens to continuously pluck and pick at choice bits of flesh. Whether frozen or warm, the black birds enjoyed their meat.

Shiverrig pushed past Malachi and removed his gloves, sticking them loose under his belt. "I am grateful to see the City of Spires still stands. There has been no trouble?"

Malachi gave a slight shrug of his shoulders. "None worth a mention. A few voiced their unfavorable opinions of the new regime. The city guard effectively quelled their noise. Any other would-be heroes have scurried back to their alleys and dirty holes beneath the city. The frontier lands paint a different picture. Maugris's demon horde has splintered since the Battle at the Last Garrison and ravages the border villages."

"Border villages," Shiverrig said with a lack of enthusiasm. He brought his heavy hand to his chin and rubbed through the stiff stubble. "They will need to fend for themselves for the time being. I cannot spare men and supplies chasing after packs of demons in the frontiers. There's a bigger threat we must focus our efforts on defeating."

Shiverrig felt the Chaos Devil rise to the surface of his thoughts like a rogue wave, swelling unchecked across the open sea. He was caught in a rush of vertigo and waved Malachi away. "I wish to be alone. Leave me. All of you."

Hilo's eyes sparkled behind Malachi's gaze. "Yes, my Aj-Kahun. I am here at your service, should the need arise."

Daku and Sess'thra knowingly glanced at Shiverrig and then each other. Sess'thra's eyes grew wide with anticipation. She took an eager step closer. "Is he here? Now?"

"I said, leave me!" Shiverrig said sharply. The succubus stopped short. She and Daku bowed and removed themselves, following Malachi out of the hall.

The sensation overtook him like a storm, and although he remained standing still, it felt as if his entire body was tossed like a rag doll in the hands of a playful child. Knife blades cut into his temples, and spots flared before his eyes. The pressure in his skull was overwhelming.

+YOU WILL NEED A BIGGER ARMY IF YOU ARE TO CONQUER THIS LAND IN MY NAME. THE PALTRY DOZENS CREATED BY YOUR SEX WITH THE SUCCUBUS WILL NOT BE ENOUGH, EVEN IF THEY HAD THE BLOOD OF XERTHOTHA FLOWING THROUGH THEIR VEINS. YOU MUST HAVE MORE, AND THE CITY OF SPIRES IS RIPE FOR CHANGE.+

Shiverrig staggered to one of the many columns supporting the vaulted ceiling of the hall. He held on to it like a life preserver to keep from drowning under the weight of Xerthotha's presence.

"Only if I want to rule over a city of the damned," Shiverrig somehow managed to say. He would lose more of himself to the devil if he didn't make a stand now. He pushed himself off the pillar and staggered on shaky legs.

"It seems this would be more to your benefit than mine," he said through gritted teeth. "If I followed your desires, there would no longer be mortal kingdoms to conquer. It would become a world of demonkind."

+HO, HO, HO! YOU MAKE AN ASTUTE OBSERVATION. AND WOULD THAT BE SO BAD? WHY NOT REIGN OVER AN ENTIRE WORLD? WHAT WOULD IT MATTER IF IT WERE FILLED WITH DEMONS INSTEAD OF HUMANS? I THINK YOUR PREFERENCE OF LOYAL SUBJECTS IS LIMITED AT THE MOMENT.+

Shiverrig found his legs and stood straight. He knew the devil was right. Sekka could call forth endless legions from Gathos, and he would never win a war of attrition against those numbers.

"All in time, Devil. Nonetheless, what you suggest is beyond my means," Shiverrig said in an even tone.

+BUT NOT BEYOND MINE. THERE ARE FASTER WAYS TO CONVERT A MORTAL SOUL INTO A CREATURE OF THE DEEP DARK.+

Shiverrig raised an eyebrow. "I'm listening."

The flickering flames of low burning candles danced on tiny wicks across a candelabra's long nest of hardened wax. Shiverrig stared for long moments at the line of small flames without blinking. The fire burning in the fireplace against the rear wall of his study did nothing to remove the chill from the air. He leaned against the back of a stiff chair, contemplating the Chaos Devil's suggestion.

Just how far are you prepared to go, Gerun? You but need to say the word, and Baroqia will forever be changed. He honestly didn't know the answer. But what choice did he have? He would not sit idly and watch his kingdom suffer Sekka's invasion.

Xerthotha knew, as well as he did, that the initial brood created with Sess'thra was inferior when measured against the strength of Sekka's troops. The half-breeds had fallen with the Knights of Gethem to Aeshmara and her sorcerous brother. He would need stronger, more resilient soldiers if he hoped to defeat the Frost Queen and her Vyzyn warlords.

It was a revolting thought, but a necessary one. Every moment Shiverrig let Sekka hold open that blasted Chaos Gate, more filth poured into his kingdom. Soon, the enemy numbers would be impossible to defeat. *I must overthrow Sekka now and worry about cleaning up the mess later.*

He bemoaned that his decisions were reactions to events out of his control rather than a carefully laid out strategy. He longed to direct his foes to the deadly ground of his choosing, but instead, he felt like he was drowning in rapids, being pulled and twisted by the whims of a wild current. He couldn't guess when the waters would slow and only hoped he could regain some semblance of control before everything was lost.

Then he scoffed at the melodrama of his musings. *I am Gerun Shiverrig. I'm always in control. I'll let Xerthotha create for me an unstoppable army to defeat Sekka, and then I'll use it to destroy the Chaos Gate.*

He rose and walked to a nearby table, pondering his decision. The city was worse than when he left. The unrest from the regime change was more than Shiverrig had expected. He sniggered to himself. Of course, it was more. His original plan had not called for Qaqal to be overrun with demonkind. He gazed down at maps detailing the smaller villages far outside the reach of the capital city.

Stacked neatly nearby were opened scrolls of Malachi's written reports, describing in detail the damage and death at the hands of marauding demons throughout the frontier. He could quickly solve that problem, but there was not enough raw material to make a difference. Even the larger towns of Oathsworth and Grennay were filled with inadequate stock. It would have to be one of the two major cities. But which one, Qaqal or Gethem?

He pushed away from the table and turned to a map hung on the wall to his left. A circle on the map marked Rachlach Fortress's location, the ruined lair of the sorcerer, Maugris, and the birthplace of the Chaos Gate.

Shiverrig clenched his jaw. *You bloody madman, Maugris. All of this could have been avoided if...if what? If I had revolted openly against King Conrad from the beginning?*

He knew that would have been a fool's errand. His military resources were slowly being sucked dry by the king's incessant decrees to deploy Gethem's troops throughout the land. House Shiverrig could not stand alone against the combined might of the remaining four great houses, and any fool could see it was only a matter of time before he became a lesser and forgotten influence in Baroqia. Maugris and his abyssal alliance had presented him with an opportunity he could not squander if he was ever to regain the throne.

Gethem or Qaqal? Gethem or Qaqal? He rubbed his rough and stubbled cheeks. His breath came out in a loud sigh. What would it mean to give the order to turn the citizens of an entire city to demonkind? Would they be more easily controlled? But by who, Shiverrig or Xerthotha?

He shook his head. A favorable decision of his making had been stripped from him by the consequences of his actions. There was no choice but to move forward. He couldn't defeat Sekka with mortal men and horses. *But the cost?* His legacy in the histories of House Shiverrig would be lost as he slowly turned Baroqia into a second Abyss. There was no honor in this decision, only overwhelming need.

No, he was not helpless to fate. This time, he would change his plight to his advantage and rewrite the histories when he had conquered the Three Kingdoms.

"I'll steal the strength and power from the demons as my forefathers did with the wild ogre tribes so long ago."

Shiverrig looked back over his maps. The decision was now obvious due to its proximity to the Chaos Gate. Qaqal would fall.

63

SEKKA

Sekka remained calm as Zizphander's horde raced towards Furia Keep. She walked with deliberate steps contemplating when to release the behemoth. Cymeryes had awoken and stirred beneath the ice, waiting to be called to battle.

"I killed you once but didn't finish the job," she said.

She scanned the immediate land surrounding Furia Keep. Azrollorza's army of fiends had been deployed as a living buffer into the Wastelands of Thresh as she had commanded. The fiends gnashed their teeth and howled at the oncoming horde. Burnt-orange banners with symbolized images of Azrollorza's seven eyes and surrounding tentacles, fluttered in the cold winds. Some of the fiends threw down their standards and started fighting amongst themselves, unable to control their rising bloodlust.

The demon prince, Kotto'gyges, had arranged his demon warriors into five companies around the keep as instructed. They would engage Zizphander's horde once it had worked its way through the fiend fodder. She was woefully short on military assets. This battle had come at the most inopportune time.

Isn't that the way of things? It's never easy, she thought.

Zizphander shot through the sky like a red comet. Sekka watched her fiend army rush the horde and do what it was made to do, die. But as she had expected, it also reduced the enemy's numbers.

The initial confrontation was a gruesome spectacle as the opposing armies clashed together in an explosion of claws, teeth, hooked beaks, and talons. Bodies were ripped apart and parts were tossed into the air.

Lord Oziax had gathered the flying Takuun into the keep and positioned them along the battlements. Now they watched and waited. Below, Kotto'gyges barked out commands to his troops. She hoped he lived up to his reputation of being a competent general.

Sekka scanned the horizon from the battlements. Zizphander's horde was endless as it circled Furia Keep. She canted a series of dark words of power and brought the wrath of the storm clouds down upon the endless horde. Silent bolts of lightning flashed into Zizphander's troops, followed by a rapid succession of thunderous booms. The enemy evaporated in great swatches of shocked air wherever the lightning struck. But it was not enough. A countless number of enemy fiends and lesser demons poured over the hills and across the frozen lake.

She called upon the deep reserves of Gathos's Elemenati magic and threw blinding snow squalls, filled with wicked ice shards the length of spears into the horde, yet on they came. Sekka spotted a red-hot beacon glowing above the battle. Zizphander was seemingly impervious to the storm swirling across the sky.

"Cymeryes!" Sekka screamed into the storm, and the ancient behemoth answered her call.

The frozen lake before Furia Keep burst open as giant pinchers and claws, each the size of a castle wall, rose into the air and then crashed down on the fiery specs still racing across the ice. Those who were not drowned like sinking lanterns in the lake's dark waters or smashed between vast chunks of ice were smeared to a pulp against the unbroken surface by Cymeryes's monstrous crab-like appendages.

Slowly, Cymeryes pulled himself from the lake and onto more stable land. His size was impossible. Eight smaller, segmented legs supported the behemoth's enormous bulk. He moved slowly, preferring to hunt under the ice where his weight was negated by the deep water.

Zizphander's fire demons swarmed over Cymeryes, trying in vain to pierce his hard outer shell, but to no avail. He was a creature of lore throughout the Abyss, and Zizphander's troops would pay dearly for disturbing his slumber.

Sekka watched as the enemy's northern attack faltered. The rise of Cymeryes had shattered the layer of ice in all directions. Thousands of fiery fiends and fire demons were swallowed under the cold waters. Reserve troops altered their route and focused their attention on the lumbering fortress of death.

+Oziax! Move the Takuun to attack the enemy along the south side of the keep. Their aerial attack will decimate Zizphander's foot troops. Let the D'xyston warriors prove their worth.+

+Yes, my Queen.+

Sekka smiled with satisfaction. It wouldn't be long now before Cymeryes changed the momentum of battle in her favor. Zizphander must have seen the same. He flashed from the sky towards the behemoth. Cymeryes raised his mighty claws to strike the comparably gnat-sized foe, but the Red Devil was too quick and deftly landed on his back.

Sekka squinted to see what was happening through the storm, but the snow and ice obscured her vision. Then brilliant flashes of light erupted above Cymeryes's head. A feeling of horrible dread crept up her spine. Something was wrong.

Sekka heard a bellow that shook the walls of Furia Keep. Cymeryes's great pinchers snapped randomly into the sky, and he moved in a crazed fashion. A second, softer wail followed. She recognized it as the cry of a dying beast. Cymeryes's pinchers dropped heavy to the ground, followed by the bulk of his enormous body.

"No, no, no! This cannot be!" Sekka cried.

Zizphander's fire demons covered the downed behemoth like a swarm of hungry insects, biting at the soft spots between joints and soon picked apart the great beast, piece by piece.

Sekka raised the broken chunks of ice floating in the lake and formed them into a tidal wave of frozen debris. She cast it mercifully over Cymeryes's body, hoping to snuff out the fires which now raged over the behemoth. *What had happened? How could the mighty Cymeryes be defeated so quickly? What power had the Chaos Devil bestowed upon Zizphander?*

Sekka saw more of Zizphander's troops charging from the eastern and western fronts. She sent blizzards of razor-sharp ice into the enemy, thinking to cut them down as they drew closer to Kotto'gyges's demon companies. The enemy miraculously survived her barrage. She scanned the sky and saw the Red Devil hovering in place.

"He is not strong enough to cancel my magic." Sekka snarled. "Only a Supreme Devil has such power." Then a horrifying thought crossed her mind. *Is Xerthotha here?*

She turned to see if Oziax had committed the Takuun to the southern front. The lesser juggernauts attacked Zizphander's horde from above with impunity. Their hanging appendages coiled around the enemy and fed them to the mouthed proboscis on the underside of their jellied heads. The D'xyston riders clad in vermillion armor hurled spears down on the hapless fire fiends. Sekka nodded thankfully that the southern front would hold.

On cue, Zizphander darted to the south, and Sekka watched as his brilliant, red wings lit up the sky. He stopped and hovered over the flying Takuun as the air vibrated around his body.

Then, like the shadow of a dragon, she saw a black pattern appear against the clouds. She recognized the rune and her devilish heart sank as the greyish-blue skies turned deep purple. A hot wind gusted past her, and she felt her flesh burn from its intense heat.

Sekka heard a high-pitched shriek, and then another, and then more. She knew what was coming as it fell from great heights through the upper cloud banks. The air over the Takuun turned bright red as globs of fiery magma plummeted down on them, bursting on impact and engulfing each juggernaut and its riders in flame.

The land boiled where the fiery goop fell, melting away thousands of years of ice and snow and creating a deep depression in the southern plains. Sekka watched Zizphander dive into one of the larger the hollow pits. "What's this now?"

Then she felt the land rumble under her feet. "No, no, no!" Sekka screamed.

Chedipe hobbled to her side. "The southern front is lost!"

The land shook with terrible force, throwing Chedipe to the battlement floor and causing Sekka to catch her balance on the crenel to her side. An eruption of reddish-black magma vomited from the ground as bedrock buried miles beneath the surface of Gathos was hurled into the sky.

"No, not again! It cannot happen again. The Dead Giant must not awaken!" Sekka shouted over the din of battle and hurried to the southern wall.

Lava flowed from the pit as more magma spewed from the bowels of Gathos. The lava gathered in a slow crawl towards Furia Keep. Zizphander appeared again, shooting out from the black smoke above the pit. He caught the thermal updrafts in his great wings and glided in a lazy circle around the pillar of smoke.

Sekka gathered the jol'goths from Furia Keep. "We march to fight for the survival of our home. Gathos is your life, and your life belongs to Gathos. Destroy the enemy.

Leave nothing alive. Go my warriors and sate your bloodlust on the fiends from the realm of fire."

With any luck, her legion of jol'goths would give her the space she needed to fight Zizphander without distraction. The Red Devil was strong. So much more potent than he had ever been. This time she knew she could not use sleight of hand to defeat him.

"Two can play this game," Sekka said as she transformed into her devilish form and marched onto the Wastelands of Thresh. A legion of her jol'goth warriors fell in line behind her. She towered over the large demon brutes with muscles rippling along her thighs, shoulders, and back. Her white mane of hair thrashed behind her in the hot winds.

+I am impressed you dared to leave your precious tower,+ Zizphander whispered in Sekka's mind. *+That was a mistake.+*

+We end this now. Fight me as equals, if you dare,+ Sekka shot back.

+Equals?+ Sekka heard the laughter of the Red Devil in her mind. *+How could you presume we were equals? You have no army to protect you. Your remaining behemoths are too distant from Gathos and cannot answer your call. You have spread yourself too thin. No longer will my Master tolerate your meddling in his affairs.+*

+You said that once before and left Gathos with your head ripped from your body. This time I will go deeper.+

But Sekka knew he was right. She had deployed too much of her military strength to other realms for future gain. Only Cymeryes had remained, and he had been destroyed with ease. Her frustration grew deadly.

"Fight me!" she screamed.

Zizphander swooped in low over her head. Purple and black sigils hovered behind his fiery hair. His handsome face flashed a wicked grin, mocking Sekka and her pending doom. The Chaos Devil's brand, eight entwined serpents, each head devouring its own tail, was engraved across his chest armor.

His magnificent, feathered wings beat gracefully, changing color from bright red to yellow and then to orange as he flew past. Flames burned across his body but left no trails of smoke. His legs were hidden beneath a long set of thin, blue spines which acted as tail feathers of a sort. As he passed, sparkling debris trailed in his wake.

+You are already defeated. The lava flow cannot be turned back. Furia Keep will be smoldering ash by the end of this day.+

Sekka sent forked lightning at Zizphander, but he deftly dodged the sizzling electricity. She next shot razor-sharp ice shards at him, but they shattered harmlessly against a protective barrier. Gale force winds could not throw him from the sky. Zizphander's laughter rang in her head as he continued towards Furia Keep.

Sekka had thrown the power of Gathos at Zizphander, and the Red Devil had pushed it aside as if it were a mild annoyance. Banners of dull, burnt-orange littered the snow along with tens of thousands of dead fiends and demons. Where was Kotto'gyges? What did it matter? She saw the end of Gathos looming before her eyes. She had one last option left to her, one that came with a terrible price.

+Azrollorza!+ Sekka's mind shot out in search of the Supreme Devil.

+MY LITTLE DEVIL HAS WASTED SUCH VALUABLE ASSETS, AND STILL, SHE CALLS FOR ME?+

+Gathos is lost. I cannot win against the strength of Xerthotha.+ Sekka pleaded. She hated admitting the truth.

+I REQUIRE MUCH TO INTERVENE.+
+Name your price.+
+A LIFE DEBT SHALL DO.+
+How much?+
+ONE MORE THAN HALF OF ME.+
She would suffer an eon of torment to fulfill that amount of life debt. *+A tenth of the half.+*
+TSK, TSK, BY NOW YOU SHOULD KNOW HOW THIS WORKS. I HAVE RAISED THE DEBT. NOW IT SHALL BE THREE MORE THAN HALF OF ME. PRAY I DO NOT EXTEND AGAIN DUE TO YOUR RUDE BEHAVIOR.+

Sekka watched as Zizphander circled Furia Keep. His northern horde had regrouped and raced towards her citadel. Her legion of jol'goths could stall their advance, but the Red Devil's numbers were too vast.

She gazed south. The heat from the unstoppable lava was like a slap across her face. It hissed mockingly at her as it slowly crawled forward to destroy Furia Keep. Desperation washed over her. Without Azrollorza's help, all that she had worked and struggled for would be lost. She could rebuild, but that would take millennia, and she would suffer the stigma of defeat from any future would-be allies. "Obliteration would be better."

The suffocating heat intensified as the lava approached. She saw her forces and those of Azrollorza strewn across the snow and ice. In the distance was the broken shell of dead Cymeryes. Sekka had never know defeat of such magnitude. She lowered her head. *+Agreed.+*

+LET IT BE KNOWN A LIFE DEBT HAS BEEN GRANTED. ANY HARM SUFFERED BY AZROLLORZA SHALL BE ABSORBED BY SEKKA, UP UNTIL THE LIFE COST OF HALF, PLUS THREE OF MY ABYSSAL LIFE, IS PAID IN FULL.+

Gathos must survive. That was all that mattered. Sekka would find a way to transfer that debt to another later. She looked to the sky. *Starting with him.*

Her gaze was drawn to the left, where a small, green spark flared against the bruised colored clouds, which formed into a little, winged creature, like a maligned, naked cherub with seven eyes. Sekka felt her knees tremble at the tremendous power of Azrollorza's avatar.

The winged cherub placed his hand on Sekka's chest and shackled her life force to its own.

"The contract is made," the warped child said. He then twisted his body in the direction of Zizphander as he flew over Furia Keep and reached out with his other hand. As his chubby fingers clenched into a tight fist, so too did Zizphander's wings curl around his body. The Red Devil dropped from the sky and landed hard outside the wall of her citadel.

"You will find him much more receptive to your attention now," the seven-eyed cherub said with a broad smile. His body flared again and was reduced to a mere spark before popping out of existence.

Sekka rushed toward the Red Devil, bounding over the dead and dying. She threw jol'goths out of her way when they dallied too long in her path. There he was, crumpled in the snow and defenseless.

Sekka drove her claws into Zizphander's chest armor, tearing through his compromised magical defense until her hands found warm flesh. She grabbed at his exposed organs, ripping them out of his body and tossing them callously over her broad shoulders and into the snow behind her.

Her jol'goth warriors arrived moments later, surrounding her, and preventing Zizphander's horde from intervening.

"How does it feel, Zizphander? How does it feel to know this is the end?" She savored the look of shock on his handsome face. "Not only the end of this fight between us but also the end of you for all time. I will not have you plaguing me for the third time."

+I will not be—+

"Yes, you will!" Sekka pounced onto his chest and dug her claws into his skull, her avian talons slashing deep gashes into his thighs and midsection. Zizphander's eyes grew wide as his body was ripped to shreds. She feasted upon his flesh, pulling out his entrails and relishing the sweet taste of victory.

The Red Devil's death was a gloriously, messy affair, but she was not finished with him, oh no, not yet.

She had defeated him in the past, but physical death was only an inconvenience for the most powerful denizens of the Abyss. Zizphander had been reborn and commanded by Xerthotha to hinder her every move. She would not make the same mistake twice.

"Gather up any loose parts you see, and toss them into a pile over his body," Sekka commanded two nearby jol'goths. Her white skin was drenched in blood and bits of colorful feathers as she rose from Zizphander's mangled remains. "Leave nothing behind."

The battle raged on around her, but she hardly noticed. With Zizphander defeated and unable to lend his magical protection to his horde, the war was all but over.

She summoned a shimmering sphere around the pile of gore and spoke a word of power. Within moments Zizphander's remains were encased in ice. She turned to the two jol'goths. "Take that back to Furia Keep. The rest of you come with me. I am still hungry for warm flesh."

+My Queen! The lava flows!+ Chedipe mentally cried out in desperation. +It has reached the walls!+

"Destroy the fire fiends!" Sekka shouted to her jol'goth legion. Then she raced back to the walls that surrounded the citadel of Furia Keep. A red glow grew above the southern ramparts. Her only hope would be to freeze the volcano back into its eternal slumber.

She called out to the storm overhead and brought down a concentrated ice blizzard to temporarily halt the lava. The molten rock slowed to a hesitant stop and crusted over. But she knew her work was far from over. She would need to harness the raw Elemenati energy of Gathos to quench the source of fire deep within the crater.

She didn't know if her demonic body could withstand such abusive heat for long. But she had no choice. With quick strides, she came to the mouth of the crater and leaped into its center. The heat was unbearable, and raw blisters immediately covered her skin. Her protective magic held, but it would not last.

Sekka willed herself deep into the core of the volcano. She had little time left and could feel the heat intensify as her aegis faltered. She called to the freezing cold of Gathos, drawing it to her, and siphoning as much as she could hold in her being. Just as her protective shield failed, she unleashed the excessive cold outwards, pumping a glacial reservoir of ice into the inferno of fire.

The ice melted as fast as it left her body, and the core of the volcano continued to churn out molten lava. Her skin boiled and burned. Fiery blisters bit deeply into her flesh. But she would not relent and gathered more Elemenati energy from the heart of Gathos.

Gathos would not die, not now, not when she had defeated her greatest rival. Sekka pleaded for more power from the primal forces of her world. And more power was given. She felt a wave of energy flow through her veins. It was exhilarating. Gathos had found her a worthy champion. Sekka became one with her realm as she absorbed more of its raw Elemenati energy.

The glacial ice flowing from her extinguished the volcano's fiery core and froze it solid. The rock shook around her, cracking ice and granite alike, but the ice would not shatter. Her home would remain a world of cold.

Sekka closed her eyes. She was exhausted. The ice around her was like a mother's womb. She wished to curl up in its cold embrace, but there was more to be done. She burrowed to the surface. Her jol'goth legion had engaged what was left of Zizphander's horde and was herding the demons and fiends away from Furia Keep.

Sekka sent her magic into the clouds and gathered the water, transforming it into heavy balls of ice, which then dropped from the sky over the enemy. The ice smashed like the fists of Gathos over the horde, pulverizing them where they ran. It was a glorious sensation, watching the last of her foe's warriors die by the power at her command.

"Let them die by the might of Gathos."

When it was finally over, she walked the Wastelands of Thresh, assessing the cost of her victory. She found the bloated form of Kotto'gyges, surrounded by heaps of dead fire fiends. Hundreds of the enemy had fallen before the demon prince had been slain. His body was charred and ruined. The five Nu Kua bodyguards lay scattered in pieces throughout the mangled flesh of the dead. They, too, had extracted a heavy toll from the enemy before they fell.

A new layer of ice covered the lake outside Furia Keep. Gathos was healing itself. A glimmer of hope formed that Cymeryes could be saved, but the behemoth was finished. His massive body burned so thoroughly that broad swatches of his shell carapace turned to ash at her touch. Tens of thousands of fire fiends lay smeared in long streaks on the ground.

Fresh snow fell and had already covered much of what remained of the battle. Soon, the Wastelands of Thresh would have a new topography. A geological trophy to remind her of this day. She had survived, and Gathos was still hers. The debt was worth the cost. She could regain what was lost over time.

Sekka idly wondered if Oziax had escaped the firestorm that brought down the Takuun Juggernauts. Her general had survived millennia of warfare, and she had a hunch he had avoided that calamity. *Though it would be just punishment for his insubordination and recent failures,* she thought.

She scanned the horizon and then gazed back at her home. Furia Keep stood proudly against the frozen landscape. The walls had been breached in several locations, and damage had been done, but nothing that couldn't be repaired.

The Chaos Gate would ensure a constant supply of souls to her realm, and the protection of Azrollorza would afford her time. The Life Debt worked both ways.

Azrollorza would want Sekka to remain alive if possible, less the Supreme Devil lose such a surplus of additional life energy.

Sekka marched back to Furia Keep. She had one last task to perform before she could cast the Red Devil into oblivion. Then she would begin the search for Aetenos in earnest. When she caught him, he would suffer the same fate at Zizphander.

64

SHIVERRIG

Shiverrig leaned heavily on the pommel of his saddle, staring at the City of Spires. Early morning light shimmered off the high towers, which gave the city its name. *This is the only way,* he thought. The guilty feeling in his gut sunk a little deeper.

His mood was somber as he waited in the cold, sharp morning air. A blustery winter's wind blew through the sparse pine trees surrounding his position. The creaking branches swayed and cracked, dislodging clumps of wet snow from dense bundles of needles. How he despised the pungent smell of sap now.

"Will it take long? How will we know it's done?" Shiverrig blurted out.

Heavy snow had fallen the night before, and the thin top layer had frozen. He was forced to squint from the glare bouncing off the surface and into his eyes—a further irritation to the morning's ride. Qaqal was in the distance, two, maybe three miles away. The black bear furs he wore canceled the chill from the wind but did nothing against the cold resting deep in his bones.

"I cannot begin to understand the ways or whims of the Chaos Devil," Sess'thra replied. "Maybe he'll whisper in your ear when all is ready."

The charcoal-spotted, chaos horse she rode pawed at the snow-covered ground and snorted in the cold air, clouding his face with steam. Shiverrig wrinkled his nose at the queer smell. The steed's mane and tail writhed as if alive, like the snakes atop the head of a long-forgotten gorgon.

Hours passed, and the city remained silent.

"Look there, to the skies above the city," Sess'thra said, calling Shiverrig back to the tree line. "Not long now, I think."

Shiverrig watched as bruised storm clouds gathered and swirled over the City of Spires. Lightning flashed across the turbulent sky, illuminating the clouds from within. Sheets of shadowy-grey rain fell to the ground, obscuring the city's buildings and towers' beautiful designs.

Gradually, a pinkish fog rose throughout the city, and all but the tallest spires were lost from view. "When will it be safe to return?" Shiverrig said impatiently, wondering what awaited him in the condemned city.

"I have never witnessed a transformation of this scale before," Sess'thra said. Her eagerness to see such an event was evident in her voice. Her eyes glistened and remained fixed on the city.

"No more waiting." Shiverrig spurred his black destrier forward. It was time to see what his ill-fated decision had spawned.

What was once Qaqal was no more. The City of Spires had undergone a horrific change. Illustrious spires now appeared as dark totems fluctuating in the blustery wind. Entire buildings had fallen to the ground, while others simply vanished and reappeared in a different location.

"What fresh new hell have I created?" Shiverrig said with a heavy sigh as he approached the entrance gate. Remarkably, it had remained relatively unchanged but left open, contrary to his orders. The pinkish mist had turned deep lavender and rolled out from between the two large doors.

Shiverrig had placed a curfew on the city the night before. Anyone walking the streets after the stroke of nine would be held for questioning until morning. The gates surrounding the city were closed, with strict orders that no one was to leave. The men he had posted at the entrance were gone. He scanned the walls, also empty.

"Where are the guards?" Shiverrig said but assumed they had died or fled. He spurred his destrier forward, but the horse bucked and refused to enter the city.

"Easy girl." He patted the horse's neck, hoping to calm down the war horse's giddiness.

The mare's eyes were giant saucers as she turned her head left and right. He had ridden this horse through countless skirmishes with brigands and barbarian marauders seeking to plunder frontier villages or ransack small towns. She was fearless in the face of death and danger. But this new madness was more than she had ever encountered in the past.

Shiverrig looked to Sess'thra for a possible explanation. She shrugged indifferently. However, a crafty smile cornered her mouth as if she knew exactly what to expect.

"Come on!" Shiverrig spurred his horse forward, drawing deep, bloody gashes at its sides. The horse jumped a step and then reluctantly trotted through the gates and into the city's tunnel.

The mist was thicker in the tunnel and filled the area with a distinct smell of lavender. It swirled in lazy spirals, outlining the currents of air flowing out of the city.

It could be worse, Shiverrig thought, until he came to the courtyard entrance and the mist cleared, revealing the bodies littering the open ground.

Hundreds of people lay about the entrance to the tunnel and across the square. Their bodies were warped into strange amalgamations of various animals of Baroqia and other things Shiverrig could not identify. Each person now had too many parts or too few. Here was a man with three other arms protruded from his chest. His three new hands were wrapped in a stranglehold around his throat.

Lying next to him was a woman with snake-patterned scales covering her face and neck. Her eyes were expanded into moist, black orbs, resembling a deep-water fish. Trails of old tears left marks down her cheeks. A stunted wing of thin, leathery membrane jutted from her hip. Her arms and legs had dissolved at her sides into smeared puddles of goo.

Shiverrig looked from one gross abomination to the next. There was no end to the freakish transformations. Then, a high-pitched shriek jarred him from his macabre observation. His destrier's legs buckled as if it had just been pierced in the side by a spear.

Shiverrig managed to spring from the saddle before the horse hit the ground. The change happened fast. Finger-sized thorns broke the thin skin across the horse's body, encasing its frame in a toothy armor. Her head and neck shook from side-to-side with such force as to cause a long tear down her right shoulder. Shiverrig watched in amazement as a second head grew from the gash.

Thick froth spewed from her two mouths and pooled on the ground. The mare shuttered violently, wailing in pain. Yet, her loyal and dutiful heart would not die, and she tried to stand again for her master. She stood one last time on wobbling legs before collapsing in an awkward heap on the ground.

The mare's eyes locked on Shiverrig's, pleading with him to end her suffering. Shiverrig drew his sword. His blade was sharp, and the end was quick.

"She was a good horse," he said, wiping the blade on a length of saddle cloth.

He surveyed the courtyard and pieced together the possible events. Many had tried to flee the city as the change had overcome them. The guards must have held them as instructed. There was a conflict, and many died. "What a mess."

Shiverrig pivoted and looked back through the tunnel. Some had escaped. He could not tell if his guards were gone or were part of the bodily refuse strewn about the courtyard. He looked back to Sess'thra and cocked his eyebrow with suspicion.

"Some mortal creatures do not accept the call of chaos as well as others," she said. "And some, not at all."

Shiverrig nodded in understanding. Something of this nature was to be expected. As his initial shock wore off, he realized the city was waking up to a new dawn. But the sounds of shop doors opening and smells of wood-burning fires, fresh bread, and brewed coffee was replaced with a strange and churning ambiance.

Buildings crumbled and were rebuilt by unseen hands. Ghostly moans echoed in the shadowed alleys tapering off from the body of the courtyard. Shiverrig heard sounds in the distance, coming from the direction of the palace. The gibbering howls grew bolder as time wore on and reminded Shiverrig of wild animals calling in the night. The scent of lavender was everywhere.

"Come, there is room on my steed for two. You can ride behind me, all the way back to the palace." She leered at him seductively.

"Slide back, succubus, I'll take the lead," Shiverrig said, taking the reins from her small hands. Sess'thra did as he commanded. She hopped nimbly out of the saddle and onto the chaos horse's rump. He then climbed into the empty saddle. "Don't you ever think of anything else?"

Sess'thra's small arms wrapped around his waist and hips. "Mm...never." She buried her head deep in the bearskin furs covering his back.

Shiverrig nudged the chaos horse forward to the rhythm of a two-beat trot. Its hooves clip-clopped over the cobblestone square. His disappointment grew as more of the changed city was revealed. To his dismay, some of the citizens still lived, trapped in warped bodies of worthless configuration.

The owner of a small tannery dragged his mangled carapace out from the entrance of his shop. Slimy pseudopods trailed behind him, where his legs once stood. The tanner's eyes held him fast with recognition as he crawled across the street, pointing a trembling finger at Shiverrig.

"The Shiverrigs of Gethem were the protectors of Baroqia. You were supposed to keep us safe."

Shiverrig heard wails of grief coming from the apartment lofts to the left. He looked up and saw the front of a body pressed up against the window. The curtains had been ripped down, and a white-haired woman pounded her hands against the glass. Her face bubbled with lesions.

Shiverrig watched her slowly slide down the face of the window and out of sight.

"This was a mistake," Shiverrig said. "There must have been a better solution."

Sess'thra took the sides of his head in her hands and directed his view back to the street.

"You must first defeat the Frost Queen if you wish to unite the Three Kingdoms under one rule. Stay true to your vision. The salvation for Baroqia and the foundation of your new empire awaits you at the palace, my Aj-Kahun."

Shiverrig harrumphed. "How will I defeat the Frost Queen's legion with this cesspool of human detritus?"

"This? Oh, you're so adorable in your ignorance. This is merely the unusable material from Xerthotha's flesh change. The inferior stock of any brood must be culled to ensure what remains of the group is strong."

"And what remains? I see only death warmed over and served on a cold platter."

"If Khalkoroth, or should I say, Daku? Well, whoever he is now, if he has followed my instructions, your army awaits in the fields beyond the palace."

Shiverrig and Sess'thra continued towards the palace. Her words gave him hope, though he remained pessimistic. They rounded a street corner and saw an entire family lay mangled on the cobblestones, covered in broken shards of glass. He looked to the upper stories and found window frames smashed outward.

These citizens had jumped, rather than live through this shame, he thought.

Shiverrig could not escape the loathsome fact that it was he who had allowed this to happen. He was responsible for the destruction of Qaqal. *Dammit, Gerun, there should have been another way.* But scolding himself now was pointless. The deed was done.

Shiverrig's military mind countered with rational and calculated logic. The succubus was right. This was a means to an end. He needed a city's worth of raw material to create an army capable of defeating Sekka's warriors, and this was the quickest path to that outcome. The longer he waited, the more time he gave Sekka to establish a strong position in his kingdom.

But how much of my humanity did I lose in the process? He glanced at his arms and legs.

"Why have I not been affected in a more obvious way?"

+OH, BUT YOU HAVE BEEN TOUCHED IN THE MOST GLORIOUS WAY POSSIBLE.+

The voice crackled through Shiverrig's mind like a bolt of electricity. He gasped audibly and shuddered in the saddle. Then he felt Sess'thra's arms hold him snugly. Her hands roamed up his chest, almost as if she knew another's presence had entered his being.

Shiverrig gripped the pommel with one leather-gloved hand to steady himself, then brought his other hand to his head. The initial pain passed, and he could think once more.

"These creatures are spawned from your fell sorcery, Devil. How will they know me?" Shiverrig said aloud as if the Chaos Devil walked beside him. He peered into dark alleyways, searching for some new manifestation of Xerthotha, though unsure of why. The Chaos Devil insisted he could not physically enter this realm, not yet.

If that was true, which to Shiverrig's thinking was doubtful, it meant he may still have a measure of leverage, however slight.

+IT WAS YOUR WILL WHICH CHANGED THEIR LIVES. YOUR HAND WHICH INITIALED THE SPELL. YOU ARE THEIR CREATOR, AND WHAT ARE YOU BUT THE CONTINUATION OF ME?+

The voice of Xerthotha pounded in his mind. Shiverrig shuddered again, and the reins slipped from his hands. His vision blurred, and darkness crept in from the sides, threatening to consume him. He barely acknowledged Sess'thra's quick reach for the reins before his senses left him.

Shiverrig ran naked through the narrow streets of Qaqal's commerce district. He was lost. The market square looked the same as in any other city, but this place was unfamiliar to him.

Butcher shops displayed prime cuts of red meat and hung de-feathered, blueish-white poultry from hooks in the open air. Maggots burrowed out of the beef and slithered on the surface. Fish stalls crowded the opposite side of the square, displaying a wide array of sea fare, which melted into long strands of slime in the sunlight.

The aroma of fresh bread wafted throughout the market. But when he looked inside the shops, he saw blotches of green and black mold covering the baked goods, not that he felt hungry in any way. The thought of food made him queasy, and he searched on weak legs for a secluded place to vomit.

Then, his body was moving, jumping over mangled bodies of the dead and dying. He saw heaps of human flesh bubble and burst into new, horrible things. Slimy tentacles erupted from open chest cavities, entangling his legs in their slithering clutches. Other bodies grew multiple heads from open wounds, which shrieked and gibbered at him, yelling fearful insults or mocking him as the all-powerful Aj-Kahun, the absolute ruler of a worthless kingdom.

Shiverrig couldn't see who or what followed him, but he could feel its moist breath on the back of his neck. He ran faster, frantically trying to outpace his invisible stalker and the cries of the transformed city folk. He turned down another street, where the smells changed abruptly. He had entered Merchant's Row.

The stone facades of the buildings were now polished and rich. The Royal Bank of Qaqal sat proudly at the north end of the street, while the Trader's Guild and export fur shops occupied the south end. Smaller money lending choices, and more ordinary services, such as blacksmiths and clothing stores, filled the buildings in between.

Shiverrig spotted a soft light glowing at the end of the street. The light called to him, and somehow, he knew it was the key to escaping this nightmare. He ran faster. The light offered salvation, and he needed to feel clean again.

But the light faded as he approached. The ground underfoot turned to deep mud, making progress impossible. Out of the corner of his eye, he saw the buildings melting into the shapes of caves and primitive huts. He peered into the sky and saw the legendary spires of Qaqal had vanished, replaced by tall, frond-topped trees. If he could just reach the light in time, he would be saved.

+WHERE ARE YOU GOING WITH SUCH HASTE, MY GOLDEN BOY?+ A new voice mingled with his thoughts. It was light and sweet and spoke with a child's innocence but carried menacing undertones. +IT IS BUT A DREAM YOU RACE TOWARD, BUT ONE SADLY THAT DOES NOT BELONG TO YOU. YOUR DESTINY LIES WITH ME.+

"No, I have listened to your lies long enough," Shiverrig spoke through heavy breaths. The light was fading faster now, pulling away from him. Abandoning him.

+COME TO MY EMBRACE INSTEAD. I OFFER YOU SALVATION AND THE FATE OF YOUR BLOODLINE. YOU HAVE BEEN CHOSEN+

"You are not real."

+AH, BUT YOU HAVE MADE ME REAL IN YOUR WORLD.+

Shiverrig came to a halt. The light was gone. He doubled over, resting his hand on his knees, panting. "Then, I unmake you."

+YOU CANNOT, FOR I AM YOU. I AM THE MANIFESTATION OF YOUR DESIRES.+

"I no longer want these things you offer. I am the Aj-Kahun. I need nothing from you." Shiverrig knew it was a lie. He couldn't hope to defeat Sekka without the Chaos Devil's help.

+YOU SEE? YOU NEED ME. IT IS WRITTEN IN THE DARKNESS OF YOUR HEART. AND WITH MY HELP, YOU SHALL BECOME A GREAT WARLORD OF CHAOS. YOU WILL LEAD MY LEGIONS INTO BATTLE. THE THREE KINGDOMS WILL BE YOURS. THE CIRCLE OF GATHOS WILL BE YOURS. SEKKA'S HEAD WILL BE YOURS.

+WE SHALL ROCK THE FOUNDATIONS OF THE SEVEN HEAVENS! BUT FIRST, YOU MUST RELINQUISH THE FOOLISH NOTION YOU PURSUE. WAKE UP. THAT DREAM IS FALSE. ONLY I AM REAL.+ The sweet voice trailed off.

+WAKE UP...WAKE UP...WAKE...+

Shiverrig was awake but kept his eyes closed. He felt his body move as unseen hands forcefully rocked him back and forth. Another voice, youthful in nature but one with a sultry tone, called to him, and it sounded impatient. "Wake up, wake up."

Shiverrig slowly opened his eyes to a new day. Sess'thra stood next to his bed. She was dressed in blueish-grey leathers, strung up tight in the front and back with crisscrossing black laces. Her hair braided in two long tails to the sides of her head.

"It's about time. You've slept long enough," she said.

Shiverrig took in his surroundings. He was in an unfamiliar bed, its sheets soaked with sweat. A fire blazed on the opposite wall. He removed the sheet, exposing his naked body to the yellow light of the fire. "How long?"

"Two full days of tossing and turning, and sadly, not the type that Sess'thra enjoys from her Aj-Kahun," Sess'thra pouted like a sad little girl. Shiverrig knew it was all for show.

His body felt invigorated, yet his mind remained sluggish. He glanced to his chest. The welts from the wounds Khalkoroth had inflicted a week ago were gone, but in their place was a symbol of sorts, branded across his broad pectoral muscles.

Eight serpents, rolling together, each eating its own tail. Was he still living through the nightmare, or was he now trapped between two worlds?

Sess'thra reached down and traced her fingers around the intertwining design. Her purple eyes followed the trail of each snake.

"I see you have finally accepted your destiny," Sess'thra said while gazing lustfully into his eyes. Then she squealed like an excited child and spun away from him. "I have the most amazing surprise for you!"

She walked to a closed window and threw the shutters open. Then she motioned for Shiverrig to join her. "Come, your army awaits. The view from the south window is particularly excellent."

He rose to his feet and walked to the window. His muscles responded ahead of his will, and he was at the window faster than he thought possible. He gasped at what he saw. An ocean of bodies filled the open fields behind the palace. The numbers were staggering.

Lord Jolla stood at the head of the immense army. When the half-breed demon saw Shiverrig in the window, he raised his spear in salute. The army followed his lead. Tens of thousands of warriors, no more, many more, raised their weapons into the air.

Shiverrig smiled a wolfish grin. His mind cleared, and his thoughts were fast and lucid. He forgot about the nightmare that plagued his sleep and the unfortunate citizens who failed the change of chaos.

His vision was sharp. He saw the face of each warrior, no matter the distance. He picked out subtle gradations of skin tones or the intricate map of veins through leathery wings. His eyes quickly counted the transformed. Five hundred and fifty-four thousand strong stood ready, awaiting orders. *Five proper legions,* he thought and chuckled softly to himself. "I told you, Conrad. I would command the Five Armies one day."

"Are there more?" Shiverrig asked though he didn't take his eyes from the field.

"More have survived the change but have been put to other tasks. Equipping and feeding a conquering army of this size is no small matter. I hate to admit it, but the worm has done a commendable job," Sess'thra said begrudgingly.

"Malachi still has his uses," Shiverrig turned from the window. "Call the squires. I will address the troops in my battle armor. It's time to settle a score with Sekka and her warlords."

+YOU HAVE NO NEED TO WORRY, MY GOLDEN BOY. YOU CANNOT BE HARMED BY ANYTHING OF THIS WORLD.+

"I'm invincible?" Shiverrig said and immediately wished he hadn't said it aloud. He nodded to the door to dismiss Sess'thra. "Leave me."

"As you wish, my Aj-Kahun," Sess'thra said through pouting lips.

The deep voice chuckled as Sess'thra closed the bed-chamber. *+AH, THE SUCCUBUS. SUCH A TASTY MORSEL THAT ONE.+* Then Xerthotha's voice rose like a strong wind.

Shiverrig braced his mind for the pain that typically followed, but this time the pressure in his head was bearable.

+THE TWO ENTRANCES OF THE CHAOS GATE MUST BE CONTROLLED AT ALL TIMES.+

"Yes, my thoughts exactly. When will you invade Gathos? Surely that is within your great power," Shiverrig said. It was a test to see if the Chaos Devil could read his every thought, for he meant to destroy the Chaos Gate, not hold it as a military asset.

+THERE ARE UNSPEAKABLE RULES THAT CANNOT BE BROKEN AT THIS TIME, AND OPEN HOSTILITIES ARE NOT ALLOWED FOR ONE SUCH AS I. BUT WHERE I AM THWARTED, YOU WILL PREVAIL.+ The voice of the child princess responded.

"I wonder if you truly are Xerthotha. Your lack of conviction makes me think otherwise."

+HO! YOU ARE BOLD. LISTEN TO MY WORDS CAREFULLY, MORTAL. YOU MUST PLAY SEKKA'S DEVOTED SLAVE UNTIL INSTRUCTED OTHERWISE. SOON, SHE WILL PROCURE TWO SMALL BAUBLES. YOU MUST RETRIEVE THESE FOR ME BEFORE THEY REACH GATHOS. THAT IS OF UTMOST IMPORTANCE.+ The warrior's voice boomed in Shiverrig's mind.

"You speak of gifts? Am I to offer Sekka this new army as a gift as well? I think not. These warriors will serve to defeat Aeshmara and her siblings. I have a debt to settle. Now is the time to strike!"

+YOU WILL DO AS I COMMAND!+

The terrible voice brought Shiverrig to his knees, and his ears rang as if a noonday bell clanged in his head. The pain was excruciating. Blood flowed freely from his nose and splashed in small puddles on the floor. And then it was gone.

+WHAT XERTHOTHA GIVES, CAN EASILY BE TAKEN AWAY, EVEN FROM YOU, MY GOLDEN BOY.+

Shiverrig managed to slowly rise to his feet. "Surely the enemy will smell your taint on me. The sorcerer, Dai-Ko-Zior knows."

+DAI-KO-ZIOR IS BUT A PLAYTHING TO FORGOTTEN GODS. YOU HAVE BEEN MARKED WITH THE FAVOR OF XERTHOTHA. NONE, NOT EVEN SEKKA, WILL KNOW WHO LIES BENEATH YOUR SKIN.+

"And the baubles you require?"

+WE SHALL SPEAK OF THEM ANOTHER TIME. FIRST YOU MUST WIN THE TRUST OF SEKKA. SHE IS THE KEY TO YOUR EVERLASTING POWER. DO AS I COMMAND, AND THE MORTAL WORLD WILL BE YOURS.+

The presence of Xerthotha faded.

"No, Devil, I will not do as you command. The Chaos Gate will be destroyed, and the filth from the Abyss will be removed."

Shiverrig frowned as the telltale smell of cinnamon and sulfur drifted past his nostrils. He knew the succubus had materialized behind him.

"I hope that doesn't include me," she said.

"I told you to leave me."

She moved in front of him, searching for his eyes with her own.

"Listen to me, my foolish love. Xerthotha's power is limitless. He's a terrible foe and a dangerous ally. His fickle mood changes as much as his shape, and you are only useful to him while you hold his fancy." She reached up with both hands to hold the sides of his face and lowered it to make sure she had his attention. Her strength was considerable.

"There is a game being played that goes beyond this world and stretches through the history of time. You are but one of many pieces being moved by the hand of the Chaos Devil. You must be mindful of every step you take from this point onward."

"You sound as if you actually care. I have no desire to be Xerthotha's pawn. I will destroy the Chaos Gate before he, or any other devil, can use it to enter my kingdom."

"That will be no easy task, even for you. A Chaos Gate is created from ancient magic, and once born, it wills itself to survive."

"Wonderful. If it lives, then it can die."

Sess'thra wrapped her arms around Shiverrig's waist. "You're not listening. If you are to survive this war, you will have to move with great skill. But with every defeat comes a valuable lesson. Now you will not underestimate the Warlords of Vyzyn. You must stay two steps ahead of Aeshmara and her siblings and miles ahead of Sekka.

"Again, I warn you, do not trust the Chaos Devil. Xerthotha will not honor any bargain he strikes with you. He will alter his persona and claim the pact did not belong to him."

"You seem to know this devil well."

"My knowledge of the Chaos Devil is my own," Sess'thra said and stared hard into Shiverrig's eyes. "Heed my warning. The stakes in this conflict have grown."

"Fine. Keep your secrets. I will play along with Xerthotha's plans until they no longer serve my purpose. Go now and bring the squires to my private armory. I will see Daku, Lord Jolla, Duke Manda, and Malachi as well. The army marches at dawn. Go."

Sess'thra gave a deep bow. "Yes, my Aj-Kahun." A wicked smile graced her dark lips when she rose. "You are a most interesting mortal. Fearless to the end."

Four squires in purple and rose attire placed and fastened gleaming armor to Shiverrig's massive legs. Each piece of war armor had been carefully molded to his body and fit perfectly over the padded gambeson under-suit. Shiverrig had donned a lightweight chainmail undershirt when Lord Jolla and Malachi came into the arming chamber. Daku shuffled in a moment later.

The last to join the group was Duke Manda. His body had changed due to Xerthotha's mist, like all the other citizens of Qaqal. Somehow, he still maintained a basic humanoid appearance, two arms, two legs, and a human head, though now his skin was covered in a colorful design of blues and yellows and shined like fish scales against the light. His eyes had grown large and dead, like the black eyes of a deep-water shark.

Still a peacock, Shiverrig thought.

"We do not have enough mounts for each warrior," Shiverrig said as his breast-plate was fastened around his upper torso. "Lord Jolla, you will instruct half of those who can fly to leave now. I want them to take up position around the Chaos Gate. Place them under Lord Vorleeth's command. Name a second commander in case there are altercations along the way.

"Then, divide two full legions into smaller divisions of spear, shield, and archers. Have them ready for a quick march, light equipment only. You will assume command.

"I will lead the cavalry division, which will stay tied to the foot soldiers during the march to the Last Garrison. There, we shall make camp in the fields and wait."

Shiverrig turned to Manda. "Your time as Finance Minister in Qaqal has ended.

Bring one half of all troops, aerial, mounted and on foot to Gethem, and fortify the new capital city."

"Your wish be done, Aj-Kahun," Manda said and respectfully bowed.

"By your will, my Aj-Kahun," Jolla said. He, too, bowed in acknowledgment. His dull blue wings folded neatly behind his back.

"Malachi, you will prepare the supply train. Load the lead wagons with immediate needs only, arms, armor, squires, blacksmiths, surgeons, cooks, and food to feed the troops. Strip Qaqal bare of whatever resources remain. The heavier equipment, war engines, and raw building material will follow later. I need speed of movement. Is that understood?"

"Without a doubt, my Aj-Kahun. It shall be done," Malachi bowed low. When he rose, Shiverrig saw the suspicious eyes of the fiend, Hilo, staring at him behind Malachi's human features. "By my estimates, that leaves roughly half of the menial workers here in Qaqal."

"Yes, it does," Shiverrig said. "Once you have supplied the soldiers' march to the Chaos Gate, you will lead the remaining citizens to Gethem. I have no desire to return to this place."

Malachi bowed again. "As the Aj-Kahun commands."

"What about me?" Daku asked. He fingered the tip of a long-spaded spear in a rack against the wall. "Do I have some role in your grand parade?"

"You'll remain at my side when we march to the Chaos Gate to join Sekka's Frost Legion. I am interested to hear the stories of Ordu. The Master Monks were said to be brilliant military strategists. I'm curious to know what you learned while tucked away at the top of your mountain retreat. I'm assuming you didn't spend all day and night contemplating the turning of the seasons."

Daku's eyes narrowed at the mention of his ruined home. "I know that every new empire was built on the ashes of the last. I suspect this one will be no different and will fall the same way."

Shiverrig chuckled. "That circlet is quite a boon, but I see it hasn't improved your attitude. Your brazen spirit is alive and well."

"The Monastery of Ordu was a sacred place, I know that now. You will not disrespect its memory with your snide remarks."

Shiverrig raised his hands in mock innocence. "I meant no harm." He looked to the others. "You have your orders. We march at once."

Snow covered the rural landscape as far as the eye could see. Small snowdrifts sparkled in the afternoon sun, as tiny ice crystals reflected chips of light. Darker clouds gathered on the horizon, though the sky overhead remained clear.

The scent of changing weather clung to winds driving down from the Hoarfrost Mountains and flowing across the northern plains of Baroqia. Fresh snow would fall before the day was done. That would hamper his movement to the Last Garrison, and they were already moving dreadfully slow.

The newly transformed half-breeds had endless endurance but were always fighting within their ranks. Shiverrig sighed in his saddle. He would train these creatures into disciplined soldiers, if he had time.

The line of troops wove behind him for over a mile. He hoped their numbers would be enough. This was to be the gamble for the kingdom, and most likely his mortal soul. He recalled Daku's history lesson of empires being built on the ashes of the old. The boy had a sharp wit and sharper tongue.

He had taken a risk with that one by letting Khalkoroth live. If he wanted to rid himself of one less dagger in the night, he would have executed the pale demon long ago. But he had to admit he liked the youngster. He appreciated a man who dared to speak his mind.

Shiverrig looked behind him and to the right. Daku slumped on the back of an oversized chaos horse. His white, hulking body was more bearlike than human and did not rest well in a saddle. Shiverrig thought it curious why Daku had chosen to ride when he easily could have kept pace with the horses, even at full gallop, and be barely winded. *Perhaps the boy longs for more familiar, human behaviors,* Shiverrig thought.

He brought his horse close to Daku's chaos horse and immediately noticed the ornate scabbard strapped to the rear packs. Tiny shards of ice crystals wafted off its surface and trailed in a mini snow flurry behind him.

"Khalkoroth hated that sword," Shiverrig said.

Daku's dark, charcoal eyes peered into Shiverrig's own. Then looked back to the road. "It's a fine blade."

"Your predecessor could not bring himself to wield it. He said it was too argumentative."

"Khalkoroth was a stupid beast with no appreciation for the subtleties of martial art. The strength of a warrior is mirrored by the protection with which he is surrounded. I learned this truth at Ordu."

Shiverrig nodded with appreciation. "You have healed well and are once more looking strong and fit, with a clear mind, no less."

"I have Khalkoroth under control if that is the true question behind your pleasantries. The circlet keeps him at bay, but the demon is still with me. He's a crafty thing, and for now, he sulks and waits."

"Plotting your demise, no doubt."

"And yours. Eventually, one of us will consume the entirety of the other. The real battle has yet to be fought."

Shiverrig looked ahead and took in the landscape. It was a beautiful land. "What do you make of all this?" Shiverrig spanned his arms around behind him. "This march, the troops, all of it."

Daku shrugged his shoulders as if he couldn't care one way or the other. "We march to the Chaos Gate to unite with the Sekka's warlords, presumably to resume the conquest of Sunne."

Shiverrig's thoughts fell into the slow cadence of heavy hoofbeats muffled by the snow.

"Yes, that is the order of things," Shiverrig said at last and waited as Daku pondered the events leading up to this moment.

Daku's bestial face took on an introspective countenance and then glanced sideways at Shiverrig. He glanced over each shoulder, checking the nearness of the closest soldier. When he was sure it was safe to speak, he slowly turned his bear-shaped head toward Shiverrig.

"You march two-fifths of your army to the Chaos Gate, to do what, hand over the most powerful standing army in Baroqia to another who would rule in your place? I don't think so."

"Oh, and why is that?" Shiverrig feigned indifference.

"Because you also march an even greater host to fortify Gethem. If, and more likely, when, things go poorly at the portal, the city of your forefathers will need to withstand a siege from Sekka's forces."

"But Daku, I am the Frost Queen's loyal servant."

"Hardly." Daku laugher was deep and guttural, but not as sinister as before when Khalkoroth had control of Daku's soul. "Does the succubus know what you intend?" Daku scratched the underside of his muzzle, thinking. "She must."

Shiverrig sized up Daku before answering. He needed allies, and Daku was bound to him by the circlet, and by extension to Xerthotha. A misstep on Daku's part would allow the pale demon to regain control. And Daku wouldn't risk that outcome.

"She knows."

"Then you have one more conspirator at your side. Until I can finally rid myself of Khalkoroth's influence, I need you and whatever powers protect you." Daku tapped the circlet on his head. "The length of your life is now tied to my own, and I have no wish to die."

Shiverrig nodded brusquely and kicked his horse forward. Sess'thra, and now Daku were his, as far as he could tell. Although loyalty was written on a thin and brittle parchment when it came to demonkind. *Power is all they understand*, thought Shiverrig, *and the fear of retribution.*

The thought amused him. He couldn't trust the human nobles any more than the demons, and they were his own kind, that is if he still considered himself human.

He bemoaned the loss of Malachi's counsel. His archvashim had foolishly partaken of Sess'thra's demon seed like some sort of heart-struck lover in a tragic romance, eager to throw his life away for his ambivalent beloved. Usually, tales of this nature ended with the unrequited lover plunging a metaphorical dagger into his heart, or a real one in his back.

His archvashim now relied more on Hilo's calculating mind as his own fell deeper into an addled, chaotic mush of contradiction and madness. *Malachi, you fool. I warned you not to go too deep, and now look at what has become of you, and of me.*

Hilo was a wildcard, but the fiend knew what pain awaited him if he betrayed his Aj-Kahun to Sekka. And the demon was more inclined towards self-preservation than self-sacrifice.

He'll play nice until he knows for sure that Sekka has won, which will also mean I'll be dead. Every move had become a life-or-death struggle.

And where was that blasted assassin? Eventually, Dax would learn Shiverrig's campaign had taken on a more sinister patron. The influence of Xerthotha would not remain hidden for long. Which meant he had little time to play out the game with Sekka before Dax came for him in the night. Best to kill the changeling when they next met and stop wondering if the troublesome creature was lurking in the shadows with a sharp blade.

But if Sess'thra could be turned by the influence of power, maybe it would be the same for the assassin as well. Dax was not born of Gathos and had more of a mercenary mindset than a loyal follower. If his gain was substantial enough, perhaps he would flip.

"I'll send Sess'thra to find him and convince him to join us," Shiverrig said to himself.

Shiverrig milled over other decisions as the army passed through another abandoned town, this one smaller than most. There were no familiar smells of wood burning in fireplaces or the sounds of children playing in the streets. No merchants called out their wares or the sounds of creaking wagons drawn by old nags.

Fresh snow had covered the ground and the tops of low buildings but couldn't hide the damage of rampaging demons. Claw marks raked across doors, and the glass was shattered in most of the windows. Shiverrig would occasionally spot a dead carcass of some otherworldly creature, though no human bodies remained in sight. Apparently, the wolves and bears of Baroqia had not the stomach for Abyssal flesh.

He was surrounded by so much death. Maugris had unleashed an avalanche of destruction when he summoned Sekka to the Mortal Realm. And no matter Shiverrig's efforts to staunch the filth coming from Rachlach Fortress, and that foul Chaos Gate, the flow of bile continued to pour out.

And you've made it worse. The voice of Shiverrig's late father haunted his thoughts. How much of this had he caused by agreeing to conspire with the sorcerer? He could have joined the king's banner and destroyed the threat from the North as a loyal son of Baroqia. And then what?

After the battle was won, King Conrad would have dismantled his ancestral home piece-by-piece.

You're wrong, father. I did what I had to do to ensure our Great House's survival and the preservation of the kingdom. If that spineless Conrad had remained on the throne, the real battle would have been lost, and the citizens of Baroqia would be marching to the Chaos Gate in chains.

Shiverrig looked at the transformed citizens of Qaqal. Hadn't he accomplished the same result? No, a city was sacrificed to save a kingdom, and possibly the entire realm. It was a hard but necessary choice, and he was the only one with enough courage to make it.

He would not let the lands of his ancestors be swallowed by the madness that vomited out of the Chaos Gate. He was the people's champion, their protector, and their savior.

This was the only way he could hope to win. He would make this right once Sekka was defeated. The kingdom would be cleansed, in time. Now, all that mattered was victory.

"We are still too far East for Sekka's warbands to care about such towns. The frontier villages offer easier prey for her soul harvest," Shiverrig said, alarmed at finding another deserted town.

Sess'thra kicked her chaos horse forward to a snow-covered hump beside the road. She prodded her mount to rear kick the mound, pushing it over and sending the snow flying. Beneath the snow covering was the body of a corpse covered in rigid spines with numerous segmented legs tucked under its body. Its head lay a few paces away.

"This creature is a Chaxu and was part of Maugris's horde unleashed from Rachlach Fortress to fight the King's Army. I believe you were preoccupied with killing the king that day to notice."

Shiverrig glared at the succubus. He didn't need a history lesson. "How many of Maugris's horde survived? Just give me your best estimate."

"It's difficult to say. After the fall of Lord Oziax by the Ever Hero, most of the horde's demons fell upon each other or simply scampered away," Sess'thra said and walked her fingers over the palm of her hand.

Daku kicked his chaos horse closer. "You mean Kasai?"

Shiverrig raised an eyebrow. Daku sounded genuinely surprised and possibly, what, jealous? That was a second emotional reference to Daku's past life as a monk of Ordu within a week. Shiverrig wondered at the implications and the possible confusion it might cause the young monk.

"Yes, your friend has grown strong," Sess'thra said. Her eyes grew wide with excitement. "Powerful."

"Strong? How strong?" Daku pressed. He kicked his mount again, harder this time.

"I'm not sure, Daku. How strong do Ever Heroes become?" Sess'thra teased.

"Ever Hero," Daku scoffed at the idea. "It's a stupid name. He's a sham."

"Enough," Shiverrig interjected. He gave Sess'thra a reprimanding stare. "We have other concerns. There has been no contact or word about any Ever Heroes or demigods walking Baroqia since the final battle at the Last Garrison. I'm sure your friend perished with everyone else at that massacre."

"He survived," Daku said and pulled back on the reins of his chaos horse. "I will see him again." He fell back into the column of regular troops as they plodded along toward the Last Garrison.

"He's not wrong you know. The young Ever Hero did survive," Sess'thra said as she directed her chaos steed back into line. "He will be an interesting player in the games to come."

The road to the Last Garrison snaked ahead of them. Days passed, and the trees and towns gave way to open fields. Thin stalks of brown, long grass poked above the snow's surface, their tips swaying in the light breeze. Months had passed since the King's Army drew swords against Maugris's horde. Small humps remained on the field and provided a frozen bounty for crows and other scavengers during the cold winter season.

"Lord Jolla set up camp here. Spread the troops out and maintain wide corridors for movement. I don't want the troops hampered by loose equipment, empty wagons, or the bodies of the dead when the call to arms is sounded."

It was an odd thing to consider laying out a camp for warriors who did not need sleep or protection from the elements. "Report to me the moment there is word from the recon scouts. I suspect Aeshmara's troops will be along in good time."

"By the will of the Aj-Kahun, it shall be done." Jolla bowed and gathered other ranking knights to carry out his orders.

"Sess'thra, Daku, you are with me. It's time I saw the infamous Chaos Gate with my own eyes."

65

DESDEMONIA

Desdemonia walked beside Kasai as Zhao Houzi led the party down a long corridor, which opened to a vast atrium of another section of the Heavenly Hall. Wingless celestials scampered across the lobby area, rushing from one office door to the next. They glided over smooth and polished, milky-white marble tiles, each perfectly laid and without chip or crack.

The celestials moved in haste, talking together, nodding their heads in unheard agreements or wagging their fingers with polite disapproval. Massive water fountains pulsed choreographed, liquid dances into the air, but never did a drop of water spray onto the floor.

Desdemonia looked to the upper stories and saw angels soaring through the open air, delivering documents or other important matters to offices higher in the complex. Long banners of white and blue hung from the balconies. They were tied at their base to not create a visual disturbance or interfere with the angels' flight.

Whether on the ground or in the air, the workers never collided with one another. They meshed seamlessly between invisible lines of traffic with ease. There was a perfect harmony of movement wherever she looked. Even the pale gold-colored walls of the atrium contained a similar, flawless design.

An even number of tall columns with inlaid grooves rose on the sides, separating one office from another. The ground columns supported the next story of offices with open balcony entrances. The second set of columns, offset from the lower group, rose from the second story.

The pattern repeated itself in a perfect spiral as it rose along the atrium's curved walls, opening to a cloudless sky. Desdemonia lost count of how many levels the atrium contained. It was all too rigid for her tastes.

"Amazing. I've never seen such wonders." Kasai arched his back, trying to take it all in.

"Yes, there is a precise mathematical symmetry between each story within the atrium. Every angle follows a specific pattern, and as it repeats, keeps the entire structure sound. The Heavenly Hall is truly a marvel of architectural design.

"The Hall simultaneously aligns with the surrounding buildings of Asher as well as the geography of the mountain. Weather, wind currents, even degrees of precipitation were considered in its design, however slight they may seem," Zhao Houzi said. "I wrote a one thousand five hundred and two-page essay on the flawlessness of the design. You can read it if you like when all this is over."

"I can see no imperfections," Desdemonia said with disappointment. She was not as awestruck as Kasai in the least.

"Oh no. Imperfections are simply not allowed. Everything is in perfect balance." Zhao Houzi placed his fingers together, making the shape of a steeple. "The structure is sound and has existed as such since the city of Asher came to be."

"How can anything grow freely here, when everything is forced to be what you want it to be, and not what it was made to be?" Desdemonia said. She kept her head down and let her hair shield her face. *Why must that light be so damn bright?*

"There is no room for imperfection in a perfect world," Zhao Houzi said. He raised a single finger into the air as if to make a simple yet straightforward point.

"Don't you miss the unpredictable nature of the jungle, Monkey?"

Zhao Houzi raised his bushy eyebrows as if remembering a forgotten memory. "The jungle?"

"So sad," Desdemonia shook her head. "You have forgotten who you are."

"But this is Paradise. Life is held at its highest point of perfection."

"Held? Seems more like grabbed tight and strangled to me. You think you live in Paradise, but it's just a pretty prison, designed to control everything. You live the same life, day after day after day. What meaning do you have now? What new experiences do you discover? Can anything new exist in a world where everything is entirely the same?

"You hold this world too tight, as a prize to be coveted. But you squeeze all the air from its lungs," Desdemonia hunched her shoulders and lowered her head into her chest.

Zhao Houzi brought his small hands up to his furry face and stroked his short beard. "I never thought of it that way. It's a most interesting point of view. I wonder what Titus would say to your bleak assessment of the Heavenly Realm?"

"Your paradise is a dead place," she said.

"Don't listen to her. The witch speaks true to her dark nature," Orin said. "Ever Hero, it is only a matter of time before she turns on us all. She will betray us to her true master. We should leave her here."

"Orin, we will need every one of us to complete the Challenge of Righteousness," Kasai said. He gave her a look of concern.

I wish he would stop doing that. I'm fine; just a bit worn out. But Desdemonia knew she was being sour and abrasive. She glanced at Kasai and noticed he was staring at her.

"What?" she said sharply.

"Des, what's going on with you?" Kasai asked tentatively.

She gave him a quick glare then lowered her head again. "Are there no clouds to block out that horrible sun?"

She felt an uneasy tension grip her as they approached a ground-level door, edged with delicate designs, curling around its frame.

"Ah, here we are. You will find your belongings inside." Zhao Houzi grabbed the handle and opened the door.

The arming chamber was neat and clean. Their clothing had been mended or replaced entirely with a newer, more luxurious version. The Kibo Gensai spent little time changing into their angelic gifts. Only Desdemonia refrained from wearing anything provided by the Heavenly Court. She made do with her worn forest clothing.

She noticed spell components and healing herbs laid out in small packets on a silver platter, some of them exceptionally rare. She found bone dust, iron filings, rose petals, bat dung, gold dust, oak bark, eggshell, snakeskin, and a few more that she wasn't sure quite how to identify. *At least one of them is thoughtful,* she thought begrudgingly as she stuffed her hidden pockets. *Though, I bet it was the little monkey man.*

"You must prepare," Zhao Houzi said to the group as he walked beside Kasai. "Remember, there's a time limit to fulfilling your mission, and you will be watched closely."

Desdemonia saw Ninziz-zida resting on a pedestal. The staff's sections, and the chain that connected them, had been polished with care. A slight flame rippled along the surface of the three segments. It traveled the length of one section and then jumping to the next. Heavy, orange robes hung nearby, along with darker colored pants and woolen socks. A new set of shoes with long cloth ties rested on the floor.

Kasai reached for the robes. Desdemonia could tell they were cut to his exact fit and were of high quality.

"You're gonna look clean and handsome on your way back to hell," Desdemonia said. She meant it as a joke, but apparently, nobody else thought so based on their dour faces.

"What? It was just a joke. Sheesh, tough crowd."

Kasai just shook his head. Then he turned to the monkey. "Thank you, Master Zhao Houzi, for all you have done."

Zhao Houzi bowed. "You have a noble heart, Soulless One. It has been my honor to serve you, even if only in the smallest of ways."

Kasai put his arms through the sleeves of the robes and let them sit on his shoulders. As she expected, it was a perfect fit. "At least we will have Aetenos by our side and at full strength in this fight," he said.

Monkey's normal jovial expression turned blank. "Yes, well, may the Heavenly Light guide you true, in all you do. I hope Lord Raguel will see the error of his ways before it's too late. Lady Illyria has done all she can on your behalf."

"There is more between those two than meets the eye," Pallo said as he cinched up his sword belt and checked the edges of his two short swords. Run-Run brought a finger to just under his lower eyelid and pulled down on the skin. He pointed back at his brother and nodded enthusiastically.

"Raguel and Illyria? Why should we care about them? We have been given back our freedom. Finally, they know our worth," Orin said. He did nothing to hide the bitterness in his words. "I'm eager to begin our search for the Devil Queen. She must pay for the murder of Airis."

Desdemonia rolled her eyes. "You're not free. That self-righteous angel holds your life on a short leash. The death sentence remains, only now we are our own executioners."

Orin sheathed his two long daggers at his hips. The blades clicked into place, like two jaws snapping shut. He glared at her as if she was the enemy. "You're mistaken."

Desdemonia just sighed. She knew she had it right. This was a suicide mission. How were they expected to succeed? They were five against an archdevil, with all the might of the Circle of Gathos behind her. No one had even mentioned Sekka's current whereabouts. She could be anywhere. And what army was left to oppose her when she returned to Baroqia in force?

"Has anyone said where we will find her?" Desdemonia asked. "Or are we supposed to just ask people as if we are looking for a missing person? Hi, excuse me, have you seen Death walking around lately? Long white hair, bad disposition, known to steal souls? No? Okay, have a nice day."

"Aetenos will know," Kasai said with confidence. "He defeated Sekka once before, during the first Frost War. He will do it again."

"Oh, I wouldn't count on it. The old monk is crazy. And has anyone seen him for that matter?" Desdemonia said discouragingly. "I have a bad feeling we're on our own in this fight."

"No one has seen him since Raguel's guards took him away after the hearing," Pallo said.

Desdemonia heard heavy boots coming closer. Soon, three Protectorates entered the arming chamber. "The Chancellor Pinnacle will see you now," said the commanding guard. He scowled at Zhao Houzi. "Not you, Monkey."

Kasai looked to Zhao Houzi for an explanation. The monkey wore a forced smile. "Oh, it's no bother. Lord Raguel must have some parting words of encouragement for you."

The Kibo Gensai left the room with the guards while Desdemonia lingered behind, waiting for Kasai.

"Soulless One," Zhao Houzi said. "You have great strength within you, more than you know. Trust in yourself and let your noble heart guide you."

The monkey's small furry face broadened into a wide smile. "Now, off you go, young master."

Desdemonia couldn't help but see the sadness behind the clever monkey's eyes.

"Could this possibly get any worse?" she mumbled to herself as she followed Kasai out of the room.

66

KASAI

"I will not repeat myself." Kasai heard a strong voice said behind a closed door. He thought it sounded like the Chancellor Pinnacle, but the voice was slightly muffled.

"You're being unreasonable," Aetenos's voice responded clearly. "I must be permitted to leave the Heavenly Realm."

Kasai was shocked at what he heard. He looked questioningly at Pallo whose worried eyes confirmed the same. The lead Protectorate knocked gently on the door.

"Enter," the strong voice called out from behind the door.

The door opened, and Kasai saw Lord Raguel sitting behind a grand desk of polished wood. Four wooden angels with outstretched arms and unfurled wings supported the thick tabletop. Light poured through seven windows lining the back wall, which cast him in a strong silhouette. Aetenos stood in front of the table. His hands were held comfortably behind his back. The room was clutter-free with no other chairs or tables.

"Don't just stand there, come in. I have little time for this matter," Raguel said. "Now, where were we? Ah yes, discussing Aetenos's forbidden deeds in your realm."

Kasai's eyes absentmindedly shifted to the aura of the archangel. The room bloomed with the light of a hundred rainbows. Kasai gasped at its intensity and quickly concentrated only on the physical form of Raguel.

"Lord Raguel, they are only children, and you send them alone against insurmountable odds. There must be another way we can prove ourselves to you."

"I'm sure there are a number of alternatives," Raguel said. His expression hardened. "But I do not trust you, any of you." He waved his hands at Kasai and his companions.

Orin took a step forward. "But you said—" Run-Run was quick to grab the feisty warrior and hold him back. Orin shucked Run-Run's hand away. He pointed an accusatory finger at Raguel.

"This isn't right."

"Orin!" Pallo grabbed Orin and pulled him back in line.

Desdemonia laughed. "The mad dog jerks eagerly against his master's rope, snapping his own neck with a crack."

Pallo fixed Desdemonia with an incredulous stare. "Please, don't make this worse."

Raguel was unmoved by the outburst. "I said you would be given the opportunity to right the wrongs you have created. The Challenge of Righteousness has justly been placed upon you."

"Please forgive my companions, Lord Raguel. We have endured much and are weary of mind and heart. I understand your concerns. We willingly accept the terms of your challenge. If I may ask one favor, not for us but for the innocent souls of Baroqia. Could you impart a pardon to the Immortal Mother, to close the Chaos Gate?"

"It would end so much unnecessary suffering," Kasai added.

"The Immortal Mother need not be troubled by such things. I but need to snap my fingers, and the Chaos Gate would collapse upon itself. Such is my power. But you are responsible for the devil you have unleashed and all of the wickedness she brings to the Mortal Realm."

Aetenos gave a half-smile at Raguel's boast. "Then close the Gate now, brother. If you can."

"Do not challenge me, monk!" Raguel boomed. Kasai and the others stepped back as if being pushed from the force of the archangel's voice. Only Aetenos held his ground.

"I jest, and I should not. Please, accept my apology," Aetenos said and respectfully bowed.

"What did you hope to accomplish by returning?" Raguel slapped his open palm on the hardwood table.

"There was more work to do in the Mortal Realm."

"I meant here," Raguel said in an exasperated tone. "Why did you return to the Heavenly Realm? Did you mean to break her heart a second time?"

Aetenos shook his head. His expression was saddened. "Let the past go, brother. Free your heart."

Raguel glared at Aetenos. Then, he leaned back in his chair, assessing Aetenos. "Only a fool would have been duped by Sekka so easily. The suffering caused by the Chaos Gate is your guilt to bear. And now you connive to bring Illyria back into the folds of your mischief. Hasn't she suffered enough by your betrayal?"

Kasai looked questioningly at Aetenos. "Betrayal?"

"Tell them how you stole Illyria's love, only to abandon her by returning to that miserable realm of mortals. You knew she could not follow you there. No True-born of the Seventh Heavens or Supreme Hell-spawn can remain there indefinitely. It breaks the rules of the Great Balance. But you insisted the mortals needed your help. The audacity!"

"They need guidance, and with no one to lead them, they can stray easily into harm's way."

"You left her broken."

"Raguel. Let it go."

Raguel clenched his jaw, and his body shimmered as it vibrated in anger. His colorful feathers bristled like splayed fingers. And almost as quickly, the archangel became calm and composed. "You're right. It's in the past. But now that I have you, I will not allow you to make the same mistakes again."

"I must be allowed to face Sekka."

"No. You will remain here, under close supervision, until the Challenge of Righteousness has been met or abandoned. This duty has now passed to your avatar."

The word *"No"* echoed in Kasai's mind. He cleared his throat, trying to think of something to say. "Lord Raguel, please forgive me. But how will we defeat Sekka without the strength of Aetenos at our side?"

Raguel smirked at Aetenos. "Isn't it obvious?" He then turned to Kasai. "Aetenos created you to continue his role of divine shepherd. Now, it's up to you to lead the flock."

"But I'm not ready," Kasai stammered.

"Then, Aetenos chose wrongly. This should serve as a lesson to him, and all who wield divine power thoughtlessly."

"Please, close the Chaos Gate. Save the innocents who will die while it exists," Kasai pleaded.

"All the more reason for you to hurry in your task."

"But you must! Please!"

"Kasai, stop. Don't give the bastard the pleasure of groveling. He may have the power to close the portal, but he doesn't care. He has no heart. It's why he lost Illyria's love in the first place," Desdemonia said and tried to pull Kasai closer to her, but he pulled away.

"But what of the stolen soul energy flowing into Gathos? You will allow Sekka to create more demons to fight in the ongoing war against you," Kasai said.

"The Seven Heavens are in no danger of being overthrown if a few more souls go to the Abyss. This will not upset the balance," Raguel said, confidently.

"You cannot forsake them," Kasai said.

"Did you not do the same when you aided Sekka against her greatest foe, and in doing so, allowed her to continue her soul harvest?"

"Raguel, listen to yourself. You represent the best in all Heavenly beings. You know in your heart you should not make this demand. Illyria will—" Aetenos was cut short.

"Do not speak of Illyria! I can and will do as I please. She holds sway in my court. That awkward display of pageantry was a distraction but gave me an idea, and that stupid monkey was kind enough to provide the popular answer."

"The Challenge of Righteousness provides the perfect scenario to have neutral beings destroy an archdevil on neutral ground. It's an opportunity I will not squander. If your Ever Hero is worthy of his title, then he will prevail. If not, well, then the fate of you and your followers is out of my hands."

"Master Aetenos, this makes no sense," Kasai said.

Aetenos merely shrugged his shoulders. "He has a black heart and a stubborn soul."

"Lord Raguel, why would you let so many people die when you can save them so easily?" Kasai said.

"Do you really need to ask?" Desdemonia interjected.

Kasai looked at her with bewilderment. "How can this be happening?"

"Because he doesn't care about the people in our realm. He's obsessed with Illyria," she said with a sharp tongue and swept her hand at the Chancellor Pinnacle. "She rejected him and chose Aetenos instead."

Raguel's eyes snapped toward Desdemonia. His brow furrowed, and the menacing glare in his eyes returned. "Watch your tongue, Wood Witch."

Kasai looked back to Aetenos. "Is this true?"

Aetenos gave a slight nod and a sigh. "True love is like a ghost, which everyone speaks of knowing, but few are lucky enough to see. Raguel once knew love. But it was not returned to him in the manner he wished."

"And so, he punishes you through us," Desdemonia said.

Kasai looked back and forth between Aetenos and Desdemonia. Raguel stood quickly, causing the wooden chair under him to buck and screech against the polished stone floor. He turned from the group and walked to one of the many windows against the back wall.

"The time limit to complete the Challenge of Righteousness has already begun. I suggest you leave with haste," Raguel said as he stared out into the cloudless sky.

"But all those people," Kasai said.

"Kasai, are you really that naive? This whole thing, the Chaos Gate, the quest into the Abyss, all of it is meaningless to him. We are expendable things caught up in a spurned lover's tantrum." Desdemonia threw her hands up in the air. Her face was red with anger. "All I wanted was to be left alone in my forest!"

"I'm sorry, Des. If I could make it right, I would," Kasai said.

"Stop trying to save me! You can't. None of you can. It's too late for that!"

He reached out to comfort her, but she flinched away.

"Don't touch me. This is all your fault. Why couldn't you just listen to me for once?" She stormed to another side of the room. The Kibo Gensai smartly moved aside to let her pass.

"Let her be, my son." Aetenos took Kasai's shoulder in his hand. "Desdemonia will find her space. She's dealing with more than you know. You must be quick with the completion of your task, or I fear you will lose her to a horrible fate."

"Raguel demands the impossible. I cannot defeat Sekka. I have tried and failed. I cannot do this without you. Now is when I need you the most."

"Now? What is now, but your time to lead?"

"But I don't have your power. I am not one with the Boundless. It slips through my fingers whenever I try to grasp it."

"Then keep your hands open and let it land on your palm." Aetenos tapped Kasai on the forehead, and then on his chest over his heart. "All you need is here, and here." A warm smile lit his face. "You will find a way, and the Fire Serpent shall help you."

"But I thought all of this was for you? You're the Divine Fist. We rescued you so you could save us from evil. That is what you do."

"No, my son. This was all for you."

"Me?"

"Yes. Now is your time. Raguel is right when he says this was why the Ever Hero exists."

"But you made me into this. You changed me."

"Me? I changed nothing. You finally decided to see the impossible as possible. It's amazing what happens when we open our eyes to the truth."

"But Lord Raguel said…"

"Never mind what that old curmudgeon said. I'm telling you now. You have always had the spirit of the Ever Hero inside you, like your brothers and sisters before you."

Aetenos turned over Kasai's hands, revealing the palms. The marks of the demigod were still there. "And I will always be with you." The design had all but faded during the trial, but now the cobalt-blue spiral design flared to the surface.

"Any deviation from the destruction of Sekka will be met with severe consequences," Raguel said from the back of the room, still facing the windows. "We shall see what you are willing to sacrifice for each other and for the innocent souls you say must be saved."

Raguel finally turned around. "Due to the uniqueness the challenge demands, I shall allow you to pick the location where you are to be sent."

"Take us to Sekka," Kasai said, though his gut told him he was making another wrong decision.

Then Desdemonia stepped forward before Raguel could respond. "No, we shall go to the Heart of Sunne. Send us to the jungle."

This elicited a raised eyebrow from Raguel. "The Heart of Sunne? An interesting choice."

"Des, what are you thinking? There's no time to go to Sunne. Didn't you hear what Raguel said? We must seek out and destroy Sekka immediately."

"I heard him." The fearless druid had returned. Desdemonia's amber eyes blazed from an inner fire. "We go to Sunne. If the arrogant angel won't help us, I'm sure there are others who will."

Kasai looked to Aetenos for advice. The Great Monk winked fast and shrugged his shoulders. "The decision is yours, Ever Hero, but keep in mind, she's a quick study."

67

SEKKA

The crisp, cold air of Gathos changed abruptly to a hot and humid atmosphere. The air reeked of the fetid smell of moist decomposition and animalistic secretions. Ancient trees towered above the ground and into the muddy-orange sky. Their twisted branches fanned out over younger competitors. Each twig of each branch fingered desperately for the dull, orange light.

Everything looked like it was smoldering. Sekka felt something squish under her foot. Its purple remains spread out under her boot. *Disgusting,* she thought.

Ropey vines, covered in colorful fungus and mold, draped down to the forest floor. Slithering tendrils peeked out from hard, mollusk-like shells attached to bark and stone, undulated in the air, feeling for food. Condensed moisture collected in beads of dirty water, covering the visible surface in a wet membrane of slick slime.

The shrieking winds of Gathos faded away, and Sekka heard angry howls, warning of trespass and pending attack. All around her were the sonorous buzzing of small, flying demons, chittering in alarm from sprawling hives built in the dense canopy overhead.

Bizarre crustacean-like fiends crawled on segmented legs across the jungle floor, searching for anything to devour. Their pinchers pierced and cracked smaller creatures' carapaces, tearing away the hard skin and picking at the soft meat. Sharp mandibles chewed through the living and dead alike. The ground level chorus was of constant chomping and munching.

She scanned the crowded fern patches and broad-leafed foliage, trying to recall the footsteps that lead to Azrollorza's lair, but the path curved in an unfamiliar way. The vegetation swelled under her gaze, growing until stalks bulged against fibrous seams and eventually split.

New plant life vomited from the seeping gashes in colorful displays of euphoric birth. And was immediately forced to survive. Everything here fought for room to grow.

It wasn't long before the silvery-blue leather armor she wore was covered in grey needles and brown pollen. With a thought, she cast the unwanted debris from her person. She would not present herself to Azrollorza as a filthy peasant.

A fist-sized creature fluttered before Sekka's eyes on thin, transparent wings. Long, segmented legs of metallic blueish-purple dangled beneath its narrow thorax. The creature quickly pounced on a smaller, unsuspecting critter, scurrying across a pockmarked leaf.

Sekka observed the leaf curl over both prey and predator, wrapping the creatures in a papery blanket. The bodies of both animals were quickly dissolved in the acidic juice secreted by the carnivorous plant. Then the leaf uncurled a moment later, revealing only the broken pieces of tough exoskeletons that were too difficult to digest.

She took in her surroundings with no small amount of disdain. Azrollorza's lair was a chaotic realm of abundant life and grisly death, entwined in a constant struggle for dominance. It was the same everywhere in the Abyss. But here, the jungle strangled itself with too much life.

Nothing that a little frost couldn't cure, she thought.

"If we are following a trail, I cannot see it," Aosoth, the captain of her guard, said. The long spear he held in two hands was rendered useless in such close quarters. His sharp, ice-blue eyes scanned the ever-changing environment for danger as he slashed apart a wall of vines that barred their way.

The honor guard of five lumbering jol'goths pounded their meaty fists in the muddy ground as they walked on all fours in single file along the unmarked path. Cries and howls from demons hidden from view but close enough to be a threat sounded within the shadows of the undergrowth.

The jol'goths' nostrils flared in angry frustration as they twisted and turned their thick necks in search of enemies that could not be seen. They gathered protectively around Sekka, crowding her space, like everything else in this damned place.

"Get off me," she said, irritated. "I will not have you bumbling into me."

Then she noticed the foliage had changed. Human appendages replaced palm fronds, broad leaves became massive, snapping jaws. Saplings rose from the moist ground composed of fleshy amalgamations of human tissue and bones. Flayed arms stretched out, forming macabre branches ending in boney fingers for leaves.

Fern fronds unraveled like open hands at her approach, their ends tipped with extending fingers, grabbing for anything that ventured too close. A hapless, winged creature was snagged from the air and crushed in a tight fist of feathery mush.

The jol'goths drew short swords and hacked at the invasive feelers, cutting away the stalks and stems of the aggressive flesh-plants. Lime-green ooze dripped from the severed digits and puddled on the jungle floor. Miniature hordes of smaller creatures from the undergrowth raced to feed on the fortunate bounty.

"Keep moving," Sekka commanded. "It must be close."

Two jol'goths trailed behind the main group. They carried the ice sphere containing the butchered remains of Zizphander. Sekka was pleased to see the orb had not melted in the sweltering heat of Azrollorza's jungle realm. A soft blue glow illuminated the sphere and cast the nearby plants, vines, and trees in a cool, drab grey.

She walked with her chin held high. Her magic was strong, even in the domain of a Supreme Devil. This time she came offering gifts instead of begging for help.

Azrollorza would see her as the force of power that she was and treat her accordingly.

Plump, finger-long larvae inched through the damp undergrowth. Their smooth bodies crawled and squirmed over roots, rocks, and the decomposing mulch found on the wet jungle floor. The jol'goths squashed hundreds of the slimy worm-like creatures into pink muck with each heavy step.

The smell of death attracted hundreds more from the shadows of decaying logs and under soggy leaves, searching to feast on the remains of their kin. Soon the jungle floor moved like an undulating sea of bloated filth.

Sekka detected a change in the air. She rubbed her human-shaped nose to wipe away a tingling itch and caught a whiff of something more acidic nearby.

"The entrance is near. Push forward. Cut through the vines and bush."

The jol'goths furiously hacked through hanging vines and tall ferns. The foliage quickly fell away. The first guard through the vine wall hard-stepped forward and sank knee-deep into a viscous quagmire of sludge covered in blue-green algae. The jol'goth immediately jumped back, trying to reclaim the solid ground, but slid back down the slick bank.

Something colossal moved under the surface, pushing waves of fetid water and surface scum to the far reaches of the swamp. Sekka smiled inwardly. Azrollorza was predictable. The Supreme Devil never failed to exhibit blatant displays of her strength.

Could it be she was secretly insecure of Sekka's rise to power? The Frost Queen's manipulative schemes had brought her to heights undreamed of by lesser devils. And now she returned to Azrollorza as a champion.

Sekka had slain Xerthotha's champion in epic fashion. What did it matter that Azrollorza had interfered at a crucial moment? It was Sekka who orchestrated that intervention from the start. The victory was hers, and hers alone.

You are already doomed. Sekka heard the taunting voice of Maugris rattle in her head like a nagging conscience. She glanced behind her at the spoils of war she brought as an offering to her shadow patron. The Red Devil would never thwart her plans again.

Not this time, she answered.

The sludge of the swamp churned and bubbled. Three thin tentacles broke the surface. Each writhed in the air as if taking in the scent of trespassers. Then darted toward the jol'goth still wading in the quagmire. In moments the tentacles coiled around the guard's legs and yanked him under the surface of the murky pond.

Startled growls came from the other jol'goths' throats. Aosoth barked out orders to the others and held his spear out, pointing at each tentacle in turn.

"Be still, you fool," Sekka commanded. Her guard fell silent. "This is nothing but another test. Lower your weapons. They will do you no good here."

"Mistress, is that wise?" Aosoth questioned, refusing to lower his spear.

Sekka's glare was more than enough to convince the white-furred captain. She took a moment to compose herself. "Azrollorza! Your champion, Sekka, has brought you a gift!"

Nine fat tentacles rose out of the swamp. Each one wrapped like a constrictor around the decomposing body of a "living" soul-slave, for what human was ever truly still alive in the Abyss?

Sludge poured from the soul-slaves' open mouths, nostrils, and ears. Their eyes were rolled back, showing only milky white orbs. Luminescent blue-green algae sparkled as it clung to their emaciated bodies. They chanted a macabre chorus of wet gurgles and coughs. Their lungs heaved with desperate memories of air they no longer needed.

+A GIFT FOR AZROLLORZA?+ Sekka heard the voice of the Supreme Devil in her mind. The voice probed and penetrated deeper. Gentle fingers traced swirling caresses in her thoughts, like sweet honey, dripped over warm butter cake. *+WHAT HAVE YOU BROUGHT FOR ME, MY LITTLE PET?+*

Sekka turned to the shimmering sphere of ice. She waved her hand, and the orb lifted from the ground, then slowly moved over the swamp.

Azrollorza's head and shoulders rose out of the sludge. The Supreme Devil's face would be considered beautiful in mortal terms, but for the seven, lidless eyes clustered about her forehead. Strands of slime clung to her arms like slick seaweed.

Her hands reached out and caught the ball of ice with ease. Azrollorza puckered her full lips and kissed the orb. The sound of the smack sounded like the slap of wet flesh.

The ice dissolved into dripping slush. Azrollorza watched the fat wad of disparate parts fall into the swamp with an unceremonious plop. Bits and pieces of undescribed flesh, feathers, and entrails disappeared under the murky surface, then bobbed back up into view. A swarm of demonic flies came fast to feed. Sekka could hear their monotonous buzzing as they hovered over the feast that was once the mighty Zizphander.

Sekka's face flushed with disappointment. Azrollorza had dissolved her ice orb without much of a thought. She scowled inwardly. "There will come a time when the spells of Sekka are not so easily dismissed," she said quietly.

The Supreme Devil's unblinking eyes grew bright. "Xerthotha's intolerable whelp, in the flesh, if one could still say such a thing of the Red Devil," Azrollorza said in a satisfied tone. Her real voice gurgling through each word.

"This is all that remains of your rival's champion," Sekka added.

"RIVAL?" the soul-slaves screamed in unison. The word boomed through the quagmire. The swamp's surface rippled away from the bulk of the Supreme Devil in thick waves. A strong wind blew through Sekka's bone-white hair, and the trees behind her shook as if they trembled in fear.

"Azrollorza has no rivals," the Supreme Devil said in a sinister tone.

"No, my Mistress. Please forgive me." Sekka could not bring herself to say the last two words, "your servant."

Azrollorza's seven eyes blazed into her. "See that you mind your tongue, slave."

"I wished only to clear the life debt owed to you. Surely, this is a worthy payment."

"SILENCE!" The mouths of the semi-living soul-slaves screamed again. This time their voices spoke off cue, echoing throughout the swamp. They jerked like toy puppets on strings in Azrollorza's tentacled grip. Sekka saw that she was being mocked.

"It's Azrollorza who will determine the value of your gift. I have not so soon forgotten the destruction of the army I delivered to you in your time of need. So much valuable soul-material wasted." Azrollorza's mouth twisted into a sour frown.

"Not wasted. Used to further your goals and mine." Sekka climbed from the bank and knelt into shallows of the sludge. She could hear the clanking of armor as her honor guard mirrored her movement. "But what was lost can be replaced." She controlled her frustration and held her tongue. *There will come a time when I am the power, and you, wretched thing, are nothing. But sadly, it is not now.*

Sekka boldly stared at Azrollorza, then she glanced down at the floating remains of Zizphander. The Supreme Devil's eyes followed Sekka's to the multicolored feathers of bright red, yellow, and deep orange floating haphazardly in the swamp. It took but a moment to distract the displeasure of the Supreme Devil with something new and shiny.

"Now, let me see what we can do with what is left of the Red Devil," Azrollorza said and licked her lips.

She waved her hands over the floating body parts and chanted fluid words in a liquid voice. Sekka's excitement grew as the swamp below her bubbled and boiled. Zizphander's remains congealed into a viscous syrup, then slowly dissolved into the murky water.

A forked tongue rolled out of Azrollorza's wide mouth and sampled the soup floating at the surface. "Ah, this is a prize worth savoring. Xerthotha had given so much to his champion, all for naught."

She submerged her body until her mouth was at surface level. Then she slurped up Zizphander's essence. Each mouthful was relished with delight. And then it was over. The last of Zizphander, the Red Devil, and Champion of Xerthotha, was no more.

Azrollorza rose to her full height and smacked her lips. "Succulent." Swamp scum clung to her massive body, and black muck slid in thin streams between her numerous breasts. Her pseudopods slopped in the shallows, drawing her closer to Sekka.

She appraised Sekka with glassy eyes. Her pupils were diluted and dull from consuming the heady draught of Zizphander's essence. "You have done well, my little pet. Now, tell me, how did you think to hide such a precious asset from me? Hmm?"

The Supreme Devil loomed over Sekka. Her head swayed gently on her shoulders. A wide wake of debris followed behind her. "Oh, don't look so surprised. I have known of the Chaos Gate since it was born."

Sekka stood knee-deep in the swamp with her neck craned back. She hoped to appear confident and strong as the murky water lapped against her thighs.

"I meant no treachery to you, Great One. I wished to reveal this gift for a more glorious occasion. I offer its use to you as payment for my ascendancy."

"Do you offer a gift or a ledger? Does Sekka of Gathos give with one hand and take with the other?"

"You misunderstand," Sekka said. "I am here to offer you a partnership with an abundance of soul-slaves as my dowry."

Azrollorza's instinctively licked her lips.

"Let me rule by your side. We shall harvest the Mortal Realm together."

Azrollorza waded a bit closer to Sekka.

"Rule?" Two slick tentacles rose from the sludge. Each one caressed Sekka's face and neck, smearing gooey slime over her skin. "By my side?"

The words came out of Azrollorza's mouth like lapping waves in a shallow lake. She chuckled with deep, bemused laughter. "Any other creature would suffer a fate worse than Zizphander's for speaking such bold and arrogant words to me. But you have managed to do what was thought to be undoable. You have created something of value to me, and I want it."

"The Chaos Gate," Sekka said knowingly. If she had to relinquish such a treasure, it would be traded for something of equal value, or she would destroy it. "And my request? You will elevate me to your side in the High Pantheon of the Abyss?"

"You are getting closer with every success." Another tentacle rose from the swamp. It curled up Sekka's torso and raised her out of the swamp. Azrollorza's mouth curled into a lascivious smile.

Sekka did not flinch.

"I shall have the soul essence of the two who are bound to the portal. All I need is but a sliver. Bring this to me," Azrollorza gurgled.

"And you will honor my request?"

Azrollorza's head swayed from side-to-side. "We shall talk of ascension when you have completed your task."

Sekka understood. The greedy always demanded more. "I have what you seek from one but not the other."

"You will get me both. And do not dally. My appetite has been aroused and craves to be satiated."

"Yes, my Queen. It shall be as you demand." Sekka said and thought, *she means to devour the essence of Aetenos and his mind-slave.*

"You are an obedient devil. This is good. Your usefulness to me grows," Azrollorza said. Her breath was pungent with the last vapors of Zizphander. The taste of peppery cinnamon touched Sekka's tongue. A jolt of ecstasy coursed through her body. If only she could have devoured the Red Devil herself, instead of offering Azrollorza such a prize. Oh, the power she could have wielded.

"But tell me, how did you ensnare the demigod on Gathos?" Azrollorza slid closer. "There is no passage through the Outer Realms. The Amaranthine Barrier seals each world tight."

"Even True-borns may fall from their lofty perch in Tanalum. It's no different in the Abyss," Sekka said.

"Bah. The condemned bird is stripped of its wings once it's cast out from the Heavenly Realm. They become nothing of importance; an empty husk, unable to influence or help the mortals."

Sekka inhaled deeply, searching the air for anything that remained of Zizphander. She yearned for just one more taste. Nothing.

"It's a perplexing riddle," Sekka said offhandedly. "I stoked Aetenos's mind with enticing imagery of his love, Illyria, imprisoned in my keep. How could he abandon her to such a fate? Though I admit, I never really believed my playful ruse would work until it did."

"Aetenos arrived unannounced. His mind was broken. I have often wondered how he skirted the Amaranthine Barrier. He must have been allowed to come."

"Allowed, you say?" Azrollorza gasped.

Sekka was released abruptly, and fell awkwardly into the swamp water. Azrollorza withdrew her tentacles as if they had been burned by fire. The decomposing marionettes plunged under the surface.

+ALLOWED.+ Azrollorza's voice drifted in Sekka's mind. +*THERE ARE RULES WHICH CANNOT BE BROKEN.*+

The Supreme Devil slid beneath the murky water until only her eyes remained above the surface. Each one rolled in its socket, searching for intruders or spies. Sekka was surprised at Azrollorza's fearful reaction. What could unnerve a Supreme Devil in such a manner?

Sekka rose from the swamp. She halfheartedly brushed off the muck from her arms. Now was not the time for pride or vanity. She needed to act quickly. The loss of Azrollorza's favor would be catastrophic to her plans in the Mortal Realm.

"A great bounty awaits you," Sekka said enthusiastically. "I can provide the soul essence of one, and soon that of the other. I shall bring you what you desire."

Sekka didn't think it necessary to explain how Aetenos and his companions had escaped her dungeon. Soon she would find them and performed the ritual on the Ever Hero. Her lackadaisical attention to detail had proven to be a costly oversight. *I should have done this the moment I had them secured. Curses on them both!*

Azrollorza's bulk rose out of the swamp. Thankfully, Sekka had her attention again. It appeared the Supreme Devil was pondering different outcomes.

"You must gather the essence of the second with all speed. There is much to gain if we act quickly."

"Yes, my Queen. I shall go myself," Sekka said.

"Remember, the Ever Hero must come to you freely, as did his mentor. The essence of his soul must remain pure. It is the only way I may leave my world."

"But that's impossible. My queen, you are forbidden. The Great Balance prevents you."

"Not this time, child."

Sekka's mind raced for answers. Had Azrollorza found a way to bypass the Immortal Mother's laws? A disturbing thought crossed Sekka's mind. *She means to usurp control of the Chaos Gate from me. I will be left with nothing.*

No realm would be safe if Azrollorza could bring her entire form to its lands. Gathos would be first, of course. *How could I have been so short-sighted?*

Azrollorza moved closer to Sekka. "What could be a more glorious gift to your Queen than direct access to the Mortal Realm? I can think of no better way to ensure your ascendancy. Bring me the means to take what I desire, and you will sit by my side in the High Pantheon."

There it was! Azrollorza had finally said the promise aloud. It was now a pact that the Supreme Devil would be bound to uphold. Rules were rules, even in the Abyss.

Sekka needed time to think. Azrollorza demanded control of the one thing that would protect her from ruin. Where was the hidden trick? What was she missing?

She turned to Aosoth. "Come, there is work to do. We go to the Mortal Realm."

Aosoth grinned a mouthful of ice-crystal teeth. "Wonderful. It's been too long since I feasted on raw, human flesh."

A dull quiet had fallen over Furia Keep. The remains of the battle for Gathos had been buried under a new blanket of snow. Her military strength had been decimated, and she had no doubt her many enemies were eyeing her territory for conquest. Only the protection of Azrollorza now held them at bay. *At least there's that*, she thought.

Sekka had commanded Chedipe to supervise the rebuilding of the Frost Legion from the souls flowing from the Mortal Realm. Unfortunately, the numbers were meager as of late. The Warlords of Vyzyn were a constant disappointment. None of the siblings had made much progress in the conquest of Sunne. Sekka realized she would need to play a more active role in the subjugation of the jungle kingdom.

"Such are my labors," she sighed as she stepped across the surface of the Chaos Gate, accompanied by Aosoth and his jol'goth guard.

A bigger concern haunted her thoughts. Gathos was now safe, but she found the lack of pending attack disturbing. She had been deeply obsessed with the advancements, feints, and aggressive posturing of Zizphander over the long years that the lack of his presence made her feel a bit empty and fearful.

An unease crept up her spine. Did a trap sit in plain sight, waiting to be sprung when she let down her guard? She chided herself for feeling safe. It was the residue of invincibility one feels after a substantial victory. Nothing in the Abyss was ever truly safe.

Attacks came in layers, and she sensed a warning hiding in the shadows of another thought, but one she couldn't yet decipher. *Bah, I'm just paranoid. When I have the mortals locked in my dungeon again, I will have Chedipe question them and see what their loose tongues divulge. If Aetenos will not talk, perhaps the boy will.*

She chanted the ritual spell to activate the portal, and within moments she arrived in the Mortal Realm with a gurgling belch from the Chaos Gate. A small army of demons surrounded the portal. They were armed and poised for attack.

"These are not of my brood," Sekka said.

Aosoth and his warriors immediately took up defensive positions around her. But the demons encircling the portal did not attack. Instead, they lowered their weapons and watched her with curious fascination, like a town of peasants gathered at the roadside to watch a parade of knights riding past on their huge warhorses.

The demons looked queer to Sekka, and she could sense something crawling under the mask of their warped faces. There was a scent in the air that was strange to her, yet oddly familiar. She recalled the smell of Azrollorza's breath after she had devoured the essence of the Red Devil. The distinct memory of tasting peppery cinnamon touched her tongue.

Sekka spotted Shiverrig across the debris of Rachlach Fortress's ruined throne room. The floor was covered with rubble and large pieces of a collapsed wall. Sess'thra was there, and Khalkoroth. The succubus was speaking to them out of the corner of her mouth.

Shiverrig nodded, then he dropped to his knee in supplication. The motion was fluid and precise. Khalkoroth followed his lead, as did the thousands of warriors surrounding the Chaos Gate.

"Move aside," Sekka said to her guards.

The stone ruins of Rachlach Fortress were covered in a fine layer of snow and ice. The voracious appetite of the Chaos Gate had eaten away most of the mountain rock that had once acted as a ceiling to the throne room. What had been the seat of power in Trosk was now nothing more than a white, powdery grave.

Sekka crossed the steaming surface of the Chaos Gate with her honor guard following closely behind. Aosoth raced past her as she approached the far side and reached the stone slate of the ruins first. He stood upright and planted the butt end of his spear onto the floor. Its spaded tip extended three feet over his head.

"Rise," Sekka said as she appraised the warlord. Shiverrig cut an impressive figure beneath the heavy bearskins draped over his broad shoulders. He was thicker than

Sess'thra's description of him. Serrated muscles rippled along his forearms and exposed neck.

She had been informed that he had killed the Three, her mewling emissary to his court. The deformed messengers were an annoying reminder of Maugris's pompous attitude of his superior might, and she was happy to have them removed. But killing them without her permission was clearly an act of defiance to her authority.

She took note of the army surrounding the Chaos Gate. She now noticed many of them bore wings. They were strong, like Shiverrig, and carried the scent of a powerful demonic spirit, which was usually absent from creations using a human's seed as its foundation.

Half-breeds of this number and quality would take years to procure. Yet, he had done it in months. Azrollorza could have assisted in their creation as a prelude to her arrival. It was possible.

Sekka narrowed her eyes at Sess'thra. "It seems I have quite an impressive force on the other side of the Chaos Gate. In fact, much more so than I would have believed possible. These troops could have been put to use when Zizphander's horde invaded Gathos."

Shiverrig stood proud. She noticed he was not swayed by her presence in the least bit. Such arrogance! Yet, it was not misplaced like that sniveling fool Maugris. Sess'thra had provided vital intel during her time in the Mortal Realm. The Shiverrigs' were conquerors who knew how to win on their own terms. And if she knew this fact, then so would others. Was Azrollorza testing her resolve and presenting to her the next adversary to defeat and prove her worth?

Bah, Shiverrig was a mere mortal with a colorful family history. She was filling the void of not having an enemy to fight. She was just edgy from her meeting with Azrollorza, nothing more.

Sekka shook off the lunacy that Shiverrig was a threat and breathed in the cold air of Trosk. The temperature was soothing. The northern winters in the Mortal Realm did not compare to Gathos' arctic climate, but the crisp air was still a relief from Azrollorza's lair's oppressive heat.

"I have brought the Frost Queen an army bred for victory," Shiverrig said. He turned his body and swept his arms to encompass the entire area. His face looked straight ahead towards the Chaos Gate, but his left eye remained locked on her at its corner. She thought she saw the iris of his eye shift and twist into something dreadful. But then his face turned back to her, and his eyes were normal.

"The conquest of Sunne awaits at your pleasure," he said.

"Yes, I see. I am delighted by your initiative," Sekka said. "My servants have been busy."

"There are more. This is but a fraction of what I offer you," Shiverrig bowed again.

"More?"

"Yes, my queen. Many more. We are two hundred thousand strong. More than enough to overwhelm the jungle-dwellers of Sunne."

Shiverrig called to one of his generals. "Lord Vorleeth remain here while I show our queen her new army. Alert me if anything more comes through the portal." A half-breed with a stork-like beak and a great fan of red and purple feathers nodded in acceptance. Sekka couldn't help but see a small resemblance to Zizphander.

Khalkoroth sulked closer to Shiverrig's side but appeared more like a protective bodyguard than a haughty adversary. This struck Sekka as strange, for she recalled the pale demon held only disdain for mortals. She noticed his hand hovered over the pommel of the fell blade, Eishorror. *And his hackles are raised as if I am the enemy.*

She looked at him with a more quizzical eye. "Khalkoroth, what is that on your head? I have never known you to partake in jeweled trinkets," Sekka said. She kept her manner overly casual.

"Khalkoroth is no more, your highness. My name is Daku. I am from the Lost Monastery of Ordu."

Sekka raised an eyebrow. "Is that so? It's no easy feat to win a battle of control over such an ancient shadow demon. Most mortals try to reject the soul-bonding and are consumed, but you have embraced it. Interesting. It appears you learned something useful in that dusty monastery."

"Ordu taught me many things," Daku said.

"And Eishorror at your hip. Today certainly is a day for surprises. Oziax will be happy to know his blade is being used well while he waits on Gathos."

"My blade, your highness." Daku's eyes remained defiant. "He'll need to challenge me for it if he wants it back."

Sekka nodded approvingly. "Yes, of course."

A messenger approached with hesitant steps from behind the pale demon. She recognized him as one of her own from Gathos.

"What is it?" Shiverrig commanded.

The messenger bowed low to Sekka first. "My queen."

"Get on with it," Shiverrig said. The irritation in his voice was evident, as was the trembling body of the messenger.

"My Aj-Kahun, a large movement of troops has approached from the south."

"What markings do they bear?"

"The banners are of Gathos. Sekka's Frost Legion has returned from Sunne." The messenger glanced nervously at her, and then his eyes quickly found the ground.

"Numbers?" Shiverrig said.

"Less than ten thousand," the messenger mumbled.

"Speak up!"

"Ten thousand, my Lord. Maybe less. A trail of humans follows in chains, joined by a high number of wounded soldiers. The returning army appears to have suffered heavy losses."

"That is too small a number to represent all of the Frost Legion in our realm. A greater force of jungle dwellers may be circling our flanks. Have scouts ride east and west to confirm we are not being duped," Daku said.

Sekka was impressed with Daku's intelligent assessment of the situation. Unlike most shadow demons who were small and sickly, Khalkoroth's bulk made him built for war and fearless in battle. But a tactician? Never.

"We have monitored the progress of the Frost Legion since the Sarribe Pass. There has been no pursuit from Sunne," the messenger said, attempting to sound dismissive in front of his queen.

A low growl resonated from Daku's throat. "Are you challenging my orders?"

The messenger's demeanor changed fast, and his voice cracked. "It shall be done, Lord Daku."

"Continue," Shiverrig said, slightly irritated by Daku's distraction.

The messenger bowed. "The ten thousand wait in the outer fields by the south-most tree line. There are three who lead them. They wait."

A sly smile crossed Shiverrig's mouth. "Excellent. The Warlords of Vyzyn have returned home. Let us give our brother and sisters a warm welcome." Shiverrig rubbed his hands together like an excited child. Sekka presumed it was to take away the nip in the air. Although, she saw eagerness in the Aj-Kahun's eyes.

"Tell Lord Jolla to prepare the troops for inspection."

"Yes, Aj-Kahun."

"Is everything in order, Shiverrig? I'm sensing some friction," Sekka said.

"Everything is exactly how it is supposed to be, my queen. Now, if you will follow me, I have something to show you," Shiverrig said. He abruptly turned to leave. The small army of half-breeds snapped to attention. All eyes locked on Sekka. They waited patiently for her to follow.

Shiverrig's reception was calculated, of course. Presenting her with his newly amassed army was a brilliant bit of showmanship. She could smell the stench of deception coming from his pores as if a thousand vile flowers bloomed at once.

The reason was apparent. Shiverrig wanted what was hers. At some point, he would move to take it by force. *Let him try, and he'll join Zizphander in oblivion.*

Her eyes wandered over the muscular frame of the pale demon who was once Khalkoroth. The beast lumbered along at Shiverrig's side. She was sure the story of how Daku bested the shadow demon was an interesting one.

I suspect he's hiding much from me. They all are, Sekka thought. Daku craned his neck to look at her as if he could feel her eyes upon him. Sekka held his gaze, and he did not flinch. She gave him a playful smile. *I'll eventually uncover Shiverrig's plans, and Daku from Ordu will be an ideal place to start. If his mind shatters in the process, well then, all the better.*

Her jol'goth guard took up positions around her. Together they followed Shiverrig to his base camp. The sounds of industry and war echoed in Sekka's ears as she descended Storm Wind Pass. Smoke rose from forges in the basin below, like black snakes curling through the air. A dry wind brought the smells of burning wood, smelted ore, and the stench of demonkind.

Shiverrig had not boasted on the numbers of warriors under his command. A vast army of tens of thousands trained with shield and sword, spear and arrow, while an equal number toiled to raise a small city within the center of the vast military camp.

Trees cut from forests to the west and south had been dragged to the basin, shaved into planks, and stacked in neat towers. Sekka saw hundreds of such deposits of building material throughout the camp. Lesser thralls marched in winding lines between the new construction. They hauled stones on their backs or lashed angrily at chaos-changed, beasts of burden struggling to pull overloaded carts.

A ring-shaped quarry dropped in the city's centermost position with the start of a small keep under construction atop the remaining central column. *The mortal has some skill outside of hacking and slashing. He has already impressed me more than those worthless Vyzyn fools. He could be an excellent placeholder for Lord Oziax in the coming wars if he survives long enough to be useful.*

"An ideal place for my new tower," Sekka said, nodding approvingly at Sess'thra. The succubus had at least followed the design she had insisted be used in construction. *Oh, and how many secret doors did you add, my little, mischievous minx?*

Sekka had expected as much foul play, if not more, from her minions. It was the way of the Abyss, and all too familiar to her. She would tame Shiverrig in time, and the succubus would need a thrashing or two to keep her in line. *Knowing Sess'thra, she'll beg for more before I'm finished.*

She looked over the progress being made in her honor. Pride filled her dark heart, and her ambition swelled. She saw herself elevated to the status of a Supreme Devil, sitting alongside Azrollorza. The two monarchs would conquer the Abyss, using the Mortal Realm's soul material to fuel their infinite armies.

The balance of power would shift in the High Pantheon. Xerthotha and Morrdilliax would grovel at her feet or be destroyed; the latter was preferable, of course. Her toes curled in her soft leather boots as her excitement grew.

Pleasurable musing quickly turned to disappointment as her gaze drifted beyond the boundaries of the camp to a pitiful show of failure. She frowned as she viewed the broken remains of her Frost Legion. The Warlords of Vyzyn had managed to reduce her glorious war machine into a laughable afterthought, fodder to soak up the advance of an enemy's well-trained army.

Sekka now seethed with anger throughout the inspection of Shiverrig's troops. His forces mocked her, albeit indirectly. The soldiers snapped to attention when they approached. Their lines were straight and crisp.

A captain barked out a series of commands, and the company moved through complicated military maneuvers for her review. The discipline they exhibited was uncanny for anything claiming to have demon blood running through its veins. The soldiers' eyes were filled with an intelligence reserved for demon lords and lesser devils.

She had seen enough. "Come, Shiverrig. Let's hear what disappointing news the Warlords of Vyzyn have brought from Sunne."

"I have prepared a carriage for your comfort." Shiverrig signaled Sess'thra and Daku to join him.

Eventually, a small procession paraded to the military camp's outer boundary en route to the remains of Sekka's depleted Frost Legion. Shiverrig assembled an armed guard of his elite warriors, mounted on chaos steeds to escort Sekka's carriage out of the military camp. Sess'thra and Daku joined him in the vanguard, while Aosoth and his jol'goth guard surrounded the carriage as it rolled at a leisurely pace behind Shiverrig's warriors.

The Warlords of Vyzyn climbed from their saddles when the procession came to a stop. The jol'goth guard formed two protective lines on either side of the carriage. The door opened, and Sekka's long legs slid from the cabin's interior, like two snakes slithering from the hollows of a tree.

Aeshmara, her sister Tazizu, and the mysterious brother, Dai-Ko-Zior, kneeled in the ankle-deep snow. Shiverrig, Sess'thra, and Daku dismounted and stood above them, waiting for Sekka.

"Why are all three of you here instead of furthering my agenda in Sunne? I specifically said I wanted more souls, and yet you return to me with this rabble in tow," Sekka said. "Where is the rest of my Frost Legion?"

Aeshmara shot up quick as a viper. One hand was on the hilt of her dagger, the other pointed an accusatory finger at Shiverrig. "My spies informed me this traitor brought an army against you. I returned with the Frost Legion in haste. My queen, I feared for your safety."

"My safety," Sekka said. "You think an army of welp half-breeds is any worry to me?"

"Please forgive my rashness, my queen. I meant no disrespect." Aeshmara shifted tactics. "It was Shiverrig who prevented me from bringing you the souls you demanded. He's a constant drain on my efforts to serve you. Dai-Ko-Zior, I command you to kill him! This time I want no excuses."

Dai-Ko-Zior bowed to Sekka and stepped backward. His face remained hidden in the cowl of his robe. "No, sister. As I have said, this man has been chosen by forgotten powers. He and the pale demon who walks as his shadow are not to be harmed. Events unfold beyond your comprehension. It is not my hand which is to slay either of them, only to ensure they reach their anointed place in time."

Sekka studied the sorcerer. What new mystery was this? Dai-Ko-Zior had always made her mildly uncomfortable, like a boil that itched just under the surface of the skin but refused to burst. His essence was like a smoky vapor, solid one moment, and then gone in the breeze the next. He was here and nowhere at once.

"Then I will do it myself." Aeshmara drew one of her double-bladed daggers. She held it pointed at Shiverrig. Daku flashed forward with a menacing growl.

"Calm your dog, Shiverrig, or I will put him down as well," Aeshmara said. "You and I will finish this now."

Shiverrig smirked. "Didn't you hear the sorcerer? I have been chosen for a higher purpose," he said with contempt. "Your bravado is misplaced. Look around you. Do you really think you could slay me out of hand and survive the consequences?" He laughed and drew his great sword from its sheath. "And with a dagger?"

"He's a traitor, my queen. He is not fit to join the Frost Legion." Aeshmara lunged at Shiverrig before Dai-Ko-Zior or Tazizu could stop her.

But Daku moved faster. Eishorror flashed from its scabbard, and he wedged the fell blade between the edges of Aeshmara's double dagger. He smoothly pivoted his entire upper body from his hips and twisted her wrist.

Sekka watched with disinterest as Aeshmara's dagger was ripped out of her hand and sailed through the air, eventually landing with a crunch through the snow.

"You will have no better luck with that doomed blade than did Oziax. It couldn't save him, and it will not save you," Aeshmara said, trying to hide her shame.

Daku edged closer, lips quivering with bloodlust, and forced Aeshmara to take a step backward. His dark eyes bore into her. "Draw your second dagger, and we'll see whose luck holds true."

Shiverrig's eyes remained locked on Aeshmara as he sheathed his sword. "This is pointless. The camp, soldiers, and workers are evidence enough that my worth and loyalty is unquestioned. Where Aeshmara's leadership has failed, mine will bring you victory."

"The Frost Legion is mine to command!" Aeshmara shouted.

"Thanks to you, there is no more Frost Legion," Shiverrig said.

"Be still, both of you," Sekka scolded. She then turned to Shiverrig. "And how will you do any better than the Warlords of Vyzyn?"

"Because they lacked the insight needed to best the Sunnese. They raced into the jungle unprepared before taking the time to know their enemy."

"He lies!" Aeshmara said. "He will fare no better against the jungle's tangled vines or stand unscathed against the magic of the Sunnese. They sneak through shadows and lay buried in the deep mud, waiting until we are vulnerable." Sekka heard desperation building in Aeshmara's voice.

"Tell me, Shiverrig, what is the secret of Sunne?" Sekka said, her voice curious and challenging.

"The campaign must be handled with subtlety and cunning. No doubt you have found your colossal beasts to be ineffective in such dense terrain. You faced an enemy who attacks without warning, then disappears into the shadows of the jungle before you can mount a proper counter-attack. Grant me command of the legions, and I will deliver a war strategy to break the Sunnese."

"You have brought me a great army, Aj-Kahun Shiverrig. I have underestimated you. My understanding of your power base was something less than the numbers presented to me." Sekka eyed Sess'thra with suspicion, yet the succubus gave no hint at duplicity or hidden schemes.

She collected her thoughts. Shiverrig was becoming an increasingly interesting asset. She was reminded of the endless numbers of Zizphander's unstoppable horde under Xerthotha's patronage. *How had this mortal amassed such an army?* A horrible thought crept into her mind and sparked her paranoia again. *Impossible. The Chaos Devil would not have the means.*

She took a hard look at the self-appointed Aj-Kahun, looking for a hint of duplicity. But the man's face was as stone-cold as his eyes. He stood like an immovable rock, with the confidence of a mountain behind him. Sekka sensed something unique about the mortal, but she could not place it. Some part of him was hidden from her, like a quick arctic fox, flashing through a fresh snowscape. Just when she thought she had the answer, it slipped away from her thoughts.

She would find it, eventually. For now, it was an intriguing riddle.

"Aj-Kahun Shiverrig, I grant you command of the new Frost Legion in this realm. Aeshmara, you will act as the Aj-Kahun's second," she said.

Aeshmara's eyes glared daggers into Shiverrig as she drew her second real dagger, pointing it at the Aj-Kahun. "This is not over."

"Oh, I think it is," he said in a dismissive tone, then turned to Sekka. "Construction has begun on special quarters for you, but in the meantime, my command tent is at your disposal.

"When you are ready, I'd like to share the initial stages of my war campaign with you, and any you deem fit to learn how to conduct a proper invasion."

"Thank you, Aj-Kahun Shiverrig. I will be along shortly. I assume Sess'thra knows the way?" she said as she glided towards the succubus and locked Sess'thra's arm in her own. "Let us ride back together in my carriage. We have much to discuss."

Aosoth and his guard followed close behind. The captain stopped briefly before Daku, and the two squared off.

"You are a quick fool with that wicked blade, half-breed. But unsheathe it again in the presence of the queen, and it will be the last thing you ever do."

"Aosoth, leave him be," Sekka said over her shoulder. "I enjoy him."

The Frost Queen then leaned her head close to Sess'thra's ear. "I am curious as to how such a vast amount of half-breeds could be created so quickly. Where did this new army come from? Your infernal magic could not convert so many in such a short amount of time."

Sess'thra's eyes quickly glanced to the Vyzyn warlords as they walked to Sekka's carriage. She spoke in a hushed, conspirator's tone. "You are correct, Mistress. When the Aj-Kahun realized his seed could not produce warriors equal to the true demon spawn of Gathos, he demanded greater numbers over strength. I introduced a liquid version of the demon seed into the water supply at Qaqal. The transformation was quick, although diluted in strength.

"Though I must admit, I do enjoy the more traditional means of creating the seeds one by one. Shiverrig is an impressive man under all that black fur."

Sekka did not detect a lie, though she knew she had not heard the entire story. Succubae were masters at manipulating the truth. She looked hard at Sess'thra and said, "I hope you have not grown overly fond of the mortal. Play with him as you will, but remember, he is a tool to be used to further my ambitions, nothing more, and nothing less. He will be discarded when his usefulness becomes stale."

"Of course, Mistress. You are the true power in this realm, and I am your loyal servant, who lives only at your desire. Shiverrig is nothing to me." The words poured from her mouth like warm honey.

Sekka heard the chime of deceit ring between each sentence. Shiverrig's hands dug deep into the soil she had meticulously tilled for her conquest of the Mortal Realm. His influence had compromised her assets. What was left of her Frost Legion held no power next to his army. He commanded at least two full legions of trained warriors. She suspected there were more hidden away. He would not show his full strength, not yet.

Khalkoroth, the ancient demon meant to dominate Shiverrig into submission, had become his protector. And now Sess'thra was his bitch in heat. Sekka wondered if the assassin, Dax was still hers to command.

She sucked at her teeth. Shiverrig had been busy during her absence. He was still no match for her, but his newfound army would be an annoying threat to her ascension plans if it turned on her.

"I have a task for you. You must locate the Ever Hero of Aetenos. I suspect by now he has made it back to this realm with delusions of stopping me. There is a message you will deliver to him on my behalf," Sekka said. "One that will bring him to me of his own accord."

The succubus looked surprised. "The boy monk has escaped Furia Keep?"

Sekka scowled. "Just find him and deliver my message."

"Yes, Mistress. Though, I do not think he will trust anything I have to say. Would it not be easier for me to bring him to you bound and gagged?"

"No, he must come to me of his own free will."

"It shall be as you command. Where shall I begin my search?"

"Use the Wood Witch as a beacon. The onyx ring she wears will guide you to her." Sekka paused for a moment, thinking. "You will deliver my message to the boy and then bring the girl to me. She should be ready."

"And the Great Monk? What of him?"

"Kill him, if you can. He's no longer important."

"I shall not fail you, Mistress."

"Of course, you won't, my dear." Sekka's smile was hollow. "There's more. You will go to Gethem and find Dax. His work in Gethem is finished, and I want him here. Though you may have some difficulty locating him. He should be deep undercover by now." *If he is still mine to control*, thought Sekka.

"Gethem?" Sess'thra's entire body slackened at this news, but she recovered quickly. She took on a casual air of indifference. "Perhaps I should return to Shiverrig's side instead. I can serve you better by whispering your desires into his ear at night and ensuring he acts according to your wishes in the morning. This is a crucial time for the mortal when he will be tempted to flex his strength. We do not want him to go astray with delusions of rebellion."

"Aeshmara will keep Shiverrig in line. He will follow my commands, or he will die," Sekka said.

She stopped in front of the carriage and pointed inside. Sess'thra pouted before she climbed into the interior. Sekka was now convinced of two things, one, there was more to the relationship between the succubus and the warlord than Sekka had initially wanted, and two, they were plotting against her.

68

SHIVERRIG

Sess'thra rushed into Shiverrig's tent on the verge of tears, which struck Shiverrig as odd and out of character. "I have been ordered to leave," she said through sniffles.

"To go where?" Shiverrig stood in front of a makeshift table. Pouring over his beloved maps and charts. He had learned from his father that every great military leader knew the lay of the land before engaging in any formal combat, be it the terrain, opponents' weapons of war, new advancements equipment or steel, or secret words whispered in the dark.

It was part of the Shiverrig tradition and art of war-making. The great sword at his hip was a testament to honoring the ways of the old. It was an ancient weapon, used by five generations of Shiverrig rulers, and could still shatter an opponent's sword with a skillful strike. Such was the art of metalsmithing and sword craft by used his ancestors.

"Will you miss your little succubus?" Sess'thra moved behind him and playfully attempted to clasp her hands across his chest. She failed.

"Answer the question." It was late, and Shiverrig was in no mood for Sess'thra's antics.

She moved in front of the table and dramatically threw her hand in a sweeping motion across the room. "She's sending me elsewhere. By the time I return, you will be gone to play your war games in the jungle."

Shiverrig frowned. "Does she suspect your duplicity?"

"She's the Archdevil of Gathos. She suspects everyone and everything of foul play."

He clenched his chiseled jaw. "I was hoping you would provide intel of Sekka's movements and motives, or at least those of her conniving warlords."

"Perhaps I will provide you with something far more valuable. Sekka seeks the Ever Hero again, and I suspect I know the reason why. Though if I am right, the game board has grown dangerously wide, and you must be overly cautious with your moves.

"An opportunity will arise to smite the Frost Queen, but you must stop thinking like a mortal. You have the potential to become the living avatar of the Chaos Devil. This is a great honor."

Shiverrig drew his head back. "What makes you think that is what I want?"

"Because if you don't, then you are a fool, and I am wasting my time," Sess'thra snapped. Then her tone softened. "But that's not you. Be patient, my dear Gerun, and you will see in time. You're just now tasting the gifts the Chaos Devil can offer you. Think of how strong you'll become once you have given yourself fully to him."

"I will not lose control. Not to you, Sekka, or that insufferable Xerthotha. I will have no master other than myself."

"Spoken like a true devil. Perhaps that is true and is why you are so interesting to me."

She sashayed back to his side now that she had his attention. "That and these lovely jewels." Her hand traveled down his midsection and rested on his loins. "You give me such shudders when I think of what you shall become, now that you are following the path of your true destiny. Such delicious and wonderful shudders. We will make a family of powerful demon princes and princesses together."

Shiverrig removed her hand and got back to studying his maps. "When do you leave?"

"I should already be gone." She deftly unbuckled his sword belt and untied the strings of his leathers.

No matter how he tried to resist her advances, he found she eventually wore down his resolve. It made him laugh. He would oppose the will of a Supreme Devil until his death but so easily succumb to the cooing and caresses of a damned succubus.

So be it.

He turned, lifted her in the air, and slammed her down on his precious maps. Her wolfish smile ignited his lust, and he thrust himself into her, over and over, and over again.

He didn't care who heard or if Sekka walked in and saw them entwined together. Seven Hells, maybe she would join in the fun. The thought of coupling with the enemy drove his excitement to new heights and caused Sess'thra to scream in delight.

When it was over, Sess'thra left without a word, as was her way. Shiverrig dressed and collected the crumpled maps that had fallen to the ground. He laid them carefully on the table and put weights at the corners. Thankfully, none were torn.

He studied the jungle terrain of Sunne and the twin rivers, Wadi Majarah and Wadi Banz-jan, as they snaked through most of the southwestern kingdom, curling around each other but never joining. Both rivers were fed from the spring thaw and hot summer air, which melted the frozen snow at the Sarribe Mountains heights. During the winter months, the flow of the rivers was mostly calm. He would use this to his advantage to transport troops.

Wadi Majarah was the larger and more aggressive of the two sisters. Her waters swelled in the late spring, causing rapids that were too dangerous to sail. But in the winter, he could move barges filled with troops and equipment down its center lane. With any luck, that would put him out of range of attack from the shores.

I need better intel on their ranged capabilities, he thought. Shiverrig rubbed the over-grown stubble on his chin. *I could send Aeshmara and her troops as reconnaissance, and if they were destroyed, I'd have one less dagger pointed at my back.*

Wadi Banz-jan was more passive than her older sister and meandered slowly along its course. She was a peaceful stream next to her boisterous sister, with no grand rapids to fret over, but plenty of hitch-back choke points where his troops would be susceptible from large swaths of shoreline. He would need a deterrent to ward off attacks from the densely packed banks where the enemy could hide and attack with impunity.

Shiverrig glanced at a bundle of weathered, leather-bound books that recently arrived from his personal library in Gethem. They represented the complete histories of Shiverrig war campaigns waged in Sunne, and their subsequent defeats, dating back to his grandsire, Overlord Baroq Shiverrig.

He had read them all, numerous times. Each war journal said the same thing, the Sunnese and the jungle were one. They fought together in a metaphoric, symbiotic fashion, where one relied on the other, overlapping defenses and mounting destructive attacks.

The secret to crippling the Sunnese was to destroy their beloved land. Leave them exposed, one-legged, and off balance. Shiverrig would force the natives to fight on the terrain of his choosing or his creation. If he could not lure them into a killing ground to his liking, he would destroy the jungle they hid behind and force them into an open fight.

He tapped the old pages of the book with two fingers. His flying corps would pepper the jungle-dwellers from above while his infantry overwhelmed them with sheer numbers. That was it. That's how he would win where his ancestors had failed.

His gaze blurred at the hectares of rain-forests, marshlands, and hilly terrain described on his maps. He understood why his predecessors had failed to conquer the fertile basin of Sunne. They could not defeat the jungle.

The strategy forming in his head was sound. If he approached the destruction of the land in a systematized way, perhaps there was a chance. Cordon off areas with rings of fire, trapping the enemy within.

His aerial warriors would then drop incendiaries from above, out of harm's way. It would be a slow process, but one that could prove effective over time. Fire over ice, Shiverrig mused. How would the Frost Queen view that tactic? All he needed was patience and the promise Aeshmara's troops would not betray him.

Two burly jol'goths pushed through the flaps of his tent and scanned the inner area for threats. Their ice-blue eyes squinted against the fluttering torchlight. A third jol'goth followed quickly inside and came to stand opposite Shiverrig at the table.

"Lord Aosoth, welcome," Shiverrig said with indifference, and returned to studying the map below him.

"The Frost Queen comes and expects to see your plan for victory," Aosoth said.

Shiverrig ignored Aosoth and traced his finger along the Wadi Majarah. He tapped an area of the map where the river stayed straight, providing the longest beachhead to support off-loading his troops. His aerial corps would arrive beforehand and raze the jungle from the air. He nodded approvingly.

Maybe he would catch some of the enemy unaware who lurked in the shadows and reported their progress along the river. The more he could drive them into specific areas, the better his odds of trapping them.

Yes, that spot will do nicely, and then the real work begins, he thought. Shiverrig lifted his head and stared into Aosoth's cold eyes. "Of course, she does."

"Sekka is all-knowing, and why she chose you to lead her Frost Legion over a true demon lord is beyond my understanding," Aosoth said, snarling and clearly provoking a challenge. He sniffed the air and his brow furrowed. "You're nothing but a weak mortal who reeks of the succubus."

Shiverrig was unmoved. He had troops and equipment to deploy. Catapults and ballistae would be ineffective in the jungle terrain. But perhaps the sorcerer could provide a more efficient way of delivering a deadly payload. He unrolled a long parchment resting on the table, which depicted troop divisions within a legion and their accompanying siege-craft.

"Is there anything else you wish to report, Captain?" Shiverrig said as he reviewed the scroll.

"Look at me when I speak to you, mortal," Aosoth growled.

Was there no end to the arrogance of demons? Shiverrig lowered the scroll. He had no doubt he could best the jol'goth with the added strength of Xerthotha, but now was not the time to reveal his secret.

"The Frost Queen comes," said one of the jol'goth sentries at the tent flaps.

Aosoth's lips curled, and he moved to the side of the table. "There will be another time, mortal."

This is the manner of their world, thought Shiverrig. *Best not to forget that and use it to my advantage.*

The two sentries pulled back the tent flaps, allowing a cold burst of night air to fill the tent. Tazizu was the first to enter. The reddish and blue-grey hides of her leather armor were battle-worn and rough. The attire hugged her slender, boyish frame.

She had carved new runes into an open space on her bald head. Blueish blood still seeped from the self-inflicted wounds. *Ugly as sin,* thought Shiverrig.

Ancient runes of mystical power covered her thin leathers, and an orange sigil spun slowly above her head. Shiverrig realized it was a display of power, as well as a liability on the battlefield. It made her an obvious target for the enemy archers. Shiverrig was surprised the witch still lived.

Tazizu gave him a slight nod and stood at a corner of the table. Apparently, she had accepted her supporting role in the campaign.

The sorcerer, Dai-Ko-Zior, entered next. His face remained hidden under his heavy cowl. He ignored the jol'goths, Shiverrig and Tazizu, standing off to the side, and in the shadows of the tent.

Shiverrig studied the sorcerer, looking for something that might indicate if he was friend or foe. The sorcerer revealed nothing of his intentions but stood motionless, seemingly fading into the darkness of the tent.

Aeshmara stalked into the tent with her hands resting on the pommels of her double-bladed daggers. "This is an insult and betrayal of our agreement," she said to her siblings. Her stormy slate-blue eyes flared. "Sekka promised us command of the Frost Legion."

Her white hair shot straight to her shoulders, and black, smoky runes trailed behind her as she approached the center of the tent. Aeshmara's subtle leathers flexed with her catlike movements, and Shiverrig could plainly see the outline of toned muscles beneath the thin material. She was tense and could spring at a moment's notice.

"You were promised command if you delivered me Sunne. I fail to see holding pens filled with the Sunnese or long lines of prisoners being marched to the Chaos Gate to feed the orthod pits on Gathos," Sekka said as she entered the tent.

The Warlords of Vyzyn, Aosoth, and his guards, all bowed.

Shiverrig carefully eyed the archdevil as she made her entrance. She was tall and sleek but radiated incredible, destructive power. Her alabaster hair was braided in an intricate pattern and coiled behind her head and down her back. She wore a silver neck gorget that tapered to a point between her breasts.

Beneath the metal choker, she donned a thinly meshed, chainmail shirt, which she belted at the waist. Her legs were covered in black leather and high boots. She cut an impressive figure if one were attending a victory gathering and not a war council. Shiverrig bowed, more with his head instead of his waist, which drew a hiss from Aeshmara.

"Shall we begin?" Shiverrig said as Sekka came to a halt at the map table. All but Dai-Ko-Zior gathered around the table to hear Shiverrig's plan.

"The mistake your shock troops made was trying to fight against an enemy who is at one with their environment. You used tactics on the Sunnese made for open terrain warfare and left them the advantage of the close confines of trees, branches, vines, and thick bush. The sharpest long sword is wasted when a short dagger is needed."

Aeshmara sucked at her teeth, scoffing at Shiverrig's opening remarks. "All of Sunne is covered in jungle. Shall we run blindly with our short blades drawn, and hope the Sunnese stand still long enough for us to bleed them?"

"No, Aeshmara, we take the jungle away from the enemy. It's a simple mathematical equation, really, and mostly dealing with subtraction. I'm surprised the combined knowledge of four, sorry, three invincible Vyzyn warlords did not deduce this logic sooner."

"Aeshmara is right, my queen. The jungle extends forever. It cannot be done," Tazizu countered.

"I agree. It cannot be done by you," Shiverrig said. "I have full reports from my own scouts of your unsuccessful forays into Sunne and the wasteful deployment of large, valuable assets. I believe you call them juggernauts."

Tazizu opened her mouth to contest him, but he cut her short.

"We do not need nor want to destroy the entire kingdom. That would be counterproductive to the aims of the campaign. We will scorch the land to create killing zones of our choosing, thereby trapping the Sunnese when we have superior numbers, and they cannot slip away through the shadows of the jungle."

Sekka looked over the map with interest. Shiverrig noticed she nodded her head slightly.

"Where do you propose we begin?"

"Our first objective will be to level this beachhead. My aerial warriors will clear us a landing area before the ships arrive to off-load troops, supplies, and the heavier equipment. Once we have established a preliminary base of operations, we will expand into the jungle."

"And the ships you speak of, how will you carry them over the Sarribe Pass? He's a fool. This is an impossible task," Aeshmara laughed. "My Queen, you cannot possibly think this mortal can—"

"The ships are being built on the southern side of the Sarribe Pass as we speak. They sit at the water's edge of the Wadi Majarah and will be ready to sail when my troops arrive."

"Why fight small jungle skirmishes when your aerial troops can simply fly to the capital and destroy them at the root?" Aeshmara challenged.

Shiverrig turned the map of Sunne around to Aeshmara. "Would you please point to the location of the capitol?"

Aeshmara scowled.

"No? That's because the Sunnese people do not operate as a normal, civilized culture. They have no central government that can surrender. Their kingdom is made up of thousands of tribes ruled by individual chieftains. It is their religion that connects them as a people, not a central leader.

"And it's their faith in a living jungle goddess which gives them their spell power. Take away the forest vines, trees, and roots and you cripple them. You must defeat the jungle if you are to conquer the people.

"Now, if would you like to embarrass yourself further, please continue," Shiverrig said.

"It's an interesting solution to a troublesome problem. You have done well, Aj-Kahun Shiverrig. Once more, I am impressed."

"Thank you, my queen." Shiverrig gave a slight bow. "I will need to know specifics of destructive spell power and elemental control of fire and wind from the magic users."

Shiverrig looked to Tazizu and Dai-Ko-Zior for a response, but both remained silent. He tilted his head to Sekka for confirmation he would receive this information.

"You will leave nothing out," Sekka commanded. "Give him what he needs. I will not tolerate any more disappointments from you three. I demand victory."

"Yes, mistress," Tazizu replied.

Dai-Ko-Zior silently nodded once.

69

KASAI

Kasai felt nauseous, and his head spun like a top. *I think I'm gonna puke,* he thought. A wet sensation seeped around his knees, and looking down, he saw that he was kneeling in muck. His body shivered, but not from being cold, for the air around him was sweltering, and heavy, and thick.

Then, the sounds of the jungle came at him hard, and fast. Squawking birds cried out in alarm, warning their jungle neighbors of intruders. Small animals hooted and screeched in the tall brush or scampered deeper into the patches of broad-leaf plants. Ground flowers swayed from dashing rodents confined to the forest floor, while frogs chirped, and toads croaked in the shallow puddles.

The noise blended like raucous laughter, except for the unmistakable presence of horseflies buzzing in his ear. Instinctively, Kasai swatted the air around his head and scratched his leg, thinking he had already been bitten.

"At least I'm still in one piece," he said, quelling the bile rising in his throat. Then, he looked around for the rest of his group. "Des? Pallo?"

He stood up fast, and his stomach lurched as the emerald-green landscape around him spun before his eyes. *Bad move.* He was sure he was going to vomit now.

Pain flooded his head, making his eyes squint. He rubbed his temples, but it did little to ease what could only be described as nails driving into his brain. Exhaling a deep breath, he tried to focus on his new environment.

A light breeze moved smoothly through the maze of boughs and smaller branches. Tiny leaves twirled to the ground like pinwheels. Colorful birds with feathers of vibrant-yellow, fire-red, and brilliant-blue flitted from one tree branch to the next or took flight in fear from the sudden arrival of the human invaders.

"Where is everyone?" he called out.

Giant fronds with drooping heads lined up like bowing, silent sentries. Thin vines with small, blue flowers crawled through the ferns and snaked up through the tree branches. Suddenly, a troop of short-haired, orange monkeys with curled, prehensile tails darted into fern patches. They jumped on and off each other's backs, howling in panic as they raced away.

Kasai thought of the dry woods he had run through as a youngster, long before Ordu. Straight white pines and broad bur oak trees covered the land for miles around the small village of his early childhood. But that forest was never as green or as lush as this one, or as wet.

And the air there was different. It was lighter somehow, and crisper, unlike this place where every breath was damp, hot, and suffocating. Kasai felt like a soggy, wool blanket had been thrown over his back and wrapped tightly around his chest.

A white egret with its head feathers raised in alarm stopped mid-step in a wide stream. The majestic bird cocked its head to one side, then leaped into the air with powerful beats of its white wings. Soon it was gone, flying along the winding waterway.

The jungle darkened as the breeze picked up, and with it came the fresh, earthy smell of rain. Kasai's mood darkened with the dimming light. *Why is this happening to me? I'm nobody, just a stupid, insignificant monk.*

He looked down at his dirty hands and saw the cobalt blue marks of Aetenos beneath smeared, black soil and bits of dried leaves. "Why did you have to choose me?"

Kasai tried to collect his thoughts, but the pounding in his head made him dizzy. He felt incredibly lost. Ordu was gone, its walls breached by *things* from his childhood nightmares. In his father's study, the old books, the ones with the pictures of angels and devils at war, had it right. The Abyss and Seven Heavens were real! And now, impossible means of travel between realms had become commonplace. "And I'm smack in the middle of a war that has no end. What a mess."

The Master Monks of Ordu should have prepared him for such things. Maybe Master Choejor had tried, towards the end, but Kasai never wanted to listen. "I wish I had your guidance now, Master," Kasai said. But Choejor was gone, too. Nothing remained the same.

Kasai shook off some small leaves that clung to his robe. He was in a small clearing, surrounded by densely packed tree trunks of hunter green, and covered at their base with blue moss and grey lichen. The trees grew tall at the edge of the shallow stream. Each reached for the sky and its nourishing sunlight.

Long vines hung from high branches, sprouting tiny leaves and finger-shaped seed pods. Smaller trees vied for space, collecting whatever sunlight filtered through the dense canopy. "I'm in the middle of nowhere," Kasai said. "Des! Pallo! Where is everyone?"

The wind picked up, sending ripples through his robe and causing thick tree branches to sway and creak. The pending rainclouds cast a blueish-grey light over the clearing, giving the forest a luminous glow. The jungle seemed quieter now and oddly serene.

"And now it's going to rain. Well, isn't that just grand. Where are they? Des!"

Kasai scanned the undergrowth again, and then the treetops searching for his companions. Finally, Pallo appeared, pushing through a patch of tall ferns that grew in clumped bundles.

"I'm here, Ever Hero," Pallo said. "A bit shaky, but still alive."

His leather tunic was covered in thousands of rust-colored hairs; presumably, the husks shed from the fronds. Run-Run came next from behind a large, moss-covered boulder, wearing an excited grinned. He was a dirty mess. Mud and bits of earthy mulch covered his clothing, and his shaggy hair was filled with tiny twigs and bright green leaflets. Kasai had no doubt that Run-Run was in his element in this type of wilderness.

The same could not be said for Orin, who repeatedly hacked at drooping vines, barring his way to the others. His hands and knee-high boots were covered in grey mud. He trudged towards Kasai, harried by flies that followed him from whatever mud patch he had fallen into soon after his arrival.

The air suddenly crackled, and the jungle lit up in a flash. A thundering boom followed. Orin looked up and scowled. The pending rain did nothing to improve his sour disposition.

Desdemonia slid from between two moss-covered trees just as the downpour washed over them. The rainwater clung to her skin and leathers, creating a vibrant sheen over her shapely figure. Kasai noticed she finally looked at ease.

"Not what you were expecting, right?" she said and gave Kasai a bit of a mischievous grin.

"I don't like it. We are too far away from our objective," Orin said as he cleaned the mud from under his belt and flicked it to the ground. Vomit still stuck to his chin. "This was a mistake."

Kasai barely heard Orin's complaining. He was mesmerized by Desdemonia. Her hair was weighed down by the water and fell from her head like streams of black oil. She was a vision of beauty, shimmering before him as the rainwater pelted her body.

"Her beauty rivals the most vibrant, jungle flower," Pallo said when he reached Kasai's side, almost as if he spoke with another man's voice. Kasai was surprised to hear such poetic words from the mouth of the stoic man. But Pallo was right. Desdemonia looked radiant. The two stared dumbfounded as she approached.

"Close your mouths boys, you're likely to swallow a fly, or worse," she said playfully.

Kasai wasn't sure, but he thought maybe she held Pallo's gaze a little too long. She tossed her head, letting thick, wet clumps of her raven hair fall over her face. The blueish, half-light of the forest cast her amber eyes in shadow, turning them dark moons of charcoal black.

"We had best find a drier place until the rains stop," Pallo said, unsuccessfully trying to hide his embarrassment. He moved to take shelter under some low hanging branches. Kasai and the others followed him to wait out the storm.

"Where are we?" Kasai asked. "I've never heard of the Heart of Sunne."

Orin wiped away the vomit from his mouth. The mud on his hands smeared grey tracks down his jaw and chin. "I don't see anything here that would be a recognizable marker for a meeting place. My gut says this is a trap."

"It's more of an idea than a place," Desdemonia said.

"An idea?" Pallo asked.

"Yes, it means to be in a safe place, surrounded by family and friends. My mother once told me, *If you are in need, seek out the Heart of Sunne.* Well, I'd say we are in deep, wouldn't you?"

"By the grace of the angels, we are lucky they understood the subtlety of your words," Pallo said.

Desdemonia's expression darkened. "The angels have no grace. They are no better than the demons of the Abyss, maybe worse. At least the demons wear their cruelty in plain sight."

"She still spits out her blasphemy, and you do nothing," Orin griped. "The Wood Witch is in liege with Sekka. She has sent us to the middle of nowhere to prevent us from fulfilling our mission. Am I the only one who sees this?"

A sudden screech caused him to spin. One of his short swords shot out, viper quick in his outstretched hand. He scanned the area for threats. A cat-sized lizard bounded from a bush and raced up a nearby tree. It twisted its neck and head to screech again, presumably at Orin, then raced up higher into the tree's foliage.

"This is a bad place," Orin said, scowling while lowering his sword. "There is only death here."

"Why are you always in such a foul mood?" Desdemonia said.

"Experience," Orin said with a sneer.

"Ever Hero, we cannot stay here long. The Chaos Gate must be closed." Pallo's voice was urgent, and his face was filled with concern. "We are far from Trosk." He scanned the trees and bush. "How far is anyone's guess."

Kasai came back to the hard reality of his impossible task. "And far from an answer to Sekka. I can't defeat her." Kasai shook his head. "She's too powerful."

"You are the Ever Hero. You will find a way," Pallo said. He placed a reassuring hand on Kasai's shoulder. "You are Aetenos's Chosen. You are the savior that was foretold."

"I'm no savior. The pebble does not outshine the moon and is lost in the open sea."

"Oh, boo hoo hoo," Desdemonia said. "Poor Kasai. Can you please find some courage? We'll figure this out. It just might take a little while."

"He chose the wrong monk. I should be dead," Kasai said sharply. "It was Aetenos who guided my hand to victory. And when I failed, it was you, Des. You and your magic. I don't deserve to be chosen for anything. I can barely grasp the true meaning of the Boundless. Sekka is beyond me. I'm not ready."

"I do not envy you, Ever Hero. You must bear the weight of suffering for those you are called to protect. It's a hero's fate. But have faith. The Kibo Gensai will not abandon you. We do not turn our back on our oaths or our friends."

"Thank you, Pallo. But Sekka and her armies are too strong for all of us. Faith and loyalty will not be enough."

"Then we too shall need an army," Pallo said.

"There are no more armies to call upon. You saw as well as I did. They were massacred on the fields of the Last Garrison. The Master Monks of the Four Orders are gone, betrayed and murdered by Maugris's shape-shifting assassin. And any surviving monks are either dead now or scattered by the four winds. There's no one left."

Run-Run squirmed his way to Pallo's side. The mute warrior gestured wildly with his hands, and his eyes bright shown with excitement. When he was done, he nodded at his brother and pointed at Kasai.

"Brother, she's not enough," Pallo said.

"What did he say?" Kasai asked.

"Run-Run says there is a woman who can help. She claimed to be a priestess of Aetenos with much influence over his followers. Run-Run told her to gather the faithful for the Ever Hero walks the land once more."

"She was unmoved at first, hesitant to believe such a miracle from a stranger. Then Run-Run described to her how you channeled the righteous light of Aetenos into saving the witch from the angry mob outside of Gethem. She, too, had heard the tale.

"When he described the marks on your hands, she was convinced you were the one. She said she would help. Run-Run will find her and anyone else she has gathered."

"He said all that?"

"Surprisingly, yes," Pallo said. "With any luck, the call has spread, and many have rallied to her summons."

"She's not right in the head," Orin said dismissively. "It's doubtful any will come to her call."

"Is it all people you despise, or just those unlike you?" Desdemonia said.

Kasai looked questioningly at Orin. "What do you mean?"

"Run-Run speaks of the Miko," Orin said, and his face scrunched up, as if the mention of her name left a bad taste in his mouth. "Airis, Kafar, and I traveled for a time with a woman called Nuna'ngy. She fancied herself something of a priestess or prophetess. But most of us just called her the Miko Nuna.

"She wasn't much more than a snake oil soothsayer to my ears. Just another untrustworthy witch, as far as I could see. But Airis took a liking to her. He found hope in her words, so we stayed.

"Together, we joined the line of soldiers marching north with the King's Army to battle the threat from Maugris. When we met Run-Run, we introduced him to Miko Nuna."

Run-Run nodded enthusiastically at Orin as water streamed down his face.

"Miko? I am unfamiliar with this name," Kasai said.

"It's not a name. Miko means crazy," Pallo said.

"Truly?" Kasai said, wiping water from his eyes.

The rain increased, and although the low branches and broad leaves of their impromptu shelter took the brunt of the storm, it wouldn't be long before they were all drenched.

"What happened to her?"

"I'm sure she died in the mouth of something horrible," Orin said. "Nobody stood a chance when the King's Army failed."

"And yet, here we are," Desdemonia said.

Run-Run stood in front of Kasai. He waved away what Orin said and boldly pointed at himself with his thumb. He then used two fingers to run in the air, nodding the entire time excitedly. He pointed to the nearby stream and moved his hand as if mirroring the slow ripples.

He then whistled through his teeth, mimicking the sound of the wind. He held his hand in the air to catch its direction, then nodded knowingly.

"Are you saying you know the way to Baroqia?" Kasai said.

Run-Run waited a moment and then quarter-turned his body. He pointed in a new direction, nodding excitely at the way he would go.

"If anyone can find Miko Nuna and the faithful that follow her, it's Run-Run," Pallo said.

"Even if he found her and she had collected the faithful together in one place, *and* he was somehow able to rally the hidden clans of Kibo Gensai, our numbers would still be paltry against Sekka's legions. It would do us no good," Orin said as he stomped grey mud from his boots. "They would die with the rest of us."

"So we had better not fail," Desdemonia said.

Run-Run raised his eyebrows, and Kasai realized he was waiting for an answer.

"I don't know Run-Run. We need all the help we can get, but until we have a better idea of where we are and how we will defeat Sekka, it's probably best to stay together. I think that is what Aetenos would want us to do."

Run-Run's face fell with disappointment, but he bowed to Kasai his acceptance and looked at Pallo with sad eyes.

"The Ever Hero is right. Now is the time to stay together. I'm sure he believes you could find your way back to Baroqia." Pallo squeezed Run-Run's arm for reassurance.

"Okay, Des, what's next?" Kasai asked. "Where do we go from here?"

"No clue. I imagine we wait." Desdemonia scanned the trees. "I think it will happen soon, though."

"Wait? What are we waiting for? I thought you had a plan," Kasai said, surprised. "What will happen soon?"

"We're waiting for the magic to arrive. The Sunnese possess an incredible innate connection to the Elemenati. We will need their strength to defeat Sekka."

"Where are they? How long will it take to reach them?" Pallo asked.

"We don't have to move from this spot. We are in the Heart of Sunne. They will find us."

"I knew this was a trap." Orin moved protectively in front of Kasai. "Who will find us, witch?" he demanded. His free hand went to his second blade, and Kasai knew there would be a fight.

70

DESDEMONIA

"My people," Desdemonia said, and she walked out of the shelter and into the rain. *If Orin pulls a knife on me one more time, I'm seriously going to end him,* she thought as she scanned the upper canopy. "I assume they're already here."

As if on cue for some mysterious performance, the rain ceased. The dark gloom was lifted. Shafts of sunlight poked through the canopy ceiling, illuminating the rocks, plants, and trees. The heat returned with the sun, and soon a sweaty mist lifted from the jungle floor.

"The name of Aetenos is known to us," a female voice spoke, though the speaker was hidden from sight, lost in the overlapping foliage of the jungle trees. She held a thick accent with flat vowels and clipped endings. "Our great fathers' fathers have fought side by side with the Divine Fist."

Desdemonia squinted through the glare of the sharp sunlight. She searched through the high branches, looking right and left, but remained calm.

"Who's there? Show yourself," Orin called out and drew his second sword. "She brings more witches to her side."

"Lower your weapons, warrior. They will only cause a faster death for you and your comrades."

Pallo and Run-Run immediately joined Orin and closed around Kasai in a protective circle, a short sword in each hand. Desdemonia stepped farther into the clearing and held her hands out wide.

"I am Desdemonia Mishi, of the village Shryse, south of the Sarribe Pass. We are also friends of Aetenos. Come, join us. Share our story."

The voice remained silent, and Desdemonia's pulse quickened. She hoped she had not made a mistake. They would either receive help from the jungle folk or die in the next few minutes. She looked back to Kasai and nodded for him to join her. If she was going to die, she would have him by her side.

"Let me through," he said and pushed through the Kibo Gensai to stand beside her in the clearing. He took hold of Ninziz-zida, and the segments of the black staff emitted a bright glow.

"You speak openly of Aetenos, yet the people of Sunne have not seen the Great Monk walking along the jungle paths for many generations."

"An archdevil has crossed over into our realm from the Abyss and opened a Chaos Gate in Trosk. Her demons spill out into the Three Kingdoms. We have been charged to destroy her. We fight in the name of Aetenos," Kasai blurted out.

"You reveal too much, Ever Hero," Orin said for all to hear. "Who knows if they can be trusted?"

"Only a fool would use the title Ever Hero so freely in such times," the female voice echoed from a different location. "And you, Desdemonia Mishi of the village Shryse, speak of the Heart of the Sunne, yet you wear an onyx ring, a devil's ring on your finger."

Desdemonia absentmindedly covered the ring with her other hand. "Reveal yourself. Hear our tale, and judge our truth for yourself," she said.

The female voice trilled through an exotic call of a bird, and the jungle came alive. Branches shook with the relief of lost weight. Leaves fluttered haphazardly in the air. Large fronds swayed aside, and thick, ropey vines parted between dark green shafted arrows, followed by the archers who held the bows taut.

Twenty dark-skinned warriors appeared from the steamy foliage of the jungle. Twenty sets of tapered shaped eyes with deep shades of green, rose, purple and blue, bore into Desdemonia. The warriors' eyes had an inner glow, like her own. At least half were female and carried the same intensity as their male counterparts. The warriors all had jet-black hair, some woven in tight braids, which hung like serpents down their backs, while others wore it cropped short.

The warriors' clothing was a seamless blend of the colors and shapes of the forest, not unlike hers. Their boots were made of soft, subtle leather, designed for quick movement over rocks and roots. Desdemonia was not surprised the Sunnese had encircled them without a sound.

A tall, slender woman stepped forward from the rest. Her cheeks rose high on the sides of her face, causing her eyes to angle upwards in a more pronounced manner. She had keen eyes, intelligent eyes, and held no visible weapon. Yet Desdemonia sensed a different type of power radiating from her; Elemenati magic.

The slender warrior's smooth, hairless scalp gleamed with wetness from the rain. Across her forehead, and continuing around to the back of her head, was a blue ban, maybe a finger's width. The ban had small, blue spirals spinning from the top edge.

"Kasai show her," Desdemonia said.

"Are you sure?"

"Just do it," she said and watched him wipe a muddy hand on his wet pant leg, exchanging the muck from one surface to the other.

The azure symbol of three spirals spinning out from its center was clear to see on his palm. The similarities were uncanny. Had this warrior been marked as one of Aetenos's Chosen as well?

Desdemonia turned to the warrior, who was now staring at Kasai.

"We are part of the same tribe," Desdemonia said.

The warrior's eyes roamed over Kasai, scrutinizing his robes and tattoos. Then, she fixed her stare on Ninziz-zida and gasped. Her gaze shot back to Kasai's eyes, her expression questioning. "Could it be true?" she said. Desdemonia thought she heard awe in the woman's voice.

Kasai raised his hand slowly, palm faced outward. He then looked over his shoulder at the Kibo Gensai. "Lower your swords. They are not the enemy."

"He bears the mark," the woman warrior said. The archers lowered their shafts to a resting position, yet their fierce stare did not change.

Desdemonia heard Kasai sigh with relief.

"I told you. This is the Heart of Sunne," she said. "We are safe now."

The woman turned to Desdemonia. "How do you know the meaning of such a thing?"

"It is known to all who hold the spirit of the jungle in their soul," Desdemonia said.

The woman gave a slight nod, as if that answer was acceptable, at least for now. "Why are you here, now, in Sunne?" the woman asked. "How could you be so deep in the jungle without being detected?"

There was no hostility in her voice, only curiosity. She looked squarely at Desdemonia, sizing her up.

"Your eyes are the honey-colored pedals of the Kodama orchid. It's a rare flower. I suspect you are an awakened child of Nayche, but I do not know the name Mishi or of the Shryse tribe."

"My tribe is gone, asleep until the day of their reawakening. Only I remain with open eyes," Desdemonia said.

"Recent times have brought much sadness to us all. A blight has come to the jungle. Creatures bred of darkness have come to raze our villages and to steal our people."

"We are late in our quest. Sekka's reach has extended into Sunne. Now, no kingdom is safe." Pallo said.

"Sekka? The archdevil's name is familiar to the histories of Sunne. Though, I speak of the Chaos Warlord, who leads a limitless army. One with the blood of man but possessed by dark chaos. He is joined by three wicked lieutenants and a hulking, white demon."

"They destroy entire villages with their fell magic. The green mist suffocates all who breathe it in, and the jungle burns and blisters under their command."

"Since you are so good at sneaking about, why not steal into his command tent and kill him in his sleep? Remove his head, and the demons under his command will come undone. Problem solved," Orin said. His tone was indignant.

The woman slowly shook her head, no. "The white demon is forever at the warlord's side. The beast slips through shadows with its master, thwarting our efforts for an ambush and a decisive kill."

"Khalkoroth," Kasai whispered.

"Easy Kasai," Desdemonia said. "You don't know that it's him. There could be other shadow walkers."

"Master Choejor will be avenged," Kasai said. "I swear it."

"I know he will. But we kill Sekka first, then the rest of them," she said. Then Desdemonia raised her voice for all to hear.

"We fight the same enemy. Together we can stop the flow of madness coming from the Chaos Gate."

The female warrior assessed Desdemonia, then the Kibo Gensai. But her eyes continued to drift to Ninziz-zida and back to Kasai. "My name is Ruith Zylris Faeharice, of the Frona tribe. I lead this war party."

"That's a tongue twister," Orin said, begrudgingly sheathing his short swords.

"I believe her name roughly translates to 'Flowery Gift' in the common tongue," Desdemonia said. "But I am unfamiliar with her dialect."

"My father named me 'Gift of the Hanging Gardens.'"

"Gift," Kasai said. "It's a name which is most welcome to us."

"If you find it easier, that is what you may call me."

Kasai bowed to the warrior woman. "I am Kasai Ch'ou from the Monastery of Ordu. This is Pallo Katan, his brother Run-Run, and the one with the viper's tongue is Orin Wyth. We need your help."

Another warrior approached Gift and stopped at her side. His hair was loose with mud, twigs, and leaves covered his clothing and skin. He held a long, hollowed reed, which he pointed first at Kasai, and then at Ninziz-zida.

Her brow furrowed as he whispered in her ear. He slashed his hand downward and held a stern expression. She gave a quick nod, but her eyes did not leave Kasai.

"We shall see, Tavian," she said and took a step forward. "Show me the staff."

Kasai was reluctant, of course, and looked to Desdemonia for guidance.

This could all go bad very quickly, she thought. "It'll be okay. They need to trust us."

"Okay, Des," Kasai said. He took a deep breath and held out Ninziz-zida in one hand.

Gift scrutinized the staff and tentatively reached out to touch it but brought her hand back instead. Her eyes followed the rippling flame as it traveled along the straight black segments and then lapped across Kasai's hand. Her mouth opened as if to say something but then close when she saw it caused him no harm.

"How do you possess such a weapon?"

"We came together due to unfortunate circumstances at Ordu."

"The winds of the jungle say the sacred monasteries of Aetenos are gone. Claimed by treachery and fire." Gift's eyes shifting thoughtfully left and right as if she was putting together the pieces of a puzzle in her head. She then stared back at Ninziz-zida.

"You hold the legendary Fire Serpent," Gift said with reverence. A few of her warriors gaped in awe. "It is said the Fire Serpent chooses her own master, and no other but the Divine Fist, or one of his awakened Ever Heroes, may clutch her sections, and live."

"This is Ninziz-zida. She and I have an understanding."

"An understanding?" Gift said incredulously. She looked questioningly into Kasai's eyes, and then to the hand that effortlessly held the legendary weapon. She turned to Desdemonia.

"And how is it that the Fire Serpent has permitted the wearer of an onyx ring to live? Is this another understanding?"

"It's a long story," Desdemonia said. "We are together in our efforts to aid the Ever Hero."

Gift raised her voice for all to hear. "I need no other proof. He who holds the Fire Serpent so freely in hand can only be an awakened Ever Hero of Aetenos. You too, Desdemonia Mishi of the sleeping Shryse tribe, shall be accepted as a friend. The Fire Serpent would not allow you to be anything but pure in her presence."

Gift looked to the Kibo Gensai. "You are all welcome to join our war party."

The warrior known as Tavian was not convinced. He spoke in hidden words to the warrior next to him, then eyed Kasai and then Desdemonia with suspicion.

"Thank you, Gift. We are honored by your trust," Kasai said and bowed low.

"Come, I am curious to hear more of your tale. We have food and shelter nearby. You are welcome to both." She turned and followed the stream to the north. Her warriors fell in line behind her.

"Kasai, I need to talk to you, away from the others," Desdemonia said and grabbed his hand. She led him in the opposite direction from the departing warriors.

"The Ever Hero should not be unprotected. I will go as well," Orin said and was quick to Kasai's side.

"Orin, it's okay. I'll be fine," Kasai said. "I wouldn't be much of an Ever Hero if I needed protection wherever I went."

"Give them some privacy, Orin. They have much to discuss," Pallo said.

Orin reluctantly backed off, but it was clear he was not in agreement. "One scratch on him, witch, and I will hold you responsible."

Desdemonia ignored him and pulled on Kasai's hand. "Come on."

She walked at a brisk pace, following what appeared to be an animal path. The jungle quickly closed around them.

"How does anyone know where they are in this place?" Kasai said. "I'm already lost."

"Tell me something I don't already know," Desdemonia said teasingly.

Bald, red-headed monkeys with shaggy, tan coats scampered along the twisting boughs overhead. The hairy beasts howled down at them from a safe distance, shaking the smaller branches violently. Desdemonia's pace quickened as she moved deeper into the jungle.

"Des, slow down. We will not be able to find our way back."

"Would that be so bad?" she said under her breath, then turned around to look into his eyes. "What if we stayed in the solitude of the jungle? Let the world solve its own problems."

"Sekka is my problem. I cannot turn my back from this responsibility, even if I wanted to, remember? We all die if I don't destroy her."

"I know, Kasai. I know. It was just a fantasy," she sighed. "We're in this together."

"It's a hopeless cause. How can the angels think I can defeat an archdevil alone?"

"Raguel never expected you to win. He wanted his hands clean of your death. But he underestimated you."

"I can't do it, Des. I need Aetenos. I need his guidance to direct me. I have barely scratched the surface of understanding the Boundless. It's all just a confusing jumble in my head. Sometimes it works, sometimes I get nothing."

"Aetenos is no longer here, so you must rely on yourself now."

"And you, Des. I can rely on you, can't I?"

"I'm not sure. I am changing. My magic has grown strong, but there is something else that stirs and writhes inside of me. It's a craving I cannot control."

She stared at Kasai and was filled with greedy desire. Her skin tingled, and she absentmindedly licked her lips. She felt like a predator on the hunt and he was the prey.

"What do you mean?" Kasai said.

She grabbed Kasai roughly with one hand by the front of the V in his robe, the other around the back of his head, and pulled him closer to kiss him. Her tongue explored his mouth in a ravenous fashion. The hand clutching the front of his robe moved up his chest and gripped him by the throat.

He did his best to return the kiss but muddled through the motions. His inexperience with women was evident. She abruptly pushed him away and wiped her mouth with the back of her sleeve. They both stared in silence at one another for long, uncomfortable moments.

"What have I done?" she said at last. "I'm so sorry. I don't know what came over me."

She rubbed her forehead and looked at Kasai, searching for an answer, and took a step backward. The taste of his awkward kiss was still on her lips, and she wanted more.

"Des?" Kasai asked softly. "What happened? You just kissed me as if your life depended on it."

Her heart thumped in her chest. Everything was unraveling too fast.

"Oh, Kasai. I'm sorry. I didn't mean to. I mean, I wanted to, but can't you see? I'm losing control."

"It's because of that ring, isn't it?"

She remained quiet and looked past Kasai into the trees and ferns. *He needs to know before it's too late.*

"Des?" he said again.

"I think we are alone." She knew she could trust him, but her pulse quickened, nonetheless.

"I want to tell you something important." She paused again, listening to the sounds of the jungle, then she continued.

"Everyone has secrets that they keep hidden, for fear revealing such a truth would destroy them. Some try to forget their secrets, or hide them under denial, or remorse, or simply to keep themselves safe from another holding power over them."

"What are you saying, Des? It was just a kiss. I won't tell the others."

"Stop talking and listen to me. I'm serious."

"Okay, okay, I'm listening."

"All things made of magic have a secret name, which holds power, especially for those who discover the hidden identity of the owner. That's why the demons and devils hide their true names from their enemies. They fear another will use it to bind them and control their actions. I suspect the angels do the same."

"I see. That would be a useful trick."

"Listen, Kasai. It's powerful magic I am talking about, not tricks!" She sighed. "We must hurry and defeat Sekka, but I fear I may not be able to stop myself from doing horrible things once the change fully has me. It will be up to you to prevent me from hurting those I love."

"It was only a kiss. It didn't hurt."

"A kiss to you, but something more lethal to others. The line between friend and foe is becoming blurred. I am acting only on my immediate desire, be it pleasure or pain, but taking it to an extreme. And I forget things.

"At first, I thought it was just fatigue. But now I know it's something different like my memories are being replaced by other experiences that are not my own. They are Sekka's memories, or memories she is forcing me to accept. I don't know. Everything keeps shifting in my head."

She took his hands into her own, and her voice was whisper soft. "I give to you freely the name given to me by my parents. It was my secret name to introduce my spirit to the Guardians of the Forest. That name is Manna'Desdevi Mishi."

Kasai looked dumbfounded for a moment.

He doesn't get it. Desdemonia watched him closely, hoping he would understand.

He frowned with disappointment. "I have no hidden name to give you. I'm just Kasai Ch'ou. Does that matter?"

She felt relieved. "It's okay. You don't need one. I know who you are to me. You're my family now—only you. Not even the angels knew my secret name, or they would have used it, those pompous bastards. You must keep it safe. Use it to stop me when I lose control."

"Don't talk like that. We will find a way to reverse the effects of that ring," Kasai said. "Maybe the angels can help."

"Oh Kasai." She just shook her head. He was trying so hard to be reassuring. She watched him look at the space around her, and she knew he was seeing her differently.

"You see it now, don't you? Sekka's blood is contaminating me."

"I can't lose you, Des. You are all I have left too. We'll fight this together."

"That's very touching," a sultry voice said.

Desdemonia spun around and felt the heat of Ninziz-zida's segments blaze on her back.

"Show yourself!" she shouted.

Sess'thra came from behind a thick tree with bright-green moss glistened at its base and leaned lazily against its green-grey trunk. Small twigs, ending in coral-colored leaves, hung down from its lower branches, partially hiding the succubus's lithe figure.

"You!" Desdemonia snarled.

"Sister, why so hostile, hmm? This is a glorious day," Sess'thra said. She pushed off the tree and approached them. She was dressed in tight, green leathers that did little to conceal the form of her sleek curves. Her pale white skin was in stark contrast to the dark shapes and shadows of the jungle. Her almond-shaped, purple eyes were gleaming and flirtatious.

Desdemonia moved slowly, away from Kasai, creating an advantage against the succubus. But Sess'thra simply stopped moving and waited patiently.

"When you're both finished, I come with a message from my mistress. One that could put an end to the war between our worlds."

Desdemonia fired three magical darts at the Sess'thra, but the succubus dismissively waved her hand, and the darts exploded in a harmless shower of blue sparks.

Sess'thra rolled her eyes. Stopppppp." She dragged the word out of her mouth. "Now, others will come, and there is less time to tell you what needs to be said."

"What do you want, demon?" Kasai said through clenched teeth.

"Such a sweet boy. There is no time for what I want just yet. But soon, we shall explore what it really means to be the Ever Hero." She smiled wickedly at Kasai, then her face became more plain.

"You cannot hope to defeat Sekka. The Frost Queen's power and influence have only grown since our last encounter on Gathos. But this earthy realm is not to her taste. Especially when there are so many other worlds to choose from in the Abyss."

"Get on with it," Kasai said. He raised the end segment of Ninziz-zida, ready to strike. "What does she want?"

Desdemonia didn't trust her, but she was genuinely curious. If there was a way to evict Sekka from the Mortal Realm without more bloodshed, maybe the Challenge of Righteousness would be fulfilled, and she and Kasai could be free of this madness.

"All of this could be over tomorrow. My mistress has a Life Debt to settle with a higher power, one of the Great Three, no less. She can absolve herself by delivering the Ever Hero as payment against her debt. But you cannot be forced to go. It must be your choice."

"How can I trust you?" Kasai said.

"Trust me? Why would you ever think you could trust me? I'm just the messenger. But your options are limited. If you refuse, this realm will suffer. Its kingdoms will fall to her Frost Legions. The people will become slaves, or worse, fodder for her twisted whims.

"What shall it be, Ever Hero? Will you sacrifice your life for the many, or instead, watch your entire world be covered in ice? Not much of a choice, I'm afraid, but a choice, nonetheless."

"It's a trick!" Desdemonia said. "You mustn't go with her. Stay and fight or let's remain in the shadows. Sekka needs you. We can use that against her. If you are captured, then it's over."

"You are changing," Sess'thra purred at Desdemonia. And slowly walked closer to her.

"Get back. You disgust me."

"Of course, I do. You see in me all the things you hate about yourself. But slowly, that hate gives way to acceptance, and then desire. I see all that you are becoming, and it's a wonderful sight."

She reached out quick as a viper and grabbed Desdemonia by the wrist. "You cannot prevent what is happening. Believe me, I know," Sess'thra said and held up Desdemonia's hand with the onyx ring. "Soon, we shall be the same."

Desdemonia tried in vain to escape Sess'thra's grip. But the succubus was too strong.

"Mother would like a word with you, Manna'Desdevi Mishi," Sess'thra said. She gave Kasai a wolfish grin, and in a fluid motion, she twirled Desdemonia into her embrace.

"Des!" Kasai shouted.

"You will find my mistress waiting for you in the fields where Lord Oziax's head fell. I'm sure you remember the place. And be quick about it, Ever Hero. My mistress is not known for her patience."

Sess'thra then vanished into thin air, taking Desdemonia with her.

71

RAGUEL

R aguel stood alone at an open window in his high tower, looking down on buildings and towers as far as the eye could see. The sun shone as a yellow king, high in a cloudless sky over the city of Asher. He basked in the sun's warmth as if its soothing rays were a personal gift from the Immortal Mother to only him.

The rooftops below reflected yellow light, casting the buildings in a sea of shimmering gold. This was his city. He was its architect and protector. A cool breeze blew across his face, and he folded his hands behind his back and under his great wings.

His brow furrowed as he looked out to the horizon. *How can it be that no matter what state of perfection I create, there will always be some that refuse to conform? How could anyone shun the light of paradise?*

Behind him, his equerry, Sonnalle, continued speaking. "I am only saying you might have exercised more caution first. A few moments of introspection may have warranted a different course of action."

Raguel turned from the sunlight and walked toward Sonnalle. The blonde-haired angel stood patiently in the meeting chamber, where the polished stone reflected his elegant attire. Precious stones were woven into the hemlines and sparkled as they caught the light.

"Since the beginning of all things, the Immortal Mother has placed a heavy burden upon my shoulders. As the Warden of Heaven, I have been charged with maintaining the purity of the Seven Heavens. At all times, I must be the Archangel of Justice, Vengeance, and Redemption. I am the Watcher of Mortals, and the bane to devils and demons alike."

"None dare refute those titles, lord. Your word is the law. I am merely saying it was risky to let the mortals live."

Sonnalle stood tall under an overhead window. His sharp cheekbones caught the noontime light and dropped long shadows down his face.

"You have created precedence for sympathy and forgiveness for the fallen. Those of the lower heavens are rallying behind this new example of empathy. They wish to save Aetenos in the same fashion and see you grant him clemency."

Raguel scowled at hearing the name of his nemesis but allowed Sonnalle to continue. His equerry was one of the few beings whose opinion Raguel respected.

"The sting from Artiya'il's banishment still bleeds in their hearts. That should have been done silently. Many now watch the movements of the mortals with keen interest. And I do not speak of only the celestials inhabiting the lower levels. There are True-borns in Tanalum who hope for the young monk and his companions' survival."

Aetenos. The mere mention of the monk's name spun Raguel's peaceful mood into agitation. His emotions had become fickle of late, ever since the arrival of the one-eyed monk to Elysian.

A memory flashed to the forefront of his mind. At the request of Illyria, Aetenos was to be plucked from the Mortal Realm to receive her divine gift, granting him the status of a living demigod. She insisted he ascend through the Seven Heavens and take his place on Tanalum.

Raguel had refused, of course. There was a natural process that all beings must adhere to when entering the Seven Heavens. But this wasn't a request from Lady Illyria, who never cared much about such rules. The Laws of Heaven only existed at her pleasure, as if she was the Immortal Mother and not one of her nine daughters.

The conversation that followed was filled with sweet words that flowed like honey when spoken from her lips. But Illyria's words also carried the sting of bees. There would be no discussion. He was to do as she commanded.

"My dear Raguel, you will do as I ask. I do not wish to ruin such a beautiful after-noon with such a trivial debate," she had said. "Make it so." And then the conversation was over. Her wishes were to be honored.

To think it was by his own hand that he created the one who had stolen her affec-tion from him. But now, the Great Monk had fallen from grace. Aetenos's demise was assured. But that pleasure seemed hollow to him now. He felt as if nothing had been gained, and worse that he had lost much in the process.

Raguel returned his thoughts to the conversation with Sonnalle. "The wards of Aetenos are a curiosity for those needing a distraction, nothing more. If I'm lucky, the young monk will fail the Challenge of Righteousness quickly. Aetenos will be swept away and forgotten. His meddling in the affairs of mortals finally ended. The dissenters will see I was just and kind for giving them a chance to redeem themselves."

Raguel walked to an assortment of fruit resting on a golden serving platter. He moved aside cherries, the color of dark burgundy and bright-red strawberries that did not meet his taste.

He eventually took hold of a full bunch of plump purple grapes and plucked one from the top. In a quick motion, he popped it into his mouth and savored its layers of succulent flavor. *Soon this will all be over and forgotten.*

His vintners had meticulously spiced together thirty unique vines to produce such an extraordinary fruit. The process of introducing each new child branch to the mother vine took a generation to adhere and stabilize before the next could be added. The result was well worth the wait, for the altered plants produced grapes of unsurpassed quality and taste.

"Tread carefully, lord. The Seven Heavens are rising to a tipping point. Turmoil and unrest are increasing. The Cloud Court fills daily with petitioners demanding the release of Aetenos," Sonnalle said.

"Things will return to normal."

"Some say you have taken your role of the warden to the extreme. I see anger on the faces of many celestials, and the word tyrant is all but spoken on their lips," Sonnalle said.

"Tyrant? Don't be absurd. Tanalum has existed in a state a of perfection for centuries. The lower levels fight for an individuality they do not understand. Perfection is absolute. There need be no other way than what I have designed."

"And if the lower levels see a different plan for themselves?"

"They will agree to comply with my Golden Path, or they will be no more. Those who transgress the Laws of Heaven must be punished. We will lead the lesser beings to paradise. How they get there is up to them. This is the wish of the Immortal Mother."

Raguel was aware of dissenters within the Seven Heavens. They leeched the strength of his righteousness with ideas of tolerance and change. Who were they to change what was already perfect? He had spent millennia honing the Way of Heaven, and his order was without reproach, yet some still did.

Small groups of protesters, made up of celestials and animal spirits, were always challenging his decrees. It didn't surprise him that those who could never claim the mantle of True-born were jealous. But their needs were beneath his concern.

"The Great Balance must remain in all things," Sonnalle said.

"The Great Balance is an antiquated idea whose time has passed. Trust me, Sonnalle. I know what I am doing. That monkey was foolish to suggest the Challenge of Righteousness. He mistakenly gave me the way to be rid of those bothersome mortals. And the timing could not have been better. The fate of Aetenos and his followers provides a significant diversion from other, more pressing areas. The future of Heaven is at a crossroads."

"Lord Raguel, if I may speak plainly. These are blasphemous thoughts. The Immortal Mother—"

"The Immortal Mother has entrusted me with the power to decide what is right and what is wrong. Perhaps what I say will not be to the liking of some, but they are necessary words to hear.

"For once, that fool Aetenos is right. The Three Realms have changed. The ideology of the Great Balance as a swinging pendulum no longer applies. The Three Realms drift towards permanent chaos. A new hierarchy must exist, and the Seven Heavens will be its pinnacle.

"We will dictate a new ideal for the other realms. It's our divine providence to provide the beacon of salvation to those lesser creatures trapped in darkness. This is the only way to hold tight the reigns of perfection."

"There will be resistance, lord. This could start a war not only in Heaven but across the Three Realms."

And divine vengeance awaits those who resist my will, Raguel thought. He pursed his lips and held his tongue in check. He had hoped to have more support from his equerry. But in time, Sonnalle would see things his way. He always did.

"The birth of the Chaos Gate has made that inevitable."

"Then you must intervene! Petition the Immortal Mother to destroy the Chaos Gate," Sonnalle said.

"I will do no such thing. The Chaos Gate offers an unprecedented opportunity, one I will exploit it to its fullest."

"Muster the Heavenly Host. Implore the Immortal Mother to grant us holy passage though the Amaranthine Barrier. We will storm through the skies of the Mortal Realm and crush the demon armies before they can do more damage and steal more souls."

"You sound like that addlebrained monk. I will see what his so-called Ever Hero can do before anything else. If the boy fails, then the naysayers will see the error of Aetenos's ways in bastardizing Illyria's divine gift, and I will be vindicated from blame.

"If he is successful in destroying Sekka, then we have the good fortune to strike a significant blow against one of the Great Three."

Sonnalle's eye widened. His surprised expression turned to a conspirator's knowing grin.

"What do you know?" he said, taking a step forward.

Raguel pivoted and walked back to the open window. His hands clasped once more behind his back. *That's it*, thought Raguel, *pique his interest but keep him wondering until you are ready to commit.*

"I will speak with the prisoner now, Sonnalle. Bring him in, and then leave us. I will call you when I am finished."

"Yes, Chancellor Pinnacle."

He heard the equerry's swift departure from the meeting chamber.

Raguel took in the shimmering sea of golden rooftops below. A flock of orange-feathered birds held his gaze until they vanished against the amber background. Moments later, new footsteps arrived.

"You have been treated well?" Raguel said.

"Yes, Raguel. The prison vistas here are glorious, unlike the drab, cold walls of Furia Keep's dungeons. Sekka could learn a thing or two from you in the way of hospitality.

He paused as if recalling a thought. "And far too many chains. No, I was never fond of the chains. Chaffed my wrists and ankles raw. Very unpleasant."

Raguel turned fast. "I am the Chancellor Pinnacle. You will address me accordingly."

Aetenos bowed. "Forgive me, Chancellor Pinnacle. I forget myself. There was once a time when we called each other friend."

"We both know that time has long passed if ever it existed. Now you are an outcast and an embarrassment to those who believed in you. You should have never returned. Do you ever think of anyone but yourself? Lady Illyria has been shamed by your roguish ways and selfish actions."

Aetenos lowered his head and remained quiet.

Raguel studied the monk. His black topknot was oiled and woven in a tight braid and hung over his right shoulder. He had been presented with a choice of more austere attire but opted instead to handmake simple robes from cobalt blue cloth. His craftmanship was mediocre at best. At least the man had bathed.

A simple, black patch covered his ruined eye. There was no beauty in the man. Nothing. Aetenos was plain and ordinary. How could this wretch have stolen Illyria's love? What could she have seen in this stray dog that was so captivating?

"You must let me return to the Mortal Realm. It should be me who challenges Sekka, not the boy. He's not ready to face such a burden alone."

"Boy or man, what does it matter? He's your *Ever Hero*. He will live or die by that marker. The fate of the Mortal Realm is now in his hands."

"Your bitterness of the past has clouded not only your judgment but also your sight. The Chaos Gate has attracted far worse than an archdevil to the doorstep of the Mortal Realm. The visions are stronger now, aren't they?"

Raguel's self-righteous attitude turned to suspicion. What did Aetenos know? Had he somehow uncovered the bargain with Xerthotha? Raguel quickly composed himself. "You are mistaken."

"Am I? Then why am I here? You need something."

"Yes, information. Sadly, you are the only one who possesses an accurate knowledge of Sekka's movements and disposition."

"You know as much as I. The archdevil has stretched herself too thin and cannot hold the Chaos Gate alone. Powerful beings have awakened. They slough from the shadow dimension to claim the portal for their own. She will need reinforcements, or she will lose. Her eternal war with Zizphander continues to drain her resources."

"Zizphander is dead."

"Oh? That could not have been easy."

Raguel watched Aetenos ponder the news. His one eye shifted side-to-side. Then the monk looked at Raguel straight on.

"You wish to know which of the Great Three she owes allegiance," Aetenos said.

"Quite so."

Aetenos looked up to the ceiling in thought. He shrugged his shoulders. "One Supreme Devil is as good or bad as another, I suppose, for a time at least."

"Time? What such time?"

"The Ancients, Raguel. They are coming. The Chaos Gate is their beacon. Maybe they have already arrived in a lesser state, waiting for the Amaranthine Barrier to collapse until they can bring their true forms to bear."

"I have time to accomplish much before their true forms can manifest. The Seven Heavens will no longer be a counterweight to the lawlessness of Chaos. I see a new path for the Three Realms. Tanalum will ascend to new heights."

Aetenos looked to the floor and shook his head. "Please, for once, do not solely look for the outcome you desire, but see the reality before you."

"You dare speak to me of reality? It was your madness that created the Chaos Gate. How could you not see such an obvious trap? If Illyria needed to be rescued, did you think I would not have petitioned the Immortal Mother to lower the Amaranthine Barrier? I would have stormed the entirety of the Abyss to retrieve her."

"And yet, it was I who was told to go, not you."

"Told to go, and not allowed? By whom?"

"It no longer matters. What has been done is done. If the Ancients find the means to dissolve the Barrier, there will be nothing separating the Three Realms."

"I'm sure it will not come to that," Raguel said. "There is still plenty of time." He tapped his finger to his lips. "Nonetheless, this is not your concern."

"Raguel, what if your timing is wrong?"

Raguel put his hand up to stop Aetenos. "You were not brought here to discuss the welfare of the Three Realms. You shall provide me with the information I need and nothing more. Now, who pulls Sekka's strings?"

"We all walk freely into the traps we are blinded by because we see them as salvation, old friend. Sekka will be betrayed, as will you."

"Me? Who will betray me?"

"Whichever of the Great Three that you think to ally with against the other two."

Raguel dismissed the comment. "I will not ask you again."

"I honestly don't know. Pick whichever one you wish. The outcome will be the same."

"Sonnalle," Raguel called out. "The prisoner will return to his chambers. I am done with him."

Raguel stepped closer to Aetenos. "I had thought you would have been more cooperative, for the Lady Illyria's sake."

"Please, old friend, think hard about what you are doing. There is still time to change your ways."

"You should never have been given the divine gift. But soon, that mistake will be rectified."

Sonnalle entered the meeting chamber. Aetenos bowed to Raguel and was led away. Raguel wasn't sure what he meant to achieve by meeting with Aetenos, but whatever it was, he had failed to accomplish it.

He could clearly hear Aetenos whistling a light-hearted tune in the distance as if all was right in the Three Realms.

"That monk and his infuriating humming and whistling! I'll not second guess myself. I know what I'm doing."

72

SEKKA

A dark tower rose from the depths of a great chasm in the center of Shiverrig's military camp. Great blocks of black hematite, lined with silver and red streaks, were quarried from the bottomless pit and raised by giant pulley systems surrounding its edge. The metallic rock was filled with densely packed impurities and acted as an excellent conductor of Elemenati energy, making it an ideal choice to lay as the foundation of her new stronghold.

Sekka stood at the opening of a large window looking out over the construction site. She spotted slave crews at the base of the tower smashing the jagged slabs into smaller, more precise building blocks. The design of the tower was of an infernal aesthetic, hereto unseen by mortal eyes. Fiends with hammer and chisel sculpted the rock into organic shapes, which curled together like writhing worms.

Wicked looking buttresses shot out from the tower's sides to spear the walls of the chasm's far perimeter. The impossible height of the design called for excessive bracing at its base. To Sekka's eyes, the supports resembled an intricate spider's web, and she enjoyed the symbolism of being the monster in the middle.

Far below the tower and its support matrix were the lower levels of her lair. The column of rock which remained as a central spoke to the pit's circle was immense. Her slaves worked tirelessly burrowing tunnels and excavating rooms from the dense stone. These areas would accommodate dungeons, holding pens, slave pits, and larger halls for grander experimentations and entertainment.

Much had been accomplished in the short months since she had returned to the Mortal Realm, but her patience had its limits, as did Azrollorza's. The Supreme Devil made a point to send a bothersome stream of gruesome cherubs via the Chaos Gate to check on Sekka's progress. She wanted the essence of the Divine Fist and his Ever Hero now.

Sekka did her best to placate the sickly messengers with assurances that she would soon have their essence's soon, before sending them away. *Oh, how I wish I could rip out their tongues and snap their little necks*, she thought.

Her gazed drifted across the once snow-covered grass plains of Baroqia. The outpost buildings of the Last Garrison had been swept away to make room for Shiverrig's army. Now, the area resembled a small city whose sole purpose was to make war on Sunne.

The man was made for war, she mused.

If only the Warlords of Vyzyn had a similar aptitude. The fools raced into Sunne with her Frost Legion at their command, only to be outmaneuvered and displaced by its natives. She shook her head with disappointment. That was the shortcoming of all lesser demons. They possessed no concept for shifting strategies that unfolded over time.

Shiverrig's efforts had already tripled the soul harvest from Sunne. Now there was a warlord she could respect. If only he wasn't such a thorn in her side. She only knew one other mortal that was more troublesome than Shiverrig, if he could still be labeled in such a way. But Aetenos had disappeared since fleeing Furia Keep's prison. It was curious that the Great Monk had not yet interfered with her plans.

"Maybe he's finally dead," she said and glanced down to see a bug scurrying across the windowsill. She let it crawl up her hand then squashed it between her thumb and index finger. "Maybe."

Her pleasant mood was enhanced by the sound of overbearing jol'goth slave masters barking out commands to lesser thralls. The ever-present crack of strong whips gave her a thrill and took her mind off the incomplete construction of the tower.

Still, she was restless. The central tower should have more height by now. She leaned out the window, craned her head upwards, and watched goblin slaves dangling from ropes attached to the uppermost construction. Some carved protective runes into the outer surface, while others splashed buckets of blood over the finished designs.

One of the diminutive workers recklessly rappelled to her left, letting blood splash out from an open sack tied to his waist. Sekka lowered her gaze to see stringy dots splattered across the thin fabric covering her chest.

She grabbed the thrall by the throat and shook his body like a rag doll gripped in the mouth of a hound. Blood splashed in all directions and drenched her in the process. She held the small humanoid creature steady. Her displeasure was evident in the thrall's mud-colored eyes.

She brought the slave's face closer to her own. Its rancid breath heightened her now foul mood. Her grip on the goblin's throat tightened. "What is taking so long?"

The most she heard as an answer was a feeble gasp for air, then the goblin's body went limp. Disgusted, she tossed the dead thing away. It pinwheeled head-over-feet until it smashed against the ground below.

Sekka then heard a marching horn sound over the din of construction. She saw Tazizu heading a long train of what could only be Sunnese captives.

"Finally, one of the Vyzyn doing something positive." Sekka ripped off her shirt and changed into something more appropriate for outside. She eventually walked to the extensive camp's edge to welcome the witch with a nod of approval.

Steam rose from the body of Tazizu's war mount. Its jaws were slathered in purplish goo, which hung like long, thin vines from its lips. The Vyzyn warlord bowed her hairless head when she passed Sekka. The blood-red, arcane tattoos stood out in stark contrast to the pale skin of her scalp.

The Sunnese captives were bound and gagged. It appeared Tazizu had sacked a village, or maybe two. The slaves shuffling past her were not warriors but the beginnings and ends of families. The young huddled close to their elders, clinging to whatever hope of protection they could along the long march north. But there would be no salvation for this lot.

Sekka sighed with mild frustration. The magic in their souls would be meager at best. At this rate, it would take longer than expected to raise another Behemoth the likes of Cymeryes.

Bringing one of Gathos's fantastic beasts to the Mortal Realm would quickly equalize the balance of power against Shiverrig's army. "Tch, another delay," Sekka grumbled.

A squad of Shiverrig's half-breeds gathered the captives into a holding pen. Another team would eventually march them north through the Hoarfrost Mountains via the Storm Wind Pass. From there, the Chaos Gate would send them to Gathos, where they would be transformed into something more useful to her.

Nonetheless, Shiverrig's tactics were bearing fruit. At last, a warlord up to the task of conquering Sunne. Lord Oziax was a ruthless commander, but he shucked discipline in favor of brute force and glory. Shiverrig's mind was a brilliant mix of tactics and organization but he couldn't be trusted. She allowed herself a small chuckle. *I'd respect him less if I could.*

She wondered how Aeshmara felt now that Shiverrig commanded the Frost Legion. Bitter, of course. But would she move against Shiverrig and regain her status of command? That brought to the surface another question, what was the Frost Legion now?

The initial legions she had bequeathed to the Warlords of Vyzyn were all but gone. A few companies remained, but her Juggernauts had fallen in Sunne due to poor battle strategy and mismanaged resources. And the war with Zizphander had left her with a fraction of her fighting force on Gathos. Shiverrig's half-breeds comprised most of the legion's shock troops, and they were loyal to him.

Aeshmara fears him. She will not stay idle. If Shiverrig cannot hold his position, then he doesn't deserve to have it, she thought. It was the way of the Abyss. Strength prevails where weakness falters.

As Sekka strolled through the military camp, she couldn't help but feel impressed. Shiverrig had left a quarter of his troops behind to facilitate the building of a city around her tower. Forges blasted hot air out of doors and windows and sent black smoke into the sky.

Armorers banged steel into protective chest plates and helms. Slaughterhouses popped up in the hundreds to keep the army fed. It was built quickly and effectively and solely to support Shiverrig's war machine. The snow covering the grasslands had been trampled and packed by hundreds of thousands of warriors. It was now as hard as thick ice.

Those who were not conscripted into the manual labor of supplying and equipping the troops spent their time training for war. Sekka observed multiple companies marching forward in unison. A shrill note sang from a signal caller's flute. Each company arranged itself into a different combat formation with overlapping points of attack and defense.

She saw that other areas were set aside for combat training. Spears thrust forward into the midsection of straw dummies hanging from wooden gibbets.

Archers pulled back on longbows nocked with black shafted arrows and released them into distant targets. The clang of steel was a constant song, sung throughout the camp.

Shiverrig's warriors had the strength of demon spawn and the thinking minds of humans. They were not brilliant, but they were not mindless either. Shiverrig had created a powerful combination. Sess'thra should have reported that such a force could exist before she had given him the tools to convert so many, and so quickly. Once again, Sekka had underestimated this mortal.

And there was something arrogant about Shiverrig's warriors. They carried a sense of entitlement as they marched in their tight-formed companies or tirelessly drilled in mock combat. Lone sentries were scattered about the camp in what was meant to be a random pattern. But she knew the look of a spy when she saw one. They watched her movements and listened to her conversations.

The half-breeds remained respectful and diligent with meeting her demands, but there was no fear in their eyes. She was sure they leered at her when they thought she looked elsewhere.

Sekka had seen the same as she waded through Zizphander's fire fiends and demons in that glorious, final battle on Gathos. She remembered the Red Devil commanding his horde forward into battle, knowing they would be butchered. Even as they fell by the tens of thousands, they still raced forward with a berserker's rage. Perhaps they reserved their fear for another, higher power?

Xerthotha. The name alone filled her with a premonition of dread. She shook it off.

"I no longer need to fear the Chaos Devil now that I have the protection of Azrollorza. And Shiverrig couldn't possibly cast more fear in these creatures than me."

Sekka's ire rose as she studied the half-breeds around her, most of whom were not even warriors tested in battle. They were mere citizens of a human city before succumbing to the demon seed. Yet, they did not quake before her either.

Shiverrig may have been their progenitor, but he simply did not have the raw power that her blood possessed. "I should have Aosoth round up a company of Shiverrig's soldiers. I'll play nicely at first, then things will change. Let the onlookers learn the extent of my nastiness." Her lips moistened at the idea of so much carnage.

Sekka thought back to her time spent in Rachlach Fortress. Hundreds of novice magic users were brought to her to be tutored in the dark arts. Each one possessed an unwavering eagerness to learn the depths of their craft. It was adorable.

But nothing quite compared to the sweetness of draining their life force using the same magic they begged her to teach them. Of course, she left out the critical component that would protect them from the spell becoming parasitic and feeding their essence to her instead. *What did they expect? I am an archdevil, after all.* Her tongue remembered the metallic tang of their blood, and her mouth watered.

Maugris thought he was strong in the ways of magic. He was a babe lost in the woods in comparison to her infernal strength. He was a glutton for a power that he had no understanding of how to control. His ego was his undoing, like so many other enemies who crossed her path.

The fool of a sorcerer had given her everything she needed for her ascension. She was now one task away from sitting at the side of Azrollorza in the High Pantheon of the Abyss. Not yet as an equal, but that would come in time. *Perhaps she would be the first to slay a Supreme Devil. Now wasn't that a tantalizing thought?*

Sekka looked to the North, happy that winter refused to relinquish its hold on the land. Snowstorms still swirled down from the Hoarfrost Mountains and covered the grasslands with fresh snow. Winter's cold was drawn to her like an amorous lover, yearning for her embrace. She welcomed the affection with open arms. There was nothing better than a winter's storm to make her feel at home.

She knew parts of Rachlach Fortress still stood, though not for much longer. The Chaos Gate was growing. It hungered for the residual magic that remained in the ruins of Maugris's keep. It devoured the rock and wood, as a carnivore feasted on flesh and bone. It had expanded by a factor of ten when she had arrived three months ago, fresh from her victory over Zizphander.

It would still be months before her new tower was completed, and Sekka was bored. She wondered if the magic she used to create her old scrying chamber had held against the hunger of the Chaos Gate. The portal devoured magic as greedily as the souls fed to it for passage.

The trek through Storm Wind Pass took little time to complete. She wore brown hunting pants tucked into high boots. Her ice-blue shirt was loosely tied in the front and billowed open with each strong wind. The chilly air caressed the skin of her chest and neck. Clothing was such an exciting accessory. She needed none, of course, for the harsh elements had no ill effect on her.

She looked out over the snowcapped mountain range. The wind blew out the loose tie holding her hair in check. Thick, white locks snapped like vipers about her face. It was a glorious sensation. She appreciated the raw power of nature. It was pure chaos, just like her.

Sekka continued toward the remains of Maugris's mountain fortress and soon spotted the Chaos Gate. It had grown far beyond her expectation to the size of a small lake.

So big.

The Chaos Gate was more than just a portal between realms. It was a living thing, like a tree, animal, or human, with its own life pattern and essence. It had needs and hungered for more of anything that it could devour.

Sekka studied the movement of its ever-changing surface. Bubbles of dissolved rock popped in rapid succession as the steaming edges of the portal continued to devour the mountain at an alarming rate. It seemed as if the Chaos Gate was preparing for the conveyance of something enormous. *Maybe it had already come through,* Sekka thought and quickly scanned the area for evidence of trespass. Nothing out of the ordinary, or nothing she could see now.

An uneasy feeling crept up her spine. What was left on Gathos to warrant such an expansion? Her armies had been decimated fighting against that wretched Zizphander. It would take years to replenish their numbers.

The few remaining Behemoths of Gathos fought in her name on distant Circles in the Abyss. As much as she wanted them here, they could not be recalled. She would lose the frail trust of her allies if she took them back. The ungrateful devils and demon lords would turn on her the moment the giant beasts were gone. Again, she cursed the name of Zizphander for the death of Cymeryes.

A thought squirmed into her mind. *"You are weak. If not for the protection of Azrollorza, you would be dead."* Sekka dismissed the idea. Nothing is gained without risk, and the Chaos Gate was worth the totality of her armies and more. She would sacrifice them a hundred times over to complete her ascension.

She recalled Azrollorza's words to her before she departed the Supreme Devil's realm.

"The essence of an innocent mortal whose soul is connected to the divine, and saturated with demonic power, is a valuable thing. The combination of such elements will allow me to travel unfettered through the portals.

"The Amaranthine Barrier has been weakened by the birth of the Chaos Gate but still holds back the greatest of devils. Only the slumbering Ancients have the power to bypass the Barrier now. We must claim this world before they awaken."

Sekka squinted her eyes at the living portal. Something was demanded access, but if not from her homeworld, then where? The Ancients? No, Azrollorza must be massing her troops on Gathos to prepare for an invasion of the Mortal Realm.

It made sense. Sekka had planted a tempting seed in her greedy mind. The Supreme Devil would be eager to satiate her hunger with such a feast of souls. It was curious why Chedipe had sent no word of their arrival.

The movement of such military might would levy a hefty tax in souls from the Chaos Gate. *Does Azrollorza expect me to pay the soul fee?* "I won't do it!" she said. "Let Azrollorza pay her own way if she intends to steal what I have paid for so dearly. Her forces will remain trapped on Gathos until my magic opens the portal."

Sekka smirked. Nothing escaped the Immortal Mother's touch. Everything had its rules, and the Chaos Gate was no different. *The Great Balance must remain.*

The act of defiance made her feel especially powerful, but only for a moment. "As if you would dare such a bold move. Azrollorza would destroy Gathos without a second thought and you along with it."

Sekka knew she stood in the middle of a slippery slope. Until she could amass a new Frost Legion on Gathos, she was defenseless to attack from any one of a thousand greater devils looking to raise their status in the Abyss. Only the protective influence of Azrollorza held the jaws of these scavengers at bay. Even now, they circled Gathos like starved wolves. She could see their shadows darting just outside the light of her astral campfire.

But the Supreme Devil had her own agenda, and Sekka was just a means to an end. Although she had a pact with the Supreme Devil, that was no guarantee Sekka would receive everything she wanted. There were always small details to be worked out in every contract.

Things would change when she delivered the soul essence of Aetenos and his Ever Hero. Sekka would lose her leverage over Azrollorza and become insignificant.

But I could stall Azrollorza's advancement into the Mortal Realm until I am ready, she thought.

A Chaos Gate was a miracle of travel if you were the originator of the portal. Sekka could pass freely from one realm to the next, retaining her full strength and magical might wherever she went. A toll must be paid, of course, and the Chaos Gate thirsted for souls.

But the portal would not allow one such as Azrollorza to pass without dire consequences. The Supreme Devils were shackled to their own Layer in the Abyss. They could influence other realms through clever subterfuge and command champions and armies to wage war in their name on distant Circles, but they could never bring their full might to bear on another Supreme Devil's home. Rules were rules.

Azrollorza, Xerthotha, or Morrdilliax would lose all but a fraction of their life force upon trespassing on another's Layer and presumably would die if she entered the Mortal Realm or Seven Heavens without the blessing of the Immortal Mother.

And if Azrollorza ventured through Sekka's portal, the Chaos Gate, would strip away her strength and devour her magic as payment for the voyage. Any vulnerability was death in the Abyss. Sekka assumed it was the same in the Seven Heavens. Loss of power meant loss of control. And oh, how those self-righteous angels needed to control everything.

She could picture that flowery and pretentious, Raguel, sitting in his office, high in the clouds on Tanalum, as he scratched out his new rules and laws for all to follow. He was called the Chancellor Pinnacle, but by any other name, he was just another despot. He boasted of a paradise made through lawful order, but she scoffed at the idea. The Seven Heavens were designed to retain control.

But Sekka knew all laws had loopholes, or breaking points, as she liked to call them. She fondly remembered the day she shattered the spell of binding Maugris held over her. Ah, to relive that wonderful instant when she was freed, and he realized he was doomed. But now was not the time for such pleasant thoughts.

A Chaos Gate was a manifestation of deep magic that existed when the slumbering Ancients were young godlings drifting through the outer realms of life and death, or so the legends went. The alignments of good and evil had not yet surfaced, and the realms existed in harmony. But desire and greed change all things over time, and the outer worlds pulled away from the middle. And so, the Immortal Mother issued rules of balance that must never be broken.

She means to deceive the Chaos Gate and bypass the portal's rules! Somehow, Azrollorza had discovered a unique coin to satisfy the heavy toll for passage. The key was buried in the stolen soul essence of Aetenos, and his Ever Hero, which acted as anchor points for the dark portal.

If this was accurate, the Supreme Devil would use ownership of their essence to deceive the dark portal into thinking she was Sekka, not Azrollorza, who passed through its gateway. It would be a smart trick, indeed, if it worked. *No, no, too risky.*

Then the realization of Azrollorza's scheme came to her. *Oh no. She will create her own portal and invade the Mortal Realm with impunity.*

Sekka thought back to her present situation. Who was to say that once Azrollorza possessed access to the Mortal Realm, she would honor her pact? She was no fool. Her resources had been depleted by constant war, and she could no longer call upon great armies to invade new lands or defend those already conquered. Without the ability to dangle something shiny in front of Azrollorza's many eyes, Sekka would be considered a broken, and useless thing.

But until Azrollorza had the essence of both souls, she and her mighty legions were effectively trapped in the Abyss. Desdemonia was the key to the Ever Hero, and Sekka had the Wood Witch. She had leverage, for the time being. She would need to keep that secret safe. For once, the Immortal Mother's damned rules worked in her favor.

"Who is to say how long it will take to reclaim the Ever Hero?" Sekka said. "With a little more time, my position here will change for the better. In the meantime, I'll convert Shiverrig's army to my own, not just in name but in loyalty as well.

"I could destroy the Chaos Gate and forsake Gathos to rule here instead." She glanced skyward with wary eyes. "Too soon. They would come, and I would not be ready."

She turned from the festering portal and climbed over the fallen rocks, broken columns, and loose debris that had once been the great hall. The spark of life provided by the sorcerer's magic had been sucked away long ago by the voracious appetite of the Chaos Gate. The portal fed indiscriminately on whatever stood in its path. The ruins were now a dead place.

Sekka located an open archway leading to an unlit corridor. She navigated her way around waist-high chunks of black stone. Whole sections of the wall had crumbled, and she was forced to use her hands to climb over loose piles of rubble.

She followed a once-familiar path through Rachlach Fortress, descending broken stairways and sloping walkways. Northern winds howled through vacant halls and empty corridors, bringing with it cold, stale air. Suddenly, the rock floor beneath her feet rolled like a wave of water.

She caught her balance against the wall as the aftershock of the quake tremble through the rock. The Chaos Gate continued to feast on whatever magic remained of Maugris's legacy. Its appetite was voracious.

Sekka heard the mountain's death rattle in the wind and falling stones echoing through the passageways. *Yes, it must be preparing to vomit something colossal into this realm. Whatever it is, it will happen soon.*

Sekka hurried along the corridor and was surprised at the number of dead bodies that littered the way. Obviously, these were slaves who failed to flee in time, and the doomed fortress took them. Most were crushed by falling rocks of unsupported ceilings, while others died of starvation. Predators had not, or would not venture so deep in this place, even for an easy meal.

Trust that which is wild to sense danger.

Sekka kicked one of the dead slaves out of her way. Its body broke apart against the impact of her boot, scattering hundreds of cave beetles from within the corpse. "At least you can enjoy one last feast."

She came to a stone bridge that traversed a deep chasm. Another violent tremor shook the mountain, and the bridge wobbled underfoot, causing Sekka to fall to her knees.

"A thousand deaths upon you!" she cursed to no one in particular.

Her eyes shot upward, fearing the ceiling might collapse. Nothing yet. She moved on and eventually located her old scrying chamber. It had somehow remained intact.

And why would it not? It was her magic that had carved the chamber out from the heart of the mountain. A token gesture of water remained at the bottom of the basin.

"Just enough," she said and dipped her finger into the shallow pool. The water turned to slush as she traced complex patterns into its surface.

She sent her mind to Gathos via the entrance of the Chaos Gate on her homeworld. The portal's surface pool bubbled and hissed in the cold snow, but curiously, it had not grown in relative proportion to the entrance in the Mortal Realm. Sekka searched the landscape for Azrollorza's troops. Nothing. The area surrounding the Gate was void of life. *What does that mean? What would cause only one of the Chaos Gate's entrances to swell with such enormity?*

Her vision moved to Furia Keep. The superficial damage to the walls and tower had been repaired. Chedipe had done well. A satisfied grin crossed her mouth. She knew her reputation would grow, and she once more felt untouchable. No other devil would dare move on her now.

+Chedipe.+ Sekka's mind called to the demon witch. The connection was instant

and crisp. Her apprehension at the mystery of the Chaos Gate subsided.

+Yes, Mistress. Your servant, Chedipe, is here.+

+You will send ten thousand more Yanari fiends through the Chaos Gate immediately. Progress is slow on my new stronghold. Shiverrig's half-breeds are not of Gathos and blunder through the simplest building tasks.+

+Yes, Mistress.+

Sekka sensed hesitancy from Chedipe. The demon witch was holding something back.

+What is it, Chedipe? You are keeping something from me.+

+There is news.+

+Speak.+ Sekka's mind raced through possible threats. She was safe. Wasn't she? Who could hope to best her now that Zizphander had been destroyed?

+Maugris has been broken. Your Chedipe flayed his mind open like overripe fruit.+

+You were to leave him alive. His torment had barely begun.+

+Chedipe obeys the Mistress. He is not dead, though he has begged for release. Chedipe mocked him for his tears and screams.+

+What did you learn?+

The voice of Chedipe's mind moaned in worrisome sobs. *+Please, do not punish poor Chedipe. Your servant only just learned of Maugris's duplicity through dribbled and distorted memories.+*

+Tell me everything.+

Chedipe's thoughts drifted. She spoke as if in a trance. *+Maugris could not hide the truth from your diligent and resourceful Chedipe. As she peeled away the layers of his memories, one by one, she discovered an unusual stench, mingled between failed fantasies of conquest and domination. Chedipe did not recognize this foul odor, and so she dug deeper.+*

+Go on.+

+Poor Chedipe's hands trembled as she worked. What's this? What's this?+ Chedipe sent a vision of pulling long, sticky threads from the sorcerer's mind. She held them in the air before her eyes, examining them.

Chedipe gasped as if experiencing the shock of her discovery for the first time. She tried in vain to remove the sticky threads, but the substance soon entangled her.

+What? What did you find?+ Sekka's command snapped Chedipe's mind back to the present.

+Possession, Mistress Sekka. The taint of the Chaos Devil had long ago been woven through the essence of the sorcerer. Maugris was a pawn.+

+Xerthotha.+ The voice of Sekka's mind said the name with loathing. *+You will tell me all you know, now!+*

+Yes, mistress. Chedipe obeys Sekka. Maugris was under the sway of Xerthotha long before he summoned you to Rachlach Fortress. It was Xerthotha magic that weakened Maugris's spell of binding, not Sekka's. He was the puppet master, pulling the puppet's strings.+

Sekka's anger rose. She quickly calculated the obvious paths of Xerthotha's influence over others in the Three Kingdoms. *+Shiverrig.+*

+Yes, mistress. Shiverrig has been compromised. What shall you do?+ Chedipe mewled like a beaten cat. Sekka needed to think and silenced the connection.

This was dire news, but not altogether unexpected. "Again, I am surrounded by foes. But this time, I know the identity of my enemy, and that makes a difference."

She tapped her index finger to her lips. What was Xerthotha's plan? Undoubtedly, the Chaos Devil would know when Maugris's mind had broken. And then what? Wait for Sekka to move against Shiverrig once she realized the truth of his allegiance?

He would know she would destroy everything he had established in the Mortal Realm. But Xerthotha would not be so careless to let an asset like Shiverrig go to waste. Why then would he keep the fool Maugris alive in the first place?

Sekka's stomach churned with the possibility that Xerthotha had masterfully led her along a path of his choosing, pulling her strings just as easily as he manipulated Maugris. Every step she took, every obvious solution to an obstacle he placed in front of her, was paced in time with a hundred, nay thousands of other events. Dammit. She was trapped. *Or am I?*

+Mistress?+ Chedipe's thoughts came back into focus in Sekka's mind.

+I should have suspected one last trick.+

+Shall I dispose of Maugris? I can think of many ways to make his torment exquisite.+ Chedipe sent her thought.

+Perhaps he may still have some use. Patch him up. Take his tongue and remove his hands. He will never need either again. But keep him alive. I will want him alert when I return.+

+Return quickly, mistress. Chedipe fears for your safety.+

+There is one last demand Azrollorza makes on me, and I must honor it.+

Sekka severed her mind connection to Chedipe. She had been played masterfully by the Chaos Devil, but to what end? Her triumph over Zizphander had meaning to Xerthotha. What would he gain by sacrificing a major archdevil to oblivion? Or worse, enabling Azrollorza to gain access to a Chaos Gate. It made no sense to Sekka. It was pure madness.

She had been so careful, or so she thought. Xerthotha had used her from the beginning. He led her like a seasoned trapper. And now she was caught in his net. Indeed, his goal was control of the Chaos Gate.

Another tremor shook the mountain, and loose debris fell from the ceiling. The Chaos Gate would soon devour the entire fortress. This scrying chamber would eventually be consumed. Her magic was strong, but not strong enough to resist the hunger of such a diabolical device indefinitely.

It mattered little to her. The tower was rising in the south, and a new scrying chamber would be ready soon enough. Sekka took in the walls of the room. It had served its purpose, but like the rest of Rachlach Fortress, it was lost.

Let Xerthotha scheme in his corner of the Abyss. Azrollorza would keep him in check for now. Then, a devious smile crossed Sekka's full, blue lips. She would command Shiverrig to triple his efforts with the soul harvest. Xerthotha's pawn would indirectly fuel her war machine. If she could stall him for long enough, her power would be unmatched. All she needed was just a little more time.

With the conquest of Sunne, she could rebuild her Frost Legion on Gathos and potentially create a second one in the Mortal Realm. Shiverrig would then be removed in the most unpleasant way possible.

But until then, she was vulnerable and therefore deemed it best to remain unpredictable. She would do nothing against Shiverrig's position until she had proper reinforcements. The formation of a plan took root in Sekka's mind.

Azrollorza must have a personal stake in creating her own Chaos Gate. If Xerthotha wants a war for the Mortal Realm, I will let Azrollorza fight it for me.

73

DESDEMONIA

Desdemonia rested her weight on the sill of an unfinished window. The opening was roughed out, and the initial mortar laid in the seams between stones. It was a sloppy job. The surface was uneven and jagged. The subtle details of polished construction had been neglected.

Desdemonia sighed. It was the same over much of the tower; haste was preferred over aesthetics during wartime.

She crossed her arms and absentmindedly tapped the palm side of her onyx ring against the bracelet she wore on her left arm. The pinging sound created a colorful melody as it mingled with the deep pounding of hammers below. She hummed a forgotten tune from a time she couldn't remember.

Peering out the window, she surveyed the construction below. The workers looked like so many little ants scurrying about their tasks. Slaves toiled night and day to raise the tower, and beyond, a vast military camp grew into a functioning city.

She leaned further out the window, and a gust of wind caused her shirt to billow like a flag. Snow swirled around her free-flowing black hair, and the chilly air felt pleasant on her face. She felt happy and alive.

By her reckoning, winter should have given way to spring by now. But winter would not release its grip on the land. Desdemonia didn't mind. The cold felt like home, at least she thought it did.

How long had she been in the tower? Since the initial construction, or at least the upper levels. She wasn't allowed to venture into any other rooms or halls below ground. Everything had become somewhat hazy since her *accident*. How long? Months? Years? It was a mystery.

She didn't feel out of place. However, another voice mingled with her thoughts, a stranger's voice, and one that sounded weak. It whispered to her of other times and other memories. All of it remained just out of reach of her understanding.

She spotted a long line of dark-haired captives from Sunne led by hulking demons covered in shaggy, white fur. Smaller creatures harassed the prisoners with whips and prods, forcing them to keep pace. The procession headed north, always north. Her sister, well half-sister really, had explained the prisoners go to the Chaos Gate in Trosk.

Desdemonia did not know what a Chaos Gate was or what passage it provided. She only knew that the people of Sunne were the sworn enemies of her adopted mother. "If the Sunnese insisted on waging war against us, then they must be punished," her mother had said.

"Curses to the jungle-dwellers," Desdemonia said. She wished her mother would let her fight alongside her sister in battle again. It was their fault her memory had been stolen from her, so said her sister.

But the Sunnese are your people and are not to blame. Desdemonia heard the thought voiced in her mind. She cast away such a ridiculous idea. "Tsk, tsk, what kind of foolish thinking is that Desdemonia?"

Mother was overly protective. She would not let Desdemonia leave the tower until her memories were fully intact. "You could get lost, and then how would I find you?" Mother had said countless times.

So, for now, she was confined to her high loft with the infrequent bird coming to roost and playful rats racing underfoot. The walls were marked with deep holes with dark soot surrounded their edges. Each had a small pile of chipped stone lying beneath it on the floor.

Mother said this was an ideal place to continue her studies. It was peaceful, with no interruptions or distractions. She conjured another ball of blue flame in her hand, then whipped her body around in a spiral-like dance.

When she had gathered enough momentum, she threw the fireball at the far wall. A black serpent tail of smoke trailed behind it until it smashed into a large stone, shattering it on impact. Bits of rock sprayed into the air around her.

Desdemonia walked to the wall to examine its surface. Blue fire smoldered around the edges of the small crater her magic had made. A skinny rat shot across the floor and huddled close to her feet. Shaking with fright.

"That's the deepest cut yet," she smiled with satisfaction.

She pushed her hand through her thick hair, clearing it from her face. Her fingers brushed up against the two small protrusions just beyond her forehead. The bumps were the beginnings of horns, just like the ones on her sister's forehead.

She was proud of her new horns and the secret of their growth that she shared with her sister. Sess'thra had told her to practice making them appear and recede from sight on command. It was a game they played together. Sess'thra was always faster and teased Desdemonia that she would never deceive anyone with such pretty horns on display.

Desdemonia willed them back into her head. Her horns vanished with a thought. "I'm getting faster," Desdemonia said to the rat who followed at her feet.

Her sister said in time her memory would return, and when it did, everything would make sense. Sess'thra was wise in such things. Her sister said the nightmares would end, too, and that was a welcome thought.

She returned to the open window, and her thoughts wandered into the wind. Where would I be without my sister? The jungle-dwellers had left me for dead, and it was Sess'thra who found me and brought me to the tower. Then, Mother's magic nursed me back to health.

What was I doing in the jungle? She wondered. Unfortunately, she could not remember anything before that time. *If I could regain my memory, then everything would be perfect*, Desdemonia thought.

She felt something glide up her back, tracing the line of her spine. Her magic flared to life, and fast as a viper, she whipped around. Electricity danced at her fingertips, while black sigils of power fanned out behind her.

Sess'thra stood less than an arm's length away, dressed in olive-green hunting leathers. Her lavender eyes were dazzling and hypnotic. Desdemonia wished she had purple eyes too, instead of just dull brown.

Sess'thra titled her head to one side, causing her black hair to flow over her shoulder and down her front.

"Jumpy?" Sess'thra's mouth held its typical smirk.

"You startled me, that's all," Desdemonia said, lowering her guard, but her magic didn't want to be relinquished. It yearned to be released.

"You should be more aware of enemies hiding in the shadows, sister. Next time, instead of a gentle caress, it might be a dagger thrust into your back," Sess'thra purred out the words, but her eyes remained intense. "You must remember, we are at war."

Desdemonia became apprehensive. Her magic whispered warnings of caution in her mind, and not for the first time, a feeling of betrayal sat heavy in her gut. As usual, she dismissed it as anxiety caused by the loss of her memory. She smothered her instincts and let the awkward feeling pass.

"You should see your face," Sess'thra said, then laughed like a little girl filled with joy.

Desdemonia half-smiled back. "You shut your mouth."

Sess'thra's laugher only increased, and then Desdemonia was laughing just as hard. She gave Sess'thra a playful shove. "I hate you."

"Come, sister. Mother wishes to have a word with you," Sess'thra said. The two left the room together, elbows locked, and giggling like schoolgirls.

Desdemonia followed Sess'thra into a large hall where her breath clouded before her face. This room was much colder than most areas in the tower. Mother wanted it that way. She said the cold made one's senses sharp.

At the end of the chamber was a dais made of five great granite slabs, laid on their bellies to create steps. Upon the platform sat a throne, carved from a single block of black ice.

Seven spokes jutted out and up from the backside of the throne. A separate ball of clear ice was embedded midway to the end of each spoke. The balls had been carved to resemble a naked eye, staring out at all who addressed Mother. Desdemonia was convinced that the eyes moved on their own, blinked even, whenever she looked away.

Dark blue and purplish light radiated from a pulsing orb of energy hovering above the throne. The sphere seemed to breathe in and out as if it were alive. It reminded Desdemonia of a swollen and bruised storm cloud. She secretly wished to see a snowstorm in Mother's throne room one day. The idea of such a thing made her smile.

Mother sat at her leisure, conversing with Aosoth, the jol'goth Commander of her guard, who stood at the base of the dais. Her bone-white hair was braided and coiled, like entwined snakes atop her head. Seven thin spikes of jade stabbed into her hair, holding it in place. The ends of the green stone created a macabre headdress resembling the shafts of arrows.

Mother wore a flowing lace shirt with a ruffle of white fur clasped around her neck. The shirt extended past her waist but left her long legs uncovered. Her white skin absorbed the orb's color above her, making her look more like a water-born creature from the deep sea.

Behind the throne were smaller granite slabs, which had been arranged in a primitive pattern to resemble a colossal crystal. The design extended in a zig-zag fashion across the back wall.

It looks like a pretty snowflake, the voice of the forgotten twin said in her head. Desdemonia shook off its lingering whisper. She didn't think that was the image Mother wanted to convey. So, she held her tongue, which was no easy task.

The irregular surface of the walls glistened from the light of the orb. The stone walls flowed like waterfalls of ice. Desdemonia was fascinated by the sight of her ever-changing reflection as she walked past. The room's furnishings were sparse but for the throne.

Mother said this was a place to make important decisions, not idle chatter.

She broke from her conversation with Aosoth and gave Desdemonia a warm smile. The special magic within her swelled when she was close to Mother, and the opposite was true when they remained apart for too long. Desdemonia experienced horrible anxiety whenever Mother left the tower.

"Hello, my daughters," Sekka said.

"Mistress," Sess'thra said and knelt at the base of the dais.

Desdemonia followed her sister's lead and bowed her head to the floor. She heard Aosoth grunt in annoyance.

"Desdemonia, your sister tells me you have dreams," Sekka said. "Bad dreams."

"Yes, Mother. But it's nothing. They will pass."

"I will not have one of my favorite children suffer needlessly. Now, tell me of these dreams."

Desdemonia stood. "Very well. Two nights past, I saw the image of a magnificent, red devil. It flew alone in a grey sky. Maybe he symbolized something from my lost memory coming to the surface of my thoughts. I don't know. I cannot recall such an event in my life."

Sekka's eyes blazed for a moment, then relaxed. Her voice was carefree. "A red devil, you say?"

"Yes, with broad feathered wings of crimson and purple. His wings beat over a barren world of ice and snow. In the distance rose a tower, black as night against a white landscape."

"And then?" Sekka's voice was soft and coaxing.

"A great power blossomed within me. My magic was more alive than I had ever hoped it could be. It demanded to be released."

"And did you smite this red devil with your magic?"

"No, Mother. The dream changed abruptly. I felt an incredible sense of failure. My knees trembled, and exhaustion took me. I fell to the ground.

The palms of my hands drove into the shallow snow, scraping hard against the frozen rock beneath. I pulled back my arms to reveal masculine hands, worn from use but still young. My skin was torn and bloody. My new hands were numb, and I didn't feel any pain.

"I was kneeling in the snow, somehow wearing the orange robes of a monk. The voice of a woman called to me from the sky. Her voice was filled with sorrow. It sounded familiar as if it were my own but a younger version, I don't know. It's all very hazy now. Sometimes I wonder if I'm retelling a story I want as a memory instead of a dream."

Desdemonia searched her memory for more of the dream. She knew there was something else just under the surface of her thoughts. Then she realized that the woman's voice in her story was the same one that had been whispering in her mind of late.

"What happened next?" Sekka said. She leaned forward on the edge of her throne.

"I scanned the sky, searching for the woman with the sad voice. But I saw only the red devil, swooping beneath heavy storm clouds.

"Then, miraculously, I flew beside him like an invisible shadow, mirroring the graceful movements of his wings. He possessed extraordinary beauty, the beauty of an angel."

Desdemonia's voice trailed off. She didn't know why she had said angel. Both Mother and Sess'thra frowned. There was a clue here to regaining her memory. It was locked somewhere in these cascading images.

"You saw a vision of Zizphander," Sekka said with confidence.

"Zizphander," Desdemonia said. She didn't recognize the name, but more of the dream came back to her. "My face was close to Zizphander's, and I saw his eyes were sad. Tears spilled from the corners and were taken by the wind. Then, he looked directly at me. I was shocked that my presence was so easily revealed.

His sad expression vanished, and his eyes now held only anger with a face twisted with malice. His mouth curled into a queer smile. Then..."

"Yes? Then?" Sekka said.

"A sound rolled into my mind. It gathered speed and took the form of a name, spoken over and over. I felt as if a great mallet smashed all other thoughts from my mind.

"I shut my eyes until the pain lessened, and when I opened them, everything was different. Gone were the clouds, the snow, the ground, and the black tower. The entire world fell upon itself like broken glass, each piece shattering into smaller pieces until nothing remained but dust."

"What name did you hear that could cause so much turmoil and destruction?" Sekka's voice became suspicious.

The answer came fast to her lips. "Kasai."

The sound of the name shot through her like a jolt of electricity. It was the first time she had said the name aloud. Was he connected to her past? He didn't feel like an enemy. Could he be a lover, perhaps? No, that didn't feel right either.

Was Kasai the one who wore the orange robes in her dream? Desdemonia couldn't be sure. She couldn't see his face. So much of her past was shrouded in fog. She nervously twisted the onyx ring on her finger.

"Kasai," Sekka said the name slowly, letting it linger in the air. She glanced at Sess'thra. "It's an interesting name, is it not?"

"Yes, mistress. My sister sees visions of the future."

"There is no such future which ends this way," Sekka said. Her mood appeared to sour.

"Yes, mistress," Sess'thra said and bowed her head. "Of course, he is nothing. I meant no offense."

Desdemonia heard a wisp of insincerity in her sister's apology, and she noticed Sess'thra's tail twitched ever so slightly, like a mischievous cat about to knock a priceless vase to the floor. Sess'thra was up to something.

"Who's Kasai?" Desdemonia said. She immediately felt uncomfortable under Mother's watchful stare.

Sekka sat back on her throne. Her long fingers came up in a steeple, and she tapped them slowly together. "Kasai is the name of the Ever Hero. He is the embodiment of the demigod, Aetenos. Do you have any recollection of this person?"

"The Ever Hero," Desdemonia said. She felt a connection to that title as well. The shape of a face formed in her mind but then faded when she heard Mother's voice.

"Well? Answer me, child."

"Mother. I don't remember him." She didn't know why she lied.

"Perhaps you will in time. That boy is the key to ending this war. There's something he has that I want. If he gives it to me freely, I will make him a Prince of Chaos and a happy addition to our little family."

Desdemonia stepped forward. "Sess'thra and I can track him down. We will bring him before you in chains, or dead if need be."

"Oh no. That won't do. Freely, I said. The Ever Hero must come to me by his own will," Sekka said. "And come, he will, but with dreams of defeating me. It's such a shame. So much could be accomplished if he would join me instead. But this is not for you to worry about now. Tell me, how are your studies coming along?"

"My abilities grow," Desdemonia said, and she swelled with pride.

"Yes, I am sure they do. Continue to learn from your sister, and you will grow in power and stature. You have a powerful connection to raw Elemenati magic, as do I. Soon, I will have Chedipe tutor you in the deeper magic of Gathos."

"Thank you, Mother," Desdemonia said and bowed her head. "I wish only to be worthy of your favor."

The voice in Desdemonia's head did not approve. She did her best to silence it with distraction. "Mother, who is Zizphander?"

The corners of Sekka's mouth rose in a confident smile. "Zizphander desired to steal my kingdom on Gathos. The fool thought he could take it from me by force. So, naturally, I destroyed him, twice even. The second time I cast him into oblivion, something I should have done centuries earlier."

"Mother, I too wish to smite your enemies. When will I be allowed to fight at my sister's side? I grow tired of being cooped up like a prisoner in this tower."

"This tower is your home, not a prison. Though, I agree, it's a bit rough around the edges. I regret construction is slower than I would like. The war taxes our resources to extremes.

"But soon, the battles with the jungle-dwellers will end, and we will be victorious. Perhaps I will make you warden of this land, and this tower shall be yours."

"Thank you, Mother. I am forever grateful for your generosity. But when may I see more of the tower? So much is happening below, yet I am prevented from being part of it."

"This is only for your protection. I know, I know, I worry far too much."

Sekka appeared thoughtful for a moment. "You may explore the new additions to the ground level, but no deeper. I forbid you to step foot in the lower levels of the chasm. They are unfinished and hazardous. You have great value to me, Desdemonia. I don't want my darling daughter damaged in any way."

"Thank you, Mother," Desdemonia said, and thought she saw Aosoth smirk at Mother's remark, but the jol'goth turned his face before she could be sure.

"Very well. If there is nothing more, you may leave us," Sekka said.

"Stay out of trouble, Sess'thra," Aosoth said. His voice was stern and parental.

"Come now, Aosoth. You know me better than that," Sess'thra said and blew the hulking warrior a kiss.

Then Desdemonia and Sess'thra bowed to Mother, turned, and walked away. Desdemonia kept her thoughts to herself until they were out of earshot.

"Well, at least now I am out of my dusty attic," she said as they walked down the corridor. Then a moment later, she blurted out, "I wish I knew more of this mysterious Kasai and what he means to Mother. Maybe if I remembered what he looked like, then I could piece together more of the puzzle."

"I bet there's a way to find out," Sess'thra whispered in the soft voice of a conspirator. "There is much to see in the caves underground."

"No chance. You heard Mother. I am not allowed."

"Do you always do what you're told? Come on, I want to show you something," Sess'thra said. The end of her tail twitched with a snap. She grabbed Desdemonia's hand, pulling her down the hallway to a series of staircases that seemed to go on forever.

From there, Sess'thra led Desdemonia through yet another rough and unfinished corridor and then more stairs which eventually opened to a corridor with walls curved to a rounded ceiling as if a giant rodent had burrowed the tunnel with its claws.

"Where are you taking me? We cannot go any farther. Mother forbids it. We're already too far below ground."

"Do you want to see his face or not?"

"I do, but..."

"Then be quiet. We're already here." Sess'thra pulled a key from a pouch at her side. "I had one of the workers make this for me when they installed the door. I hope Mother hasn't laid any potent spells yet..."

Sess'thra unlocked the door with the key and pushed it open. "Success!" She pointed to a basin standing in the center of a room. "Do you know where you are?"

"This is Mother's scrying chamber," Desdemonia said.

"That it is. I've been keeping my eyes on the progress of its completion. I believe it's finally ready for use."

"Forget it. I cannot use my magic to see through time or distance."

"But you have interesting visions that speak of the past and reveal the future."

"They're just dreams."

Sess'thra was at the basin before Desdemonia could stop her. "No, stop! Sess'thra, wait! Don't you dare! Mother will know!"

Sess'thra swirled her index finger in the bowl's clear water. "I admit, I'm not the best suited for this. My talents lie elsewhere. But I'll try to get us started."

She gave Desdemonia a wink. Then she spoke strange words into the air.

"*Bor' nu siah.*" The water turned to slush. "You'll need to learn the language of Gathos if you want to operate this device."

Her finger drew an intricate pattern on its surface. With a mischievous grin, she deftly plucked a long strand of Desdemonia's hair and tossed it into the center of the design. It sunk beneath the slush as if it were a white-hot ember. Sess'thra spoke again, and the slush dissolved into a smooth, transparent surface.

"*Bla'in bludeudu xoltus du'* Kasai Ch'ou," Sess'thra said. The words crawled out of her mouth like bloated worms. The smooth surface on the basin turned green. Leaves and vines crowded into the viewing space. Then they receded, and an image of a young man came into focus. His scalp was smooth, but for a long braid that grew from the back of his head. Tattoos marked his visible skin. The rest of his body was covered in burnt orange robes.

"The robes of a monk," Desdemonia whispered in awe. Her heart beat faster. "Is that him? Is that Kasai?" She didn't need to ask the question, and the voice in her head confirmed as much.

"He's a handsome lad. Oh, I like him. If you don't want him, I'll take him," Sess'thra said and leaned in closer to get a better look.

Desdemonia pulled her sister away from the basin. "He's mine, Sess'thra. You will not touch him!" She was surprised at how possessive she sounded, and the voice in her head rejoiced.

74

KASAI

"Des! Des!" Kasai yelled frantically. The noise of the jungle swallowed up his shouts and added their own. She was gone. Vanished. The succubus had stolen into their private moment and ripped her away from him. Nothing of Desdemonia remained. Not a broach or a piece of clothing, nothing.

Kasai couldn't even smell her scent through the bold fragrances of the jungle. The sweet bouquet of the blooming flowers masked everything. Where was she now? Did Sess'thra take her back to the Abyss to be tortured? Was she a captive of Sekka's in Baroqia or imprisoned in Trosk?

"Desdemoniaaaaaaaaaaa!"

The Kibo Gensai crashed through the underbrush.

"What happened? We thought you were following us?" Orin said. His short swords hacked through vines barring his way. Pallo was next to emerge from the bush. The older warrior bounded through the foliage, followed by his brother at his heels. Gift and two of her warriors came last.

"Where's Desdemonia?" Pallo said.

Kasai dropped to his knees, and the jungle seemed to crowd in around him. It was suffocating. The trees loomed over him like angry giants, mocking him. The green hues of their leaves turned to black shadows.

He felt empty and alone. His fire xindu ignited as his anger swelled, and he pounded his fists into the soft soil. "Why does this always happen to me? Why is everything I love stolen from me?"

Pallo knelt next to Kasai. "Ever Hero, what happened? Where is she?"

"She's gone."

"Gone? Gone where?" He scanned the area looking for signs of the direction she had run.

"Sess'thra stole her."

"The succubus? Here?" Pallo said, and his eyes searched the trees for the demon. "Stolen? How?"

"We are good to be rid of her. The Wood Witch was evil," Orin said as he approached Kasai. He wore the face of a man about to say, I told you so. "She's where she belongs."

Kasai's fire xindu coursed through his body. He flashed to his feet with Ninziz-zida gripped tight in one hand. He thrust the end of it just under Orin's throat. Orange flame rippled in a spiral around the hand that held the sections together. "Not one more word, Orin, or I'll let Ninziz-zida have you. I'm sick and tired of hearing your voice."

Orin stood stone still. He stared down at the ancient weapon with fearful eyes.

"Nod once if you understand?" Kasai edged the compressed staff closer. Ninziz-zida rattled in his hand.

Orin nodded quickly.

Kasai's anger would not ebb. He heard Ninziz-zida whisper in his mind. *She was worthy. Let him burn.*

Pallo placed his weathered hand on Kasai's arm and slowly lowered Ninziz-zida away from Orin's throat. His voice was soft and caring. "He's not the enemy."

Kasai looked at Pallo with lost eyes. The fire within him subsided as fast as it had risen.

"Des wasn't the enemy, either. She needed my help. The ring was evil, not her."

Kasai's shoulders slumped. He felt as if all the happiness within had been ripped away, leaving him empty and hollow. "It doesn't matter anymore. I can't do it alone."

"Ever Hero, I too, was fond of Desdemonia. Sadly, we must assume she's lost to the enemy. But the fight goes on."

"It's a hopeless task. It's too big for me, even with your help."

"It's not the size of the task ahead of us that matters or whether we think we can accomplish it or not. What matters is that we must carry on. There is no other option. The Chaos Gate must be destroyed."

"I have no chance. Sekka is too strong," Kasai said. "Let someone else fight her."

"You are the Ever Hero. You will find a way!" Pallo said. "You must!"

"I'm not a hero! I'm just a stupid monk!" Kasai shouted back. "I don't know what I am doing!"

Pallo's voice softened. "I don't see a stupid monk in front of me. I see a boy who quickly grew into a man. And that man tended to his Master's needs and led him across a hostile wilderness to seek a remedy for his sickness.

"And when the King's Army fell to disarray on the battlefields of the Last Garrison, and soldiers ran for their lives from merciless demons, slaughtering at will, it was that same man who walked calmly into the heaviest fighting to face their warlord in single combat and won!

"It was you who agreed to journey into the Abyss on a quest to save a demigod. And you would have willingly gone alone when others would have turned the other way, and rightly so. For whom could even conceive of what horrors awaited you in the Deep Dark?"

"You went too," Kasai said.

"But only because I followed your courage. These are your deeds. You must own them. There is always a chance for victory, even for a stupid monk, if you keep fighting for what is right."

"What does any of that matter now? I tried to kill her once and she toyed with me."

Kasai walked away. He wiped the sweat from his brow. "I never wanted any of this. I said it wasn't for me. I said I wasn't ready for such responsibility. I said no from the start."

"Who is ever ready for such a burden?" Pallo said, trailing behind him.

Kasai stopped. His head hung low. "My skills are feeble when compared to what Sekka can do. She's too strong."

Gift approached Kasai. She turned over his palms to show him the outward spirals designating the Mark of Aetenos. "You bear the mark of greatness, and while you still draw breath, nothing is hopeless."

Kasai's body slumped. "I'm just a simple monk. I'm far from being one with the Boundless. I never completed my training."

"Your deeds proceed you. You lived them but refuse to believe they are true. You are the Ever Hero of Aetenos, whether you want to be or not. You must put to sleep Kasai the simple monk and let your greater self-awaken."

Kasai heard Gift's words, but they held no meaning for him. He just didn't care what happened anymore. "I can't do it without her. I can't do it alone."

NOT ALONE! Ninziz-zida came to life in his hand. *Why have you so quickly forgotten ME? Trust in me as I have put my trust in you. I am the weapon, and you are my wielder.*

Together we will avenge all who have fallen to the treachery of evil. You are stronger than you know. Together we are stronger still.

She coiled around Kasai's xindu energy like a mother snake protecting her eggs. She lit his fire xindu first and then touched upon his dormant air, water, and earth energies—each one pulsed like a heartbeat in his spirit.

The warmth of her touch melted away his reluctance to see the truth. It was an odd sensation not to feel afraid. Doubt and fear had been his constant companions since as far back as he could remember. They followed him like shadows, affecting his decisions and holding him back.

The emptiness caused by their absence left him off-balance and lightheaded, as if he stepped down but felt no ground beneath his feet, only air. A wave of exhaustion swept over his body, and Kasai drifted into a trance.

He felt like he was floating into a great open sky, one without walls or barriers. If he had wings, he would soar like an angel. But at the same time, a part of him was drowning in a cold, unforgiving ocean. The blackness of its depth paralyzed him, and he felt insignificant and invisible. He could no longer sense where he existed between the air and water.

His mind expanded into a new space as the boundaries of his body faded from recognition. He felt uncertain and lost without a Master to guide him. There was no one to tell him if what he was feeling was real or that it was safe. He pulled his mind back into the confines of his body. The space closed. Jungle trees and the worried faces of his companions came back into focus.

Kasai gritted his teeth and let his anger rise again. It gave him purpose. *To the Abyss with feeling afraid. If I must face Sekka, I will do so with honor. I will avenge all those who had been taken from me, or I'll die trying. Most likely, the latter will be my fate. And that will be fine.*

"I will find her and bring her back," Kasai said with conviction.

"Your courage is admirable. But I fear there is more to this abduction than meets the eye," Gift said. "Why take only the girl when you are so valuable?"

Orin opened his mouth to respond, but Kasai's eyes shot daggers at him that would penetrate steel. The Kibo Gensai warrior lowered his head and walked away, muttering to himself.

"She's waiting for me," Kasai said.

"Who, Desdemonia?" Pallo said. "Where?"

Kasai shook his head, no. "The succubus relayed a message before she vanished. My life in exchange for the lives of everyone else. I can end the war if I surrender myself to Sekka."

"The honey-coated words of the devil cannot be trusted," Pallo said.

"But if there is a chance to end the war, I should at least consider it as an option."

The anger he held in his heart dissipated as he remembered Desdemonia's face just before she was taken from him. She reached for him with her frantic eyes. *"Save me,"* they said. But he reacted to slowly and Sess'thra got away. He had failed Desdemonia, and now she was gone.

"What? Absolutely not. Surrender is not an option!" Pallo said.

"Ever Hero," Gift said. Her voice was firm but also filled with care. "We must kill the cutthroat in our hut before we can route out the band of thieves in their den. It's Sekka's warlord who must be defeated first."

Yessss...listen to the warrior-mage. She is wise and strong. Take the fight to the enemy you can see. Avenge her, my son. Avenge them all!

"We will need more than twenty warriors," Kasai said. "Brave as you are."

"We are more. This is but a scouting party. We are one hundred strong in total."

Enough to fight in the confines of the jungle and slip away quickly, but not enough to stand against a horde of demons in open combat, Kasai thought. He turned to Run-Run. "How many of the Kibo Gensai are there?"

Run-Run began counting on his fingers. One, two, three...

"Just give him a number," Pallo said and sighed with irritation. He wiped the sweat from his forehead and face. The heat was unbearable.

Run-Run raised his eyebrows, and his mouth formed in the shape of an "O." He thought for a moment, then pounded a fisted hand three times into the palm of his hand.

"Three thousand?" Pallo said.

Run-Run nodded. He put his finger to his eye and pointed at his older brother. He then circled the air above his head.

"Maybe more?" Pallo asked.

Run-Run clasped his hands together as if in prayer, then shucked his shoulders.

"Or maybe less," Pallo said. He nodded his understanding, disappointing as it was.

"Three thousand will not be enough. Sekka commands legions," Kasai said.

"Our numbers will grow. There is the Miko Nuna to consider," Pallo said. "Run-Run, are you sure you can find her?"

Run-Run nodded enthusiastically.

Kasai wore a hopeful expression for the others, though he knew their numbers were akin to a misguided stone thinking it could hold back the raging waters of a flood. He appreciated Pallo's faith in him, but they had both seen the horrors a demon horde was capable of inflicting on normal men. Fear stole the courage of battle-hardened warriors when they discovered their nightmares were real.

Kasai knew what he must do, though he did not hope to trust the succubus's promise. Eventually, he would need to confront Sekka and defeat her if he could.

The shadow of doubt crept back into his thoughts. His resolve clouded, and he could not see a way past her to victory.

To climb the tallest mountain begins with the smallest step, Master Choejor's words echoed in his mind. He wasn't truly alone. Master Choejor was with him, as was Ninziz-zida. Kasai felt a drop of hope splash on the dry, desert ground of his uncertainty.

"Run-Run, you will find the Miko. Tell her of our need. Bring the faithful to the Fields of the Last Garrison. The rest of us will seek out Sekka's Chaos Warlord and slay him," Kasai said. "That is our goal."

"Run-Run will not reach the border alive," Gift said with certainty. "Without a blessing, you would not be allowed to pass."

She approached Run-Run. "I will mark you as a friend of the jungle." She muttered strange words Kasai didn't understand, then kissed him on both cheeks. The shape of vermillion-colored lips lingered on his rough skin and then faded.

Run-Run bowed to Gift. He glanced at his brother with a smug expression and raised his eyebrows twice.

"Yes, Run-Run, I think she likes you too," Pallo said.

"But you will not go alone. Ertu and Aika shall travel with you. Both are swift of feet and will speak on my behalf to the other war chiefs. You will need to be granted permission to travel through their territories," Gift said.

She turned to her warriors. "Tell those you meet to save hope. The Ever Hero walks once more with the people of Sunne. Let the message spread like the monsoon wind."

Gift waved her hand, and the three departed into the jungle. Barely a leaf moved in their wake.

"Come, my village is not far," Gift said and motioned for her warriors to follow.

The village was buzzing with activity, but it was of a peaceful nature. The flow of movement from its inhabitants was like the easy sway of a summertime breeze. Kasai could scarcely believe the war had come to these people based on their calm and peaceful mannerisms.

Just like Ordu, until the demons climbed over the walls.

Merchants called out their ware of fruits and meats in the market stalls. Buyers haggled over the weight of a chicken or the ripeness of bananas. A carpenter's hammer pounded on a wooden peg, securing a new piece of wood to a broken fence, while another laid down new thatch to the roof of a nearby hut.

A herd of goats darted across the dirt street, bleating out their annoyance at yapping dogs nipped at their heels. Cows tied to posts driven into the ground chewed grass at a slow and methodical churn, indifferent to the warriors' arrival.

The village buildings were modest in size but made with expert craftsmanship with intricate patterns woven into the doors. Each hut was raised on short stilts to prevent the summertime rains from flooding the homes. The designs expressed an aspect of the jungle. Here was the image of a tree, there a clump of fern fronds, another door held the picture of a mountain range.

Kasai heard the panicked cackle of scurrying chickens. A flock of black-feathered and red-breasted fowl scattered in different directions from the side of the street. Two groups of children raced through the crowds on either side of the road, eager to be the first to see the strangers. Conversations came to a halt, and villagers stared in curious bewilderment as Kasai, Pallo, and Orin walked through the village at Gift's side.

"Des once described to me the village she grew up in. It sounded a lot like this one," Kasai said.

Gift nodded her understanding and then pointed to an empty hut. "You will take rest there. Food and drink have already been placed inside. We shall meet in the Chieftain's Lodge as the sun sets across the jungle. I will send for you."

"Who lives there now?" Kasai said.

"The war has taken them, and their spirits now sleep through the long night, awaiting the day of their reawakening. Their families would be honored to have the Ever Hero and his companions stay there as their guests."

"It is we who are honored. Thank you, Gift," Kasai said, then bowed. Pallo and Orin did likewise.

"Rest now. There is much to discuss and plan."

Kasai, Pallo, and Orin entered the hut. It was spacious and well kept. A picture of water, a bowl of fruit, and dried meats had been placed on a table to the right. Kasai suddenly realized how hungry he was. Pallo poured a cup of water for each, and they dug into the food.

Kasai tried the dried meat but found it too salty for his palate. He chose a melon-shaped fruit instead. The peel came off with ease. The fruity pulp inside was sweet and delicious, and juice ran from the sides of his mouth as he bit deeply into its center. It had a unique taste, like the kiss he shared with Desdemonia.

Oddly, the fruit juice made him thirsty, and he drank two full cups of water and then sat back on one of four cots in the room—one for each of them, plus an extra. *One cot for Des*, Kasai thought.

He laid back to rest, but although his body was exhausted, his mind wouldn't let him sleep. *Where is she now? I'm going to find her and save her.*

The Chieftain's lodge was much bigger than the other dwellings in the village, and the dimly lit interior reminded Kasai of the Meditation Hall of Ordu. He wondered if he would ever see his home again and if he should. *It's ruins now, thanks to me.*

Kasai pushed the bleak memory from his thoughts. The destruction of Ordu and the deaths of his Brothers were in the past, and he couldn't wallow in guilt, or he would be of no help to the people whose lives he could still protect. *Still, Aetenos could have chosen a better-prepared champion.*

Seated at the entrance of the lodge were families who provided food and trade for the village. Farmers, tanners, blacksmiths, carpenters, and healers all came to hear the village elder's words and took part in the decisions of the tribe.

Kasai stood behind Gift at the entrance to the lodge, with Pallo and Orin flanking his sides. The villagers parted to create a path down the lodge's center, which led to a raised platform against the back wall. Upon the platform sat a small woman with a shawl of brightly colored feathers covering her hunched back. There were four empty sitting mats set to her right.

The interior became darker still when the door was shut, and the walls were lost in shadow. Kasai saw the dark shapes of warriors who sat on either side of the central aisle. Gift had said earlier that military matters would be discussed at this meeting, and their voices would be heard first.

Kasai remembered a scene from his old life. "Still the last one to the hall," he said softly.

"Follow me," Gift said, and she marched purposefully to the platform.

Kasai had thought Gift was more handsome than pretty when they first met. She had hard features, and her expression was always stern. He could see she was fierce like Desdemonia, but there was no hop in her step, and she didn't seem like the dancing and playful gypsy type.

When Gift reached the platform, she pointed to the empty mats. "You will sit here," she said, though she remained standing.

The room held a low din of murmurs until Gift raised her hands and silenced the crowd. Kasai saw she commanded the same respect of the villagers as she did from her warriors.

"We of the Sunne are a peace-loving race. Our people do not look for war or conquest against the northern kingdoms. Instead, we strive for harmony with all things. Sadly, an enemy that wishes only to kill and destroy has invaded our lands. They steal our people and leave our villages in ruin.

"Our magic is strong, but we can no longer push this enemy back. No individual village is safe from the Chaos Warlord."

Gift turned to Kasai. "But there is hope. Nayche, the Mother Goddess, who gives birth to all things, has guided one who can turn away this foe. This monk is the Ever Hero of our age and has come to fight by our side."

The room came alive with an equal volume of cheers and denials. Kasai could feel the villagers' keen eyes on him like he was a target for their arrows and spears.

Many villagers looked away in disappointment as if Gift had dangled the hope of salvation before them, only to present them with a fool of a monk who had not seen his twentieth summer. Many waved their hands dismissively in the air as if this could not be.

"Proof! What proof is there that this boy is the avatar of Aetenos?"

The warrior who spoke now stood. Kasai recognized him from Gift's war party and remembered his name was Tavian.

Gift took a torch from the platform and encouraged Kasai to stand. "Show them," she said and held the torch in front of him.

Kasai stood and raised both hands to the crowd, exposing his palms in the torch-light for all to see. He was doubtful the villagers could discern the Marks of Aetenos from this distance, but this had been what Gift suggested he do first.

"His body is covered with tattoos. Why should his hands be any different?" Tavian said.

"Tavian refuses to believe, as is his right," Gift shouted so every villager could hear.

Then, she muttered to Kasai under her breath. "He has the ear of many warriors in the tribe. We must convince him first for the rest to follow."

"Any of us could show the same by crushing berries of the azulla bush," Tavian joked and sat back down on his mat. A few of the warriors next to him nodded their agreement.

Another warrior stood, emboldened by Tavian's words. "He is a foreigner. He does not belong here."

Another stood. "How do we know the monk is not a spy for the enemy?"

"We all know of Aetenos the Protector, and no one may doubt the righteousness of his deeds. Our people have shared friendship and trust with his Master Monks of the Four Orders of Light. During times of need, the Ever Heroes of Aetenos have come to battle at our side. Now is no different."

Kasai wondered what else he could do to prove his connection to the demigod. Was it a miracle they needed? *Good luck with that,* he thought. His link to the Boundless seemed like a frail thing filled with gaps and blind spots, especially now that Desdemonia was gone. He just felt numb and disconnected from everything.

He looked at Gift with uncertainty, and she pointed at Ninziz-zida. He understood and took the three-sectioned staff from his sash, then raised it to the crowd.

"Who among you would dare to wield the Fire Serpent of legend without being chosen?" Gift raised her voice.

A hush filtered through the crowd. Ordinary villager and warrior alike shook their head, no—all except for one. Tavian stood once more.

"Why should we believe this is the holy weapon of Aetenos? It is but three black sticks connected by a cord through its center. A child's toy." This time laugher followed the warrior's remarks.

Ninziz-zida vibrated in Kasai's hands, and he felt her anger rise. A raspy hiss coiled around his thoughts.

I AM NINZIZ-ZIDA! I am the eternal Fire Serpent! Let the first non-believer step forward and feel my flame.

"Now is not the time. We need friends, not more enemies," Kasai whispered under his breath. His eyes scanned the room. More of the warriors took up the laughter, and Ninziz-zida blazed to life.

I will not be mocked!

The room blossomed with orange light, and her angry hiss was unmistakable for all to hear within the lodge. Never had her voice manifested itself in such a way. The crowd pulled back in superstitious awe. Kasai was in as much shock as they were, but he stood firm.

He held the end sections of Ninziz-zida out wide. Her flames leaped from the end of one segment to the other. Each orange tongue twisted and swirled in the air like a skillful acrobat. The laughter ceased.

"Behold, Ninziz-zida!" Gift said. "Who but the Divine Fist or one of his Ever Heroes may wield the Fire Serpent with such ease?"

Kasai saw a sea of wide eyes and open mouths staring back at him. Some villagers bowed their heads in respect. Tavian remained standing, shaking his head, no.

"I too, can conjure pretty fire." With a word, orange flames spread across his hands. He waved his arms in a playful gesture to accentuate the movement of the fire.

Then, with a shrug, he spread his arms to encompass the lodge. "Even the less gifted of us can do the same. We learn this trick in our youth."

Kasai worried he would need to do something more drastic to convince the warriors of who he was and what he held. The villagers looked uncertain, and Ninziz-zida grew angrier in his hands. She wanted a fight. He sensed the restlessness of his companions.

Kasai locked eyes with Orin, who was already scowling. "Not a word from you."

"But?" Orin said. He held his hands out in mock innocence. "What did I do?" He looked to Pallo for support and received none.

"Tavian, please step forward." The elder covered in the shawl of feathers had spoken. She was old, older than a person should be and still live. Her body was small, almost childlike.

She had unkempt hair that had turned the color of grey smoke long ago but still held its length. Her face was puckered with fat wrinkles, but her eyes held the wisdom from experience and not embellished stories.

"Gladly, Great Mother," Tavian said as he made his way past the seated villagers. His face was filled with the confidence of a man who knew he was right. When Tavian reached the back of the lodge, he bowed in deference to the elder.

"You wish to refute the legitimacy of this young man's claim?" the Great Mother said.

"I do. I have looked into the monk's eyes and saw only a lost boy, who stared back at me in fear. He is not the Ever Hero of Aetenos."

Kasai could see Tavian was proud and aggressive, like Daku. He was the kind of man who would press his point until the other person backed down or simply lost interest in the argument. Either way, Tavian would consider himself the winner and prove he was right.

Tavian turned to Kasai. "Do you claim the power of the Ever Hero?"

Kasai flinched at answering such a straightforward question. "Well, I," he stammered.

"Yes or no?" Tavian said quickly.

Kasai could not escape the question. *I'm no hero. I'm just a stupid monk.* Then he heard Desdemonia's voice in his head as clear as if she stood right next to him.

Why do you doubt yourself so much? His heart leaped but then sank. She wasn't there. It was just his imagination.

Kasai looked out to the people gathered in the lodge, and he saw desperation. Now was the time for courage, if not for himself, then for the innocent lives that looked to him for help.

"Yes or no? Tavian insisted.

"I do."

"Take the weapon from the monk," the Great Mother said.

Tavian smirked at Kasai and held out his hand, waiting.

"Great Mother, with due respect, this is not wise," Kasai said. He felt Ninziz-zida stir eagerly in his hands. "There must be another way."

Tavian approached him with a smug expression. He was taller than Kasai and older. His hair was braided in three long coils that fell down his back. "Are you afraid I will break your little toy? Place the weapon in my hand, or must I take it from you?"

Ninziz-zida responded with an angry hiss.

Be kind. He's not evil, only misguided, Kasai thought. He could only hope Ninziz-zida felt the same way.

I will show him the error of his ways.

Kasai placed Ninziz-zida in Tavian's hands. Her fire was immediately extinguished.

Tavian turned to the audience of villagers with Ninziz-zida held above his head in one hand. "You see? Just a trick. The monk is false."

Murmurs grew louder from the crowd, and Tavian swiveled his head to Kasai. "You are not the Ever hero. You are a fraud."

"Do not release the staff," the Great Mother said from behind Tavian. "Hold it."

"An easy task, Great Mother. May I keep it? It would make an excellent gift for my—"

Tavian's dark skin became pale in the hut's torchlight, and the arm which held Ninziz-zida aloft began to shake as if burdened by a heavy bucket of water for too long.

"Hold it," the Great Mother said.

Tavian's eyes grew wide in wonder. They darted back and forth as if he bore witness to a horror which only his eyes could see. He gasped and quickly raised his other hand to support the staff. His cocksure attitude faded. "Great Mother...I cannot..."

"Hold it."

His legs trembled. One faltered, and then the other, dropping him to his knees. Tavian would not, or could not, lower Ninziz-zida to the platform.

"I cannot...bear...to see...anymore."

His eyes were wide with fright, and his body twisted unnaturally towards Kasai. He bowed so low that his chin brushed against the floor while keeping Ninziz-zida raised high in the air.

"Please. Take her. I am unworthy to hold one such as she."

Kasai took Ninziz-zida from Tavian's shaking hands with ease. Then orange flames ignited along Ninziz-zida's three sections. The fire swirled around Kasai's forearm and brought a welcome sense of warmth and completeness to him.

He did not suffer much.

Tavian lay flat on the floor and moaned softly.

"Tavian, what is your opinion of the young monk now?" the Great Mother said.

"I am humbled. The boy is true." He gazed up at Kasai with searching eyes. "How?"

Kasai lowered his hand in friendship to the warrior. "It's a long story for another time, my friend."

Tavian accepted Kasai's hand and rose. All hubris had been burned away from the warrior. His eyes held the same look of fanaticism that Kasai saw in the eyes of his Kibo Gensai companions.

"I was shown more than a man should see in this lifetime or the next. I was mistaken. You are not lost, nor do you carry the eyes of a coward. I would be honored to fight by your side if you would have me."

Kasai smiled warmly. "We are brothers against a common foe, and your help is most appreciated."

Tavian smiled back. He gave a short nod, then turned to the crowd.

"Let it be known. Tavian Vivi of the Frona was wrong. The monk is true! The Ever Hero of Aetenos walks again with the people of Sunne."

Gift approached. "The monks of Ordu are said to be military geniuses, masters of strategy and combat. We will hear from Master Kasai of the ways of war. He will instruct us on the correct strategy to defeat the Chaos Warlord."

"Me?" Kasai's stomach lurched. He had led monks in training exercises at Ordu and the odd expedition outside the monastery walls, but he knew nothing of warfare. Since leaving the monastery, his decisions seemed to just make things worse.

"Please, no. I didn't even reach the level Capu to the junior monks at Ordu, let alone the rank of Master. I've never led warriors into battle. You speak of the Master Monks who have spent their long lives studying the battles of history."

Gift frowned. The look of disappointment she wore on her face was nothing compared to the eyes that bore into Kasai's uncertainty. "Your true spirit has awakened. You have been named Ever Hero in the presence of elder, warrior, and villager of the Frona Tribe. You are no longer Kasai 'the stupid, simple monk.' You *are* Master Kasai, the Ever Hero of Aetenos."

She was a hard woman and would not relent. "Now, how do we defeat the enemy, Master Kasai?"

Kasai understood. This was the role the monks of the Four Pillars of Light accepted when there was great need throughout the Three Kingdoms. With or without a strong connection to the Boundless, he still needed to help, and lead them if he could.

"Sadly, I'm ignorant of the strengths and weaknesses of your magic. How have you fought in the past?" he said, trying to discover if there was something he could exploit on their behalf against the demons.

"Nayche is mother to all who live under the great canopy of the jungle. She gives freely to her children," Gift said. 'It is through her gifts that we fight the enemy."

"Nayche?" Kasai said. The name wasn't familiar. He wished he had studied more of the Sunnese histories at Ordu. "Does she rule Sunne? Will I meet her? Is she far?"

"Nayche is not a queen. She is everywhere and everything. She is the flowing river and stagnant swamp. She is the monsoon wind that bends the trees and the light breeze that spins the leaves. She is the rock that forms hill and mountain or the water that polishes the smallest stone.

"Nayche is every plant and every animal that lives beneath her great canopy of green and blue. She is all of this and more. She is life itself. It's her gift that we share."

Tavian leaned closer to Kasai. "When we are young children, we begin to feel a connection to her gifts. Fire magic is the easiest to conjure. It's fueled by emotion. Air magic and water magic follow as we mature. Only a few of us reach mastery of earth magic, for it's the most difficult to control. One must have a calm heart and tranquil mind to move the stones of the earth."

"Nayche asks in return that we live in harmony with all things in her great kingdom. All things are equal in her eyes," Gift said.

"You are describing xindu energy. Do you know of the Boundless?" Kasai asked, hopefully.

"Nayche is known by many names. Perhaps they are the same."

"Perhaps. I confess I have yet to understand the depth of the Boundless. I know it's the combination of all things, but still, it remains nothing. It's an elusive thing," Kasai said.

"I would like to hear more of your Boundless," Gift said. "There is much we can share together."

"At a later time. Now we must focus on eliminating Sekka's warlord. Your village looks untouched by the enemy. You must be doing something right," Kasai said.

He purposefully shifted the conversation away from the Boundless. He knew so little of something that now had become so important. Unfortunately, without the help of a true Master Monk, Kasai doubted he would ever fully understand the mysteries of the Boundless.

"This is but one of the villages of the Frona Tribe. Other locations have felt the blade of the enemy and perished. When we first encountered the creatures of cold, they were unorganized. There was no finesse to their attacks. Wave after wave of brute force came at us, but we melted into the jungle and escaped with few to no losses.

"We used our fire magic to burn them. We swallowed them in the earth and raise the rivers to deter their attacks. Our magic was too strong for them to overcome. But the coming of the Chaos Warlord changed that," she said solemnly.

"The death magic of the enemy kills the forest and saps our strength. Their numbers have increased a ten thousand-fold with each attack. Entire villages have been lost," Tavian added.

Kasai listened intently to the description of so much magic. Life magic. Death magic. Earth and fire magic. It stacked up like so many bad memories of his early childhood. *Think! There must have been something I learned at Ordu that can help these people.*

He searched his memories. Nothing. Kasai absentmindedly gazed at the designs woven into the walls of the lodge. In the half light, he saw the tall trees of the jungle and behind them the tops of great mountains. He remembered gazing at snow-covered mountain tops as he swept steps at dusk at the monastery.

His mind continued to wander, sweeping so many steps, even those that ended in stone walls. Master Choejor said these were the most important steps to keep clean. *No wonder I was always late for dinner.*

Kasai pondered the misleading steps for a moment longer. There were so many hidden, overlapping layers of defenses built into the Monastery at Ordu. Only a person with a keen knowledge of the grounds' layout could navigate through without getting themselves lost or trapped.

"Have you thought of overlapping your attacks? Use the strength of your warriors and magic in layers," Kasai said.

"How do you mean?" Gift asked.

"Your warriors can move unseen through the jungle. Let them be seen and make the enemy give chase and lead them into magical traps designed to confuse, maim and kill," Orin said.

"We have done this. The enemy cuts off our retreat with fell magic. A ring of decay surrounds us. The green mist kills the jungle and steals the strength of Nayche's gift. Once trapped, winged horrors fly overhead and drop balls of fire from the sky."

"Then the jungle must change," Kasai said aloud, though it was the voice of Master Choejor that he heard in his head.

Gift titled her head to the side. Looks of bewilderment stared back at Kasai from the villagers and warriors in the lodge.

"Seek to place the enemy on deadly ground, while you remain on living ground, before attacking. If no living ground exists, you must change the ground or die," Kasai said.

His mind latched onto an idea. He took a few steps, thinking aloud while he walked.

"The power of the jungle is your greatest strength, and perhaps, your greatest weakness. The enemy knows of your reliance on the living jungle for shelter, stealth, and magical power. It's as much a part of you as the air you breathe. That's why he kills it.

"By removing the trees, brush, and vines during a battle, he breaks your limbs and steals your power. He uses the jungle against you."

Many of the Sunnese nodded in agreement. "But the land cannot be changed. The jungle is eternal," Gift said. "As is our bond to it."

"I suspect the warbands of the Frona Tribe have been fighting in isolated groups, and not as a greater force with other tribes."

"We are a people united by the jungle, not a singular ruler. Each tribe holds and protects its own territory. This is our way," the Great Mother said, and the villagers agreed.

"Yes, I understand, but this we must change."

The villagers gasped, and Kasai heard moans of denial from the warriors on the side of the lodge.

"We will engage the enemy in the smallest of conflicts. Find their weaknesses and exploit them," Kasai said, hoping to elicit support.

"They travel in a rolling horde and are too big to engage," Tavian said.

"Then we will hit the stragglers or use the terrain against them when they come to uneven ground. The rivers and marshes will be our allies. When the timing is right, we attack in force for the briefest of moments. We will be like the sudden downpour of an afternoon rainstorm. Then we retreat."

"The enemy will counter," Gift said.

"Precisely. Let the enemy believe they have us and pray they give chase. As their numbers spread, the horde will thin. Then more rain will fall elsewhere, diverting the enemy's attention."

"I don't understand. You think the rain will stop the enemy?" Tavian said. Kasai realized his example was lost in translation.

"He means the first group acts to bait the trap," Orin said, shaking his head. "They will know it's a ruse. I would."

"Orin, you are not helping," Pallo said.

"I'd rather not help now and save our skin than blindly follow a flawed plan."

"It's ok, Pallo," Kasai said, still putting together the pieces of a strategy. He moved to the dirt floor of the lodge. He used the end of one of Ninniz-zida's segments to draw a large circle.

"This is the horde." Then he drew a smaller circle outside the first. "This is the first war band. We attack here. Once the enemy has committed themselves to battle, a second war band will strike with strength from hiding here.

"And then a third, here, and a fourth, here. Our numbers must be hidden until the moment of attack. This will keep the enemy off-balance. In this way, we determine the ground of life and death."

"If it were only that simple," Pallo said. "We must consider the coordination of the attacks. Communication between the warbands will be critical, and I don't see how we can relay orders without flags or horns to signal the other groups."

"See? Listen to Pallo," Orin said.

"We will set up shorter relays and use the sounds of the jungle to communicate commands," Tavian interjected. He shrugged his shoulders. "This is not difficult."

"Excellent, Tavian. That's what we'll do," Kasai said.

"What you describe will require thousands of warriors. The Frona Tribe's numbers no longer carry such strength," Gift said.

"That is why we will need the warriors from neighboring tribes."

Gift simply shook her head, no. "You have a courageous heart, but you cannot change a thousand generations of tradition. This cannot be done."

"You're right. Kasai, the stupid monk, cannot change an entire kingdom's will, but maybe the Ever Hero can convince enough tribes to make a difference. Our goal is to defeat the Chaos Warlord, and to do this, we'll need their help."

"The victories will be too small. The enemy's numbers are limitless. How will this make a difference? We will lose too much," Gift said, shaking her head. "They will destroy everything that remains of the Frona Tribe."

"A village can be rebuilt. It's the people we must protect," Pallo said.

Kasai noticed the Great Mother remained silent. Their eyes met, and she nodded for him to continue.

"Sekka's warlord cannot be everywhere at once. We will strike at the sub-commanders that lead their raiding parties. Without a leader, the lone demon is left to his own chaotic behavior. He will attack an ally if it's easier to kill."

"The Ever Hero is right. The demon's lust for killing is only held at bay by their leader's strength. We can use this to our advantage," Pallo said.

"As I have said, we have tried and failed to kill the Chaos Warlord. He is surrounded by thousands and thousands of demons. Or, if we by chance find him separated from his troops, he escapes into the shadows when we draw close."

"Then we must change the sun," Kasai said with confidence. A plan formed in his head, and for once, he believed it could work.

The sound of a commotion from the entrance turned the heads of the villagers.

"I must be allowed to speak with the Great Mother!" A young boy pushed through the people standing at the entrance. He was small and skinny, and his hair was a tangled mess of sticks and leaves. Dirt rolled down his body in streams of sweat. Seated villagers rose to give him a path to the platform.

"The enemy comes!" The boy placed his hands on his knees. His chest heaved as he tried to catch his breath.

"Corbetjak, what have you seen?" the Great Mother said. She pushed her way past Kasai and Gift.

"The Parpurish Tribe, beyond Vine Ridge, has been taken by the horde. The devil's death magic melts the trees and chokes the village." The boy spoke between deep breaths. "The survivors are marched north. Jacjon follows them. I returned to warn the village."

"They go to the Fields of the Last Garrison in Baroqia," Kasai said. "And then to the Chaos Gate in Trosk."

"How do you know?" Gift said.

"Sekka is there, waiting for me. She lures me closer with offers of peace while yanking a tight leash around my throat. She will end this suffering if I willingly surrender myself to her. The Three Kingdoms are saved by one sacrifice."

"She lies," Gift said.

"You don't understand. I am responsible for the Chaos Gate."

"Ever Hero, we must intercept them before they leave the jungle," Pallo said. "These people are just as important as our own in Baroqia."

"Their numbers would help our cause," Orin added.

Kasai nodded his agreement. "Still, we will need more. We must unite the other tribes," Kasai said and looked to Gift. "We must try."

"They will not come. One does not merely ask a war chief to relinquish their authority of their tribe to another. Now more than ever, the tribes are looking to their own safety," Gift said.

"Then we must show them there's strength through unity," Kasai said. He hoped enough rain would fall. One hundred warriors from one tribe were but a drizzle. It would not be enough, but it was a start.

A stench of decay seeped into the lodge, and more villagers rose with uncertainty. They covered their noses and mouths, but the stench still made their faces scrunch with disgust. Kasai knew the smell well, and his fire xindu spiked. A cry of warning came from outside the lodge.

"The enemy has found us!"

75

RAGUEL

Raguel called for order, again. He stood with his back to the edge of an open rotunda high atop one of his private towers in Asher. Eleven arched windows circled the chamber, meeting at two shimmering golden doors. Rays of sunshine bathed the room in warm light.

Spotless rose-gold columns gleamed as the light bounced from shiny floor tiles and lit their cylindrical forms. Raguel's perfect city was in upheaval, as were other cities on each of the seven levels of Heaven. The unrest throughout the Seven Heavens was growing, and it now affected the daily machinations and administrative duties of his orderly paradise, which was unacceptable. *Damn that Aetenos! Must I end him myself to be finally rid of his influence?*

Raguel had expected unhappiness from some of the inhabitants of the lower levels. There were always some dissenters who were never satisfied, no matter what form of perfection you placed before their eyes. But he had not expected anything like this.

The Chancellor Pinnacle raised his hands in the air, attempting to quell the rising tension among the True-born he had gathered to this small audience chamber. The angels before him each held the highest position of authority in the Administration and were responsible for governing one of the six lower Heavenly levels.

He had personally groomed and appointed each of them to their lofty roles. But instead of seeing heads nodding in affirmation to his orders, he saw faces filled with bitterness and resentment. And now they were pushing back against his will.

Raguel knew their angst was fear-based, specifically the fear of change. And in many ways, that fear was good. The mentality of a frightened herd was easier to control than the individual freethinker. And what was Heaven but the perfect state of control?

But his angels were turning on him.

Were my actions too rash? he wondered. *Perhaps the public banishment of Artiya'il was a mistake. All of this would have been avoided if the True-born's punishment was sentenced behind closed doors. Artiya'il would have become an afterthought instead of a martyr.*

Raguel frowned at the thought. He was the first and highest of the Immortal Mother's divine creations. *I do not make mistakes. We are exactly where I meant for us to be. A bit of unrest is healthy if the overall perfection is maintained.* It was a paradox he toyed with from time-to-time. The abstract thought of a duality existing simultaneously to benefit the greater ideal kept his mind sharp.

"I will have silence!" Raguel's voice filled the chamber. His rainbow-colored wings fanned out behind his back. "You will not behave like ill-mannered mortals."

The rioters filling the streets of Asher was a testament that even the tempers of celestials could flare with enough provocation. Cadres of dissenters formed in packs like wild dogs and proclaimed the unjust treatment of Artiya'il. They moved through the pristine streets, defacing priceless architecture and destroying idyllic parks to symbolize their discontent. They demanded his safe return to Tanalum, or the destruction would continue.

These shortsighted rabble-rousers disgusted Raguel. Riots indeed! How outlandish and uncouth. How dare they undermine his authority. And now, this business with Aetenos and his Ever Hero gave them a second banner to rally behind.

He knew they watched the journey of the Ever Hero with keen interest. Each day more celestials became sympathetic to the fate of Kasai, the soulless monk. It would only be a matter of time before he was pushed too far and was forced to put down the rabid dogs. *They deserve no less treatment if they continue to act like animals.*

The six angels finally became silent.

"Thank you," Raguel said. "Now—" He was distracted by the sight of the golden doors swinging open in the front of the room. A furry animal scampered in on all fours, wearing a red vest trimmed with silver frills. His knuckles scraped the floor as they bore the forward weight of his small body.

Raguel was at first incredulous, then his anger flared as the diminutive creature made his way to the front of the group. The True-born angels just stared with mild curiosity at the arrival of the monkey, Zhao Houzi.

"Please forgive my tardiness. I was only just informed of this important meeting," Zhao Houzi said. He raised himself on his hind legs to appear taller.

"That is because you were not invited," Raguel said.

"Oh, I am rarely invited to grand appointments these days. But today, I come at the request of Lady Illyria. She wishes the animal spirits of Elysian be represented at your most important meeting and any other spirits who need representing, I suppose. She was not clear in this regard. Surely you would not shun her wishes."

Raguel did nothing to hide his disappointment. Illyria was up to her typical tricks. She would spite him while remaining innocent of any wrongdoing. He knew that to act against the daughter of the Immortal Mother would only cause him more problems.

"If you must be here, then stand to the side out of the way," Raguel said, then quickly added, "And be quiet."

Raguel waited until Zhao Houzi had settled before continuing. "As I was saying, the Heavenly Host will only intervene if the Ever Hero of Aetenos fulfills the demands of the Challenge of Righteousness. Kasai Ch'ou must defeat Sekka. That is his penance."

"But in the meantime, you leave an active Chaos Gate open, my lord Raguel. As we speak, the archdevil of Gathos steals the souls of the mortals destined for the Seven Heavens. She will upset the balance of power between the Heavenly Realm and the Abyss."

Raguel recognized the voice of the angel, Patriciana, who governed from Canaan, the caretakers of the Seven Heavens. Her heart was kind, and Raguel thought she was too soft when exercising his laws of punishment.

"Bah. It's but for a moment in time. We have soul reserves enough to weather this storm. The loss of soul energy will be inconsequential to our power standing against the devils of the Abyss."

"But what of the innocent souls you condemn to an eternity of suffering by this brass action?" she said.

"They're only mortals. The Seven Heavens have other, more pressing concerns to deal with at this time."

"But, like all of us here, you hope the young master succeeds in eliminating Sekka and thus closing the Chaos Gate forever," Zhao Houzi said. "Right?"

"Yes, this is my hope." The lie came quickly to Raguel's lips.

"And if he fails? Will the Lords of Heaven simply shrug their shoulders and conduct their daily duties as if nothing had happened?" the angel Marduke said. He was the warden of Eden, the second level of Heaven. There was an echo of guilt in his tone.

Raguel's wings twitched ever so slightly, causing a crimson feather to float to the floor.

"The Challenge of Righteousness is set. You are forbidden to offer divine interference. The human child must face this test alone, and if he fails, Aetenos and his line of avatars will finally end."

"And the end of one moment allows for the beginning of another," Sonnalle said.

Raguel gave his equerry a thankful nod. "Sonnalle is right. We are in a most auspicious time. I am glad we are all here together, my most trusted brothers and sisters. I wish to tell you of my plans.

"Long have the devils and demons stolen the soul energy that could and should be used for divine purposes. Think of how much more we could accomplish with the soul energy from the entirety of the Mortal Realm, and not just a portion?

"It's time for a change. I will make a Heavenly Pyramid that will encompass all three realms under one rule. But to do this, a new order must grow from the foundation we have perfected over millennia.

"And we will go beyond the Three Realms and spread the word of the Immortal Mother to the outer worlds. The Seven Heavens shall be the pinnacle of law and order. Tanalum will be a beacon of light in the cosmos."

Raguel saw the angels' stunned expressions and glanced at his equerry. This was the moment they had rehearsed.

"Do not fear for the souls of the Mortal Realm, for I do not intend to forsake them. The innocent and worthy shall be welcomed into Heaven's warm embrace," Raguel said.

"Lord Raguel is right. The infernal born are vermin and should be exterminated as such! They have proven to be undeserving of the Immortal Mother's divine light since the beginning of all things. They have been given countless opportunities to change, but they will not.

"There is much to gain by controlling the soul energy from the Mortal Realm. We should look to influence other, less fortunate realms. It's our privilege and responsibility to bring them the blessing of the Immortal Mother's will," Sonnalle said.

"Are you speaking of conquest, Lord Raguel?" Zhao Houzi said.

"Conquest? No, no, no. We will not bring the ways of the Immortal Mother with blade and whip. We intend only to influence those in need of direction, as is our way."

"You mean like following the ways of Aetenos and Artiya'il?" Monkey asked.

I should have disposed of that monkey long ago, thought Raguel.

"Monkey, you misunderstand. There are variations," Raguel said.

"I have thought the same as Lord Raguel for some time. The Heavenly Path must be altered," Lord Samal interjected. The warrior angel from Arcadia brought his fist to his chest. "The Heavenly Host is ready to enforce the will of the Chancellor Pinnacle."

Raguel smiled with relief. He suspected the warrior caste would be easiest to convert. Warriors needed battle. It was in their blood. But what of the others? He waited patiently. The angels pondered in silence.

"It makes sense. A pyramid is the most stable structure," Patriciana said.

Good, good, Raguel thought.

"Only if you use the three-dimensional thought of a mortal. Erode the base of any physical structure, and the top will fall," Zhao Houzi interjected. "A metaphysical sphere is true stability, for at no point can it fall in space or time. It spins uniformly with the flow of the cosmos."

"Then, Heaven shall be the outer embrace of the sphere. Let the devils and their kin dwell in the core. The Immortal Mother favors the True-borns over all others. The rest were meant to serve or were mistakes, created irresponsibly from the remains of perfection," Sonnalle said.

"But before you look to 'spread the light of the Immortal Mother's will to unknown realms,' as you say, shouldn't we secure what is already known? We are pledged to protect the Mortal Realm if the balance with the Abyss is tipped out of proportion. It is written! I have proof!"

Monkey reached into a pocket in his vest and took out a golden parchment, which he held above his head.

"Whatever proof you believe you have is irrelevant. I will not close the Chaos Gate or unleash the Heavenly Host into the Mortal Realm until the condition of the Challenge of Righteousness has been met. Sekka must die at the hands of the Ever Hero. There is nothing more to discuss. The Heavenly Law cannot be broken or altered. The mortals must atone for their sins."

"I am only a simple monkey, but even I can see that the Chaos Gate must be destroyed."

Raguel saw the heads of the angels nodding in agreement. He clenched his jaw in frustration.

"Must I remind you, Monkey, that the creation of a Chaos Gate is no slight misdemeanor to be swept under the rug and forgotten for good behavior? The mortals must learn there is a price to dishonoring the divinity within their souls."

"No one here disagrees with you on that fact, lord," Patriciana said. "But the monkey is right. The Chaos Gate must be closed. The Great Three have long awaited the opportunity to skirt the Amaranthine Barrier and invade the Mortal Realm."

"The actions of one mortal soul cannot possibly bear the weight of all others," Marduke added.

"We must tread carefully, Lord Raguel. The Seven Heavens are at a tipping point. Turmoil and unrest are increasing," Vayani, the angel mystic from Paradise, said with a deep and ominous voice. "The movements of the Ever Hero are watched by more than the Far Seers of Paradise. If he fails—"

"Then the world of mortals will be consumed," Zhao Houzi said. "Lord Raguel, this is an illogical gamble you are pursuing so adamantly. One must ask the question, why?"

"The Heavenly Host must be released! The devils will claim the Mortal Realm while we do nothing. Implore the Immortal Mother to lower the Amaranthine Barrier," Samal said. "We will fight!"

"The Far Seers have seen worse than legions of demons infesting the Mortal Realm. The Ancients have awakened from their sleep. They come!" Vayani said.

"They cannot cross the Amaranthine Barrier," Patriciana said. There was worry in her words. "Can they?"

"The Chaos Gate has created a tear in the barrier. It is unknown what might slip through," Vayani said.

Curse that little monkey. I'm losing them.

"The Chaos Gate will remain open until the Ever Hero completes his task. I will not repeat myself again."

"We must fight!" Samal came forward. His face was filled with determination.

"The Heavenly Host cannot be summoned without proper sanction from the Immortal Mother," Zhao Houzi said.

"If the Immortal Mother lowers the Amaranthine Barrier to allow the Heavenly Host to pass through, then will it not also provide a big enough opening in the Abyss? As the Great Balance remains in all things, we would inadvertently provide legions of devils and demons access to the mortals. This cannot be allowed to happen," Patriciana said. "Why will you not simply close the Gate, Lord Raguel?"

"If the Ever Hero fails, and the Chaos Gate becomes fixed, what then? The Supreme Devils will win the Mortal Realm," Marduke said.

Raguel sighed. His plans were quickly unraveling. "Brothers. Sisters. Do you think I move forward with blind eyes? I have assurances that the legions of the Great Three will remain where they belong. We have nothing to fear from them."

"You sound overly confident," Zhao Houzi said.

"I do not need to explain myself to any of you, least of all you, Monkey. You must trust me as you have done since the beginning of all things."

"To what end? The secrets you keep only serve to undermine the trust you demand," Patriciana said.

"Is it not plain to see? Lord Raguel intends to invade the Abyss, though my small monkey brain cannot deduce why? For such an act is forbidden. Does our Chancellor Pinnacle now wish to usurp the will of the Immortal Mother?"

The room went deathly still. Raguel watched as the faces of the True-borns turned to expressions of shock.

"I only say aloud what you have all been wondering. My guess is Lord Raguel has made a deal with one or more of the Supreme Devils. If I was a betting monkey, I would put my coin on Xerthotha. Am I right?"

Raguel's ire rose as he watched the little monkey hop from one foot to the next. But now was not the time for anger, and he quickly mastered his emotion.

"Monkey, you have a mind quick as a hummingbird, which flutters briskly from flower to flower. But alas, unlike the hummingbird, you do not stop long enough to savor the nectar. And thus, the secrets of the flower remain hidden to you," Raguel said.

Raguel scanned the True-borns' faces and saw they looked back at him with suspicious eyes. He had no choice but to reveal his true motives, or he would lose their support.

"Reluctantly, I am forced to say out of a courtesy what should be told later. It is my will to issue in a new hierarchy of Heavenly supremacy. The Seven Heavens will shepherd in the next epoch of existence. Positions of influence will shift.

"Long have we been forced to watch the destruction of lower realms. The Abyss and Mortal Realm destroy their own through war, deception, and cruelty. It's a never-ending cycle of chaos. I have seen enough to know it's time for peace.

"Xerthotha and I have an agreement of mutual service. I will help the Chaos Devil defeat Azrollorza before she can pass through the Chaos Gate. Her demise will lessen the soul strength of the Abyss by a third. This will be enough to shift influence in his favor."

"Removal of one of the Great Three would upset the balance of power in the Abyss," Marduke said. "The fall out of this event, and the eventual wars that follow will quickly spill into the Mortal Realm, perhaps even reach the Heavenly Gates of Elysian."

"Marduke, your worry is unfounded, for I intend to remove the remaining Supreme Devils from existence. The Abyss will serve the Seven Heavens as a penal world."

"And the Mortal Realm, lord? What of the humans?" Zhao Houzi said.

"Their souls will be cultivated according to the Heavenly Path. They will contribute their soul energy to our great cause. Those who will not abide by the Heavenly Laws will be sent elsewhere until their soul energy matures into usable stock."

"Lord Chancellor Pinnacle, with all due respect to you and your position, I see now that the Lady Illyria's fears are true. Your views are no longer aligned with the will of the Immortal Mother. You speak boldly with words laced with heresy," Zhao Houzi said.

Raguel nodded to Sonnalle, who took up position behind the monkey.

"Monkey, you have no right to say such things. Lord Raguel's position cannot be questioned. He is and shall always be the highest and best of us. So says the Immortal Mother," Sonnalle said.

Zhao Houzi craned his neck to see the equerry. "When did she say this, Lord Sonnalle? Was it whispered in Lord Raguel's ear as a babe when all things were yet to be? Who else was there when this grand proclamation was announced? Truly, I would like to know. That would be a most excellent conversation."

Raguel glared at Zhao Houzi but was helpless to punish the animal spirit since the lesser creature held the protection of Illyria, at least today in this room. *But when the dissenters are collected and removed from my paradise, Monkey will be the first to go.*

A broad smile came to Raguel's lips, and his gaze swept the entire room. "Brothers and sisters, we must not bicker and quibble like children over things which have no relevance to our order. Until the Immortal Mother says otherwise, you shall adhere to my will. I am the Chancellor Pinnacle."

Nothing could touch him. He could eliminate the entire first level of Heaven, and who would stand against him? Over time things would settle, and the angels would see things his way, or they'd be replaced.

"Lord Raguel, the Chaos Gate must be closed. Send the Heavenly Host to stop Sekka. Nothing more can be accomplished by waiting," Patriciana said. The heads of many angels nodded their agreement. "The Great Balance must remain."

Raguel scowled. That phrase irked him more than any other string of words uttered by celestial lips in his long years of existence. He would no longer let it shackle his ambition.

"The Great Balance *will* remain," Raguel said with exasperation. His patience had ended. "The Heavenly Host will remain ready but will not act until I have sanctioned its use. I will see the completion of the Challenge of Righteousness. The mortal must prove his innocence. That is my final decision."

"Lord Raguel is right. We are not to interfere needlessly. The Mortal Realm must remain neutral ground. If the Supreme Devils invade, we must be prepared to intervene. But until that time, the stipulations of the Challenge of Righteousness must be observed," the angel Sonja said.

She came from Erewhon, the fourth level of Heaven, where mages harnessed the soul energy from the inhabitants of the Seven Heavens.

"What of the Great Three? The Supreme Devils must also know that a Chaos Gate lives between two realms. Reports from the Far Seers tell us that Sekka has aligned with Azrollorza.

"And if one Chaos Gate can be made, so can another. If Azrollorza births a portal on her homeworld, nothing will stop her from rushing to invade the Mortal Realm. Such an influx of mortal soul energy will upset the balance of the Abyss, and the Seven Heavens will be vulnerable," Patriciana said.

The woman will not relent, Raguel thought. He would need to have Sonnalle find a replacement for her soon.

"I have commanded Xerthotha to intervene. He has been instructed to prevent Azrollorza and her legions from entering the Mortal Realm. At this moment, he moves his armies to block her advancement," Raguel said.

"This is folly. The Chaos Devil cannot be commanded to do anything that is not in his interest," Marduke countered.

"In this, you are correct. The rivalry between Xerthotha and Azrollorza has reached its apex. They will engage in a war of such colossal magnitude that it will shake the very foundations of the Seven Layers of the Abyss and shatter the orbiting Circles. When they have exhausted their resources, the Heavenly Host will sweep them both away in one quick stroke."

"The presence of Morrdilliax will prevent such a war between the two titans. It's his role to be the fulcrum between the other two opposing powers."

"Not this time. I have promised Morrdilliax rulership of the Abyss for his cooperation and neutrality during this conflict."

Zhao Houzi jumped in excitement from one foot to the next. "How do you propose to send the Heavenly Host to the Abyss? Passing into the Mortal Realm is one thing. Gaining access to the Abyss is something completely different. The Immortal Mother would never allow—"

"Why, through the Chaos Gate, of course."

Zhao Houzi's monkey eyes grew wide in surprise. "You made a promise to release the souls of Aetenos and his Ever Hero when the Challenge of Righteousness was completed. This can only be accomplished with the destruction of the portal."

"The child Ever Hero must win through legions of demons to destroy an archdevil. What hope was there that this would be achieved by one so young and inexperienced?"

"Aetenos's boy is finding his strength," Patriciana said.

"He would be dead but for the interference of Ninziz-zida," Sonnalle said. "But this time, he will surely fail. The strength of the ancient fire elemental is lost in such inexperienced hands."

"And yet, the venerable Ninziz-zida stays by the boy's side. Azrollorza and Xerthotha have chosen their champions, yet you do nothing to support Heaven's champion," Zhao Houzi said.

"Such an idea as the Ever Hero is a blasphemous thing. Aetenos had no right to create what should be mine to decide." Raguel's brows knit together. He had thought this would be easier. "As I have said, my decision is final."

Raguel watched Zhao Houzi ease away from the angels and point at him with a tiny, wrinkled finger. "Lord Raguel, your logic has become unsound. You stray too far from the path of the Great Balance. I have no choice but to report your words of heresy to the Lady Illyria."

Raguel had heard enough. "Sonnalle, seize the traitor. His invitation to Tanalum has been revoked."

Zhao Houzi dashed to the front of the room quicker than a thought, but Sonnalle reached the doors faster and slammed them shut before the monkey spirit could escape. Zhao Houzi spun and darted for a window. He leaped into the air with Sonnalle's open hand just behind him, but this time, the equerry was too slow, and the monkey spirit vanished over the ledge.

"Do not fear my friends. Monkey will be found and dealt with accordingly," Raguel said. "His soul energy has ever been ill-suited to mesh with the purity of Heaven. Like all dissenters, as their boldness grows, they act as if it's their right to be in paradise. They are mistaken," Raguel said. Then continued. "Eventually, the Chaos Gate will be closed, and the Seven Heavens will prosper like no other time in our existence. Trust me, I have taken care of everything."

"The Chancellor Pinnacle has spoken," Sonnalle said. "Go in peace."

The equerry returned to the golden doors and opened them. The True-borns slowly left the chamber, huddled in their private thoughts.

"Shall I hunt for the monkey?" Sonnalle said when the last True-born had left.

"He's probably already at Lady Illyria's heels by now. No, let the creature be. I don't want another martyr on my hands. That will be all, Sonnalle."

Sonnalle closed the doors behind him. Raguel took a moment to reflect on his current path. He had hoped for more support from those who owed him favors, but just the opposite had occurred. No matter. Rule of the Seven Heavens was his and his alone. Its armies would move according to his plan. Aetenos and his Ever Hero were insignificant when compared to the expansion of the Heavenly Realm.

He could close the Chaos Gate at any time, but for now, it was a tantalizing carrot to encourage an unlikely ally. Xerthotha would unwittingly play his part in Heaven's triumph over the Abyss. He congratulated himself on such a brilliant strategy.

The infernal portal presented an opportunity not seen since the creation of the Amaranthine Barrier. No longer would his Heaven be isolated in the cosmos. Now was the time to expand. Now was the time to build a new empire. He would worry about the Ancients later.

He stared out the window that had granted Zhao Houzi's escape and saw the speck of a dark rain cloud forming in the distance of his perfect sky.

76

KASAI

"Let me through!" A village sentry pushed his way into the lodge. He was panting as he stumbled through the last inner row of standing villagers. His back was covered in greenish blisters. "Great Mother, the jungle is dying!" *The enemy is here.* Ninziz-zida's words echoed in Kasai's mind.

"Pallo, Orin, with me, now!" Kasai said and leaped off the small platform. He raced to the entrance of the lodge but was waylaid by the frantic villagers. Ninziz-zida rattled with excitement in his hand.

Shouts of alarm rang through the hut. Confusion and panic overcame the villagers. They jostled past one another attempting to be first to escape the confines of the lodge. Children clutched their mothers' breasts in fear. Gone was the tranquility Kasai had marveled at when he first arrived at the village.

Gift's warriors jumped to their feet, and Kasai saw flashes of orange, blue, and gold igniting in their hands. The villagers jammed through the lodge entrance like mad beasts, fleeing through an opening of a narrow pen.

It was no use. Kasai could not get through the mass of bodies. Then the screams of villagers outside the lodge halted those within.

"Warriors with me! Everyone else stays inside the lodge!" Kasai shouted and continued to squeeze his way through panic-stricken bodies. He hoped he could get outside in time to make a difference.

"Move aside for the Ever Hero!" Gift yelled from the back of the room. Miraculously, an opening formed, enough for Kasai, Pallo, and Orin to squeeze through.

The sun had set, leaving only an after-glow of its warmth in the air. Torches had been lit around the village to provide light against the coming darkness. Shadows darted between huts, and strange shapes raced across the dirt streets. Villagers unlucky enough to be caught unaware were struck down, or worse, dragged into the jungle. Their muffled pleas for help eventually silenced.

"How did they get so close without warning?" Orin said. He drew his two short swords in a fluid motion as he ran.

Gift finally emerged from the lodge with a handful of warriors at her side. "Impossible! This cannot be!"

"Fell magic has kept the demons from their eyes," Pallo said while running stride for stride with Kasai.

Gift's warriors raced to the right to intercept a rolling mass of burly arms, segmented appendages, and malformed heads with snapping jaws. It was difficult to determine if different creatures were tumbling together or it was one colossal monstrosity.

The undulating heap of demon body parts slammed into the feeble wall of defense set up by the unorganized warriors. No amount of fiery hands or spear points could keep the monster at bay. Its hideous form swelled high above the line of defenders and crashed down over their heads.

Kasai heard their screams as he leaped into the fray. Ninziz-zida whirled with incredible speed, attacking repeatedly and immolating demons with each strike. His hands were her hands, and soon he had pushed the mass of demons back.

The group separated into individual creatures but were no less repulsive. Pallo and Orin were at his side. Their blessed short swords sliced through demon flesh as if it were thick cream.

Kasai saw a flash of light to his left. Tavian's hands spewed orange flame just behind him. A demon howled in pain as the fire blazed across his body. Somehow the creature had gotten inside Kasai's blind spot.

Tavian's eyes flickered quickly at Kasai before he unleashed more fire on a flying, bat-like demon. The smaller creature pirouetted to the ground, leaving a trail of smoke as its rancid flesh burned.

Kasai saw bright green and yellow sigils fan out behind the Sunnese warriors as they unleashed their magic into the demon horde. Balls of fire burst around him, but the demons were everywhere, overwhelming lone warriors who were mauled by three and four monsters at once.

Walls of fire sprang from the ground, allowing the Frona warriors to regroup. Ninziz-zida's spirit slid within Kasai like a snake, gliding with fluid grace through calm waters. The line separating weapon and wielder blurred and eventually vanished.

Kasai leaped into battle though he felt like a spectator, floating high above the conflict. Fiery shapes swirled around him, like long, blue tongues, whipping in the wind. Ninziz-zida's essence burst from the confines of the mundane staff as her blue flames leaped into the air, coalescing into the shape of something serpentine and ferocious.

Kasai saw himself within the center of a blue inferno. The fires that swirled around him took form, recoiling back like a wicked, blue viper, preparing to strike.

Be free, Ninziz-zida, Kasai thought, though he may have said the words aloud as well. It was difficult to tell in the chaos of battle.

Ninziz-zida hissed with triumph, and her flames struck with blinding speed. A dozen demons snapped to ash. Then his mind was back in his body as he spun and kicked a demon, pushing it backward.

Ninziz-zida's segments struck demons at will. His fists followed her strikes, smashing through the chest of one demon, and whipping back around to shatter the skull of another. Together, they were a furious tempest of destruction.

No longer will they take from us. We will avenge the fallen. Ninziz-zida fed his emotions with her fire xindu, and he grew angrier with each step.

"Together! For Desdemonia!" Kasai yelled out.

The enemy fell back. They were nothing against the might of the Ever Hero and the wrath of the Fire Serpent in his hands. Kasai snapped her burning segments into the fleeing monsters. Ninziz-zida's shrieks of glee vibrated through the air as each demon combusted to a powdery cloud of ash. The cinders of their demise covered his body as he ran. It was glorious.

Kasai lost sight of Pallo and Orin. Nor was he aware of Tavian or any of the other Frona warriors. The righteous bliss of Ninziz-zida's fire xindu flowed through him. Wielder and weapon were of a singular purpose. Together they would eradicate evil from this village. They would cleanse the land of this blight. They would not stop until the last of them was destroyed.

The heat of Ninziz-zida's fire was intense, and though he was not burned, Kasai's eyes still blurred with watery tears. He squeezed them shut and saw a flash vision of Desdemonia in his mind. She was skipping along a path in a forest, humming a happy tune. She turned her head back to him, and her dark hair flowed around her face. Then, she winked playfully at him.

Kasai's heart leaped as Desdemonia jumped on a stump and curtsied to him. *"Aren't you going to ask me to dance?"*

The entire scene had taken place in the span of three running steps. Kasai opened his eyes, and Desdemonia was gone. The loss he felt was like a sharp kick to the gut.

"I'm going to save you," Kasai said. Ninziz-zida's flame grew brighter and bolder. She coiled around him, protectively while seeking more targets to strike.

Together.

Kasai ran toward another pack of demons surrounding a group of defenseless villagers. Ninziz-zida attacked with a furious flurry of strikes, and the demons sizzled and popped like bugs trapped in burning logs.

The ashes of their remains were caught in the vortex of Ninziz-zida's swirling movements. It became difficult for Kasai to see clearly, but it didn't matter. Ninziz-zida was his eyes now.

I shall guide you. We are one.

Kasai knew the ancient force within the three-sectioned staff spoke true. Demons fled from him but failed to outrun Ninziz-zida's whipping strikes, which now flew well beyond the staff's physical constraints. Kasai felt invincible with the Fire Serpent in his hands. Sekka would pay for all the harm she had caused. He was going to win!

The blast hit him hard in the chest, twisting his body awkwardly in midair. Kasai bounced once off the ground once before sliding to a stop. He wiped the dirty sweat sticking to his face and spat out the bloody grit of a broken tooth from his mouth.

Kasai rose too fast and was rewarded with a sharp spasm of pain in his right side. A bright light flashed before his eyes, and he collapsed down to one knee. Ribs moved on their own as he tried to breathe.

He wiped his face on the sleeve of his robe, then tightened his grip on Ninziz-zida. *What hit me?* His robes were covered in the stench of old muck and decay. The clash of battle crashed over him in a deafening wave of confusion. Intangible voices of Sunnese warriors shouted war cries. The death howls from mortal and monster alike filled his ears.

He squinted, half-blind, scanning the battleground, and searching for the enemy. Dark ash drifted in the wind, obscuring his sight in the torchlight. Then the shape of a wiry woman, wearing dark hides, slowly materialized through the ash and sauntered toward him. A wicked smile played on her lips.

Small childlike creatures with brownish-purple, moldy skin fanned out behind her. Their hunched backs forced them to walk awkwardly on all four limbs. They gibbered to one another in gleeful gurgles with mouths dripping with yellow drool.

The strange woman waved her hand and sent her minions into the village. The grotesque children scurried off in a joyous frenzy to frolic in their new playground. Then the woman looked him over with contempt.

One of her hands glowed with energy the color of swamp-green muck, while the other held a whip with three, long lashes, dangling from the handle. Each lash ended in a cruel-looking barb. She swung the handle in a playful, figure-eight motion, and shards of ice tumble to the ground with each swish.

Kasai rose slowly, favoring his right side. Then, he felt the reassuring warmth of the Fire Serpent pulse through his body.

There stands a Warlord of Vyzyn. Destroy her and hurt the enemy as they have hurt you, Ninziz-zida whispered in his mind.

"You are a strange one amongst so many dark skins. But no matter. Sekka's Orthod Pits will feed on your soul just the same," the woman said.

The hides she wore was a patchwork of reddish and blue-grey material. It was covered in thinly-lined runes of mystical power, and each rune glowed a different shade of violet.

Her black eyes were nestled in narrow slits that sloped unnaturally high on her face. An orange sigil spun slowly above her head, while tendrils of dark energy snaked and snapped in the air behind her. Kasai saw blood-red symbols had been tattooed on her hairless head.

Around her neck was a pendant and at its center was a smooth, onyx orb. The black stone reminded Kasai of the ring Sekka had given to Desdemonia. The ring she was forced to accept to save his life. His anger rose. Ninziz-zida coiled around his fire xindu and gave him strength. The pain in his ribs dulled.

Kasai maintained his focus on the warlord as she prepared a spell. He didn't care. His eyes roamed over her body, marking the spots where Ninziz-zida's strikes would do the greatest damage.

Yesssss, Ninziz-zida hissed in his mind. *We see with the same eyes. Let your fire xindu blaze.*

"Ever Hero!" A voice shouted his name to his left. It was Tavian. He raced past Kasai with an orange fire glowing in his hands, lighting his way to the warlord. Midstep, he leaped into the air and used his body's momentum to spin full circle. His extended arm followed, whipping a small ball of fire straight at the woman.

The warlord slapped it away without much thought and continued to speak twisted words of fell magic. Kasai shouted a warning, but Tavian refused to heed it. The warrior ran at her like a mad bull.

The three cables of her whip lashed out at him from an impossible distance. Tavian's momentum carried him into the lashes and somehow, he managed to dodge the barbs. The fire burned bright on his hands once more, and his face was set with determination.

"Not this time, witch!"

Kasai saw the warlord's mouth curl in a wicked sneer. She snapped her whip's cables back and deftly hooked the weapon to her side. A crackle of energy filled the area, and Kasai felt as if a thousand insects crawled over his skin.

The warlord inhaled a deep breath, sucking the ash-filled air into her lungs. Then, quick as lightning, she was gone. A swirling ball of black ash remained where she once stood. Kasai stood open-mouthed in disbelief while Tavian continued to run toward where she last stood.

A cloud of dark air burst opened in front of Tavian, and the warlord materialized within his guard. Her legs wrapped around his waist and locked behind his back, while her free hands closed firmly under his chin. They ran together as lovers with her lips firmly pressed to his. He tried in vain to push her off, but his burning hands proved ineffective against her grip.

When she finally tore her mouth away, a murky, greenish-fog spilled from his mouth. Tavian's eyes were wide with shock and pain as his face bubbled and blistered. His screams fell silent as thick slabs of flesh sloughed off his bright, white skull.

The warlord leaped to the side as Tavian's momentum carried him a few more steps before his burning body stumbled to the ground.

Kasai watched her spring to her feet like a cat. A sly smile lit her face. "So, this is the elusive Ever Hero." The tone of her words mocked him. "I shall finally receive the honor I deserve. It will be Tazizu, not Aeshmara or that sniveling runt, Dai-Ko-Zior, who delivers you to the Frost Queen."

Kasai didn't know who Tazizu or the others were, nor did he care. He was going to end her. Ninziz-zida's segments rattled in his hands; her blue flames leaped from the staff and swirled around him in a cyclone of rage.

Tazizu took the whip from her side. She jogged the handle, making the lashes curl like snakes, then shot them toward him. Kasai was already a blur of motion, and the Fire Serpent struck with astonishing speed. Each barb was shattered in turn by Ninziz-zida's fiery segments.

Tazizu jumped back a few paces, astonished her strike had failed. She tossed the broken whip to the ground and snarled at him. Ninziz-zida shrieked in victory as her fiery cyclone grew around Kasai. It twisted one way and then darted another.

Tazizu paused. She seemed mesmerized by the motion of Ninziz-zida's fiery rage. Kasai loathed the sight of her and everything she represented. He stepped forward, and her black eyes locked onto his.

Then she mouthed the words of a spell and vanished. Kasai spun in place, anticipating her attack and trying to protect every side at once.

"Where is she?" Kasai shouted.

Close. Ninziz-zida responded in his thoughts.

Kasai took three steps to the right, and then two more straight ahead. Ninziz-zida howled a warning in his mind. He spun around to his backside, and Tazizu's wicked face was inches from his own. Her foul breath made him gag.

He felt the icy grip of her boney fingers tighten around his throat. Tazizu whispered cursed words into his ears, and his strength faded.

"Release the staff," she said. Her pupil-less eyes bore into him. Kasai meant to resist and tried to hold Ninziz-zida tighter, but his muscles went soft.

His fire xindu cooled, and he no longer knew why he wanted to fight her. Defeat was perfectly acceptable. He dropped Ninziz-zida to the ground.

Nooooooooo! Ninziz-zida's objection was a distant echo in his mind.

"You see? That wasn't so difficult," Tazizu said and kicked Ninziz-zida away. The Fire Serpent's blue fire sputtered out as it spun in the dirt.

Tazizu took one hand away from Kasai's throat and grabbed his wrist, twisting it to examine his palm. Excitement shone on her face. "The mark is true. You shall be a worthy prize for the Frost Queen."

Kasai's vision dimmed in the evening darkness. Black soot-covered everything and his mouth was dry and tasted of ash. It seemed blacker than a moonless night or a raven's dark wing. He was lightheaded and needed peace from so much suffering.

Visions of kinder memories drifted before his eyes. He saw thick hair flowing in the wind. A sparkle of amber shown in the darkness. It lit a mischievous, playful smile. His stomach leaped in somersaults of anticipation for what would come next.

"Desdemonia," he whispered. Secret words spoke softly in his mind—*a hidden name in exchange for a forbidden kiss.*

Heartache and sadness flooded through him, drowning him in sorrow. The weight of his newfound powers mocked him, constricting his chest with each breath. *You are unworthy*, they said.

Desdemonia's name echoed in his mind, haunting him. It was his fault, all of it; Ordu Master Choejor, the Chaos Gate, and now Desdemonia. He had failed them all.

"Not much fight in you, is there?" Tazizu said with no small amount of disappointment. "Why are you such a prize to the Frost Queen, I wonder? Perhaps you are not the one she seeks."

Kasai heard Desdemonia's voice echo in his mind. *You cannot quit. Let go of your pain. Let go of your sorrow and guilt. Fight! Fight for me!*

Kasai's fire xindu sparked back to life, and he boiled away the sadness and the guilt. He would fight! But anger was a hollow feeling, and he did not have an angry heart, not like Daku.

The voice of Master Choejor came to him. *Anger is not the answer when you seek salvation.* Kasai listened and released his choler. Oddly, his fire xindu grew brighter.

A new sensation entered his perception. He barely noticed it at first. Like the petals of a morning flower, it opened slowly, warmed by the first rays of sunlight after a cold night. Ninziz-zida had shown him something similar, but he had turned away from it in fear. This time the sensation called to him as if it were a truth of his own making.

Kasai felt a new space open within his spirit as he released his anger, grief, and guilt. It pulled him closer and expanded as he floated nearer. The open space was peaceful, calm, and inviting.

His fire xindu raced into the open space like a flash fire thirsting for more oxygen. It rose higher and higher, as it grew with the ever-expanding area. The sensation of a familiar summertime shower washed over him. It was cool and cleansing. His emotional pain vanished and was replaced with focused determination.

Kasai surrendered himself to the ever-expanding space, and his mind filled with knowledge. Fire xindu was not based on anger or fear. Those emotions were merely the easiest way to bring it to life. Fire xindu was movement and momentum and was a way to begin. It was the spark that lit a greater power.

Kasai's remaining xindu energies bloomed to life. His air xindu swept up from deep chasms of unlocked memories. He envisioned Desdemonia swimming in a lagoon. The sheen of water over her body sparkling in the warm sun. He remembered the bond of trust they shared while fighting and watching each other's back.

His water xindu rose through his spirit like a geyser trapped underground for too long. He felt his uncertainty wash away. Gone was the distraction of *I can't do it*. He felt relaxed and calm while his fire xindu mixed with his air and water xindu. Each strand of energy wrapped around the other, forming a tighter bond.

His earth xindu heaved like molten rock. It oozed like a slow flow of lava, then hardened around his spirit like the mountain which bore it. His earth xindu supported the expansion of his fire, air, and water xindu energies like the flying buttresses lining a great cathedral's outer walls, raised to honor the Immortal Mother. His xindu energies continued to grow as one into the ever-expanding space.

The infinite sky and bottomless ocean within him combined into one. He surrendered his spirit self and physical self to the truth of an unlimited, higher power. His xindu energies were not a fickle oddity that hid deep within him and remained elusive to his mental grasp.

Nor were they raw elements from the outside world he was meant to manipulate. Xindu energy was a merging between both worlds. It was a relationship to be shared and a bond to be honored. It was the Boundless.

In his mind's eye, he could see his four xindu energies flowing together, entwined in hoops that circled his body in a spinning sphere. He felt no anger or fear, and sorrow held no power over him. He focused on what he would do and how he would do it. He gathered his xindu energies together and channeled their power into his hands.

Kasai's mortal eyes sprang open.

What had seemed like hours of contemplation were mere moments in the real world. Tazizu's face roamed over his own as she sniffed him like a hound. Her skin was drawn tight over sharp cheekbones. The two uneven gashes on her nose flared open with each breath, and her teeth were brown and cracked. She wore a smug expression, then something caught her eye. She looked down in surprise.

White energy flowed like waterfalls from Kasai's vibrating palms.

"Stop!" She commanded. The crackle of her voice betrayed her fear.

Kasai's air xindu flowed through his limbs. He drew back both elbows and shifted his right leg back to take the weight of his body. Then his earth xindu anchored his foot to the ground. With a thought, his fire xindu exploded outwards, sending his open palms into Tazizu's chest. She flew backward with her arms and legs trailing like pennants in the wind.

Kasai wasted no time snatching Ninziz-zida up from the ground. The Fire Serpent blazed to life in his hands.

You see now with open eyes.

He remained oddly calm as Tazizu rose on unsteady legs. Her body shivered in the blue light from Ninziz-zida's fire. Kasai watched her exposed flesh ripple like the surface of a lake caressed by an autumn breeze. It was a poetic thought for a gruesome deed.

Tazizu gritted her rotten teeth as she fumbled for a discarded whip that was no longer at her hip. Blood bubbled from her mouth, distorting the words of a malformed spell that dribbled out of her quivering lips.

She is finished, Ninziz-zida hissed, not with anger, but with certainty. *There is more work to do.*

But Kasai waited. The release of so much energy left him weary and panting for breath. One of Tazizu's hands went to her chest, then the other went to her abdomen as her torso shook with uncontrollable force. Her eyes raised to Kasai in shock. She tried to speak, but only mumbled sounds came from her blood-stained mouth.

She fell to her knees, screamed once, then keeled over into the dirt. The seams of the hides she wore split. Tazizu stared up at Kasai one last time with eyes filled with hate just as her chest and back exploded in a fountain of gore.

"Horrible," Kasai said. He took a moment to steady his trembling legs. Fierce fighting sounded nearby. Tired as he was, Ninziz-zida was right. There was still more to do.

Let the fires of wrath sustain you.

"Not wrath, but purpose."

Ah, you have learned a new truth. Then let us go and cleanse this place with purpose.

Kasai felt Ninziz-zida's raw energy flow into him. The heat of her fire xindu was like a blast from an iron worker's furnace, and the tang of smelted steel lingered on his tongue.

"We must help the others."

Follow the trail of death, and we will find our foes.

Kasai ran deeper into the village. An orange and yellow fire burned multi-legged carcasses, interlocked with the bodies of mangled villagers. He heard a series of deafening booms detonating around the corner of a large hut with its roof ablaze. Black smoke pumped into the sky as the fire spread. The village was burning around him.

He turned the corner of the building and saw a mass of demons surrounding a small group of villagers. They were pinned with their backs to a long, weathered hut with nowhere to run.

Gift stood boldly between the demons and the villagers, rapidly conjuring fist-sized fireballs and hurling them into the horde. She couldn't miss, but there were too many demons for her to fight alone. The monsters closed in on her position, knocking the burning bodies of their brethren aside, and careless of the raw blisters they received.

The enemy will burn.

"Yes, they will," Kasai spun the ends of Ninziz-zida in two fiery pinwheels, and blue fire leaped into the sky. He raced forward, and she hissed her elation as they entered the fray of battle.

The first demons were struck down unaware, and their bodies exploded in clouds of ash. The righteous might of Ninziz-zida's flame was more than their Abyssal forms could endure.

A demon turned fast and lashed out at Kasai with a barbed, mantis-like arm. He ducked the blow and swept Ninziz-zida low, snapping three of the demon's legs in a crippling strike. Ninziz-zida's outer section spun around and smashed in the side of the demon's head as he fell. Only a cloud of ash was left where the demon once stood.

"Come on!" he yelled, whirling the Fire Serpent faster and shifting the demon's attention from the villagers to him.

His xindu energies swirled together as most of demons turned toward him. Ninziz-zida hissed in his hands. *Give yourself to the Boundless, for we are one within its abundance.*

Kasai surrendered more of himself to the ever-expanding space between the vast sky and deep ocean in his mind. The connection to Ninziz-zida become stronger. She was there with him in the Boundless as a ring of blue fire, swirling around him.

A splinter of memory flashed in his thoughts. Desdemonia was there, and her long hair flowed past his eyes like a river. His nose caught the earthy smell of her leathers. She turned with a crafty smile on her lips and a sparkle in her amber eyes. Then she was gone. Ripped from his thoughts. He felt a longing in his heart and knew he would give anything to have her back.

She will be avenged!

Ninziz-zida's words gave him focus, and he released his combined xindu energies into the fiery ring. The more he gave willingly to the Fire Serpent, the more her shape shifted into something more organic and recognizable.

"What are you?" he said just as his mortal eyes opened in the real world and saw a spinning vortex of fire swirling around him. Smoke and debris whipped together, obscuring his view. He thought he saw a great serpent's form rise into the air, just before he flashed with unnatural speed into action.

His hands glowed with power as Ninziz-zida segments snapped at demons like the end of a bullwhip. Nothing could stop her fury, and he didn't care. The destruction of the enemy was all that mattered. He barely noticed the fire leaping into the air and burning everything it touched. Flames soon spread over thatched rooftops and into trees.

All of it must burn. The taint of evil must be vanquished!

Kasai's mind was pulled back to the ever-expanding space. He saw a mirror image of himself becoming smaller, drifting into the distance. Ninziz-zida's protective ring of fire grew around him, whirling like a tempest.

A warning flashed in his mind. Ninziz-zida's fury was out of control.

Kasai forced his perception back into his physical reality and saw only the ashes of demon death drifting in the air. The enemy had been destroyed.

"Ninziz-zida, you must cease your fury."

They must burn! I will allow nothing to harm you. Stay with me in the Boundless.

"I am the wielder. You must come back to me." Kasai asserted more control. "The enemy has been defeated, and those that remain are allies that will help us reach our ultimate goal."

Sekka, Ninziz-zida hissed.

"Yes, Great Fire Serpent. Sekka. She must be stopped. Quell your passion. This battle is won but the war is not over."

Kasai ceased the flow of his fire, earth, and air xindu into Ninziz-zida and let his water xindu cool her fiery spirit. "Be calm, Ninziz-zida."

Together, as weapon and wielder, all is possible. Alone there is nothing.

Kasai felt Ninziz-zida's fury recede. He was back in control and exhaled a weary breath. His shoulders slumped with exhaustion. Gift stepped away from him, her eyes still wide.

"It's okay. Ninziz-zida has recognized you for the friends you are."

Her body remained tense. "Master Kasai, I have never seen such a thing. Within the cloud of ash, I beheld a great serpent of light," Gift said.

"The Fire Serpent has risen from its slumber," a villager said from the long, weathered hut. He was an older man, frail, but spoke with the confidence of experience.

A group of warriors approached. "The demons have scattered like rats," a bald man said. He pointed with his spear into the jungle. "They fled this way after their leader fell to Master Kasai."

"Let them go. We must regroup. I will not be caught blind again," Gift said.

A villager approached Kasai hesitantly. She held out a trembling hand and touched Kasai lightly on the back of his hand. "The Ever Hero walks among us," she said in awe.

She then knelt on the ground. The other villagers followed, supplicating themselves in front of him.

"The prophecy reveals itself," Orin said like a ghost at Kasai's side.

"The tongues of foreign voices will speak the words of his arrival. They will claim him as their own," Pallo said. He stood opposite Orin. Had either of them ever left his side?

Pallo bowed to Kasai. His face was covered in smears of soot and blood. He cleaned black ichor from his blades before returning them to their scabbards.

More villagers and warriors came to stand by Gift, and Kasai saw adulation in their eyes. One by one, they knelt to the ground.

"Please, no. Get up. You mustn't do that," Kasai pleaded. "The village is burning. We must put out the fires. Bring water!"

"You have saved our people." Gift said.

"But I have destroyed your village. I couldn't control Ninziz-zida's flame."

"The fires you see are pure and right. They will cleanse the death and decay the enemy has brought to this land. The buildings of this village will sleep. When the time is right, our homes will reawaken."

"But..." Kasai stammered.

"We do not attach ourselves to the gifts of Nayche. She gives and takes as is needed."

Kasai watched the fires spread. Black smoke rose into the air, while dark ash settled across the village like a dusting of black snow. More warriors joined Gift. Their eyes were sharp though their bodies were weary from combat. Ash clung to their hair and skin as they stepped reverently around the dead.

"Very few remain," Kasai said.

The small figure of the Great Mother walked into the clearing. She surveyed the burning buildings and the bodies scattered throughout the street. A gathering of villagers followed her.

"I am grateful to have seen the miracle of the Ever Hero before I sleep the long slumber," the Great Mother said.

"I'm so sorry. I could not control the flames. Your village is lost," Kasai said.

She looked deeply into his eyes. "What you say has been lost has been returned to Nayche. She will look after those who have fallen until their time of awakening."

The villagers bowed their heads and whispered silent prayers.

"We will find new rivers filled with fish. We will hunt and harvest new lands. Our carpenters and masons shall rebuild. Life will continue. Nayche will provide all we need."

Kasai was about to say more, but the Great Mother put her hand up to silence him.

"The Frona Tribe is grateful to the Ever Hero of Aetenos. You and your companions have earned the bond of trust. You will remain members of our tribe until your time of sleep."

"Ever Hero," Pallo said. He leaned in towards Kasai. "The Chaos Gate."

"I know," Kasai said in a low voice. He bowed to the Great Mother. "My friends and I are honored to be accepted into your tribe. We thank you. But we must go north. That is where we will find Sekka. I mean to end this."

"What of her Chaos Warlord? What of the captives of the Parpurish Tribe? Will we abandon our brothers and sisters to a fate worse than we experienced here?" Gift said. "Great Mother, Master Kasai is right. We must change our ways if we are to survive. If we must give help to receive help, then that is our path.

"Bring the young and old to the Hiraka Tribe and seek refuge. Tell them we follow the Ever Hero and go to save the Parpurish Tribe. Our three tribes have shared a peaceful coexistence for many generations, and now is the time for us to unite as one people. Together we will take the fight to the enemy." Gift's eyes blazed with passion.

The Great Mother smiled warmly at her and nodded her head in understanding. "You will make an excellent Great Mother one day. Your words speak the truth of our time. Change is upon us."

Kasai was about to interject when Pallo leaned in again. "We can use their numbers. And a guide north would be helpful."

The Great Mother waved her hands and gathered the survivors to her. "Let it be known that the Frona Tribe was first to break from tradition, not from weakness or despair, but from the strength of choice.

"We follow the Ever Hero of our time. The Sunnese people must change what is unchangeable for our people to survive." Her voice carried over the snap and crackle of flames.

"We were lucky the enemy's numbers were few," Orin said. "They fight with passion, but a greater force would have taken the entire village."

Pallo rubbed the thick stubble on his jaw. "We will not succeed if we do not have the cooperation of the other tribes. This would be an opportunity to win the trust of others."

"Agreed," Kasai said. His eyes met those of the warriors waiting for instruction. "We will start small, and our numbers will grow. It's the best we can hope for now."

When Kasai, Pallo, Orin, and the warriors of the Frona Tribe arrived at the Parpurish village, they saw the wooden huts had melted into a soupy, black goo. The scattered remains of burnt thatched roofs were covered in mold. Heaps of fly-infested flesh lay strewn about the ground. A thriving village had been turned into a quagmire of death.

It was not difficult for Gift to pick up the trail of the Parpurish captives. A northernly path grew wider as greyish-green muck continued to dissolve the foliage and shrubs at its edges. The hunters wasted no time following the trail.

Kasai was amazed at the warriors' stamina. They had been running at a quick pace for two days since leaving Gift's village. Kasai's training at Ordu had prepared his body for lengthy periods of endurance. By noon of the third day and he was hard-pressed to keep pace with the Frona warriors' fastest runners. All the while, a slow breeze carried a steady smell of rancid decay through the jungle trees.

Kasai wondered how his companions fared. The last time he checked, Pallo's hair was drenched with sweat. The older warrior ran at a forced gait. Every other step was more of a stumble forward than a purposeful stride. His eyes were determined, and Kasai knew the man would not stop until Gift called for the next rest.

Orin complained endlessly about biting bugs and bothersome trees. The insects seemed particularly drawn to him, and no other warrior found so many hidden roots.

When Gift finally called a halt for the day, her warriors took no time setting up a small encampment. They cleared brush and erected small shelters against the nightly rain. Kasai did what he could to help but was politely deterred. The warriors fawned over him like a revered holy man. Some prostrated themselves before him as he walked past. He just smiled awkwardly and moved on.

His head swam in the dizzying fatigue of the forced run. Images of skies and seas and the nothingness in between came in and out of focus. He tried to relive moments of his fight against Tazizu. But the battle was now a haze of jumbled sensations. He mostly remembered the horrible stench of rotted teeth.

But something had changed within him, and the world was somehow crisper to his senses. The Boundless was real. He had experienced a taste of its abundance, enough to convince himself that everything his Masters had told him at Ordu was true. But try as he might, he could not reestablish his connection to the expanding space.

He forced his mind to concentrate on the events that led to his initial awareness of the Boundless. Logically, the pathway should be open to him since he had earned the right of passage. But the harder he sought the doorway into the ever-expanding space, the more elusive the entrance became. He demanded his xindu energies to weave together again into an unbreakable bond. Each rose and fell, independent of the others, but would not merge. He had lost the key to their harmony.

I'm just too tired.

He found Gift conferring with Pallo and Orin. A fourth warrior was at her side and explained something to the other three, but Kasai was too far away to hear. Gift listened intently to the warrior's words. She looked hopeful. When the warrior was finished, she gave him a brisk nod in agreement.

Gift saw Kasai approaching and halted the conversation until he was closer. He was eager for news.

"Master Kasai. We are gaining on the enemy. Their progress has slowed," she said.

"Have the scouts returned?" Kasai asked.

"Only Jorraih," Pallo said and nodded to the warrior at Gift's side. "He says the other scouts will return shortly if stealth and luck travel with them."

"Maybe Des is with them, too," Kasai said hopefully.

Pallo and Orin exchanged a concerned look. "Ever Hero, do not torment yourself with false hope. You must assume she is lost," Pallo said.

"You don't know that! I can still save her," Kasai barked, frustrated that his companion had already given up on her. If there was a way to save Des, he would find it. *I won't lose her forever.*

Pallo bowed respectfully. "Truly, I am sorry. I know you cared for her."

"We are all sorry for your loss and the loss of all who have fallen to the enemy. But the fight goes on. We must plan for the coming battle. It will not be long now," Gift said. "We will hear Master Kasai's council when we know more of the strength of the enemy. For now, we will rest."

Gift's words were hard, but she was right. The fight must go on. It only ended with the defeat of Sekka, and they were counting on him to lead them, to save them. He read it in Gift's eyes, as he did with the other warriors in the camp. They saw him as their *savior*. He was beginning to hate the sound of that word.

Kasai sulked away and looked for a place to meditate. He sat with his back against a tree and Ninziz-zida resting on his lap. There must be something he could use from his lessons on warfare at Ordu.

The history of the Three Kingdoms of Hanna was filled with stories of conquest and bloodshed. He knew of countless battles fought between the armies of long-dead kings and could retell glorious moments of genius when a commander's deceptive feint allowed his troops to occupy the living ground of battle and defeat their enemy with one decisive blow. But stories read in scrolls and books were scrubbed clean of the usable details he needed to be sure of victory.

Keep your strategy simple, he thought. When the battle began, chaos would ensue. The easier the plan was to remember, the easier it would be to execute. He remembered the slaughter on the fields of the Last Garrison. The horror of battle could not be underestimated.

He would need to be mindful of where and when he attacked the enemy. Only then could he hope to keep the losses to a minimum. But how to defeat Sekka? The eventuality of that battle still loomed on the horizon. Whether he had a brilliant plan or not, he was still helpless against the archdevil and her legions. He rubbed the top of his head. *I still need an army.*

He scanned the camp. There were what, maybe thirty warriors ready to fight? He could pick off stragglers falling behind the bulk of the enemy horde with such numbers or ambush smaller war parties in the jungle, but that didn't get him any closer to defeating Sekka on a larger scale.

And while the Chaos Gate remained opened, it wouldn't matter how many of the demons he destroyed in the jungles of Sunne, or eventually in the forests of Baroqia. *She can simply snap her fingers, and more will appear.*

He thought of two grand armies clashing together, with his emerging victorious. Then Kasai shook his head. *It'll never happen that way. Confronting Sekka, army to army would be a disaster. Des was right. It's an impossible task.*

You will find a way, Ninziz-zida voiced encouragingly.

Think! There must be a way. Remember, keep it simple. What am I overlooking? Kasai thought.

He exhaled slowly and tried to calm his thoughts. If his limited experience of battle had taught him anything, it was that a leaderless army was vulnerable. He would need to concentrate on the commanders. At least now there was one less warlord to worry about. The Boundless had seen to the destruction of Tazizu.

No, it was you who harnessed the Boundless. Ninziz-zida's flame rippled along the three segments. *The Boundless showed you what was already within you.*

"I cannot find my way back, Great Fire Serpent. The Boundless has closed itself to me."

Surrrrrrrrenderrrrr, Ninziz-zida hissed in his mind. *You must surrender all that you know and all that you are. Let go of what you hold too tightly.*

"I'm trying!" Kasai said in frustration. "The Boundless won't listen to me."

He heard some commotion across the camp. Another scout had arrived. Kasai got to his feet and jogged to where a small group had gathered. Pallo, Orin, and Gift were already there.

"We have found the Parpurish Tribe. The Chaos Warlord has stopped his march north," the scout said.

"Show me," Gift said.

The scout drew a rough map in the soil. "We are here. The enemy is but a day's run ahead of us." He looked up at Gift. "They are waiting in the belly of the Shallow Salamander."

"Shallow Salamander?" Pallo asked.

"A ravine, which is empty now, but floods with the late spring rains," Gift said.

"His creatures pound spears into the ground, then sharpen the ends," the scout said.

"He intends to sacrifice the Parpurish," Orin said.

The scout gave a quick nod. "He has divided his forces into thirds. Two companies of demonkind have departed, traveling north. He remains with the captives and a smaller force."

"He has grown overconfident," Gift said.

Kasai listened carefully to the scout's report. He wondered why such a skillful leader would put himself on such difficult ground to defend. Deadly ground.

"Now is the time to strike!" the scout said.

Orin shook his head in disagreement. "It's a trap. He knows you are eager for a victory and expects you will run to the aid of your people," Orin said. "We should not engage him at this time."

"But the Parpurish will die," the scout said.

"And the Frona will live to fight another day," Orin said. "Ever Hero, we are but a handful against what could still be hundreds, maybe even thousands."

Defeat her Warlord, and you will cripple the devil, Ninziz-zida hissed in his mind.

Kasai continued to study the crude map drawn in the dirt. He agreed with Orin's assessment of the scout's report. The Sunnese were desperate, and the Chaos Warlord had given them just the right lure to entice them to strike. He would spring his trap when they raced to claim his head.

But what if I could snag him in his own trap? "You have drawn your map in a curious manner. The ravine edges are narrow here and much wider in this area. Is this accurate?"

"Yes. The ravine tapers together at this point," the scout said. "It's a barren place. Scorched by the high noon sun."

"High noon sun...hmm." Kasai removed a leaf from the map on the ground, which threw a shadow over one of the ravine sides.

A warrior ran to Gift's side and spoke with animated words in the Sunnese tongue. Kasai glanced up momentarily but then brought his concentration back to the primitive map. He traced some lines in the dirt, of possible troop movement and attack points, but then shook his head.

"Orin's right. We must find another way until we have more warriors."

"Master Kasai!" Gift's voice was filled with surprise.

Kasai looked up fast. "What is it, Gift? Are we under attack?"

Gift pointed to the south. "The Hiraka Tribe has arrived. A thousand warriors strong."

"A thousand, you say?" Kasai looked back to the map and placed stone markers in the dirt. He drew lines of additional troop movement with his finger, then knelt back and studied his marks. "That might just be enough."

"Ever Hero, you must reconsider. We are rushing into battle blind and do not have accurate intel on what remains of the enemy," Orin said. "It's a trap. Can't you see this? Pallo, tell him."

Kasai stood. "You have the right of it, Orin. It's a trap. The Chaos Warlord is clever. He expects pursuit from the Sunnese to save the captives and knows the imminent deaths of the Parpurish will force rash action from his pursuers. What better way to entice a vengeful warband into a fight than to wait at the base of a poorly defended ravine?

"But he has revealed the true nature of his deception by appearing too vulnerable. He hasn't dismissed his troops. I suspect they wait in ambush here, and here." Kasai pointed at two small stones he had placed on either side of the ravine.

"He extends his neck just enough to tempt the Sunnese to strike," Pallo said.

"Exactly," Kasai said. "He assumes you will attack predictably. Which is exactly what we will do. I have a plan."

77

SHIVERRIG

A waning crescent moon shone directly overhead, gently bathing the shallow valley in soft blue light. A muggy haze clung to the rocks at the base of a gradual slope leading up to an open ridgeline. The night's air was still and did nothing to relieve the suffocating heat.

Shiverrig swatted away a large fly, then another. He wondered how anyone would willingly live in such an inhospitable environment. If it wasn't sweltering heat, it was torrential downpours, and then more heat. But this was war, and war required sacrifices the strong made without a second thought.

"This heat be damned," he said as he sat straighter in his saddle, shifting the stiffness in his lower back to his legs.

He then kicked his chaos horse forward. Snake-scale patterns wound around a once flawless chestnut roan's body, like thin worm trails through swamp muck. The frenetic lines shimmered from the flickering flames of torches at the edge of the slope.

One hundred and eighty-nine poles pointed into the night sky, the ends of each sharpened to a ruinous tip. The number of stakes was given to him by Dai-Ko-Zior, who had been specific about the exact placement of each shaft, which now formed an outward spiral. It all seemed arbitrary to Shiverrig; numbers, shapes, the time of day, what did it matter? But he conceded he was not versed in the ways of sorcery and had his half-breeds do as the sorcerer requested. *What do I care if it yields the desired results?*

He looked to the east and west slopes where his loyal half-breeds lined the two ridges. They stood like stone totems to long-forgotten gods in the soft moonlight, bearing witness to the procession of captives below.

Shiverrig twisted in his saddle as Daku's hulking body approach with Eishorror strapped across his back. The pale demon led a long line of Sunnese warriors inside the torch ring, and there he corralled them into a large group.

Each warrior was bound tightly at the wrist, and a short rope was tied to each ankle. The more troublesome ones had their mouths stuffed with cloth, which was then held tight by a rough chord around their head.

Shiverrig thought the bait tempting enough. The screams of the dying Sunnese would draw the enemy in close, and in numbers. He grew tired of so many small skirmishes with little to no reward of captives.

He gazed at captive warriors without much of a thought. Their fate was sealed. They were a means to an end. Shiverrig was impressed that none of the jungle-dwellers pleaded for their lives. That would change, of course, once the first was impaled and the smell of death hit their nostrils.

His chaos horse's tail switched at black flies attempting to land on its flanks. Shiverrig swatted one, gorging itself on his exposed neck. He wiped the smeared remains on a saddle cloth.

"Bloody mess. Don't these creatures sleep?"

A robed figure stood in the center of the unwinding spiral of posts. Dai-Ko-Zior wore a grey cloth frock, covered in vermillion runes. As Shiverrig's chaos horse trotted forward, he heard cryptic mumblings snaking through the sharpened stakes as if ghosts haunted the spiral.

The sorcerer's grey hood remained over his head, hiding his eyes and nose from the moonlight. His entire body swayed like a hooded snake, following the musical movements of a snake charmer. The sorcerer seemed oblivious to the oppressive heat, and Shiverrig wished he could be so lucky.

Dai-Ko-Zior's hands were lost in the folds of his sleeves. Only his mouth moved within the shadows of his hood, chanting sounds queer to human ears. Shiverrig waited, mesmerized by the sound of the sorcerer's eerie homage to appease his otherworldly masters.

Then, the echo of Dai-Ko-Zior's chanting trailed off like a whisper in the wind as the last syllable of his worship left his dry lips.

"All is ready," Dai-Ko-Zior said in a weak voice.

"Very well."

Shiverrig motioned to a pair of demons, milling in a larger group. Two citizens, previously of Qaqal and transformed by Xerthotha's chaos change, eagerly bounded forward. Their human faces had extended into broad snouts. Frothing slobber lined their black and purple lips, which curled upwards in wicked smiles.

The half-breeds wore heavy, padded armor with an image of a three-headed mastiff branded over the left chest. Thin-membraned wings poked from the backs and remained folded behind them.

"Bring the first," Shiverrig ordered, pointing to the group of captives.

The two half-breeds waded into the group of captives and grabbed a warrior. The demons' wings then extended, and with powerful downward thrusts, they rose into the air with the struggling prisoner.

The man's legs kicked and jerked, trying to escape his captors' grips as he hovered above a sharp spike.

"Until my day of reawakening!" he shouted into the night air. The remaining captives bowed their heads in reverence. The demons shrieked in delight, yanking him back and forth between them.

Shiverrig gestured to drop the captive. The man twisted awkwardly in the air and impaled himself chest first over the stake. His instant death caused Shiverrig to frown. It was over too quickly. The raucous howls of half-breed demons died down, and they looked dumbfounded at each other. Eventually, they turned their wet muzzles to the remaining captives.

"The rest of you do the same," Shiverrig commanded. "I want the jungle-dwellers following us to hear their cries. Those who fail to keep the warriors alive longer than this one will suffer the same fate,"

The demons didn't wait for more instruction. They pounced in pairs on the helpless captives and carried them over the waiting spikes. The Sunnese who survived the initial impalement remained fixed in place, moaning deeply as their lifeblood coated the deadly shafts.

"Better. That should get their attention," Shiverrig said. He pulled on the reins of his chaos horse, turning to Dai-Ko-Zior. "They are yours, sorcerer. May your dark gods savor their souls."

"The Ancients favor you, Gerun Shiverrig," Dai-Ko-Zior said. "Your gift has been accepted."

Shiverrig smirked. "Whatever you say."

Dai-Ko-Zior walked to the nearest body. The captive was still breathing, but barely. The sorcerer placed a thin hand on the man's leg and resumed his chanting. The body shuddered as dark magic slithered over bruised skin and ripped clothing.

Shiverrig jerked the reins again, this time turning his chaos horse to his base camp. He fell into the rhythm of the horse's gait. His thoughts drifted back to his plan and the risk he was taking. *But the worm must be juicy enough to attract the biggest fish.* Now, he would wait.

Shiverrig paced the floor of his command tent. Nighttime had passed into the late morning without any respite from the heat. Sleep had avoided him, as it usually did on the eve of battle. Sweat flowed freely under his chest armor as he paced from one section of the tent to another. A small swarm of black gnats followed his every move, darting just out of eyesight but never far from his ears.

He swatted aimlessly into the air. "These damned flies," he said through gritted teeth. His irritation grew with each word. Even with the tent's flaps down and tied off, he could not prevent the bothersome insects from gaining entrance.

The invasion of Sunne was progressing effectively, albeit slowly. The destruction of the jungle had been a great boon in weakening the jungle-dwellers' ability to wage war. The Sunnese drew power from the vast stores of life the jungle offered. But once Shiverrig took that advantage away from them, their magic became less potent.

He was no fool and assumed the jungle-dwellers would adapt to his scorched earth strategy soon enough. Much of the night was spent envisioned possible countermeasures the Sunnese might take to turn the advantage he had gained against him. What would he do if a hostile force invaded his land, using superior manpower and weapons of mass destruction? He paused and lowered his gaze at Aeshmara. *What would I do, indeed?*

The Vyzyn warlord sat at the central table covered with maps and uneaten food. One of her legs draped over the armrest of her wooden chair. Her bone-white hair remained cropped short and hung straight just above her shoulders. She lifted a mug of dark mead from the table and brought it to her lips, while her slate-blue eyes glared back at him, holding his gaze as she drained the cup.

"You look troubled, Shiverrig," she said and then wiped her mouth clean with the back of her wrist.

Shiverrig ignored her taunt and resumed his slow walk to a cluster of boxes and crates at the end of the tent. The bins held an assortment of weapons collected from recent victories over the jungle-dwellers. His fingers idly sifted through the relics, indiscriminately tossing them back-and-forth.

Thin bladed swords rattled against blowpipes and finely-crafted bows. These trinkets of war held little interest for Shiverrig. *I must have more souls*, he thought. The conversion of Qaqal had been a show of strength and power, but to win a full-scale engagement against Sekka, he would need double or triple the amount of new warriors. Possibly more. The Chaos Gate was the equalizer. Without it, she would be helpless.

But how to control it? Or better yet, destroy it? Each battle in its own time, he thought.

"Are your reports confirmed by the secondary scouts?" Shiverrig asked his First Scout and spy, Pathias. He didn't bother to turn around.

"As I have said, my lord, they have not yet returned," Pathias said.

Shiverrig heard the confidence in Pathias's voice. Or was it swagger? He turned to face the scout. "Not yet returned, or dead?"

Pathias merely shrugged his shoulders. "They were Frost Legion, lord. Chosen by General Aeshmara and not under my command. I cannot account for their whereabouts or actions, only that they did not return."

The First Scout stood at ease to the side of the closed tent flaps. His mousebrown hair was straight and thin, and he wore it slicked back over his head. Pathias had always maintained a calm and collected demeanor.

Shiverrig stroked the stubble that grew long on his face. He hated relying on the Vyzyn warlords for anything. Of the three siblings, he felt he could trust the sorcerer the most, which was just shy of not at all. Dai-Ko-Zior traveled along a mysterious path. He came and went more often than Sess'thra, and with the same lack of forewarning or explanation. He was gone again, claiming higher powers demanded his attention elsewhere.

In comparison, Pathias was loyal without compromise. He was born from a lowtiered, farming family, who worked as fiefs on a small plot of land outside the walls of Volkerrum Keep, the ancestral home of the Shiverrig clan. Pathias had found his stride in the wilderness, first as a child, hunting small game for Shiverrig's kitchens. Later, as a successful tracker for his duke's seasonal hunts. Shiverrig liked Pathias. He was a scrapper.

Shiverrig's thoughts drifted back to his strategy. He was wary of committing his troops without proper recon. Pathias was good. The scout could go deep into enemy territory and remain unseen, but he was one man and couldn't see the entirety of enemy movement on his own. The secondary scouts were to sweep Pathias's inner quadrant, specifically the ridgeline, and then report that the rear quadrant was clear.

Shiverrig turned to the remaining figure in the tent, who stood stoically in the shadows. The great fan of red and purple feathers covering Lord Vorleeth's head reminded Shiverrig of the primitive headdresses worn by the natives he was currently slaughtering. The demon's ruby-colored wings hung loosely behind his back.

Shiverrig recalled when young Prince Dane was forced to take the demon seed. A sad day for the only son of the late King Conrad. He casually wondered if Prince

Dane was enjoying his imprisonment within the possession of the demon, Vorleeth. The boy's blood was weak, just like his father's, and Shiverrig despised weakness.

"The Sky Reavers are assembled, Lord Vorleeth," Shiverrig said, breaking himself out of his reverie. It was a statement. He already knew the answer.

"Yes, my Aj-Kahun. We await your orders," Vorleeth said. The human voice that spoke from the demon's long, stork-like beak was twanged with the sound of a crow's caw.

"My lord, the Captain of the Second Scouts has arrived," a guard's voice announced from the other side of the tent flap.

"Let him pass," Shiverrig said.

The flaps pulled open, and a sickly, humanoid creature emerged from the bright morning light. The scout scampered quickly into the tent, bowed low to Shiverrig, and then to Aeshmara.

He wore no clothing but instead was covered in a shaggy coat of creamy, coarse hair, better suited for work on the ice flows of Gathos, rather than the tropical jungle of Sunne.

To Shiverrig's eyes, he resembled something akin to a forest monkey, with long arms and legs, ending in dexterous fingers and toes. His body was covered in dried mud, broken twigs, and bits of leaves. The scout stood panting in the center of the tent with worried eyes, appearing unsure of himself in the presence of the assembled warlords.

Shiverrig caught a condescending smirk on Pathias's lips.

"Report," Shiverrig commanded.

The scout bowed again and moved to the map covering the command table to the right.

"Three Sunnese war parties advance, converging on our current location. They are small, my lord, and barely a full company when combined. They will take advantage of our weak position while we remain at the base of the ravine. We will be trapped if they take the ridgeline.

"There is thin access in or out at the southern end, with easier movement to the north. The ravine sides are not steep but still lend an advantage to whoever holds the high ground."

The scout looked questioningly to Aeshmara. She waved her hand, dismissing whatever question was to follow.

"I am familiar with the geography," Shiverrig said, not bothering to hide his irritation. "Only three war parties? Pathias, your previous reports had indicated a larger assemblage of the enemy in this area."

"Yes, my Aj-Kahun. I saw them with my own eyes, at least five companies strong, possibly six. They may have moved on to support positions attacked by General Tazizu to the South or Lord Jolla in the East."

"This is disappointing. I had hoped for more," Shiverrig said. Then he turned to Aeshmara. "Your brother has done his part. Are your troops in place?"

"We'll be ready," she replied casually as if the answer were truly unimportant. She rose from her chair with a playful grin and searched through a supply box. "Is there no more of this weak mead? I'm still parched."

"That is not what I asked. You were to have placed full companies on either side of the ridge to hold the Sunnese from circling behind our position."

Aeshmara turned quick. Her playful grin turned to a wicked sneer. "And I said we will be ready."

He held her gaze, refusing to back down from the smallest of challenges. They were not allied, nor would they ever be. This campaign would be a test of wills, and only one would survive the subterfuge of the other.

"The ridge support is in place," Shiverrig would not relent. "Let me hear you say the words."

"Yes, yes. All is as you instructed, mighty Aj-Kahun. The ridge support was placed before I came to this awe-inspiring war council." The sarcasm dripped from her thin lips. "But it's a fool's plan. Few have come. We should move on to another village. The Frost Queen grows impatient for more souls."

The heat grated on Shiverrig's every nerve, but not more than Aeshmara's insubordination. Her days were numbered.

Lasting leadership was not passed by decree with demons. Instead, it was earned through mortal combat. Failure was not tolerated. Succession came by way of death of the weak, and Aeshmara had proven herself a capable enough commander. What was left of the Frost Legion still gave her their loyalty.

Her victories against the frontier villages in Baroqia were shallow, but nonetheless, reinforced her position of command in Sekka's soldiers' infernal eyes. Aeshmara could not be replaced, but she could be slain. *When the time is right, it will be my hands around her throat or, better yet, my steel through her back.*

"Very well, then. Lord Vorleeth bring the Sky Reavers off the ridgeling and assemble them in the rear guard. The rest of you have your orders," Shiverrig said, hiding his annoyance.

Aeshmara sauntered out of the tent as if she had won a significant battle. His retaliation would be all the sweeter the more Aeshmara thought she had the better of him.

Pathias was the last to leave the tent and bowed respectfully before he closed the flaps behind him. Shiverrig walked to the command table and studied the map a final time. His finger circled the marker at the base of the ravine. He was surprised more of the enemy had not come out of hiding to save their brethren.

"We have longer to wait before we can fully engage them. All the while, Sekka continues to fill her tower with filth from Gathos," Shiverrig said to a dark corner of the tent.

Daku materialized from the shadows. "It's the way of the Sunnese to stay hidden. They only fight when cornered."

"This campaign is taking too long," Shiverrig said. "Aeshmara bides her time to strike. One misstep and she will pounce."

"Be done with her then. Slay her for all to see. Or let me do it," Daku said. He drew Eishorror from the sheath on his back and drove it forward. "One quick thrust, and it's over."

Shiverrig pursed his lips and slowly nodded. "She will die. But not today. I have more to do. Leave me."

"As you wish," Khalkoroth said and left the tent in the same manner he entered, through the shadows.

The sun blazed overhead when Shiverrig finally stepped outside into the noonday heat. The dirt at the base of the ravine was cooked and cracked. It peeled upwards as if in homage to the sun. The morning shadows and rain clouds had been driven away by the bright, yellow orb, which reigned supreme in the sky.

"Daku, with me," Shiverrig called as he rode toward Aeshmara. Daku loped like a feral wolf behind him.

Aeshmara waited at the head of a corridor separating two companies. She wore no helm, and her bone-white hair marked her as an easy target. *Foolish*, he thought, then realized his helm was still fastened to his saddle. *Curse this blasted heat.*

She rode on the back of a fearful creature, dredged up from some nether region of the Abyss. Her mount had a sleek upper body and head, resembling a large hunting cat. Smooth skin, the color of ash, covered the long frame of the beast. Lean muscles flexed and rippled when it moved.

"The jungle-dwellers approach," Shiverrig said. He pointed to the south. A war party of twenty-five spears fanned out, blocking the southern passage.

"I say again, you're ruse has fooled no one. You've attracted some curiosity seekers and nothing more. This is not worth my time, or my soldiers," Aeshmara said and nodded at Daku. "Send your dog instead."

"Two companies are needed," Shiverrig said in a definitive tone, wanting to settle the matter.

"To what end?" Aeshmara glared at Shiverrig. The frustration of her words was mirrored in her clenched fists. "I will not be mocked. You divvy out morsels of information, keeping me blind to your plans. I am a Warlord of Vyzyn and a General of Sekka's Frost Legion. I demand to be treated as such."

"Warlord of Vyzyn, I said advance." Shiverrig pointing again in the direction of the oncoming Sunnese warriors.

Daku straightened his back to his full height. He stood at eye level to Aeshmara on her steed. A low growl resonated from his throat as he slid Eishorror from its scabbard with an icy screech. A flurry of ice crystals fell from the fell blade, which not even the heat of the noonday sun could melt.

Aeshmara defiantly held her ground.

Shiverrig looked to the sloping ridges on either side of the ravine. "The jungle-dwellers think to hold us at the southern passage where our numbers will count for less." He drew his black-bladed sword, sweeping it across the opposing ridgelines. "Their aim is to surround us while our backs are turned. The Sunnese war parties advancing along the ridgeline is the real threat."

"However, the troops you have hidden in the forest will cut off their advance before they can gain position, thereby forcing them into the ravine. At which point, you will pivot. My Sky Reavers will attack from above, sealing the fate of the attackers."

Shiverrig intertwined his fingers, closing his two brawny hands together like a carnivorous plant.

Aeshmara scowled. "You should have told me more from the beginning."

"Frankly, I assumed the strategy to be obvious. Now, do as I command."

Aeshmara jerked the reins of her mount to the left. "Ho ha!" she shouted and dug her heels into its ribs. Shiverrig saw the glimmer of excitement in her slate-blue eyes.

The woman has the devil's eyes. She's up to something.

Daku was right. Aeshmara would need to be dealt with sooner rather than later. She would need to be broken. Shiverrig rubbed his chin as he watched her leave. Much of the success of this trap depended on her ability to follow his orders.

Shiverrig kicked his mount towards the rear position. Ahead of him were the soiled posts in Dai-Ko-Zior's spiral sacrifice. The sharp spikes of wood were stained red, blue, and maroon, but otherwise vacant.

Beneath him, the chaos horse's hooves splashed through a gooey muck that had once been the flesh and bone of the Sunnese captives. It was impossible to tell where one ended and another began, so complete was Dai-Ko-Zior's sorcery.

The spell of toxic mist he had conjured the night before had dissolved the flesh of the captives like an alchemist's acid poured over a soft peach. Now, only harmless, orange vapors rose off greasy puddles of viscous juice.

War was ugly business, and the coin of their souls was the only value to their lives.

He absentmindedly rubbed his chin again. Something was missing, something he couldn't quite put his finger on. *I saw them with my own eyes.* Pathias's words whisper through his thoughts. Where were the rest of Sunnese? The sacrifices should have brought them in droves to avenge their tortured brethren.

"Daku, come," Shiverrig commanded as his chaos horse trotted forward to where Lord Vorleeth waited patiently. The winged half-breed stood proud in front of his company of Sky Reavers. Shiverrig put the question behind him for now. He would need better reconnaissance in the future.

"The Sky Reavers await your orders, my Aj-Kahun," Lord Vorleeth said.

Shiverrig merely nodded his approval and spun his mount to face the south. Aeshmara would be engaging the enemy by now.

"The Sunnese war party cannot hold its position in the South. This will be over quickly," Daku said.

"Not too quickly, I hope. The Sunnese approaching along the ridgeline must be given time to come to their comrades' aid," Shiverrig responded. He scanned the ridgeline—still nothing.

"What are they waiting for? Now would be an ideal time for them to take the ridge and attack from the sides," Daku said.

"Yes, it would," Shiverrig said. The feeling of unease he had moved to his gut. "So why aren't they?"

The troops Aeshmara had hidden in the jungle suddenly rushed to the edge of the ridgeline, ready to fight a foe that was not there. Some looked confused, while others raced down the sides of the ravine without stopping at the ledge.

Battle lust quickly overcame those who remained at the ridge, and they rumbled down the slopes to join with those advancing on the southern position.

"What's this?" Shiverrig said aloud. "No, no, no!"

"The Sunnese didn't take the bait. They have abandoned their brothers and fled," Daku surmised.

"I think not." Shiverrig scanned the slopes to either side of his position. Empty. The same was true behind Lord Vorleeth's Sky Reavers. "They're still in the jungle, waiting. Lord Vorleeth split the Reavers into two groups. Fly beyond the jungle's edge, and drop your incendiaries there, there and there. Do the same on the opposite side. We will flush the jungle rats out of their holes."

"Yes, my Aj-Kahun. By your will." Within moments the company of winged demons was airborne.

Shiverrig heard blasts of magic bursting at the southern passage. The small group of Sunnese warriors had grown. Many more now lined the opposing ridges of the gap. The jungle-dwellers hurled magic into Aeshmara's warriors. Bright-blue missiles streaked at the two companies of demons but caused little damage.

"There are your missing war parties," Daku said. "They have reformed their numbers to hold the southern passage. Let's join the fight."

Shiverrig became pensive. "Something's not right. Aeshmara's concealed troops came out of hiding much too soon. They would have done so only if provoked or because they had been ordered to do so."

His gaze went to the Vyzyn warlord as she commanded the two companies to the south. As if she heard their conversation, Aeshmara turned in her saddle toward him. He could not see her face, but the wave of her hand was unmistakable. She was saying good-bye.

The hair on Shiverrig's neck stiffened. *She has consolidated her troops and left me defenseless. I've been outplayed.*

A purple bolt of energy flashed into the sky above him, and Daku uttered a low growl as hundreds of Sunnese warriors appeared along the ridge on the eastern side of the ravine. An equal number appeared on the western side.

Aeshmara's scout had lied about the actual numbers of Sunnese approaching the ravine. Dark-skinned warriors shouted war cries from both sides of the ridge. He was trapped.

Shiverrig turned to give orders to the few remaining troops at his side, only to watch each cut down by missiles of blue flame or engulfed by orange fireballs. Their bodies crumbled into broken cinders as they fell to the ground. Somehow, the magic of the Sunnese had grown stronger.

Both sides of the ravine were teeming with Sunnese warriors. He would be overwhelmed soon. Lord Vorleeth and the Sky Reavers had flown too far away and were oblivious to his plight. They would not return in time.

He glanced to the northern passage of the ravine, where it curved to the right. A fourth and fifth war party had filled the only exit and now raced towards him, intent on being first to claim his head as their prize. Retreat was now impossible.

Shiverrig spotted a lone figure, clad in burnt orange robes, at the head of the Sunnese charge. *The boy monk?* But then the war cries from the ridge snapped his attention back to immediate needs.

"Damn that Vyzyn whore." Shiverrig gritted his teeth. This was a delay, nothing more.

His troops at the southern passage could handle these natives. He just needed to reach them. Shiverrig scanned the southern position. Aeshmara and her troops were pushing forward but not engaging the enemy. They were leaving the battlefield.

"Daku, we must leave. Shadow walk us away from this place," Shiverrig said. He clenched his strong jaw, then sighed. "Sloppy, Shiverrig. Very sloppy."

His mount stumbled as the hard ground under her cloven hooves turned to mud. The chaos horse panicked, and the mud greedily sucked her down deeper into the earth. Shiverrig had no choice but to jump clear of his steed. He cursed as he sunk chest-deep into the soft, wet earth and clawed his way to where Daku stood on solid ground. "Dammit, Daku! Pull me out!"

Daku grabbed Shiverrig's hand and dragged him free.

"It's time to leave," Shiverrig said.

"I cannot shadow walk with no shadows!" Daku's said. "The noon sun washes everything out." Shiverrig heard a tinge of panic in the pale demon's voice. Daku's dark eyes wavered between browns and pinks. He was losing control.

"How much do you need?" Shiverrig said.

"More than what's here!"

Shiverrig gave a quick glance to the southern troops. They were all but gone.

He could hear Aeshmara's vindictive laugher in his head as he tightened his grip on the hilt of his black blade. If this was to be his end, he would die with his honor intact.

78

DESDEMONIA

esdemonia silently crept down the frozen hallway leading to Mother's scrying chamber. Fossilized bones of fantastic beasts dredged up from Gathos lined the walls. The irregular-sized, skeletal cavities supported the twisting corridors and doorways. Mother was continually bringing mementos from the ice world to her new tower in Baroqia. She said it made the place homier.

The ice corridor's sub-zero temperature was soothing. She hadn't seen a thrall working on construction in some time since the tower's infrastructure had been completed, and their presence was no longer needed. Desdemonia assumed they had already been slaughtered. Unfortunately, those who possessed knowledge of the secret chambers and their locations were building their own tombs.

The luckier thralls who carved out the central tunnels and finished off rooms were moved to another worksite. They, too, would be killed when the construction of the tower was complete. Mother said the tower required proper sacrifice to remain healthy and strong.

She was always offering helpful tidbits and advising her on increasing the potency of her magic, that and being overprotective with everything Desdemonia wanted to do.

"*Nothing must harm you, my precious daughter. Your value to me is immeasurable. I would burn kingdoms to the ground to see you safe.*"

Mother was fond of saying such things. But Desdemonia didn't want to be safe. She needed to run free and go where she wanted to go.

She recalled her last conversation with Mother in the throne room, and Desdemonia played out her dream events again. Dark clouds shrouded the sky as the Red Devil soared through the turbulent air.

Her body flew beside his, and she saw the sadness in his eyes. Tears rolled freely off the side of his face. Then he saw her. The queer smile on his lips still unnerved her.

"*Zizphander is dead. I destroyed him as I do all of my enemies,*" Mother had said, but somehow, Desdemonia still felt the Red Devil was important. He had a message for her, and like most of her memories, it remained just out of reach.

"One less devil in the world. And one more to replace him," the voice in her head whispered. Desdemonia absentmindedly touched the burgeoning horns on her forehead.

"Shush! What do you know, anyway?" Desdemonia said to the voice, and then she giggled. "I'm spending too much time alone."

She started humming a festive tune, and her thoughts turned to the mysterious Kasai. Desdemonia wasn't sure why, but she felt a strange connection to the young monk whenever she was calm or happy. A memory of his face flashed in her mind. *He has such charming eyes,* she thought. *They are the color of sage in direct sunlight and olive green in the shade.* Desdemonia stopped short. "How could I know that?"

She started walking again and convinced herself it was just her imagination. But thinking of Kasai put her at ease. It was so different from how she felt around Mother. Being close to her made Desdemonia feel aggressive, on edge, and eager to unleash her magic.

Kasai was the key to regaining her memory. She just knew it.

"But who is he to me?" The question continued to vex her. She felt joyful saying his name aloud in step with a skip and a twirl down the hall. "Kasai. Kasai. Kasai!"

But there were also feelings of sadness and loss, and sometimes she felt angry and frustrated. Her emotions leaped and tumbled over one another like marsh frogs, squirming together in a deep wooden bucket.

"I knew you couldn't stay away. How did you expect to get in without a key?"

Startled, Desdemonia spun around and saw Sess'thra walking towards her. She was dressed in her typical dark green and black hunting leathers, blending effortlessly into the shadows.

"Oh, it's only you," Desdemonia said, somewhat relieved. "I honestly didn't expect to get this far. Most times, I turn back before even getting to the tunnels."

"I know, I've seen you," Sess'thra said. The tone of her voice almost sounded condescending. Then she gave Desdemonia a broad smile. "That monk has you all wound up. You're singing and dancing like a wild gypsy."

"You're right. I cannot stop wondering who he is."

"That's to be expected after all you have shared."

"Do you know something? Sess'thra, tell me!" she said as the succubus joined her side.

"All right. But you mustn't tell Mother I told you. Promise me."

"I promise!"

"Kasai was once your most trusted companion. Can you believe it? Your bond together was strong. One might even say you loved him, if only for a brief while."

"I loved him?" Desdemonia said. Her body stopped short, and she gave a sour expression, albeit halfheartedly. Something in her heart told her Sess'thra spoke the truth.

"But he's the enemy. I would never betray Mother like that," she said it in a dismissive tone and hoped Sess'thra would believe her.

"Actually, the two of you were innocent bystanders who got dragged into this silly war by unfortunate events. When the time to choose sides came, Kasai joined with the Sunnese. But the jungle-dwellers only wanted him, not you. They saw you as something corrupt, a dangerous witch who wielded chaos magic."

Sess'thra scoffed, "Those silly fools know nothing of real magic. They would not accept you in their tribes. Tempers flared, and in a heated moment, they struck you down.

"Kasai had the opportunity to save you, but he didn't. He turned his back on you and left you for dead." Sess'thra's eyes flared. Then, her demeanor turned more casual as she took an interest in a design carved into the corridor's stone and traced it with her finger. "It was mere luck that I found you when I did."

"Why was I not told of this earlier?"

"Mother forbade it. She fears him. And there's more. Just as she predicted, your Kasai marches north with an army of natives to overthrow her."

"We cannot let that happen. Sister, we could go now to stop him. Come on." Desdemonia reached out and took Sess'thra by the wrist, pulling her to follow as she walked in the direction of the upper.

A part of Desdemonia was determined to keep Mother safe, while another part yearned to see Kasai in the flesh, to touch his skin, to see the forest colors in his eyes. She couldn't tell which part was truly motivating her to action.

"No," Sess'thra said. She twisted her wrist from Desdemonia's grip. "Mother needs Kasai alive. He must come to her of his own free will."

"What? Why?"

"Mother said he is the Ever Hero of this age. He's the key to stopping this war."

"How can he be the Ever Hero? That's insane. He's just a kid."

"Oh, he's old enough," Sess'thra said with a sly smile. "Curious that you would know his age."

Desdemonia tried to collect her thoughts. Kasai seemed to be part of everything in her life. "There's still more, isn't there? More to my loss of memory and my relationship with Kasai."

Sess'thra paused. She looked to the ground, appearing to weigh the implications of the information she held. "It's secret and I shouldn't say."

"Tell me, Sess'thra." Desdemonia leaned into her sister. "Tell me now."

"I can't. Mother will punish me if she finds out I told you."

"I won't say a word. You can trust me. We're sisters! Please!"

Sess'thra's eyes glanced left and then right. "Mother has not been altogether truthful with you."

"How do you mean?"

"Look around you," Sess'thra's arms went wide. Her head and eyes rolled to encompass their surroundings. "This tower is meant to be more than just a haven for us in this realm. Its stones are infused with ancient magic from Gathos. You can smell it seeping through the rock and wood. Part of its purpose is to keep you blind. It acts as a buffer to your past."

"Why?"

"Because of Kasai. Your visions hold a prophecy foretelling of Mother's downfall. Not only in the Mortal Realm, but in all realms. It's all in your dream."

"How do you know this? What prophecy?"

"I have been part of these games for an extremely long time. I have heard the voices of powerful beings whispered on the winds of memory and thought. They dangle visions of conquest in the minds of mortals.

"Mother is right to fear this Ever Hero and those connected to him. He will bring about great change through the Three Worlds, maybe even beyond."

"Then we must do something to stop him."

"We will when the time is right," Sess'thra said, "The Ever Hero must be brought to Gathos before he reaches his full potential. Mother says it will prevent the fulfillment of the prophecy. That's why she waits for him now."

Desdemonia was torn. She absentmindedly twisted the onyx ring on her finger, trying to put all the puzzle pieces together in her head. "I don't want Mother harmed in any way. If Kasai must be brought to Gathos, then let us bring him here ourselves. My magic is strong enough."

"There are requirements for his capture and rules that must be observed."

"Whose rules?" Desdemonia threw her hands in the air. "Listen, if you won't help me, I'll do it myself."

"You are a dutiful daughter. But there is more to the story. Mother fears for your safety as well as her own. She worries the strain of seeing him outside the tower's influence would be too much for you. She fears the sight of him could erase your remaining memories and even your magic."

"But my magic is within me. It's who I am."

"Is it? You've said yourself your magic wanes when Mother travels far from the tower."

"Not all my magic."

"It's the part that matters which vanishes. Without Mother's influence, your magic is but a drop of water when it rains and no longer the storm."

Desdemonia sulked. "I'm not that weak."

"You are most important to Mother. That's why she keeps you safe. It will be up to you to convince the Ever Hero to join us." Sess'thra came closer to Desdemonia.

"Will he join us?" Desdemonia said.

"Maybe, if you do the things I've taught you," Sess'thra said.

The idea intrigued her. A yearning grew within her, and she felt a strong desire to do...what? Her thoughts were confused and erratic, fluttering over an idea she could not make complete in her mind. *Kasai. Kasai. Kasai!*

There was no reason to be confused. Kasai was the enemy, and she had her duty to Mother. But he was also the key to her past. *Ugh, he is such a bother.*

Desdemonia then felt Sess'thra's fingers walk up the sleeve of her upper arm and then traced the contours of her neck.

"Sess'thra, what are you doing?" she said as she felt Sess'thra's cold breath on her skin.

"You are also important to me, sister."

Sess'thra raised her lithe body higher, their mouths almost touching, and without thinking, Desdemonia closed her eyes. Her lips parted, slightly quivering with uncertain excitement as her heart thumped in her chest, boom, boom, boom.

Her body trembled with giddy nervousness. It was the same when she first met Kasai in the meadow. The lost memory flashed before her eyes, but this one she caught before it was gone.

Kasai. Desdemonia gently pushed Sess'thra away. *Kasai.*

Sess'thra's eyes narrowed. She smirked, then quickly turned away. "Come on then. Let's find out what your obsession is doing. Mother's scrying chamber isn't far."

When Desdemonia and Sess'thra arrived at the scrying chamber, the door was shut tight. Desdemonia approached it with hesitation. She could feel her magic swelling within her as if she were preparing for a fight. Her eyes went wide when she heard the voices on the other side.

"She's already there! We must leave immediately." Desdemonia said in a dire whisper. She backpedaled from the door.

"Mother's inside? Who is she talking to? That's not Chedipe. Wait, Desdemonia. I want to hear."

"No, it's forbidden. We should've been more careful."

Sess'thra wore a crafty smile, and her eyes sparkled with mischief. "You worry too much about everything. No one will know we're here."

"We must go." Desdemonia tried to pull Sess'thra away from the door.

"Stop it. I want to listen." Sess'thra stood fast. The tip of her tail snapped back and forth.

"This is a bad idea," Desdemonia said. But she reluctantly joined Sess'thra at the door. Her curiosity getting the better of her caution.

When she reached the door, the voices had gone silent. Desdemonia feared the worst and wanted to run. Then a voice gurgled out words as if spoken through a mouthful of water.

"When will you have what I have demanded? The mind slave of Aetenos must be mine."

"Soon, very soon, Great One. There are other, more pressing considerations to address before this task can be fulfilled," Sekka said. Her voice was confident.

"What could be more important than what Azrollorza desires?"

Desdemonia gasped, then heard what appeared to be great waves of water splashing against the walls of the inner chamber.

"You speak boldly, but your hubris is misplaced. The favor of Azrollorza can be taken away just as easily as it was given."

"I meant no disrespect, Great One. There is the matter of Xerthotha which must be addressed."

"Ho, ho, ho. Is that pompous fool sulking now that his welp, Zizphander, has been cast to oblivion? I can still taste his sweet essence on my tongue."

"Your gift may not hold such a savory taste after I tell you my news. While we were occupied with the destruction of the Red Devil, Xerthotha took possession of the human, Shiverrig."

"Bah, what is that to me? The possession of a human is a trivial thing," Azrollorza countered.

"Xerthotha has outmaneuvered us. He controls Shiverrig like a puppet, and through him commands a great army in the Mortal Realm."

"Then prove your worth and take back what you've lost. Kill the mortal and be done with it. Command of his army will then be yours."

"You are not listening, Great One. Shiverrig's army is loyal only to Xerthotha. Killing the mortal will do no good. It will take years to rebuild the Frost Legion to a strong enough force to defeat such a foe."

"This is not my problem."

"Great One, I believe I understand Xerthotha's strategy. Shiverrig wars in Sunne in my name, but in secret, he searches the jungles for the boy monk. Xerthotha has commanded him to destroy the Ever Hero of Aetenos."

"What? What's this? You must prevent that at all costs! The Ancients have awoken from their ageless sleep with a hunger that drives them to the Mortal Realm. All will be lost if they arrive before me."

"Of course, Great One. You must protect your interests or hand them over uncontested to Xerthotha," Sekka said.

A gurgled moan resonated from the scrying chamber. It bubbled and popped as it grew louder. Then something heavy bounced off the inner side of the wooden door, and Desdemonia heard Mother groan in pain.

"You must claim the Ever Hero before Shiverrig finds him. If you fail, you will be destroyed. Am I understood?" Azrollorza gurgled.

"Yes, Great One," Sekka said softly. "And the troops to protect your new realm?"

"You shall have more than you need. Now rise, Sek'Kiyohime."

"You cannot know that name!" Sekka said, shocked.

Azrollorza's choked out a malicious chuckle. "I have told you, my sweet pet, the reach of Azrollorza is vast. Now go. Do as your queen commands."

"The Ever Hero will be yours. It's only a matter of time."

"Time is a luxury you no longer have."

Azrollorza's voice trailed off. The sound of splashing water echoed in the air, then it too faded.

"Sess'thra, we must go!" Desdemonia whispered.

Sess'thra nodded. "Come, this way."

The hall branched out three ways. Sess'thra took the left-most passage. They walked in silence for a time until Desdemonia heard Sess'thra mumbling to herself. "Indeed, Shiverrig is a sneaky one, isn't he, Mistress Sekka? My man is slippery as an eel."

"What's that?" Desdemonia said.

"Hmm? Oh, I just thought that Mother has more enemies than a mangy mutt has fleas," Sess'thra said.

"Shiverrig. You said Shiverrig, didn't you? I remember that name," Desdemonia said excitedly. "Does Mother mean Duke Shiverrig of Gethem?"

A crooked smile turned up the right corner of Sess'thra's mouth. "Yes, the same but no longer a duke. My lord Gerun Shiverrig has risen to the lofty status of Aj-Kahun. He now rules all of Baroqia and Trosk." Sess'thra added a light skip to her step, mimicking Desdemonia's earlier dance. "And Sunne will fall within the year."

A deep voice boomed out from the end of the corridor. "Stop!"

Desdemonia froze, but Sess'thra turned around casually as if she had expected to be found.

"What are you two doing here?"

Desdemonia recognized Aosoth's voice. The commander of Sekka's jol'goth guard approached quickly.

"My sister became lost, and Mother sent me to find her," Sess'thra said quickly. "What is it to you, jol'goth?"

"Your words reek of deceit. You are forbidden to be here."

"Don't presume to tell me where I can and cannot go," Sess'thra said.

A broad grin crossed the jol'goth's face. "Is today the day, little one? I have waited long for this moment." Aosoth grabbed Sess'thra roughly by the collar. "I heard you like it rough."

"Don't touch her!" Desdemonia shouted as her magic flared to life. A ball of blue fire punched Aosoth in the chest. He staggered back a step, releasing his hold on Sess'thra's soft, and now stretched, leather shirt.

"You ruined my favorite shirt!" Sess'thra said.

"It is time you two spoiled brats learned some respect."

He lunged at Sess'thra, but she ducked his blow quick as a cat. Desdemonia tossed a small ball of fire into his face, which glanced off the side, leaving raw marks of burned skin and singed hair. She then dashed to the side, avoiding his sweeping fist.

Laughing, Aosoth smothered the fire with his hand. "Do you think a little fairy fire can harm me?"

Then, Sess'thra was on his back and brought the tip of her dagger to his oversized throat.

"No, but it's a clever distraction. My dagger hasn't tasted jol'goth blood in some time, Aosoth. Now, there's plenty of poison coating this blade, so I'll give you just the tip."

Aosoth put his hands in the air in frustration. "Poison is a weak warrior's weapon."

"Run along now. Playtime is over," Sess'thra said.

"Mistress Sekka will hear about this. She does not like to be interrupted during her private moments," Aosoth said as he lumbered away.

Desdemonia's heart thumped in her chest. "What a big baby. But I swear, I was ready to destroy the brute."

"Aosoth is no worry. He's been confined to the tower for too long and needs something to kill."

"I know how he feels."

"Come on. Let's leave this dreary place."

Sess'thra locked her arm with Desdemonia's at the elbow and prattled on about many things as they walked together. Each subject tumbled into the next, but Desdemonia was too preoccupied to pay attention.

She meant what she had said about Aosoth. Her next blast would have gone straight through him. But more surprising than her desire to end the jol'goth's life was the realization that she had just heard Sekka's true name.

Funny, I didn't refer to her as Mother, she thought as she walked.

"Nor should you," the annoying voice in her head said.

79

KASAI

"The Hiraka tribe demands the first strike on the Chaos Warlord. We will accept no other honor," Aruka said. The warrior towered over Kasai like a dark mountain. He glared at Gift as he folded his lanky yet muscular arms across his chest. This was a challenge for her leadership.

Orin chuckled softly. "I wouldn't want to be the first meat for the grinder either." Pallo elbowed Orin in the side. "Be still."

Gift raised her chin and thrust her chest forward. "Nayche knows our truth. The Ever Hero of Aetenos came to the Frona tribe before all others. We are forever bonded as family and tribe. It is Master Kasai who commands us now. We can speak of glory and honor when the war is over, and the Kingdom of Sunne stands victorious."

Kasai was thankful for the trust Gift had in him, and with more suffering to come, he hoped his decisions would keep the sacrifices of the Sunnese to a minimum. Never in his wildest dreams did he imagine leading armies into battle, nor had he considered himself worthy of such a position. That was always a role for the Master Monks of legends. But he was the Master now, or so the people around him thought, and they were counting on him.

Just keep everything simple, he thought for the hundredth time, and then carefully laid out his plan of attack with Gift and Aruka.

"The completion of each stage of the attack is crucial to the next. If one link in the chain fails, the chain no longer serves its purpose," Kasai said. "The timing of the attack must be precise. Remain hidden until the enemy commits on the southern position. Advance only when you see the signal."

"We will have our revenge!" Aruka said, and he clenched his fists together. Kasai saw many of the Hiraka warriors do the same. He didn't blame them.

"Concentrate your fight on the Chaos Warlord," Kasai said to Aruka. "Get him isolated. That is your goal and greatest challenge."

Kasai knew it was a lot to ask of two separate tribes who had never battled side by side against a common enemy. He hoped they would follow his plan, and with any luck, they would catch the warlord unaware. The entire operation was a long shot. They all knew it, but it was the best option they had short of surrender and death.

They traveled in silence for the rest of the night. When they reached the ravine, the companies broke apart to go to their respective positions. Aruka was to take half of his warriors farther south and cross the dried riverbed undetected. They would trek back to the warlord's position while darkness still hid their movement.

Kasai prayed the prideful Aruka did not encounter the enemy's long-range sentries.

"Avoid them if you can, kill them if you must, but do not let them escape to sound the alarm," he said to the tall warrior.

"Do not worry, Ever Hero. None shall live to see the morning."

Gift took a small group of Frona warriors to where the ravine passage narrowed in the south. They were the bait to separate the enemy troops from their leader. Somehow, he knew she would survive the battle, though his mind questioned his optimism.

Kasai then took his company of Frona warriors north to where the ravine curled at a right angle. The land sloped upwards in a gentle rise, and from this vantage point, he could see the entirety of the Chaos Warlord's camp. Pallo and Orin were shadows at his sides.

He watched the bobbing torchlights of demon sentries patrolling the ridgeline. Luckily, or intentionally, the enemy coverage was light. Either way, he and his warriors were committed to the plan of attack. Now they would wait in hiding until the daylight evened the odds.

Kasai crouched within the thick brush that grew in broad swatches beneath the trees. His thighs ached from cramps from being in one position for too long. Broad leaves drooped from the surrounding tree's lower branches and provided another layer of camouflage. He imagined Aruka's warriors creeping closer to the ravine's edge like the shadow cats of the Sarribe Mountains. The time was drawing near to fight, and he hoped they had reached their appointed spots.

The combined numbers of the Frona and Hiraka tribes could never stand against the might of Sekka. The horrors of Gathos were countless. But it was a start. He could stall the war in Sunne if he could remove the Chaos Warlord. Hopefully, this would give him time to unite the remaining tribes, if that was possible. If not...well, he'd worry about the "if not" later.

It was already a hot day and threatened to get hotter. Sweat covered his body and dripped down his forehead, stinging his eyes. There was little wind, and the air surrounding the ravine sat stale with a repulsive smell. Kasai felt like it coated him in a filthy second skin. He gently pushed a broad leaf to the side and peered through the narrow opening, which gave him a clear view of the enemy and their movements.

A snarling, three-headed mastiff with bared teeth was easily visible on the still banners. Kasai counted approximately two full companies of demons. Some of them had wings. The foot soldiers were in heavy armor the color of soot, while the winged horrors sported rose-colored padded leather on their chests and thighs.

Then he saw Khalkoroth. His white fur stood out like a bright light against the dark armor of the other demons. Kasai's fire xindu flared red hot, and he felt the guilt of Master Choejor's death heavy on his conscience.

The killer of the Master dies today, Ninziz-zida whispered in Kasai's mind. He could almost taste the venom in her words. *When the moment to strike is revealed, you must not hold back.*

"Our target is the Chaos Warlord, Great Serpent. There will be another time to confront Khalkoroth," Kasai whispered. He also yearned for revenge, though he wished it were otherwise. "Daku, you stupid fool."

Your friend is gone. He cannot be saved. Let go or be shackled to his doom. The Boundless calls.

"I know. I know. When the time comes, I will put an end to that *thing*. But the Chaos Warlord must come first."

Kasai felt Ninziz-zida's fire xindu mix with his own. Her passion for battle was intoxicating. He fought hard to resist the urge to leap from his hiding place and race into the ravine to strike down the pale demon. But reason forced him to focus on the mission, and he slowed his breathing.

"Be calm, Ninziz-zida. Our time approaches, but not yet."

Kasai watched the enemy's movements. He then spotted the Chaos Warlord leaving his tent dressed in shining armor from the neck down and wearing deep purple and rose colors.

"He's human?" Kasai said, surprised. Somehow, he had assumed the leader of Sekka's forces would be another great demon lord like Oziax.

The Chaos Warlord is more than he seems. I sense a great evil in this place.

"There is no shortage of that these days," Kasai said.

His eyes scanned the ravine again and rested once more on the numerous wooden spikes pointing skyward. Orange vapors continued to rise from the thin, reddish muck at their base, which could only be the remains of the Parpurish tribe.

The warriors in his group repeated silent prayers to Nayche throughout the morning, and murmurs of revenge were whispered like growls of hidden animals around him.

The jungle canopy was dense, and everything around him was covered in shadow. He had sent three warriors to climb a nearby tree and relay the sun's position back to the group. When it was high in its apex, the attack would begin. Kasai waited for the signal and slightly shifted his weight to relieve some of the aching in his legs.

The hard clay and small river rocks were bleached bone-white, and deep cracks created a buckled patchwork along the parched ground. There was not a shadow in sight.

"Ever Hero, the enemy is separating. It begins," Orin whispered on Kasai's left.

"It won't be long now, Des," Kasai said. Somehow, her name just slipped out, and his stomach sank.

"Ever Hero?" Pallo whispered to his right.

"Nothing. Just be ready to move. It will happen soon."

Kasai watched most of the enemy forces move to the southern passage. He could hear their howls of bloodlust as they first marched and then ran to engage Gift's warriors.

"They've taken the bait," Orin said. "For once, being at your side, Ever Hero is not the worst place to be in the Three Kingdoms."

Approximately thirty of the winged horrors, plus what appeared to be an additional honor guard of twenty demons, remained behind, surrounding the Chaos

Warlord and standing at attention. Khalkoroth paced in a tight circle, just like Daku used to do before a sparring match.

Kasai said a silent prayer that the Hiraka warriors would remain hidden until the demons he assumed were hiding on the ridgeline grew restless. He gambled that their lack of discipline would cause them to join what they thought to be an easy slaughter at the southern passage.

Suddenly, a demon sentry came into full view in front of Kasai's hiding place. Then a second barked out a command and joined him. A few moments later, a third stood at their side. Kasai's heart pounded in his chest. This was bad.

The enemy will die quickly in my fire, Ninziz-zida hissed in Kasai's mind.

+*Calm your flame, Great Fire Serpent, for your fire would blaze too bright, and we would be discovered too early. We must choose a different way,*+ Kasai mentally responded back.

Pallo tapped on Kasai's right shoulder, then pointed to himself and Orin, and then to the three sentries. He slowly drew his short sword. Orin raised himself to a crouching position and nodded that he was ready.

Kasai trusted the stealth of the Kibo Gensai. They were trained to move in silence. But the crack of a hidden dry twig underfoot would alert the enemy to their present danger. Kasai held his companions back. *Think! For once, make a smart decision.*

The sounds of magical explosions bursting at the southern passage caught the sentries' attention. Green and gold feathered birds high in the branches above squawked in alarm and leaped into the air. Gift had attacked from the southern position.

Everything was happening now, and the timing of the attacks was crucial. Kasai's group had to move into position. He should be the one to remove the sentries while their backs were turned. Ninziz-zida would make short work of them now that he didn't need to worry about an alarm.

He started to rise when a slender reed eased through the jungle cover over Kasai's left shoulder. Kasai hadn't even heard the Frona warrior's movement from behind. The warrior blew three darts in rapid succession. The bright-feathered bits that guided the darts through the air were the only trace of their flight.

Seconds later, the demons dropped awkwardly to the ground. Kasai nodded his thanks over his shoulder, then looked back to the ridgeline to see a great commotion moving through the smaller trees. Branches jostled as if shaken by a great wind. Kasai heard the howls and shrieks of demons as they burst through the foliage and gathered momentarily at the ravine's edges before racing down the slopes.

Thankfully, the Hiraka remained in hiding. Kasai was impressed with the Sunnese warriors' discipline, and he was reminded of better times with his Brothers at Ordu. Sad memories flooded his thoughts, and as usual, they found their way back to his friend Daku. He watched the beast, Khalkoroth, prowl by his new master's side.

Is this who you were inside? How could I have been so blind? Kasai thought. *It was the same with Reese. If I had just listened to Des, none of this would have happened.* He knew he would need to face his old friend before this madness was over. *And I'll deal with that damn succubus, too.*

He looked back to the Chaos Warlord, who was now frantically pushing his hand forward in the air as if to say, stop! But the demons racing down the slopes ignored him.

Kasai heard the warriors around him grow restless.

"Hold position," he whispered.

Then the Chaos Warlord directed his winged demons into the sky. They leaped into the air and divided into two groups while airborne. One group flew east, and the other flew west. Kasai watched them go until the foliage blocked his view.

"That's it. Fly, fly, fly away," Kasai whispered.

Then, Kasai heard the high-pitched shriek of magic missiles being fired in the distance. Gift was following the battleplan and was harrying the enemy with a peppering barrage of fire. Just enough to keep them occupied but not directly engage them in combat. Not yet.

"Ok, let's move!" Kasai said.

His group emerged from the jungle and raced down the slope. The southern passage was lit with lines of streaking blue fire. Gift's warriors held the high positions on either side of the ridge, with a small group forming a wall at its base. Together they blasted the demons relentlessly.

The demons surged forward to attack Gift's warriors. But instead of fighting, they just ran past them and continued along the ravine. It made no sense. *Are they running away?* Kasai wondered.

"Now!" he yelled.

The warrior by his side shot a bolt of purple energy into the sky. It was the signal for the hidden Hiraka to attack. Within moments the ridgeline was filled with dark-skinned warriors, who pulled back on longbows and launched arrows tipped with brilliant blue fire at the demons surrounding the Chaos Warlord.

Other warriors gathered the jungle's life magic and hurled glowing balls of orange flame into the ravine base. The impacts of the fireballs were deafening. Boom! Boom! Boom!

Aruka and his Hiraka warriors wasted no time racing down the eastern and western slopes with curled blades held high above their heads. The chaos of battle filled the base of the ravine as steel clashed against steel.

A barrage of fireballs flew toward the Chaos Warlord and exploded into bits of harmless embers when they hit his body. Soon the shapes of friend and foe were distorted by fire and smoke, and Kasai momentarily lost sight of his target.

This entire attack would be in vain if the enemy leader managed to escape. Kasai heard shouts of triumph and horrible wails of pain as he ran into the heart of the battle. He squinted his eyes from the stinging smoke and brushed away dirty tears. There! The Chaos Warlord had lost his steed and now fought on foot.

Demons were falling to the Hiraka warriors' might and magic. Kasai held his breath and dared to believe his plan would work. Ninziz-zida's flame ignited along her three sections as he engaged the enemy. Pallo and Orin's blades flashed and slashed as they fought next to him.

Kasai dispatched his demon attacker, then watched in anguish as the Chaos Warlord cleaved mercilessly with his great black blade through every warrior he encountered. Off to the left, Khalkoroth moved like a white whirlwind through the Hiraka warriors. Their mundane weapons couldn't harm him, and his razor-sharp claws ripped mercilessly through the dark-skinned warriors.

"It's up to us, Ninziz-zida," Kasai said, and with a silent prayer, he sought the Boundless, but the path was congested with conflicting emotions. He tried again, this time with desperation, and the connection completely vanished.

Not now! Kasai thought. He couldn't hope to win against the Chaos Warlord if he couldn't join the ever-expanding space. +*The Boundless still rejects me. It knows I'm a fraud.*+

Not a fraud. The Boundless shares my faith in you, but you must surrender yourself to its embrace.

+*I'm trying!*+

You must be patient. Be less of Kasai and more of everything.

+*There's no time to be patient! I need the Boundless now.*+

Patience, Ninziz-zida whispered in his mind. *Let go.*

Kasai slowed his run as he approached the Chaos Warlord. A demon attacked from the right, but Pallo quickly intervened. Orin had his hands full with two others to the left. Ahead of him was a wall of fighting and in the center of it was Khalkoroth, or whatever the thing called itself now.

Kill that which killed the Master, Ninziz-zida's ancient voice whispered. She was eager for revenge. Kasai looked to the Chaos Warlord, then to the pale demon slashing his way through the helpless Hiraka.

The warlord was the priority, but Khalkoroth was the immediate threat. A memory of Master Choejor's kind smile flashed before his eyes, and he heard the old man's wise voice in his head. *Doing the right thing is not always the easiest to do, but that does not make it wrong.*

Kasai knew what he must do. He would destroy Khalkoroth today. Now.

Yessssssss, Ninziz-zida hissed in Kasai's mind. *Listen to the Master. The shadow demon will not escape us this time.*

Kasai set his sights on Khalkoroth, who had slowed to a stop. His white fur was now covered in dirt and Hiraka blood. It heaved with exertion as he looked for more warriors to kill. Then, the demon's massive, bear-shaped head swiveled toward Kasai, and a wicked smile of needle teeth widened across his face.

"I see you," Khalkoroth said and pointed a long, blood-stained finger at Kasai. The pale demon lumbered forward with his face scrunched in anger. "Face me, so-called Ever Hero, if you dare!"

Khalkoroth's voice struck Kasai in the chest like the rear kick from an angry mule. "That was Daku," Kasai said.

A trick, Ninziz-zida warned. *You must let go of the past.*

The Hiraka from the ridgeline had added their numbers to the ground attack. Kasai caught sight of the Chaos Warlord spinning fast and cutting down a warrior attacking from his backside. The dead Hiraka crumpled to the ground. Suddenly, the field of vision to the Chaos Warlord was clear.

"Look at his face. That's Duke Shiverrig of Gethem," Pallo said through huffs of hard breathing. He was somehow still at Kasai's side. "Much has changed since we have been gone."

"Has it?" Orin questioned, rejoining the two. "The high and mighty are never far from the dirty water circling the drain."

Kasai barely heard them. His mind was clouded with confusion. Could Daku still be fighting for his soul?

The time to strike the beast draws near.

"Right!" Kasai said and steeled his resolve. He knew he shouldn't hold on to hope that Daku could still be saved. But hope was there, nonetheless.

"Spread out," Kasai said to Pallo and Orin. "Leave Khalkoroth to me."

The Kibo Gensai fanned out to either side as Kasai whirled Ninziz-zida into a spiral eight pattern in front of his body. Khalkoroth loped forward with a devil's feral hunger.

Kasai heard a tremendous voice bellow across the battlefield. Khalkoroth stopped abruptly and snarled in frustration. Then reluctantly turned back to Shiverrig's position like an obedient dog.

"Another time, little brother!" he said over his shoulder.

Kasai watched as Shiverrig grabbed the bodies of two fallen Hiraka warriors, one in each hand, and lift the dead men over his head. Khalkoroth joined him and drew together what little shadow he could. But it was enough. A black mist rose quickly from the ground at their feet.

Kasai broke into a run. "No!" Kasai yelled. "Stop him!"

Pallo and Orin each threw one of their short swords at the pale demon. The blessed blades spun end over tip through the air and found their mark. Khalkoroth's otherworldly wail was a mixture of surprise and agony.

The hulking demon stared menacingly at Kasai as he pulled the blood-coated steel from his side and tossed blades to the ground in contempt. For a moment, Kasai thought he caught a resemblance of Daku as the bear-shaped face twisted away.

Just the smoke, he thought. *It's not Daku.*

Khalkoroth and the Chaos Warlord vanished in the dead Hiraka warriors' shadows, who then fell heavily to the ground.

The Chaos Warlord had escaped, and Kasai stuttered to a stop. It was over. And Daku... He looked about the ravine to assess the damage of his failed attack and saw the Hiraka had suffered heavy losses. Their bodies lay in a gruesome ring round where the Chaos Warlord once stood.

Kasai then scanned the ridgeline and spotted squadrons of aerial demons hovering in the distance. Orin saw them too. "What are they waiting for? Why don't they attack?" he said.

As if receiving a silent command, the winged demons abruptly flew north.

"They retreat," Orin said with relief. Then his face scrunched in pain as he held his hand over a wound at his side.

"They go to their leader," Kasai said.

"Shiverrig, or worse, the archdevil," Pallo added as he walked to Orin's side. "Let's have a look at that cut. You don't want infection setting in."

"I'm fine. I don't need you to baby me. Others had a worse time of it. Go mother them," Orin said gruffly, but let Pallo examine his side, nonetheless. The cut was deep and would require stitches and bandaging.

"The Hiraka are victorious!" Aruka ran toward them with his curved sword raised high. It wasn't long before Gift, and her warriors joined Kasai's small group.

"Gift, what news of the southern passage?" Kasai asked.

"Your suspicion was correct, Ever Hero. The enemy came at us in force once we exposed ourselves at the narrow passage. Then, more joined from the ridgeline, and their armor's silver and black became a river of steel.

"The warlord with cloud white hair gave a high-pitched command, and the demons charged. But instead of attacking, they raced through us. It was an odd thing. But who can understand the minds of such creatures? We destroyed those we could and sent scouts to follow the rest."

Gift looked expectantly at the others. "And the Chaos Warlord?"

"We failed. He escaped," Kasai said.

"Do not feel disheartened. This is a day of triumph," Aruka interjected. "The enemy fled in fear. We have proven we can defeat the great warlord and scatter his devil warriors like scared mice."

The nearby Hiraka warriors cheered and brandished their swords and spears. But Kasai didn't feel victorious.

"Aruka is right. The isolated tribes of the Sunnese are strong, but when united, we are invincible," Gift said.

"She's right. Hopefully, more tribes will follow after word of this victory spreads," Pallo said as he poured canteen water over Orin's wound to wash away the blood, then took out a small needle and thread from a belt pocket.

"Let's hope so," Orin said and winced as Pallo stitched his wound closed. "We'll not see such luck a second time."

"What now, Ever Hero? Do we give chase to the demons who escaped to the south?" Pallo said.

Kasai thought for a moment. "Send out the swiftest runners to the northern villages. Go in pairs, one warrior from the Frona tribe, one from the Hiraka. Let them see the unity of your people. Tell the war chiefs we fight as one to save all of Nayche's children."

He then turned to Gift. "Send a small group to follow the enemy. But they are to remain out of sight. Something doesn't add up. Their tactics reek more of betrayal rather than fear. I suspect the Chaos Warlord may have more enemies than just us."

"We could only be so lucky," Pallo said.

"The rest of us will go to the Sarribe Pass. The Chaos Warlord must regroup to gather his strength, and that is the most likely place to replenish his troops."

"We are going to need warmer clothing to pass over the mountains," Orin said. "And I doubt we will find a warm summer's sun awaiting us in Baroqia. Sekka will be there and in force. I suspect her reach has grown far while we have been away."

"No doubt," Kasai said. "She's waiting for me south of the Hoarfrost, and that's our eventual destination."

"Ever Hero, even with all the tribes united and fighting as one, it would be a fool's gambit to attack her at her base," Pallo said. "Remember the defeat of the King's Army. Another way must be found."

Kasai knew Pallo had it right. Sekka was the end game, but to force a battle against her with so few numbers was insanity.

"If we could somehow destroy the Chaos Gate first, that might help even the odds," Pallo said.

"I wish it were that easy. But who knows how to destroy such a thing? Plus, the Challenge of Righteousness demands I destroy her before the angels intervene. Only then will they come and clean up this mess."

"If they deem us worthy enough to help," Orin said. "I'm not sure they recognize friend from foe."

Kasai sadly agreed. *Angels, what a disappointment*, he thought, then looked to his companions. "We will draw the queen out of her hive. And this time, I'll be the bait."

80

SEKKA

"The mortal certainly knows the way to an infernal's black heart. I can now understand Sess'thra's obsession with the man," Sekka said as she gazed out over Shiverrig's military camp from an upper balcony of her tower. What was once a sprawling mass of lumber mills, forges, and butcheries a few short months ago had transformed into a stronghold city designed for one purpose: to make war.

Since Shiverrig's return from the jungle campaign, the city had bustled with increased industry. His mere presence was enough to inspire his army of half-breeds to new levels of production. He was still a thorn in her side, but she could appreciate the man's competence, especially when the fruits of his labors were more human souls.

"Winter's Fury seems like an apt name for my new city," she said with an air of satisfaction as she watched a company of half-breed demon troops in freshly minted armor marching over packed snow. The crunch of their footsteps was lost in the din of machines cranking through gears and hoisting large quantities of raw materials from one location to another.

Fires flickered atop furnace chimneys while the incessant clang of hammer and steel rang across the land. Winged half-breeds dove past her position, drilling through complex strafing maneuvers against moving ground targets.

Her tower was a pillar of malice with a permanent snow squall swirling like a mad tempest around its apex. Sheets of icy rain fell on the city below from turbulent thunderstorms churning in the sky. Flashes of jagged electricity lit her tower like a beacon across the flat landscape of the surrounding snow-covered plains.

"Just like home," she mused.

Sekka had a clear view of the city's layout from the upper reaches of the tower. Her eyes were better attuned in the icy sheen of winter's light, and she could pick out the tiniest of details from afar. She spotted a parade of priests approaching the southeastern gate. They were clad in blood-red cloaks.

One of the lead priests carried a banner that billowed in the sharp winds. An image of a chaos sphere fluttered at its center. The ball was impaled by nine arrows pointing in various directions over its surface.

"Ah, it seems the Disciples of Mor have arrived with a new crop of devotees. How excellent. More souls for the Orthod Pits."

An ornate litter carried by a dozen over-sized men came next. It jostled left and right as it followed the parade of priests through the gate. The litter bearers' shirtless bodies gleamed a metallic copper when the lightning flashed above as if their skin was covered in reptilian scales.

Surrounding the litter was an escort of Shiverrig men. Soldiers who wore the three-headed mastiff across their chest plate. Behind them, a trail of zealots followed in a line extending far into the distance. They march naked through the snow, oblivious to the cold, with wicked renditions of chaos spheres engraved in their chests and backs.

Sekka saw Shiverrig, accompanied by an escort of winged demons, halt the litter. Daku was at his side, sitting back on his haunches like a faithful hound. The litter bearers lowered the carriage and opened the ornate door for Eto Vyliche, the Reverend Grandmaster of Eternity of the Temple of Illumination at Gethem.

The two leaders exchanged more than just pleasantries. Though Sekka could not hear from this distance, she was sure she would not like what they said.

A war horn pealed. Sekka looked in the direction of the alarm. An aerial squadron of half-breeds circled over the southwestern gate. She squinted to get a better view. A ragged company of demons broke through the distant tree line and ran in retreat towards the city. Aeshmara was among them. Her numbers were few and scattered.

Pursuing them were more than a hundred Sunnese warriors, who raced out of the forest but skidded to a stop when they saw the city standing like a harbinger of doom in the middle of the plains.

"Another failure," Sekka sighed. She left the balcony with her pleasant mood turning sour with every step. She hailed an attendant outside her chamber. "Fetch Shiverrig, the high priest, that Vyzyn half-wit and her siblings, if they still exist, and bring them to the throne room."

Eto Vyliche sauntered into Sekka's throne room as if his counsel was the reason the dark powers had gathered. He moved with the swagger of authority and an arrogance of one who was meant to keep others waiting. Four tall and muscular, red-robed priests, all with heads hooded in cowls, were split to each side of the Grandmaster.

"It's an odd summer's wind that blows such a deep chill through the border villages and covers them in snow. Not particularly to my tastes," the Grandmaster said.

Sekka raised an eyebrow at the comment. She sat upon her ice throne, impatiently tapping her fingers on the armrest. Her pale skin shown in stark contrast to the black leather corset she wore, which flowed into a thin cotton gown, slit on one side to reveal the flesh of one long, white leg.

"Treacherous scum," Aeshmara said with disdain. "We don't need his kind here."

Shiverrig ignored Aeshmara's comment and took a step towards the Grandmaster. "May the Gethem sun still warm your bones, Old Father. How fairs the city of my ancestors?"

"Aj-Kahun Shiverrig," the Grandmaster gave a curt bow. "Gethem is braced for war, per your instructions."

He's oblivious to the imposter before him, Sekka thought.

Daku loped over to Vyliche. He growled at the Grandmaster's bodyguards before sniffing the Grandmaster's chest and face. *"Harrumph.* Reveal yourself, assassin. You may be able to hide from a mortal nose, but mine has the benefit of both worlds."

The Grandmaster shrugged his shoulders. "As you wish." His body shimmered and transformed into the shape of Daxzulz Thrum. *"Better?"*

Sekka noticed that Shiverrig was not surprised by the transformation, though he appeared disappointed. "I gave no orders for the removal of the real Grandmaster," he said.

"And alive, he remains. The rabble I picked up along the way required a figurehead of Mor to encourage them to leave the outskirts of Gethem. The Grandmaster seemed a fitting choice," Dax replied.

"Are you finished?" Sekka said, annoyed, all the while studying Dax's reaction to Shiverrig. She had yet to determine where the assassin's loyalties were fixed. Dax was smart and a survivor. He wouldn't over commit one way or the other. Not yet.

She then scanned the assembled warlords. Her eyes rested first on Aeshmara and then her sullen brother, Dai-Ko-Zior, who stood to the left of the throne. Shiverrig, Daku, and Dax were to the right, with Sess'thra and Desdemonia stood between them.

"I seem to be missing a beloved child. Where is Tazizu?"

"She either continues the fight in the jungles or has fallen," Shiverrig said. His matter-of-fact attitude of the obvious grated on Sekka's nerves.

"I'll wager she's dead. She was sloppy and unfit to lead the simplest of missions," Aeshmara said. There was no hiding her contempt for her sister. Aeshmara glared menacingly at Shiverrig. "Sloppiness is a weakness that must be weaned from command."

Sess'thra moved closer to Shiverrig's side, but still within striking range if Aeshmara did something stupid. Daku's hackles raised, and his lips curled.

Sekka gave a sideways glance to Desdemonia and wondered what the Wood Witch would do if Shiverrig and Aeshmara came to blows. Desdemonia remained still and said nothing, but Sekka could see she was observing everything. Her expression changed from attentive to reflective as if finally remembering a lost thought.

Then, just as Sekka's vision moved back to her warlords, she caught Desdemonia's eyes narrow, and her fists clenched.

"Desdemonia—" Sekka started but was interrupted by a harrowing wail that entered the room. The dark blue and purplish orb which permanently hovered over Sekka's throne pulsated rapidly.

Sekka stood from her throne and moved to the floor as eight slimy tentacles oozed from the orb. The tentacles were dark violet and covered with bright orange blotches. Each had rows of suction cups lining its underside.

The coiling limbs reached for open-air and somehow pulled the rest of its invertebrate body into the room, where it fell unceremoniously in a slimy heap of oozing flesh over Sekka's throne.

The thing took shape as a mutated octopus, and its tentacles quickly found purchase on the structure and clung to it for support.

"What wonderful timing. You must be here to deliver the troops I was promised, yes?" Sekka said. Now Shiverrig would get a taste of real power. Nothing could stand up to the combined might of Sekka and Azrollorza. Nothing. "Come now. Speak up."

"Azrollorza's attentions are required elsewhere." The creature's voice sounded like viscous bubbles slowly popping at the surface of a swamp.

It twisted to see the warlords below. "The legions of Xerthotha have been released. His armies march on all realms controlled by Azrollorza. The Chaos Devil claims a war debt must be paid for the unwarranted destruction of Zizphander."

Sekka stiffened and immediately assumed the worst. Xerthotha would march to Gathos first, and the Chaos Gate was unprotected. Her eyes darted right and left, but she maintained her composure. She didn't want Shiverrig or the others to know her homeworld was woefully unarmed.

"And what of Gathos?" she said casually.

"Azrollorza has cut off all access to Gathos. Your world of ice remains safe for now. Azrollorza honors her promise, albeit in her own fashion."

"The Great One reminds you, devil, to fulfill her demand. The Ever Hero must be hers." The slimy thing then melted into a gooey substance and drooled down the sides of the throne. The spark of life that had lit the creature went dim.

"And from oblivion, the Red Devil strikes one last time to even the score," Aeshmara said with a sarcastic chuckle as she side-stepped a growing puddle of the thing's gooey remains.

"You should be more mindful of the dirty words that dribble from your traitorous lips," Shiverrig snarled.

Aeshmara shrugged her shoulders. "If you cannot handle a few jungle-dwellers on your own, well then what is there to do? I can't hold your hand through every battle."

"You abandoned your superior commander! I will have your head on a spike for your insubordination." Shiverrig's hand was at the hilt of his sword. Sess'thra's tail twitched in anticipation of conflict.

Sekka moaned. Her plans of ascension continued to be waylaid by Xerthotha, and now this.

What have I done to deserve such attention from the Chaos Devil? Champions of the Great Three were slain as a matter of course in the Abyss. Yes, there were repercussions, but to declare total war on another Supreme Devil over the death of one such as Zizphander? Unheard of!

She needed quicker results and was tempted, not for the first time, to let Sess'thra bring the Ever Hero to her in a sack. She wondered how much of his essence's potency would be diminished if he came to her in shackles. Some rules could be bent, if not broken, but this was one she could not manipulate. The stakes were too high. The Ever Hero must come on his own accord.

And if the potency was less than needed, and Azrollorza couldn't make her own portal... wouldn't that solve another problem? Don't be a fool. You would be the first thing she destroyed, Sekka thought.

She sighed and assessed her warlords, knowing she would need to play this game carefully. Sess'thra was a fickle trollop, and for now, Shiverrig held her fancy. It had happened before; she was only a succubus after all. Daku had clearly sided with the man. She would break his will soon enough and let Khalkoroth run free. But not yet. When she had the Ever Hero in hand, their childhood friendship could prove to be useful tool for leverage. And Shiverrig was winning the war in Sunne, and that benefitted her.

Aeshmara would never lead the Frost Legion again. Her failures in Sunne would not be tolerated. But she was a thorn in Shiverrig's side, and that alone had its worth. Sekka assumed Tazizu was dead, not that it mattered. Tazizu was always a follower, never a leader.

Dai-Ko-Zior was a competent wielder of death magic and could lay waste to hundreds of the enemy with the wave of his hand. But the loss of soul energy from such irresponsible displays of power was disconcerting, especially now.

And apparently, the sorcerer knew something interesting about Shiverrig so-called destiny. In time she would squeeze that information out of him and see if she could use it against Xerthotha. Then she would rip the sorcerer's tongue out for not telling her sooner. *It'll be fun*, she mused.

The half-breed demon army was a powerful asset and represented the evolution of demonic armies. Each of Shiverrig's warriors was bonded by its creator's blood and possessed of a mortal's thinking mind. But this lot held no fear of her, or rather, they feared their master more.

Then there was Dax. He had yet to report to her anything meaningful of Shiverrig's assets in Gethem or give her an accurate account of its real strength. And now Azrollorza had abandoned her. *Must I do everything myself*, she thought?

"Enough!" Sekka shouted. "I didn't summon you here to listen to you bicker. Give me a report on the enemy position and numbers."

"My scouts count forty-five to fifty thousand Sunnese warriors traveling north over the Sarribe Pass. The numbers were difficult to count in the jungle. Somehow, they have miraculously banded together as a cohesive fighting force," Shiverrig said. "This is worrisome."

"Don't be such a little boy. The cattle have come to slaughter," Aeshmara said with overconfidence. "The Frost Legion will butcher them all within a day."

"No more than fifty thousand Sunnese? This rabble is all that has stood against the might of Gathos?" Sekka said. She was furious and pointed a long, tapered finger at Aeshmara. "You had four full legions of my finest soldiers, and you squandered them! Now, the Sunnese have united, and I have a handful of broken things as a result."

"Poor leadership brings death and defeat," Shiverrig said.

"For once, the annoying mortal is right. If you want to know why the Frost Legion failed, raise my dead brother Sitrix and talk to him. He's responsible for the loss of your soldiers, not me. I was busy harvesting souls throughout the border villages, as you commanded me to do."

"Your Ever Hero appears to be creating trouble," Shiverrig said to Sekka. "The boy should be removed."

"It will not be so easy as you say," Dai-Ko-Zior interjected. "The Ever Hero has walked between the realms of what is seen and unseen. He has harnessed the elemental powers of the beyond and commands the inferno of a great fire serpent."

"Are you telling me the Boundless is real?" Daku said.

Sekka rolled her eyes. "Yes, you fool. The Boundless, as you call it, is real. Now shut up," Sekka said and paced a few steps across the throne, minding not to step in the now fetid remains of Azrollorza's messenger.

"Kasai is with them. He's coming here?" Desdemonia said. Her voice was hesitant but eager.

Sekka placed a gentle hand on her cheek. "Yes, my dear. The Ever Hero has come to our home. I will need your help."

"Anything, Mother."

Daku eyed Desdemonia with suspicion. "Can she be trusted?"

Shiverrig gave a shrug of his broad shoulders. "What does one Wood Witch matter?"

Sekka turned to address her warlords. "As I have said before, the boy must reach me, unharmed. Is that understood?"

"If he does not come willingly, I shall lay his cold body at your feet," Aeshmara said. She took three bold steps forward.

"I said unharmed!" Sekka slapped Aeshmara hard, sending her to the floor. "Aj-Kahun Shiverrig, I will hear your thoughts."

"We have superior numbers, and they cannot hope to best us in a direct fight. We could empty the city and give chase, but they will scatter into the forest, and you will lose your precious Ever Hero again. The only way I see to bring him here is to entice him to come. Present an invitation he cannot refuse."

Sekka furrowed her eyebrows. "Desdemonia must remain with me."

"You misunderstand, my queen. I mean for the Ever Hero to come for you, not the witch. Undoubtedly, the monk knows he must defeat you to save the Three Kingdoms. He's not coming all this way for Aeshmara's head or mine, for that matter.

"The monk has shown some tactical skill, and he's intelligent. He won't waste time or resources laying siege to a city he cannot break. If you are not seen on the battlefield, he will return to the jungle and solidify his position. With the tribes united, the war against the Sunnese has become a completely different campaign and one that will take much more time to execute to its finality. He must not be allowed to escape back to Sunne."

"The Ever Hero has Shiverrig spooked," Aeshmara said from her knees. "He's unqualified to lead."

"When have I been wrong during this entire campaign?" Shiverrig said. Sekka thought he might kick her like a beaten dog, and she was tempted to do the same.

Shiverrig continued, "We will meet them in the field with a fraction of our strength. I have already marched the rest to the base of the Hoarfrost Mountains. Let them see you in plain sight with inadequate protection and give the Sunnese confidence to engage. They will think you are overconfident and vulnerable."

"And then?" Sekka asked.

"Allow the forward lines to collapse, creating an open corridor for the Ever Hero to reach you. Once he draws near, hidden reserves will attack from the sides. We will crush his followers and capture him."

"Your strategy promotes weakness. Have you learned nothing of demonkind? Your warriors will turn on you rather than knowingly allow the enemy to advance," Aeshmara said as she rose, rubbing her red cheek.

"My warriors will do as I command," Shiverrig said.

"My queen, this fool knows nothing. We finally have the enemy together. We must strike like a storm at sea and drown them without mercy. Allow me to lead, and I will leave nothing but death in my wake."

"I'm sure the queen is more interested in capturing soul-slaves than hearing your bold declaration of death and destruction. The time of chest-thumping is over," Shiverrig said.

"I demand trial by conflict and challenge this spineless coward for command of the legions," Aeshmara said.

Daku's hackles rose, and Sess'thra hissed. Shiverrig's hearty laugh echoed in the room.

"A coward with two hundred thousand strong awaiting his orders and never yours. What do you command again? That's right, nothing."

"Shiverrig, make ready for war. When the battle is over, I want your promised lines of prisoners marching to Gathos, and not fields of dead souls," Sekka said. She gave Shiverrig a rueful look. "Do not fail me."

Shiverrig nodded once and left the room. His reaction was stoic and reveled nothing of his intension. She expected as much. He was in control of his emotions, which was more than she could say for Aeshmara. The Vyzyn seethed where she stood, her eyes filled with hate.

Sekka doubted Aeshmara would live to see the end of this battle, which was fine by her.

81

KASAI

This is where it will all end, Kasai thought. He looked across the snow-covered field and the high stone walls surrounding Sekka's demon city. And rising from its center was a black tower. He was astounded at how much the landscape had changed in less than a year.

Chimney smoke pumped high in the air, mingling with dark clouds and falling snow. The sound of industry constantly banged in his ears, as did the screams of tortured innocents and the howls of their tormentors. He shook his head. This is all my fault.

Word of his victories against the enemy had spread like wildfire throughout the jungle. What started as a handful of warriors fighting by his side had grown into a small army. And more tribes arrived every day.

"It will be my greatest honor to die fighting by your side," each said as they pledged their sword, spear, and magic to him.

He scanned the walls again, looking for any weakness that might help him save lives in the coming battle, but all he saw was hard stone and cold death. A brisk wind swept up from the fields and into the tree line. As it billowed through his robes, he caught the scent of worn leathers and jasmine oil, the kind Desdemonia would dab into her hair to keep it in place. This suffering could have been avoided if I had just listened to her, he thought.

His heart sunk. She's somewhere behind those walls, wondering where I am and why I haven't rescued her yet. Maybe she thinks I've abandoned her.

He heard someone crunching through the ground snow over his shoulder and turned to see Pallo approaching. The cheeks of his weathered face were rosy and white breath clouded his face.

"Amazingly, Run-Run and the Miko have returned with the faithful," the older warrior said.

"That is amazing. How many have come?"

"Too few, though their numbers have been bolstered by bands of Kibo Gensai.

Run-Run managed to find a few forest clans that have rallied to the call of the Ever Hero. Hopefully, more will come."

"There won't be time. This will end rather quickly once it starts. I don't see a long siege in our future," Kasai said. "Where are they now?"

"They kept to the eastern woods, north of the road leading to the Last Garrison. Run-Run will use them to draw the southeastern flank of the enemy away from the central battlefield."

Pallo's eyes were drawn to Sekka's city as he spoke. "Impossible. A city of evil raised faster than a shadow cat disappears in the darkness of night."

"And we'll take it down just as fast," Kasai said.

"From your mouth to the Immortal Mother's ears, Ever Hero. I hope you have the same special connection to the goddess as you do with that staff."

"We'll find a way. Let's join the others and figure out what happens next."

They walked to a small clearing where Orin was already arguing with Aruka of the Hiraka tribe. His voice was near shouting when Kasai reached them.

"There's a lot of ground to cover even before we reach that gate, and recon has that wall built high around the entire city," Orin said. His face was red from shouting. "Scaling it isn't an option."

"Maybe not for one as small as you," Aruka leaned his lanky frame over Orin. "And not blessed with the magic hands of the Hiraka Tribe."

Orin shook his head in frustration. "They would surround us while we tried to get our numbers over the other side. It would be a massacre."

"Run-Run and the Miko have returned," Pallo said.

"I heard," Orin said, clearly unimpressed.

"They will give us time," Pallo added.

"Time for what? They are farmers, butchers, and blacksmiths from remote villages. Maybe we'll find a random noble house or two among that rabble that wasn't consumed by Shiverrig's coup for power. They have nothing left but the currency of their lives, and they will spend it cheaply this day."

"Do not lose the battle before the fight, Orin," Kasai said, clearly disappointed by Orin's summation, though, how often had he felt the same way?

Orin looked to the others and saw the same expression. He threw his hands up in frustration. "I'm only stating the obvious. We will lose too many warriors trying to win the gate. And none of us know what lies beyond those walls."

He looked in the direction of the open fields. "It's a numbers game, Pallo. And our numbers say we lose."

"Yet, we will never have a better opportunity to strike the heart of the beast. There are no more armies to collect nor time to do so. The Challenge of Righteousness has set a short time to complete this task. We must make do with what we have and bring the fight to her," Pallo said.

Gift stepped forward. "Never before has such a unity been created in the Kingdom of Sunne. The chieftains of the northern tribes have joined the call of the Ever Hero. This is an auspicious moment. We have pushed the enemy back to their lair. Now is the time to strike!"

"One warrior of the Hiraka tribe is worth ten of the enemy. The odds are in our favor," Aruka said boastfully.

His passion was fierce, and Kasai didn't doubt his courage. But to race headlong toward the gate was a suicide run. Orin was right. There was just too much open field between the trees and the walls of the city.

"I believe the enemy has lured us here, to this place, and time. Our scouts have said their numbers stretch beyond sight. Look through the trees and tell me what you see? Where are the hundreds of thousands of demons gathered in the fields before the walls? And where are the demons flying overhead to assess our strength of numbers and weapons of war? They know we are here yet have barely prepared for battle."

"Nayche has gifted us with stealth and surprise," Aruka said.

"They show us just enough to whet our appetites and give us hope," Orin said and looked deeply into Kasai's eyes. "There *must* be another way."

"Have faith, Orin. The Ever Hero walks with you," Pallo said. His stoic resolve would not waver.

"Faith is not enough!" Orin said, exasperated.

"If you have no hunger for battle, then I suggest you find something else to do. There is no room for those with weak hearts in this war council," Aruka said.

"How dare you!" Orin bristled. "You know nothing of me."

Aruka towered over the shorter man, but Kasai knew Orin to fight like a cornered badger when he felt he was right, which was always. He was the same way with Desdemonia.

"Settle down, both of you," Kasai said. He was in no mood to break up another fight between "friends" in the company of allies.

"Orin, we won't need to enter the city. Sekka wants me here and will meet me in the open field. She needs me for something and will not want to see me harmed. I'd wager I could walk to the gate myself and be greeted with open arms."

"Surrender is not an option, Ever Hero," Pallo said. "We have gone over this often enough. If Sekka needs you for one of her sinister schemes, we must take that option away. You're too valuable."

"I only need to reach her."

"You're not listening to me! You cannot throw your life away based on the lies of a succubus. This is a trap!"

"I know it is Pallo. But maybe if I get close enough, I can at least free Des."

"She's gone!" Pallo stared at him in disbelief. Then his eyes softened. "Ever Hero, I know you are in pain, but you must let her go. If she's still alive, then Sekka has turned her into an agent of evil. You must let her memory be at rest in your heart."

"I can't," Kasai said and lowered his head. "I won't."

"If the devil falls, the rest will follow. It's the way of demonkind," Gift said after a long moment of silence. "When she takes the field, we will take her head."

Aruka nodded fiercely. "The Hiraka will shield you from her horde." He pounded his chest. "We pledge our blood and magic to the Ever Hero."

"Witches and devils," Orin said and spit in the snow. "This is a folly. The northern flank will collapse on us as we move towards the center. No speed will be fast enough to get to Sekka before they engage us," Orin said.

"Then we must do what we can to keep that flank occupied," Pallo said. "Run-Run will engage the southern flank and bleed their strength."

"It's a small window, but maybe enough for one lethal strike," Kasai said. "And we'll only get one chance. So, we must make the best of it."

Sekka had been over his shoulder like a bad dream for as long as he could remember. He wished he had a brilliant solution to destroy the archdevil, and one that would save the lives of the warriors at his side. But he had nothing more than to get in close and strike hard and fast.

"Ever Hero, you must decide," Pallo urged.

Kasai wondered what Aetenos would do if he were here now. *Probably say something ridiculous, slap me on the shoulder, and say, "Have fun. Let me know how it turns out."*

"Sekka is beyond all of you, and probably me as well. But if I can get through her guard, then Ninziz-zida and I may have a chance, slim as it is, to destroy her."

"My warriors will draw away her guard," Aruka said with confidence.

"The northern flank must be prevented from attacking our exposed side," Orin reminded everyone.

"Orin's right. We must find a way to get close enough to those gates without losing our warriors across the field," Kasai said. "We need a diversion."

"The Frona Tribe have ways of remaining hidden," Gift said. "We will strike the unsuspecting quail like the invisible forest hawk. The way will be clear."

She related her plan to the others. All eyes looked to Kasai as a war horn blared in the far distance.

"Run-Run's position has been exposed. It's now or never," Pallo said.

The group of warriors ran to the edge of the forest. There was movement to the south as the enemy turned to engage an unseen foe.

Kasai looked back to the city. More movement. The troops guarding the gate parted, allowing a group of hulking jol'goths to move past the front ranks. He saw the glint of armor in the distance catch the cold sunlight.

"She's here."

He took hold of Gift's arm. "Everything depends on you. May Nayche protect us."

82

SHIVERRIG

Shiverrig's chaos steed trotted to a sloping knoll outside the walls of Winter's Fury. The natural incline gave him an unobstructed view of the intended battlefield as cold winds rippled along the black bear fur covering the shoulders of his long cloak. He sat stoically in the saddle, pondering troop movements.

He could see clearly across the plains and picked out the markings of different warrior groups flirting with taking on his army themselves as they dashed in and out of the tree line. His sight enhancement was a fortunate bonus from his agreement with Xerthotha.

"At least there's that," he grumbled and craned his neck to look back at Sekka's tower, "One devil at a time."

There were more of the jungle-dwellers than he had initially anticipated, but the numbers that had come against him were an annoyance at best. He lamented committing most of his troops to the foothills of the Hoarfrost Mountains. He could have destroyed the Sunne in one fell swoop, then marched into the jungles for a more formal conquest.

"But she needs the boy alive. So, we play the loyal bastard until the time is right to end this charade. Still, I should have kept more in reserves."

He removed the heavy leather glove from his right hand to wipe the perspiration from his brow and noticed it trembling as if he were a sick and feeble old man. A flash sweat covered his body, leaving his skin feeling clammy and wet under his clothing and armor.

His lower back muscles groaned with a deep fever ache, and he shifted in his saddle to find a more comfortable position. A queer sensation crept up his spine, then searing pain lit into his head. A whispering voice came into his thoughts and grew into a roar.

+TIME MOVES QUICKLY, MY GOLDEN CHILD.+ Xerthotha's mind voice expanded as it entered his consciousness.

Shiverrig brought his opposite hand to his forehead. He massaged his temples with his thumb and index finger, but the pain would not abate, so he squeezed harder. If he was going to be in pain, he would control it.

He sensed Dai-Ko-Zior drawing near, huddled in the saddle of his own chaos steed. It would be unfortunate for the sorcerer to see him in a weakened condition. Luckily, the sorcerer's face remained hidden and unmoving under his cowl. Shiverrig assumed he was communing with whatever specters haunted his delusional thoughts.

+MUCH HAPPENS UNDER THE SURFACE OF YOUR WORLD. WAR HAS COME TO THE ABYSS.+

"So, I've heard. Go on then, enjoy your war and leave me to mine. Win or lose, the outcome of your fate is not my concern."

+OH, BUT OUR FATES ARE INTERTWINED. SOON YOUR GREATER PURPOSE WILL BE REVEALED. ALL HAS BEEN MADE READY FOR YOUR ASCENSION.+

"Get out of my head!" Shiverrig said a bit too loudly. Still, Dai-Ko-Zior showed no interest in his one-sided conversation.

+SEKKA SEEKS THE ONE CALLED EVER HERO. YOU MUST FIND HIM FIRST. KEEP THE MONK SAFE. I REQUIRE HIM FOR SOMETHING SPECIAL.+

"And why should I help you? You are a fickle patron at best and make your deals when I have no other recourse but to accept."

+A FRIEND OWES A FRIEND A FAVOR. NOW IS MY TIME TO COLLECT.+

"He's nothing but a boy."

+ALL THE MORE REASON YOU MUST KEEP HIM SAFE FOR ME. DO THIS, AND THE MORTAL REALM SHALL BE YOURS.+

Xerthotha's voice drifted away, and the haze swirling through his mind cleared. Shiverrig leaned heavily on the pommel of his saddle as his gut churned with nausea. He puked over the side of his chaos steed, then wiped his mouth clean of chunky spittle.

"I will not be your pawn."

Aeshmara approached, riding on the back of her chaos steed. The beast was long and streamlined and moved like a jungle cat. Her short-cropped hair fluttered in the wind like thin fingers tapping across her face. A company of elite foot soldiers trailed behind her.

Frost Legion, Shiverrig thought with disdain.

She stopped at his side and nodded for her warriors to continue to their predetermined destination.

"Can't hold your mud before a real battle?" she said with a smirk.

"Aeshmara," Shiverrig said with scarce enthusiasm.

A sliver of darkness expanded between them, and Daku stepped into the cold light. He rose on his back legs to his full height, imposing himself between Shiverrig and the Vyzyn warlord.

"Move along, traitor," Daku said.

Aeshmara scowled at the pale demon. "Muzzle your pet, Shiverrig. I do not take kindly to mongrel dogs."

"I'm not overly concerned with what you want or not," Shiverrig said. "Do you have something of value to report?"

"Have you heard the news from Furia Keep? Maugris is dead," she said.

"Maugris died in his fortress months ago. You're needed elsewhere," he said and waved her away. "See if you can follow orders for once."

Aeshmara laughed. "Not just a fool, but a blind one as well. The sorcerer has been in Sekka's keeping since the birth of the Chaos Gate. Apparently, the crone, Chedipe, pried some rather interesting information out of his worthless brain before she was done."

Shiverrig saw she was looking for a reaction. He gave her none, "Is that it?"

"That is enough for now. Your shaggy dog will not always be at your side in times of need. When he is not, I will be there."

Daku growled and slid Eishorror from its sheath; ice crystals leaked from its edges. Aeshmara eyed the wicked blade and sucked at her teeth in distaste. Her stormy eyes slowly moved back to Shiverrig, and a wry smile crossed her face.

"Come with me, Brother. The fighting will be more exciting at the northern flank."

Dai-Ko-Zior brooded in silence beneath his hood.

"Suit yourself. The glory of this battle will be mine when this day is done." Aeshmara kicked her mount, and the beast lurched away. Daku followed behind at a slow chase.

Shiverrig's eyes narrowed as he watched her leave. Maugris's death concerned him greatly. This *was* news to him.

Did you throw one last boastful barb at the devil before she ended you? Sekka must know of my alliance with Xerthotha. My army of half-breeds is proof enough. Damn you, Maugris! In life and in death, damn you.

But why would Sekka reveal such coveted information to the Vyzyn? She would know Aeshmara would not hesitate to flaunt such knowledge in front of me. She must have heard it from another source.

Shiverrig realized the timetable to overthrow Sekka had become dangerously short.

"My sister doesn't like you," Dai-Ko-Zior said.

Shiverrig had almost forgotten the sorcerer was still there.

"Hmm. No, I think not."

His mind still wrestled with the death of Maugris. *What is Sekka waiting for,* he wondered? *Why not send the assassin in the night? Or maybe she's just lying to get under my skin before battle. Unnerve me, so I make a mistake.*

A squad of half-breeds jogged past him. They were his troops, citizens of Qaqal, warped through the chaos change. He wondered not for the first time how the self-proclaimed Protector of the Realm had aligned himself with such allies.

"I am honor-bound to this land. I will do what I must to safeguard the survival of its people." The oath sounded hollow when he spoke it aloud.

Dai-Ko-Zior's forced a dry chuckle through his wheezing breath. The sorcerer's back was bent and hunched over the pommel of his saddle. His face remained hidden beneath the hood of his cowl. "So says all who taste power and find it to their liking."

"Something to say, sorcerer?"

Dai-Ko-Zior prodded his chaos steed closer to Shiverrig's mount. "Your proud boast of loyalty to the land of your forefathers is misplaced and meaningless. Your destiny follows a different path. This has been preordained."

Shiverrig rolled his eyes. "I don't believe in cryptic prophecies or obscure destinies determined for me by soothsayers and mystics. I was born to rule this land. And rule it, I shall."

"I do not think the Frost Queen would like to hear such words coming from her

First General. Those who mistakenly challenged her reign have been punished by death."

Shiverrig could almost feel the sly smile crossing Dai-Ko-Zior's thin lips.

"Sekka doesn't frighten me. One only needs to look deeply into her soulless eyes to see she fears me. She knows I will not allow her invasion of my kingdom to go unchecked for much longer.

"The troops she needed from Azrollorza are not coming. The Frost Legion has been decimated in the jungles of Sunne, and there are no more she can spare from Gathos, or they would already be here. She hides in her tower, pretending to rule a kingdom she has yet to claim. Sekka is weak and afraid."

"Are you so sure of your assessments of the Frost Queen? She has survived for thousands of years in a realm filled with hostility and treachery, the likes of which you cannot fathom. All the while proving herself a worthy champion of chaos. Many have thought to destroy her and take what she has earned through conquest, only to have their hopes and dreams dashed upon the cold ground of defeat. She has my respect, if not my loyalty."

"It was easy enough to outmaneuver her once I had the manpower."

"You think you outmaneuvered her?" His laugher was higher this time and sounded girlish. "You are moved by the Chaos Devil, who is, in turn, being moved by my masters."

"The Chaos Devil?" Shiverrig laughed. "Again, you claim knowledge of me with no evidence to—"

"I have known everything about you from the moment you became the chosen of Xerthotha. Ho, you are a blind man walking, indeed, Gerun Shiverrig. I have often wondered what the Higher Powers see in you. But such wisdom is not mine to know."

Shiverrig grunted. He recalled his first meeting with the Dai-Ko-Zior at Aeshmara's camp along the Sarribe Pass. The sorcerer had said it clearly enough then, too. At this point, what did he have to lose?

"Circumstances revealed unlikely partnerships which worked to my advantage."

"Your secret, as obvious as it is to me, remains safe. Though Maugris may not have been as discreet," Dai-Ko-Zior wheezed through another small laugh.

Shiverrig had his doubts about the integrity of both mages. He was never comfortable with magic or those who wielded it. The craft was dishonest. Give him a sword and shield, and he would reveal the truth in a man.

"Sekka's end draws near. All her maneuvering and scheming comes down to one small thing: a young monk with an over-inflated title. Remove him, and the balance of power shifts drastically out of her favor."

Dai-Ko-Zior nodded under his hood. "Sekka's destiny begins and ends with the Ever Hero. She used him to open the Chaos Gate, and because of him, she will lose everything. Two of the three Supreme Devils race toward Gathos. Each means to claim the entrance to the portal for their own. The Abyss has not known such conflict in eons. But their wars are pointless. The same is true of this war, for my masters have already arrived."

"Whatever you say, sorcerer."

"The coming of an Ever Hero has always been the harbinger of great change across the Three Realms. He is a catalyst for growth and destruction. He is an anomaly whose influence shapes not only the Mortal Realm but also the Abyss and Seven Heavens.

"This time, he will be the spark by which this world will be destroyed. All has been foretold."

Warning horns blared along the walls guarding the city. Dai-Ko-Zior's chaos steed shifted its weight, and its cloven hooves clicked on the frozen ground. Daku loped back to Shiverrig's side. His face bore an eager, childlike expression.

"She ran like a scared rabbit," he said.

Shiverrig gave a short nod but sat in silence. He mindlessly watched troops hurry into battle formations. The enemy had revealed themselves in greater numbers against the tree line.

Aeshmara was indeed quick to her northern position. Her chaos steed raced along the front line of her warriors, most likely screaming out blood oaths of revenge against the jungle-dwellers. For all her arrogance and complaining, he admired her as a warrior. She was fearless. Nonetheless, his sword would take her head before the day was done.

He swiveled in his saddle toward Sekka's tower. A new peel of horns signaled that the devil had left her lair. From his elevated position, he spotted the city gates opening. Sekka had chosen to remain in her human form, wearing sapphire-colored leathers with a silver breastplate encasing her torso.

The sheen of her armor's surface caught the cold winter's light and flashed as she moved through the gate entrance. Her alabaster hair whipped in the air, mirroring the blizzard of snow that circled the upper reaches of her tower.

She was surrounded by jol'goths with Sess'thra and the Wood Witch walking at her sides. That was to be expected. He considered those two women more potent than Sekka's entire guard.

He was suddenly struck by the ridiculousness of this engagement. All these warriors surrounding Winter's Fury acting as her shield wall, and for what? *She could rip through the enemy army without assistance or worry of harm.*

Shiverrig surveyed the open field beyond the outer wall of the city again. The Sunnese remained spread out along the forest's edge, and he noticed they wore proper clothing against the cold. Someone on the other side had some foresight or simply good reconnaissance.

He looked back at Sekka's progress. She had passed the agreed-upon position she was meant to hold and went straight to the open field.

"Where is she going?" Daku said.

"Blast! Will not one of these infernal creatures follow my orders?" Shiverrig said.

The Sunnese forces swelled forward then receded back into the forests, reminding Shiverrig of ocean waves rolling in on the morning tide. It was difficult to judge their strength of numbers, for each time they returned to sight, they presented a greater or lesser array of warriors.

"Jungle magic." Shiverrig rubbed his eyes and grunted.

"It will begin soon," Dai-Ko-Zior said.

Daku's purple lips dripped with saliva. "It's about time."

"It's a shame Tazizu isn't here to enjoy the battle," Shiverrig said. His manner was casual though he knew there wasn't any real familial bond between the Vyzyn brood.

"My sister's magic was misguided. It was her fate to fail in this realm. She mistakenly devoted herself to those who would never answer her call when her need was greatest."

"I see her loss affects you deeply," Shiverrig said with a chuckle.

"I care nothing for Tazizu," Dai-Ko-Zior said and waved his bony hand across the battlefield. "Nor any of this. You are all beneath my contempt. Sekka and her ambitions are insignificant before the might of my masters. I am here to render a service and gain favor by ensuring you live through this time. You are a means to an end for me, nothing more."

"No doubt," Shiverrig said. His eyes were on the outer edge of the forest. The Sunnese were there, and their numbers had grown again. The boy monk walked just outside the line of trees and into the field. He was soon joined by three other warriors.

"The Ever Hero has arrived," Shiverrig said. He watched the expression on Daku's bestial face darken.

"Bah, don't call him that," Daku said. The pale demon pointed a sharp-clawed finger at his long-ago friend. "It's only Kasai. He's no champion. I've bested him countless times at Ordu."

"Sekka wants him alive for reasons I cannot fathom. As does Azrollorza and the Chaos Devil. But I see no reason to advance any of their schemes. Kill him," Shiverrig said and glanced at Dai-Ko-Zior. The sorcerer didn't seem concerned either way at the fate of the Ever Hero.

"With pleasure." Daku raced off without looking back.

Even with the majority of Shiverrig's troops withdrawn to the base of the Hoarfrost Mountains, his army still outnumbered the jungle-dwellers three to one. And he held the defensible position. He reconsidered his earlier lament of sending so many troops to the mountain. Now he felt he should have removed more.

"What hope do they have? What could they possibly be thinking?"

Shiverrig heard the peel of a familiar war horn sounding from the rear of his command. His troops stirred as a second force came out of the western forest.

Ragtag knights wearing the weathered and torn colors of King Conrad's army burst through the trees on horseback. Somehow, they had survived the massacre of the Battle at the Last Garrison and regrouped. Running behind the knights were leather-clad foot soldiers. A scattering of orange and brown-robed monks added to their numbers.

"Conrad's remaining rabble," Shiverrig grumbled as his half-breeds turned to face the new foe.

"Let them go alone. It's time we pass into the mist of this realm."

The hairs on the back of Shiverrig's neck rose like the hackles of a wild dog.

"Your riddled words give me little comfort, sorcerer." He instinctively gripped the hilt of his sword. "Be straight. Are you the assassin Sekka has sent?"

The cowl covering Dai-Ko-Zior's head swiveled towards Shiverrig. "Soon, this battlefield will be covered in the ash of the fallen. And it is not your destiny to be counted among those numbers. At least, not today."

"You cannot know such things. The jungle-dwellers have no hope of victory. This day will see the collapse of Sunne and the end of that monk. With any luck, your miserable sister dies today as well."

"Their fates, like yours, have already been written. Now come."

"Do you expect me to leave my soldiers and abandon Winter's Fury to Sekka's rule?"

"If the city you have infested with your half-breeds still stands when we return, then we shall make use of it."

Shiverrig laughed. "I imagine that goes for Gethem and Qaqal as well?"

"These places you hold dear are irrelevant through time. The arrival of my masters will change this world forever. You, Gerun Shiverrig, will usher the survivors into a new age."

"What of Daku? Was it not his destiny to survive as well?" Shiverrig said, challenging the sorcerer's foresight.

"Whether it was Khalkoroth or Daku in possession of that demon's form, his path was less important. Someone or some*thing* was needed to keep you safe until the appointed hour, and now he has served his purpose. That is enough."

"I'm unconvinced. I have forged my own destiny from the beginning and have no need of your prophetic gibberish. Go if you must. I care not. But I will remain with my men."

"When you are blinded by a light greater than the sun, you will see the error in your decision. Until that time, I am needed elsewhere." Dai-Ko-Zior pulled the reins of his chaos steed and trotted in the opposite direction. His image blurred and then vanished behind a flurry of snow.

"I hate sorcerers," Shiverrig said. Then bellowed out, "On me. Keep the line tight and slow." He'd finish the legacy of King Conrad himself. And then, turn his attention to Sekka. He glanced back in her direction and saw a third army materialize midfield, racing toward her. They had been hidden with Sunnese magic, and the warriors at the tree line were just a distraction.

"Clever boy. Now it becomes interesting."

He looked to see what Aeshmara's reaction would be, and predictably, she drove her host into the lines of the newly arrived warriors. Shiverrig shook his head. "Fool. Her bloodlust knows no end. She strengthens the center."

"Dammit! Daku, be quick about it," Shiverrig called out, but the pale demon was already gone.

83

KASAI

Gift's surprise attack had done its part, and her warriors engaged the northern flank of the enemy before they could stop Kasai and the remaining Sunnese from rushing past.

"Keep running! There's no time stop!" Kasai shouted. They all knew their window of opportunity was closing fast.

He silently thanked her and her warriors for their sacrifice. Once Gift's clandestine offensive was revealed, the northern flank drove hard into them. The clash of battle was fierce with deafening screams of madness and mayhem. Moments later, the demons before the walls surged forward in a massive sea of cold flesh, horns, and whip-like tails.

Ninziz-zida blazed to life, and then the demon horde was upon them. It happened faster than Kasai could have anticipated. He lost sight of Pallo and Orin within the first few moments of fighting. No doubt, his twin shadows were nearby but staying outside the range of Ninziz-zida's burning segments.

The enemy was everywhere. Like moths drawn to a bright flame, they came at Kasai from all sides. He stood alone, surrounded by horrors. The shouts of the injured and screams of the dying filled his ears. A death stench rose from the ground as warriors fell bloody into the snow.

Ninziz-zida hissed with each strike, exploding demons into thick, black ash. But where one dissolved, three more advanced. Aerial demons swarmed overhead. They reached for him with gnarled fingers or snapped at him with oversized claws.

Ninziz-zida flew up to shatter a swooshing arrow before Kasai knew the danger was upon him. He moved with the intimacy of the wooden arrow's shards and twisted away from the flying debris, but not before the broken shaft nicked his cheek. His assessment of Sekka's intention for him was wrong. She never wanted him alive. Dead would be just as fine. The demons pressed in closer and tried to rip him apart.

Kasai clenched his jaw. *I'm done with this.*

He felt his fire xindu bloom in his spirit. But rather than letting his emotional anger shoot like a geyser, Kasai focused the energy into determination and channeled his fire xindu into his hand, then dropped to one knee and slapped his open palm to the ground.

"Get back!" he shouted. A fiery dome of raw energy expanded around him. The snow trapped within evaporated, leaving behind a swatch of black and smoldering grass.

Kasai's blast immolated the pressing demons as the expanding edge of the dome past through them. Lightheaded, he drew a deep breath to steady himself and stood slowly. The energy strike was short-lived but had served its purpose. He stood alone at the center of a blackened circle.

"Nice trick, little brother."

As the swirling ash of demon death cleared, Kasai saw Khalkoroth standing at the edge of the charred grass.

"Did Master Choejor teach you that one while I was away?" Khalkoroth said in the voice of Daku. "The Masters always kept the best things from me."

"That hook has lost its worm, demon. My Brother, Daku, is dead," Kasai said and felt the reassuring presence of Ninziz-zida pulsing in his hands. Her blue fire rippled along each of her segments.

"Much has changed since Ordu. I have finally found myself. The beast Khalkoroth is gone. Only I remain," Daku said.

Kasai could now see more of the demon's face. Daku's image shifted under the bearlike muzzle and fur. *It's just another trick*, Kasai thought.

"Let me help you. I can save you," Kasai said. The words just slipped out.

Daku laughed and slid Eishorror from its scabbard in response, then swung it in a chopping X motion at Kasai. He shook his bear-shaped head. "You know, everywhere I go, they call you Ever Hero. But we both know that's not true."

"Daku, wait."

Daku spat a wad of phlegm on the ground. "Even now, with the Fire Serpent in your hands, you're still afraid. That's always been your problem, Kasai. And that's why I always won. Just like I will today."

Daku came at him with the force of a charging bull. He hacked down repeatedly with Eishorror, but his strikes lacked finesse, and Ninziz-zida easily deflected each blow.

The pale demon jumped backward and held the fell blade out wide in his hand. In a flash, he swept it down and low, seeking Kasai's midsection. Ninziz-zida quickly blocked the strike, but then with surprising agility, Daku whipped his body around and sent a kick slamming into Kasai's side.

Kasai's eyes bulged from the pain of the impact. He was sure a rib or two had fractured.

"See? Nothing has changed since Ordu. You're still an easy target," Daku taunted.

Kasai dropped into a flexible defensive posture. Ninziz-zida hissed her frustration in his mind.

Strike!

"Patience, Great Serpent. He's overconfident and will make him make," Kasai said. "He always does."

"This time, you die!" Daku roared and lunged forward.

But Kasai was ready. He shot Ninziz-zida's end segment out like the butt end of a spear and connected with a crack over Daku's brow, leaving a bloody gash. The pale demon regained his senses quickly as Ninziz-zida's blue fire rippled over his head, leaving raw blisters in its wake.

Daku roared and pressed forward, swinging Eishorror in a berserker's fury. Kasai shuffled backward, avoiding the blade's reach. He compressed Ninziz-zida together, tucking her in a coiled snake hold under his arm. Each time Daku advanced, Kasai snapped Ninziz-zida out at him, effectively keeping the demon at a distance.

Daku paused. His chest heaved as he wiped the blood flowing from his brow. "You're nothing without that staff," he said with a sneer.

"You're probably right. But I'm still faster than you," Kasai said, and for a moment, the lighthearted jab made Kasai think of other times and the banter he and Daku had shared while sparring at Ordu.

"Put it down and let's see who you really are," Daku said.

Maybe it was due to nerves, but Kasai couldn't help but laugh at the outrageous statement. "You're kidding, right?"

Daku growled in frustration and lunged with the point of Eishorror aimed at Kasai's chest but leaving Daku open to an easy counterstrike.

Strike! Ninziz-zida hissed in his mind.

But Kasai held back. His emotions were jumbled and confused. *There must be a way to save him*, Kasai thought. *I can't lose everyone.*

"Ha! You're still weak! Just like during the competitions at Ordu. You never had the guts to do what was necessary to win," Daku said and attacked Kasai repeatedly. "Weak! Weak! Weak!" The fell blade came at him fast and from different angles, but Ninziz-zida anticipated every strike and deflected them to the side.

Kasai could feel her wrath increasing as the blue flame that burned on her segments rose into the air. He knew she wanted to hurt this thing that had taken the life of Master Choejor.

Daku pressed forward, backing Kasai out of the blackened circle where he tripped over the body of a dead warrior. Kasai gasped as Daku raised Eishorror over his head and smirked.

"Time to die, Kasai."

Before the blade fell, Daku's eyes grew wide in shock, then he howled in pain. Pallo came from around the demon's backside, stabbing his two short swords repeatedly into the beast's white fur. The blessed blades plunged easily into the demon's flesh.

Pallo's clothing was torn, and his face was scratched and bloody. Daku roared and spun fast, connecting with a backhanded blow that sent the aged warrior into the air and outside of the charred circle. He landed heavy and didn't move.

Daku covered his wounds with his hand and laughed. "It will take more than pins and needles to stop me."

Kasai looked to the left and saw Orin untangle himself from a bloody melee of Sunnese warriors and fish-scaled demons. He came in fast, throwing one of his swords at Daku, which the pale demon deflected with ease.

"Missed. But I won't," Daku said and drew back Eishorror to strike.

"Orin! No!" Kasai cried as he rose to his feet.

The Kibo Gensai warrior lunged low and pushed Kasai out of the way as Eishorror fell and struck the ground. Daku cursed in frustration and grabbed Orin by the pant leg and dragged him closer.

"I remember you," Daku said, glaring at Orin. He then turned to face Kasai as he thrust Eishorror through Orin's back. "You're *all* weak."

Frost bloomed over Orin's body. The din of battle subsided enough for Kasai to hear the last wheeze of life leave Orin's body. Daku howled in laughter then ripped the blade out.

"Monster!" Kasai said.

"Isn't that obvious?" Daku said with a wide grin.

Whatever Kasai had been holding onto regarding the memory of his friend dissolved. Daku had made his choice and was beyond redemption. Bright, white energy collected in his hands.

Yesssss. Let the Boundless flow. Destroy the darkness. Kill the creature.

Kasai wanted his revenge. He could taste it mingling with the coppery tang of blood in his mouth. But to unleash such power would mean the end of Daku in the most horrible way.

"Not like this, Great Serpent. Daku has suffered enough," he said and released the energy from his hands. "Brother, I know you're still in there somewhere. Ninziz-zida and I will find you and set you free."

"Spare me your theatrics," Daku scoffed. "The Fire Serpent should have been mine. If the Masters weren't so stingy with their gifts, maybe things would have been different." He raised Eishorror, tracing the blade's sharp edge with his eyes as he would a lover's body.

"Then again, maybe not."

Destroy him.

Kasai snapped Ninziz-zida forward fast as a striking viper, shattering Daku's wrist. Blue fire crackled through white fur, and the wicked blade fell to the ground. Daku stood dumbfounded as his hand flopped over, limp and useless at the end of his burning forearm.

Kasai collapsed Ninziz-zida into one hand, and with the other, he struck Daku with a blow to the chest. His air xindu gave his fist speed and strength. Daku stumbled ten steps backward, and Kasai followed quickly, loading his legs with fire xindu. He leaped, spinning in the air, and connected his heel to the side of Daku's chin.

Again! Again!

Kasai landed solidly on the ground. The pain in his ribs was forgotten. "Now, we take him," he said and let Ninziz-zida have her lead.

Her wrath exploded over Daku like a thousand snakes, striking mercilessly with sharp fangs and a whiplike tail. He was defenseless. Blow after fiery blow landed against white fur, burning flesh and breaking bones. Kasai didn't hesitate to press the attack with spinning, hurricane kicks as Ninziz-zida coiled back before striking again.

Kasai pitied Daku, almost. The demon thing couldn't hope to withstand the fury of Ninziz-zida and her blinding strikes and sharp thrusts. She left him a wreckage of shattered bones and raw, blistering flesh.

"Do it!" Daku screamed with his face inches from the disheveled ground. "Finish me!"

Kasai gained his breath. The falling snow created an eerie juxtaposition of serenity against the chaotic backdrop of the battle raging around the two onetime friends.

Daku's mouth was half-burrowed in the wet dirt. Kasai could see he was sobbing. "The staff should have been mine. I was always better."

"No, Daku, Ninziz-zida never would have accepted you. You turned your back on everyone, including me, your only friend. You were the only one who thought you were the best."

"You can't win." Daku coughed his words into the mud. "Sekka will kill you, or worse, make you her slave. That's what she does." His heavy head lowered into the muddy slush and went still. His dark eyes slowly closed.

Kasai stared at the wreckage of his old friend. Surprisingly, he had no more remorse. The last shred of brotherhood was finally gone. There was nothing more to do. The nightmare that was Daku was over.

"I know, Brother. But still, I must try." Kasai turned away. The falling snow tapered off, and the ground layer swirled in small whirlwinds as he looked to the gates. He knew Sekka was there, waiting for him. Around him, the Sunnese raced past, shouting triumphant war cries. The demons had pulled back.

"And so, the endgame begins." Kasai drew a deep breath and followed his allies, most likely to his doom.

"Master Kasai! Look! The way is clear. They are fleeing. We have them!" Gift had somehow managed to find him in the chaos of battle. She veered toward him as she ran. Her sharp green eyes were lit with excitement.

"I don't know. Maybe. Orin is dead, but Pallo may need help. Please get him away safely."

Gift looked at him questioningly. "Now? Is there time? We must strike before they reform their lines."

Kasai tried to give her a warm smile. "We must save as many as we can." He squeezed Gift's shoulder. "Thank you. I could never have gotten this far without your help. But now I must do what I came here to do."

Gift seemed to understand. "May Nayche watch over you as she does all of her children."

"Thank you, Gift. Now please, help Pallo."

"It will be done. I will bring him there." She pointed to where the Sunnese had gathered in numbers.

The field of battle opened before Kasai. Bodies of slain Sunnese warriors littered the ground. The demon equivalent had been turned to ash by Sunnese magic. The smell of their demise lingering in the air. It stunk of rotten eggs or curdled milk.

Together, Ninziz-zida whispered in his mind. *Always together.*

Kasai eventually came to the rear of the Sunnese warriors standing in a loose gathering. They had stopped their progress and fanned out in a sweeping curve. Kasai moved through the center.

Warriors from various tribes saluted him as he walked past. Some gave Kasai proud nods, while others reached out and placed their hand on his shoulders as if he were a divine being.

Would they be so proud to know I just killed my best friend?

Kasai took a deep, steady breath. He sought the connection to the ever-expanding space, but as usual, the passage remained elusive in the storm of his turbulent emotions, first because of his refusal to let Daku go, and now for Desdemonia.

He had never known love before, not like this, and when he met her, it kicked him in the chest like an angry mule. Now, he wished he could have looked upon her gypsy smile just one more time before the end.

Kasai trudged past the bodies of warriors he didn't know. All of them thinking he was their savior. He walked with heavy steps as he remembered the losses he had suffered. Each one cried for attention in his head and his heart. They were wrong to put so much trust in him. *I failed them all.*

Let them go, Ninziz-zida voiced in his mind, and Kasai did. The bodies faded from his sight as his mind drifted outside of his body. He was just Kasai; he was nothing.

Yessssss. Release yourself from your world of suffering. Let go of what is and be filled with what is not. There you will find me. There you will find the Boundless.

Kasai sank deeper into his walking trance. The infinite sky and bottomless sea formed before him. He let go of his material-self and walked towards the horizon. The guilt he held for the death of his parents left him. The betrayal of Daku faded from his thoughts. He saw Master Choejor at peace. The love he felt for Desdemonia was filled with happiness and joy rather than sadness and loss.

He moved past it all without thought or emotion, and the Boundless opened before him as a blossoming lotus, stretching across the horizon. Its cream-colored petals were infused with white light. They faded before Kasai's eyes to reveal the coiled body of a serpent, wound in a tight ball of blue flames.

You have finally come to me.

"You are Ninziz-zida?"

Yessssss. She welcomed him into her embrace, and Kasai felt no fear as the fire elemental wrapped around his ethereal body.

"We must finish this now."

Always together. Never alone.

Kasai realized five xindu powers, not four, existed as his consciousness was filled with the Boundless's raw energy. His fire, water, air, and earth xindu rose to join with his spirit xindu to create something new. Each one was formless, but he could feel the pulse of their vibrations and direct them to his will. He was as ready as he would ever be.

His eyes focused back on the battlefield, and he realized he had come to the frontline of the Sunnese warriors. Aruka had managed to stay alive and stood at his side.

"We await your signal, Ever Hero. May this day carry over into the awakened lives of all Sunnese."

Kasai gave him a brief smile of acknowledgment, but his mind was focused on Sekka. He could see her clearly now. She had moved away from her guard and stood alone. Her demon horde waited behind her.

"You must give me your word; you will do nothing unless I fall. If I can defeat Sekka now, then perhaps no more lives will be lost."

"We will do as you say, Ever Hero," Aruka said. He clasped Kasai's forearm in a warrior's embrace. "I will have my men send word to the other chieftains."

"Thank you, my friend."

Kasai gripped Ninziz-zida tightly. So quiet was the battlefield that he could hear the mud sucking at his boots as he walked toward Sekka. Snow fell in soft whispers around him when he finally stopped some thirty feet from her position.

Sekka gave him a cruel smiled. "The Ever Hero has finally come. Look about you.

Do you really want to watch them die?" She waved her hand to encompass the remaining Sunnese warriors.

"I have no wish for that, either. They have much better uses. Let us have peace between our realms," Sekka said in an insincere voice. Her jol'goth guard stood in a tight circle behind her. They snorted and shifted hostile with battle lust.

"You're a liar," Kasai said.

"Perhaps. But just think if I am telling you the truth. You'll be a dark prince of Gathos with a princess at your side," Sekka said and signaled for someone to come forward.

A figure in battle leathers walked out from the jol'goth guards and stood to the left of Sekka.

"This princess," Desdemonia said.

Kasai's heart skipped a beat. She was dressed in the enemy's colors and bloodied. Her beauty was shocking and startling at once. Raven hair blew like wildfire in the wind. Kasai stood stunned in the snow, unable to speak. She looked at him with charcoal-colored eyes, distant and unfamiliar.

"Hello, Kasai," Desdemonia said.

"Des. Y-you're alive," Kasai stammered. "I thought I lost you."

She walked toward him, but there was no softness in her expression, no recognition of what they had shared.

"Why won't you do as Mother says? All of this suffering and death can end," she said. "I remember sacrificing everything to keep you safe. Will you not do the same for me? Will you not choose me now instead of them?"

"There is no choice to make," Kasai said and pointed to Sekka. "She's evil."

"There's always a choice," Sess'thra purred as she materialized at Desdemonia's side. "This one is simple. The exchange of one Ever Hero for the lives of all these cattle. It's a fair trade, is it not?"

"Am I not worth it?" Desdemonia said. "Don't you love me?"

"Perhaps, sister, he would like the companionship of two. We can all be together if you like, Ever Hero. You see? There are so many easy choices for you this day."

He knew better than to believe Sekka's offer, but his desire to be with Desdemonia clouded his judgment. "Will she honor her promise if I go with you? Will all of this be over?"

"Mother says you can be one of us. Don't you want to be together again?"

Kasai took an involuntary step forward. He wanted to believe her, but there wasn't any warmth in her eyes, and her words came out cold. "I do, but..."

Lies! The hiss of Ninziz-zida's voice brought Kasai back to his senses.

"Des, Sekka is not your mother. She's the enemy!"

Desdemonia's face turned dark and small horns sprouted from her forehead. She gave Kasai a lascivious smile. "Enemy or not, you're coming with me."

Her narrow hips swayed as she came intimately close. She held out her hand to him.

"Come with me, Kasai. Take my hand. We shared something special once. I can feel it."

Kasai held his hand back. "I cannot go with you. Can't you see? I must save you."

Her expression changed from cold to hostile. "Then it's you that is the enemy."

Kasai fell backward as the blast of dark magic hit him in the gut like a sucker punch. He raised himself off the ground and steadied himself.

"That was just a warm-up. It's gonna get worse," Desdemonia said with a wink.

Attack! Ninziz-zida hissed in his mind, but Kasai held her three segments compressed together in one hand.

"I won't fight you, Des."

"Well, that's not very smart."

She threw another bolt at him, and he let it hit him squarely in the chest. She was right. This one was worse than the first.

"Fight!" She hit him again in the chest, then once more in the shoulder. Each shot tore through his robes and burned into his flesh. Kasai crumpled to the cold ground and let Ninziz-zida fall from his grasp.

"I'd rather die," Kasai said.

"What trickery is this?" Sekka shouted as she came closer. She shoved Desdemonia to the side and grabbed him by the chin to look deeply into his eyes.

"You have come this far of your own will. I'm sure that will be enough to satisfy the requirements of the ritual. You only need to be alive when I take your essence. The level of life is inconsequential," Sekka said and threw his chin to the side.

Kasai knew he was bleeding, badly. "Des, it's me, Kasai. You saved me once. When we first met. Help me again. Please."

She circled him like a predator, watching him and enjoying his suffering. "Why would I do that? You left me for dead in the jungle."

"No. That's another lie."

"And why should I believe you? What proof do you have except the words of a beaten boy, unwilling to fight for his life? How could I have ever loved you? You're pitiful."

"Hold it tight. Keep it safe," Kasai said. His words were no louder than a whisper.

Desdemonia stopped short, then leaned in close to Kasai's face. "What's that? What are you saying? Speak up."

"I know who you truly are, Manna'Desdevi Mishi."

Kasai raised his head from his chest to look at her. She stared back at him, wide-eyed and stone still. He heard Sess'thra laughing from somewhere nearby. The succubus's voice sounded sinister and innocent at once.

"Well, what will you do now, sister?" she said.

Kasai searched for the succubus and finally found her standing at Sekka's side. The archdevil looked on with amusement. A perfect moment of calm fell over the battlefield.

Desdemonia looked baffled. Her eyes scanned the ground, searching for answers, then she lifted her head. Kasai watched her eyes narrow when she saw Sekka and her face fill with disgust.

She looked back at him, and the charcoal black of her eyes turned bright amber. Sigils of green and yellow fanned out behind her back. Kasai saw that her hands glowed with a bright blue light.

"Miss me, handsome?"

Kasai smiled. He then looked past her to where Sekka and Sess'thra stood. A twisted and almost flirtatious smile appeared on Sess'thra's mouth as she moved deliberately away from Sekka's side.

"Daughter?" Sekka said in a bemused tone. "What are you doing? Collect the boy and bring him to the tower."

Desdemonia spun in a gypsy dance and shot blue bolts from her palms. They struck Sekka in the face, blinding her with blue fire. The archdevil cursed and brushed them away with her hand.

Desdemonia grabbed Ninziz-zida and thrust the three-segmented staff into his hands, unphased by the heat of the weapon. "You're going to need her."

She then pulled him up by the front of his robes. "By the way, you look horrible."

"I feel horrible," Kasai said. "You could have gone easy on me."

"Oh, don't be such a baby. They were love taps," she said. "And I hope you learned some new tricks while I was away. We're gonna need them."

Call me from the Boundless. I will fight by your side, and together we shall prevail, Ninziz-zida said in his mind as if she had heard Desdemonia's human voice.

Kasai looked at the staff, confused. He was unsure of what she meant.

Call me!

"Ninziz-zida! Come!" Kasai shouted without another thought.

The blue fire rippling along the sectional staff coiled around his body then rose high into the air, forming into a magnificent serpent of fire. Kasai felt an intimate connection to the elemental beast. He knew they were separate in life but the same within the Boundless. Whatever would happen next, they would do it together.

"I am Ninziz-zida! I am reborn!" Ninziz-zida's voice bellowed across the battlefield in a long hiss. A viper's tongue darted from her mouth, assessing the threat from the circling demons. Sekka's jol'goth guard closed in fast with open mouths filled with needle-sharp teeth and eyes blazing with hatred.

"Aosoth, stop," Sekka commanded. "I need the boy alive."

She slowly snuffed out the last of the blue flames on her hair and face. Then hideous laughter filled with contempt erupted from her mouth.

"I see we are playing a different game, then. It's time we settled this, snake."

The female form of Sekka's perfect human body changed. Horns grew from her head, followed by gnashing tusks. Sharp talons ribbed from her booted feet, and her height tripled as Kasai watched the beast of Gathos become whole before his eyes.

"You will not defeat me a second time, Ninziz-zida. That boy is not Aetenos. Without the Divine Fist to ground you, you are nothing. Let me show you."

Sekka bounded forward and lashed out at Kasai with her sharp claws. The blow raked across his chest, ripping his robe from his body and left four deep furrows in his flesh. Kasai had never felt such pain. Blood gushed from his wounds, but somehow, he managed to hold his grip on the staff.

"Kasai!" Desdemonia said in alarm.

Ninziz-zida flashed forward. Her open mouth was filled with fire and fury as she bit down on the gap between Sekka's neck and shoulder. The archdevil screamed in pain and scratched at the fire serpent's face. Ninziz-zida held her jaws tight and quickly coiled her body around Sekka like a constrictor. Blue fire burned mercilessly over the archdevil.

Kasai's sight blurred in and out with the throbbing pain in his chest. The ground temperature suddenly dropped. He felt like he was turning to ice. Kasai focused on Ninziz-zida's blue flame. It was fading within a miniature blizzard of snow and ice swirling with raged around the two titans.

Feed me your strength! Ninziz-zida commanded.

Kasai's chest burned with pain, and blackness pushed in from the edges of his sight. "I'm dying," he mumbled.

Kasai tried desperately to cling to life as more of his lifeblood poured out of him with each tortured breath. His connection to the Boundless slipped from his grasp, and Ninziz-zida's fiery form dissolved from reality.

"Not until I'm done with you, you aren't," Sekka said and gave him a wicked grin as she emerged from the snow squall.

"Kasai! Get up!" Desdemonia shouted. "This isn't over yet."

But it was over. Sekka was too strong, even against the righteous might of Ninziz-zida.

+You have failed the Fire Serpent as you have failed so many others.+ Sekka's voice pounded in his head. *+You see it now, don't you? You cannot win against me.+*

Desdemonia fired more fiery bolts at Sekka, but she deflected each harmlessly away. Sekka's body morphed back into her human form, and she moved with smooth grace over the trampled ground.

"I do so enjoy the delicate sensitivity of this body," Sekka said. "Seeing you broken and on your knees is so much satisfying with these mortal eyes."

Ninziz-zida's attack had not left her unscarred. An ugly bite had torn away the flesh at the corner of her neck and shoulder. Her alabaster hair clotted around the wound but could not prevent syrupy blue blood from flowing down her chest, coating her breasts and abdomen. Winding around her body was a trail of raw, purplish flesh, burnt crisp at the edges.

Desdemonia stood protectively in front of him and quickly glanced over her shoulder. "I can't do this without you! Get up!" she shouted. Then she turned to Sekka. "You will not touch him again."

"Oh, I think I will," Sekka said.

The archdevil struck fast, and Kasai barely registered the blur of Desdemonia's dark leather and black hair as she was tossed to the side. He heard her groan in pain when she hit the ground. Sekka then leered seductively at him. "Now, where were we?"

"No, you won't," Desdemonia said in a frail voice.

Kasai's head lolled to the side and he saw a kaleidoscope of greens, yellows, and blues—jungle colors, bathing her body in a protective light. Sigils of power, weak as they were, blossomed above her body as she raised a trembling open hand at Sekka.

"Sek'Kiyohime!" she said and snatched at the air, closing her hand into a fist. "Weakness!"

Sekka's steps faltered, and she stumbled to the ground. She looked at Desdemonia with astonishment. "You dare!"

"She's vulnerable. Kasai, fight," Desdemonia said in a strained voice.

"Stupid girl. Shatter," Sekka said.

The onyx stone encased in the ring on Desdemonia's finger shattered in a cloud of black mist. Desdemonia cried out but still managed to keep her fist closed, holding the debilitating magic on Sekka in place. Her eyes widened as she tried to swallow large gulps of air.

Fight! Ninziz-zida shouted in his mind.

His will to fight got him to one knee. *I won't let her win.* The pain was excruciating, but that was inconsequential now. He would die later. Ninziz-zida's fire rippled along the segments of the staff.

Kasai searched for a strength that could not be found in muscle or bone or through the mystical weapon. His heart would not let him quit, but that would not be enough either.

"I give what is left of myself to the Boundless. Take it all. Sekka must be stopped."

His spirit xindu opened, and the Boundless flowed into him. The view of the world around him shifted from one of physical things to elements of pure vibration. Desdemonia's magical command was siphoning layers of protection away from Sekka's human form. Holes appeared across her body, growing larger and seeping out smokey darkness.

Kasai collapsed Ninziz-zida and thrust her into what remained of his sash. He would do this deed on his own. Sekka watched him with a bemused smile. The Boundless was alive within him now, and he filled his lungs with invigorating air and breathed out slowly.

He channeled the strength and purity of the Boundless into his fists, causing Sekka to raise her forearms to shield her eyes from the clean and bright energy.

He moved purposefully toward her, without caution or fear.

"Open her up," he said and commanded his xindu energies to pry apart the holes spreading across her body. On his third step, he shot his fists into Sekka's chest. The force of the blow ripped through her and pulverizing her heart, before exploding out her back.

He was face to face with her when she gasped. Her mouth hung open, but she couldn't speak. Kasai withdrew his gory arms and fists, then stepped away. Sekka dropped to her knees, then fell forward, dead.

Her body turned to black ash and collected in a small pile until the wind blew the bits and pieces out of sight.

Kasai stumbled to the lifeless form of Desdemonia. He knelt at her side and pulled her body close to his. She was cold. He plucked loose strands of hair from her face and used the torn sleeve of his other arm to wipe away the tears streaming from his eyes.

His body felt numb and was covered in a patchwork of scratches and bruises. The horrible gashes across his chest had stopped bleeding. The Boundless was sustaining him now in a way he never thought possible.

The demon horde howled in a combination of rage and glee and quickly renewed their attack on the Sunnese or each other, whichever adversary was closer.

Aosoth roared. He stormed forward with his polearm pitched and at a downward angle. The jol'goths around him raced a step behind their leader. Kasai looked up but didn't care. Desdemonia was gone.

Sess'thra materialized before him and casually spun in a delicate pirouette. Her black wings followed like soft, velvet flags, rippling in the air. She uttered words Kasai couldn't understand, but the effect was profound. The rampaging Aosoth and his jol'goth guards were held fast in mid-stride. It was as if the succubus had frozen time.

Kasai gave Sess'thra a nod of defeat. He knew he was finished. The succubus could kill him now however she wished. He didn't care; his work was done.

He felt the dead weight of Desdemonia's body on his own.

"Soon, I'll join you, Des," Kasai said. Then he noticed a warm light growing in the cold, grey sky over Sess'thra's shoulder. A bell chimed from above, lost in the distant storm clouds.

He heard the bell chime again. This time it rang clear and sharp.

Sess'thra bent over, grabbed him by the chin, and kissed him passionately, biting his bottom lip. She gave him a pirate's smile as she withdrew her embrace. Her lips and tongue left his mouth tasting metallic and sweet.

"There's just no time for more, my little crush. But there will be another time. There's always another time."

Sess'thra unfurled her leathery wings and leaped upwards. The air popped, and she was gone. Kasai pulled Desdemonia's shattered body closer to his.

"Don't go, Des. We still have roads to travel. I wanted to show you Ordu. I thought we could restore it together." But there were no playful jabs from the frolicking gypsy or hard words from the stoic druidess.

A thunderclap's deafening sound filled the battlefield. The heavy storm clouds vibrated as if they would shatter. Kasai glanced at Aosoth, who had taken another step but then faltered and stumbled. The rest of his group tumbled into him as they, too, moved freely again.

There was a second great boom, and the sky was set on fire.

Kasai and all those around him stared into the heavens and saw a sight that could not be unseen. A bright-yellow glow from a fiery comet descended over the city and fields, evaporating the storm clouds with the heat of a second sun.

Kasai saw thousands upon thousands of winged silhouettes emerging from the light. Long, shadowed wings beat in unison as they swooped from the heavens onto the battlefield. The sky sparkled from the gleam of golden armor and the shine of steel blades.

Spheres of bright light flashed around Kasai, momentarily blinding him. Lesser thunderclaps boomed across the battleground. An earthy smell of burning mulch and heavy rain filled his nose. When his vision cleared, Kasai saw the grasslands filled with armed ranks of wingless warriors. Arcs of forked lightning roamed over their flawless armor, and the spear tips of their long halberds crackled with jagged energy. The golden soldiers moved with the speed of the wind and the precision of a flawless arrow.

The angels had arrived.

Lord Raguel swooped down close to where Kasai held Desdemonia. The archangel was accompanied by a superfluous honor guard. Aetenos stood nearby, no longer in chains and wearing a proud smile.

Kasai gazed in wonder at the spectacle unfolding around him. He thought he caught a glimpse of a small monkey riding a giant black horse and throwing fiery magic into the scattering demon horde.

Then the majestic figure of Lord Raguel towered over him. He held a golden sword blazing with yellow fire in his hand. The archangel opened his wings in a victorious stretch, eclipsing the light of the second sun.

Kasai was unimpressed. Raguel's wings mimicked a pale rainbow when juxtaposed across the bodies of the dead and dying. He was speaking, but Kasai wasn't listening. He didn't care about Raguel or his words of accomplishment. None of it mattered.

"You could have come anytime," Kasai eventually said and clutched Desdemonia's lifeless body to his own.

84

KASAI

Kasai's tongue stuck to the roof of his dry mouth, and his skin felt like it was baking under a hot desert sun. He looked up to see what had scorched the air and saw seven columns of Heavenly fire falling from the sky. Each touched down over the enemy's positions and tore through the horde of demons now scattered across the battlefield.

The holy tornados moved across the land, seemingly directed by an unseen conductor. Angels circled overhead and threw balls of vibrant electricity that splattered into multiple chains upon hitting the ground, frying demons to ash.

The winged demons took flight and engaged the angels in aerial combat. But they were too few, and the angels controlled the higher air. They were each destroyed in turn.

Kasai sat and watched in disbelief. He shielded Desdemonia's body from the ash storm of demon death that choked the air. As unbelievable as it seemed, he saw Aosoth and his group of jol'goths rise and rush Lord Raguel.

The archangel merely gave a look of bothered disappointment. Before Aosoth and his jol'goth guard were in striking range, a company of winged angels materialized around them in balls of crackling lightning.

Aosoth and the others were skewered on the angels' long halberds like so many wild pigs. It was the same wherever Kasai looked. Angels wielding powerful magic slaughtered the leaderless demons with ease. Fire and lightning burned everything unholy, but miraculously, left the humans unscathed, or so it seemed.

Sour ash filled his mouth, and Kasai coughed violently. His watery eyes looked toward Sekka's city, which now blazed within an inferno that touched the sky. A geyser of fire spun inside the walls, burning everything. Even the distant Hoarfrost Mountains were ablaze as columns of fire roved over the jagged peaks.

Where's Shiverrig? Kasai idly wondered. *I hope he's dead, too.*

"This area will be cleansed shortly. Aetenos, you will attend to me. I don't want you wandering off and getting into trouble," Raguel said and moved to another area of the battlefield.

Aetenos came to Kasai and briefly looked at Desdemonia with a sad eye. "I'm sorry, my boy. She had a good soul."

"Aetenos!" Raguel said.

"We'll talk later. It's best to stay on that one's good side. At least until this mess is cleaned up."

Kasai just shook his head in bewilderment. The war which had spanned months and cost tens of thousands of lives had ended, seemingly within minutes. He hugged Desdemonia tight and rocked her back and forth.

"They could have come anytime, Des. Anytime."

Sometime later, a group of angels came to Kasai and tended to his wounds. They wrapped his chest with a moist cloth, then bundled him in a warm cloak. He immediately felt the soothing comfort of the medicine laced within the fabric. They took Desdemonia and told him they would prepare her body for a hero's funeral.

"Bring her to Gift, of the Sunnese. They will know how to prepare her body so she may sleep peacefully until the day of her awakening," Kasai said. He choked out the words, and reluctantly agreed and let her go.

Kasai's eyes wandered aimlessly over the battlefield. The land was charred, and smoke rose into the air from a thousand small fires. The snow was gone, and not one puddle of water could be seen anywhere. He realized he was incredibly thirsty as he walked through the desolation, searching for his friends.

"What I wouldn't give for some water."

He returned to the spot where Pallo and Orin had fallen against Daku. Warm sunlight reflected off the steel of discarded weapons and empty armor that somehow hadn't melted in the holy inferno. Pallo wasn't there, and he prayed Gift had gotten him out of harm's way. Orin's body was gone as well, and Kasai assumed it had been taken by the fire.

The Sunnese had suffered significant losses by the time the Heavenly Host arrived. The thought of their grand entrance infuriated him.

Anytime.

Kasai had not seen Run-Run since he left the jungle in search of the Miko Nuna. He heard from passing Sunnese that the brave warriors holding the southern flank were overwhelmed by the Chaos Warlord and his half-breed demons.

So much lost, he thought.

Death and misery were everywhere. Kasai could feel the pain and sadness of the survivors.

If I had only...only what? Surrendered to Sekka and her diabolical plan? Kasai heaved his shoulders. His deep sigh turned bitter. "I did what I had to do. I did what was expected of the Ever Hero," he said bitterly. He had saved the land, but he felt like a casualty of war.

What do I do now? The Monastery of Ordu was destroyed. His Brothers and the Master Monks were gone. If any monks survived the massacre, they were scattered by the wind now.

Kasai kept walking. The field had been groomed over by the survivors, and he saw the Sunnese moving the bodies of their fallen to more hallowed grounds where angels had blessed the land. Gift had once explained to him the dead would sleep the long dream and await the time of their reawakening. *Des hated sleep. She was always in motion.*

Then, Kasai was ripped from his musings by a magnificent, black stallion charging toward him with a small monkey in decorative armor riding on its back. The stallion came up fast and halted with great precision. He snorted, seemingly happy to see Kasai.

"You see, Titus, we have found our hero. It didn't take as long as you expected," Zhao Houzi said.

Titus snorted again, this time with a bit of fuss over the monkey's remark.

"Hello, Zhao Houzi. Hello, Titus." Kasai respectfully bowed to each of the celestial animal spirits.

"And a good day to you, Ever Hero. We have been sent to retrieve you for a most urgent meeting. Titus would be honored to carry you. If you would just climb aboard, we will be on our way."

Zhao Houzi turned Titus in the direction of the Hoarfrost Mountains.

"Lord Raguel has found the Chaos Gate?" Kasai asked.

"Yes."

"Finally, this nightmare will end."

Kasai noted the monkey's expression wasn't very reassuring as he hoisted himself up on Titus's back.

"Hold tight. Titus likes to run."

Kasai wasn't sure what he was supposed to hold on to, so he reached around Zhao Houzi's small body and grabbed a bunch of hair from Titus's mane. Then the three raced towards the Hoarfrost Mountains and the location of the diabolical portal.

Seven choirs of angels stood at equidistant positions around the Chaos Gate. Their voices filled the air with divine melodies. The music slowly dispelled the forever cold of Sekka's reign. The springtime breezes carried from the base of Storm Wind Pass brought the scent of smokey air and burnt things through Rachlach Fortress's ruins.

The ground below Titus's hooves remained harsh and desolate. It would always carry the scars of an evil mind's thirst for power and the intense heat of Heavenly fire.

"At least people will remember what happened here," Kasai said.

"We can only hope," Zhao Houzi said.

Kasai then spotted Lord Raguel. A small group of angelic figures stood around the archangel. They were huddled in deep conversation. Kasai recognized the six judges that had presided over his trial in the Cloud Court.

Aetenos was there as well, clothed in a simple blue robe. Kasai saw a line of prisoners held in chains to the side. They sat on the damp ground with their heads hung low. Armored angels stood stoically behind them with weapons held ready.

Kasai slid off Titus's back. The fighting had made his entire body was sore with muscles that he didn't know he had. Then the monkey leaped off Titus and rolled as if it were a game, causing a stir of irritation from the judgmental angels. Raguel took notice and stopped speaking as they approached.

A fake smile graced his face as he opened his arms in a warm greeting. Kasai didn't feel the uplifting grace he felt when in the presence of Illyria. His gut told him Lord Raguel couldn't be trusted.

Anytime, he thought. *They could have come anytime and stopped this madness before it began.*

"You have exceeded expectations," Raguel said. "Sekka has been banished to Gathos."

"Banished? She's not dead?" *How can I be so dense? Of course, she was only banished. It was the same with Lord Oziax.*

Kasai then looked fearfully to the festering Chaos Gate. "She'll return."

"Not for a thousand of your years, Ever Hero," Zhao Houzi said in a proper and sagely fashion.

"I'm not convinced," Kasai said and took a knee before Lord Raguel. "I have done what was asked of me. We all did. Those who are not present have suffered, many with their lives."

Raguel's smile widened. "Yes, the Challenge of Righteousness has rooted out the evil and revealed the truth. The innocent live, and the guilty are dead. Balance has been restored."

"We were all innocent," Kasai said. "This can't be right. How can such a divine being not see the truth?"

Raguel's wings unfurled, and the feathers absorbed the sunlight, casting a radiant glow behind his back. He gave Kasai a liar's smile and turned around to better address his celestial entourage.

"Let it be known. The Challenge of Righteousness has been satisfied. The Cloud Court absolves this mortal from any allegiance to the archdevil, Sekka."

"This is fantastic news," Zhao Houzi said gleefully. "Now Lord Raguel will destroy the portal. Oh, I've been looking forward to this moment. I can't wait to see how it's done."

"Not today." Raguel's broad smile creased to a fine line.

Kasai wasn't sure he heard correctly. He looked to Aetenos for confirmation. The Great Monk's face was unreadable.

Kasai got up and stood in front of Raguel. "Please forgive me. I don't understand. We have done as you asked."

"Yes. A fine job. And I have acquitted you from any guilt in this matter."

"But—" Kasai stammered.

"The Chaos Gate shall remain functional until I see fit to close it."

"But you promised!"

Raguel's amiable demeanor dissolved. "Do not question the integrity of the Chancellor Pinnacle. The Chaos Gate will serve the Seven Heavens until I see fit to destroy it."

"This can't be," Kasai said softly. The nightmare would not end.

"I am sorry, young one," Zhao Houzi said, trying to console Kasai. "The outcomes of our honest toils are not always what we expect."

Kasai stared at the ground. "He's a liar."

The snow was gone, and a thin layer of soot covered the blackened rock. It was filthy and ugly. He vaguely listened to Raguel talking to another group of people and heard the word prisoner mentioned.

"Gerun Shiverrig of Gethem, you and the rest of the possessed have been judged. You are guilty of the highest crime committed by a mortal. You have forfeited the divine essence of your soul to the whims of darkness and evil. According to your due, you shall be punished by death."

"I was forced to participate in Sekka's invasion, though I fought to thwart her plans from the onset. Your divine sight will see I am innocent!"

"So says all who are guilty," Raguel said.

"I have, and always will be the champion of Baroqia!" Shiverrig's voice rose in anger as he was prodded to his feet by the angelic guard.

"Quiet! You reek of the Abyss. You are to be slain without mercy on the ground you have defiled. Take him away," Raguel said then moved back to the center of the gathered angels. They spoke quietly amongst themselves.

"My Lord Raguel. This is not right," Kasai said.

"Aetenos, console your young ward. Give him a sweet if you must," Raguel said over his shoulder. "You are free to go, as well. Pray, I do not see you in the Seven Heavens for at least an age or two."

"The boy has it right, Raguel," Aetenos said.

"You will address me—"

"This is not the Way of Heaven," Aetenos interrupted.

"You are in no position to give me a sermon on right and wrong." Raguel fully turned to face Aetenos. The anger in his expression was sharp.

"Close the Chaos Gate, Raguel," Aetenos said, this time more sternly.

"I will not."

"You will." A voice echoed over the ruins of Rachlach Fortress. It was majestic and demanded unwavering obedience.

Kasai felt like he was being suffocated by the sheer power of the voice. His legs quivered, and he dropped slowly to the ground. The angels bowed down to one knee with their heads held low on their chests.

Only Raguel deigned not to grovel. He bowed from the waist, then stood straight, his chin held high. A whirlwind gathered, changing into a throbbing white sphere of energy. Electricity crackled and struck the ground, shattering rocks into dust.

The raw energy dissipated, and Illyria stepped forward. Kasai felt like the wind had been knocked from him, and he struggled to regain his breath. Eventually, he raised himself to his knees.

"I have been sent by the Immortal Mother to serve as her word," Illyria said. Electricity riddled through her golden hair, and sparks snapped off her sleek body. She was nature's energy in physical form. Kasai had never seen such beauty be so terrible to behold.

"Lady Illyria. What a welcome surprise," Raguel said. Though Kasai could clearly see the worry in his eyes. "What news do you bring of the Immortal Mother's wishes?"

"Promises made will be delivered in full. The Chaos Gate will be destroyed, and the souls of the Great Monk and his Ever Hero will be returned."

"All will be done as you say. But the completion of my great work shall come first. There is still much to accomplish," Raguel said.

"Now," Illyria said. The sound of her voice shook the ground.

She then floated beside Raguel and whispered something only for his ears. Raguel's wings stiffened, and Kasai saw the archangel's hand move to the pommel of his sword. Rather than grab it, his fingers thoughtfully tapped the hilt.

Kasai was unsure what would happen next. A heavy tension silently sat between the two ancient divinities.

"As you wish," Raguel said. The liar's smile returned quickly to his face.

The process was relatively straightforward. Raguel brought Aetenos and Kasai together and uttered a string of complex syllables and words. Illyria then added to Raguel's chant with her own melodic song.

She placed her hand on Aetenos's chest, and the Chaos Gate shuddered. It boiled and tossed as if it would erupt in a geyser of muck and infernal flotsam. Kasai could hear distant screams riding on echoes of wintery winds.

Then Illyria placed her hand on Kasai's chest, and the perimeter of the portal began to shrink. A residual, oily slime mixed with melting rock remained as the edges were drawn into its center. The molten stew reeked of dead things. And then it was over.

"It is done," Raguel said.

"That's it?" Kasai stood, flabbergasted. He expected to feel something different. "How?"

"A living Chaos Gate must first be bonded to a powerful infernal being, one who can wield the deep magic that is needed to anchor the unique combination of a divine sou and mortal soul to its birth. Stripping the portal of its anchoring souls caused the bridge between two realms to collapse," Illyria said. Her bright, blue eyes were round saucers floating in porcelain clouds. Kasai just stared. His mouth held agape in awe.

"I am proud of you, Kasai Ch'ou. You are more than you once believed you could be. Yet, I see many questions still fill your heart."

"I cannot begin to understand the ways of angels," Kasai said.

"We are all works in progress. Good or evil, it's all the same in the Great Balance. We are each driven to the ultimate versions of ourselves. That is the scale that must remain even."

Illyria looked to Raguel. "Some have lost their way and wish to burden the scale with selfish agendas."

Kasai noticed Raguel's bravado seemed deflated as if a portion of his former glory and grandeur had been stripped away. Aetenos turned to Kasai and laid a hand on each of his shoulders. His one good eye looked deeply into Kasai's own.

"It is time, my son."

"You're leaving."

Aetenos nodded. "My time in this realm has ended, and there are other roads to travel."

"But we need you, now more than ever. The Three Kingdoms need your guidance."

Aetenos slowly shook his head. "Not mine, yours."

"Mine?"

"Of course, yours," Aetenos said in an exasperated tone. "Haven't you been paying attention? You're the Divine Fist now. The Three Kingdoms need a symbol to galvanize their souls and uplift the people to a greater purpose. I can think of no other than you to bring them hope."

"Me? What am I supposed to do?" Kasai wasn't sure he wanted to know.

"That is always the hardest question. Start with what you know. Rebuild what was destroyed."

"Ordu?"

Aetenos shrugged his shoulders. "It's as good as any place to start, though a bit stuffy for my tastes."

Kasai chuckled. "I know what you mean. I was always late...for everything."

"Me too," Aetenos said with a warm smile.

"Come, my darling. Our time draws near," Illyria said. She took Aetenos's hand into her own.

"Lady Illyria, could I ask a request of you before you leave?" Kasai said.

"Yes, Ever Hero. What is it?"

"Can you bring Desdemonia back to me?"

"I am sorry. The Great Balance must have its due."

Kasai's heart sank, but he nodded respectfully. "What will become of her soul?"

"Do not fear, Ever Hero. The soul of Manna'Desdevi Mishi burns brightly still."

EPILOGUE

Kasai, Zhao Houzi, and Titus returned to the scorched and scarred lands of the battlefield.

"The Three Kingdoms are torn, and there is much healing to be done," Kasai said.

"In this summation, you are right, Ever Hero. I fear nothing shall grow on these grounds for generations to come. It will be up to you to unite this land in harmony," Zhao Houzi said.

"It's a long way back to Ordu," Kasai said as he slid off Titus's back.

"Indeed. Perhaps you will have company along the way." Zhao Houzi smiled. "We bid you farewell, Ever Hero. Until our paths cross again."

Titus nuzzled his great head into Kasai's neck and almost caused him to stumble. "Okay, okay, Titus." Kasai patted the horse's cheek. "I'll miss you, too."

"Titus is fond of you. He's looking forward to watching your progress. As am I. Now, we shall leave you to your own." Titus sprang forward, and soon the two vanished back towards the Hoarfrost Mountains.

Kasai watched them go for a time, then turned and walked to the camps set up to care for the wounded and bury the dead. It wasn't long before he came to the first Sunnese encampment and found the bodies of the fallen lying in neat rows.

When able, their arms were folded across their chest, and a weapon lay by their side. Kasai noticed many had a colored cloth draped across their eyes.

"At least they look at peace," he said.

Kasai walked along the rows, trying to identify warriors he had befriended, even if he couldn't remember their names. Eventually, he saw a warrior with small scars notched across his skin. For once, the warrior's face was relaxed.

"Goodbye, Orin," Kasai said, relieved the faithful warrior would receive a proper burial. "Thank you for all you did for me. I wish you could have seen the good in Desdemonia's heart before the end."

"Not everyone has the sight to see what is real, even if it's directly in front of them."

Kasai turned and saw Gift walking toward him. "He was a brave warrior and will be mourned by the Frona Tribe, as will all of the members of our family that have taken the deep sleep."

"Have you any word of Pallo and his brother, Run-Run?" Kasai asked and was instantly relieved to see her smile.

"Yes, Pallo was brought to the healers, as you requested. His brother miraculously found him soon after. He's a wonder, that one. I've never seen a northerner with such an amazing sense of direction."

Kasai chuckled. "That's Run-Run, alright."

"Would you like to see them?"

"Maybe later. Have you seen Desdemonia? Is she here?" Kasai said.

"Yes, but she is being kept separate and safe. She sacrificed so much to see us win through this day. She is a true hero."

"Why separately?"

"Too many winged warriors, asking too many questions. We of the Frona Tribe protect our own. They will not find her."

"Thank you, Gift. She would have appreciated that," Kasai said and looked to the dead bodies. "What will happen to them?"

"Many will be brought back to the jungle where they will become one with the land and trees. The rest, we will burn here and carry their ashes to their families."

Kasai was thoughtful for a moment. "Des didn't have any family."

"Of course, she did. She had you, Master Kasai, and then she had us. Desdemonia will come back to Sunne with me, and I will personally perform the ritual of deep sleep for her. You are welcome to join me and stay with us in the jungle."

"That would be nice. Perhaps I can stay for a time. But I will need to return to Ordu. There is much to rebuild."

Gift nodded. "Yes, much to rebuild everywhere. Come, let us check on your other friends."

Kasai looked in what he thought was the direction of Ordu. *Yes, lots to rebuild*, he thought.

Shiverrig trudged through knee-high snow. The winds blowing off the Hoarfrost Mountains stung the skin of his exposed face. He was clad in the clothing of a nomadic barbarian of some unremarkable northern tribe. Dai-Ko-Zior hovered at his side. The sorcerer remained huddled beneath the cowl of his thick robes.

"Is there no other direction we can go but north? I have had my fill of ice and cold," Shiverrig grumbled.

"Would you prefer a pleasant stroll through a pit of fire, watching the flesh melt from your body? Perhaps you would like to exchange positions with the one I placed in your stead?" Dai-Ko-Zior said.

"I'm surprised the angels didn't immediately see through such a glamour. You're sure it will hold?"

"The angels are blind to many truths. They see only what they want to see. Raguel's plans have been thwarted. He will need to punish someone. It won't matter which mortal dies, as long as one, or many, perish under his sword."

"Why haven't we returned to Gethem. I now have the largest standing army in the Three Kingdoms. I suspect the angels will not stay in this realm long. When they fly off, I shall claim Baroqia, then invade Sunne. Properly this time.

Dai-Ko-Zior wheezed through a dry chuckle.

"What humors you, sorcerer?"

"You do. You *once* had a mighty army, crafted by excellent stock and no small amount of the Chaos Devil's infernal magic. But no longer. The Heavenly Host was thorough when exterminating your half-breeds from the Mortal Realm. Gethem and Qaqal have suffered the same fate as Winter's Fury and have been burned to cinders. Your legions are no more.

"Perhaps some random creatures remain, sulking in the depths of Sekka's tower, but none of consequence."

"I will regroup. Sess'thra will find me. I'm sure that clever minx made her exit long before the skies opened, and the angels descended to ruin everything."

Dai-Ko-Zior drew his heavy cloaks closer instead of responding.

They moved on in silence, listening to the howling wind. At least it drowned out the ringing in his ears. He had not felt the presence of Xerthotha in many days.

Maybe the arrival of the angels broke the connection to the Chaos Devil. If that's true, then their appearance was a great boon instead of a setback. Blast this cold, he thought.

"Where are we going?" Shiverrig called ahead to Dai-Ko-Zior, who had hovered to a stop and waited for Shiverrig to catch up.

"The Northern Vortex," Dai-Ko-Zior said.

"Never heard of it."

"Most mortals have not, for it's a forgotten place. It's there that you will rebuild and grow strong under the guidance of my masters."

"Not without me," Daku said. The body of the pale demon materialized from a shadowed crevasse in the mountain path. His pale-colored fur was covered in dried blood and filth. The wicked blade, Eishorror, was strapped across his back in a makeshift scabbard. Daku moved awkwardly as if broken bones had mended poorly.

"Figured you to be dead," Shiverrig said. He only raised his head slightly in acknowledgment of the pale demon. The ice and snow were annoyingly blinding.

Daku scoffed. He limped into line behind Shiverrig. "A round goes to Kasai, nothing more. Next time he will not be so lucky."

"The Ever Hero has found his power. This is good. He will make a fitting sacrifice," Dai-Ko-Zior said.

"Ever Hero. It's a stupid name," Daku grumbled.

Shiverrig didn't bother with a reply. He couldn't decide if he hated the cold of the mountains more than the heat of the jungle. One was just as miserable of a climate as the other. Pulling his furs closer to his chest, he scanned the horizon and saw endless mountain tops.

"Sorcerer! Can you not teleport us to this mysterious place?"

"The angels would detect such a spike of dark magic. They must remain blind to our movement."

Shiverrig trudged on through deep snow. "Fucking Hell. This cold is definitely worse."

. . .

Sekka opened her sore and stinging eyes. The world around her was blurred but familiar. She was in the rejuvenation pits on Gathos. "Home," she sighed.

The memory of her defeat returned. "Damn that Aetenos and his miserable brood. A thousand curses upon that boy. Next time they all die fast."

Sekka retained the human form she had perished in during her fight against the Ever Hero and climbed naked and wet out of the slushy waters of the pit. She ran her hands over her flesh, wiping away icy goo. Her human form had healed, and she was pleased.

She took in her surroundings. Chedipe had made some changes in her absence, most notably the temperature of the chamber. And the air felt heavy. A sticky, humid warmth clung to her body.

"What is this blazing heat? Chedipe! Do you mean to melt all of Gathos?"

Sekka cleared away the last bit of slimy membrane covering her face. When she opened her eyes, she saw Lord Oziax's head mounted on a wall above his slumped body on the floor. Dread filled her newly formed heart. "Oh no."

"Ah, you're finally awake. Splendid." A deep baritone voice echoed through the chamber.

Sekka spun around. A young princess stood before her. She held the broken body of Chedipe by the neck like a ragdoll. The juxtaposition of forms was unnerving.

"Who are you?" Sekka said. She trembled as a rush of primal fear filled her body.

"Tsk, tsk, you know who I am." The princess's voice was filled with power.

"Azrollorza protects me!" Sekka said.

"Azrollorza is not here. Nor will she ever attempt to step foot on Gathos again. This realm of ice is now mine. Claimed as a prize wrought from victory. I know you know all about those little rules."

"Let me serve you, Lord Xerthotha," Sekka begged. "I shall grant you passage to the Mortal Realm. A world of fresh souls shall be yours."

Xerthotha transformed into a giant, encased in fiery armor. The stylized face of a growling lion with curling tusks made up the front grill. He tossed the broken body of Chedipe against the far wall.

"Ho, ho, ho. Your Chaos Gate is no more. It has been snuffed out by so many little birds."

"No, no, no. It can't be!"

"Yes, it can, and I am most displeased. But let's get back to you. You've been a naughty, little devil, haven't you? It's not wise to tamper with the deep magic that even a Supreme Devil will not touch. One can never be too sure what will step out of the darkness when you play with forbidden power."

"What do you want of me?"

The warrior transformed again, this time into a pair of twins, each with the Ever Hero's face. They both gave Sekka a polite smile filled with black teeth.

"I believe you owe Azrollorza a Life Debt," one boy said as he took Sekka by the hand.

"Come along now," the other said in the same, childlike voice. He took Sekka's other hand in his own. "We will start working off that debt through your flesh. Then we can move on to other, more interesting areas."

"We assume you have time?" the twins said in unison, then they giggled and laughed like little boys.

Sekka hung her head low as the dual nightmares lead her away to her penance. She knew there was nothing she could do to resist the might of the Chaos Devil. For now, she accepted her punishment but vowed she would take her revenge.

Sekka would find a way to survive. She always did. Always.

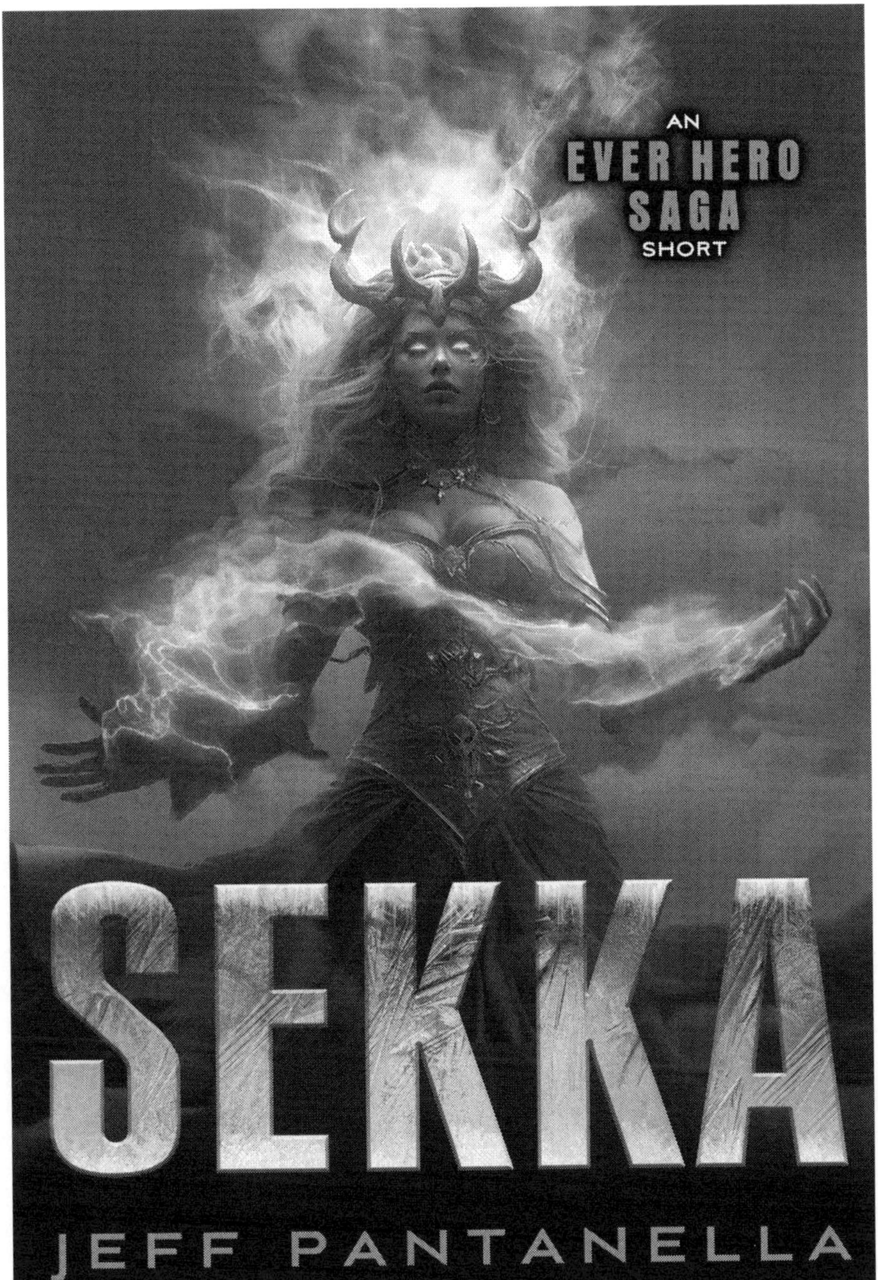
AN
EVER HERO
SAGA
SHORT
SEKKA
JEFF PANTANELLA

JEFF PANTANELLA

SEKKA

AN
EVER HERO
SAGA
SHORT

SEKKA
ARCHDEVIL OF GATHOS

PROLOGUE

I n the beginning, there was only hunger and thirst in an infinite void of mindless wandering.

She opened her eyes, though to perceive them as eyes was a mortal misconception, for she was an Ancient and could see through the dimensions of space and time using senses incomprehensible to humans.

Images of a long-forgotten time, when she and her family devoured whole realms for the sustaining nourishment they provided passed across the horizon of her mind. She watched as her siblings descended as gods on unsuspecting worlds and proceeded to leech the lands dry of the vital life-energy they supplied. Then they would depart, leaving the world a hollow husk, a scrap of cosmic debris never to sustain living matter again.

But after eons of feasting, worlds with enough life-energy to satiate their hunger became scarce. It was decided the youngest and strongest of them would travel through distant space in search of new crops to plunder and call to the others when more food was found. In the meantime, the elders would sleep.

She was chosen to seek new territories to exploit, while the others drifted into deep hibernation. On and on, she traveled into the void, until she could no longer be seen or heard by her brothers and sisters.

The isolation of the void was vast, and over eons of exploration, she forgot her responsibilities to her family and thought of herself as a singular entity. She dreamt of the creations of worlds, rather than their destruction. These ideas took hold in her mind and festered to become obsessions.

Each world would be a self-sustaining system whose inhabitants would nourish her through devotion, sacrifice, or worship, for she was the Creator, the Destroyer, and the Great Balance to all living things. From the raw essence of her being, she brought forth into the void two worlds that existed in complete opposition to each other, and then a third, which she placed in the middle to act as a fulcrum for balance. And thus, the Three Realms were born.

She knew pure chaos would provide a dynamic path to propel her worlds into a limitless future, but realized that law and order would be just as essential to keep the way firm enough for life to grow and prosper. The two forces were woven together in eternal conflict as one strove to tear-free, while the other remained steadfast and rigid. Such was the great paradox of life.

Therefore, the first law of her worlds was that the Great Balance must remain. Neither of the two outer realms would ever be allowed to overthrow the middle and gain an overwhelming advantage over its adversary.

The first of her progeny were perfect creatures of beauty and grace. They called her the Immortal Mother and referred to their world of paradise as the Seven Heavens. There, the True-borns, as they called themselves, set down strict laws for order and lived in eternal happiness.

Then she turned to the opposite realm of ever-changing landscapes of fire, frost, murky swamp, and arid desert, and filled them with horrors. Three impossibly powerful beasts were molded from the stuff of chaos to rule over the harsh world, which was named the Abyss.

The third world was called the Mortal Realm, and to all living things born to this place, she gave a unique soul, which contained the spark of her raw essence, and its power would be used as the fuel for the machinations of divine power, or sinister dark magic.

The human soul was intentionally born without alignment, a blank slate that would be colored according to the holder's life choices. Each man or woman was given free will to choose their path, for good or for evil, or a combination of both. Their lives would dictate where the life-energy continued its journey, be it in the lofty skies of the Seven Heavens, or the deep dark of the Abyss.

Souls secured in the Seven Heavens' cloudless realms provided the energy needed to create wondrous things and gifted the True-born angels with divine might. But not all souls traveled a righteous path, and those rooted in evil were cast down into the Abyssal Layers where their suffering would be used to evoke sinister and dark magic or give birth to nightmarish abominations.

The Abyss was divided into Layers and then again into smaller and smaller parts by seven to the seventh power, creating a sprawling, twisting jumble of lesser worlds that fought eternally against one another. The greatest of these subdivisions were called Circles, which often provided bridges or gateways to other Layers during their constant rotational orbits.

All creatures of the Abyss were obsessed with power, which was attained in only one way, the constant accumulation of mortal souls. A soul allowance was given quarterly to any creature who securely held significant territory; the more land, the more souls.

Those unfortunate to be born into the Abyss without holdings had to indenture themselves to higher powers, hire themselves as mercenaries, or steal it.

Presiding over much of the Abyss were the three original beasts created by the Immortal Mother, who took the names Xerthotha, Azrollorza, and Morrdilliax, respectively, and collectively these Supreme Devils were referred to as the Great Three.

The mere existence of the Great Three created a triangular truce of power, a stalemate of relative stability that kept the Abyss from tearing itself apart in war.

None of the Great Three ever moved directly against a rival for fear of retribution from the third. Nonetheless, each sought to trick the others into a misstep, which would cause them to forfeit territory. They sent the devils and demons under their rule to undermine war campaigns through clever subterfuge. Alliances of convenience were made and then quickly broken when new opportunities for further gain were at hand. And so, it had been since the dawn of all things.

Xerthotha sat uncharacteristically still within an undefinable structure that continuously changed in size, shape, and composition. Architectural facades rose around him then crumbled moments later before coming to completion. Then, a new structure would form, this time from organic matter rather than stone and mortar. It, too, would fall to be rebuilt again, using yet another building material to complete its design.

Stones walls changed to flowing sheets of water with intricate relief patterns of screaming faces, which dropped into collections of slushy ice puddles, only to boil and rise into the air into steaming domes, and then condense into fiery rocks that rained down around him. The cycle of change was endless.

Four legs jutted from Xerthotha's lower body, interlocking and crossed like a disciplined monk lost in deep meditation. His eyes were closed, and the Supreme Devil appeared to be at peace as infernal glyphs of deep orange and purple floated a lazy circle around his rigid body.

He was clad in a ceremonial mawashi around his waist and loins, leaving his broad, hairless chest and four legs exposed. He wore a full helmet of gold with wing-tipped sides and a facemask of a snarling lion. A swarm of bright-blue butterflies fluttered above his head like a floating halo. The air remained heavy and humid, causing sweat to drip down from his helmeted head and onto his chest.

"Enter, Zizphander," Xerthotha commanded in a booming voice.

Zizphander, the Red Devil of Naraka, hovered at the entrance of the ever-changing hall. He folded his blood-red, feathered wings behind his back and grew eight segmented appendages that resembled the legs of a wasp from the Mortal Realm. The Red Devil had a handsome, human face with fiery hair burning atop his head. The flames danced as he moved through the warped chamber.

His slender build was wrapped in toned muscles formed from red-hot embers that glowed across his body. He took a few steps forward and bowed low before Xerthotha.

"You have returned sooner than expected," Xerthotha said. "I am pleased."

He sent a charge of electricity dancing through the butterflies, and they fell to the floor like fist-sized stones, then melted into puddles of magma.

+I have removed the devil, Mogwai, as you commanded. His mind was weak, and his thoughts easily mastered. It was little trouble to dispose of him.+

Zizphander's mouth had never been an adequate mechanism for speech. It was too slow, and the psionist's mind was powerful enough to convey his thoughts directly into the mind of the great Chaos Devil.

"You sound as if defeating a devil of Mogwai's status was simple."

+He was a simpleton, unworthy of the world he ruled.+

"And now that world is yours." Xerthotha let the words linger in the air.

Zizphander's beautiful face became smug. Then his eyes shifted to the Xerthotha.

+I offer you the world of Taarne as a gift to honor your patronage.+ Zizphander voiced his thoughts using only his mind.

Xerthotha chuckled at the presumption of patronage. "Lesser devils never cease to amuse me. The territory you offer is insignificant to me, though when one is in the service of Xerthotha, one should know that all plunder is already mine. But today, I am feeling generous. Keep the land as your own."

+You want nothing more?+

"I always want more. Perhaps you will show me what waits in the hall, or must I guess?"

+Yes, of course, Great Xerthotha. I meant no disrespect. I bring another gift, perhaps something more satisfying.+

Zizphander looked over his shoulder and nodded to six burly demons, also glowing red from the fires that burned within their bodies. Each held an extended limb of a barely conscious and broken devil.

+If it pleases you, I bring you the still living Mogwai. His essence is yours to devour.+

"Now that was thoughtful. Azrollorza will be furious. You risk much bringing me one of her known champions. She is a vengeful Supreme Devil."

+Xerthotha is the only Supreme Devil! May his will reign uncontested in the Abyss.+

Xerthotha chuckled again as his body transformed into the shape of a middle-aged woman. She stood wearing a pretty gown with red roses imprisoned within a maze of thorny vines. Her straight, peppered hair was tied up in an intricate bun, held in place by two extraordinarily long and thin chopsticks. She approached Zizphander barefoot, but now on only two, shapely legs.

"Flattery will get you everywhere," she said with a demure smile. "If it is my patronage you seek, then there is more for you to do. But first, I will gladly accept your gift."

Xerthotha spat in her hand and squeezed her fist tight. When she opened it, there was a small pearl resting in her palm. She casually tossed it at the outstretched Mogwai, and the pearl expanded into a transparent bubble. It floated slowly towards the semi-conscious devil and his handlers. Larger and larger it grew until it encased them within its perimeter. Zizphander's demons looked at their master with concern from inside.

"There we are," Xerthotha said and waved her hand over the bubble.

The howls from Zizphander's demons echoed within the hardening ball and then were silent.

"I must say, in years of existence that extend back to the beginning of all things, I never tire of such a melodic chorus."

Xerthotha pinched her thumb and forefinger together, and the pearl shrank back to its original size. She picked it off the floor and tossed it in her mouth.

"Ah, succulent!"

Zizphander bowed low again. *+I only wish to please the great Chaos Devil.+*

"You are proving yourself to be a worthy asset. I am pleased with your progress," Xerthotha said.

+I must be allowed to ascend! Make me an Archdevil. I grow stronger each day.+

"You grow strong, yes, but only at my pleasure. Displease me, and you will return to the insignificant fiend you were before I graced you with a few devilish powers."

Xerthotha pointed to her pretty head as a reminder.

+*Yes, my Master.*+

Xerthotha then transformed into the shape of a small, human girl with long straight hair and almond-shaped eyes. "Now rise, my Red Devil. Go and make Taarne a realm of fire. If you can hold it without my assistance, I will see that you are worthy to ascend. Know that I shall be watching. In the meantime, let us discuss other thorns you can place in Azrollorza's meaty side."

SEKKA

CHAPTER 1

Sekka's long white hair fell across her back in a tangled and frayed mess. The mortal form she preferred to take during peaceful times was stiff, cut, and bruised. The acute pain she felt was a sharp reminder never to let her guard down. Betrayal was a way of life in the Abyss, and enemies lurked within every shadow, waiting for an opportunity to strike.

She limped awkwardly across the room, feeling the memory of every spear thrust, slashing claw, and sharp bite that discolored her once perfectly unmarred, pale skin. But she was alive, which is more than could be said for those who had attacked her. She wore a soft leather shirt, brown breeches, and boots, though it all still chaffed her healing wounds.

The devil hobbled across a scarcely furnished room that was as cold and somber as her mood. She looked through a glassed window and gazed out over the barren tundra of her burgeoning kingdom of Nilas, and found it lacking. She had suffered much to protect the pitiful lands bequeathed to her at birth. And now there was hardly anything left of them.

She tapped the glass of the window with a long, sharp fingernail, careful not to shatter the costly material. "They think I am weak, and their attacks will now come with greater regularity. And they're not wrong," she said with a sullen expression. "Damn that Badderrash and his insatiable greed."

A territorial dispute between a neighboring devil's kingdom had turned into a full-fledged war, one that had left her weak and depleted of elite forces. It would take her centuries of soul harvesting to return her ranks to their former glory, not that they were ever anything significant.

No sooner had she finally destroyed the last of Badderrash's armies, and took his head for her troubles, than she was forced to defend herself against a surprise attack from a roving band of greater demons calling themselves the Horrid Five.

She was outnumbered, fighting with injured and worn out troops, and away from her defensible stronghold. The timing of the attack couldn't have been worse for her.

The Horrid Five hailed from the first Abyssal Layer called Purgio and had secured territory on one of its seven Circles. Crossing into the second Abyssal Layer of Arcoxia had been a bold move, attacking Sekka on her home ground had been even more daring. Their strategy had been simple, take advantage of her vulnerable condition, destroy her remaining warriors, and assume control of her lands. And they had almost succeeded.

Sekka didn't care for their unimaginative name nor which one of Purgio's Circles had spawned them, but the combined strength of the five demon warlords and the number of their warriors was worrisome. She remembered watching a vast horde of fiends and lesser demons amassed against her with a tinge of dread.

"Rogue demons," she said with contempt. "The cowards would never think to challenge me at any other time."

But she was not without daring and resolve. She consolidated her injured troops and broken war engines into a ragtag battalion and commanded them to hold a precarious position on a poorly defended ice flow. With luck, the enemy horde would find such an easy target too tempting to resist. If they marched on her stronghold instead, her remaining troops would be hard-pressed to repel their overwhelming attack.

"But risks must be taken, and sacrifices made to climb the ladder of power," she reminded herself.

When the trap was set, she waited for the Horrid Five to make their move. Demons were predictable in their bloodlust, and the horde took the bait. While her troops fell to the Horrid Five's warriors' and teeth, she used her innate infernal magic to melt the entirety of the ice flow beneath their feet.

There was some pleasure in watching the last look on the warlords' startled faces as the frigid sea claimed them and their hopes of conquest. But one must know the ground on which one fights. Unfortunately, the troops she had lost in the gambit brought her overall forces to terrifyingly low levels.

It was the only way she would have survived against the horde. But now, she was placed in a dire predicament. She could no longer fight wars of attrition and would be unlikely to hold her territory with the remaining troops under her command.

Sekka took one last, disappointing look at her territory. The land was not blessed, or cursed, depending on one's point of view, with innate magical energy. It was dead ground, and to some, this did not matter if it provided enough soul allowance to its owner. But she overleveraged her quarterly quota with too many wars and shaky alliances that failed to buffer her from attack. Now, she was desperately low of souls.

Newly formed land meshed together from fragments of wild chaos took time to soak up the mortal soul energy sacrificed on its surface. Only then would it become a reservoir of power for the one who ruled over it. But the frozen ground of Nilas was too new to be anything more than a barren wasteland.

She caught the reflection of her scowl in the window before it fogged. The current state of her kingdom was an embarrassment to her pedigree as a devil of the higher Circles of Arcoxia. She knew it, as did those who thought her weak. She wondered if another attack was just over the horizon.

"Such a waste of valuable territory. Gone in an instant, but still holding a debt that will take me centuries to pay off."

And now, payment was coming due to the Chaos Warden, Lord Auzdioz, and she had little reserves to squander. She would need to replenish the troops of her depleted legions and find a supplemental source of energy to fuel her most complex spells. Turning from the window, she contemplated her plight.

Auzdioz was a greedy, ancient devil whose sole purpose in the Abyss was to convert unformed lands into new territory. The area she had just destroyed had only recently been deeded to her. If the desire moved him, he would spray the virgin lands with his seed, planting acres of fiends and lesser demons, who rose into existence and formed warbands to fight against one another for dominance.

"If you can hold it, I will give you more," he had said with what appeared to be a sly grin.

She hated the little hobgoblin of a devil. He knew what he was doing when he made the outrageous offer for new lands. The war with Badderrash was turning against her, and she needed reinforcements fast. What could she do but swallow the bitter pill and worry about its payment later?

"That little hobgoblin took advantage of me."

"Mistress?"

Sekka was interrupted from her musings by the demon witch, Chedipe, who stood at the open door. She was the offspring of a greater demon and a mortal witch. The desire for such a union was not uncommon as humans lusted for power over their rivals the same as demonkind and would often make pacts together for mutual benefit. The humans gained a dash of infernal power in the Mortal Realm, and the demons received souls sacrificed in their name. Love certainly had nothing to do with the arrangement.

But the actual birth of such a liaison was rare. There were myriad travel restrictions between the realms and the large allotment of soul stock required to attempt such a journey. There was also the added risk that the child would go mad during maturity, and the totality of the investment would be lost.

The offspring would intentionally be born in the Abyss, for a hybrid demon in the Mortal Realm would attract too much attention from the Angelic Watchers. The intervention of the Heavenly Host would ruin years of scheming, not to mention the soul cost of such an endeavor.

The Angelic Watchers had been obnoxiously diligent with their observations in recent decades, but Sekka knew their watchful eye was a passing phase. Raguel, the Chancellor Pinnacle of the Seven Heavens, often grew bored with humans' fate and would reallocate his resources to other, more divine pursuits.

The practice continued, for it was said that the human mind was evolutionarily more advanced than most demons. If the offspring could withstand the duality of species, it would be an important asset, especially to a full-fledged devil, such as Sekka.

Chedipe has somehow defied the odds and survived her birth and maturity into a young woman. She was acquired by Sekka when she was still an adolescent, and the demon witch had not lost any of the vibrancy of her youth. By human standards, she would be considered alluring.

Her reddish hair was the color of a fiery Autumn and reached the base of her back and narrow waist. She wore a long frock, which hid her shapely legs and womanly figure. But to Sekka, Chedipe's beauty lay in her wicked mind. The demon witch had a gift for inflicting pain and a real talent for soothsaying, though she was not the most courageous creature and often prophesized the more negative side of an ever-changing future.

Sekka appreciated the balance she received from Chedipe's predictions over her other seers, who were mere sycophants promising her victory at every step, no matter how ludicrous. Sekka did not suffer incompetence, and many of the latter found themselves bound to a torturer's rack, and under Chedipe's knife.

"The perimeter needs repairs, my Queen," Chedipe said. "Souls are due to arrive, but much of them are owed elsewhere." She had a list and raised the tablet for Sekka to see.

"There is no sense in building a permanent stronghold here. This ice flow spreads for hundreds of miles, but it is a dead territory and will remain so for centuries," Sekka said with irritation. "And my incompetent benefactors can wait to receive anything more from me. Renegotiations are in order. The Horrid Five should never have gotten that close to Nilas."

Lord Oziax, the General of her armies, or what was left of them, strode boldly into the room, pushing Chedipe to the side. He was in his mortal form, as per Sekka's command, and dressed in an off-white armor with hundreds of abrasive barnacles covering its surface. His hair was singed, and a terrible scar traveled down the side of his face.

"Here's a hot mess," Sekka said bitterly, remembering why the leader of her armies looked battered and bruised.

"It's nothing," Lord Oziax replied. He possessed a unique ability to regenerate tissue, albeit slowly, and survived the most grievous wounds if given time to heal.

"I have the final tally of losses."

"Oh, do tell, and brighten my day," Sekka said sarcastically.

"We suffered the loss of a third of our infantry when the ice flow melted. They drowned with the enemy."

"I can replace them with the next soul allowance," she said and gazed back out the window.

"There's more," Lord Oziax said. "Chedipe has calculated the numbers according to the remaining land, soul debts owed, and what we can expect from your vassals. You will not be able to rebuild immediately."

"I know. She has already informed me of this wonderful news."

Sekka turned to the demon witch, who looked to the floor and remained silent and shaking.

"When?" Sekka commanded.

"With the current territory under your command, your allowance barely covers your debt to the Chaos Warden. The lesser devils under your banner have asked for a postponement of payment lasting six rotations. The war against Badderrash has dried up their soul reserves and made them paupers, or so they claim. They have nothing to give this quarter."

"How long?" Sekka's eyes rolled with anger. "How...long...Chedipe?"

"Just under two centuries to pay the soul debt to the Chaos Warden, if you maintain your soul agreements to the demon lords."

"Impossible. I will be dead within a year!"

"The demon lords will turn on you," Lord Oziax said, matter-of-factly.

"Obviously!" Sekka screamed.

"You must be more defensively minded until you can stockpile souls. Currently, there is nothing left to use as raw material to build reinforcements," Chedipe said and took an uncertain step backward.

Lord Oziax stood in the center of the room. His white mane of hair was braided in spots and held finger bones of enemies at the tip. At his hip was the sword, Eishorror. The fell blade was nestled in a frost-covered scabbard. He held his arms behind his back, and he waited patiently at attention.

"What are your orders, my queen?"

Centuries earlier, she had recruited the greater demon lord and his jol'goth followers to wage war in her name. They had successfully conquered smaller, leaderless tribes, which she piecemealed together to form a patchwork of territory to rule —anything to grant her more mortal souls.

But now she was far too weak even to contemplate engaging another devil of merit for more land. She was trapped in a pitiful state of existence that would take centuries to overcome.

She knew the eyes of her rivals watched her, waiting for her to make one critical mistake, then they would pounce. If she survived the defeat, she would be enslaved like a base fiend and paraded as a showpiece to exemplify the victor's power.

But she promised herself that would not be her fate.

"Luckily, Lord Auzdioz has generously gifted to you more territory to exploit, which comes with a healthy stock of minions, ready to earn the praise of their new master," Lord Oziax said. "My jol'goth enforcers will weed out the challengers and dissenters, while the rest are assimilated into your army."

"What land do you think was destroyed, you brute?" Chedipe said, throwing her arms in the air. "How can you be so dense?"

Sekka's black-on-black eyes narrowed. "That disgusting gremlin, Auzdioz, shackles me to his so-called gifts. The more he gives, the more I must sacrifice to please his sordid whims. He knows I will need more by giving me worthless ice and dirt. It will take me millennia to gain enough power to accomplish the most trivial of things. But I cannot afford the cost of new land."

"Then steal it, Mistress," Sess'thra said in a playfully seductive voice. The heady perfume of cinnamon and sulfur preceded her as she clip-clopped on hooved feet into the room. The succubus had ink-black hair that flowed down her front side like an untended oil slick, partially covering her chest and midsection. Her leathery wings were tucked into her flesh, but she let her smooth tail flow behind her with the ease of a hunting cat.

Sess'thra's childlike innocence deceived any that did not understand her true nature. She was a killer.

"It is not so easy as that. There is always a price in the Abyss, always."

Sess'thra shrugged her narrow shoulders. "Then let another pay the price while you reap the benefits. It's simple, see?"

Behind her lumbered a bearish demon covered with short white fur. Sess'thra held him in check by a chained leash that ended in a shackle around his throat. A black vapor trailed from its body as it moved.

The demon was massive, standing eight feet tall, with a stout muzzle filled with needle-shaped teeth. Instead of front paws, the beast had hands ending in long fingers, tipped with black claws. His pink, rat-shaped eyes moved in erratic, sharp glances at each of the room's occupants.

"What is that?" Lord Oziax asked.

Sess'thra spun like a child performing a pirouette. "Do you like him? He is a shadow demon called Khalkoroth and can shift his body to a separate location at will. All he needs is a bit of darkness. Isn't that wonderful?"

"Yes, it's a handy trick," Sekka said dismissively.

Khalkoroth snarled at Lord Oziax, which earned him a backhanded slap from the demon lord. "Do not think to challenge me, Pale One, or you will find yourself on the wrong side of my blade."

Sekka looked warily at the naïve succubus. Shadow demons were known for their duplicitous nature and self-serving agendas. They were small-minded, untrustworthy thieves, who would not think twice about betraying a master if a stronger one presented itself.

But the succubus was crafty, and Khalkoroth had the body of a warrior, rather than a sneak. Perhaps he would prove himself worthy enough to stay alive.

"Sess'thra, you know better than to bring mongrel demons past the walls of the stronghold," Sekka said in almost a motherly tone, almost. The succubus was more than seven hundred years old.

Sekka's gaze fell on Sess'thra's lithe body, small, curling horns, and playful tail. She had been a gift of sorts from a young devil in hopes of keeping a fragile peace. Sekka suspected deception at the time, and therefore, killed the devil, but kept the gift.

Over the years, the succubus had proven to be a trusted asset and a keen assassin. Sekka had been wrong about the devil's intentions after all, and shrugged her shoulders. She was not infallible.

Sess'thra continued to dance about the room as if she was the center attraction as Sekka's irritation grew worse. No one should be cheerful while their queen was miserable.

"Enough of your antics. Have the new souls arrived?"

Sess'thra stopped immediately and became serious. "Yes, Mistress. I watched the imps dumping your soul allowance into the respective pits. They are ready to be transmuted into new creations at your leisure."

Not fiends or loyal demons bonded to her will, but imps! She was a devil who commanded imps, Sekka thought furiously. The notion disgusted her and only served to darken her already foul mood.

"Fine, if you have nothing else to report, you will go to the Orthod Pits and instruct the handlers to ready their herd. And take that thing with you. It stinks."

"Well, there is one small thing of interest you might like to know. While Khalkoroth the *thing* and I were playing elsewhere," Sess'thra giggled at the new title of her pet, "we stumbled across the most amazing thing. Guess what it was!"

"Sess'thra." Sekka glared at the succubus. "I'm not in the mood for your childish games."

"Okay, okay, I'll just tell you, then. The Red Devil of Naraka has taken Taarne!"

Sekka and Lord Oziax looked at Sess'thra, expecting more.

Sess'thra returned their stare, and eventually raised her eyebrows for emphasis. "Isn't that grand?"

"The devil, Mogwai, rules the world of Taarne and is strong. You are mistaken, succubus child," Chedipe said and waved the notion away that a lesser devil such as Zizphander could overthrow one as mighty as Mogwai. "Zizphander is young. He would not have the military might to do as you say."

"Mogwai has been defeated! We saw it with our own eyes. It was an epic battle of

Zizphander's fire fiends clashing against Mogwai's demon drakes. The Red Devil soared high above it all on his mighty red wings, until Mogwai drew down lightning from the skies and battered him with sizzling electricity."

Sess'thra curled and wriggled her fingers to emulate the lightning strikes.

"But Zizphander remained aloof and would not engage Mogwai on the ground. The sly Red Devil forced Mogwai to mount one of his dragons and fight him in the sky," Sess'thra said with wide, storytelling eyes.

"Zizphander hovered calmly in the air as Mogwai flew higher and higher, and then, the oddest thing happened. Mogwai turned his sword on himself, thrusting it clean through his chest. He didn't make a sound as he plummeted to the ground."

"It appears Zizphander is a Psion. He fights with the mind instead of the sword," Chedipe added.

"Anyways," Sess'thra said, annoyed at being interrupted by the demon witch and ruining her story's mystery. "Zizphander now holds Taarne and plans to awaken the Dead Giant. Once it erupts, lava will flow and cover the lands in fire."

"And what do you hope to achieve by burdening me with such a story? Do you seek to further my displeasure by reminding me of my present shortcomings?" Sekka said.

"No, of course not, Mistress. But did you know, the land of Taarne is saturated with raw Elemenati energy?"

"Is it now? How do you know such things?" Sekka asked suspiciously.

"Oh, I traded a little of this for a little of that and got the information I needed," she said with a wink as she waved her hands over her toned body.

"Be assured, Mistress, the soil, the water, I bet even the air is filled with Elemenati energy. What flows through the core of Taarne is worth ten times the soul allowance it provides for one such as you."

"My dear child, you have done exceptionally well."

"Thank you, Mistress." Sess'thra curtsied.

"Defeating Mogwai was no small feat, and I suspect that arrogant Zizphander is very weak now. He will need time to nurse his wounds and rebuild his armies," Sekka said as her mind churned through different scenarios of how best to exploit this fortuitous news.

"It would be an ideal time to steal his soul plunder!" Lord Oziax said.

"But if we lose, we will be completely defenseless," Chedipe said as she tossed a handful of runestones on the floor. "Chedipe peers into the future and sees..."

"What? What do you see, witch?" Oziax impatiently growled.

Chedipe brushed all but three stones to the side. "This is strange. The stones speak of a time lost in the future, and a human soul split between mortal life and a divine spirit, but its two parts remain the same. The identity of this being is hidden beneath layers of secrecy, though your destinies are forever entwined."

She threw the stones again, and this time quickly looked up to Sekka with fearful eyes.

"The stones show an impossible victory followed by an agonizing defeat, both caused by the hands of the unseen hero. My Queen, you must reconsider a blood feud with Zizphander, for once you set foot on this path, you will not be able to alter your fate."

"Roll them again, witch. You are confused," Oziax said and made to scoop up the stones with his hand.

"No! Only Chedipe must touch the stones. You will anger those who grant her the secret knowledge of foresight. The Daughters of the Whispering Spirits will only twist their truth out of spite. The stones have spoken. There is no more Chedipe can say."

Sekka turned away from the others and stared out the window to the bleak landscape of her useless territory. Chedipe's talents were not to be second-guessed or cast aside as meaningless, but they were often laced in unsolvable riddles until the actual events happened.

"I will not have another opportunity to take such a vast amount of territory this quickly, and so infused with Elemenati magic. What would be useless to that psychic deviant is priceless to me. My power base will increase a thousand-fold once Zizphander is removed."

"But Chedipe knows not how with so few troops. Do not disregard the warning of the stones, Mistress," Chedipe said, shaking her head and imploring Sekka to choose a different path.

"Never use your forces when someone else's will do just as well," Sekka said, giving Sess'thra a knowing nod. "I have an idea."

SEKKA
CHAPTER 2

Sekka journeyed to Vortexx, the Third Circle of Arcoxia, and the land currently held by the Demon Lord, Akkoro. Shrieking air ripped through wind tunnels in the canyon below as she climbed the last leg of the bluff, which served as the designated meeting place. She was taking a risk being away from her lands during a time when it was known she was vulnerable, but she would not cower in her stronghold and wait idly for the end to come.

Accompanying Sekka was Lord Oziax and a small escort of his jol'goth guard. The massive demons lumbered behind her like enormous white boulders, standing fifteen feet high, covered in dense fur, though their heads were covered in stretched skin, smeared with charcoal grey streaks. Their purple lips curled back in growls and snarls, revealing crystal-shaped teeth as they approached Lord Akkoro and his party.

Sekka's hair whipped around her head in the wind and repeatedly stung her face, but she paid it no mind. Her focus was set on saving her kingdom and her life. She sized up the demon lord. He was available, if not an ideal, partner to achieve both.

Akkoro's face was covered in black feathers and shaped like a streamline raptor ending in a hooked beak. His eyes were placed on the sides of his face and he cocked his head to the side to observe Sekka. Where feathered wings should have grown from his back were iridescent, vaporous ribbons, flashing shades of green and purple, billowing behind him as he swayed in the air.

His long arms were folded across his lean chest, and his thin, black, avian legs hovered just above the ground. The physical mass he presented to her was nothing but the elaborate disguise of a thief. Akkoro was a Djinn'jinn, an elemental demon of the air, and his body could dissipate into thin air at a moment's notice.

He wore a light, transparent vest open in the front, which dropped to his thighs and was covered in shiny baubles and small trinkets, displaying mementos of past victories or stolen plunder. Akkoro was an obsessive collector of rare and unique objects, and by many accounts, he held a vast trove of cursed items, any one of them a lethal surprise to his enemies.

But today, he came unarmed. It was a subtle message, but one Sekka understood immediately. He was not afraid of her, or at least he attempted to appear that way. She scoffed at the idea. All demonkind had an inherent fear of devils. It was in their blood, and Akkoro was a coward at heart.

She had no doubt he was an opportunistic parasite of the Abyss, the type who attacked his allies when their backs were turned. She had no doubt he would attempt to betray her. *Let him try*, she thought.

His willowy body constantly jostled in the gusty air, rushing up from the base of the ravine. It was a bothersome quirk that annoyed Sekka, forcing her eyes to follow his movements just to see him squarely. She wanted to reach out and grab him and make him stay still.

Floating in a semi-circle behind Akkoro were his bodyguards. Each bobbed in the air like the demon lord but sported a mini-tornado swirling beneath their waists. The guards were smaller in stature but no less aggressive. They were fast and agile and would swarm to attack if they feared their master was in danger. It was a good show, but Sekka wasn't interested in their pageantry, only their strength of arms.

"Lord Akkoro, thank you for accepting my invitation to meet," Sekka said with as much of a gracious smile as she could muster.

Akkoro gave a hoot and nodded his head three times. "It was more curiosity than generosity that allowed you to trespass my lands."

He turned his bird head from side-to-side to see her more clearly with each eye. "I wondered how a devil looked when she was groveling for scraps."

The high-pitched screech that came from Akkoro's throat, posing as laughter, grated on Sekka's nerves.

"You dare!" Lord Oziax unsheathed his blueish-white blade, Eishorror, and his jol'goth guards roared their outrage at the insult to their queen. Their coarse hair bristled along their oversized backs. Akkoro squawked in alarm but did not take flight.

"Lord Oziax, lower your blade. Lord Akkoro is in a playful mood."

Akkoro settled his ruffled feathers back into place and eyed Oziax's sword with desire.

"What do you need?" he said. "Though I don't know why I ask. You seem to be in short supply of anything I might want in return," he said boldly, yet kept a wary eye on the fell blade in Lord Oziax's hand.

Sekka held back a sneer. She could rip this demon peasant apart before he could shift into thin air. But that would not help her achieve her goal.

"The Circle of Vortexx is uniquely positioned between the second and third Abyssal Layers. Your territory is practically a bridge between the two, and I need passage."

Akkoro shrugged his shoulders. "Many high-ranking, powerful devils cross my lands into the Land of Sorrows via its Seventh Circle without any thought of payment to me for their trespass. The strong prey on the weak everywhere across the Abyss. I accept this, for such is the way of things. But you are weak, Sekka. Why should I grant you anything?"

"I can pay."

"With what? You of all devils should know secrets here do not remain hidden for long. Information travels faster than the Cromian Winds throughout the Circles of the Abyss, and the wars of devils are of interest to many. Those who collect and provide information are paid handsomely. Luckily, I am in a position to provide both services."

"Bah, that scuffle with Badderrash cost me next to nothing. I have already recouped my losses," Sekka said off-handedly.

Akkoro clucked again. "Your forces have dwindled, and your soul debts grow. Many lesser devils seek your head for their banners. Not for that dead patch of ice you call home, but because they are eager to see you removed. And why wouldn't they? The head of a defeated devil is a symbol of power and commands respect among demonkind."

"Be careful, Akkoro. My patience with you is evaporating rapidly." Sekka sneered out the words.

The bold confidence drained from Akkoro's raptorlike face. Lord Oziax took a menacing step forward. Ice shards fell from Eishorror as it shivered in his grip. Akkoro's guard spun higher into the air, taking up defensive positions around their lord.

"Lord Oziax, be still. We are here as friends, perhaps even partners. I see a day when Lord Akkoro parades Zizphander's head atop the pole of a victory banner. How high would your status rise among your kin then, I wonder?" Sekka said in a conspirator's tone.

"The Red Devil is the one you wish to overthrow?" Akkoro did nothing to hide his incredulous expression. "Are you mad? It is rumored he is being groomed for an elevated position, but who knows who starts such rumors? Maybe Akkoro, eh?"

"But he is weak. Now is the time to strike!"

Akkoro chirped and chattered in a what could only be assumed was an amused chuckle.

"Why would I want to risk all that I have conquered by joining you on this suicidal crusade? Zizphander is too strong, with too many powerful allies. Only a fool would get in his way. And I am not a fool."

"No, you are an opportunist and a collector of many things, and would not the head of a devil before he ascends be the ultimate trophy?"

"Bah, you are only here because you think you can use me like every other devil that has trespassed through my land. I know of Zizphander's recent victory over Mogwai, and his current strength. He is weak, yes, but not enough to be destroyed."

Sekka took an eager step forward. "Think of the vast territory you and I would control together. Who would trespass on Akkoro when retribution from the Archdevil, Sekka, and her Frost Legions would be swift and deadly?"

"Archdevil, you say?"

"My ascension would be obvious."

"Interesting, but still, no," Akkoro said with a bit of a snicker. "You have nothing of value to offer me that would justify helping you achieve this foolhardy venture. Your star is falling, your alliances are crumbling, and this is your one last gasp at survival. Maybe I should be kind and put you out of your misery, instead."

"I would have your head before you took flight, coward," Lord Oziax roared.

"Oziax, enough," Sekka said sternly.

"We are finished here, my Queen," Lord Oziax said with contempt. "He has no ambition for power."

"Unfortunately, you are right," Sekka responded. "Come, Lord Oziax, we will make our offer of partnership elsewhere. Perhaps Lord Narthoth will be more receptive to becoming a Major Demon." She turned to Akkoro. "You should have been more open-minded to what we could accomplish together."

"Wait! Wait, wait, wait, my friends. There is always room to negotiate."

"Go on," Sekka said.

"You would ascend me to the status of Major Demon? Is that possible?"

"Certainly. I will have enough territory under my control to grant you a fiefdom with a constant supply of mortal souls."

"How many souls?" Akkoro's interest was piqued.

"A tenth of the soul allowance of Taarne."

"A tenth is a rather generous amount, and the extra souls will be an enjoyable distraction, but they are worthless to me as no demon can transmute souls into infernal beings."

"But I can," Sekka said with a wicked grin. "You will need superior warriors if you are to conquer more land in my name."

"Ah, I see, now we come to it. You offer yourself as a Shadow Patron."

"Yes, with a vested interest in your gains."

"And if you fail to deliver me my due? What then? I will need an unbreakable pact."

"What do you wish?"

"If you fail to ascend me, I will own you. Indefinitely!"

"Own me indefinitely?" That got her eyebrows raised. She almost laughed.

"Yes!" said Akkoro with more chirping and excited squawking.

"My dear Akkoro, I will give you a thousand years of service if I renege on my offer."

"Three thousand."

"You will take less if you ask for more again."

"A thousand years then. Akkoro wins either way. And one more thing. I will take that blade from Oziax as a deposit. It will make a lovely addition to my collection."

Lord Oziax growled deeply. "Why not ask for the head of one of the Great Three while you wish for impossible things? Eishorror would devour your mind the moment you held it in your dainty hands."

"Lord Oziax will need his blade for the coming battle. You may have it afterward if you still desire it."

Akkoro took stock of the sword and reconsidered his request. The demon lord was wary of the fell blade for a good reason for one cut would freeze him solidly as stone.

"So be it, keep your foul weapon. But I will need an assurance of your commitment to succeed. I will take the land you promised now."

"Impossible."

"Then I will take your miserable ice flow as a down payment, or the equivalent if that is easier to stomach. I must be given something to make this idiotic enterprise of yours worthwhile."

"No."

"Then we are finished here." Akkoro's body dissolved into nothingness. His guard followed a moment later.

"You cannot trust Akkoro. He will steal what will not be given freely," Lord Oziax said, slamming Eishorror back into its sheath.

"I know what I am doing," Sekka responded and turned to descend the high bluff, and the journey back to her stronghold.

SEKKA

CHAPTER 3

Sekka teleported to another location on the outer edge of Arcoxia with her demon witch consort, Chedipe, and Lord Oziax. The three were in search of the Chaos Warden, Lord Auzdioz. The ancient devil was created at the beginning of all things and tasked with forming new lands from the raw stuff of pure Chaos.

Only the unique talents of a Chaos Warden could transmute the ever-changing, raw aether to a substance that held to a fixed set of laws. He was said to grant favors of unclaimed territory to any who could pay his exorbitant fee of mortal souls if they could find him.

Lord Auzdioz was a hermit and drifted with the tides of the Chaos Seas in his floating tower. He shunned the world and wanted nothing to do with the needs of devils and demons unless they could offer him something to occupy his depraved mind. But that, too, was a guessing game, and to guess wrong would negate any previous negotiations for new, uncharted lands.

Sekka took in their new surroundings. The solid ground was soon lost under a dense fog wall filled with cascading colors. She searched for a tower but only found thick mist butting up against undulating land that rolled like the waves of an underground sea.

"The witch is wrong again, the old hermit is not here," Lord Oziax griped.

"And you are sure he is here, now?" Sekka said. Like Oziax, her irritation grew with each near miss as they chased the last locations of the Chaos Warden across the perimeter of Arcoxia.

"Chedipe has seen many things through stones and bones. The Warden of Chaos is not here now but will be soon!" Chedipe said and scanned the land nervously.

"He will be here but will not remain for long. Much new territory is required for hungry devils such as great Sekka."

"He had better, or you will find yourself under my knives when we return to the stronghold," Oziax said.

"Chedipe knows! She knows! Look, mighty Sekka, look! The tower has arrived." Her hand shot out eagerly with a finger pointing to the left.

Sekka turned to see a lone tower materialize at the edge of the mist. It was modest in size and rather shoddy in appearance. There were no raised merlons or battlements of any kind to grace its walls, though it looked as if it had endured many hardships or neglect. Perhaps the owner simply did not care to uphold unnecessary pretenses considering his reclusive nature.

"Lord Auzdioz's fortress, my queen," Chedipe said, vindicated at last.

"I can see that," Sekka sneered.

The tower stood at the edge of the divide between what was real and what was yet to be. It was balanced between two realms and somehow refrained from being consumed in the nothingness of the churning mist. One half of the tower seemed to be without form, a mere whisper of the continuation of the material walls from the other side, which was a high pillar of crumbling stones black as soot, ugly and broken.

Sekka wondered what form of ancient magic held the derelict structure together. A massive iron door at the base of the tower screeched open as the metal slowly scraped against the stony ground. Then, a tiny figure shuffled from the darkness to the outside.

He was a mess of dirt and slop. Loose skin sagged from his cheeks, arms, and legs where it wasn't covered in hair filled with grime or gunk. Tired, orange eyes shimmered from sunken sockets placed abnormally far apart on his face.

Lord Auzdioz appeared to be no more than a disgusting hobgoblin, something to be squashed underfoot on a whim. She watched the devil in envy as he went about his business without a care or worry of being attacked, for Lord Auzdioz was considered untouchable in the Abyss, as were the six other Chaos Wardens.

"Greetings, Lord Auzdioz," Sekka chirped with eagerness. Lord Oziax and Chedipe followed a step behind her.

"You, again, so soon?" Lord Auzdioz said from his rodent-shaped snout. "Have you lost what I have already given you? The soul debt is still owed to me, whether you hold the land or not."

"You will have your payments as they come due. I am here for more," Sekka said confidently.

"More," he chuckled. "There is no more for you. Do you think you are the only devil to request my services? There is a long line before you, begging for my favor."

"There must be something you would like in return for a special favor to me," Sekka said.

She felt molested by the hobgoblin's lustful stare until his orange eyes drifted to Chedipe, and he licked his bloated lips. "Perhaps we can make a side agreement for the witch. Half-human, is she? Such a rare treat, and one that looks very tasty."

Chedipe's eyes grew wide. "My queen, do not forsake your Chedipe to this creature."

"Hush. You will do as you are told," Sekka said, relieved it would not be her who sullied her body with this wretched toad.

"Creature?" Auzdioz's rheumy eyes narrowed. "I was made when the Great Three were born. I am the oldest of the Chaos Wardens and have brought the entirety of Arcoxia into existence. Though I am treated as a servant to the Supreme Devils, without me and my ilk, they would still be floating helplessly in the void. Who are you to call me 'creature'?"

Auzdioz walked towards the edge of solid ground. "Leave me. I have nothing for you now. Return in a hundred years, and maybe I will reconsider."

"Chedipe," Sekka said through clenched teeth. Then, "Lord Auzdioz, please, pay no mind to my ignorant servant. She will be punished accordingly for insulting you."

Auzdioz turned and raised his bushy eyebrows. "Oh? And how will she suffer? Will she be drained of blood or will she lose of all the pretty digits of her hands? Tell me!"

"I will allow you to watch if that is your desire after we have agreed to terms."

"You have my attention, young devil."

His face was more hair than skin, but Sekka could still see the shyster's smile crease his lips. "What do you want?"

"Land, you fool! Is that not obvious?" Oziax said. His hand drifted to the hilt of Eishorror.

Auzdioz glared at Oziax, and then a thin, amused smiled crossed his face. "Careful, dog. Your life exists only at my pleasure."

Sekka stepped in front of Oziax, hoping to relieve the mounting tension between the two.

"Lord Auzdioz, I am in great need," Sekka pleaded.

"No doubt, you are, but you must be patient. Power in the Abyss is earned over time, and you are still but a babe. There are no short cuts, and debts must be paid in full before more can be borrowed. Even here, the Great Balance must remain."

"My lack of available resources puts me at a clear disadvantage against my rivals. To be blunt, I need your help if I am to survive."

"Then, perhaps, you will die. This is not my concern."

"Then your soul debt dies with me," Sekka countered. "And I wouldn't want that."

Sekka approached the dwarf-sized devil. She twirled a bit of his mangy hair through her fingers. "Can't you just make this one little exception for me?"

"You will attract more attention than you wish. The Great Three will know of your land grab, for nothing escapes their ever-watchful eyes. It will displease them to learn you have taken what was not earned through conquest. Eventually, they will know it was me who grafted the land, and I will be punished."

"Punished? How dare they think they could do anything to one of your royal blood? You are all equals, are you not?"

"You are an ambitious devil, Sekka, with the flickering tongue of a silver snake. Your desire for more will be your undoing."

"So, you agree!"

Lord Auzdioz crossed his arms over his chest. "I have said nothing of the sort. I will need something more for the risk I take in this endeavor of yours. I will take six times the soul fee from your last land grab, quarterly."

"Six times and quarterly! That is just under equal the amount of souls granted for such land. The debt will never be paid," Chedipe wailed. "My Queen, you mustn't."

"Quiet!" Sekka scolded Chedipe and cuffed her upside her head. "Or I will add you into the deal as a bonus."

She turned to Auzdioz. "Surely, we can come to more favorable terms."

"Take it or leave it. I'll have your answer now. There is much work for me to do, and you have already set my schedule back."

Lord Auzdioz waited a moment longer, then turned his back and walked towards the multi-colored wall of fog.

"Decide," he said over his shoulder.

"I'll take it all," Sekka said without delay.

"Then you are a desperate fool, Sekka of Nilas. No devil in their right mind would agree to such terms."

"Thank you for your concern, Lord Auzdioz. But I was not made to wait patiently as other devils leap ahead of me in power from conquered lands. I will not suffer millennia of mediocrity while waiting for some arbitrary amount of time to receive what I want. The Great Balance is flawed! One is not given power, Lord Auzdioz. One takes it!"

The ancient devil raised his bushy eyebrows and gave a quick look to the sky. "The Immortal Mother would not take so kindly to such words."

"Bah, she no longer cares for us or these worlds of her making."

Lord Auzdioz couldn't help but laugh. "Oh, Sekka, you are priceless entertainment. And a lonely devil such as myself enjoys the distraction you offer from the dreary monotony of my existence."

"I'm happy to make you happy. Now, do we have a deal?"

He beckoned her closer to tell her a great secret. "Did you know that countless devils have stood where you stand now, sparring with me over their unsurpassed greatness? Some even dared to think they could one day topple one of the Great Three and become a Supreme Devil in the High Pantheon of Chaos.

"They thought as you do now, but their gamble did not pay off, and they spent their long lives as slaves to greater powers, or worse, obliterated and never to reform."

"That will not be my fate."

Lord Auzdioz laughed again. "So said all those who thought to cheat their way through their ascension. The upper ranks must be earned over millennia, not by sleight-of-hand and trickery. I know you do not have the means to repay the soul debt for such a request, and I do not need to tell you that you are not well-liked among your peers. It is doubtful your lopsided alliances will last when it is known you are without a supply of souls to fuel your war machine."

"Will you give me what I want, or not? There are other Chaos Wardens who would offer better terms."

"Not on Arcoxia. Only I can form the virgin lands on this Layer. But the Abyssal Layers are not peeled back like an onion. They twist and turn and overlap one another to form a swirling ball of chaos. You would need to trespass over the domain of other devils on other Layers to reach another Chaos Warden. And I don't think you want to do that if you are here begging me for more land. Therefore, I am your only option, my dear Sekka."

"So, you say. Do we have a deal then? I will take all of this period's bounty and more if you have it."

"I could give you enough new land to choke on, and, as a bonus, I would seed it with a host of demonkind, ready for war. All at no extra charge."

He winked at Chedipe, who cringed in disgust. "But I won't. Those who help you now doom themselves to certain death, or worse, oblivion."

"You sound afraid," Oziax chimed into the exchange.

"Bah, fear has nothing to do with it. I enjoy my solitude. I am unbothered and unmolested. You already have a considerable soul debt owed to me. You cannot afford more."

"You'll get your damn souls. Now release the lands to me, and I will be on my way."

"I will not. Remember this day, for it is the day that I saved you from yourself."

Auzdioz turned to the wall of fog and began to extract rocks and boulders from the mist, which fell on the solid ground behind him. Sekka picked up a stone that had tumbled her way from the excess. She wanted to hurl it at the slovenly imp, but she tossed it in her hand instead. The rock turned insubstantial in the air, then returned to solid matter when it hit her hand.

"I will double your outrageous debt on the new land and double the remaining quarter's payment if you grant me what I need now."

"I have told you already, my answer is no."

"You'll give her the land she needs, or Eishorror will slice you in half," Lord Oziax shouted.

Auzdioz glanced over his shoulder. "Leash your dog, Sekka. If he threatens me again, you will be ended." Lord Auzdioz waved his hand over the ground, and a hundred pairs of colossal eyes flashed opened across its surface.

"My Chaos Golems savor devil meat most of all. Now leave me to my work. I have nothing more for you until your original soul debt is paid."

"I had thought you more receptive to negotiations."

"Then, you thought wrong. And be warned, young devil, if you fail to deliver me the demanded souls when I call my past debt due, then you'll receive an unwanted visit from my golems. They are not bothered by a little ice and snow."

SEKKA

CHAPTER 4

Sekka returned to the top of the designated bluff and waited impatiently for Akkoro to arrive. Vortexx's mountainous landscape stretched out beneath her, and she fantasized of snowstorms raging over the peaks, frozen waterfalls, and the ravines filled with ice. She checked the markers for the designated location one more time, and she was in the right spot. The Djinn'jinn was late.

"Typical," Sekka grumbled under her breath. "When this is over, I will have that cocky demon's head."

The air above her head vibrated as numerous winged creatures manifested into more physical forms. A cacophony of squawking and sharp cries echoed in her ears as Lord Akkoro and his guards made their appearance.

"Do you think it wise to come alone?" Lord Akkoro said as he swirled into being in front of Sekka.

"Lord Oziax and Sess'thra remain with my jol'goth army in the valley below, ready to invade the Circle of Taarne. Why should I fear to tred in the land of my new warlord?"

"You must have reconsidered my proposal and now have the land I requested, yes? Please, tell me it isn't that dismal ice flow you have been defending all these years. The cold winds are too harsh on my plumage," Akkoro said and chirped and clucked in laughter.

"An agreement has been made, and I have secured the lands you require."

"Excellent! When can I see the new addition to my territory?"

Sekka produced the small stone of raw chaos that she lifted from Lord Auzdioz's worksite. The rock constantly shifted between hard matter and mist as it lay in the palm of her hand.

"What is that?" Akkoro said, curious but also skeptical that Sekka had lied about the promised land.

"This is a symbol of your down payment. Lord Auzdioz will produce new land at your discretion," she said. The lie came easy and left her lips as quickly as her mind had conceived it.

"What trickery is this, devil? Where is my land?"

"Surely, you can understand that claiming uncharted territory from raw chaos takes time. Your land has not been created yet."

"Then the answer is still, no," Akkoro said.

"I thought you might say that, which is why I have instead secured Lord Narthoth's acceptance of the same offer. All I need to do is bring him this chaos stone, and our pact will be binding."

Sekka clenched the stone and tucked it away.

"Lord Narthoth would never agree to attack Zizphander on Taarne for a future stake in unmade land. The Valgothi is many things, but he is not stupid."

"You're right. Narthoth balked at my offer until I told him that I would help him conquer the Circle of Vortexx once I possessed Taarne. And who do you think was the first of his rivals he wanted to destroy?"

"You're a wicked beast."

"Then, the agreement is satisfactory?"

"Agreed," Akkoro's beak snapped. "Give me the stone."

When Sekka presented it once more, he grabbed it fast from her outstretched hand, tapped it with his beak, squawked, and then threw the stone to one of his guards.

"Done," Sekka said without hesitation. "Your terms have been accepted, and the pact is now binding. Lord Oziax will brief you on the particulars of battle and when you are to attack. When the Circles of Vortexx and Taarne align, we will cross the gap."

"A bridge of sorts will form when the Circles intersect. You must move your troops across quickly. Though it will last for many days, any creature that remains on the crossover when the Circles separate will be lost forever."

"Today shall be a day remembered in the histories of the Abyss. Come, let us go and claim our destinies, Lord Akkoro," Sekka said.

"Yes, let's," Akkoro said and leaped into the sky and flew to where the edges of Vortexx and Taarne would soon collide.

The Circle of Vortexx's high cliffs and thermal updrafts shifted into a land of fire and ash as Sekka and her army crossed into the Circle of Taarne. The sky was dark, and the rivers of red lava flowed across the land. Waves of stifling, dry air gusted into her face and made her skin feel raw. She felt like she was melting under her form-fitting armor.

"This will never do," she said as she turned her gaze to a distant volcano and watched the mountain top belch fiery magma into the sky. Hot lava flowed down its jagged sloped, forming rivers of fire and burning everything in its path.

Zizphander had awakened the Dead Giant and meant to transform the land into a realm of fire. A blazing inferno lit the top of the mountain and churned charcoal smoke into the sky. Hot ash and flaming boulders spewed from the mouth of the open crater.

Tall geysers of fire erupted across the flatlands as the land was ripped apart by underground gaseous pressures, long suppressed, and seeking a final release. Lakes boiled, and smaller rivers and streams evaporated into scolding steam.

"He did not wait long," Lord Oziax said as he trotted beside Sekka on a fiendish mount. He wore his traveling armor colored bleached coral. It was thin and not meant to withstand heavy blows.

"All the better. Zizphander will be exhausted. Psions are not known for their innate spellcasting ability. Waking the Dead Giant will have cost him much of his strength."

"My skin itches," Sess'thra complained. "Can we please hurry this up? Chop, chop, and we are done."

"If it were only that easy," Sekka replied. "Lord Akkoro, you seemed overly confident you knew of Zizphander's whereabouts, but we have been marching for days."

"Maybe he is bathing in the lava flow. Do you think I enjoy this heat any more than you do? The sooner we are done with this madness, the better."

"Akkoro, you are sure Zizphander does not suspect an attack?" Oziax said, perusing the fiery landscape. "The terrain ahead is ideal for an ambush."

"Do you question my trustworthiness on the edge of battle?"

"Yes," he said emphatically.

"Then where are the hordes of fire fiends waiting for your grand arrival? My spies have confirmed Zizphander and his horde are nursing their wounds from the war with Mogwai. If we fight him now, we are assured of victory!"

"First, we must find them."

"The road ahead is clear and beyond that is higher ground. We can establish a war camp there and assess our next move," Akkoro squawked.

The armies took the road Akkoro suggested. Sekka's troops plodded along the long and narrow strip as lava steadily rose on each side. Lord Akkoro's warriors flew on ahead to the small mount.

"We are not equipped for a long engagement," Oziax said, "We don't have the strength to lay siege to a castle or keep, and a prolonged ground battle will see us ruined."

"Do you see any such thing as a stronghold here? The entire land is not but fire and ash!" Sekka snapped. She glanced behind her as the Circle of Vortexx finally separated from Taarne and the gateway between the two worlds dissolved. Her keen eyes scanned the landscape. Nothing seemed amiss, for now.

"We are committed," she said. "I intend to make this quick. Zizphander is hurt, and his armies must surely be a fraction of their previous strength. With a quick strike, we will neutralize his ability to wage war."

"Well, where are they, then?" Oziax's frustration was increasing. "Why haven't they noticed our arrival? Something is not right here. If this is your doing, Djin-n'jinn, I will have your head."

"Those under my whip are loyal to me," Akkoro said boastfully. "Do not fret, Lord Oziax. Zizphander is still oblivious to our arrival."

The lava continued to rise on either side of the strip.

"Then who or what is that?" Sess'thra said, pointing to an orange comet streaking across the charcoal red sky. As it approached, feathered wings colored ruby red unfurled and flapped with strong strokes like a great bird of prey.

"Finally," Sekka said with no small amount of satisfaction.

"I go to the hill and will organize my warriors. Courage and strength to us all,"

Akkoro said and took to the air. He was soon addressing his warriors and arranging them into formation.

Zizphander shrieked in the sky, and the sound crawled up her back like a bad dream. Sekka eyed the rising lava flow with concern. It was swelling at an alarming rate and would soon overflow into the road.

"Race to the hill! Sess'thra, stay with me," she commanded and spurred her mount forward.

"The horde rises! Akkoro has been duped!" Oziax shouted as thousands of fire fiends rose from the lakes of fire on either side of the strip. "To arms! The enemy attacks!"

Oziax shouted orders to form ranks with the jol'goth brutes moving to the sides while the lesser demon archers remained behind their protective wall. Akkoro sounded a shrill call from the hill and drew his sword. He flew into the air with the rest of his warriors behind him.

Fire fiends leaped out of the lava and smashed into the jol'goth lines. Wherever the wall was weak or yet to close, the fiends raced forward, slaughtering Sekka's archers with their claws and teeth. Whole platoons went up in flames as their bodies caught fire.

The jol'goths howled in pain as fiery hands tore into them and set them ablaze. Soon, vast swatches of jol'goth warriors were consumed in enormous fireballs of flesh and fur. Oziax's lines were breaking.

"Fall back and retreat to the hill!" Oziax yelled out to his troops. Eishorror's icy-blue glow lighted the way like a beacon. "To the hill! To the hill!"

The jol'goths swatted away Zizphander's fiends with their war clubs or impaled them on the spiked points of their long pikes. Once the archers had reached higher ground, they were able to provide support to the retreating jol'goths.

Sekka watched the battle unfold from the highest point on the hill. The initial surprise attack of the smaller fiends had been absorbed, and now the jol'goths' superior strength pushed Zizphander's soldiers back. Their long swinging arms swept the double-axed polearms into the mass of fiends and cleaved them apart. The archers let fly their black arrows and dropped hundreds of fiends collecting in the strip's rearguard.

Oziax reached the beginning of the incline with a dozen jol'goths at his side. Gangs of fire fiends gathered on the hill's right and left sides, attempting to surround the small group. Oziax leaped from his mount and unsheathed Eishorror, stabbing it into the ground, while the enemy jostled and jumped over each other in a mad rush to reach him.

Oziax shouted a word of dark magic, and the runes of power covering his light-weight armor glowed briefly before the suit faded from sight. Then, his mortal body quickly transformed into its infernal form.

His human face changed into a snarling lion's head with long coarse hair. One hand gripped the hilt of Eishorror. The other had mutated into five long tentacles that curled and coiled at his side. He shook his white mane and unleashed a mighty roar at the enemy mob surrounding him and his jol'goth guard.

The fire fiends advanced as a great mass of bodies, arms, legs, claws, and teeth. The jol'goths pounded the ground, and their bodies shook with rage, so eager were they to rend and tear the smaller creatures apart.

Eishorror's frosty blade struck out in a blur of motion, and countless fiends were frozen where they stood or sliced open with the ease of a surgeon's knife. Oziax kicked a frozen fiend into a thousand smaller pieces of ice and pointed his sword to the rest, challenging them to attack. And on came the mob.

There seemed to be no end to the numbers of Zizphander's horde. The fire fiends continued to leap from the lava flow without end. Sekka watched as Zizphander circled back around in a wide loop. An uneasy realization crept up her spine. Something was not right.

"Zizphander knew we were coming. His losses were grossly exaggerated, or his warriors have somehow been miraculously replaced."

"Mistress?" Sess'thra said.

"It was too easy to get to this point, this exact location," Sekka said. "Where is that traitor, Akkoro?"

Zizphander screeched again in the sky above her head. Oziax let the jol'goth hammer into the fiends and got to where he could be seen by the archers still on the strip leading to the hill. He shouted to them to fire on Zizphander. Sekka took a few hesitant steps towards her General's position as hundreds of arrows shot into the sky. Zizphander banked to the left, easily avoiding the shafts.

Oziax barked out a new set of orders, and successive volleys flew at the Red Devil, leaving him nowhere to fly. Sekka shouted in glee, assuming some of the arrows would find their mark. But Zizphander's mocking laugher said otherwise as he masterfully wove between the flights of arrows.

"Fight me!" Oziax shouted in frustration.

Zizphander swooped in low and buzzed over Oziax's head but remained a sword's length out of reach. Lord Oziax grabbed a spear from a nearby jol'goth and threw it at the winged devil. Somehow, it caught him on the side, just under his wing.

The Red Devil screamed in pain and twisted his head towards Oziax, who fell to his knees. Eishorror tumbled from his sword hand's grip, while the tentacles of his other arm wrapped around his head. He bellowed in agony. Sekka watched in dread as the jol'goths under Oziax's command stopped fighting and wandered away from the battle. The fire fiends swarmed over them, setting their bodies ablaze with their flaming touch.

"Akkoro, Mistress!" Sess'thra said when she spotted the Djinn'jinn appear in the air over the prone Oziax. As the fire fiends continued to overrun Oziax's forces on the hill, Akkoro dropped behind Oziax with his sword drawn.

He caught Sekka's eye as he grabbed the top of Oziax's mane and pulled his head back. Then, he rammed his sword into her General's back. The point ripped through his chest and glistened with black blood.

Akkoro shoved Oziax's body into the dirt and reached down to grab Eishorror. He raised the fell blade into the air and gave Sekka a mock salute before ripping the scabbard from Oziax's waist. His head bobbed three times as if in laughter, then he whistled to his flock of warriors and one-by-one, they whipped into small, spinning tornadoes which eventually dispersed into nothingness against in the ash-filled sky.

"Betrayed!" Sekka said, snarling out the word.

SEKKA

CHAPTER 5

"The coward flees!" Sess'thra yelled as the last of Akkoro forces vanished from the battlefield.

"Find him. Bring me his head," Sekka said, seething. "Now!"

"Yes, my Mistress," Sess'thra said, leaping into the air on leathery wings and teleporting away.

Sekka's eyes narrowed on Zizphander as he flew erratically through the charcoal red clouds. Oziax's spear still jutted from his side and hampered his movements. Even from this distance, she saw his handsome face filled with pain. It wasn't an unpleasant sight.

Then, she watched in keen interest as an arm grew from under his wing and worked the shaft free.

"That's new," she said.

He wailed like a babe when the spearhead was finally dislodged. She lost sight of the mutated arm as Zizphander banked towards her. The fire burning across his body shifted through a bright array of blues, purples, oranges, and yellows as his mighty wings beat towards her.

"That's it. Come to me, you, arrogant peacock," Sekka said.

He did not make her wait long. Zizphander circled lower until he hovered above her, but still high enough away to be safe from immediate danger. She knew he was assessing her and the degree of the threat she represented.

A pleasing sensation caressed her body as a whispering thought crossed her mind, which quickly turned into a condescending slap.

+*Come to me, flightless beast.*+

The Red Devil's high-pitched, horrible laughter rang over the deep rumbles of the Dead Giant as it continued to belch fire and black smoke into the sky. His cowardice and arrogance infuriated her in equal measure as he taunted her but remained out of reach.

Lord Akkoro was the airpower she had hoped would ground Zizphander, but that was now a failed option. Teleportation was too risky and imprecise when trying to align with moving objects. Now, she could only stare helplessly at the winged devil.

"Blast that scheming Djinn'jinn!"

Then an uplifting sight caught her eye. Weeping magma dripped like burning blood from Zizphander's side. His wound was not healing. Sekka had assumed correctly, Zizphander's magic was weak. She allowed herself a small smile, knowing this was something she could exploit.

"Time to bring you closer."

With a word, her armor melted from her flawless body as she transformed into her Abyssal form. Four horns curled out of her skull, followed by four hooked teeth. Sekka grew three times her mortal form's height and towered over the tiny fire fiends scurrying to get closer. Coarse, white fur sprouted from her back as hard muscles rippled across her body.

Her human-shaped legs buckled backward and formed into the avian equivalent, which ended in raptor talons, and dug into the rocky ground. She clenched and unclenched her clawed hands, then shrieked her fury at the approaching enemy.

The fire fiends surrounding the body of Oziax took notice and raced up the hill towards her. They swarmed around her feet like mortal hornets gone haywire. Their fiery touch did little to stop her from wreaking havoc through their ranks. She barely felt the heat of the flames, singing her hair and scorching her skin. Her devilish flesh's outer surface was mostly resistant to fire, and the discomfort she felt only added fuel to her rage. But over time, her resistance would become overtaxed and fail. She could not win a war of attrition against such numbers.

Nonetheless, Sekka waded through the mass of fire fiends, intent on reaching Lord Oziax. She swatted eight of the little brutes with one hand, sending them into the air and crashing into others rushing up the hill. She grabbed three at once and squeezed them to a pulp in her fist. One leaped at her neck and managed to dig its claws into her flesh. She tore it from her body and swallowed it whole.

She killed relentlessly. The fiends were nothing to her individually, insects to be stomped and squashed, but as their numbers swelled, she understood the unseen power of the horde.

Finally, she reached Oziax's crumpled body and cleared the immediate area of fiends.

"Get up," she shouted and kicked him in the side.

Oziax moaned but remained motionless. With any luck, he would live long enough to be useful, but only if he wasn't burned to cinders by the horde, which was now circling their position, their numbers continually increasing as more spawned from the lava flow and leaped into the fray of battle.

Sekka plowed forward like a ram, trampling ten, twenty, thirty, or more under her feet as she made her way closer to her remaining army. The numbers between them were too high, and she was forced to stop. The horde followed like a mad shadow and circled her backside, surrounding her and closing in.

Those in the rear pushed the front lines forward, forcing their brethren to engage Sekka's waiting claws. She swept her hands with splayed fingers, gouging horrible rents across the bodies of countless fiends. Her hands and arms became raw and scorched from such constant exposure to the flames. Her resistance was failing.

The fiends' bodies were so tightly packed that many climbed on the backs of their comrades to reach her, or jumped from shoulders, hoping to gain higher purchase on her body. She grabbed the first few who leaped at her, but soon, the fiends increasingly landed on her back, arms, and head.

At once, the horde swelled around her like a rising tide of flesh and fire. Her claws and talons reaped a deadly tally of death into the mindless mob, but soon she was overwhelmed. They covered her like starving rats feasting on rotten meat. She felt her skin sizzle against their hot bodies as slashing claws tore into her skin and biting teeth sank deeply into her flesh.

A deep, guttural growl resonated from her throat. She called upon her innate frost magic and froze everything within a thirty foot diameter around her body. The residual magic seeped into the fiends swarming over the hill, causing their bodies to turn black and useless from severe frostbite. She shook her body like a wet beast, tossing off the fiends clinging to her like deformed icicles. Their bodies shattered on the ground.

On the narrow slip between the lava flow, her soldiers howled and raged at the fire fiends blocking them from rejoining their queen. No matter how many were put down by arrow or by a blade, the horde's numbers were replenished from the magma. Fire fiends jumped on the backs of jol'goths closest to the lava flow and ignited their bodies into walking infernos.

She sent another burst of frost magic into the enemy, pushing them back down the hill. She glanced into the sky, searching for the Red Devil.

"Come on, come on, I haven't all day to wait for you," she said, clenching her teeth in frustration.

Then a mild tingle caressed her mind as if playful fingers danced across the surface of her brain. Zizphander was probing her, looking for a way past her mental defenses. The more she resisted, the more incessant his touch became. Soon he was pounding on her skull, demanding entrance.

Her mind clouded, and her will to fight lessened just as he came into view. He glided closer to her position, and she heard a voice grow in her mind that was filled with arrogance and conceit.

+*On your knees, insignificant thing.*+

Laced between each word was more of his mocking laughter. His psionic attack was numbing. Sekka couldn't resist his compulsion to obey, and she dropped to one knee, and then the other.

+*Akkoro is but one of My Master's loyal retainers. Your feeble attempt to rest this world from me was doomed from the start.*+

Sekka's will to fight slipped away, and she struggled to remain conscious. Zizphander floated closer, gloating as he watched her suffer.

+*Look at you, a simple creature of cold and ice. How could you hope to win against an entire realm of fire and flame? You are anathema here. But it matters not now. Your existence will soon end as my Master slowly devours your essence. Only oblivion waits for you now.*+

Her strength melted out of her body like the lava flowing from the Dead Giant. Sekka bent over and supported herself with one arm. Blood collected in her mouth, and she spat it out defiantly onto the steaming ground.

+*Everything burns, and you will too, even if I must start from the inside.*+

She looked up, and Zizphander's face was inches from her own. Through watery eyes, she saw the smug expression on his beautiful face just as his body flared with bright flames. She ground her teeth against the fire that burned in her mind. With all her remaining strength, she dug her claws into the solidified lava, searching for the reservoir of Elemenati energy Sess'thra claimed saturated this land.

She called it, pleaded with it to answer her. And it did.

Like a rejoining of two parts of the same soul, a rush of Elemenati energy flowed into her and meshed effortlessly with her magic. It coiled around her and gave her strength enough to clear her mind from Zizphander's mental attack.

She stared defiantly into his sapphire blue eyes and uttered the last syllable of a frozen contingency spell she had prepared for this exact moment. His haughty expression changed to one of mild confusion as a wicked smile curled up the corners of her mouth. Then, she watched in silent satisfaction as a sphere of darkness formed in the air over him.

"Now," she whispered.

Khalkoroth's deafening roar shattered the intimate moment between the two rivals as he bounded through the darkness and onto Zizphander's back. With a berserker's madness, his black claws ripped through feathers and tore deeply into charred flesh.

The Red Devil immediately shot skywards, hoping to dislodge the pale demon from his back. Khalkoroth looped one arm in a stranglehold around Zizphander's neck, and bit ferociously into the shoulder of one wing, tearing away a large chunk of burning muscle, and ruining his ability to fly.

Sekka managed to stand as Zizphander's hold on her mind faded. She happily watched as her champion continued to tear away flaming chunks of Zizphander's savaged back. But then Khalkoroth's body went suddenly limp, and the pale demon tumbled off Zizphander's back, falling like a stone to the burning ground.

Zizphander's broken body followed as it spiraled out of the clouds and landed awkwardly near Khalkoroth. She knew she had one chance and rushed to her fallen foe.

"So frail," she said with contempt.

Her sharp claws were inches from her face when Zizphander's eyes snapped open, and he regained his mental control.

+*STOP! You will stop!*+

His arrogant expression returned as eight chitinous legs grew from his underside and lifted him off the ground. His husky, mocking laughter echoed in Sekka's mind, but this time it was shallow. She knew he was hurt. She could see it in his eyes, which was where she focused her will.

+*You are nothing! You will not defeat me!*+

"Yes, I will," Sekka said with renewed confidence as the Elemenati energy pulsing through the land flowed through her now like fresh blood. This world had accepted her as a lost daughter. It was invigorating.

Sekka brushed away his last, weak attempts to control her mind and pressed her hand forward until her claws found the soft pulp of Zizphander's eyes. The Red Devil's chin dropped, and his mouth hung silently open as she buried her claws deep into his soft brain matter.

Sekka quickly maneuvered behind his body and gripped his skull through the ruined eye sockets. With a sharp jerk, she cracked Zizphander's neck like a dry twig, leaving his head hanging unnaturally on his chest.

The horde flew into an unbridled rage. Sekka lifted his limp body over her head and threw it at the swarming fiends, racing too late to save their lord. The beaten and broken body skidded through them until it rolled to an unceremonious stop, breaking apart like a log too long in the armorer's fire. Charred bits of smoldering coals and glowing ash scattered as if swept away by an unseen hand.

Khalkoroth was on his feet. His pink eyes were milky, and his steps were laborious, but he still issued a growling challenge to any of the fiends who thought to continue the attack.

"Blood of the Abyss, there is no end to them," he said as he came to her side.

Sekka called upon her innate magic, now fueled by the Elemenati energy at her feet, and sent a blizzard of ice into the lava flow on either side of the narrow strip of land where her army still fought. Within moments the ground hardened, preventing any more of Zizphander's fiends from respawning.

Those fire fiends that remained came at her with the madness of a rampaging mob. But without reinforcements, they could not stand against Sekka and her deep reservoir of magic.

The mop-up work was most satisfying.

SEKKA
CHAPTER 6

I t took months of intricate spell work, fused with layers of Elemenati energy, and more than fifty thousand sacrificed soul slaves to quell the fiery rage vomiting from the Dead Giant.

Luckily for Sekka, she eventually found a soul cache in a sealed cavern, presumably hidden by Mogwai before he was defeated by Zizphander. Now those souls were hers, and she put them to good use by lulling the massive volcano back to sleep.

She suspected there were more and had search parties scouring the cooling lands to find them before blizzards swept across Taarne and covered vast portions of the terrain in deep snow.

The reason why Zizphander had so desperately wanted Taarne still eluded her. She had been an opportunist striking when her enemy was weakest, but he had confronted Mogwai on much more unfavorable terms, with fiends, no less. How could such a young devil have hoped to win such a lopsided war? Yet, he had done so with a masterful blow.

Regardless of Zizphander's psionic might, he could not harness the Elemenati energy saturating the land. The conquest of Taarne seemed overly bold, reckless even, with a reward paling in comparison to the risk. It made no sense to Sekka's reckoning.

"Why here?" she said as she gazed out over the vastness of her new territory from the topmost platform of scaffolding, which surrounded her newly constructed tower. "Surely, to do more than to watch it burn."

A nagging suspicion something was not as it seemed fluttered across the forefront of her thoughts. As much as she prided herself in her wicked cunning, the victory seemed overly easy.

"There must have been something more at stake for him to risk so much," she said into the wind. "Or, the simple answer is that flying peacock made a mistake and I capitalized on it."

. . .

Snow and bits of ice whipped across her smiling face. She leaned over the platform and stared straight down into the dark chasm that swallowed her new tower's lower reaches. The foundation of her stronghold was set to where the currents of Elemenati energy were the strongest and flowed like underground rivers through the bedrock.

So much had changed in such a brief time. One quarter's soul allowance of holding Taarne was more than fifty years' worth of what she received from the pitiful ice flow she once ruled on Nilas. And oddly, she had Zizphander to thank for depleting Mogwai's forces in their initial battle. Opportunity had its rewards.

She watched the trail of residual smoke slowly churning from the smoldering, yet cooling crater. Volcanic ash choked the air throughout the Circle, turning the skies black, and robbing it of what would be considered sunlight in the Mortal Realm. Fierce winds spun dirty rain clouds into swirling tempests, and spit showers of hail from their swollen and bruised darkness.

The climate changed rapidly as the heat from the volcano's fire was expelled from the land, and temperatures dropped to sub-zero, much to her comfort and delight. She had no fondness for excessive hotness, especially from the flames that blistered and burned her skin.

"Soon, the permafrost will take hold, and the land will be forever frozen," she mused with no small amount of pride, then shouted, "And all will know it was Sekka, the Frost Queen of Nilas that conquered the Circle of Taarne."

Her words were caught by the racing winds and echoed across the wastelands, churning and twisting into the wailing, mournful cries of a thousand lost souls. It was a fitting motif, for all who trespassed in her realm would despair.

"But that name carries with it the stigma of defeat, for too many have recently held this territory only to lose it to a greater power. This land will need a different name, one that declares a warning to any who think to challenge me and my new empire. I shall call it Gathos, the Wasteland of Weeping Winds."

+*This is not finished. My Master will see you destroyed, and I shall return to claim what is mine.*+ Zizphander's voice whispered in her mind like a haunting specter.

Sekka spun quickly, scanning the horizons, but saw nothing. There was no red comet streaking through the sky, or a fiery horde cresting the mountains preparing to invade her domain. The wind had its fun with her, and she laughed along with it, unphased by the threat of the Red Devil's ghost. This world was hers now.

Lord Narthoth would arrive soon, and it was time to extend and strengthen the borders of her conquered territory. She agilely climbed from the platform and traveled indoors to the more finished areas of her stronghold. The main chambers, halls, and corridors had been blocked out, but there was no refinement to their surfaces. There would be plenty of time to decorate the walls with the bones of her enemies and to freeze soul slaves into columns permanently.

Her descent through the multiple levels of the keep took no small amount of time as she carefully studied the load-bearing structures and the spells laid into their seams to give them additional support. Her calculating eyes measured the exact dimensions of summoning chambers and rejuvenation pits. She was obsessed over the smallest detail of the construction of her stronghold. Everything would be done to her exact specifications, or heads would roll.

She walked down a series of corridors, making mental notes as to the twists and turns of their routes and how they related to the hundreds of other similar stretches throughout the tower. If seen from above, the overlapping map of the walkways created a blended sigil of power. The design served to circulate the Elemenati energy drawn from the deep bedrock and pass it into the halls and chambers of her tower like blood flowing through the veins of a living creature.

Eventually, she arrived in her temporary throne room. The temperature was noticeably colder here. A sharp mind was awake with the crispness of cold, rather than dulled into idle thought by heat. The room was basic in form and decoration, but it would serve her needs, for now.

She walked confidently to her throne, which had been carved from a massive block of ice. Lord Oziax stood to one side of the chair. His long, white hair was tied back in long strands of black leather, matching his pants, boots, and shirt. He remained stoic and still with his strong arms held across his chest. A bluish silver medallion hung from his neck and sparkled when it caught the light.

"I see you are finally on your feet and ready for service. I was worried you needed more time to nurse your wounds," Sekka said with a tinge of playful sarcasm.

Oziax harrumphed. "I'm fine. That backstabbing thief, Akkoro will not be so lucky when I find him."

"If you can find him."

Oziax turned to face Sekka, "I will find him. He owes me a war debt that I intend to squeeze out of him, starting with his neck."

"I'm sure you will."

Khalkoroth's rumbling chuckle from the opposite side of the throne drew Oziax's ire. Chedipe stood to his right, a silent shadow in an unflattering black frock, cinched at the waist. Her auburn hair was bound above her head and held in place with the small reddish bones of Zizphander's fire fiends. One hand protectively guarded a small satchel, which hung at her side.

"Do not provoke me, Pale One. You still exist only at the queen's pleasure. Why she allows Sess'thra to keep you as her dog is beyond me."

"It's a shame your face was buried in the dirt when I made my grand entrance onto the battlefield. Had you not been so indisposed, you would know the queen is quite pleased with me."

Chedipe swatted Khalkoroth's muzzle like a disobedient dog. Wisps of black mist rose from his coarse hair, and his lips trembled into a snarl.

"Behave yourself. Lord Oziax is not one to offend," Chedipe scolded.

"Chedipe, do you have any news while we await the arrival of Lord Narthoth?" Sekka said.

Chedipe walked to the front of the throne and bowed to Sekka. "Your servant, Chedipe, has been most successful, my queen. The demon seed is ready for a more robust trial."

"Excellent." She turned to where Khalkoroth stood. His attention was now occupied, trying to catch a snow mite that zipped back and forth across his face. "Shadow demon, come to where I can see you better."

Khalkoroth groaned in irritation and snapped one last time at the victorious snow mite. He then lumbered into the center of the room, where he stood next to Chedipe. Khalkoroth looked askance at the demon witch before turning his attention to Sekka. "What is it?"

"I have a special reward for you," Sekka said, then she nodded to Chedipe, who produced a small translucent pearl from the satchel at her side.

"What is that?" he said suspiciously. "Am I to be punished for my deeds? If not for me, Zizphander would have melted you all to slag!"

"Quiet, beast," Lord Oziax said.

Sekka gave him a mild smile. "I said, this is a reward."

Khalkoroth remained unconvinced. "I am no fool. Choose another to be consumed by your Oblivion Pearl. Give it to Oziax as a reward for surviving Akkoro's blade."

"My dear shadow demon, I would never want to destroy one as valuable as you. As Chedipe has said, that is a demon seed. It will hold your essence until another host is available for you to possess."

"I prefer me as I am. I refuse."

"You will do what the queen tells you to do," Oziax growled.

"What if I told you that the intended host was to be a human in the Mortal Realm?"

"You can do that?"

"I can do anything now," she said with absolute confidence.

Khalkoroth wore a hungry grin. "Well then, I would like that very much."

Sekka heard stomping boots of a large procession coming towards the throne room. She waved Khalkoroth and Chedipe to the side as the captain of her jol'goth guard enter. "We shall talk about this later."

Captain Aosoth was clad in a ceremonial breastplate with Sekka's mark of eight spearheads outwardly arrayed from a central point across his chest. He was a massive jol'goth with curling, transparent horns and dense, white fur, covering the entirety of his body, except for his mottled, hairless head. The blotchy, reddish-purple streaks of his skin gave his face a permanent, angry expression.

His shoulders dipped with each step as he plodded into the room. Behind him followed his jol'goth guard, and together they surrounded a black-winged figure with a bat-faced head.

Lord Narthoth of Vortexx strode into the throne room as if he owned it. He carried himself in a regal fashion upon the hind legs of a predatory cat. A thick mane of white hair bristled from the back of his head and traveled between two leathery wings, which he kept folded across his back. Braids were woven in his locks that ended in various bones and the fleshy digits of defeated enemies.

He had powerful shoulders and arms, ending in oversized hands tipped with claws meant for rending and tearing flesh. Circling his torso were five smaller arms with crablike pinchers instead of hands, which clacked and snapped in the air like the mouths of hungry little birds.

When his beady eyes saw Lord Oziax, his face contorted as if presented with a bad smell, and his long tail swished aggressively over the polished stone floor.

"Ah, the humbled and defeated Oziax, who was brought low by that conniving bird, Akkoro. I had thought you a more able warrior," he said in a haughty demeanor.

His eyes then met Sekka's, "When you are ready to upgrade the General of your armies, Narthoth will be ready."

Lord Oziax merely scowled but said nothing, purposefully ignoring the challenge and infuriating Narthoth at the same time.

"Lord Narthoth, thank you for accepting my invitation. Welcome to Gathos," Sekka said, steering the conversation back to her agenda.

"Gathos? It's quite a catchy name," Lord Narthoth chuckled. "But only to you. The rest of the Abyss will continue to call the third Circle of the Land of Sorrow by its original name, Taarne. There will be another to take your place soon enough. This Circle has always been rife with conflict."

"Indeed. I suppose it does hold a significant strategic positioning between the Third and Fourth Layers, which is why you are here. I wish to open negotiations for your fealty."

"My fealty? Why do I need you? My greatest rival has vanished into thin air. None have heard the whereabouts of that swindler, Lord Akkoro, and those annoying spinning flies he calls warriors."

"What do you think happened to him?"

"I assume that thieving bird stole from the wrong bag and got his wings clipped. But what does it matter? With Akkoro gone, I rule Vortexx uncontested."

"Not so fast. I think it important for you to realize the gift you have been given and how easily it can be taken away."

Narthoth's bat-like face scrunched, and his nostrils flared. "What's your game, devil? You called me here, and I assumed it was to create a mutually beneficial alliance. Let's get on with it. What do you offer?"

"Offer?" Sekka laughed out loud and was joined by the rest of her court. "I'm taking Vortexx."

"Never!" Narthoth took an aggressive stance.

"Now, before you get all riled up, I'm perfectly happy to let you play there to your heart's content if you pledge your allegiance to me. In return, you will receive a hundredth of the Circle's yearly soul allowance, a battalion of my finest warriors, plus a division of my newly created juggernauts."

"And if I refuse?"

Sekka searched the air above Narthoth. "Sess'thra, would you please show Lord Narthoth what awaits him if he is difficult?"

The room filled with the taste of cinnamon and the smell of sulfur before the telltale crackle of air ripping open from a teleportation entry sounded directly behind Narthoth. Sess'thra appeared holding a sack in one hand and the sword, Eishorror, safely in its sheath, in her other hand. She jabbed the blunt end between Narthoth's wings to get his attention.

Narthoth spun around, ready to attack, though Sess'thra held her ground and merely gave him an amused smile. She deftly flipped the sack upside down and grabbed its bottom as the contents fell to the floor with a splat. Lord Akkoro's severed head landed at Narthoth's feet.

"You may have that head as a trophy for your banner. It will serve as a warning to your enemies and a reminder to you of where you got it. If you do as you are told, a greater world will open to you. Betray me and suffer the same consequences as Akkoro," Sekka said with casual ease.

Sess'thra walked to Lord Oziax and handed him his sword, which he grabbed impatiently.

"He was mine to kill," Oziax said gruffly.

"And had you not needed months to recover from being impaled like a pig on his nasty sword, I'm sure you would have found him, and killed him just as I did. Trust me when I say his death was uneventful and most unsatisfying, except for the crying."

"I see where your dog learned his manners," Oziax said as he buckled the scabbard's belt around his waist.

Narthoth grunted at the exchange between the two demons. His beady eyes scanned the makeshift throne room, fell on Captain Aosoth and the jol'goth guards surrounding him. He then presented Sekka with a friendly smile. "What are these juggernauts you speak of?"

"I'm so glad you asked. Stroll with me outside, and I will show you. Captain Aosoth, lead the way. Sess'thra, with me, and bring the head. The rest of you have duties elsewhere."

Aosoth's guards opened the final courtyard doors that lead outside. Heavy snow was falling over the blinding, white landscape. The small party marched along through shin-deep snow until they reached the edge of a large, excavated pit.

Below, forty or more quadruped demons with the upper torsos of mortal men, and the lower extremities of muscular lions, milled or sprinted about in their makeshift pen. The juggernauts towered thirty feet high, though their height was compromised by the depth of the pit.

The creatures had boar-shaped heads with enormous tusks jutting from their oversized mouths. Lips slathered in mucus dripped ropey drool past their jutting chins, as hot breath clouded the air before their faces. Each had two long tails, glistening with iridescent scales that snapped in the air or swished over the hard ground.

Occasionally, two grappled together, establishing the natural hierarchy of the herd. Those nearby snipped and brayed but shuffled away as the two adversaries squared off. Great roars thundered across the pit as powerful blows fell. Eventually, one would concede defeat, or receive a mortal blow and drop dead on the snow-packed floor.

"Giants," Narthoth said with reluctant admiration.

"And mighty giants at that," Sekka commented. "They stand as tall as siege towers and have the strength of twenty jol'goths."

Narthoth eyed Aosoth and stroked his tiny chin. "Impressive. But how are they controlled?"

"Control flows to the most dominant. If you maintain a strong whip, they will obey. If you are weak, they will crush you," Aosoth said matter-of-factly.

Narthoth took a step forward, as if to get a better look. He shook his head in disbelief, then turned back to Sekka. "You cast a long shadow, devil, and draw much attention to your actions. This will not go unnoticed by the Great Three."

"I've heard such warnings before, and yet here we are. But this is nothing," Sekka said dismissively. "I have harnessed the power of Gathos and shaped it to my will. These beasts are just the latest steppingstone to something truly awe-inspiring."

"It should be ready to hatch, Mistress," Sess'thra said with a wicked grin as she twirled the sack containing Akkoro's severed head.

"Hatch?"

"Splendid. Come along," Sekka said enthusiastically.

They traveled across the open plain to the dried-out depression of what was once a great lake. Nestled within the open cavity, and covered in a crisscrossing, fibrous membrane, was what appeared to be an enormous shell.

"Is that an egg?" Narthoth said in disbelief.

"Of a kind, yes," Sekka responded.

"It's as big as my castle-keep. The soul cost must have set you back centuries."

The surface membrane of the egg sack dissolved, revealing the monstrous form underneath. Crablike claws cut through the sticky remains as the creature slowly moved out of its birthing pit on eight segmented legs. Narthoth's bravado was swept away with the cold winds shrieking across the plain.

"Its size is impossible," Narthoth gasped. The dark complexion of his skin turned a sickly pallor.

"He is Cymeryes, the first of my behemoths."

A great clicking, chittering echoed over the barren plains as the remaining membrane sloughed off Cymeryes's shell as he took another thunderous footstep. Sess'thra dropped the sack and clapped her hands in glee.

"You've done it!"

"Is it wise to blatantly create such an overwhelming force? This will certainly attract the attention of the Great Three," Narthoth said nervously. "They will assume you wish to rival their power."

"They know and can do nothing," Sekka said with amusement. "The Great Three are trapped within the boundaries of their kingdoms, forever watching and scheming but still prisoners under the weight of their greatness. The Immortal Mother has her rules, after all."

"Yes, but," Narthoth stammered.

"But nothing. The time has come to decide. I would rather take Vortexx without bloodshed, but if you insist on your claim, we will settle things in a more hostile manner," Sekka said.

On cue, Cymeryes bellowed out a second call, causing the ground to rumble for miles.

Narthoth glance once at Sess'thra, whose eyes lit with wild excitement, and then back to Sekka. He took a knee and bowed his head low, stopping just above the snow.

"A new power rises from the frozen wastelands, and I, Narthoth of Vortexx, pledge my fealty to Sekka, the Frost Queen of Gathos."

"And you will not be the last to do so," Sekka said.

PLEASE LEAVE A REVIEW!

If you have enjoyed this book, it would be tremendous if you could leave a review wherever you purchase your books.

Reviews help me get noticed and they can bring my books to the attention of other readers who may enjoy them. Thank you for your support!

Jeff Pantanella

BOOK 1 IN THE EVER HERO SAGA

AVAILABLE NOW

Kasai Ch'ou has the power to challenge the gods. He just doesn't know it yet.

Enter the archdevil, Sekka hellbent on conquest and lacking but one final piece to guarantee her victory; the soul of the Ever Hero. Will Kasai find his power in time and with it, the courage to defeat the legions of the Abyss?

A century has passed since the disappearance of the demigod, Aetenos, savior and protector of the Mortal Realm. As whispers of war echo across the Three Kingdoms of Hanna, fate follows in the footsteps of two unlikely companions, a novice mystic monk on the run, and a feisty wood witch with a troubled past.

This series is packed with mysticism, magic, vengeance, and salvation. It does not disappoint with a full cast of mad sorcerers, fiery witches, corrupt dukes, weak kings, sinister devils, a succubus thrown in for good measure. Just wait until the angels arrive as the series gets on a roll.

Perfect for fans of Fans of George R.R. Martin's, A Game of Thrones, Brandon Sanderson's, Mistborn series, John Gwynne's, Bloodsworn Trilogy, Harmon Cooper's, Pilgrim series, and The Fatemarked Epic, by David Estes.

If you are looking for a propulsive, epic fantasy series opener that brings mystical martial-arts action, magic, and political intrigue to the forefront, as awkward companions come of age against the eternal forces of good and evil, then this book is for you.

Buy **The Chaos Gate** now to enjoy this exciting new series today!

Pantanella pours a dark, cinematic foundation in this first volume of his epic fantasy series as a singular hero rises to face both militaristic and demonic enemies. A propulsive fantasy that brings revenge, forbidden attraction, and heroism to the forefront.
"They were physically wrong as if their bodies had been stuffed into human skin a size too small."
~ Kirkus Reviews

BOOK 2 IN THE EVER HERO SAGA

AVAILABLE NOW

Save an imprisoned demigod, kill an archdevil on her home turf, and somehow reclaim his soul. Simple, right?

Captured by the archdevil, Sekka, Kasai must defeat her archnemesis, the devil, Zizphander and his legion of fire fiends at her gate in the hopes she will honor her promise and let his companions live.

Meanwhile back in the Mortal Realm, the fate of the Three Kingdoms is at stake, and without the power of the Ever Hero, all seems lost.

Kasai must finally accept his role as Aetenos's next Ever Hero and save the land he loves from the diabolical, Frost Legion, rampaging across the continent. But to do this, he must rely on the help from his closest companions, a witch with an identity crisis, who is torn between using her powers for good or evil, and a sentient three-sectioned staff, that may seek to possess him before his work is done.

But what does any of that matter while the devil, Sekka, holds his soul in her frosty grip?

Kasai must connect to the ethereal Boundless to tap into the powers of the Ever Hero, but without a mentor or master to guide him, his odds for success seem remote. Nonetheless, he must find the courage to crush the darkness. Afterall, he is the Chosen One, whether he wants the title or not.

This epic fantasy series will be especially enjoyed by fans of Brandon Sanderson, Robert Jordan, Michael J. Sullivan, Edward W. Robertson, Patrick Rothfuss, and Michael Wisehart.

Buy **The Foe Wars** now and continue to enjoy this exciting new story today.

BOOK 3 IN THE EVER HERO SAGA

AVAILABLE NOW

Why have the angels forsaken us when demons and devils destroy our world?

Kasai and Desdemonia escape the Abyss and travel to the Seven Heavens in hopes of salvation, only to be accused of consorting with the enemy and imprisoned for treason on their arrival. Meanwhile, a new threat from beyond time wakes, driven mad by the scent of fresh souls leaking from the Chaos Gate. The Ancients are coming, and they are hungry.

All the while, the Three Kingdoms are left defenseless to Sekka's rampaging hordes of demons. The Soul War has begun, and the Ever Hero is needed like never before. However, Kasai's fate and that of the Mortal Realm, will be decided by

Raguel, the archangel with a personal vendetta against Aetenos. And how better to enact his revenge on the demigod than to destroy his progeny?

If you enjoy an engaging story, pitting the underdog against overwhelming odds, with dark powers turning would-be heroes into finger puppets, and mad ambition which throws worlds into conflict, you'll love the third installment in Jeff Pantanella's page-turning Ever Hero Saga.

A perfect fit for epic fantasy fans of Brandon Sanderson, Robert Jordan, Michael J. Sullivan, Edward W. Robertson, Patrick Rothfuss, and Michael Wisehart.
Buy **The Divine Fist** now and continue to enjoy this exciting new series today!

BOOK 4 IN THE EVER HERO SAGA

AVAILABLE NOW

What could be worse than a cosmic, world destroying, vampire hungry to drain the Mortal Realm of all life? How about two of them?

The stakes rise to cataclysmic proportions and with the Seven Heavens and Abyss preoccupied with internal war, defense of the Mortal Realm falls to the Ever Hero, a broken and recluse man.

Six years have passed since the defeat of Sekka at the hands of the Ever Hero. The Heavenly Host has departed, leaving the lands a charred, ash-ladened dystopia. Kasai Ch'ou has returned to the ruins of Ordu, seeking solace, but finding none.

Enter Cyrus Wraith, a mysterious Master Monk of Lost Symmetu, who promises to guide the famed Ever Hero back to the elusive Boundless and help him rebuild the Four Orders of Aetenos. But Cyrus has a hidden agenda, and his obsession with the ancient staff, Ninziz-zida, quickly becomes problematic.

Kasai must rekindle the fire in his soul but in the process, starts down a path that will force him to do the unthinkable to the one person he holds most dear or watch helplessly as the Three Worlds are consumed, literally.

A perfect fit for epic fantasy fans of Brandon Sanderson, Robert Jordan, Michael J. Sullivan, Edward W. Robertson, Patrick Rothfuss, and Michael Wisehart

Buy, *The Forgotten Gods* now and enjoy the fourth installment in Jeff Pantanella's page-turning Ever Hero Saga.

BOOK 5 IN THE EVER HERO SAGA

AVAILABLE NOW

Kazumi was born to slay demons, until the fateful day she became one.

Kazumi is a teenaged ninja warrior eager to prove she is ready to ascend to the vaulted rank of Night Blade; an elite group of female demon slayers. Denied by her mother, the High Priestess of the Yoru Ya-iba clan to complete her training, Kazumi sets off on her own to prove her mother wrong.

But chance and fate have other plans for young Kazumi when she is attacked by a monstrous chaos beast in the forest and left for dead, or so she thinks. Soon after, Kazumi realizes the horrible truth: she has become the one thing she has spent her life training to kill.

Outcast from her home, wandering the countryside, Kazumi meets a stranger named Sunny, who joins the young ninja warrior in her quest to find an antidote. Sunny promises Kazumi answers to her unique condition but carries a dark secret of her own. Whether Sunny is friend or foe, only time will decide.

BOOK 6 IN THE EVER HERO SAGA

AVAILABLE NOW

Misfits, outcasts, loners; who could ask for better heroes?

In a world hovering on the brink of eternal darkness, Kazumi, the fearless teenaged demon slayer, and her companion, Sunny, the enigmatic fox-devil, emerge as humanity's final shield against the malevolent House D'Vross; sinister vampire lords ruling over Gethem.

Fueled by vengeance and burdened with the weight of her ancestors, Kazumi, the newly anointed High Priestess of her clan, seeks justice for her fallen family, wielding her razor-sharp katana and lightning-fast wakizashi. All the while, Lily, the demon spirit sharing her soul, offers dark bargains for freedom.

Within a city cloaked in shadows and ancient mysteries, Kazumi and Sunny join Sophia Jolla, a young noblewoman with a shattered birthright and a hidden agenda. Together, they mount a last-ditch effort to stop the D'Vross nightmare from spreading. The question lingers: who poses a greater threat, the would-be tyrants or the young maiden claiming innocence?

In this enthralling sequel, witness Kazumi and Sunny's determined resolve and unwavering friendship face the ultimate tests of betrayal and heartbreak when a haunting truth lurking beneath the surface of lies is uncovered.

"**Crouching Tiger, Hidden Demon!**" An anime and manga inspired action romp set within the world of the Ever Hero Saga. Buy Book Two: *KAZUMI, Wicked Fox* now and read the continuing story of a teenaged ninja warrior with a dark secret. Book Two in the Night Blades Series, an Ever Hero Saga Story.

BOOK 7 IN THE EVER HERO SAGA

AVAILABLE NOW

The hunted becomes the hunter!

Kazumi and Amos turn the tables on their pursuers and take the fight to the enemy. The quest to free Kazumi's and Lily's soul from the chaos beast connecting them encounters a deadly snare; now those professing to be healers want Kazumi's blood for their own nefarious schemes.

Meanwhile, a new threat enters the conflict, one who could cast the Mortal Realm into everlasting chaos. The Dark King has risen, and he wants Kazumi dead.

"Crouching Tiger, Hidden Demon!" An anime and manga inspired action romp set within the world of the Ever Hero Saga. Buy Book Seven: KAZUMI, Vampire Hunter now and read the continuing story of a teenaged ninja warrior with a dark secret. Book Two in the Night Blades Mini-Series, an Ever Hero Saga Story.

BAND OF EVER HEROES

Join my Band of Ever Heroes to receive free or discounted books like this one as part of my Advance Reader Team.

It's completely free to sign up and you will never be spammed by me. (Because Ever Heroes respect your privacy) You can opt out easily at any time.

Click HERE to join my Band of Ever Heroes!

ABOUT THE AUTHOR

Jeff Pantanella is a Rhode Island School of Design (RISD) graduate, Guggenheim Fellow, fine art painter, video game maker, and fantasy novel author. He can't remember names or dates and was told there'd be no math in writing fiction, so, here we are.

"I've always been drawn to the complexities confronted by being the hero in any story. Whom do you save, and what if you can't? The "Ever Hero Saga" is my debut series into the world of dark fantasy fiction, and I explore just how challenging it can be when you are indeed that hero or you're not and think you are."

Welcome to the Three Kingdoms of Hanna and your introduction to the life and times of the Ever Hero. Follow Kasai's adventures, spanning different lands, realms, and worlds as he does his best to fight the forces of evil, that unknowingly, he lets loose on the Mortal Realm.

I hope you have as much fun reading my novels as I had writing them.

Author photo by Asian Yen

Made in the USA
Columbia, SC
28 October 2024

44845414R00430